TORTS

ASPEN CUSTOM PUBLISHING SERIES

TORTS

Principles and Practice

Charles A. Palmer

Kathleen C. Butler

Mark Anthony Dotson

Wolters Kluwer
Law & Business

Published by Wolters Kluwer Law & Business in New York.

Wolters Kluwer Law & Business serves customers worldwide with CCH, Aspen Publishers, and Kluwer Law International products. (www.wolterskluwerlb.com)

To contact Customer Service, e-mail customer.service@wolterskluwer.com, call 1-800-234-1660, fax 1-800-901-9075, or mail correspondence to:

> Wolters Kluwer Law & Business
> Attn: Order Department
> PO Box 990
> Frederick, MD 21705

Printed in the United States of America.

2 3 4 5 6 7 8 9 0

ISBN 978-1-4548-0726-1

About Wolters Kluwer Law & Business

Wolters Kluwer Law & Business is a leading global provider of intelligent information and digital solutions for legal and business professionals in key specialty areas, and respected educational resources for professors and law students. Wolters Kluwer Law & Business connects legal and business professionals as well as those in the education market with timely, specialized authoritative content and information-enabled solutions to support success through productivity, accuracy and mobility.

Serving customers worldwide, Wolters Kluwer Law & Business products include those under the Aspen Publishers, CCH, Kluwer Law International, Loislaw, Best Case, ftwilliam.com and MediRegs family of products.

CCH products have been a trusted resource since 1913, and are highly regarded resources for legal, securities, antitrust and trade regulation, government contracting, banking, pension, payroll, employment and labor, and healthcare reimbursement and compliance professionals.

Aspen Publishers products provide essential information to attorneys, business professionals and law students. Written by preeminent authorities, the product line offers analytical and practical information in a range of specialty practice areas from securities law and intellectual property to mergers and acquisitions and pension/benefits. Aspen's trusted legal education resources provide professors and students with high-quality, up-to-date and effective resources for successful instruction and study in all areas of the law.

Kluwer Law International products provide the global business community with reliable international legal information in English. Legal practitioners, corporate counsel and business executives around the world rely on Kluwer Law journals, looseleafs, books, and electronic products for comprehensive information in many areas of international legal practice.

Loislaw is a comprehensive online legal research product providing legal content to law firm practitioners of various specializations. Loislaw provides attorneys with the ability to quickly and efficiently find the necessary legal information they need, when and where they need it, by facilitating access to primary law as well as state-specific law, records, forms and treatises.

Best Case Solutions is the leading bankruptcy software product to the bankruptcy industry. It provides software and workflow tools to flawlessly streamline petition preparation and the electronic filing process, while timely incorporating ever-changing court requirements.

ftwilliam.com offers employee benefits professionals the highest quality plan documents (retirement, welfare and non-qualified) and government forms (5500/PBGC, 1099 and IRS) software at highly competitive prices.

MediRegs products provide integrated health care compliance content and software solutions for professionals in healthcare, higher education and life sciences, including professionals in accounting, law and consulting.

Wolters Kluwer Law & Business, a division of Wolters Kluwer, is headquartered in New York. Wolters Kluwer is a market-leading global information services company focused on professionals.

To Georgia Palmer, Emma Palmer, and Kenley Palmer Schmidt

May our legacy be yours

C.A.P.

To Bill Butler and Elaine Shoben

K.C.B.

To Etta (my mom), Lala, Kel, Ryan, Cam and Kai,
my friends at Quarles & Brady, John Michaud (the ultimate legal resource),
Rich Henke, and all the students who every day
remind me of what it means to love a job

M.A.D.

SUMMARY OF CONTENTS

CONTENTS

PREFACE

The student should understand that the authors have edited the principal cases in this book. Some footnotes have been omitted. Many of the citations in the opinions have also been omitted because the student will not need them to understand the relevant portions of the opinion. Since the cases presented here illustrate certain essential points about the law of torts, discussion of other issues in the cases has been removed.

The contents indicate that the book has been separated into two parts, one for a first semester course, Torts I, and another for a second semester course, Torts II. Separating the course into two parts is not essential but, for those who do so, the separation will be helpful.

The authors hope that students will carefully consider the questions after the cases to be sure they are ready to discuss the cases in class. A student who cannot answer the questions is not ready for class. Students should also work the problems in the reading to ready themselves for their short-term goal of succeeding on exams and long-term goal of being able to analyze and advocate like lawyers.

C.A.P.
K.C.B.
M.A.D.

July 2011

TORTS

TORTS I

Chapter 1

The Stages of a Tort Claim

A. THE INITIAL INTERVIEW

A person who is injured as a result of someone's negligence has a perilous journey to reach the point when he or she will receive money from the party who caused the injury. There are many gates or filters designed to weed out the frivolous or unworthy claimants. It is only those claims worthy enough to survive all the gates that eventually result in the recovery of money. And the first gate, maybe the one that filters out the most claims, is the initial conference with a lawyer.

1. Getting the Facts

The personal injury claimant's lawyer faces a daunting task at the initial interview. First, he or she must get the facts. It's important that the claimant feel that the lawyer cares and there is no better way to do this than to listen. What is the injury, and what does it mean to the claimant? Some of the important facts may be embarrassing and the client may not want to disclose them in a professional setting. Some clients can't read, many have embarrassing maladies brought about by their injury, and many have backgrounds that they don't want to share with a respected professional, but a good interview will discover these problems without the cost of expensive investigations.

The attorney is not obligated to take the case at the initial conference. More often than not, the attorney will chose not to take the case because liability is doubtful or the damages are just not large enough to justify the time the attorney will have to spend on the case. The attorney will develop a preliminary impression of the case at the initial interview, but more investigation will have to be done before determining whether to take the case. Someone will have to obtain the medical records of the claimant's injury. Sometimes a nurse or doctor will be retained to read and interpret the medical records. Other experts may be used to further investigate the case but ultimately, the attorney must decide to take the case or not. If the attorney isn't going to take the case, the client has to be unequivocally informed that the attorney will not be representing the injured party.

2. The Contingency Fee

In most personal injury lawsuits, the claimant does not have enough money to pay the attorney an hourly fee. Many claimants have been seriously injured. They are not working or earning a living anymore so there is no money to pay a lawyer. Even those who are working usually don't have enough money to pay an attorney an hourly fee. The claimant's attorney may agree to forego an hourly fee but instead take a percentage of the net recovery (33⅓% in Michigan). There is a risk for the claimant's attorney in this deal. The attorney will work on the case, often for several years, without being paid, only to recover one lump sum at the end.

There is another problem; the claimant often does not have enough money to pay the expenses of the lawsuit. There will be filing fees, deposition fees, and expert witnesses, like doctors, which have to be paid; all in order to get the case to the fact finder. These costs can run from $1,000 to $100,000. The attorney is not allowed to pay the expenses for the claimant but often, in order for the case to proceed, the attorney will have to loan money to the client for the expenses. Those expenses will be deducted from the claimant's recovery at the time of recovery. So, the claimant's attorney does not get paid for work done on the case while the case is awaiting trial, the attorney often pays the expenses of the case out of his or her pocket, and the payment of expenses is a loan so they are not deductible as expenses on the attorney's income taxes. If the jury should return a verdict of no cause of action, the claimant and the attorney will recover no contingency fee, nothing for the time spent on the case, and no money to pay back the loan for expenses. Obviously the claimant's attorney has to be cautious about accepting contingency fee cases. Consequently, the attorney's decision to take the case on a contingency fee basis is the first and maybe most significant gate for the claimant to pass. The claimant is going to have to convince an attorney to take the case, and that will be difficult. Much will depend upon the extent of the damages. The attorney must see enough profit in the case to justify his or her time, money, and risk.

The contingency fee has been maligned in the media, but it has both good points and bad points for the civil justice system. First, and importantly, the contingency fee allows poor people to go to court and often with the best personal injury lawyers available in the community. Criminal defendants have the state to pay for their lawyers at bargain basement fees, those seeking a divorce have Legal Aid if they're lucky, but the significantly injured personal injury claimant will be welcome at any personal injury law firm. When critics of the contingency fee argue that eliminating it will cut down on claims, they are correct. But they will do that by driving the poor, and the seriously injured, out of the court system.

The contingency fee system also cuts down on frivolous claims. Given the discussion above, it is clear that the claimant with a weak claim is not going to find an attorney to take his or her case. An attorney is going to have to anticipate a substantial return to justify the time and risk involved in a contingencyfee arrangement. Cases in which high damage awards are anticipated, like those involving death, paraplegia, and brain injuries, will often find attorneys, but those that anticipate low damage awards will rarely justify the time, expense, and risk of an attorney paid by a contingency fee. But the contingency-fee system has real downsides also.

It can be argued that the contingency-fee system presents too much incentive to attorneys. Watch the advertisements of attorneys on television. How many of them are asking for divorce, criminal, or corporate claims? Most are asking for contingency fee personal injury cases. That's because they can pay for the costs of their advertising with contingency fee cases. In any review of the highest paid attorneys in the United States, the personal injury lawyers usually lead the pack. A one-third contingency fee is common. If the claimant recovers a million dollars, a not uncommon award in the sort of cases attorneys take on contingency, the attorney makes around $333,333 for one case. That's why the attorneys are advertising for personal injury cases.

In re Abrams & Abrams P.A.
605 F.3d 238 (4th Cir. 2010)

WILKINSON, C.J.

After winning their disabled client an $18 million personal injury settlement that will pay for his care for the rest of his life, the attorneys in this case saw their compensation slashed by the district court from the thirty-three percent provided in their contingency fee agreement to a mere three percent. While a district court does possess discretion in approving fee awards, particularly when its power to protect minors or the disabled is involved, we hold that the court here abused that discretion by improperly applying the standards we have established for determining whether an attorney's fee is reasonable. As a result, we vacate and remand.

I.

On New Year's Eve 2005 in Raleigh, North Carolina, twenty-six year old Mark Pellegrin was struck by a truck driven by his friend, Kelly McKiernan, who had been drinking. Pellegrin hit his head on the pavement, and paramedics found him unconscious and unable to breathe as a result of his injuries. The bleeding, swelling, and lack of oxygen that resulted caused permanent, severe brain damage. Pellegrin spent 112 days in the hospital and can no longer walk, talk, or even roll over. He is completely dependent on others for feeding, dressing, washing, and toileting. He is, however, partially conscious and can communicate through facial reactions. If Pellegrin lives to full life expectancy, his future care and medical expenses are estimated to cost approximately $17 million.

At the time of his injury, Mark Pellegrin worked for KCI Technologies as a crew leader for communications tower inspections, and McKiernan was one of his crew members. Because the tower inspections frequently required travel, KCI provided company trucks to many of its employees, including McKiernan. KCI had a written policy prohibiting employees from operating its equipment while intoxicated.

On December 31, 2005, Pellegrin asked McKiernan to come to his house to check equipment for an upcoming inspection. McKiernan drove his KCI truck to Pellegrin's home. After working for a while, Pellegrin and McKiernan began drinking to celebrate New Year's Eve. Eventually McKiernan decided to leave but was prevented by Pellegrin, who told him he could not drive. When Pellegrin left the room, however, McKiernan said that he:

> took the keys and . . . ran. I was just trying to get out of there. And that's when I walked down to the truck. Basically, I put it in reverse, went to a stop and put it in drive. Of course I've got to mess with the radio. . . . Why couldn't I see him? And I-I-I hit him. I'm sure he was just coming down to tell me, you know, man, what are you doing. Kelly, you're drunk, dude.

McKiernan called 911, and when police arrived he told them to "just put me in handcuffs. You know, I'm drunk. I accidentally hit my buddy who was just trying to stop me from leaving." Police officers found human hair on the truck's front grill. McKiernan later pled guilty to driving while intoxicated and has never denied that he was responsible for the accident.

Pellegrin's father, Jerry, was appointed as his son's General Guardian in North Carolina some two months after the accident and remains Pellegrin's primary caregiver. Because the Pellegrins are from Louisiana, Jerry Pellegrin retained attorney Charles Bourque of the Louisiana law firm St. Martin, Williams and Bourque to attempt to recover for his son's injuries. The retainer agreement Jerry Pellegrin signed agreed to pay Bourque's firm thirty-three percent of any gross recovery, plus litigation expenses. With Jerry Pellegrin's consent, Bourque then retained the North Carolina firm of Abrams & Abrams, P.A., agreeing to split any contingency fee equally.

Before Jerry Pellegrin even signed the agreement, KCI's insurer, National Union Fire Insurance Company of Pittsburgh, Pennsylvania, transmitted a "reservation of rights" letter to McKiernan, denying coverage for the accident. Although KCI carried $21 million in insurance, National Union claimed it was not obligated to pay because McKiernan violated KCI's internal rules by driving while intoxicated.

The insurance policy, however, did not incorporate KCI's internal rules, and Pellegrin's counsel believed that North Carolina courts had already rejected a similar defense in United Services Automobile Association v. Rhodes, 577 S.E.2d 171 (N.C. App. 2003). In that case, an insurance company was required to cover expenses arising from an accident involving a rental car driven by an intoxicated driver, even though the rental agreement prohibited drunk driving. Pellegrin's counsel thus filed suit in North Carolina court against Kelly McKiernan on July 19, 2007, after some six months of investigation.

National Union not only again disclaimed any coverage but also refused even to defend McKiernan. Under North Carolina law, if an insurer improperly refuses to defend a claim, it is estopped from denying coverage and must pay any reasonable settlement—even if it made an honest mistake in its denial. . . . Because Pellegrin's counsel drafted their complaint against McKiernan to state only that McKiernan negligently struck Mark Pellegrin with a KCI vehicle he was operating with the company's "knowledge, consent and permission," the complaint triggered National Union's duty to defend the suit, which is based on facts alleged in pleadings and is broader than the duty to indemnify. Waste Mgmt. of Carolinas, Inc. v. Peerless Ins. Co., 340 S.E.2d 374, 377 (N.C. 1986).

Without National Union, McKiernan could not afford counsel and instead defended himself. Several depositions were taken and a trial date set, but McKiernan did not appear at trial. As a result, the district court entered a $75 million judgment against him. McKiernan obviously lacked the funds to satisfy such a judgment, and counsel filed a second complaint against National Union within the thirty day time limit provided in North Carolina law to alter or amend a judgment. That complaint contained a description of the McKiernan suit and attached a copy of the judgment. It sought a declaration that National Union was liable for the full $75 million judgment against McKiernan because of its insurance coverage and its failure to defend the earlier suit, and it designated Pellegrin as a third-party beneficiary.

At this point, National Union removed the suit to federal court, invoking federal diversity jurisdiction. A one-day mediation took place on August 28, 2008, at the end of which National Union agreed to pay $18 million to resolve all claims. Of that amount, $6 million went into a Special Needs Trust designed to supplement Pellegrin's care. The next $6 million purchased a structured annuity that was guaranteed to make monthly payments for Pellegrin's support for at least thirty years and would continue to pay after that point for the duration of his life. Over the first thirty years, the annuity was guaranteed to pay $12.1 million, and if Pellegrin lived to 78, his life expectancy if he were healthy, it would pay $29.9 million. The final $6 million was to be paid outright and used to satisfy the retainer agreement. There is no dispute that the settlement agreement will provide amply for Pellegrin throughout his life.

Because Pellegrin was incompetent, National Union and Jerry Pellegrin jointly moved for court approval of the settlement. The district court questioned Pellegrin's attorneys about their work, demanding to know how many hours they had spent on the case. At first, Douglas Abrams of Abrams & Abrams, P.A. replied that the firm did not keep hourly records because it only took contingency cases. When pressed, he guessed that "our firm alone has a thousand hours" and that Bourque's firm "has at least a thousand hours." Bourque estimated his firm's time as "something well in excess of a thousand hours." No other evidence about hours was presented.

At the close of the hearing, Pellegrin's father and guardian addressed the court. He said:

> I'd like to state that I'm not a big fan of lawyers myself. However, these people Abrams, Chuck Bourque, have shown me and my son more compassion and help and I do not begrudge them anything. I think they earned everything. I was proud of them and we're all tired and ready for this to be over.

In spite of this request, the district court reduced the lawyers' compensation from $6 million to $600,000, or from thirty-three percent down to three percent of the settlement. The $5.4 million balance reverted to Pellegrin. The court reached this number by taking what it termed counsel's "pure speculation" as to the number of hours worked and multiplying it by a $300 per hour rate that it believed was "a high hourly rate for a similarly-situated lawyer in North Carolina." This appeal by Pellegrin's counsel followed. We appointed amicus counsel to defend the district court's fee decision as National Union had no stake in the outcome on appeal.

II.

In this case, "[w]e review a district court's award of attorney's fees for abuse of discretion." Grissom v. The Mills Corp., 549 F.3d 313, 320 (4th Cir. 2008). As an initial matter, the district court in this case properly noted that courts evaluate attorney's fees under a reasonableness standard. Pellegrin's lawyers contend that they are entitled to have their contingency fee agreement enforced unless the resultant fees are "clearly excessive." As they see it, only agreements that are so excessive that no ethical attorney could sign them should be cast aside. That standard presents its problems, however, because it allows approval of fees that are unreasonable and excessive just so long as they are not clearly so.

The simpler standard of "reasonableness" is one that Congress and many courts have adopted. For instance, in the fee-shifting context under 42 U.S.C. §1988(b), which applies to certain civil rights suits, a "court, in its discretion, may allow the prevailing party, other than the United States, a *reasonable* attorney's fee." 42 U.S.C. §1988(b) (emphasis added). Nor is the reasonableness standard limited to the fee-shifting context. As we noted in *Bergstrom v. Dalkon Shield Trust (In re A.H. Robins Co.)*, "the law of this circuit has long been clear that federal district courts have inherent power and an obligation to limit attorneys' fees to a reasonable amount." 86 F.3d 364, 373 (4th Cir. 1996). In particular, "[t]he district courts' supervisory jurisdiction over contingent fee contracts for services rendered in cases before them is well-established." Allen v. U.S., 606 F.2d 432, 435 (4th Cir. 1979). Here too the review of fee arrangements is for reasonableness.

Indeed, it is difficult to imagine why any different standard would be warranted. In a case like this involving a minor or disabled individual, a district court plainly enjoys discretion to protect those who come in front of it. In general, "infant[s] and other incompetent parties are wards of any court called upon to measure and weigh their interests." Dacanay v. Mendoza, 573 F.2d 1075, 1079 (9th Cir. 1978). As a result, "[i]t has long been established that the court in which a minor's claims are being litigated has a duty to protect the minor's interests." Salmeron v. U.S., 724 F.2d 1357, 1363 (9th Cir. 1983). This duty is intended to protect those who may be especially vulnerable to manipulation or who may be unable to protect themselves. Id.

Integral to this protective judicial role is ascertaining whether attorney fee agreements involving minors or incompetents are reasonable. "Independent investigation by the court as to the fairness and reasonableness of a fee to be charged against a minor's estate or interest is required." Dean v. Holiday Inns, Inc., 860 F.2d 670, 673 (6th Cir. 1988) Moreover, the public reputation of the profession would deservedly suffer if attorneys were seen to be gouging those least able to fend for themselves. Consistent with this charge, the local rules of the Eastern District of North Carolina state that in approving a settlement, "the court shall approve or fix the amount of the fee to be paid to counsel for the minor or incompetent parties." E.D.N.C.L.R. 17.1(c).

The parties spend a great deal of time and energy debating whether the review of attorney's fees is a federal or state question, whether North Carolina or Louisiana law applies, and what exactly the laws of each jurisdiction may or may not be. We are not convinced, however, that the law of either state is so different from the federal standard as to make a difference. And we are persuaded that the virtues of simplicity and straightforwardness counsel against adopting different standards with different shades and nuances in different contexts. The district court therefore did have the discretion to review the settlement here, including the contingency fee, for reasonableness.

III.

The district court's discretion is by no means unguided, however. District courts should look at the twelve factors first set forth in Johnson v. Georgia Highway Express, Inc., 488 F.2d 714, 717-19 (5th Cir. 1974), and adopted by this court in *Barber*, 577 F.2d at 226, and *Allen*, 606 F.2d at 436 n.1. In *Allen*, we stated the factors as follows:

> (1) the time and labor required in the case, (2) the novelty and difficulty of the questions presented, (3) the skill required to perform the necessary legal services, (4) the preclusion of other employment by the lawyer due to acceptance of the case, (5) the customary fee for similar work, (6) the contingency of a fee, (7) the time pressures imposed in the case, (8) the award involved and the results obtained, (9) the experience, reputation, and ability of the lawyer, (10) the "undesirability" of the case, (11) the nature and length of the professional relationship between the lawyer and the client, and (12) the fee awards made in similar cases.

Id.[3] Though *Barber* upheld an award in a Truth in Lending Act fee-shifting case under 15 U.S.C. §1640(a)(3), *Allen* was a contingency fee case and noted that "[t]hese factors . . . apply even where the fee request is based on a private fee agreement." *Allen*, 606 F.2d at 435-36.

Although the district court correctly recognized that some factors may not have much, if anything, to add in a given case, the factors that do apply should be considered. "We cannot afford effective appellate review unless we have before us the district court's reasons for finding a particular award appropriate." Particularly when such a steep and indeed drastic reduction from the fee provided in the retainer agreement was ordered, some care in explanation might be expected. The district court here neglected to consider several critically important factors in its analysis. For example, it failed to adequately address the contingency of the fee (factor 6), the award involved and the results obtained (factor 8), and the fee awards made in similar cases (factor 12). We consider these factors in turn.

---

3. The district court relied upon *Barber*'s formulation of factor six, which addresses "the attorney's expectations at the outset of the litigation." *Allen* rephrased this factor to address "the contingency of a fee" While both formulations address the basic question of how an attorney anticipates being paid, we have recognized that *Allen*'s version is superior for cases like the present one "because it deals with contingent fees and places upon the district court the obligation to limit such fees to a reasonable amount."

A.

The chief error in the district court's analysis was its failure to recognize the significance of the contingency fee in this case. The court obviously knew that a contingency fee was involved, but it did not give that fact the weight it was due in the decisional calculus. After quoting language from *Allen* stating that contingency agreements are subject to supervision by courts for reasonableness the court merely stated that it "must consider the other relevant *Barber* factors in order to determine the reasonableness of the contingency fee requested by Plaintiff's Counsel." It then proceeded to apply an hourly rate calculation based on dubious estimations of the applicable hours and rates with no further consideration of the relevance of the contingency fee agreement. Fixing a lodestar fee in this contingency case was error and threatens to nullify the considerable advantages of contingency arrangements.

1.

As an initial matter, contingency fees provide access to counsel for individuals who would otherwise have difficulty obtaining representation. Sadly, a plaintiff sometimes has little to offer a lawyer other than his personal plight. As an advocate before the Kentucky Supreme Court noted as early as 1823, in the absence of contingency fees a client "may not have any thing else to give, and without the aid of the matter in the contest, he can never sue for his right, not having otherwise the means to employ counsel).

Nor has that rationale changed with time. The Second Circuit has explained that, "[m]any claimants . . . cannot afford to retain counsel at fixed hourly rates . . . yet they are willing to pay a portion of any recovery they may receive in return for successful representation. Ignoring reasonable contingent fee agreements or automatically reducing them would impair claimants' ability to secure representation." While the various amici in this case debate whether contingency fees encourage or discourage insubstantial suits where the chance of recovery is slight, that ongoing argument is beyond the power of this court to resolve. The point remains that contingency fees are an acknowledged feature of our legal landscape, approved by legislative and judicial bodies alike that help secure for the impecunious access both to counsel and to court. See, e.g., 28 U.S.C. §2678 "[A]ccepting reasonable contingency agreements . . . increases the likelihood that a claimant can find an attorney sufficiently committed and skilled to litigate successfully."

The facts of this case illustrate precisely the type of situation in which a contingency fee may be the only way an individual can protect his interests. Yet the district court's analysis made no mention of the role that contingent compensation played in providing the Pellegrins with access to court. Mark Pellegrin's father and guardian, Jerry, faced a tough financial situation. His son was horribly injured, and he certainly did not have the estimated $17 million needed over a lifetime of care. At the same time, neither did he have the resources to retain lawyers on an hourly basis to pursue a large insurance company in court, especially after National Union denied any coverage at all. The money to solve the problems was available in National Union's $21 million insurance policies, but it could only be obtained if someone else was willing to front the funds for attorneys and fees. The contingency agreement was, as the saying goes, the key to the courthouse door that allowed Jerry Pellegrin to retain the attorneys who eventually provided for his son's ongoing needs. The district court erred in failing to consider the access to the legal system that contingency fees like the ones herein provide.

2.

Nor did the district court consider the related point that contingency fee agreements transfer a significant portion of the risk of loss to the attorneys taking a case. Access to the courts would be difficult to achieve without compensating attorneys for that risk. The risks a lawyer assumes are not dissimilar to those undertaken, for example, by a realtor on commission, who accepts the possibility of no sale as well as the potential reward of a quick transaction. In addition, it may be necessary to provide a greater return than an hourly fee offers to induce lawyers to take on representation for which they might never be paid, and it makes sense to arrange these fees as a percentage of any recovery. "[M]any attorneys are unwilling to accept the risk of nonpayment without a guaranteed contingency percentage of the recovery." In other words, plaintiffs may find it difficult to obtain representation if attorneys know their reward for accepting a contingency case is merely payment at the same rate they could obtain risk-free for hourly work, while their downside is no payment whatsoever.

Conversely, an attorney compensated on a contingency basis has a strong economic motivation to achieve results for his client, precisely because of the risk accepted. As the Seventh Circuit has explained, "[t]he contingent fee uses private incentives rather than careful monitoring to align the interests of lawyer and client. The lawyer gains only to the extent his client gains." Kirchoff v. Flynn, 786 F.2d 320, 325 (7th Cir. 1986). A contingency fee "automatically handles compensation for the uncertainty of litigation" because it "rewards exceptional success, and penalizes failure." Because the district court's ruling failed to recognize that contingency fees provide attorneys due consideration for the risk they undertake, it reduced counsel's fee to a level that few attorneys would have accepted at the outset of litigation, when success was by no means assured and the size of any settlement or judgment was unpredictable.

Indeed, there were a number of sticky problems with the present suit when counsel undertook the representation, problems which Pellegrin's attorneys managed to overcome. The difficulties included National Union's reservation of rights letter to McKiernan based on his violation of KCI's alcohol policy and the prospect of securing a verdict against a judgment-proof defendant once coverage was denied. Additionally, North Carolina is a contributory negligence state where the failure to exercise due care by a plaintiff operates as a complete bar to recovery. Contributory negligence was an obvious defense in a case involving an intoxicated plaintiff who ran in front of a moving vehicle driven by a friend he knew had also been drinking. . . . Finally, Pellegrin's attorneys faced the task of triggering coverage under a company insurance policy that only covered company-authorized travel without transforming the suit into an exclusive worker's compensation claim under the North Carolina co-employee immunity doctrine, which prevents employees injured during employment from suing co-workers. The district court's failure to consider such risks and the fact that contingency fees "are set to account for the risk of nonrecovery" was error.

B.

The district court also overlooked another important *Barber/Allen* factor — "the award involved and the results obtained." We have noted that "the most critical factor in determining the reasonableness of a fee award is the degree of success obtained." While that statement came in a fee-shifting case, there is no reason why it should be inapplicable in a contingency situation. After all, the job of an advocate is to achieve beneficial outcomes for a client, and success is every bit as important to the prevailing party in a contingency case as under a fee-shifting statute. It was error therefore for the district court to fail to recognize that an $18 million settlement served the client well by any standard and particularly in light of National Union's $21 million policy limit. While amicus argues that the district court did consider the settlement amount, the fact that it mentioned the $18 million sum briefly in its statement of the facts, and again while analyzing a different *Barber/Allen* factor, does not constitute the full consideration of the significant results obtained by counsel that *Barber/Allen* requires.

Notably, Jerry Pellegrin, Mark Pellegrin's guardian, was satisfied with the results obtained by the lawyers he retained. He asked both the district court and this court in no uncertain terms to uphold the parties' contingency contract. Indeed, after the district court's order created a $5.4 million conflict between Jerry Pellegrin and his lawyers due to the fact that Mark Pellegrin would receive any funds not awarded as attorney's fees, Jerry Pellegrin retained his own counsel to request reversal of the district court's fee reduction and reinstatement of the contingency agreement. To be sure, "a court must independently investigate and evaluate any compromise or settlement of a minor's claims to assure itself that the minor's interests are protected, even if the settlement has been recommended or negotiated by the minor's parent or guardian ad litem." Nonetheless, we cannot ignore the fact that Jerry Pellegrin not only made no objection to the thirty-three percent contingency fee but also actively supported it, both as a point of personal honor and in recognition of the manner in which his son's lawyers provided for the lifetime needs of their severely disabled client.

Nor was the district court correct in discounting the obstacles Pellegrin's attorneys faced and ultimately overcame. Because the suit against McKiernan was undefended and because National Union settled quickly once it was sued, the district court concluded that "[t]he uncontested nature of this action strongly implies that Plaintiff's Counsel did not expend a great deal of time in the handling of this case and that a fee in the amount Plaintiff's Counsel seeks would be an unjustified windfall."

That view, however, considers the litigation only from the point at which National Union awoke to the peril it faced due to a combination of its own decisions and trial strategy by Pellegrin's counsel. Pellegrin's lawyers should hardly be penalized for comprehending the strategic implications of National Union's decision to refuse to represent McKiernan, which due to the breadth of the duty to defend under North Carolina law conceivably left National Union on the hook for the full amount of the judgment obtained against McKiernan in National Union's absence. By the time mediation and settlement occurred, the case may well have appeared open and shut, but that was only because Pellegrin's attorneys had spent almost two years laying the groundwork to secure their client's interests. As noted above, the suit faced potential problems including the National Union reservation of rights letter, the reality that McKiernan was judgment-proof, the fact that any contributory negligence on Pellegrin's part would operate as a bar to recovery in North Carolina, and the need to obtain payment from a company insurance plan that provided coverage only for company-authorized acts without triggering worker's compensation under North Carolina's co-employee immunity doctrine. Successful outcomes often make risks seem less risky in hindsight than they were at the time, and the court should not have ignored those risks merely because at some later point in litigation the defendant found it in its interest to settle.

C.

Finally, the district court did not properly analyze the twelfth *Barber/Allen* factor, the customary fee for such work. Its analysis consisted of deciding with no real supporting evidence that $300 per hour was "a high hourly rate for a similarly-situated lawyer in North Carolina." In doing so, the district court again overlooked the important fact that this case was a contingency fee case. The proper question involved, not some hourly rate in the abstract, but whether thirty-three percent was an acceptable fee for the contingency-based personal injury work performed by Pellegrin's counsel. In this regard, a number of respected North Carolina and Louisiana lawyers submitted affidavits stating that a thirty-three percent fee was actually lower than the forty percent they would have demanded to undertake Pellegrin's case. If the affidavits are to be disregarded in favor of contrary evidence, the trial court must explain why, without disregarding the contingent nature of the fee. While court-appointed amicus attempts to discredit the submissions by claiming that they are "cookie-cutter affidavits" based on "conclusory statements," the affidavits properly recognized that the customary fee for such work is based on contingency agreements. The district court should have based its analysis on a similar recognition.

IV.

It should be apparent from our discussion of the above facts and circumstances that the district court's reduction of attorney's fees from
thirty-three percent to a mere three percent was much too steep a decrease.
Upon remand, the district court's discretion must be guided by a more
rigorous analysis of the applicable *Barber/Allen* factors, and especially
by recognition of the important role played by contingency fees in this
type of litigation. Because the district court failed to consider that significant factor as well the other considerations discussed above, the judgment
must be vacated and remanded for further proceedings consistent with this
opinion.

VACATED AND REMANDED.

PREPARING FOR CLASS

1. What is a "lodestar" fee? What's wrong with the lodestar approach in this
    case? In what kinds of cases would the lodestar approach be used more
    appropriately?

2. Considering the facts as set forth by the court, what do you think is an
    appropriate fee in the *Abrams & Abrams* case?

3. Can the court prevent Jerry Pellegrin from paying the total attorney fee
    requested by Abrams & Abrams, i.e., can't Pellegrin just give Abrams &
    Abrams the money that exceeds the approved attorney fee?

INCREASING YOUR UNDERSTANDING

1. The Pellegrins retained Charles Bourque, who practiced law in Loui-
    siana. Bourque then referred the case to Abrams & Abrams in North
    Carolina, agreeing to "split any contingency fee equally." Do you think
    that Bourque is entitled to half of the considerable attorney fee? What
    does the sharing of the fee say about Abrams & Abrams's argument that
    the total contingency fee is fair?

2. The Pellegrins purchased a structured annuity with $6 million from the
    settlement. This is a complex subject, especially for the beginning of
    your study of law, but it does mean that Mark Pellegrin will receive
    regular payments from a life insurance company for 30 years.

3. The Abrams & Abrams law firm evidently did not keep track of the
    hours they spent on the case. Was that wise? Why don't you think
    they kept track of their hours?

Hypothetical

John Prentiss makes an appointment at the office of your personal injury law firm. Mr. Prentiss enters your office with noticeable difficulty with his left hip and leg. He does not walk well. His right eye and mouth seem to droop somewhat so that he has some trouble talking.

Mr. Prentiss says that he was injured in an automobile accident at the intersection of State and Main in the City of Arkansas. He says that he has only a limited memory of what happened but does remember that he was heading to work when another vehicle ran into him at this intersection. He says that there is a red light at the intersection. He is well aware that the light is there since he drives through that intersection every day, and is quite sure that he would not have driven through there unless the light facing him was green. Nevertheless, on the morning in question, he was driving through the intersection when a truck owned by the Memphis Trucking Company also entered the intersection and ran into Mr. Prentiss on the driver's side door.

Mr. Prentiss says that the collision caused numerous injuries including a badly broken hip and leg and neurological injuries to his head and face, which have not been totally assessed at this time.

Mr. Prentiss says that he heard that the Memphis truck driver claims that the light was green for him when he entered the intersection. He has been told by the police that witnesses were not sure who had the green light since the light was changing, or seemed to be, at the time of the accident. Mr. Prentiss finds this all very confusing but feels that he has been injured by the fault of someone else and should be compensated for it. That's why he came to your office.

PREPARING FOR CLASS

The senior partner in the firm you join shortly after law school has interviewed this potential client with you. She's not sure whether the firm should accept this new client or not. She has estimated that it will cost about $10,000 to get this case to the jury. She wants your opinion on this matter. Should the firm investigate further at a cost of around $1,000 for the investigation? Is this the sort of case the firm will want to take if the investigation confirms the client's version of the facts? Explain your reasoning.

B. THE INVESTIGATION

The next task is to more thoroughly investigate the facts in preparation for settlement negotiations and trial. The attorney's understanding of the law shapes investigation of the facts. Lawyers read legal opinions to find out what they must prove and where the potential weaknesses of the cases are. Reading opinions makes the lawyer sensitive to the kinds of questions to ask and what must be investigated. The client doesn't know all of the facts and may be biased about the facts she thinks she knows. Accident records of the automobile accident and all of the medical records must be obtained. These records may have to be interpreted by experts in the field. Accident reconstruction experts will be necessary for automobile accident cases, and doctors or nurses are necessary to interpret medical records. With all of this information, the attorney, with the client, will have to come up with a claim—a claim that will prevail in court.

C. DEMAND LETTER AND NEGOTIATIONS

The next major step is to tell the person who committed the tort about the claim. This can be done by writing a letter to the tortfeasor. A letter allows the parties to negotiate before the formal case begins.

PREPARING FOR CLASS

Before deciding whether to take the case, the senior partner turns the file over to you for further investigation. She tells you that we don't need every piece of information, that would be too expensive, but we need all of the important information to go to court.

1. What do you plan to investigate?

2. What documents will you obtain?

3. Approximately how much is this discovery going to cost?

4. How will you obtain these documents before the case begins?

D. STARTING THE CASE IN COURT

1. *Filing the Complaint*

The claimant goes to court by filing a complaint in the court clerk's office. The complaint must give a short and plain statement of the court's jurisdiction or power to rule in the case, a short and plain statement of the claim showing that the claimant is entitled to relief, and a demand for judgment, usually money damages. Notice to the defendant is the essence of the initial pleadings; the claimant must tell the respondent enough information so the respondent may answer and have some idea of how to defend the claim. It doesn't take a long or formal pleading to make sufficient allegations to satisfy the requirements of a complaint.

The defendant is usually insured. He or she will contact the insurance company, and it will hire a lawyer to defend the case. Part of the contract of insurance is the obligation to defend the insured.

PREPARING FOR CLASS

1. The senior partner in the law firm says that she understands that you are just out of law school, but can you put together a rough outline of the facts and theories that should be in the complaint about the hypothetical? She will put together the final draft from your outline, but what is the basic theory of the case, i.e., what did the defendant do wrong?

2. Do you have any preliminary ideas about how much this case may be worth, i.e., if the defense calls to settle, how much should we ask for?

2.   Motion to Dismiss the Complaint

Sometimes, the claimant does not make sufficient allegations to satisfy the requirements of a complaint either because the claimant's attorney is incompetent or because there are not enough facts to justify an award to the claimant. The defendant may make a motion to dismiss the complaint so that the case may be ended without the necessity of expensive discovery or a trial.

In the motion to dismiss, the judge will accept as true the allegations of the complaint as well as all reasonable inferences that can be drawn from them. The question is, looking just at the complaint, has the claimant made sufficient allegations which, if true, would justify a remedy? Usually, even if the complaint is insufficient, the judge will give the claimant a period of time (usually 30 or 60 days) to amend it. So, although the motion to dismiss sounds like a significant "gate" or limitation on the claimant's ability to proceed, it rarely is in a tort case.

3.   The Answer

If the motion to dismiss is denied, as it usually is, the respondent will file an answer, either admitting, denying, or refusing to admit or deny each of the allegations in the complaint. Actually, the respondent rarely admits and rarely denies, the safer response being to neither admit nor deny but leave the claimant to his or her proofs. The answer will tell the claimant as little as possible; why should the defendant tell the claimant anything? The only revealing part of the answer is the affirmative defenses, which are new allegations that justify the defendant's conduct or present a reason to dismiss the case. Self-defense, comparative fault, and the running of the statute of limitations are all examples of affirmative defenses. These affirmative defenses do not necessarily deny the plaintiff's allegations but plead additional facts that justify or excuse the defendant's actions. The affirmative defenses must be raised in the answer or they will be lost as a defense for the rest of the case.

4.   Discovery

Each party will want to use the help of the court to uncover more evidence, especially the evidence in the possession of the other party. There are three essential ways to do this. The most common is the deposition. Shortly after the case begins, the defendant will want to ask the plaintiff questions about the case. That can be done by bringing the plaintiff before a court reporter who swears him or her to tell the truth and then makes a record of the plaintiff's responses to the attorneys' questions. Other witnesses, including the defendant, will also be deposed. Each party may request documents, like medical reports, from the other side. And, finally, each party may seek answers to written questions called interrogatories. In large personal injury cases, discovery can be extensive and expensive.

PREPARING FOR CLASS

The senior partner reminds you that we can get most of the information necessary to litigate the case just by asking for it on behalf of the claimant, for example, medical records. Is there any information that we must obtain from the defense with the use of a court-ordered discovery process?

5.   Motion for Summary Disposition

After discovery is complete, there is a fundamental question for the court: Do we need to have a trial? Juries determine facts; judges determine the law. If there are no disputed issues of fact, then there is no need for a trial. The judge can rule on the law and issue an appropriate judgment in the matter. So, after discovery is complete, there is the question whether there are any disputed facts that require a jury trial. Often the defendant will want to avoid a trial and will file a motion for summary disposition contending that there are no disputed issues of fact and the judge can rule in the case. The standard for deciding a motion for summary disposition is whether there are any disputed facts to be determined by a jury. The party who claims that there are disputed facts will have to show those disputes usually in the form of facts developed during discovery. The judge will look at the depositions, witness affidavits, answers to interrogatories, admissions of the parties, and any other matters properly before the court, which the parties through their attorneys cite to the court to determine whether there are any disputed facts. The court will not determine the credibility of the witnesses, which is a matter for the jury as fact finder, but will look to see if there is any conflict in the evidence that requires a jury trial.

In a motion for summary disposition, there will be two essential questions to be determined: Are there disputed issues of "material" fact to be determined and, if not, does the law require a ruling in favor of one of the parties? A dispositive ruling, a ruling that ends the case with a judgment for one side or the other, may be appealed. The summary disposition of a case is a drastic resolution of the case. Summary disposition means there will not be a trial. There will be no witnesses in court and no jury to hear them. So the losing party often appeals to a higher court insisting on their right to a trial. Some jurisdictions do not favor summary disposition, preferring instead to have the case decided at a full trial with all of the witnesses before the court. Some of the federal district court cases in this casebook will be rulings on motions for summary judgment but, more often, you will read state appellate court rulings on the granting of summary judgment in the trial court.

It is important for you to notice the difference between disposition of the case on the pleadings in a motion to dismiss and the disposition of the case after discovery on a motion for summary disposition. These are different motions, coming at different times during the trial, and should not be confused.

Barbre v. Indianapolis Water Company
400 N.E.2d 1142 (Ind. App. 1980)

Buchanan, C.J.

Case Summary

Plaintiff-appellant Brett Barbre (Brett) appeals a summary judgment entered against him claiming that because there were material issues of fact involved in the controversy the trial court erred in granting summary judgment.

We affirm.

Facts

The facts[1] necessary to our disposition of this appeal are:
On July 3, 1975, Brett and five other companions planned a swimming expedition and traveled from their home in Anderson, Indiana, to Morse

---

1. Extensive pretrial discovery was conducted motions, memoranda, affidavits, answers to interrogatories, and depositions.

Reservoir, near Cicero in Hamilton County. Brett was 17 at this time and had completed his junior year of high school. He testified in his deposition that this was his first visit to this particular area of Morse Reservoir, the place where he and his friends selected for their swim.

As Brett walked towards the lake he saw no signs prohibiting swimming or trespassing nor any fences or wires constructed to keep people out. He did see other cars parked nearby and observed people swimming in the lake.

. . . In describing the water, Brett stated he realized the water was deeper towards the center of the reservoir and shallower along the banks.

After swimming for approximately one-half hour, Brett decided to dive into the water from a cliff (he had previously seen one other person dive into the water from a different location along the shore). Unfortunately he dove into shallow water and struck his head on the bottom of the reservoir. He remained conscious as several friends pulled him out of the water and laid him on the shore. His statement was that after he hit the bottom of the reservoir he had no feeling below his armpits.

As a result of this injury, Brett became a quadriplegic and spent many months in several hospitals.

On March 19, 1976, Brett filed a complaint against the Indianapolis Water Co. (Water Co.) in Hamilton Superior Court and on May 6, 1976, was allowed to amend his complaint to add Shorewood Corporation (Shorewood) as an additional defendant.[2] The complaint alleged that the negligence of either the Water Co. or Shorewood, or both, was the proximate cause of his injury.

The trial court entered summary judgment for both Water Co. and Shorewood.

ISSUES

Brett presents one issue for our consideration:

Were there genuine issues of material fact thereby rendering granting of summary judgment improper?

DECISION

PARTIES' CONTENTIONS

Brett contends there were material issues of fact as to the negligence of the defendants.

The Water Co. and Shorewood respond that they owed no duty to Brett as a trespasser (or at best a licensee) and therefore Brett took the conditions of the land as he found them.

---

2. Upon investigation after the accident, Brett discovered that defendant-appellee Water Co. owned the lake itself and defendant-appellee Shorewood owned the land surrounding the lake.

Conclusion

Because the Water Co. and Shorewood owed no duty to Brett, there were no material issues of fact in controversy. So summary judgment was proper.

The function of a summary judgment proceeding is to expedite the disposition of disputes in which there is no genuine issue of fact material to the claim involved and a party is entitled to judgment as a matter of law.

Because the effect of this procedure is to deprive the non-moving party of the right to a trial; strict standards have been established which a moving party must meet in order to prevail.

The burden is on the proponent to establish that no genuine issue as to any material fact exists. Accordingly, for purposes of determining whether to grant the motion: (a) facts set forth by the opponents' affidavits will be taken as true; (b) the depositions, admissions, etc. are to be liberally construed in favor of the opponent; and (c) any doubt as to the existence of a genuine issue as to a material fact must be resolved against the proponent of the motion. Even in cases in which the trial judge believes that the proponent of a motion for summary judgment is likely to prevail at trial, motion for summary judgment is inappropriate if any genuine issue of fact exists.

And what is a material issue of fact? It is one which may be dispositive of the case. In almost every case there are factual issues upon which the parties may disagree; a summary judgment is proper only if the resolution of these factual issues would have no bearing upon the resolution of the legal issues and the ultimate determination of the case. The facts which Brett claims are in dispute, e.g., whether the defendants knew or should have known that there was swimming in this area, whether there were fences or signs to deter swimmers, whether Brett or the defendants had acted in a reasonable fashion, go to the issue of negligence. So we must determine if the defendants, or either of them, owed a duty to Brett. There can be no negligence without breach of a duty owed to the plaintiff.

A person entering upon the land of another comes on to the land either as an invitee, a licensee, or a trespasser. The status of the person on the land determines the duty owed by the landowner to him. The facts most favorable to Brett show unequivocally that he was not an invitee. An invitee is a person who goes on to the land of another at the express or implied invitation of the owner or occupant either to transact business or for the mutual benefit of the invitee and the owner or occupant.

But is Brett a licensee or a trespasser? Even though the admitted facts do not conclusively establish Brett's legal status upon the land, the resolution of this factual question is superfluous because either as licensee or trespasser no duty was owed him.

A licensee is one who enters the premises of another for his own convenience, curiosity or entertainment. He takes the land of the owner as he finds it. The owner of the land is not liable for any defects in the condition of the land and he does not have the duty to maintain his premises in a safe condition

The only affirmative duty a land owner owes to a licensee is to refrain from willfully or wantonly injuring him or acting in a way which would increase the licensee's peril. A showing by the licensee of mere negligence on the part of the land owner will not be enough to insure him recovery. The unfortunate accident which befell Brett was not caused by any willful or wanton act of Shorewood or the Water Co. Although man-made, Morse Reservoir reflected the conditions of a natural lake. Inherent in the conditions of bodies of water are the dangers of varying depths, sharp drop offs and shallow shorelines. Because Brett testified that he was a normal 17 year old at the time of the accident, he is deemed as a matter of law, to be familiar with these dangers. Indiana case law has clearly established that even young children are presumed to understand and appreciate the dangers common to bodies of water.

Our decision here is not changed or influenced by the well-recognized doctrine of attractive nuisance or the less settled principle that a land owner owes a higher duty to a child licensee than to an adult licensee. These cases deal with infants or children of tender years and do not contemplate application to a 17 year old, one year short of graduation from high school. Brett was sui juris and the duty owed to him was that of a reasonable adult.

And so it becomes apparent from the material facts not in controversy that the defendants as landowners did not owe Brett (as a licensee or trespasser) a duty as a matter of law, and the facts in controversy are not material to resolution of the ultimate question of landowner liability. In this state it has long been the law that a showing by a licensee (or a trespasser) of defects in the land or negligence on the owner's part does not entitle him to recovery. Thus we are compelled to affirm the summary judgment.

Affirmed.

PREPARING FOR CLASS

1. The court says "Even in cases in which the trial judge believes that the proponent of a motion for summary judgment is likely to prevail at trial, motion for summary judgment is inappropriate if any genuine issue of fact exists." Why would a judge allow a case to go to trial that the judge believes is unlikely to prevail at trial?

2. What if there is no genuine issue of fact but the facts indicate the plaintiff should prevail?

3. If the claimant is entitled to a jury trial and demands a jury trial, how can a judge decide the case without a trial?

4. When should the defendant move for summary disposition: after filing the complaint, after completing discovery, or just before trial?

UNDERSTANDING THE LAW

Many jurisdictions call the pretrial dispository motion a motion for summary judgment, as in the *Barbre* case above, but other jurisdictions call it a motion for summary disposition. The motions may have slightly different rules, but they are essentially the same.

APPLYING THE LAW

Consider the hypothetical from earlier in this chapter. If you limit your consideration to the facts stated there, is summary judgment appropriate? Explain your answer. What evidence will the plaintiff seek in order to avoid summary disposition?

E. TRIAL

1. *The Trial and Motion for a Directed Verdict*

If there are disputed, material facts, then a judge or jury must resolve the disputes at a trial. The claimant will be given an opportunity at the trial to call all of the witnesses he or she desires to prove the case. The defendant may then cross-examine each witness. The defendant may also object to the admission of evidence. This may be done prior to trail in a motion in limine, i.e., a motion to prevent the opposing party from trying to admit evidence at the trail or by objecting to the admission of evidence at trial. The judge's ruling on these matters will be subject to review on appeal.

At some point in the trial, claimant will be done; the claimant will have presented all the evidence he or she has. The claimant's attorney will tell the judge that "the plaintiff rests," i.e., the plaintiff has no more evidence to present. This brings about one of the most dramatic moments of the trial. The defendant will move to dismiss since, the defendant will almost always contend, the plaintiff has not produced sufficient evidence to justify an award to the plaintiff. The defendant will argue in the motion for a directed verdict that if the judge makes all reasonable inferences in favor of the plaintiff, a reasonable juror could not find that the plaintiff has proven his or her case by a preponderance of the evidence. If not, then the defendant is entitled to the dismissal of the case. Often, the defendant will make this motion simply to preserve a right to appellate review. The appellate court will not review the wisdom of the jury verdict, but it will review whether the judge should have allowed the case to go to the jury if the motion for a directed verdict is made and denied. This is the last gate or roadblock before the jury's verdict, and it is a critical one.

If the judge denies the motion for a directed verdict, then the defense will have its turn to present evidence. After the defense presents its evidence and the claimant is given a chance for rebuttal, the proofs are closed and it is time to instruct the jury on the law that they will apply in reaching a verdict.

2.   Jury Instructions

Juries determine facts while judges determine the law, so this is the occasion for the judge to determine the law and instruct the jury. Most states have "pattern jury instructions," which have previously been determined to be proper on each particular subject by the state supreme court. Each side will propose certain jury instructions from the pattern instructions during a hearing outside the presence of the jury. It will then be up to the judge to determine which instructions to give to the jury. For instance, the claimant will insist that the jury be instructed on the lesser (preponderance of the evidence) burden of proof since the jurors will most likely have sat as jurors in criminal trials when the "beyond a reasonable doubt" standard was used. If you get a chance during your law school years, go to a trial, especially to see the judge give jury instructions. They often take an hour or more to read to the jury and are often so dull as to be incomprehensible. Yet this is one of the most common areas for reversal on appeal. If the law is misstated or an important instruction for the jury's understanding is omitted, the appellate court will have to consider whether the case must be reversed on appeal. You will see many decisions in this book when the appellate court examines the jury instruction decisions of the trial courts below.

3.   Post-Trial Motions

Following the trial, the prevailing party prepares a judgment to be signed by the judge, which gives legal effect to the jury's decision. There are then two motions that may be filed in the trial court before the matter is appealed.

The losing party may file a motion for j.n.o.v. (judgment non obstante veredicto), which asks the judge to reverse the jury's decision on the grounds that no reasonable jury could have reached this verdict.

A losing party may also make a motion for a new trial, contending that errors were made at the trial which makes the jury's decision fundamentally unfair. A motion for new trial is also made when the defendant contends that the jury's verdict is excessive.

4.   The Appeal

The losing parties in tort litigation are usually entitled to appeal the judge's decision to an appellate court as a matter of right. But they are limited in their ability to appeal to matters of law rather than the factual decisions of the jury and are further generally limited to appealing decisions that the parties objected to in the trial court below. So, the first step after filing the notice of appeal is to order the appellate record. Usually this is done by having the court reporter make a transcript of everything that was said during the trial. After the transcript is prepared, the appellant or party taking the appeal is given a certain amount of time to prepare a written brief of the appellate arguments, which the appellant contends justify a reversal on appeal. The appellee is then given a period of time to respond with its own brief. Following the submission of briefs, the appellate court sets the matter for oral argument if the parties request it. Following oral argument, the judges decide the case in a written opinion, which may or may not be released for publication. The threat of a reversal on appeal gives the parties reason to negotiate a settlement of the case.

The parties may appeal to the state supreme court after the decision of the first appellate court, but that appeal is not a matter of right; the parties must seek leave to appeal in the state supreme courts and in the U.S. Supreme Court.

Most of the decisions in this casebook are appellate court decisions; however, the decisions that are cited as Federal Supplement are usually not appellate court decisions but the decisions of the federal trial courts. Also note that different jurisdictions list the parties in the headings differently. Many list the appellant's name first, i.e., they change the order of the parties in the heading so the appealing party's name comes first. Others, including the federal system, do not change the heading on appeal, so the appellant may be the first or second name in the heading.

The printed decisions in this casebook are not usually the whole opinion of the appellate court. Most have been edited to show the legal points considered in the chapter.

F. COLLECTION

Even after the claim has survived these many gates or restrictions to winning the case and obtaining a judgment, there is still another hurdle. A judgment is not self-collecting. Someone—the claimant's attorney, usually—has to force the defendant to pay. If the defendant has liability insurance, this will be fairly easy since the insurance companies have adequate assets and usually pay without having to resort to collection procedures. If the defendant does not have insurance and has no assets, or his or her assets are exempt from collection (see tenancy by the entireties in your Property course), then the defendant will take the judgment to bankruptcy court for discharge of the obligation in the case. For those defendants with collectible assets and no insurance, collection procedures may be instituted. Garnishment of wages, seizure of assets, and debtor discovery subpoenas may be necessary to collect an unpaid judgment.

Chapter 2

Intentional Torts

A. INTRODUCTION

Cases in this chapter document the theories of liability for intentional acts. The claims covered will include battery, assault, false imprisonment, intentional infliction of emotional distress, trespass to chattel/land, and conversion. Each cause of action is unique in the elements that must be proved as well as the intrusion that the law attempts to protect against. Each element can be viewed as a means to not only define the cause of action but also as a way of promoting or discouraging recovery. Recognizing the right to be free of certain intentional intrusions is a reflection of how the law expects those in society to comport themselves. Liability is imposed to conform conduct, more specifically, to discourage conduct deemed antisocial and in some instances criminal.

Common to all of the intentional torts is the requirement that the defendant have acted intentionally. The requisite intent that must be proven is tailored to the specific claim. The first few cases will assist in honing an understanding of how the law of *intent* has developed and established rules that are common to all intentional tort claims. They will be followed by cases that address issues unique to the stated cause of action.

As is normally the case, the plaintiff carries the burden of proving each element that is required by law. Defenses/privileges to the intentional torts will be taken up in the next chapter.

B. INTENT

Bennight v. Western Auto Supply Co.
670 S.W.2d 373 (Tex. Ct. App. 1984)

POWERS, Justice.

Joe Bennight and his minor daughter, Jennifer Bennight, appeal from a judgment of the trial court that denies them recovery in their suit against Western Auto Supply Company. Their claims arose from personal injuries sustained by Cathy Bennight, their wife and mother respectively, in the course of her employment with the company. We will reverse the judgment of the trial court that Joe Bennight take nothing, rendering judgment that he recover against Western Auto in the amount found by the jury as his damages. We will affirm the judgment of the trial court that Jennifer Bennight take nothing by her suit.

THE CONTROVERSY

The rear, or warehouse area, of the Western Auto retail store where Cathy Bennight worked was shown to be infested with bats, a fact known to the manager of the store who refused to have them removed after being requested several times by employees to do so. The manager knew the bats posed a serious risk of rabies should one bite an employee, a fact pointed out to him by employees and a local health official whom employees called to the store shortly before the incident giving rise to the present suit.

Cathy Bennight was fearful of the bats, a fact communicated repeatedly to the manager. On several occasions, he nevertheless required her, over her protests, to enter the bat-infested area in the course of her work. On one particular day, she was "attacked" by bats three times while in the rear of the store. She was not bitten although one became briefly entangled in her hair. The next working day, she was bitten by a bat when the manager required that she go again to the rear of the store on a business errand. The bite necessitated anti-rabies treatment.

In the course of treatment, Cathy reacted adversely to a prescribed vaccine, becoming permanently blind and emotionally disturbed. She asserted against Western Auto a worker's compensation claim that was ultimately settled and compromised pursuant to the Workers' Compensation Act, Tex. Rev. Civ. Stat. Ann. arts. 8306-8309f (1967 & Supp.1982).

Alleging that the manager had committed an intentional tort, Joe Bennight sued Western Auto for loss of consortium. Under similar allegations, Jennifer sued for harms allegedly sustained by her as a result of her mother's injuries. These harms are discussed in more detail below.

Before trial, the district court rendered summary judgment that Jennifer take nothing by her suit. The judgment rests, in this respect, upon the ground that Jennifer possessed no cause of action of the kind alleged by her. The parties proceeded to trial on Joe Bennight's claim for loss of consortium. At the conclusion of the trial, the jury returned the following verdict in answer to special issues submitted to them:

1. Do you find from a preponderance of the evidence that on the occasion in question [the manager] required Cathy Bennight to work in the warehouse area against her will with the intention of causing her to be bitten by a bat or to be otherwise exposed to rabies?
Answer: We do not.

* * *

3. Do you find from a preponderance of the evidence that [Western Auto], through its manager, intentionally maintained an unsafe place to work?
Answer: We do.
4. Do you find from a preponderance of the evidence that on the occasion in question [the manager] required Cathy Bennight to work in the loft against her will when he knew that such place was an unsafe place to work?
Answer: We do.
5. Do you find from a preponderance of the evidence that the action described in Special Issue No. 4 was a proximate cause of physical or emotional harm to Cathy Bennight?
Answer: We do.
6. What sum of money, if any, if paid now in cash, do you find from a preponderance of the evidence would fairly and reasonably compensate Joe Bennight for loss of consortium, if any, suffered by him in the past and which, in reasonable probability, will be suffered by him in the future, resulting from physical and emotional harm sustained by Cathy Bennight, if any. By "loss of consortium" is meant the mutual right of a husband and wife to that affection, solace, comfort, companionship, society, assistance, and sexual relations necessary to a successful marriage.
Answer: $87,500.00.

The trial court rendered judgment on the verdict that Joe Bennight take nothing. This appeal ensued.

THE APPEAL OF JOE BENNIGHT

If the injury sustained by Cathy Bennight in her employment was an "accidental injury," Joe Bennight's loss of consortium is not compensable because his claim, being derivative of his wife's claim, is barred by the exclusive-remedy provision contained in the Workers' Compensation Act. If, on the other hand, Cathy's injury was the result of an *intentional* tort by the manager, her husband's claim for loss of consortium is not barred by the Act, for the bar extends only to "accidental injuries." By Cathy's settlement and compromise under the act, she is estopped from further recovery against Western Auto. The parties concede the foregoing rules. Their dispute is whether the jury's verdict establishes that Cathy's injury was accidental or intentional.

The parties' respective contentions center upon the nature of the intent required in order that a tort might be classified as "intentional." Joe Bennight argues that the requisite intent refers to an intentional breach of a duty owed by an employer to his employee, here the duty of furnishing a safe place to work, so that an "intentional tort" results when such a breach of duty is the proximate cause of harm to some legally protected interest of the employee. Western Auto argues, on the other hand, that the intent required for an "intentional tort" is more circumscribed—that nothing short of an actual intent by the employer to injure the employee will suffice; and, moreover, the employer must intend to injure the employee: (1) in the precise way in which he was in fact injured and (2) in the specific legally protected interest in which he was in fact injured. Given their respective positions in argument, the parties are able to assign opposite meaning and effect to the jury's verdict in the present case.[1]

Joe Bennight contends that Western Auto was under a duty to furnish his wife a safe place to work. Tex. Rev. Civ. Stat. Ann. art. 5182a, §3(a) (1971). He argues that the verdict establishes a breach of that duty by the manager when he intentionally maintained the workplace in an unsafe condition and required Cathy to work there, as the jury found in answer to special issues 3 and 4. Therefore, when the jury's answers as to proximate cause and damages are coupled with those in response to special issues 3 and 4, Joe Bennight contends that the verdict establishes an intentional tort for which he was entitled to judgment on the verdict, notwithstanding the jury's answer to special issue 1.

Western Auto urges the terms of section 8A, Restatement (Second) of Torts (1965). That section provides:

> The word "intent" is used throughout the Restatement of this Subject to denote that the actor desires to cause the consequences of his act, or that he believes that the consequences are substantially certain to result from it.

---

1. . . . Western Auto urges a theory that narrows even further what we have called the "prevailing view": not only must the employee prove that the actor intended actually to injure him, he must prove that the actor intended to injure him *in a specific way* and *in a specific legally protected interest.* While some decisions in other jurisdictions involve factual situations where the employee *could* only have been injured in one way, and in only one legally protected interest, we find no authority for the rule advanced by Western Auto.

Joe Bennight argues that an employee need prove only that the actor intentionally breached a duty owed to the employee. . . .

The trial court decided the case by applying to the jury verdict the severely restricted version of the prevailing view advanced by Western Auto. As noted in the text of this opinion, Western Auto's variation of the prevailing view is contrary to that view considered in its entirety. More importantly, Western Auto's variation would require that we reject the principle of the Texas precedents discussed in the text of this opinion, a principle that forbids the variation advanced by Western Auto without rejecting the prevailing view mentioned above. Conversely, that principle requires that Bennight recover on the jury verdict even under the prevailing view, a view necessarily applied as well by the trial court because it constitutes the foundation upon which Western Auto erects the more constrictive extension for which it contends. *The principle is, of course, that an actor's intent to injure by his unlawful act extends by operation of law to consequences which, while unintended, are legally caused by his act.* Under this principle, the jury's verdict harmonizes itself and requires that Bennight recover, whether under the prevailing view or under Bennight's theory. This principle is long-established in Texas jurisprudence as discussed in the text of this opinion.

The comments under the section give further meaning to the foregoing black-letter statement. The word "intent" refers "to the consequences of an act rather than the act itself" and "is limited, wherever it is used, to the consequences of the act." However, "intent" to cause particular consequences is not limited to those consequences which the actor "desires," but includes those which he knows are certain, or substantially certain, to result from his act. The charge to the jury defined "intent" substantially in the sense supplied by section 8A and the comments thereunder.

Based upon the foregoing definition of "intent," Western Auto points to the jury's answer to special issue 1 and argues that it confirms that the manager did *not* commit an intentional tort because the jury's answer establishes that: (1) the manager did not intend the particular consequences (that is, being bitten by a bat and exposed to rabies) which followed from his requiring Cathy Bennight to work in the warehouse; and (2) those consequences were not certain or substantially certain to result from the manager's act.

We believe Western Auto's position to be unsound because it leaves no room for a legal principle well-established both in the Restatement itself and in several Texas decisions. The principle is this: the unlawful and intentional invasion of *one* legally protected interest of another will supply the intent necessary to hold the actor liable for the unintended consequences of his act when some *other* legally protected interest of the victim is harmed in consequence of the act. The jury's answer to special issue 1 establishes only that the manager did not intend that Cathy be bitten by a bat and exposed to rabies; it does *not* establish, as a matter of law, that he committed no intentional tort against Cathy, for as we will discuss below, the jury's answer to the remaining special issues established that he intentionally committed an assault against her and his intent in *that* regard is imputed *by operation of law* to the actual harm which did occur with catastrophic results.

Section 8A of the Restatement must, of course, be interpreted in conjunction with other related sections. Section 16, entitled "Character of Intent Necessary," referring to the intentional tort of "battery," illustrates the imputation of intent to the harm which actually resulted, although the actor intended by his act an invasion of some other legally protected interest.

> (1) If an act is done with the intention . . . of putting another in apprehension of either a harmful or offensive bodily contact, and such act causes a bodily contact to the other, the actor is liable to the other for a battery although the act was not done with the intention of bringing about the resulting bodily harm.

See also section 435B of the Restatement, entitled "Unintended Consequences of Intentional Invasions." We turn then to *whether* the jury's answers to the remaining special issues established the infliction of an intentional tort against Cathy by the manager.

The jury found in answer to special issues 3 and 5 that the manager intentionally failed to provide Cathy a safe place to work and required her to work there "against her will." The jury also found affirmatively on the issue of proximate cause and established the amount of damages necessary to compensate Joe Bennight for his loss of consortium. The phrase "against her will," as used in special issue 3, establishes that the manager intentionally placed Cathy Bennight in apprehension of being bitten or otherwise attacked *again* by a bat if she were required to work in the loft. The phrase can have no other meaning under the pleadings and the evidence. Intentionally placing Cathy in such fear was an "assault," an invasion of her personality, and an independent intentional tort in and of itself. More to the point for our present purposes, the manager's intention to place Cathy in such apprehension extends by operation of law to the specific additional injury which she did receive and for which she sought recovery, *whether or not* the manager in fact intended that additional and subsequent harm.

Notwithstanding the fiction employed — whether the intent be "imputed," "presumed," "implied," "constructive," or even "transferred" — various Texas decisions illustrate the principle. *Hill v. Kimball*, 76 Tex. 210, 13 S.W. 59 (1890) (defendant liable to bystander, a pregnant woman who miscarried, for injuries sustained by her if proximately caused by defendant's intentional and wrongful beating of others in her presence); *City of Garland v. White*, 368 S.W.2d 12 (Tex. Civ. App. 1963, writ ref'd n.r.e.) (defendant who intentionally and wrongfully shot plaintiff's dog liable for unintended injuries to plaintiff in form of mental pain and suffering and physical damage to his house caused by the shotgun blast);*Whitehead v. Zeiller*, 265 S.W.2d 689 (Tex. Civ. App. 1954, no writ) (defendant who intentionally and wrongfully removes lateral support from land owned by plaintiff is liable for unintended consequences of soil erosion, destruction of trees, and deprivation of use); *Morrow v. Flores*, 225 S.W.2d 621 (Tex. Civ. App. 1949, writ ref'd n.r.e.) (defendant liable for injury to plaintiff when defendant intended by his act to commit battery against third person).

The jury found in answer to special issues 3 and 4, under the interpretation we have given them, that the store manager intentionally placed Cathy Bennight in apprehension of a harmful or offensive bodily contact with a bat. We hold, accordingly, that the jury's verdict established that the manager committed against Cathy Bennight an "intentional tort" and that the trial court erred in its judgment that Joe Bennight take nothing by his suit. We render judgment for him in the sum of $87,500.00, the amount found by the jury as his damages proximately caused by the manager's intentional tort.

The Appeal of Jennifer Bennight

Jennifer Bennight sued Western Auto for money damages as compensation for three categories of harm allegedly sustained by her as a result of the store manager's intentional tort against her mother: (1) mental anguish resulting from Jennifer's observing her mother's injuries and suffering; (2) loss and impairment of certain intangible aspects of her relationship with her mother, that is, her mother's affection, solace, comfort, companionship, society, and assistance; and (3) impairment of Jennifer's legal right to receive from her mother financial support.

We hold that Jennifer's petition did not state a cause of action allowable under the laws of this State. We therefore affirm the judgment of the trial court that she take nothing by her suit.

It is difficult "on the basis of natural justice to reach the conclusion that this type of action will not lie." The difficulty issues from the obvious reality of such injuries to a child when a parent suffers injuries such as those sustained by Cathy Bennight. One should think that in the ordinary case each family member would probably suffer a loss in much the same way. The difficulty arises as well from the incongruity of allowing certain family members, but not others, to recover for substantially the same harm suffered by each. May it logically be said that Joe Bennight's relationship with Cathy Bennight was harmed in this instance but Jennifer's relationship with the same person was not, assuming the proof showed a normal family relationship? Is Jennifer's interest less deserving of legal protection than that of Joe Bennight?

Quite obviously, the cause of action for which Jennifer contends would require the adjustment of several established legal principles. For example, one not present at the scene of injury to another is ordinarily not entitled to recover for mental anguish occasioned by the other's injury. Ordinarily, the perpetrator of an intentional tort is not liable for loss of support sustained by those dependent upon the victim. A primary purpose of the Workers' Compensation Act is to supply the injured employee money damages in compensation for his lost earning capacity, posing the obvious possibility of double recovery if those dependent upon the employee may recover for their loss of support in actions based upon intentional torts. There are other difficulties as well. On the other hand, the difficulty of proving the reality of injury and attendant money damages and the possibilities of speculation by the fact finder would appear to present no barrier in such a cause of action, given that such harms are routinely compensated in actions under the wrongful death statute.

We deal not merely with allowing a certain element of damages to be recovered by a plaintiff—to hold Western Auto to answer for Jennifer's allegations would require the establishment of a new duty in favor of a new class of persons. In *Garza v. Garza*, 209 S.W.2d 1012 (Tex. Civ. App. 1948, no writ), minor children sued "the other woman" for alienation of their father's affection, by reason of which they lost his affection and support. In reversing a judgment for the children, the appellate court declined to create in the children a new common law right of action, expressly basing its decision upon deference to the Legislature. This is the only pertinent Texas decision we have found; other jurisdictions are divided in various ways on the matter. It is not the role of an intermediate appellate court to create a new cause of action. We too must leave the matter to the Legislature or the Supreme Court of Texas.

See Sanchez v. Schindler, 651 S.W.2d 249 (Tex. 1983). We therefore affirm the judgment of the trial court as to the claim of Jennifer Bennight.

The judgment of the trial court is reversed insofar as it orders that Joe Bennight take nothing by his suit. We render judgment that he recover from Western Auto the sum of $87,500, together with post-judgment interest, from the date of the judgment below, as provided by law.

Reversed and Rendered in Part and Affirmed in Part.

PREPARING FOR CLASS

Typically in tort actions, liability is determined by what is foreseeable or directly traceable to the tortious conduct. Within these standards there arguably lies the right for close relatives to recover for the harm to the relationship they had with the party who was directly injured by the defendant. These claims (Joe's and Jennifer's) are called derivative as they are derived from the wrong to someone (Cathy) other than the party seeking recovery. These claims will be discussed in more detail in Torts II, as will the Workers' Compensation laws.

INCREASING YOUR UNDERSTANDING

1. We start the intentional tort discussion with *Bennight* for one prominent reason: to illustrate the scope of liability for intentional torts, which then sets the proper context for the discussion on intent that follows. Paying damages is the end game to liability, something that defendants want to avoid whenever possible. But compensating the injured and deterring conduct are the two prominent goals behind tort law, so whenever a liability rule is fashioned, courts (or legislators) seek to harmonize the rules with the goals.

2. Scope of intentional tort liability. The rule in *Bennight* is the rule followed in most courts; the intentional tortfeasor is liable for all harm that flows from the wrongdoing notwithstanding the lack of strict "foreseeability." This means that trespassing defendants may be liable for a heart attack that ensues after an argument with the plaintiff over the trespass (Baker v. Shymkiv, 6 Ohio St. 3d 151, 451 N.E.2d 811 (1983)), a trespassing defendant who fails to remove a stake to a fence leads to the death of the operator of a lawn mowing machine is liable in wrongful death (Rogers v. Board of Road Comm'rs for Kent County, 319 Mich. 661, 30 N.W.2d 3588 (Mich. 1947)), and a defendant is liable for causing a pregnant bystander to miscarry after she witnessed the defendant's intentional and wrongful beating of others (Hill v. Kimball, 76 Tex. 210, 13 S.W. 59 (1890)).

3. The Supreme Court of Texas later recognized a cause of action by a child for loss of a parent's consortium in Reagan v. Vaughn, 804 S.W.2d 463 (Tex.1990).

Garratt v. Dailey
46 Wash. 2d 197, 279 P.2d 1091 (Wash. 1955)

HILL, Justice.

The liability of an infant for an alleged battery is presented to this court for the first time. Brian Dailey (age five years, nine months) was visiting with Naomi Garratt, an adult and a sister of the plaintiff, Ruth Garratt, likewise an adult, in the back yard of the plaintiff's home, on July 16, 1951. It is plaintiff's contention that she came out into the back yard to talk with Naomi and that, as she started to sit down in a wood and canvas lawn chair, Brian deliberately pulled it out from under her. The only one of the three persons present so testifying was Naomi Garratt. (Ruth Garratt, the plaintiff, did not testify as to how or why she fell.) The trial court, unwilling to accept this testimony, adopted instead Brian Dailey's version of what happened, and made the following findings:

> "... that while Naomi Garratt and Brian Dailey were in the back yard the plaintiff, Ruth Garratt, came out of her house into the back yard. Some time subsequent thereto defendant, Brian Dailey, picked up a lightly built wood and canvas lawn chair which was then and there located in the back yard of the above described premises, moved it sideways a few feet and seated himself therein, at which time he discovered the plaintiff, Ruth Garratt, about to sit down at the place where the lawn chair had formerly been, at which time he hurriedly got up from the chair and attempted to move it toward Ruth Garratt to aid her in sitting down in the chair; that due to the defendant's small size and lack of dexterity he was unable to get the lawn chair under the plaintiff in time to prevent her from falling to the ground. That plaintiff fell to the ground and sustained a fracture of her hip, and other injuries and damages as hereinafter set forth.
>
> "IV. That the preponderance of the evidence in this case establishes that when the defendant, Brian Dailey, moved the chair in question *he did not have any wilful or unlawful purpose* in doing so; that *he did not have any intent to injure the plaintiff, or any intent to bring about any unauthorized or offensive contact with her person* or any objects appurtenant thereto; that the circumstances which immediately preceded the fall of the plaintiff established that the defendant, *Brian Dailey, did not have purpose, intent or design to perform a prank or to effect an assault and battery upon the person of the plaintiff.*" (Italics ours, for a purpose hereinafter indicated.)

It is conceded that Ruth Garratt's fall resulted in a fractured hip and other painful and serious injuries. To obviate the necessity of a retrial in the event this court determines that she was entitled to a judgment against Brian Dailey, the amount of her damage was found to be $11,000. Plaintiff appeals from a judgment dismissing the action and asks for the entry of a judgment in that amount or a new trial.

The authorities generally, but with certain notable exceptions, see Bohlen, "Liability in Tort of Infants and Insane Persons," 23 Mich. L. Rev. 9, state that when a minor has committed a tort with force he is liable to be proceeded against as any other person would be.

In our analysis of the applicable law, we start with the basis premise that Brian, whether five or fifty-five, must have committed some wrongful act before he could be liable for appellant's injuries.

The trial court's finding that Brian was a visitor in the Garratt back yard is supported by the evidence and negatives appellant's assertion that Brian was a trespasser and had no right to touch, move, or sit in any chair in that yard, and that contention will not receive further consideration.

It is urged that Brian's action in moving the chair constituted a battery. A definition (not all-inclusive but sufficient for our purpose) of a battery is the intentional infliction of a harmful bodily contact upon another. The rule that determines liability for battery is given in 1 Restatement, Torts, 29, §13, as:

> "An act which, directly or indirectly, is the legal cause of a harmful contact with another's person makes the actor liable to the other, if
>
> "(a) the act is done with the intention of bringing about a harmful or offensive contact or an apprehension thereof to the other or a third person, and
>
> "(b) the contact is not consented to by the other or the other's consent thereto is procured by fraud or duress, and
>
> "(c) the contact is not otherwise privileged."

We have in this case no question of consent or privilege. We therefore proceed to an immediate consideration of intent and its place in the law of battery. In the comment on clause (a), the Restatement says:

> "*Character of actor's intention.* In order that an act may be done with the intention of bringing about a harmful or offensive contact or an apprehension thereof to a particular person, either the other or a third person, the act must be done for the purpose of causing the contact or apprehension or with knowledge on the part of the actor that such contact or apprehension is substantially certain to be produced."

See, also, Prosser on Torts 41, §8.

We have here the conceded volitional act of Brian, *i.e.*, the moving of a chair. Had the plaintiff proved to the satisfaction of the trial court that Brian moved the chair while she was in the act of sitting down, Brian's action would patently have been for the purpose or with the intent of causing the plaintiff's bodily contact with the ground, and she would be entitled to a judgment against him for the resulting damages.

The plaintiff based her case on that theory, and the trial court held that she failed in her proof and accepted Brian's version of the facts rather than that given by the eyewitness who testified for the plaintiff. After the trial court determined that the plaintiff had not established her theory of a battery (*i.e.*, that Brian had pulled the chair out from under the plaintiff while she was in the act of sitting down), it then became concerned with whether a battery was established under the facts as it found them to be.

In this connection, we quote another portion of the comment on the "Character of actor's intention," relating to clause (a) of the rule from the Restatement heretofore set forth:

> "It is not enough that the act itself is intentionally done and this, even though the actor realizes or should realize that it contains a very grave risk of bringing about the contact or apprehension. Such realization may make the actor's conduct negligent or even reckless but unless he realizes that to a substantial certainty, the contact or apprehension will result, the actor has not that intention which is necessary to make him liable under the rule stated in this section."

A battery would be established if, in addition to plaintiff's fall, it was proved that, when Brian moved the chair, he knew with substantial certainty that the plaintiff would attempt to sit down where the chair had been. If Brian had any of the intents which the trial court found, in the italicized portions of the findings of fact quoted above, that he did not have, he would of course have had the knowledge to which we have referred. The mere absence of any intent to injure the plaintiff or to play a prank on her or to embarrass her, or to commit an assault and battery on her would not absolve him from liability if in fact he had such knowledge. Without such knowledge, there would be nothing wrongful about Brian's act in moving the chair and, there being no wrongful act, there would be no liability.

While a finding that Brian had no such knowledge can be inferred from the findings made, we believe that before the plaintiff's action in such a case should be dismissed there should be no question but that the trial court had passed upon that issue; hence, the case should be remanded for clarification of the findings to specifically cover the question of Brian's knowledge, because intent could be inferred there from. If the court finds that he had such knowledge the necessary intent will be established and the plaintiff will be entitled to recover, even though there was no purpose to injure or embarrass the plaintiff. If Brian did not have such knowledge, there was no wrongful act by him and the basic premise of liability on the theory of a battery was not established.

It will be noted that the law of battery as we have discussed it is the law applicable to adults, and no significance has been attached to the fact that Brian was a child less than six years of age when the alleged battery occurred. The only circumstance where Brian's age is of any consequence is in determining what he knew, and there his experience, capacity, and understanding are of course material.

From what has been said, it is clear that we find no merit in plaintiff's contention that we can direct the entry of a judgment for $11,000 in her favor on the record now before us.

Nor do we find any error in the record that warrants a new trial.

. . . The cause is remanded for clarification, with instructions to make definite findings on the issue of whether Brian Dailey knew with substantial certainty that the plaintiff would attempt to sit down where the chair which he moved had been, and to change the judgment if the findings warrant it.

Remanded for clarification.

PREPARING FOR CLASS

1. There are two distinct versions of what happened on the day of the injury that gave rise to the lawsuit. Make sure you give consideration to both.

2. Unlike negligent actions, it is generally understood that there is no minimum age for intentional tortfeasor liability. States, though, often require that children have reached a certain age before there can be liability for their negligent actions.

3. Rarely will defendants accused of intentional torts admit that they intended the intrusion of which they are accused. Often, courts and juries will have to look into the circumstances to determine if the defendant acted with the requisite intent. The task becomes more difficult when children are involved because of their lack of experience/intelligence/education, and frankly because of the societal resistance in believing that a child might act in such a way.

4. To avoid litigation costs, it is common practice for the trial court to answer the damages question even if it finds that the defendant was not liable. In the event of a retrial, only the liability issue will have to be resolved. In this case, upon reconsideration and substantial guidance from the Washington Supreme Court, the trial court entered a judgment for the plaintiff.

APPLYING THE LAW

Defendant, intoxicated after an evening of heavy drinking, strikes a pedestrian crossing the street while driving home. Is she liable for battery?

INCREASING YOUR UNDERSTANDING

The Restatement (Second) of Torts §8A provides:

> "The word "intent" is used . . . to denote that the actor desires to cause consequences of his act, or that he believes that the consequences are substantially certain to result from it."

It would more useful to replace the word consequences with intrusion, as courts are disinterested for the most part in what the defendant's state of mind was beyond whether he intended to improperly intrude upon the plaintiff. As such for battery in *Dailey*, the question is not whether Brian intended to fracture Garratt's hip but instead did he intend the contact that eventually resulted in her injuries. The next case reiterates this approach.

Masters v. Becker
22 A.D.2d 118, 254 N.Y.S.2d 633 (N.Y. App. Div. 1964)

Christ, J.

The single question is whether, with respect to a cause of action for assault, the definition of intent given by the trial court in its charge and in its ruling on an exception and a request to charge constituted reversible error. The court stated that the plaintiffs were required to establish that the infant defendant intended the act that resulted in injury, that she intended to commit an injury, and that she intended the very injury sustained by the infant plaintiff. The court also posed the question: "Can a nine-year old, by her action, intend the injury which resulted in this case?" To all this plaintiffs' counsel took an exception and requested the court to charge that plaintiffs were required to establish only that "the act was done with intent to inflict an offensive bodily contact." The court refused such request to charge and adhered to its previous instructions.

When the injury occurred, the infant plaintiff Susan Masters was about six years of age and the infant defendant Claudia Becker was about nine years of age. They, together with Claudia's sister, were playing on a motor truck in an empty lot, and Susan was standing on a narrow ledge on the outside of the truck's tailgate. Claudia told or at least urged Susan to get off; and Susan refused and cried, saying she was frightened. Then Claudia pried Susan's fingers off the tailgate and Susan fell to the ground, sustaining severe injuries. Claudia's testimony indicated that the reason for her act was to force Susan to give Claudia and her sister their turns to get onto the ledge so that they could jump off.

The correct rule as to intent is set forth in the American Law Institute's Restatement of the Law (Restatement, Torts, vol. 1, §16, subd. [1]), namely: that intent is established "If an act is done with the intention of inflicting upon another an offensive but not a harmful bodily contact or of putting another in apprehension of either a harmful or offensive bodily contact, and such act causes a bodily contact to the other . . . although the act was not done with the intention of bringing about the resulting bodily harm."

The law as thus stated has been followed in *Baldinger v. Banks* (26 Misc. 2d 1086) which case was approved by this court in a subsequent connected case (*Baldinger v. Consolidated Mut. Ins. Co.*, 15 A.D.2d 526, affd).

A plaintiff in an action to recover damages for an assault founded on bodily contact must prove only that there was bodily contact; that such contact was offensive; and that the defendant intended to make the contact. The plaintiff is not required to prove that defendant intended physically to injure him. Certainly he is not required to prove an intention to cause the specific injuries resulting from the contact.

Hence, the trial court's rulings and instructions were not in harmony with the law. On the facts a jury could well find that Claudia intended only to force Susan off the truck, without any thought of injuring her. It could also find that Claudia intended the bodily contact she was forcing upon Susan; and that, although this was not harmful in itself, it was offensive to Susan. Under a correct instruction, findings of the presence of such intent would be sufficient for holding Claudia responsible for the ensuing injury. In requiring plaintiffs to establish that Claudia in fact intended an injury and even the very injury that Susan sustained, the trial court was in error. Such instruction imposed on plaintiffs an excessive burden and made it highly improbable that the jury would find in favor of plaintiffs.

In *Baldinger v. Banks* (supra), where the correct rule was applied, liability was found against an even younger child than Claudia. There, the act of a six-year-old boy was not significantly dissimilar to Claudia's. He resented the four-year-old infant plaintiff's presence on a lawn where he was playing and he pushed her. She fell to the ground and sustained severe injuries. A substantial recovery was awarded against the boy.

As the error in the instant case was highly prejudicial, the judgment should be reversed on the law, and a new trial granted, with costs to plaintiffs to abide the event.

PREPARING FOR CLASS

Improper jury instructions often are subjects of appeals by parties who lose at the trial-court level. Most states have "Model Jury Instructions," which have either been articulated by the state's supreme court or legislature. If an improper instruction has been given and the court of appeals finds that the failure to give the correct instruction may have caused the jury to come to an improper decision, the trial court's error is deemed "reversible" and a new trial will likely be ordered. This is not to say that the next jury won't come to exactly the same conclusion, it just means that whatever conclusion is eventually arrived at will have involved the right process.

Shaw v. Brown & Williamson Tobacco Corp.
973 F. Supp. 539 (D. Md. 1997)

WALTER E. BLACK, JR.

Plaintiffs allege the following facts. Robert T. Shaw was employed as a long distance truck driver with the Kelly-Springfield Tire Company from 1968 to 1991. From May 1, 1973 to November 14, 1984, Shaw routinely traveled in an enclosed truck with a co-worker who smoked Raleigh cigarettes, which are manufactured, produced, and distributed by Brown & Williamson. Shaw did not smoke cigarettes at any time during his employment with Kelly-Springfield. Nevertheless, Shaw was diagnosed with lung cancer in 1992. Shaw and his wife allege that he developed lung cancer as a result of his exposure to second-hand or environmental tobacco smoke (hereinafter "ETS") emitted from the Raleigh cigarettes.

Defendant challenges plaintiffs' ability to establish that Brown & Williamson had the intent necessary to commit a battery. Under Maryland law, "[a] battery is the 'unpermitted application of trauma by one person upon the body of another person.'"

"[T]he tort of battery requires intent by the actor 'to bring about a harmful or offensive contact. . . . [It is] confined to intentional invasions of the interests in freedom from harmful or offensive contact.'" Accidental contact does not constitute a battery because "[w]here an accident occurs, . . . the actor would not have *intended* to invade the other's interest." A defendant in a battery action need not have intended to do harm, however, as the crux of a battery claim is an absence of consent on the part of the plaintiff. *Ghassemieh v. Schafer*, 52 Md. App. 31, 38, 447 A.2d 84 (1982). Nevertheless, he must have done some affirmative act and must have known that an unpermitted contact was substantially certain to follow from that act. Indeed, it is this intent that separates battery from mere negligence:

> "In negligence, the actor does not desire to bring about the consequences that follow, nor does he know that they are substantially certain to occur, or believe that they will. There is merely a risk of such consequences, sufficiently great to lead a reasonable man in his position to anticipate them, and to guard against them. If an automobile driver runs down a man in the street before him, with the desire to hit him, or with the belief that he is certain to do so, it is an intentional battery; but if he has no such desire or belief, but merely acts unreasonably in failing to guard against a risk which he should appreciate, it is negligence."

Id. at 41, 447 A.2d 84 (quoting Prosser, *Law of Torts* §31, at 145 (4th ed. 1971)).

Plaintiffs argue that the intent requirement is satisfied by Brown & Williamson's intentional manufacture, marketing, and distribution of Raleigh cigarettes, on the basis that such acts "set[ ] in motion the inevitable series of events leading to plaintiff Robert Shaw's injuries." The Court disagrees.

In *Pechan v. DynaPro, Inc.*, 251 Ill. App. 3d 1072, 190 Ill. Dec. 698, 622 N.E.2d 108 (1993), a plaintiff alleged that her former employer was liable for her exposure to second-hand cigarette smoke in the workplace. The appellate court affirmed the dismissal of plaintiff's battery count, finding that the employer could not, as a matter of law, have had the intent necessary to commit a battery. The *Pechan* court reasoned that "[s]moking is a legal activity and not an act of battery because, generally, smokers do not smoke cigarettes with the intent to touch nonsmokers with secondhand smoke." Similarly, Brown & Williamson does not manufacture, market, or distribute cigarettes for the purpose of touching non-smokers with second-hand smoke. Furthermore, Brown & Williamson did not know with a substantial degree of certainty that second-hand smoke would touch any particular non-smoker. While it may have had knowledge that second-hand smoke would reach some non-smokers, the Court finds that such generalized knowledge is insufficient to satisfy the intent requirement for battery. Indeed, as defendant points out, a finding that Brown & Williamson has committed a battery by manufacturing cigarettes would be tantamount to holding manufacturers of handguns liable in battery for exposing third parties to gunfire. Such a finding would expose the courts to a flood of farfetched and nebulous litigation concerning the tort of battery. It is unsurprising that neither plaintiffs nor the Court have been able to unearth any case where a manufacturer of cigarettes or handguns was found to have committed a battery against those allegedly injured by its products.

Accordingly, dismissal is appropriate with respect to [plaintiff's battery claim].

PREPARING FOR CLASS

1. Cigarette manufacturers have been frequent targets in tort litigation, with causes of actions against them ranging from products liability to intentional torts. Plaintiffs have been creative in their prosecution of the companies, with some of the creativity resulting from juries being unwilling to find liability under traditional theories because of how the plaintiff was voluntarily involved in the decision to smoke. Though not a smoker, Robert Shaw might be found contributorily negligent for riding in an enclosed vehicle with a smoker and, as such, might be barred from recovering unless the defendant was found to have acted intentionally.

2. Is the actual smoker a batterer? What additional facts would help in your determination?

APPLYING THE LAW

Human-Immunodeficiency-Virus-infected (HIV) man has sex with woman who then contracts the virus. Can she prove intent for battery? What additional facts would help in reaching a decision?

INCREASING YOUR UNDERSTANDING

If Brown & Williamson didn't intend for people to smoke, what was its intent behind selling cigarettes? Is it really a stretch to conclude that Brown & Williamson wasn't at least substantially certain that non-smokers would come in contact with cigarette smoke? Here the court construed strictly the intent requirement because of the potential ramifications should it rule in favor of the plaintiffs on their theory. At a minimum, courts require something more than a voluntary act; the act complained of must have been done with the intent to intrude upon someone consistent with the theory of one of the intentional torts.

Ranson v. Kitner
31 Ill. App. 241 (Ill. App. Ct. 1889)

CONGER, J.

This was an action brought by appellee against appellants to recover the value of a dog killed by appellants, and a judgment rendered for $50.

The defense was that appellants were hunting for wolves, that appellee's dog had a striking resemblance to a wolf, that they in good faith believed it to be one, and killed it as such.

Many points are made, and a lengthy argument filed to show that error in the trial below was committed, but we are inclined to think that no material error occurred to the prejudice of appellants.

The jury held them liable for the value of the dog, and we do not see how they could have done otherwise under the evidence. Appellants are clearly liable for the damages caused by their mistake, notwithstanding they were acting in good faith.

We see no reason for interfering with the conclusion reached by the jury, and the judgment will be affirmed.

Judgment affirmed.

PREPARING FOR CLASS

1. A good weight of intentional tort law has developed in cases involving conduct that either was criminal or came to the edges of criminality. As

such, it should not surprise that some defendants have attempted to avoid liability by relying on the lack of evil motive or intent.

2. What is the defendant asking the court to do? Privilege his acts, or create an intent rule that would favor him in this case? If the latter, what do you think the defendant is proposing?

Talmage v. Smith
101 Mich. 370, 59 N.W. 656 (Mich. 1894)

MONTGOMERY, J.

The plaintiff recovered in an action of trespass. The case made by plaintiff's proofs was substantially as follows: On the evening of September 11, 1891, some limekilns were burning a short distance from defendant's premises, in Portland, Ionia County. Defendant had on his premises certain sheds. He came up to the vicinity of the sheds, and saw six or eight boys on the roof of one of them. He claims that he ordered the boys to get down, and they at once did so. He then passed around to where he had a view of the roof of another shed, and saw two boys on the roof. The defendant claims that he did not see the plaintiff, and the proof is not very clear that he did, although there was some testimony from which it might have been found that he was within his view. Defendant ordered the boys in sight to get down, and there was testimony tending to show that the two boys in defendant's view started to get down at once. Before they succeeded in doing so, however, defendant took a stick, which is described as being two inches in width, and of about the same thickness, and about 16 inches long, and threw it in the direction of the boys; and there was testimony tending to show that it was thrown at one of the boys in view of the defendant. The stick missed him, and hit the plaintiff just above the eye with such force as to inflict an injury which resulted in the total loss of the sight of the eye. Counsel for the defendant contends that the undisputed testimony shows that defendant threw the stick without intending to hit anybody, and that under the circumstances, if it in fact hit the plaintiff—defendant not knowing that he was on the shed—he was not liable. We cannot understand why these statements should find a place in the brief of defendant's counsel. George Talmage, the plaintiff's father, testifies that defendant said to him that he threw the stick, intending it for Byron Smith—one of the boys on the roof—and this is fully supported by the circumstances of the case. It is hardly conceivable that this testimony escaped the attention of defendant's counsel.

The circuit judge charged the jury as follows: "If you conclude that Smith did not know the Talmage boy was on the shed, and that he did not intend to hit Smith, or the young man that was with him, but simply, by throwing the stick, intended to frighten Smith, or the other young man that was there, and the club hit Talmage, and injured him, as claimed, then the plaintiff could not recover. If you conclude that Smith threw the stick or club at Smith, or the young man that was with Smith—intended to hit one or the other of them—and you also conclude that the throwing of the stick or club was, under the circumstances, reasonable, and not excessive, force to use towards Smith and the other young man, then there would be no recovery by this plaintiff. But if you conclude from the evidence in this case that he threw the stick, intending to hit Smith, or the young man with him—to hit one of them—and that that force was unreasonable force, under all the circumstances, then Smith, you see (the defendant), would be doing an unlawful act, if the force was unreasonable, because he has no right to use it. Then he would be doing an unlawful act. He would be liable then for the injury done to this boy with the stick, if he threw it intending to hit the young man Smith, or the young man that was with Smith on the roof; and the force that he was using, by the throwing of the club, was excessive and unreasonable, under all the circumstances of the case, if it was, and then the stick went on and hit the boy, as it seems to have hit him, if it was unreasonable and excessive, then he would be liable for the consequences of it, because he was doing an unlawful act in the outset; that is, he was using unreasonable and unnecessary force—excessive force—against Smith and the young man, to get them off the shed." We think the charge a very fair statement of the law of the case. The doctrine of contributory negligence could have no place in the case. The plaintiff, in climbing from the shed, could not have anticipated the throwing of the missile, and the fact that he was a trespasser did not place him beyond the pale of the law. The right of the plaintiff to recover was made to depend upon an intention on the part of the defendant to hit somebody, and to inflict an unwarranted injury upon some one. Under these circumstances, the fact that the injury resulted to another than was intended does not relieve the defendant from responsibility. The cases cited in defendant's brief, we think, support this rule. The case is to be distinguished from a case of negligence on the part of defendant. The act is found by the jury to have been a willful act.

The judgment will be affirmed, with costs.

PREPARING FOR CLASS

1. A trespass by contact to a person is a battery.

2. Rules are fashioned by the authorities when motivated to affect change in behavior or afford avenues of redress. You therefore will occasionally hear that "extreme or bad facts make bad law." This is not to say that the doctrine of "transferred intent" is valueless, simply to say that it would have been tremendously difficult for the *Talmage* court to leave young Mr. Smith with no remedy as against someone who conducted himself the way Talmage did.

3. What of Talmage's claim that he had no intent to hit the plaintiff; where does it find its legal basis?

4. There would have been no liability had Talmage been reasonably defending his property against the trespassers. Don't let the status of

the youths as trespassers, therefore, cloud your ability to receive the rule and evaluate the appropriateness of it.

APPLYING THE LAW

Plaintiff attempts to break up fight between parties when one, attempting to hit the other, strikes the plaintiff. Can intent be established?

INCREASING YOUR UNDERSTANDING

1. Another manifestation of a common theme. The courts have consistently rejected arguments by intentional tortfeasors that legal intent should somehow require a subjective mental component. Courts have not yielded to the plea that an inquiry should be made into the consequences desired by the defendant or who was intended to be the victim of the act. The defendant is no less deserving of punishment when he intends one wrong though accomplishing another.

2. At a minimum, the doctrine of "transferred intent" allows for intent to transfer (person to person; claim to claim) in all cases involving the original trespass claims: battery, assault, false imprisonment, trespass to land and chattel. This leaves intentional infliction and conversion as two intentional tort claims where intent may not transfer. The reluctance to transfer under an IIED theory has been universally accepted with hardly any dissent. But it's hard to justify why intent would transfer in the cases of trespass to land or chattel but not in the case of conversion, beyond an adherence to an old set of rules.

Banks v. Dawkins
339 So. 2d 566 (Miss. 1976)

SMITH, Justice, for the Court:

This was an action begun by Mack Elmore Banks against Merdith Preston Dawkins, Jr., in the Circuit Court of Lowndes County and subsequently transferred to the Circuit Court of Noxubee County. Banks sought damages for personal injuries inflicted upon him by Dawkins by shooting him in the head and face with a shotgun. The appeal is from a verdict and judgment for Dawkins.

Banks was the proprietor of a so-called "supper club" at Crawford. On the night of Banks' injury, he had forced Dawkins to leave the club earlier that same evening because of alleged misconduct on the part of the latter. In the course of ejecting Dawkins there had been a fight and Dawkins claims to have been struck in the head by Banks with "brass knucks."

Dawkins' defense is that he was completely "blacked out" and remembered nothing whatever after he was forced out of the club by Banks. He testified that he did remember the fight and having been compelled to leave the club by Banks. Dawkins' wife testified that Dawkins had driven home in his pickup truck where he was seen by his wife to have blood on his head and face and was, as she said, "raving." It is contended that Dawkins then drove himself back to the club in his pickup, carrying a shotgun. When he arrived at the club Banks and several others were inside and Banks was attending to his own business.

Whatever effect Dawkins' condition may have had upon his recollection of events, apparently it had little or none upon his ability to drive his truck home, drive it back to the club, go to a window through which he thrust the gun and, from among the several persons who were in the club, single out his adversary Banks and shoot him in the face. As the result, Banks sustained the loss of an eye and other injuries.

It appears that the next day Dawkins consulted a doctor, his purpose in doing so and the treatment he received, if any, is not clear, although it does appear that in the fight he had sustained some cuts or abrasions about the face. There is no evidence of skull or brain damage, other than Dawkins' own claim not to remember the events after he left the club and, although the doctor's office was about 15 miles from the place of trial, the doctor was not subpoenaed or called by Dawkins as a witness. There was no explanation by Dawkins of his failure to call him.

It is the general rule in this and other states that, although a person may be suffering from a mental condition so as to be insane, nevertheless he is required to respond in compensatory damages for injuries resulting from his torts.

Dawkins' claim that he lost his memory during the critical times involved is unsupported and inconsistent with his actions.

It was error for the trial court to instruct the jury that, before Banks would be entitled to recover compensatory damages, the jury must find that Dawkins had shot Banks "knowingly." Even if it is established that at the time of the shooting Dawkins was, in fact, insane to such an extent that he did not know or appreciate the nature or consequences of his act and did not know that it was wrong to shoot Banks, the latter was entitled to recover damages to compensate him for his injuries.

If Dawkins shot Banks "knowingly," that is, intentionally and while sane, Banks would be entitled to recover punitive damages also. There was no claim of self-defense nor defense of any kind (save the claim of memory loss) offered by Dawkins for the shooting.

Dawkins' claim that he lost his memory is unsupported and weak and the injuries he inflicted upon Banks were grievous and severe. We think the verdict of the jury was against the overwhelming weight of the evidence and that the case should be reversed and remanded for another trial.

REVERSED AND REMANDED.

PREPARING FOR CLASS

1. Dawkins is not arguing in favor of an affirmative defense called insanity. Instead, he appeals to the court to allow his state of inebriation to militate his ability to sufficiently intend to shoot Banks. In short, Dawkins attempts to align his drunkenness with those who are mentally incapacitated.

2. You have to assume that Dawkins was liquored to the point of mental impairment in order to appreciate the broader rule. Similarly, temporarily disregard those facts that cut against his claim of insanity.

APPLYING THE LAW

Defendant, who suffers from Tourette's Syndrome, a nervous disorder characterized by involuntary movements and words, plays basketball for his high-school team. While sitting on the bench during a game, he raises his arm, striking a teammate. Is he liable for battery?

INCREASING YOUR UNDERSTANDING

1. Almost without exception, the general rule is that a defendant who suffers from a mental disorder will be just as liable for his intentional acts as an unimpaired or sane person would. It matters not the specific disorder or its alleged mental impairment characteristics; the law has consistently treated them all the same. Over the years, several justifications have been offered for this rule; included among them are the desire not to have each intentional tort case turn into a battle of experts from the field of psychology and the difficulty in having the jury smoke out those who are feigning mental illness.

2. Distinguish the acts of a person whose "insanity" genuinely prevents her from knowing right from wrong and a person whose insanity may create a misguided belief as to the need to intentionally intrude on the plaintiff. It is generally agreed that the latter will not prevent a finding of intent. For example, if D, as a result of an insane delusion, unreasonably believes that P is a domestic terrorist and therefore confines him until the authorities arrive, D is liable for false imprisonment, assault, and any other claims that might be brought against a sane person.

3.   Miscellaneous insanity matters. The insane defendant is civilly liable even in circumstances where his insanity may avoid criminal liability. See Polmatier v. Russ, 206 Conn. 229, 537 A.2d 468 (Conn. 1988) (Defendant who beat and shot decedent is liable for wrongful death, even though he was insane and his intention was not rational and though he was incapable of forming the intent necessary for criminal responsibility); and Delahanty v. Hinckley, 799 F. Supp. 184 (D.D.C. 1992). (Defendant who shot at President Reagan but missed and struck bystanders liable for compensatory damages though later found not guilty criminally by reason of insanity). And while a defendant's insanity does not mitigate the compensatory damages allowable for injuries caused by him, it may make a punitive award inappropriate. Phillips' Committee v. Ward's Adm'r, 241 Ky. 25, 43 S.W.2d 331 (Ky. App. 1931).

C.   BATTERY AND/OR ASSAULT

Restatement (Second) of Torts §13 Battery: Harmful Contact

An actor is subject to liability to another for battery if

(a) he acts intending to cause a harmful or offensive contact with the person of the other or a third person, or an imminent apprehension of such contact, and

(b) harmful contact with the person of the other directly or indirectly results.

Restatement (Second) of Torts §18 Battery: Offensive Contact

(1) An actor is subject to liability to another for battery if

(a) he acts intending to cause a harmful or offensive contact with the person of the other or a third person, or an imminent apprehension of such contact, and

(b) an offensive contact with the person of the other directly or indirectly results.

(2) An act which is not done with the intention stated in Subsection (1, a) does not make the actor liable to the other for a mere offensive contact with the other for a mere offensive contact with the other person although the act involves an unreasonable risk of inflicting it and, therefore, would be negligent or reckless if the risk threatened bodily harm.

Restatement (Second) of Torts §21 Assault

(1) An actor is subject to liability to another for assault if

(a) he acts intending to cause a harmful or offensive contact with the person of the other or a third person, or an imminent apprehension of such contact, and

(b) the other is thereby put in such imminent apprehension.

(2) An action which is not done with the intention stated in Subsection (1, a) does not make the actor liable to the other for an apprehension cause thereby although the act involves an unreasonable risk of causing it and, therefore, would be negligent or reckless if the risk threatened bodily harm.

Picard v. Barry Pontiac-Buick, Inc.
654 A.2d 690 (R.I. 1995)

Lederberg, Justice.

This case came before the Supreme Court on the appeal of Jesse Silvia (defendant) from a judgment against him for assault and battery, for compensatory damages in the amount of $60,346, and for punitive damages in the amount of $6,350, plus interest and costs. We affirm the judgment in respect to the assault and battery but sustain the defendant's appeal in respect to damages. We vacate the award of damages and remand the case to the Superior Court for a new trial on damages.

Facts and Procedural History

This case began eight years ago with a broken signal light. The plaintiff, Victorie A. Picard, brought her mother's car to Barry Pontiac-Buick, Inc. (Barry Pontiac) in Newport, Rhode Island, where the car had been purchased, to have the light repaired. While the car was being repaired, plaintiff decided to have its annual inspection performed as well. The car failed this inspection because, according to a Barry Pontiac representative, the brakes needed to be replaced. The plaintiff brought the car to Kent's Alignment Service (Kent's Alignment), also located in Newport, where the car passed inspection.

The plaintiff then contacted a local television news "troubleshooter" reporter, presumably to report her experience at the two inspection sites. Shortly after Kent's Alignment had inspected plaintiff's car, Barry Pontiac phoned Kent's Alignment to ask that the car be checked again and the sticker removed because the brakes "were bad." Accordingly Edward Kent (Kent), the owner of Kent's Alignment, set January 27, 1987, as the date that plaintiff, accompanied by her goddaughter Kristen Ann Seyster (Seyster), returned with the car to Kent's garage.

Kent's Alignment was divided into a garage area separated by a glass partition from an office area. At the time of the incident at issue in this case, Seyster was in the office, while plaintiff was in the garage. After Kent inspected the car, he told plaintiff that he had been asked to call Barry Pontiac which also wished to inspect the brakes. Ray Stevens (Stevens), the service manager at Barry Pontiac arrived at Kent's Alignment, accompanied by defendant, who was employed by Barry Pontiac.

The defendant began to inspect the brakes. He and plaintiff gave vastly different descriptions of what next happened. The plaintiff said she began to take a picture of defendant as he was facing away from her, presumably as evidence for the troubleshooter report. The plaintiff testified that she *did* intend to photograph defendant although the photograph was not intended to identify defendant. The photograph did, however, clearly show defendant fully facing the camera, standing upright while pointing his index finger at plaintiff. After the camera snapped, the events that gave rise to this case occurred.

The plaintiff testified that defendant "lunged" at her and "grabbed [her] around around [*sic*] the shoulders,"[2] although plaintiff did not experience any pain. The plaintiff then testified on cross-examination that after defendant grabbed her by both her shoulders, she and defendant "spun around wrestling." According to plaintiff, defendant released her after someone said, "let her go." The plaintiff then left the garage with her goddaughter.

Seyster and Stevens also testified at trial, and Kent's deposition was admitted into evidence. Seyster, who had remained in the office area, testified that she saw defendant "grab her [plaintiff's] left shoulder and try to get the picture with his other hand," but defendant did not touch either the photograph or the camera. Seyster further testified that defendant had reached for plaintiff with only one arm, not two, and that plaintiff was not spun around, shaken, picked up or thrown against a wall. Stevens testified that he did not see what transpired because his back was turned. He did, however, remember defendant "hollering" that he did not want his picture taken. Kent stated that after plaintiff came out of the office and attempted to photograph defendant, he heard defendant say something such as "don't take my picture." Kent then saw defendant reach for the camera and touch it, but saw no contact between plaintiff and defendant, nor did he see defendant lift plaintiff.

The defendant testified that as he was looking at the car, plaintiff had come up behind him and aimed the camera toward him. He then pointed at plaintiff and said, "who gave you permission to take my picture?" then walked around the car to plaintiff, placed his index finger on the camera and again asked, "who gave you permission to take my picture?" The defendant denied grabbing plaintiff, touching her body, threatening her or making any threatening gestures, scuffling with her or reaching for the photograph. He also testified that he did not intend to cause plaintiff any bodily harm.

The plaintiff testified that although she did not experience any pain immediately after the incident, she did experience numbness in her hips and legs. However, about a week after the incident, plaintiff visited William E. Kenney, M.D. (Kenney) because of "pain radiating down my right leg . . . ," pain that reportedly continued periodically up to the time of trial. Kenney examined

---

2. In a statement describing the incident to the Newport Police, plaintiff stated, "HE GRABBED MY COAT[.] I LUNGED BACKWARD HURTING MY BACK[.]" In a Social Security Administration "Reconsideration Disability Report" dated March 20, 1987, plaintiff stated that she had been "attack [*sic*] by a merchanic [*sic*] from Barry Pontiac" and that she had been "[t]hrown against a wall at Kents [*sic*] garage [.]" The plaintiff testified at trial that, notwithstanding the Disability Report, she had not been thrown against a wall.

plaintiff and advised a CAT scan. W.R. Courey, M.D., of St. Anne's Hospital in Fall River, Massachusetts, prepared a radiology report on April 17, 1987, that described "[g]eneralized degenerative bulging of the annulus at [L-3-L-4, L-4-L-5, and L-5-S-1]." Kenney himself saw plaintiff five times in his office between January 30, 1987, and May 26, 1987, each time with a $30 charge.

On April 28, 1987, Kenney wrote a "To Whom it May Concern" letter, in which he stated:

> "This patient had had a ruptured intervertebra disc on the left which was apparent in October or earlier of 1985. She had not complained of her right lower extremity, however, on 1/30/87 she was seen with a history that she had been assaulted on 1/22/87 and had pain in the right lower extremity. The CAT scan taken at St. Anne's Hospital on 4/17/87 reveals nerve root pressure on the right at L5-S1 level. Therefore, this change is probably causally related with the assault."

On June 1, 1987, Kenney wrote a second "To Whom it May Concern" letter, stating: "The question has been raised as to whether or not the pain in the right leg is permanent. *The answer is that it is probably not permanent*, but there is no way that I have of knowing for sure whether it is permanent or not." (Emphasis added.) But, twenty-four days later, with no evidence of an intervening examination of plaintiff, Kenney, on June 25, 1987, wrote to plaintiff's attorney:

> "It is apparent that the patient sustained a ruptured disc on the right at L5-S1 found by CAT scan on 4/17/87, following an assault on 1/22/87. *The ruptured disc at L5-S1 on the right is a permanent injury*." (Emphasis added.)

The injured area identified by Kenney was the right L5-S1 region of the spinal column. The defendant introduced into evidence a Newport Hospital Report dated March 26, 1985, which showed a left-sided disc herniation at the L5-S1 locus. The plaintiff confirmed at trial that she had had a history of back problems for at least ten years prior to her encounter with defendant.

. . . The plaintiff prevailed at trial and was awarded compensatory damages in the amount of $60,346. Because the trial justice found that defendant's conduct was "sufficiently egrigious [*sic*]," punitive damages in the amount of $6,350 were imposed, for a total judgment of $66,696, plus interest and costs. The defendant appealed the judgment, arguing (1) that plaintiff failed to prove an assault and battery.

STANDARD OF REVIEW

The findings made by a trial justice, sitting without a jury, are accorded great weight. These findings will not be disturbed on appeal absent a determination that the trial justice misconceived or overlooked relevant evidence or was otherwise clearly wrong.

ASSAULT AND BATTERY

The defendant contended that plaintiff failed to prove the occurrence of an assault because plaintiff was not placed in reasonable fear of imminent bodily harm. Further, defendant argued that plaintiff failed to prove a battery because the evidence failed to establish that defendant intended to inflict an unconsented touching of plaintiff. We disagree with both contentions.

Assault and battery are separate acts, usually arising from the same transaction, each having independent significance. *Proffitt v. Ricci*, 463 A.2d 514, 517 (R.I. 1983). "An assault is a physical act of a threatening nature or an offer of corporal injury which puts an individual in reasonable fear of imminent bodily harm." *Id.* It is a plaintiff's apprehension of injury which renders a defendant's act compensable. *Id.; see also* W. Page Keeton et al., *Prosser and Keeton on the Law of Torts* §10, at 43 (5th ed. 1984) ("[t]he damages recoverable for [assault] are those for the plaintiff's mental disturbance, including fright, humiliation and the like, as well as any physical illness which may result from them"). This apprehension must be the type of fear normally aroused in the mind of a reasonable person. *Keeton et al., supra*, at 44.

The plaintiff testified that she was frightened by defendant's actions. A review of the attendant circumstances attests that such a reaction was reasonable. The defendant admitted approaching plaintiff, and the photograph taken that day clearly showed defendant pointing his finger at plaintiff as defendant approached her. Because plaintiff's apprehension of imminent bodily harm was reasonable at that point, plaintiff has established a prima facie case of assault.

We have defined battery as an act that was intended to cause, and in fact did cause, "an offensive contact with or unconsented touching of or trauma upon the body of another, thereby generally resulting in the consummation of the assault. . . . An intent to injure plaintiff, however, is unnecessary in a situation in which a defendant willfully sets in motion a force that in its ordinary course causes the injury." *Proffitt*, 463 A.2d at 517.

In the instant case, defendant contended that a battery did not occur because defendant did not intend to touch or injure plaintiff. Rather, defendant argued, the evidence showed that he intended to touch plaintiff's *camera*, not plaintiff's person, and therefore the contact was insufficient to prove battery. With this contention we must disagree. Even if this court were to accept defendant's characterization of the incident, a battery *had* nonetheless occurred. The defendant failed to prove that his actions on January 22, 1987, were accidental or involuntary. Therefore, defendant's offensive contact with an object attached to or identified with plaintiff's body was sufficient to constitute a battery. As noted in the comments to the Restatement (Second) Torts §18, comment c at 31 (1965):

> "Unpermitted and intentional contacts with anything so connected with the body as to be customarily regarded as part of the other's person and therefore as partaking of its inviolability is actionable as an offensive contact with his person. *There are some things such as clothing or a cane or, indeed, anything directly grasped by the hand which are so intimately connected with one's body as to be universally regarded as part of the person.*" (Emphasis added.)

The defendant's contact with the camera clutched in plaintiff's hand was thus sufficient to constitute a battery. We conclude, therefore, that plaintiff has proven the elements of assault and battery.

PREPARING FOR CLASS

1. Try your best to avoid comparing criminal assaults and/or batteries with the civil variety; it will only confuse.

2. Both assault and battery are described as dignitary claims, which means that the law considers the intrusions significant enough to allow for liability even in the absence of tangible physical harm.

3. The law of battery seeks to protect the plaintiff from contact that is either harmful or offensive, while the right to be free of apprehension of harmful or offensive contact is sought to be protected by the law of assault.

4. What common items qualify as being intimately connected when in the possession of or being used by a person?

APPLYING THE LAW

While plaintiff sits in her car with the doors locked and windows closed, defendant approaches and in a menacing fashion balls his fist at her and eventually bangs on the car with his hands. Is the defendant liable for assault and/or battery?

INCREASING YOUR UNDERSTANDING

Both the laws of battery and assault attempt to protect a party from intrusions that are not consented to. As the principle case indicates, they are distinct claims, though they often both arise under the same facts.

Battery gravamen. There can be no battery without some form of harmful or offensive contact. "A bodily contact is offensive if it offends a reasonable sense of *personal dignity*." Restatement (Second) of Torts §19 (emphasis added). Offensiveness is therefore judged under the circumstances, influenced by the governing societal morals. It is an objective standard and therefore not judged by those who might be described as overly sensitive. So an African-American mathematician, who while attending a buffet had a plate snatched from him by an employee shouting racial epithets at him, was battered though he never feared for his safety nor was harmed by the incident beyond being humiliated or embarrassed. Fisher v. Carrousel Motor Hotel, Inc., 424 S.W.2d 627 (Tex. 1967). And a radio talk show guest stated sufficient facts in support of a "battery" claim against the radio host by alleging that, at host's urging, second host repeatedly blew cigar smoke in guest's face, as the incident could be found to be "disagreeable or nauseating or painful because of outrage to taste and sensibilities or affronting insultingness." Leichtman v. WLW Jacor Communications, Inc., 92 Ohio App. 3d 232, 634 N.E.2d 697 (Ohio App. 1 Dist. 1994). But a paralegal, who upon trying to enter his boss's office without knocking had the door closed on him, forcing him into the hall, failed to state an "offensive-battery claim" as a matter of law on the grounds that an "ordinary person . . . not unduly sensitive as to his personal dignity intruding upon a private conversation in [plaintiff's] manner would not have been offended by [the defendant's] response to the intrusion." Wishnatsky v. Huey, 584 N.W.2d 859 (N.D. App. 1998).

Holloway v. Wachovia Bank & Trust Co., N.A.
109 N.C. App. 403, 428 S.E.2d 453 (N.C. Ct. App. 1993)

In April 1985, plaintiff Hallie Holloway purchased a car financed by defendant Wachovia Bank & Trust Co., N.A. (hereinafter "Wachovia"). She defaulted on the loan. On 21 May 1986, defendant Jean Dawson, an employee of defendant Wachovia, attempted to repossess the car in the parking lot outside of a Durham laundromat. At the laundromat with Hallie Holloway were: 1) Sue Holloway, who is Hallie Holloway's mother; 2) Swanzett Holloway, who is Hallie Holloway's 10 year old niece; and 3) Damien Holloway, who is Hallie Holloway's 4 month old son. Plaintiffs left the scene driving the car defendant Dawson sought to repossess.

In their 27 April 1988 complaint, plaintiffs alleged that defendant Dawson aimed a gun at them in her attempt to repossess the car. Each plaintiff sought recovery for assault, for intentional infliction of emotional distress, and for violations of G.S. 75-51 and G.S. 75-56 (hereinafter "G.S. Chapter 75 claims"). Additionally, plaintiffs Hallie Holloway and Damien Holloway sought recovery for battery arising from defendant Dawson's touching them while "reach[ing] through the window of the car" to take the car keys from the ignition.

At trial, directed verdicts in favor of defendants were entered on Damien Holloway's battery claim and both Swanzett Holloway's and Damien Holloway's assault claims. Plaintiffs appeal.

EAGLES, Judge.

Plaintiffs bring forward fifteen assignments of error. We affirm in part and reverse in part.

VII.

In their tenth assignment of error, plaintiffs argue that the trial court erred by granting defendants' motions for directed verdict. As to Damien Holloway's assault claim, we affirm. As to Damien Holloway's battery claim and Swanzett Holloway's assault claim, we reverse and remand for a new trial on these two claims only.

A.

Regarding the tort of assault, this Court has stated:

> The interest protected by the action for assault is freedom from apprehension of a harmful or offensive contact with one's person. In *Dickens v. Puryear*, 302 N.C. 437, 445, 276 S.E.2d 325, 330 (1981), our Supreme Court stated assault requires the plaintiff's reasonable apprehension of an immediate harmful or offensive contact. The *Dickens* Court further quoted the Comment to Section 29(1) of Restatement (Second) of Torts (1965): "[T]he apprehension created must be one of imminent contact, as distinguished from any contact in the future. Imminent does not mean immediate, in the sense of instantaneous contact . . . it means rather that there will be no significant delay." 302 N.C. at 445-46, 276 S.E.2d at 331.

. . . At trial, plaintiff Hallie Holloway answered "yes" to the question "throughout this he [Damien Holloway] was either asleep or too young to understand what was going on throughout this confrontation; isn't that correct?" Plaintiffs have failed to show that the infant Damien experienced any apprehension of harmful or offensive contact. Accordingly, we find no merit in plaintiffs' argument.

B.

However, there was sufficient evidence to permit a jury to consider the infant Damien Holloway's battery claim. "The elements of battery are intent, harmful or offensive contact, causation, and lack of privilege. As with assault, a showing of actual damage is not an essential element of battery.

Hallie Holloway testified that while she was sitting in the driver's seat of the automobile, she had the infant Damien "up on my chest". She further testified that as defendant Dawson reached to take the keys from the ignition on the right hand side of the steering wheel, defendant Dawson "had her elbow in my baby's back. She was trying to pull my hands off the key."

Defendants argue that the trial court "allowed a directed verdict on Damien Holloway's battery claim because there was clearly no intent to touch Damien. Rather his touching was inadvertent, incidental, and unintentional." However, "[t]he gist of the action for battery is not the hostile intent of the defendant, but rather the absence of consent to the contact on the part of the plaintiff." *McCracken*, 40 N.C. App. at 216-17, 252 S.E.2d at 252. See *416 N.C. Farm Bureau Mut. Ins. Co. v. Stox*, 330 N.C. 697, 707, 412 S.E.2d 318, 324 (1992) ("'[t]he intent with which tort liability is concerned is not necessarily a hostile intent, or a desire to do any harm. Rather it is an intent to bring about a result which will invade the interests of another in a way that the law forbids.' Prosser, [Law of Torts] §8, p. 36 [(5th ed. 1984) (hereinafter "Prosser")].") Based upon the record before us, the issue of whether the infant Damien was entitled to recover upon a claim of battery should have been submitted to the jury.

C.

Next, we address Swanzett Holloway's assault claim. "An assault is an offer to show violence to another without striking him." "The elements of assault are intent, offer of injury, reasonable apprehension, apparent ability, and imminent threat of injury. Plaintiff establishes a cause of action for assault upon proof of these technical elements without proof of actual damage.

At the time that Jean Dawson had the gun in her hand, Swanzett Holloway was sitting in the back seat of the automobile. At trial, Swanzett Holloway gave the following testimony:

Q   [Plaintiffs' counsel]: Did you see the gun?
A   [Swanzett Holloway]: Yes.
Q: And how did you see the gun?
A: It was in her [defendant Dawson's] hand.
Q: All right. And where did she have — where was she when you saw her with the gun?
A: She was outside the car on the driver's side.
Q: On the driver's side. Where did she have it pointed?
A: Toward Hallie [Holloway] and her baby [Damien Holloway]. . . .
Q: Now, but for Hallie would the gun have been pointed at you the way you described it on here?
A: Yes.

Mr. Hoof [defendants' counsel]:   Objection to leading.
Court: Sustained.

Q: Could you see the barrel of the gun?
A: Yes, I saw the gun, black and brown.
Q: ... What did you think or what did you feel when you saw the gun?
A: I was scared.
Q: What were you afraid of?
A: She could have shot either one of us.
Q: ... Were you afraid of being shot?
A: Yes.

Since Swanzett Holloway testified that the gun was not pointed directly at her, she relies on the concept of transferred intent to recover on this assault claim. The Restatement (Second) of Torts explains the concept of transferred intent as follows: "If an act is done with the intention of affecting a third person ... but puts another in apprehension of a harmful or offensive contact, the actor is subject to liability to such other as fully as though he intended so to affect him." *Id.* §32(2). *See generally,* Prosser, §8, pp. 37-39; Daye and Morris, North Carolina Law of Torts §2.31.2, pp. 8-10 (1991) (hereinafter "Daye and Morris").

Our research indicates that the concept of transferred intent has not been applied in a civil case in North Carolina. However, at least four criminal cases have tacitly recognized transferred intent principles.

"North Carolina follows common law principles governing assault and battery. ... Common law principles of assault and battery as enunciated in North Carolina law are also found in the Restatement (Second) of Torts (1965)."*Dickens,* 302 N.C. at 444-45, 276 S.E.2d at 330-31. Prosser notes that the concept of transferred intent existed at common law, first appearing

> in criminal cases at a time when tort and crime were still merged in the old trespass form of action. It represents an established rule of the criminal law, in cases in which shooting, striking, throwing a missile or poisoning has resulted in unexpected injury to the wrong person. The criminal cases have been understandably preoccupied with moral guilt, and the obvious fact that if the defendant is not convicted there is no one to hold liable for the crime. *But the same rule was applied to tort cases arising in trespass*[, which "was the progenitor not only of battery, but also of assault and false imprisonment"]. This may possibly have been due to a considered feeling that the defendant could not sustain a burden of proof of freedom from fault when the defendant had at least intended to injure another person. But a better explanation may lie in nothing more than the mere proximity of the criminal law to the trespass action, with its criminal tradition and the similarity of the fact situations. It is quite probable, however, that the persistence of the principle has been due to a definite feeling that the defendant is at fault, and should make good the damage. The defendant's act is characterized as "wrongful," and the fault is regarded as absolute toward all the world, rather than relative to any one person. Having departed from the social standard of conduct, the defendant is liable for the harm which follows from the act, although this harm was not intended.

Prosser, §8, pp. 37-38 (emphasis added) (footnotes omitted). Since the concept of transferred intent was recognized at common law, we hold that on the facts presented in this case, the issue of whether Swanzett Holloway was entitled to recover for a claim of assault should have been submitted to the jury.

Affirmed in part; reversed in part and remanded.

INCREASING YOUR UNDERSTANDING

1. *Assault gravamen.* The law of civil assault only protects against reasonable apprehension of an imminent battery. All apprehensions thus are not protected, only reasonable ones are. Furthermore, the law does not require the plaintiff to prove that he was fearful of the contact, just that he was aware of the possibility of being offended or harmed. Restatement (Second) of Torts §21, comment (1)c. Consider the following for reasonableness:

   a. Defendant places telephone calls to plaintiff threatening that "I'm going to find out where you live and I'm going to kick your ass," and to "cut you in your sleep. . . ." *Held*: Threats found insufficient to support an assault claim: "Although calls threatened action in future, threat was not in imminent future, and there were no circumstances indicating that caller was in position to reach plaintiff and inflict physical violence almost at once." Brower v. Ackerley, 88 Wash. App. 87, 943 P.2d 1141 (Wash. App. Div.1 1997).

   b. Neighbors are in dispute over use of a trail that runs between their properties. Plaintiff-neighbor had his fill of the rowdiness attendant to the trail's use and decided to fell a tree across to limit its usefulness. In retaliation, a group arrived at the plaintiff's property, at which time plaintiff perched himself in the tree. "Bring on the chainsaws!" one of the defendant-neighbors cried. The sawyers began to cut around the tree, but after noticing plaintiff's resolve, stopped when it was clear that he would not budge. *Held*: Act of dismembering tree provided sufficient facts for jury to find that assault had occurred.

   c. Robed members of the Ku Klux Klan gather on a shrimp boat and journey down a water way on the first day of fishing season in an area heavily populated with Vietnamese fishermen. The KKK members openly bore arms and fired a cannon during the boat ride. There was conflicting testimony over the purpose behind the boat ride; some claimed it was an effort to intimidate, while others claimed that it was done simply to gain media attention. *Held*: "As a rule . . . , the defendant's act must amount to an offer to use force, and there must be an apparent ability and opportunity to carry out the threat immediately. There is no assault where the defendant is too far away to do any harm. . . . Although there were several armed persons on this 'boat ride,' there was no testimony that any of these individuals were in close enough proximity to any of the plaintiffs to actually commit a battery." Plaintiffs, though, would be allowed to supplement the record and provide the court with evidence in an attempt to meet the requirements of the offense. Vietnamese Fishermen's Ass'n v. Knights of Ku Klux Klan, 518 F. Supp. 993 (D.C. Tex. 1981).

2. *Battery vs. assault and awareness.* Assault liability requires proof that, at the time of the intentional act, the plaintiff was placed in apprehension of an imminent battery. On the other hand, the touchstone for a battery claim is harmful or offensive contact, which allows for a claim to be brought even if the plaintiff is not aware of the contact at the time it occurs. "[T]he actor's liability is based upon an intentional invasion of the others dignitary interest in the inviolability of the person . . . this affront is as keenly felt by one who knows after the event that an indignity has been perpetrated upon him as by one who is conscious of it while it is being perpetrated." Restatement (Second) of Torts §18, comment d (1965).

D. FALSE IMPRISONMENT

RESTATEMENT (SECOND) OF TORTS §35 FALSE IMPRISONMENT (1965)

   (1) An actor is subject to liability to another for false imprisonment if
      (a) he acts intending to confine the other or a third person within boundaries fixed by the actor, and
      (b) his act directly or indirectly results in such confinement of the other, and
      (c) the other is conscious of the confinement or is harmed by it.
   (2) An action which is not done with the intention stated in Subsection (1,a) does not make the actor liable to the other for a merely transitory or otherwise harmless confinement, although the act involves an unreasonable risk of imposing it and, therefore, would be negligent or reckless if the risk threatened bodily harm.

Eilers v. Coy
582 F. Supp. 1093 (D. Minn. 1984)

MACLAUGHLIN, District Judge.
   The plaintiff in this case, William Eilers, has moved the Court to enter a directed verdict against the defendants on his claim that the defendants falsely imprisoned him.

After careful consideration the Court has decided as follows:

... Plaintiff's motion for a directed verdict on the issue of false imprisonment is granted and the Court holds, as a matter of law, that plaintiff William Eilers was falsely imprisoned without legal justification.

FACTS

The evidence in this case has established the following facts. The plaintiff William Eilers and his pregnant wife Sandy were abducted from outside a clinic in Winona, Minnesota in the early afternoon of Monday, August 16, 1982, by their parents and relatives and by the defendant deprogrammers who had been hired by the parents of the plaintiff and his wife. The plaintiff was 24 years old at the time and his wife Sandy was 22. The couple was living on a farm near Galesville, Wisconsin and had traveled to Minnesota for Sandy's pre-natal examination.

At the time of the abduction, Bill and Sandy Eilers were members of the religious group Disciples of the Lord Jesus Christ. There is ample evidence that this group is an authoritarian religious fellowship directed with an iron hand by Brother Rama Behera. There is also evidence that Bill Eilers' personality, and to some extent his appearance, changed substantially after he became a member of the group. These changes were clearly of great concern to members of the plaintiff's family. However, other than as they may have affected the intent of the parents of Bill and Sandy Eilers in the actions they took in seizing Bill and Sandy, the beliefs and practices of the Disciples of the Lord Jesus Christ should not be, and are not, on trial in this case.

While leaving the Winona Clinic on August 16, 1982 the plaintiff, who was on crutches at the time due to an earlier fall, was grabbed from behind by two or more security men, forced into a waiting van, and driven to the Tau Center in Winona, Minnesota.[1] Forcibly resisting, he was carried by four men to a room on the top floor of the dormitory-style building. The windows of this room were boarded over with plywood, as were the windows in his bathroom and in the hallway of the floor. The telephone in the hallway had been dismantled.

The plaintiff was held at the Tau Center for five and one-half days and subjected to the defendants' attempts to deprogram him. Shortly after his arrival at the Tau Center, and after a violent struggle with his captors, the plaintiff was handcuffed to a bed. He remained handcuffed to the bed for at least the first two days of his confinement. During this initial period, he was allowed out of the room only to use the bathroom, and was heavily guarded during those times. On one occasion, the plaintiff dashed down the hall in an

---

1. After dropping the plaintiff at the Tau Center, one of the family members drove the van to a location eight miles outside of Winona and left it there.

attempt to escape, but was forcibly restrained and taken back to the room. After several days of resistance, the plaintiff changed tactics and apparently pretended to consent to his confinement.

The defendants and the plaintiff's relatives had agreed in advance of the abduction that the plaintiff would be kept at the Tau Center for one week, regardless of whether the plaintiff consented to their actions. At no time during the week was the plaintiff free to leave the Tau Center, nor at any time were reasonable means of escape available to him. Three of the eight people hired by the parents were designated "security men." These individuals, described by witnesses as at least six feet tall and weighing over 200 pounds, guarded the exits on the floor at all times.

On the evening of Saturday, August 21, 1982, as the plaintiff was leaving the Tau Center to be transported to Iowa City, Iowa for further deprogramming, he took advantage of his first opportunity to escape and jumped from the car in which he was riding. Local residents, attracted by the plaintiff's calls for help, assisted the plaintiff in making his escape and the police were summoned.

The evidence has also shown that within three weeks before the abduction occurred, the plaintiff's relatives had contacted authorities in Trempealeau County, Wisconsin in an attempt to have the plaintiff civilly committed. Family members have testified that they believed the plaintiff was suicidal because of a letter he had written to his grandmother before joining the Disciples of the Lord Jesus Christ in which he wrote that demons were attacking his mind and telling him to kill himself rather than go to the Lord. Joyce Peterson, a psychiatric social worker, interviewed the plaintiff in person on July 26, 1982. After interviewing the plaintiff and consulting with the Trempealeau County Attorney, Peterson informed the plaintiff's relatives that no legal grounds existed in Wisconsin for confining the plaintiff because he showed no signs of being a danger to himself or to others. The defendants in this case were aware of that information at the time they abducted and held the plaintiff.

Discussion

In considering the plaintiff's motion for a directed verdict, the Court is required to view the evidence in the light most favorable to the defendants and to resolve all conflicts in the evidence in the defendants' favor. A directed verdict motion should be granted only when reasonable jurors could not differ as to the conclusions to be drawn from the evidence.

The plaintiff has alleged two main causes of action against the defendants: false imprisonment and conspiracy to deprive the plaintiff of his constitutional rights in violation of 42 U.S.C. §1985(3). These claims will be discussed separately.

A. FALSE IMPRISONMENT

The plaintiff's first claim is that the defendants' conduct in confining him at the Tau Center constituted false imprisonment for which the defendants had no legal justification. False imprisonment consists of three elements:

1) words or acts intended to confine a person;

2) actual confinement; and

3) awareness by the person that he or she is confined.

Blaz v. Molin Concrete Products Co., 309 Minn. 382, 385, 244 N.W.2d 277, 279 (1976); Restatement (Second) of Torts §35 (1965).

The evidence in this case has overwhelmingly established each of the elements of false imprisonment. By their own admission, the defendants intended to confine the plaintiff for at least one week. While the defendants maintain that their purpose was to help the plaintiff, it is not a defense to false imprisonment that the defendants may have acted with good motives. Malice toward the person confined is not an element of false imprisonment.

There is also no question that the plaintiff was actually confined. Relying on the Minnesota Supreme Court's decision in *Peterson v. Sorlien*, 299 N.W.2d 123, 129 (Minn. 1980), *cert. denied*, 450 U.S. 1031, 101 S. Ct. 1742, 68 L. Ed. 2d 227 (1981), the defendants contend that there was no actual confinement because there is evidence that the plaintiff consented to the defendants' actions, at least by the fourth day of his confinement.[3] The plaintiff, in contrast, has testified that he merely pretended to consent in order to gain an opportunity to escape. The plaintiff's apparent consent is not a defense to false imprisonment. Many people would feign consent under similar circumstances, whether out of fear of their captors or as a means of making an escape. But in this case, unlike the *Peterson* case relied on by the defendants, it is undisputed that the plaintiff was at no time free to leave the Tau Center during the week in question, nor were any reasonable means of escape available to him. Under these circumstances, the Court finds, in agreement with many other authorities, that the plaintiff's apparent consent is not a defense to false imprisonment. The Court therefore holds, as a matter of law, that the plaintiff has proven the necessary elements of false imprisonment.

Accordingly, the Court rules as a matter of law that the plaintiff was falsely imprisoned without justification. The issue of what amount of damages, if any, the plaintiff suffered from this false imprisonment is a question for the jury.

---

3. In *Peterson*, the parents of 21-year-old Susan Jungclaus Peterson engaged deprogrammers to extricate their daughter from The Way Ministry. Peterson resisted the deprogramming for two or three days, but from then on stayed with her deprogrammers willingly for the next 13 days. At the end of the 16-day period, Peterson returned to The Way Ministry, apparently at the urging of her fiance who was also a member of the group.

Based on the foregoing, IT IS ORDERED that the plaintiff's motion for a directed verdict is granted as to his claim for false imprisonment.

PREPARING FOR CLASS

1. A directed verdict is essentially a motion for summary judgment at trial and subject to the same standard. Either party can make the motion at trial with the argument being that there are no material issues of fact remaining and, therefore, it's unnecessary to have the jury deliberate. Are you convinced the facts only point in favor of the plaintiff?

2. With the liability issue resolved, the case will go forward only on the issue of compensatory damages. What would you award in this case?

APPLYING THE LAW

Joe attempts to enter a tavern but is denied entrance because he is mistakenly identified as a patron who started a fight in the bar the week before. Does Joe have a claim for false imprisonment?

Wal-Mart Stores, Inc. v. Cockrell
61 S.W.3d 774 (Tex. Ct. App. 2001)

DORSEY, Justice.

Wal-Mart Stores, Inc., appeals from a judgment, following a jury verdict, finding that it had assaulted and falsely imprisoned a suspected shoplifter, Karl Cockrell. Based upon these findings the jury awarded Cockrell $300,000 for past mental anguish. The question raised on appeal is whether the evidence is legally and factually sufficient to support the verdict. We affirm.

I. FACTS

On November 6, 1996, Karl Cockrell and his parents went to the layaway department at a Wal-Mart store. Cockrell stayed for about five minutes and decided to leave. As he was going out the front door Raymond Navarro, a loss-prevention officer, stopped him and requested that Cockrell follow him to the manager's office. Once in the office Navarro told him to pull his pants down. Cockrell put his hands between his shorts and underwear, pulled them out, and shook them. Nothing fell out. Next Navarro told him to take off his shirt. Cockrell raised his shirt, revealing a large bandage which covered a surgical wound on the right side of his abdomen. Cockrell had recently had a liver transplant. Navarro asked him to take off the bandage, despite Cockrell's explanation that the bandage maintained a sterile environment around his surgical wound. On Navarro's insistence Cockrell took down the bandage, revealing the wound. Jay Garrison and Nancy Suchomel, both Wal-Mart employees, were in the office when Cockrell lifted his shirt. Afterwards Navarro apologized and let Cockrell go.

II. Discussion

By issues one and two Wal-Mart attacks the legal and factual sufficiency of the evidence to support the jury's findings that it had assaulted and falsely imprisoned Cockrell.

A. FALSE IMPRISONMENT

The elements of false imprisonment are: (1) a willful detention; (2) performed without consent; and (3) without the authority of law. A person may falsely imprison another by acts alone or by words alone, or by both, operating on the person's will.

In a false-imprisonment case if the alleged detention was performed with the authority of law then no false imprisonment occurred. The plaintiff must prove the absence of authority in order to establish the third element of a false-imprisonment cause of action.

A case which helps to decide this issue is *H.E. Butt Grocery Co. v. Saldivar*, 752 S.W.2d 701 (Tex. App.-Corpus Christi 1988, no writ). In that case Saldivar was shopping at an H.E.B. store when a clerk told Isabel Lopez, an assistant manager, that "a lady" had taken a pair of sunglasses and removed the sales tag. Lopez did not see Saldivar take the sunglasses. As Saldivar walked outside the store, an armed security guard stopped her, accused her of theft, and told her to come to a back room with him. At that point Lopez approached her and displayed a sales tag she had found which she claimed Saldivar had removed from the sunglasses. The security guard guided Saldivar back into the front of the store where she remained for several minutes. She was released after the manager determined that she had not stolen the sunglasses.

Saldivar sued H.E.B. for false imprisonment. At trial, she testified that after she and the security guard entered the store she did not leave because she "didn't feel like [she] could." She stated that she never went near the sunglass display. A jury returned a verdict in her favor. We affirmed, finding that the facts supported a willful detention without consent and that a rational jury could have found that H.E.B. did not "reasonably believe" a theft had occurred and therefore lacked authority to detain her. *Id.* at 702-04.

Analysis

1. Willful Detention and Consent

Here Ray Navarro, the loss-prevention officer, testified that Cockrell was in his custody at the point when he escorted him to the office. When Cockrell's counsel asked Navarro, "Was it your decision as to when he [Cockrell] could leave?" he replied, "I guess." Navarro testified that he probably would have let Cockrell leave after seeing that he did not have anything under his shirt.

Cockrell testified that he was not free to leave when Navarro stopped him and that Navarro was not going to let him go. He also testified that Navarro and two other Wal-Mart employees accompanied him to the office. When counsel asked Cockrell why he did not leave the office, he replied, "Because the impression I was getting from him, I wasn't going no place."

We conclude that these facts are sufficient to support the jury's finding that Cockrell was willfully detained without his consent.

2. Authority of Law

Question One asked the jury whether Wal-Mart falsely imprisoned Karl Cockrell. "Falsely imprison" was defined to mean "willfully detaining another without legal justification. . . ." The court instructed the jury on the "shop-keeper's privilege." This instruction stated: "when a person reasonably believes that another has stolen or is attempting to steal property, that person has legal justification to detain the other in a reasonable manner and for a reasonable time to investigate ownership of the property." Thus the jury could only find false imprisonment if it found no justification for Wal-Mart's actions.

A. Reasonable Belief

Neither Raymond Navarro nor any other store employee saw Cockrell steal merchandise. However Navarro claimed he had two reasons to suspect Cockrell of shoplifting. First he said that Cockrell was acting suspiciously, because he saw him in the women's department standing very close to a rack of clothes and looking around. Later he saw Cockrell looking around and walking slowly by the cigarette aisle and then "pass out of the store." Second he saw a little "bulge" under Cockrell's shirt.

Cockrell testified that he had done "nothing" and that there was "no way" a person could see anything under his shirt. We conclude that a rational jury could have found that Navarro did not "reasonably believe" a theft had occurred and therefore lacked authority to detain Cockrell. *See Saldivar*, 752 S.W.2d at 704.

B. Reasonable Manner

The extent to which Wal-Mart searched Cockrell compels us to address the reasonable manner of the detention. The "shopkeeper's privilege" expressly grants an employee the authority of law to detain a customer to investigate the ownership of property in a *reasonable manner*.

At least one appellate court has stated that when a store employee has probable cause to arrest a person for shoplifting, the employee may do so and make a "contemporaneous search" of the person and the objects within that person's control. *See Raiford v. The May Dep't Stores Co.*, 2 S.W.3d 527, 531 (Tex. App.-Houston [14th Dist.] 1999, no pet.). As authority for this precept the *Raiford* Court relied in part on *Douglas v. State*, 695 S.W.2d 817 (Tex. App.-Waco 1985, pet. ref'd). In that case a private citizen, Melvin Jodie, discovered that someone had burglarized his home and stolen his property. A police officer told Jodie that he thought he knew who had committed the crime and that the suspect lived in a house on a certain street. Jodie went to the house, found Douglas with the stolen property, and delivered him into the officer's custody. Douglas was convicted of burglary and on appeal asserted that Jodie's citizen's arrest was illegal. The appellate court stated that article 18.16 of the Texas Code of Criminal Procedure authorized a private citizen to make a warrantless arrest of a thief when the stolen property is found in the thief's possession. *Id.* at 820. The court further stated that because Douglas's warrantless arrest was lawful, Jodie was authorized to conduct a contemporaneous search of his person and of the area within Douglas's immediate control. *Id.*

We therefore hold that when a store employee has probable cause to arrest a person for shoplifting, the employee may do so and make a contemporaneous search of the person and objects within that person's immediate control. The contemporaneous search is limited to instances in which a search of the body is reasonably necessary to investigate ownership of property believed stolen. Accordingly Navarro's contemporaneous search was unreasonable in scope, because he had no probable cause to believe that Cockrell had hidden any merchandise under the bandage. Removal of the bandage compromised the sterile environment surrounding the wound. Having found the evidence sufficient with respect to each of the essential elements of false imprisonment we overrule issue one.

B. ASSAULT

Question Two asked whether Wal-Mart assaulted Cockrell. The jury answered affirmatively. The trial court instructed the jury that a person commits an assault "if he intentionally or knowingly causes physical contact with another, when he knows or should reasonably believe that the other will regard the contact as offensive or provocative."[1] Cockrell's testimony was that as he was going out the outer set of front doors Navarro put his hands on his back and shoulder and "twisted" him around. He thought that Navarro was going to rob him. Navarro did not believe that he had touched Cockrell. We conclude that a rational jury could find that Navarro knew or should have reasonably

---

1. The trial court did not instruct the jury on any defensive theories.

believed that Cockrell would regard the contact as offensive or provocative. We hold that the evidence is legally and factually sufficient to support the jury's finding that Wal-Mart assaulted Cockrell. We overrule issue two.

C. MENTAL ANGUISH

By issue three Wal-Mart asserts that there is no evidence to support the $300,000 award for past mental anguish. Alternatively Wal-Mart argues that the award is against the great weight and preponderance of the evidence. We conclude that there is evidence to support the award.

In *Parkway Co. v. Woodruff*, 901 S.W.2d 434, 444 (Tex. 1995) the court held that a mental anguish damages award requires evidence of a "high degree of mental pain and distress" that is "more than mere worry, anxiety, vexation, embarrassment, or anger." To recover for mental anguish a plaintiff must offer "direct evidence of the nature, duration, and severity of their mental anguish, thus establishing a substantial disruption in the plaintiffs' daily routine," or other evidence of "'a high degree of mental pain and distress' that is 'more than mere worry, anxiety, vexation, embarrassment, or anger.'" Courts should "closely scrutinize" awards of mental anguish damages. There must also be evidence that the amount of mental anguish damages awarded is fair and reasonable, and the appellate court must perform a "meaningful evidentiary review" of the amount found.

Evidence of Cockrell's mental anguish comes largely from the following testimony: Counsel asked Cockrell to describe his demeanor when he took down his bandage in the manager's office. He stated that Navarro:

> made me feel like I was scum, like . . . I was no part of society, that I had no say-so in the matter, that—just made me feel like a little kid on the block, like the bully beating the kid up and saying, "Well, I didn't catch you with nothing; but I'm going to humiliate him, twist a knife a little bit more into them."

When counsel asked Cockrell how he felt when people looked at the scar he said, "Humiliated. . . . Your dignity has been stripped, been raped. All your rights have been—might as well have been taken away at that time because I had no rights back there. . . . [E]ven after it was over with, I felt like I had no rights."

Cockrell testified that after Navarro let him go he was shaking, crying, nervous, scared, and looking around to make sure no one else was trying to stop him. When he got home his demeanor was about the same.

Cockrell's parents saw him in the Wal-Mart store immediately after he was let go. They said he was upset, nervous, had tears in his eyes, and looked scared, pale, and badly shaken up. When he arrived at home he was crying, nervous, and still "pretty well shook up." His mother said that he stayed upset for a "long time" and would not go out of the house or go anywhere with his parents. She explained that

> he won't go out hardly. And if he does, he just goes with us. And he's always looking around if we go in a store, like he's looking over his shoulder to see if anybody's following him. And he's self-conscious of his stomach, and he feels like everybody knows it. . . .

His father said that:

> Before this happened, he [Cockrell] and I, we were real good buddies. We went places together, you know, and we'd go to the Dairy Queen and we'd go down to the pawn shop and just shop around, you know. And after that, he was—he really didn't want to go nowhere. And I asked him one time, "Why?" He said, "I just don't want to go." And a lot of times—sometimes he might go and sometimes he might sit in the car and I go do what I want to do. But after that, he—he has just recently got out of it, really. . . . [W]e're a member of the lodge and he didn't even want to go to the lodge with me because he was so embarrassed that he might meet someone down there that would confront him with what had happened out there. And he just—recently, we'll go places together now since I retired and he's not been working for a long time. And just got buddy-buddy again, and he's finally come out of it some. But he's still not like he was.

On cross-examination his father said that in 1997 he and Cockrell began going to the Dairy Queen sometimes once or twice a day to socialize.

This is direct evidence of the nature, duration, and severity of Cockrell's mental anguish, thus establishing a substantial disruption in his daily routine. His mental pain and distress was more than mere worry, anxiety, vexation, embarrassment, or anger.

We hold that the evidence is legally and factually sufficient to support the award of mental anguish damages. We overrule issue three.

We AFFIRM the trial court's judgment.

PREPARING FOR CLASS

The case is not terribly complicated but does provide a good discussion of many of the issues that are often associated with false imprisonment claims that arise in a retail setting. Often the injury in these cases is emotional in nature (humiliation; embarrassment; defamation), and the jury will be allowed to decide the dollar figure to assign to each loss. Here we potentially have harm caused by both the assault and the false imprisonment, and it would have been interesting to see what the special verdict form looked like as the jury assigned damages. Damages will be discussed in detail in both Torts II and Remedies, so your consideration here should be minimal and more so to complete the picture than anything else. Privileges, such as the one claimed here, will follow in the next chapter.

INCREASING YOUR UNDERSTANDING

1. Recovery in false imprisonment cases starts with a consideration of the emotional harm caused from being confined. Don't trivialize it, as it is legitimate enough for the courts to impose liability when a person has been civilly "kidnapped." Recovery is not limited, however, to emotional damages; these cases often give rise to a punitive award as well as other compensatory damages that may have flowed from the confinement.

2. There also may be liability for false imprisonment on the person who intentionally provides misleading information to authorities which leads to the plaintiff being detained for investigation or in some cases arrested. "A private citizen at whose request, direction, or command a police officer makes an arrest without a warrant is liable if the arrest turns out to be unlawful." Blackwood v. Cates, 297 N.C. 163, 254 S.E.2d 7 (N.C. 1979). See also McGillivray v. Siedschlaw, 278 N.W.2d 796 (S.D. 1979). (Roommate, who gave police officer pill found on floor of apartment that she shared with plaintiff and who informed police officer that plaintiff was a drug user and then encouraged investigation of plaintiff, which led to plaintiff being arrested, was found liable for false imprisonment). Merely reporting facts, however, to a police officer, and leaving it to that officer's discretion whether to make an arrest, does not subject the reporter to liability for false arrest. See Highfill v. Hale, 186 S.W.3d 277 (Mo. 2006).

Richardson v. Costco Wholesale Corp.
169 F. Supp. 2d 56 (D. Conn. 2001)

EGINTON, Senior District Judge.
This action concerns defendant Costco Wholesale Corporation's employment practice of locking employees in the store during its closing collection procedure. Plaintiffs Elaine Richardson and Heather Antedomenico allege that defendant's lock-in procedure violates the Connecticut General Statutes and the federal Fair Labor Standards Act [(FLSA)], and constitutes false imprisonment Defendant has filed a motion for summary judgment.

BACKGROUND

The parties have submitted briefs, statements of facts pursuant to Local Rule 9(c), and supporting exhibits. These materials reveal the following undisputed facts.

Defendant Costco hired plaintiff Elaine Richardson in September, 1993, at its Waterbury, Connecticut store. She began her career with defendant as a part time cashier and was made a full time cashier in 1994. In 1996, she was transferred to the defendant's warehouse in Brookfield, Connecticut, where she worked as a cashier until her employment terminated in January, 1999.

In 1998, Richardson began having work-related problems. On January 22, 1998, Richardson was asked by a front-end supervisor to sign off on a front-end supervisor checklist. She refused to do so. Richardson was issued a counseling notice for this incident which she refused to sign. On April 29, 1998, Richardson left work without authorization, and received verbal counseling for this violation of Costco policy. On August 22, 1998, Richardson left work 1.2 hours prior to the end of her shift with a line of waiting members at her register. On August 25, 1998, Richardson received a counseling notice and was suspended for three days without pay for this violation of Costco policy.

Plaintiff Heather Antedomenico began her employment with defendant as a seasonal part time employee in September, 1991, working as a membership clerk on a part time basis. In January, 1992, she became a permanent part-time employee. At present, she is employed in this position.

Since February, 1997, Antedomenico has worked 30 hours per week; prior to that time, she worked 20 hours per week. She has not worked more than 40 hours per week since 1994.

At the conclusion of an employee's scheduled work shift, the employee leaves her work station, logs out on defendant's computerized time clock, collects any personal belongings in the employee locker area. An employee may then leave the warehouse unless the collection procedure has commenced. If an employee who has already clocked out does not leave the warehouse prior to the collection procedure, that employee remains in the warehouse until the conclusion of that procedure.

The collection procedure begins after the last customer member leaves Costco's Brookfield warehouse, the member's exit door is closed and locked, and the employee exit door is closed and alarmed. Generally, the collection procedure begins within five minutes after the employee exit door is alarmed.

No employee is allowed to leave the warehouse until the collection procedure is completed. Employees who have completed their shifts have been locked inside the warehouse during the collection procedure. At completion of the procedure, a manager disengages the alarm on the employee door so that any employee whose shift has ended can leave the warehouse. A manager then resets the security alarm on the employee door.

During the collection procedure one person takes tills from the cash registers and brings them to the vault. Another person takes the jewelry and brings it to a merchandise pickup room. A total of 36 cash till and money bags are collected during this process. Once in the vault, the manager signs a log showing the time that the cash was placed in the vault.

Plaintiffs assert that the collection procedure has taken up to 40 minutes on nights when they have been locked in the store. Plaintiffs also state that the collection procedure can take as little as ten minutes.

Neither plaintiff has records reflecting when or how often they remained in the warehouse during closing procedures. Antedomenico claims that she has remained in the warehouse during closing procedure once or twice since March, 1998.

Employees may leave the warehouse during closing procedures during an emergency situation. However, employees leaving for reasons other than an emergency could be subject to disciplinary action.

This action was commenced in Connecticut superior court on March 2, 1998, and removed to federal court on March 18, 1998.

DISCUSSION

A motion for summary judgment will be granted where there is no genuine issue as to any material fact and it is clear that the moving party is entitled to judgment as a matter of law. "Only when reasonable minds could not differ as to the import of the evidence is summary judgment proper."

COUNT THREE

In count three, plaintiffs assert that the lock-in procedure constitutes false imprisonment. Defendant argues that plaintiffs cannot prove the prima facie case of false imprisonment.

To establish liability for false imprisonment, plaintiffs must prove each of the following elements: (1) their physical liberty was actually restrained; (2) the defendant intended to confine them; (3) they were conscious of the confinement; (4) they did not consent to the confinement; and (5) the confinement was not otherwise privileged. False imprisonment can only be based upon circumstances that include actual restraint, threat of force or the assertion of legal authority.

In this instance, plaintiffs cannot prove that they were physically or actually restrained because a safe avenue of escape existed through the employee exit. *See* Restatement (Second) of Torts §36 (1965). The evidence demonstrates that Richardson and Antedomenico understood that they could exit through the employee door during the closing procedures. The fact that opening the employee exit door would result in an alarm sounding and possible employee discipline does not give rise to an inference that actual confinement or threatening conduct took place. Moral pressure or threat of losing one's job does not constitute a threat of force sufficient to establish that plaintiffs' were involuntary restrained. Testimony that two managers once ran after an employee who exited during closing procedures and informed her that she would be suspended for her conduct does not establish a threat of force.

Plaintiffs argue that the employee exit was not a reasonable means of egress because it would entail triggering an alarm. A reasonable means of escape does not exist if the circumstances are such as to make it offensive to a reasonable sense of decency or personal dignity. Restatement (Second) of Torts, §36(2), Comment a. However, the Restatement elaborates that it is unreasonable to refuse to utilize a means of escape because it entails "a slight inconvenience or requires him to commit a technical invasion of another's possessory interest. . . ." For example, as illustrated by the Restatement, it is unreasonable to require an unclothed individual to exit into a room of people, or to require an individual to use an exit that would cause material damage to her clothing. Exiting through an alarmed door in this instance does not rise to the level of offensiveness contemplated by the Restatement. The court will enter summary judgment on count three.

SO ORDERED.

PREPARING FOR CLASS

1. Given these economic times, would a failure for plaintiffs to leave under these circumstances still be considered a voluntary act, compelled by moral pressure? Should a threat of losing one's job always be considered, as a matter of law, insufficient to constitute the restraint necessary to prevail on a false imprisonment claim?

2. Liability for false imprisonment will only follow if the confinement results from the defendant's intentional acts. The burden lies with the plaintiff to prove all of the elements of the claim. Sometimes plaintiffs who have been wronged lose because the facts aren't helpful.

APPLYING THE LAW

Girlfriend, in jealous rage, locks boyfriend in bedroom after they return from sorority formal. Boyfriend, who is the star running back for the football team, has no clothes available to him except the tuxedo he wore for the evening. Window in girlfriend's second floor bedroom is right above a trash dumpster. Does the law require that he take the plunge?

INCREASING YOUR UNDERSTANDING

Confined or inconvenienced? Courts have no interest in hearing claims of false imprisonment in cases where the plaintiff could have, through reasonable efforts, avoided being confined. However, one unlawfully confined by another is not required to attempt an escape if he has a reasonable belief that an attempt would involve the risk of personal injury or insult. Titus v. Montgomery Ward & Co., 232 Mo. App. 987, 993, 123 S.W.2d 574.

Parvi v. City of Kingston
Court of Appeals of New York, 1977
41 N.Y.2d 553, 362 N.E.2d 960, 394 N.Y.S.2d 161 (N.Y. App. Div. 1977)

FUCHSBERG, Justice.

This appeal brings up for review the dismissal, at the end of the plaintiff's case, of two causes of action, both of which arise out of the same somewhat unusual train of events. One is for false imprisonment and the other for negligence. The judgment of dismissal was affirmed by the Appellate Division by a vote of three to two. The issue before us, as to each count, is whether a prima facie case was made out. We believe it was.

Bearing in mind that, at the procedural point at which the case was decided, the plaintiff was entitled to the benefit of the most favorable inferences that were to be drawn from the record we turn at once to the proof. In doing so, for the present we rely in the main on testimony plaintiff adduced from the defendant's own employees, especially since plaintiff's own recollection of the events was less than satisfactory.

Sometime after 9:00 P.M. on the evening of May 28, 1972, a date which occurred during the Memorial Day weekend, two police officers employed by the defendant City of Kingston responded in a radio patrol car to the rear of a commercial building in that city where they had been informed some individuals were acting in a boisterous manner. Upon their arrival, they found three men, one Raymond Dugan, his brother Dixie Dugan and the plaintiff, Donald C. Parvi. According to the police, it was the Dugan brothers who alone were then engaged in a noisy quarrel. When the two uniformed officers informed the three they would have to move on or be locked up, Raymond Dugan ran away; Dixie Dugan chased after him unsuccessfully and then returned to the scene in a minute or two; Parvi, who the police testimony shows had been trying to calm the Dugans, remained where he was.

In the course of their examinations before trial, read into evidence by Parvi's counsel, the officers described all three as exhibiting, in an unspecified manner, evidence that they "had been drinking" and showed "the effects of alcohol." They went on to relate how, when Parvi and Dixie Dugan said they had no place to go, the officers ordered them into the police car and, pursuing a then prevailing police "standard operating procedure," transported the two men outside the city limits to an abandoned golf course located in an unlit and isolated area known as Coleman Hill. Thereupon the officers drove off, leaving Parvi and Dugan to "dry out." This was the first time Parvi had ever been there. En route they had asked to be left off at another place, but the police refused to do so.

No more than 350 feet from the spot where they were dropped off, one of the boundaries of the property adjoins the New York State Thruway. There were no intervening fences or barriers other than the low Thruway guardrail intended to keep vehicular traffic on the road. Before they left, it is undisputed that the police made no effort to learn whether Parvi was oriented to his whereabouts, to instruct him as to the route back to Kingston, where Parvi had then lived for 12 years, or to ascertain where he would go from there. From where the men were dropped, the "humming and buzzing" of fast-traveling, holiday-bound automobile traffic was clearly audible from the Thruway; in their befuddled state, which later left Parvi with very little memory of the events, the men lost little time in responding to its siren song. For, in an apparent effort to get back, by 10:00 P.M. Parvi and Dugan had wandered onto the Thruway, where they were struck by an automobile operated by one David R. Darling. Parvi was severely injured, Dugan was killed.

THE CAUSE OF ACTION FOR FALSE IMPRISONMENT

With these facts before us, we initially direct our attention to Parvi's cause of action for false imprisonment. Only recently, we had occasion to set out the four elements of that tort in Broughton v. State of New York, 37 N.Y.2d 451, 456, 373 N.Y.S.2d 87, 93, 335 N.E.2d 310, 314, where we said that "the plaintiff must show that: (1) the defendant intended to confine him, (2) the plaintiff was conscious of the confinement, (3) the plaintiff did not consent to the confinement and (4) the confinement was not otherwise privileged."

Elements (1) and (3) present no problem here. When the plaintiff stated he had no place to go, he was faced with but one alternative arrest. This was hardly the stuff of which consent is formed, especially in light of the fact that Parvi was, in a degree to be measured by the jury, then under the influence of alcohol. It is also of no small moment in this regard that the men's request to be released at a place they designated was refused. Moreover, one of the policemen testified that his fellow officer alone selected the location to which Parvi was taken; indeed, this was a place to which the police had had prior occasion to bring others who were being "run out of town" because they evidenced signs of intoxication. Further, putting aside for the time being the question of whether such an arrest would have been privileged, it can hardly be contended that, in view of the direct and willful nature of their actions, there was no proof that the police officers intended to confine Parvi.

Element (2), consciousness of confinement, is a more subtle and more interesting subissue in this case. On that subject, we note that, while respected authorities have divided on whether awareness of confinement by one who has been falsely imprisoned should be a sine qua non for making out a case, *Broughton*, supra, has laid that question to rest in this State. Its holding gives recognition to the fact that false imprisonment, as a dignitary tort, is not suffered unless its victim knows of the dignitary invasion. Interestingly, the Restatement of Torts 2d (§42) too has taken the position that there is no liability for intentionally confining another unless the person physically restrained knows of the confinement or is harmed by it.

However, though correctly proceeding on that premise, the Appellate Division, in affirming the dismissal of the cause of action for false imprisonment, erroneously relied on the fact that Parvi, after having provided additional testimony in his own behalf on direct examination, had agreed on cross that he no longer had any recollection of his confinement. In so doing, that court failed to distinguish between a later recollection of consciousness and the existence of that consciousness at the time when the imprisonment itself took place. The latter, of course, is capable of being proved though one who suffers the consciousness can no longer personally describe it, whether by reason of lapse of memory, incompetency, death or other cause. Specifically, in this case, while it may well be that the alcohol Parvi had imbibed or the injuries he sustained, or both, had had the effect of wiping out his recollection of being in the police car against his will, that is a far cry from saying that he was not conscious of his confinement at the time when it was actually taking place. And, even if plaintiff's sentient state at the time of his imprisonment was something less than total sobriety, that does not mean that he had no conscious sense of what was then happening to him. To the contrary, there is much in the record to support a finding that the plaintiff indeed was aware of his arrest at the time it took place. By way of illustration, the officers described Parvi's responsiveness to their command that he get into the car, his colloquy while being driven to Coleman Hill and his request to be let off elsewhere. At the very least, then, it was for the jury, in the first instance, to weigh credibility, evaluate inconsistencies and determine whether the burden of proof had been met.

Accordingly, the order of the Appellate Division should be reversed.

BREITEL, Chief Judge (dissenting).

I dissent. On no view of the facts should plaintiff, brought to causing his own serious injury by his voluntary intoxication, be allowed to recover from the City of Kingston for damages suffered when he wandered onto the New York State Thruway and was struck by an automobile. His attack is the familiar one on the good Samaritan, in the persons of two police officers, for not having, in retrospect, done enough.

... So long as Parvi did not remain out in public, intoxicated, creating a public nuisance, and endangering his own life, the officers had no wish to interfere with Parvi's freedom of movement. Since Parvi could suggest no suitable place where the officers might take him, the officers chose another site. Apparently, Parvi and Dugan were pleased with the choice. And it should not matter that Parvi testified, although he could recall nothing else, that he was ordered into a police car "against (his) will". (On cross-examination, he said he recalled nothing that day.) Parvi's "will" was to stay where he was, intoxicated, in public. In order to deprive him of that one choice, which the officers could do without subjecting themselves to liability for false imprisonment, the officers had to transport Parvi some place else. He was given a choice as to destination. He declined it, except for his later suggestion of an unsafe place, and the officers made the choice for him. There was no confinement, and hence no false imprisonment.

Moreover, plaintiff has failed even to make out a prima facie case that he was conscious of his purported confinement, and that he failed to consent to it. His memory of the entire incident had disappeared; at trial, Parvi admitted that he no longer had any independent recollection of what happened on the day of his accident, and that as to the circumstances surrounding his entrance into the police car, he only knew what had been suggested to him by subsequent conversations. In light of this testimony, Parvi's conclusory statement that he was ordered into the car against his will is insufficient, as a matter of law, to establish a prima facie case.

PREPARING FOR CLASS

1. Assuming he was falsely imprisoned, Parvi would probably be able to recover under the Restatement rule that allows recovery when one suffers injury as a result of the confinement.

2. Indentify the acts of confinement by the police officers.

3. Remember that while Parvi's recall deficiency might limit his damages for the stress of being confined, even a nominal award might support a claim for punitive damages.

E. INTENTIONAL INFLICTION OF EMOTIONAL DISTRESS

Eckenrode v. Life of America Ins. Co.
470 F.2d 1 (7th Cir. 1972)

KILEY, Circuit Judge.
Plaintiff, a resident of Pennsylvania, filed this three count diversity complaint to recover damages for severe emotional injury suffered as a result of the deliberate refusal of Life of America Insurance Company (Insurer), of Chicago, to pay her the proceeds of Insurer's policy covering the life of her husband. The district court dismissed the suit. Plaintiff has appealed. We reverse.

. . . In Count II she sought compensatory damage for Insurer's "outrageous conduct" in refusing to pay her the policy proceeds when its duty was clear and when it knew of plaintiff's and her family's financial distress. In Count III she sought compensatory and punitive damages 1) because Insurer allegedly defrauded decedent into the insurance contract by its promise of payment of benefits immediately upon proof of the insured's death from "accidental causes," while at the time its practice was not to pay meritorious claims; and 2) because Insurer allegedly sought by "economic coercion" to compel plaintiff—so increasingly financially distressed—to accept less than the face value of the policy or be forced to sue for payment of the proceeds.

The district court dismissed Counts II and III as stating no claim on which relief could be granted. . . .

I.

Taking the allegations, properly pleaded in Counts II and III, as true, the following facts are stated: Defendant's life insurance policy covering plaintiff's husband issued September 22, 1967. Under the policy Insurer agreed to pay plaintiff $5,000 immediately upon due proof of death from "accidental causes." On December 17, 1967, insured was an accidental victim of a homicide. Plaintiff met all conditions of the policy and repeatedly demanded payment, but Insurer refused to pay. Decedent left plaintiff with several children, but no property of value. She had no money, none even for the funeral expenses. Denied payment by Insurer, she was required to borrow money to support her family, while her financial condition worsened. The family was required to live with, and accept charity from, relatives.

Further: Insurer knew or should have known of the death of decedent from accidental causes and of plaintiff's dire need of the policy proceeds. Yet Insurer repeatedly and deliberately refused her demands for payment, and as a proximate result she was caused to suffer "severe distress and disturbance of [her] mental tranquility." Instead of paying her the proceeds of the policy, and being fully aware of the accidental cause of decedent's death and of plaintiff's financial distress, Insurer breached the policy promise to pay immediately upon proof of death. Insurer, knowing full well that plaintiff needed the proceeds of the policy to provide necessaries for her children, applied "economic coercion" in refusing to make payment on the policy, and in "inviting" plaintiff to "compromise" her claim by implying it (Insurer) had a valid defense to the claim.

II.

The issue before us with respect to Counts II and III is whether plaintiff— beneficiary of her husband's life insurance policy—may on the foregoing "facts" recover damages for severe mental distress allegedly suffered as a result of Insurer's conduct. Illinois law controls our decision, and, in anticipation that the Illinois Supreme Court would hold as we do, we decide the issue in favor of plaintiff.

We have no doubt, in view of Knierim v. Izzo, 22 Ill. 2d 73, 174 N.E.2d 157 (1961), that the Illinois Supreme Court would sustain plaintiff's complaint against Insurer's motion to dismiss.

In *Knierim*, plaintiff filed a wrongful death action alleging, inter alia, that defendant Izzo threatened her with the murder of her husband, carried out the threat, and thereby proximately caused her severe emotional distress. The trial court dismissed her complaint, but the Illinois Supreme Court reversed and held that plaintiff had stated a cause of action for an intentional causing of severe emotional distress by Izzo's "outrageous conduct."

The court recognized the "new tort" of intentional infliction of severe emotional distress, following similar recognition by an "increasing number of courts," and cited several state decisions. 174 N.E.2d at 163. The court rejected reasons given by other courts not recognizing the "new tort." As to the reason that mental disturbance is incapable of financial measurement, the court pointed out that "pain and suffering" and "mental suffering" are elements of damage, respectively, in personal injury and malicious prosecution cases. 174 N.E.2d at 163. As to the reason that mental consequences are too evanescent for the law to deal with, the court noted that psychosomatic medicine had learned much in the past "thirty years" about the bodily effects of man's emotions, and that symptoms produced by "stronger emotions" are now visible to the professional eye. 174 N.E.2d at 164. As to the reason that recognizing the "new tort" would lead to frivolous claims, the court observed that triers of fact from their own experiences would be able to draw a line between "slight hurts" and "outrageous conduct." *Id.* And finally, as to the reason that mental consequences vary greatly with the individual so as to pose difficulties too great for the law, the court adopted an objective standard against which emotional distress could be measured. The court thought that the standard of "severe emotional distress to a person of ordinary sensibilities, in the absence of special knowledge or notice" would be a sufficient limit for excluding "mere vulgarities . . . as meaningless abusive expressions." 174 N.E.2d at 165. The court noted that the "reasonable man" is well known to triers of fact who are also well acquainted with "the man of ordinary sensibilities."

The court added a cautionary note, expressing confidence that Illinois trial judges would not permit litigation to introduce "trivialities and mere bad manners" under the cloak of the "new tort." The court concluded—with implications from the famous Warren-Brandeis article on the "new tort" or privacy—that peace of mind is a personal interest of sufficient importance to receive the law's protection against intentional invasion by "outrageous conduct," and that the allegations in Mrs. Knierim's complaint stated a cause of action.

In *Knierim* the court, inter alia, relied upon State Rubbish Collectors Association v. Siliznoff, 38 Cal. 2d 330, 240 P.2d 282 (1952), and Restatement,

Torts §46 (1948 Supp.). In *Siliznoff* the California Supreme Court, in an opinion by Justice Roger Traynor, recognized the "new tort" for the first time and held that Siliznoff could recover from the cross-defendant Rubbish Collectors Association for mental distress caused by the Association's severe threats to beat him up, destroy his truck and put him out of business unless Siliznoff offered to pay over certain proceeds to the Association. Later, the California Supreme Court *en banc* affirmed a trial court judgment against an insurance company, including $25,000 for mental suffering caused by the insurance company's earlier unreasonable refusal to accept a settlement within the limits of the liability policy. Crisci v. Security Ins. Co. of New Haven, 66 Cal. 2d 425, 58 Cal. Rptr. 13, 426 P.2d 173 (1970). There Mrs. Crisci's mental distress claim was in addition to her loss of property caused by the insurance company's failure to settle. The court thought that where there were substantial damages apart from the mental distress, the danger of fictitious claims was reduced. Subsequently in Fletcher v. Western National Life Ins. Co., 10 Cal. App. 3d 376, 89 Cal. Rptr. 78 (1970), an appellate court relying upon *Siliznoff* and *Crisci*, held that the defendant insurance company's threatened and actual bad faith refusals to make payments under the disability policy were essentially tortious in nature and could legally be the basis for an action against the company for intentional infliction of emotional distress. The decision rested on the finding that the refusals were maliciously employed by the company in concert with false and threatening communications directed to the badly injured plaintiff-insured for the purpose of causing him to surrender his policy or disadvantageously settle a nonexistent dispute. 89 Cal. Rptr. at 93. The court found sufficient evidence showing emotional distress of the "requisite severity" (*i.e.*, outrageousness), and thus affirmed the trial court's denial of judgment N.O.V.

We think that the California court in *Fletcher, supra*, set out correctly the elements of a prima facie case for the tort of "intentional infliction of severe emotional distress":

(1) Outrageous conduct by the defendant;

(2) The defendant's intention of causing, or reckless disregard of the probability of causing emotional distress;

(3) The plaintiff's suffering severe or extreme emotional distress; and

(4) Actual and proximate causation of the emotional distress by the defendant's outrageous conduct.

See *Knierim, supra*; Restatement 2d Torts, §46(1); Prosser, Torts §11 (3d Ed. 1964).

It is our view that were this case before the Illinois Supreme Court, that court would find the foregoing elements substantially correct; and that plaintiff here has sufficiently pleaded the elements.

It is recognized that the outrageous character of a person's conduct may arise from an abuse by that person of a position which gives him power to affect the interests of another; and that in this sense extreme "bullying tactics" and other "high pressure" methods of insurance adjusters seeking to force compromises or settlements may constitute outrageous conduct. It is also recognized that the extreme character of a person's conduct may arise from that person's knowledge that the other is peculiarly susceptible to emotional distress by reason of some physical or mental condition or peculiarity.

Here Insurer's alleged bad faith refusal to make payment on the policy, coupled with its deliberate use of "economic coercion" (*i.e.*, by delaying and refusing payment it increased plaintiff's financial distress thereby coercing her to compromise and settle) to force a settlement, clearly rises to the level of "outrageous conduct" to a person of "ordinary sensibilities."

Furthermore, it is common knowledge that one of the most frequent considerations in procuring life insurance is to ensure the continued economic and mental welfare of the beneficiaries upon the death of the insured. The very risks insured against presuppose that upon the death of the insured the beneficiary might be in difficult circumstances and thus particularly susceptible and vulnerable to high pressure tactics by an economically powerful entity. In the case before us Insurer's alleged high pressure methods (economic coercion) were aimed at the very thing insured against, and we think that the insurance company was on notice that plaintiff would be particularly vulnerable to mental distress by reason of her financial plight.

In deciding as we do, we note that insurance business affects a great many people, is subject to substantial governmental regulation and is stamped with a public interest. We also note that insurance contracts are subject to the same implied conditions of good faith and fair dealing as are other contracts.

It is true that settlement tactics may be privileged under circumstances where an insurer has done no more than insist upon his legal rights in a permissible way. But we do not think that a refusal to make payments based on a bad faith insistence on a non-existent defense is privileged conduct against the complaint here.

III.

We hold, however, that plaintiff may not recover punitive damages because in our view *Knierim v. Izzo, supra,* will not support an anticipation that the Illinois Supreme Court would sustain a judgment allowing punitive damages. In *Knierim* the Illinois Supreme Court stated:

> We believe, nevertheless, that punitive damages cannot be sanctioned as an additional recovery in such an action. Since the outrageous quality of the defendant's conduct forms the basis of the action, the rendition of compensatory damages will be sufficiently punitive.

The court then went on to hold effectually that the trial court did not err in dismissing the "portions of Counts III and IV that related to . . . punitive damages."[6] We fail to see, in the face of that language how we can anticipate that punitive damages are permissible in an action under the "new tort" in Illinois.

For the reasons given, the judgment of the district court dismissing Counts II and III of plaintiff's complaint is hereby reversed.

PREPARING FOR CLASS

1. Plaintiffs have both a contract and tort claim under these facts. The remedy for the contract claims would likely be limited to recovering the policy amounts plus interest as the emotional distress (special or consequential) damages would not be recoverable in a contract action. The tort claim is therefore appealing because of the considerable emotional angst that emanated from the defendant's conduct. But the plaintiffs are going to have to first convince the court that it should recognize this "new tort."

2. Since the case was suited in federal court, but brought as a state law claim, the court had to predict how the Illinois Supreme Court would respond to such a claim were it brought before it—not a comfortable task given that there was only one other case that seemed to be on point. In short, state, not federal law, governed this dispute.

3. Historically there has been a distinct judicial bigotry when it comes to mental or emotional matters, whether it involve attempts to recover for emotional distress **alone** or pleas from insane defendants that allowances should be made for acts committed while mentally impaired. Pay particular attention to how this court justifies accepting plaintiffs' invitation to recognize an intentional infliction of emotional distress claim.

INCREASING YOUR UNDERSTANDING

1. *Historical limitations.* Tort law has from its inception primarily been contoured to provide redress for physical injuries that resulted from tortious conduct. Recovery for emotional distress damages would be allowed when parasitic to another recognized claim, i.e., one of the other common law intentional torts. So it was possible for a plaintiff to recover for the apprehension from an assault or false imprisonment, provided all the requirements could be met, but the plaintiff would be

---

6. In this respect the Illinois court stopped short of the California courts which approve punitive damages in the "new tort." 89 Cal. Rptr. at 95.

denied recovery for emotional distress damages if his claim was incapable of being attached to one recognized under the common law.

2. Numerous justifications have been offered for why the plaintiff whose sole injury is emotional alone should be denied judicial redress, and most of them are cited by the *Eckenrode* court, though the shadow of reluctance lingers. The American Law Institute (ALI) in the First Restatement of Torts took the following position:

> "The interest in mental and emotional tranquility and, therefore, in freedom from mental and emotional disturbance is not, as a thing in itself, regarded as of sufficient importance to require others to refrain from conduct intended or recognizably likely to cause such a disturbance. . . ." Restatement (First) of Torts §46 (Conduct Intended To Cause Emotional Distress Only) cmt. C (1934).

Soon thereafter, the ALI reversed itself and eventually re-articulated §46 in the version cited in *Eckenrode*.

3. *Intentional or reckless behavior.* The defendant must act for the purpose of causing emotional distress or in a manner where she knows that her actions are substantially certain to cause it. Restatement (Second) of Torts §46, comment i. Recklessness can be described generally as acting indifferently in the face of a known risk. Since the doctrine of transferred intent has not been extended to intentional infliction of emotional distress (IIED) claims, the plaintiff must in all circumstances show that the defendant's acts were directed toward her. The following case, *GTE*, addresses the other elements of the claim.

GTE Southwest, Inc. v. Bruce
998 S.W.2d 605 (Tex. 1999)

Justice ABBOTT delivered the opinion of the Court.

In this case we determine whether three GTE Southwest, Incorporated employees may recover damages for intentional infliction of emotional distress based on the workplace conduct of their supervisor. The trial court rendered judgment for the employees on the jury verdict, and the court of appeals affirmed. We affirm the judgment of the court of appeals.

I. FACTS

Three GTE employees, Rhonda Bruce, Linda Davis, and Joyce Poelstra, sued GTE for intentional infliction of emotional distress premised on the constant humiliating and abusive behavior of their supervisor, Morris Shields. Shields is a former U.S. Army supply sergeant who began working for GTE in 1971. Between 1981 and May 1991, Shields worked as a supervisor in GTE's supply department in Jacksonville, Arkansas. During his tenure there, four of Shields's subordinate employees (none of the employees involved in this case) filed formal grievances against Shields with GTE, alleging that Shields constantly harassed them. As a result of these complaints, GTE investigated Shields's conduct in 1988 and 1989, but took no formal disciplinary action against him.

In May 1991, GTE transferred Shields from Jacksonville to Nash, Texas, where he became the supply operations supervisor. The supply department at Nash was small, consisting of two offices and a store room. There were approximately eight employees other than Shields. Bruce, Davis, and Poelstra ("the employees") worked under Shields at the Nash facility. Like the GTE employees in Jacksonville, Bruce, Davis, and Poelstra complained to GTE of Shields's conduct, alleging that Shields constantly harassed and intimidated them. The employees complained about Shields's daily use of profanity, short temper, and his abusive and vulgar dictatorial manner. The employees complained that, among other offensive acts, Shields repeatedly yelled, screamed, cursed, and even "charged" at them. In addition, he intentionally humiliated and embarrassed the employees.

GTE investigated these complaints in April 1992, after which GTE issued Shields a "letter of reprimand." After the reprimand, Shields discontinued some of his egregious conduct, but did not end it completely.

Eventually, Bruce, Davis, and Poelstra sought medical treatment for emotional distress caused by Shields's conduct. In March 1994, the employees filed suit, alleging that GTE intentionally inflicted emotional distress on them through Shields. The employees asserted no causes of action other than intentional infliction of emotional distress. The jury awarded $100,000.00 plus prejudgment interest to Bruce, $100,000.00 plus interest to Davis, and $75,000.00 plus interest to Poelstra.

III. Intentional Infliction of Emotional Distress

An employee may recover damages for intentional infliction of emotional distress in an employment context as long as the employee establishes the elements of the cause of action. *See Wornick Co. v. Casas*, 856 S.W.2d 732, 734 (Tex. 1993). To recover damages for intentional infliction of emotional distress, a plaintiff must prove that: (1) the defendant acted intentionally or recklessly; (2) the conduct was extreme and outrageous; (3) the actions of the defendant caused the plaintiff emotional distress; and (4) the resulting emotional distress was severe. *Standard Fruit & Vegetable Co. v. Johnson*, 985 S.W.2d 62, 65 (Tex. 1998). In addition, "[a] claim for intentional infliction of emotional distress cannot be maintained when the risk that emotional

distress will result is merely incidental to the commission of some other tort."
Id. at 68. Accordingly, a claim for intentional infliction of emotional distress
will not lie if emotional distress is not the intended or primary consequence of
the defendant's conduct. *Id.*

GTE contests its liability for intentional infliction of emotional distress on
several grounds. First, GTE argues that the alleged conduct does not rise to the
level necessary to constitute extreme and outrageous conduct. Second, GTE
argues that the employees did not prove that GTE, as opposed to Shields, had
the requisite intent. And, third, GTE contends that the employees have not
shown that they suffered severe emotional distress. We consider these arguments in turn.

A. EXTREME AND OUTRAGEOUS CONDUCT

GTE first argues that Shields's conduct is not extreme and outrageous.
To be extreme and outrageous, conduct must be "so outrageous in character,
and so extreme in degree, as to go beyond all possible bounds of decency, and
to be regarded as atrocious, and utterly intolerable in a civilized community."
Generally, insensitive or even rude behavior does not constitute extreme and
outrageous conduct. Similarly, mere insults, indignities, threats, annoyances,
petty oppressions, or other trivialities do not rise to the level of extreme and
outrageous conduct.

In determining whether certain conduct is extreme and outrageous, courts
consider the context and the relationship between the parties. "The extreme
and outrageous character of the conduct may arise from an abuse by the actor
of a position, or a relation with the other, which gives him actual or apparent
authority over the other, or power to affect his interests." Restatement (Second)
of Torts §46 cmt. e (1965).

In the employment context, some courts have held that a plaintiff's status as
an employee should entitle him to a greater degree of protection from insult
and outrage by a supervisor with authority over him than if he were a stranger.
This approach is based partly on the rationale that, as opposed to most casual
and temporary relationships, the workplace environment provides a captive
victim and the opportunity for prolonged abuse.

In contrast, several courts, including Texas courts, have adopted a strict
approach to intentional infliction of emotional distress claims arising in the
workplace. These courts rely on the fact that, to properly manage its business,
an employer must be able to supervise, review, criticize, demote, transfer, and
discipline employees. Although many of these acts are necessarily unpleasant
for the employee, an employer must have latitude to exercise these rights in a
permissible way, even though emotional distress results. We agree with the
approach taken by these courts.

Given these considerations, Texas courts have held that a claim for intentional infliction of emotional distress does not lie for ordinary employment
disputes The range of behavior encompassed in "employment disputes" is

broad, and includes at a minimum such things as criticism, lack of recognition, and low evaluations, which, although unpleasant and sometimes unfair, are ordinarily expected in the work environment. Thus, to establish a cause of action for intentional infliction of emotional distress in the workplace, an employee must prove the existence of some conduct that brings the dispute outside the scope of an ordinary employment dispute and into the realm of extreme and outrageous conduct. Such extreme conduct exists only in the most unusual of circumstances.

GTE contends that the evidence establishes nothing more than an ordinary employment dispute. To the contrary, the employees produced evidence that, over a period of more than two years, Shields engaged in a pattern of grossly abusive, threatening, and degrading conduct. Shields began regularly using the harshest vulgarity shortly after his arrival at the Nash facility. In response, Bruce and Davis informed Shields that they were uncomfortable with obscene jokes, vulgar cursing, and sexual innuendo in the office. Despite these objections, Shields continued to use exceedingly vulgar language on a daily basis. Several witnesses testified that Shields used the word "f——" as part of his normal pattern of conversation, and that he regularly heaped abusive profanity on the employees. Linda Davis testified that Shields used this language to get a reaction. Gene Martin, another GTE employee, testified that Shields used the words "f——" and "motherf——er" frequently when speaking with the employees. On one occasion when Bruce asked Shields to curb his language because it was offensive, Shields positioned himself in front of her face, and screamed, "I will do and say any damn thing I want. And I don't give a s——who likes it." Another typical example is when Gene Martin asked Shields to stop his yelling and vulgarity because it upset the female employees, and Shields replied "I'm tired of walking on f——ing eggshells, trying to make people happy around here." There was further evidence that Shields's harsh and vulgar language was not merely accidental, but seemed intended to abuse the employees.

More importantly, the employees testified that Shields repeatedly physically and verbally threatened and terrorized them. There was evidence that Shields was continuously in a rage, and that Shields would frequently assault each of the employees by physically charging at them. When doing so, Shields would bend his head down, put his arms straight down by his sides, ball his hands into fists, and walk quickly toward or "lunge" at the employees, stopping uncomfortably close to their faces while screaming and yelling. The employees were exceedingly frightened by this behavior, afraid that Shields might hit them. Linda Davis testified that Shields charged the employees with the intent to frighten them. At least once, another employee came between Shields and Poelstra to protect her from Shields's charge. A number of witnesses testified that Shields frequently yelled and screamed at the top of his voice, and pounded his fists when requesting the employees to do things. Bruce testified that Shields would "come up fast" and "get up over her"—causing her to lean back—and yell and scream in her face for her to get things for him. Shields included vulgar language in his yelling and screaming. Bruce stated that such conduct was not a part of any disciplinary action against her. Further, the incidents usually occurred in the open rather than in private. Bruce testified that, on one occasion, Shields began beating a banana on his desk, and when he jumped up and slammed the banana into the trash, Bruce thought he would hit her. Afterwards, Shields was shaking and said "I'm sick."

Bruce also told of an occasion when Shields entered Bruce's office and went into a rage because Davis had left her purse on a chair and Bruce had placed her umbrella on a filing cabinet in the office. Shields yelled and screamed for Bruce to clean up her office. Shields yelled, "If you don't get things picked up in this office, you will not be working for me." He later said that Bruce and Davis would be sent to the unemployment line and "could be replaced by two Kelly girls" that were twenty years old. On another occasion, Shields came up behind Bruce and said, "You're going to be in the unemployment line." Once he told Bruce that he had been sent to Nash to fire her. Another time, he typed "quit" on his computer and said, "That's what you can do." Davis testified that Shields threatened to "get them" for complaining about his behavior. And both Bruce and Martin testified that Shields had stated that "he was in a position to get even for what [the employees] had done."

Bruce also testified that Shields called her into his office every day and would have her stand in front of him, sometimes for as long as thirty minutes, while Shields simply stared at her. Bruce was not allowed to leave Shields's office until she was dismissed, even though Shields would periodically talk on the phone or read papers. This often occurred several times a day. Bruce testified that it made her nauseated and intimidated her. On one occasion, Shields backed Bruce into a corner, leaned over her, and said, "Rumor has it that you know how to get anything you want out here." During an annual review, Shields said to Bruce, "You're mean and you're deadly, very deadly." Davis also testified that Shields would stand over her desk and stare at her.

Shields required Bruce and Davis, both general clerks at GTE, to purchase vacuum cleaners with company funds and to vacuum their offices daily, despite the fact that the company had a cleaning service that performed janitorial services such as vacuuming. The purpose of this seemed not to clean, but to humiliate. Bruce testified that she was ridiculed by other employees. Shields also yelled and screamed when he discovered a spot on the carpet; he made Bruce get on her hands and knees and clean the spots while he stood over her yelling. Poelstra testified that Shields required her to clean tobacco stains from a wall in the warehouse. Poelstra testified that, after she forgot her paperwork for a driving test, Shields ordered her to wear a post-it note on her shirt that said, "Don't forget your paperwork." Other witnesses corroborated the employees' testimony about Shields's conduct.

In considering whether the evidence establishes more than an ordinary employment dispute, we will also address GTE's argument that because none of Shields's acts standing alone rises to the level of outrageous conduct, the court of appeals erred in holding that, considered cumulatively, the conduct was extreme and outrageous.

As already noted, the employees demonstrated at trial that Shields engaged in a course of harassing conduct directed at each of them, the totality of which caused severe emotional distress. It is well recognized outside of the employment context that a course of harassing conduct may support liability for intentional infliction of emotional distress. In such cases, courts consider the totality of the conduct in determining whether it is extreme and outrageous. *See id.* (analyzing creditor's entire course of conduct, including repetitive threatening phone calls and letters).

Similarly, in the employment context, courts and commentators have almost unanimously recognized that liability may arise when one in a position of authority engages in repeated or ongoing harassment of an employee, if the cumulative quality and quantity of the harassment is extreme and outrageous.

When such repeated or ongoing harassment is alleged, the offensive conduct is evaluated as a whole. In addition to the court of appeals in this case, at least two other Texas courts of appeals have followed this approach. *See Qualicare, Inc. v. Runnels*, 863 S.W.2d 220, 223 (Tex. App.-Eastland 1993, no writ) (considering as a whole evidence that supervisor made repeated threats and phone calls, surveilled the employees, and sent a black floral arrangement as a death threat); *American Med. Int'l, Inc. v. Giurintano*, 821 S.W.2d 331, 340-42 (Tex. App.-Houston [14th Dist.] 1991, no writ) (considering as a whole evidence that hospital administrators spread rumors, yelled at, cursed, and insulted plaintiff as part of conspiracy to engage plaintiff in confrontations and use his responses to oppose his appointment). GTE cites no cases to the contrary

We agree with the overwhelming weight of authority in this state and around the country that when repeated or ongoing severe harassment is shown, the conduct should be evaluated as a whole in determining whether it is extreme and outrageous. Accordingly, we hold that the court of appeals did not err in doing so.

We now consider whether Shields's conduct, taken as a whole, amounts to extreme and outrageous conduct. "It is for the court to determine, in the first instance, whether the defendant's conduct may reasonably be regarded as so extreme and outrageous as to permit recovery. . . ." When reasonable minds may differ, however, it is for the jury, subject to the court's control, to determine whether, in the particular case, the conduct has been sufficiently extreme and outrageous to result in liability. Restatement (Second) of Torts §46 cmt. h. To support liability for intentional infliction of emotional distress, it is not enough that the defendant has acted with an intent that is tortious, malicious, or even criminal, or that he has intended to inflict emotional distress. *Id.* §46 cmt. d. Although the defendant's intent is relevant, the conduct itself must be extreme and outrageous to support liability.

GTE argues that the conduct complained of is an ordinary employment dispute because the employees' complaints are really that Shields was a poor supervisor with an objectionable management style. GTE also contends that the actions are employment disputes because Shields committed the acts in the course of disciplining his employees.

We recognize that, even when an employer or supervisor abuses a position of power over an employee, the employer will not be liable for mere insults, indignities, or annoyances that are not extreme and outrageous. But Shields's ongoing acts of harassment, intimidation, and humiliation and his daily obscene and vulgar behavior, which GTE defends as his "management style," went beyond the bounds of tolerable workplace conduct. The picture painted by the evidence at trial was unmistakable: Shields greatly exceeded the necessary leeway to supervise, criticize, demote, transfer, and discipline, and created a workplace that was a den of terror for the employees. And the evidence showed that all of Shields's abusive conduct was common, not rare. Being purposefully humiliated and intimidated, and being repeatedly put in fear of one's physical well-being at the hands of a supervisor is more than a mere triviality or annoyance.

Occasional malicious and abusive incidents should not be condoned, but must often be tolerated in our society. But once conduct such as that shown here becomes a regular pattern of behavior and continues despite the victim's objection and attempts to remedy the situation, it can no longer be tolerated. It is the severity and regularity of Shields's abusive and threatening conduct that brings his behavior into the realm of extreme and outrageous conduct. Conduct such as being regularly assaulted, intimidated, and threatened is not typically encountered nor expected in the course of one's employment, nor should it be accepted in a civilized society. An employer certainly has much leeway in its chosen methods of supervising and disciplining employees, but terrorizing them is simply not acceptable. If GTE or Shields was dissatisfied with the employees' performance, GTE could have terminated them, disciplined them, or taken some other more appropriate approach to the problem instead of fostering the abuse, humiliation, and intimidation that was heaped on the employees. Accordingly, the trial court properly submitted the issue to the jury, and there was some evidence to support the jury's conclusion that Shields's conduct was extreme and outrageous.

B. INTENT

GTE argues that the employees failed to establish that GTE, as opposed to Shields, possessed the requisite intent to support GTE's liability. The jury found that Shields intentionally inflicted emotional distress on the employees. The jury further found that Shields was acting in the scope of his employment. GTE contends that these findings are insufficient to support

GTE's liability because the jury never found that GTE acted with the requisite intent. GTE relies on the fact that the jury failed to find that GTE ratified Shield's intentional infliction of emotional distress and failed to find that GTE acted "with malice." GTE further contends that the jury's finding that Shields was acting in the scope of his employment is insufficient for liability because, GTE argues, an employer is never liable for an employee's intentional or malicious acts that are unforeseeable considering the employee's duties, and there was no finding that Shields's intentional acts were foreseeable by GTE.

Generally, a master is vicariously liable for the torts of its servants committed in the course and scope of their employment. This is true even though the employee's tort is intentional when the act, although not specifically authorized by the employer, is closely connected with the servant's authorized duties. If the intentional tort is committed in the accomplishment of a duty entrusted to the employee, rather than because of personal animosity, the employer may be liable. Shields's acts, although inappropriate, involved conduct within the scope of his position as the employees' supervisor. GTE admitted as much when it argued that Shields's acts were "mere employment disputes." GTE has cited no evidence that Shields's actions were motivated by personal animosity rather than a misguided attempt to carry out his job duties. The jury concluded that Shields's acts were committed in the scope of his employment, and there is some evidence to support this finding. Thus, GTE is liable for Shields's conduct.

C. SEVERE EMOTIONAL DISTRESS

GTE next contends that any distress the employees suffered was not severe. GTE argues that the employees' complaints of embarrassment, fear, stomach aches, loss of sleep, and headaches "are problems that are normally dealt with by each of us in every day life."

Emotional distress includes all highly unpleasant mental reactions such as embarrassment, fright, horror, grief, shame, humiliation, and worry. Severe emotional distress is distress that is so severe that no reasonable person could be expected to endure it. The employees testified that, as a result of being exposed to Shields's outrageous conduct, they experienced a variety of emotional problems, including crying spells, emotional outbursts, nausea, stomach disorders, headaches, difficulty in sleeping and eating, stress, anxiety, and depression. The employees testified that they experienced anxiety and fear because of Shields's continuing harassment, especially his charges and rages. Each employee sought medical treatment for these problems, and all three plaintiffs were prescribed medication to alleviate the problems. An expert witness testified that each of them suffered from post-traumatic stress disorder. This evidence is legally sufficient to support the jury's finding that the employees suffered severe emotional distress.

* * *

We conclude that there is legally sufficient evidence to support the jury's verdict against GTE on each of the employees' claims for intentional infliction of emotional distress. Accordingly, we affirm the court of appeals' judgment.

Justice OWEN filed a concurring opinion.

PREPARING FOR CLASS

1. This "new tort" required some tinkering, and special rules were created to meet the challenges of special situations. Thus was the case where employees brought IIED claims based on work-related conduct. See how the court modifies the standards to make the "new tort" acceptable in the workplace.

2. GTE is held vicariously liable, which means it is being held responsible for the acts of someone else. There is little to support a finding that GTE itself did anything directly wrong toward the plaintiffs. Vicarious liability and workers and compensation for work-related injuries will be addressed in Torts II.

INCREASING YOUR UNDERSTANDING

1. *Extreme and outrageous standard.* This difficult-to-meet standard is intentionally employed for two related reasons: first, to limit claims to those involving the most extreme conduct; and second, to have confidence that plaintiff's claimed emotional distress is legitimate. As was the case in *GTE*, while assessing defendant's conduct for extremeness, courts will often identify special contexts where, because of the relationship between the plaintiff and defendant, special liability rules are warranted. The employment context has created a legal paradox: Some states have severely restricted liability that stems from traditional employment decisions or acts, but these same courts will cite the disparity in power between the employee and employer as a reason why the conduct may be extreme. It is typically stated that the court first will decide whether there is sufficient evidence to submit this issue to the jury, with the jury receiving the question where there is some doubt as to whether a particular defendant acted in an extreme manner. Experience has shown that in IIED cases, judges are especially dutiful, as many of the cases are dismissed on this issue as a matter of law.

2. *Only the most distressed need apply.* Recovery under IIED is limited to the most damaged, and the cases have yet to establish a clear standard for what type of emotional harm qualifies as severe. As such, and given

this is an objective standard, the cases have yielded inconsistent results. A boilerplate instruction might describe severe emotional distress as the type of distress that "no reasonable person should be expected to endure." Restatement (Second) of Torts §46, comment j. The jury then will declare how mentally tough we are expected to be.

F. TRESPASS TO LAND/CHATTEL

Hawke v. Maus
141 Ind. App. 126, 226 N.E.2d 713 (Ind. Ct. App. 1967)

FAULCONER, Judge.
Appellee brought this civil action against appellants for damages to real estate resulting from a collision of appellant's (Associated Truck Lines, Inc.) truck with the trees of appellee, and based upon the alleged trespass of appellants to the realty of appellee.

Appellee alleged that he was the owner and in possession of certain real estate on the southwest corner of the intersection of State Highway 16 and United States Highway 31 in Miami County, Indiana, and that there were growing on said real estate three maple trees; that a 1963 tractor truck being driven by defendant-appellant's agent, Gerald S. Hawke, "wrongfully came upon the Plaintiff's (appellee's) said real estate and collided with Plaintiff's said maple trees, completely destroying one maple tree and breaking limbs from the other two, tore up the grass and soil and otherwise injured and damaged said real estate." Appellee alleged damages and demanded judgment in the sum of $1,000.

Appellants' demurrer for want of sufficient facts was overruled, after which appellants filed their answer in general denial. Trial was to the court without a jury, and judgment entered for appellee.

Appellants' motion for new trial specified that the decision of the court is not sustained by sufficient evidence and is contrary to law; and that the court erred in sustaining objections to certain questions propounded by appellants, and in overruling defendants-appellants' motion for finding at the close of plaintiff-appellee's evidence and in overruling defendants-appellants' motion for leave to amend their answer by filing a second paragraph.

The overruling of appellants' motion for new trial is the sole error assigned on appeal.

The question which objections were made and sustained would have elicited testimony to the effect that appellant-Associated's truck, while proceeding south on United States Highway 31 through the intersection with State Road 16, was struck by an automobile proceeding west on State Road 16, which automobile had run a red light, knocking the left front wheel loose and breaking the axle of appellant's truck, thus causing appellant-Hawke to lose control of the truck whereby it entered upon appellee's real estate. Such questions would have further elicited testimony that appellant-Hawke had no control over said truck after the impact, that he had no intention of entering appellee's real estate, nor was such entry his voluntary act.

> No issue is here presented concerning ownership, agency or amount of damage since all were stipulated at the trial.
> "The most important of the trespass rules to survive was that which imposed liability for invasions of property which were neither intended nor negligent. The defendant was not liable so long as he had done no voluntary act, as where he was carried onto the plaintiff's land by others against his will." (Emphasis supplied.) Prosser, Torts, §13, p. 63 (3d Ed. 1964).
> "So long as the invasion was due to any kind of volitional act on the part of the actor, there was a wrong, and if the damage was direct, trespass was the appropriate action. If, however, there was no act of volition by the actor, he was not liable, as where one is cast on another's land by third persons."
> "The early English common law seems to have imposed liability upon one whose act directly brought about an invasion of land in the possession of another, irrespective of whether the invasion was intended, was the result of reckless or negligent conduct, or occurred in the course of an abnormally dangerous activity, or was a pure accident, and irrespective of whether harm of any sort resulted to any interest of the possessor. All that seems to have been required was that the actor should have done an act which in fact caused the entry. At the present time, however, except in the case of one carrying on an abnormally dangerous activity, an unintentional and non-negligent entry or remaining on land in the possession of another or causing a third person or thing so to enter or remain is not a trespass on land and imposes no liability upon him."

It is true that in an action of trespass the intention of the defendant in making the entry or intrusion is immaterial. This proposition is strongly urged by appellee who cites two Indiana cases as authority. There are many decisions in Indiana setting forth this cardinal principle of trespass. However, a careful reading of these decisions will disclose that in each the entry was based upon a voluntary act of the defendant. This distinction is best described by the scholars.

> "In order to be liable for a trespass on land under the rule stated in §158, it is necessary only that the actor intentionally be upon any part of the land in question. It is not necessary that he intend to invade the possessor's interest in the exclusive possession of his land and, therefore, that he know his entry to be an intrusion."
> "The intention which is required to make the actor liable under the rule stated in this Section is an intention to enter upon the particular

piece of land in question, irrespective of whether the actor knows or should know that he is not entitled to enter."

"Although it is not necessary that the trespasser intend to commit a trespass or even that he know that his act will constitute a trespass, it is required for trespass that there be an intentional act and an intent to do the very act which results in the trespass."

"(T)he driver of an automobile who suddenly loses control of his car because he is seized with a heart attack, a stroke, a fainting spell, . . . is not liable unless he knew that he was likely to become ill . . . , in which case he is to be found negligent in driving the car at all. The same conclusions are reached when the defendant's car is struck by another vehicle and thrown out of control. . . ." Prosser, Torts, §29, pp. 143-44 (3d Ed. 1964).

The question we are called upon to decide in this cause is whether the evidence in the record before us is admissible under the general denial and, if not, whether the trial court was in error in refusing to allow appellants to file their written second paragraph of answer at the close of plaintiff's (appellee's) case.

. . . In an action of trespass quare clausum fregit, it is necessary for the plaintiff to prove only that he was in possession of the land and that the defendant entered thereon without right, such proof entitling the plaintiff to nominal damages without proof of injury, and upon additional proof of injury to products of the soil, the plaintiff is entitled to compensatory damages.

Appellants argue that since their excluded evidence would show that appellant-Hawke entered appellee's property through no fault on his part and that he had no intent to so enter and did no voluntary act which would cause or result in such entry, such evidence, going to defeat the cause of action, was admissible under the general denial. Appellee contends such evidence goes only to proof of a justification and, therefore, must be pleaded by special answer. We can see the merit of these contentions. Without specifically deciding the issue as to the admissibility of such evidence under the general denial, we are of the opinion that justice in this cause would be better served by allowing appellants to file their second paragraph of answer.

Whether or not appellants' evidence which they would introduce under the second paragraph of answer would have been sufficient to defeat appellee's cause of action is, of course, not for us to determine, but justice, in our opinion, requires their opportunity to do so. It was brought out at oral argument that appellants did not become aware of the court's attitude concerning admissibility of such evidence under the general denial until the close of appellee's case and the denial of appellants' motion for a directed verdict. Therefore, in our opinion the facts and circumstances of this case warrant a reversal for failure to allow appellants to file their second paragraph of answer.

Cause reversed with instructions to grant appellant's motion for new trial.

PREPARING FOR CLASS

The case sets forth the elements for trespass to land, which can be described as an intentional interference with a person's exclusive right to the possession of land. As the case explains, conduct that might be deemed only as negligent is insufficient to meet the intent requirement. In this respect, *Hawke* takes us back to where we started.

APPLYING THE LAW

A walks his dog along the same path every day, and just about every time, the dog leaves a form of waste on B's yard. A, being a good neighbor, always has his pooper scooper in hand and immediately removes any waste that he can. B sues in trespass. Who wins and why?

INCREASING YOUR UNDERSTANDING

1. Strict liability offense? As long as the actor intentionally enters the property of another without the other's consent, he is viewed in the eyes of the law as a trespasser. In so far as being labeled a trespasser is concerned, it matters not how long he is on the property, whether he causes any tangible harm, or that he has a reasonable belief that his actions are proper; the wrong is established by the intentional, unconsented entry onto the land of the other.

2. Liability. The trespasser is liable for all the harm that results from his trespass and nominal damages should he cause no actual harm. Any person rightfully in possession has standing to sue.

City of Newark, N.J. v. Eastern Airlines, Inc.
159 F. Supp. 750 (D.N.J. 1958)

William F. SMITH, District Judge.

This is a civil action in which the plaintiffs: the Cities of Newark, Elizabeth and Linden, and the Townships of Hillside and Union, and six individuals, seek to enjoin: first, "the airborne operations of (the named) airlines to and from Newark Airport to the extent that the same constitutes a public and/or a private nuisance," and second, to enjoin "the continued airborne operations of said airlines to and from Newark Airport to the extent that the said constitutes a trespass on the property of the plaintiffs."

The plaintiffs, in response to the Court's request, filed a "Memorandum of Relief Sought" in which they prayed that the "defendant airlines" be restrained "from operating any of their airplanes over the congested residential sections of Newark, Elizabeth, Hillside and Union at an altitude of less than Twelve Hundred Feet from the Ground." (Emphasis by the Court). The term "congested residential sections" is defined therein as "those locations" in which the witnesses reside. The prayer for relief is admittedly based on the "Noise Abatement Procedures" recommended by the National Air Transport Coordinating Committee, a voluntary group having no official status.

DEFENDANT AIRLINES

Each of the defendants is the holder of an "Air Carrier Operating Certificate" issued to it by the Civil Aeronautics Administrator, pursuant to the provisions of §40.10, et seq., of the Civil Air Regulations, 14 C.F.R., and particularly §40.13, of the said Regulations, 14 C.F.R. Each of the defendants is required by the express terms of the said certificate to conduct "all operations . . . in accordance with the terms and provisions of the Operations Specification," prescribed by the Civil Aeronautics Administrator, the "Civil Aeronautics Act, and the Civil Air Regulations." These specifications are subject to amendment by the Administrator, pursuant to the authority vested in him by §40.21 of the Civil Air Regulations, 14 C.F.R.

There can be no doubt that the defendant airlines, like all certificated air carriers, are subject to an elaborate and uniform system of regulations and controls. They operate under the authority granted by the Civil Aeronautics Board and are under the obligation to conduct their operations in compliance with the regulations promulgated by the Board under the authority vested in it by the Civil Aeronautics Act. They may operate only under the terms and conditions prescribed by the Civil Aeronautics Administrator and embodied in the operations specifications.

FEDERAL REGULATION OF AIR COMMERCE

The enactment of the Civil Aeronautics Act, 49 U.S.C.A. §401 et seq., was a proper exercise by Congress of the power granted by the Commerce Clause of the Constitution, Article I, Section 8, Clause 3. This legislation clearly evidenced the intent of Congress to preempt the exclusive power of regulation and control in the field of interstate air commerce. There was created there under a Civil Aeronautics Board, 49 U.S.C.A. §421, charged with the responsibility of, and vested with the authority to: first, encourage and develop in the public interest "an air-transportation system properly adapted to the (present and future) needs of the foreign and domestic commerce of the United States, of the Postal Service, and of the national defense"; and second, regulate "air commerce in such manner as to best promote its development and safety." See Declaration of Policy, Section 2 of the Act, 49 U.S.C.A. §402; see also

Section 601 of the Act, 49 U.S.C.A §551. The Board was empowered to supervise and control by rule, regulation and order the entire field of interstate air commerce. Section 205 of the Act, 49 U.S.C.A. §425. It was also made the final arbiter of the public interest.

Section 3 of the Act, 49 U.S.C.A. §403, provides: "There is recognized and declared to exist in behalf of any citizen of the United States a public right of freedom of transit in air commerce through the navigable airspace of the United States." The term "navigable airspace" is defined in general terms in Section 10 of the Air Commerce Act of 1926, 49 U.S.C.A. §180, as follows: ". . . the term 'navigable airspace' means airspace above the minimum safe altitudes of flight prescribed by the Civil Aeronautics Authority. . . ." The term is not otherwise defined by statute, but is defined by regulation.

The Civil Aeronautics Board, pursuant to the authority vested in it to prescribe and revise from time to time "air traffic rules governing the flight of . . . aircraft, including rules as to safe altitudes of flight," Section 601(a)(7) of the Act, 49 U.S.C.A. §551(a)(7), promulgated §§60.17, 14 C.F.R., which prescribed minimum safe altitudes. This rule defined the "navigable airspace" in the manner contemplated by the statutes hereinabove cited.

The pertinent provisions of the applicable regulation read as follows:

> "§60.17 Minimum safe altitudes. Except when Necessary for Take-Off or Landing, no person shall operate an aircraft below the following altitudes. (Emphasis by the Court).
>
>> "(a) Anywhere. An altitude which will permit, in the event of the failure of a power unit, an emergency landing without undue hazard to persons or property on the surface;
>>
>> "(b) Over congested areas. Over the congested areas of cities, towns or settlements . . . an altitude of 1,000 feet above the highest obstacle within a horizontal radius of 2,000 feet from the aircraft."

The rule seems to recognize impliedly that in the glide path which must be followed in both take-off and landing, the minimum altitude of 1,000 feet cannot be maintained.

It necessarily must be presumed that these rules, like the related air traffic rules, are intended to promote safety of operations in air commerce.

We are of the opinion that the term "navigable airspace," as thus defined, includes not only the space above the minimum altitude of 1,000 feet prescribed by the regulation but also that space below the fixed altitude and apart from the immediate reaches above the land. The latter limits are not defined with mathematical certainty but by a formula which, as the Civil Aeronautics Board explains, "applies the standard of necessity to accomplish specified ends and in so doing produces the maximum flight paths for climb and descent that are consistent with the safest operating techniques and practices." It has been held that this airspace is in the public domain. United States v. Causby, 1946, 328 U.S. 256, 266, 66 S. Ct. 1062, 90 L. Ed. 1206;

Allegheny Airlines v. Village of Cedarhurst, 2 Cir., 1956, 238 F.2d 812, 815; Hinman v. Pacific Air Transport, 9 Cir., 1936, 84 F.2d 755, 758, certiorari denied 1936, 300 U.S. 654, 57 S. Ct. 431, 81 L. Ed. 865.

SECOND COUNT

There are contained in the second count the individual claims of the plaintiffs for damages and for injunctive relief predicated upon an alleged trespass to realty. These claims are jointly pleaded but for the purposes of adjudication must be regarded as separate and distinct claims. The claims present common questions of law and fact of which identical principles are determinative. It might be well, therefore, to first consider these principles.

There no longer can be any doubt that the public enjoys a "right of freedom of transit in air commerce through the navigable airspace of the United States." Section 3 of the Aeronautics Act, supra. The right was recognized by the Supreme Court in the case of *United States v. Causby*, supra, at pages 260 and 261 of 328 U.S., at page 1065 of 66 S. Ct., wherein it is stated: "It is ancient doctrine that the common law ownership of the land extended to the periphery of the universe—Cujus est solum ejus est usque ad coelum. But that doctrine had no place in the modern world. The air is a public highway, as Congress has declared. Were that not true, every transcontinental flight would subject the operator to countless trespass suits. Common sense revolts at the idea. To recognize such private claims to the airspace would clog these highways, seriously interfere with their control and development in the public interest, and transfer into private ownership that to which only the public has a just claim." It was therein held, 328 U.S. at page 266, 66 S. Ct. at page 1068: "The airspace, apart from the immediate reaches above the land, is part of the public domain." (Emphasis by the Court.)

It was further held in the *Causby* case, 328 U.S. at page 264, 66 S. Ct. at page 1067: "The landowner owns at least as much of the space above the ground as he can occupy or use in connection with the land." The Supreme Court cited with approval *Hinman v. Pacific Air Transport*, supra, in which it was held, at page 758 of 84 F.2d: the landowner owns "so much of the space above the ground as (he) can occupy or make use of, in connection with the enjoyment of (the) land. This right is not fixed. It varies with (the) varying needs and is coextensive with them." The rule, as we interpret it, is that the landowner owns not only as much of the space above the ground as he occupies but also as much thereof as he may use in connection with the land. The airspace which lies above the immediate reaches of his land as thus defined is in the public domain and may be used by the public as navigable airspace. It follows "that the flight of aircraft across the land of another cannot be said to be a trespass without taking into consideration the question of altitude."

The rule as established by the federal courts appears to be consistent with the rule contained in the Uniform Aeronautics Law as enacted by the New Jersey Legislature, R.S. 6:2-6, N.J.S.A., which reads as follows: "Flight in aircraft over the lands and waters of this state is lawful, unless at such a low altitude as to interfere with the then existing use to which the land or water, or the space over the land or water, is put by the owner, or unless so conducted as to be imminently dangerous to persons or property lawfully on the land or the water beneath."

The principles do not foreclose the right of the landowner to maintain an action for trespass to realty in a proper case but the action may not rest on evidence that the aircraft in flight passed across his land in the navigable airspace above the immediate reaches thereof. There must be evidence not only that the aircraft passed over his lands from time to time but also that there was an unlawful invasion of the immediate reaches of his land; in other words, there must be evidence that the aircraft flights were at such altitudes as to interfere substantially with the landowner's possession and use of the airspace above the surface.

The evidence offered by the plaintiffs in support of their individual claims must be examined in the light of these recognized principles. When thus examined, the insufficiency of the evidence to support the claims becomes apparent.

CLAIM OF ANNA BIONDI

This plaintiff lives at 444 Schiller Street, Elizabeth, N.J., in a house which she occupies with her husband, son and mother. The mother is admittedly the owner of the house, which is located approximately 14,700 feet from the start of the take-off run. She testified generally that planes coming from the airport flew "low" over the house and that she and the members of her family were disturbed by the noise and vibration. She further testified that it was necessary to replace two ceilings in the house, but there was no evidence which would support a determination that there was any causal relation between the damage to the ceiling and the flight of aircraft over the house.

Neither this plaintiff, nor any witness on her behalf, ventured an approximation of the altitudes at which planes passed over the house. There is clearly no evidence which will support a determination that aircraft passed below the navigable airspace and within the immediate reaches of the land. The lack of such evidence is fatal to the claim for relief.

We find in the case of this plaintiff, as in the case of the City of Newark, an additional deficiency in the evidence. Even if we assume that there was a trespass over the lands, there is no evidence which will support a determination that the defendant airlines were the ones guilty. There is no evidence which will enable the Court to establish the identity of the offenders. What has been said concerning the claim of the City of Newark is equally applicable to the claim of this plaintiff.

It further appears that this plaintiff lacks the possessory interest in the land sufficient to qualify her to maintain her claim under the second count. The plaintiff is an occupant of the property, but with her mother, who is admittedly the owner thereof; it would appear from her testimony that the plaintiff is neither the owner nor a tenant in exclusive possession of the property. It follows that the cause of action under the second count, based upon a trespass to realty, could have been asserted only by the mother. It appears that she is the real party in interest.

The claim for injunctive relief asserted by this plaintiff under the second count must be dismissed for the reasons herein stated.

CLAIM OF IRVING S. JAY

This plaintiff lives at 333 Itaska Street, Hillside, N.J., in a house which is more than three and a half miles from the start of the take-off run. He testified generally that he and the members of his family were, and are, disturbed by the noise and vibration caused by planes which pass over his house.

He was asked, "Will you tell us just what happened and what you saw?" He answered: "Yes. During the period .that I am home I noticed that there are anywhere from thirty to fifty planes until one o'clock it the morning, that is, the period from six o'clock at night to one o'clock in the morning. Some near, some far, some very, very close. These planes come over, both coming from the Airport and going to the Airport. They come over with a terrible roar; they come over, they shake the house; they have caused cracks in the ceiling, they have caused the dishes to jingle in the cupboard, they have caused us to wake up at night. They disturb my sleep and my family's sleep." When asked as to the identity of the planes, he answered: "American, Eastern, TWA and several others like that." When pressed further, he added: "United," and "Mohawk." It appears from his testimony that these identifications were made during the summer months. When asked, "how many of the planes that come over from 6 P.M., to 8 A.M., did you identify?", apparently referring to observations made by the plaintiff during the winter months, he answered, "I couldn't identify any." The testimony was otherwise so indefinite that it would be impossible for the Court to determine with any reasonable degree of certainty the frequency with which any one or more of the aircraft of any one or more of the defendant airlines passed over the property of the plaintiff.

A deficiency of evidence, common to the claims of the other plaintiffs, is present here. A careful examination of the plaintiff's testimony discloses that he did not venture an approximation of the altitudes at which planes crossed his property. There is clearly no evidence which will support a determination that aircraft passed below the navigable airspace and within the immediate reaches of the land, a determination of fact which is necessary if the Court is to adjudge any one or more of the defendants guilty of a trespass to realty.

We do not mean to suggest that the plaintiff must prove with mathematical exactitude the altitudes at which aircraft ordinarily passed over his property;

this might very well be an impossible task. There must be some evidence, however, which will enable the Court to make a determination that the aircraft flights were at altitudes below the navigable airspace, which is in the public domain, and within the superadjacent airspace immediately above the land. The ultimate determination must be predicated upon a consideration of aircraft altitudes, and therefore some evidence as to altitudes, for example, well-grounded approximations, is necessary. A determination that there has been a continuing trespass may not rest on mere speculation and conjecture.

The claim for injunctive relief asserted by this plaintiff under the second count must, therefore, be dismissed because of the insufficiency of the evidence.

The defendants shall prepare and submit to the Court, on notice to the plaintiffs, an appropriate order of dismissal.

PREPARING FOR CLASS

An injunction is a court order requiring the defendant to perform a specific act or refrain from acting in a certain way. Injunctions are often issued to avoid harm and/or remediate harm previously caused by the defendant. Courts, though, only enjoin illegal acts, so a party seeking an injunction must at a minimum convince the court that the defendant is likely to commit a tort—in this case, a trespass.

INCREASING YOUR UNDERSTANDING

How far up? Courts have recognized a right to exclusive possession in areas above and below the ground. *City of Newark* tests the limits of the possessory rights. The Restatement (Second) of Torts §159 Intrusions Upon, Beneath, and Above Surface of Earth provides:

> (1) Except as stated in Subsection (2), a trespass may be committed on, beneath, or above the surface of the earth.
> (2) Flight by aircraft in the air space above the land of another is a trespass if, but only if,
> (a) it enters into the immediate reaches of the air space next to the land, and
> (b) it interferes substantially with the other's use and enjoyment of his land.

The hunter who shoots a gun across the property of his neighbor is liable in trespass. See Herrin v. Sutherland, 74 Mont. 587, 241 P. 328, 42 A.L.R. 937 (1925). A tree branch overhanging a landowner's property line is a technical trespass, which he may alleviate by trimming the encroaching branches without regard to the degree of physical harm done to their property; the redressable harm caused by the trees is that of the trespass onto the landowner's property, not physical damage done to his land. Jones v. Wagner, 425 Pa. Super. 102, 624 A.2d 166 (Pa. Super. 1993).

CompuServe Inc. v. Cyber Promotions, Inc.
962 F. Supp. 1015 (S.D. Ohio 1997)

GRAHAM, District Judge.

This case presents novel issues regarding the commercial use of the Internet, specifically the right of an online computer service to prevent a commercial enterprise from sending unsolicited electronic mail advertising to its subscribers.

Plaintiff CompuServe Incorporated ("CompuServe") is one of the major national commercial online computer services. It operates a computer communication service through a proprietary nationwide computer network. In addition to allowing access to the extensive content available within its own proprietary network, CompuServe also provides its subscribers with a link to the much larger resources of the Internet. This allows its subscribers to send and receive electronic messages, known as "e-mail," by the Internet. Defendants Cyber Promotions, Inc. and its president Sanford Wallace are in the business of sending unsolicited e-mail advertisements on behalf of themselves and their clients to hundreds of thousands of Internet users, many of whom are CompuServe subscribers. CompuServe has notified defendants that they are prohibited from using its computer equipment to process and store the unsolicited e-mail and has requested that they terminate the practice. Instead, defendants have sent an increasing volume of e-mail solicitations to CompuServe subscribers. CompuServe has attempted to employ technological means to block the flow of defendants' e-mail transmissions to its computer equipment, but to no avail.

This matter is before the Court on the application of CompuServe for a preliminary injunction which would extend the duration of the temporary restraining order issued by this Court on October 24, 1996 and which would in addition prevent defendants from sending unsolicited advertisements to CompuServe subscribers.

For the reasons which follow, this Court holds that where defendants engaged in a course of conduct of transmitting a substantial volume of electronic data in the form of unsolicited e-mail to plaintiff's proprietary computer equipment, where defendants continued such practice after repeated demands to cease and desist, and where defendants deliberately evaded plaintiff's affirmative efforts to protect its computer equipment from such use, plaintiff has a viable claim for trespass to personal property and is entitled to injunctive relief to protect its property.

I.

The Court will begin its analysis of the issues by acknowledging, for the purpose of providing a background, certain findings of fact recently made by another district court in a case involving the Internet:

1. The Internet is not a physical or tangible entity, but rather a giant network which interconnects innumerable smaller groups of linked computer networks. It is thus a network of networks. . . .

2. Some networks are "closed" networks, not linked to other computers or networks. Many networks, however, are connected to other networks, which are in turn connected to other networks in a manner which permits each computer in any network to communicate with computers on any other network in the system. This global Web of linked networks and computers is referred to as the Internet.

3. The nature of the Internet is such that it is very difficult, if not impossible, to determine its size at a given moment. It is indisputable, however, that the Internet has experienced extraordinary growth in recent years. . . . In all, reasonable estimates are that as many as 40 million people around the world can and do access the enormously flexible communication Internet medium. That figure is expected to grow to 200 million Internet users by the year 1999.

4. Some of the computers and computer networks that make up the network are owned by governmental and public institutions, some are owned by non-profit organizations, and some are privately owned. The resulting whole is a decentralized, global medium of communications—or "cyberspace"—that links people, institutions, corporations, and governments around the world. . . .

11. No single entity—academic, corporate, governmental, or non-profit—administers the Internet. It exists and functions as a result of the fact that hundreds of thousands of separate operators of computers and computer networks independently decided to use common data transfer protocols to exchange communications and information with other computers (which in turn exchange communications and information with still other computers). There is no centralized storage location, control point, or communications channel for the Internet, and it would not be technically feasible for a single entity to control all of the information conveyed on the Internet.

Internet users often pay a fee for Internet access. However, there is no per-message charge to send electronic messages over the Internet and such messages usually reach their destination within minutes. Thus electronic mail provides an opportunity to reach a wide audience quickly and at almost no cost to the sender.

It is not surprising therefore that some companies, like defendant Cyber Promotions, Inc., have begun using the Internet to distribute advertisements by sending the same unsolicited commercial message to hundreds of thousands of Internet users at once. Defendants refer to this as "bulk e-mail," while plaintiff refers to it as "junk e-mail." In the vernacular of the Internet, unsolicited e-mail advertising is sometimes referred to pejoratively as "spam."

CompuServe subscribers use CompuServe's domain name "CompuServe. com" together with their own unique alpha-numeric identifier to form a distinctive e-mail mailing address. That address may be used by the subscriber to exchange electronic mail with any one of tens of millions of other Internet users who have electronic mail capability. E-mail sent to CompuServe subscribers is processed and stored on CompuServe's proprietary computer equipment. Thereafter, it becomes accessible to CompuServe's subscribers, who can access CompuServe's equipment and electronically retrieve those messages.

Over the past several months, CompuServe has received many complaints from subscribers threatening to discontinue their subscription unless CompuServe prohibits electronic mass mailers from using its equipment to send unsolicited advertisements. CompuServe asserts that the volume of messages generated by such mass mailings places a significant burden on its equipment which has finite processing and storage capacity. CompuServe receives no payment from the mass mailers for processing their unsolicited advertising. However, CompuServe's subscribers pay for their access to CompuServe's services in increments of time and thus the process of accessing, reviewing and discarding unsolicited e-mail costs them money, which is one of the reasons for their complaints. CompuServe has notified defendants that they are prohibited from using its proprietary computer equipment to process and store unsolicited e-mail and has requested them to cease and desist from sending unsolicited e-mail to its subscribers. Nonetheless, defendants have sent an increasing volume of e-mail solicitations to CompuServe subscribers.

In an effort to shield its equipment from defendants' bulk e-mail, CompuServe has implemented software programs designed to screen out the messages and block their receipt. In response, defendants have modified their equipment and the messages they send in such a fashion as to circumvent CompuServe's screening software. Allegedly, defendants have been able to conceal the true origin of their messages by falsifying the point-of-origin information contained in the header of the electronic messages. Defendants have removed the "sender" information in the header of their messages and replaced it with another address. Also, defendants have developed the capability of configuring their computer servers to conceal their true domain name and appear on the Internet as another computer, further concealing the true origin of the messages. By manipulating this data, defendants have been able to continue sending messages to CompuServe's equipment in spite of CompuServe's protests and protective efforts.

Defendants assert that they possess the right to continue to send these communications to CompuServe subscribers. CompuServe contends that, in doing so, the defendants are trespassing upon its personal property.

IV.

This Court will now address the second aspect of plaintiff's motion in which it seeks to enjoin defendants Cyber Promotions, Inc. and its president Sanford Wallace from sending any unsolicited advertisements to any electronic mail address maintained by CompuServe.

CompuServe predicates this aspect of its motion for a preliminary injunction on the common law theory of trespass to personal property or to chattels, asserting that defendants' continued transmission of electronic messages to its computer equipment constitutes an actionable tort.

Trespass to chattels has evolved from its original common law application, concerning primarily the asportation of another's tangible property, to include the unauthorized use of personal property:

> Its chief importance now, is that there may be recovery . . . for interferences with the possession of chattels which are not sufficiently important to be classed as conversion, and so to compel the defendant to pay the full value of the thing with which he has interfered. Trespass to chattels survives today, in other words, largely as a little brother of conversion.

Prosser & Keeton, *Prosser and Keeton on Torts*, §14, 85-86 (1984).

Both plaintiff and defendants cite the Restatement (Second) of Torts to support their respective positions. In determining a question unanswered by state law, it is appropriate for this Court to consider such sources as the restatement of the law and decisions of other jurisdictions.

The Restatement §217(b) states that a trespass to chattel may be committed by intentionally using or intermeddling with the chattel in possession of another. Restatement §217, Comment e defines physical "intermeddling" as follows:

> . . . intentionally bringing about a physical contact with the chattel. The actor may commit a trespass by an act which brings him into an intended physical contact with a chattel in the possession of another[.]

Electronic signals generated and sent by computer have been held to be sufficiently physically tangible to support a trespass cause of action. It is undisputed that plaintiff has a possessory interest in its computer systems. Further, defendants' contact with plaintiff's computers is clearly intentional. Although electronic messages may travel through the Internet over various routes, the messages are affirmatively directed to their destination.

Defendants, citing Restatement (Second) of Torts §221, which defines "dispossession," assert that not every interference with the personal property of another is actionable and that physical dispossession or substantial interference with the chattel is required. Defendants then argue that they did not, in this case, physically dispossess plaintiff of its equipment or substantially interfere with it. However, the Restatement (Second) of Torts §218 defines the circumstances under which a trespass to chattels may be actionable:

> One who commits a trespass to a chattel is subject to liability to the possessor of the chattel if, but only if,
>   (a) he dispossesses the other of the chattel, or
>   (b) the chattel is impaired as to its condition, quality, or value, or
>   (c) the possessor is deprived of the use of the chattel for a substantial time, or
>   (d) bodily harm is caused to the possessor, or harm is caused to some person or thing in which the possessor has a legally protected interest.

Therefore, an interference resulting in physical dispossession is just one circumstance under which a defendant can be found liable. Defendants suggest that "[u]nless an alleged trespasser actually takes physical custody of the property or physically damages it, courts will not find the 'substantial interference' required to maintain a trespass to chattel claim." To support this rather broad proposition, defendants cite only two cases which make any reference to the Restatement. In *Glidden v. Szybiak*, 95 N.H. 318, 63 A.2d 233 (1949), the court simply indicated that an action for trespass to chattels could not be maintained in the absence of some form of damage. The court held that where plaintiff did not contend that defendant's pulling on her pet dog's ears caused any injury, an action in tort could not be maintained. *Id.* 63 A.2d at 235. In contrast, plaintiff in the present action has alleged that it has suffered several types if injury as a result of defendants' conduct. In *Koepnick v. Sears Roebuck & Co.*, 158 Ariz. 322, 762 P.2d 609 (1988) the court held that a two-minute search of an individual's truck did not amount to a "dispossession" of the truck as defined in Restatement §221 or a deprivation of the use of the truck for a substantial time. It is clear from a reading of Restatement §218 that an interference or intermeddling that does not fit the §221 definition of "dispossession" can nonetheless result in defendants' liability for trespass. The *Koepnick* court did not discuss any of the other grounds for liability under Restatement §218.

A plaintiff can sustain an action for trespass to chattels, as opposed to an action for conversion, without showing a substantial interference with its right to possession of that chattel. Harm to the personal property or diminution of its quality, condition, or value as a result of defendants' use can also be the predicate for liability.

> An unprivileged use or other intermeddling with a chattel which results in actual impairment of its physical condition, quality or value to the possessor makes the actor liable for the loss thus caused. In the great majority of cases, the actor's intermeddling with the chattel impairs the value of it to the possessor, as distinguished from the mere affront to his dignity as possessor, only by some impairment of the physical condition of

the chattel. There may, however, be situations in which the value to the owner of a particular type of chattel may be impaired by dealing with it in a manner that does not affect its physical condition. . . . In such a case, the intermeddling is actionable even though the physical condition of the chattel is not impaired.

The Restatement (Second) of Torts §218, comment h. In the present case, any value CompuServe realizes from its computer equipment is wholly derived from the extent to which that equipment can serve its subscriber base. Michael Mangino, a software developer for CompuServe who monitors its mail processing computer equipment, states by affidavit that handling the enormous volume of mass mailings that CompuServe receives places a tremendous burden on its equipment. Defendants' more recent practice of evading CompuServe's filters by disguising the origin of their messages commandeers even more computer resources because CompuServe's computers are forced to store undeliverable e-mail messages and labor in vain to return the messages to an address that does not exist. To the extent that defendants' multitudinous electronic mailings demand the disk space and drain the processing power of plaintiff's computer equipment, those resources are not available to serve CompuServe subscribers. Therefore, the value of that equipment to CompuServe is diminished even though it is not physically damaged by defendants' conduct.

Next, plaintiff asserts that it has suffered injury aside from the physical impact of defendants' messages on its equipment. Restatement §218(d) also indicates that recovery may be had for a trespass that causes harm to something in which the possessor has a legally protected interest. Plaintiff asserts that defendants' messages are largely unwanted by its subscribers, who pay incrementally to access their e-mail, read it, and discard it. Also, the receipt of a bundle of unsolicited messages at once can require the subscriber to sift through, at his expense, all of the messages in order to find the ones he wanted or expected to receive. These inconveniences decrease the utility of CompuServe's e-mail service and are the foremost subject in recent complaints from CompuServe subscribers. Patrick Hole, a customer service manager for plaintiff, states by affidavit that in November 1996 CompuServe received approximately 9,970 e-mail complaints from subscribers about junk e-mail, a figure up from approximately two hundred complaints the previous year. Approximately fifty such complaints per day specifically reference defendants. Defendants contend that CompuServe subscribers are provided with a simple procedure to remove themselves from the mailing list. However, the removal procedure must be performed by the e-mail recipient at his expense, and some CompuServe subscribers complain that the procedure is inadequate and ineffectual.

Many subscribers have terminated their accounts specifically because of the unwanted receipt of bulk e-mail messages. Defendants' intrusions into CompuServe's computer systems, insofar as they harm plaintiff's business reputation and goodwill with its customers, are actionable under Restatement §218(d).

The reason that the tort of trespass to chattels requires some actual damage as a *prima facie* element, whereas damage is assumed where there is a trespass to real property, can be explained as follows:

> The interest of a possessor of a chattel in its inviolability, unlike the similar interest of a possessor of land, is not given legal protection by an action for nominal damages for harmless intermeddlings with the chattel. In order that an actor who interferes with another's chattel may be liable, his conduct must affect some other and more important interest of the possessor. Therefore, one who intentionally intermeddles with another's chattel is subject to liability only if his intermeddling is harmful to the possessor's materially valuable interest in the physical condition, quality, or value of the chattel, or if the possessor is deprived of the use of the chattel for a substantial time, or some other legally protected interest of the possessor is affected as stated in Clause (c). *Sufficient legal protection of the possessor's interest in the mere inviolability of his chattel is afforded by his privilege to use reasonable force to protect his possession against even harmless interference.*

Restatement (Second) of Torts §218, Comment e (emphasis added).

Defendants argue that plaintiff made the business decision to connect to the Internet and that therefore it cannot now successfully maintain an action for trespass to chattels. Their argument is analogous to the argument that because an establishment invites the public to enter its property for business purposes, it cannot later restrict or revoke access to that property, a proposition which is erroneous under Ohio law. On or around October 1995, CompuServe notified defendants that it no longer consented to the use of its proprietary computer equipment. Defendants' continued use thereafter was a trespass.

Based on the foregoing, plaintiff's motion for a preliminary injunction is GRANTED.

It is so ORDERED.

PREPARING FOR CLASS

1. Having won the injunction, CompuServe can move on and sue the defendants for damages.

2. The defendants' argument that a trespass to chattel requires dispossession is borderline frivolous, but they didn't have much to provide as a defense.

3. Count the ways that CompuServe has been harmed.

4. Why is harm required in chattel cases but not in land cases?

APPLYING THE LAW

B, a law student, sees his roommate's draft of a research and writing paper lying on the kitchen table and copies it while roommate is at the gym. When roommate returns, the paper is sitting in the same position as it was when he left. B incorporates much of what was contained in roommate's draft into his final paper for the class and gets an A grade. Roommate's effort only garners a B grade. Does roommate have a trespass claim?

INCREASING YOUR UNDERSTANDING

As the principal case indicates, a person is not a trespasser to chattel unless the interference harms the plaintiff. The court will not presume harm nor award nominal damages for the inconvenience. Relying on Restatement (Second) of Torts §218, the *CompuServe* court charts the many ways a chattel owner might satisfy the harm requirement.

G. CONVERSION

RESTATEMENT (SECOND) OF TORTS §222A WHAT CONSTITUTES CONVERSION

(1) Conversion is an intentional exercise of dominion or control over a chattel which so seriously interferes with the right of another to control it that the actor may justly be required to pay the other the full value of the chattel.

(2) In determining the seriousness of the interference and the justice of requiring the actor to pay the full value, the following factors are important:

(a) the extent and duration of the actor's exercise of dominion or control;

(b) the actor's intent to assert a right in fact inconsistent with the other's right of control;

(c) the actor's good faith;

(d) the extent and duration of the resulting interference with the other's right of control;

(e) the harm done to the chattel;

(f) the inconvenience and expense caused to the other.

Wiseman v. Schaffer
115 Idaho 537, 768 P.2d 800 (Idaho Ct. App. 1989)

WANSTROM, Judge.

Larry and Freda Wiseman sued David Schaffer, alleging that he committed a tort when, without authorization, he towed their pickup to a location where it ultimately was stolen. A jury in the magistrate division found for Schaffer and a judgment dismissing the Wisemans' action was entered. The judgment was affirmed on the Wisemans' appeal to the district court. Appealing further, the Wisemans contend . . . that the jury verdict was not supported by the evidence. We vacate in part and we remand for a new trial.

The essential facts are as follows. The Wisemans left their Ford pickup parked at the Ross Point Husky Truck Stop in Post Falls, Idaho, while they were doing some long haul trucking. During their absence an imposter, identifying himself as Larry Wiseman, telephoned Schaffer and asked him to tow the Ford pickup at the Husky Truck Stop to the yard of a local welding shop. The imposter told Schaffer that $30 for the towing charge had been left on top of the sunvisor in the pickup. Schaffer located the pickup and the cash. He then towed the pickup to the welding shop as directed. Sometime later, the pickup was stolen.

The Wisemans filed this action alleging trespass or conversion, and negligence on the part of Schaffer.

Jury Verdict

When reviewing a jury verdict on appeal, the evidence adduced at trial is construed most favorably to the party who prevailed at trial and the verdict will not be set aside if supported by substantial evidence. However, when it appears to the reviewing court that there is no substantial evidence to support the verdict, the verdict cannot stand. A new trial is in order whenever the jury's verdict is not supported by the evidence.

Presumably, the jurors considered the facts and the law under both the theory of conversion and the theory of negligence when they rendered their verdict. Construing the evidence most favorably to Schaffer, including the testimony of the two tow truck operators, there is substantial evidence to support a verdict on the issue of negligence. However, a verdict for Schaffer on the issue of conversion is not supported by the evidence.

Conversion traditionally has been defined as "any distinct act of dominion wrongfully exerted over another's personal property in denial or inconsistent with his rights therein, such as a tortious taking of another's chattels, or any wrongful exercise . . . over another's goods, depriving him of the possession, permanently or for an indefinite time." *Klam v. Koppel*, 63 Idaho 171, 179-80, 118 P.2d 729, 732-33 (1941) (quoting *Schlieff v. Bistline*, 52 Idaho 353, 357, 15 P.2d 726, 728 (1932)). More recently, conversion has been described as an intentional exercise of dominion or control over a chattel which so seriously interferes with the right of another to control it that the actor may justly be required to pay the other the full value of the chattel. Restatement (Second) of Torts §222A (1965) (hereinafter Restatement) *cited in Gissel v. State*, 111 Idaho 725, 727 P.2d 1153 (1986).

The instruction on conversion used here was patterned after Idaho Jury Instruction (IDJI) 450, which for authority relies upon *Klam v. Koppel, supra,* and other earlier cases. Under this instruction, the jury was required to determine, first, whether Schaffer exercised dominion over the Wisemans' pickup without a right to do so, and second, whether the Wisemans had been "consequently deprived of possession" of their pickup. Finally, if the foregoing two elements were found to exist, the jury had to find the "nature and extent of the damages."

The evidence shows that Schaffer exercised dominion or control over the Wisemans' pickup inconsistent in fact with the Wisemans' right of ownership. This satisfied the first element of conversion. The jury could have found otherwise only if they postulated a "right" to exercise dominion upon the consent given by the imposter. No such "right" was embodied in the jury's instructions. Indeed, the law of conversion does not relieve an actor of liability due to his belief, because of a mistake of law or fact not induced by the other, that he has the consent of the other. Furthermore, to create liability for conversion it is not necessary that the actor intends to commit a trespass or a conversion; and the actor may be liable where he has in fact exercised dominion or control, although he may be quite unaware of the existence of the rights with which he interferes.

The evidence shows the second element of conversion was also satisfied. Schaffer's interference with the Wisemans' right of control ultimately resulted in the loss of the Wisemans' pickup. The jury could have found otherwise only if they postulated that the deprivation of possession did not follow "consequently" from Schaffer's actions because the pickup apparently was stolen by an unknown third party. Such reasoning by the jury might have been consistent with the judge's instructions—and defense counsel's arguments—on the *negligence* theory of liability, but it was not appropriate under the conversion theory. The judge's instruction on conversion did not excuse liability if property were lost due to theft by a third party after the defendant wrongfully exercised dominion. Consequently, the jury's verdict is not supported by the evidence. The judgment must be vacated on the issue of Schaffer's liability for conversion.

On remand, we direct the trial court's attention to the *Gissel* case and the applicable sections of the Restatement. We suggest that these sources of law be used in fashioning jury instructions supplemental to, or in substitution for, IDJI 450. *See* I.R.C.P. 51(a)(2). Restatement §222 A, for example, cited in *Gissel,* relates important factors for the jury to consider in deciding whether Schaffer's conduct amounts to conversion. If the jury affirmatively answers that question, "the measure of damages is the full value of the chattel[s], at the time and place of the tort." Restatement §222 A, comment c.

The district court's appellate decision upholding the judgment in the magistrate division is vacated in part. The case is remanded for a new trial on the issue of conversion. Costs to the Wisemans. No attorney fees on appeal.

PREPARING FOR CLASS

1. A conversion action is a forced sell; the premise being that since the defendant has acted in a way that expresses ownership it's only just that he purchase it. It wouldn't be inappropriate to view a conversion as a more extreme form of trespass, though this analogy has its limitations.

2. What possibly led the jury to rule for the defendant? Jury nullification?

APPLYING THE LAW

A is away on a weekend vacation and has *B* housesit for her. While housesitting, *B* notices the keys to *A*'s Mercedes-Benz Coupe lying on the table and decides to go for a ride. *B* smokes cigarettes while on the joy ride but returns the car within an hour without incident. Upon returning, *A* detects the smell of smoke and confronts *B*, who admits to the joy riding. *A*, allergic to cigarette smoke, takes the car to the dealer, who informs her that it will cost about $500 to have the car detailed, though it can't guarantee that remnants of cigarette smoke won't linger. The car has a Blue Book value of $35,000. Is *B* a converter?

INCREASING YOUR UNDERSTANDING

The considerations of §222A are not exclusive and are weighed individually according to how one perceives the conduct and values the consideration with one conclusion in mind; if found to be a converter, the defendant is forced to purchase the chattel. Anything less is possibly a trespass.

Chapter 3

Consent and Defenses to Intentional Torts

A. CONSENT

O'Brien v. Cunard S.S. Co.
154 Mass. 272, 28 N.E. 266 (1891)

KNOWLTON, J.

This case presents two questions: First, whether there was any evidence to warrant the jury in finding that the defendant, by any of its servants or agents, committed an assault on the plaintiff; secondly, whether there was evidence on which the jury could have found that the defendant was guilty of negligence towards the plaintiff. To sustain the first count, which was for an alleged assault, the plaintiff relied on the fact that the surgeon who was employed by the defendant vaccinated her on ship-board, while she was on her passage from Queenstown to Boston. On this branch of the case the question is whether there was any evidence that the surgeon used force upon the plaintiff against her will. In determining whether the act was lawful or unlawful, the surgeon's conduct must be considered in connection with the surrounding circumstances. If the plaintiff's behavior was such as to indicate consent on her part, he was justified in his act, whatever her unexpressed feelings may have been. In determining whether she consented, he could be guided only by her overt acts and the manifestations of her feelings. . . . It is undisputed that at Boston there are strict quarantine regulations in regard to the examination of emigrants, to see that they are protected from smallpox by vaccination, and that only those persons who hold a certificate from the medical officer of the steam-ship, stating that they are so protected, are permitted to land without detention in quarantine, or vaccination by the port physician. It appears that the defendant is accustomed to have its surgeons vaccinate all emigrants who desire it, and who are not protected by previous vaccination, and give them a certificate which is accepted at quarantine as evidence of their protection. Notices of the regulations at quarantine, and of the willingness of the ship's medical officer to vaccinate such as needed vaccination, were posted about the ship in various languages, and on the day when the operation was performed the surgeon had a right to presume that she and the other women who were vaccinated understood the importance and purpose of vaccination for those who bore no marks to show that they were protected. By the plaintiff's testimony, which, in this particular, is undisputed, it appears that about 200 women passengers were assembled below, and she understood from conversation with them that they were to be vaccinated; that she stood about 15 feet from the surgeon, and saw them form in a line, and pass in turn before him; that he "examined their arms, and, passing some of them by, proceeded to vaccinate those that had no mark"; that she did not hear him say anything to any of them; that upon being passed by they each received a card, and went on deck; that when her turn came she showed him her arm; he looked at it, and said there was no mark, and that she should be vaccinated; that she told him she had been vaccinated before, and it left no mark; "that he then said nothing; that he should vaccinate her again"; that she held up her arm to be vaccinated; that no one touched her; that she did not tell him she did not want to be vaccinated; and that she took the ticket which he gave her, certifying that he had vaccinated her, and used it at quarantine. She was one of a large number of women who were vaccinated on that occasion, without, so far as appears, a word of objection from any of them. They all indicated by their conduct that they desired to avail themselves of the provisions made for their benefit. There was nothing in the conduct of the plaintiff to indicate to the surgeon that she did not wish to obtain a card which would save her from detention at quarantine, and to be vaccinated, if necessary, for that purpose. Viewing his conduct in the light of the surrounding circumstances, it was lawful; and there was no evidence tending to show that it was not. The ruling of the court on this part of the case was correct.

PREPARING FOR CLASS

1. Why did plaintiff bring this claim, and what happens if the court finds that consent was lacking?

2. What facts support a finding of consent?

3. What if plaintiff is unfamiliar with the vaccination practice?

4. Small pox is a viral disease thought to be totally eradicated in the early 1980s. Currently there appears to be no cure though the vaccine has been very effective in preventing spread of the disease. It remains a bioterrorism concern.

Mohr v. Williams
95 Minn. 261, 104 N.W. 12 (Minn. 1905)

Defendant is a physician and surgeon of standing and character, making disorders of the ear a specialty, and having an extensive practice in the city of St. Paul. He was consulted by plaintiff, who complained to him of trouble with her right ear, and, at her request, made an examination of that organ for the purpose of ascertaining its condition. He also at the same time examined her left ear, but, owing to foreign substances therein, was unable to make a full and complete diagnosis at that time. The examination of her right ear disclosed a large perforation in the lower portion of the drum membrane, and a large polyp in the middle ear, which indicated that some of the small bones of the middle ear (ossicles) were probably diseased. He informed plaintiff of the result of his examination, and advised an operation for the purpose of removing the polyp and diseased ossicles. After consultation with her family physician, and one or two further consultations with defendant, plaintiff decided to submit to the proposed operation. She was not informed that her left ear was in any way diseased, and understood that the necessity for an operation applied to her right ear only. She repaired to the hospital, and was placed under the influence of anaesthetics; and, after being made unconscious, defendant made a thorough examination of her left ear, and found it in a more serious condition than her right one. A small perforation was discovered high up in the drum membrane, hooded, and with granulated edges, and the bone of the inner wall of the middle ear was diseased and dead. He called this discovery to the attention of Dr. Davis—plaintiff's family physician, who attended the operation at her request—who also examined the ear, and confirmed defendant in his diagnosis. Defendant also further examined the right ear, and found its condition less serious than expected, and finally concluded that the left, instead of the right, should be operated upon; devoting to the right ear other treatment. He then performed the operation of ossiculectomy on plaintiff's left ear; removing a portion of the drum membrane, and scraping away the diseased portion of the inner wall of the ear. The operation was in every way successful and skillfully performed. It is claimed by plaintiff that the operation greatly impaired her hearing, seriously injured her person, and, not having been consented to by her, was wrongful and unlawful, constituting an assault and battery; and she brought this action to recover damages therefor. The trial in the court below resulted in a verdict for plaintiff for $14,322.50. Defendant thereafter moved the court for judgment notwithstanding the verdict, on the ground that, on the evidence presented, plaintiff was not entitled to recover, or, if that relief was denied, for a new trial on the ground, among others, that the verdict was excessive; appearing to have been given under the influence of passion and prejudice. The trial court denied the motion for judgment, but granted a new trial on the ground, as stated in the order, that the damages were excessive. Defendant appealed from the order denying the motion for judgment, and plaintiff appealed from the order granting a new trial.

1. It is contended on plaintiff's appeal that the trial court erred in granting a new trial of the action; that the order should be reversed, and the verdict reinstated. The new trial was granted, as already stated, on the ground that the verdict was excessive, appearing to have been given under the influence of

passion and prejudice; and the point made is that the evidence, as contained in the record, does not sustain this conclusion, within the limits of the rule applicable to motions for a new trial based upon that ground. Considerable confusion has existed with reference to the proper rule guiding this court in reviewing orders of this kind ever since the decision in Nelson v. West Duluth, 55 Minn. 487, 57 N.W. 149, wherein it was said that the rule of Hicks v. Stone, 13 Minn. 434 (Gil. 398), did not apply. Several decisions involving the same question have since been filed, and the bar is apparently in some doubt as to the true rule upon the subject. We are not disposed to review the former decisions of the court, but, for future guidance, take this occasion to say (that there may be no further controversy in the matter) that in actions to recover unliquidated damages, such as actions for personal injuries, libel, and slander, and similar actions, where the plaintiff's damages cannot be computed by mathematical calculation, and are not susceptible to proof by opinion evidence, and are within the discretion of the jury, the motion for new trial on the ground of excessive or inadequate damages should be made under the fourth subdivision of section 5398, Gen. St. 1894; and in such cases the court will not interfere with the verdict unless the damages awarded appear clearly to be excessive or inadequate, as the case may be, and to have been given under the influence of passion or prejudice. On the other hand, in all actions, whether sounding in tort or contract, where the amount of damages depends upon opinion evidence, as the value of property converted or destroyed, the nature and extent of injuries to person or property, the motion for new trial should be made under the fifth subdivision of the statute referred to; and in cases of doubt, or where both elements of damages are involved, under both subdivisions. But in any case, whether a new trial upon the ground of excessive or inadequate damages should be granted or refused, or whether the verdict should be reduced, rests in the sound judicial discretion of the trial court in reviewing which this court will be guided by the general rule applicable to other discretionary orders. We applied this rule at the present term in Epstein v. Ry. Co. (recently decided) 104 N.W. 12. Where the damages are susceptible of ascertainment by calculation, and the jury return either an inadequate or excessive amount, it is the duty of the court to grant unconditionally a new trial for the inadequacy of the verdict, or, if excessive, a new trial unless plaintiff will consent to a reduction of the amount given by the jury. Applying the rule stated to the case at bar, we are clear the trial court did not abuse its discretion in granting defendant's motion for a new trial, and its order on plaintiff's appeal is affirmed. We cannot adopt the suggestion of counsel for plaintiff that this court now reduce the verdict to a proper amount, for there is no verdict upon which such an order could act. It was set aside by the trial court.

2. We come then to a consideration of the questions presented by defendant's appeal from the order denying his motion for judgment notwithstanding the verdict. It is contended that final judgment should be ordered in his favor for the following reasons: (a) That it appears from the evidence received on the trial that plaintiff consented to the operation on her left ear. (b) If the court

shall find that no such consent was given, that, under the circumstances disclosed by the record, no consent was necessary. (c) That, under the facts disclosed, an action for assault and battery will not lie; it appearing conclusively, as counsel urge, that there is a total lack of evidence showing or tending to show malice or an evil intent on the part of defendant, or that the operation was negligently performed.

We shall consider first the question whether, under the circumstances shown in the record, the consent of plaintiff to the operation was necessary. If, under the particular facts of this case, such consent was unnecessary, no recovery can be had, for the evidence fairly shows that the operation complained of was skillfully performed and of a generally beneficial nature. But if the consent of plaintiff was necessary, then the further questions presented become important. This particular question is new in this state. At least, no case has been called to our attention wherein it has been discussed or decided, and very few cases are cited from other courts. We have given it very deliberate consideration, and are unable to concur with counsel for defendant in their contention that the consent of plaintiff was unnecessary. The evidence tends to show that, upon the first examination of plaintiff, defendant pronounced the left ear in good condition, and that, at the time plaintiff repaired to the hospital to submit to the operation on her right ear, she was under the impression that no difficulty existed as to the left. In fact, she testified that she had not previously experienced any trouble with that organ. It cannot be doubted that ordinarily the patient must be consulted, and his consent given, before a physician may operate upon him. It was said in the case of Pratt v. Davis, 37 Chicago Leg. News, 213, referred to and commented on in Cent. Law J. 452: "Under a free government, at least, the free citizen's first and greatest right, which underlies all others—the right to the inviolability of his person; in other words, the right to himself—is the subject of universal acquiescence, and this right necessarily forbids a physician or surgeon, however skillful or eminent, who has been asked to examine, diagnose, advise, and prescribe (which are at least necessary first steps in treatment and care), to violate, without permission, the bodily integrity of his patient by a major or capital operation, placing him under an anaesthetic for that purpose, and operating upon him without his consent or knowledge." 1 Kinkead on Torts, §375, states the general rule on this subject as follows: "The patient must be the final arbiter as to whether he will take his chances with the operation, or take his chances of living without it. Such is the natural right of the individual, which the law recognizes as a legal one, Consent, therefore, of an individual, must be either expressly or impliedly given before a surgeon may have the right to operate." There is logic in the principle thus stated, for, in all other trades, professions, or occupations, contracts are entered into by the mutual agreement of the interested parties, and are required to be performed in accordance with their letter and spirit. No reason occurs to us why the same rule should not apply between physician and patient. If the physician advises his patient to submit to a particular operation, and the patient weighs the dangers and risks incident to its performance, and finally consents, he thereby, in effect, enters into a contract authorizing his physician to operate to the extent of the consent given, but no further. It is not, however, contended by defendant that under ordinary circumstances consent is unnecessary, but that, under the particular circumstances of this case, consent was implied; that it was an emergency case, such as to authorize the operation without express consent or permission. The medical profession has made signal progress in solving the problems of health and disease, and they may justly point with pride to the advancements made in supplementing nature and correcting deformities, and relieving pain and suffering. The physician impliedly contracts that he possesses, and will exercise in the treatment of patients, skill and learning, and that he will exercise reasonable care and exert his best judgment to bring about favorable results. The methods of treatment are committed almost exclusively to his judgment, but we are aware of no rule or principle of law which would extend to him free license respecting surgical operations. Reasonable latitude must, however, be allowed the physician in a particular case; and we would not lay down any rule which would unreasonably interfere with the exercise of his discretion, or prevent him from taking such measures as his judgment dictated for the welfare of the patient in a case of emergency. If a person should be injured to the extent of rendering him unconscious, and his injuries were of such a nature as to require prompt surgical attention, a physician called to attend him would be justified in applying such medical or surgical treatment as might reasonably be necessary for the preservation of his life or limb, and consent on the part of the injured person would be implied. And again, if, in the course of an operation to which the patient consented, the physician should discover conditions not anticipated before the operation was commenced, and which, if not removed, would endanger the life or health of the patient, he would, though no express consent was obtained or given, be justified in extending the operation to remove and overcome them. But such is not the case at bar. The diseased condition of plaintiff's left ear was not discovered in the course of an operation on the right, which was authorized, but upon an independent examination of that organ, made after the authorized operation was found unnecessary. Nor is the evidence such as to justify the court in holding, as a matter of law, that it was such an affection as would result immediately in the serious injury of plaintiff, or such an emergency as to justify proceeding without her consent. She had experienced no particular difficulty with that ear, and the questions as to when its diseased condition would become alarming or fatal, and whether there was an immediate necessity for an operation, were, under the evidence, questions of fact for the jury.

3. The contention of defendant that the operation was consented to by plaintiff is not sustained by the evidence. At least, the evidence was such as to take the question to the jury. This contention is based upon the fact that she was represented on the occasion in question by her family physician; that the condition of her left ear was made known to him, and the propriety of an operation thereon suggested, to which he made no objection. It is urged

that by his conduct he assented to it, and that plaintiff was bound thereby. It is not claimed that he gave his express consent. It is not disputed but that the family physician of plaintiff was present on the occasion of the operation, and at her request. But the purpose of his presence was not that he might participate in the operation, nor does it appear that he was authorized to consent to any change in the one originally proposed to be made. Plaintiff was naturally nervous and fearful of the consequences of being placed under the influence of anaesthetics, and the presence of her family physician was requested under the impression that it would allay and calm her fears. The evidence made the question one of fact for the jury to determine.

4. The last contention of defendant is that the act complained of did not amount to an assault and battery. This is based upon the theory that, as plaintiff's left ear was in fact diseased, in a condition dangerous and threatening to her health, the operation was necessary, and, having been skillfully performed at a time when plaintiff had requested a like operation on the other ear, the charge of assault and battery cannot be sustained; that, in view of these conditions, and the claim that there was no negligence on the part of defendant, and an entire absence of any evidence tending to show an evil intent, the court should say, as a matter of law, that no assault and battery was committed, even though she did not consent to the operation. In other words, that the absence of a showing that defendant was actuated by a wrongful intent, or guilty of negligence, relieves the act of defendant from the charge of an unlawful assault and battery. We are unable to reach that conclusion, though the contention is not without merit. It would seem to follow from what has been said on the other features of the case that the act of defendant amounted at least to a technical assault and battery. If the operation was performed without plaintiff's consent, and the circumstances were not such as to justify its performance without, it was wrongful; and, if it was wrongful, it was unlawful. As remarked in 1 Jaggard on Torts, 437, every person has a right to complete immunity of his person from physical interference of others, except in so far as contact may be necessary under the general doctrine of privilege; and any unlawful or unauthorized touching of the person of another, except it be in the spirit of pleasantry, constitutes an assault and battery. In the case at bar, as we have already seen, the question whether defendant's act in performing the operation upon plaintiff was authorized was a question for the jury to determine. If it was unauthorized, then it was, within what we have said, unlawful. It was a violent assault, not a mere pleasantry; and, even though no negligence is shown, it was wrongful and unlawful. The case is unlike a criminal prosecution for assault and battery, for there an unlawful intent must be shown. But that rule does not apply to a civil action, to maintain which it is sufficient to show that the assault complained of was wrongful and unlawful or the result of negligence.

The amount of plaintiff's recovery, if she is entitled to recover at all, must depend upon the character and extent of the injury inflicted upon her, in determining which the nature of the malady intended to be healed and the beneficial nature of the operation should be taken into consideration, as well as the good faith of the defendant.

Order affirmed.

PREPARING FOR CLASS

1. What support does defendant have for his consent claim?

2. If the evidence shows that plaintiff has benefitted from the surgery, where does the harm stem from?

3. Is there really any doubt that if asked, plaintiff would have consented to the surgery?

4. Reconcile *O'Brien* and *Mohr*.

INCREASING YOUR UNDERSTANDING

1. What does consent add to the liability discussion? Consent can be manifested expressly or implicitly by the circumstances, and the answer to the consent question must depend on the facts of each case. *O'Brien* and *Mohr* both involved cases where the defendant claimed the consent should be implied by plaintiff's conduct, in an attempt to avoid liability for the alleged intentional tort. The court's emphasis on the defendant's argument might mislead one to believe that consent is an affirmative defense. It is not. The lack of consent does not excuse the tort; there is no tort if plaintiff consented to the intrusion. As such, plaintiff carries the burden of persuading the court that she did not consent to the intrusion. Otherwise, how can it be claimed that the defendant is a wrongdoer?

2. Plaintiff not only controls the appearance of consent but also its scope, and defendant must remain within the permission granted by the plaintiff to avoid liability. In short, plaintiff is authorized to define the consent parameters and also withdraw any consent granted previously.

3. Generally, consent may be vitiated (void) in four specific circumstances:

   Plaintiff lacked the capacity to consent. The analysis here often involves a consideration of whether the plaintiff has the capability to sufficiently evaluate the circumstances and weigh the risks that exist at the time of the tort. In some situations, lack of maturity or age will be the focus of the inquiry. Other situations involve adults who through intoxication or mental defect are unable to weigh the circumstances in the way that an ordinary person would.

   Plaintiff is involved in the type of conduct that the law forbids consenting to. The tortuous conduct may also violate a penal or criminal law and the question that has to be resolved by the court is to what extent it should be influenced by the conduct also being criminal in nature. Most cases have held that consent, even to illegal conduct, is valid as it would frustrate the criminal laws should plaintiff be allowed to recover damages. "Except as stated . . . consent is effective to bar recovery in a tort action although conduct consented to is a crime." Restatement (Second) of Torts §892C(1). The authorities, however, show a contrary result where the plaintiff is particularly vulnerable. So, while in limited cases the defendant who has sex with an underaged minor is a criminal but not a civil-batterer (see Barton v. Bee Line, 238 A.D. 501, 265 N.Y.S. 284 (N.Y.A.D. 2 Dept. 1933) "Instead of incapacity to consent being a shield to save, it might be a sword to desecrate. The court is of the opinion that a female under the age of eighteen has no cause of action against a male with whom she willingly consorts, if she knows the nature and quality of her act."), when it comes to minors and sex, most opinions have held that the policies behind imposing criminal liability mandate a rule that discourages such conduct. Therefore, consent will be ineffective to deny civil liability. "If conduct is made criminal in order to protect a certain class of persons irrespective of their consent, the consent of members of that class to the conduct is not effective to bar a tort action." Restatement (Second) of Torts §892C(2).

Plaintiff was coerced into consenting. The premise here is simple: Effective consent must be voluntarily obtained or given; otherwise, it should not be forced on the plaintiff.

Defendant either misrepresented the circumstances that led to the intrusion or was aware that plaintiff misunderstood and acted in the face of the misunderstanding. This will be discussed in the next case.

4. Medical care, emergencies, and consent.

   a. *Adults.* The prospect of legal liability and the goal of promoting the right of personal integrity have led to the development of an entire collection of cases, rules, and liability issues falling within the category of "informed consent." Informed consent, better styled as the failure to obtain proper consent, as a cause of action will be discussed in detail later in Negligence. In fact, most of the battery cases in the medical context have been converted to "informed consent" claims out of a desire to avoid stigmatizing medical personnel as "batterers." Assuming, however, that the case remains within the intentional tort arena, it is sufficient for now to say that medical practitioners are required, whenever possible, to obtain consent expressly from patients before administering care or otherwise face tort liability for a "medical battery." Consent can only properly be obtained if the patient is first advised of the risks associated with the medical care. There may be circumstances, however, (intoxication, mental or physical incapacity) where the requisite consent cannot be obtained expressly, yet medical care is ostensibly required. In these circumstances it may be reasonable to imply consent which that essentially allows the medical practitioner to substitute her judgment for the patient—the judgment influenced, of course, by what the practitioner knows about the particular patient. So, a male nurse may have committed a battery when he participated in the delivery of the plaintiff's baby if previously informed that her religious and moral views prevented her from being seen unclothed by a member of the opposite sex. Cohen v. Smith, 269 Ill. App. 3d 1087, 648 N.E.2d 329 (Ill. App. 5 Dist. 1995). And a physician who performs a quadrantectomy (removal of outer-quarter of breast) in the absence of a malignancy diagnosis has committed a battery as a matter of law where the patient's consent authorized the procedure only if cancer had been found. Hernandez v. Schittek, 305 Ill. App. 3d 925, 713 N.E.2d 203 (Ill. App. 5 Dist. 1999). Factual disputes on the meaning to give to ambiguous consent language should be resolved by the jury. Id.

b. *Minor children.* In most circumstances, minor children, as a matter of law, lack the capacity to expressly consent to medical treatment, and in these circumstances, courts require consent from a parent in order for the treatment to be legally authorized. The law that has developed in this regard is meaty and complex, perhaps for no other reason than the inherent conflict between what the parents may consent to and the desire of physicians to treat and cure to the best of their ability. Any medical compulsion to treat must be subordinated to the express dictates of the patient—otherwise civil liability may follow. If consent is refused, the safer course is for the medical practitioner to appeal to the court and seek a declaration on whether it is proper to proceed in the absence of consent. It is common for the court to rule favorably on the petition, particularly where the situation involves a serious or life-threatening condition. See Jehovah's Witnesses in State of Wash. v. King County Hospital Unit No. 1 (Harborview), 278 F. Supp. 488 (D.C. Wash. 1967) (State may intervene in name of health and welfare in the indoctrination and participation of children in religion . . . right to practice religion freely does not include liberty to expose child to ill health or death.), and Crouse Irving Memorial Hosp., Inc. v. Paddock, 127 Misc. 2d 101, 485 N.Y.S.2d 443 (N.Y. Supp. 1985) (Hospital and attending physicians were entitled to give blood transfusions to save baby's life and health despite parents' objections based on their religious beliefs, in view of state's vital interest in welfare of children).

c. *Emergencies.* In circumstances where the need to provide immediate medical care is necessary to avoid serious injury or death, consent for the care will be implied. This is true with respect to adults and minor children, but conditioned on the medical provider lacking any information that would indicate that the patient wishes not to consent.

De May v. Roberts
46 Mich. 160, 9 N.W. 146 (Mich. 1881)

MARSTON, C.J.

The declaration in this case in the first count sets forth that the plaintiff was at a time and place named a poor married woman, and being confined in child-bed and a stranger, employed in a professional capacity defendant De May who was a physician; that defendant visited the plaintiff as such, and against her desire and intending to deceive her wrongfully, etc., introduced and caused to be present at the house and lying-in room of the plaintiff and while she was in the pains of parturition the defendant Scattergood, who intruded upon the privacy of the plaintiff, indecently, wrongfully and unlawfully laid hands upon and assaulted her, the said Scattergood, which was well known to defendant De May, being a young unmarried man, a stranger to the plaintiff and utterly ignorant of the practice of medicine, while the plaintiff believed that he was an assistant physician, a competent and proper person to be present and to aid her in her extremity.

The second and third counts while differing in form set forth a similar cause of action.

The evidence on the part of the plaintiff tended to prove the allegations of the declaration. On the part of the defendants evidence was given tending to prove that Scattergood very reluctantly accompanied Dr. De May at the urgent request of the latter; that the night was a dark and stormy one, the roads over which they had to travel in getting to the house of the plaintiff were so bad that a horse could not be rode or driven over them; that the doctor was sick and very much fatigued from overwork, and therefore asked the defendant Scattergood to accompany and assist him in carrying a lantern, umbrella and certain articles deemed necessary upon such occasions; that upon arriving at the house of the plaintiff the doctor knocked, and when the door was opened by the husband of the plaintiff, De May said to him, "that I had fetched a friend along to help carry my things;" he, plaintiff's husband, said all right, and seemed to be perfectly satisfied. They were bid to enter, treated kindly and no objection whatever made to the presence of defendant Scattergood. That while there Scattergood, at Dr. De May's request, took hold of plaintiff's hand and held her during a paroxysm of pain, and that both of the defendants in all respects throughout acted in a proper and becoming manner actuated by a sense of duty and kindness.

Some preliminary questions were raised during the progress of the trial which may first be considered. The plaintiff when examined as a witness was asked, what idea she entertained in reference to Scattergood's character and right to be in the house during the time he was there, and answered that she thought he was a student or a physician. To this there could be no good legal objection. It was not only important to know the character in which Scattergood went there, but to learn what knowledge the plaintiff had upon that subject. It was not claimed that the plaintiff or her husband, who were strangers in that vicinity, had ever met Scattergood before this time or had any knowledge or information concerning him beyond what they obtained on that evening, and it was claimed by the defendant that both the plaintiff and her husband must have known, from certain ambiguous expressions used, that he was not a physician.

We are of opinion that the plaintiff and her husband had a right to presume that a practicing physician would not, upon an occasion of that character, take with him and introduce into the house, a young man in no way, either by education or otherwise, connected with the medical profession; and that something more clear and certain as to his non-professional character would be required to put the plaintiff and her husband upon their guard, or remove such presumption, than the remark made by De May that he had brought a friend along to help carry his things. The plaintiff was not bound however to rest her case upon this presumption, however strong it might be considered, but had a right to prove what she supposed was the fact, and this she could do by showing anything said at the time having such a tendency, or in the absence thereof what she actually believed to be the fact.

The question asked the plaintiff's husband as to what he had stated under oath in an affidavit was properly overruled. This court has repeatedly pointed out the proper practice in such cases. Hamilton v. The People, 29 Mich. 198, and cases cited.

The question asked the witness Dr. Monfort[*] as to the custom among physicians in such cases as to calling assistance was not objectionable, besides the answer given could in no way have injured the defendants. In either event therefore they cannot complain.

It yet remains to consider the principal questions raised in the case. They relate to the sufficiency of the declaration, to which the general issue was pleaded, and further that admitting the facts to be true as claimed by the plaintiff she was not entitled to recover. We need not consider the question as to what the effect would be had the jury found that the plaintiff knew the non-professional character of the defendant Scattergood and made no objection or

---

[*] The testimony of Dr. Monfort was as follows: Question. "You say you have been in practice about eight years; what is the custom among physicians called upon to do the necessary duties attending cases of midwifery? Answer. I suppose that would depend somewhat upon the circumstances under which the case existed; usually it is not the custom to have assistance, unless the case demands it; after it is ascertained that assistance is required, it is customary and proper to call medical assistance; in an urgent case, perhaps most any kind of assistance; but medical if it could be obtained."

consented to his remaining in the house or rendering such assistance as was demanded. Upon this branch of the case the court charged the defendants would be justified in doing what they did, if the plaintiff or her husband consented to Scattergood being there, with a full understanding of, or with good reason to believe or know of the character in which he was there. This certainly was placing the matter in a sufficiently favorable position for the defendants.

A few facts which were undisputed may assist in more clearly presenting the remaining question. Upon the morning of January 3d Dr. De May was called to visit the plaintiff professionally which he did at her house. This house was 14 by 16 feet. A partition ran partly across one end thus forming a place for a bed or bedroom, but there was no door to this bedroom. Next to this so-called bedroom, and between the partition and side of the house, there was what is known and designated as a bed sink, here there was a bed with a curtain in front of it, and it was in this bed the doctor found Mrs. Roberts when he made his first visit. On their way to the house that night De May told Scattergood, who knew that the plaintiff was about to be confined, "how the house was; that she was in the bed sink lock, and there was a curtain in front of her, and told him he need not see her at all." When the defendants got to the house they found Mrs. Roberts "had moved from the bed sink and was lying on the lounge near the stove."

I now quote further from the testimony of Dr. De May as to what took place: "I made an examination of Mrs. Roberts and found no symptoms of labor at all, any more than there was the previous morning. I told them that I had been up several nights and was tired and would like to lie down awhile; previous to this, however, some one spoke about supper, and supper was got and Scattergood and myself eat supper, and then went to bed. I took off my pants and had them hung up by the stove to dry; Scattergood also laid down with his clothes on. We lay there an hour or more, and Scattergood shook me and informed me that they had called me and wanted me. Scattergood got my pants and then went and sat down by the stove and placed his feet on a pile of wood that lay beside the stove, with his face towards the wall of the house and his back partially toward the couch on which Mrs. Roberts was lying. I made an examination and found that the lady was having labor pains. Her husband stood at her head to assist her; Mrs. Parks upon one side, and I went to the foot of the couch. During her pains Mrs. Roberts had kicked Mrs. Parks in the pit of the stomach, and Mrs. Parks got up and went out doors, and while away and about the time she was coming in, Mrs. Roberts was subjected to another labor pain and commenced rocking herself and throwing her arms, and I said catch her, to Scattergood, and he jumped right up and came over to her and caught her by the hand and staid there a short time, and then Mrs. Parks came up and took her place again, and Scattergood got up and went and took his place again, back by the stove. In a short time the child was born. Scattergood took no notice of her while sitting by the stove. The child was properly cared for; Mrs. Roberts was properly cared for, dressed and carried and placed in bed. I left some medicine to be given her in case she should suffer from pains."

Dr. De May therefore took an unprofessional young unmarried man with him, introduced and permitted him to remain in the house of the plaintiff, when it was apparent that he could hear at least, if not see all that was said and done, and as the jury must have found, under the instructions given, without either the plaintiff or her husband having any knowledge or reason to believe the true character of such third party. It would be shocking to our sense of right, justice and propriety to doubt even but that for such an act the law would afford an ample remedy. To the plaintiff the occasion was a most sacred one and no one had a right to intrude unless invited or because of some real and pressing necessity which it is not pretended existed in this case. The plaintiff had a legal right to the privacy of her apartment at such a time, and the law secures to her this right by requiring others to observe it, and to abstain from its violation. The fact that at the time, she consented to the presence of Scattergood supposing him to be a physician, does not preclude her from maintaining an action and recovering substantial damages upon afterwards ascertaining his true character. In obtaining admission at such a time and under such circumstances without fully disclosing his true character, both parties were guilty of deceit, and the wrong thus done entitles the injured party to recover the damages afterwards sustained, from shame and mortification upon discovering the true character of the defendants.

Where a wrong has been done another, the law gives a remedy, and although the full extent and character of the injury done may not be ascertained or known until long after, yet in an action brought damages therefor may be fully awarded. This is true both in cases of tort and crime as well as in actions for breach of contract. The charge of the court upon the duty and liability of the defendants and the rights of the plaintiff was full and clear, and meets with our full approval.

It follows therefore that the judgment must be affirmed with costs.

PREPARING FOR CLASS

1. What's the harm to plaintiff?

2. Didn't the husband consent, and is that sufficient to deny liability?

3. Dr. De May is now a batterer, something that might not set well given the nature of the relationship he and other doctors have with their patients. This area of law is largely now controlled by the law of informed consent.

Defendant is out sunbathing with plaintiff. While sunbathing, defendant places a sunscreen on plaintiff that he knows a large percentage of the population is allergic to but does not know that plaintiff is ignorant of its effects. Is defendant liable for battery?

INCREASING YOUR UNDERSTANDING

1. In Torts II we will discuss misrepresentation as a cause of action, something that always looms when the defendant has taken advantage of a party as a result of the party's misunderstanding of the circumstance. The misrepresentation action dovetails into consent as there have been cases where the misrepresentor commits an intentional tort and later claims the plaintiff consented. Consistent with Restatement (Second) of Torts §892B(2), a mistaken plaintiff's consent will be effective unless the actor knows that the plaintiff is mistaken or the actor, through her conduct, has created the mistaken circumstance (fraudulently or innocently).

2. It would mislead to suggest that fraud (lying) is required to vitiate consent. Indeed, *De May* involved no such conduct and often, defendants have no intention to mislead. In cases, however, where the defendant has intentionally misled, for the consent to be ineffective the misrepresentation must have gone to the essential character of the claim, not to a collateral matter. If, for example, a battery is claimed following a misrepresentation ("I'll give you a part in my next movie if you'll have sex with me") and defendant affords no part in any movie after sex, the operative question is whether the promise went to a collateral matter or to the essence why the sex act was offensive or harmful. And while it's unlikely that a battery claim will exist in this situation, there is always the prospect of a misrepresentation claim.

B. SELF-DEFENSE, PROVOCATION

Poliak v. Adcock
2002 WL 31109737

WILLIAM C. KOCH, JR., J.

This appeal involves a dispute between a father and his adult daughter's live-in boyfriend. The boyfriend filed a personal injury suit against his girlfriend's father in the Circuit Court for Davidson County after the father assaulted him with a piece of two-by-four. The father admitted that he had assaulted his daughter's boyfriend but asserted the defenses of self-defense, provocation, and defense of property. In response to the boyfriend's motion for partial summary judgment, the trial court determined that the father had failed to produce evidence to substantiate any of these defenses. The father perfected this appeal after the trial court certified its order as final in accordance with Tenn. R. Civ. P. 54.02. We have determined that the trial court was correct when it determined that the father's evidence regarding the circumstances surrounding the assault could not, as a matter of law, support his affirmative defenses. Accordingly, we affirm the trial court.

I.

James M. Adcock and his wife own a house in Nashville. Their adult daughter, Anna Michelle Adcock-Butler, and her two children live with them. Ms. Adcock-Butler's boyfriend, Matthew Poliak was a frequent visitor in the Adcock home. Despite at least one run-in with Mr. Adcock in early 1998, Mr. Poliak moved his clothing and other personal effects into Mr. Adcock's house several months later and apparently began spending significant amounts of time there. Even though Mr. Adcock was not pleased with Mr. Poliak's actions, he never directly opposed or protested Mr. Poliak's presence in his house after Mr. Poliak moved back in.

By mid-1998 Mr. Adcock decided he could not permit Mr. Poliak to live in his house any longer. On the afternoon of July 11, 1998, armed with a piece of two-by-four, Mr. Adcock entered his daughter's bedroom where he found Mr. Poliak lying alone on the bed. As Mr. Poliak began to arise from the bed, Mr. Adcock, without warning, struck him with the two-by four. He told Mr. Poliak that he was going to leave the house for a while and that he would kill Mr. Poliak if he was still there when he returned. Mr. Poliak sustained severe injuries and was taken by ambulance to the hospital.

In July 1999, Mr. Poliak sued Mr. Adcock for assault and battery in the Circuit Court for Davidson County, seeking $150,000 in compensatory damages and $150,000 in punitive damages. Mr. Adcock responded by admitting that he had struck Mr. Poliak with a two-by-four. He also asserted that he had been provoked and that he was acting in self-defense because Mr. Poliak was a younger and larger man. After taking Mr. Adcock's discovery deposition, Mr. Poliak moved for a partial summary judgment seeking dismissal of Mr. Adcock's affirmative defenses of provocation, self-defense, and protection of property. The trial court granted Mr. Poliak's motion because Mr. Adcock had failed to demonstrate that he would be able to provide material evidence to support his affirmative defenses. Mr. Adcock has now appealed.

II. Standard of Review

The standards for reviewing an order granting a summary judgment are well-settled. A summary judgment is proper in virtually any civil case where the moving party demonstrates that no genuine issues of material fact exist and that it is entitled to a judgment as a matter of law. Because a summary judgment involves an issue of law rather than an issue of fact, *Planters Gin Co. v. Federal Compress & Warehouse Co.*, 78 S.W.3d 885, 889 (Tenn. 2002), an order granting a summary judgment is not entitled to a presumption of correctness on appeal.

III. Mr. Adcock's Affirmative Defenses

Mr. Adcock does not dispute that he assaulted Mr. Poliak with a two-by-four. However, he has undertaken to deflect liability for Mr. Poliak's injuries by asserting three affirmative defenses—provocation, self-defense, and defense of property. After taking Mr. Adcock's deposition, Mr. Poliak moved for a summary judgment on the ground that Mr. Adcock would be unable to prove the essential elements of these defenses at trial. Mr. Adcock responded by insisting that the testimony he gave in his deposition is sufficient to support each of his defenses.

A. SELF-DEFENSE

Self-defense is a complete defense to a civil action for battery. Thus, persons who can prove that they were acting in self-defense when they assaulted another person will be absolved from liability for the injuries they may have caused.

The elements of the defense are essentially the same in civil and criminal cases. Restatement (Second) of Torts §63 (1965). The defense reflects the principle that persons are entitled to defend themselves when they reasonably believe they are about to be seriously injured. Restatement (Second) of Torts §§63, 65 (1965); Tenn. Code Ann. §39-11-611(a) (1997). However, persons are entitled to use force to defend themselves only as long as the threat of injury continues, and may use only as much force as is necessary to defend themselves.

The Restatement provides fact-finders with factors for determining whether the amount of force used by a person acting in self-defense was reasonable. These factors include: (1) the amount of force the defender exerted, (2) the means or the object by which the defender applied the force, (3) the manner or method used by the defender to apply the force, and (4) the surrounding circumstances under which the defender applied the force. Restatement (Second) of Torts §70 cmt. b. Using similar factors, this court has upheld a trial court's conclusion that a person who threw an aggressor to the ground and repeatedly hit him had used more force than was reasonably necessary.

According to Mr. Adcock, he and Mr. Poliak had at least one previous confrontation. However, even though Mr. Poliak is the younger and larger man, there is no evidence in the record that Mr. Poliak had ever attempted to intimidate or harm Mr. Adcock. Nonetheless, Mr. Adcock armed himself with a two-by-four and entered the room where Mr. Poliak was sleeping with the settled intention to strike Mr. Poliak over the head to dissuade him from resisting Mr. Adcock's ultimatum to leave his house. When Mr. Adcock entered the room cursing at Mr. Poliak, Mr. Poliak's only actions before Mr. Adcock struck him were to mumble something and to begin to get out of bed. Viewing Mr. Adcock's own testimony in a light most favorable to him, the only conclusions that a reasonable person can draw are that on the afternoon of July 11, 1998, Mr. Adcock had no reasonable basis to fear that Mr. Poliak was about to injure him seriously and that Mr. Adcock's attack on Mr. Poliak was clearly disproportionate to Mr. Poliak's conduct. Accordingly, the trial court correctly held that Mr. Poliak was entitled to a summary judgment striking Mr. Adcock's defense of self-defense because Mr. Adcock had failed to demonstrate that he would be able to substantiate this defense at trial.

B. PROVOCATION

In Tennessee, provocation is a theory used to mitigate damages rather than an affirmative defense. It does not completely absolve a defendant from liability like the defense of self-defense does. Instead, it enables defendants to reduce the amount of damages a plaintiff receives by demonstrating that the plaintiff provoked the defendant into the injury-causing conduct.

The theory of provocation stems from the belief that persons should not be permitted to benefit from their own wrongful conduct. It arises in circumstances where the plaintiff's conduct is so provocative that it "heat[s] the blood or arouse[s] the passion of a reasonable man." However, a person attempting to mitigate damages by asserting that he or she was provoked must demonstrate (1) that the plaintiff's conduct was truly provocative, (2) that his or her response to the provocation was not wholly disproportionate to the offense offered, and (3) that not enough time had elapsed for the effect of the provocative conduct to dissipate.

The courts have not laid down a definitive test for determining whether a plaintiff's actions are sufficiently provocative to mitigate a defendant's forceful reactions to them. These inquiries are fact-specific. Thus, whether the plaintiff's conduct was truly provocative and whether the defendant's response was disproportionate must be determined on a case-by-case basis in light of all the circumstances.

Mr. Adcock claims that Mr. Poliak provoked the July 11, 1998 assault by continuing to live in his home after he had asked Mr. Poliak to leave. As we understand Mr. Adcock's testimony, Mr. Poliak had been living in his house for a number of weeks, if not months, before July 11, 1998. While a reasonable person could be upset by the presence of an unwanted guest in his or her home, the presence of such a guest, especially one who has been invited into the home by one of the other persons residing there, is not the sort of conduct that heats the blood or arouses the passions of reasonable persons to the point where they feel compelled to assault the unwanted guest with a two-by-four. Thus, the trial court properly determined that Mr. Poliak's mere presence in Mr. Adcock's home was not the sort of provocative conduct that provides a basis for claiming provocation as a justification for mitigating damages.

The events of July 11, 1998 likewise fail to provide a factual basis for a provocation argument. Viewing the evidence in the light most favorable to Mr. Adcock, Mr. Poliak did nothing on July 11, 1998 to provoke Mr. Adcock's violent attack. In fact, Mr. Adcock essentially admits that he had decided to hit Mr. Poliak with the two-by-four before he entered the room. As far as this record shows, Mr. Poliak's actions in response to Mr. Adcock entering his room were to mumble something and to begin to get out of bed. No reasonable person would view these actions as being so provocative that they warranted being struck on the head with a two-by-four. Accordingly, there is no evidence in the record to support Mr. Adcock's claim that he was provoked into attacking Mr. Poliak with a two-by-four on July 11, 1998.

C. DEFENSE OF PROPERTY

Property owners may use as much force as is reasonably necessary to prevent another from unlawfully coming onto their property or to remove another who is trespassing on their property. To raise the defense of property defense, a property owner must prove (1) that the plaintiff was trespassing on his or her property, (2) that he or she reasonably believed that the force used on the trespasser was necessary to get the trespasser off or to keep the trespasser off his or her property, and (3) that he or she first asked the trespasser to leave and that the trespasser refused or that he or she reasonably believed that any such attempt would have been useless or would have caused substantial harm. Restatement (Second) of Torts §77 (1965). Property owners can never use force that endangers human life or inflicts serious bodily harm.

Mr. Adcock's testimony in his deposition fails to substantiate any of the ingredients of a defense of property defense. Mr. Poliak was not an uninvited guest in Mr. Adcock's house. He was living there at the invitation of Mr. Adcock's adult daughter, who was a resident of the home. After his daughter invited Mr. Poliak to live with her, Mr. Adcock did not express dissatisfaction about Mr. Poliak's presence. His silence over a period of months, as a matter of law, must reasonably be construed as permission for Mr. Poliak to remain in the house. Restatement (Second) of Torts §892 (1965) (stating that inaction can be construed as consent if the circumstances would make a reasonable person believe that he or she had consent to be on the property).

Similarly, Mr. Adcock's testimony does not demonstrate that striking Mr. Poliak with a two-by-four was immediately necessary to prevent or terminate Mr. Poliak's trespass or that the assault did not cause serious bodily harm. Months earlier, Mr. Adcock had ordered Mr. Poliak out of the house when he discovered Mr. Poliak in bed with his daughter and granddaughter. Mr. Poliak had complied with this demand making further force or threats of force unnecessary. Accordingly, the record provides no basis for concluding that Mr. Adcock was required to resort to violence on July 11, 1998 to remove Mr. Poliak from his house. There is certainly no factual justification for seriously injuring Mr. Poliak. If Mr. Adcock wanted Mr. Poliak to leave his house on July 11, 1998, he should have asked him to leave. The circumstances as described by Mr. Adcock do not provide a justification for using force to defend his house. Accordingly, the trial court properly concluded that Mr. Adcock would have been unable to substantiate a defense of property defense had this case gone to trial.

IV.

We affirm the partial summary judgment foreclosing Mr. Adcock's affirmative defenses as a matter of law and remand the case to the trial court for further proceedings consistent with this opinion. We tax the costs of this appeal to James H. Adcock and his surety for which execution, if necessary, may issue.

PREPARING FOR CLASS

Position yourself as counsel for Adcock, how do you prepare him for his deposition? In other words, how do you describe the law to him, and what questions do you ask?

APPLYING THE LAW

Bully is 6'4" and 250 pounds, while Meek is 5'6" and 150 pounds but very fast—in fact, the star sprinter on the track team. Bully has a history of harassing Meek and on this particular day confronts Meek in a field with his fists balled and saying "if you even sneeze I'm going to knock you out." Meek sneezes and then gives Bully a shot of pepper spray. Is Meek liable for battery?

INCREASING YOUR UNDERSTANDING

1. A person is privileged to use reasonable force to defend herself from a harmful intrusion provided she is reasonable in her belief (even if the belief is mistaken) that force is necessary to avoid the intrusion. The amount of force authorized to defend is measured by the magnitude of the threat that looms. Generally, the privilege will exist even in circumstances where the use of non-deadly force could have been avoided by retreating (Restatement (Second) of Torts §63), and the courts are split on whether retreating is required before becoming privileged to use deadly force. The prominent rule, however, is that you aren't required to retreat from your home before using force, but again, some courts

would require it if the only alternative is the use of deadly force. For example, in a case where a woman after she killed her husband in their home later claimed self defense, one court answered the "whether one has to retreat from the home" question as follows:

> "Privilege not to retreat, premised on maxim that every man's home is his castle which he is entitled to protect from invasion, did not apply where both defendant and her husband had equal rights to be in the "castle" and neither had legal right to eject the other. State v. Bobbitt, 415 So. 2d 724 (Fla. 1982).

2. What about my friend? Similarly, a person is privileged to use reasonable force to protect a third party from a harmful intrusion in the same manner that she would be allowed to protect herself. The actor is privileged even if mistaken as to the need to intervene. Restatement (Second) of Torts §76 cmt. d

3. Provocation is a variation of the contributory negligence defense, which will be discussed later in the term. It's black letter law that contributory negligence is not a defense to an intentional tort claim. However, there is a long line of cases that have allowed for the plaintiff's damages to be reduced when the plaintiff sufficiently "provoked" the intentional intrusion in the first place. It also should be clear that provocation involves a different conduct, and different legal consideration, than consent.

Katko v. Briney
183 N.W.2d 657

MOORE, Chief Justice.

The primary issue presented here is whether an owner may protect personal property in an unoccupied boarded-up farm house against trespassers and thieves by a spring gun capable of inflicting death or serious injury.

We are not here concerned with a man's right to protect his home and members of his family. Defendants' home was several miles from the scene of the incident to which we refer infra.

Plaintiff's action is for damages resulting from serious injury caused by a shot from a 20-gauge spring shotgun set by defendants in a bedroom of an old farm house which had been uninhabited for several years. Plaintiff and his companion, Marvin McDonough, had broken and entered the house to find and steal old bottles and dated fruit jars which they considered antiques.

At defendants' request plaintiff's action was tried to a jury consisting of residents of the community where defendants' property was located. The jury returned a verdict for plaintiff and against defendants for $20,000 actual and $10,000 punitive damages.

After careful consideration of defendants' motions for judgment notwithstanding the verdict and for new trial, the experienced and capable trial judge overruled them and entered judgment on the verdict. Thus we have this appeal by defendants.

I. In this action our review of the record as made by the parties in the lower court is for the correction of errors at law. We do not review actions at law de novo. Rule 334, Rules of Civil Procedure. Findings of fact by the jury are binding upon this court if supported by substantial evidence. Rule 344(f), par. 1, R.C.P.

II. Most of the facts are not disputed. In 1957 defendant Bertha L. Briney inherited her parents' farm land in Mahaska and Monroe Counties. Included was an 80-acre tract in southwest Mahaska County where her grandparents and parents had lived. No one occupied the house thereafter. Her husband, Edward, attempted to care for the land. He kept no farm machinery thereon. The outbuildings became dilapidated.

For about 10 years, 1957 to 1967, there occurred a series of trespassing and housebreaking events with loss of some household items, the breaking of windows and "messing up of the property in general." The latest occurred June 8, 1967, prior to the event on July 16, 1967 herein involved.

Defendants through the years boarded up the windows and doors in an attempt to stop the intrusions. They had posted "no trespass" signs on the land several years before 1967. The nearest one was 35 feet from the house. On June 11, 1967 defendants set "a shotgun trap" in the north bedroom. After Mr. Briney cleaned and oiled his 20-gauge shotgun, the power of which he was well aware, defendants took it to the old house where they secured it to an iron bed with the barrel pointed at the bedroom door. It was rigged with wire from the doorknob to the gun's trigger so it would fire when the door was opened. Briney first pointed the gun so an intruder would be hit in the stomach but at Mrs Briney's suggestion it was lowered to hit the legs. He admitted he did so "because I was mad and tired of being tormented' but 'he did not intend to injure anyone." He gave to explanation of why he used a loaded shell and set it to hit a person already in the house. Tin was nailed over the bedroom window. The spring gun could not be seen from the outside. No warning of its presence was posted.

Plaintiff lived with his wife and worked regularly as a gasoline station attendant in Eddyville, seven miles from the old house. He had observed it for several years while hunting in the area and considered it as being abandoned. He knew it had long been uninhabited. In 1967 the area around the house was covered with high weeds. Prior to July 16, 1967 plaintiff and McDonough had been to the premises and found several old bottles and fruit jars which they took and added to their collection of antiques. On the latter date about 9:30 P.M. they made a second trip to the Briney property. They entered the old house by removing a board from a porch window which was without glass. While McDonough was looking around the kitchen area plaintiff went to another part of the house. As he started to open the north bedroom door the shotgun went off striking him in the right leg above the ankle bone. Much of his leg, including part of the tibia, was blown away. Only by McDonough's assistance was plaintiff able to get out of the house and after crawling some distance was put in his vehicle and rushed to a doctor and then to a hospital. He remained in the hospital 40 days.

Plaintiff's doctor testified he seriously considered amputation but eventually the healing process was successful. Some weeks after his release from the hospital plaintiff returned to work on crutches. He was required to keep the injured leg in a cast for approximately a year and wear a special brace for another year. He continued to suffer pain during this period.

There was undenied medical testimony plaintiff had a permanent deformity, a loss of tissue, and a shortening of the leg.

The record discloses plaintiff to trial time had incurred $710 medical expense, $2056.85 for hospital service, $61.80 for orthopedic service and $750 as loss of earnings. In addition thereto the trial court submitted to the jury the question of damages for pain and suffering and for future disability.

III. Plaintiff testified he knew he had no right to break and enter the house with intent to steal bottles and fruit jars therefrom. He further testified he had entered a plea of guilty to larceny in the nighttime of property of less than $20 value from a private building. He stated he had been fined $50 and costs and paroled during good behavior from a 60-day jail sentence. Other than minor traffic charges this was plaintiff's first brush with the law. On this civil case appeal it is not our prerogative to review the disposition made of the criminal charge against him.

IV. The main thrust of defendants' defense in the trial court and on this appeal is that "the law permits use of a spring gun in a dwelling or warehouse for the purpose of preventing the unlawful entry of a burglar or thief." They repeated this contention in their exceptions to the trial court's instructions 2, 5 and 6. They took no exception to the trial court's statement of the issues or to other instructions.

In the statement of issues the trial court stated plaintiff and his companion committed a felony when they broke and entered defendants' house. In instruction 2 the court referred to the early case history of the use of spring guns and stated under the law their use was prohibited except to prevent the commission of felonies of violence and where human life is in danger. The instruction included a statement breaking and entering is not a felony of violence.

Instruction 5 stated: "You are hereby instructed that one may use reasonable force in the protection of his property, but such right is subject to the qualification that one may not use such means of force as will take human life or inflict great bodily injury. Such is the rule even though the injured party is a trespasser and is in violation of the law himself."

Instruction 6 stated: "An owner of premises is prohibited from willfully or intentionally injuring a trespasser by means of force that either takes life or inflicts great bodily injury; and therefore a person owning a premise is prohibited from setting out 'spring guns' and like dangerous devices which will likely take life or inflict great bodily injury, for the purpose of harming trespassers. The fact that the trespasser may be acting in violation of the law does not change the rule. The only time when such conduct of setting a 'spring gun' or a like dangerous device is justified would be when the trespasser was committing a felony of violence or a felony punishable by death, or where the trespasser was endangering human life by his act."

Instruction 7, to which defendants made no objection or exception, stated: "To entitle the plaintiff to recover for compensatory damages, the burden of proof is upon him to establish by a preponderance of the evidence each and all of the following propositions:

'1.   That defendants erected a shotgun trap in a vacant house on land owned by defendant, Bertha L. Briney, on or about June 11, 1967, which fact was known only by them, to protect household goods from trespassers and thieves.

'2.   That the force used by defendants was in excess of that force reasonably necessary and which persons are entitled to use in the protection of their property.

'3.   That plaintiff was injured and damaged and the amount thereof.

'4.   That plaintiff's injuries and damages resulted directly from the discharge of the shotgun trap which was set and used by defendants.' "

The overwhelming weight of authority, both textbook and case law, supports the trial court's statement of the applicable principles of law.

Prosser on Torts, Third Edition, pages 116-118, states:

"... the law has always placed a higher value upon human safety than upon mere rights in property, it is the accepted rule that there is no privilege to use any force calculated to cause death or serious bodily injury to repel the threat to land or chattels, unless there is also such a threat to the defendant's personal safety as to justify a self-defense. . . . [S]pring guns and other mankilling devices are not justifiable against a mere trespasser, or even a petty thief. They are privileged only against those upon whom the landowner, if he were present in person would be free to inflict injury of the same kind."

Restatement of Torts, section 85, page 180, states: "The value of human life and limb, not only to the individual concerned but also to society, so outweighs the interest of a possessor of land in excluding from it those whom he is not willing to admit thereto that a possessor of land has, as is stated in §79, no privilege to use force intended or likely to cause death or serious harm against another whom the possessor sees about to enter his premises or meddle with his chattel, unless the intrusion threatens death or serious bodily harm to the occupiers or users of the premises. . . . A possessor of land cannot do indirectly and by a mechanical device that which, were he present, he could not do immediately and in person. Therefore, he cannot gain a privilege to install, for the purpose of protecting his land from intrusions harmless to the lives and limbs of the occupiers or users of it, a mechanical device whose only purpose is to inflict death or serious harm upon such as may intrude, by giving notice of his intention to inflict, by mechanical means and indirectly, harm which he could not, even after request, inflict directly were he present."

In Volume 2, Harper and James, The Law of Torts, section 27.3, pages 1440, 1441, this is found: "The possessor of land may not arrange his premises intentionally so as to cause death or serious bodily harm to a trespasser. The possessor may of course take some steps to repel a trespass. If he is present he may use force to do so, buy only that amount which is reasonably necessary to effect the repulse. Moreover if the trespass threatens harm to property only—even a theft of property—the possessor would not be privileged to use deadly force, he may not arrange his premises so that such force will be inflicted by mechanical means. If he does, he will be liable even to a thief who is injured by such device."

In Hooker v. Miller, 37 Iowa 613, we held defendant vineyard owner liable for damages resulting from a spring gun shot although plaintiff was a trespasser and there to steal grapes. At pages 614, 615, this statement is made: "This court has held that a mere trespass against property other than a dwelling is not a sufficient justification to authorize the use of a deadly weapon by the owner in its defense; and that if death results in such a case it will be murder, though the killing be actually necessary to prevent the trespass. The State v. Vance, 17 Iowa 138." At page 617 this court said: "[T]respassers and other inconsiderable violators of the law are not to be visited by barbarous punishments or prevented by inhuman inflictions of bodily injuries."

The facts in Allison v. Fiscus, 156 Ohio 120, 110 N.E.2d 237, 44 A.L.R.2d 369, decided in 1951, are very similar to the case at bar. There plaintiff's right to damages was recognized for injuries received when he feloniously broke a door latch and started to enter defendant's warehouse with intent to steal. As he entered a trap of two sticks of dynamite buried under the doorway by defendant owner was set off and plaintiff seriously injured. The court held the question whether a particular trap was justified as a use of reasonable and necessary force against a trespasser engaged in the commission of a felony should have been submitted to the jury. The Ohio Supreme Court recognized plaintiff's right to recover punitive or exemplary damages in addition to compensatory damages.

In Starkey v. Dameron, 96 Colo. 459, 45 P.2d 172, plaintiff was allowed to recover compensatory and punitive damages for injuries received from a spring gun which defendant filling station operator had concealed in an automatic gasoline pump as protection against thieves.

In Wilder v. Gardner, 39 Ga. App. 608, 147 S.E. 911, judgment for plaintiff for injuries received from a spring gun which defendant had set, the court said: "A person in control of premises may be responsible even to a trespasser for injuries caused by pitfalls, mantraps, or other like contrivances so dangerous in character as to imply a disregard of consequences or a willingness to inflict injury."

In Phelps v. Hamlett, Tex. Civ. App., 207 S.W. 425, defendant rigged a bomb inside his outdoor theater so that if anyone came through the door the bomb would explode. The court reversed plaintiff's recovery because of an incorrect instruction but at page 426 said: "While the law authorizes an owner to protect his property by such reasonable means as he may find to be necessary, yet considerations of humanity preclude him from setting out, even on his own property, traps and devices dangerous to the life and limb of those whose appearance and presence may be reasonably anticipated, even though they may be trespassers."

In United Zinc & Chemical Co. v. Britt, 258 U.S. 268, 275, 42 S. Ct. 299, 66 L. Ed. 615, 617, the court states: "The liability for spring guns and mantraps arises from the fact that he defendant has . . . expected the trespasser and prepared an injury that is no more justified than if he had held the gun and fired it."

In addition to civil liability many jurisdictions hold a land owner criminally liable for serious injuries or homicide caused by spring guns or other set devices.

In Wisconsin, Oregon and England the use of spring guns and similar devices is specifically made unlawful by statute.

The legal principles stated by the trial court in instructions 2, 5 and 6 are well established and supported by the authorities cited and quoted supra. There is no merit in defendants' objections and exceptions thereto. Defendants' various motions based on the same reasons stated in exceptions to instructions were properly overruled.

PREPARING FOR CLASS

1. What does *de novo* review mean?

2. What choices did the Brineys have to protect their property?

3. Find the merit in the holding despite your distaste for Katko.

Neighbor, in upscale community, sees burglars break into house across the street. Upon seeing burglars exit house with bags in their hands, neighbor grabs his shotgun and decides to confront the burglars. Confrontation ends with both burglars being shot dead, one in the back? Privileged?

INCREASING YOUR UNDERSTANDING

1. *Katko* expresses the prevailing law; one is not allowed to use deadly force to protect property alone. This conclusion is reached primarily from

examining the same principles that govern liability in circumstances where the landowner was physically present and decided to use force. An owner of property is not justified in inflicting harm upon a trespasser by means of traps, spring guns, or other instrumentalities of destruction, unless the owner would have been justified, had he been personally present, in using the same force. The *Katko* rule though is not absolute: Ciarmataro v. Adams, 275 Mass. 521, 176 N.E. 610 (Mass. 1931) (Owner of premises held not liable for death of trespasser killed by shot from concealed spring or trap gun set up by caretaker without knowledge of owner); Allison v. Fiscus, 156 Ohio St. 120, 100 N.E.2d 237 (Ohio 1951) (Defendant's belief that amount of dynamite defendant planted and way defendant planted dynamite would result only in frightening intruder and not cause injury, were for jury, and defendant was not as a matter of law liable to plaintiff); Scheuermann v. Scharfenberg, 163 Ala. 337, 50 So. 335 Ala. 1909 (Owner of store is not liable to a would-be burglar shot by a spring gun, where such intrusion would constitute a felony).

2. In summation. Use of deadly force or force intended to inflict serious injury to protect property will rarely be authorized. Defendants like the Brineys will surely lose unless they convince the court that threat of personal injury was the real motivation behind the force employed.

The next case, *Bobb*, expands on this discussion.

Bobb v. Bosworth
2 Litt. Sel. Cas. 81, (Ky. 1808)

Opinion of the Court, by Judge TRIMBLE.

This was an action of assault and battery, brought by Bosworth against Bobb, in which "not guilty" was pleaded, with leave to give special matter in evidence. A verdict having been found for the plaintiff, a new trial was moved for by the defendant, which was overruled. Whereupon he filed a bill of exceptions, containing the whole evidence given on both sides, and appealed to this court, in which he hath assigned for error, that a new trial ought to have been granted.

One wrongfully dispossessed of his goods, may retake them wherever he can find them.

The recaption must not be in a riotous or forcible manner.

This will depend upon the question, in what cases, and in what manner can the right of recaption be lawfully exercised? There is no doubt, but that one having either the general or a special right of property in personal chattels, may, if wrongfully dispossessed thereof, retake them wherever he can find them, provided he can obtain peaceable possession; but the law more highly regards the public peace, than the right of property of a private individual, and therefore forbids recaption to be made in a riotous or forcible manner. The law, however, permits the possessor of property to maintain his possession by force, where force is used in attempting to divest his possession; the law, in that case, permits the party in possession to oppose violence to violence. It is material, whether the violence has been used to regain a possession which had been previously lost, or whether it has been used to maintain a present possession. In the former, it is unlawful; in the latter, lawful.

A possessor of property may lawfully repel by force, a forcible attempt to divest his possession.

If A. attempts to retake his goods by force, B. resists the recaption, and in the affray A. wounds B. a civil suit will lie against A. for the battery. In such case it is not material whether A. or B. had the better claim to the property.

In the case now before the court, it appears that Bosworth, at the time the assault and battery was committed, was in possession of the slave, which was the subject of dispute between the parties; that Bobb came with others to retake him out of Bosworth's possession in a violent and forcible manner, which was resisted by Bosworth; and, in the scuffle, Bobb broke the arm of Bosworth. It is not material, whether Bobb or Bosworth had the better right to the negro. Bosworth was in actual possession; Bobb could not lawfully use violence and force in regaining possession. Having broken the peace, and used force, where he was forbidden by law to do so, he must be answerable for the consequences.

Upon "not guilty," with leave to give the special matter in evidence, in trespass, assault and battery, anything which amounted to a justification might be given in evidence; but circumstances not amounting to a legal justification, could not be thereby permitted to be given in evidence.

The leave to give special matter in evidence under the general issue, authorized Bobb to prove any thing, which if pleaded, would have made a good justification in law; but the circumstances made out in proof by him, did not amount to a legal justification. We are, therefore, of opinion a new trial was properly refused.

Judgment affirmed with damages and costs.

PREPARING FOR CLASS

1. What method should Bobb have used to reclaim his property?

2. What additional facts would assist you in determining whether the recapture attempt was reasonable here?

3. Should the law be more flexible and allow force to be used during recapture, especially if the property is valuable or there is a real threat of it being made unavailable?

APPLYING THE LAW

A has a going away party for B, who is leaving the next day and returning home to Israel. During the party, A brought B to his room to show him the engagement ring he had just purchased for his fiancée. When A returned to his room after the party, he discovered that the ring was missing and suspected that B had stolen it. A immediately drives over to B's home and knocks on his door, but there is no answer, though B's car is in the driveway. A travels around to the back of B's home, peers in the window to his bedroom, and sees the box for the ring sitting on B's dresser. A breaks the window, enters, and retrieves the ring. In the trespass suit brought by B, is A liable?

INCREASING YOUR UNDERSTANDING

The law grants a privilege to recapture property wrongfully taken provided that certain conditions are met. The failure to meet these conditions will result in the disposed being liable for any injuries inflicted during the attempt to recapture and also potentially liable for conversion if mistaken as to who has proper title. A replevin action is the proper recourse where the owner fails to meet the recapture requirements. The conditions for proper recapture can be described as requiring:

1.   Fresh pursuit. "The actor is not privileged to use force against another for the purpose of reception unless he acts promptly after dispossession or after timely discovery of it." Restatement (Second) of Torts §103. The cases have interpreted this language to require "fresh pursuit" of the wrongfully taken chattel but without establishing any consistent parameters. At a minimum, the disposed party must act with urgency upon being notified of dispossession—urgency with respect to apprehending the defendant and with respect to ascertaining the fact that he has been disposed.

2.   Keeping the peace. *Bobb* holds that recapture will not be privileged if recapture involves "breaching the peace." Others have ruled similarly, though perhaps describing it in different terms. "Secured party's right to take self-help possession of its collateral upon default is limited by breach of the peace rule . . . if his attempt to take possession results in breach of the peace . . . because the debtor resists, he faces consequences of its use of force." Nixon v. Halpin, 620 So. 2d 796 (Fla. App. 4 Dist. 1993). The Restatement, however, authorizes the use of non-serious force, seemingly even if it disturbs the peace.

3.   Demand. The authorities consistently have required that the person seeking repossession first articulate a demand before taking recapture actions. Where the demand is rejected, reasonable force may be authorized to secure the property and defend one's own person.

C. DETENTION

Gortarez By and Through Gortarez v. Smitty's Super Valu, Inc.
140 Ariz. 97 (1984), 680 P.2d 807

FELDMAN, Justice.

Petitioner, Ernest Gortarez, Jr., and his parents (plaintiffs) bring this petition for review to contest the trial court's disposition of their claims against respondents, Smitty's Super Value, Inc., and its security officer, Daniel Gibson (defendants). Plaintiffs brought suit against defendants for false arrest, false imprisonment, and assault and battery after Gortarez and his cousin, Albert Hernandez, were detained in the parking lot of Smitty's.

Finding that the circumstances in the case gave reasonable cause for detention, the trial court directed a verdict on the count of false imprisonment and false arrest. The assault and battery count went to the jury, which returned a verdict for defendant Gibson. The court of appeals affirmed by memorandum decision. We accepted review to examine the extent and application of the "shopkeeper's privilege" and because the facts of this case indicate an improper and, we believe, dangerous tendency to extend the statutory grant of the privilege in question.

FACTS

We view the facts in a light most favorable to the party against whom the verdict was directed.

Ernest Gortarez, age 16, and his cousin, Albert Hernandez, age 18, went to Smitty's store on January 2, 1979, around 8:00 P.M. They visited the automotive department, where Hernandez selected a power booster which cost $22.00. While Hernandez was paying for the power booster, Gortarez picked up a 59-cent vaporizer used to freshen the air in cars. Gortarez asked if he could pay for it in the front of the store when he finished shopping. The clerk said yes, but decided that the request was suspicious and had a "hunch" that Gortarez would try to leave the store without paying for the item.

The two cousins wandered through the store, looking at other merchandise, and finally left the store through an unattended check-out aisle. The clerk, Robert Sjulestad, had followed the two through the store, in aisles parallel to where the young men were walking, so that there were occasions when he could not observe Gortarez below shoulder level. Since Sjulestad did not see them dispose of or pay for the vaporizer, he concluded that Gortarez or Hernandez took the item without paying for it.

Sjulestad then told the assistant manager and the security guard, Daniel Gibson, that "[t]hose two guys just ripped us off." According to Gibson's testimony, Sjulestad explained that "they had picked up a vaporizer and asked to pay for it in the front, and then didn't pay for it, as I watched them walk through, and they obviously did not pay for anything at that time."

Gibson and Scott Miller, the assistant manager, along with two other store employees, then ran out of the store to catch the two young men as they were about to get inside their car in the parking lot. Miller went to the passenger side to intercept Gortarez, while Gibson went for Hernandez, who was about to open the car door on the driver's side. Gibson said that he identified himself "as an officer" by showing his badge as he ran up to Hernandez. (Gibson was an off-duty police officer working as a security guard for Smitty's.) Gibson told Hernandez: "I believe you have something you did not pay for." He then seized Hernandez, put his arms on the car and began searching him. Hernandez offered no resistance even though Gibson did not ask for the vaporizer, nor say what he was looking for. In cross-examination, Gibson admitted that Hernandez did nothing to resist him, and, as Gibson searched him, Hernandez kept repeating that he did not have anything that he had not paid for.

Meanwhile, on the other side of the car, flanked by Miller, Gortarez saw Gibson grab Hernandez, push him up against the car, and search him. Gortarez was outraged at this behavior and used strong language to protest the detention and the search—yelling at Gibson to leave his cousin alone. According to Gortarez, he thought the men were looking for the vaporizer because he heard Gibson tell the others to watch out for the bottle, and to look under the car for the bottle. Gortarez testified that he told the men that Hernandez did not have the vaporizer—it was in the store. No one had stopped to check at the counter through which the two exited, where the vaporizer was eventually found in one of the catch-all baskets at the unattended check-out stand.

Seeing Gibson "rousting" Hernandez, Gortarez came to the defense of his cousin, ran around the front of the car and pushed Gibson away. Gibson then grabbed Gortarez and put a choke hold around Gortarez' neck until he stopped struggling. Both Hernandez and Gortarez testified that the first time that Gibson identified himself to them was after he had restrained Gortarez in a choke hold. There was testimony that Gortarez was held in the choke hold for a period of time even after Gortarez had advised the store employees that he had left the vaporizer in the store. When a carry-out boy told the store employees that he had found the vaporizer in a basket at the check-out stand, the two cousins were released.

Gortarez later required medical treatment for injuries suffered from the choke hold. Plaintiffs sued Smitty's and Gibson for false arrest, false imprisonment, and assault and battery. The case was tried before a jury. At the close of all the evidence, the court directed a verdict for the defendants on the false imprisonment and false arrest count. The assault and battery claim went to the jury, with an instruction on self-defense; the court refused plaintiffs' instruction on withdrawal. The jury returned a verdict for defendant Gibson. The court of appeals affirmed, and plaintiffs petition this court for review.

FALSE IMPRISONMENT AND FALSE ARREST

HISTORICAL PERSPECTIVE

At common law, a private person's privilege to arrest another for a misdemeanor was very limited. The Restatement (Second) of Torts describes the circumstances under which a private person may arrest another without a warrant:

a) if the other has committed the felony for which he is arrested, or

b) if an act or omission constituting a felony has been committed and the actor reasonably suspects that the other has committed such act or omission, or

c) if the other, in the presence of the actor, is committing a breach of the peace or, having so committed a breach of the peace, he is reasonably believed by the actor to be about to renew it, or

d) if the actor has attempted to commit a felony in the actor's presence and the arrest is made at once or upon fresh pursuit, or

e) if the other knowingly causes the actor to believe that facts existed which would create in him a privilege to arrest under the statement in Clauses (a) to (d).

Arizona has codified the common law. So far as relevant here, the statute provides that a private person may make an arrest for a misdemeanor when the person to be arrested has committed a misdemeanor amounting to a breach of the peace in the presence of the person making the arrest. §13-3884, 5A A.R.S. Thus, at common law and by statute, the privilege to arrest for misdemeanors without a warrant is limited to those misdemeanors which constitute a breach of the peace.[3] In the case of misdemeanors such as shoplifting, there is no breach of the peace, and no common law privilege to arrest. Therefore any common law privilege would exist only for recapture of chattel. There is a limited privilege for an owner whose property has been wrongfully taken, while in fresh pursuit, to use reasonable force to recapture a chattel. Prosser, *supra*, §22 at 117. An important caveat to this privilege is that the actor must be correct as to the facts which he believes grant him the privilege, and faces liability for damages resulting from any mistake, however reasonable. *Id.* The force privileged must be reasonable under the circumstances, and not calculated to inflict serious bodily harm. Ordinarily, the use of any force at all will not be justified until there has been a demand made for the return of the property. *Id.*

---

3. A mistaken belief that a breach of the peace has been committed does not confer a privilege under Clause (c). Restatement (Second) of Torts, §119 Comment (o). (A peace officer is privileged under §121(c) where the one arrested is a participant in an affray.)

Thus, privileges for misdemeanor arrest traditionally available at common law recognize no privilege to arrest for ordinary "shoplifting." Under this rule a shopkeeper who believed that a customer was shoplifting was placed in an untenable position. Either the shopkeeper allowed the suspect to leave the premises, risking the loss of merchandise, or took the risk of attempting to recapture the chattel by detaining the customer, facing liability for the wrongful detention if the person had not stolen merchandise. *Id.* §22 at 121.

As Prosser noted, shoplifting is a major problem, causing losses that range into millions of dollars each year. *Id.*; *see also Kon v. Skaggs Drug Centers, Inc.*, 115 Ariz. 121, 563 P.2d 920 (App. 1977). There have been a number of decisions which permit a business person for reasonable cause, to detain a customer for investigation. Prosser, *supra* at 122. This privilege, however, is narrow; it is

> confined to what is reasonably necessary for its limited purpose, of enabling the defendant to do what is possible on the spot to discover the facts. There will be liability if the detention is for a length of time beyond that which is reasonably necessary for such a short investigation, or if the plaintiff is assaulted, insulted or bullied, or public accusation is made against him, or the privilege is exercised in an unreasonable manner. . . .

Id.

The developing, common law "shopkeeper's privilege" described by Prosser was incorporated into the second Restatement of Torts with the addition of section 120A—Temporary Detention for Investigation:

> One who reasonably believes that another has tortiously taken a chattel upon his premises, or has failed to make cash payment for a chattel purchased or services rendered there, is privileged, without arresting the other, to detain him on the premises for the time necessary for a reasonable investigation of the facts.

Comment (a) states that this section is necessary to protect shopkeepers from the dilemma we have just described. Comment (d) explains that the privilege differs from the privilege to use reasonable force to recapture a chattel, because it protects the shopkeeper who has made a reasonable mistake regarding the guilt of the suspect. As noted in Comment (g), the privilege is one of detention only.

We have not had occasion to pass upon the applicability of the Restatement rule. Instead Arizona has adopted the shopkeeper's privilege by statute, which provides in pertinent part:

> C. A merchant, or his agent or employee, *with reasonable cause, may detain* on the premises *in a reasonable manner and for a reasonable time*

any person suspected of shoplifting . . . *for questioning or summoning a law enforcement officer.*

D. Reasonable cause is a defense to a civil or criminal action against a peace officer, merchant or an agent or employee of such merchant for false arrest, false or unlawful imprisonment or wrongful detention.

A.R.S. §13-1805 (emphasis supplied).

The trial court was evidently of the view that by the terms of subsection D, reasonable cause, alone, was a defense. We disagree; we believe that the statutory shopkeeper's privilege, like that described in the Restatement, involves all of the elements noted in subsection C. Subsections C and D of §13-1805 must be read together. Applying subsection (D) by recognizing the privilege defense upon a showing of "reasonable cause" without the limitations contained in subsection (C), would render the latter meaningless. Where the language of the statute is susceptible of several interpretations, the court will adopt one which is reasonable and avoids contradictions or absurdities. Also, we must construe a statute as a whole and give effect to all its provisions.

To invoke the privilege, therefore, "reasonable cause" is only the threshold requirement. Once reasonable cause is established, there are two further questions regarding the application of the privilege. We must ask whether the purpose of the shopkeeper's action was proper (*i.e.*, detention for questioning or summoning a law enforcement officer). The last question is whether the detention was carried out in a reasonable manner and for a reasonable length of time. If the answer to any of the three questions is negative, then the privilege granted by statute is inapplicable and the actions of the shopkeeper are taken at his peril. If the shopkeeper is mistaken and the common law recapture privilege is therefore also inapplicable, the seizure is tortious.

REASONABLE CAUSE

Under statutes permitting the detention of suspected shoplifters, "reasonable cause" generally has the same meaning as "probable cause." Our court of appeals has held that reasonable cause under this statute is the "reasonable cause standard of arrest." We agree that for the purposes of this privilege, reasonable cause and probable cause seem equivalent.

Reasonable cause is not dependent on the guilt or innocence of the person, or whether the crime was actually committed. *Tota v. Alexander's*, 63 Misc. 2d 908, 314 N.Y.S.2d 93, 95 (1968). In *Tota*, the court stated that one may act on what proves to be an incorrect belief provided the facts show that the belief was reasonable. *Id.* As our court of appeals properly stated in *Kon*, the "reasonable cause" clause is inserted in the statute generally to cover those situations where no one actually sees the theft. 115 Ariz. at 123, 563 P.2d at 922.

Reasonable cause is generally held to be a question of law to be determined by the court. Annot. *supra* §2(b). In *Kon*, the court of appeals held that the issue of reasonable cause to detain a shoplifter is a matter of law for the court to decide. 115 Ariz. at 123, 563 P.2d at 922. It would be more correct to say that reasonable cause is a question of law for the court *where the facts or inferences from them are not in dispute.* When there is a dispute, then the issue of reasonable cause becomes a mixed question of law and fact, and it is for the jury to determine the disputed facts.

In the case at bench, the facts supporting reasonable cause are as follows: the clerk saw Gortarez with the item when he asked if he could pay for it at the front. The clerk followed the two young men through the store, and did not see them either deposit the item or pay for it as they left. Although the question of reasonable cause in the instant case may have been close we defer to the trial court's better opportunity to see and judge the credibility of witnesses and uphold it on the specific finding that conflicting inferences could not be drawn from the facts and that reasonable cause existed as a matter of law.

PURPOSE OF THE DETENTION

The statute provides this privilege for the express and limited purpose of detention for investigation by questioning or summoning a law enforcement officer. A finding of detention for the proper purpose could not have been made as a matter of law on the state of the evidence before the trial judge, since there was no evidence of either questioning or summoning of officers. At best, this was a question for the jury, because although there was no questioning, it is possible that the intent of the employee was to question or call officers.

REASONABLENESS OF THE DETENTION

Assuming there was reasonable cause for the detention, and that the detention was for a proper purpose, the privilege still may not attach if the merchant does not detain in a reasonable manner and for a reasonable time. As with the question of reasonable cause, the issue of reasonableness of the detention is one for the court to decide as a matter of law where there is no conflict in the evidence as to the length of time or the circumstances under which the plaintiff was held. Where the facts are in dispute or where different inferences may be drawn from undisputed facts, it is for the jury, under proper instructions from the court, to determine the reasonableness of the detention.

Comment (h) to §120A of the Restatement (Second) of Torts states that the use of force is never privileged unless the resistance of the suspected thief makes the use of such force necessary for the actor's self-defense.

> Reasonable force may be used to detain the person; but ... the use of force intended or likely to cause serious bodily harm is never privileged for the sole purpose of detention to investigate, and it becomes privileged only where the resistance of the other makes it necessary for the actor to

use such force in self-defense. In the ordinary case, the use of any force at all will not be privileged until the other has been requested to remain; and it is only where there is not time for such a request, or it would obviously be futile, that force is justified.

Id. The Arizona statute is essentially a codification of the common law shopkeeper's privilege. The limitations on the use of force are obviously wise. We hold that the principle quoted is applicable to our statutory requirement that the detention be carried out in a "reasonable manner."

Under the restrictions given above, there was a question whether the use of force in the search of Hernandez, and, more importantly, in the restraint of Gortarez, was reasonable. There was no request that the two young men remain. No inquiry was made with regard to whether Hernandez had the vaporizer. Gibson testified that Hernandez gave no indication of resistance and made no attempt to escape. The possible theft of a 59 cent item hardly warrants apprehension that the two were armed or dangerous. There was, arguably, time to make a request to remain before Gibson seized Hernandez and began searching him. Also, there is no indication that such a request would *obviously* have been futile. The evidence adduced probably would have supported a finding that the manner of detention was unreasonable as a matter of law. At best, there was a question of fact; there was no support for the court's presumptive finding that as a matter of law the detention was performed reasonably.

The court directed a verdict for defendants on the false arrest and imprisonment counts. In so doing, it necessarily found as a matter of law that there was reasonable cause, and that the seizure and detention were undertaken for a proper purpose and in a reasonable manner. We hold that the court erred in its findings with respect to both the purpose and manner of detention. This requires reversal and retrial. At the new trial evidence on the three issues should be measured against the principles set forth in this opinion.

We therefore reverse and remand for new trial on all counts.

GORDON, V.C.J., and HAYS and CAMERON, JJ., concur.

HOLOHAN, Chief Justice, dissenting.

If the case at issue had involved a claim by Albert Hernandez, the cousin of the plaintiff, much of what is written in the majority opinion would be acceptable. The vital factor is that Hernandez is not the plaintiff, but the majority opinion ignores this fact by setting forth legal principles which have no application to the facts as applied to the plaintiff Gortarez.

The law applicable to the issues of false arrest and false imprisonment is purely statutory. A.R.S. §13-1805, the applicable statute, is broader in scope than the rule advanced by the Restatement, a fact which is acknowledged by the majority but relegated to a footnote. The provisions of the statute material to this case and in effect at the time provided:

"C. A merchant, or his agent or employee, with reasonable cause, may detain on the premises in a reasonable manner and for a reasonable time any person suspected of shoplifting as defined in subsection A for questioning or summoning a law enforcement officer.

"D. Reasonable cause is a defense to a civil or criminal action against a peace officer, merchant or an agent or employee of such merchant for false arrest, false or unlawful imprisonment or wrongful detention."

Focusing on the action taken by the defendant security guard against the non plaintiff Hernandez, the majority holds that unreasonable force against Hernandez resulted in his false arrest and imprisonment, which in turn also resulted in the false arrest and imprisonment of the plaintiff. It is conceded by the majority that plaintiff Gortarez was initially not touched by the defendant's agent. Apparently by some theory of transferred intent or otherwise any unreasonable restraint of the non plaintiff became unreasonable as to the plaintiff.

The agents of the defendant had reasonable cause to detain the plaintiff and his cousin, a position which the majority concedes. Since the defendant's agents had reasonable cause to detain the plaintiff, this must of necessity include the authority to keep him from leaving the parking lot; thus any action against the plaintiff's driver adds nothing to the issue of the right to detain the plaintiff. He was subject to detention irrespective of any action taken to detain or release his cousin.

The individual who had picked up the items thought to have been stolen was the plaintiff. Under A.R.S. §13-1805(C) the defendant's employees were entitled to detain the plaintiff in a reasonable manner and for a reasonable time for questioning or summoning a law enforcement officer. There is absolutely no evidence in the record that any unreasonable action was directed against the plaintiff. He was not touched or restrained in any manner. This is borne out by the record which shows that no agent of the defendant company sought to stop the plaintiff from leaving the passenger's side of the automobile to approach and challenge the security guard who was searching his cousin. Any restraint of the plaintiff, actual or by implication, was accomplished in a reasonable manner.

The directed verdict on the claim for false arrest and false imprisonment should be affirmed.

As the case was tried in the superior court and based on the issues presented to the Court of Appeals, I believe that the Court of Appeals was correct in affirming the judgment of the superior court. I dissent from the opinion of the court.

PREPARING FOR CLASS

1. Identify the various intentional torts and the factual support for each claim.

2. Do you agree with the dissenting opinion that Gortarez was never detained?

3. In this circumstance, what would a reasonable detention consist of?

APPLYING THE LAW

Johnny, a local television personality, is shopping at a department store when he gets a call from his pregnant wife informing him that she is in labor. Johnny immediately sprints out of the store but is confronted outside by a security guard who ushers him back into the store for questioning in front of a line of customers who are checking out. After 15 minutes of questions Johnny is allowed to go, but the delay causes him to miss the birth of his first son. What, if anything, can Johnny sue for, and how do you expect the store to respond?

INCREASING YOUR UNDERSTANDING

1. *"The shopkeeper's privilege."* Either by judicial decision or legislation, most jurisdictions authorize business owners to detain those that they have reasonable cause to believe are involved in theft. The privilege has two interlinking requirements: The suspicion of theft must be reasonable, and the detention must be as well. "Statutory provision allowing for a shopkeeper's defense to false arrest or false imprisonment claims based upon a reasonable belief that the plaintiff was shoplifting or that the manner of the detention or arrest was reasonable has been read in the conjunctive, despite the use of disjunctive language." K Mart Corp. v. Adamson, 192 Ga. App. 884, 386 S.E.2d 680 (1989). It does not matter that the business owner was wrong in the suspicion as long as the suspicion was reasonably acquired. The question on reasonableness, as it is in most cases, will be answered by the trier of fact.

2. *Scope of the privilege.* The privilege allows generally for a reasonable detention, with the circumstances shaping what is reasonable. A detention for an unreasonable period will lose the protection of the privilege, as will an unreasonably intrusive manner of investigation. What once may have been a legitimate basis to detain may escalate to an unauthorized detention necessitating a distinction between the harm that occurred during the privileged detention and what occurred later. Again, the privilege simply permits a storekeeper time to investigate a suspected shoplifter but does not "confer the power of intimidation by holding a person incommunicado until a confession is signed, without reasonable effort to ascertain the true facts." Wilde v. Schwegmann Bros. Giant Supermarkets, Inc., 160 So. 2d 839 (La. App. 1964).

D. TRESPASS, INTRUSION, PUBLIC/PRIVATE NECESSITY

South Dakota Dept. of Health v. Heim
357 N.W.2d 522 (1984)

HENDERSON, Justice.

PROCEDURAL HISTORY/FACTS

This is an appeal from a judgment of December 21, 1983, after trial to the court, denying compensation from the State of South Dakota for the destruction of a diseased elk herd. We affirm.

A skin test administered to appellant's elk in September 1981, indicated the presence of bovine tuberculosis. The animals were placed under quarantine and on October 2, 1981, a Complaint for Abatement of a Public Health Hazard was filed.

A similar suit was pending in the Eighth Judicial Circuit concerning the elk herd of James and Dwight Owen, which had been purchased from appellant. On December 8, 1981, the litigants herein stipulated that they would be bound by the decision of Judge Tschetter, Eighth Judicial Circuit, with regard to Owen's herd. The Heim animals remained in quarantine during this period. No further action was taken.

Judge Tschetter's decision to destroy the Owen's elk came on May 13, 1982. This order was subsequently amended on August 18, 1982. A warrant to destroy appellant's herd was issued on August 19, 1982, by Circuit Judge Vernon Evans, Third Judicial Circuit. Appellant's elk were again administered the skin test. Those reacting positively were destroyed. Appellant brought action for compensation of the destroyed elk, claiming the State acted pursuant to its power of eminent domain.

ISSUE

DID THE STATE DESTROY THE HEIM ELK HERD PURSUANT TO ITS POWER OF EMINENT DOMAIN?

DECISION

In *City of Rapid City v. Boland*, 271 N.W.2d 60 (S.D. 1978), we established certain rules concerning the duty of the government to compensate owners of property damaged or destroyed by the government.

From the general rule requiring compensation, we delineated the following specific exceptions:

> There are three important exceptions to the requirement of compensation where, without the owner's consent, private property is intentionally, purposefully or deliberately taken or damaged for the public use, benefit or convenience. They are the taking or destruction of property (1) during actual warfare; (2) to prevent an imminent public catastrophe; and (3) to abate a public nuisance. In each instance, the power to "take or damage" without compensation is based upon the public necessity of preventing an impending hazard which threatens the lives, safety, or health of the general public.
>
> The public necessity privilege is an extension of every individual's privilege to take whatever steps appear reasonable to prevent an imminent public disaster.

Boland, 271 N.W.2d at 65 (footnote omitted). Based upon the record herein, it is clear that the destruction of appellant's diseased animals falls within the third exception to compensation found in *Boland.*

This case is also governed by our holding in *South Dakota Dep't of Health v. Owen*, 350 N.W.2d 48 (S.D.1984). As stated in *Owen*, 350 N.W.2d at 50,

> [i]t is the generally accepted rule of law that destruction by health authorities of animals suffering from a contagious disease, where such destruction is necessary to prevent the spread of the disease, does not deprive the owner of property without due process of law. It is not a taking of property for public use within the meaning of the constitutional provisions requiring compensation for such use. (Footnote and citations omitted.)

Here, the trial court specifically found:

3. The hazard to human health, welfare and safety created by the Defendant's elk herd was of sufficient gravity to require its abatement for the protection of the general public of the State of South Dakota.

4. The form of abatement . . . was through the destruction of the animals which had a positive reaction to the tuberculosis skin test performed by the Department.

5. The only adequate and recognized method of controlling Mycobacterium bovis in animals is through the destruction of the animals that have a positive reaction to the tuberculosis skin test.

These findings constituted a determination that the diseased elk herd was a public nuisance. *Owen*, 350 N.W.2d 48. Conclusions of Law numbers 2 and 3 provided:

2.   The Defendant's elk, as a "cause of sickness," within the meaning of SDCL 34-16-7, were a public nuisance.

3.   The Defendant's elk, which were a "cause of sickness," and a public nuisance, presented a continuing threat to human health and safety and were imminently hazardous to the public health, safety and welfare.

We cannot hold that this was clearly erroneous.

Appellant concedes in its reply brief "that the only effective and economical means of eliminating tuberculosis in an animal herd is to destroy the entire herd." As destruction of the herd was a summary abatement of a nuisance imminently hazardous to the public health, safety, or welfare, appellant is not entitled to compensation. *See Owen*, 350 N.W.2d 48.

Appellant insists that the one-year lapse between the discovery of the disease and its abatement indicates these animals were not a public nuisance and were taken under the State's power of eminent domain. The record indicates, however, that the time lapse was due to continuances urged and agreed to by appellant and not to any lack of diligence on the part of the State.

We need not reach just compensation, incidental damages, or consequential damages due to our basic holding herein.

Affirmed.

PREPARING FOR CLASS

1.   Identify and articulate the public necessity.

2.   What is the rule, and what intentional intrusion might be protected by the rule?

APPLYING THE LAW

Joe Citizen suspects his neighbor is on the verge of meeting with a group of home-grown terrorists who are plotting to blow up an abortion clinic. Joe slits the tires of the neighbor's car before he can depart. Turns out, Joe was wrong. Is Joe liable in trespass/conversion?

INCREASING YOUR UNDERSTANDING

Resting on the maxim, *necessitas inducit privilegium quod jura privata*, courts have extended a privilege to those whose heroic efforts have averted a "public disaster" as long as the do-gooder reasonably believed intervention was necessary and the threat of harm imminent. The "public necessity" privilege absolutely protects society's defender from liability for the harm that is caused by his intentional acts. Typically, the actors are employees of the government, so most of the cases in this regard have discussed the privilege in claims brought against the government where property had been destroyed. Much debate has focused on whether the privilege should be limited to government actors and circumstances where property has been destroyed, but the authorities that do so are unpersuasive; the unpaid private actor is perhaps nobler in his efforts, and any privilege should start with him.

Rossi v. DelDuca
344 Mass. 66 (1962), 181 N.E.2d 591

SPALDING, Justice.

Although the declaration contains thirteen counts against several defendants, we are now concerned with only the first and seventh. The plaintiff in the first count (hereinafter called the plaintiff) is Patricia Rossi, a minor, who seeks by her next friend to recover for injuries inflicted upon her by two dogs owned by the defendant, Ernest V. DelDuca. In the seventh count John Rossi, Patricia's father, seeks to recover for medical expenses incurred by him on behalf of his daughter. Both counts were submitted to the jury who returned verdicts for the plaintiffs. The case comes here on the defendant's exception to the denial of his motion for a directed verdict on each count.

There was evidence of the following: The plaintiff lived with her parents on Oak Street, Methuen. Oak Street runs north and south. In order to reach the Rossi house coming from the south it is necessary to pass Cambridge Street which joins Oak Street from the east. On the east side of Oak Street starting at the junction of Cambridge and Oak streets and proceeding northward there are three houses occupied by the defendant and members of his family. The first house (No. 105) is owned and occupied by Arthur DelDuca, a brother of the defendant. To the north of, and next to, Arthur's house is a house (No. 119) owned and occupied by Samuel DelDuca, also a brother of the defendant. Next to and north of Samuel's house is the defendant's house (No. 121). At 70 Cambridge Street (on the north side of the street) is a garage owned by the defendant's wife, which the defendant uses in his contracting business. There is a small shed near the back of the garage, slightly to the west, which is also used in the business. Cambridge Street is a dead-end street to the east of the garage, and there are no streets running off Oak Street north of Cambridge Street. In connection with his business, the defendant owned and maintained bulldozers, graders, and equipment which he kept outdoors on a field owned by his father, Vincenzo, located east of 105, 119, and 121 Oak Street, and north of the garage at 70 Cambridge Street. "Going north of the east side of Oak Street starting at Cambridge Street there were no fences between the houses. The field on the east side of Oak Street was to the north of 70 Cambridge Street and east of . . . [the defendant's] land at 121 Oak Street. The land was all open in there." On this field, the defendant, with the permission of his father, had erected a pen to house two great Dane dogs which he owned. The defendant's brother Arthur was the owner of a purplish-gray German Weimaraner dog.

In September, 1955, Ida Celia and the plaintiff, both aged eight, were students in the third grade of the Ashford school. In the afternoon of September 26, school having closed, they started walking up Oak Street toward their homes. As they reached the corner of Cambridge Street, they saw the German Weimaraner ahead of them on Oak Street. The dog started to come toward them, and, as the plaintiff testified, "We got frightened so we . . . ran down Cambridge Street . . . [and the dog was] [f]ollowing us." Realizing that Cambridge Street was a dead-end street, the girls left Cambridge Street on the north side, passing around the garage at 70 Cambridge Street and the shed. The dog continued to follow them. After they passed the shed, they ran along a path in the field belonging to the defendant's father. The plaintiff then saw, for the first time, a black great Dane. "[T]he dog was on its hind legs and it was going to jump on her. It did jump on her. She doesn't remember after that, and then she remembers two black dogs on her. She didn't feel anything but they were biting her neck. She shouted for help." The plaintiff's father observed the defendant's great Dane dogs in the field. They "were worrying some object" which he learned was his daughter Patricia who was "crouched down on her knees . . . with her hands on her face." He picked her up and took her to the hospital.

The defendant testified that on September 26, 1955, he owned two "black Dane dogs." The dogs were "trained to stay in the field to the rear of this defendant's home where his equipment was kept. . . . He had a lot of equipment and was concerned about it." The defendant's arrangement with his father regarding this land was that the "defendant could use all of that property for parking his equipment and doing anything he wanted with it in connection with his business. . . . He had full control of the field."

1. It is clear both from the pleadings and the evidence that the plaintiff seeks to recover under G.L. c. 140, §155, which, as amended by St. 1934, c. 320, §18 reads: "If any dog shall do any damage to either the body or property of any person, the owner or keeper, or if the owner or keeper be a minor, the parent or guardian of such minor, shall be liable for such damage, unless such damage shall have been occasioned to the body or property of a person who, at the time such damage was sustained, was committing a trespass or other tort, or was teasing, tormenting or abusing such dog." Under this statute, unlike the common law, "the owner or keeper of a dog is liable . . . for injury resulting from an act of the dog without proof . . . that its owner or keeper was negligent or otherwise at fault, or knew, or had reason to know, that the dog had any extraordinary, dangerous propensity, and even without proof that the dog in fact had any such propensity." It is to be noted that the strict liability imposed by the statute is of no avail to a plaintiff if at the time of his injury he "was committing a trespass or other tort, or was teasing, tormenting or abusing such dog." And it is incumbent upon a plaintiff to plead and prove that he has done none of these things.

The defendant contends that the plaintiff is barred from recovery because on her own testimony—and there is no evidence more favorable to her—she was committing a trespass at the time the defendant's dogs attacked her. We assume that, although the field where the plaintiff was attacked was owned by the defendant's father, the defendant had possessive rights in the property sufficient to render the principle enunciated in Sarna v. American Bosch Magneto Corp., 290 Mass. 340, 195 N.E. 328, inapplicable. We are of opinion, nevertheless, that the jury could have found that the plaintiff was not a trespasser, as that word is used in the statute. A finding was warranted that the plaintiff, an eight year old girl, was frightened by the German Weimaraner dog which was between her and the only means of access to her house; that she turned and ran down a side street; and that because this was a dead-end street she went north across the field in the rear of the defendant's house in order to get home, the Weimaraner following her all the while. This evidence brings the case, we think, within the principle that one is privileged to enter land in the possession of another if it is, or reasonably appears to be, necessary to prevent serious harm to the actor or his property. Restatement 2d: Torts, Tent. draft no. 2, 1958, §197. This privilege not only relieves the intruder from liability for technical trespass but it also destroys the possessor's immunity from liability in resisting the intrusion. "The important difference between the status of one who is a trespasser on land and one who is on the land pursuant to an incomplete privilege is that the latter is entitled to be on the land and therefore the possessor of the land is under a duty to permit him to come and remain there and hence is not privileged to resist." Restatement 2d: Torts, Tent. draft no. 2, 1958, §197, comment k. We assume that the statute evidences a legislative recognition of the right of a possessor of land to keep a dog for protection against trespassers. Nevertheless, we do not believe that the Legislature intended to bar recovery in a case like the present.

Exceptions overruled.

PREPARING FOR CLASS

1. Was Patricia Rossi a trespasser?

2. How does the privilege here differ from the one previously discussed in *Helm*, and how is Patricia "protected/privileged"?

APPLYING THE LAW

Plaintiff has a license allowing him to dock his boat at defendant's business until 5 P.M. A sudden storm descends on the area preventing plaintiff from leaving. The violence of the storm creates a powerful splashing of water, which is causing damage to the dock because of the boat's attachment.

To avoid any additional damage and believing he is authorized by plaintiff's trespass to do so, defendant undocks the boat where it is lost to the storm. What result?

INCREASING YOUR UNDERSTANDING

1. "One is privileged to enter or remain on the land in the possession of another if it is or reasonably appears to be necessary to prevent serious injury to

   a. the actor, or his land or chattels, or

   b. the other or a third person, or the land or chattels of either, unless the actor knows or has reason to know that the one for whose benefit he enters is unwilling that he shall take such action." Restatement Second of Torts §197.

   Unlike the public necessity privilege, "private necessity" is an incomplete one, as the actor is liable for any harm that results from his intrusion.

2. "I'm lost on what is privileged." The actor intentionally tortfeases because of the necessity and is liable for the harm that results. But during the time of tortfeasing, the person upon whom the actor is intruding loses the right to treat the actor as a tortfeasor and is liable for any harm he causes in his attempt to overcome or ignore the privilege. So the actor is privileged by virtue of being able to take certain liberties with another's property in the attempt to avoid harm to himself.

Chapter 4

Negligence — Breach of Duty

A. INTRODUCTION

Determining whether the defendant has breached his or her duty involves two fundamental questions: (1) What should the defendant have done under the circumstances; and (2) what did the defendant do? The first question depends upon whether the defendant's conduct has imposed a socially unacceptable risk on others. Most conduct imposes a risk of harm on others, but we are looking at what amount of risk is too much. For example, when you drive on the expressway at 60 mph, there is a clear risk that you are going so fast that you will be unable to stop for another auto or an unexpected pedestrian on the roadway. But that risk is an acceptable one, i.e., we do not expect the defendant to slow down. When the defendant increases his or her speed from 60 mph to 70 mph, and then to 80 mph, he or she eventually goes too fast, i.e., he or she is imposing a socially unacceptable risk upon others. Consider the following hypothetical:

Hypothetical

Tom is driving a tanker truck around 4 P.M. filled with 9,000 gallons of highly flammable gasoline as it begins to rain. Tom is delivering the gasoline to a service station about 50 miles away that has called to tell the gasoline company that they are just about out of gasoline for the evening rush hour. The truck is being driven on a four-lane road that is not limited access and has a few stoplights. There are many other cars and trucks on the road, with most cars going 75 mph and the trucks going around 65 mph. There is an elementary school about ten miles ahead and a large factory in another ten miles. Strip malls and repair shops border most of this road. Tom calls you on his cell phone. How fast can he drive under these conditions before he is negligent? What should he consider in making this decision?

1. Would it make any difference if Tom were 16 years old?

2. Would it make any difference if Tom has just one eye and, thus, has a lack of depth perception?

3. Would it make any difference if Tom has an IQ that is significantly below average?

In this chapter, we consider cases that will assist you in solving this problem. We will first consider the factors courts and juries look at in determining whether the actor's conduct imposed too much risk on those around them. Then, we will examine how we judge the actor's conduct, i.e., will the actor's conduct be judged by a reasonable person in the circumstances or just by a reasonable person standard. Next we will look at this reasonable person, i.e., who is he or she, and what particular characteristics of the reasonable person standard match the characteristics of the defendant. Might the reasonable person be blind, like the defendant, or mentally-ill like the defendant?

First, we present one of the most recognized negligence cases, a case where Judge Learned Hand sets out a formula to determine how much risk is too much.

United States v. Carroll Towing Co.
159 F.2d 169 (2d Cir. 1947)

Hand, J.
[This case involves the sinking of the barge "Anna C" on January 4, 1944, in the New York Harbor. The Conners Company owned the barge and chartered it to the Pennsylvania Railroad, which included the services of a bargee limited to the hours of 8 A.M. to 4 P.M. The Grace line was the charterer of the tug, Carroll, which was owned by Carroll Towing. The Anna C was moored to one of the piers in the New York Harbor with a load of flour when it broke away as a result of the negligence of the Carroll and drifted down the harbor and into a tanker moored at another pier. The propeller of the tanker broke a hole in the Anna C causing the barge to tip and dump its cargo of flour. The relevant part of this appeal involves the liability of the Anna C for failing to have a bargee on board during the evening hours.]

It appears from the foregoing review that there is no general rule to determine when the absence of a bargee or other attendant will make the owner of the barge liable for injuries to other vessels if she breaks away from her moorings. However, in any cases where he would be so liable for injuries to others obviously he must reduce his damages proportionately, if the injury is to his own barge. It becomes apparent why there can be no such general rule, when we consider the grounds for such a liability. Since there are occasions when every vessel will break from her moorings, and since, if she does, she becomes a menace to those about her; the owner's duty, as in other similar situations, to provide against resulting injuries is a function of three variables: (1) The probability that she will break away; (2) the gravity of the resulting injury, if she does; (3) the burden of adequate precautions. Possibly it serves to bring this notion into relief to state it in algebraic terms: if the probability be called P; the injury, L; and the burden, B; liability depends upon whether B is less than L multiplied by P: i.e., whether B less than PL. Applied to the situation at bar, the likelihood that a barge will break from her fasts and the damage she will do, vary with the place and time; for example, if a storm threatens, the danger is greater; so it is, if she is in a crowded harbor where moored barges are constantly being shifted about. On the other hand, the barge must not be the bargee's prison, even though he lives aboard; he must go ashore at times. We need not say whether, even in such crowded waters as New York Harbor a bargee must be aboard at night at all; it may be that the custom is otherwise, as Ward, J., supposed in "The Kathryn B. Guinan," and that, if so, the situation is one where custom should control. We leave that question open; but we hold that it is not in all cases a sufficient answer to a bargee's absence without excuse, during working hours, that he has properly made fast his barge to a pier, when he leaves her. In the case at bar the bargee left at five o'clock in the afternoon of January 3rd, and the flotilla broke away at about two o'clock in the afternoon of the following day, twenty-one hours afterwards. The bargee had been away all the time, and we hold that his fabricated story was affirmative evidence that he had no excuse for his absence. At the locus in quo—especially during the short January days and in the full tide of war activity—barges were being constantly "drilled" in and out. Certainly it was not beyond reasonable expectation that, with the inevitable haste and bustle, the work might not be done with adequate care. In such circumstances we hold—and it is all that we do hold—that it was a fair requirement that the Conners Company should have a bargee aboard (unless he had some excuse for his absence), during the working hours of daylight.

PREPARING FOR CLASS

1. Explain the burden in this case. What does the plaintiff want the Anna C to do?

2. Explain the probability in this case. What facts, mentioned in the opinion, affect the probability in *United States v. Carroll Towing*?

3. Explain the severity of the injury in this case. There was no personal injury threatened, was there? If the bargee had been on board the barge, as the plaintiff argues, then personal injury to the bargee was possible, wasn't it? How does that affect the calculations in this case?

4. Who has the burden of proof of the *Carroll Towing* factors?

5. Who decides whether the probability multiplied by the severity exceeds the burden?

INCREASING YOUR UNDERSTANDING

1. The burden of the *Carroll Towing* formula not only involves the inconvenience to the defendant, but also the harm to society. Thus, doctors contend that the burden of medical malpractice litigation affects medical care in general, i.e., doctors are forced out of practice by high medical malpractice premiums and are forced to increase the costs of medical care when they must undertake additional procedures to avoid being sued for medical malpractice.

2. Theoretically, the defendant considers probability, severity, and burden before taking action. But the jury necessarily considers these factors in retrospect. So, in driving down a residential street, a motorist must consider the probability of a child running out before the car. But, at the trial, we know the child ran out before the oncoming car and was injured. In fact, the injured child is in the courtroom before the jury. How does this affect the weighing of the factors?

Dobson v. Louisiana Power and Light Co.
567 So. 2d 569 (La. 1990)

Dennis, J.

This is a wrongful death action by the surviving spouse and five minor children of a tree trimmer, Dwane L. Dobson, who was electrocuted on April 24, 1985 when his metallically reinforced safety rope contacted an uninsulated 8,000 volt electric power distribution line. The trial court awarded the widow and her children $1,034,054.50 in damages, after finding the deceased free of fault and holding the Louisiana Power & Light Company liable in negligence for failure to maintain its right of way, insulate its high voltage distribution line, or give adequate warnings of the line's dangerous nature. The court of appeal affirmed the decree as to the power company's negligence, but reversed in part, reducing the plaintiff's recovery by 70% based on a finding that the deceased had been guilty of fault to that degree.

The facts, as the trial judge found them, were as follows: Dwane L. Dobson, a 29 year old tree trimmer, was electrocuted while attempting to remove a pine tree from the backyard of a house owned by a Mrs. Davidge in Hammond, Louisiana. The tree was located near the rear property line, which was adjacent to a right of way for LP & L's uninsulated high voltage distribution lines serving an apartment complex. Dobson was wearing a safety line he had made by inserting a metal wire inside a 13 foot nylon rope. He used the safety line to lash himself to the tree while cutting with his chain saw, and he had inserted the wire in the rope to prevent it from being accidentally severed by the saw. Just prior to the accident, Dobson had cut a section from the top of the tree and had lowered it with the help of his coworkers below. As he descended to cut another section, his safety line touched one of the uninsulated distribution lines and he was electrocuted.

The LP & L high voltage distribution lines behind Mrs. Davidge's property were installed in 1968 to carry electricity 315 feet from Wardline Road to the University Apartments. The lines were elevated from the road to a point behind the Davidge house and placed underground from there to the apartments. LP & L originally intended that the entire span be buried to serve other commercial purposes but those developments did not occur.

Mrs. Davidge complained many times to LP & L about hazards created by the condition of the elevated lines and the right of way behind her house. She complained about transformers blowing up, limbs falling into the wires, fires caused by trees falling on the lines, and having to call the city fire department to extinguish the blazes. Some time prior to the accident she asked LP & L to remove a pine tree behind her house because it was "spindly" and overhanging the power lines. This was the same tree she later hired Dobson to remove. LP & L rejected her requests because the base of the tree was in her backyard and not in LP & L's right of way. LP & L never came to inspect or remove the tree. During this time LP & L suffered from the lack of adequate funds to properly trim trees in its rights of way in the Hammond area. Also, LP & L had no regular team or program devoted exclusively to the inspection of its lines and rights of way but relied on its employees to watch for dangers as they performed other duties.

Dobson had started his tree trimming service several months before his death. He had no formal training but was learning from hard work, experience and talking with other local tree trimmers. After he accidentally damaged a single residence service line at another location in Hammond, an LP & L representative informed him that LP & L would lower such single unit service lines to facilitate tree trimming and that LP & L would assist him generally in the future. The LP & L representative did not inform Dobson that some of its major distribution lines, unlike its single residence service lines, were uninsulated or that LP & L would lower or de-energize major distribution lines for his tree trimming jobs. The day before Dobson's death he was successful in getting LP & L to lower a single consumer service line during his work.

However, because Dobson had no reason to believe that LP & L would have lowered or deenergized the major distribution lines serving the apartment complex to facilitate his removal of the pine tree for Mrs. Davidge, he did not request LP & L to do so.

The trial judge concluded that LP & L was guilty of several negligent acts or omissions that caused the fatal accident: Despite LP & L's constructive and actual knowledge of the dangers created by its uninsulated lines and right of way conditions, it failed to perform adequate inspections of its electric lines, trim or remove the tree or trees creating the hazard, provide insulated covering of dangerous parts of the lines, or place adequate warnings of the high voltage electricity on or near its uncovered wires. Furthermore, the trial judge found that even though LP & L had actual knowledge that Dobson was an inexperienced tree trimmer who would be working near its uninsulated distribution lines in Hammond, the company failed to warn Dobson of the dangers associated with its high voltage distribution lines. With respect to Dobson, the trial judge ultimately found that he did not know of or appreciate the special danger created by the uninsulated overhead high voltage distribution lines; and further that Dobson was not negligent because he was unaware of the extreme danger.

The trial court's purely factual findings were free of clear or manifest error. For example, its resolution of the most hotly contested factual issue—whether Dobson was unaware that the distribution lines were not insulated—was based on reasonable inferences of fact and evaluations of credibility.

As an important background fact, the evidence clearly established the great disparity of danger between "distribution" lines and "service" lines. "Distribution" lines are uninsulated wires used to deliver very high voltage electricity-as much as 8,000 volts-throughout the community. In contrast, "service" lines are insulated with nonconductive covering and used to transfer much lower voltage electricity from distribution lines to individual dwellings. Despite this great difference in danger, distribution lines carry no special markings or warnings but are black in color and similar in appearance to service lines. Dobson's coworkers and relatives testified that they thought the distribution lines were insulated both because they appeared to have black covering and because birds and squirrels traversed them without harm. Thus, the trier of fact reasonably could have inferred that the distribution line's appearance belied its lethally uninsulated nature and made it difficult for an untrained person to appreciate its fatally dangerous character.[1]

The evidence was in conflict regarding whether Dobson had knowledge of the dangers of the distribution lines. On the one hand, Dobson's coworkers and relatives testified that he was ignorant of the deadly conductivity of the

---

1. The Supreme Court of Utah has stated:

"A high tension transmission wire is one of the most dangerous things known to man. Not only is the current deadly, but the danger is hidden away in an innocent looking wire ready at all times to kill or injure anyone who touches it or comes near to it. For the average citizen there is no way of knowing whether the wire is harmless or lethal until it is too late to do anything about it."

distribution lines, and the plaintiffs' experts were of the opinion that his actions prior to the accident indicated that he was unaware of the danger. On the other hand, a power company trouble-shooter testified that he had talked to Dobson on two occasions prior to the accident and that it was his habit to warn tree trimmers of such dangers and to offer to drop or deenergize power lines for them. In the aggregate, however, the trouble-shooter's testimony was equivocal as to whether he had warned Dobson, specifically, of the absence of insulation on distribution lines or had definitely offered to deenergize them for Dobson's operations. Moreover, these conversations occurred only because Dobson had accidentally knocked down service lines at two dwellings and the company representative had come to inspect the damage and to repair the service lines. Thus, the service line incidents involved only property damage to insulated service lines and had no direct relationship to the risk of personal injury or death created by uninsulated distribution lines or the need for precautions against such hazards. Additionally, there is no evidence that prior to the accident Dobson had ever had any first hand experience with uninsulated distribution lines or had received any demonstrative instruction in how to identify and guard against their dangers. Therefore, the evidence is easily susceptible to the reasonable inference that the trouble-shooter's discussions with Dobson focused primarily on the prevention of future damage to the company's insulated service lines rather than on Dobson's safety while working around uninsulated distribution lines. This inference bolsters the trial court's reasonable decision to credit the testimony of the plaintiffs' witnesses to the effect that Dobson was unaware of the extreme danger of the uninsulated distribution lines before the accident. Where there are factual issues upon which the evidence is in conflict, reasonable evaluations of credibility and reasonable inferences of fact by the trial court should not be disturbed on review.

Nevertheless, we agree with the court of appeal that the trial court made a reversible mistake in concluding that Dobson was free of any fault that caused the accident. Although the trial court did not commit any manifest error or clearly wrong determination in its purely factual findings, it fell into what was essentially an error of law in its approach to the question of whether Dobson was negligent. The crucial mistake was its assumption that, because Dobson had no actual notice or knowledge of the true nature of the uninsulated distribution lines, or the extraordinary hazard they created, he was not required by law to recognize this danger. Any person is required by law to recognize that his conduct involves a risk of causing harm to himself if a reasonable person would do so while exercising such attention, perception of the circumstances, memory, and knowledge of other pertinent matters, intelligence and judgment as a reasonable person would have. A reasonable person who has an ordinary amount of exposure to the facts of modern life in America should be treated as though he knows that any electrical line could be dangerous. In addition to the knowledge with which people generally may be charged, any reasonably prudent person who engages in an occupation such as tree trimming which requires that he work close to electric lines is under a peculiar obligation to acquire the knowledge and ability required to identify uninsulated power lines and to take precautions against the extreme dangers they pose. Consequently, Dobson was required to recognize that his conduct near the uninsulated power lines created a risk of physical harm to himself, and his failure to take precautions to avoid the risk of which he should have known amounted to negligence.

We see no error in the Court of Appeal's conclusion that LP & L was guilty of negligence that caused Dobson's death and should be held at least partially responsible for the damages occasioned by the accident. But we granted certiorari because the percentages of fault assigned by the Court of Appeal seemed out of line. Also, we felt called upon to further elaborate a method for determining the degree or percentage of negligence attributable to a person for purposes of reducing recovery due to comparative fault.

Under our Civil Code, every act of a person that causes damage to another obliges the one by whose fault it happened to repair it. If a person dies due to the fault of another, suit may be brought by the surviving spouse and children of the deceased to recover damages which they sustained as a result of the death. For purposes of this liability, a person's fault includes his negligence, imprudence or want of skill. When contributory negligence is applicable to a claim for damages, and a person suffers death as the result partly of his own negligence and partly as a result of the fault of another person or persons, the claim for damages shall not thereby be defeated, but the amount of damages recoverable shall be reduced in proportion to the degree or percentage of negligence attributable to the person suffering the death.

The generally accepted view is that negligence is defined as conduct which falls below the standard established by law for the protection of others against an unreasonable risk of harm. The test for determining whether a risk is unreasonable is supplied by the following formula. The amount of caution "demanded of a person by an occasion is the resultant of three factors: the likelihood that his conduct will injure others, taken with the seriousness of the injury if it happens, and balanced against the interest which he must sacrifice, or the cost of the precaution he must take, to avoid the risk." If the product of the likelihood of injury multiplied times the seriousness of the injury exceeds the burden of the precautions, the risk is unreasonable and the failure to take precautions or sacrifice the interest is negligence. The foregoing conception has been referred to by legal scholars as the "Hand formula," the "Learned Hand test" or the "risk-benefit" balancing test.

We believe that the Hand formula also may be used to measure and compare the negligence or fault of one person with that of another. Indeed, Judge Hand, the author of the test, invoked it to help measure whether a driver's negligence had been gross or ordinary under the Vermont "guest-occupant" law. The authors of Harper, James & Gray, *The Law of Torts*, cogently observe that "[t]he same risk, furthermore, may be avoidable at different sacrifices or other costs by different actors, and the reasonableness or unreasonableness of a failure to avoid that risk may vary correspondingly among those actors." By the same token, Professor David Sobelsohn has argued persuasively that, "[i]f 'fault' means a 'departure from a standard of conduct required of a person by society for the protection of his neighbors,' 'comparing fault' ought to mean a comparison of the extent to which each party deviated from the applicable standard of conduct."

In *Watson v. State Farm Fire & Cas. Ins. Co.*, 469 So. 2d 967 (La. 1985) this court adopted the practice of looking to the Uniform Comparative Fault Act for a checklist of some of the various factors that may be relevant in determining the percentage or degree of fault to be assigned to each party. In its comment to §2, the Uniform Act provides:

> [t]he conduct of the claimant or of any defendant may be more or less at fault, depending upon all the circumstances including such matters as (1) whether the conduct was mere inadvertence or engaged in with an awareness of the danger involved, (2) the magnitude of the risk created by the conduct, including the number of persons endangered and the potential seriousness of the injury, (3) the significance of what the actor was seeking to attain by his conduct, (4) the actor's superior or inferior capacities, and (5) the particular circumstances, such as the existence of an emergency requiring a hasty decision.

Unif. Comparative Fault Act §2, comment (1979), 12 U.L.A. 39 (1990).

The Hand formula provides a method for accommodating and weighing all of these factors including the more subjective factors, such as the existence of an emergency, a party's capacity, or his awareness of the risk. The Hand formula, or balancing process, moreover, helps to "center attention upon which one of the factors may be determinative in any given situation."

It assists us to concentrate here on the costs of the precautions necessary to avoid the accident because the magnitude of the danger caused by the conduct of either Dobson or LP & L was extreme. If the risk that a person might come into contact with the bare high voltage distribution line were to take effect, the anticipated gravity of the loss was of the highest degree. Dobson's conduct in lowering himself down the tree trunk with a metallically reinforced safety line dangling below near the electric wires substantially increased the possibility of such an accident. But so did LP & L's conduct in transmitting high voltage electricity through its uninsulated distribution lines in a residential subdivision without regular inspection of its equipment and right of way, regular maintenance of its right of way by trimming unsafe trees and limbs, insulation of its lines in close proximity to trees, or installation of adequate warnings of the dangerous uninsulated condition of the distribution lines. The chances of an accident were further increased when LP & L, by refusing to respond to Mrs. Davidge's complaints, encouraged her to take it upon herself to remove the limbs and trees in close proximity to the uninsulated distribution lines. The odds of an electrocution were raised again when LP & L failed to warn Dobson specifically of the uninsulated distribution lines although the company had knowledge that he was a new, inexperienced tree trimmer working in the neighborhood where the lines were located.

Confining ourselves to the factor of the cost of taking an effective precaution to avoid the risk, it appears to us that the cost or burden of eliminating the danger would have been greater for Dobson than for LP & L. As we have indicated, the power company had a number of relatively inexpensive, efficacious precautions available to it, e.g., inspection, maintenance, partial insulation, public education and visible warnings. Moreover, there was one particularly effective way in which LP & L could have eliminated the risk at little or no cost-by explicitly warning Dobson about the uninsulated high voltage distribution lines and telling him how to distinguish them from the insulated dwelling service lines. On the other hand, the cost to Dobson, who was ignorant of the characteristics of the uninsulated distribution lines and therefore unaware of their special danger, exceeded the cost to a person with superior capacity and knowledge. An actor with "inferior" capacity to avoid harm must expend more effort to avoid a danger than need a person with "superior" ability. A person about to cause injury inadvertently must expend much more effort to avoid the danger than need one who is at least aware of the danger involved. For this reason courts have traditionally cited "awareness of danger" as a factor distinguishing mere negligence from the higher state of culpability commonly known as "recklessness" or "willful and wanton conduct."

In conclusion we believe that, while the magnitude of the risk of harm created by either Dobson or LP & L was great, under the circumstances of the present case, the cost of taking effective precautions to avoid the risk was greater for the tree trimmer than for the power company. This disparity is heightened by the fact that LP & L was clearly in a superior position to avoid the danger. Because the cost of taking effective precautions was significantly less for LP & L than for Dobson, the fault of LP & L was the greater of the two. We do not think that the unreasonableness of LP & L's conduct was so great as to be double the fault of Dobson. But we conclude that a palpable majority of the fault should be attributed to the power company in order to achieve substantial justice in this case. Accordingly, we attribute 60% of the negligence herein to LP & L and 40% to Dobson. Consequently, the recovery of plaintiffs, the surviving spouse and five minor children, will be reduced by 40%.

The decree will be modified as follows. The judgment of the trial court is reinstated except that the principal amount of the judgment, $1,034,054.50, shall be reduced by 40% and all court costs shall be assessed to the defendant.

Affirmed in part; Amended in part.

PREPARING FOR CLASS

1. The court, in this case, seems to assume that Dobson has a right to work as a tree trimmer without any training. The courts says that Dobson is "learning from hard work." Should Dobson be learning about power

lines by "hard work"? Would you suggest that a new automobile driver "learn by hard work"? Doesn't the court's language—"learning by hard work"—suggest the result in this case?

2. What about the burden to insulate the power lines? The court never considers how much it would cost the power company to insulate all of its power lines. Should the court have considered the costs to insulate the power lines, which are high in the air where people on the ground cannot touch them?

3. How does the *Carroll Towing* formula relate to the percentage of fault?

4. Couldn't the power company use special, colored lines to show that the lines are dangerous? Isn't it negligent to have uninsulated power lines that look just like insulated power lines?

INCREASING YOUR UNDERSTANDING

Many negligence cases, especially cases dealing with proximate causation, refer to the reasonable foreseeability test. That "reasonable foreseeability" is the probability of harm multiplied by the severity of harm of *Carroll Towing*.

APPLYING THE LAW

1. What is the probability of harm in the hypothetical from the beginning of this chapter?

2. What is the severity of harm in the hypothetical?

3. What is the burden of care in the hypothetical?

B. THE CIRCUMSTANCES

The reasonable person standard does not change except in certain limited circumstances. But the reasonable person always acts under the circumstances that are not under his or her control. This allows the standard to be flexible. A reasonable person in a sudden, blinding rainstorm on the road will be held to a different standard than a driver in the middle of a beautiful afternoon or a person in a light rain storm. So, the reasonable person in difficult circumstances may still breach the standard of care of a reasonable person.

Should the judge instruct the jury on the standard of care in an emergency if the judge has already instructed the jury to consider the defendant's actions under the circumstances? Isn't that redundant or, even worse, doesn't that suggest that the defendant is unlikely to be negligent in an emergency? The judge doesn't instruct the jury that the defendant had plenty of time to consider his or her actions, so why instruct on an emergency? Consider the following case.

Young v. Clark
814 P.2d 364 (Colo. 1991)

VOLLACK, J.

We granted certiorari to review the court of appeals unpublished decision, *Young v. Clark*, No. 89CA0421 (Colo. App. Mar. 22, 1990). The issue to be resolved is whether the trial court's submission of a "sudden emergency" instruction in this automobile collision case was improper. The court of appeals held that the trial court did not err by so instructing the jury. We affirm.

I.

This case arose from a rear-end collision on February 6, 1987, at approximately 10:30 A.M. The plaintiff, John Young (Young), and the defendant, Holly Clark (Clark), were both traveling eastbound in the center lane on Colorado Highway 36. Construction on the highway caused all traffic to slow to an estimated thirty-five to forty-five miles per hour. One unidentified driver, who was four to five cars ahead of Young, pulled out of the center lane into the right-hand lane and then swerved abruptly back into the center-lane traffic, forcing all drivers behind him to apply their brakes. At that time, Clark had looked over her shoulder while attempting to change lanes. Her passenger, Susan Baldwin, yelled to Clark upon seeing that all traffic ahead had stopped. Clark applied her brakes and swerved to the left, but was unable to avoid colliding with the rear of Young's car.

Young filed suit against Clark on June 11, 1987, claiming that he sustained personal injuries as a result of the accident that was caused by Clark's negligent operation of her car. Young's complaint was later amended to add a loss of consortium claim on behalf of Young's wife. Clark denied that she was negligent and designated the unidentified driver as a nonparty, claiming that he was responsible for causing the accident.

The trial court submitted the issues of Clark's negligence, John Young's contributory negligence, and the negligence of the designated nonparty to the jury. Included in the court's instructions to the jury was an explanation of the "sudden emergency" doctrine. The trial court submitted this instruction over the objection of the Youngs' attorney based on its finding that the sudden emergency doctrine remained valid under Colorado law and that the instruction served both parties "because both were confronted with the same sudden emergency."

The jury found that the Youngs' injuries were not caused by any negligence on Clark's part, and consequently never determined whether John Young was negligent or whether the nonparty driver was negligent. The court of appeals held that the trial court did not err by instructing the jury on the sudden emergency doctrine. We granted certiorari to determine whether the trial court's submission of a "sudden emergency" instruction was improper, either under the circumstances of this particular case, or because the instruction should no longer be given.

II.

The sudden emergency doctrine was developed by the courts to recognize that a person confronted with sudden or unexpected circumstances calling for immediate action is not expected to exercise the judgment of one acting under normal conditions. See W.P. Keeton, D. Dobbs, R. Keeton & D. Owen, *Prosser and Keeton on the Law of Torts* §33, at 196 (5th ed. 1984) [hereinafter *Prosser and Keeton*].

[T]he basis of the special rule is merely that the actor is left no time for adequate thought, or is reasonably so disturbed or excited that the actor cannot weigh alternative courses of action, and must make a speedy decision, based very largely upon impulse or guess. Under such conditions, the actor cannot reasonably be held to the same accuracy of judgment or conduct as one who has had full opportunity to reflect, even though it later appears that the actor made the wrong decision, one which no reasonable person could possibly have made after due deliberation.

The doctrine does not, however, impose a lesser standard of care on a person caught in an emergency situation; the individual is still expected to respond to the situation as a reasonably prudent person under the circumstances. The emergency is merely a circumstance to be considered in determining whether the actor's conduct was reasonable. *Id.* At 196-97. See also *Restatement (Second) of Torts* §296(1) comment b (1977) ("Among the circumstances which must be taken into account is the fact that the actor is confronted with [a sudden] emergency. . . ."). Thus, a person may be found negligent if his actions are deemed unreasonable, despite the emergency. *Prosser and Keeton* §33, at 197. The sudden emergency doctrine is available in a number of emergency situations and is used by both plaintiffs and defendants to counter charges of contributory and primary negligence. It is most commonly applied in the context of claims arising from motor vehicle accidents, as in the present case.

A.

In this automobile collision case, the trial court submitted to the jury Colorado's pattern "sudden emergency" instruction, which states: "A person who, through no fault of his or her own, is placed in a sudden emergency, is not chargeable with negligence if the person exercises that degree of care which a reasonably careful person would have exercised under the same or similar circumstances." The Youngs first contend that the trial court erred by giving this instruction under the circumstances of this case because, they argue, the sudden emergency confronting Clark arose from a common, and thus foreseeable, traffic problem, and because Clark's own negligence caused the emergency situation.

This court has approved of giving an instruction on the sudden emergency doctrine where sufficient evidence exists that a party acted in an emergency situation not caused by the party's own negligence. In all of these cases, it was deemed appropriate to give a sudden emergency instruction in the context of an automobile collision.

In *Davis v. Cline*, 177 Colo. 204, 493 P.2d 362 (1972), an accident occurred when the defendant bus driver moved into the plaintiff's lane of traffic, forcing the plaintiff to steer sharply to the right to avoid colliding with the bus. The plaintiff subsequently struck a high curb and was thrown against the steering wheel, resulting in the aggravation of a previous back injury. This court held that the trial court committed prejudicial error by refusing to instruct the jury on the sudden emergency doctrine when there was competent evidence to justify giving the instruction. In so holding, the court noted that the sudden emergency doctrine "has long been recognized in Colorado as a valid principle" based on the rationale "that in an emergency there is no time for cool reflective deliberation during which alternative courses of action might be considered and explored; but rather, the situation demands [a] speedy decision based largely upon the actor's perception of the compelling circumstances." The court further viewed the doctrine "as an evidentiary guideline by which a trier of fact may properly apply the prudent [person] rule in evaluating the evidence of negligence being considered." Finally, the *Davis* court instructed that it was for the trier of fact to determine whether an emergency existed and, if so, whether the party's conduct was reasonable under the circumstances.

This court has also ruled it proper to give the sudden emergency instruction in automobile accidents involving a rear-end collision, as in the present case. In both *Daigle v. Prather*, 152 Colo. 115, 380 P.2d 670 (1963), and *Cudney v. Moore*, 163 Colo. 30, 428 P.2d 81 (1967), the evidence indicated that the defendants each experienced brake failure while attempting to stop their vehicles prior to hitting the rear-end of the plaintiffs' cars. In *Daigle*, the defendant testified that the suddenness of the brake failure prevented her from using her emergency brake or from veering to the left or right, and in *Cudney*, the defendant testified that "everything went so fast" that he was unable to reach his emergency brake in time and did not have room enough to swerve around the plaintiff's car. Under these circumstances, this court found that the defendants in both cases were entitled to a sudden emergency instruction.

C.R.C.P. 51.1(1) states: "In instructing the jury in a civil case, the court shall use such instructions as are contained in Colorado Jury Instruction (CJI) as are applicable to the evidence and the prevailing law." Moreover, "[a]n instruction should not be given to the jury unless there is evidence introduced to support that instruction." We conclude that, by using the approved pattern instruction in CJI-Civ. 2d 9:10 to advise the jury on the sudden emergency doctrine, the trial court properly followed the prevailing law of this state favoring the use of this instruction when, as here, sufficient evidence of an emergency is presented.

The Youngs contend that it was improper to give the instruction because the rear-end collision was caused by Clark's lack of attention and failure to maintain a safe distance from Young's car. While it is true that the sudden emergency instruction is not available where a defendant, or a plaintiff, is obviously guilty of negligence, the question of whether an emergency arose because of some negligence by Clark was not so clear. No evidence was presented to show that Clark was following too closely to Young's car or that she was driving too fast under the circumstances. In fact, John Young testified that he never saw how close Clark's car was to his or how fast she was driving just prior to the accident. Clark's passenger, Susan Baldwin, testified that Clark was not following Young's car too closely and that she was not speeding or "going faster than the regular flow of the traffic." The factual dispute as to whether Clark was at fault for causing the accident was therefore appropriately submitted to the finder of fact. Indeed, under CJI-Civ. 2d 9:10, the jury's application of the sudden emergency doctrine is explicitly conditioned on a finding that the actor was not placed in a perilous predicament through any fault of his or her own.[2]

Further, it was Clark's theory that the negligence of the unknown driver caused the accident when the driver pulled out of the center lane of traffic and then abruptly reentered the lane several cars ahead of Young, precipitating the sudden stopping of all the cars behind the driver. Young conceded that he had to brake "hard" to avoid hitting the car in front of him and that the unknown driver probably shared some fault in causing the accident between Young and Clark. In our view, the sudden and unexpected reentry of the unknown driver into the flow of traffic provided sufficient evidence to support giving the sudden emergency instruction. *See Restatement* (Second) of Torts §296(1) comment a (1977) (the sudden emergency doctrine applies "where the sudden emergency is created in any way other than by the actor's own negligent conduct, as where it is created by the unexpected operation of a natural force or by the innocent or wrongful act of a third person") (emphasis added). We therefore conclude that the trial court did not act improperly in instructing the jury on the sudden emergency doctrine under the circumstances of this case.

---

2. The language of CJI-Civ.2d 9:10, "[a] person who, through no fault of his or her own, is placed in a sudden emergency" (emphasis added), calls upon the finder of fact to make the initial determination as to whether the emergency situation was created by the actor's own conduct.

B.

The Youngs further urge this court to follow the lead of those jurisdictions that have abolished, or curtailed the use of, the sudden emergency doctrine. These courts generally have denounced the usefulness of the sudden emergency instruction based upon a perceived "hazard" that the doctrine tends "to elevate its principles above what is required to be proven in a negligence action," reasoning that "[e]ven the wording of a well-drawn instruction intimates that ordinary rules of negligence do not apply to the circumstances constituting the claimed 'sudden emergency.'" *Knapp*, 392 So. 2d at 198. See also *Simonson*, 713 P.2d at 989 ("The instruction adds nothing to the law of negligence and serves only to leave an impression in the minds of the jurors that a driver is somehow excused from the ordinary standard of care because an emergency existed.").

Such reasoning, in our view, is based on unfounded assumptions about how jurors perceive an instruction explaining the relatively simplistic sudden emergency doctrine. The pattern instructions used by Colorado courts, are a clear statement of the doctrine and obligate the finder of fact to do nothing more than apply the objective "reasonable person" standard to an actor in the specific context of an emergency situation. It thus does not operate to excuse fault but merely serves as an explanatory instruction, offered for purposes of clarification for the jury's benefit.

The sudden emergency doctrine is a long-established principle of law in this jurisdiction. We choose to leave the doctrine intact, and continue to uphold the propriety of giving the sudden emergency instruction where competent evidence is presented that a party was confronted with a sudden or unexpected occurrence not of the party's own making. We affirm the court of appeals judgment.

Lohr, J. dissenting:

I conclude that the court's instruction to the jury on sudden emergency was erroneous and prejudicial as applied to the facts of this case. Furthermore, I would disapprove of the use of this instruction for the future because it is unnecessary, confusing, and places undue emphasis on only a portion of the relevant facts in a negligence action. Accordingly, I respectfully dissent.

I recognize that we have approved the use of sudden emergency instructions on many occasions in the past. In recent times, however, some courts have determined that such an instruction has little utility but significant potential for prejudice and have withdrawn their approval of such instructions. I believe that a fresh consideration of special emergency instructions in the context of the present case demonstrates the wisdom of the course chosen by those courts that have discontinued or severely limited the use of such instructions.

Properly understood, the sudden emergency instruction describes the reasonably careful person standard which governs negligence actions. The Colorado sudden emergency pattern jury instruction, which was given in this case, explains: "A person who, through no fault of his or her own, is placed in a sudden emergency, is not chargeable with negligence if the person exercises that degree of care which a reasonably careful person would have exercised under the same or similar circumstances." CJI-Civ. 2d 9:10. Emergency circumstances are merely one of several factors to consider in determining whether a person acted with the degree of care that would have been exercised by a reasonably careful person. The sudden emergency doctrine is simply a specific application of the reasonably careful person standard.

This instruction provides little guidance beyond that offered by other standard jury instructions. The instructions on both negligence, CJI-Civ. 2d 9:4, and reasonable care, CJI-Civ. 2d 9:6, each of which was given in this case, also direct the jury to compare the party's conduct against that of a reasonably careful person acting under the same or similar circumstances. The general negligence and reasonable care instructions provide sufficient guidance for the jury to apply the reasonably careful person standard. Furthermore, counsel, in closing argument, can discuss the standard and explain the application of that standard under the evidence presented in a particular case. The sudden emergency instruction merely restates the reasonably careful person standard. The instruction, therefore, has minimal utility.

Several states have reconsidered the sudden emergency instruction and have abolished or severely restricted its use. In *Knapp v. Stanford*, 392 So. 2d 196 (Miss.1980), the Mississippi Supreme Court prospectively abolished the sudden emergency doctrine. The court recognized the doctrine's "tendency to elevate its principles above what is required to be proven in a negligence action." Although the same standard of care applies in all negligence actions, "[e]ven the wording of a well-drawn [sudden emergency] instruction intimates that ordinary rules of negligence do not apply to the circumstances constituting the claimed 'sudden emergency.'" *Id.* Applying uniform principles of negligence under all circumstances would be the best procedure. . . . In *Simonson v. White*, 713 P.2d 983 (Mont. 1986), the Montana Supreme Court banned the sudden emergency instruction in all automobile accident cases. The instruction adds nothing to standard negligence law but leaves the impression that an emergency excuses the duty of ordinary care. Similarly, the Hawaii Supreme Court discourages the use of the sudden emergency instruction. I agree that the prejudice and confusion engendered by the instruction outweigh its utility.

A serious flaw in the instruction is its failure to apprise the jury that it must resolve certain factual prerequisites before applying the sudden emergency doctrine. In the present case, the evidence creates issues about the existence of an emergency and whether Clark was at fault in creating it.

The accident occurred on a stretch of Highway 36 on which construction was being performed. Clark observed a truck with lighted arrows indicating that traffic was to merge right. The alleged emergency was an unidentified car merging into traffic, a potential hazard that Clark was warned about. Arguably, drivers exercising ordinary care should anticipate that such traffic conditions are likely to arise. The Youngs also argued that Clark's inattentiveness to traffic conditions caused her to collide with the Youngs. Clark turned her head—to look at the construction and then to see if she could merge right—for an indefinite time before looking ahead to see the unidentified car merging. A jury could have determined that Clark was at fault in engendering the alleged emergency, which would have prevented her from invoking the sudden emergency doctrine. See CJI-Civ. 2d 9:10; *Restatement (Second) of Torts* §296(2) (1977). The jury was required to decide these questions of fact concerning the existence of an emergency and whether Clark was at fault in causing it before the sudden emergency doctrine could be applied. Whether an emergency actually existed is a question of fact for the jury to decide.

The jurors, however, were not instructed that they must decide the existence of an emergency and Clark's responsibility for creating the emergency. The majority contends that the sudden emergency instruction is explicitly conditioned on a finding that the actor was placed in a perilous predicament through no fault of her own. The existence of an emergency and Clark's responsibility for it, however, are not posed as factual prerequisites for jury determination. Rather, reference to those matters in the sudden emergency instruction appears to explain to the jurors why they must consider the emergency circumstances when evaluating Clark's conduct. The sudden emergency instruction abstractly discusses the standard of care applicable to emergency circumstances. The instruction can be easily interpreted as an instruction by the court that an emergency existed, that Clark was without fault in creating it, and that a special standard of care for that situation is to be applied. The jurors, believing that they have heard the court instruct that an emergency existed and that Clark was without fault in its creation, may therefore apply the doctrine even though they did not address its factual prerequisites as the law requires. I conclude that this acute potential for misinterpretation, coupled with the absence of an instruction that the jury must determine whether an emergency existed and whether Clark was at fault for creating it, caused prejudicial error.

The instruction's redundant recital of the reasonably careful person standard, while adding little to the jury understands of that standard, creates potential confusion. As the third reference to the importance of the circumstances—supplementing the instructions on negligence and reasonable care—the instruction overly emphasizes this aspect of the case. "[I]t is error to give two instructions, virtually the same, which would tend to confuse the jury by overly emphasizing a defense." As we said in a similar context, the instruction "serves only to twice tell the jury that the plaintiff cannot recover unless he proves negligence."

The instruction also implies that a sudden emergency invokes a different standard of care. A separate instruction for sudden emergencies suggests to the jury that sudden emergencies give rise to different standards of conduct; otherwise there would be no need for a separate instruction. The instruction can readily be understood by jurors to connote that a sudden emergency excuses ordinary negligence instead of simply being one of the circumstances to be considered in determining whether the person confronted with an emergency acted as a reasonably careful person would.

Moreover, the emphasis on the emergency tends to focus the jury on the party's conduct during and after the emergency rather than examining the conduct before, during and after the emergency. "[W]here there is definite evidence of negligence on the part of the defendant, the weight of such evidence might be entirely destroyed by an instruction on sudden emergency. Such an instruction might well cause the jury to lose sight of the negligence which caused the emergency." In the present case, the jury's attention is channeled to focus on Clark's actions after the unidentified car attempted to merge back into traffic and to ignore the evidence that Clark may have been inattentive or otherwise negligent before the alleged emergency arose. Yet, the entirety of Clark's conduct, before, during, and after the unidentified car merged into traffic must be considered in determining whether Clark was negligent.

These problems illustrate the serious danger of misapplication of the sudden emergency instruction. The instruction has only marginal utility but creates serious risk of misapplication and confusion. The instruction does not inform the jurors that they must decide whether an emergency exists and the party's role in causing it. In addition, the instruction suggests a different standard for emergency situations and gives undue prominence to the emergency circumstances. These problems have led other state courts to abolish or severely restrict the use of the instruction. Rather than leave the matter for the trial court's discretion to permit use of the instruction in those circumstances where it might have some limited value, I would abolish it.[3]

If I were persuaded that the instruction did not prejudice the plaintiff, I would concur in the majority's judgment but express the view that the instruction should be disapproved for future use. The difficult factual issues concerning whether an emergency existed and if so whether it came about through no fault of Clark, coupled with the absence of an instruction that these issues are to be determined by the jury and the implication instead that the court had already resolved them, convince me that the instruction was highly prejudicial. Accordingly, I dissent and would remand the case for a new trial.

PREPARING FOR CLASS

1. In the American system of justice, the judge determines issues of law and the jury determines facts. The majority in this decision does not

---

3. In *Knapp*, 392 So. 2d at 198, the Mississippi Supreme Court observed that during the prior twenty-five years it had considered approximately twenty-seven cases involving the sudden emergency instruction and had reversed twenty because the instruction was erroneous in its language or application.

contend that emergency instructions should be given in every case. How will a judge determine when to give an emergency instruction without determining the facts in the case?

2. If the judges are going to instruct about an emergency situation, shouldn't they also instruct on situations when a party has more than adequate time to prepare for the decision. Why don't the judges give that instruction?

3. Does the "sudden emergency instruction" actually add anything to the jury's understanding? If your answer is yes, what is added?

INCREASING YOUR UNDERSTANDING

1. Many states have Good Samaritan laws that give health care providers special protections when they render care in certain emergencies. Do you think these statutes are necessary, i.e., would you take a case on contingency against a Good Samaritan who made a mistake in rendering care? These cases seem to be rare.

2. Many states extend the protections of the Good Samaritan laws to in-hospital emergencies. These statutes provide immunity rather than instructions on special situations like the case above.

APPLYING THE LAW

1. If you represented the plaintiff in Mississippi and the defendant was arguing that the amount of recovery should be reduced due to the plaintiff's negligence in an emergency situation, would you request an emergency instruction? (Look at footnote 3 of the opinion above.)

2. An automobile driver is driving at an excessive rate of speed and passing a bus when the bus suddenly and wrongfully pulls into the passing lane. Is the auto driver entitled to a "sudden emergency" instruction?

Gibson v. Shelby County Fair Ass'n
65 N.W.2d 433 (Iowa 1954)

OLIVER, Justice.
Plaintiff, Max Gibson, then aged seventeen years, while a spectator at automobile races on the track at the fair grounds of defendant Shelby County Fair Association, was permanently paralyzed by a wheel which became detached from a speeding racer, broke through a wire fence beside the track and struck him. He brought this action for damages, by his father and

next friend. Although officers and directors of the Fair Association are named defendants with it, the association appears to be the only actual defendant. A former appeal in this case, decision reported in 241 Iowa 1349, 44 N.W.2d 362, involved the sufficiency of the petition only. Upon remand, trial to a jury resulted in verdict and judgment for defendant and this appeal by plaintiff.

Defendant leased the fair grounds for October 23, 1949, to Dale Swanson for "hot rod" and "stock car" automobile races. Swanson testified the term "hot rod" means an engine with increased horsepower and a "hot rod" is a racing machine built from a stock car block and body, usually without much regular racing equipment. The gears of the rear wheels are locked so the differential does not operate. This increases the stresses on the axles at the turns. Defendant's track is a dirt, half-mile oval, originally built for horse races. Swanson testified it had since been made a little wider and a little more sloping at the ends.

Plaintiff lived in a neighboring town. He was not familiar with the fair grounds and had never attended an automobile race. He testified he purchased a ticket and entered the gate; no one was there directing traffic nor were there signs directing patrons where to go; he looked ahead and did not see anyone in that direction; he saw people standing nearby "all up and down" a fence watching the races; he walked over "where all the people were standing," and stood eight or ten feet behind the fence which was alongside the track. There were no warning signs in the vicinity.

Witnesses estimated there were from thirty to two hundred people in this area, watching the races, among who were women, babies and children. This fence was the only barrier between the race track and spectators. There was evidence it consisted of a strip of woven wire 26 to 36 inches in width, above which were several strands of barbed wire. It was in poor repair. Some of the wooden posts were broken and the wire was rusty and loose. Plaintiff testified he saw one race and some time trials and was injured during the next race. He didn't see the detached wheel rolling toward him but the people who were standing in front of him "faded away" and he was struck by it. A spectator who stood at the fence in front of plaintiff saw the wheel come off the racer and travel in his direction. He knelt in an effort to escape it. The wheel burst through the fence, injured his hand and continued its course.

Defendant introduced evidence of warnings, over the loud speaker, to spectators to keep away from the fence and come to the grandstand. Plaintiff testified he could faintly hear the loud speaker but could not understand what was said. Swanson testified he went to the fence in person, warned spectators the place was dangerous and ordered them out but many of them called him vile names and refused to move. There were highway patrolmen assisting at the track. Swanson testified he continued with the races. Plaintiff testified no one talked to him or others in his hearing about leaving the place.

Plaintiff had pleaded defendant was negligent in that the track and appurtenances were unsuitable, inadequate and dangerous to spectators, and the wire fence barrier adjacent to it, maintained for the protection of spectators from dangers inherent in the races, was wholly unsuitable and inadequate for that purpose and had been permitted to become dilapidated and in a ruinous condition.

He assigns as error the refusal of the Court to permit him to show the usual, customary and approved methods of construction of barricades, walls and fences, on tracks of this type, for the protection of spectators at automobile and hot rod races.

Plaintiff first attempted to show this by Abe Slusky, the operator, for some years, of Playland Stadium, an automobile race track in Council Bluffs.

> Q. Are you familiar with the usual and customary construction of race tracks used for automobile racing?
> Objection.
> The Court: Sustained.
> Q. Do you know what the usual and customary standards are with reference to the maintenance of automobile race tracks where the track is maintained and used for public amusement, and are you acquainted with the usual and customary standards of protective devices, used on such tracks for the protection of the public who attend . . . ?
> Objection.
> The Court: Sustained.
> Q. Are there among automobile race track owners certain customary methods and approved methods of construction of barriers, walks, fences and barriers around such tracks for the protection and safety of the spectators?
> Objection.
> The Court: Sustained.

Plaintiff then offered to prove "that there are certain customary and approved methods of construction of barricades, walls, fences and barriers on tracks of similar character and nature . . . which barricades, walls, fences and so forth, are erected for the protection and safety of spectators invited to view . . . automobile racing. . . ." The profit referred also to the practice of providing guard rails, safety zones, additional high and strong fences, etc., "and that such practice is (and was in 1949) commonly adopted and used in tracks of such character in this vicinity. . . ." An objection by defendant was sustained.

Subject to certain exceptions not here applicable, the rule is well settled that evidence of the custom or common usage of a business or occupation is generally admissible on the question of negligence, although it is not a conclusive test, since the standard of care is ordinary care under the circumstances and the standard of custom cannot be substituted for it.

Kuemmel v. Vradenburg, Tex. Civ. App., 239 S.W.2d 869, 872, was an action by a minor spectator at "hot rod" races for injuries sustained when struck by a racing automobile which went out of control and burst through a barrier behind which plaintiff was standing with other spectators and from which spectators had been warned to stay away. Much of the evidence centered upon the inquiry whether the customary fence or barrier had been maintained. The decision states:

"... The jury has here found, supported by evidence, that there was nonconformity with the customary precaution used at 'hot-rod' races. Just as conformity with custom may evidence freedom from negligence, nonconformity may evidence the presence of negligence."

Blake v. Fried, 173 Pa. Super. 27, 95 A.2d 360, 364, was an action by a spectator at stock car races, against the race track operators, for injuries suffered when a wheel became detached from a speeding racer, bounced 24 feet into the air, cleared a protective fence 14 feet high and fell into the grandstand. There was no allegation or proof that the precautions were substandard or defective. The decision states:

"In this case plaintiff adduced no evidence whatever as to the height of protective fences at other race tracks which the jury could use as a basis of comparison to determine whether or not defendants were negligent in not having erected a higher one. While customary methods do not furnish a conclusive or controlling test of negligence or justify a practice obviously laden with danger, they are nevertheless to be considered as factors of measurement of due care."

Atlantic Rural Exposition v. Fagan, 195 Va. 13, 77 S.E.2d 368, 375, was an appeal, by a track owner and the track lessee, from a judgment for injuries to a spectator when a wheel became detached from a speeding racer, struck a guard rail, bounced over a 3 ½ foot fence, passed under a suspended chain, bounded into the bleachers and struck plaintiff. Appellants complained there was no expert evidence to establish a standard of care to be followed in the erection of protective facilities. The court held such evidence was not necessary under the circumstances, and stated:

"... But here evidence was offered that distinctly tended to show that freed wheels are recognized hazards and that they at times hurdle fences at high or even higher than the one maintained and travel hundreds of feet. No expert testimony was necessary to show that this fence was known or should have been known to experienced race track operators to be insufficient protection for spectators within the area provided for them."

In 65 C.J.S., Negligence, §16, p. 404, the rule is stated in bold-face:

"The common usage of a business or occupation is a test of care or negligence, and is a proper matter for consideration in determining whether or not sufficient care has been exercised in a particular case, at least where the conduct in question is not inherently dangerous; but customary methods or conduct do not furnish a test which is conclusive or controlling on the question, and negligence may exist notwithstanding the conduct pursued or the methods adopted were in accordance with those customarily pursued or adopted."

38 Am. Jur. 1015, 1016, states:

> "The degree of care which is required of a person either to prevent injury to another or to protect himself is reasonable care under the circumstances. Although subject to certain qualifications, the rule is that upon the issue of negligence or contributory negligence, evidence of the ordinary practice or of the uniform custom, if any, of persons in the performance under similar circumstances of acts like those which are alleged to have been done negligently is generally competent evidence. Evidence of custom is admissible to prove negligence as well as to disprove it."

It is clear the proffered evidence was competent.
Reversed.

PREPARING FOR CLASS

1. Many other spectators stood near the fence at the races; does that mean that they weren't negligent?

2. How widespread does the practice have to be in order to be a custom? If one other track owner testifies that he did the same thing, does that mean there is a custom? If not one, how many?

3. Explain to a judge or jury just what custom proves.

4. If there is a widespread custom, i.e., everyone in the industry does the same thing, how can a jury or fact finder overrule that custom?

INCREASING YOUR UNDERSTANDING

1. Custom evidence may be used as a sword or as a shield, i.e., it can be used to show the customary standard of care that the defendant failed to comply with or it can be used to show that the defendant's actions were like everyone else's and, therefore, not negligent.

2. Custom generally must be widespread. When it is not, it must, at least, exist in the geographic area where it is used.

3. A course of conduct that is not widespread is often called a practice. A practice may be introduced to show that that conduct is feasible or that the feared harm is foreseeable.

4. Custom establishes a standard of care for doctors. Can you anticipate why custom would establish a standard of care for them and not for the rest of us?

APPLYING THE LAW

1. A tug boat did not have a radio to talk to other boats in the area. Most of the other tugs in the area did not have radios either. The tug boat was hauling barges along the coast when a large storm hit, sinking the barges. If the tug had had a radio it probably would have heard of the approaching storm in order to avoid it. However, the tug did not learn of the storm until it was too late, causing the barges to sink. If the tug is sued for negligence in not having radios on the barge, how should the court rule on the admissibility and effect of the custom of not having radios on the boats?

2. The General Railroad had an internal rule that no freight train of more than ten cars should go over 50 mph. One of the General Railroad trains of 20 cars was traveling 60 mph and ran into a car at an intersection. Accident reconstruction experts indicate that the accident would not have happened if the train was going less than 50 mph. There is no conclusive evidence of how fast other railroads' freight trains travel. Is the internal rule of General Railroad relevant? Why should it be?

3. All of the taxicabs in Placerville have been yellow for the last 20 years. The city did not require the yellow color, but all of the cab companies thought that it would be easier for customers to spot the cabs if they were all yellow. A pedestrian was crossing the street, failed to see the oncoming red cab, and was struck. The pedestrian claims that he would have noticed the cab if it were yellow. The pedestrian has sued the cab company for negligence. The pedestrian wants to introduce evidence that the other cabs are yellow. Is that admissible as a customary standard of care?

C. THE PARTICULAR CHARACTERISTICS OF THE REASONABLE PERSON

Now we move on to determine the particular characteristics of the reasonable person. Does the reasonable person, that person whose conduct is used as a standard in a negligence case, vary according to the particular characteristics of the defendant in the case? If the defendant is blind, should we hold the defendant to the standard of care of an ordinary person or a blind person?

Merkley v. Schramm
142 N.W.2d 173 (Wisc. 1966)

Respondent Maxine Schramm owns and operates a rooming house on Wells Street in the city of Milwaukee. Respondent Richard Schramm and appellant Laura Merkley each rented a room on the second floor of the building. The hallway on the second floor is approximately 30 feet long and runs in a north-south direction. Schramm's room (No. 22) is located at the south end and appellant's (No. 26) is on the west side of the hall. A bathroom, which was shared by all the roomers, was at the north end. The distance between the door to appellant's room and the end of the hallway near Schramm's was roughly 20 feet. The only light fixture in the hall hung from the ceiling just above the hallway directly outside of appellant's door. There were no windows in the hall. The walls and ceiling of the hall were painted a dark color and there was a dark carpet on the floor.

Respondent Richard Schramm suffered from an eye disease known as retinitus pigmentosa (known as "tunnel vision"), which reduced his peripheral vision to 15 degrees in each eye. This means, according to the testimony of Dr. Arthur Bussey, a specialist in ophthalmology, that:

"Outside of this 15 degree central vision he is blind. He doesn't see anything unless he points his head in this direction and brings those 15 degrees around to were he wants to look. He can't see where he is stepping and points like a telescope and points at what he is going to see. He won't know if he is going to fall into a hole or what."

In addition, the condition caused Schramm to have difficulty in seeing in darkened areas or in distinguishing dark objects. Schramm wore glasses but this did not correct the peripheral vision defects; rather the glasses only improved his sight within the 15-degree range to 20/80 in the right eye and 20/60 in the left eye.

At about 11:00 A.M. on March 16, 1963, respondent was reading in his room when a shaving cream dispenser began to leak. He scooped up a handful of the foam in his right hand, went into the hall, and began moving toward the bathroom at a normal or brisk pace, feeling the wall with his left hand to guide him. After walking approximately 20 feet he bumped into appellant, who was bent over in her open doorway in the process of removing her boots, and caused her to fall to the floor. Appellant, who was eighty-six years old, sustained serious injuries. Respondent was wearing his glasses at the time but testified that he did not see the appellant at any time before colliding with her. Appellant neither saw nor heard respondent approaching. The light in the hall was lit. Appellant was wearing dark clothes.

Appellant (who has since died) brought suit against respondent Maxine Schramm for an alleged safe-place violation and common-law negligence and against respondent Richard Schramm for alleged negligence.

Immediately on the close of the trial to the court on December 10, 1964, the trial court dismissed plaintiff's action against the defendant Richard Schramm.

Its decision on the case against Maxine Schramm was entered on May 10, 1965. Appeal is taken from a judgment dismissing plaintiff's actions against both respondents.

Wilkie, Justice.

Negligence of Richard Schramm

Because Richard Schramm was visually handicapped, he was obliged to conduct himself as an ordinary prudent person with the same disability would under the same or similar circumstances. This does not mean that he was required to exercise a greater degree of care, but rather that he must do more or put forth greater effort in order to attain the standard of ordinary care. There was testimony that he was either moving at his normal or a slightly brisker speed. He knew the physical layout of the hall, and guided himself by feeling the west wall with his left hand. In regard to his lookout, Schramm testified that he "tried to scan the hallway in the general direction" he was going. He explained that he turned his "eyes from side to side up and down and from side to side." Thus Schramm attempted to ascertain whether his path was clear before navigating down the corridor. He admitted that he did not see her at any time prior to the accident. Either he must have looked and failed to see what was there or he must have failed to focus his tunnel vision at the precise time and spot where the plaintiff was bent low partly in the doorway to her room, dressed in dark clothing.

Considering the entire record a majority of the court is of the opinion that the evidence supports a finding that this defendant exercised sufficient effort to meet the standard of care required of him and that the trial court's finding of no negligence on the part of Richard Schramm is, therefore, not against the great weight and clear preponderance of the evidence.

Judgment affirmed.

PREPARING FOR CLASS

1. Richard Schramm walked down a hallway and ran into Laura Merkley, who was directly in front of him. How can you justify that?

2. Why should we have a different standard of care for disabled persons?

3. Would a person with one leg be held to a different standard of care?

4. What will be the standard of care for a person in a wheelchair? How will the ordinary, lay jury know what the standard of care is for a person in a wheelchair?

INCREASING YOUR UNDERSTANDING

1. If the actor reasonably knows, or should know, of the possible sudden onset of a disability, then the actor must act accordingly. Thus, the person who realizes that he or she suffers from epileptic seizures and desires to drive a car may be required to take medication to prevent those seizures, must not drive a car when a seizure is suspected, and must stop driving immediately when the sudden onset of a seizure is suspected. But, if the seizure is unforeseeable, then the person will be held to the standard of an ordinary person.

2. The special standard of care for the disabled rule requires the disabled person to use other abilities to overcome the disability if a reasonable disabled person would do that.

3. Should a different standard of care apply to people with special abilities?

4. The defendant, who is not disabled, has an obligation as a reasonable person to anticipate persons with disabilities in certain situations. For instance, if the defendant has hired a disabled person, then the defendant must act accordingly, realizing that he or she is dealing with a blind person or a deaf person. On the other hand, a reasonable person who has no special knowledge of the presence of a disabled person has only the ordinary reasonable person's duty to anticipate a disabled person.

5. Obviously, voluntary intoxication is not a disability, but the sudden, unanticipated onset of an intoxicated state may have to be taken into consideration. For instance, the defendant who is, without his or her knowledge, given intoxicating substances is entitled to the ordinary person standard of care.

APPLYING THE LAW

1. If you represented the plaintiff, Laura Merkley, in the above case, what would be your best argument for liability, or that Richard Schramm was negligent?

2. What would be the standard of care of an Alzheimer's patient? Is Alzheimer's disease a physical disability?

Hudson-Connor v. Putney
86 P.3d 106 (Or. App. 2004)

BREWER, J.

Plaintiff appeals a judgment on a jury verdict for defendant in this action for negligent entrustment of a golf cart. Plaintiff, a 16-year-old girl, was injured when she was struck by a golf cart driven on private property by an 11-year-old boy. Defendant, who was 14 years old at the time, owned the golf cart and had allowed the boy to operate it.[1] The trial court instructed the jury that defendant was subject to the duty of care toward other persons that generally applies to minors. On appeal, plaintiff argues, among other things, that the court erred in giving that instruction because defendant was subject to the more stringent adult standard of care. Plaintiff contends that both the entrustment and operation of a golf cart require adult qualifications and, accordingly, minors who engage in those activities must be held to the adult standard of care. We review for errors of law, and affirm.

Defendant lived in central Oregon with her grandparents. In 1998, when she was 12 years old, defendant's grandfather purchased a motorized golf cart and gave it to her. The golf cart's maximum speed was approximately 12 miles per hour. Before making the purchase, defendant's grandfather spent several days teaching her how to drive a golf cart. Defendant was permitted to drive the golf cart around her grandparents' property. Other than to specify the boundaries within which the cart could be used on their property, defendant's grandparents did not restrict its use. Defendant was permitted to allow other children from the neighborhood to drive the cart on the property. However, defendant established her own rules about who could drive the cart and under what conditions. One of her rules was that no person under the age of 12 could drive the cart unaccompanied.

Plaintiff and defendant were neighbors and friends. On June 15, 2000, they had been driving the golf cart around the property. They were standing near the cart when they were approached by Billy and Bobby, two brothers who also lived in the neighborhood. Bobby, who was 11 years old at the time, asked defendant if he could drive the golf cart. Defendant previously had allowed Bobby to drive the cart, but she had always accompanied him. This time, though, defendant did not want to ride on the cart with Bobby, so she refused his request. Bobby began to beg, and defendant eventually relented. Bobby drove the cart up the driveway, turned around, and drove back toward the other children. As he was approaching them, he attempted to stop the golf cart but stepped on the accelerator pedal instead of the brake. He drove directly into defendant and plaintiff. Plaintiff's left femur was fractured and required surgery to repair.

After the parties rested, defendant moved for a directed verdict. She argued that Bobby's age, by itself, was insufficient to permit the jury to find that defendant negligently had entrusted the golf cart to him. The trial court denied the motion.

---

1. Because of their minority, plaintiff and defendant appeared before the trial court through guardians ad litem. Plaintiff no longer is a minor and, therefore, she is the actual appellant. For ease of reference, we refer to the actors themselves as plaintiff and defendant.

Before submitting the case to the jury, the trial court discussed the parties' proposed jury instructions with counsel. Defendant requested UCJI 22.04, which provides:

"In considering charges of negligence against a minor, you are instructed that it is the duty of a minor to use the same care that a reasonably prudent person of the same age, intelligence, and experience would use under the same or similar circumstances."

Plaintiff objected to that instruction, arguing that, by permitting other people to operate the golf cart, defendant had engaged in an adult activity and must be held to an adult standard of care. The court gave UCJI 22.04 to the jury despite plaintiff's objection. The jury found that defendant was not negligent and, based on the jury's verdict, the trial court entered judgment in defendant's favor.

On appeal, plaintiff argues that the trial court erred in giving UCJI 22.04. Specifically, she contends that all motorized vehicles, including golf carts, are inherently dangerous instrumentalities and that their operation is an adult activity for which it is appropriate to hold minors to an adult standard of care. She also asserts that the adult standard of care should apply when a minor entrusts another person with the operation of a motorized vehicle. In response, defendant contends that minors can be held to an adult standard of care only in the operation of automobiles on roads or premises that are open to the public. Defendant cross-assigns error to the trial court's denial of her motion for a directed verdict.

A party is "entitled to have his [or her] theory of the case presented to the jury if there was evidence to support it and the proposed instruction was a correct statement of the law." *State v. Thaxton*, 79 P.3d 897 (2003). Thus, here, we consider whether, on this record, the trial court's jury instruction correctly stated the standard of care applicable to defendant's conduct.[2]

Generally, in a negligence action, an adult is held to the standard of care that a reasonable adult of ordinary prudence would exercise in the same circumstances. Minors, by contrast, generally are held to the lower standard of care enunciated in UCJI 22.04. However, the adult standard may apply when a minor engages in an adult activity.

An "adult activity" is one that is "normally undertaken only by adults, and for which adult qualifications are required." *Restatement* at §283A Comment c. If either of those requirements is not met, the *Nielsen* exception does not apply. Whether conduct constitutes an "adult activity" is a question of law, determined on a case-by-case basis, depending on the facts in evidence relating to the nature of the activity.

---

2. Plaintiff did not assign error to the trial court's failure to instruct the jury that defendant was subject to the adult standard of care. However, because that instruction and the instruction that the trial court gave—that defendant was subject to the standard of care for minors—necessarily are mutually exclusive, the question whether the latter is a correct statement of the law necessarily also answers the question whether the former is an incorrect statement. In addition, as discussed below, the same facts are pertinent to each of those inquiries.

Here, plaintiff focuses her argument exclusively on the adult qualifications requirement. We therefore first consider that requirement. However, as explained below, the evidence in this case did not satisfy either requirement necessary to support the conclusion that defendant engaged in an adult activity.

The *Nielsen* court did not explain precisely what factors constitute "adult qualifications." Citing the *Restatement* and cases from other jurisdictions, however, the court discussed such factors as skill, knowledge, competence, experience, judgment, and "conscious realization of the probable consequences of [the action]." The court also noted that applying the exception to the operation of automobiles on public highways was consistent with public safety considerations implicit in the statutory requirements for that activity, in which no distinction was made between minors and adults.

All of the described considerations are sensible, and we agree with them. An activity logically demands adult qualifications if its safe performance requires a level of skill and judgment not typically associated with children. Further, the level of skill and judgment required to perform an activity safely increases in proportion to the danger to persons that the activity poses. Thus, where the risk of harm is low, an activity may be less likely to be treated as an adult activity.

With the foregoing principles in mind, we turn to plaintiff's specific arguments on appeal. We first briefly address plaintiff's contention that the entrustment of a golf cart to another person is inherently an adult activity. According to plaintiff, a minor who entrusts the use of a motorized vehicle to another person should be held to the same standard of care as if he or she actually had operated it. Plaintiff relies on *Ardinger v. Hummell*, 982 P.2d 727, 731 (Alaska 1999). In that case, the Alaska Supreme Court held that, because the entrustment of an automobile requires an exercise of dominion and physical control, entrustment is equivalent to the operation of the vehicle. Accordingly, the court concluded that the adult standard of care was applicable to the act of entrustment. Plaintiff argues that the "reasoning of the Alaska court is sensible, and a contrary approach would create an unreasonable distinction between a negligent minor driver before and after she hands the wheel over to her minor friend." Plaintiff may well be correct. However, the question remains whether the operation of a golf cart on premises that are not open to the public is, itself, inherently an adult activity. We turn to that issue.

Plaintiff asserts that *all* motorized vehicles are inherently dangerous and therefore require adult qualifications to operate. It follows, plaintiff reasons, that the *Nielsen* exception applies here, and the court erred in giving the challenged instruction. Again, however, whether an activity requires adult qualifications such as adult levels of skill and judgment depends on the nature of the activity. We turn to the evidence on that point.

The parties do not dispute that ORS 801.295 defines "golf cart," in part, as a motor vehicle that is "designed to be and is operated at not more than 15 miles per hour." The evidence showed that the maximum speed of defendant's golf cart was approximately 12 miles per hour. Plaintiff offered no evidence that golf cart accidents commonly occur on premises that are not open to the public or that they often result in fatal or serious injury. Further, there is no evidence in the record, and we may not take judicial notice of the proposition, that having a motor alone makes an instrumentality inherently dangerous. Thus, the evidence does not support plaintiff's contention that operation of a golf cart requires adult qualifications.

Plaintiff protests that, like automobiles, motorized golf carts pose inherent risks of harm to persons if not properly operated. We may take judicial notice of the fact that automobile accidents frequently result in fatalities and serious injuries. In addition, the evidence permitted the inference that the same rudimentary skills are needed to propel, maneuver, and stop both a golf cart and an automobile with an automatic transmission. However, placing undue emphasis on those similarities understates the significance of the differences between them. For example, there are statutory restrictions on where a golf cart may be operated that are not applicable to automobiles. With limited exceptions, golf carts may be driven only on private property. Equally important, in order to operate an automobile on the public highways a driver must master a more demanding set of skills, including understanding the traffic laws and traffic signs and signals, judging road surface conditions, traffic conditions, safe stopping distances, and myriad other safe driving practices. To obtain a license to operate an automobile on the highways, a driver must demonstrate mastery of those skills by passing a knowledge test, a driving skills test, and, if the driver is under the age of 18, a safe driving practices test. No such license is required to operate a motorized golf cart on premises that are not open to the public. Significantly, there is no evidence in the record that the operation of golf carts on private premises and automobiles on premises open to the public requires similar driving skills beyond the most rudimentary level. In short, on the factual record before us, we conclude that the operation of a motorized golf cart on private premises does not require adult qualifications.

Finally, even if plaintiff had shown that adult qualifications are required for the operation of a motorized golf cart, there was no evidence that such instrumentalities normally are operated only by adults. Because operation of a golf cart is not an adult activity, it follows that entrustment of a golf cart to another also is not an adult activity. The trial court did not err in giving UCJI 22.04 to the jury.

PREPARING FOR CLASS

1. Would a 10-year-old child with an intellectual disability be held to a different standard of care than a 10-year-old child of average intelligence? What would be the standard of care of a 10-year-old with an intellectual disability?

2.   What about the standard of care of a particularly intelligent child? Could a child be so capable that the child would be held to an adult standard of care?

3.   Is the child standard of care objective or is it really a subjective standard of care?

4.   Who decides whether to use the adult or child standard of care—the judge as a matter of law or the jury as a matter of fact?

INCREASING YOUR UNDERSTANDING

1.   A few states have a doctrine called "the rule of sevens." In those states, a child under 7 years old is not capable of negligence, a child between 7 and 14 years of age is presumptively incapable of negligence, and a child over 14 is presumed to be capable of negligence. Notice that this gives immunity to children under 7 years old and establishes the burden of proof for those over 7. But a judge in New York (A non-rule of sevens state) held that a 4-year-old child on a bicycle who ran into an elderly lady could be held liable for negligence. Alan Feuer, *4-Year-Old Can Be Sued, Judge Rules in Bike Case,* N.Y. Times, Oct. 28, 2010

2.   Tort law is often influenced by the availability of insurance. Children usually do not have insurance, but adults usually do. How do you think this influences litigation when children are involved?

APPLYING THE LAW

1.   Jerome, a 15-year-old who grew up on a farm, was driving a tractor on the farm. Unfortunately, Jerome drove the tractor into a pickup on the farm, which resulted in injuries to its occupant, Betty. Betty has sued Jerome for negligence. What is Jerome's standard of care?

2.   Would a court use the adult standard or the child standard for the following activities:

Deer hunting

Setting a campsite fire

Tackle football

Setting poison traps for animals

A 16-year-old riding a bicycle

Ramey v. Knorr
124 P.3d 314 (Ct. App. Wash. 2005)

Cox, C.J.

Insanity and other mental incapacities are not generally recognized as defenses to a claim of negligence. Some jurisdictions permit a limited exception to this rule by permitting sudden mental incapacity as a defense for a tortfeasor. This defense requires a defendant to establish "(1) [they had] no prior notice or forewarning of [their] potential for becoming disabled, and (2) the disability renders [them] incapable of conforming to the standards of ordinary care." We hold that there is no legally sufficient evidentiary basis for a jury to find that Nancy Knorr ("Knorr") was entitled to the defense of sudden mental incapacity. Thus, the trial court properly granted Lanette Ramey's motion for judgment as a matter of law. We also hold that the trial court correctly denied Knorr's motion for summary judgment as well as her alternative post-trial motions. We affirm.

This personal injury action arises from a head-on automobile collision on I-405. While in a delusional state, Knorr turned her car around towards oncoming traffic, removed her seatbelt, and drove head-on into Ramey's car. At the time of the incident, Knorr believed she was the object of a conspiracy to attack her. She was trying to commit suicide.

Ramey suffered substantial injuries from the collision. She sued Knorr for negligence. Knorr raised the defense of sudden mental incapacity.

Pre-trial, the trial court denied Knorr's motion for summary judgment. At the close of all the evidence at trial, both Knorr and Ramey moved for directed verdicts. The trial court granted a directed verdict for Ramey, ruling that as a matter of law, Knorr's sudden mental incapacity defense could not be sustained on the basis of the evidence. The jury returned a verdict for Ramey in the amount of $497,578.00. The trial court denied Knorr's post-trial motion for judgment as a matter of law or, alternatively, a new trial.

Following entry of judgment on the jury verdict, Knorr appealed.

MOTIONS

Knorr argues that the trial court erred in denying her motions for a judgment as a matter of law and in granting Ramey's motion for a directed verdict. We disagree.

INSANITY AND OTHER MENTAL DEFICIENCIES AS DEFENSES

Both for historical and other reasons, insanity or other mental deficiencies generally are not recognized as defenses to negligence. Washington, along with the majority of states, holds the mentally ill to the standard of a reasonable person under like circumstances.

Traditionally, courts have relied on several rationales to hold the mentally ill to an objective standard of liability for negligence. The most common justification is that innocent victims should be compensated for their injuries. Another common reason is that the existence and degree of one's mental illness can be difficult to measure and is a major obstacle for applying a mental deficiency defense. Other rationales include the belief that liability of the mentally ill will encourage caretakers to look after them and the difficulty of drawing a line between mental illness and variations of temperaments, intellect, and emotional balance.

Knorr expressly disclaims an insanity defense or an argument that mental illness alone is a defense to negligence. Instead, she maintains that "a driver who suffers an acute psychotic episode, which incapacitates the driver, is not chargeable with negligence." While noting that Washington has not addressed this issue, Knorr primarily relies on authority from the state of Wisconsin, *Breunig v. American Family Ins. Co.*, 173 N.W.2d 619. Accordingly, we consider whether that case is applicable to the matter before us.

"SUDDEN MENTAL INCAPACITY" DEFENSE

In *Breunig*, the defendant, Erma Veith was driving her car when she believed that God was taking control of the steering wheel and directing her car. Believing she could fly "because Batman can," Mrs. Veith stepped on the gas and collided with an oncoming truck. At trial, a psychiatrist testified that Mrs. Veith was unable to operate the vehicle with her conscious mind. A jury returned a verdict in the plaintiff's favor.

The Wisconsin Supreme Court in Breunig recognized an exception for sudden mental incapacity and adopted a two part test stating,

> [the] disorder must be such as to [1(a)] affect the person's ability to understand and appreciate the duty which rests upon him to drive his car with ordinary care, or [1(b)] if the insanity does not affect such understanding and appreciation; it must affect his ability to control his car in an ordinarily prudent manner. And . . . [2] there must be an absence of notice or forewarning to the person that he may be suddenly subject to such a type of insanity or mental illness.

The *Breunig* test was further explained by the same court in *Jankee v. Clark County*, 612 N.W.2d 297. Sudden mental incapacity is a "rare exception [and] applies only when two conditions are met: (1) the person has no prior notice or forewarning of his or her potential for becoming disabled, and (2) the disability renders the person incapable of conforming to the standards of ordinary care."

The *Breunig* court upheld the jury's verdict, finding Mrs. Veith did have knowledge or forewarning that her hallucinations could affect her driving. Mrs. Veith had previously experienced delusional visions and should have known she posed a risk to others if she drove. The Wisconsin Supreme

Court later limited the *Breunig* rule stating, "'[a]ll we hold is that a sudden mental incapacity equivalent in its effect to such physical causes as a sudden heart attack, epileptic seizure, stroke, or fainting should be treated alike and not under the general rule of insanity.'"

ABSENCE OF NOTICE OR FOREWARNING

Whether Knorr had notice or forewarning that her paranoia could affect her driving is the more difficult question presented. In order to meet the first prong of sudden mental incapacity, the defendant must have "no prior notice or forewarning of his or her potential for becoming disabled."

The standard of whether a defendant had notice or forewarning of the mental incapacity depends on whether the defendant had any forewarning or knowledge of a prior mental disability or disorder that incapacitates him from conforming his conduct to the standard of care. The driver must have been incapable of knowing that a mental incapacity could occur while driving, preventing the driver from avoiding a collision.

Whether a person has knowledge or forewarning of their condition is based on an objective standard. When the occurrence of an illness or loss of consciousness should have been reasonably foreseen by a person of ordinary intelligence and prudence, the driver of a motor vehicle is negligent as a matter of law. "The negligence is not in the manner of driving but rather in driving at all, if the person should reasonably have foreseen that the illness or lack of consciousness might occur and affect the person's manner of driving."

The Wisconsin cases provide several examples defining notice and forewarning. In *Jankee*, the court declared that forewarning exists when a person is under the treatment of medication. The court discussed *Stuyvesant Assoc. v. John Doe*, 534 A.2d 448, to illustrate when forewarning is satisfied with regard to taking medication. In *Stuyvesant Assoc.*, a schizophrenic man was receiving injections every other week for his illness and knew if he missed an injection, deterioration would result. The defendant also knew of the risks he posed if he fell into a psychotic state. The defendant missed an appointment for his medication and committed vandalism while in a psychotic state. "The court held the defendant to an objective standard of care and found him liable, reasoning that the patient was cognizant of his condition and the risks posed by refraining from the medication. . . ."

In *Johnson v. Lambotte*, 363 P.2d 165, the defendant was being treated for "chronic schizophrenic state of paranoid type" when she left the hospital and having little or no apparent control of her vehicle, collided with another car. In *Breunig*, the court stated that "*Johnson* is not a case of sudden mental seizure with no forewarning [because the] defendant knew she was being treated for a mental disorder and hence would not have come under the nonliability rule herein stated."

In addition, symptoms of a mental disability provide adequate notice and forewarning. In *Breunig*, Mrs. Veith was found to have had notice and forewarning of her mental condition because she had previously experienced delusional visions. The issue of forewarning went to the jury in *Breunig* because there was not substantial evidence whether Mrs. Veith had knowledge or forewarning. Mrs. Veith was not previously treated for a mental disorder and her friends testified that she was normal for some months prior to the accident.

In the case at hand, Knorr does not meet the test of sudden mental incapacity because the evidence clearly establishes she had notice and forewarning of her mental condition. The testimony at trial showed that in 1994, Knorr had a mental breakdown and was hospitalized for ten days. During that period, Knorr believed the person she worked for was conspiring to steal her and her husband's assets, was going to kill them, and was poisoning her. She also had concerns about her brother being a murderer. The delusions escalated to a point where she believed the neighbors were part of this scheme of "taking them out." Knorr was diagnosed with possible delusional disorder, was put on medication, and was advised to see a psychiatrist.

When Knorr was released from the hospital she was given Lithium along with other medication, which helped end her delusional thoughts. The hospital directed Knorr to see a psychiatrist and she saw Dr. McConnaughy. After three months, Knorr quit seeing Dr. McConnaughy and quit taking her medication. Knorr testified at trial that in July of 1994, she "started to get real anxious again" and had to go back to the hospital. At the admittance office, Knorr "started snapping out of it" and decided to go back home and see how she felt. When Knorr returned home she felt fine and no longer had anxiety or other symptoms until 2001.

The testimony at trial further showed that beginning in March 2001, Knorr's delusional thoughts about her brother being a murderer came back. Knorr and her family testified that by November 2001, her thoughts escalated and Mr. Knorr tried to get her to agree to go to the hospital. Knorr wanted to wait until after the holidays to go to the hospital and had an appointment scheduled for two days after the accident.

The day before the accident Knorr believed intruders were coming to her house and were going to kidnap her and her husband and rape them. The morning of the accident a friend offered to take Knorr to the hospital, but she refused to go. At trial, Dr. Young testified that people with delusional beliefs almost never believe something is wrong with them. He further testified that on the day of the accident, Knorr's delusional beliefs caused her to panic, and "it's at that point that erratic or dangerous behavior can occur." Dr. Young testified that Knorr's delusional beliefs that caused her to panic were "relatively sudden."

The trial court concluded that under *Breunig* and *Johnson*, Knorr had forewarning because she knew she had been treated for a mental condition in 1994 and chose not to continue with the medication, and therefore did not fall within the sudden mental incapacity exception. We agree. We note further that the episodes continued and existed in this case as recently as the day preceding the auto collision. The record shows that Knorr was forewarned of the condition that again arose on the day of the accident.

Knorr heavily relies on the expert testimony of Dr. Young, which she describes as "unrebutted." However, the question before the court at the time of the motions was whether there was a legally sufficient evidentiary basis to allow the defense. The court was neither required to only consider the evidence of the expert nor to believe that evidence.

More importantly, when one views the testimony by Dr. Young and the other witnesses in the light most favorable to Knorr, there is substantial evidence to conclude that Knorr had knowledge and forewarning of her mental disorder. Knorr was treated for delusional beliefs in 1994, decided to stop that treatment, including taking her medication, began experiencing delusions again almost a year prior to the accident, and had ample opportunity to go to the hospital and seek help. Knorr also agreed to go to the hospital, which further supports her knowledge of her mental disorder. Therefore, the trial court properly granted a directed verdict in favor of Ramey.

Although Knorr had no history of being dangerous or violent, or any problems with her driving, that is not required under *Breunig*. Knorr experienced delusional beliefs for several months prior to the accident and believed the night before the accident that intruders were going to come into her family's home and rape and kill them. Under an objective standard, a reasonable person would have foreseen that Knorr's mental condition could affect her driving. Therefore, Knorr's mental incapacity while driving was foreseeable.

INCAPABLE OF CONFORMING TO STANDARDS OF ORDINARY CARE

Addressing the other prong of sudden mental incapacity, the *Breunig* court stated:

> [the] disorder must be such as to affect the person's ability to understand and appreciate the duty which rests upon him to drive his car with ordinary care, or if the insanity does not affect such understanding and appreciation, it must affect his ability to control his car in an ordinarily prudent manner.

The court in *Jankee* later clarified the rule from *Breunig* and stated "the disability [must] render the person incapable of conforming to the standards of ordinary care."

Ramey argues that because Knorr did not lose physical control of her vehicle, she does not meet the second prong of *Breunig*. However, lack of ordinary care does not only require loss of physical capacity. Lack of ordinary care occurs when there is either an inability to understand and appreciate the duty to drive with ordinary care, or an inability to control the vehicle with ordinary care. Although Knorr was in physical control of her vehicle, her delusional beliefs prevented her from understanding and appreciating her duty to drive with ordinary care. Because Knorr was mentally incapable of conforming to the standards of ordinary care while driving, she meets the second prong of *Breunig*.

Knorr relies, in part, on Washington authority that holds that, "[a] driver who becomes suddenly stricken by an unforeseen loss of consciousness, and is unable to control the vehicle, is not chargeable with negligence." In *Kaiser v. Suburban Transp. Sys.*, 398 P.2d 14, the doctor did not warn the driver of a bus of the side effects of drowsiness or lassitude, and the court held the driver could not be liable for negligence unless he had "knowledge of the pill's harmful qualities." The general rule from *Kaiser* applies only to a sudden physical incapacity or loss of consciousness that is unforeseeable, and has never applied to a mental incapacity with no loss of consciousness. *Kaiser* is not applicable to the case before us because Knorr remained in physical control of her vehicle and never lost consciousness.

To summarize, the trial court properly denied Knorr's summary judgment motion because there were then genuine issues of material fact. At the close of the evidence at trial, the court properly granted the motion. There was no need to either adopt or reject the *Breunig* exception in ruling on that motion, and we decline to do either here. The trial court properly refused the instructions proposed by Knorr and the instructions the court gave were proper. The motion was properly denied. We affirm the trial court rulings in all respects.

PREPARING FOR CLASS

1. Nancy Knorr intended to commit suicide. Are Knorr's actions negligence or intentional torts? Does it make any difference? What is the standard for mentally ill people who attempt an intentional tort like battery?

2. What if a person shows clear signs of mental illness but that person, due to mental illness, does not realize that he or she is mentally ill? Does that person have notice of mental illness?

3. John was shot in the head and sustained significant brain damage as a result. John's brain damage caused him to close his eyes to sunlight. John did not realize that he had this disability. John was exercising by running on a track when the sun came out. John closed his eyes and ran into another runner, knocking the runner down. Does John have a mental or physical disability? How should John's actions be judged?

INCREASING YOUR UNDERSTANDING

1. Will the mental disability of a child be considered in judging the child's conduct? See Restatement (Second) of Torts §283B.

2. What would be the standard of care for a person with an intellectual disability? Do you think that a jury would follow the court's instructions

about holding a person with an intellectual disability to the standard of care of an ordinary person?

APPLYING THE LAW

1. If Nancy Knorr had not had any advance notice of her mental illness, what would be her standard of care?

2. Bernard had an incident of paranoia lasting one hour in 2009. Bernard recovered without seeking treatment. Bernard did not believe that he had been mentally ill but believed that he had been under attack from forces. One year later, Bernard had another incident, but this time he ran out the door of his apartment to get away from his imaginary attackers and ran into a lady walking down the hallway. Bernard claims this was the sudden onset of mental illness. Is Bernard correct?

Chapter 5

Negligence — Proving Breach of Duty with Circumstantial Evidence

---

A. INTRODUCTION

The plaintiff has the burden of proof to show that the most likely inference from the facts introduced at the trial is the negligence of the defendant. It is not enough to show that two cars ran into each other, or that the plaintiff suffered injury, or that the defendant was involved; the plaintiff must show a combination of facts that justify an inference of negligence.

In proving negligence, the courts divide the proofs into direct and circumstantial evidence. Direct evidence is when a witness testifies to observing the facts. When a witness watches a car fail to stop for a stop sign and run into someone in the intersection, that is direct evidence of negligence. On the other hand, if the witness arrives at the scene shortly after the accident and sees that the car proceeding past the stop sign has run into the side of the car with the right-of-way, that is circumstantial evidence of negligence. There was no direct observation of the accident, but the witness did see facts that may lead to a conclusion that there was negligence. There is nothing inherently wrong with circumstantial evidence, but the courts continually struggle with the question of how much circumstantial evidence is enough. How much circumstantial evidence is necessary to allow a jury to decide the case? How much is necessary to convince a jury that negligence is more likely than not?

Hypothetical

John Couch was driving his parents' car on a Sunday afternoon with his girlfriend, Megan Smith, as a passenger. John's parent's car was two years old and had been rigorously maintained by John's father.

199

John was driving on Haney Road at two o'clock in the afternoon. There were no other cars on Haney Road at that time and no witnesses when John's car suddenly swerved off the road and into a woods nearby. There were no skid marks on the road. The car struck a tree, and both John and Megan were killed in the crash. The crash was so severe that the metal in the front of the car was crushed. Auto mechanics were unable to reach any conclusions about the condition of the car before the accident since the car was so badly damaged. Accident reconstruction experts were also unable to determine why the car swerved off the road. A check with the National Weather Service indicated that the weather was sunny and warm at the time of the accident. The police report indicated that the cause of the accident was "inconclusive."

Megan Smith's parents come to your law office to talk about suing the estate and insurance company of John Couch for negligence. They say they think "that's the least we can do for poor Megan."

PREPARING FOR CLASS

Consider the following questions:

1. What other possible evidence, if any, should your office investigate?

2. Will you take this case on a one-third contingency fee basis? Explain your answer.

3. What if you cannot find any other evidence and present the facts as set forth above at trial? The attorney for the estate of John Couch makes a motion for directed verdict during the trial. The attorney argues that the plaintiff has not presented any evidence whatsoever of what John Couch did wrong. Is a judge likely to grant a motion to dismiss this case and take it away from a jury?

B. CIRCUMSTANTIAL EVIDENCE

Winn Dixie Stores v. White
675 So. 2d 702 (Fla. App. 4 Dist. 1996)

GUNTHER, Chief Judge.

Appellant, Winn Dixie Stores, Inc., defendant below, seeks review of the jury verdict rendered in a slip-and-fall case. On appeal, Winn Dixie asserts that the trial court erred in denying its motion for a directed verdict. We agree.

The evidence adduced at trial reveals that the appellee slipped and fell in Winn Dixie, sustaining personal injuries. A man with a buffer was observed near the location of appellee's fall; however, no witness had seen the man buff the particular area where appellee fell. Although the floor surface was shiny, appellee found no wetness or other cause for her accident when she looked after falling. Moreover, a witness who noticed appellee's fall experienced no slipperiness on the floor.

Winn Dixie's store manager testified that the buffing takes place regularly and does not leave the floor surface slippery or wet. Furthermore, an examination of the area shortly after the accident revealed nothing on the floor. At the close of the evidence, the trial court denied Winn Dixie's motion for directed verdict.

In considering a motion for directed verdict, all inferences of fact should be construed most strictly in favor of the non-moving party. Negligence, however, may not be inferred from the mere happening of an accident alone. Circumstantial evidence "will not support a jury inference if the evidence is purely speculative and, therefore, inadequate to produce an inference that outweighs all contrary or opposing inferences." In order to find Winn Dixie liable in the instant case, the jury would have to necessarily infer that there was a dangerous condition at the site of the fall and that Winn Dixie had actual or constructive knowledge thereof. Such inferences could not be properly drawn from the evidence adduced. Rather, they could only be drawn from speculation and conjecture.

Accordingly, the trial court erred in denying Winn Dixie's motion for a directed verdict. As such, the instant case is reversed and remanded with directions to the trial court to enter a verdict in favor of Winn Dixie.

PREPARING FOR CLASS

1. "A man with a buffer was observed near the location of appellee's fall." Can you argue that this is enough evidence to allow a jury to conclude that negligence is more likely than not?

2. What if this case came to your law office? Sarah White wants you to represent her. You have an investigator in your office to do further investigation. What do you want your investigator to look for? What kind of evidence is likely to establish a case for White?

INCREASING YOUR UNDERSTANDING

1. The gathering of evidence in slip and fall cases favors the store owners. The plaintiff has been injured by the fall, is in pain, and will often be taken away for medical care. The store owners are often experienced in

these cases. They will assist the plaintiff but then remain at the scene to gather evidence. Who do you think examined the floor shortly after White's fall? Who concluded that the shiny spot was not slippery?

2. Should the jury be instructed about this imbalance in gathering evidence? How would you do that?

Spiers v. Martin
58 N.W.2d 821 (Mich. 1953)

DETHMERS, Chief Justice.

Plaintiffs, aged four and nine years of age respectively, were standing on the sidewalk at the southwest corner of the intersection of Jos. Campau Avenue, a 46-foot, paved, north and south street, and Charlevoix Avenue, a 26-foot, paved through street, running east and west, in the City of Detroit. The district was residential, the pavements dry and the afternoon bright and clear. Defendant Martin drove south on Jos. Campau and stopped in response to a stop sign before entering Charlevoix. Although he told police at the time that he had seen no vehicle approaching, he testified, on trial, that when he stopped he saw defendant Atwell's taxicab approaching the intersection from the east about 400 or 500 feet distant (at another time he fixed the distance at a half block, which the physical facts showed to be 132 feet); that he waited a couple of seconds and then started into the intersection. Martin's testimony was conflicting on this and other points, but he testified that when he started into the intersection the taxicab was about 500 feet, or a half block (132 feet), distant and "he was far enough so I figured for me to go across." Martin further testified that his car stalled or jerked somewhat and that he choked it and proceeded into the intersection at a rate of speed of five or ten miles per hour; that when his car had reached about the center of Charlevoix, which he was crossing, its left front fender and wheel were struck hard by the taxicab, causing his car to go up onto the sidewalk and to strike the plaintiff children and roll over on its top. Physical evidence indicated that the collision between the two vehicles occurred in the northwest quadrant of the intersection. Both vehicles came to rest entirely outside and to the south of the intersection. Martin's car lay on its top, headed south on the sidewalk along the west side of Jos. Campau, 35 feet from the point of impact. The taxicab stood south of the intersection, headed northeast, with its left rear wheel on the west curb of Jos. Campau, 21 feet from the point of impact. The front and of the Checker cab was badly damaged and crushed in and there was damage to its entire right side from end to end. The left front of Martin's car was damaged.

It is conceded that plaintiffs were not guilty of contributory negligence. They sustained serious injuries resulting from the accident. On trial defendant Atwell, owner of the taxicab, moved for a directed verdict and, after verdict for plaintiffs, for a judgment non obstante veredicto, which was denied.

He appeals, asking for reversal of the judgment for plaintiffs without a new trial, and contends that a verdict should have been directed for him on the ground that there was no proof of any actionable negligence attributable to him.

Negligence may be established by circumstantial evidence as well as by direct proof and they are equally competent, their relative convincing powers being for the jury to determine. Negligence may be inferred from circumstances which place the case within the field of legitimate inferences from established facts, and when, as here, appeal is from denial of defendant's motion for directed verdict, that testimony and those legitimate inferences which may be drawn therefrom which are most favorable to plaintiff, must be accepted.

Defendant places reliance on *Manley v. Potts*, and *Weil v. Longyear*. Both are distinguishable. In Manley nothing more was shown than that plaintiff was struck by a cab, with no proof of where the cab came from or how. In the *Weil* Case testimony affirmatively disclosed that defendant Longyear had operated his truck and conducted himself in a manner which was free from negligence. Such was not the situation at bar. Here there was testimony which, if believed by the jury, warranted the conclusion that defendant Martin stopped for the intersection and then proceeded into it when defendant Atwell's taxicab was 400 or 500 feet, or 132 feet, distant, that the view was unobstructed, the day clear and the pavements dry, that the cab traversed that entire distance, through a residential district, While Martin's car proceeded into the intersection at a rate of speed of five or ten miles per hour and crossed half of 26-foot wide Charlevoix Avenue, that the front of the cab then struck the left side of Martin's car hard and with sufficient force, combined with the relatively slow speed of Martin's car, to carry both vehicles to the respective positions and to inflict the consequent damage, above noted. There was evidence, which, when viewed in the light most favorable to plaintiffs, sufficed to support and warrant a finding of facts by the jury from which it could reasonably and legitimately have inferred that the taxicab driver (1) failed to maintain a reasonable and proper lookout ahead, (2) traveled at an unreasonable rate of speed in a residential zone, (3) failed to have his taxicab under reasonable control and, hence, was guilty of negligence which was a proximate cause of plaintiffs' injuries.

Affirmed, with costs of plaintiffs.

PREPARING FOR CLASS

1. Who had the right-of-way in the intersection? Should the taxicab be under an obligation to anticipate that Martin would not yield the right-of-way? How can the court rely on Martin's testimony if it "was conflicting on this and other parts"?

2. The appellate court seems to rest its conclusions on "circumstantial evidence," but Martin testified to the actions of his car and of the taxicab. Is this circumstantial evidence?

INCREASING YOUR UNDERSTANDING

1. The plaintiff must prove that negligence is the most likely explanation of the events. There may be other explanations of the accident, but the plaintiff is not obligated to disprove all other explanations. In the case above, the accident may have been caused by Martin's negligence. Martin did not have the right-of-way and evidently stalled his car in the intersection. But the court evidently believed that the negligence of the taxicab was a more likely explanation. Why?

2. When the court denies a motion for directed verdict, the court is not ruling that the defendant was negligent; the court is ruling that negligence is a permissible inference in the case. In other words, the jury will determine whether the plaintiff has proven negligence.

3. The plaintiff has demanded a right to a jury trial under the state or federal constitution, but if the court directs a judgment for the defendant on a motion for a directed verdict, there will be no jury trial. How can that ruling be justified?

4. Courts rarely direct a verdict for the plaintiff. Why is that?

C. RES IPSA LOQUITUR

Negligence is not a fact but the evaluation of the facts about a party's conduct. Those facts must be relatively specific in order to allow a jury to draw an inference of negligence. A jury will have a difficult time evaluating whether the defendant's conduct threatened harm to others or whether the threatened harm of the defendant's conduct outweighed the utility of the conduct if the jury doesn't know with some specificity what the defendant did. The jury cannot reach a fair inference of negligence from the fact that two cars ran into each other. More details, like the speed and direction of the cars, are needed. This is one of the central questions in a negligence trial, i.e., how specific must the plaintiff be in proving what the defendant did? The following cases deal with that issue.

Curtis v. Lein
239 P.3d 1078 (Wash. 2010)

Stephens, J.
 . . . Petitioner, Tambra Curtis, lived on a farm owned by the respondents, Jack and Claire Lein. Curtis was injured on the farm when a dock on which she was walking gave way beneath her. The Leins had the dock destroyed

shortly after the incident, so there is no evidence as to the dock's condition at the time of the accident. Curtis brought a negligence suit against the Leins, who moved for summary judgment. Curtis invoked res ipsa loquitur to fill in the evidentiary gaps caused by the dock's destruction. The lower courts held the doctrine did not apply. We reverse the Court of Appeals and hold that at trial, Curtis may rely upon res ipsa loquitur as evidence of negligence.

FACTS AND PROCEDURAL HISTORY

Jack and Claire Lein bought Willow Creek Farm in 1978 and took up residence there around 1980. Claire Lein raised thoroughbred horses on the farm. The property included a small pond, which the Leins enlarged. In the late 1980s the Leins had a wooden dock built over the pond in order to facilitate access to the pond's drainage pipe. The pond and dock were open to the farm's residents and, although the pond was primarily decorative, the Leins' grandchildren sometimes swam in it.

Around 2001, the Leins sold the farm, though they continued living on it until 2004 along with their son Mike, his wife Donna, and their children. Also living on the farm in housing provided by the Leins was Michael Stewart, who was hired as the farm manager in 2001, and Stewart's girl friend, Tambra Curtis, and their son. Curtis did not work on the farm.

On April 25, 2004, Curtis walked out onto the dock over the pond for the first time since she began living on the farm. A couple of steps onto the dock, the boards underneath her feet gave way, and her left leg plunged through the dock up to her hip. As a result of the fall, Curtis suffered a hairline fracture to her tibia.

When Claire Lein learned of the accident, she instructed Stewart to remove the dock. Knowing the farm's new owners planned to level the property to build a school, she saw no reason to replace the dock. As a result of the dock's destruction, there is no evidence as to what about the dock caused Curtis's fall. Claire and Mike Lein testified that they had no reason to believe the dock was in need of repair or unsafe. Curtis does not recall the condition of the dock on the day she stepped out onto it, but in an interrogatory response she noted that her son told her he was instructed by the Leins' grandchildren that the dock was not safe to play on.

Curtis brought a personal injury action against the Leins and Willow Creek Farms, Incorporated. The Leins moved for summary judgment, which the trial court granted. The trial court held that res ipsa loquitur did not apply because causes other than negligent maintenance of the dock could have been at play in Curtis's fall. On appeal, the Court of Appeals also concluded that res ipsa loquitur did not apply, though on different grounds. The Court of Appeals reasoned that, while res ipsa loquitur could be invoked as evidence of negligence, it did not relieve Curtis of the burden of proving that the dock's defect was discoverable. Curtis petitioned for review, which we granted.

ANALYSIS

This case requires us to determine whether summary judgment was properly granted as to the application of res ipsa loquitur in a premises liability suit. An overview of these concepts is helpful.

Whether res ipsa loquitur applies in a given context is a question of law. Res ipsa loquitur means "'the thing speaks for itself.'" Generally, it "provides nothing more than a permissive inference" of negligence. It is "ordinarily sparingly applied, 'in peculiar and exceptional cases, and only where the facts and the demands of justice make its application essential.'" Tinder v. Nordstrom, Inc., 84 Wash. App. 787, 792, 929 P.2d 1209 (1997) (quoting Morner v. Union Pac. R.R. Co., 31 Wash. 2d 282, 293, 196 P.2d 744 (1948)).

> The doctrine of res ipsa loquitur spares the plaintiff the requirement of proving specific acts of negligence in cases where a plaintiff asserts that he or she suffered injury, the cause of which cannot be fully explained, and the injury is of a type that would not ordinarily result if the defendant were not negligent. In such cases the jury is permitted to infer negligence. The doctrine permits the inference of negligence on the basis that the evidence of the cause of the injury is practically accessible to the defendant but inaccessible to the injured person.

Curtis argues that because the dock was destroyed following her accident, it is impossible to know what precisely about the dock caused her fall. She therefore relies upon res ipsa loquitur, contending that a wooden dock does not ordinarily give way unless the owner has negligently failed to maintain the structure. The trial court granted the Leins' motion for summary judgment, reasoning that res ipsa loquitur did not apply to Curtis's claim because the court could conceive of "multiple other causes which could have caused the failure of the step on the dock," such as improper construction or defective materials. The Court of Appeals affirmed the trial court, reasoning that while wooden docks do not ordinarily give way in the absence of negligence (thus implicating res ipsa loquitur), the doctrine could not be used to infer that dangerous docks exhibit discoverable defects. Rather, Curtis retained the burden under premises liability of proving the Leins knew or should have known of the dock's faulty condition.

We reject this analysis. A plaintiff may rely upon res ipsa loquitur's inference of negligence if (1) the accident or occurrence that caused the plaintiff's injury would not ordinarily happen in the absence of negligence, (2) the instrumentality or agency that caused the plaintiff's injury was in the exclusive control of the defendant, and (3) the plaintiff did not contribute to the accident or occurrence. The first element is satisfied if one of three conditions is present:

> "'(1) When the act causing the injury is so palpably negligent that it may be inferred as a matter of law, i.e., leaving foreign objects, sponges,

scissors, etc., in the body, or amputation of a wrong member; (2) when the general experience and observation of mankind teaches that the result would not be expected without negligence; and (3) when proof by experts in an esoteric field creates an inference that negligence caused the injuries.' "

Curtis relies upon the second scenario: general experience and observation teaches that a wooden dock does not give way under foot unless it is negligently maintained. The Court of Appeals agreed with this argument but concluded that it "does not follow that dangerous docks ordinarily exhibit discoverable defects," and therefore res ipsa loquitur could not apply. The Court of Appeals explained that Curtis could not rely on res ipsa loquitur to meet her "burden of showing that the dock's defect was discoverable."

The Court of Appeals erred when it parsed out the inference of negligence that can be drawn from res ipsa loquitur. When res ipsa loquitur applies, it provides an inference as to the defendant's breach of duty. It therefore would apply an inference of negligence on the part of the Leins generally: what they knew or reasonably should have known about the dock's condition is part of the duty that they owed to Curtis. What the Leins knew or reasonably should have known about the dock is exactly the sort of information that res ipsa loquitur is intended to supply by inference, if the inference applies at all.

The only question remaining is whether res ipsa loquitur applies at all, a premise the trial court rejected. As noted, res ipsa loquitur applies where the injury-producing event is of a type that would not ordinarily occur absent negligence, the injury-producing agency or instrumentality is in the exclusive control of the defendant, and the plaintiff did not contribute to the injury. The Leins conceded during their motion for summary judgment before the trial court that Curtis was not at fault. The inquiry has since focused on the first two elements.

Taking the element of exclusive control first, the Leins argue that Curtis "failed to cite any legal authority in which courts have found that a wooden dock on a pond constitutes an 'instrumentality' and/or that ownership, alone, of the dock would be considered 'exclusive control' of such instrumentality." It cannot be seriously debated that the dock was not an injury-producing instrumentality in this instance. As for exclusive control, the Leins do not argue that anyone else had responsibility for the dock. The Leins have offered no evidence that the dock was not in their exclusive control prior to Curtis's accident.

That leaves the first element: whether an accident of this sort ordinarily occurs in the absence of negligence. As noted, the Court of Appeals concluded that docks do not normally give way if properly maintained, but Curtis still had to prove the dock had obvious defects. As explained, the latter half of this reasoning was in error. However, the Court of Appeals was correct when it reasoned that general experience tells us that wooden docks ordinarily do not give way if properly maintained. That is, "[i]n the general experience of mankind," the collapse of a portion of a dock "is an event that would not be expected without negligence on someone's part."

The trial court concluded that res ipsa loquitur did not apply because "there are multiple other causes [than negligence] which could have caused the failure of the step on the dock," such as improper construction or defective wood. This analysis misses the mark. A plaintiff claiming res ipsa loquitur is "not required to 'eliminate with certainty all other possible causes or inferences' in order for res ipsa loquitur to apply." Instead, "res ipsa loquitur is inapplicable where there is evidence that is completely explanatory of how an accident occurred and no other inference is possible that the injury occurred another way." The rationale behind this rule lies in the fact that res ipsa loquitur provides an inference of negligence.

> [T]he res ipsa loquitur doctrine allows the plaintiff to establish a prima facie case of negligence when he cannot prove a specific act of negligence because he is not in a situation where he would have knowledge of that specific act. Once the plaintiff establishes a prima facie case, the defendant must then offer an explanation, if he can. " 'If then, after considering such explanation, on the whole case and on all the issues as to negligence, injury and damages, the evidence still preponderates in favor of the plaintiff, plaintiff is entitled to recover; otherwise not.' "

As with any other permissive evidentiary inference, a jury is free to disregard or accept the truth of the inference. The fact that the defendant may offer reasons other than negligence for the accident or occurrence merely presents to the jury alternatives that negate the strength of the inference of negligence res ipsa loquitur provides. The trial court therefore erred when it concluded that res ipsa loquitur was inapplicable as a matter of law due to the possibility that reasons other than negligence accounted for the dock's collapse.

In sum, Curtis has shown each of the elements necessary for relying upon res ipsa loquitur in a jury trial: (1) she has shown the accident is of a type that would not ordinarily happen in the absence of negligence because general experience counsels that properly maintained wooden docks do not give way under foot; (2) there is no evidence before us that the dock was not in the exclusive control of the Leins; and (3) it is uncontested that Curtis herself did not contribute in any way to the accident. We therefore hold that Curtis may rely upon res ipsa loquitur in presenting her case to a jury. Whether the inference of negligence arising from res ipsa loquitur will be convincing to a jury is a question to be answered by that jury.

Conclusion

The injury here was caused by an event that would not normally happen in the absence of negligence, and the Leins have not shown they did not have exclusive control of the dock. Thus, the elements at issue for application of res ipsa loquitur to this case are satisfied. We reverse the trial court and the Court of Appeals, and remand this case for trial.

PREPARING FOR CLASS

1. Isn't it likely that the jurors have little or no experience maintaining a dock? If that is the case, how can they determine whether certain facts are associated with negligent maintenance of a dock?

2. "The Leins had the dock destroyed shortly after the accident." Does this affect the application of res ipsa loquitur? Should it?

3. The Court of Appeals thought there was not enough evidence that the Leins had notice of the defective condition of the dock. How was this requirement shown in the Washington Supreme Court?

INCREASING YOUR UNDERSTANDING

1. Res ipsa loquitur depends upon a conclusion that the "injury is of a type that would not ordinarily result if the defendant were not negligent." It is a matter of probabilities that when this event occurs, it is usually caused by negligence. It is easy to confuse this requirement with the fact that the event is unusual. For instance, it is unusual for a baby to die when the child is lying alone in a crib, but that event does not suggest negligence on the part of the parents. On the other hand, it is unusual for doctors or nurses to leave a sponge in a patient after an operation, but this is an event that is associated with negligence.

2. Res ipsa loquitur cases are different than a circumstantial evidence case. Circumstantial evidence is used to show indirectly specifically what happened in a case. For instance, skid marks and metal testing may be used to show the speed of a car at the time of impact and prior to impact. That is circumstantial evidence of negligence, but the evidence points to a specific theory of what the defendant did wrong. In the case of the Lein's dock, there is no evidence pointing specifically to the Lein's negligence. This is a case where the court is willing to proceed without specificity of just what the Leins did wrong.

3. Most res ipsa loquitur cases deal with an instrument of harm. The defendant has control of an instrument of harm that causes an accident. But not all res ipsa loquitur cases fit that mode. Sometimes the defendant is a caretaker or custodian, like a day care center, a surgeon, or a nursing home attendant, who fails to protect the defendant. Res ipsa loquitur is sometimes applied in those circumstances. See Dan Dobbs, The Law of Torts, p. 375.

4. Res ipsa loquitur, in most jurisdictions, permits a jury to find negligence. It does not require that conclusion but only furnishes a permissible inference of negligence when the specificity of the defendant's conduct cannot be shown. So, res ipsa loquitur gets the plaintiff past a motion for summary disposition and a motion for directed verdict, even when the plaintiff cannot show specifically what the defendant did.

APPLYING THE LAW

1. On the day before Easter, John woke in his mobile home to find that there was no heat, i.e., the furnace was not working. John had to go to work, so he called Mel's Heating. John told Mel's about his heating problem and asked them to take a look at it as soon as possible. Someone from Mel's Heating called John around 11 A.M. and told John that he had been to his mobile home and fixed the furnace. Later that afternoon, John got a call from the Fire Marshall, who told him that his mobile home was burning. John's mobile home and its contents were a total loss. John sued Mel's for his loss. At the trial, the worker from Mel's testified that he went to John's home and performed the required work on John's furnace in a proper and workman like manner. John had no more specific evidence than his mobile home burned down approximately 3 hours after the worker from Mel's left. Mel's has moved to dismiss the case. How should the court rule? Can a court reject the sworn testimony of Mel's worker that he did nothing wrong? Explain.

2. Cattle ran onto the highway in a rural area and caused an auto accident. The occupants of the car want to sue the farmer/owner of the cattle for his negligence in allowing the cattle to escape. The farmer testifies to extensive maintenance of the fence around the cattle. No one can find where the cattle escaped. Will res ipsa loquitur be applied in a rural court against the farmer?

Morgan v. Children's Hospital
480 N.E.2d 464 (Ohio 1985)

On August 3, 1978, plaintiff-appellant Jerome Morgan (hereinafter "appellant") underwent a surgical procedure known as a thymectomy, the removal of the thymus gland, as treatment for myasthenia gravis, a rare muscle disease. The thymus gland is located under the sternum. The operation involved the opening of appellant's chest and splitting the sternum to reach the gland.

Appellant's general anesthesia was administered by defendant-appellee, Dr. John Garvin, and his agent, Jean Marshall, a certified registered nurse anesthetist. The anesthesia was introduced at 12:30 P.M. and the chart Marshall kept during the operation shows that appellant's vital signs remained normal until approximately 1:45 P.M. At 1:45, appellant's rate of respiration increased from twenty breaths per minute to forty breaths per minute. Marshall administered succinylcholine to paralyze appellant's muscles and demerol for the pain. These drugs prevented appellant from breathing on his own. The drugs were administered because the increase in the respiration rate showed that pain was penetrating the anesthetized level of the patient. With appellant's muscles paralyzed, Marshall was required to breathe for appellant by squeezing a bag which forced oxygen and anesthetic into his lungs.

At 2:40 P.M., as Dr. Catalano, the surgical resident, was closing appellant's chest, bradycardia, a slowing of appellant's heart rate, occurred. There is conflicting testimony in the record between Dr. Catalano and Marshall as to exactly when the bradycardia was noticed. However, after such condition was noticed, Dr. Catalano administered closed cardiac massage, followed by open cardiac massage, while an anesthesiologist, one of appellee's associates, and the nurse anesthetist administered drugs to speed the heart rate and stabilize the heart muscle.

Dr. Catalano again closed the chest and appellant was taken to the intensive care unit at approximately 3:20 P.M. While in the intensive care unit appellant suffered grand mal seizures. Appellant never awoke from the anesthesia and, at the time of trial, remained in a comatose, vegetative state from which he is never expected to emerge. At the time of his operation appellant was twelve years old.

The expert witnesses agree that the appellant suffered diffused or global brain damage as a result of oxygen deprivation (hypoxic encephalopathy). However, appellants' expert witnesses asserted the oxygen deprivation resulted from the failure of Marshall to adequately ventilate appellant, whereas appellee's expert witnesses explained the damage was caused by an air emboli or bubbles of air, which blocked the blood vessels carrying oxygen to the brain.

At trial, the appellants, Jerome and his mother, Geneva Morgan, requested an instruction to the jury on res ipsa loquitur. The trial court refused to give this instruction.

After presentation of all the evidence the jury returned a verdict for the appellee. Appellants appealed to the court of appeals which affirmed the trial court's decision rejecting the requested jury instruction on res ipsa loquitur. The appellate court reasoned that when expert testimony is required, as in this case, the jury may not be instructed on res ipsa loquitur since the lay person cannot "as a matter of common knowledge" tell that the injury is one which does not normally occur if due care had been exercised.

CLIFFORD F. BROWN, Justice.

It must be noted at the outset of this opinion that the doctrine of res ipsa loquitur is only a rule of evidence which allows the trier of fact to draw an inference of negligence from the facts presented. The trier of facts is permitted, but not compelled, to find negligence.[1] This rule is set forth in *Jennings Buick, Inc. v. Cincinnati.*

"The doctrine of res ipsa loquitur is not a substantive rule of law furnishing an independent ground for recovery; rather, it is an evidentiary rule which permits, but does not require, the jury to draw an inference of negligence when the logical premises for the inference are demonstrated. . . .

"The doctrine of res ipsa loquitur does not alter the nature of the plaintiff's claim in a negligence action; it is merely a method of proving the defendant's negligence through the use of circumstantial evidence. The only way in which a defendant might conceivably be prejudiced by the invocation of the doctrine is where only a specific allegation of negligence is pleaded, and the inference to be drawn from the plaintiff's proof is inconsistent with the theory of negligence set forth in the complaint. . . ."

The two prerequisites which must be met to warrant an instruction to the jury on res ipsa loquitur, which have been set forth by this court in Hake v. Wiedemann Brewing Co. (1970), 262 N.E.2d 703 [52 O.O.2d 366], are as follows:

"To warrant application of the rule a plaintiff must adduce evidence in support of two conclusions: (1) that the instrumentality causing the injury was, at the time of the injury, or at the time of the creation of the condition causing the injury, under the exclusive management and control of the defendant; and (2) that the injury occurred under such circumstances that in the ordinary course of events it would not have occurred if ordinary care had been observed."

In the present case appellants assert that the instrumentality causing the injury to Jerome Morgan was the failure of appellee's agent to properly ventilate the appellant during the operation. This alleged failure caused oxygen deprivation to the brain, thereby resulting in the injuries which appellant suffered causing his present vegetative state. The appellate court in this case concluded that even if the appellants are presumed to have met the first prerequisite for the instruction of res ipsa loquitur, that they are unable to meet the second prerequisite because it is essential in a medical malpractice case that expert testimony be used to establish the standard of ordinary care. Therefore, the court reasoned that the doctrine of res ipsa loquitur cannot be applied in medical malpractice cases because a lay person cannot say "as a

---

1. See Prosser & Keeton, Law of Torts (5 Ed. 1985) 257-258, Section 40, which reads in pertinent part:

"In the ordinary case, absent special circumstances or some special relation between the parties, the great majority of the American courts regard res ipsa loquitur as no more than one form of circumstantial evidence. 'Where there is no direct evidence to show cause of injury, and the circumstantial evidence indicates that the negligence of the defendant is the most plausible explanation for the injury, the doctrine applies.' The inference of negligence to be drawn from the circumstances is left to the jury. They are permitted, but not compelled to find it. The plaintiff escapes a nonsuit, or a dismissal of his case since there is sufficient evidence to go to the jury; but the burden of proof is not shifted to the defendant's shoulders nor is any 'burden' of introducing evidence usually cast upon the defendant except in the very limited sense that if he fails to do so, he runs the risk that the jury may very well find against him."

matter of common knowledge" that the injury is one which would not have ordinarily occurred in the course of events had ordinary care been observed.

The appellate court, relying on *Yandrich v. Blair*, sets forth a rigid rule that when expert testimony is necessary to explain that an injury is the result of a lack of due care, then the injury does not speak for itself. Such a rigid rule excludes the doctrine of res ipsa loquitur from nearly all medical malpractice cases.

The reasoning of the lower court concerning res ipsa loquitur in medical malpractice cases is not compelling. Numerous other jurisdictions when faced with this same question have found that expert testimony can be used in medical malpractice cases to establish that the injury occurred under such circumstances that in the ordinary course of events it would not have occurred if ordinary care had been observed, thereby allowing an instruction on res ipsa loquitur to be given to the jury.

This court enunciated in *Oberlin v. Friedman* the proposition that the underlying circumstances necessary to sustain a request for a res ipsa loquitur instruction to a jury may be established by expert testimony. This court set forth three basic rules to be utilized in making such a determination on the application of res ipsa loquitur in medical malpractice cases.

First, the doctrine cannot be "based solely upon the fact that the treatment was unsuccessful or terminated with poor or unfortunate results." Second, the doctrine applies "only where the instrumentality causing the injury was under the exclusive management and control of the defendant." Third, the plaintiff's offering of evidence to prove specific acts of negligence does not preclude the application of the doctrine of res ipsa loquitur if there is proof presented in support of application of the doctrine. Thus, even though the appellants have presented expert testimony as to possible specific acts of negligence on the part of appellee or appellee's agents, such offerings would not preclude the instruction of res ipsa loquitur if otherwise justified by the circumstantial evidence adduced at trial.

The use of expert testimony in a medical malpractice case to establish that the injury occurred under such circumstances that in the ordinary course of events it would not have occurred if ordinary care had been observed does not disqualify such case from the application of the doctrine of res ipsa loquitur. See Note, Malpractice and Medical Testimony (1963), 77 Harv. L. Rev. 333, 349, which states in pertinent part: "While lay knowledge is normally insufficient to say that the injury indicates negligence, it does not follow that expert knowledge is similarly incapacitated. Much as the courts have implemented the malpractice standard of care through expert testimony, the court can adapt res ipsa loquitur to malpractice by requiring expert testimony that the injury bespeaks negligence."

The appellee also argues that res ipsa loquitur is inapplicable in the present case because he has presented evidence which rebuts the inference of appellee's negligence. This evidence is embodied in the defense theory of an air embolism which caused the oxygen deprivation to appellant's brain. It is a well-established principle that a court may not refuse as a matter of law to instruct on the doctrine of res ipsa loquitur merely upon the basis that the defendant's evidence sufficiently rebuts the making of such an inference. In addition, this court made quite clear in *Fink v. New York Central RR. Co.* (1944), when we stated in paragraph three of the syllabus that:

"The trial court, in a jury trial, in a case which calls for the application of the rule of res ipsa loquitur, is without authority to declare, as a matter of law, that the inference of negligence which the jury is permitted to draw, has been rebutted or destroyed by an explanation of the circumstances offered by the defendant, and such action on the part of the trial court is an invasion of the province of the jury."

Because of the error in not applying the doctrine of res ipsa loquitur to the facts presented in the present case we are compelled to reverse the judgment of the court of appeals and remand this cause to the trial court for a new trial.

Judgment reversed and cause remanded.

CELEBREZZE, C.J., and SWEENEY and DOUGLAS, JJ., concur.

LOCHER, HOLMES and WRIGHT, JJ., dissent.

HOLMES, Justice, dissenting.

I dissent herein because a reading of the record readily establishes that the evidence adduced at trial does not warrant the trial court giving a jury instruction on the doctrine of res ipsa loquitur. The majority opinion quite accurately summarizes the law applicable to the doctrine of res ipsa loquitur by citing *Jennings Buick, Inc. v. Cincinnati* (1980), but, unfortunately misapplies the law in relation to the evidence adduced by both parties in this case. Case law dictates that two vital elements must first be established by the evidence before a party can avail itself of the doctrine. It must be demonstrated that at the time of the injury, the instrumentality or the occurrence which produced the injury was under the exclusive management and control of the defendant. Second, it must be established that the injury would not have occurred in the absence of negligence.

In my view, neither element was firmly established within the presentation of this case for various reasons. First, although recognizing that the anesthesia equipment was under the exclusive control of the defendant, it was not established that this instrumentality, or its use, actually produced the injury. Second, and intertwined with the first, the evidence was insufficient to prove that the injury would not have occurred in the absence of negligence.

In Jennings, this court cited with approval *Loomis v. Toledo Railways & Light Co.* (1923), as follows:

"'The maxim res ipsa loquitur ... does not apply where there is direct evidence as to the cause, or where the facts are such that an inference that the accident was due to a cause other than defendant's negligence could be drawn as reasonably as that it was due to his negligence'. . ."

The issue involved within this appeal is whether the plaintiffs have offered an evidentiary foundation at trial to warrant submission of the res ipsa loquitur doctrine to the jury. I submit that the plaintiffs have not done so.

At trial, each expert witness questioned on the subject agreed that a number of causes exist for a global hypoxia such as that suffered by Jerome Morgan. Dr. Eric Grossman, the first of plaintiffs' anesthesia experts, agreed that anything which prevents oxygenated blood from reaching the brain cells would produce hypoxia, including an obstruction in the small arteries of the brain itself. Dr. David Bachman, a neurologist, mentioned four possible conditions which could have occasioned the injury, i.e., (1) heart stoppage, (2) stoppage of breathing or lung failure, (3) drop in blood pressure providing insufficient blood to brain, and (4) blockage of the blood vessels to the brain by clot, or air, or other emboli. There is no testimony presented from any of the expert witnesses which disputed Dr. Bachman's analysis of these possibilities.

Further testimony adduced by both the plaintiffs and the defendant then narrowed the four possibilities down to two probabilities. The plaintiffs' anesthesia experts, Dr. Grossman and Dr. Mervyn Jeffries, testified that in their opinion the damage to the patient had been occasioned by under-ventilation, and they attributed this occurrence to the failure of the nurse-anesthetist to squeeze the breathing bag on the anesthesia machine for a period of time. In my view, this portion of the record does not reflect that these expert witnesses testified that the injuries could not have occurred without negligence. The plaintiffs' witnesses were merely testifying to the effect that although there may have been other possible causes for the injury, it was their expert opinion that the most probable cause was the underventilation occasioned by the nurse's failure to squeeze the bulb of the equipment.

In response to the testimony advanced by the plaintiffs' witnesses, the defendant called two anesthesia experts, Dr. John D. Michenfelder and Dr. William Hamelberg. Both of these physicians testified that in their opinion the most probable cause of the injury was the remaining potential mechanism, an obstruction of the arteries to the brain. Dr. Michenfelder stated that in his opinion Jerome Morgan was, for a significant period of time, subjected to an unrecognizable, but ongoing, air embolism, whereby an amount of air entered his circulation through his surgical wound and traveled to his brain, obstructing the small arteries of the brain with air and thus producing the brain damage. Dr. Hamelberg agreed that the most likely cause of Jerome Morgan's brain damage was an air embolism to the arteries of the brain.

Given the state of the evidence in which both sides produced diametrically opposed expert opinions as to the specific cause of Jerome Morgan's injury, it would have been error for the trial court to have charged the jury on the doctrine of res ipsa loquitur. The doctrine is founded upon an absence of specific proof concerning acts or omissions which would constitute negligence. It also has been stated that the doctrine can only be applied when the "thing speaks for itself." Here, as noted, there was evidence adduced by the plaintiff relating to the defendant's negligence. Also, Jerome Morgan's injury cannot be deemed to speak for itself where complex technical and medical testimony was required to explain the result, and which evidence produced conflicting opinions as to the more probable cause of the injury.

It became a jury question to choose the more probable cause of the injury and, after considering all of such evidence, the jury did just that, accepting the defendant's theory that the injury was occasioned by some embolism and apparently rejecting the plaintiff's theory of underventilation. To have submitted this case to the jury accompanied with the charge of res ipsa loquitur would have invited the lay jury to speculate on some alternative theory concerning the injury not suggested by the evidence of either party. Such application of the utilization of the doctrine of res ipsa loquitur would be an allowance of an inference of negligence based simply upon the occurrence of an unfortunate medical result. This court has not only frowned upon but prohibited the utilization of the doctrine in such a manner in *Oberlin v. Friedman* (1965), where paragraph three of the syllabus states:

"Generally, the doctrine of res ipsa loquitur is not applicable in malpractice actions in which its claimed applicability is based solely upon the fact that the treatment was unsuccessful or terminated with poor or unfortunate results."

This court should continue to prohibit the use of the doctrine under circumstances as presented by this case.

Accordingly, I would affirm the court of appeals.

Locher and Wright, JJ., concur in the foregoing dissenting opinion.

PREPARING FOR CLASS

1. How would the majority respond to the dissent, i.e., where is the proof that the anesthesia equipment caused the injury, and where is the proof that the injury would not have occurred in the absence of negligence?

2. The plaintiff does not complain of a summary disposition or a directed verdict but rather complains about the trial court's failure to give a jury instruction. There are many jury instructions in a negligence case; do you think that the failure to give an instruction on the use of this evidence could have been so prejudicial that the plaintiff is entitled to try the case over again?

3. If you were the plaintiff's attorney in this case, what questions would you ask a medical expert to establish res ipsa loquitur? Would your medical expert have to cite statistical studies to justify his or her opinion?

INCREASING YOUR UNDERSTANDING

1. One of the difficult questions in applying res ipsa loquitur to medical malpractice cases is when the medical procedure confronts a known but worthwhile and uncontrollable risk. Thus when the adverse but rare result comes about, the courts should not apply res ipsa loquitur.

2. Most medical malpractice res ipsa loquitur cases require expert medical opinion. But there are some medical errors that are so apparent that the courts have not required an expert opinion. When the surgeon leaves a sponge inside the patient's body or when the patient is injured in a part of the body that was not operated on, the courts have been willing to apply res ipsa loquitur without the necessity of an expert opinion.

APPLYING THE LAW

1. Following surgery, a patient acquires a rare bacterial infection that causes serious injury to the patient. A doctor testifies that those infections rarely occur. Should the court apply res ipsa loquitur? What, if any, further evidence is required?

2. An expert in a medical malpractice case testifies that the injury in this case is usually caused by the wrong method of treatment. Is this enough to justify the application of res ipsa loquitur?

D. IDENTIFYING THE RESPONSIBLE PARTY

Ybarra v. Spangard
154 P.2d 687 (Cal. 1945)

GIBSON, Chief Justice.

This is an action for damages for personal injuries alleged to have been inflicted on plaintiff by defendants during the course of a surgical operation. The trial court entered judgments of nonsuit as to all defendants and plaintiff appealed.

On October 28, 1939, plaintiff consulted defendant Dr. Tilley, who diagnosed his ailment as appendicitis, and made arrangements for an appendectomy to be performed by defendant Dr. Spangard at a hospital owned and managed by defendant Dr. Swift. Plaintiff entered the hospital, was given a hypodermic injection, slept, and later was awakened by Drs. Tilley and Spangard and wheeled into the operating room by a nurse whom he believed to be

defendant Gisler, an employee of Dr. Swift. Defendant Dr. Reser, the anesthetist, also an employee of Dr. Swift, adjusted plaintiff for the operation, pulling his body to the head of the operating table and, according to plaintiff's
testimony, laying him back against two hard objects at the top of his shoulders,
about an inch below his neck. Dr. Reser then administered the anesthetic and
plaintiff lost consciousness. When he awoke early the following morning he
was in his hospital room attended by defendant Thompson, the special nurse,
and another nurse who was not made a defendant.

Plaintiff testified that prior to the operation he had never had any pain in, or
injury to, his right arm or shoulder, but that when he awakened he felt a sharp
pain about half way between the neck and the point of the right shoulder. He
complained to the nurse, and then to Dr. Tilley, who gave him diathermy
treatments while he remained in the hospital. The pain did not cease but
spread down to the lower part of his arm, and after his release from the hospital
the condition grew worse. He was unable to rotate or lift his arm, and developed paralysis and atrophy of the muscles around the shoulder. He received
further treatments from Dr. Tilley until March, 1940, and then returned to
work, wearing his arm in a splint on the advice of Dr. Spangard.

Plaintiff also consulted Dr. Wilfred Sterling Clark, who had X-ray pictures
taken which showed an area of diminished sensation below the shoulder and
atrophy and wasting away of the muscles around the shoulder. In the opinion
of Dr. Clark, plaintiff's condition was due to trauma or injury by pressure or
strain applied between his right shoulder and neck.

Plaintiff was also examined by Dr. Fernando Garduno, who expressed the
opinion that plaintiff's injury was a paralysis of traumatic origin, not arising
from pathological causes, and not systemic, and that the injury resulted in
atrophy, loss of use and restriction of motion of the right arm and shoulder.

Plaintiff's theory is that the foregoing evidence presents a proper case for the
application of the doctrine of res ipsa loquitur, and that the inference of negligence arising therefrom makes the granting of as nonsuit improper. Defendants take the position that, assuming that plaintiff's condition was in fact the
result of an injury, there is no showing that the act of any particular defendant,
nor any particular instrumentality, was the cause thereof. They attack plaintiff's action as an attempt to fix liability "en masse" on various defendants, some
of whom were not responsible for the acts of others; and they further point to
the failure to show which defendants had control of the instrumentalities that
may have been involved. Their main defense may be briefly stated in two
propositions: (1) that where there are several defendants, and there is a division
of responsibility in the use of an instrumentality causing the injury, and the
injury might have resulted from the separate act of either one of two or more
persons, the rule of res ipsa loquitur cannot be invoked against any one of
them; and (2) that where there are several instrumentalities, and no showing
is made as to which caused the injury or as to the particular defendant in
control of it, the doctrine cannot apply. We are satisfied, however, that
these objections are not well taken in the circumstances of this case.

The doctrine of res ipsa loquitur has three conditions: "(1) the accident must be of a kind which ordinarily does not occur in the absence of someone's negligence; (2) it must be caused by an agency or instrumentality within the exclusive control of the defendant; (3) it must not have been due to any voluntary action or contribution on the part of the plaintiff." It is applied in a wide variety of situations, including cases of medical or dental treatment and hospital care.

There is, however, some uncertainty as to the extent to which res ipsa loquitur may be invoked in cases of injury from medical treatment. This is in part due to the tendency, in some decisions, to lay undue emphasis on the limitations of the doctrine, and to give too little attention to its basic underlying purpose. The result has been that a simple, understandable rule of circumstantial evidence, with a sound background of common sense and human experience, has occasionally been transformed into a rigid legal formula, which arbitrarily precludes its application in many cases where it is most important that it should be applied. If the doctrine is to continue to serve a useful purpose, we should not forget that "the particular force and justice of the rule, regarded as a presumption throwing upon the party charged the duty of producing evidence, consists in the circumstance that the chief evidence of the true cause, whether culpable or innocent, is practically accessible to him but inaccessible to the injured person." In the last-named case, where an unconscious patient in a hospital received injuries from a fall, the court declared that without the doctrine the maxim that for every wrong there is a remedy would be rendered nugatory, "by denying one, patently entitled to damages, satisfaction merely because he is ignorant of facts peculiarly within the knowledge of the party who should, in all justice, pay them."

The present case is of a type which comes within the reason and spirit of the doctrine more fully perhaps than any other. The passenger sitting awake in a railroad car at the time of a collision, the pedestrian walking along the street and struck by a falling object or the debris of an explosion, are surely not more entitled to an explanation than the unconscious patient on the operating table. Viewed from this aspect, it is difficult to see how the doctrine can, with any justification, be so restricted in its statement as to become inapplicable to a patient who submits himself to the care and custody of doctors and nurses, is rendered unconscious, and receives some injury from instrumentalities used in his treatment. Without the aid of the doctrine a patient who received permanent injuries of a serious character, obviously the result of some one's negligence, would be entirely unable to recover unless the doctors and nurses in attendance voluntarily chose to disclose the identity of the negligent person and the facts establishing liability. If this were the state of the law of negligence, the courts, to avoid gross injustice, would be forced to invoke the principles of absolute liability, irrespective of negligence, in actions by persons suffering injuries during the course of treatment under anesthesia. But we think this juncture has not yet been reached, and that the doctrine of res ipsa loquitur is properly applicable to the case before us.

The condition that the injury must not have been due to the plaintiff's voluntary action is of course fully satisfied under the evidence produced herein; and the same is true of the condition that the accident must be one which ordinarily does not occur unless some one was negligent. We have here no problem of negligence in treatment, but of distinct injury to a healthy part of the body not the subject of treatment, nor within the area covered by the operation. The decisions in this state make it clear that such circumstances raise the inference of negligence and call upon the defendant to explain the unusual result.

The argument of defendants is simply that plaintiff has not shown an injury caused by an instrumentality under a defendant's control, because he has not shown which of the several instrumentalities that he came in contact with while in the hospital caused the injury; and he has not shown that any one defendant or his servants had exclusive control over any particular instrumentality. Defendants assert that some of them were not the employees of other defendants, that some did not stand in any permanent relationship from which liability in tort would follow, and that in view of the nature of the injury, the number of defendants and the different functions performed by each, they could not all be liable for the wrong, if any.

We have no doubt that in a modern hospital a patient is quite likely to come under the care of a number of persons in different types of contractual and other relationships with each other. For example, in the present case it appears that Drs. Smith, Spangard and Tilley were physicians or surgeons commonly placed in the legal category of independent contractors; and Dr. Reser, the anesthetist, and defendant Thompson, the special nurse, were employees of Dr. Swift and not of the other doctors. But we do not believe that either the number or relationship of the defendants alone determines whether the doctrine of res ipsa loquitur applies. Every defendant in whose custody the plaintiff was placed for any period was bound to exercise ordinary care to see that no unnecessary harm came to him and each would be liable for failure in this regard. Any defendant who negligently injured him, and any defendant charged with his care who so neglected him as to allow injury to occur, would be liable. The defendant employers would be liable for the neglect of their employees; and the doctor in charge of the operation would be liable for the negligence of those who became his temporary servants for the purpose of assisting in the operation.

In this connection, it should be noted that while the assisting physicians and nurses may be employed by the hospital, or engaged by the patient, they normally become the temporary servants or agents of the surgeon in charge while the operation is in progress, and liability may be imposed upon him for their negligent acts under the doctrine of respondeat superior. Thus a surgeon has been held liable for the negligence of an assisting nurse who leaves a sponge or other object inside a patient, and the fact that the duty of seeing that such mistakes do not occur is delegated to others does not absolve the doctor from responsibility for their negligence.

It may appear at the trial that, consistent with the principles outlined above, one or more defendants will be found liable and others absolved, but this should not preclude the application of the rule of res ipsa loquitur. The control at one time or another, of one or more of the various agencies or instrumentalities which might have harmed the plaintiff was in the hands of every defendant or of his employees or temporary servants. This, we think, places upon them the burden of initial explanation. Plaintiff was rendered unconscious for the purpose of undergoing surgical treatment by the defendants; it is manifestly unreasonable for them to insist that he identify any one of them as the person who did the alleged negligent act.

The other aspect of the case which defendants so strongly emphasize is that plaintiff has not identified the instrumentality any more than he has the particular guilty defendant. Here, again, there is a misconception which, if carried to the extreme for which defendants contend, would unreasonably limit the application of the res ipsa loquitur rule. It should be enough that the plaintiff can show an injury resulting from an external force applied while he lay unconscious in the hospital; this is as clear a case of identification of the instrumentality as the plaintiff may ever be able to make.

An examination of the recent cases, particularly in this state, discloses that the test of actual exclusive control of an instrumentality has not been strictly followed, but exceptions have been recognized where the purpose of the doctrine of res ipsa loquitur would otherwise be defeated. Thus, the test has become one of right of control rather than actual control. In the bursting bottle cases where the bottler has delivered the instrumentality to a retailer and thus has given up actual control, he will nevertheless be subject to the doctrine where it is shown that no change in the condition of the bottle occurred after it left the bottler's possession, and it can accordingly be said that he was in constructive control Moreover, this court departed from the single instrumentality theory in the colliding vehicle cases, where two defendants were involved, each in control of a separate vehicle. Finally, it has been suggested that the hospital cases may properly be considered exceptional, and that the doctrine of res ipsa loquitur "should apply with equal force in cases wherein medical and nursing staffs take the place of machinery and may, through carelessness or lack of skill, inflict, or permit the infliction of injury upon a patient who is thereafter in no position to say how he received his injuries."

In the face of these examples of liberalization of the tests for res ipsa loquitur, there can be no justification for the rejection of the doctrine in the instant case. As pointed out above, if we accept the contention of defendants herein, there will rarely be any compensation for patients injured while unconscious. A hospital today conducts a highly integrated system of activities, with many persons contributing their efforts. There may be, e.g., preparation for surgery by nurses and interns who are employees of the hospital; administering of an anesthetic by a doctor who may be an employee of the hospital, an employee of the operating surgeon, or an independent contractor;

performance of an operation by a surgeon and assistants who may be his employees, employees of the hospital, or independent contractors; and post surgical care by the surgeon, a hospital physician, and nurses. The number of those in whose care the patient is placed is not a good reason for denying him all reasonable opportunity to recover for negligent harm. It is rather a good reason for re-examination of the statement of legal theories which supposedly compel such a shocking result.

We do not at this time undertake to state the extent to which the reasoning of this case may be applied to other situations in which the doctrine of res ipsa loquitur is invoked. We merely hold that where a plaintiff receives unusual injuries while unconscious and in the course of medical treatment, all those defendants who had any control over his body or the instrumentalities which might have caused the injuries may properly be called upon to meet the inference of negligence by giving an explanation of their conduct.

The judgment is reversed.

PREPARING FOR CLASS

1. The final sentence of the opinion places the burden "to meet the inference of negligence" on all those "who had control over his body." How will the plaintiff's counsel establish who has control over the plaintiff's body? If the plaintiff/patient is conscious throughout the operation on her knee, does anyone have control over her body? Who has control over her body if the patient is put under general anesthesia for an operation on the patient's throat?

2. The opinion also places a burden "to meet the inference of negligence" on all those who had control over the instrumentality that "might" have caused the injury. Aren't there a lot of instruments that might cause injury? What instrument "might" have caused harm in the *Ybarra* case? What is the burden to show that the instrument might have caused harm? The operating table might have caused harm, so is the hospital who owns and controls the table obligated to meet the inference of negligence?

3. There is also an element of this case, isn't there, that involves the obligation of all those who can observe the negligence to come forward and report what they saw? How significant is this requirement? What if there were medical student observers in the operating room; would they have a legal obligation to come forward with what they saw? Would they have to meet the inference of negligence?

4. The opinion says that assisting physicians and nurses "engaged by the patient" would become the "temporary servants or agents" of the surgeon. Is that fair? What if there is more than one surgeon?

INCREASING YOUR UNDERSTANDING

1. This opinion also talks about a doctrine sometimes known as the "captain-of-the-ship" doctrine, which would make the chief surgeon responsible for the negligence of all others in the operating room regardless of the surgeon's fault. The surgeon would be vicariously liable, i.e., liable regardless of fault. Notice that this would not hold the nurse or anesthesiologist liable, so they would not have to meet any inference of negligence.

2. There is another vicarious liability doctrine closely analogous to the captain-of-the-ship doctrine. Many courts hold that the provision of medical services in the operating room is a "non-delegable duty" and the hospital is liable for the negligence of all of the health care providers in the operating room, including its employees and independent contractors. This doctrine makes the hospital liable but does not put a burden on any of the doctors or nurses to come forward with an explanation.

APPLYING THE LAW

1. The Simpson Elementary School P.T.A. asked mothers and fathers to bake chocolate chip cookies for the school bake sale. The cookies were baked by ten parents in their homes, mixed together at the school, and sold at the P.T.A. sale? Twelve out of 200 of the cookies were not adequately baked and caused food poisoning. Those who suffered poisoning were seriously injured and want to sue each of the ten parents since the school P.T.A. has immunity from suit. Will the *Ybarra* case require the parents to meet "an inference of negligence"? Explain.

2. John went to an outpatient center for a colonoscopy. When he arrived, he was greeted by an admitting nurse who had John fill out a number of forms for the procedure. John then went to the pre-operating room where two nurses took his clothes, hooked him to an IV tube, and talked to him until he was taken to the operating room. There was a doctor, an anesthetist, and a nurse in the operating room where John was put under general anesthesia and lost consciousness. John was taken to a post-op room where he was attended by two nurses and recovered consciousness after about ten minutes. John was taken home by his wife but discovered a severe burn on his lower leg when he got home. The burn required surgery and further hospitalization. Who will have the burden of meeting "an inference of negligence"?

Chapter 6

Negligence—Breach of Duty as a Matter of Law

A. INTRODUCTION

Who determines whether the defendant's activities pose too much risk and are, therefore, negligent? That is one of the fundamental questions of negligence law. Most of the time, the parties have a right to a have a jury make that determination as a matter of fact. But sometimes the appellate court will determine as a matter of law what the reasonable person would do in a particular situation, and sometimes the legislature will pass a statute setting forth what a reasonable person would do. When that happens, there are a number of significant issues.

Hypothetical

Terry was driving home at night when his vehicle collided with a horse that ran into the road. The horse had escaped from its corral and wandered into the road. The horse and corral were owned by Simon, a local farmer. A municipal ordinance provides:

> No person owning or keeping any animal, other than an ordinary domesticated house cat, shall fail to keep said animal on the premises of the owner or keeper unless the animal is:
>
> A. On a leash, cord or chain held by a person who is physically able to control the animal; or
>
> B. Within a vehicle, or similarly physically confined, and without access to passers-by.

Simon says that he had a hayride for local school children the night of the accident and believes that one of the children must have gone into the corral to pet the horse and failed to properly latch it when he left. Simon has checked the corral and gate and has not found any holes in the corral or problems with latching the gate. Terry contends that the ordinance makes it a criminal offense to allow an animal to escape, therefore it must be negligence.

PREPARING FOR CLASS

1. Should this ordinance be used to establish a standard of care in a suit against Simon?

2. Should this ordinance establish negligence as a matter of law, or should the jury just take it into consideration when considering the standard of care?

3. What about Simon's excuse that the school children might have left the gate open? Could that excuse violation of the ordinance?

4. Does it make any difference that Simon is accused of violating an ordinance rather than a statute?

B. JUDGE-MADE RULES

Theisen v. Milwaukee Automobile Mutual Insurance Company
118 N.W.2d 140 (Wisc. 1963)

HALLOWS, Justice.

This is a case of a sleeping driver. On the evening of November 16th, 1960, the plaintiff and Shepherd participated in the Arcadia high school senior class play in which Shepherd had the leading role. The play was over about 10:15. The members of the cast and those associated with the production, numbering in all about 30, were invited to a party at the home of Alfred Service, father of one of the members of the cast. Service lived about seven miles west of Arcadia on Highway 95. After the play, the young folks went to a cafe in Arcadia, then to a dancehall and danced, and about midnight started for the Service home. Upon arriving there, the girls prepared a lunch. The party then went on a hayride for about an hour, and upon returning to the house, played the piano, danced and talked. Shepherd brought a fifth of liquor to the house. At the party, beer or sloe gin, or both, were consumed, but there is no evidence anyone became intoxicated. Some of the girls testified the liquor could not be felt or not very much, or made them tired or sleepy or drowsy. The only evidence concerning Shepherd's drinking is by one of the girls who said she saw him with a drink in his hand.

About 3:00 A.M. the party broke up and five girls, including the plaintiff, got into Shepherd's car for the ride home. The plaintiff sat in the rear left seat. These girls testified they were tired and one stated the car was warm which just naturally made them drowsy. About four miles from the Service home the Shepherd car, as it was traveling east toward Arcadia on a straight level stretch of Highway 95, gradually veered from its right lane to the left lane and onto the shoulder of the road. At this time, at least all the girls were asleep or dozing. When the car left the pavement, one of the girls in the front seat woke up and shouted, "Louis, lookout" but there was no reaction; she thought Louis was asleep. Another girl hollered "Louie" but Shepherd did not move. The car proceeded on its course 270 feet until it hit a large tree stump on the north side of the road about 10 feet from the edge of the blacktop.

Normally no harm will be done if one falls asleep reading the newspaper after dinner or this opinion. In the horse and buggy days, one might have fallen asleep while driving and the horse quite likely would have had enough horse sense to stop or even to take the driver home through habit and instinct quite safely. But falling asleep behind a wheel of an auto propelled by 200 or 300 mechanical horses having no horse sense is entirely a different matter in terms of your duty to others. We recently pointed out the increase in the frequency and in the seriousness of the consequences of automobile accidents today resulting from modern, high-powered vehicles. The increase in risks and hazards of driving an automobile on public highways demands greater skill and attention than 40 years ago. When one is under a duty to use care not to injure another, he cannot fulfill the duty by falling asleep.

We must approach a sleeping driver case on the premise the driver has the duty to stay awake while he drives and it is within his control either to stay awake, to cease driving, or not to drive at all when sleepy. Up to now no decision has gone beyond the limits of the well established rule that the fact the driver of an automobile goes to sleep while driving is a proper basis for an inference of negligence sufficient to make a prima facie case and support a verdict for recovery if no circumstances tending to excuse or justify such conduct are proven. The inference of negligence which arises from "sleeping at the wheel" is based on the judicial recognition that sleep ordinarily does not occur without some notice and to fall asleep while driving is the usual result of negligence in failing to heed the warning.

Whatever the medical and scientific basis may be for the inference, we find no justification in the common experience of mankind for one's falling asleep with his foot on the accelerator, his hands on the wheel and his auto transformed into an instrument of destruction. The process of falling asleep—normal and healthy sleep—is a matter of common experience and usually attended by premonitory warnings or is to be expected. Such warnings or reasonable expectations of sleep are especially accentuated when one is conscious of his duty to stay awake while driving and the failure to heed such warnings and permitting oneself to fall asleep while driving an automobile must be deemed negligence as a matter of law. If while driving a car one is in such a state of exhaustion that he falls asleep without any premonitory warning, he is chargeable with the knowledge of any ordinarily prudent man that such exhaustion is reasonably likely to cause sleep while driving. Although it has been argued the liability of a sleeping driver should be absolute on the grounds of an extra hazardous activity, we do not base our decision on that ground but hold that falling asleep at the wheel is negligence as a matter of law because no facts can exist which will justify, excuse or exculpate such negligence. The language in earlier Wisconsin cases that falling asleep while driving may be excusable is overruled.

We exclude from this holding those exceptional cases of loss of consciousness resulting from injury inflicted by an outside force or fainting or heart attack, epileptic seizure, or other illness which suddenly incapacitates the driver of an automobile and when the occurrence of such disability is not attended with sufficient warning or should not have been reasonably foreseen. When, however, such occurrence should have been reasonably foreseen, we have held the driver of a motor vehicle negligent as a matter of law, as in the sleep cases.

The party claiming the driver fell asleep while driving has the burden of proving the driver in fact fell asleep. If the evidence whether direct or by permissible inference, tends to establish the fact, such evidence casts a burden upon the party seeking to excuse the driver's loss of consciousness—the burden of showing the greater probability that the loss of consciousness is excusable on some nonactionable basis.

The trial court excluded an offer of proof made by the defendant which would have shown Shepherd was not an habitual user of alcoholic beverages and was physically exhausted from the loss of considerable sleep for some six weeks prior to the accident practicing for the play, getting to bed later than his normal bedtime and continuing his usual farm chores. It was not error of the trial court to reject this evidence offered to prove a justification for going to sleep. On the contrary, such proof would have tended to show Shepherd should have known, as a reasonable prudent man, he was likely to have fallen asleep. Such offer of proof, of course, is immaterial under our holding that falling asleep while driving is negligence as a matter of law.

PREPARING FOR CLASS

1. What does a jury do, if anything, after a court establishes what a reasonable person would do as a matter of law, i.e., what issues does the jury determine and what issues does the judge determine?

2. What are the advantages of determining what the reasonable person would do as a matter of law? What are the disadvantages? In Baltimore & Ohio R. Co. v. Goodman, 275 U.S. 66 (1927), Justice Oliver Wendell

Holmes said "the question of due care very generally is left to the jury. But we are dealing with a standard of conduct, and when the standard is clear it should be laid down once and for all by the courts." Justice Holmes then went on to hold that when a motorist approaches a train intersection and the intersection is partially blocked, "In such circumstances it seems to us that if a driver cannot be sure otherwise whether a train is dangerously near he must stop and get out of his vehicle, although obviously he will not often be required to do more than to stop and look." What do you think of that as a standard of conduct? What happens to the defendant who approaches a blocked train intersection, stops to look down the tracks, does not see an oncoming train, and is later struck by the train. Justice Cardozo took a dim view of this decision in Pokora v. Wabash Ry. Co., 292 U.S. 98, when he said "Standards of prudent conduct are declared at times by courts, but they are taken over from the facts of life. To get out of a vehicle and reconnoiter is an uncommon precaution, as everyday experience informs us. Besides being uncommon, it is very likely to be futile, and sometimes even dangerous." How does the *Pokora* case influence your view of a standard of care made by the judiciary? But is the standard of care set forth in the *Theisen* case uncommon, futile, or dangerous?

INCREASING YOUR UNDERSTANDING

1. How would this ruling affect the admissibility of evidence at the trial? What if the defendant claims that he was the only sober person at the house and another party goer needed medical attention, would that be admissible?

2. What if the defendant contends that he fell asleep for only a matter of seconds but that the car swerved because of horseplay in the car, which hit the steering wheel?

APPLYING THE LAW

1. Should the driver who fails to wear a seat belt be found to have negligently aggravated her injuries as a matter of law?

2. How does a rule that every defendant who falls asleep while driving assist the plaintiff in proving his case? Is this ruling ever a disadvantage to the plaintiff?

3. If you were an appellate court judge, would you rule that a driver who cannot stop his car within the range of his headlights is negligent as a matter of law?

C. VIOLATION OF STATUTE

Rains v. Bend of the River
124 S.W.3d 580 (Ct. App. Tenn. 2003)

William C. Koch, Jr.
This appeal involves an eighteen-year-old who committed suicide with his parents' .25 caliber handgun. The parents filed suit in the Circuit Court for Putnam County against the retailer who sold their son ammunition for the handgun shortly before his death. They later amended the complaint to seek loss of consortium damages for themselves and their son's surviving siblings. The trial court denied the retailer's motion for summary judgment regarding the wrongful death claims, as well as the retailer's motion to dismiss the loss of consortium claims. Thereafter, the trial court granted the retailer permission to seek a Tenn. R. App. P. 9 interlocutory appeal from its refusal to dismiss the wrongful death and loss of consortium claims. We granted permission to appeal and have now determined that the trial court erred by denying the retailer's Tenn. R. Civ. P. 56 and 12.02(6) motions because, based on the undisputed facts, the suicide was not reasonably foreseeable and was the independent, intervening cause of the young man's death.

I.

Aaron Rains was one of three children of Bobby Wayne Rains and Sandra Gail Rains. In July 1995, when he was sixteen, Mr. Rains and his parents moved from Mississippi to Cookeville, Tennessee. He made new friends, attended school, and, like many teenage boys, found a series of part-time jobs to earn some spending money. Mr. Rains was an active member of the local Police Explorers post and sang in his church's youth choir. He was also particularly close to his mother's older brother who worked as a deputy sheriff with the Putnam County Sheriff's Department and frequently rode with his uncle on patrol. Mr. Rains had aspirations to continue his education following high school and to pursue a career in either law enforcement or forestry.

Mr. Rains's father had always owned firearms and had taught his son to shoot at a young age. He forbade his son to use the firearms unless he was present to supervise. In addition to several rifles and shotguns, Mr. Rains's father owned a .25 caliber handgun that he had purchased while the family lived in Mississippi. He stored the handgun and the other weapons in a locked gun case in his home, and he kept the key to the gun case in his wife's jewelry box. Mr. Rains and his father had frequently used to the .25 caliber handgun and a .22 caliber rifle for target practice while they lived in Mississippi. They did not have target practice after moving to Cookeville because they lacked a suitable place to shoot.

Mr. Rains turned eighteen in mid-January 1997. At some point on July 16, 1997, Mr. Rains found the key to his father's gun case and removed the .25 caliber handgun. He closed and locked the case and then returned the key to his mother's jewelry box where he had found it. Then, he set out to find ammunition for the pistol because his father did not have any ammunition in the house. His first stop was the sporting goods department at a local K-Mart. He inquired about the minimum age for purchasing .25 caliber ammunition and was told that buyers of that ammunition must be at least twenty-one years old. Mr. Rains showed the clerk his driver's license and commented, "Oh, I'm only eighteen." Rather than purchasing the ammunition, Mr. Rains purchased a package of BBs and left K-Mart.

After leaving K-Mart, Mr. Rains drove to Bend of the River Shooting Supplies, a store in Cookeville selling firearms, shooting supplies, and ammunition. While at Bend of the River, Mr. Rains purchased a box of Winchester .25 ACP automatic caliber 50 gr. full metal jacket cartridges. The store clerk did not ask Mr. Rains for proof of his age and accepted Mr. Rains's personal check in the amount of $11.85 in payment for the ammunition. There is no evidence that Mr. Rains's conduct and demeanor while he was at Bend of the River were out of the ordinary.

Sometime later, either on July 16, 1997 or early July 17, 1997, Mr. Rains drove his car to Walker Hollow Road and parked. He loaded his parents' pistol with the ammunition he had purchased at Bend of the River and fatally shot himself. The box of ammunition bearing Bend of the River's price tag was found in his car. It is undisputed that Mr. Rains used the .25 caliber handgun and ammunition to commit suicide. It is equally undisputed that neither Mr. Rains's parents nor any other family members had any sort of warning that Mr. Rains was planning to take his own life. From all outward signs, he was a happy, well-adjusted young man.

Mr. Rains's mother and sister were away at a church camp on July 16, 1997. His father was not alarmed when Mr. Rains did not return home that evening. Nor was he concerned when he discovered that his .25 caliber handgun was missing from the gun case. However, on the morning of July 17, 1997, Mr. Rains's father called his brother-in-law to report that his son had not come home. Mr. Rains's father and uncle searched his room looking for some clue about his whereabouts and found the K-Mart bag containing the BBs and the sales slip from Bend of the River. They went to both K-Mart and Bend of the River and then drove around looking for Mr. Rains and talking to his friends about where he might be.

Ms. Rains returned home when the news of her son's disappearance reached her. She and her husband distributed fliers around Putnam County, and the members of their church mobilized to help the Putnam County Sheriff's Department look for Mr. Rains. On Sunday morning, July 20, 1997, Ms. Rains's brother received word that Mr. Rains had been found dead in his automobile. He asked his sister and brother-in-law to meet him at the sheriff's office and when they arrived, he informed them of their son's death. Several days later, the funeral director returned Mr. Rains's personal effects, including his wallet, to his family. Mr. Rains's father found a suicide note in the wallet. The note shed no light on the basis for Mr. Rains's decision to take his own life.

On July 15, 1998, Mr. Rains's parents filed a wrongful death lawsuit seeking actual and punitive damages from Bend of the River premised on two theories-negligence per se and negligent entrustment. They asserted that Bend of the River was negligent per se because it had sold handgun ammunition to a person who was less than twenty-one years of age in violation of the Gun Control Act [18 U.S.C. §922(b)(1) (2000)]. They also asserted that Bend of the River should not have entrusted handgun ammunition to an "18-year-old child." Bend of the River filed an answer denying liability and, in July 1999, moved for a summary judgment.

B. THE NEGLIGENCE PER SE CLAIM

In Tennessee, the common-law standard of conduct to which a person must conform to avoid being negligent is the familiar "reasonable person under similar circumstances" standard. As a general matter, this standard requires a person to exercise reasonable care under the circumstances to refrain from conduct that could foreseeably injure others. This standard is flexible, and its contours are inherently fact-sensitive. Therefore, determinations regarding whether particular conduct conforms to the common-law standard of conduct are made on a case-by-case basis.

However, the common law is not the only source of legal duties or standards of conduct in negligence cases. In addition to the general duty to act reasonably to avoid harming others, more specific duties governing particular situations and relationships may be imposed by the General Assembly. Legislatively created legal duties arise in two ways. First, the General Assembly may create a legal duty and then provide a civil cause of action for its breach. Second, the General Assembly may enact a penal statute that does not explicitly provide a civil remedy, and the courts may then derive a civil legal duty from the penal statute. "Negligence per se" is the term used to describe one of the two doctrines associated with the latter process.

The negligence per se doctrine enables the courts to mold standards of conduct in penal statutes into rules of civil liability. The process has been analogized to "judicial legislation," and its governing principles and their application vary considerably from jurisdiction to jurisdiction. Still, a consensus exists regarding many of the doctrine's basic precepts.

The negligence per se doctrine does not create a new cause of action. Rather, it is a form of ordinary negligence that enables the courts to use a penal statute to define a reasonably prudent person's standard of care. Negligence per se arises when a legislative body pronounces in a penal statute what the conduct of a reasonable person must be, whether or not the common law would require similar conduct.

The negligence per se doctrine is not a magic transformational formula that automatically creates a private negligence cause of action for the violation of every statute. Not every statutory violation amounts to negligence per se. To trigger the doctrine, the statute must establish a specific standard of conduct. Restatement (Second) of Torts §874A cmt. e ("The common law tort of negligence is not changed, but the expression of the standard of care in certain fact situations is modified; it is changed from a general standard to a specific rule of conduct."). Many states require the statutory standard of conduct to differ from the ordinary prudent person standard of conduct. Invoking the negligence per se doctrine is unnecessary and redundant if the statute requires only the ordinary reasonable person standard of conduct.

The effect of declaring conduct negligent per se is to render the conduct negligent as a matter of law. Thus, a person whose conduct is negligent per se cannot escape liability by attempting to prove that he or she acted reasonably under the circumstances. However, a finding of negligence per se is not equivalent to a finding of liability per se. Plaintiffs in negligence per se cases must still establish causation in fact, legal cause, and damages.

The fact that the General Assembly has enacted a statute defining criminal conduct does not necessarily mean that the courts must adopt it as a standard of civil liability. Decisions regarding the proper civil standard of conduct rest with the courts. Thus, the courts must ultimately decide whether they will adopt a statutory standard to define the standard of conduct of reasonable persons in specific circumstances. Restatement (Second) of Torts §874A cmt. e ("[I]t is the court that adopts and utilizes the statutory rule in substitution for the general standard and . . . [the court] may exercise its sound discretion as to when this should be done.").

The courts consider a number of factors to determine whether the violation of a statute should trigger the negligence per se doctrine. The two threshold questions in every negligence per se case are whether the plaintiff belongs to the class of persons the statute was designed to protect and whether the plaintiff's injury is of the type that the statute was designed to prevent. Restatement (Second) of Torts §286.[10] Affirmative answers to these questions do not end the inquiry. Courts also consider (1) whether the statute is the sole source of the defendant's duty to the plaintiff, (2) whether the statute clearly defines the prohibited or required conduct, (3) whether the statute would impose liability without fault, (4) whether invoking the negligence per se doctrine would result in damage awards disproportionate to the statutory violation, and (5) whether the plaintiff's injury is a direct or indirect result of the violation of the statute.

We have substantial doubt that the illegal sale of handgun ammunition to an eighteen-year-old purchaser who used it to commit suicide should trigger the negligence per se doctrine. Congress did not undertake to create a private, civil cause of action for these sorts of violations of the Gun Control Act of 1968. In addition, the Act does not contain a clearly defined standard of conduct with

---

10. The Restatement points out that the courts should not adopt a standard of conduct defined by legislation if the legislation's exclusive purpose is (1) to protect a class of persons other than the one whose interests are invaded, (2) to protect an interest other than the one invaded, (3) to protect against other harm than that which has resulted, or (4) to protect against other hazards than that from which the harm has resulted. Restatement (Second) of Torts §288(d)-(g).

regard to the sale of ammunition to persons who may be intending to use it for self-destructive purposes. Finally, it is far from clear that Congress intended to protect adults from self-destructive acts when it enacted the Gun Control Act.

The courts that have addressed the question of whether various violations of the Gun Control Act of 1968 trigger liability under the negligence per se doctrine have reached inconsistent results. However, the Tennessee Supreme Court has, over the years, been quick to invoke the negligence per se doctrine with regard to violations of penal statutes designed to protect the public. In addition, another panel of this court has implied that the sale of handgun ammunition to a person under twenty-one years of age is negligence per se under Tennessee law. Accordingly, for the purpose of reviewing the trial court's denial of Bend of the River's motion for summary judgment, we will presume that the sale of handgun ammunition to an eighteen-year-old purchaser in violation of 18 U.S.C. §922(b)(1) is negligence per se.

[The court went on to determine that the suicide of Aaron Rains was an independent, intervening cause of his death and, thus, cut off liability of Bend of the River.]

PREPARING FOR CLASS

1. The legislature could pass a statute that specifically creates a cause of action for damages for its violation. Most state dramshop statutes specifically create a cause of action for that statute's violation. Why should a court find a cause of action for violation of a statute when the legislature does not provide for a cause of action in negligence?

2. Who determines whether a statute establishes a standard of conduct — the judge as a matter of law or the jury as a matter of fact? It appears that Bend of the River committed a criminal act by selling ammunition to someone who was under the age of 21. Why should a court be concerned about whether such criminal acts are negligent? Won't they always be negligent?

3. Is Aaron Rains in the class of persons this statute was meant to protect? Explain.

4. Is suicide the type of harm this statute was meant to protect against? Explain.

INCREASING YOUR UNDERSTANDING

1. Statutes are not the only legislation that may be adopted by the courts as a standard of care. Courts may also adopt ordinances and administrative regulations as a standard of care.

2. Statutes may also lower the standard of care for certain activities. Good Samaritan statutes relieve health care providers from the professional standard of care when rendering care in emergency situations. Recreational use statutes excuse landowners of ordinary care standards toward recreational users of their land.

3. Some statutes, such as the federal Occupational Safety and Health Act (OSHA), expressly provide that its standards and regulations do not affect common law rights (25 U.S.C.A. §651 et seq.).

4. Some federal statutes may set a standard of care and preempt or exclude a state standard of care. The federal statute requiring warnings on cigarette packages expressly bars state-mandated warnings. Cipollone v. Liggett Group, 505 U.S. 504 (1992).

APPLYING THE LAW

1. Suppose a statute prohibits the use of alcoholic beverages while driving. The defendant's attention is diverted from his driving while he attempts to open his first beer of the day. His car swerves and runs into an oncoming car. Can the statute be used to establish a standard of care in a tort suit against the defendant?

2. A statute requires driving and parking on the right side of the road. Jason pulls his car to the left shoulder of the road to park and talk to his friend, Bert. When Jason pulled away, he ran into Bert's young son who was standing beside the car. Bert, through his representative, sued Jason. Does the statute establish a standard of care?

Perry v. S.N. and S.N.
973 S.W.2d 301 (Texas 1998)

PHILLIPS, Chief Justice.

This is a suit for injuries arising out of the abuse of children at a day care center. Plaintiffs filed suit individually and as next friends of their two children, alleging that defendants witnessed the abuse and failed to report it to the police or child welfare officials. The sole issue before us is whether plaintiffs may maintain a cause of action for negligence per se based on the Family Code, which requires any person having cause to believe a child is being abused to report the abuse to state authorities and makes the knowing failure to do so a misdemeanor. The trial court granted summary judgment for defendants, but the court of appeals reversed and remanded plaintiffs' negligence per se and gross negligence claims for trial. We reverse the judgment of the court of appeals and render judgment that plaintiffs take nothing. Because plaintiffs did not preserve their common law negligence claims, we do not decide whether there should be a common law duty to report child abuse in some circumstances.

B.N. and K.N. attended a day care center operated by Francis Keller and her husband Daniel Keller from March 25, 1991, to August 28, 1991. Their parents, S.N. and S.N., allege that during that period, Daniel Keller regularly abused B.N. and K.N. and other children at the center both physically and sexually. Mr. and Mrs. N. brought suit against the Kellers and three of the Kellers' friends, Douglas Perry, Janise White, and Raul Quintero. Plaintiffs claim that Francis Keller confided in White at an unspecified time that Daniel Keller had "abusive habits toward children." They further allege that on one occasion in August 1991, while visiting the Kellers, defendants Perry, White, and Quintero all saw Daniel Keller bring a number of children out of the day care center into the Kellers' adjoining home and sexually abuse them. The record does not indicate whether B.N. and K.N. were among these children. According to plaintiffs, Perry, White, and Quintero did not attempt to stop Daniel Keller from abusing the children or report his crimes to the police or child welfare authorities.

Mr. and Mrs. N. alleged only that Perry, White, and Quintero were negligent per se because they violated a statute requiring any person who "has cause to believe that a child's physical or mental health or welfare has been or may be adversely affected by abuse" to file a report with the police or the Department of Protective and Regulatory Services. Plaintiffs also asserted gross negligence and common law negligence claims. They claimed that Perry, White, and Quintero's failure to report the abuse proximately caused them harm by permitting the day care center to remain open, thus enabling Daniel Keller to continue abusing the children at the center. They sought damages for pain, mental anguish, and medical expenses, as well as loss of income when they could not work outside the home because of B.N. and K.N.'s injuries.

The trial court granted Perry, White, and Quintero's motions for summary judgment and severed plaintiffs' claims against those three defendants from their suit against the Kellers, which is not before us. Because defendants' motions for summary judgment argued only that plaintiffs failed to state a cognizable claim, the trial court's judgment can be upheld, if at all, only on that ground. When the ground for the trial court's decision is that plaintiffs failed to state a cause of action, we must take the allegations in the pleadings as true in determining whether a cause of action exists.

"It is fundamental that the existence of a legally cognizable duty is a prerequisite to all tort liability." The court of appeals found a duty in the following mandatory child abuse reporting provisions of the Texas Family Code:

> A person having cause to believe that a child's physical or mental health or welfare has been adversely affected by abuse or neglect by any person shall immediately make a report as provided by this subchapter.

(a) A person commits an offense if the person has cause to believe that a child's physical or mental health or welfare has been or may be adversely affected by abuse or neglect and knowingly fails to report as provided in this chapter.

(b) An offense under this section is a Class B misdemeanor.

Tex. Fam. Code §261.101

The court [of appeals] concluded that these provisions create a "statutory duty" to report child abuse, and that a violation of this duty is negligence per se. See 944 S.W.2d at 730.

All persons have a duty to obey the criminal law in the sense that they may be prosecuted for not doing so, but this is not equivalent to a duty in tort. "It is well-established that the mere fact that the Legislature adopts a criminal statute does not mean that this court must accept it as a standard for civil liability." "The considerations which warrant imposing tort liability are not identical with those which warrant criminal conviction," and we will not apply the doctrine of negligence per se if the criminal statute does not provide an appropriate basis for civil liability.

Before we begin our analysis of whether section 261.109 of the Family Code is an appropriate basis for tort liability, we emphasize that we must look beyond the facts of this particular case to consider the full reach of the statute. We do not decide today whether a statute criminalizing only the type of egregious behavior with which these defendants are charged — the failure of eyewitnesses to report the sexual molestation of preschool children — would be an appropriate basis for a tort action. That is not the statute the Legislature passed. Rather, the issue before us is whether it is appropriate to impose tort liability on any and every person who "has cause to believe that a child's physical or mental health or welfare has been or may be adversely affected by abuse or neglect and knowingly fails to report."

The threshold questions in every negligence per se case are whether the plaintiff belongs to the class that the statute was intended to protect and whether the plaintiff's injury is of a type that the statute was designed to prevent. Texas's first mandatory child abuse reporting statute, from which Family Code section 261.101(a) is derived, stated that "[t]he purpose of this Act is to protect children who[ ] . . . are adversely affected by abuse or neglect." Similarly, the current Family Code provision governing the investigation of reports of child abuse states that "[t]he primary purpose of the investigation shall be the protection of the child."

B.N. and K.N. are within the class of persons whom the child abuse reporting statute was meant to protect, and they suffered the kind of injury that the Legislature intended the statute to prevent. But this does not end our inquiry. The Court must still determine whether it is appropriate to impose tort liability for violations of the statute. This determination is informed by a number of factors, some discussed by the court of appeals in this case and others derived from past negligence per se decisions of Texas courts and from scholarly analyses. These factors are not necessarily exclusive, nor is the issue properly resolved by merely counting how many factors lean each way. Rather, we set out these considerations as guides to assist a court in answering the ultimate question of whether imposing tort liability for violations of a criminal statute is fair, workable, and wise.

We first consider the fact that, absent a change in the common law, a negligence per se cause of action against these defendants would derive the element of duty solely from the Family Code. At common law there is generally no duty to protect another from the criminal acts of a third party or to come to the aid of another in distress. Although there are exceptions to this no-duty rule, this case does not fall within any of the established exceptions, and Mr. and Mrs. N. have not asked this Court to impose on persons who are aware of child abuse a new common law duty to report it or take other protective action.

In contrast, the defendant in most negligence per se cases already owes the plaintiff a pre-existing common law duty to act as a reasonably prudent person, so that the statute's role is merely to define more precisely what conduct breaches that duty. For example, the overwhelming majority of this Court's negligence per se cases have involved violations of traffic statutes by drivers and train operators—actors who already owed a common law duty to exercise reasonable care toward others on the road or track.

When a statute criminalizes conduct that is also governed by a common law duty, as in the case of a traffic regulation, applying negligence per se causes no great change in the law because violating the statutory standard of conduct would usually also be negligence under a common law reasonableness standard. But recognizing a new, purely statutory duty "can have an extreme effect upon the common law of negligence" when it allows a cause of action where the common law would not. In such a situation, applying negligence per se "bring[s] into existence a new type of tort liability." The change tends to be especially great when, as here, the statute criminalizes inaction rather than action.

Some commentators contend that the term "negligence per se" does not even apply when the statute on which civil liability is based corresponds to no common law duty. While our definition has never been so restrictive, this Court in fact has created a new duty by applying negligence per se on only one occasion. In Nixon v. Mr. Property Management Co., 690 S.W.2d 546, 549 (Tex. 1985), a third party dragged the plaintiff into an unlocked vacant apartment owned by the defendant and raped her. Because the plaintiff was a trespasser according to traditional premises liability categories, the defendant landowner owed her no common law duty. Although two members of this Court would have recognized a new common law duty of reasonable care toward trespassers, at least in certain cases, a plurality instead found a duty only in a city ordinance requiring landowners to keep vacant buildings locked. But in our next major negligence per se case, we returned to the norm of deriving duty from the common law and looking to the statute only for the standard of conduct. Only after we created a new common law duty not to sell alcohol to intoxicated persons, did we adopt a relevant section of the Alcoholic Beverage Code as "the attendant standard of conduct." Thus, based on both this Court's past practice and the observations of noted scholars, we conclude that the absence of a relevant common law duty should be considered in deciding whether to apply negligence per se to the Family Code's reporting provision.

The court of appeals in this case listed several factors to consider in deciding whether to apply negligence per se. According to the court of appeals, the principal factors favoring negligence per se are that the Legislature has determined that compliance with criminal statutes is practicable and desirable and that criminal statutes give citizens notice of what conduct is required of them. As considerations against negligence per se, the court of appeals cautioned that some penal statutes may be too obscure to put the public on notice, may impose liability without fault, or may lead to ruinous monetary liability for relatively minor offenses. The first of these factors is not helpful because it points the same way in every case: the very existence of a criminal statute implies a legislative judgment that its requirements are practicable and desirable. The court of appeals' remaining factors, however, are pertinent to our analysis.

On the question of notice, this Court has held that one consideration bearing on whether to apply negligence per se is whether the statute clearly defines the prohibited or required conduct. The Family Code's reporting requirement is triggered when a person "has cause to believe that a child's physical or mental health or welfare has been or may be adversely affected by abuse or neglect." In this case, defendants allegedly were eyewitnesses to sexual abuse. Under these facts, there is no question that they had cause to believe abuse was occurring, and thus that the statute required them to make a report. In many other cases, however, a person may become aware of a possible case of child abuse only through second-hand reports or ambiguous physical symptoms, and it is unclear whether these circumstances are "cause to believe" that such conduct "may be" taking place.[6] A statute that conditions the requirement to report on these difficult judgment calls does not clearly define what conduct is required in many conceivable situations.

The next factor the court of appeals considered was whether applying negligence per se to the reporting statute would create liability without fault. We agree with the court of appeals that it would not, because the statute criminalizes only the "knowing[ ]" failure to report. This characteristic of the statute weighs in favor of imposing civil liability.

Our next consideration is whether negligence per se would impose ruinous liability disproportionate to the seriousness of the defendant's conduct. In analyzing this factor, the court of appeals treated child abuse as the relevant

---

6. Determining whether abuse is or may be occurring in a particular case is likely to be especially difficult for untrained laypersons. Texas is one of a minority of states that require any person who suspects child abuse to report it. . . . Most states place such a requirement only on professionals who may be expected to know more than the average person about recognizing child abuse and who have a professional relationship with and responsibility for children. . . . The Texas Family Code contains a separate mandatory reporting provision, not relevant here, specifically directed to members of certain professions. See Tex. Fam. Code §261.101(b).

conduct. The conduct criminalized by section 261.109, however, is not child abuse but the failure to report child abuse. Through its penal laws, the Legislature has expressed a judgment that abuse and nonreporting deserve very different legal consequences. The abuser in this case committed the offense of aggravated sexual assault on a child under the age of fourteen, a first degree felony carrying a penalty of five to ninety-nine years in prison and a fine of up to $10,000. Almost all of the other acts of abuse and neglect covered by the reporting requirement are also felonies. Even the lowest level of felony is punishable by 180 days to two years in jail and a $10,000 fine, and automatically deprives the offender of certain civil rights such as the franchise, eligibility for public office, and the right to own a firearm. By contrast, failure to report abuse or neglect, no matter how serious the underlying crime, is a class B misdemeanor punishable by no more than six months in jail and a $2,000 fine. This evidence of legislative intent to penalize nonreporters far less severely than abusers weighs against holding a person who fails to report suspected abuse civilly liable for the enormous damages that the abuser subsequently inflicts. The specter of disproportionate liability is particularly troubling when, as in the case of the reporting statute, it is combined with the likelihood of "broad and wide-ranging liability" by collateral wrongdoers that we condemned.

Finally, in addition to the factors discussed by the court of appeals, we have also looked to whether the injury resulted directly or indirectly from the violation of the statute. In *Carter v. William Sommerville & Son, Inc.*, we refused to apply negligence per se liability to a provision of the Texas Motor Carrier Act making it a misdemeanor to aid and abet any violation of the Act. We concluded that the aiding and abetting section was "too far removed to be adopted as a standard" for civil liability, in part because "[i]t is only by first finding a violation of some other section of the Act that the court may then find a violation" of that provision.

The lack of direct causation is not in itself dispositive; we have imposed civil liability for some statutory violations that caused the plaintiff's injury by facilitating the tort of a third party. But a reporting statute by definition places a fourth party between the defendant and the plaintiff: the person or agency to whom the defendant is required to make the report. Thus, the connection between the defendant's conduct and the plaintiff's injury is significantly more attenuated in a case based on failure to report than in Nixon or El Chico. We are not aware of any Texas case applying negligence per se to a statute that, like the child abuse reporting provision, interposes not one but two independent actors between the plaintiff and the defendant.

We conclude by noting that for a variety of reasons, including many of those we have discussed, most other states with mandatory reporting statutes similar to Texas's have concluded that the failure to report child abuse is not negligence per se.

In summary, we have considered the following factors regarding the application of negligence per se to the Family Code's child abuse reporting provision: (1) whether the statute is the sole source of any tort duty from the defendant to the plaintiff or merely supplies a standard of conduct for an existing common law duty; (2) whether the statute puts the public on notice by clearly defining the required conduct; (3) whether the statute would impose liability without fault; (4) whether negligence per se would result in ruinous damages disproportionate to the seriousness of the statutory violation, particularly if the liability would fall on a broad and wide range of collateral wrongdoers; and (5) whether the plaintiff's injury is a direct or indirect result of the violation of the statute. Because a decision to impose negligence per se could not be limited to cases charging serious misconduct like the one at bar, but rather would impose immense potential liability under an ill-defined standard on a broad class of individuals whose relationship to the abuse was extremely indirect, we hold that it is not appropriate to adopt Family Code section 261.109(a) as establishing a duty and standard of conduct in tort. Therefore, Mr. and Mrs. N. and their children may not maintain a claim for negligence per se or gross negligence based on defendants' violation of the child abuse reporting statute. Because plaintiffs did not appeal the court of appeals' adverse decision on their common law negligence claims, we do not consider whether Texas should impose a common law duty to report or prevent child abuse.

For the foregoing reasons, we reverse the judgment of the court of appeals and render judgment that plaintiffs take nothing.

PREPARING FOR CLASS

1. The plaintiff did not preserve the common law negligence claim. Do you think there would be a common law negligence claim in this case that would survive a motion to dismiss and a motion for directed verdict? Did plaintiff's counsel make a mistake in not preserving this cause of action?

2. Is this court ruling that this statute is so unclear that it cannot be used for tort purposes but it can be used in a criminal case to send someone to jail? What would you do if you were representing someone charged with a criminal offense of violating this statute?

3. Do you think the Texas Supreme Court would have approved the application of this statute if its application had been limited to "professionals"?

INCREASING YOUR UNDERSTANDING

1. The U.S. Supreme Court has held that the government has a duty under the civil rights laws when it has custody of a person. When the government has custody of a prisoner, Estelle v. Gamble, 429 U.S. 307 (1976), and when it has custody of a mental patient, Youngberg v. Romeo, 457 U.S.

307 (1982), it owes legal duties, for example, health care, to those in its custody. In a subsequent case, the county department of social services took temporary custody of a small child, Joshua, because they believed that he had been physically abused by his father. But the department returned the custody of Joshua to his father while retaining the right to monitor Joshua's safety. After Joshua was returned there were numerous reports that Joshua was being physically abused, but the department left Joshua in his father's custody. Joshua's father finally beat him so severely that he caused extensive brain damage. Joshua sued the state department of social services, but the U.S. Supreme Court held that the department did not have the kind of custody of Joshua that caused it to have a duty under the civil rights laws to protect him, DeShaney v. Winnebago County Dept. of Social Service, 489 U.S. 189 (1989). How do you think the Supreme Court would rule if the child was in a government youth home? How about if the child was taken from his parents' home and placed in a foster home?

2. The court in the *Perry* case was concerned about an expansive application of the statute but did not seem to be as concerned about applying the statute to the case before it. Why didn't the court just limit the statute to the facts before it?

APPLYING THE LAW

Consider the hypothetical at the beginning of this chapter. Should a court adopt the ordinance as the standard of care in a negligence case? Explain.

Zeni v. Anderson
243 N.W.2d 270 (Mich. 1976)

Williams, Justice.

I—Facts

The accident which precipitated this action occurred one snowy morning, March 7, 1969, when the temperature was 11° F, the sky was clear and the average snow depth was 21 inches. Plaintiff Eleanor Zeni, then a 56-year-old registered nurse, was walking to her work at the Northern Michigan University Health Center in Marquette. Instead of using the snow-covered sidewalk, which in any event would have required her to walk across the street twice to get to her job, she traveled along a well-used pedestrian snowpath, with her back to oncoming traffic.

Defendant Karen Anderson, a college student, was driving within the speed limit in a steady stream of traffic on the same street. Ms. Anderson testified that she had turned on the defroster in the car and her passenger said she had scraped the windshield. An eyewitness whose deposition was read at trial, however, testified that defendant's windshield was clouded and he doubted that the occupants could see out. He also testified that the car was traveling too close to the curb and that he could tell plaintiff was going to be hit.

Defendant's car struck the plaintiff on the driver's right side. Ms. Anderson testified she first saw the plaintiff between a car parked on the right-hand side of the road and defendant's car, and that she did not hear nor feel her car strike Ms. Zeni. The eyewitness reported seeing plaintiff flip over the fender and hood. He said when he went over to help her his knees were on or inside the white line delineating a parking space. A security officer observed blood stains on the pavement approximately 13 feet from the curb.

Ms. Zeni's injuries were serious and included an intra-cerebral subdural hematoma which required neurosurgery. She has retrograde amnesia and therefore, because she does not remember anything from the time she began walking that morning until sometime after the impact, there is no way to determine whether she knew defendant was behind her. Following an extended period of convalescence, plaintiff, still suffering permanent disability, could return to work on only a part-time basis.

Testimony at trial indicated that it was common for nurses to use the roadway to reach the Health Center, and a security officer testified that in the wintertime it was safer to walk there than on the one sidewalk. Apparently, several days before the accident, Ms. Zeni had indeed fallen on the sidewalk. Although she was not hurt when she fell, the Director of University Security was hospitalized when he fell on the walk.

Defendant, however, maintained that plaintiff's failure to use that sidewalk constituted contributory negligence because, she said, it violated MCLA 257.655; MSA 9.2355, which requires:

"Where sidewalks are provided, it shall be unlawful for pedestrians to walk upon the main traveled portion of the highway. Where sidewalks are not provided, pedestrians shall, when practicable, walk on the left side of the highway facing traffic which passes nearest."

The trial court instructed the jury on this point:

"Now, it is for you to decide whether on the evidence presented in this case, sidewalks were provided for the plaintiff, Mrs. Zeni, to go from parking lot 'X' (where she parked her car before beginning her walk) to her place of work. Then, as to this statute, you shall then decide whether or not it was practicable for her to walk on the left side of the highway facing traffic which passes nearest. If you find that the plaintiff, Mrs. Zeni, violated this statute before or at the time of the occurrence, then Mrs. Zeni was negligent as a matter of law, which, of course, would bar her claim under Count I, providing that her negligence was a proximate contributing cause of the occurrence."

The Court of Appeals, in a thorough opinion, Zeni v. Anderson, 224 N.W.2d 310 (1974), found first it was a question of fact whether MCLA 257.655; MSA 9.2355 relating to failure to use a sidewalk applied to the case, and whether if Ms. Zeni were found to be negligent, such negligence was a proximate cause of her injuries.

We granted leave to appeal January 29, 1975.

II—EFFECT OF VIOLATION OF STATUTE

An analysis of the Michigan cases indicates that the real Michigan rule as to the effect of violation of a penal statute in a negligence action[6] is that such violation creates only a prima facie case from which the jury may draw an inference of negligence. It is true that a number of passages in cases speak of negligence per se almost in terms of strict liability, but closer examination of the application of the rule reveals that Michigan does not subscribe to such a harsh dogma.

A. VIOLATION OF STATUTE AS REBUTTABLE PRESUMPTION

In a growing number of states, the rule concerning the proper role of a penal statute in a civil action for damages is that violation of the statute which has been found to apply to a particular set of facts establishes only a prima facie case of negligence, a presumption which may be rebutted[7] by a showing on the part of the party violating the statute of an adequate excuse[8] under the facts and circumstances of the case. The excuses may not necessarily be applicable in a criminal action, since, in the absence of legislatively-mandated civil penalties, acceptance of the criminal statute itself as a standard of care in a civil action is purely discretionary.

Michigan cases have in effect followed this rule. For example, over a 65-year period, cases concerning the effect in a negligence action of violation of the statute requiring vehicles to keep to the right side of the road have almost

---

6. Such a statute is relevant to a civil case "even though the statute does not, as is normally the case, contain a provision respecting civil liability." This is true whether the issue is the negligence of defendant, or the contributory negligence of plaintiff.

7. "This latter view is a specific application of the hornbook rule of procedure that a trial judge may direct a verdict on an issue on which reasonable jurors cannot differ. Substantively, this view is also recognition that prudent men do not break the criminal law without justification. The assurance with which a trial judge may direct a verdict against a defendant who has offered no proof tending to justify his breach of the criminal law is based on the warning qualities of penal statutes and on the legislature's opportunity to investigate before enacting proscriptions." Morris, The Role of Criminal Statutes in Negligence Actions, 49 Colum. L. Rev. 21, 35 (1949).

8. Although not intended to be exclusive, the Restatement Torts, 2d, suggests some possible excuses:

"(a) (T)he violation is reasonable because of the actor's incapacity;
"(b) he neither knows nor should know of the occasion for compliance;
"(c) he is unable after reasonable diligence or care to comply;
"(d) he is confronted by an emergency not due to his own misconduct;
"(e) compliance would involve a greater risk of harm to the actor or to others." 2 Restatement of Torts 2d, §288A, p. 33.

consistently adopted a rebuttable presumption approach, even though the language of the statute is not written in terms of a presumption.

Thus, in Tyler v. Nelson, 109 Mich. 37, 41, 66 N.W. 671, 673 (1896), we approved a charge to the jury that even though the "law of the road" required driving to the right, "if, under all the circumstances, it was apparently safer for him to turn to the left, and he did only what a man of ordinary prudence would have done under similar circumstances, then he had a right to disregard the law of the road in that particular, and his turning to the left would not in itself be negligence." (Emphasis added.)

Again, in Buxton v. Ainsworth, 138 Mich. 532, 536, 101 N.W. 817, 818 (1904), although the statute was not specifically mentioned, we said:

"As an abstract proposition, the driver of a vehicle about to meet another team is presumptively at fault if he fails to turn to the right of the center of the wrought portion of the highway; *but if the presumption that he is thus at fault is overcome by the evidence of circumstances,* or if it appears that the fault, if found, did not essentially contribute to the injury, the fact that he may have been in a sense out of place does not place him beyond the protection of the law." (Emphasis added.)

By the time we decided Corey v. Hartel, 216 Mich. 675, 680, 185 N.W. 748, 749 (1921), it was clear that the law was,

"While a driver who does not keep to the right of the center is presumptively at fault, *the circumstances attending such meeting may be such as to overcome the presumption,* or the evidence may establish the fact that such act of negligence did not essentially contribute to the injury." (Emphasis added.)

The Michigan rebuttable presumption approach is not restricted to these statutes. The Standard Jury Instruction covering the effect of the violation of any penal statute on a negligence case, asks the jury to consider possible excuses if such evidence is presented. Although the text of the instruction is couched in terms of the emergency exception, the Note on Use provides that the instruction "should be modified for other categories of excused violations." For such possible excuses, the Comment refers to the five categories of excuses suggested by the Restatement. The Restatement itself has suggested that this list is not all-inclusive.

We think the test of the applicable law was well stated by our brother Justice Fitzgerald when he was a judge on the Court of Appeals. In Lucas v. Carson, 38 Mich. App. 552, 196 N.W.2d 819 (1972), he analyzed a case where, in spite of defendant's precautions, her vehicle "inexplicably slid into the rear of plaintiff's stopped car" where plaintiff was waiting at a traffic signal. Plaintiff alleged that defendant violated the assured clear distance statute, as well as MCLA 257.643; MSA 9.2343[16] and MCLA 257.402; MSA 9.2102.[17]

---

16. "The driver of a motor vehicle shall not follow another vehicle more closely than is reasonable and prudent. . . ."

17. "In any action, in any court in this state when it is shown by competent evidence, that a vehicle traveling in a certain direction, overtook and struck the rear end of another vehicle proceeding in the same direction, or lawfully standing upon any highway within this state, the driver or operator of such first mentioned vehicle shall be deemed prima facie guilty of negligence."

Although the language of the latter two statutes raises the possibility of excuse, we think our review of the precedents indicates Lucas was correct in not distinguishing among the statutes as to acceptable standards of excuse, and in not restricting the acceptable gamut of excuse possibilities.

First, in analyzing whether the presumption of negligence attributed to a rear-end collision had been rebutted in the case before them, the Court of Appeals acknowledged that the usual grounds for rebuttal, sudden emergency, did not appear in this case. In effect accepting defendant's contention that the doctrine of sudden emergency was not the sole basis for rebutting a presumption of negligence, the Court held:

"The general rule appears to be that evidence required to rebut this presumption *as a matter of law* should be positive, unequivocal, strong, and credible. In the case at bar, defendant driver contended that she was at all times driving in a reasonable and prudent manner. . . . [T]here was sufficient evidence at least to generate a jury question regarding rebutting of the presumption." 38 Mich. App. 552, 557, 196 N.W.2d 819, 822 (citations omitted; emphasis by the court).

As to the other alleged statutory violations, Justice Fitzgerald observed:

"Whereas, at one time, the application of the statute (assured clear distance) was strictly construed and applied as evidenced by the rule in the case of Lewis v. Yund, 339 Mich. 441, 64 N.W.2d 696 (1954), recent cases indicate that the statute must be reasonably construed and exceptions to the statutory edict have been created to accomplish justice, including bringing the assured clear distance rule to qualification by the test of due or ordinary care, exercised in the light of the attending conditions.

"See Hendershot v. Kelly, 11 Mich. App. 173, 160 N.W.2d 740 (1968). The qualification applying to the assured-clear-distance statute as enunciated in the above quotation is also applicable to the rule against following too closely. *Hendershot v. Kelly*, supra.

"Since there was at least some evidence that defendant driver was operating her vehicle in a reasonable and prudent manner prior to the accident, the question of whether or not defendant violated one or both of these statutes was properly a factual one for the jury to resolve." 38 Mich. App. 552, 558, 196 N.W.2d 819, 823 (emphasis added).

This is the approach we follow today. For one, it recognizes that the Legislature has spoken in a particular area, and that,

"The legislative process includes opportunities to arrive at informed value judgments superior to the opportunities of judges and jurors. Furthermore the legislative judgment is pronounced in advance and tends to educate the public." 49 Col. L. Rev. 21, 47.

Particularly in the area of health and safety regulations, we find ourselves attempting "to further the ultimate policy for the protection of individuals which they find underlying the statute." Prosser, supra, 191.[18] Then, too, it

---

18. However, Prosser calls such an implied intent to provide for tort liability "(i)n the ordinary case . . . pure fiction concocted for the purpose." Prosser, 191.

is felt that "the reasonably prudent man usually tries to comply" with the criminal law. 49 Col. L. Rev. 21, 33.[19]

Another attraction of this approach is that it is fair. "If there is sufficient excuse or justification, there is ordinarily no violation of a statute and the statutory standard is inapplicable." It would be unreasonable to adhere to an automatic rule of negligence "where observance would subject a person to danger which might be avoided by disregard of the general rule."

The approach is logical. Liability without fault is not truly negligence, and in the absence of a clear legislative mandate to so extend liability, the courts should be hesitant to do so on their own. Because these are, after all, criminal statutes, a court is limited in how far it may go in plucking a statute from its criminal milieu and inserting it into the civil arena. The rule of rebuttable presumption has arisen in part in response to this concern, and in part because of the reluctance to go to the other extreme and in effect, discard or disregard the legislative standard.

B. VIOLATION OF STATUTE AS NEGLIGENCE PER SE

While some Michigan cases seem to speak of negligence per se as a kind of strict liability, an examination indicates that there are a number of conditions that attempt to create a more reasonable approach than would result from an automatic application of a per se rule.

The first such condition is that the penal standard does not have to be applied in the civil action. Absent explicit legislative language creating civil liability for violation of a criminal statute, a court is free to exercise its discretion and either adopt the legislative standard,[21] or retain the common law reasonable person standard of care. By its interpretation of the statutory

---

19. Still another rationale is that the criminal statute establishes "a standard of care greater than that required by the common law" and is therefore a more accurate test. 57 Am. Jur. 2d, Negligence, §242, p. 626.

21. Thus, 2 Restatement Torts (2d), §286, comment d, p. 26, observes:

"(T)he initial question is whether the legislation or regulation is to be given any effect in a civil suit. Since the legislation has not so provided, the court is under no compulsion to accept it as defining any standard of conduct for purposes of a tort action.

"Where criminal legislation, although constitutional, is entirely unreasonable or inappropriate—as where, for example, there is an automobile speed limit of six miles an hour, enacted in 1908 and never repealed—the court has no choice, in a criminal prosecution, but to apply the law so laid down. But since it is under no such compulsion in a civil suit, it may still treat the provision as inapplicable for the purposes of defining negligence in such a suit. In doing so, it may rely on the justification that the legislature has indicated no intention that it shall be so applied, since nothing more than a criminal penalty has been provided. . . .

"On the other hand, the court is free, in making its own judicial rules, to adopt and apply to the negligence action the standard of conduct provided by such a criminal enactment or regulation. This it may do even though the provision is for some reason entirely ineffective for its initial purposes, as where a traffic signal is set up under an ordinance which never has been properly published and so for the purposes of a criminal prosecution is entirely void. *The decision to adopt the standard is purely a judicial one, for the court to make. When the court does adopt the legislative standard, it is acting to further the general purpose which it finds in the legislation, and not because it is in any way required to do so. . . .*" (Emphasis supplied.)

purpose[22] a court may in effect excuse an individual from the consequences of violating a statute. For example, the court may find the statute's purpose was not to protect the person allegedly injured, or, even if it was, that the harm suffered was not what the Legislature designed the statute to do.

Once this threshold is crossed and the court determines that the statute is applicable to the facts in the case before it, liability still does not attach unless the finder of fact determines that the violation of the statute is the proximate cause of the injury.

Despite such limitations, the judge-made rule of negligence per se has still proved to be too inflexible and mechanical to satisfy thoughtful commentators and judges. It is forcefully argued that no matter how a court may attempt to confine the negligence per se doctrine, if defendant is liable despite the exercise of due care and the availability of a reasonable excuse, this is really strict liability, and not negligence. Since it is always possible that the Legislature's failure to deal specifically with the question of private rights was not accidental, and that there might have been no legislative intent to change the law of torts, such treatment of the statute may well be a gross perversion of the legislative will. It is troublesome too, that "potentially ruinous civil liability" may follow from a "minor infraction of petty criminal regulations," 49 Col. L. Rev. 21, 23, or may, in a jurisdiction burdened by contributory negligence, serve to deprive an otherwise deserving plaintiff of a much-needed recovery.

The rule, too, may have unfortunate effects on the administration of justice.[26] Justice Talbot Smith suggests that adoption of the statutory standard improperly takes from the jury its function of setting the standard of care. He also suggests that in order to avoid what may be an unfair result, courts may attempt to distort one of the negligence per se conditions, and create instead a negligence per se loophole. This is particularly true, he contends, of element of proximate cause.

---

22. This is usually done by applying the statutory purpose doctrine:

> "The court may adopt as the standard of conduct of a reasonable man the requirements of a legislative enactment or an administrative regulation whose purpose is found to be exclusively or in part
>> "(a) to protect a class of persons which includes the one whose interest is invaded, and
>> "(b) to protect the particular interest which is invaded, and
>> "(c) to protect that interest against the kind of harm which has resulted, and
>> "(d) to protect that interest against the particular hazard from which the harm results."

> "This instruction should be given only if:
>> "1. the statute is intended to protect against the injury involved; and
>> "2. the plaintiff is within the class intended to be protected by the statute; and
>> "3. the evidence will support a finding that the violation was a proximate cause of the occurrence."

This remains true for plaintiff, except that "the statute is intended to protect against the result of the violation." Note on Use, SJI 12.03.

26. The doctrine of negligence per se purports to rob the judge of judicial functions. It places responsibilities on a legislature that could not possibly conceive of all cases to which its proscription might apply and that has not provided for civil liability, and that, therefore, surely has not considered proper limitations and excuses. At times violation of the criminal law is not unreasonable. If the doctrine of negligence per se is applied obdurately to reasonable violators their liability can be justified only on some basis other than fault—if at all." 49 Col. L. Rev. 21, 29.

C. VIOLATION OF STATUTE AS EVIDENCE OF NEGLIGENCE

Just as the rebuttable presumption approach to statutory violations in a negligence context apparently arose, at least in part, from dissatisfaction with the result of a mechanical application of the per se rule, a parallel development in our state with respect to infractions of ordinances and of administrative regulations, has been that violations of these amount to only evidence of negligence.

We have not, however, chosen to join that small minority which has decreed that violation of a statute is only evidence of negligence. In view of the fairness and ease with which the rebuttable presumption standard has been and can be administered, we believe the litigants are thereby well served and the Legislature is given appropriate respect.

D. APPLICATION OF STATUTORY STANDARD TO THIS CASE

We have seen, therefore, that while some of our Michigan cases seem to present negligence per se as an unqualified rule, the fact of the matter is that there are a number of qualifications which make application of this rule not really a per se approach at all. Not only must the statutory purpose doctrine and the requirement of proximate cause be satisfied, but the alleged wrongdoer has an opportunity to come forward with evidence rebutting the presumption of negligence.

An accurate statement of our law is that when a court adopts a penal statute as the standard of care in an action for negligence, violation of that statute establishes a prima facie case of negligence, with the determination to be made by the finder of fact whether the party accused of violating the statute has established a legally sufficient excuse. If the finder of fact determines such an excuse exists, the appropriate standard of care then becomes that established by the common law. Such excuses shall include, but shall not be limited to, these suggested by the Second Restatement of Torts, §288A, and shall be determined by the circumstances of each case.

In the case at bar, moreover, the statute itself provides a guideline for the jury, for a violation will not occur when it is impracticable to use the sidewalk or to walk on the left side of a highway. This is ordinarily a question for the finder of fact, and thus the statute itself provides not only a legislative standard of care which may be accepted by the court, but a legislatively mandated excuse as well.

In the instant case the court charged the jury:

"Now, it is for you to decide whether on the evidence presented in this case, sidewalks were provided for the Plaintiff, Mrs. Zeni, to go from parking lot 'X' to her place of work. Then, as to this statute, you shall then decide whether or not it was practicable for her to walk on the left side of the highway facing traffic which passes nearest. If you find that the Plaintiff Mrs. Zeni, violated this statute before or at the time of the occurrence, then Mrs. Zeni was negligent as a matter of law, which, of course, would bar her claim under Count I, providing that her negligence was a proximate contributing cause of the occurrence."

Thus, we find the jury was adequately instructed as to the effect of the violation of this particular statute on plaintiff's case.

PREPARING FOR CLASS

1. How would this case be decided if the court used the negligence per se approach to the statute? Explain.

2. How would this case be decided if the court used the evidence of negligence approach to the statute? Explain.

3. What excuse will Eleanor Zeni argue? Will that excuse justify Mrs. Zeni walking in the road in the morning where she is likely to be struck by a car?

4. Who has the burden of proof to show an excuse for violation of a statute?

INCREASING YOUR UNDERSTANDING

1. Sometimes if the court does not believe that the harm suffered was the kind to be protected by the statute, the court will still cite the statute as some evidence of negligence. Galloway v. State, 654 So. 2d 1345 (1995); Dan Dobbs, The Law of Torts, §134, p. 317.

2. Negligence per se is often used in motor vehicle accident cases when the defendant is speeding or making prohibited turns. Martin v. Herzog, 126 N.E. 814 (1920).

3. Some states treat violations of local ordinances or regulations as evidence of negligence while treating statutes as negligence per se. Griglione v. Martin, 525 N.W.2d 810.

APPLYING THE LAW

A state statute requires operating smoke detectors in all residential rentals. A fire breaks out in the Harlow Apartments in that state and one of the tenants, Ms. Cynthia Morris, died as a result of smoke inhalation. The Fire Inspector found smoke detectors in Ms. Morris's apartment but believes that the smoke detectors did not work. The owner of the apartments says that it provided smoke detectors for the apartment but the tenant must have taken the batteries out for other uses.

1. Explain how this statute will apply in negligence per se jurisdiction.

2. Explain how this statute will apply in a presumption of negligence jurisdiction.

3. Explain how this statute will apply in an evidence of negligence jurisdiction.

4. You represent the tenant in the cause of action against the landlord in the above case. The jurisdiction has not ruled on how to apply an applicable statute. What standard will you advocate? Why is that a preferable standard for your client? How would you argue for this standard?

Chapter 7

Negligence—Breach of Duty and the Professional

A. INTRODUCTION

We saw in the previous chapter that the courts are willing to change the reasonable person standard to accommodate the disability of the defendant. But there are certain other situations when the courts change the reasonable person standard to take into consideration the special abilities of the defendant, i.e., the defendant will be held to a higher standard than the reasonable person. How can this be justified?

B. WHO ARE PROFESSIONALS?

Powder Horn Nursery, Inc. v. Soil and Plant Laboratory, Inc.
579 P.2d 582 (Ariz. Ct. App. 1978)

In this appeal we must determine the proper standard of care a soil and plant laboratory must use in furnishing information to its customers.

The plaintiff/appellant Powder Horn Nursery, Inc. (Nursery) argues that the "reasonable man" test is the proper standard of care to be applied to this case. The defendant/appellee Soil and Plant Laboratory (Lab) takes the position that a plant laboratory is in a class of professional consultants and that any negligence claim against them must be measured by the professional standard of care existing within the community.

The Nursery, which conducts a commercial plant nursery in Scottsdale, Arizona, sued the Lab, located in Santa Clara, California, for $233,966.51 in damages arising from a plant loss allegedly caused by the negligence of the Lab. The Lab was awarded summary judgment against the Nursery claim and was also awarded the sum of $245.37 on its counterclaim for services rendered. The trial court rendered the judgment upon the following grounds:

...It is the view of the Court that the Plaintiff must establish that the Defendant failed to conform with a standard of care existing within the community. There is absolutely no evidence brought to the Court's attention indicating any opinion by a qualified expert that the advice given by Defendant breached any existing standard of care. Absent such an opinion, there is no evidence showing a breach of duty owed by the Defendant to the Plaintiff.

The Nursery appeals from this judgment and the denial of its motion for reconsideration. The Nursery claims the court erred in granting summary judgment for the following reasons:

1. The proper standard of care by which the Lab's negligence should be judged is the reasonable man test and not the more demanding test of the prevailing community standard as applied in professional malpractice cases.

2. The conflict in the professional opinions by the respective party experts relative to the proper method of diagnosing the particular plant disease raised a genuine issue of material fact which bars the granting of a motion for summary judgment.

3. The Nursery under the provisions of the Restatement (Second) of Torts §552 established a prima facie case of negligence against the Lab when it failed to inform the Nursery on the proper methods to combat a condition known as "iron toxicity" which was destroying the Nursery's potted plants.

The facts necessary for the determination of this appeal disclose that the Nursery is in the business of raising plants for commercial sale, with an operation of approximately 5,000 containers and some field grown stock. The Lab provides professional assistance to nurserymen and offers a wide variety of professional services ranging from soil, plant and water analysis to field calls and extended area visitations. The parties had a prior business relationship dating back to 1967 or 1968, whereby the Lab provided recommendations on proper fertilization and soil mix for the Nursery's container stock. The problem which triggered this litigation arose when the Nursery, by a letter dated May 25, 1970, asked the Lab for advice on the prevention of yellowing leaves in the Nursery's container grown stock. The Lab replied by letter dated June 8, 1970, with a pertinent recommendation that iron chelate be added to the fertilizer solution. The iron chelate was implemented with the watering on June 10, 1970, and approximately one week later the plants began looking more unhealthy.

On June 25, 1970, the Lab was advised by phone that the Nursery was encountering leaf burn problems. The Lab recommended leaching the plants with clear water to remove any contaminants and requested soil and leaf samples for examination. The Lab received a soil sample from the Nursery on June 29, 1970, and leaf and water samples were received the following day. The Lab report, dated July 1, 1970, found the problem "which you have recently encountered appears to be due to sudden and extreme rate of fertilizer application with nitrogen being the primary element found in excess. The formula which has been provided and presumably has been in use could not possibly result in values in the range found, if the proportioner is operating in a normal manner." The report further stated:

Although the incidence of injury coincided in some degree with the application of iron, we cannot feel that this was responsible in view of the data obtained. It appears quite certain from data and our past experience that the problem is one of extreme concentration of fertilizer being applied. (We hope you will be able to figure out how this could have occurred and certainly avoid any further repetition.)

The results of the leaf and water supply analysis were compiled in a letter dated July 6, 1970. After studying the soil samples further, the Lab issued another report in a letter dated July 11, 1970. The results of these tests, as reported to the Nursery, indicated that sodium toxicity was the primary cause of the plant decline.

The plants continued to decline, resulting in considerable damage to the Nursery's potted plants. The Nursery then instituted suit, alleging the negligence of the Lab caused the plant damage.

The decisive issue is whether the court was justified in granting the Lab's motion for a summary judgment on the basis of the Nursery's failure to establish the requisite standard of care and a departure therefrom.

In order to show negligent conduct, there must be:

1.   A duty, or obligation, recognized by the law, requiring the actor to conform to a certain standard of conduct, for the protection of others against unreasonable risks.

2.   A failure on his part to conform to the standard required . . . W. Prosser, Handbook of the Law of Torts, §30 at 143 (4th ed. 1971) (footnote omitted).

The Lab argues that §299A of the Restatement (Second) of Torts gives indication that the drafters of the Restatement intended to adopt the professional standard rather than the reasonable man standard of care in determining the negligence duty question in this case. This section, in commenting upon the standard of conduct, reads:

UNDERTAKING IN PROFESSION OR TRADE

Unless he represents that he has greater or less skill or knowledge, one who undertakes to render services in the practice of a profession or trade is required to exercise the skill and knowledge normally possessed by members of that profession or trade in good standing in similar communities.

It is our opinion that the pertinent portions of the Restatement dealing with the question before us indicate that the Lab owed the Nursery the duty to exercise the skill and knowledge normally possessed by members of the plant laboratory trade in similar communities.

In our opinion, the proper standard of care to be applied to the facts of this case was set forth in Kreisman v. Thomas 469 P.2d 107 (1970). In *Kreisman* the plaintiff claimed he got an ear infection as a result of the defendant's negligence in failing to properly adjust loaner hearing aids. This court, on appeal, affirmed the order of the trial court directing a verdict for the defendant. This court found the plaintiff had failed to establish the requisite community professional standard of care and the defendant's departure therefrom. In addressing the issue, the court stated:

Where, as here, the duty which the law recognizes arises because the defendant has held himself out to be trained in a particular trade or profession, the standard required for the protection of others against unreasonable risks is that the defendant exercise the skill and knowledge normally possessed by members of that trade or profession in good standing in similar communities. Restatement (Second) of Torts §299A (1965);

There is no dispute in this case that the Lab held itself to be an experienced and trained professional laboratory which provided advisory services for the growing of plants. As such, the law placed a duty upon the Lab to exercise the skill and knowledge normally possessed by members of that trade or profession.

The burden of establishing both the standard of care and the Lab's departure there from fell upon the Nursery. As we stated in *Kreisman*:

The plaintiff has the burden of establishing what conduct this standard of care requires and that the defendant has failed to comply therewith. . . . The requirement that there be proof of the requisite standard of conduct means that even if we assume that defendant provided plaintiff with a set of unfitted hearing aids which irritated plaintiff's ears, and that an infection developed because of this irritation, the existence of such assumed facts alone cannot make defendant liable to plaintiff for the damages caused by such infection. There must be an additional showing that because of the relationship between the parties there was a duty or obligation imposed upon defendant requiring him to do something which he did not do; that is, that he failed to conform to a certain standard of conduct required in this particular transaction with plaintiff.

Where, as here, the duty which the law recognizes arises because the defendant has held himself out to be trained in a particular trade or profession, the standard required for the protection of customers against unreasonable risks must be established by specific evidence. It cannot be left to conjecture nor be established by argument of counsel. In the absence of evidence establishing the requisite standard of care and that defendant's conduct failed to meet that standard, there was no basis upon which the jury could have found defendant liable to the plaintiff, and therefore the trial court did not commit error in refusing to submit the matter to the jury.

In the depositions of the Nursery's two experts, neither could express any opinion of whether the Lab had failed to exercise that degree of care normally possessed by members of that trade. The Nursery's principal expert was Dr. Wallace H. Fuller, a professor and biochemist employed by the University of Arizona. It was his opinion that the plant damage "(w)as associated with the period of application of iron chelate Fe 330." When questioned relative to the Lab's standard of care and deviations therefrom, Dr. Fuller gave the following pertinent testimony:

> Q.   You can't say then that they failed to exercise care and competence, can you?
> A.   I have not made that accusation, no sir.

The only deviation of care testified to by Dr. Fuller was his statement that he personally would not want to make a plant diagnosis in such a case without an on-site inspection. When further questioned along these lines, he stated:

> Q.   You can't say here today then either that Soil and Plant Lab failed to exercise the degree of care that would be the standard of care under all the circumstances that existed at the time?
> A.   No, I can't answer that one way or the other. I have an opinion, and my opinion is that I wouldn't undertake business this way.

All parties agree it is easier to make an accurate diagnosis with an on-site inspection. The Lab offered on-site inspections at an additional fee to its customers. The fact that Dr. Wallace H. Fuller who is hired by a state agency, would prefer to diagnose only after an on-site inspection cannot reasonably set the inspection standard of care fixed upon a commercial plant laboratory. It is unrealistic to force a commercial plant laboratory located in California to come to Arizona for on-site inspection unless its customer requests such a service and is willing to pay the additional fee.

Mr. Lowell True, who works with the University of Arizona Agricultural Extension Service, was the Nursery's other expert. Mr. True lacked sufficient information and background to express an opinion on whether the advice from the Lab caused the damage to the Nursery's plants. He could not say that the Lab engaged in wrongful or negligent conduct or that the Lab failed to exercise care and competence in obtaining and communicating relevant information to the Nursery.

The standard of care issue is determinative of this appeal. After a review of the law and the evidence, it is our opinion that the Nursery failed to establish the requisite standard of care and the Lab's departure from such standard.

Affirmed.

PREPARING FOR CLASS

1. Why was the plaintiff required to call an expert witness in this case?

2. What should the plaintiff's counsel ask the expert?

3. What qualifications should the plaintiff's counsel look for in an expert witness in this case?

4. The court says that it is not practical for a laboratory in California to come to Arizona for an on-site inspection. How would the plaintiff reply to that argument? Explain.

5. The expert will rarely be a witness to the negligence. So what does the expert know that will assist the court in deciding the case?

6. Why should a court limit the standard of care to professionals in "similar communities"?

INCREASING YOUR UNDERSTANDING

1. There are two standards of care for professional conduct. Some courts hold the defendant to a reasonable professional standard of care. Other courts hold the defendant to a reasonable person standard of care but consider the need for professional abilities as the circumstances of the case. See Corpus Juris Secundum, §163, Professional Standard of Care.

2. Violation of an ethical rule of a profession is generally not sufficient to establish negligence. See Bala v. Powers Ferry Psychological Associates, 491 S.E.2d 380 (1997).

3. What if the plaintiff intended to retain a doctor and the plaintiff thought the doctor was a general practitioner? However, unknown to the plaintiff or the public, the doctor was a specialist in treating plaintiff's affliction. What would be the standard of care of the doctor? What are the issues?

APPLYING THE LAW

1. What would be the standard of care for a plumber?

2. What would be the standard of care for a doctor driving home from the office?

3. What would be the standard of care for a truck driver? Would the standard of care of a truck driver then differ from the standard of care for an automobile driver driving next to him or her? How about the standard of care for a cab driver?

4. What would be the standard of care for a greeter at a large department store?

5. What would be the standard of care for a chiropractor who is asked to treat a serious spinal injury, possibly requiring surgery?

Hypothetical

On April 15, Sam Kennedy went to Dr. Nixon, a podiatrist, for pain in his heel. Podiatrists are not medical doctors but separately licensed and trained specialists in the study, diagnosis, and treatment of the foot, ankle, and lower leg. Orthopedists are medical doctor specialists in the foot and ankle. Dr. Nixon put Mr. Kennedy's foot in a soft cast and prescribed pain medication but not anti-inflammatory medication. On April 22, Mr. Kennedy went back to Dr. Nixon complaining of discoloration and pain in his heel. Dr. Nixon put on a different soft cast and told Mr. Kennedy to continue with his present medication. But the pain and discoloration continued. Mr. Kennedy sought the advice of a medical doctor.

Mr. Kennedy had an appointment to see Dr. Harold, M.D., an orthopedist, on May 17, but the problems with his heel had become so severe that he canceled his appointment. On May 20, Mr. Kennedy was taken to the emergency room with severe discoloration and pain in his heel. Dr. Harold saw him in the emergency room and determined that nothing could be done, i.e., Mr. Kennedy's foot must be removed.

Mr. Kennedy comes to your law office. He wants to consider filing a malpractice suit against Dr. Nixon. Dr. Harold has told him that his foot had to come off or he would have contracted gangrene and possibly died. Dr. Harold said that if he had treated Mr. Kennedy, he would have prescribed anti-inflammatory drugs and procedures for his foot in a cast. Dr. Harold also believes that there is a good chance the cast on Mr. Kennedy's foot was too tight.

You decide to investigate Mr. Kennedy's possible malpractice claim.

1. Do you need an expert witness in this case?

2. If you need an expert, what kind of expert, i.e., a medical doctor of any kind, a medical doctor who specializes in the treatment of the foot, or a podiatrist?

3. Dr. Harold says that if he had treated Mr. Kennedy, he would have prescribed anti-inflammatory drugs. Is that enough, i.e., can Mr. Kennedy simply rely on Dr. Harold's testimony?

4. Do you have to seek podiatric experts or medical doctor experts in the area or can you look for experts nationwide?

C. MEDICAL PROFESSIONAL STANDARD
OF CARE

Sheeley v. Memorial Hospital
710 A.2d 161 (R.I. 1998)

GOLDBERG, Justice.

This case is before the court on the appeal of Joanne Sheeley (Sheeley) from the directed verdict entered against her in the underlying medical malpractice action. Specifically Sheeley asserts that the trial justice erred in excluding the testimony of her expert witness, which exclusion resulted in the entry of the directed verdict. For the reasons set forth below, we hold that the trial justice erred in excluding the testimony and reverse the judgment from which the appeal was taken. Furthermore, we take this opportunity to reexamine the proper standard of care to be applied in medical malpractice cases and, in so doing, abandon the "similar locality" rule, which previously governed the admissibility of expert testimony in such actions. The facts insofar as are pertinent to this appeal are as follows.

On May 19, 1987, Sheeley delivered a healthy child at Memorial Hospital (hospital) in Pawtucket, Rhode Island. At the time of the birth Sheeley was under the care of Mary Ryder, M.D. (Dr. Ryder), then a second-year family practice resident. Brian Jack, M.D. (Dr. Jack), was the faculty member responsible for the supervision of Dr. Ryder.

In conjunction with the delivery process Dr. Ryder performed an episiotomy on Sheeley. This procedure entails a cut into the perineum of the mother, the purpose being to prevent tearing during the delivery. After the baby had been delivered, Dr. Ryder performed a repair of the episiotomy, stitching the incision previously made into the perineum.

After her discharge from the hospital Sheeley developed complications in the area in which the episiotomy had been performed and ultimately developed a rectovaginal fistula. This condition, which consists of an opening between the vagina and the rectum, required corrective surgery. Notwithstanding the surgery, however, Sheeley continued to experience pain and discomfort at the site of the episiotomy. Sheeley, together with her husband Mark Sheeley, then filed suit against the hospital, Dr. Ryder, and Dr. Jack (collectively defendants), alleging that defendants were negligent in performing the episiotomy incision and repairing the same properly.

At the trial on the malpractice action, Sheeley sought to introduce the expert medical testimony of Stanley D. Leslie, M.D. (Dr. Leslie), a board certified obstetrician/gynecologist (OB/GYN). Doctor Leslie planned to testify about Dr. Ryder's alleged malpractice and the applicable standard of care as it relates to the performance of an episiotomy. The defendants objected and filed a motion in limine to exclude the testimony, arguing that Dr. Leslie, as an

OB/GYN, was not qualified under G.L.1956 §9-19-41[3] to testify against a family practice resident who was performing obstetric and gynecological care. A hearing on the motion was conducted, at which time it was disclosed that Dr. Leslie had been board certified in obstetrics and gynecology since 1961 and recertified in 1979. Doctor Leslie testified that board certification represents a level of achievement of skill and knowledge as established by a national standard in which the standard of care is uniform throughout the medical specialty. Doctor Leslie is currently a clinical professor of obstetrics and gynecology at the Hill-Science Center, State University, College of Medicine in Syracuse. He is a member of the New York Statewide Professional Standards Review Council, which reviews disputes between doctors and hospitals regarding diagnosis and management, and the Credentials and Certification Committee at the Crouse-Irving Hospital, where his responsibilities include drafting standards for family practice physicians. It was further revealed that Dr. Leslie has in the course of his career delivered approximately 4,000 babies and that even though he has been retired from the practice of obstetrics since 1975, he has maintained his familiarity with the standards and practices in the field of obstetrics through weekly conferences, active obstetric work, professorial responsibilities, and continuing education.

Nevertheless, relying on Soares v. Vestal, 632 A.2d 647 (R.I. 1993), defendants maintained that §9-19-41 requires a testifying expert to be in the same medical field as the defendant physician. In *Soares* this court upheld the trial justice's decision to exclude the testimony of the plaintiff's expert witness in a situation in which the expert was board certified in neurology and internal medicine, and the underlying malpractice action involved a family practitioner performing emergency medicine. Agreeing that *Soares* was determinative, the trial justice here granted defendants' motion, stating: "I fail to see where this case is distinguishable from *Soares*. I don't quarrel with the doctor's background and qualifications. I think he's the inappropriate expert to testify in this case." Sheeley did not have any other experts prepared to testify, nor was she able to procure one within the two-day period allowed by the trial justice. Consequently defendants' motion for a directed verdict was granted. This appeal ensued.

On appeal Sheeley argues that the trial justice's ruling constitutes an abuse of discretion and is clearly wrong because Dr. Leslie was amply qualified to testify concerning the alleged malpractice. The defendants respond by arguing that Sheeley's appeal should be summarily dismissed for her failure to make an adequate offer of proof. Furthermore defendants assert that Sheeley's expert is

---

3. General Laws 1956 §9-19-41 states:

"In any legal action based upon a cause of action arising on or after January 1, 1987, for personal injury or wrongful death filed against a licensed physician, hospital, clinic, health maintenance organization, professional service corporation providing health care services, dentists or dental hygienist based on professional negligence, only those persons who by knowledge, skill, experience, training or education qualify as experts in the field of the alleged malpractice shall be permitted to give expert testimony as to the alleged malpractice."

not competent to offer expert testimony on the appropriate standard of care because he has more specialized training than Dr. Ryder and because he lacks any recent experience in providing obstetric care.

"The determination of the competency of an expert witness to testify is within the discretion of the trial justice." This court will not disturb that decision in the absence of clear error or abuse. In fairness to the trial justice, we note that in making her determination with respect to the admissibility of the expert's testimony, she was without the benefit of our decisions in Marshall v. Medical Associates of Rhode Island, Inc., 677 A.2d 425 (R.I. 1996), and more importantly Buja v. Morningstar, 688 A.2d 817 (R.I. 1997), which have distinguished *Soares* and limited its holding to situations in which the physician-expert lacks knowledge, skill, experience, or education in the same medical field as the alleged malpractice. Nevertheless, after a review of these cases, we find it clear that the trial justice did in fact abuse her discretion and commit reversible error in excluding the testimony of Dr. Leslie.

In *Buja* the plaintiffs brought a medical malpractice action against their family practitioners when their child suffered severe medical complications, including cerebral palsy and mental retardation, after having been deprived of oxygen just prior to birth. At trial, the plaintiffs sought to introduce testimony of a board certified obstetrician. The trial justice, however, excluded the testimony and stated that testimony concerning the standard of care required of a family practitioner practicing obstetrics had to be introduced by an expert in family medicine, not an expert in OB/GYN. Relying on our previous holding in *Marshall*, this court reversed the trial justice and stated that even though the proposed expert did not practice in the same specialty as the defendants, he clearly had the prerequisite "knowledge, skill, experience, training or education . . . in the field of the alleged malpractice." (quoting §9-19-41 and citing *Marshall*, 677 A.2d at 427). The *Buja* court held that nothing in the language of §9-19-41 requires the expert to practice in the same specialty as the defendant. "Such an additional requirement is unnecessary and is in contravention to the General Assembly's clear intentions, as expressed in §9-19-41." In view of this holding and the striking factual similarities of the instant matter to *Buja*, there can be little doubt that we must reverse the decision of the trial justice and remand the case for a new trial.

Yet in spite of our holdings in *Buja* and *Marshall*, defendants continue to insist that Dr. Leslie is not qualified to testify. In essence defendants argue that Dr. Leslie is overqualified, stating that a board certified OB/GYN does not possess the same knowledge, skill, experience, training, or education as a second-year family practice resident performing obstetrics in Rhode Island. Furthermore defendants argue that because Dr. Leslie has not actually practiced obstetrics since 1975, his experience in providing obstetrical care is "clearly outdated" and he is therefore not competent to testify concerning the appropriate standard of care as it applied to the performance of an episiotomy and the repair of the same—even while they acknowledge that the standard of care relative to the procedures involved in the alleged malpractice have changed little over the last thirty years. Finally defendants assert that pursuant to the limitations of the "similar locality" rule, Dr. Leslie must be disqualified because he lacks any direct knowledge about the applicable standard of care for a family practice resident providing obstetric care in Rhode Island. The defendants suggest that Dr. Leslie, although he has attended national conferences and studied medical journals and treatises in addition to his national certification, is not qualified to testify about the applicable *local* standard of care. In light of these arguments and with a view toward preventing any further confusion regarding the necessary qualifications of an expert testifying about the proper standard of care in medical malpractice actions, we take this opportunity to revisit our position on the appropriate standard of care.

For over three-quarters of a century this court has subscribed to the principle "that when a physician undertakes to treat or diagnose a patient, he or she is under a duty to exercise 'the same degree of diligence and skill which is commonly possessed by other members of the profession who are engaged in the same type of practice in similar localities having due regard for the state of scientific knowledge at the time of treatment.'" This "same or similar locality" rule is a somewhat expanded version of the "strict locality" rule, which requires that the expert testifying be from the same community as the defendant. The rationale underlying the development of the "strict locality" rule was a recognition that opportunities, experience, and conditions may differ between densely and sparsely populated communities.

This restrictive rule, however, soon came under attack in that it legitimized a low standard of care in certain smaller communities and that it also failed to address or to compensate for the potential so-called conspiracy of silence in a plaintiff's locality that would preclude any possibility of obtaining expert testimony. Furthermore, as this court noted in *Wilkinson*, the locality rule is somewhat of an anachronism in view of "[m]odern systems of transportation and communication." Thus many jurisdictions, including our own, adopted the "same or similar locality" rule, which allows for experts from similarly situated communities to testify concerning the appropriate standard of care. Nevertheless, even with this somewhat expanded view, the medical malpractice bar has continually urged a narrow application of the rule, arguing the need for similar, if not identical, education, training, and experience. The obvious result of such an application, however, is to reduce the pool of qualified experts to its lowest common denominator. This is a consequence that we have never intended.

The appropriate standard of care to be utilized in any given procedure should not be compartmentalized by a physician's area of professional specialization or certification. On the contrary, we believe the focus in any medical malpractice case should be the procedure performed and the question of whether it was executed in conformity with the recognized standard of care, the primary concern being whether the treatment was administered in a reasonable manner. Any doctor with knowledge of or familiarity with the

procedure, acquired through experience, observation, association, or education, is competent to testify concerning the requisite standard of care and
whether the care in any given case deviated from that standard. The resources
available to a physician, his or her specific area of practice, or the length of
time he or she has been practicing are all issues that should be considered by
the trial justice in making his or her decision regarding the qualification of an
expert. No one issue, however, should be determinative. Furthermore, except
in extreme cases, a witness who has obtained board certification in a particular
specialty related to the procedure in question, especially when that board certification reflects a national standard of training and qualification should be
presumptively qualified to render an opinion.

This court is of the opinion that whatever geographical impediments may
previously have justified the need for a "similar locality" analysis is no longer
applicable in view of the present-day realities of the medical profession. As the
Shilkret court observed:

> "The modern physician bears little resemblance to his predecessors. As
> we have indicated at length, the medical schools of yesterday could not
> possibly compare with the accredited institutions of today, many of
> which are associated with teaching hospitals. But the contrast merely
> begins at that point in the medical career: vastly superior postgraduate
> training, the dynamic impact of modern communications and
> transportation, the proliferation of medical literature, frequent seminars
> and conferences on a variety of professional subjects, and the growing
> availability of modern clinical facilities are but some of the develop-
> ments in the medical profession which combine to produce
> contemporary standards that are not only much higher than they were
> just a few short years ago, but are also national in scope.
>
> "In sum, the traditional locality rules no longer fit the present-day
> medical malpractice case."

Shilkret, 349 A.2d at 252.

We agree. Furthermore, we note that in enacting §9-19-41, the Legislature
failed to employ any reference to the "similar locality" rule. We conclude that
this omission was deliberate and constitutes recognition of the national
approach to the delivery of medical services, especially in the urban centers
of this country, of which Rhode Island is certainly one.

Accordingly we join the growing number of jurisdictions that have repu-
diated the "same or similar" communities test in favor of a national standard
and hold that a physician is under a duty to use the degree of care and skill that
is expected of a reasonably competent practitioner in the same class to which
he or she belongs, acting in the same or similar circumstances. In this case the
alleged malpractice occurred in the field of obstetrics and involved a procedure and attendant standard of care that has remained constant for over thirty

years. Doctor Leslie, as a board certified OB/GYN with over thirty years of experience, a clinical professor of obstetrics and gynecology at a major New York hospital, and a member of the New York Statewide Professional Standards Review Council, is undoubtedly qualified to testify regarding the appropriate standard of care.

For the foregoing reasons the plaintiff's appeal is sustained, and the judgment appealed from is reversed. The papers in the case are remanded to the Superior Court with our decision endorsed thereon for a new trial in accordance with this opinion.

PREPARING FOR CLASS

1. What is the justification for the local, community standard of care? What would the defendant's attorney argue to justify the local, community standard of care?

2. Plaintiff's expert testifies that "I wouldn't do it that way" when testifying about the defendant doctor's alleged malpractice. Is that enough to establish that the defendant's actions were malpractice? What questions would you ask the expert if you were representing the plaintiff?

3. Would the national standard of care include an expert from Windsor, Canada?

4. What about a surgeon who testifies that he or she does not do anesthesiology but does know what anesthesiologists in the community do since they work together in surgery. Would you allow the surgeon to testify about the anesthesiologists' community standard of care?

INCREASING YOUR UNDERSTANDING

1. Presenting the testimony of an expert doctor in a medical malpractice case is one of the greatest challenges for the trial attorney. First, the plaintiff's attorney must qualify the expert, i.e., the plaintiff's attorney must ask the witness questions establishing that the witness has sufficient training, skill, or knowledge to assist the court in determining facts at issue in the trial. The attorney should ask the witness about where the witness went to college, medical school, specialty training, board certification, practical experience, etc. The attorney asks these questions to convince the judge to recognize the witness as an expert and thus to allow the witness to testify to his or her opinion. The attorney also asks these questions to convince the jury or fact finder that the witness is not only minimally qualified but should be followed in determining the standard of care in the community.

2. It must be remembered that most of the trial experts did not see the malpractice so they are not fact witnesses; these experts cannot testify about what happened, only what should have happened. This is usually done with the use of a hypothetical question, i.e., "witness, assume the following facts to be true" followed by a recitation of the facts that the attorney believes he or she will be able to prove. The facts for the hypothetical must be carefully drafted. If the attorney cannot prove the assumed facts, then the testimony of the expert will no longer apply to the case on trial.

D. MEDICAL INFORMED CONSENT

Woolley v. Henderson
418 A.2d 1123 (Me. 1980)

GLASSMAN, Justice.

The plaintiffs, Linda E. Woolley and her husband, Brandon Woolley, appeal from a judgment of the Superior Court, Somerset County, entered on April 13, 1979 following a jury verdict in favor of the defendant, Dr. Lester K. Henderson. On appeal in this medical malpractice action, the plaintiffs challenge rulings of the Superior Court Justice regarding . . . the striking of an implied contract count in the complaint, the denial of a motion to add a battery claim to the complaint and the jury instructions concerning informed consent and the defendant's right to practice medicine. We vacate the judgment.

Linda Woolley suffered from a history of back problems and associated sciatic pain in her right leg. In 1965 she had back surgery for a ruptured disc at the interspace between her fourth and fifth lumbar vertebrae (L 4, 5). Experiencing renewed back pain, the plaintiff, in January of 1976, consulted the defendant, an orthopedic surgeon practicing in Skowhegan, who diagnosed a ruptured disc at the L 4, 5 vertebral interspace. When conservative treatment failed to alleviate the plaintiff's pain, the defendant performed a lumbar myelogram, a diagnostic procedure involving the use of dye and x-ray. On the basis of this test, the defendant recommended surgery. The extent to which he apprised the plaintiff of the risks of the proposed surgery is unclear.

In February of 1976, the defendant operated on the plaintiff, performing a laminectomy and foraminotomy at what he thought to be the L 4, 5 interspace. The defendant urged at trial, however, that because of the plaintiff's transitional vertebra, a congenital abnormality of the spine that makes counting and ascertaining the vertebral levels difficult, he in fact operated at the L 2, 3 and L 3, 4 interspaces, performing the surgical procedures at L 3, 4 rather than at

L 4, 5. There was also evidence that the area of previous surgery was in fact L 3, 4 and not L 4, 5.

During the course of this operation, the defendant inadvertently made a rent in the dura, arachnoid and pia, the protective tissues encasing the spinal cord, while removing a small bone attached to epidural scar tissue. As a result, spinal fluid leaked from the plaintiff's spinal cord. Medical experts for both sides testified that a dural tear was a normal risk of this type of surgery, especially for a patient who had previous surgery at the location, and that a dural tear could occur at the hands of the most careful and competent surgeon.

Following surgery, the plaintiff's low back and radiating leg pain intensified. The defendant did not order further x-rays or myelograms, choosing to treat these symptoms with pain medication. Because her condition failed to improve, the plaintiff consulted another physician who, following examination and myelogram, removed protruding disc material at the L 4, 5 interspace in July of 1976. Although this surgical treatment alleviated the plaintiff's radiating leg pain, her back pain continued and subsequently intensified because she began to suffer from chronic adhesive arachnoiditis, an inflammation and thickening of the spinal cord that causes intractable back pain.

In a four-count complaint filed in the Superior Court on November 8, 1977, Linda Woolley alleged the defendant had breached an implied contract to perform surgery "in a good, workmanlike, professional, and skillful manner"; the defendant had failed adequately to inform the plaintiff of the risks of surgery; and the defendant had been negligent in operating at the wrong level of the plaintiff's lumbar spine, in causing a dural tear, in his postoperative care and otherwise in his diagnosis and treatment of the plaintiff. Brandon Woolley included a claim for loss of consortium.

II. Informed Consent

At trial the plaintiffs seasonably objected to the jury instruction of the presiding Justice that the defendant's obligation to apprise Linda Woolley of the risks of the proposed surgery was limited to those disclosures which would be made by a reasonable medical practitioner. In Downer v. Veilleux, Me., 322 A.2d 82 (1974), this Court recognized the doctrine of informed consent as an actionable species of medical negligence:

> The doctrine is based on the general principle of law that a physician has a duty adequately to disclose to his patient the proposed diagnostic, therapeutic or surgical procedure to be undertaken, the material risks involved therein and the alternatives available, if any, so that a patient of ordinary understanding, confronted with these disclosures and faced with a choice of undergoing the proposed treatment, or selecting an alternative process, or preferring refusal of all medical relief, may, in

reaching a decision, intelligently exercise his judgment by balancing the probable risks against the probable benefits. Id. at 90-91.

Our decision in Downer raised, but expressly left unresolved, the scope of the physician's duty to disclose and the test applicable in determining proximate causation. We are now called upon to determine these questions, which go to the core of the informed consent doctrine.

A. SCOPE OF DISCLOSURE DUTY

Although it is well settled that the law imposes on a physician a general duty reasonably to disclose to his patient significant information concerning treatment, jurisdictions differ on the scope of this disclosure obligation. Many courts hold that the duty of a physician to make adequate disclosure is, as in other cases of medical malpractice, measured by the standard of the reasonable medical practitioner under the same or similar circumstances. Under this "professional" disclosure standard, therefore, whether and to what extent a physician has an obligation to disclose a particular risk must in most cases be determined by expert medical testimony establishing the prevailing standard of practice and the defendant's departure therefrom. On the other hand, an increasing number of courts hold that because a physician's obligation to disclose therapeutic risks and alternatives arises from the patient's right of physical self-determination, the disclosure duty should be measured by the patient's need for information rather than by the standards of the medical profession. These courts reason that physicians have a legal obligation adequately to disclose risk and option information that is material to the patient's decision to undergo treatment and that expert testimony as to medical standards is not required to establish this duty. Under this "material-risk" standard, although expert medical testimony may be necessary to establish the undisclosed risk as a known danger of the procedure, the jury can decide without the necessity of a medical expert whether a reasonable person in the patient's position would have considered the risk significant in making his decision.

A basic principle of medical malpractice law is that the physician is not an insurer. "A poor result, standing alone, is insufficient to establish liability. Thus, under no view of the doctrine of informed consent can liability be found for every failure to disclose a risk that has later materialized; despite solicitude for the informational needs of patients, liability for nondisclosure must still be based on fault. Underlying the conflict in the cases is a disagreement over the fundamental question whether fault in informed consent actions should be predicated on deviation from the professional standard of care or on interference with a patient's interest in physical self-determination. Consistent with our view of informed consent as a form of professional malpractice, we believe that fault must be measured by reference to the reasonable medical practitioner in the same branch of medicine and not according to some variable lay standard of "materiality."

When a patient alleges that an unrevealed hazard has caused him injury, the jury must determine whether, under the facts of the case, the physician has deviated from the standard of care of the reasonable practitioner. Although the unreasonableness of a particular nondisclosure may be " 'sufficiently obvious as to lie within common knowledge . . . ,' " in most cases expert medical testimony is just as necessary to establish negligence in failing adequately to disclose as it is to prove negligence in diagnosis or treatment. Whether the physician has acted unreasonably is often a question of professional judgment. In determining whether and how much he should disclose, the physician must consider the probable impact of disclosure on the patient, taking into account his peculiar knowledge of the patient's psychological, emotional and physical condition, and must evaluate the magnitude of the risk, the frequency of its occurrence and the viability of alternative therapeutic measures. "This determination involves medical judgment as to whether disclosure of possible risks may have such an adverse effect on the patient as to jeopardize success of the proposed therapy, no matter how expertly performed." Aiken v. Clary, 396 S.W.2d 668, 674 (Mo. 1965).[7] Conceivably, full disclosure under some circumstances could constitute bad medical practice.

Moreover, a rule that allows a plaintiff to establish the existence and extent of the defendant-physician's disclosure obligation without regard to medical standards hardly diminishes the importance of expert medical testimony or absolves the plaintiff from producing such evidence on other issues in the case. The courts that have adopted this rule recognize the necessity, in the usual case, of medical evidence to identify the known risks of treatment, the nature of available alternatives and the cause of any injury or disability suffered by the plaintiff, and would allow the defendant to show by expert testimony that his conduct comported with medical standards,[8] Furthermore, when the patient also claims negligent diagnosis or treatment, he will have secured medical experts to testify to the applicable standard of care. It certainly adds little to the burden of the plaintiff on his informed consent claim to require him to produce medical evidence that the physician's nondisclosure departed from prevailing standards of practice.

---

7. Courts that have rejected the need for medical evidence on the disclosure obligation nevertheless acknowledge that valid medical reasons may warrant nondisclosure. These courts posit that a physician has a "privilege" to withhold information for justifiable therapeutic reasons. Just how the concept of a "privilege" fits into a negligence action is unclear, but the net effect is to place upon the physician the burden of showing the reasonableness of his conduct. Presumably, the physician would raise this privilege by way of expert medical testimony.

8. Even these courts recognize limits on a physician's disclosure obligation. "The physician need not deliver a 'lengthy polysyllabic discourse on all possible complications. A mini-course in medical science is not required(.)' " Sard v. Hardy, supra, 379 A.2d at 1022, quoting Cobbs v. Grant, supra, 502 P.2d at 11. In addition, "disclosure is not required where the risk is either known to the patient or so obvious as to justify presumption of such knowledge, nor is the physician under a duty to discuss the relatively remote risks inherent in common procedures, when it is common knowledge that such risks inherent in the procedure are of very low incidence."

Nevertheless, these limitations on the disclosure duty are unlikely to afford a physician much guidance in his daily interactions with patients. Rather than relying on his professional judgment, a physician practicing in a "material-risk" jurisdiction may well feel compelled at his peril to disclose every imaginable risk and alternative to treatment.

In addition, we are not unmindful of the practical implications of dispensing with the requirement of expert medical testimony to establish the existence and extent of the disclosure duty in a given case. Inherent in such a rule is the potential danger that a jury, composed of laymen and gifted with the benefit of hindsight, will divine the breach of a disclosure obligation largely on the basis of the unfortunate result. In *Bly v. Rhoads*, supra, the Virginia court expressed a similar concern:

> The matters involved in the disclosure syndrome, more often than not, are complicated and highly technical. To leave the establishment of such matters to lay witnesses, in our opinion, would pose dangers and disadvantages which far outweigh the benefits and advantages a "modern trend" rule would bestow on patient-plaintiffs. In effect, the relaxed "modern trend" rule permits lay witnesses to express, when all is said and done, what amounts to a medical opinion. 222 S.E.2d at 787.

Finally, we believe that legal principles designed to provide compensation to persons injured by bad professional practice should not unduly intrude upon the intimate physician-patient relationship. Although the "material-risk" theory may make it easier for some plaintiffs to recover, it does so by placing good medical practice in jeopardy. The physician's attention must be focused on the best interests of his patient and not on what a lay jury, unschooled in medicine, may, after the fact, conclude he should have disclosed. As a North Carolina court noted,

> (t)o adopt the ("material-risk" standard) would result in requiring every doctor to spend much unnecessary time in going over with every patient every possible effect of any proposed treatment. The doctor should not have to practice his profession with the knowledge that every consultation with every patient with respect to future treatment contains a potential lawsuit and his advice and suggestions must necessarily be phrased with the possible defense of a lawsuit in mind. This would necessarily result in the doctor's inability to give the best interest of his patient primary importance. Butler v. Berkeley, 213 S.E.2d 571, 581-82 (1975).

We hold, therefore, that the scope of a physician's duty to disclose is measured by those communications a reasonable medical practitioner in that branch of medicine would make under the same or similar circumstances and that the plaintiff must ordinarily establish this standard by expert medical evidence.

B. CAUSATION

All courts recognizing the doctrine of informed consent as a species of medical negligence require the plaintiff to prove proximate causation by a preponderance of the evidence. Otherwise, the physician's omission, however wrongful, is legally inconsequential. As we noted in *Downer v. Veilleux*, supra, to establish a proximate causal relationship between the nondisclosure and the untoward result, the plaintiff must show not only that the undisclosed risk materialized causing him harm but also that had he been informed of the risk he would not have submitted to the treatment. The question we left open in *Downer* and which we now address is whether this second causation requirement is to be judged by a subjective test—whether the particular plaintiff would have undergone the treatment had he been adequately informed or by an objective test—whether a reasonable person in the plaintiff's position would have submitted to the procedure had there been adequate disclosure. In the instant case, the presiding Justice instructed the jury, without objection, that it was to apply the objective causation standard.

We believe that the subjective test is an unsatisfactory gauge for determining causality in informed consent actions and, therefore, in accord with those courts that have squarely addressed this issue, we hold that causation should be judged by an objective standard. The Maryland court in *Sard v. Hardy*, persuasively summarized the rationale in support of the objective standard:

> (I)f a subjective standard were applied, the testimony of the plaintiff as to what he would have hypothetically done would be the controlling consideration. Thus, proof of causation under a subjective standard would ultimately turn on the credibility of the hindsight of a person seeking recovery after he had experienced a most undesirable result. Such a test puts the physician in "jeopardy of the patient's hindsight and bitterness." 281 Md. at 449, 379 A.2d at 1025. (Citations omitted).

Under the objective test, a causal connection exists between the defendant's failure to disclose and the plaintiff's injury only if a reasonable person in the position of the plaintiff would have declined the treatment had he been apprised of the risk that resulted in harm "(T)he patient's hindsight testimony as to what he would have hypothetically done, though relevant, is not determinative of the issue." Sard v. Hardy, 379 A.2d at 1025.

III. BATTERY CLAIM

After the close of evidence, the plaintiffs moved to amend their complaint to add a battery theory of recovery on the ground that evidence in the case tended to show that the defendant actually had performed surgery at the L 2, 3 and L 3, 4 interspaces rather than the surgery at the L 4, 5 interspace to which Mrs. Woolley had consented. The presiding Justice denied this motion, ruling that the plaintiffs' "wrong-level" theory had not been tried by the express or implied consent of the parties as required by M.R. Civ. P. 15(b). We have no occasion to consider the propriety of this ruling however, because even if the amendment had been allowed it would not have stated an actionable claim of battery on the facts of this case.

Although the decisions from which the informed consent doctrine developed were cases that imposed liability for unauthorized treatment on a theory of battery, it is now settled, as we recognized in *Downer v. Veilleux*, supra, that despite the jurisprudential roots of the doctrine actions based on lack of informed consent sound in negligence and not in battery. We noted that the modern approach confines the battery theory to cases where "the treatment is either against the patient's will or substantially at variance with the consent given."

The plaintiffs' allegation that the defendant operated at the wrong lumbar interspace does not come within the narrow area in which physicians remain liable for battery in their treatment of patients. Here, Linda Woolley authorized the defendant to operate on her lumbar vertebrae in an attempt to relieve her discomfort. The defendant did not perform this surgery against the will of the plaintiff. Nor did the defendant perform an operation which he knew was substantially different from that to which the plaintiff had consented. In such egregious circumstances, the conscious disregard of the patient's interest in his physical integrity carries the physician's conduct outside of the physician-patient relationship.[11]

We reject any shopworn doctrine that would impose liability for a battery on physicians whose treatment deviated from that agreed to, however slight the deviation and regardless of the reasonableness of the physician's conduct. It places form over substance to elevate what is essentially a negligence action to the status of an intentional tort based on the fortuity that touching is a necessary incident to treatment in a relationship which is consensual in nature. Therefore, as in other areas of professional liability, when a physician, acting in good faith and in what he believes to be the best interests of his patient, deviates from the proposed procedure or surgery, the issue is ordinarily whether under the circumstances the physician exercised due care in deviating from the proposed treatment and not whether he exceeded the scope of the patient's consent. We believe that such a rule best accords with modern principles of medical malpractice favoring a single basis of liability predicated on fault and with the realities of the physician-patient relationship.

IV. IMPLIED CONTRACT COUNT

Prior to trial, the defendant moved under M.R. Civ. P. 12(b)(6) to dismiss Count I of the plaintiffs' complaint on the ground that the breach of contract allegation failed to state a claim upon which relief could be granted. The

---

11. Obviously, a physician, like anyone else, may be liable for a battery if contact is wholly unauthorized or if he engages in flagrant misconduct toward another person. 1 D. Louisell & H. Williams, Medical Malpractice P 8.09 (1977). We are concerned here only with the viability of a battery theory for conduct which does not transcend the physician-patient relationship.

presiding Justice denied this motion, concluding that Maine law recognized a breach of implied contract as a theory of recovery for medical malpractice. Nevertheless, he ordered Count I stricken sua sponte on the ground that it was redundant in view of the negligence claim contained in Count III of the complaint. On appeal, the plaintiffs challenge the action of the presiding Justice, arguing that breach of implied contract is an independent theory of recovery in medical malpractice actions and that such a claim was not duplicative of the negligence count.

In support of these contentions, the plaintiffs rely, as did the presiding Justice, on a frequently cited passage in Coombs v. King, 78 A.468 (1910), defining a physician's legal responsibility:

> He contracts with his patient that he has the ordinary skill of members of his profession in like situation, that he will exercise ordinary or reasonable care and diligence in his treatment of the case, and that he will use his best judgment in the application of his skill to the case. Id. at 378, 78 A. at 468.

Although *Coombs* and other early cases framed a physician's duty in terms of an implied representation that he possessed and would exercise a reasonable level of professional competence it is now clear that the implied contract theory merely imposes a duty that tort law would in any event require. With the development of modern tort principles, the majority of courts, usually in the context of whether contract or tort limitation or venue statutes govern the action, have come to recognize that although the physician-patient relationship is typically consensual in nature the existence of this relationship imposes a duty of due care which arises in negligence rather than in contract.

Illustrative of the modern view holding that malpractice actions are squarely grounded in principles of tort law is the leading case of Kozan v. Comstock, 270 F.2d 839 (5th Cir. 1959), in which the Fifth Circuit Court persuasively reasoned:

> It is the nature of the duty breached that should determine whether the action is in tort or in contract. To determine the duty one must examine the patient-physician relationship. It is true that usually a consensual relationship exists and the physician agrees impliedly to treat the patient in a proper manner. Thus, a malpractice suit is inextricably bound up with the idea of breach of implied contract. However, the patient-physician relationship, and the corresponding duty that is owed, is not one that is completely dependent upon a contract theory. There are instances in which the relationship exists though there is clearly no contractual relationship between the patient and the physician. Thus, the patient may be incapable of contracting or a third person may have contracted with the physician for the treatment of the patient. Even in these instances in which no contract is present the physician still owes a

duty to the patient. The duty of due care is imposed by law and is something over and above any contractual duty. Certainly, a physician could not void liability for negligent conduct by having contracted not to be liable for negligence. The duty is owed in all cases, and a breach of this duty constitutes a tort. On principle then, we consider a malpractice action as tortious in nature whether the duty grows out of a contractual relation or has no origin in contract. Id. at 844-45.

In addition to the inadequacy of implied contract as a comprehensive liability base in malpractice actions, we discern additional reasons for eschewing any reliance upon a theory that a physician has breached an implied contractual duty of due care. First, the reasonableness of a physician's conduct can be adequately determined under familiar tort principles without the necessity of importing into malpractice actions commercial concepts with traditionally distinct rules as to theory, proof, damages, limitation periods and venue. Second, and related to the foregoing, recognizing the continued vitality of implied contract as an independent cause of action would be fundamentally inconsistent with the modern view that malpractice actions should be predicated on a single basis of liability—deviation from the professional standard of care—with the application of common evidentiary and procedural rules.

We are not here concerned with a breach of an express contract between a physician and his patient. A physician may be liable in contract for breach of an express agreement to effect a cure or to achieve a particular result. We hold only that where a plaintiff claims he has suffered personal injury as the result of a physician's faulty diagnosis or mistreatment his remedy lies in a complaint for negligence, not in an action based on an implied contract to exercise due care. In the instant case, the presiding Justice should have granted the defendant's motion to dismiss although his action in striking the count had the same effect.

The entry is:

Appeal sustained.

Judgment vacated.

Remanded to the Superior Court for further proceedings consistent with the opinion herein.

PREPARING FOR CLASS

1. The plaintiffs argue that the defendant operated on the wrong vertebral interspaces. How does the court deal with that argument, or does it? Should the doctor have warned the plaintiff that "I might operate on the wrong vertebral interspace"?

2. The court says that the standard for informed consent is the "reasonable" medical practitioner. What does the word "reasonable" add to the test?

3. The court says that the standard of causation is whether the reasonable patient would have changed his or her mind when told of the additional risk. But the doctor is recommending the medical procedure. When would the reasonable patient refuse a medical procedure that the expert medical person recommends?

4. What is the advantage of the "professional" disclosure standard?

INCREASING YOUR UNDERSTANDING

1. Some states have statutes establishing panels or administrators to set forth standard warnings to be given for certain medical procedures. What are the advantages and disadvantages of this procedure?

2. The courts have placed the burden of informed consent on the doctor, not on the patient. Therefore, the courts have not allowed the doctor to plead the contributory negligence of the patient's failure to investigate or become informed about the risks of the medical procedure, even in an age of computer medical information.

3. Under *Carroll Towing*, there is little burden of providing warnings. How does this affect the determination of negligence in an informed consent case?

4. Sometimes there will be no medical custom because the procedure is new or unusual. What will the courts expect in those circumstances?

APPLYING THE LAW

1. Must a doctor who is going to perform surgery disclose that he or she has tested positive for HIV?

2. Must a doctor who is going to perform a medical procedure disclose his or her record of past performance with this procedure?

3. A doctor is going to perform open heart surgery on a patient. The doctor provides the patient with 35 single-spaced pages of risks. What do you think of the adequacy of this disclosure?

4. What if the patient is a Jehovah's Witness who, because of a sincere religious conviction, refuses to consent to blood transfusions? The doctor determines that the Jehovah's Witness patient is bleeding to death. The doctor informs the patient of all possible risks and alternatives to the medical procedure, but the patient refuses. What should the doctor do?

5. The patient consents to surgery by doctor A. Doctor B performs the surgery. Is doctor A or B, or both liable?

E. INFORMED CONSENT AND CONFLICT OF INTEREST

Moore v. Regents of the University of California
793 P.2d 479 (Cal. 1990)

PANELLI, Justice.

We granted review in this case to determine whether plaintiff has stated a cause of action against his physician and other defendants for using his cells in potentially lucrative medical research without his permission. Plaintiff alleges that his physician failed to disclose preexisting research and economic interests in the cells before obtaining consent to the medical procedures by which they were extracted. The superior court sustained all defendants' demurrers to the third amended complaint, and the Court of Appeal reversed. We hold that the complaint states a cause of action for breach of the physician's disclosure obligations, but not for conversion.

II. FACTS

Moore first visited UCLA Medical Center on October 5, 1976, shortly after he learned that he had hairy-cell leukemia. After hospitalizing Moore and "withdr[awing] extensive amounts of blood, bone marrow aspirate, and other bodily substances," Golde confirmed that diagnosis. At this time all defendants, including Golde, were aware that "certain blood products and blood components were of great value in a number of commercial and scientific efforts" and that access to a patient whose blood contained these substances would provide "competitive, commercial, and scientific advantages."

On October 8, 1976, Golde recommended that Moore's spleen be removed. Golde informed Moore "that he had reason to fear for his life, and that the proposed splenectomy operation . . . was necessary to slow down the progress of his disease." Based upon Golde's representations, Moore signed a written consent form authorizing the splenectomy.

Before the operation, Golde and Quan "formed the intent and made arrangements to obtain portions of [Moore's] spleen following its removal" and to take them to a separate research unit. Golde gave written instructions to this effect on October 18 and 19, 1976. These research activities "were not intended to have . . . any relation to [Moore's] medical . . . care." However, neither Golde nor Quan informed Moore of their plans to conduct this research or requested his permission. Surgeons at UCLA Medical Center, whom the complaint does not name as defendants, removed Moore's spleen on October 20, 1976.

Moore returned to the UCLA Medical Center several times between November 1976 and September 1983. He did so at Golde's direction and based upon representations "that such visits were necessary and required for his health and well-being, and based upon the trust inherent in and by virtue of the physician-patient relationship. . . ." On each of these visits Golde withdrew additional samples of "blood, blood serum, skin, bone marrow aspirate, and sperm." On each occasion Moore traveled to the UCLA Medical Center from his home in Seattle because he had been told that the procedures were to be performed only there and only under Golde's direction.

"In fact, [however,] throughout the period of time that [Moore] was under [Golde's] care and treatment, . . . the defendants were actively involved in a number of activities which they concealed from [Moore]. . . ." Specifically, defendants were conducting research on Moore's cells and planned to "benefit financially and competitively . . . [by exploiting the cells] and [their] exclusive access to [the cells] by virtue of [Golde's] on-going physician-patient relationship. . . ."

Sometime before August 1979, Golde established a cell line from Moore's T-lymphocytes. On January 30, 1981, the Regents applied for a patent on the cell line, listing Golde and Quan as inventors. "[B]y virtue of an established policy . . . , [the] Regents, Golde, and Quan would share in any royalties or profits . . . arising out of [the] patent." The patent issued on March 20, 1984, naming Golde and Quan as the inventors of the cell line and the Regents as the assignee of the patent. (U.S. Patent No. 4,438,032 (Mar. 20, 1984).)

The Regent's patent also covers various methods for using the cell line to produce lymphokines. Moore admits in his complaint that "the true clinical potential of each of the lymphokines . . . [is] difficult to predict, [but] . . . competing commercial firms in these relevant fields have published reports in biotechnology industry periodicals predicting a potential market of approximately $3.01 Billion Dollars by the year 1990 for a whole range of [such lymphokines]. . . ."

With the Regents' assistance, Golde negotiated agreements for commercial development of the cell line and products to be derived from it. Under an agreement with Genetics Institute, Golde "became a paid consultant" and "acquired the rights to 75,000 shares of common stock." Genetics Institute also agreed to pay Golde and the Regents "at least $330,000 over three years, including a pro-rata share of [Golde's] salary and fringe benefits, in exchange for . . . exclusive access to the materials and research performed" on the cell line and products derived from it. On June 4, 1982, Sandoz "was added to the agreement," and compensation payable to Golde and the Regents was increased by $110,000. "[T]hroughout this period, . . . Quan spent as much as 70 [percent] of her time working for [the] Regents on research" related to the cell line.

Based upon these allegations, Moore attempted to state 13 causes of action.[4] Each defendant demurred to each purported cause of action. The superior court, however, expressly considered the validity of only the first cause of

---

4. (1) "Conversion"; (2) "lack of informed consent"; (3) "breach of fiduciary duty"; (4) "fraud and deceit"; (5) "unjust enrichment"; (6) "quasi-contract"; (7) "bad faith breach of the implied covenant of good faith and fair dealing"; (8) "intentional infliction of emotional distress"; (9) "negligent misrepresentation"; (10) "intentional interference with prospective advantageous economic relationships"; (11) "slander of title"; (12) "accounting"; and (13) "declaratory relief."

action, conversion.[5] Reasoning that the remaining causes of action incorporated the earlier, defective allegations, the superior court sustained a general demurrer to the entire complaint with leave to amend. In a subsequent proceeding, the superior court sustained Genetics Institute's and Sandoz's demurrers without leave to amend on the grounds that Moore had not stated a cause of action for conversion and that the complaint's allegations about the entities' secondary liability were too conclusory. In accordance with its earlier ruling that the defective allegations about conversion rendered the entire complaint insufficient, the superior court took the remaining demurrers off its calendar.

With one justice dissenting, the Court of Appeal reversed, holding that the complaint did state a cause of action for conversion. The Court of Appeal agreed with the superior court that the allegations against Genetics Institute and Sandoz were insufficient, but directed the superior court to give Moore leave to amend. The Court of Appeal also directed the superior court to decide "the remaining causes of action, which [had] never been expressly ruled upon."

III. Discussion

A. BREACH OF FIDUCIARY DUTY AND LACK OF INFORMED CONSENT

Moore repeatedly alleges that Golde failed to disclose the extent of his research and economic interests in Moore's cells[6] before obtaining consent to the medical procedures by which the cells were extracted. These allegations, in our view, state a cause of action against Golde for invading a legally protected interest of his patient. This cause of action can properly be characterized either as the breach of a fiduciary duty to disclose facts material to the patient's consent or, alternatively, as the performance of medical procedures without first having obtained the patient's informed consent.

Our analysis begins with three well-established principles. First, "a person of adult years and in sound mind has the right, in the exercise of control over his own body, to determine whether or not to submit to lawful medical treatment." Second, "the patient's consent to treatment, to be effective, must be an informed consent." Third, in soliciting the patient's consent, a physician has a fiduciary duty to disclose all information material to the patient's decision.

These principles lead to the following conclusions: (1) a physician must disclose personal interests unrelated to the patient's health, whether research or economic, that may affect the physician's professional judgment; and (2) a

---

5. The superior court did not reach (a) any defendant's general demurrer to the causes of action numbered 2 through 13; (b) any defendant's demurrer on the ground of the statute of limitations; (c) Golde's, Quan's, and the Regents' demurrers on the grounds of governmental immunity; or (d) Genetics Institute's and Sandoz's numerous demurrers for uncertainty.

6. In this opinion we use the inclusive term "cells" to describe all of the cells taken from Moore's body, including blood cells, bone marrow, spleen, etc.

physician's failure to disclose such interests may give rise to a cause of action for performing medical procedures without informed consent or breach of fiduciary duty.

To be sure, questions about the validity of a patient's consent to a procedure typically arise when the patient alleges that the physician failed to disclose medical risks, as in malpractice cases, and not when the patient alleges that the physician had a personal interest, as in this case. The concept of informed consent, however, is broad enough to encompass the latter. "The scope of the physician's communication to the patient . . . must be measured by the patient's need, and that need is whatever information is material to the decision."

Indeed, the law already recognizes that a reasonable patient would want to know whether a physician has an economic interest that might affect the physician's professional judgment. As the Court of Appeal has said, "[c]ertainly a sick patient deserves to be free of any reasonable suspicion that his doctor's judgment is influenced by a profit motive." The desire to protect patients from possible conflicts of interest has also motivated legislative enactments. Among these is *Business and Professions Code* section 654.2. Under that section, a physician may not charge a patient on behalf of, or refer a patient to, any organization in which the physician has a "significant beneficial interest, unless [the physician] first discloses in writing to the patient, that there is such an interest and advises the patient that the patient may choose any organization for the purposes of obtaining the services ordered or requested by [the physician]." Similarly, under Health and Safety Code section 24173, a physician who plans to conduct a medical experiment on a patient must, among other things, inform the patient of "[t]he name of the sponsor or funding source, if any, . . . and the organization, if any, under whose general aegis the experiment is being conducted."

It is important to note that no law prohibits a physician from conducting research in the same area in which he practices. Progress in medicine often depends upon physicians, such as those practicing at the university hospital where Moore received treatment, who conduct research while caring for their patients.

Yet a physician who treats a patient in whom he also has a research interest has potentially conflicting loyalties. This is because medical treatment decisions are made on the basis of proportionality—weighing the benefits to the patient against the risks to the patient. As another court has said, "the determination as to whether the burdens of treatment are worth enduring for any individual patient depends upon the facts unique in each case," and "the patient's interests and desires are the key ingredients of the decision-making process." A physician who adds his own research interests to this balance may be tempted to order a scientifically useful procedure or test that offers marginal, or no, benefits to the patient.[8] The possibility that an interest extraneous

---

8. This is, in fact, precisely what Moore has alleged with respect to the postoperative withdrawals of blood and other substances.

to the patient's health has affected the physician's judgment is something that a reasonable patient would want to know in deciding whether to consent to a proposed course of treatment. It is material to the patient's decision and, thus, a prerequisite to informed consent.

Golde argues that the scientific use of cells that have already been removed cannot possibly affect the patient's medical interests. The argument is correct in one instance but not in another. If a physician has no plans to conduct research on a patient's cells at the time he recommends the medical procedure by which they are taken, then the patient's medical interests have not been impaired. In that instance the argument is correct. On the other hand, a physician who does have a preexisting research interest might, consciously or unconsciously, take that into consideration in recommending the procedure. In that instance the argument is incorrect: the physician's extraneous motivation may affect his judgment and is, thus, material to the patient's consent.

We acknowledge that there is a competing consideration. To require disclosure of research and economic interests may corrupt the patient's own judgment by distracting him from the requirements of his health.[9] But California law does not grant physicians unlimited discretion to decide what to disclose. Instead, "it is the prerogative of the patient, not the physician, to determine for himself the direction in which he believes his interests lie." "Unlimited discretion in the physician is irreconcilable with the basic right of the patient to make the ultimate informed decision. . . ."

Accordingly, we hold that a physician who is seeking a patient's consent for a medical procedure must, in order to satisfy his fiduciary duty[10] and to obtain the patient's informed consent, disclose personal interests unrelated to the patient's health, whether research or economic, that may affect his medical judgment.

---

9. A related problem may arise with excessive disclosure of the risks of medical treatment. As we recognized in *Cobbs v. Grant*, supra, disclosure of risks in some cases can "so seriously upset the patient" as to affect the patient's ability to weigh "dispassionately . . . the risks of refusing to undergo the recommended treatment. Under those circumstances, "[a] disclosure need not be made beyond that required within the medical community. . . ." (Ibid.)

However, we made that statement in the context of a physician-patient relationship unaffected by possible conflicts of interest. *Cobbs v. Grant*, supra, permits a physician acting solely in the patient's best interests to consider whether excessive disclosure will harm the patient. Disclosure of possible conflicts of interest raises different considerations. To illustrate, a physician who orders a procedure partly to further a research interest unrelated to the patient's health should not be able to avoid disclosure with the argument that the patient might object to participation in research. In some cases, however, a physician's research interest might play such an insignificant role in the decision to recommend a medically indicated procedure that disclosure should not be required because the interest is not material. By analogy, we have not required disclosure of "remote" risks that "are not central to the decision to administer or reject [a] procedure."

10. In some respects the term "fiduciary" is too broad. In this context the term "fiduciary" signifies only that a physician must disclose all facts material to the patient's decision. A physician is not the patient's financial adviser. As we have already discussed, the reason why a physician must disclose possible conflicts is not because he has a duty to protect his patient's financial interests, but because certain personal interests may affect professional judgment.

1. Dr. Golde

We turn now to the allegations of Moore's third amended complaint to determine whether he has stated such a cause of action. We first discuss the adequacy of Moore's allegations against Golde, based upon the physician's disclosures prior to the splenectomy.

Moore alleges that, prior to the surgical removal of his spleen, Golde "formed the intent and made arrangements to obtain portions of his spleen following its removal from [Moore] in connection with [his] desire to have regular and continuous access to, and possession of, [Moore's] unique and rare Blood and Bodily Substances." Moore was never informed prior to the splenectomy of Golde's "prior formed intent" to obtain a portion of his spleen. In our view, these allegations adequately show that Golde had an undisclosed research interest in Moore's cells at the time he sought Moore's consent to the splenectomy. Accordingly, Moore has stated a cause of action for breach of fiduciary duty, or lack of informed consent, based upon the disclosures accompanying that medical procedure.

PREPARING FOR CLASS

1. Is there a cause of action under the *Moore* case even when the information withheld is not material to the patient's decision?

2. Managed care plans have become popular in the United States today. These plans use a variety of techniques to reduce the costs of health care. Would a doctor who is part of a managed care plan and advising a patient to pursue a cheaper treatment have to advise the patient that the doctor and the plan could benefit if the patient adopts the cheaper treatment?

INCREASING YOUR UNDERSTANDING

1. What if the doctor recommends that the patient do nothing, or the doctor does nothing to the patient, for example, the doctor does not test a pregnant woman in her first trimester of pregnancy for genetic defects of her fetus? Does that require informed consent?

2. Henrietta Lacks was diagnosed with cervical cancer in 1951. During the course of her treatment, cells of the cancer were removed for research purposes without her knowledge or permission. Ms. Lacks eventually died of her cancer in 1951, but her cells, which were reproduced in a petri dish, would become the HeLa (Henrietta Lacks) cells, which are commonly used in biomedical research throughout the world today. These cells were used by Dr. Jonas Salk when he was researching the

eventual cure for polio. It is estimated that there are now 20 tons of HeLa cells in the world and over 11,000 patents that have been derived from research on HeLa cells. Ironically, many of Henrietta Lacks's relatives cannot afford health care today. For further reading on this subject, see Rebecca Skloot, The Immortal Life of Henrietta Lacks (Crown Publishers, 2010).

Chapter 8

Duty and Limitations—Physical Injury

In the last chapter we considered various ways plaintiffs can demonstrate that defendants were negligent. The broad question was whether the defendant had failed to act like a reasonable and prudent person in the same or similar circumstances. But sometimes unreasonable, imprudent behavior that causes harm will not support a cause of action—because sometimes the law has not imposed an obligation on the defendant to act with care for the plaintiff's benefit. Although we think of the defendant who took an unreasonable risk as a negligent defendant, technically, a defendant is negligent only if he breached a legally imposed duty of care. A defendant with no duty cannot be negligent in the legal sense, no matter how unreasonably risky his behavior.

The first element of a plaintiff's negligence case is a duty of care owed by the defendant. (We looked at breach first because doing so gives us a sense of what obligations arise from duties, an often important consideration in determining whether a duty should be imposed.) The existence of a duty is a question of law for the judge, and in most cases, duty is a given. Generally, when lack of care in an activity presents a foreseeable, unreasonable risk of harm to people or their property, the person engaging in the activity has a duty to exercise reasonable care. The driver of a car has a legal obligation, a duty, to drive it with reasonable care because carelessly driven cars pose a foreseeable and unreasonable risk of ramming into property or running over people. The arborist trimming branches high in a tree has a duty to those below to exercise care because if he does not there's a foreseeable and unreasonable risk branches will fall and injure them. So, in most negligence cases, the defendant clearly owed a duty and will not try to contend otherwise.

Even though the plaintiff has the burden of proving that the defendant owed her a duty of care and defendants often concede duty, the duty element is nonetheless an important part of a defendant's arsenal. Because duty is a question of law for the judge, the defendant in a negligence case may move for summary judgment on the ground that he owed no duty to the plaintiff. If that motion succeeds, the defendant has achieved a defendant's primary goal: keeping the case from the jury. And keeping the case from the jury on summary judgment is even better than keeping it from the jury with a directed verdict. The defendant will not have to go to trial at all. That means no more negotiations, no more discovery and investigation, no trial preparation, no expert testimony fees, no settlement, no more financial exposure. And it may mean establishing a precedent that wards off future lawsuits. That said, duty may not always be resolved on summary judgment. Discovery may have produced contradictory facts relevant to the duty issue, and then duty will be resolved at trial, often upon defendant's motion for directed verdict or judgment notwithstanding the verdict.

In this chapter and the next, we will consider cases in which defendants contended that they owed the plaintiffs no duty of care. We will be searching for bases for no-duty motions and considering how plaintiffs can respond to those motions. In the first section of this chapter, we will look at cases where the defendants contended that they owed no affirmative duty to rescue, aid, or protect the plaintiffs or to control third parties dangerous to plaintiffs.

A.   NO-AFFIRMATIVE-DUTY RULES

1.   Acts and Omissions

Satterfield v. Breeding Insulation Co.
266 S.W.3d 347 (Tenn. 2008)

KOCH, JR., J.
[Doug Satterfield worked at Alcoa, an international manufacturer of aluminum and aluminum by-products, in a job that exposed him to asbestos. Alcoa had known since the 1930s that the asbestos used in their manufacturing endangered employees and since the 1960s that the asbestos fibers employees took home on their clothes endangered their families. Since 1972, OSHA had prohibited employers from letting workers exposed to asbestos take their work clothes home to be laundered. Alcoa knew that the levels of asbestos fibers on its workers' clothes were extremely high but violated this and a number of other OSHA regulations designed to educate employees of the dangers of asbestos exposure and to protect them and their families from those dangers.]

On September 7, 1979, Amanda Nicole Satterfield was born to Mr. Satterfield and Donna Satterfield . . . [and] from the day of her birth, Ms. Satterfield was exposed to the asbestos fibers on her father's work clothes.

Ms. Satterfield was eventually diagnosed with mesothelioma. On December 8, 2003, she filed suit against . . . Alcoa. . . . She alleged that mesothelioma is a highly lethal form of cancer that is almost exclusively caused by exposure to asbestos and that she contracted mesothelioma as a direct result of the negligent acts and omissions of . . . Alcoa. . . . Ms. Satterfield died from mesothelioma on January 1, 2005.

[Her father was substituted as the personal representative of her estate. Alcoa filed a motion for judgment on the pleadings. It contended that it owed Ms. Satterfield no duty. The trial court concurred and dismissed the case. Mr. Satterfield appealed, and the court of appeals reversed the dismissal of the complaint.]

We have determined that the trial court erred by dismissing Ms. Satterfield's complaint and that the Court of Appeals properly reversed the trial court's dismissal of the complaint. Based on the facts alleged in the complaint, Alcoa owed a duty of reasonable care to Ms. Satterfield.

In its most succinct form, the pivotal question in this case is whether, under the facts alleged in Ms. Satterfield's complaint, Alcoa owed a duty of reasonable care to Ms. Satterfield. Alcoa asserts that it did not owe a duty to Ms. Satterfield. It contends that imposing such a duty on it would improperly create an affirmative obligation to act despite the absence of any special relationship between Alcoa and either Ms. Satterfield or her father. On the other hand, Mr. Satterfield insists that his daughter's complaint is premised on the assumption that Alcoa owed Ms. Satterfield a duty of reasonable care because it created an unreasonable and foreseeable risk of harm to her. . . .

Duty is a legal obligation to conform to a reasonable person standard of care in order to protect others against unreasonable risks of harm. As a general rule, persons have a duty to others to refrain from engaging in affirmative acts that a reasonable person "should recognize as involving an unreasonable risk of causing an invasion of an interest of another" or acts "which involve[ ] an unreasonable risk of harm to another." Restatement (Second) of Torts §§284, 302, at 19, 82 (1965). Thus, if an individual "acts at all, [he or she] must exercise reasonable care to make his [or her] acts safe for others." Restatement (Second) of Torts §4 cmt. b, at 8. The core of negligence is the violation of this requirement by engaging in "behavior which should be recognized as involving unreasonable danger to others."

These rules do not, however, require that persons always act reasonably to secure the safety of others. . . .

Dean Keeton and Dean Prosser explained . . . :

> In the determination of the existence of a duty, there runs through much of the law a distinction between action and inaction. . . . [T]here arose very early a difference, still deeply rooted in the law of negligence, between "misfeasance" and "nonfeasance"—that is to say, between active misconduct working positive injury to others and passive inaction or a failure to take steps to protect them from harm. The reason for the distinction may be said to lie in the fact that by "misfeasance" the defendant has created a new risk of harm to the plaintiff, while by 'nonfeasance' he has at least made his situation no worse, and has merely failed to benefit him by interfering in his affairs.

. . . The distinction between misfeasance and nonfeasance can be easily misunderstood. One can be led astray by thinking that a defendant's negligent act must be characterized "as an affirmative act for a duty to exist, rather than appreciating that it is the defendant's entire course of conduct that must constitute an affirmative act creating a risk of harm and that negligence may consist of an act or omission creating an unreasonable risk." A classic illustration of this point is the example of a driver who fails to apply his or her brakes to avoid hitting a pedestrian walking in a crosswalk. Even though the driver's negligent act—failing to apply the brakes—is an omission, the "driver's careless failure to apply the brakes is negligent driving, not negligent failure to rescue." Accordingly, distinguishing between misfeasance and nonfeasance can best be accomplished, not by focusing on whether an individual's "specific failure to exercise reasonable care is an error of commission or omission," but rather by focusing on whether the individual's entire course of conduct created a risk of harm. Thus, even though the specific negligent act may constitute an omission, the entirety of the conduct may still be misfeasance that created a risk of harm.

The distinction between misfeasance and nonfeasance is far from academic. It has practical significance, and Tennessee's courts regularly employ it when called upon to decide whether a duty exists. With regard to misfeasance, this Court has held that "all persons have a duty to use reasonable care to refrain from conduct that will foreseeably cause injury to others." As for nonfeasance, Tennessee's courts generally have declined to impose a duty to act or to rescue. Simply stated, persons do not ordinarily have a duty to act to protect others from dangers or risks except for those that they themselves have created.

Tennessee's general rule with regard to nonfeasance is consistent with the Restatement's position that "[t]he fact . . . the actor realizes or should realize that action on his part is necessary for another's aid or protection does not of itself impose upon him a duty to take such action." Restatement (Second) of Torts §314, at 116. This general and long-standing principle of tort law, often termed either the "no duty to act rule" or the "no duty to rescue rule" has been subject to considerable and enduring criticism.

A compelling argument in opposition to the no duty to act or to rescue rule rests comfortably "on the perception that, as a matter of inarticulate common sense, it is wrong for one person to stand by as another suffers an injury that could easily be prevented." An expert swimmer who stands on the shore watching a child drown or a passerby on the bridge who cannot be bothered to throw a rope to a person in distress in the waters below stand as illustrations that demonstrate the unreasonableness that can be exemplified by a failure to rescue. Even staunch defenders of the no duty to act or to rescue rule must concede that failure to do so may, in certain circumstances, not only be unreasonable, a normal measure for negligent conduct, but actually "outrageous."

Nevertheless, common-law courts, including Tennessee's courts, have preserved, though not inviolably, the no duty to act or to rescue rule. The reason is not intransigency or lack of consideration. Quite to the contrary, the rule survives because its limitations continue to be of considerable importance and value. Imposing a duty to act or to rescue strays dangerously into interference with individual liberty. By adhering to a no duty to act or to rescue rule, the courts are not rendering the common law amoral but instead are prioritizing liberty over altruism in circumstances where the defendant did not create the risk of harm. While a person who fails to act may well be subject to public censure, not all failures to act should be prohibited or punished by force of law. Failure to leave sufficient space outside the dictates of the law may have an adverse effect on the exercise of private judgment which is critical to the development of a person's moral capacities.

. . . In addition, it has been asserted that recognizing a duty to act or to rescue rule could create problems of comprehensibility, verifiability, and conformability, as well as administrative difficulties, to such an extent that maintaining the current no duty to act or to rescue rule, while not perfect, is still the superior course.

Searching for reasonable ground between the competing viewpoints surrounding the no duty to act or to rescue rule, Tennessee's courts have maintained the general rule but have carved out exceptions to mitigate against some of its harshest applications. These exceptions arise when certain special relationships exist between the defendant and either the person who is the source of the danger or the person who is foreseeably at risk from the danger. These relationships create an affirmative duty either to control the person who is the source of the danger or to protect the person who is endangered.

. . . While there are many potential justifications for these departures from the general rule, among the most straightforward of justifications is that the nature of the particular relationship creates a sufficiently significant obligation that there is an enforceable expectation of reasonable action rather than unreasonable indifference. . . .

Courts across the country have disagreed as to how these broad principles of tort law should be used to determine whether an employer owes a duty to persons who develop asbestos-related illnesses after exposure to asbestos fibers on its employees' clothing. . . .

The opinions of many state courts contain well-reasoned and insightful analyses of the legal principles implicated in these so-called "take-home" asbestos exposure cases. Even though the outcomes in these cases differ, their principled disagreements are captured and synthesized in two particularly edifying recent cases.

Last year, the Michigan Supreme Court addressed the question presently before this Court. The majority of the court held that no liability could be imposed on the employer in the absence of a relationship between the plaintiff and the employer. In re Certified Question from Fourteenth Dist. Ct. App. of Tex., 740 N.W.2d 206, 213 (2007). The majority reasoned that the

> defendant, as owner of the property on which asbestos-containing products were located, did not owe to the deceased, who was never on or near that

property, a legal duty to protect her from exposure to any asbestos fibers carried home on the clothing of a member of her household who was working on that property as the employee of independent contractors, where there was no further relationship between defendant and the deceased.

In re Certified Question from Fourteenth Dist. Ct. App. of Tex., 740 N.W.2d at 222. In a vigorous dissent, Justice Michael F. Cavanagh offered the following rebuttal:

> [T]he majority's severely curtailed view of "relationship" seems to be based on its view of premises liability law rather than on the principles of ordinary negligence. Under the latter (and the former as well, although that is not at issue here), a harmed person need not visit the property of the injuring party. This case involves an employer who exposed a worker to asbestos, knowing that the asbestos fibers were toxic and could be carried home, thus exposing the worker's family to asbestos. Under these circumstances, I have no difficulty concluding that the relationship—that a jury found defendant had to [the employee]—extended to [the step-daughter]. To conclude otherwise, as does the majority, ignores basic negligence principles and gives employers carte blanche to expose workers to communicable toxic substances without taking any measure whatsoever to prevent those substances from harming others. This I cannot do. Indeed, as discussed later in this dissent, our government also refuses to grant this free pass.

In re Certified Question from Fourteenth Dist. Ct. App. of Tex., 740 N.W.2d at 225 (Cavanagh, J., dissenting).

Also within the past year, the Washington Court of Appeals addressed the argument that "employer liability does not extend to employees' spouses and homes, and premises liability does not extend outside the premises." Rochon v. Saberhagen Holdings, Inc., No. 58579-7-I, 2007 WL 2325214, at *3 (Wash. Ct. App. Aug.13, 2007). The court noted that the employer's argument missed the central point of the case because the plaintiff's cause of action did not depend on premises liability principles or on the employer's duty to protect the plaintiff from the acts of third parties. Rather, as the court noted, the plaintiff's claim was based on the employer's own unreasonably risky acts—operating its factory in an unsafe manner—that directly and proximately caused her injuries. The court also held that the employer had a duty to prevent the foreseeable injuries caused by its misfeasance because its operation of its plant created an unreasonable risk of harm of asbestos exposure to others who came in regular contact with its employees. While the courts, like the Michigan Supreme Court, that have found, as a matter of law, that employers have no duty in take-home asbestos exposure cases, rely upon the absence of a special relationship, this argument is misplaced under Tennessee tort law as it has developed over the years. This Court has recognized that a duty of reasonable care arises whenever a defendant's conduct poses an unreasonable and foreseeable risk of harm to persons or property. Thus, like the drafters of the new Restatement (Third) of Torts containing the principles applicable to liability for physical harm, we are of the view that

> [e]ven when the actor and victim are complete strangers and have no relationship, the basis for the ordinary duty of reasonable care ... is conduct that creates a risk to another. Thus, a relationship ordinarily is not what defines the line between duty and no-duty; conduct creating risk to another is.

Restatement (Third) of Torts §37, Reporter's Note, cmt. c, at 721. . . .

According to Ms. Satterfield's complaint, Alcoa's employees worked with materials containing asbestos on a daily basis. Employees, including Mr. Satterfield, worked under improper and unsafe conditions which violated internal safety requirements and OSHA standards. As a result, the employees' clothes collected significant amounts of asbestos fibers. Even though Alcoa was aware of the dangerous amounts of asbestos on its employees' clothes, Alcoa did not inform its employees that the materials that they were handling contained asbestos or of the risks posed by asbestos fibers to the employees or to others. The danger was compounded even further because Alcoa dissuaded its employees from using on-site bathhouse facilities, and it failed to provide coveralls or to wash its employees' work clothes at the factory. Under the facts alleged in Ms. Satterfield's complaint, Alcoa's alleged misfeasance created a significant risk of harm to Ms. Satterfield.

Despite Alcoa's protestations to the contrary, this is not a failure to act case wherein a defendant "declined to interfere, . . . was in no way responsible for the perilous situation, . . . did not increase the peril, . . . took away nothing from the person in jeopardy, [but instead] . . . simply failed to confer a benefit." The rules establishing no duty to protect, to rescue, or to control the conduct of third parties, the underlying basis of Alcoa's argument, are all subsets of the same no affirmative duty to act absent a special relationship rule. That rule, however, is inapplicable to this case. Instead, this case involves a risk created through misfeasance. Thus, . . . the outcome of this case does not turn on a failure to act or on the act of a third party, but instead, it turns on the employer's own misfeasance—its injurious affirmative act of operating its facility in such an unsafe manner that dangerous asbestos fibers were transmitted outside the facility to others who came in regular and extended close contact with the asbestos-contaminated work clothes of its employees. . . .

[The court then explained that misfeasance was not, of itself, sufficient to establish a duty and considered public policy factors that weighed in favor of finding a duty in the case. The threshold inquiry was the foreseeability of harm. Justice Holder concurred in the result and the clarification of issues presented here but found that the majority's discussion of foreseeability trod upon jury territory of breach or proximate cause.]

PREPARING FOR CLASS

1. How, apparently, did Alcoa's attorneys persuade the trial court to dismiss the case against their client?

2. Why did the Tennessee Supreme Court believe that these arguments were inapt and the dismissal was improper?

3. What is the difference between misfeasance and nonfeasance? Why will it matter whether the incident was misfeasance or nonfeasance?

4. What is the difference between omissions and nonfeasance?

5. The Michigan Supreme Court considered a similar case, In re Certified Question from Fourteenth Dist. Ct. App. of Tex., but resolved it differently from the Tennessee Supreme Court. What is the difference between the logic of the two courts? Do you think that different logic led to different conclusions or that the desire to reach different conclusions led to different logic?

6. What policy reasons justify the seeming harshness of no-duty rules? Do you find them persuasive?

APPLYING THE LAW

1. Residents of a neighborhood had all set out their garbage cans for pickup the next morning when a heavy storm blew their cans into the street. One man went out and retrieved his can from the street. Although another neighbor's cans were within reach, he left them there. The power was out, and the street was dark. A woman was injured when she drove her car into the can that the man had left behind when he retrieved his own. The woman sued him for negligence. How will the man's attorneys argue for dismissal of the case? How will the woman's attorneys respond? How is the judge likely to rule?

2. A college student attended an annual sophomore class picnic, planned with the aid of a faculty supervisor, who co-signed the check used to purchase approximately seven half-kegs of beer by the underage class president. Most of the sophomore class was under the state drinking age, and university rules prohibited underage drinking, but the college duplicating center reproduced the beer-mug decorated flyers that the party organizers posted throughout campus to advertise the picnic. The college provided no transportation, leaving the underage drinkers to find their own ways to and from the off-campus grove where the party was held. The faculty sponsor did not attend the picnic or send anyone in his place. The student did not drive and was depending on his friend, another student, for a ride back to campus after the party.

The friend became drunk at the party and on the drive home lost control of his car, severely injuring the student. If the student sues the college, how would counsel for the college argue that it is entitled to summary judgment? How would the student's lawyer respond? How is the judge likely to rule?

INCREASING YOUR UNDERSTANDING

The unforeseeable plaintiff. The Tennessee Supreme Court in *Satterfield* stated, "This Court has recognized that a duty of reasonable care arises whenever a defendant's conduct poses an unreasonable and foreseeable risk of harm to persons or property." Notice that the court does not say a "risk of harm to plaintiff or plaintiff's property." Do defendants owe duties to the world at large to be careful? Or do they owe duties simply to the foreseeable victims of their carelessness? The most famous debate on this question occurred in Palsgraf v. Long Island R.R. Co., 48 N.Y. 339 (N.Y. App. 1928), which appears in Chapter 11. For now, know that the first and second Restatements of Torts adopted the view that defendants did not owe duties to unforeseeable plaintiffs. The current draft of the third Restatement, however, does not include language limiting duty to foreseeable plaintiffs. Just what that may mean is discussed in Joseph W. Little, *Palsgraf Revisited (Again)*, 6 Pierce L. Rev. 75 (2007).

Yania v. Bigan
155 A.2d 343 (Pa. 1959)

JONES, J.

A bizarre and most unusual circumstance provides the background of this appeal.

On September 25, 1957 John E. Bigan was engaged in a coal strip-mining operation. . . . On the property being stripped were large cuts or trenches created by Bigan when he removed the earthen overburden for the purpose of removing the coal underneath. One cut contained water 8 to 10 feet in depth with side walls or embankments 16 to 18 feet in height; at this cut Bigan had installed a pump to remove the water.

At approximately 4 P.M. on that date, Joseph F. Yania, the operator of another coal strip-mining operation, and one Boyd M. Ross went upon Bigan's property for the purpose of discussing a business matter with Bigan, and, while there, were asked by Bigan to aid him in starting the pump. Ross and Bigan entered the cut and stood at the point where the pump was located. Yania stood at the top of one of the cut's side walls and then jumped from the side wall—a height of 16 to 18 feet—into the water and was drowned.

Yania's widow, in her own right and on behalf of her three children, instituted wrongful death and survival actions against Bigan contending Bigan was responsible for Yania's death. Preliminary objections, in the nature of demurrers, to the complaint were filed on behalf of Bigan. The court below sustained the preliminary objections; from the entry of that order this appeal was taken.

Since Bigan has chosen to file preliminary objections, in the nature of demurrers, every material and relevant fact well pleaded in the complaint and every inference fairly deducible therefrom are to be taken as true. . . . Bigan stands charged with three-fold negligence: (1) by urging, enticing, taunting and inveigling Yania to jump into the water; (2) by failing to warn Yania of a dangerous condition on the land, i.e., the cut wherein lay 8 to 10 feet of water; (3) by failing to go to Yania's rescue after he had jumped into the water. . . .

Appellant initially contends that Yania's descent from the high embankment into the water and the resulting death were caused "entirely" by the spoken words and blandishments of Bigan delivered at a distance from Yania. The complaint does not allege that Yania slipped or that he was pushed or that Bigan made any physical impact upon Yania. On the contrary, the only inference deducible from the facts alleged in the complaint is that Bigan, by the employment of cajolery and inveiglement, caused such a mental impact on Yania that the latter was deprived of his volition and freedom of choice and placed under a compulsion to jump into the water. Had Yania been a child of tender years or a person mentally deficient then it is conceivable that taunting and enticement could constitute actionable negligence if it resulted in harm. However, to contend that such conduct directed to an adult in full possession of all his mental faculties constitutes actionable negligence is not only without precedent but completely without merit. . . .

[I]t is urged that Bigan failed to take the necessary steps to rescue Yania from the water. The mere fact that Bigan saw Yania in a position of peril in the water imposed upon him no legal, although a moral, obligation or duty to go to his rescue unless Bigan was legally responsible, in whole or in part, for placing Yania in the perilous position. Restatement, Torts, §314. *Cf.* Restatement, Torts, §322. The language of this Court in Brown v. French, 104 Pa. 604, 607, 608, is apt: "If it appeared that the deceased, by his own carelessness, contributed in any degree to the accident which caused the loss of his life, the defendants ought not to have been held to answer for the consequences resulting from that accident. . . . He voluntarily placed himself in the way of danger, and his death was the result of his own act. . . . That his undertaking was an exceedingly reckless and dangerous one, the event proves, but there was no one to blame for it but himself. He had the right to try the experiment, obviously dangerous as it was, but then also upon him rested the consequences of that experiment, and upon no one else; he may have been, and probably was, ignorant of the risk which he was taking upon himself, or knowing it, and trusting to his own skill, he may have regarded it as easily superable. But in either case, the result of his ignorance, or of his mistake, must rest with himself—and cannot be charged to the defendants." The complaint does not aver any facts which impose upon Bigan legal responsibility for placing Yania in the dangerous position in the water and, absent such legal responsibility, the law imposes on Bigan no duty of rescue.

Recognizing that the deceased Yania is entitled to the benefit of the presumption that he was exercising due care and extending to appellant the benefit of every well pleaded fact in this complaint and the fair inferences arising therefrom, yet we can reach but one conclusion: that Yania, a reasonable and prudent adult in full possession of all his mental faculties, undertook to perform an act which he knew or should have known was attended with more or less peril and it was the performance of that act and not any conduct upon Bigan's part which caused his unfortunate death.

Order affirmed.

Weirum v. RKO Radio General, Inc.
539 P.2d 36 (Cal. 1975)

[KHJ, a popular radio station with a large teenage audience, conducted a contest that rewarded the first person to find a disc jockey, "the Real Don Steele," who was traveling in a conspicuous red car to various locations in the Los Angeles metropolitan area. Two teenagers tracking Steele raced each other along the freeway at 80 mph. They forced another car off the road, and it overturned, killing the driver. (One of the teenagers actually caught Steele and collected a prize.) The driver's family sued the owner of the radio station as well as the teenagers. The jury returned a verdict for the plaintiffs, and KHJ appealed the denial of its motion for judgment notwithstanding the verdict. Judge Mosk of the California Supreme Court affirmed:]

Defendant, relying upon the rule stated in section 315 of the Restatement Second of Torts, urges that it owed no duty of care to decedent. The section provides that, absent a special relationship, an actor is under no duty to control the conduct of third parties. As explained hereinafter, this rule has no application if the plaintiff's complaint, as here, is grounded upon an affirmative act of defendant which created an undue risk of harm.

The rule stated in section 315 is merely a refinement of the general principle embodied in section 314 that one is not obligated to act as a "good samaritan." This doctrine is rooted in the common law distinction between action and inaction, or misfeasance and nonfeasance. Misfeasance exists when the defendant is responsible for making the plaintiff's position worse, i.e., defendant has created a risk. Conversely, nonfeasance is found when the defendant has failed to aid plaintiff through beneficial intervention. As section 315 illustrates, liability for nonfeasance is largely limited to those circumstances in which some special relationship can be established. If, on the other hand, the act complained of is one of misfeasance, the question of duty is governed by the standards of ordinary care discussed above.

Here, there can be little doubt that we review an act of misfeasance to which section 315 is inapplicable. Liability is not predicated upon defendant's failure to intervene for the benefit of decedent but rather upon its creation of an unreasonable risk of harm to him.

PREPARING FOR CLASS

1. Thinking about *Yania v. Bigan.*

    a. As plaintiff's lawyer, how would you have tried to characterize Bigan's conduct as misfeasance? (And do you know why you would have tried to characterize it that way?)

    b. The court suggests Bigan had a moral obligation to Yania. Why is that moral obligation not enough to create a duty?

    c. What if Bigan had believed the water was safe and enticed a ten-year-old neighbor child into the water? Would he have had a duty to rescue the child if the child began to drown?

    d. Does this case mean that plaintiffs who behave stupidly are not owed duties of care by others?

2. Thinking about all three cases you've just read.

    a. Superficially, how is the *Weirum* case like the *Yania* case? How might the defendant in *Weirum* have argued that the rule in *Yania* supported a no-duty finding in its favor? How would the plaintiff have distinguished the two cases?

    b. Is *Weirum* more like *Yania* or *Satterfield*? How is the logic in the *Weirum* case like the logic in the *Satterfield* case?

APPLYING THE LAW

Two friends, Bob and Al, had been drinking at their lodge. Bob was driving Al home in Bob's pick-up truck. As Bob was driving down the highway, Al tried to climb out the passenger-side window (for some unknown reason that made sense to him in his inebriated state). Bob saw what Al was doing, but he did not attempt to stop the truck or restrain Al until Al had fallen out the window. If Al sues Bob for negligence, does Bob have a basis for a summary judgment motion? Is the motion likely to be granted? Would it matter whether Bob was speeding? Would it matter whether Bob had dared Al to climb out the window?

INCREASING YOUR UNDERSTANDING

1. The no-duty rules are often described as no duty to protect, rescue, or aid the plaintiff and no duty to control third parties dangerous to the plaintiff.

    a. *No duty to protect.* Restatement (Second) Torts §314, cmt. c, states, "A sees B, a blind man, about to step into the street in front of an approaching automobile A could prevent B from so doing by a word or touch without delaying his own progress. A does not do so, and B is run over and hurt. A is under no duty to prevent B from stepping into the street, and is not liable to B."

In Patterson v. DeMatteo, 21 So. 3d 1094 (La. App. 2009), a man was shot several times by an unknown assailant in a parking lot. The defendant owned the property, but the property was leased to someone else. The court found that the defendant owed the man no duty because "Generally, there is no duty to protect others from the criminal activities of third persons."

A case involving the failure to protect the plaintiff from third-party criminal behavior might also be characterized as a failure to control third parties dangerous to the plaintiff. Distinguishing the two theories will matter when trying to determine if a duty did exist. The defendant, for example, might owe protection to the plaintiff but not owe the plaintiff control over the third party. When you read about special relationships, see if you can make the distinction between these theories and understand what different requirements must be satisfied under them.

b. *No duty to rescue or aid.* In Estate of Cilley v. Lane, 985 A.2d 481 (Me. 2009), the defendant's on-again, off-again boyfriend accidentally shot himself in her trailer. (He was off-again at the moment and a trespasser, a fact you will care about when you read the section on premises liability.) She heard the gunshot and saw him fall to the floor but did not see any blood and did not investigate or attempt to find out whether he was hurt. Instead, she went to a friend's trailer and told her friends that the boyfriend had just pretended to shoot himself. The friends returned and checked the boyfriend's condition and called 911. The delay in obtaining help caused his death. Summary judgment was granted the defendant and upheld on appeal on the ground that the defendant owed her boyfriend no duty of rescue. It did not matter that his situation was serious and that it would have taken little effort to help him. (As you read the next section, ask yourself whether the outcome would have changed if she had been his wife.)

c. *No duty to control dangerous third parties.* In McCloskey v. Mueller, 446 F.3d 262 (1st Cir. 2006), an armed robber contacted the FBI to surrender. He told his intentions to an agent and told him where to find him, but the agent disconnected the call and made no attempt to reconnect it, investigate it, or report it to any other law enforcement officer. The armed robber waited a few hours for the FBI to arrive and then went on a killing spree. The estate of one of his victims filed suit against the FBI. The court determined that the FBI did not owe the victim a duty because there is "no duty to control the conduct of a third person as to prevent him from causing physical harm to another" and no relevant exceptions applied.

2. *Creating the peril.* The no-duty rules are triggered by situations in which the defendant was not the source of the danger to the plaintiff. Therefore, one way to defend a summary judgment motion premised on "no duty to act" is to contend that the defendant was indeed the source of the danger. In *Satterfield* and *Weirum*, the no-duty rules were simply irrelevant because the active misconduct of the defendants created the danger. Their misfeasance supported a duty. A court may also find a duty when the defendant has created the peril even innocently. Consider the following sections from the Restatement (Second) of Torts:

§321. Duty to Act When Prior Conduct Is Found to Be Dangerous
   (1) If the actor does an act, and subsequently realizes or should realize that it has created an unreasonable risk of causing physical harm to another, he is under a duty to exercise reasonable care to prevent the risk from taking effect.
   (2) The rule stated in Subsection (1) applies even though at the time of the act the actor has no reason to believe that it will involve such a risk.

Illustrations:
   1. A is playing golf. He sees no one on or near a putting green and drives to it. While the ball is in the air, B, another player, suddenly appears from a bunker directly in the line of A's drive. A is under a duty to shout a warning to B.
   3. A, carefully driving his truck, skids on an icy road, and his truck comes to rest in a position across the highway where he is unable to move it. A fails to take any steps to warn approaching vehicles of the blocked highway. B, driving his automobile with reasonable care, does not see the truck, skids on the ice and collides with it, and is injured. A is subject to liability to B.

Could this rule have provided an argument to the plaintiff in *Yania*?

§322. Duty to Aid Another Harmed by Actor's Conduct
   If the actor knows or has reason to know that by his conduct, whether tortious or innocent, he has caused such bodily harm to another as to make him helpless and in danger of further harm, the actor is under a duty to exercise reasonable care to prevent such further harm.

Illustration 2.
   A, a "hit and run driver," negligently or innocently runs over B, inflicting serious wounds. Although A knows B's condition, he drives

away and leaves B lying in the road. The weather is exceedingly cold, and B, unable to move, contracts pneumonia from the exposure. A is subject to liability to B for the illness, whether or not he would have been liable for the original wounds.

§314, CMT. D.

[The rule that a duty does not arise simply from awareness that action is necessary to aid or protect another] applies only where the peril in which the actor knows that the other is placed is not due to any active force which is under the actor's control. If a force is within the actor's control, his failure to control it is treated as though he were actively directing it. . . .

ILLUSTRATION 2.

A, a factory owner, sees B, a young child or a blind man who has wandered into his factory, about to approach a piece of moving machinery. A is negligent if he permits the machinery to continue in motion when by the exercise or reasonable care he could stop it before B comes in contact with it.

2. *Special Relationships*

Usually, a court referring to a no-affirmative-duty rule will state that there is "no duty to rescue absent a special relationship," "no duty to protect absent a special relationship." Indeed, the tight connection between "no duty" and "no special relationship" has occasionally misled courts into ruling that a defendant not in a special relationship with the plaintiff or dangerous third party owed no duty, even though the defendant had clearly engaged in active wrong-doing and should have been found to owe a duty based on that misfeasance. The absence of a special relationship matters in nonfeasance cases only. (Courts just don't always understand that.) When a plaintiff sues a defendant who failed to intervene and protect her from a danger that he did not create, a special relationship between the plaintiff and the defendant or between the defendant and a dangerous person who injured plaintiff can support the necessary duty.

a.   With the Plaintiff

§314A Restatement (Second) Torts. Special Relations Giving Rise to Duty to Aid or Protect

(1) A common carrier is under a duty to its passengers to take reasonable action

(a) to protect them against unreasonable risk of physical harm, and

(b) to give them first aid after it knows or has reason to know that they are ill or injured, and to care for them until they can be cared for by others.

(2) An innkeeper is under a similar duty to his guests.

(3) A possessor of land who holds it open to the public is under a similar duty to members of the public who enter in response to his invitation.

(4) One who is required by law to take or who voluntarily takes the custody of another under circumstances such as to deprive the other of his normal opportunities for protection is under a similar duty to the other.

Caveat:

The Institute expresses no opinion as to whether there may not be other relations which impose a similar duty.

Lawson v. Superior Court
180 Cal. App. 4th 1372 (Cal. App. 2010)

RICHARDS, J.

Denisha Lawson was incarcerated in a community-based correctional facility . . . where she resided with her infant daughter, Esperanza. . . .

The Complaint alleges that on April 25, 2007, Esperanza developed severe respiratory problems, later diagnosed as double pneumonia. Over the course of eight to 11 days, Lawson allegedly asked personnel at the facility to obtain treatment for Esperanza. The request was repeatedly denied, despite Esperanza's "green discharge . . . , labored breathing, and increasingly more ashen complexion" and the fact that Esperanza had ceased breathing on at least three occasions. According to the Complaint, one of the employees at the facility ultimately defied her supervisors and took Esperanza to the hospital. Because of the delay in obtaining medical care, Esperanza allegedly suffered "hypoxia, double pneumonia requiring double intubation, cardiac arrest, scarring and injury to both lungs, causing permanent injury which will cause future medical problems." . . .

Lawson and Esperanza, by and through her guardian ad litem, filed this action based on the physical injuries to Esperanza. . . .

The central issue is whether, as a matter of law, [defendants] would have a legal duty to obtain medical care for Esperanza under the circumstances described in the Complaint. "Under traditional tort law principles, a person is . . . under no duty to protect another person from harm. An affirmative duty to protect another from harm may arise, however, where a 'special relationship' exists. Such a special relationship is typically where the plaintiff is particularly vulnerable and dependent upon the defendant who, correspondingly, has some control over the plaintiff's welfare."

Case law holds that "there is a special relationship between jailer and prisoner, imposing on the former a duty of care to the latter." "[I]mportant factors in determining whether a relationship is 'special' include vulnerability and dependence. Prisoners are vulnerable. And dependent. Moreover, the relation-ship between them is protective by nature, such that the jailer has control over the prisoner, who is deprived of the normal opportunity to protect himself from harm inflicted by others." Although, as we have explained, a child residing in a facility established under the PPWASPA [Pregnant and Parenting Women's Alternative Sentencing Program Act] is not a prisoner, such a child is in the same situation of dependence and vulnerability as a prisoner. According to the facts described in the Complaint, because Esperanza's mother, Lawson, was confined in the facility and unable to take Esperanza to the hospital or another medical facility, Esperanza was solely dependent on personnel at the facility to obtain the medical care that she required. We conclude that in such a situation—where Esperanza had no other means to obtain medical care—a special relationship arose that created a duty of care on the part of jailers at the facility to protect Esperanza from harm by obtaining needed medical care.

PREPARING FOR CLASS

1. What do the four relationships cited in Restatement (Second) Torts §314A have in common? Is it possible that there are more special rela-tionships? What will a court probably look for when deciding whether to expand the list?

2. How is *Lawson* a nonfeasance case?

3. How might the defendants in *Lawson* have argued that they were not in a special relationship with Esperanza?

4. Why does the court conclude that Esperanza was in a special relation-ship with the defendants?

5. If Esperanza had been a child visiting her mother in jail on visiting day and had fallen and injured herself, would the court have found that the jail owed her a duty of care?

6. If Esperanza had been a child at a week-long camp and had become sick on the second night, would the camp have owed her a duty of care?

APPLYING THE LAW

A 16-year-old high school student began part-time employment at a business as part of a work-study program offered at her school. The business executed a "Cooperative Education Agreement" with the school. This agreement required the employer to design a training program for the student, provide adequate supervision for her, and periodically evaluate her progress. She would earn course credits and wages. The business became aware that one male employee who often worked with the girl touched her more frequently than was appropriate, but no one told him to stop. Eventually, the girl was assigned to work alone with the man who had been touching her. He forced himself on her sexually, and she sued the business. The business contends that it had no duty to protect her from the male employee. How would the plaintiff argue that under *Lawson* the business owed her a duty? Is that argument likely to prevail? (As you continue reading the chapter, look for another plaintiff's argument.)

INCREASING YOUR UNDERSTANDING

1. The generally recognized categories for special relationships are businesses and their invitees, which includes carrier and passenger, and innkeeper and guest, and sometimes includes landlord and tenant; custodian and ward, which includes jailers and prisoners and caretakers and people institutionalized with severe physical or mental disabilities; schools and students (although some states limit that to grade schools and students, and others find high school and student special); spouses; parents and children; and employers and their employees (within the course of employment and when the employee does not appear to be able to care for himself).

2. Most of these special relationships between defendant and plaintiff impose a duty to exercise reasonable care to protect, rescue, or aid the plaintiff. They do not impose a duty to exercise control over third parties dangerous to the plaintiffs. The special relationship between custodian and ward, however, can impose a duty to control dangerous third parties. According to the Restatement (Second) Torts §320:

   > One who is required by law to take or who voluntarily takes the custody of another under circumstances such as to deprive the other of his normal power of self-protection or to subject him to association with persons likely to harm him, is under a duty to exercise reasonable care so to control the conduct of third persons as to prevent them from intentionally harming the other or so conducting themselves as to create an unreasonable risk of harm to him, if the actor
   >
   >   (a) knows or has reason to know that he has the ability to control the conduct of the third persons, and
   >
   >   (b) knows or should know of the necessity and opportunity for exercising such control.

3. Special relationships have been rejected in the following categories. Consider how plaintiffs may have tried to argue that the relationships were special and why the court rejected those arguments.

In Ouch v. Khea, 963 A.2d 63 (R.I. 2009), the Rhode Island Supreme Court ruled that the relationship between the defendant and his fellow gang members was not a special relationship that supported a duty to drive his car with the care necessary to avoid gunfire from rival gang members.

In Ryan Transportation, Inc. v. M and G Assocs. 832 A.2d 1180 (Conn. 2003), the Connecticut Supreme Court ruled that the relationship between commercial co-tenants was not special. An arsonist destroyed the building in which the parties were commercial co-tenants. The defendant was aware of an earlier, unsuccessful arson attempt, but did not warn the plaintiff about it.

In Patton v. U.S.A. Rugby Football, 851 A.2d 566 (Md. App. 2004), the court ruled that the relationship between the organizers of a rugby tournament and spectators and participants in the tournament was not special, so that no duty was owed to protect them from lightning.

In Thompson v. Baniqued, 741 So. 2d 629 (Fla. App. 1999), the court ruled that the relationship between a woman and a neighbor child who was playing in her yard as she gardened was not special. The woman knew the child was there playing with her children and occasionally looked up from her gardening to make sure her children did not go into the street. At some point she told all the children not to go into the street. One child did go into the street and was hit by a car, but she did not owe him a duty of care.

4. Courts generally reject the relationship between a college and a student as being special per se, but they will sometimes recognize that in a particular situation the relationship is functioning like another special relationship such as landlord and tenant or business and customer. See Kathleen Connolly Butler, *Shared Responsibility: The Duty to Legal Externs*, 106 W. Va. L. Rev. 51 (2003).

5. The exceptions to the no-duty rules, such as the special-relationship exceptions, do not create absolute duties to protect, rescue, aid, or control. They simply create duties to exercise reasonable care to protect, rescue, aid, or control.

b. With the Dangerous Third Party

Volpe v. Gallagher
821 A.2d 699 (R.I. 2003)

FLANDERS, J.

"Who knew?" In essence, that was the defense to the charge of negligence in this lawsuit. The plaintiffs, Raymond Volpe and Joyce Almonte, accused the homeowner-defendant, Sara Gallagher (defendant), of negligently allowing her adult son, James Andrew Gallagher (Gallagher), who was mentally ill, to keep guns and ammunition on her property. On July 3, 1994, Gallagher misused these firearms to shoot and kill Ronald Volpe (victim), the plaintiffs' next of kin and the defendant's next-door neighbor. But the defendant asserted that she did not know that her son kept guns or ammunition on her property, much less could she have foreseen that he would use them to murder their next-door neighbor.

As of July 3, 1994—the date of the murder—Gallagher had lived with defendant in her small North Providence ranch house for the entire thirty-four years of his life. A jobless and practically friendless loner who was plagued by hallucinations, imaginary conversants, and a paranoid distrust of others, Gallagher had suffered for many years from an increasingly severe and delu-sional mental illness. Nevertheless, while he was living in defendant's house, he also kept on the premises a shotgun, a pistol, boxes of ammunition, and related gun paraphernalia. On the date in question, for no known reason, Gallagher suddenly emerged from the basement of defendant's home—a place where he spent long hours by himself—with his loaded shotgun in hand. The victim, his next-door neighbor, apparently was trimming the hedge between their two houses. After discharging the shotgun three times into the victim's head and body, Gallagher returned, shotgun in hand, to his lair in the basement of defendant's home, leaving the victim's dead body facedown in the hedges. . . .

According to plaintiffs, defendant knew or should have known that, by allowing her mentally ill son to possess guns and ammunition while he was residing with her at her house and exhibiting paranoid and delusional behav-ior, she created an unreasonable risk of bodily harm to others. In effect, they maintained, by permitting Gallagher to combine what his psychologist sister believed was "paranoid schizophrenia" with gun possession on her property, defendant concocted a sure-fire recipe for disaster, for which she functioned as the de facto mixmaster. Although she grudgingly admitted at trial to knowing that her son was mentally disturbed ("I knew he wasn't right. I just didn't know what was wrong with him;" "[he] just wasn't acting right. He always wanted to be alone in darkness. . . . He was acting peculiar."), defendant insisted that she had no idea that he possessed any guns or ammunition, much less that he kept such firearms in her house. According to defendant, "I just wouldn't allow anybody to have guns in the house. I was afraid of them, and didn't want them." Moreover, she argued, because her son had no history of violence, she could not have foreseen that one day he would shoot their next-door neighbor to death using any of the guns and ammunition that he kept at her house. . . .

In this case, the trial justice believed that she had committed an error of law that constituted grounds for a new trial. She had instructed the jury pursuant to the legal standards set forth in the Restatement (Second) Torts §318 (1965) (restatement),[1] and the jury then found defendant liable. But absent a track record of violence for Gallagher, the trial justice reasoned, no such legal duty existed in these circumstances. Therefore, she ruled, she should not have let this case go to the jury because it was not foreseeable that defendant's son would use any of the guns and ammunition he kept on defendant's property in such a violent and deadly manner.

For the reasons enumerated below, we respectfully disagree and, consequently, reverse the granting of defendant's motion for new trial. . . .

In this case, the trial justice correctly instructed the jury on both a land possessor's liability under the legal principles set forth in §318 of the restatement—which we hereby adopt and apply to the circumstances in this case—and on a landowner's traditional liability to visitors and to those outside the property for maintaining dangerous conditions on their land.

> A special relationship under Section 318 [of the restatement] may arise between the possessor of land and those allowed on the land because of the possessor's power of control over those allowed to enter. . . . If so, the possessor has a duty to exercise reasonable care for the protection of others, including "the power of control of expulsion which his occupation of the premises gives him over the conduct of a third person who may be present, to prevent injury to the visitor at his hands." . . .

Under §318 of the restatement, when possessors of property allow one or more persons to use their land or personal property, they are, if present, under a conditional duty to exercise reasonable care to control the conduct of such users to prevent them from intentionally harming others or from conducting themselves on the possessors' property in a manner that would create an unreasonable risk of bodily harm to others. . . . Two conditions, however, must exist for this duty to arise: the possessors of the property must (1) know or have reason to know that they have the ability to control the person(s) using their land, and (2) know or should know of the necessity and opportunity for exercising such control. . . .

In this case, defendant was the possessor and owner of a tiny lot containing a small ranch house in a densely settled, residential neighborhood of similarly

---

1. Section 318 of the restatement entitled, "Duty of Possessor of Land or Chattels to Control Conduct of Licensee," provides:

> "If the actor permits a third person to use land or chattels in his possession otherwise than as a servant, he is, if present, under a duty to exercise reasonable care so to control the conduct of the third person as to prevent him from intentionally harming others or from so conducting himself as to create an unreasonable risk of bodily harm to them, if the actor
>
> (a) knows or has reason to know that he has the ability to control the third person, and
> (b) knows or should know of the necessity and opportunity for exercising such control." 4 Restatement (Second) Torts §318 at 126-27 (1965).

sized lots and houses. Specifically, as of July 1994, she was the sole owner of the seven-room ranch house on Whipple Court in North Providence where she and her son had lived for all thirty-four years of his life. Gallagher, who was defendant's adult son, apparently used her property for many years to possess and store guns, ammunition, and related gun paraphernalia. He engaged in this activity on defendant's property when the house was in defendant's possession and while he was living there with her.

Thus, defendant was "present" within the meaning of that term as it is used in §318 of the restatement because she was there when her son engaged in the conduct that created an unreasonable risk of harm to others: namely, using defendant's house for possessing and storing his guns and ammunition.[2]

The jury was entitled to conclude that defendant also knew or had reason to know that she had the ability to control her son with respect to this use of her property. First, he was living at her house only with her permission; indeed, he had no right to do so without her permission. Second, defendant virtually conceded that she had the ability to control her son's possession of guns and ammunition on her property when she testified that, if she had known about any gun, "I would have told him to get rid of it. If he didn't, I would have." Based on these circumstances, the jury was entitled to conclude that defendant knew or had reason to know that she had the ability to control her son's maintenance of guns and ammunition on her property. . . .

If, contrary to the facts in this case, the evidence had suggested that Gallagher had dominated defendant or otherwise compromised her ability to control his possession of guns on her property—for example, by threatening her, by physically or psychologically abusing her, or by intimidating her in such a manner that she feared even attempting to curtail his gun-possession activity in her own house—then the jury might well have concluded that she did not know or have reason to know that she could control her son's conduct in this respect. But the jury heard no such evidence in this case. On the contrary, it heard defendant assert that if she had known about the guns, she would have gotten rid of them in one way or in another.

In any event, both the knowledge and the control issues were factual questions that the trial justice properly submitted to the jury for its determination. . . .

After the police arrived and obtained defendant's consent to search the property, they found the shotgun box lying on top of the refrigerator in the basement, a place that was in plain view of defendant and of anyone else who went down the stairs to enter the basement. They also found the shotgun behind the boiler in this same basement where defendant regularly did her laundry.

---

2. The mere fact that, at the precise moment of the shooting, defendant was reading her newspaper in the living room of her house and was oblivious to the fact that her son was outside the house stalking their neighbor with his loaded shotgun does not preclude liability under §318. Rather, because she was present in the house when Gallagher engaged in his dangerous gun-possession activity, and when he also was exhibiting various symptoms of a delusional and paranoid mental illness, defendant had a duty to exercise reasonable care to prevent him from engaging in this activity if she knew or should have known that she was able to control him in this respect by causing the removal of the guns from the premises.

They retrieved ammunition and spent shell casings from drawers in the base-ment and from Gallagher's bedroom on the first floor of defendant's house. Boxes of ammunition, a gun-cleaning kit, and ammunition clips completed the inventory of gun paraphernalia seized from her house. Finally, defendant signed a statement for the police, prepared by one of her daughters, indicating that Gallagher suffered from mental illness. . . .

The defendant, however, steadfastly denied having any knowledge that her son possessed any guns or ammunition at her house. . . . But given the close confines of the small house that she and her son shared; the fact that her weekly cleaning, laundry, and vacuuming chores brought her in regular contact with those areas in the house where her son kept the guns, his various caches of ammunition, and the related boxes of shotgun shells and other gun parapher-nalia; and the fact that, after the murder, the shotgun and ammunition boxes, as well as the .32-caliber gun that her daughter was so quick to retrieve from Gallagher's bedroom [before the police arrived], were all found throughout the house in easily observable or locatable places, the jury was entitled to conclude that she either knew or should have known about her son's possession of these dangerous instrumentalities on her property.

Because defendant knew about her son's mental illness but nevertheless, as the jury apparently concluded, allowed him to possess and to store guns and ammunition on her property, we are of the opinion that she had "a duty to exercise reasonable care so to control the conduct of Gallagher as to prevent him from intentionally harming others or from so conducting himself as to create an unreasonable risk of bodily harm to them[.]" . . .

At trial, no evidence suggested that Gallagher ever previously had deployed the guns that he kept in defendant's house to harm anyone else before he shot the victim to death on July 3, 1994. Nevertheless, we hold, the absence of a violent past did not excuse defendant's conduct in failing to exercise control over her property to prevent such a mentally ill person from using her house as an ordnance depot. If a property owner allows a person who she knows is suffering from a delusionary and paranoid mental illness to use her property for the storage and maintenance of firearms and ammunition—despite real-izing that this person has a history of talking to himself and to imaginary others; of harboring paranoid suspicions about other people; of not taking medication for his mental problems; and of not improving after receiving medical treat-ment for his mental illness—then that property owner is taking a foreseeable risk that a third party in close proximity of that dangerous activity will be hurt or killed as a result of allowing such an unstable individual to use her property in this careless manner. Thus, "if one in possession of land permits a third person to conduct an activity on it which is highly dangerous unless great care is taken, he [or she] may properly be required to exercise constant vigilance to be able to exercise his [or her] control over the third person when and if the occasion for it arises." Restatement (Second) Torts §318, cmt. c, at 128. . . .

In sum, we conclude that the trial justice erred as a matter of law in granting a new trial on the basis that "no evidence was ever presented that the defendant knew or should have known that her son would use a firearm in a violent manner." . . . [T]he jury was entitled to conclude that a reasonably prudent and informed homeowner, such as this defendant, should not have allowed such a mentally unstable person to keep and maintain deadly weapons on her property because she should have known that, even without a violent past history, he was not the type of individual who was capable of possessing and using such dangerous instrumentalities in a reasonably safe manner. . . .

Possessors of property, we hold, are not entitled to take a legal mulligan when they are negligent. Thus, they should not obtain the benefit of one free act of negligence merely because the foreseeable consequences of their negligence did not materialize in the precise form and manner of the particular injury in question until the occurrence of the injury-causing incident itself. When negligence occurs, we are simply unwilling to sacrifice the first victims' rights to life and liberty upon the altar of an inflexible prior-similar-incidents rule. Nor are we prepared to slavishly adhere to the notion that at least one prior criminal act of violence must have occurred before a property possessor can be held liable for a licensee's otherwise foreseeable misuse of the possessor's property to harm another. . . . To be sure, previous conduct is one factor to weigh when assessing foreseeability, but it should not be a sine qua non when, as here, other circumstances are present that should have alerted the property possessor of the necessity to control the activity in question. Accordingly, given the duty-triggering circumstances that were present in this case, only the general risk of harm need be foreseen from the circumstances, not the specific mechanism or manner of the injuries actually suffered by the victims. . . .

Otherwise, possessors of residential property would have carte blanche to allow third-party users of their property, including those who are mentally ill or unstable, to engage in such inherently dangerous activities as possessing guns and ammunition, playing with fire, storing dynamite and other explosives, experimenting with volatile chemicals such as nitroglycerin, harboring poisonous snakes or other deadly or potentially life-threatening animals, or undertaking any number of other unreasonably dangerous activities on the possessors' property, and thereby needlessly exposing their neighbors and other innocent parties to wrack and ruin, let alone serious bodily injury and death. Such a rule of law would be intolerable in a civilized society. Allowing the mentally ill to use one's property must be subject to the same common-sense criterion that applies whenever possessors of property allow third parties to use their property: the practical responsibility to take reasonable care that such users do not engage in inherently dangerous activities, such as keeping guns and ammunition there, that create unreasonable risks of bodily harm to others. . . .

Finally, given the unusual circumstances of this case, we would caution against any hasty extrapolation of the legal principles discussed in this opinion to different factual scenarios. For example, the relevant considerations might be markedly different in landlord-tenant matters, in commercial-property or governmental contexts, in situations not involving guns, and in cases that do not involve this type of severe mental illness (paranoid schizophrenia)—to name just a few of the factual elements that might warrant a different analysis and outcome.

For these reasons, we sustain the plaintiffs' appeal, vacate the trial justice's order granting a new trial, and remand this case for entry of a judgment in favor of the plaintiffs consistent with the jury's verdict.

Justice Shea dissented. . . . Parents are now faced with a weighty decision. Either they must reject their troubled children whose actions they are expected to control, or else face harsh legal consequence even in the absence of any previous incidents. . . .

PREPARING FOR CLASS

1. Why did the trial judge reverse herself?

2. Why would a trial judge instruct the jury on a duty rule if duty is a question of law for the judge?

3. Did the Rhode Island Supreme Court determine that the trial judge applied the wrong law or that she applied the right law incorrectly?

4. What special relationship does this case involve? Is the special relationship in itself sufficient to impose a duty? If not, what else is required?

5. What was the defense argument that no duty was owed? Why did the Rhode Island Supreme Court reject that analysis? What different facts could have led to a different result?

6. Isn't it persuasive that the defendant did not know of the need to control her son because he had never acted violently before? Why does the court not require prior acts of violence to impose a duty in cases like this?

APPLYING THE LAW

A 22-year-old man broke up with his girlfriend, with whom he lived, and moved back into his parents' home. He was in therapy for depression and obsessive compulsive disorder (OCD) and was on medications for his depression and OCD. He engaged in self-mutilation. He dressed all in black and had tattoos of a pentagram, a skull, and Marilyn Manson. He owned knives, a set of brass knuckles, a 12 gauge shot gun, and a hand gun. The walls of his room at home were decorated with a swastika, the numbers "666," and the words "Lucifer is God." He also owned a satanic bible and books about witchcraft. One morning, he left his parents' home and drove to his former girlfriend's apartment where he strangled her to death. He then shot himself. The girlfriend's parents sued the young man's parents for negligence. If *Volpe* applies, will the young man's parents succeed with a motion for summary judgment on the grounds they did not owe the former girlfriend a duty of care?

INCREASING YOUR UNDERSTANDING

1. *Reaction to* Volpe *in the psychiatric community.* The opinion has been criticized as dependent upon prejudices against the mentally ill that presume that anyone psychotic is likely to be violent, when previous violent behavior is really the best predictor of violence. According to the critics, families should be encouraged to provide homes for mentally ill members, and letting these prejudices harden into law will discourage this kind of family support and increase the dangers to the mentally ill and others. See Paul S. Appelbaum, *Law & Psychiatry: One Madman Keeping Loaded Guns: Misconceptions of Mental Illness and Their Legal Consequences,* Psychiatric Services, Oct. 2004, *available at* http://psychservices.psychiatryonline.org/cgi/content/full/55/10/1105.

2. *Parents and children.* The son in *Volpe* was an adult, so plaintiffs relied on a relationship between a possessor of land and her licensee. Parents with minor children have a duty to control them because of the special parent-child relationship, but only when they know or have reason to know they can control the child and know or should know of the necessity and opportunity for exercising such control. See Restatement (Second) Torts §316 (1965).

3. *Employers and employees.* Similarly, the special relationship between an employer and an employee can impose a duty to control the dangerous employee, but only when certain other conditions are met. The employee must either be on premises in the employer's possession or on land the employee is privileged to enter only as the employee, or be using the employer's chattel. The employer—like the parent or possessor of land—must know or have reason to know he can control the employee and must know or have reason to know of the necessity and opportunity for controlling the employee. See Restatement (Second) Torts §318 (1965).

   According to K.M. v. Publix Super Markets, 895 So. 2d 1114 (Fla. App. 2005), "An employer does not owe a duty to persons who are injured by its employees while the employees are off duty, not then acting for the employer's benefit, not on the employer's premises, and not using the employer's equipment." In that case, a Publix employee arranged for another Publix employee to babysit her daughter. The store manager was aware of the babysitting arrangement and aware that the babysitting employee was on parole for a conviction for attempted sexual battery of a minor under 12. The store manager did nothing. The babysitting employee molested his co-worker's daughter. The court found that Publix did not owe a duty of care to the child because the criminal attacks did not occur at the store or involve its property. The mother had arranged for her co-worker to babysit to be able to work the hours her manager had scheduled for her. Was the babysitting, then, "acting for the employer's benefit"? Did the court get this wrong? Think back to the work-study student in the Applying the Law section following *Lawson v. Superior Court*. Could her attorney convince the judge that a special relationship between the employer and the employee who forced himself on her was a special relationship supporting a duty?

4. *People in charge of dangerous people.* As stated in §319 of the Restatement (Second) of Torts, "One who takes charge of a third person whom he knows or should know to be likely to cause bodily harm to others if not controlled is under a duty to exercise reasonable care to control the third person to prevent him from doing such harm."

Tarasoff v. Regents of University of California
551 P.2d 334 (Cal. 1976)

Tobriner, J.

On October 27, 1969, Prosenjit Poddar killed Tatiana Tarasoff. Plaintiffs, Tatiana's parents, allege that two months earlier Poddar confided his intention to kill Tatiana to Dr. Lawrence Moore, a psychologist employed by the Cowell Memorial Hospital at the University of California at Berkeley. They allege that on Moore's request, the campus police briefly detained Poddar, but released him when he appeared rational. They further claim that Dr. Harvey Powelson, Moore's superior, then directed that no further action be taken to detain Poddar. No one warned plaintiffs of Tatiana's peril.

Concluding that these facts set forth causes of action against neither therapists and policemen involved, nor against the Regents of the University of California as their employer, the superior court sustained defendants' demurrers to plaintiffs' second amended complaints without leave to amend. This appeal ensued. . . .

Plaintiffs' first cause of action, entitled 'Failure to Detain a Dangerous Patient,' alleges that on August 20, 1969, Poddar was a voluntary outpatient receiving therapy at Cowell Memorial Hospital. Poddar informed Moore, his therapist, that he was going to kill an unnamed girl, readily identifiable as Tatiana, when she returned home from spending the summer in Brazil. Moore, with the concurrence of Dr. Gold, who had initially examined Poddar, and Dr. Yandell, Assistant to the director of the department of psychiatry, decided that Poddar should be committed for observation in a mental hospital. Moore orally notified Officers Atkinson and Teel of the campus police that he would request commitment. He then sent a letter to Police Chief William Beall requesting the assistance of the police department in securing Poddar's confinement.

Officers Atkinson, Brownrigg, and Halleran took Poddar into custody, but, satisfied that Poddar was rational, released him on his promise to stay away from Tatiana. Powelson, director of the department of psychiatry at Cowell Memorial Hospital, then asked the police to return Moore's letter, directed that all copies of the letter and notes that Moore had taken as therapist be destroyed, and "ordered no action to place Prosenjit Poddar in 72-hour treatment and evaluation facility."

Plaintiffs' second cause of action, entitled "Failure to Warn On a Dangerous Patient," incorporates the allegations of the first cause of action, but adds the assertion that defendants negligently permitted Poddar to be released from police custody without "notifying the parents of Tatiana Tarasoff that their daughter was in grave danger from Posenjit Poddar." Poddar persuaded Tatiana's brother to share an apartment with him near Tatiana's residence; shortly after her return from Brazil, Poddar went to her residence and killed her. . . .

The second cause of action can be amended to allege that Tatiana's death proximately resulted from defendants' negligent failure to warn Tatiana or others likely to apprise her of her danger. Plaintiffs contend that as amended, such allegations of negligence and proximate causation, with resulting damages, establish a cause of action. Defendants, however, contend that in the circumstances of the present case they owed no duty of care to Tatiana or her parents and that, in the absence of such duty, they were free to act in careless disregard of Tatiana's life and safety.

In analyzing this issue, we bear in mind that legal duties are not discoverable facts of nature, but merely conclusory expressions that, in cases of a particular type, liability should be imposed for damage done. As stated in Dillon v. Legg (1968) 68 Cal. 2d 728, 734, 69 Cal. Rptr. 72, 76, 441 P.2d 912, 916: "The assertion that liability must . . . be denied because defendant bears no 'duty' to plaintiff 'begs the essential question-whether the plaintiff's interests are entitled to legal protection against the defendant's conduct. . . . (Duty) is not sacrosanct in itself, but only an expression of the sum total of those considerations of policy which lead the law to say that the particular plaintiff is entitled to protection." (Prosser, *Law of Torts* (3d ed. 1964) at pp. 332-333.) . . .

Although . . . under the common law, as a general rule, one person owed no duty to control the conduct of another nor to warn those endangered by such conduct, the courts have carved out an exception to this rule in cases in which the defendant stands in some special relationship to either the person whose conduct needs to be controlled or in a relationship to the foreseeable victim of that conduct. Applying this exception to the present case, we note that a relationship of defendant therapists to either Tatiana or Poddar will suffice to establish a duty of care; as explained in section 315 of the Restatement Second of Torts, a duty of care may arise from either "(a) a special relation . . . between the actor and the third person which imposes a duty upon the actor to control the third person's conduct, or (b) a special relation . . . between the actor and the other which gives to the other a right of protection."

Although plaintiffs' pleadings assert no special relation between Tatiana and defendant therapists, they establish as between Poddar and defendant therapists the special relation that arises between a patient and his doctor or psychotherapist. Such a relationship may support affirmative duties for the benefit of third persons. Thus, for example, a hospital must exercise reasonable care to control the behavior of a patient which may endanger other persons. A doctor must also warn a patient if the patient's condition or medication renders certain conduct, such as driving a car, dangerous to others. . . .

We recognize the difficulty that a therapist encounters in attempting to forecast whether a patient presents a serious danger of violence. Obviously we do not require that the therapist, in making that determination, render a perfect performance; the therapist need only exercise "that reasonable degree of skill, knowledge, and care ordinarily possessed and exercised by members of (that professional specialty) under similar circumstances." Within the broad range of reasonable practice and treatment in which professional opinion and judgment may differ, the therapist is free to exercise his or her own best judgment without liability; proof, aided by hindsight, that he or she judged wrongly is insufficient to establish negligence.

In the instant case, however, the pleadings do not raise any question as to failure of defendant therapists to predict that Poddar presented a serious danger of violence. On the contrary, the present complaints allege that defendant therapists did in fact predict that Poddar would kill, but were negligent in failing to warn.

Amicus contends, however, that even when a therapist does in fact predict that a patient poses a serious danger of violence to others, the therapist should be absolved of any responsibility for failing to act to protect the potential victim. In our view, however, once a therapist does in fact determine, or under applicable professional standards reasonably should have determined, that a patient poses a serious danger of violence to others, he bears a duty to exercise reasonable care to protect the foreseeable victim of that danger. . . .

The risk that unnecessary warnings may be given is a reasonable price to pay for the lives of possible victims that may be saved. We would hesitate to hold that the therapist who is aware that his patient expects to attempt to assassinate the President of the United States would not be obligated to warn the authorities because the therapist cannot predict with accuracy that his patient will commit the crime.

Defendants further argue that free and open communication is essential to psychotherapy; that "Unless a patient . . . is assured that . . . information (revealed by him) can and will be held in utmost confidence, he will be reluctant to make the full disclosure upon which diagnosis and treatment . . . depends." (Sen. Com. on Judiciary, comment on Evid. Code, §1014.) The giving of a warning, defendants contend, constitutes a breach of trust which entails the revelation of confidential communications.

We note, moreover, that Evidence Code section 1024, enacted in 1965, established that psychotherapeutic communication is not privileged when disclosure is necessary to prevent threatened danger. We cannot accept without question counsels' implicit assumption that effective therapy for potentially violent patients depends upon either the patient's lack of awareness that a therapist can disclose confidential communications to avert impending danger, or upon the therapist's advance promise never to reveal nonprivileged threats of violence. . . .

The revelation of a communication under the above circumstances is not a breach of trust or a violation of professional ethics; as stated in the Principles of Medical Ethics of the American Medical Association (1957), section 9: "A physician may not reveal the confidence entrusted to him in the course of medical attendance. . . . Unless he is required to do so by law or unless it becomes necessary in order to protect the welfare of the individual or of the community." We conclude that the public policy favoring protection of the confidential character of patient-psychotherapist communications must yield to the extent to which disclosure is essential to avert danger to others. The protective privilege ends where the public peril begins.

Our current crowded and computerized society compels the interdependence of its members. In this risk-infested society we can hardly tolerate the further exposure to danger that would result from a concealed knowledge of the therapist that his patient was lethal. If the exercise of reasonable care to protect the threatened victim requires the therapist to warn the endangered party or those who can reasonably be expected to notify him, we see no sufficient societal interest that would protect and justify concealment. The containment of such risks lies in the public interest. For the foregoing reasons, we find that plaintiffs' complaints can be amended to state a cause of action against defendants Moore, Powelson, Gold, and Yandell and against the Regents as their employer, for breach of a duty to exercise reasonable care to protect Tatiana. . . .

Turning now to the police defendants, we conclude that they do not have any such special relationship to either Tatiana or to Poddar sufficient to impose upon such defendants a duty to warn respecting Poddar's violent intentions. Plaintiffs suggest no theory, and plead no facts that give rise to any duty to warn on the part of the police defendants absent such a special relationship. They have thus failed to demonstrate that the trial court erred in denying leave to amend as to the police defendants.

WRIGHT D.J., and SULLIVAN and RICHARDSON, JJ., concur.

Thompson v. County of Alameda
616 P.2d 728 (Cal. 1980)

RICHARDSON, J.

. . . Plaintiffs, husband and wife, and their minor son lived in the City of Piedmont, a few doors from the residence of the mother of James F. (James), a juvenile offender. Prior to the incident in question, James had been in the custody and under the control of County and had been confined in a county institution under court order. County knew that James had "latent, extremely dangerous and violent propensities regarding young children and that sexual assaults upon young children and violence connected therewith were a likely result of releasing (him) into the community." County also knew that James had "indicated that he would, if released, take the life of a young child residing in the neighborhood." (James gave no indication of which, if any, young child he intended as his victim.) County released James on temporary leave into his mother's custody at her home, and "(a)t no time did (County) advise and/or warn (James' mother), the local police and/or parents of young children within the immediate vicinity of (James' mother's) house of the known facts . . . ." Within 24 hours of his release on temporary leave, James murdered plaintiffs' son in the garage of James' mother's home.

[The plaintiffs sued the county. One theory was that the county breached a duty to warn "parents of young children within the immediate vicinity" of James's mother's home that James was being released. The trial court dismissed the complaint, and the California Supreme Court affirmed.]

Unlike members of the general public, in *Tarasoff* . . . the potential victims were specifically known and designated individuals. The warnings which we therein required were directed at making those individuals aware of the danger to which they were uniquely exposed. The threatened targets were precise. In such cases, it is fair to conclude that warnings given discreetly and to a limited number of persons would have a greater effect because they would alert those particular targeted individuals of the possibility of a specific threat pointed at them. In contrast, the warnings sought by plaintiffs would of necessity have to be made to a broad segment of the population and would be only general in nature. In addition to the likelihood that such generalized warnings when frequently repeated would do little as a practical matter to stimulate increased safety measures, as we develop below, such extensive warnings would be difficult to give.

[The court also ruled that imposing liability for failure to warn the neighborhood] might substantially jeopardize rehabilitative efforts both by stigmatizing released offenders and by inhibiting their release. It is also possible that, in addition, parole or probation authorities would be far less likely to authorize release given the substantial drain on their resources which such warnings might require. A stated public policy favoring innovative release programs would be thwarted. . . .

PREPARING FOR CLASS

1. *Tarasoff v. Regents*

    a. What role did the defendants play in causing the injury in this case?

    b. As Poddar was the source of danger, why would counsel for plaintiffs believe a duty could be established?

    c.   What societal interests would be protected by refusing to find a duty? What societal interests are protected by imposing a duty? What interests does the court find weigh more heavily? Why?

    d.   How does the court try to shape a duty that is not too difficult to satisfy?

2. *Thompson v. County of Alameda*

    a.   As plaintiff's attorney in *Thompson*, how would you have tried to argue that *Tarasoff* was applicable?

    b.   Why did the court find that it was not?

APPLYING THE LAW

An attorney had a client who retired in his thirties because of a head injury. The client was receiving a pension, but because he had made poor financial decisions, control of the pension was given to an administrator. The client sought the attorney's help in regaining control over his money. One day, the client telephoned the attorney and told her that he had decided he was going to go to the bank where the money was held (she knew what bank that was) and demand his money. He said he was going to take a gun, but it wouldn't be a robbery because he was going to ask only for the money in his own account. The lawyer explained to the client that this would not help convince the court of his mental competence and could go horribly wrong. At a minimum, he'd be jailed. At a maximum, he'd be shot. They talked for an hour, at the end of which the attorney felt convinced her client had really called her to blow off steam and be talked out of his appealing fantasy of getting the money at gun point. At the end of the call, she recounted the phone call to a senior partner to ask his advice about what she should do. How should the partner advise her?

INCREASING YOUR UNDERSTANDING

Some state statutes impose a version of a *Tarasoff* duty. Also, most courts presented with the opportunity to impose a similar duty have done so. See, e.g., Emerich v. City of Philadelphia Center for Human Development, Inc., 720 A.2d 1032 (Pa. 1998). The *Tarasoff* case is not followed in all jurisdictions. The Illinois Supreme Court recently rejected it in Tedrick v. Community Resource Center, 920 N.E.2d 220 (2009).

3. Assumed Duties

Marsalis v. LaSalle
94 So. 2d 120 (La. App. 1957)

McBride, J.

[The plaintiffs were shopping in the defendants' store when the defendants' Siamese cat bit or scratched Mrs. Marsalis. Mr. Marsalis asked the defendant to keep the cat locked up for the 14-day incubation period for rabies because the local paper had reported a high incidence of rabid cats. The defendants agreed to keep an eye on the cat over that period and not to let it out. But the cat did escape and was gone about a month, so Mrs. Marsalis's physician advised her to undergo the Pasteur treatment for rabies, to which she turned out to be highly allergic. The cat was subsequently found and was not rabid. Mr. and Mrs. Marsalis sued the shopkeepers.]

Unless a man is responsible for another person's injury or distress, ordinarily he is under no legal duty or obligation of giving him aid, help or assistance, or to go to his relief. . . .

But there is a rule of law which is just as well recognized:

> . . . that one who voluntarily undertakes to care for, or to afford relief or assistance to, an ill, injured, or helpless person is under a legal obligation to use reasonable care and prudence in what he does. In such case the measure of the duty assumed is to exercise ordinary or common humanity, or to exercise with reasonable care such competence and skill as he possesses, or to exercise such care in the treatment of the injured person as the circumstances will allow; and the person who undertakes the care is liable if the existing injuries are aggravated or other injuries are caused by a lack of this measure of care. 65 C.J.S., Negligence, §58, p. 551.

In Restatement of the Law of Torts, Vol. 2, p. 881, the rule is stated thus:

> One who gratuitously undertakes with another to do an act or to render services which he should recognize as necessary to the other's bodily safety and thereby leads the other in reasonable reliance upon the performance of such undertaking
>
> (a) to refrain from himself taking the necessary steps to secure his safety or from securing the then available protective action by third persons, . . . is subject to liability to the other for bodily harm resulting from the actor's failure to exercise reasonable care to carry out his undertaking.
>
> Comment:
>
> a. The actor may undertake to do an act or to render services either by an express promise to do so or by a course of conduct which the actor

should realize would lead the other into the reasonable belief that the act would be done or the services rendered. . . .

This principle has been given application by the courts of several jurisdictions in a variety of cases. . . .

Our belief is that the . . . rule with respect to the duties of one who voluntarily undertakes to care for or to afford relief or assistance to an injured or distressed person is broad enough to have full application to the instant case. Perhaps the defendant, LaSalle, initially owed no duty whatever to Mrs. Marsalis, but when he once agreed to restrain and keep the cat under observation, he was bound to use reasonable care and prudence in doing so and to assume and exercise reasonable care and common humanity. It may be that Mrs. Marsalis had open to her some other course by which she could have had the cat incarcerated and examined in order to determine if it was rabid, but she unquestionably and in good faith relied upon defendant to carry out the agreement which he voluntarily made, thus foregoing such other possible available protection. It was of extreme importance to know if the cat had rabies so she could regulate her course of conduct with reference to the injury. We do not doubt for one moment that both defendant and his wife were fully cognizant that such injuries could be quite serious and exceedingly dangerous in the event the offending animal was infected with rabies. In fact we feel sure of our ground in saying this because of the statement of Mrs. LaSalle: "I have got that much sense to know that if a cat ever scratches anybody [not to let it out]."

LaSalle's liability would then depend on whether he used reasonable care with reference to keeping the cat, for as it developed later the Pasteur treatment was entirely unnecessary and the escape of the cat was the direct and proximate cause of the necessity for the injections and the ill effects which Mrs. Marsalis suffered as a result thereof.

Neither defendant nor his wife took any especial steps or means to prevent the cat from straying from their premises. The cat, which was three years old, had always been kept in the basement and was allowed access to the yard from time to time. No change whatever in the animal's usual routine was undertaken and we must hold that defendant failed to use ordinary or reasonable care to see to it that the animal was kept secure, and, hence, defendant is liable unto plaintiffs for whatever damages they sustained as a result of such lack of care. . . .

Amended and affirmed.

Marquez v. Home Depot
154 F. Supp. 2d 152 (D. Mass. 2001)

Ponsor, D.J.

Plaintiff Hilario Marquez has sued Home Depot, a home improvement store, seeking damages for injuries suffered when defective twine that defendant gave plaintiff broke as he was tying merchandise to his car. Defendant has moved for summary judgment on the grounds that it had no duty to protect plaintiff from the sort of accident that occurred here, and that there is insufficient evidence to suggest that it breached any duty of reasonable care.

With some reluctance, the court will deny defendant's motion for summary judgment. While the facts suggesting negligence may be weak, defendant did owe a duty of reasonable care to plaintiff, and a rational jury could find that it breached that duty. . . .

On June 1, 1997, plaintiff Hilario Marquez went to Home Depot in West Springfield, Massachusetts with his daughter, Rosanna Oliver and his son-in-law, Francisco Oliver. They purchased five doors and some other supplies, and brought the doors outside to lash them to plaintiff's truck. Rosanna Oliver then asked a Home Depot employee for something with which to tie down the load. The employee offered her a length of "hemp" style twine. From past experience there, Ms. Oliver knew that Home Depot usually supplied a stronger nylon twine to its customers free of charge, so she asked for it, explaining that her family had a heavy load. The employee said that the store had run out of the nylon twine. Ms. Oliver took the hemp twine, returned to the vehicle and gave it to plaintiff.

Plaintiff threaded the twine around the doors, which had been laid on the roof, and through a ring on the bottom of the truck. He then squatted and pulled on the twine to tighten the load. As he pulled, the twine snapped, causing him to fall backward to the ground from a squatting position. The fall caused a tear in plaintiff's rotator cuff.

For approximately ten years prior to the accident, Home Depot had routinely provided its customers with twine for tying loads to cars. In general, the store handed out a brand of nylon twine known as Polypro Q550. It was not Home Depot's usual practice to hand out hemp-style twine.

Plaintiff filed his one-count complaint of negligence. . . . Defendant . . . has moved for summary judgment. . . .

Defendant's primary line of attack is the argument that it had no duty to protect plaintiff from this accident. . . .

Plaintiff . . . argues that when Home Depot gave him the twine, it voluntarily assumed a duty—that of helping him lash his merchandise to the truck—but failed to perform it in a reasonably safe manner. It is settled in this Commonwealth that "a duty voluntarily assumed must be performed with due care."

One who undertakes, gratuitously or for consideration, to render services to another which he should recognize as necessary for the protection of the other's person or things, is subject to liability to the other for physical harm resulting from his failure to exercise reasonable care to perform his undertaking, if (a) his failure to exercise such care increases the risk of such harm, or (b) the harm is suffered because of the other's reliance upon the undertaking. [Restatement (Second) of Torts §323 (1965).]

Plaintiff's theory is that the hemp twine provided in lieu of the usual nylon twine was not reasonably safe to do the job of securing heavy materials to cars. Handing Ms. Oliver the weaker twine, plaintiff says, increased the risk not only that the load would come off the roof while on the highway, but that someone tightening the load would break the twine and injure himself.

Plaintiff points to an analogous case, Brady v. Great Atl. & Pac. Tea Co., 336 Mass. 386, 145 N.E.2d 828 (1957), where a supermarket violated its duty of care by providing a shopping cart with a defective baby seat. In that case, a mother put her baby in a baby seat and tightened its strap around the child's stomach. While she was looking away, the child fell out of the seat and was injured. After the fall, the child's mother noticed that the strap was frayed at one end and had broken away from the side of the seat. The court held that the act of providing the seat was properly found to be negligent—indeed, the jury could consider it a case of res ipsa loquitur, where the circumstances of the accident themselves established defendant's negligence.

Although this case emphatically is not one of res ipsa loquitur, Brady supports plaintiff's argument that defendant had a duty of care to protect plaintiff from this accident. Once defendant offered to help customers tie down merchandise to their cars, it was required to do so in a reasonably safe manner.

Like the strap in the *Brady* case, the twine defendant provided to plaintiff had to be reasonably safe to do its job—here, tying down heavy doors to vehicles. It seems obvious that if, for example, the Home Depot employee had tied down the doors to plaintiff's truck and the twine had snapped in traffic, causing the doors to slide off and damage plaintiff's (or another's) car, defendant could not evade its duty of care. The nature of plaintiff's injury here, viewing the facts in the light most favorable to him, is just another consequence of that sort of breach of duty. . . .

PREPARING FOR CLASS

1. *Marsalis v. LaSalle*

   a. If the defendants had not agreed to keep an eye on the cat, would they have owed Mrs. Marsalis a duty?

   b. Is the agreement alone sufficient to impose a duty?

   c. If, when the cat was finally captured, it was found to be rabid, would the plaintiffs have had a case?

2. *Marquez v. Home Depot*

   a. Does the plaintiff in this case establish an assumed duty the same way as the plaintiffs in *Marsalis*?

   b. How was providing twine an act "necessary for the protection of the other's person or things"?

    c.   How is the shopping cart case analogous? How does the assumed duty rule apply to it?

    d.   How does the second part of the rule apply here?

    e.   The judge thinks the negligence case is weak, yet he denies the summary judgment motion. Why is that?

APPLYING THE LAW

1.   A woman bought landscaping materials from the defendant's store. The woman asked the cashier if an employee could help her lower the tailgate of her truck and load the materials because she was worried she was not strong enough and might injure herself. The cashier told the woman to drive her pickup truck to a secured area where another employee would load her truck for her. The woman did as the cashier told her but after about 15 minutes, no employee had shown up, so the woman decided to load the merchandise herself. She attempted to open the tailgate, but it would not open. She tugged on it, and she fell backward when it opened. She hit her head on the ground and suffered a concussion and bruises on her hip and the side of her leg. She filed a negligence action against the store. The store moved for summary judgment on the grounds it did not owe her a duty of care. What result?

2.   Beth Smith, a 14-year-old girl, was sad that her friend, Ann, had moved away, so her parents arranged for Ann to come for a visit. Ann's father stressed that his daughter was not to be in a car with any young, male drivers. Mrs. Smith, agreed, saying, "Don't worry. I promise we'll take good care of her." Mrs. Smith dropped the girls off at the mall and left them unsupervised. When the girls were ready to come home, Beth phoned her mother and let her know they were getting a ride home with Nate, a 17-year-old boy known to the Smiths for reckless driving. Mrs. Smith said, "That's fine. Have him drive you home now. Don't hang around any more." Nate drove too fast and crashed the car. Ann died. Ann's parents have filed a wrongful death suit sounding in negligence against Beth's parents, who have filed motions for summary judgment. Should their motions be granted?

INCREASING YOUR UNDERSTANDING

To summarize, assuming a duty will require some sort of undertaking understood as necessary for plaintiff's safety and physical harm to the plaintiff because either the defendant increased the risk of harm (a common example is by preventing aid from others) to the plaintiff or the plaintiff relied on the undertaking. A defendant who has assumed a duty need only exercise reasonable care and is not required to succeed in making the plaintiff safe. Also, the assumed duty is limited by the scope of the undertaking. In other words, liability will be limited to the risks that the undertaking was meant or reasonably expected to prevent. For example, a jogger asks a friend to drive his car in front of him to protect him from oncoming traffic. A tree branch falls on the jogger. The assumed duty was meant to protect the jogger from traffic, not overhead hazards, and the driver would not owe a duty of protection from the tree.

B. THE PRIVITY LIMITATION

H.R. Moch Co. v. Rensselaer Water Co.
159 N.E. 896 (N.Y. App. 1928)

CARDOZO, C.J.

The defendant, a waterworks company under the laws of this state, made a contract with the city of Rensselaer for the supply of water during a term of years. Water was to be furnished to the city for sewer flushing and street sprinkling; for service to schools and public buildings; and for service at fire hydrants, the latter service at the rate of $42.50 a year for each hydrant. Water was to be furnished to private takers within the city at their homes and factories and other industries at reasonable rates, not exceeding a stated schedule. While this contract was in force, a building caught fire. The flames, spreading to the plaintiff's warehouse near by, destroyed it and its contents. The defendant, according to the complaint, was promptly notified of the fire, "but omitted and neglected after such notice, to supply or furnish sufficient or adequate quantity of water, with adequate pressure to stay, suppress, or extinguish the fire before it reached the warehouse of the plaintiff, although the pressure and supply which the defendant was equipped to supply and furnish, and had agreed by said contract to supply and furnish, was adequate and sufficient to prevent the spread of the fire to and the destruction of the plaintiff's warehouse and its contents." By reason of the failure of the defendant to "fulfill the provisions of the contract between it and the city of Rensselaer," the plaintiff is said to have suffered damage, for which judgment is demanded. A motion, in the nature of a demurrer, to dismiss the complaint, was denied at Special Term. The Appellate Division reversed by a divided court.

Liability in the plaintiff's argument is placed on one or other of three grounds. The complaint, we are told, is to be viewed as stating: (1) A cause of action for breach of contract within Lawrence v. Fox, 20 N.Y. 268; (2) a cause of action for a common-law tort, within MacPherson v. Buick Motor Co., 217 N.Y. 382. . . .

(1) WE THINK THE ACTION IS NOT MAINTAINABLE AS ONE FOR BREACH OF CONTRACT.

No legal duty rests upon a city to supply its inhabitants with protection against fire. That being so, a member of the public may not maintain an action under *Lawrence v. Fox* against one contracting with the city to furnish water at the hydrants, unless an intention appears that the promisor is to be answerable to individual members of the public as well as to the city for any loss ensuing from the failure to fulfill the promise. No such intention is discernible here. On the contrary, the contract is significantly divided into two branches: One a promise to the city for the benefit of the city in its corporate capacity, in which branch is included the service at the hydrants; and the other a promise to the city for the benefit of private takers, in which branch is included the service at their homes and factories. In a broad sense it is true that every city contract, not improvident or wasteful, is for the benefit of the public. More than this, however, must be shown to give a right of action to a member of the public not formally a party. The benefit, as it is sometimes said, must be one that is not merely incidental and secondary. It must be primary and immediate in such a sense and to such a degree as to bespeak the assumption of a duty to make reparation directly to the individual members of the public if the benefit is lost. The field of obligation would be expanded beyond reasonable limits if less than this were to be demanded as a condition of liability. A promisor undertakes to supply fuel for heating a public building. He is not liable for breach of contract to a visitor who finds the building without fuel, and thus contracts a cold. The list of illustrations can be indefinitely extended. The carrier of the mails under contract with the government is not answerable to the merchant who has lost the benefit of a bargain through negligent delay. The householder is without a remedy against manufacturers of hose and engines, though prompt performance of their contracts would have stayed the ravages of fire. "The law does not spread its protection so far." (Robins Dry Dock & Repair Co. v. Flint, 275 U.S. 303,).

So with the case at hand. By the vast preponderance of authority, a contract between a city and a water company to furnish water at the city hydrants has in view a benefit to the public that is incidental rather than immediate, an assumption of duty to the city and not to its inhabitants. . . . An intention to assume an obligation of indefinite extension to every member of the public is seen to be the more improbable when we recall the crushing burden that the obligation would impose. The consequences invited would bear reasonable proportion to those attached by law to defaults not greatly different. A wrongdoer who by negligence sets fire to a building is liable in damages to the owner where the fire has its origin, but not to other owners who are injured when it spreads. The rule in our state is settled to that effect, whether wisely or unwisely. If the plaintiff is to prevail, one who negligently omits to supply sufficient pressure to extinguish a fire started by another assumes an obligation to pay the ensuing damage, though the whole city is laid low.

A promisor will not be deemed to have had in mind the assumption of a risk so overwhelming for any trivial reward. . . .

(2) WE THINK THE ACTION IS NOT MAINTAINABLE AS ONE FOR A COMMON-LAW TORT.

"It is ancient learning that one who assumes to act, even though gratuitously, may thereby become subject to the duty of acting carefully, if he acts at all." (Glanzer v. Shepard, 233 N.Y. 236, 239.) The plaintiff would bring its case within the orbit of that principle. The hand once set to a task may not always be withdrawn with impunity though liability would fail if it had never been applied at all. A time-honored formula often phrases the distinction as one between misfeasance and nonfeasance. Incomplete the formula is, and so at times misleading. Given a relation involving in its existence a duty of care irrespective of a contract, a tort may result as well from acts of omission as of commission in the fulfillment of the duty thus recognized by law. . . .

The plaintiff would have us hold that the defendant, when once it entered upon the performance of its contract with the city, was brought into such a relation with every one who might potentially be benefited through the supply of water at the hydrants as to give to negligent performance, without reasonable notice of a refusal to continue, the quality of a tort. . . . We are satisfied that liability would be unduly and indeed indefinitely extended by this enlargement of the zone of duty. The dealer in coal who is to supply fuel for a shop must then answer to the customers if fuel is lacking. The manufacturer of goods, who enters upon the performance of his contract, must answer, in that view, not only to the buyer, but to those who to his knowledge are looking to the buyer for their own sources of supply. Everyone making a promise having the quality of a contract will be under a duty to the promisee by virtue of the promise, but under another duty, apart from contract, to an indefinite number of potential beneficiaries when performance has begun. The assumption of one relation will mean the involuntary assumption of a series of new relations, inescapably hooked together. Again we may say in the words of the Supreme Court of the United States, "The law does not spread its protection so far." . . .

The judgment should be affirmed, with costs.

PREPARING FOR CLASS AND APPLYING THE LAW

1. Could the failure to supply water be characterized as misfeasance? If so, how might that be significant? Is it nonfeasance? Does the court characterize it that way?

2. Could the water supply contract be characterized as an assumed duty or undertaking? How would we characterize the undertaking? Was protecting against fire within the undertaking?

3. How does the court justify not imposing a duty to the townspeople? What would be the consequences of imposing a duty?

4. A woman hires a tree service to trim dead branches from the trees on her property, and the tree trimmer drops branches onto a passing pedestrian, who sues the woman. The pedestrian is not a party to the contract. Does this mean that the tree trimmer did not owe the pedestrian a duty of care?

5. What policy grounds may underlie the *Moch* decision? Does the court explicitly base the decision on public policy grounds?

INCREASING YOUR UNDERSTANDING

The privity bar is a highly eroded concept, generally considered to have originated in Winterbottom v. Wright, 10 M. & W. 109, 152 Engl. Rep. 402 (Exch. Pl. 1842). Under a contract with the Postmaster-General, the defendant was to supply mail coaches and keep them in good repair. The plaintiff, a coachman on one of the coaches, was injured when the coach broke down, allegedly because the defendant did not fulfill the repair obligation under the contract. The court held that the plaintiff had no action on the contract because he was not a party to the contract, but dictum about the need to "confine the operation of such contracts as this to the parties who entered into them" to prevent "the most absurd and outrageous consequences, to which I can see no limit" was interpreted to bar tort actions as well as contract actions in such situations.

Winterbottom can be regarded as a nonfeasance case. The defendant was guilty of inaction—not repairing the coaches. The only reason the plaintiff was looking to the defendant was the contract. If the contract is the only source of the duty, the plaintiff should be a party to that contract or be a third-party beneficiary. (As Professor Dobbs notes in his hornbook, when the defendant agrees to protect the plaintiff from physical harm under a contract with X, the defendant should owe the plaintiff a duty of care. Dan B. Dobbs, *The Law of Torts*, §321.) But for a long time, *Winterbottom* operated to dismiss suits over any misperformance of a contract—misfeasance cases—brought by third parties. Yet badly performed contracts are misfeasance, and a duty should arise in those cases from the foreseeability of harm from careless behavior. Courts generally recognize that distinction now, making privity of little importance in current law.

The most important case in the "fall of privity" is MacPherson v. Buick Motor Co., 111 N.E. 1050 (N.Y. App 1916). The plaintiff, driving a friend to the hospital, was injured when the defective wooden wheel of his Buick "crumbled into fragments." Buick contended that it owed the plaintiff no duty because it was in a contractual relationship with the dealership and not with the plaintiff. In a highly anticipated decision (manufacturers liked the privity barrier, after all), Justice Cardozo wrote: "We have put aside the notion that the duty to safeguard life and limb, when the consequences of negligence may be foreseen, grows out of contract and nothing else. We have put the source of the obligation where it ought to be. We have put its source in the law." Therefore, manufacturers did have a duty to the ultimate consumers of their goods if those goods were "things of danger," ("reasonably certain to place life and limb in peril when negligently made"), and the manufacturer knew the goods would be used by people other than the purchaser (which meant the intermediary between manufacturer and consumer) and without new testing. *MacPherson* is set out in full in Chapter 15.

C. PREMISES LIABILITY—DUTY LIMITED BY ENTRANT'S STATUS ON LAND

1. *Traditional Categories*

a. Trespassers

Haskins v. Grybko
17 N.E.2d 146 (Mass. 1938)

RONAN, J.
   This is an action of tort brought . . . by a public administrator to recover for the death of his intestate. . . . The defendant excepted to the ruling that the plaintiff could recover for ordinary negligence although the intestate was a trespasser as to the defendant or to some third person.
   The defendant was in possession, as lessee, of a tract of land containing about twenty acres. . . . The land was used to raise squash, and the defendant's crop had suffered from the ravages of woodchucks. The defendant went to the northwesterly corner of his lot on the evening of July 7, 1933, for the purpose of shooting woodchucks. It was dusk. He was standing beside his automobile on his own lot when he heard a rustling noise in the brush about fifty feet away, and then saw a moving object about eighteen inches high in the brush. Believing that the object was a woodchuck, he shot at it. After staying a few minutes he left the tract. When he returned the next morning, he discovered the body of the intestate.
   The legal duty owed by the defendant to the intestate depended upon the relation of the intestate to him at the time of the shooting. If the intestate was merely a trespasser upon the land of a third person, then the defendant was bound to exercise reasonable care so that no harm would be incurred by the intestate on account of the defendant's negligence. If the intestate was a trespasser upon the defendant's land, the latter was not liable for mere negligence.

He was, however, under an obligation to refrain from intentional injury and from wilful, wanton and reckless conduct. As the plaintiff failed to show that his intestate was not a trespasser upon the defendant's land when the shooting occurred, he was not entitled to recover by proving that the defendant was guilty of mere negligence, and the ruling in favor of the plaintiff was erroneous. . . .

PREPARING FOR CLASS

1. Why would the defendant have been required to exercise care for a trespasser on someone else's land but not on his own land?

2. Shouldn't someone shooting a gun always exercise reasonable care? Why, then, was this defendant allowed to shoot carelessly?

3. Why didn't the principle in this case protect the Brineys from liability to Katko?

Herrick v. Wixom
80 N.W. 117 (Mich. 1899)

MONTGOMERY, J.

[The plaintiff snuck into the circus without a ticket.] A part or feature of the entertainment consisted in the ignition and explosion of a giant firecracker attached to a pipe set in an upright position in one of the show rings. This was done by one of the clowns. There is testimony to show that plaintiff sat 30 or 40 feet from the place where the cracker was exploded, but when the same was exploded a part of the firecracker flew and struck plaintiff in the eye, putting it out, whereby he lost the sight and use of the eye. For this injury action was brought against defendant for damages as a result of defendant's negligence in permitting a dangerous explosive to be used in a dangerous manner, which subjected those present to hazard and risk of injury. Upon the trial of the cause a verdict of no cause for action was rendered, and judgment for the defendant entered accordingly. Plaintiff brings error. [The plaintiff contended that the trial judge had improperly instructed the jury that:]

". . . If he was a mere trespasser, who forced his way in, then the defendant owed him no duty that would enable him to recover under the declaration and proofs in this case."

[Reversing and remanding for a new trial, the Michigan Supreme Court wrote:]

It is true that a trespasser who suffers an injury because of a dangerous condition of premises is without remedy. But, where a trespasser is discovered upon the premises by the owner or occupant, he is not beyond the pale of the law, and any negligence resulting in injury will render the person guilty of negligence liable to respond in damages. In this case the negligent act of the defendant's servant was committed after the audience was made up. The presence of plaintiff was known, and the danger to him from a negligent act was also known. The question of whether a dangerous experiment should be attempted in his presence, or whether an experiment should be conducted with due care and regard to his safety, cannot be made to depend upon whether he had forced himself into the tent. Every instinct of humanity revolts at such a suggestion. For this error the judgment will be reversed, and a new trial ordered.

PREPARING FOR CLASS

Why was the trespasser in this case, unlike the trespasser in *Haskins*, entitled to reasonable care?

Bennett v. Stanley
748 N.E.2d 41 (Ohio 2001)

Pfeifer, J.

In this case we are called upon to determine what level of duty a property owner owes to a child trespasser. We resolve the question by adopting the attractive nuisance doctrine set forth in Restatement of the Law 2d, Torts (1965), Section 339. . . .

When Rickey G. Bennett, plaintiff-appellant, arrived home in the late afternoon of March 20, 1997, he found his two young daughters crying. The three-year-old, Kyleigh, told him that "Mommy" and Chance, her five-year-old half-brother, were "drowning in the water." Bennett ran next door to his neighbors' house to find mother and son unconscious in the swimming pool. Both died.

The Bennetts had moved next door to defendants-appellees, Jeffrey and Stacey Stanley, in the fall of 1996. The Stanleys had purchased their home the previous June. At the time of their purchase, the Stanleys' property included a swimming pool that had gone unused for three years. At that time, the pool was enclosed with fencing and a brick wall. After moving in, the Stanleys drained the pool once but thereafter they allowed rainwater to accumulate in the pool to a depth of over six feet. They removed a tarp that had been on the pool and also removed the fencing that had been around two sides of the pool. The pool became pond-like: it contained tadpoles and frogs, and Mr. Stanley had seen a snake swimming on the surface. The pool contained no ladders, and its sides were slimy with algae.

Rickey and Cher Bennett . . . rented the house next to the Stanleys. The houses were about one hundred feet apart. There was some fencing with an eight-foot gap between the two properties.

The Stanleys were aware that the Bennetts had moved next door and that they had young children. They had seen the children outside unsupervised. Stacey Stanley had once called Chance onto her property to retrieve a dog. The Stanleys testified, however, that they never had any concern about the children getting into the pool. They did not post any warning or "no trespassing" signs on their property. . . .

Kyleigh told her father that she and Chance had been playing at the pool on the afternoon of the tragedy. The sheriff's department concluded that Chance had gone to the pool to look at the frogs and somehow fell into the pool. His mother apparently drowned trying to save him.

[Bennett sued the Stanleys for negligence. He alleged "that appellees' pool created an unreasonable risk of harm to children who, because of their youth, would not realize the potential danger." The trial court found that the decedents were trespassers whom the Stanleys owed only a duty "to refrain from wanton and willful misconduct." Therefore, the court granted the Stanleys' motion for summary judgment. Because Bennett's attorney had only alleged a violation of ordinary care, the trial court found for the Stanleys as a matter of law. The appellate court affirmed the decision.]

Ohio has long recognized a range of duties for property owners vis-à-vis persons entering their property. . . . Today, we face the issue of whether child trespassers should become another class of users who are owed a different duty of care.

This court has consistently held that children have a special status in tort law and that duties of care owed to children are different from duties owed to adults:

"[T]he amount of care required to discharge a duty owed to a child of tender years is necessarily greater than that required to discharge a duty owed to an adult under the same circumstances. This is the approach long followed by this court and we see no reason to abandon it. 'Children of tender years, and youthful persons generally, are entitled to a degree of care proportioned to their inability to foresee and avoid the perils that they may encounter. . . . The same discernment and foresight in discovering defects and dangers cannot be reasonably expected of them, that older and experienced persons habitually employ; and therefore the greater precaution should be taken, where children are exposed to them.'" Di Gildo v. Caponi, 247 N.E.2d 732, 734 (Ohio 1969).

Recognizing the special status of children in the law, this court has even accorded special protection to child trespassers by adopting the "dangerous instrumentality" doctrine:

"The dangerous instrumentality exception [to nonliability to trespassers] imposes upon the owner or occupier of a premises a higher duty of care to a child trespasser when such owner or occupier actively and negligently operates hazardous machinery or other apparatus, the dangerousness of which is not readily apparent to children." McKinney v. Hartz & Restle Realtors, Inc., 510 N.E.2d 386, 390 (Ohio 1987). . . .

Despite the fact that in premises liability cases a landowner's duty is defined by the status of the plaintiff, and that children, even child trespassers, are accorded special protection in Ohio tort law, this court has never adopted the attractive nuisance doctrine. The doctrine as adopted by numerous states is set forth in Restatement of the Law 2d, Torts (1965), Section 339:

> A possessor of land is subject to liability for physical harm to children trespassing thereon caused by an artificial condition upon land if:
>
> (a) the place where the condition exists is one upon which the possessor knows or has reason to know that children are likely to trespass, and
> (b) the condition is one of which the possessor knows or has reason to know and which he realizes or should realize will involve an unreasonable risk of death or serious bodily harm to such children, and
> (c) the children because of their youth do not discover the condition or realize the risk involved in intermeddling with it or in coming within the area made dangerous by it, and
> (d) the utility to the possessor of maintaining the condition and the burden of eliminating the danger are slight as compared with the risk to children involved, and
> (e) the possessor fails to exercise reasonable care to eliminate the danger or otherwise to protect the children. . . .

Ohio is one of only three states that have not either created a special duty for trespassing children or done away with distinctions of duty based upon a person's status as an invitee, licensee, or trespasser. . . .

Adopting the attractive nuisance doctrine would be merely an incremental change in Ohio law, not out of line with the law that has developed over time. It is an appropriate evolution of the common law. While the present case is by no means a guaranteed winner for the plaintiff, it does present a factual scenario that would allow a jury to consider whether the elements of the cause of action have been fulfilled.

We therefore use this case to adopt the attractive nuisance doctrine contained in Restatement of the Law 2d, Torts (1965), Section 339. In doing so, we do not abandon the differences in duty a landowner owes to the different classes of users. In this case we simply further recognize that children are entitled to a greater level of protection than adults are. We remove the "distinctions without differences" between the dangerous instrumentality doctrine and the attractive nuisance doctrine. Whether an apparatus or a condition of property is involved, the key element should be whether there is a foreseeable, "unreasonable risk of death or serious bodily harm to . . . children." Restatement, Section 339(b).

The Restatement's version of the attractive nuisance doctrine balances society's interest in protecting children with the rights of landowners to enjoy their property. Even when a landowner is found to have an attractive nuisance on his or her land, the landowner is left merely with the burden of acting with ordinary care. A landowner does not automatically become liable for any injury a child trespasser may suffer on that land.

The requirement of foreseeability is built into the doctrine. The landowner must know or have reason to know that children are likely to trespass upon the part of the property that contains the dangerous condition. See Section 339(a). Moreover, the landowner's duty "does not extend to those conditions the existence of which is obvious even to children and the risk of which should be fully realized by them." *Id.* at Comment *i*. Also, if the condition of the property that poses the risk is essential to the landowner, the doctrine would not apply:

> The public interest in the possessor's free use of his land for his own purposes is of great significance. A particular condition is, therefore, regarded as not involving unreasonable risk to trespassing children unless it involves a grave risk to them which could be obviated without any serious interference with the possessor's legitimate use of his land. *Id.* at Comment *n*.

We are satisfied that the Restatement view effectively harmonizes the competing societal interests of protecting children and preserving property rights. In adopting the attractive nuisance doctrine, we acknowledge that the way we live now is different from the way we lived in 1907, when [the court held . . . that "[i]t is not the duty of an occupier of land to exercise care to make it safe for infant children who come upon it without invitation but merely by sufferance"]. We are not a rural society any longer, our neighbors live closer, and our use of our own property affects others more than it once did.

Despite our societal changes, children are still children. They still learn through their curiosity. They still have developing senses of judgment. They still do not always appreciate danger. They still need protection by adults. Protecting children in a changing world requires the common law to adapt. Today, we make that change. . . .

[Reversed and remanded. Concurring and dissenting opinions omitted.]

PREPARING FOR CLASS

1. Are the dangerous instrumentality doctrine and the attractive nuisance doctrine really "distinctions without differences"?

2. Why do many courts impose greater duties of care towards trespassing children? Isn't this unduly burdensome on property owners?

3. Was the pool an attractive nuisance that imposed a duty?

4. Why is this case "by no means a guaranteed winner"?

APPLYING THE LAW

Mr. Green owned a single-family home on an eight-acre lot in a residential area where the average lot size was three acres. His front yard contained a 30-foot by 25-foot sewage aeration pond, which was four feet deep at its deepest point. When Mr. Green purchased the property, the pond was surrounded by a fence, meant to keep animals out, but the fence was in disrepair, so Mr. Green removed it. He had purchased materials to build a new fence but had not yet begun the project when a child drowned in the pond. The two-year-old boy had been attending a graduation party with his grandmother at the home of Mr. Green's neighbor. The grandmother lost track of the boy when she was talking with other guests. The boy's parents have sued Mr. Green for negligence. They claim he should have built a fence or wall around the pond. Mr. Green has filed a motion for summary judgment on the ground that he owed the boy no duty of care. How will the parties argue the motion? Who is likely to prevail?

b. Licensees & Invitees

Carter v. Kinney
896 S.W.2d 926 (Mo. 1995)

ROBERTSON, J.

... Ronald and Mary Kinney hosted a Bible study at their home for members of the Northwest Bible Church. Appellant Jonathan Carter, a member of the Northwest Bible Church, attended the early morning Bible study at the Kinney's home on February 3, 1990. Mr. Kinney had shoveled snow from his driveway the previous evening, but was not aware that ice had formed overnight. Mr. Carter arrived shortly after 7:00 A.M., slipped on a patch of ice in the Kinneys' driveway, and broke his leg. The Carters filed suit against the Kinneys.

The parties agree that the Kinneys offered their home for the Bible study as part of a series sponsored by their church; that some Bible studies took place at the church and others were held at the homes of church members; that interested church members signed up for the studies on a sheet at the church, which actively encouraged enrollment but did not solicit contributions through the classes or issue an invitation to the general public to attend the studies; that the Kinneys and the Carters had not engaged in any social interaction outside of church prior to Mr. Carter's injury, and that Mr. Carter had no social relationship with the other participants in the class. Finally, the parties agree that the Kinneys received neither a financial nor other tangible benefit from Mr. Carter in connection with the Bible study class.

They disagree, however, as to Mr. Carter's status. Mr. Carter claims he was an invitee; the Kinneys say he was a licensee. And the parties dispute certain facts bearing on the purpose of his visit, specifically, whether the parties intended a future social relationship, and whether the Kinneys held the Bible study class in order to confer some intangible benefit on themselves and others.

On the basis of these facts, the Kinneys moved for summary judgment. The trial court sustained the Kinney's summary judgment motion on the ground that Mr. Carter was a licensee and that the Kinneys did not have a duty to a licensee with respect to a dangerous condition of which they had no knowledge. This appeal followed. . . .

As to premises liability, "the particular standard of care that society recognizes as applicable under a given set of facts is a question of law for the courts." Harris v. Niehaus, 857 S.W.2d 222, 225 (Mo. banc 1993). Thus, whether Mr. Carter was an invitee, as he claims, or a licensee is a question of law and summary judgment is appropriate if the defendants' conduct conforms to the standard of care Mr. Carter's status imposes on them. . . .

Historically, premises liability cases recognize three broad classes of plaintiffs: trespassers, licensees and invitees. All entrants to land are trespassers until the possessor of the land gives them permission to enter. All persons who enter a premises with permission are licensees until the possessor has an interest in the visit such that the visitor "has reason to believe that the premises have been made safe to receive him." That makes the visitor an invitee. The possessor's intention in offering the invitation determines the status of the visitor and establishes the duty of care the possessor owes the visitor. Generally, the possessor owes a trespasser no duty of care, the possessor owes a licensee the duty to make safe dangers of which the possessor is aware, and the possessor owes invitees the duty to exercise reasonable care to protect them against both known dangers and those that would be revealed by inspection. The exceptions to these general rules are myriad, but not germane here.

A social guest is a person who has received a social invitation. Though the parties seem to believe otherwise, Missouri does not recognize social guests as a fourth class of entrant. In Missouri, social guests are but a subclass of licensees. The fact that an invitation underlies a visit does not render the visitor an invitee for purposes of premises liability law. This is because "[t]he invitation was not tendered with any material benefit motive" . . . and "[t]he invitation was not extended to the public generally or to some undefined portion of the public from which invitation, . . . entrants might reasonably expect precautions have been taken, in the exercise of ordinary care, to protect them from danger." Thus, this Court held that there "is no reason for concluding it is unjust to the parties . . . to put a social guest in the legal category of licensee."

It does not follow from this that a person invited for purposes not strictly social is perforce an invitee. As [case law] clearly indicates, an entrant becomes an invitee when the possessor invites with the expectation of a material benefit from the visit or extends an invitation to the public generally. See also Restatement (Second) of Torts, §332 (defining an invitee for business purposes [as "a person who is invited to enter or remain on the land for a purpose directly or indirectly connected with business dealings with the possessor of the land."]) and 65 C.J.S. Negligence, §63(41) (A person is an invitee "if the premises are thrown open to the public and [the person] enters pursuant to the purposes for which they are thrown open."). Absent the sort of invitation from the possessor that lifts a licensee to invitee status, the visitor remains a licensee as a matter of law.

The record shows beyond cavil that Mr. Carter did not enter the Kinneys' land to afford the Kinneys any material benefit. He is therefore not an invitee under the definition of invitee contained in Section 332 of the Restatement. The record also demonstrates that the Kinneys did not "throw open" their premises to the public in such a way as would imply a warranty of safety. The Kinneys took no steps to encourage general attendance by some undefined portion of the public; they invited only church members who signed up at church. They did nothing more than give permission to a limited class of persons—church members—to enter their property.

Mr. Carter's response to the Kinneys' motion for summary judgment includes Mr. Carter's affidavit in which he says that he did not intend to socialize with the Kinneys and that the Kinneys would obtain an intangible benefit, albeit mutual, from Mr. Carter's participation in the class. Mr. Carter's affidavit attempts to create an issue of fact for the purpose of defeating summary judgment. But taking Mr. Carter's statement of the facts as true in all respects, he argues a factual distinction that has no meaning under Missouri law. Human intercourse and the intangible benefits of sharing one's property with others for a mutual purpose are hallmarks of a licensee's permission to enter. Mr. Carter's factual argument makes the legal point he wishes to avoid: his invitation is not of the sort that makes an invitee. He is a licensee.

The trial court concluded as a matter of law that Mr. Carter was a licensee, that the Kinneys had no duty to protect him from unknown dangerous conditions, and that the defendants were entitled to summary judgment as a matter of law. In that conclusion, the trial court was eminently correct. . . .

The judgment of the trial court is affirmed.

PREPARING FOR CLASS

1. How are licensee and invitee status similar? How are they different?

2. What is the logic behind imposing greater responsibilities to one's invitees than to one's licensees?

3. What was Carter's status? Why? What care, then, was he owed?

4. Would this case have had a different outcome if the Kinneys had known ice had formed overnight?

APPLYING THE LAW

1. Daniel was the treasurer of a club that met monthly at the community center. Dues were payable every four months at the January, May, and September meetings. Daniel told club members that they could drop the dues off at his house any evening of the week if that was more convenient than bringing dues to the meeting. Paul was unable to attend the September meeting, so he brought his dues to Daniel's house, where he was injured when his foot went through a weakened board in the front steps. What was Paul's status? What duties was he owed?

2. Delia was a member of the board of a charity that helped women on welfare find employment. Every year, the charity held a fashion show to raise money to help the women find proper interview clothing. Penny saw a poster for the fashion show, thought it looked like fun and like a good cause, so she called the number on the poster to arrange to buy tickets. She spoke with Delia and arranged to go to Delia's home to buy tickets. When Penny arrived, Delia invited her in for a cup of coffee. Penny drank the coffee, bought her tickets, and left. On her way out, she slipped and fell on a non-obvious defect in Delia's sidewalk. What was Penny's status? What duties did Delia owe her?

INCREASING YOUR UNDERSTANDING

1. Most courts still following traditional premises liability rules would *not* agree with the statement in this opinion that "the possessor owes a licensee the duty to make safe dangers of which the possessor is aware." Generally, licensors do not have a duty of reasonable care to ensure that their premises are safe for licensees. They owe any duties owed to trespassers, plus they must warn of any dangers known to them but hidden from their licensees. In a sense, the licensee takes the property as the owner or possessor takes it—without repairs but with knowledge of its dangers.

2. Although licensees are not owed reasonable care to keep the premises in safe condition, just warnings of known, hidden dangers, they are owed reasonable care in any activities on the property.

3. Invitees can be business invitees, who are on the property by invitation for the business purposes of the possessor, or public invitees, who are on land held open to the public in a way consistent with the public invitation. So the person visiting the exhibits at a free museum or stopping off at McDonald's just to use the restroom is a public invitee. They are invitees, though, only within the scope of their invitation. Outside the scope, the plaintiff becomes a licensee or trespasser, depending upon

the circumstances. (Similarly, licensees can go outside the scope of their invitation and become trespassers.) In Nicoletti v. Westcor, Inc. 639 P.2d 330 (Ariz. 1982), the court found that although the plaintiff was an invitee in a mall parking lot, the invitation did not include a shortcut through a flower bed (where plaintiff was injured by an obstruction, possibly a wire). In that case, though, the court did not explain what status the plaintiff had in the flower bed. What do you think it should have been? Why do you think the court found no duty without determining whether the plaintiff had become a licensee or trespasser?

Posecai v. Wal-Mart Stores, Inc.
752 So. 2d 762 (La. 1999)

Marcus, J.

Shirley Posecai brought suit against Sam's Wholesale Club ("Sam's") in Kenner after she was robbed at gunpoint in the store's parking lot. On July 20, 1995, Mrs. Posecai went to Sam's to make an exchange and to do some shopping. She exited the store and returned to her parked car at approximately 7:20 P.M. It was not dark at the time. As Mrs. Posecai was placing her purchases in the trunk, a man who was hiding under her car grabbed her ankle and pointed a gun at her. The unknown assailant instructed her to hand over her jewelry and her wallet. While begging the robber to spare her life, she gave him her purse and all her jewelry. Mrs. Posecai was wearing her most valuable jewelry at the time of the robbery because she had attended a downtown luncheon earlier in the day. She lost a two and a half carat diamond ring given to her by her husband for their twenty-fifth wedding anniversary, a diamond and ruby bracelet and a diamond and gold watch, all valued at close to $19,000.

When the robber released Mrs. Posecai, she ran back to the store for help. The Kenner Police Department was called and two officers came out to investigate the incident. The perpetrator was never apprehended and Mrs. Posecai never recovered her jewelry despite searching several pawn shops.

At the time of this armed robbery, a security guard was stationed inside the store to protect the cash office from 5:00 P.M. until the store closed at 8:00 P.M. He could not see outside and Sam's did not have security guards patrolling the parking lot. At trial, the security guard on duty, Kenner Police Officer Emile Sanchez, testified that he had worked security detail at Sam's since 1986 and was not aware of any similar criminal incidents occurring in Sam's parking lot during the nine years prior to the robbery of Mrs. Posecai. He further testified that he did not consider Sam's parking lot to be a high crime area, but admitted that he had not conducted a study on the issue.

The plaintiff presented the testimony of two other Kenner police officers. Officer Russell Moran testified that he had patrolled the area around Sam's from 1993 to 1995. He stated that the subdivision behind Sam's, Lincoln

Manor, is generally known as a high crime area, but that the Kenner Police were rarely called out to Sam's. Officer George Ansardi, the investigating officer, similarly testified that Lincoln Manor is a high crime area but explained that Sam's is not considered a high crime location. He further stated that to his knowledge none of the other businesses in the area employed security guards at the time of this robbery.

An expert on crime risk assessment and premises security, David Kent, was qualified and testified on behalf of the plaintiff. It was his opinion that the robbery of Mrs. Posecai could have been prevented by an exterior security presence. He presented crime data from the Kenner Police Department indicating that between 1989 and June of 1995 there were three robberies or "predatory offenses" on Sam's premises, and provided details from the police reports on each of these crimes. The first offense occurred at 12:45 A.M. on March 20, 1989, when a delivery man sleeping in his truck parked in back of the store was robbed. In May of 1992, a person was mugged in the store's parking lot. Finally, on February 7, 1994, an employee of the store was the victim of a purse snatching, but she indicated to the police that the crime was related to a domestic dispute.

In order to broaden the geographic scope of his crime data analysis, Mr. Kent looked at the crime statistics at thirteen businesses on the same block as Sam's, all of which were either fast food restaurants, convenience stores or gas stations. He found a total of eighty-three predatory offenses in the six and a half years before Mrs. Posecai was robbed. Mr. Kent concluded that the area around Sam's was "heavily crime impacted," although he did not compare the crime statistics he found around Sam's to any other area in Kenner or the New Orleans metro area.

Mrs. Posecai contends that Sam's was negligent in failing to provide adequate security in the parking lot considering the high level of crime in the surrounding area. Seeking to recover for mental anguish as well as for her property loss, she alleged that after this incident she had trouble sleeping and was afraid to go out by herself at night. After a bench trial, the trial judge held that Sam's owed a duty to provide security in the parking lot because the robbery of the plaintiff was foreseeable and could have been prevented by the use of security. A judgment was rendered in favor of Mrs. Posecai, awarding $18,968 for her lost jewelry and $10,000 in general damages for her mental anguish. [The appellate court upheld the defendant's liability but reallocated the damages.]

The sole issue presented for our review is whether Sam's owed a duty to protect Mrs. Posecai from the criminal acts of third parties under the facts and circumstances of this case. . . .

This court has never squarely decided whether business owners owe a duty to protect their patrons from crimes perpetrated by third parties. It is therefore helpful to look to the way in which other jurisdictions have resolved this question. Most state supreme courts that have considered the issue agree that business owners do have a duty to take reasonable precautions to protect invitees from foreseeable criminal attacks.

We now join other states in adopting the rule that although business owners are not the insurers of their patrons' safety, they do have a duty to implement reasonable measures to protect their patrons from criminal acts when those acts are foreseeable. We emphasize, however, that there is generally no duty to protect others from the criminal activities of third persons. This duty only arises under limited circumstances, when the criminal act in question was reasonably foreseeable to the owner of the business. Determining when a crime is foreseeable is therefore a critical inquiry.

Other jurisdictions have resolved the foreseeability issue in a variety of ways, but four basic approaches have emerged. The first approach, although somewhat outdated, is known as the specific harm rule. According to this rule, a landowner does not owe a duty to protect patrons from the violent acts of third parties unless he is aware of specific, imminent harm about to befall them. Courts have generally agreed that this rule is too restrictive in limiting the duty of protection that business owners owe their invitees.

More recently, some courts have adopted a prior similar incidents test. Under this test, foreseeability is established by evidence of previous crimes on or near the premises. The idea is that a past history of criminal conduct will put the landowner on notice of a future risk. Therefore, courts consider the nature and extent of the previous crimes, as well as their recency, frequency, and similarity to the crime in question. This approach can lead to arbitrary results because it is applied with different standards regarding the number of previous crimes and the degree of similarity required to give rise to a duty.

The third and most common approach used in other jurisdictions is known as the totality of the circumstances test. This test takes additional factors into account, such as the nature, condition, and location of the land, as well as any other relevant factual circumstances bearing on foreseeability. As the Indiana Supreme Court explained, "[a] substantial factor in the determination of duty is the number, nature, and location of prior similar incidents, but the lack of prior similar incidents will not preclude a claim where the landowner knew or should have known that the criminal act was foreseeable." The application of this test often focuses on the level of crime in the surrounding area and courts that apply this test are more willing to see property crimes or minor offenses as precursors to more violent crimes. In general, the totality of the circumstances test tends to place a greater duty on business owners to foresee the risk of criminal attacks on their property and has been criticized "as being too broad a standard, effectively imposing an unqualified duty to protect customers in areas experiencing any significant level of criminal activity."

The final standard that has been used to determine foreseeability is a balancing test, an approach which has been adopted in California and Tennessee. This approach was originally formulated by the California Supreme Court in Ann M. v. Pacific Plaza Shopping Center in response to the perceived unfairness of the totality test. See 6 Cal.4th 666, 25 Cal. Rptr. 2d 137, 863 P.2d 207, 214-15 (1993). The balancing test seeks to address the interests of both business proprietors and their customers by balancing the foreseeability of harm against the burden of imposing a duty to protect against the criminal acts of third persons. The Tennessee Supreme Court formulated the test as follows: "In determining the duty that exists, the foreseeability of harm and the gravity of harm must be balanced against the commensurate burden imposed on the business to protect against that harm. In cases in which there is a high degree of foreseeability of harm and the probable harm is great, the burden imposed upon defendant may be substantial. Alternatively, in cases in which a lesser degree of foreseeability is present or the potential harm is slight, less onerous burdens may be imposed." McClung [v. Delta Sq. Ltd. Partnership], 937 S.W.2d at 902. Under this test, the high degree of foreseeability necessary to impose a duty to provide security, will rarely, if ever, be proven in the absence of prior similar incidents of crime on the property.

We agree that a balancing test is the best method for determining when business owners owe a duty to provide security for their patrons. The economic and social impact of requiring businesses to provide security on their premises is an important factor. Security is a significant monetary expense for any business and further increases the cost of doing business in high crime areas that are already economically depressed. Moreover, businesses are generally not responsible for the endemic crime that plagues our communities, a societal problem that even our law enforcement and other government agencies have been unable to solve. At the same time, business owners are in the best position to appreciate the crime risks that are posed on their premises and to take reasonable precautions to counteract those risks.

With the foregoing considerations in mind, we adopt the following balancing test to be used in deciding whether a business owes a duty of care to protect its customers from the criminal acts of third parties. The foreseeability of the crime risk on the defendant's property and the gravity of the risk determine the existence and the extent of the defendant's duty. The greater the foreseeability and gravity of the harm, the greater the duty of care that will be imposed on the business. A very high degree of foreseeability is required to give rise to a duty to post security guards, but a lower degree of foreseeability may support a duty to implement lesser security measures such as using surveillance cameras, installing improved lighting or fencing, or trimming shrubbery. The plaintiff has the burden of establishing the duty the defendant owed under the circumstances.

The foreseeability and gravity of the harm are to be determined by the facts and circumstances of the case. The most important factor to be considered is the existence, frequency and similarity of prior incidents of crime on the premises, but the location, nature and condition of the property should also be taken into account. It is highly unlikely that a crime risk will be sufficiently foreseeable for the imposition of a duty to provide security guards if there have not been previous instances of crime on the business' premises.

In the instant case, there were only three predatory offenses on Sam's premises in the six and a half years prior to the robbery of Mrs. Posecai. The first of these offenses occurred well after store hours, at almost one o'clock in the morning, and involved the robbery of a delivery man who was caught unaware as he slept near Sam's loading dock behind the store. In 1992, a person was mugged while walking through the parking lot. Two years later, an employee of the store was attacked in the parking lot and her purse was taken, apparently by her husband. A careful consideration of the previous incidents of predatory offenses on the property reveals that there was only one other crime in Sam's parking lot, the mugging in 1992, that was perpetrated against a Sam's customer and that bears any similarity to the crime that occurred in this case. Given the large number of customers that used Sam's parking lot, the previous robbery of only one customer in all those years indicates a very low crime risk. It is also relevant that Sam's only operates during daylight hours and must provide an accessible parking lot to the multitude of customers that shop at its store each year. Although the neighborhood bordering Sam's is considered a high crime area by local law enforcement, the foreseeability and gravity of harm in Sam's parking lot remained slight.

We conclude that Sam's did not possess the requisite degree of foreseeability for the imposition of a duty to provide security patrols in its parking lot. Nor was the degree of foreseeability sufficient to support a duty to implement lesser security measures. Accordingly, Sam's owed no duty to protect Mrs. Posecai from the criminal acts of third parties under the facts and circumstances of this case. . . .

PREPARING FOR CLASS

1. Courts will often state, as this court did, that parties in the defendant class are "not insurers" of the safety of parties in the plaintiff class. What does that mean?

2. Why do courts that impose on businesses a duty to protect against third-party crime require more than an invitee-invitor relationship?

3. Why did the court reject the approaches it rejected?

4. Isn't the balancing test the court adopted a risk-burden test? Isn't that a test for breach? Why is it a proper test for duty?

5. Did the plaintiff satisfy the balancing test?

APPLYING THE LAW

Vic was the assistant manager of a pizza place. At 1:30 in the morning, he went to FirstBank to deposit the evening's receipts and operating cash in the FirstBank night deposit box. He was attacked by a thief who shot him in the collarbone and then escaped into the woods immediately behind the bank. Vic was shot at the Hilltop branch, one of four FirstBank branches in Springfield, Michiana. The Hilltop branch, which had been open for 11 years, is in the area with the second highest crime rate in the county and the highest crime rate in Springfield. Before Vic's shooting, two armed robberies had occurred at the Hilltop branch. Both were in daylight, during banking hours, and tellers were the targets. In both instances, the robbers escaped through the woods behind the bank. Michiana crime statistics show that night deposit crimes are less frequent than daytime robberies, employee thefts, and ATM crime. A banking industry newsletter had repeatedly reported, however, the increasing frequency of serious attacks on customers at night deposit boxes (shot in face, doused with gasoline, and robbed under threat of being ignited, e.g.) and warned of the need for surveillance, adequate lighting, and clear visibility without hiding places. Vic alleges that FirstBank had none of these precautions, but FirstBank contends it owed him no duty. Would FirstBank succeed in a motion for summary judgment on no-duty grounds?

2. Rejecting or Modifying the Categories

Heins v. Webster County
552 N.W.2d 51 (Neb. 1996)

CONNOLLY, J.

The question presented is whether this court should abolish the common-law classifications of licensee and invitee and require a duty of reasonable care to all nontrespassers. . . .

[On the day of a] heavy snowfall . . . Heins, accompanied by his wife, Ruth, and daughter Jill, visited the Webster County Hospital. The evidence is disputed concerning the nature of this trip. Webster County claims that Heins was merely paying a social visit to his daughter Julie Heins, who was the director of nursing for the hospital. Heins claims that his visit was not only social, but also to coordinate plans for him to play Santa Claus for the hospital staff during the upcoming Christmas season. During their visit with Julie, Roger, Ruth, and Jill made plans to have lunch with Julie and a friend at a local restaurant.

While Roger, Ruth, and Jill were exiting the hospital through the main entrance, Roger fell. At trial, Roger testified that he held the front entrance door open for his wife and daughter and then started to step out onto the landing himself. At this point, Heins testified, he slipped and "went down into a pretzel, you might say, and I was hanging on to the door, and my behind hit the landing." Both Jill and Heins claim to have seen a patch of ice on the landing after Heins fell, and attribute the cause of his fall to the ice.

Heins [claimed] that Webster County was negligent (1) in failing to properly inspect the above-described entrance prior to inviting the public to use the entrance, (2) in failing to warn Heins of the existence of a dangerous condition, (3) in allowing the ice and snow to accumulate, and (4) in failing to remove the ice and snow.

Following a bench trial, the district court found that Heins "went to the Webster County Hospital to visit his daughter who was an employee of the hospital." Furthermore, the court concluded that Heins was a licensee at the time of his fall and that the county did not act willfully or wantonly or fail to warn of known hidden dangers unobservable by Heins. Thus, the court entered judgment in favor of Webster County. Heins appeals. . . .

This appeal questions the continued validity of the common-law classifications of licensee, invitee, and trespasser for the purposes of determining the duty of a landowner in premises liability cases. . . .

In fact, a number of jurisdictions have decided that the common-law classifications have outlived their usefulness, and have either partially or completely abandoned the common-law classifications.

In 1957, England statutorily abolished the common-law distinction between licensees and invitees and imposed upon the occupier a "common duty of care" toward all persons who lawfully enter the premises. Shortly thereafter, in 1959, the U.S. Supreme Court decided that the classifications would not apply in admiralty law, stating that the classifications created a "semantic morass." See, Kermarec v. Compagnie Generale, 358 U.S. 625 (1959). In 1968, the Supreme Court of California decided the landmark case Rowland v. Christian, 443 P.2d 561 (Cal. 1968), which abolished the traditional duty classification scheme for licensees, invitees, and trespassers and replaced it with ordinary negligence principles.

A number of jurisdictions have followed California in abandoning all classifications, including that of trespasser. [The court cites cases from Hawaii, Colorado, Rhode Island (two from this state, which first abandoned the categories and then restored trespasser status), New York, New Hampshire, Louisiana, Alaska, Illinois (with regard to child entrants), Montana, and Nevada.]

A number of states have abolished the distinctions between licensees and invitees but retained limited duties to trespassers. . . . [The court cites cases from Minnesota, Massachusetts, Wisconsin, North Dakota, Maine, Oregon, Tennessee, Wyoming, Kansas, and New Mexico.]

Other states have passed legislation altering the common-law categories. Connecticut was the first state to do so by providing that the landowner owed the same duty of care to social guests as he owed to invitees. Other states have given the social guest the status of an invitee. Illinois eliminated the classifications by statute in 1984.

However, the majority of states have retained the common-law distinctions. Thirty-six states and the District of Columbia have reconsidered the common-law classification scheme. Of the 37 jurisdictions reconsidering, 23 have abolished either some or all of the categories. Fourteen states have expressly retained the categories. Another 14 jurisdictions have simply continued to apply the common-law classifications without specifically addressing their continuing validity. We have been among the states continuing to follow the distinctions without specifically rejecting them. . . .

A number of policy reasons have been asserted for either abandoning or retaining the common-law classifications. Among the jurisdictions retaining the categories, most find value in the predictability of the common law. Some courts rejecting change have reasoned that replacement of a stable and established system of loss allocation results in the establishment of a system devoid of standards for liability. It also has been suggested that the harshness of the common-law rules has been ameliorated by the judicial grafting of exceptions and that creation of subclassifications ameliorated the distinctions between active and passive negligence. These states have concluded that abandoning the established system of liability in favor of a standard of reasonable care would decrease predictability and ensure that each case would be decided on its facts. Therefore, these states claim that landowners would be less able to guard against risks. . . .

The most common reason asserted for abandoning the categories is that an entrant's status should not determine the duty that the landowner owes to him or her. As the California Supreme Court stated in Rowland v. Christian, 443 P.2d 561, 568 (1968):

> A man's life or limb does not become less worthy of protection by the law nor a loss less worthy of compensation under the law because he has come upon the land of another without permission or with permission but without a business purpose. Reasonable people do not ordinarily vary their conduct depending upon such matters, and to focus upon the status of the injured party as a trespasser, licensee, or invitee in order to determine the question whether the landowner has a duty of care, is contrary to our modern social mores and humanitarian values. The common law rules obscure rather than illuminate the proper considerations which should govern determination of the question of duty.

In abolishing the invitee-licensee distinction, the Massachusetts Supreme Judicial Court recognized:

> It no longer makes any sense to predicate the landowner's duty solely on the status of the injured party as either a licensee or invitee. Perhaps, in a rural society with sparse land settlements and large estates, it would have been unduly burdensome to obligate the owner to inspect and maintain distant holdings for a class of entrants who were using the property "for their own convenience" . . . but the special immunity which the licensee rule affords landowners cannot be justified in an urban industrial society.

Mounsey v. Ellard, 297 N.E.2d 43, 51 (Mass. 1973).

Another justification for abandoning the classifications is to eliminate the complex and unpredictable state of the law necessitated by the harsh nature of the common-law rules. As the U.S. Supreme Court proclaimed,

> courts have found it necessary to formulate increasingly subtle verbal refinements, to create subclassifications among traditional common-law categories, and to delineate fine gradations in the standards of care

which the landowner owes to each. Yet even within a single jurisdiction, the classifications and subclassifications bred by the common law have produced confusion and conflict.

Kermarec v. Compagnie Generale, 358 U.S. 625, 630-31 (1959). The Court recognized that the "distinctions which the common law draws between licensee and invitee were inherited from a culture deeply rooted to the land, a culture which traced many of its standards to a heritage of feudalism." Referring to the judicial interpretation of the common-law distinctions as a "semantic morass," the Court declined to adopt them into admiralty law.

Those states abandoning the distinctions argue that instead of the entrant's status, the foreseeability of the injury should be the controlling factor in determining the liability of the landowner. Many jurisdictions that have abandoned the common-law classifications as determinants of liability have found that they remain relevant in determining the foreseeability of the harm under ordinary negligence principles. . . .

The present case illustrates the frustration inherent in the classification scheme. In many instances, recovery by an entrant has become largely a matter of chance, dependent upon the pigeonhole in which the law has put him, e.g., "trespasser," "licensee," or "invitee." When he was injured, Heins was exiting a county hospital, using the main entrance to the hospital, over the lunch hour. If Heins had been on the hospital premises to visit a patient or purchase a soft drink from a vending machine, he could have been classified as an invitee. However, he came to visit his daughter and was denied recovery as a matter of law.

Thus, Heins was denied the possibility of recovering under present law, merely because on this trip to the hospital he happened to be a licensee rather than an invitee. In the instant case, the hospital would undergo no additional burden in exercising reasonable care for a social visitor such as Heins, because it had the duty to exercise reasonable care for its invitees. A patient visitor could have used the same front entrance at which Heins fell and would have been able to maintain a negligence action; however, Heins has been denied the opportunity to recover merely because of his status at the time of the fall.

Modern commercial society creates relationships between persons not contemplated by the traditional classifications. Yet we have continued to pigeonhole individuals as licensees or invitees as a convenient way to ascertain the duty owed by the landowner. For instance, in Presho v. J.M. McDonald Co., 151 N.W.2d 451 (Neb. 1967), a customer of a retail store was injured when she entered a back room of the store with the permission of the store manager, in order to retrieve an empty box. We held the customer to be a licensee rather than an invitee because "[s]he was on an errand personal to herself, not in any way connected with the business of the defendant." We recognized that while she was in the store proper, she was an invitee. However, we found her to be a licensee when she entered the back room, despite the fact that the ladies' restroom was located in this back room area and was used by customers to the store.

The common-law status classifications should not be able to shield those who would otherwise be held to a standard of reasonable care but for the arbitrary classification of the visitor as a licensee. We find no merit in the argument that the duty of reasonable care is difficult for a fact finder to understand or apply, because it has been used successfully with regard to invitees and is the standard used in almost all other tort actions.

We conclude that we should eliminate the distinction between licensees and invitees by requiring a standard of reasonable care for all lawful visitors. We retain a separate classification for trespassers because we conclude that one should not owe a duty to exercise reasonable care to those not lawfully on one's property. Adopting this rule places the focus where it should be, on the foreseeability of the injury, rather than on allowing the duty in a particular case to be determined by the status of the person who enters upon the property.

Our holding does not mean that owners and occupiers of land are now insurers of their premises, nor do we intend for them to undergo burdens in maintaining such premises. We impose upon owners and occupiers only the duty to exercise reasonable care in the maintenance of their premises for the protection of lawful visitors. Among the factors to be considered in evaluating whether a landowner or occupier has exercised reasonable care for the protection of lawful visitors will be (1) the foreseeability or possibility of harm; (2) the purpose for which the entrant entered the premises; (3) the time, manner, and circumstances under which the entrant entered the premises; (4) the use to which the premises are put or are expected to be put; (5) the reasonableness of the inspection, repair, or warning; (6) the opportunity and ease of repair or correction or giving of the warning; and (7) the burden on the land occupier and/or community in terms of inconvenience or cost in providing adequate protection.

Although we have set forth some of the factors to be considered in determining whether a landowner or occupier has exercised reasonable care for the protection of lawful visitors, it is for the fact finder to determine, on the facts of each individual case, whether or not such factors establish a breach of the duty of reasonable care....

We determine that the invitee-licensee distinction should be abandoned and the new rule applied in the instant case. Considering that other litigants may have relied on our previous rule and incurred time and expense in prosecuting or defending their claims, we conclude, with the exception of the instant case, that the rule announced today shall be applied only to all causes of action arising after this date. We reverse, and remand for a new trial.

Reversed and remanded for a new trial.

FARNBRUCH, Justice, dissenting.

... The majority opinion dismantles longstanding common law by eliminating the concept of licensee, thereby forcing a landowner to treat a person who is allowed to enter or remain upon premises with the same standard of care as a person who is invited onto the premises for the mutual benefit of both landowner and invitee.

Under the majority opinion, a landowner owes a duty of reasonable care to an individual who becomes injured by conducting activities on the premises without the landowner's express permission or knowledge. From this moment on, public and private institutions, as well as residential homeowners, must be especially aware of unknown, uninvited individuals who take advantage of their land and facilities.

In McCurry v. Young Men's Christian Assn., 313 N.W.2d 689 (Neb. 1981), an individual brought an action against a Young Men's Christian Association (YMCA) as a result of an injury which arose from a fall while the individual was playing basketball on an outdoor asphalt playground owned by the YMCA. The plaintiff was not a member of the YMCA and had not obtained any express permission to use the playground. This court held that the plaintiff was a licensee and affirmed the trial court's directed verdict in favor of the YMCA. Under the majority's opinion, YMCA's and like institutions will be subject to lawsuits which hold them to a duty to treat such uninvited users of their facilities with the same standard of care as the paying members of the institution.

This court should not enact public policy which, in effect, socializes the use of privately owned property to the extent that the landowner owes the same duty to all, except trespassers, who enter the owner's land. It is not the function of the court to create a liability where the law creates none.

Under the majority's opinion, a homeowner would have potential liability for any number of not only uninvited but unwanted solicitors or visitors coming to the homeowner's door.

CAPORALE, J., joins in this dissent.

PREPARING FOR CLASS

1. What are the rationales for and against abolishing the legal distinctions based on entrant status?

2. If you were the judge in this case, would you have abolished the traditional categories?

3. Lessor-Lessee

Pagelsdorf v. Safeco Insurance Co.
284 N.W.2d 55 (Wis. 1979)

CALLOW, J.

We dispose of this appeal by addressing the single issue of the scope of a landlord's duty toward his tenant's invitee who is injured as a result of defective premises. Abrogating the landlord's general cloak of immunity at common law, we hold that a landlord must exercise ordinary care toward his tenant and others on the premises with permission.

The defendant Richard J. Mahnke owned a two-story, two-family duplex. There were four balcony porches: one in front and one in back of each flat. Mahnke rented the upper unit to John and Mary Katherine Blattner... [While helping Mrs. Blattner move some furniture, Pagelsdorf, the plaintiff, leaned against the railing of the second-floor front balcony, and it gave way. Pagelsdorf fell to the ground and was injured. Pagelsdorf sued the landlord. The trial court instructed the jury on the duties owed to a licensee. By special verdict, the jury found that the landlord had no knowledge of the defective condition of the railing. The court entered judgment on the verdict and dismissed the complaint.]

... [W]ith certain exceptions, a landlord is not liable for injuries to his tenants and their visitors resulting from defects in the premises. The general rule of nonliability was based on the concept of a lease as a conveyance of property and the consequent transfer of possession and control of the premises to the tenant. There are exceptions to this general rule of nonliability. The landlord is liable for injuries to the tenant or his visitor caused by a dangerous condition if he contracts to repair defects, or if, knowing of a defect existing at the time the tenant took possession, he conceals it from a tenant who could not reasonably be expected to discover it. Additionally, the general rule is not applicable where the premises are leased for public use, or are retained in the landlord's control, or where the landlord negligently makes repairs. The rule of nonliability persists despite a decided trend away from application of the general rule and toward expansion of its exceptions.

None of the exceptions to the general rule are applicable to the facts of this case. The premises were not leased for public use, nor was the porch within Mahnke's control, nor did he negligently repair the railing. The plaintiffs argue that Mahnke contracted to repair defects; but according to Mrs. Blattner's testimony, Mahnke's promise extended only to items the Blattners reported as being in disrepair. Therefore, error cannot be predicated on the trial court's failure to give an instruction concerning Mahnke's constructive knowledge where the asserted contract was to repair defects of which Mahnke actually knew. Finally, the concealed-defect exception does not apply because there was no evidence that the dry rot existed in 1969 when the Blattners moved in. . . .

Therefore, if we were to follow the traditional rule, Pagelsdorf was not entitled to an instruction that Mahnke owed him a duty of ordinary care. We believe, however, that the better public policy lies in the abandonment of the general rule of nonliability and the adoption of a rule that a landlord is under a duty to exercise ordinary care in the maintenance of the premises.

... Issues of notice of the defect, its obviousness, control of the premises, and so forth are all relevant only insofar as they bear on the ultimate question: Did the landlord exercise ordinary care in the maintenance of the premises under all the circumstances?

Judgment reversed and cause remanded for proceedings consistent with this opinion.

PREPARING FOR CLASS

1. What was the traditional rule regarding landlord liability? What was the rationale behind it?

2. What changes to the facts would have permitted Pagelsdorf to win under the traditional rule?

3. What rule does the Wisconsin Supreme Court adopt? Why?

Kline v. 1500 Massachusetts Ave. Apartment Corp.
439 F.2d 477 (D.C. Cir. 1970)

WILKEY, C.J.

The appellee apartment corporation states that there is "only one issue presented for review . . . whether a duty should be placed on a landlord to take steps to protect tenants from foreseeable criminal acts committed by third parties." The District Court as a matter of law held that there is no such duty. We find that there is, and that in the circumstances here the applicable standard of care was breached. We therefore reverse and remand to the District Court for the determination of damages for the appellant.

The appellant, Sarah B. Kline, sustained serious injuries when she was criminally assaulted and robbed at approximately 10:15 in the evening by an intruder in the common hallway of an apartment house at 1500 Massachusetts Avenue. This facility . . . is a large apartment building with approximately 585 individual apartment units. . . . At the time the appellant first signed a lease a doorman was on duty at the main entrance twenty-four hours a day, and at least one employee at all times manned a desk in the lobby from which all persons using the elevators could be observed. . . .

By mid-1966, however, the main entrance had no doorman, the desk in the lobby was left unattended much of the time, the 15th Street entrance was generally unguarded due to a decrease in garage personnel, and the 16th Street entrance was often left unlocked all night. The entrances were allowed to be thus unguarded in the face of an increasing number of assaults, larcenies, and robberies being perpetrated against the tenants in and from the common hallways of the apartment building. . . . The landlord had notice of these crimes and had in fact been urged by appellant Kline herself prior to the events leading to the instant appeal to take steps to secure the building. . . .

In this jurisdiction, certain duties have been assigned to the landlord because of his control of common hallways, lobbies, stairwells, etc., used by all tenants in multiple dwelling units. This Court in Levine v. Katz, 407 F.2d 303, 304 (1968), pointed out that:

> It has long been well settled in this jurisdiction that, where a landlord leases separate portions of property and reserves under his own control the halls, stairs, or other parts of the property for use in common by all tenants, he has a duty to all those on the premises of legal right to use ordinary care and diligence to maintain the retained parts in a reasonably safe condition.

While *Levine v. Katz* dealt with a physical defect in the building leading to plaintiff's injury, the rationale as applied to predictable criminal acts by third parties is the same. The duty is the landlord's because by his control of the areas of common use and common danger he is the only party who has the power to make the necessary repairs or to provide the necessary protection.

As a general rule, a private person does not have a duty to protect another from a criminal attack by a third person. We recognize that this rule has sometimes in the past been applied in landlord-tenant law, even by this court. Among the reasons for the application of this rule to landlords are: judicial reluctance to tamper with the traditional common law concept of the landlord tenant relationship; the notion that the act of a third person in committing an intentional tort or crime is a superseding cause of the harm to another resulting therefrom; the oftentimes difficult problem of determining foreseeability of criminal acts; the vagueness of the standard which the landlord must meet; the economic consequences of the imposition of the duty; and conflict with the public policy allocating the duty of protecting citizens from criminal acts to the government rather than the private sector.

But the rationale of this very broad general rule falters when it is applied to the conditions of modern day urban apartment living, particularly in the circumstances of this case. The rationale of the general rule exonerating a third party from any duty to protect another from a criminal attack has no applicability to the landlord-tenant relationship in multiple dwelling houses. The landlord is no insurer of his tenants' safety, but he certainly is no bystander. And where, as here, the landlord has notice of repeated criminal assaults and robberies, has notice that these crimes occurred in the portion of the premises exclusively within his control, has every reason to expect like crimes to happen again, and has the exclusive power to take preventive action, it does not seem unfair to place upon the landlord a duty to take those steps which are within his power to minimize the predictable risk to his tenants. . . .

[I]nnkeepers have been held liable for assaults which have been committed upon their guests by third parties, if they have breached a duty which is imposed by reason of the innkeeper guest relationship. By this duty, the innkeeper is generally bound to exercise reasonable care to protect the guest from abuse or molestation from third parties, be they innkeeper's employees, fellow guests, or intruders, if the attack could, or in the exercise of reasonable care, should have been anticipated.

Liability in the innkeeper-guest relationship is based as a matter of law either upon the innkeeper's supervision, care, or control of the premises, or by reason of a contract which some courts have implied from the entrustment by the guest of his personal comfort and safety to the innkeeper. In the latter analysis, the contract is held to give the guest the right to except a standard of treatment at the hands of the innkeeper which includes an obligation on the part of the latter to exercise reasonable care in protecting the guest.

Other relationships in which similar duties have been imposed include landowner-invitee, businessman-patron, employer-employee, school district-pupil, hospital-patient, and carrier-passenger. In all, the theory of liability is essentially the same; that since the ability of one of the parties to provide for his own protection has been limited in some way by his submission to the control of the other, a duty should be imposed upon the one possessing control (and thus the power to act) to take reasonable precautions to protect the other one from assaults by third parties which, at least, could reasonably have been anticipated. . . .

As between tenant and landlord, the landlord is the only one in the position to take the necessary acts of protection required. He is not an insurer, but he is obligated to minimize the risk to his tenants. Not only as between landlord and tenant is the landlord best equipped to guard against the predictable risk of intruders, but even as between landlord and the police power of government, the landlord is in the best position to take the necessary protective measures. Municipal police cannot patrol the entryways and the hallways, the garages and the basements of private multiple unit apartment dwellings. They are neither equipped, manned, nor empowered to do so. In the area of the pre-dictable risk which materialized in this case, only the landlord could have taken measures which might have prevented the injuries suffered by appellant.

We therefore hold in this case that the applicable standard of care in providing protection for the tenant is that standard which this landlord himself was employing in October 1959 when the appellant became a resident on the premises at 1500 Massachusetts Avenue. The tenant was led to expect that she could rely upon this degree of protection. While we do not say that the precise measures for security which were then in vogue should have been kept up (e.g., the number of people at the main entrances might have been reduced if a tenant-controlled intercom-automatic latch system had been installed in the common entryways), we do hold that the same relative degree of security should have been maintained. . . .

Having said this, it would be well to state what is not said by this decision. We do not hold that the landlord is by any means an insurer of the safety of his tenants. His duty is to take those measures of protection which are within his power and capacity to take, and which can reasonably be expected to mitigate the risk of intruders assaulting and robbing tenants. The landlord is not expected to provide protection commonly owed by a municipal police department; but as illustrated in this case, he is obligated to protect those parts of his premises which are not usually subject to periodic patrol and inspection by the municipal police. We do not say that every multiple unit apartment house in the District of Columbia should have those same measures of protection which 1500 Massachusetts Avenue enjoyed in 1959, nor do we say that 1500 Massachusetts Avenue should have precisely those same measures in effect at the present time. Alternative and more up-to-date methods may be equally or even more effective. . . .

The landlord is entirely justified in passing on the cost of increased protective measures to his tenants, but the rationale of compelling the landlord to do it in the first place is that he is the only one who is in a position to take the necessary protective measures for overall protection of the premises, which he owns in whole and rents in part to individual tenants.

Reversed and remanded to the District Court for the determination of damages.

PREPARING FOR CLASS

1. Would adopting the rule in *Pagelsdorf* be sufficient to impose liability in this case?

2. Could an assumed duty approach support a duty here?

3. Does the duty of care with regard to common areas as stated in *Levine v. Katz* impose a duty here? If not, how is this case different? How is *Levine* useful in determining whether a duty is owed in this case?

4. Why have courts been reluctant to require landlords to protect tenants from crime? Why are those rationales unpersuasive to this court?

5. What analogies make a duty appropriate here?

6. What is the scope of the duty the court imposes?

Chapter 9

Duty—Non-Physical Injury

The typical negligence case involves a careless defendant causing physical injury or property damage to a plaintiff who may also, as a result, suffer emotional harm and incur costs. The grocery store fails to clear a spill, and the plaintiff falls and breaks her elbow and her designer glasses. She cannot play tennis or work out at the gym, and this leads to depression. She misses work, losing pay, and has doctor and hospital bills and prescription costs, as well as the cost of new glasses. In other cases, though, the plaintiff suffers no underlying physical injury or property damage. In those cases, when the defendant has interfered only with a plaintiff's non-physical interests, courts are less protective of the plaintiff. These limitations on recovery are handled as duty questions.

A. NEGLIGENT INFLICTION OF EMOTIONAL DISTRESS

Physical injuries often lead to emotional harms. For example, the injured person may fear events like the one that injured him, worry about his ability to support his family because of the injury, feel embarrassed by scars or disability, or suffer depression because of the limitations the injury has put on him. The emotional harms that come from negligently caused physical injuries are called "parasitic damages" because they are attached to the physical injury, and that attachment to the physical injury makes them compensable in a negligence cause of action. But the negligent infliction of emotional distress suit is not about parasitic damages.

In these cases, the defendant has not inflicted physical injury on the plaintiff, but her negligence has caused the plaintiff emotional distress. Plaintiffs in negligent infliction of emotional distress cases are suing for purely emotional harm. They allege no physical injury (other than, in some cases, physical manifestations of their purely emotional harm). We have seen that plaintiffs can

351

recover for purely emotional harm in assault and intentional infliction of emotional distress cases. Although purely emotional harm is also recoverable in negligence cases, plaintiffs have to make some special proofs at the duty stage, and those proofs vary from state to state. The duty rules in cases of purely emotional harm are not meant to notify potential defendants of when they must be careful of other people's emotional states. Instead, the reason that courts limit duty in negligent infliction of emotional distress is that duty is a judicial inquiry, which permits courts to act as gatekeepers to the jury in these cases that the law still holds a little suspect. The court ruling on duty in such a case is determining whether this is a case worthy of a jury's attention, not whether this is a defendant who should have been careful.

Plaintiffs in negligent infliction of emotional distress cases fall into two categories—direct victims and bystanders. The direct victim is suing because of something the defendant did to him: told him falsely that his wife had died, failed to strap him into an amusement park ride, drove so close to him that he was almost hit. The bystander is suing over emotional harms from seeing someone else physically injured by the defendant's negligence: He witnesses an automobile accident that causes injury or a fire that kills someone.

1. Direct Victims

Robb v. Pennsylvania Railroad Co.
210 A.2d 709 (Del. 1965)

HERRMANN, J.

The question before us for decision is this: May the plaintiff recover for the physical consequences of fright caused by the negligence of the defendant, the plaintiff being within the immediate zone of physical danger created by such negligence, although there was no contemporaneous bodily impact?

[The rear wheels of the plaintiff's car became lodged in a rut that the defendant railroad company had permitted to form at a railroad crossing. She could not free her car. Seeing a train coming down the tracks, she jumped from her car with moments to spare. When she was just a few feet from the tracks, the train hit and demolished her car. She did not suffer any physical injuries but claimed she suffered great fear and nervous shock that physically interfered with her ability to nurse her child and engage in her work as a horse breeder. The trial judge granted summary judgment to the defendant because the plaintiff could not satisfy the impact rule. The plaintiff appealed.]

The question is still an open one in this State. Two reported Delaware cases and one unreported case border upon the field of inquiry, but none really enter it. . . . First, it is accepted as settled that there can be no recovery for fright alone, not leading to bodily injury or sickness, arising from the negligence of another. The plaintiff here concedes that proposition, stating however that she does not seek to recover for fright alone but for the physical consequences thereof. Secondly, we are not here concerned with the situation . . . wherein fright arose from the peril of another and the plaintiff was not in the path of the danger created by the negligence asserted. . . .

The two schools of thought in the matter at hand evolved from cases originating about the turn of the century. . . . The impact rule is based, generally speaking, upon three propositions expounded in [Mitchell v. Rochester R. Co., 45 N.E. 354 (1896), and Spade v. Lynn & Boston R. Co., 47 N.E. 88 (Mass. 1897)]:

1) It is stated that since fright alone does not give rise to a cause of action, the consequences of fright will not give rise to a cause of action. This is now generally recognized to be a non sequitur, want of damage being recognized as the reason that negligence causing mere fright is not actionable. It is now generally agreed, even in jurisdictions which have adopted the impact rule, that the gist of the action is the injury flowing from the negligence, whether operating through the medium of physical impact or nervous shock.

2) It is stated that the physical consequences of fright are too remote and that the requisite causal connection is unprovable. The fallacies of this ground of the impact rule, viewed in the light of growing medical knowledge, were well stated by Chief Justice Maltbie in Orlo v. Connecticut Co., 128 Conn. 231, 21 A.2d 402 (1941). It was there pointed out that the early difficulty in tracing a resulting injury back through fright or nervous shock has been minimized by the advance of medical science; and that the line of cases permitting recovery for serious injuries resulting from fright, where there has been but a trivial impact in itself causing little or no injury, demonstrate that there is no insuperable difficulty in tracing causal connection between the wrongdoing and the injury via the fright.

3) It is stated that public policy and expediency demand that there be no recovery for the physical consequences of fright in the absence of a contemporaneous physical injury. In recent years, this has become the principal reason for denying recovery on the basis of the impact rule. In support of this argument, it is said that fright is a subjective state of mind, difficult to evaluate, and of such nature that proof by the claimant is too easy and disproof by the party charged too difficult, thus making it unsafe as a practical matter for the law to deal with such claims. This school of thought concludes that to permit recovery in such cases would open a 'Pandora's box' of fictitious and fraudulent claims involving speculative and conjectural damages with which the law and medical science cannot justly cope. . . .

In considering the expediency ground, the Supreme Court of Connecticut said in the *Orlo* case, supra:

> . . . There is hardly more risk to the accomplishment of justice because of disparity in possibilities of proof in such situations than in those where mental suffering is allowed as an element of damage following a physical injury or recovery is permitted for the results of nervous shock provided there be some contemporaneous slight battery or physical injury. Certainly it is a very questionable position for a court to take, that because of the possibility of encouraging fictitious claims compensation

should be denied those who have actually suffered serious injury through the negligence of another. . . .

It is our opinion that the reasons for rejecting the impact rule far outweigh the reasons which have been advanced in its support. The cause of action and proximate cause grounds for the rule have been discredited in the very jurisdictions which first gave them credence. . . . If more were needed to warrant a declination to follow the cause of action and the proximate cause arguments, reference to the fictional and mechanical ends to which the impact rule has been carried would suffice for the purpose. The most trivial bodily contact, itself causing little or no injury, has been considered sufficient to take a case out of the rule and permit recovery for serious physical injuries resulting from the accompanying fright. Token impact sufficient to satisfy the rule has been held to be a slight bump against the seat, dust in the eyes, inhalation of smoke, a trifling burn, jostling in an automobile, indeed any degree of physical impact, however slight.

This leaves the public policy or expediency ground to support the impact rule. We think that ground untenable.

It is the duty of the courts to afford a remedy and redress for every substantial wrong. Part of our basic law is the mandate that "every man for an injury done him in his . . . person . . . shall have remedy by the due course of law. . . ." Del. Const. Art. 1, §9, Del. C. Ann. Neither volume of cases, nor danger of fraudulent claims, nor difficulty of proof, will relieve the courts of their obligation in this regard. None of these problems are insuperable. Statistics fail to show that there has been a "flood" of such cases in those jurisdictions in which recovery is allowed; but if there be increased litigation, the courts must willingly cope with the task. As to the danger of illusory and fictional claims, this is not a new problem; our courts deal constantly with claims for pain and suffering based upon subjective symptoms only; and the courts and the medical profession have been found equal to the danger. Fraudulent claims may be feigned in a slight-impact case as well as in a no-impact case. Likewise, the problems of adequacy of proof, for the avoidance of speculative and conjectural damages, are common to personal injury cases generally and are surmountable, being satisfactorily solved by our courts in case after case. . . .

We recognize that "[e]xpediency may tip the scales when arguments are nicely balanced," Woolford Realty Co. v. Rose, 286 U. S. 319, but, in our view, such nice balance no longer exists as to the subject matter.

We hold, therefore, that where negligence proximately caused fright, in one within the immediate area of physical danger from that negligence, which in turn produced physical consequences such as would be elements of damage if a bodily injury had been suffered, the injured party is entitled to recover under an application of the prevailing principles of law as to negligence and proximate causation. Otherwise stated, where results, which are regarded as proper elements of recovery as a consequence of physical injury, are proximately caused by fright due to negligence, recovery by one in the immediate zone of physical risk should be permitted. . . .

We conclude, therefore, that the Superior Court erred in the instant case in holding that the plaintiff's right to recover is barred by the impact rule. The plaintiff claims physical injuries resulting from fright proximately caused by the negligence of the defendant. She should have the opportunity to prove such injuries and to recover therefor if she succeeds. The summary judgment granted in favor of the defendant must be reversed and the cause remanded for further proceedings.

PREPARING FOR CLASS

1. What did the plaintiff seek to be compensated for?

2. What is the impact rule?

3. What rationales support the impact rule? According to the court, are those rationales still valid?

4. What kinds of impact had courts found sufficient to meet the rule? How is that significant to the court?

5. What policies are promoted by rejecting the impact rule?

6. What rule does the court adopt? Do you think the plaintiff would be able to satisfy that rule on remand?

Gammon v. Osteopathic Hospital of Maine, Inc.
534 A.2d 1282 (Me. 1987)

ROBERTS, J.
[The defendants are a hospital and a funeral home. Linwood Gammon's father died in the hospital. Gammon asked the funeral home to make arrangements. Instead of sending Gammon his father's personal effects, the funeral home sent him a bag that contained a] bloodied leg, severed below the knee and bluish in color. He yelled "Oh my God, they have taken my father's leg off." He ran into the kitchen where he leaned against the refrigerator for support, and said, "Guess what I found in the bathroom. I found my father's leg." In the words of Gammon's aunt, "He was as white as a ghost."
    Gammon later found a label located on the outside of the inner bag that identified the leg as a pathology specimen that had been removed from someone other than his father. . . . Thereafter, Gammon began having nightmares for the first time in his life, his personality was affected and his relationship with his wife and children deteriorated. After several months Gammon's emotional state began to improve, although his wife testified that he still had occasional nightmares and Gammon testified that he still sees the leg in his mind two or three times a week. He did not seek medical or psychiatric evaluation or treatment and no medical evidence was offered at trial.

The trial court granted the defendants' motions for a directed verdict on Gammon's claim for negligent infliction of severe emotional distress. . . .

The issue is whether, in these circumstances, Gammon has established a claim, in tort, for negligent infliction of severe emotional distress. A person's psychic well-being is as much entitled to legal protection as is his physical well-being. We recognize as much and provide compensation when the emotional distress is intentionally or recklessly inflicted, when the emotional distress results from physical injury negligently inflicted, or when negligently inflicted emotional distress results in physical injury. In order to ensure that a claim for emotional distress without physical injury is not spurious, we have previously required a showing of physical impact, objective manifestation, underlying or accompanying tort, or special circumstances. In the case before us, we conclude that these more or less arbitrary requirements should not bar Gammon's claim for compensation for severe emotional distress. [The court then reviewed eight emotional distress cases from Maine.]

No useful purpose would be served by more detailed analyses of our prior decisions or by consideration of whether the holdings of these cases follow a consistent trend. They demonstrate in a variety of ways the difficulty courts have had dealing with psychic injury.[5] They also demonstrate the frailty of supposed lines of demarcation when they are subjected to judicial scrutiny in the context of varying fact patterns. Moreover, these cases disclose our awareness of the extensive criticism aimed at the artificial devices used by courts to protect against fraudulent claims and against undue burden on the conduct of defendants.

The analyses of commentators and the developing trend in caselaw encourage us to abandon these artificial devices in this and future tort actions and to rely upon the trial process for protection against fraudulent claims. In addition, the traditional tort principle of foreseeability relied upon in [two previous cases] provides adequate protection against unduly burdensome liability claims for emotional distress. Jurors or trial judges will be able to evaluate the impact of psychic trauma with no greater difficulty than pertains to assessment of damages for any intangible injury. We do not foresee any great extension of tort liability by our ruling today. We do not provide compensation for the hurt feelings of the supersensitive plaintiff—the eggshell psyche. A defendant is bound to foresee psychic harm only when such harm reasonably could be expected to befall the ordinarily sensitive person.[8]

We have previously recognized that courts in other jurisdictions have allowed recovery for mental distress alone for negligent mishandling of corpses. In recognizing that Gammon has made out a claim in the instant

---

5. When discussing this type of injury, the courts of other jurisdictions and the commentators have used as the adjective either "emotional, mental, nervous or psychic" together with the noun "distress, pain, injury, harm, trauma, disturbance or shock." These phrases have not become words of art although each, with varying degrees of accuracy, seems to refer to non-tactile trauma resulting in injury to the psyche.

8. We described serious mental distress in *Culbert* as being "where a reasonable person, normally constituted, would be unable to adequately cope with the mental stress engendered by the circumstances of the event."

case, we do not find it necessary to rely on an extension of this exception. Instead, we look to the rationale supporting the exception. Courts have concluded that the exceptional vulnerability of the family of recent decedents makes it highly probable that emotional distress will result from mishandling the body. That high probability is said to provide sufficient trustworthiness to allay the court's fear of fraudulent claims. This rationale, it seems, is but another way of determining that the defendant reasonably should have foreseen that mental distress would result from his negligence. By the same token, on the record before us, a jury could conclude that the hospital and the mortician reasonably should have foreseen that members of Linwood Gammon's family would be vulnerable to emotional shock at finding a severed leg in what was supposed to be the decedent's personal effects. Despite the defendants' argument to the contrary, we hold that the evidence in this case would support a jury finding that either or both defendants failed to exercise reasonable care to prevent such an occurrence.

Although the analysis in the instant case may impact upon the rationale of our recent cases, we do not find it necessary to overrule those cases. We do not hold that any prior case was wrongly decided. Rather, we recognize that the elimination of some barriers to recovery for negligent infliction of severe emotional distress may compel further evaluation of other policy considerations. . . .

On the facts and circumstances of the case before us, however, we find no sound basis to preclude potential compensation to Gammon. We hold, therefore, that the trial court erred in directing a verdict on Gammon's claim for negligent infliction of severe emotional distress. Accordingly, we vacate the judgment in favor of the defendants on Count I.

Remanded for further proceedings consistent with the opinion herein.

PREPARING FOR CLASS

1. What had Maine courts previously required for plaintiffs to recover for the negligent infliction of emotional distress? Why had the courts imposed these requirements?

2. What approach does the Maine Supreme Court adopt instead? How does the court justify this decision?

3. The court says it does not provide compensation for "the eggshell psyche." What does this mean?

4. Couldn't the court simply have treated this as one of the special circumstances cases where recovery is allowed — as a kind of corpse mishandling case? Why didn't the court do that?

5. Did the defendants owe the plaintiff a duty?

INCREASING YOUR UNDERSTANDING

The *Gammon* decision represents a trend towards using foreseeability principles that apply in other torts cases to establish a duty in direct-victim suits for negligent infliction of emotional distress. Some states, however, still require more. Common approaches include:

1. *The impact rule.* Very few states continue to use this rule, but examples can be found. The Indiana Supreme Court has recently affirmed its "modified impact" rule, which "requires a claimant to demonstrate a direct physical impact resulting from the negligence of another. Where the physical impact is slight, or the evidence of the physical impact is tenuous, we evaluate the alleged emotional distress to determine whether it is not likely speculative, exaggerated, fictitious, or unforeseeable." Atlantic Coast Airlines v. Cook, 857 N.E.2d 989 (Ind. 2006). In R.J. v. Humana of Florida Inc., 652 So. 2d 360 (Fla. 1995), the defendant negligently diagnosed the plaintiff as HIV positive, and plaintiff lived with this belief for 18 months until he was retested. The Florida Supreme Court held that plaintiff could recover only if he had been harmed by treatments or injections because his "emotional distress suffered must flow from physical injuries the plaintiff sustained in an impact."

2. *The physical manifestation or physical consequences rule.* Under this rule, no touching is necessary, but plaintiff's emotional distress must show itself with objectively verifiable physical symptoms. Some courts have interpreted "physical" broadly, however. The court in Petition of United States, 418 F.2d 264 (1st Cir. 1969), wrote, "The term 'physical' is not used in its ordinary sense for purposes of applying the 'physical consequences' rule. Rather, the word is used to indicate that the condition or illness for which recovery is sought must be one susceptible of objective determination. Hence, a definite nervous disorder is a 'physical injury' sufficient to support an action for damages for negligence."

3. *The zone of danger rule.* If the plaintiff is in a location where defendant's carelessness risks physical danger to the plaintiff, so that the defendant owes the plaintiff a duty to exercise care for the plaintiff's physical safety, the defendant will also owe the plaintiff a duty of care for plaintiff's emotional safety. Most states further require under this rule, as Delaware did in *Robb*, that the distress manifest itself with physical symptoms. The court in Corso v. Merrill, 406 A.D.2d 300 (N.H. 1979) wrote, "The emotional harm must be a painful mental experience with lasting effects. This latter requirement guarantees that the emotional injury is sufficiently serious to be afforded legal protection. In other words, the harm for which plaintiff seeks to recover must be

susceptible to some form of objective medical determination and proved through qualified medical witnesses."

APPLYING THE LAW

1.   A ten-year-old girl skiing with her family was placed in a lift chair by a ski resort employee. The employee negligently failed to fasten the belt meant to secure the girl in the chair, so she spent the entire ride up the mountainside terrified that she would fall from the chair. She suffered emotional distress as a result and her parents, on her behalf, have sued the ski resort for its negligence. Can she recover in any jurisdiction?

2.   In Quill v. Trans World Airlines, 361 N.W.2d 438 (Minn. App. 1985), the plaintiff was a passenger in an airplane that plunged 34,000 feet in a tailspin before the pilots regained control. For 40 minutes thereafter, until an emergency landing could be made, the plane continued to shake and shudder. After that, the plaintiff was terrified of flying. The Minnesota Appellate Court permitted him to recover. Why?

3.   In Lawson v. Management Activities, Inc., 81 Cal. Rptr. 2d 745 (Cal. App. 1999), the employees of a Honda dealership saw a falling plane and were afraid it would crash into them. The plane, though, fell nearby and did not physically injure them. Do you think the California Appellate Court permitted recovery for their fear? If *Quill* is precedent, does it help the plaintiff? Or is this case distinguishable?

2.   Bystanders

Portee v. Jaffee
417 A.2d 521 (N.J. 1980)

PASHMAN, J.

We are asked to determine whether a parent can recover damages for the emotional anguish of watching her young child suffer and die in an accident caused by defendant's negligence. In Falzone v. Busch, 214 A.2d 12 (N.J. 1965), this Court imposed liability for such infliction of mental or emotional distress when negligence created the potential, but not the occurrence, for physical harm to the traumatized individual. The question presented here is whether liability should exist where there was no potential for personal injury, but distress resulted from perceiving the negligently inflicted injuries of another. . . .

Plaintiff's seven-year-old son, Guy Portee, resided with his mother in a Newark apartment building. Defendants Edith Jaffee and Nathan Jaffee owned and operated the building. On the afternoon of May 22, 1976, the youngster became trapped in the building's elevator between its outer door and the wall of the elevator shaft. The elevator was activated and the boy was dragged up to the third floor. Another child who was racing up a nearby stairway to beat the elevator opened it, saw the victim wedged within it, and ran to seek help. Soon afterwards, plaintiff and officers of the Newark Police Department arrived. The officers worked for four and one-half hours to free the child. While their efforts continued, the plaintiff watched as her son moaned, cried out and flailed his arms. Much of the time she was restrained from touching him, apparently to prevent interference with the attempted rescue. The child suffered multiple bone fractures and massive internal hemorrhaging. He died while still trapped, his mother a helpless observer.

After her son's death plaintiff became severely depressed and seriously self-destructive. On March 24, 1979, she attempted to take her own life. She was admitted to East Orange General Hospital with a laceration of her left wrist more than two inches deep. She survived and the wound was repaired by surgery, but she has since required considerable physical therapy and presently has no sensation in a portion of her left hand. She has received extensive counseling and psychotherapy to help overcome the mental and emotional problems caused by her son's death.

On December 2, 1976, plaintiff brought suit against the Jaffees and the two elevator companies. The complaint was premised on defendants' negligence in failing to provide a safe elevator. As both general administratrix and administratrix ad prosequendum of the estate of Guy Portee, plaintiff asserted survival and wrongful death claims. She also sued individually seeking damages for her mental and emotional distress caused by observing her son's anguish and death.

[The trial court granted the defendants summary judgment on the negligent infliction of emotional distress claims. The New Jersey Supreme Court here reviews that dismissal directly.]

Since plaintiff had concededly not been subjected to any risk of physical harm caused by defendants' alleged negligence, the trial court found that plaintiff's claims for psychological injury did not meet the requirements of *Falzone*. . . .

On many occasions, the law of negligence needs no other formulation besides the duty of reasonable care. Other cases, however, present circumstances rendering application of that general standard difficult, if not impossible. Without adequate guidance, juries may impose liability that is not commensurate with the culpability of defendant's conduct.

This difficulty has been recognized when courts considered liability for mental and emotional distress. We have noted the traditional argument, rejected by this Court in *Falzone*, that the imposition of such liability unoccasioned by any physical impact would lead to "mere conjecture and speculation." Even where the causal relationship between conduct and emotional harm was clear, courts would deny liability unless the fault of defendant's conduct could be demonstrated by the occurrence of physical harm to the plaintiff. Under *Falzone*, it became clear that the creation of a risk of physical harm would be a sufficient indication that defendant's conduct was unreasonable. Without such an indication, it might be argued that a jury could not form a reliable judgment regarding negligence. The question now before us is whether we are left to "mere conjecture and speculation" in assessing the culpability of conduct that creates neither the risk nor the occurrence of physical harm.

The task in the present case involves the refinement of principles of liability to remedy violations of reasonable care while avoiding speculative results or punitive liability. The solution is close scrutiny of the specific personal interests assertedly injured. By this approach, we can determine whether a defendant's freedom of action should be burdened by the imposition of liability. In the present case, the interest assertedly injured is more than a general interest in emotional tranquility. It is the profound and abiding sentiment of parental love. The knowledge that loved ones are safe and whole is the deepest wellspring of emotional welfare. Against that reassuring background, the flashes of anxiety and disappointment that mar our lives take on softer hues. No loss is greater than the loss of a loved one, and no tragedy is more wrenching than the helpless apprehension of the death or serious injury of one whose very existence is a precious treasure. The law should find more than pity for one who is stricken by seeing that a loved one has been critically injured or killed.

Courts in other jurisdictions which have found liability in the circumstances before us have placed limits on this type of negligence liability consistent with their view of the individual interest being injured. In Dillon v. Legg, 68 Cal. 2d 728, 441 P.2d 912, 69 Cal. Rptr. 72 (1968) (in bank), the California Supreme Court identified three factors which would determine whether an emotional injury would be compensable because "foreseeable":

> (1) Whether plaintiff was located near the scene of the accident as contrasted with one who was a distance away from it. (2) Whether the shock resulted from a direct emotional impact upon plaintiff from the sensory and contemporaneous observance of the accident, as contrasted with learning of the accident from others after its occurrence. (3) Whether plaintiff and the victim were closely related, as contrasted with an absence of any relationship or the presence of only a distant relationship.

. . . We agree that the three factors described in *Dillon* together create a strong case for negligence liability. In any given case, as physical proximity between plaintiff and the scene of the accident becomes closer, the foreseeable likelihood that plaintiff will suffer emotional distress from apprehending the physical harm of another increases. The second requirement of "direct . . . sensory and contemporaneous observance" appears to reflect a limitation of the liability rule to traumatic distress occasioned by immediate perception. The final criterion, that the plaintiff be "closely related" to the injured person, also embodies the judgment that only the most profound emotional interests should receive vindication for their negligent injury.

Our analysis of the specific emotional interest injured in this case a fundamental interest in emotional tranquility founded on parental love reveals where the limits of liability would lie. Addressing the *Dillon* criteria in reverse order, we find the last the existence of a close relationship to be the most crucial. It is the presence of deep, intimate, familial ties between the plaintiff and the physically injured person that makes the harm to emotional tranquility so serious and compelling. The genuine suffering which flows from such harm stands in stark contrast to the setbacks and sorrows of everyday life, or even to the apprehension of harm to another, less intimate person. The existence of a marital or intimate familial relationship is therefore an essential element of a cause of action for negligent infliction of emotional distress. In the present case, the instinctive affection of a mother for her seven-year-old son would be a sufficiently intimate bond on which to predicate liability.

The second requirement that the plaintiff witness the incident which resulted in death or serious injury is equally essential. We recognize that to deny recovery solely because the plaintiff was not subjected to a risk of physical harm would impose an arbitrary barrier that bears no relation to the injury to his basic emotional stability. Yet avoiding arbitrary distinctions does not entail that a cause of action should exist for all emotional injuries to all the close relatives of the victim. This expansive view would extend judicial redress far beyond the bounds of the emotional interest entitled to protection. To avoid imposing liability in excess of culpability, the scope of recovery must be circumscribed to negligent conduct which strikes at the plaintiff's basic emotional security.

Discovering the death or serious injury of an intimate family member will always be expected to threaten one's emotional welfare. Ordinarily, however, only a witness at the scene of the accident causing death or serious injury will suffer a traumatic sense of loss that may destroy his sense of security and cause severe emotional distress. . . . Such a risk of severe emotional distress is present when the plaintiff observes the accident at the scene. Without such perception, the threat of emotional injury is lessened and the justification for liability is fatally weakened. The law of negligence, while it redresses suffering wrongfully caused by others, must not itself inflict undue harm by imposing an unreasonably excessive measure of liability. Accordingly, we hold that observing the death or serious injury of another while it occurs is an essential element of a cause of action for the negligent infliction of emotional distress.

The first factor discussed in *Dillon*—that the plaintiff be near the injured person—embodies the same observations made concerning the other requirements of direct perception and close familial relationship. Physical proximity may be of some relevance in demonstrating the closeness of the emotional bond between plaintiff and the injured family member. For example, one would generally suppose that the risk of emotional distress to a brother who is halfway across the country is not as great as to a mother who is at the scene of the accident. The proximity of the plaintiff to the accident scene increases the likelihood that he will witness the event causing the death or serious injury of a loved one. Yet it appears that if the plaintiff must observe the accident that causes death or serious injury, a requirement of proximity is necessarily satisfied. The risk of emotional injury exists by virtue of the plaintiff's perception of the accident, not his proximity to it.

An additional factor yet undiscussed is the severity of the physical injury causing emotional distress. The harm we have determined to be worthy of judicial redress is the trauma accompanying the observation of the death or serious physical injury of a loved one. While any harm to a spouse or a family member causes sorrow, we are here concerned with a more narrowly confined interest in mental and emotional stability. When confronted with accidental death, "the reaction to be expected of normal persons," is shock and fright. We hold that the observation of either death or this type of serious injury is necessary to permit recovery. Since the sense of loss attendant to death or serious injury is typically not present following lesser accidental harm, perception of less serious harm would not ordinarily result in severe emotional distress. Thus, the risk of an extraordinary reaction to less serious injury is not sufficient to result in liability. To impose liability for any emotional consequence of negligent conduct would be unreasonable; it would also be unnecessary to protect a plaintiff's basic emotional stability. Therefore, a cause of action for emotional distress would require the perception of death or serious physical injury.

The cause of action we approve today for the negligent infliction of emotional distress requires proof of the following elements: (1) the death or serious physical injury of another caused by defendant's negligence; (2) a marital or intimate, familial relationship between plaintiff and the injured person; (3) observation of the death or injury at the scene of the accident; and (4) resulting severe emotional distress. We find that a defendant's duty of reasonable care to avoid physical harm to others extends to the avoidance of this type of mental and emotional harm.

For the foregoing reasons, the judgment of the Superior Court, Law Division, is reversed.

PREPARING FOR CLASS

1. How is this case different from *Falzone*? What new issue does it present?

2. What competing policy concerns does this case present?

3. What is the rule in *Dillon v. Legg*?

4. Why does the court adopt *Dillon*? How does the court change the rule?

5. Does the court find that the plaintiff can satisfy *Dillon* as stated by the California court? Can the plaintiff satisfy it as stated in New Jersey?

INCREASING YOUR UNDERSTANDING

1. California courts no longer apply the rule in *Dillon v. Legg*. In Thing v. La Chusa, 771 P.2d 814 (Cal. 1989), the California Supreme Court rejected the "foreseeability plus guidelines" approach of *Dillon*. In *Thing*, a child was hit by a car. His mother was near but not at the scene and did not hear or see the accident. She was, however, told about it, and she hurried there and saw her child bloody and unconscious in the road. Some lower courts had been emphasizing the foreseeability aspect of *Dillon* and not always requiring every guideline to be met. Such an approach might have permitted recovery in *Thing*. The court ruled, however, that the guidelines were absolute requirements. "Experience has shown that, contrary to the expectation of the *Dillon* majority, . . . there are clear judicial days on which a court can foresee forever and thus determine liability but none on which that foresight alone provides a socially and judicially acceptable limit on recovery of damages for that injury." In replacing foreseeability and guidelines with requirements, the court refined the rule:

> We conclude, therefore, that a plaintiff may recover damages for emotional distress caused by observing the negligently inflicted injury of a third person if, but only if, said plaintiff: (1) is closely related to the injury victim; (2) is present at the scene of the injury-producing event at the time it occurs and is then aware that it is causing injury to the victim; and (3) as a result suffers serious emotional distress—a reaction beyond that which would be anticipated in a disinterested witness and which is not an abnormal response to the circumstances.

   Regarding element (1), the court wrote, "absent exceptional circumstances, recovery should be limited to relatives residing in the same household, or parents, siblings, children, and grandparents of the victim." Regarding element (2), viewing consequences of an accident was not enough.

2. Two 1992 decisions applied the *Thing* rule. The plaintiff in Wilks v. Hom, 2 Cal. App. 4th 1264 (1992), was living in a rented home with her three daughters. She was vacuuming the living room. Her three-year-old was with her. The vacuum cleaner was plugged into the outlet in the seven-year-old's bedroom. When the plaintiff finished vacuuming, she called out to the seven-year-old to unplug the vacuum. The daughter

responded, "Yes, Mom." Immediately, there was the sound of a loud explosion. The force of it blew the mother and three-year-old out of the house. The mother tried to get in the front door but was repelled by the heat. She managed to get in the side of the house and pull the nine-year-old free. Then she pulled out the seven-year-old, who later died. The nine-year-old suffered severe burns. The landlord's negligent maintenance of the propane system was responsible for the explosion. Regarding the mother's claim for negligent infliction of emotional distress, the defendant contended it was error to instruct the jury on negligent infliction of emotional distress because the mother was not in the room with either the seven-year-old or the nine-year-old and therefore did not contemporaneously perceive that the explosion was injuring her daughters. The appellate court upheld the trial court. The contemporaneous awareness need not be visual. The mother heard her daughters' voices, knew where they were, knew they were close to the explosion, and had to have known they were experiencing injury. Interestingly, the issue of whether another room in the same house is "on the scene" was not even addressed.

The plaintiff who brought In re Air Crash Disaster Near Cerritos, California, On August 31, 1986, 967 F.2d 1421 (9th Cir. 1992), left her home before breakfast to go to the grocery store. When she left the house, her husband was in the living room reading the paper in his pajamas. Three of the children were still in bed. Returning from the store, she saw, heard, and felt a big explosion. Although she did not know it at the time, a passenger airliner had just crashed into her home. Within minutes, she managed to get through the debris and arrive at her home to find it engulfed in flames. She was surrounded by burning homes, cars, and debris. In her negligent infliction of emotional distress case, the defendant argued that she was neither present at the scene of the injury-producing event nor aware that it was causing injury to her family. The court disagreed.

> The injury-producing event was the fire. Since Estrada was present at the scene of the fire, she was present at the scene of the injury-producing event.
>
> The district court correctly found that Estrada knew her husband and children were being injured by the fire. Estrada's case is very different from *Thing* and *Fife*, in which the plaintiffs did not know until the accidents were over that their children were the victims of the accidents. Estrada's experience is similar to the situations in *Wilks* and *Krouse*, in which the plaintiffs saw or heard their relatives shortly before the injury-producing events, and therefore were aware that their relatives were being injured. Estrada left her house briefly to go to the store, leaving her husband in his pajamas in the living room and her children

asleep in bed. There could be very little doubt in Estrada's mind that her husband and children were in the house that she saw engulfed in flames.

Estrada's emotional distress did not stem merely from the knowledge that her husband and children had died. Estrada understandably experienced great emotional distress as a result of watching helplessly as flames engulfed her home and burned her family to death.

3. Although California has rejected *Dillon*, other states continue to use the rule or some variant of it, as seen in *Portee*.

4. Some states will use the zone-of-danger rule in bystander cases. In New York, it applies only to members of the "immediate family" who were in the zone of physical danger themselves. In Bovsun v. Sanperi, 461 N.E.2d 843 (N.Y. 1984), the court wrote:

> The zone-of-danger rule, which allows one who is himself or herself threatened with bodily harm in consequence of the defendant's negligence to recover for emotional distress resulting from viewing the death or serious physical injury of a member of his or her immediate family, is . . . premised on the traditional negligence concept that by unreasonably endangering the plaintiff's physical safety the defendant has breached a duty owed to him or her for which he or she should recover all damages sustained including those occasioned by witnessing the suffering of an immediate family member who is also injured by the defendant's conduct. Recognition of this right to recover for emotional distress attributable to observation of injuries suffered by a member of the immediate family involves a broadening of the duty concept but—unlike the *Dillon* approach—not the creation of a duty to a plaintiff to whom the defendant is not already recognized as owing a duty to avoid bodily harm. In so doing it permits recovery for an element of damages not heretofore allowed. Use of the zone-of-danger rule thus mitigates the possibility of unlimited recovery, an overriding apprehension expressed in [an earlier case rejecting *Dillon*], by restricting liability in a much narrower fashion than does the *Dillon* rule. Additionally, the circumstances in which a plaintiff who is within the zone of danger suffers serious emotional distress from observing severe physical injury or death of a member of the immediate family may not be altogether common.

The court also required the emotional distress to be "serious and verifiable."

APPLYING THE LAW

1. The defendant construction company's negligence caused a bulldozer
    to crash into a woman's home, collapsing it with her inside. The local
    news station covered the story. The woman's mother was watching the
    news and recognized her daughter's house and heard the reporter state,
    "Rescue crews as of yet have been unable to free the homeowner from
    the rubble." The mother became hysterical and suffered emotional
    distress from watching the broadcast. Could she recover against the
    construction company in any jurisdiction for her emotional distress?

2. Negligent security measures at a bank's night deposit led to the mugging
    and shooting of a bartender depositing the night's receipts. The sound of
    the shot and the bartender's screams of pain quickly brought the bar
    manager to the scene, which was just two doors down from the bar. He
    called the paramedics and the bartender's mother, who arrived within
    minutes of the shooting, just after the paramedics. When she arrived,
    her son was lying in a pool of his blood, his body shaking all over, and his
    face lined with tears. The paramedics were just beginning to cut his
    clothes off to attend to him. The bartender said, "I love you, Mom,"
    and reached out to her. She held his hand until he was put in the ambu-
    lance. The bartender died nine hours later. His mother underwent ther-
    apy for several months with a psychiatric nurse to help overcome the
    traumatic emotional effects of waiting with her son at the site of his
    shooting. Could she recover in any jurisdiction for her emotional
    distress?

B. ECONOMIC HARM

532 Madison Avenue Gourmet Foods, Inc. v. Finlandia Center, Inc.
750 N.E.2d 1097 (N.Y. 2001)

KAYE, C.J.

The novel issues raised by these appeals — arising from construction-related
disasters in midtown Manhattan — concern first, a landholder's duty in negligence where plaintiffs' sole injury is lost income and second, the viability of
claims for public nuisance.

Two of the three appeals involve the same event. On December 7, 1997, a
section of the south wall of 540 Madison Avenue, a 39-story office tower, partially collapsed and bricks, mortar and other material fell onto Madison
Avenue at 55th Street, a prime commercial location crammed with stores
and skyscrapers. The collapse occurred after a construction project, which

included putting 94 holes for windows into the building's south wall, aggravated existing structural defects. New York City officials directed the closure of 15 heavily trafficked blocks on Madison Avenue—from 42nd to 57th Street—as well as adjacent side streets between Fifth and Park Avenues. The closure lasted for approximately two weeks, but some businesses nearest to 540 Madison remained closed for a longer period.

In 532 *Madison Ave. Gourmet Foods v. Finlandia Ctr.*, plaintiff operates a 24-hour delicatessen one-half block south of 540 Madison, and was closed for five weeks. The two named plaintiffs in the companion case, *5th Ave. Chocolatiere v. 540 Acquisition Co.*, are retailers at 510 Madison Avenue, two blocks from the building, suing on behalf of themselves and a putative class of "all other business entities in whatever form, including but not limited to corporations, partnerships and sole proprietorships, located in the Borough of Manhattan and bounded geographically on the west by Fifth Avenue, on the east by Park Avenue, on the north by 57th Street and on the South by 42nd Street." Plaintiffs allege that shoppers and others were unable to gain access to their stores during the time Madison Avenue was closed to traffic. Defendants in both cases are Finlandia Center (the building owner), 540 Acquisition Company (the ground lessee) and Manhattan Pacific Management (the managing agent).

On defendants' motions in both cases, [the trial court] dismissed plaintiffs' negligence claims on the ground that they could not establish that defendants owed a duty of care for purely economic loss in the absence of personal injury or property damage, and dismissed the public nuisance claims on the ground that the injuries were the same in kind as those suffered by all of the businesses in the community. In *5th Ave. Chocolatiere*, plaintiffs' additional claims for gross negligence and negligence per se were dismissed on the ground that plaintiffs could not establish a duty owed by defendants, and their private nuisance cause of action was dismissed on the ground that they could not establish either intentional or negligent wrongdoing.

Goldberg Weprin & Ustin v. Tishman Constr. involves the July 21, 1998 collapse of a 48-story construction elevator tower on West 43rd Street between Sixth and Seventh Avenues—the heart of bustling Times Square. Immediately after the accident, the City prohibited all traffic in a wide area of midtown Manhattan and also evacuated nearby buildings for varying time periods. Three actions were consolidated—one by a law firm, a second by a public relations firm and a third by a clothing manufacturer, all situated within the affected area. Plaintiff law firm sought damages for economic loss on behalf of itself and a proposed class "of all persons in the vicinity of Broadway and 42nd Street, New York, New York, whose businesses were affected and/or caused to be closed" as well as a subclass of area residents who were evacuated from their homes. Plaintiff alleged gross negligence, strict liability, and public and private nuisance.

Noting the enormity of the liability sought, including recovery by putative plaintiffs as diverse as hot dog vendors, taxi drivers and Broadway productions, [the trial court] concluded that the failure to allege personal injury or property damage barred recovery in negligence. The court further rejected recovery for strict liability, and dismissed both the public nuisance claim (because plaintiff was unable to show special damages) and the private nuisance claim (because plaintiff could not show that the harm threatened only one person or relatively few).

The Appellate Division affirmed dismissal of the *Goldberg Weprin* complaint, concluding that, absent property damage, the connection between defendants' activities and the economic losses of the purported class of plaintiffs was "too tenuous and remote to permit recovery on any tort theory." The court, however, reinstated the negligence and public nuisance claims of plaintiffs 532 *Madison* and *5th Ave. Chocolatiere*, holding that defendants' duty to keep their premises in reasonably safe condition extended to "those businesses in such close proximity that their negligent acts could be reasonably foreseen to cause injury" (which included the named merchant plaintiffs) and that, as such, they established a special injury distinct from the general inconvenience to the community at large. Two Justices dissented, urging application of the "economic loss" rule, which bars recovery in negligence for economic damage absent personal injury or property damage. The dissenters further concluded that the public nuisance claims were properly dismissed because plaintiffs could not establish special injury.

We now reverse in 532 *Madison* and *5th Ave. Chocolatiere* and affirm in *Goldberg Weprin & Ustin*.

Plaintiffs contend that defendants owe them a duty to keep their premises in reasonably safe condition, and that this duty extends to protection against economic loss even in the absence of personal injury or property damage. Defendants counter that the absence of any personal injury or property damage precludes plaintiffs' claims for economic injury.

The existence and scope of a tortfeasor's duty is, of course, a legal question for the courts, which "fix the duty point by balancing factors, including the reasonable expectations of parties and society generally, the proliferation of claims, the likelihood of unlimited or insurer-like liability, disproportionate risk and reparation allocation, and public policies affecting the expansion or limitation of new channels of liability." At its foundation, the common law of torts is a means of apportioning risks and allocating the burden of loss. In drawing lines defining actionable duty, courts must therefore always be mindful of the consequential, and precedential, effects of their decisions.

As we have many times noted, foreseeability of harm does not define duty. Absent a duty running directly to the injured person there can be no liability in damages, however careless the conduct or foreseeable the harm. This restriction is necessary to avoid exposing defendants to unlimited liability to an indeterminate class of persons conceivably injured by any negligence in a defendant's act.

A duty may arise from a special relationship that requires the defendant to protect against the risk of harm to plaintiff. Landowners, for example, have a duty to protect tenants, patrons and invitees from foreseeable harm caused by the criminal conduct of others while they are on the premises, because the special relationship puts them in the best position to protect against the risk. That duty, however, does not extend to members of the general public. Liability is in this way circumscribed, because the special relationship defines the class of potential plaintiffs to whom the duty is owed.

In Strauss v. Belle Realty Co. (482 N.E.2d 34) we considered whether a utility owed a duty to a plaintiff injured in a fall on a darkened staircase during a citywide blackout. While the injuries were logically foreseeable, there was no contractual relationship between the plaintiff and the utility for lighting in the building's common areas. As a matter of policy, we restricted liability for damages in negligence to direct customers of the utility in order to avoid crushing exposure to the suits of millions of electricity consumers in New York City and Westchester.

Even closer to the mark is Milliken & Co. v. Consolidated Edison Co. (644 N.E.2d 268), in which an underground water main burst near 38th Street and 7th Avenue in Manhattan. The waters flooded a subbasement where Consolidated Edison maintained an electricity supply substation, and then a fire broke out, causing extensive damage that disrupted the flow of electricity to the Manhattan Garment Center and interrupting the biannual Buyers Week. Approximately 200 Garment Center businesses brought more than 50 lawsuits against Con Edison, including plaintiffs who had no contractual relationship with the utility and who sought damages solely for economic loss. Relying on Strauss, we again held that only those persons contracting with the utility could state a cause of action. We circumscribed the ambit of duty to avoid limitless exposure to the potential suits of every tenant in the skyscrapers embodying the urban skyline.

A landowner who engages in activities that may cause injury to persons on adjoining premises surely owes those persons a duty to take reasonable precautions to avoid injuring them. We have never held, however, that a landowner owes a duty to protect an entire urban neighborhood against purely economic losses. A comparison of Beck v. FMC Corp. (385 N.Y.S.2d 956, affd. 369 N.E.2d 10) and Dunlop Tire & Rubber Corp. v. FMC Corp. (385 N.Y.S.2d 971) is instructive. Those cases arose out of the same incident: an explosion at defendant FMC's chemical manufacturing plant caused physical vibrations, and rained stones and debris onto plaintiff Dunlop Tire's nearby factory. The blast also caused a loss of electrical power—by destroying towers and distribution lines owned by a utility—to both Dunlop Tire and a Chevrolet plant located one and one-half miles away. Both establishments suffered temporary closure after the accident. Plaintiffs in Beck were employees of the Chevrolet plant who sought damages for lost wages caused by the plant closure. Plaintiff Dunlop Tire sought recovery for property damage emanating from the blast and the loss of energy, and lost profits sustained during the shutdown.

In Dunlop Tire, the Appellate Division observed that, although part of the damage occurred from the loss of electricity and part from direct physical contact, defendant's duty to plaintiffs was undiminished. The court permitted plaintiffs to seek damages for economic loss, subject to the general rule requiring proof of the extent of the damage and the causal relationship between the negligence and the damage. The *Beck* plaintiffs, by contrast, could not state a cause of action, because, to extend a duty to defendant FMC would, "like the rippling of the waters, [go] far beyond the zone of danger of the explosion," to everyone who suffered purely economic loss.

Plaintiffs' reliance on People Express Airlines v. Consolidated Rail Corp. (495 A.2d 107) is misplaced. There, a fire started at defendant's commercial freight yard located across the street from plaintiff's airport offices. A tank containing volatile chemicals located in the yard was punctured, emitting the chemicals and requiring closure of the terminal because of fear of an explosion. Allowing the plaintiff to seek damages for purely economic loss, the New Jersey court reasoned that the extent of liability and degree of foreseeability stand in direct proportion to one another: the more particular the foreseeability that economic loss would be suffered as a result of the defendant's negligence, the more just that liability be imposed and recovery permitted. The New Jersey court acknowledged, however, that the presence of members of the public, or invitees at a particular plaintiff's business, or persons traveling nearby, while foreseeable, is nevertheless fortuitous, and the particular type of economic injury that they might suffer would be hopelessly unpredictable. Such plaintiffs, the court recognized, would present circumstances defying any appropriately circumscribed orbit of duty. We see a like danger in the urban disasters at issue here, and decline to follow *People Express*.

Policy-driven line-drawing is to an extent arbitrary because, wherever the line is drawn, invariably it cuts off liability to persons who foreseeably might be plaintiffs. The *Goldberg Weprin* class, for example, would include all persons in the vicinity of Times Square whose businesses had to be closed and a subclass of area residents evacuated from their homes; the *5th Ave. Chocolatiere* class would include all business entities between 42nd and 57th Streets and Fifth and Park Avenues. While the Appellate Division attempted to draw a careful boundary at storefront merchant—neighbors who suffered lost income, that line excludes others similarly affected by the closures—such as the law firm, public relations firm, clothing manufacturer and other displaced plaintiffs in *Goldberg Weprin*, the thousands of professional, commercial and residential tenants situated in the towers surrounding the named plaintiffs, and suppliers and service providers unable to reach the densely populated New York City blocks at issue in each case.

As is readily apparent, an indeterminate group in the affected areas thus may have provable financial losses directly traceable to the two construction-related collapses, with no satisfactory way geographically to distinguish among those who have suffered purely economic losses. In such circumstances, limiting the scope of defendants' duty to those who have, as a result of these events, suffered personal injury or property damage—as historically courts have done—affords a principled basis for reasonably apportioning liability.

We therefore conclude that plaintiffs' negligence claims based on economic loss alone fall beyond the scope of the duty owed them by defendants and should be dismissed. . . .

PREPARING FOR CLASS

1. Why have three separate cases involving two different events been joined as one case on appeal?

2. What harms do the various plaintiffs allege? Are these harms foreseeable from the defendants' negligence?

3. Why did the trial court dismiss all three cases? Why did the appellate court reinstate two of them?

4. What policy concerns do these cases raise?

5. The court cites a number of cases. Consider how each is factually similar to or different from the cases before the court. Consider how each guides the court's decisionmaking:

   a. *Strauss v. Belle Realty Co.*

   b. *Milliken & Co. v. Consolidated Edison Co.*

   c. *Beck v. FMC Corp.*

   d. *Dunlop Tire & Rubber Corp. v. FMC. Corp.*

   e. *People Express Airlines v. Consolidated Rail Corp.*

6. Do you suppose the defendants in the three cases joined here were liable to anyone?

INCREASING YOUR UNDERSTANDING

When personal injury or property damage leads to doctor bills, lost wages, repairs, and other costs, these economic losses are compensable in a tort action. The limitation in 532 *Madison* applies to cases of pure economic loss not arising from any personal injury or property damage. Pure economic loss is not recoverable. (In Torts II, however, we will study negligent misrepresentation, which is an exception, a tort that compensates pure economic harm.)

As you could tell from reading 532 *Madison*, this is a largely policy-driven position. In economic-loss cases where the parties were in a bargaining relationship, the plaintiff had an opportunity to allocate the loss by contract. Because the action is based on a risk that should have been contractually resolved, the courts refuse to permit a tort action to make up for that oversight.

In cases that did not involve a bargaining opportunity, courts want to prevent fraudulent claims or liability that is either limitless or out of proportion to the defendant's fault. Courts will also consider the role of insurance. Pure economic loss is highly unpredictable, and insurers cannot confidently predict the risks to insure against. Courts also point out that plaintiffs are in a better position to insure against their losses because they know what those losses could be. See Marshall S. Shapo, *Basic Principles of Tort Law,* ¶¶ 64.01, et seq.

APPLYING THE LAW

1. An accident at a nuclear power plant caused the release of large amounts of radiation. Because of the danger, the nearby municipality shut down its offices for several days to avoid exposing workers. As a result of the accident, the city had economic losses for lost use of the buildings, cost of emergency responders, and lost employee work time. Did the nuclear power plant owe a duty to prevent these losses?

2. One January, a water main burst because of negligent maintenance by the city. Two city blocks were flooded. Cars parked along the streets were damaged, and two restaurants were flooded. Other stores and restaurants were not flooded, but the two months of repair made reaching these businesses difficult, so that they lost significant amounts of money. Which injured parties have cases against the city?

C.   UNBORN CHILDREN

Endresz v. Friedberg
248 N.E.2d 901 (N.Y. 1969)

FULD, C.J.
. . . The plaintiff, Janice Endresz, seven months pregnant, was injured in an automobile accident in the winter of 1965 and two days later was delivered of stillborn twins, a male and a female. Four actions in negligence were brought against the persons assertedly responsible for the accident. In the first two actions—one for the wrongful death of each child—the plaintiff Steve Endresz, Janice's husband, suing as administrator, seeks damages of $100,000 by reason of the distributees' "loss of anticipated . . . care, comfort and support during the minority and majority" of each infant and for "medical, hospital and funeral expenses incurred by reason of the death" of the children. . . .

On motion of the defendants, the court at Special Term . . . dismissed the first two suits for wrongful death. . . .

This court has already decided that a wrongful death action may not be maintained for the death of an unborn child. This view is held by the courts of a number of other jurisdictions and, although there is authority to the contrary, further study and thought confirm the justice and wisdom of our earlier decisions.

Section 5-4.1 of the EPTL (L. 1966, ch. 952, eff. Sept. 1, 1967), reenacting, without substantive change, former section 130 of the Decedent Estate Law, declares, insofar as pertinent, that "The personal representative . . . of a decedent who is survived by distributees may maintain an action to recover damages for a wrongful act, neglect or default which caused the decedent's death against a person who would have been liable to the decedent by reason of such wrongful conduct if death had not ensued." Before there may be a "decedent," there must, perforce, be birth, a person born alive, and, although the statute, enacted in 1847 (L.1847, ch. 450), is silent on the subject, it is fairly certain that the Legislature did not intend to include an "unborn" foetus within the term "decedent." Indeed, it was not until 1951, more than 100 years later, that this court—overruling a long-standing decision—decided that "a child viable but in utero, if injured by tort, should, when born, be allowed to sue." (Woods v. Lancet, 102 N.E.2d 691, 693) If, before *Woods*, a child so injured had no right of action, still less was such an action intended to lie on behalf of one who, never seeing the light of day, was deprived of life while still in its mother's womb.

Our decision in the *Woods* case does not require us, as suggested, to reinterpret the wrongful death statute to provide compensation to the distributees of a stillborn foetus for "pecuniary injuries" resulting from its death apart from those sustained by the mother and father in their own right. The *Woods* decision, as the court recognized in *Matter of Logan*, 144 N.E.2d 644, simply brought the common law of this State into accord with the demand of natural justice which requires recognition of the legal right of every human being to begin life unimpaired by physical or mental defects resulting from the negligence of another. The considerations of justice which mandate the recovery of damages by an infant, injured in his mother's womb and born deformed through the wrong of a third party, are absent where the foetus, deprived of life while yet unborn, is never faced with the prospect of impaired mental or physical health.

In the latter case, moreover, proof of pecuniary injury and causation is immeasurably more vague than in suits for prenatal injuries. . . .

Beyond that, since the mother may sue for any injury which she sustained in her own person, including her suffering as a result of the stillbirth, and the father for loss of her services and consortium, an additional award to the "distributes" of the foetus would give its parents an unmerited bounty and would constitute not compensation to the injured but punishment to the wrongdoer. A leading law review article on the subject has clearly pointed up the differences in the two situations (Gordon, *The Unborn Plaintiff*, 63 Mich. L. Rev. 579, 594-595):

> The hardship of many of the decisions denying relief (in prenatal injury cases) lay in the fact that they required an infant to go through life . . . bearing the seal of another's fault. There is no such justification in the wrongful death situation. . . .
>
> A fundamental basis of tort law is the provision for compensation of an innocent plaintiff for the loss he has suffered. Tort law is not, as a general rule, premised upon punishing the wrongdoer. It is not submitted that the tortious destroyer of a child in utero should be able to escape completely by killing instead of merely maiming. But it is submitted that to compensate the parents any further than they are entitled by well-settled principles of law and to give them a windfall through the estate of the fetus is blatant punishment.

. . . [E]ven if, as science and theology teach, the child begins a separate "life" from the moment of conception, it is clear that, "except in so far as is necessary to protect the child's own rights" the law has never considered the unborn foetus as having a separate "juridical existence" or a legal personality or identity "until it sees the light of day." . . .

It is argued that it is arbitrary and illogical to draw the line at birth, with the result that the distributees of an injured foetus which survives birth by a few minutes may have a recovery while those of a stillborn foetus may not. However, such difficulties are always present where a line must be drawn. To make viability rather than birth the test would not remove the difficulty but merely relocate it and increase a hundredfold the problems of causation and damages. Thus, one commentator aptly observed that (Wenger, *Developments in the Law of Prenatal Wrongful Death*, 69 Dickinson L. Rev. 258, 268), "since any limitation will be arbitrary in nature, a tangible and concrete event would be the most acceptable and workable boundary. Birth, being a definite, observable and significant event, meets this requirement."

In light of all these considerations, then, we do not feel that, on balance and as a matter of public policy, a cause of action for pecuniary loss should accrue to the distributees of a foetus stillborn by reason of the negligence of another; the damages recoverable by the parents in their own right afford ample redress for the wrong done. Decidedly applicable here is the rule that "(l)iability for damages caused by wrong ceases at a point dictated by public policy or common sense." . . .

The order appealed from should be affirmed, without costs.

BURKE, J. (dissenting in part).

. . . The illogicalness of the majority's position was aptly demonstrated by the Supreme Court of Wisconsin, in the analogous case of Kwaterski v. State Farm Mut. Auto. Ins. Co., 148 N.W.2d 107, 110, in these terms: "If no right of action is allowed, there is a wrong inflicted for which there is no remedy. Denying a right of action for negligent acts which produce a stillbirth leads to very incongruous results. For example, a doctor or midwife whose negligent acts in delivering a baby produced the baby's death would be legally immune from a lawsuit. However, if they badly injured the child they would be exposed to liability. Such a rule would produce the absurd result that an unborn child who was badly injured by the tortious acts of another, but who was born alive, could recover while an unborn child, who was more severely injured and died as the result of the tortious acts of another, could recover nothing." . . .

In summary, I am of the opinion that it is both illogical and unreasonable to distinguish between injuries wrongfully inflicted upon a viable foetus which result in death just prior to the infant's separation from the mother and those which cause either permanent injuries or death itself, but at some short interval after birth has occurred. I, therefore, dissent from that portion of the majority opinion which affirms the dismissal of the wrongful death actions by the personal representatives of these stillborn foetuses.

PREPARING FOR CLASS

1. Is this just a case about applying the statute?

2. What influences how the court construes the statute? What distinctions is the court careful to make?

3. How do the majority and minority judges see the line-drawing process differently?

INCREASING YOUR UNDERSTANDING

Sometimes a woman who did not want to become pregnant does become pregnant because a physician has negligently performed a sterilization procedure on her or her partner. Sometimes a woman who does want a child has one with serious birth defects after a physician negligently failed to tell her that the fetus had genetic defects. As much as she wanted a child, she wishes this one had not been born. These women, and sometimes their partners, will sue the physician because he has taken from them the ability to avoid or terminate pregnancy.

1. *Wrongful pregnancy or wrongful conception.* The doctor negligently failed to prevent conception of a child—usually with a failed tubal ligation or vasectomy. Although such claims are recognized, courts are not generally willing to grant the reluctant parents child-rearing expenses. The court may explain that having a healthy child is not an injury. Other courts will state that the damages are speculative. Courts that

do permit child-rearing expenses will offset those with the benefits of raising a child. What, then, can be recovered in such a suit? Courts will permit the mother to recover for her pain and suffering in pregnancy and delivery, the costs of the failed sterilization procedure, medical expenses from the pregnancy, and lost wages. Courts are split on whether to permit recovery for emotional distress.

2. *Wrongful birth.* The mother asserts that but for the physician's negligent counsel or testing she would have terminated her pregnancy so as not to have a child with serious birth defects. Although most courts have permitted some kind of recovery in cases like this, others do deny such claims. The commonly cited rationales for rejecting these claims are that human life cannot be a legal wrong and that parents will, simply, be tempted to perjure themselves and say that they would have terminated the pregnancy had they known. Courts that do recognize these claims will allow for extraordinary child-rearing expenses arising from the child's special needs, and a few will allow for all child-rearing expenses. As this is the parent's claim and not the child's, some courts limit recovery to only those years when the child is a minor. Courts are split on whether to allow for emotional distress.

Procanik by Procanik v. Cillo
478 A.2d 755 (N.J. 1984)

POLLOCK, J.

The primary issue on this appeal is the propriety of a grant of a partial summary judgment dismissing a "wrongful life" claim brought by an infant plaintiff through his mother and guardian ad litem. That judgment, which was granted on the pleadings, dismissed the claim because it failed to state a cause of action upon which relief may be granted.

The infant plaintiff, Peter Procanik, alleges that the defendant doctors . . . negligently failed to diagnose that his mother, Rosemary Procanik, had contracted German measles in the first trimester of her pregnancy. As a result, Peter was born with congenital rubella syndrome. Alleging that the doctors negligently deprived his parents of the choice of terminating the pregnancy, he seeks general damages for his pain and suffering and for "his parents' impaired capacity to cope with his problems." He also seeks special damages attributable to the extraordinary expenses he will incur for medical, nursing, and other health care. The Law Division granted defendants' motion to dismiss, and the Appellate Division affirmed in an unreported opinion.

We granted certification. We now conclude that an infant plaintiff may recover as special damages the extraordinary medical expenses attributable to his affliction, but that he may not recover general damages for emotional distress or for an impaired childhood. Consequently, we affirm in part and reverse in part the judgment of the Appellate Division, and remand the matter to the Law Division.

Accepting as true the allegations of the complaint, the complaint discloses the following facts. . . .

On June 9, 1977, during the first trimester of her pregnancy with Peter, Mrs. Procanik consulted the defendant doctors and informed Dr. Cillo "that she had recently been diagnosed as having measles but did not know if it was German measles." Dr. Cillo examined Mrs. Procanik and ordered "tests for German Measles, known as Rubella Titer Test." The results "were 'indicative of past infection of Rubella.'" Instead of ordering further tests, Dr. Cillo negligently interpreted the results and told Mrs. Procanik that she "had nothing to worry about because she had become immune to German Measles as a child." In fact, the "past infection" disclosed by the tests was the German measles that had prompted Mrs. Procanik to consult the defendant doctors.

Ignorant of what an accurate diagnosis would have disclosed, Mrs. Procanik allowed her pregnancy to continue, and Peter was born on December 26, 1977. Shortly thereafter, on January 16, 1978, he was diagnosed as suffering from congenital rubella syndrome. As a result of the doctors' negligence, Mr. and Mrs. Procanik were deprived of the choice of terminating the pregnancy, and Peter was "born with multiple birth defects," including eye lesions, heart disease, and auditory defects. The infant plaintiff states further that "he has suffered because of his parents' impaired capacity to cope with his problems," and seeks damages for his pain and suffering and for his "impaired childhood."

In April 1983, while this matter was pending in the Appellate Division, Peter moved to amend the first count to assert a claim to recover, as special damages, the expenses he will incur as an adult for medical, nursing, and related health care services. In its opinion, the Appellate Division denied without prejudice leave to amend. . . .

In this case we survey again the changing landscape of family torts. Originally that landscape presented a bleak prospect both to children born with birth defects and to their parents. If a doctor negligently diagnosed or treated a pregnant woman who was suffering from a condition that might cause her to give birth to a defective child, neither the parents nor the child could maintain a cause of action against the negligent doctor. Gleitman v. Cosgrove, 49 N.J. 22, 227 A.2d 689 (1967).

Like the present case, *Gleitman* involved a doctor who negligently treated a pregnant woman who had contracted German measles in the first trimester of her pregnancy. Reasoning from the premise that the doctor did not cause the infant plaintiff's birth defects, the *Gleitman* Court found it impossible to compare the infant's condition if the defendant doctor had not been negligent with the infant's impaired condition as a result of the negligence. Measurement of "the value of life with impairments against the nonexistence of life itself" was, the Court declared, a logical impossibility. Consequently, the Court rejected the infant's claim.

The Court denied the parents' claim for emotional distress and the costs of caring for the infant, because of the impossibility of weighing the intangible benefits of parenthood against the emotional and monetary injuries sustained by them. Prevailing policy considerations, which included a reluctance to acknowledge the availability of abortions and the mother's right to choose to terminate her pregnancy, prevented the Court from awarding damages to a woman for not having an abortion. Another consideration was the Court's belief that "[i]t is basic to the human condition to seek life and hold on to it however heavily burdened."

In the seventeen years that have elapsed since the *Gleitman* decision, both this Court and the United States Supreme Court have reappraised, albeit in different contexts, the rights of pregnant women and their children. The United States Supreme Court has recognized that women have a constitutional right to choose to terminate a pregnancy. Roe v. Wade, 410 U.S. 113, 93 S. Ct. 705, 35 L. Ed. 2d 147 (1973). Recognition of that right by the high court subsequently influenced this Court in Berman v. Allan, 80 N.J. 421, 404 A.2d 8 [1979].

In *Berman*, the parents sought to recover for their emotional distress and for the expenses of raising a child born with Down's Syndrome. Relying on *Roe v. Wade*, the Court found that public policy now supports the right of a woman to choose to terminate a pregnancy. That finding eliminated one of the supports for the *Gleitman* decision—i.e., that public policy prohibited an award for depriving a woman of the right to choose whether to have an abortion. Finding that a trier of fact could place a dollar value on the parents' emotional suffering, the *Berman* Court concluded "that the monetary equivalent of this distress is an appropriate measure of the harm suffered by the parents."

Nonetheless, the Court rejected the parents' claim for "medical and other expenses that will be incurred in order to properly raise, educate and supervise the child." The Court reasoned that the parents wanted to retain "all the benefits inhering in the birth of the child—i.e., the love and joy they will experience as parents—while saddling defendants with enormous expenses attendant upon her rearing." Such an award would be disproportionate to the negligence of the defendants and constitute a windfall to the parents.

The *Berman* Court also declined to recognize a cause of action in an infant born with birth defects. Writing for the Court, Justice Pashman reasoned that even a life with serious defects is more valuable than non-existence, the alternative for the infant plaintiff if his mother chose to have an abortion.

More recently we advanced the parents' right to compensation by permitting recovery of the extraordinary expenses of raising a child born with cystic fibrosis, including medical, hospital, and pharmaceutical expenses. Schroeder v. Perkel, 432 A.2d 834. No claim on behalf of the infant was raised in that case, and we elected to defer consideration of such a claim until another day. That day is now upon us, and we must reconsider the right of an infant in a "wrongful life" claim to recover general damages for diminished childhood and pain and suffering, as well as special damages for medical care and the like.

The terms "wrongful birth" and "wrongful life" are but shorthand phrases that describe the causes of action of parents and children when negligent medical treatment deprives parents of the option to terminate a pregnancy to avoid the birth of a defective child. In the present context, "wrongful life" refers to a cause of action brought by or on behalf of a defective child who claims that but for the defendant doctor's negligent advice to or treatment of its parents, the child would not have been born. "Wrongful birth" applies to the cause of action of parents who claim that the negligent advice or treatment deprived them of the choice of avoiding conception or, as here, of terminating the pregnancy.

Both causes of action are distinguishable from the situation where negligent injury to a fetus causes an otherwise normal child to be born in an impaired condition. In the present case, the plaintiffs do not allege that the negligence of the defendant doctors caused the congenital rubella syndrome from which the infant plaintiff suffers. Neither do plaintiffs claim that the infant ever had a chance to be a normal child. The essence of the infant's claim is that the defendant doctors wrongfully deprived his mother of information that would have prevented his birth.

Analysis of the infant's cause of action begins with the determination whether the defendant doctors owed a duty to him. The defendant doctors do not deny they owed a duty to the infant plaintiff, and we find such a duty exists. In evaluating the infant's cause of action, we assume, furthermore, that the defendant doctors were negligent in treating the mother. Moreover, we assume that their negligence deprived the parents of the choice of terminating the pregnancy and of preventing the birth of the infant plaintiff.

Notwithstanding recognition of the existence of a duty and its breach, policy considerations have led this Court in the past to decline to recognize any cause of action in an infant for his wrongful life. The threshold problem has been the assertion by infant plaintiffs not that they should not have been born without defects, but that they should not have been born at all. The essence of the infant's cause of action is that its very life is wrongful. Resting on the belief that life, no matter how burdened, is preferable to non-existence, the *Berman* Court stated that the infant "has not suffered any damage cognizable at law by being brought into existence." Although the premise for this part of the *Berman* decision was the absence of cognizable damages, the Court continued to be troubled, as it was in *Gleitman*, by the problem of ascertaining the measure of damages.

The courts of other jurisdictions have also struggled with the issues of injury and damages when faced with suits for wrongful life. Although two intermediate appellate courts in New York and California recognized an infant's claim for general damages, those decisions were rejected by the courts of last resort in both jurisdictions. . . .

Other courts have uniformly found that the problems posed by the damage issues in wrongful life claims are insurmountable and have refused to allow the action on behalf of the infant. . . .

Even when this Court declined to recognize a cause of action for wrongful life in *Gleitman* and *Berman*, dissenting members urged recognition of that claim. . . .

Recently we recognized that extraordinary medical expenses incurred by parents on behalf of a birth-defective child were predictable, certain, and recoverable. [*Schroeder*]. . . .

When a child requires extraordinary medical care, the financial impact is felt not just by the parents, but also by the injured child. As a practical matter, the impact may extend beyond the injured child to his brothers or sisters. Money that is spent for the health care of one child is not available for the clothes, food, or college education of another child.

Recovery of the cost of extraordinary medical expenses by either the parents or the infant, but not both, is consistent with the principle that the doctor's negligence vitally affects the entire family. . . .

Law is more than an exercise in logic, and logical analysis, although essential to a system of ordered justice, should not become an instrument of injustice. Whatever logic inheres in permitting parents to recover for the cost of extraordinary medical care incurred by a birth-defective child, but in denying the child's own right to recover those expenses, must yield to the inherent injustice of that result. The right to recover the often crushing burden of extraordinary expenses visited by an act of medical malpractice should not depend on the "wholly fortuitous circumstance of whether the parents are available to sue."

The present case proves the point. Here, the parents' claim is barred by the statute of limitations. Does this mean that Peter must forego medical treatment for his blindness, deafness, and retardation? We think not. His claim for the medical expenses attributable to his birth defects is reasonably certain, readily calculable, and of a kind daily determined by judges and juries. We hold that a child or his parents may recover special damages for extraordinary medical expenses incurred during infancy, and that the infant may recover those expenses during his majority. . . .

In restricting the infant's claim to one for special damages, we recognize that our colleagues, Justice Schreiber and Justice Handler, disagree with us and with each other. From the premise that "man does not know whether non-life would have been preferable to an impaired life," Justice Schreiber concludes that a child does not have a cause of action for wrongful life and, therefore, that is "unfair and unjust to charge the doctors with the infant's medical expenses." Justice Handler reaches a diametrically opposite conclusion. He would allow the infant to recover not only his medical expenses, but also general damages for his pain and suffering and for his impaired childhood.

We find, however, that the infant's claim for pain and suffering and for a diminished childhood presents insurmountable problems. The philosophical problem of finding that such a defective life is worth less than no life at all has perplexed not only Justice Schreiber, but such other distinguished members of this Court as Chief Justice Weintraub, Justice Proctor, and Justice Pashman.

We need not become preoccupied, however, with these metaphysical considerations. Our decision to allow the recovery of extraordinary medical expenses is not premised on the concept that non-life is preferable to an impaired life, but is predicated on the needs of the living. We seek only to respond to the call of the living for help in bearing the burden of their affliction.

Sound reasons exist not to recognize a claim for general damages. Our analysis begins with the sad but true fact that the infant plaintiff never had a chance of being born as a normal, healthy child. For him, the only options were non-existence or an impaired life. Tragically, his only choice was a life burdened with his handicaps or no life at all. The congenital rubella syndrome that plagues him was not caused by the negligence of the defendant doctors; the only proximate result of their negligence was the child's birth.

The crux of the problem is that there is no rational way to measure non-existence or to compare non-existence with the pain and suffering of his impaired existence. Whatever theoretical appeal one might find in recognizing a claim for pain and suffering is outweighed by the essentially irrational and unpredictable nature of that claim. Although damages in a personal injury action need not be calculated with mathematical precision, they require at their base some modicum of rationality.

Underlying our conclusion is an evaluation of the capability of the judicial system, often proceeding in these cases through trial by jury, to appraise such a claim. Also at work is an appraisal of the role of tort law in compensating injured parties, involving as that role does, not only reason, but also fairness, predictability, and even deterrence of future wrongful acts. In brief, the ultimate decision is a policy choice summoning the most sensitive and careful judgment.

From that perspective it is simply too speculative to permit an infant plaintiff to recover for emotional distress attendant on birth defects when that plaintiff claims he would be better off if he had not been born. Such a claim would stir the passions of jurors about the nature and value of life, the fear of non-existence, and about abortion. That mix is more than the judicial system can digest. We believe that the interests of fairness and justice are better served through more predictably measured damages—the cost of the extraordinary medical expenses necessitated by the infant plaintiff's handicaps. Damages so measured are not subject to the same wild swings as a claim for pain and suffering and will carry a sufficient sting to deter future acts of medical malpractice.

As speculative and uncertain as is a comparison of the value of an impaired life with non-existence, even more problematic is the evaluation of a claim for diminished childhood. The essential proof in such a claim is that the doctor's negligence deprives the parents of the knowledge of the condition of the fetus. The deprivation of that information precludes the choice of terminating the pregnancy by abortion and leaves the parents unprepared for the birth of a defective child, a birth that causes them emotional harm. The argument proceeds that the parents are less able to love and care for the child, who thereby suffers an impaired childhood.

Several considerations lead us to decline to recognize a cause of action for impaired childhood. At the outset, we note the flaw in such a claim in those instances in which the parents assert not that the information would have prepared them for the birth of the defective child, but that they would have used the information to prevent that birth. Furthermore, even its advocates recognize that a claim for "the kind of injury suffered by the child in this context may not be readily divisible from that suffered by her wronged parents." Berman v. Allan, 404 A.2d 8 (Handler, J., concurring and dissenting). We believe the award of the cost of the extraordinary medical care to the child or the parents, when combined with the right of the parents to assert a claim for their own emotional distress, comes closer to filling the dual objectives of a tort system: the compensation of injured parties and the deterrence of future wrongful conduct. . . .

The judgment of the Appellate Division is affirmed in part, reversed in part, and the matter is remanded to the Law Division. The infant plaintiff shall have leave to file an amended complaint asserting a claim for extraordinary medical, hospital, and other health care expenses.

Chapter 10

Harm and Actual Causation

The third element of plaintiff's negligence cause of action is actual causation. This requires a factual determination whether the plaintiff was injured the way the plaintiff claims because of the defendant's negligence. Therefore, considering causation involves looking ahead to the final element, some sort of personal injury or property damage. We begin the chapter with a look at that requirement.

A. THE HARM REQUIREMENT

Preston v. Cestaro
28 Conn. L. Rptr. 711 (Conn. Super. 2001)

PITTMAN, J.

When one car negligently hits another car but no injury occurs to the second car's occupants, what is the correct form that a judgment should take? That is the issue for the court in this case.

The plaintiff John Preston was a passenger in a State of Connecticut bus when it was bumped slightly by a car driven by the defendant John Cestaro. . . .

The court concludes from the evidence that the plaintiff was not injured as a result of the collision. True, he complained about back pain shortly after the accident. But the evidence suggests that it is more likely than not that his back pain resulted from an incident that occurred some days or weeks before when he fell or jumped to the floor from a top bunk bed. Moreover the court finds that the slight force of the car backing into the large bus was insufficient to produce any injury to the plaintiff.

So under the circumstances, does this finding result in a judgment for the defendants, or must the court nonetheless find for the plaintiff and award at least nominal damages because of the previous summary judgment on liability in plaintiff's favor?

At common law, the elements of a cause of action for negligence were the following: duty; breach of duty; causation; and injury. Without proof of each of these, a plaintiff's cause would fail entirely and a plaintiff was not entitled to have the question of damages considered by the trier of fact. This was so because conduct that was merely negligent was not considered to be a significant interference with the public interest such that there was any right to complain of it, or to be free from it, without proof of an actual injury.

Nor was this merely the old-fashioned view. No less a contemporary authority than the Restatement of Torts, Second, adopts the position that nominal damages are not available in a negligence action where no actual injury is proved, since actual injury is an element of the cause of action. Restatement of Torts, Second §907, comment a.

But Connecticut began to stray from this principle. The path to apostasy can be traced to Schmeltz v. Tracy, 177 A. 520 (Conn. 1935). There a female plaintiff sued a male surgeon for common law assault as a result of his performing an unauthorized operation on her to remove certain moles. Common law assault, unlike common law negligence, has no requirement that actual injury be proved in order to recover damages, at least nominal damages. In *Schmeltz v. Tracy*, the trial court had erroneously instructed the jury that the plaintiff had to prove her actual injuries in order to prevail. The Supreme Court, correctly, said no: "This was erroneous, for if the lack of consent was established, the removal of the moles was in itself a trespass and had the legal result of an assault." The court went on: "Even if it be shown that the substantial injuries which the plaintiff suffered are due to her own improper conduct, this is not a defense to a charge of assault; the issue is whether the assault was committed. Proof of the assault entitles the plaintiff to a verdict for at least nominal damages and to such special damages in addition as the plaintiff has alleged, and proved to have proximately resulted from the assault. A violation of a legal right like that alleged in the instant case, imports damage."

Unfortunately, the concept that a "violation of a legal right" avails a plaintiff of nominal damages, correctly applied to a case of common law assault, is picked up and incorrectly applied in the case of Keller v. Carone, 85 A.2d 489 (Conn. 1951), an ordinary negligence case. There the defendants admitted "liability" for striking the rear end of the car in which the plaintiff was riding. Damages were disputed. Finding the plaintiff not credible on the subject of her injuries, the trier of fact found for the defendants and judgment was entered in their favor.

On appeal, the Supreme Court, citing *Schmeltz v. Tracy*, said the following:

> It is true that the effect of the defendants' admission of liability was to establish the fact that a technical legal injury had been done by them to

the plaintiff, and this entitled the plaintiff to at least nominal damages. This court, however, will not reverse for a mere failure to award nominal damages if substantial justice has been done. Inasmuch as the plaintiff failed to prove any actual damage, it was not reversible error to enter judgment for the defendants.

[The court discusses another Connecticut case taking this position.]

Can these basic common law principles and the more recent Supreme Court pronouncements be reconciled? Not by this trial court. But this court can use the actual holdings of the cases both to heed the principles of the extant common law and to avoid error. The cases hold that when the negligence of the defendant has not been proved to be a proximate cause of any injuries to the plaintiff, it is not reversible error for the trier to find for the defendant and to award zero damages. This court so finds in the instant case.

The court enters judgment for the defendants.

PREPARING FOR CLASS

1. How did courts misunderstand the significance of *Schmeltz v. Tracy*? What kind of harm does an assault case require? How is that different from the kind of harm required in a negligence case?

2. What are nominal damages? Why are they not available in negligence cases?

3. What policies are served by denying recovery in a case like *Preston*?

INCREASING YOUR UNDERSTANDING

1. In Torts I, we're interested in damage as an essential part of the plaintiff's negligence case but not in "damages," the compensation plaintiffs receive for their injuries. Without personal injury or property damage, the plaintiff has no case. With a broad call of the question about whether the plaintiff could recover in a negligence claim against the defendant you will write, after discussing causation, something simple like, "The plaintiff must also demonstrate harm, which she can because her leg was broken," or "Was the plaintiff damaged? Yes, her house was destroyed," but you should not consider in a Torts I essay how the plaintiff will be compensated for those losses or how a lawyer would argue for the recovery of money for medical bills, lost wages, pain and suffering, disfigurement, etc. Those are Torts II topics.

2. Personal injury that would satisfy the harm requirement is some kind of bodily harm (broken bones, tissue damage, scars, internal injuries,

disease, disability, e.g.) or emotional injury (depression, humiliation, fear, e.g.) caused by the tort. Property damage is harm to plaintiff's personal property (car fender dented, clothing destroyed, e.g.) or real property (building burns, house windows shatter, e.g.).

APPLYING THE LAW

Professor Butler had a client who came to her because he wanted to sue the garage that put new tires on his car. The garage had mixed radial and non-radial tires, which is dangerous. The client had realized the error as soon as he returned home.

> Professor B: Did you contact the garage?
> Client: Yes.
> Professor B: What did they do?
> Client: They had me come in, and they replaced the tires.
> Professor B: So what's the problem?
> Client: I could have been in an accident.
> Professor B: But you weren't in an accident.
> Client: But I could have been.
> Professor B: But you weren't. How were you harmed by this?
> Client: (*leaning forward, tapping two fingers to his temple, speaking in a serious tone*) Emotional distress.

Did the client have a claim?

B.   ACTUAL CAUSATION

1.   *Primary Tests for Causation*

a.   But-For

According to *Prosser and Keeton on Torts*, 5th ed., §41, "An act or omission is not regarded as a cause of an event if the particular event would have occurred without it. . . . [M]any courts have derived a rule, commonly known as the 'but for' or 'sine qua non' rule, which may be stated as follows: The defendant's conduct is a cause of the event if the event would not have occurred but for that conduct; conversely, the defendant's conduct is not a cause if the event, if the event would have occurred without it."

Stacy v. Knickerbocker Ice Co.
54 N.W. 1091 (Wis. 1893)

[Defendant ice company was cutting and removing ice from a lake to put into ice houses. Defendant hired plaintiff's horses to do this. Clifford and Newton were hitching the horses on the ice when the horses became frightened and ran in the opposite of the intended direction. Although Clifford and Newton tried vigorously and persistently to control the horses, they could not. Therefore, the horses] reached a place from which the ice had recently been removed, over which two or three inches of ice had again formed. The whole surface of the lake was covered by a recent fall of snow, so that the line between such thin ice and the adjoining thick ice was not visible, and no fence, guards, or other signals had been put there to indicate the place from which the ice had been removed. The horses broke through the thin ice, and both were drowned. This action is to recover the value of such horses. At the close of the testimony, which conclusively established the facts above stated, the court directed a verdict for the ice company. A motion by plaintiff for a new trial was denied, and judgment for defendant entered pursuant to the verdict thus directed. Plaintiff appeals from such judgment.

LYON, C.J., (after stating the facts).
. . . It is maintained that the ice company was negligent in three particulars, which negligence caused or contributed to the loss of the horses. These are: (1) It failed to indicate the location of the thin ice by a fence, as required by [statute]; (2) it failed to notify Clifford of the location of the thin ice; and (3) it failed to have ropes and appliances at the place of the accident to be used in getting the horses out of the water before they drowned. The testimony has been carefully examined, and we think it demonstrates that, had all these precautions been taken, they would not have saved the horses.

I. They were uncontrollable, were rearing and plunging, and getting away from the place where they became frightened as rapidly as they could. The fence of the statute (which is a single fence board nailed on 2 by 4 inch posts, 3 ½ feet from the surface upon which the posts stand) would have been but gossamer before those powerful horses, frantic with fright, upon whom two strong men could make no impression. . . .

II. Exact knowledge by Clifford of the location of the thin ice is not a possible factor in the loss of the horses, for, had he been fully advised where the thin ice commenced, he was powerless to prevent the horses going upon it. He went into the water with them, and was rescued. Were he suing the plaintiff for negligence, we would have a case where the fact that he had not such knowledge might be material, but we do not regard it material here.

III. We are aware of no rule of law which required the ice company to have, at the place and time of the accident, ropes and appliances suitable for use in hauling the horses out of the water. Moreover, had such ropes and appliances been there at the time, the proof is quite conclusive that they would have been of no avail. The horses fell into deep water and went under the ice, and were undoubtedly dead when the bystanders had succeeded in rescuing Clifford, who came near being drowned. . . .

The judgment of the circuit court must be affirmed.

PREPARING FOR CLASS

Why wasn't the defendant's negligence the actual cause of the loss of the horses?

INCREASING YOUR UNDERSTANDING

Applying the but-for rule requires the jury to imagine an alternate reality in which the defendant is not negligent—one in which the defendant does what the plaintiff thinks the defendant should have done. For example, a traveling dance troupe is negligent because it does not take on tour a portable floor used to protect dancers from poor conditions on the stages they travel to. In a sliding movement, a dancer is jabbed by a large wooden splinter from the stage floor. Imagine the company is not negligent. Imagine it takes the floor. Now, the splinter is covered by the portable floor and does not go into the dancer's leg. Failure to take the portable floor is the actual cause of the dancer's injury. On the other hand, imagine a woman riding in a friend's car. Approaching a toll road, the friend has her head down below the dashboard, looking for change in the ashtray. The driver in the car ahead slams on his brakes, and the friend rear-ends the car, injuring her passenger. The woman does not want to sue her friend, so she sues the driver ahead because his brake lights weren't working. Imagine the brake-slammer is not negligent. Imagine his brake lights come on. Does this change things? No. The friend still has her head down below the dashboard and does not see the brake lights, and she still runs into him. His negligence in maintaining his brake lights is not the actual cause of her injury.

APPLYING THE LAW

1. A director of a college play negligently decided to use a real knife in a climactic stabbing scene. The knife-wielding actor was supposed to strike a protective stab pad hidden in an actress's costume, but on opening night he missed the stab pad and punctured the actress's lung. The actress sued the director. Her theory of negligence was that he did not use a prop knife, which would have a plastic blade that disappeared into the shaft on impact. Was the director's negligence the actual cause of the actress's injury?

2. Off-duty police officers were engaging in target practice at an abandoned farm. A statute required them to post warning signs at the farm entrance, but they did not post signs. A three-year-old boy who had gotten lost while camping with his family wandered onto the farm and was shot. Was the officers' negligent failure to post the warning signs the actual cause of the boy's injuries?

Hill v. Edmonds
270 N.Y.S.2d 1020 (N.Y. 1966)

Memorandum by the Court.

In a negligence action to recover damages for personal injury, plaintiff appeals from a judgment of the Supreme Court . . . which dismissed the complaint as against defendant . . . upon the court's decision at the close of plaintiff's case upon a jury trial.

Judgment reversed, on the law, and new trial granted, with costs to appellant to abide the event. No questions of fact have been considered.

At the close of plaintiff's case the court dismissed the complaint against the owner of a tractor truck who on a stormy night left it parked without lights in the middle of a road where the car in which plaintiff was a passenger collided with it from the rear. From the testimony of the driver of the car the court concluded that she was guilty of negligence and was solely responsible for the collision. That testimony was that she saw the truck when it was four car lengths ahead of her and that she saw it in enough time to turn. . . . Assuming, arguendo, that she was negligent, the accident could not have happened had not the truck owner allowed his unlighted vehicle to stand in the middle of the highway. Where separate acts of negligence combine to produce directly a single injury each tortfeasor is responsible for the entire result, even though his act alone might not have caused it. Accordingly, the complaint against the truck owner must be reinstated and a new trial had.

PREPARING FOR CLASS

1. Why did the trial court dismiss the case? Form your answer to this question in causation terms, not fault terms.

2. Was this the correct decision? Why or why not?

3. Apply the but-for test to the truck driver only. Is the truck driver's negligence the but-for cause? Now apply the but-for test to the car driver only. Is the car driver's negligence the but-for cause?

4. Is it possible for an injury to have two causes?

INCREASING YOUR UNDERSTANDING

This case involves concurrent causes, what we'll call "Type 1 concurrent causes." With Type 1 concurrent causes, no one cause is enough to cause the injury by itself. The other cause is (or the other causes are) required. For example, at the end of the day, a road crew leaves an exposed hole in a residential street. A driver comes down that street without headlights, although it is dusk. Because he does not have headlights, he does not see the hole, and he drives into it, injuring his passenger. Neither cause is enough by itself. The hole in the road does not cause injury unless the driver does not have his headlights on and does not see it. Driving without headlights does not cause the accident unless the hole is in the road. Type 1 concurrent causes don't present a problem. When you see multiple potential causes, you simply apply the but-for test to them individually, one at a time. The Type 1 concurrent causes will all satisfy the test.

b.   Substantial Factor

Pieper v. Neuendorf Transp. Co.
274 N.W.2d 674 (Wis. 1979)

ABRAHAMSON, J.

[Pieper was a mechanic at a Sunoco station. Along with his employer (Rolling), two fellow employees, and a driver for Neuendorf Transportation, Pieper unloaded a 1,200 pound pipe-bending machine from a Neuendorf truck. Rolling did not have the proper equipment to unload the machine and so did it by stacking tires under the tailgate of the truck and attempting to glide the machine off the truck and onto the tires. Pieper knew this was a dangerous idea but participated anyway and was injured in the process.]

Special verdict questions were submitted to the jury, and the jury concluded that Rolling, Pieper and Neuendorf (through its driver) were negligent with respect to the unloading of the truck and that the negligence of Rolling and of the Neuendorf driver caused Pieper's injuries. The jury responded that Pieper's negligence was not a cause of his injuries. The jury attributed the causal negligence as follows: Neuendorf Transportation Company (by its driver), 50 percent; Rolling 50 percent; Pieper 0 percent. . . .

The trial court concluded that if the jury found Pieper negligent as to the unloading of the truck, his negligence was a cause of his injuries as a matter of law. . . .

Because the jury made no comparison of Pieper's negligence, the trial court set aside the verdict and granted a new trial on the issue of negligence.

We agree with the trial court that the jury's finding cannot stand. Pieper's negligence was causal as a matter of law.

This court has frequently stated the rule that negligence is causal if it is a substantial factor in producing the harm. The phrase "substantial factor" denotes that the conduct has such an effect in producing the injury as to lead a reasonable person to regard it as a cause, using that word in the popular sense. There may be several substantial factors in any given case. Under the substantial factor test, Pieper's negligence, to wit, his voluntary participation in unloading the truck with knowledge of an open and obvious danger, clearly was one substantial factor in causing his injury.

In Sampson v. Laskin, 224 N.W.2d 594 (1975), the employees fell while straddling an open gap in an elevator shaft which they had bridged with a steel plate. One employee had grease on the bottom of his shoes. The jury found both employees negligent with respect to their own safety because they voluntarily placed themselves in a position of peril. However, the jury found that the negligence was not causal. Setting aside the jury answer as to lack of causation, this court concluded that the employees "(were) as a matter of law . . . guilty of contributory negligence, meaning negligence that contributed to their falling as a substantial factor in causing the falling." . . .

Pieper, citing Leatherman v. Garza, 159 N.W.2d 18 (1968), correctly argues that this court cannot set aside the jury verdict if there is any credible evidence in the record which supports the jury's answer. However, Pieper fails to point out any evidence in the record which supports the jury's finding that while Pieper was negligent, his negligence was not a substantial factor in producing the injury. No such evidence can be found in the record. The trial court's decision to grant a new trial of the issue of the comparison of negligence must be affirmed. . . .

PREPARING FOR CLASS

1. How is the substantial-factor test different from the but-for test? Does it appear harder or easier to satisfy?

2. Would the substantial-factor test have produced a different result in *Hill*? Would the but-for test have produced a different result here?

3. The court writes, "The trial court concluded that if the jury found Pieper negligent as to the unloading of the truck, his negligence was a cause of his injuries as a matter of law." Does this mean that under the substantial-factor test once a jury finds negligence, it must find that the negligence is causal?

INCREASING YOUR UNDERSTANDING

This casebook sharply distinguishes the but-for and substantial-factor tests, but some state courts are not so precise. You may, in your life as a lawyer, come across opinions that mix and blur the two ideas. For example, in Doe v. Boys Clubs of Greater Dallas, Inc., 907 S.W.2d 472 (Tex. 1995), the court wrote,

"The test for cause in fact is whether the negligent 'act or omission was a substantial factor in bringing about injury,' without which the harm would not have occurred." Something "without which the harm would not have occurred" is a but-for cause, but it is also the Texas Supreme Court's definition of substantial factor. At this stage of your legal education, keep the ideas separate, while knowing the boundaries between them may not be rigid in practice.

Anderson v. Minneapolis, St. Paul, & Sault Ste. Marie Railway
179 N.W. 45 (1920)

LEES, C.

This is a fire case, brought against the defendant railway company and the Director General of Railroads. . . . Plaintiff had a verdict. The appeal is from an order denying a motion in the alternative for judgment notwithstanding the verdict or for a new trial. . . .

Plaintiff's case in chief was directed to proving that in August, 1918, one of defendant's engines started a fire in a bog near the west side of plaintiff's land; that it smoldered there until October 12, 1918, when it flared up and burned his property, shortly before it was reached by one of the great fires which swept through Northeastern Minnesota at the close of that day. Defendant introduced evidence to show that on and prior to October 12th fires were burning west and northwest of, and were swept by the wind towards, plaintiff's premises. It did not show how such fires originated, neither did it clearly and certainly trace the destruction of plaintiff's property to them. . . .

[The defendant's appeal contended that the following jury instruction was in error.]

"If the plaintiff was burned out by some fire other than the bog fire, which other fire was not set by one of defendant's engines, then, of course, defendant is not liable. If plaintiff was burned out by fire set by one of defendant's engines in combination with some other fire not set by one of its engines, then it is liable. . . .

"If you find that other fires not set by one of defendant's engines mingled with one that was set by one of defendant's engines, there may be difficulty in determining whether you should find that the fire set by the engine was a material or substantial element in causing plaintiff's damage. If it was, the defendant is liable; otherwise, it is not. . . .

"If you find that bog fire was set by defendant's engine, and that some greater fire swept over it before it reached plaintiff's land, then it will be for you to determine whether the bog fire . . . was a material or substantial factor in causing plaintiff's damage. If it was, defendant was liable. If it was not, defendant was not liable. If the bog fire was set by one of defendant's engines, and if one of defendant's engines also set a fire or fires west of Kettle River, and those fires combined and burned over plaintiff's property, then the defendant is liable." . . .

The following proposition is stated in defendant's brief and relied on for a reversal:

"If plaintiff's property was damaged by a number of fires combining, one being the fire pleaded, and the others being of no responsible origin, but of such sufficient or superior force that they would have produced the damage to plaintiff's property, regardless of the fire pleaded, then defendant was not liable."

This proposition is based upon Cook v. M., St. P. & S.S.M. Ry. Co., 74 N. W. 561. . . . If the *Cook* case merely decides that one who negligently sets a fire is not liable if another's property is damaged, unless it is made to appear that the fire was a material element in the destruction of the property, there can be no question about the soundness of the decision. But if it decides that if such fire combines with another of no responsible origin, and after the union of the two fires they destroy the property and either fire independently of the other would have destroyed it, then, irrespective of whether the first fire was or was not a material factor in the destruction of the property, there is no liability, we are not prepared to adopt the doctrine as the law of this state. If a fire set by the engine of one railroad company unites with a fire set by the engine of another company, there is joint and several liability, even though either fire would have destroyed plaintiff's property. But if the doctrine of the *Cook* case is applied, and one of the fires is of unknown origin, there is no liability. . . . [T]here [should] be liability in such a case. We therefore hold that the trial court did not err in refusing to instruct the jury in accordance with the rule laid down in the *Cook* Case. . . .

We find no error requiring a reversal, and hence the order appealed from is affirmed.

PREPARING FOR CLASS

1. Why did the defendant object to the jury instruction?

2. Apply the but-for test to the defendant. What result? Apply the but-for test to the fire of unknown origin. What result? Do these results fairly reflect the defendant's responsibility for plaintiff's losses? Do they fairly treat the plaintiff?

3. What various ways could *Cook* be interpreted? What interpretation does the court reject? Why?

4. What rule would the court apply in a case like this? (What is "a case like this"?) What result under that rule?

INCREASING YOUR UNDERSTANDING

This case involves Type 2 concurrent causes. With Type 2, either cause is enough by itself to cause the harm. The plaintiff cannot prove actual causation with Type 2 concurrent causes if the but-for test is applied. Do you understand why? (That's what the case was about.) How should a judge instruct the jury on causation if the case involves Type 2 concurrent causes? (That's also what the case was about.)

APPLYING THE LAW

Parker saw a beautiful young woman, Helen, in the stacks of the university library, and he began to flirt with her. Helen was friendly in return, so Parker leaned in and kissed her. She slapped him and stormed out. Having coffee in the student union that evening, Helen told her friends, David and Derek, that she thought Parker was a jerk for trying to kiss her and was really angry about it, but she also confessed that the kiss was great and she enjoyed it. David and Derek dislike Parker, but they dislike Helen's boyfriend, Troy, even more because they think he is jealous, possessive, and dangerously hot-tempered. Later that night, David went to Troy's dorm room and negligently (considering the likelihood Troy would do something violent) told him about Parker's pass at Helen. He emphasized how angry Helen was at Parker and didn't mention that she liked the kiss. Immediately after David left, Derek, unaware of David's visit, called Troy on his cell and negligently told him about the library incident, but he omitted the fact that Helen was angry and just told Troy how much she had enjoyed the kiss. A furious Troy went to Parker's dorm room and beat him with a baseball bat. Parker has sued David and Derek for their negligence. In his deposition, Troy was asked, "Which thought made you want to beat up Parker? The idea that he had upset Helen, or the idea that she liked being kissed by him?" Troy replied, "I guess it could have been either one. I mean both made me furious, like, I hadn't even, like sorted through what David said when Derek called. I don't know. It could have been one or the other. Either's enough to push you over. You know what I mean?" Can Parker prove that either David or Derek was the cause-in-fact of his being beaten by Troy?

2.   *Sufficiency of Proof*

Reynolds v. Texas & Pac. Ry. Co.
37 La. Ann. 694 (La. App. 1885)

FENNER, J.
[The plaintiff and his wife sued the defendant railroad company for injuries the wife suffered falling down a staircase.]

The train was behind time. Several witnesses testify that passengers were warned to "hurry up." Mrs. Reynolds, a corpulent woman, weighing two hundred and fifty pounds, emerging from the bright light of the sitting-room, which naturally exaggerated the outside darkness, and hastening down these unlighted steps, made a misstep in some way and was precipitated beyond the narrow platform in front and down the slope beyond, incurring the serious injuries complained of. . . .

[The defendant] contends that, even conceding the negligence of the company in [not providing lights or a handrail], it does not follow that the accident to plaintiff was necessarily caused thereby, but that she might well have made the misstep and fallen even had it been broad daylight. We concede that this is possible, and recognize the distinction between post hoc and propter hoc. But where the negligence of the defendant greatly multiplies the chances of accident to the plaintiff, and is of a character naturally leading to its occurrence, the mere possibility that it might have happened without the negligence is not sufficient to break the chain of cause and effect between the negligence and the injury. Courts, in such matters, consider the natural and ordinary course of events, and do not indulge in fanciful suppositions. The whole tendency of the evidence connects the accident with the negligence. . . .

Judgment affirmed.

PREPARING FOR CLASS

1. How, apparently, did the defendant contend that it was not the cause of Mrs. Reynolds's fall?

2. In the face of explanations other than the defendant's negligence, how could a jury find that the defendant's negligence caused plaintiff's injuries?

APPLYING THE LAW

A bank was located in a high-crime, commercial area. The security camera at the night deposit box had been smashed by vandals and never repaired, and there were no lights other than a street light. At 2:30 A.M., an employee of the pizza place across the street was depositing the night's cash when he was shot and seriously injured by a mugger waiting for him in the dark behind a shrub next to the deposit box. Assume the bank was negligent. Was that negligence the actual cause of the pizza employee's injuries?

New York Central R.R. v. Grimstad
264 F. 334 (2d Cir. 1920)

WARD, C.J.

. . . The charge of negligence is failure to equip the barge with proper life-preservers and other necessary and proper appliances, for want of which the decedent, having fallen into the water, was drowned.

... The tug Mary M, entering the slip between Piers 1 and 2, bumped against the barge. The decedent's wife, feeling the shock, came out from the cabin, looked on one side of the barge, and saw nothing, and then went across the deck to the other side, and discovered her husband in the water about 10 feet from the barge holding up his hands out of the water. He did not know how to swim. She immediately ran back into the cabin for a small line, and when she returned with it he had disappeared. ...

On the second question, whether a life buoy would have saved the decedent from drowning, we think the jury were left to pure conjecture and speculation. A jury might well conclude that a light near an open hatch or a rail on the side of a vessel's deck would have prevented a person's falling into the hatch or into the water, in the dark. But there is nothing whatever to show that the decedent was not drowned because he did not know how to swim, nor anything to show that, if there had been a life buoy on board, the decedent's wife would have got it in time, that is, sooner than she got the small line, or, if she had, that she would have thrown it so that her husband could have seized it, or, if she did, that he would have seized it, or that, if he did, it would have prevented him from drowning.

The court erred in denying the defendant's motion to dismiss the complaint at the end of the case.

Judgment reversed.

PREPARING FOR CLASS

1. Don't juries make inferences all the time? How is this different?

2. How is the inference of causation here different from the inference in *Reynolds*?

Kramer Service v. Wilkins
186 So. 625 (Miss. 1939)

GRIFFITH, J.

[Plaintiff/appellee was injured when he opened his hotel room door and a piece of a glass from a broken transom fell and hit his head.]

[T]here is plain and serious error in the matter of the amount of the damages. The wound on the temple did not heal, and some months after the injury appellee was advised by his local physician to visit a specialist in skin diseases, which he did ... about two years after the injury, and it was then found that at the point where the injury occurred to appellee's temple, a skin cancer had developed, of which a cure had not been fully effected at the time of the trial, some three years after the injury first mentioned.

Appellee sued for a large sum in damages, averring and contending that the cancer resulted from the stated injury; and the jury evidently accepted that contention, since there was an award by the verdict in the sum of twenty thousand dollars. Appellant requested an instruction to the effect that the cancer or any prolongation of the trouble on account thereof should not be taken into consideration by the jury, but this instruction was refused.

Two physicians or medical experts, and only two, were introduced as witnesses, and both were specialists in skin diseases and dermal traumatisms. One testified that it was possible that a trauma such as appellee suffered upon his temple, could or would cause a skin cancer at the point of injury, but that the chances that such a result would ensue from such a cause would be only one out of one hundred cases. The other testified that there is no causal connection whatever between trauma and cancer, and went on to illustrate that if there were such a connection nearly every person of mature age would be suffering with cancer. . . .

It seems therefore hardly to be debatable but that appellant was entitled to the requested instruction as regards the cancer; and since, except as to that element, the verdict could not have been large, the verdict and judgment must be reversed on the issue of the amount of the damages.

There is one heresy in the judicial forum which appears to be Hydra-headed, and although cut off again and again, has the characteristic of an endless renewal. That heresy is that proof that a past event possibly happened, or that a certain result was possibly caused by a past event, is sufficient in probative force to take the question to a jury. Such was never the law in this state, and we are in accord with almost all of the other common-law states. . . .

Post hoc ergo propter hoc is not sound as evidence or argument. Nor is it sufficient for a plaintiff, seeking recovery for alleged negligence by another toward the plaintiff, to show a possibility that the injury complained of was caused by negligence. Possibilities will not sustain a verdict. It must have a better foundation. . . .

Taking the medical testimony in this case in the strongest light in which it could be reasonably interpreted in behalf of the plaintiff, this testimony is that as a possibility a skin cancer could be caused by an injury such as here happened, but as a probability the physicians were in agreement that there was or is no such a probability.

And the medical testimony is conclusive on both judge and jury in this case. That testimony is undisputed that after long and anxious years of research the exact cause of cancer remains unknown—there is no dependably known origin to which it can be definitely traced or ascribed. If, then, the cause be unknown to all those who have devoted their lives to a study of the subject, it is wholly beyond the range of the common experience and observation of judges and jurors, and in such a case medical testimony when undisputed, as here, must be accepted and acted upon in the same manner as is other undisputed evidence; otherwise the jury would be allowed to resort to and act upon nothing else than the proposition post hoc ergo propter hoc, which, as already mentioned, this Court has long ago rejected as unsound, whether as evidence or as argument.

In all other than the exceptional cases now to be mentioned, the testimony of medical experts, or other experts, is advisory only; but we repeat that where the issue is one which lies wholly beyond the range of the experience or observation of laymen and of which they can have no appreciable knowledge, courts and juries must of necessity depend upon and accept the undisputed testimony of reputable specialists, else there would be no substantial foundation upon which to rest a conclusion. . . .

Affirmed as to liability; reversed and remanded on the issue of the amount of the damages.

PREPARING FOR CLASS

1. What evidence did the plaintiff present of the causal connection between the cut and his cancer?

2. Why shouldn't the jury be permitted to evaluate the plaintiff's evidence? Isn't that their job?

3. What kind of evidence would the plaintiff have had to produce to make it to the jury?

4. What is "post hoc ergo propter hoc"? How would submitting the case to the jury invite that kind of false logic?

INCREASING YOUR UNDERSTANDING

Proving a scientific connection generally requires expert testimony that this kind of incident can produce plaintiff's kind of injury and that, to a reasonable degree of medical certainty, the incident did produce plaintiff's harm in this case. So, if a woman sued her cell phone manufacturer for her brain tumor, she would need evidence that cell phone usage causes brain tumors and that, in her case, the expert believes to a reasonable degree of medical certainty that using defendant's cell phone caused the woman's brain tumor. Sometimes, though, the scientific connection is within common knowledge and expert testimony will not be necessary. For example, Kramer would not have needed expert evidence that the falling glass scarred his temple. People know that cuts cause scars.

Herskovits v. Group Health Cooperative of Puget Sound
664 P.2d 474 (Wash. 1983)

Dore, J.
This appeal [of the trial court's grant of summary judgment to the defendant] raises the issue of whether an estate can maintain an action for

professional negligence as a result of failure to timely diagnose lung cancer, where the estate can show probable reduction in statistical chance for survival but cannot show and/or prove that with timely diagnosis and treatment, decedent probably would have lived to normal life expectancy.

Both counsel advised that for the purpose of this appeal we are to *assume* that the respondent Group Health Cooperative of Puget Sound and Dr. William Spencer negligently failed to diagnose Herskovits' cancer on his first visit to the hospital and *proximately* caused a 14 percent reduction in his chances of survival. It is undisputed that Herskovits had less than a 50 percent chance of survival at all times herein. . . .

At hearing on the motion for summary judgment, plaintiff was unable to produce expert testimony that the delay in diagnosis "probably" or "more likely than not" caused her husband's death. The affidavit and deposition of plaintiff's expert witness, Dr. Jonathan Ostrow, construed in the most favorable light possible to plaintiff, indicated that had the diagnosis of lung cancer been made in December 1974, the patient's possibility of 5-year survival was 39 percent. At the time of initial diagnosis of cancer 6 months later, the possibility of a 5-year survival was reduced to 25 percent. Dr. Ostrow testified he felt a diagnosis perhaps could have been made as early as December 1974, or January 1975, about 6 months before the surgery to remove Mr. Herskovits' lung in June 1975. [He died on March 22, 1977.] . . .

This court has held that a person who negligently renders aid and consequently increases the risk of harm to those he is trying to assist is liable for any physical damages he causes. Brown v. MacPherson's, Inc., 545 P.2d 13 (Wash. 1975). In *Brown*, the court cited Restatement (Second) of Torts §323 (1965), which reads:

> One who undertakes . . . to render services to another which he should recognize as necessary for the protection of the other's person or things, is subject to liability to the other for physical harm resulting from his failure to exercise reasonable care to perform his undertaking, if (a) his failure to exercise such care increases the risk of such harm. . . .

This court heretofore has not faced the issue of whether, under §323(a), proof that the defendant's conduct increased the risk of death by decreasing the chances of survival is sufficient to take the issue of proximate cause to the jury. Some courts in other jurisdictions have allowed the proximate cause issue to go to the jury on this type of proof. These courts emphasized the fact that defendants' conduct deprived the decedents of a "significant" chance to survive or recover, rather than requiring proof that with absolute certainty the defendants' conduct caused the physical injury. The underlying reason is that it is not for the wrongdoer, who put the possibility of recovery beyond realization, to say afterward that the result was inevitable.

Other jurisdictions have rejected this approach, generally holding that unless the plaintiff is able to show that it was more likely than not that the harm was caused by the defendant's negligence, proof of a decreased chance of survival is not enough to take the proximate cause question to the jury. These courts have concluded that the defendant should not be liable where the decedent more than likely would have died anyway.

The ultimate question raised here is whether the relationship between the increased risk of harm and Herskovits' death is sufficient to hold Group Health responsible. Is a 36 percent (from 39 percent to 25 percent) reduction in the decedent's chance for survival sufficient evidence of causation to allow the jury to consider the possibility that the physician's failure to timely diagnose the illness was the proximate cause of his death? We answer in the affirmative. To decide otherwise would be a blanket release from liability for doctors and hospitals any time there was less than a 50 percent chance of survival, regardless of how flagrant the negligence.

We are persuaded by the reasoning of the Pennsylvania Supreme Court in Hamil v. Bashline[, 392 A.2d 1280 (Pa. 1978)]. While *Hamil* involved an original survival chance of greater than 50 percent, we find the rationale used by the *Hamil* court to apply equally to cases such as the present one, where the original survival chance is less than 50 percent. The plaintiff's decedent was suffering from severe chest pains. His wife transported him to the hospital where he was negligently treated in the emergency unit. The wife, because of the lack of help, took her husband to a private physician's office, where he died. In an action brought under the wrongful death and survivorship statutes, the main medical witness testified that if the hospital had employed proper treatment, the decedent would have had a substantial chance of surviving the attack. The medical expert expressed his opinion in terms of a 75 percent chance of survival. It was also the doctor's opinion that the substantial loss of a chance of recovery was the result of the defendant hospital's failure to provide prompt treatment. The defendant's expert witness testified that the patient would have died regardless of any treatment provided by the defendant hospital.

The *Hamil* court reiterated the oft-repeated principle of tort law that the mere occurrence of an injury does not prove negligence, but the defendant's conduct must be a proximate cause of the plaintiff's injury. The court also referred to the traditional "but for" test, with the qualification that multiple causes may culminate in injury. The court then cited Restatement (Second) of Torts §323 (1965) as authority to relax the degree of certitude normally required of plaintiff's evidence in order to make a case for the jury. The court held that once a plaintiff has introduced evidence that a defendant's negligent act or omission increased the risk of harm to a person in plaintiff's position, and that the harm was in fact sustained, "it becomes a question for the jury as to whether or not that increased risk was a substantial factor in producing the harm."

The *Hamil* court distinguished the facts of that case from the general tort case in which a plaintiff alleges that a defendant's act or omission set in motion a force which resulted in harm. In the typical tort case, the "but for" test, requiring proof that damages or death probably would not have occurred "but for" the negligent conduct of the defendant, is appropriate. In *Hamil* and the instant case, however, the defendant's act or omission failed in a *duty* to protect against harm from *another source*. Thus, as the *Hamil* court noted, the fact finder is put in the position of having to consider not only what did occur, but also what might have occurred.

Such cases by their very nature elude the degree of certainty one would prefer and upon which the law normally insists before a person may be held liable. Nevertheless, in order that an actor is not completely insulated because of uncertainties as to the consequences of his negligent conduct, Section 323(a) tacitly acknowledges this difficulty and permits the issue to go to the jury upon a less than normal threshold of proof. The *Hamil* court held that once a plaintiff has demonstrated that the defendant's acts or omissions have increased the risk of harm to another, such evidence furnishes a basis for the jury to make a determination as to whether such increased risk was in turn a substantial factor in bringing about the resultant harm.

In Hicks v. United States[, 368 F.2d 626 (4th Cir. 1966)], the Court of Appeals set forth the rationale for deviation from the normal requirements of proof in a case such as the one presently before us. The following quotation from *Hicks* is frequently cited in cases adopting loss of a chance because it succinctly defines the doctrine: "Rarely is it possible to demonstrate to an absolute certainty what would have happened in circumstances that the wrongdoer did not allow to come to pass. The law does not in the existing circumstances require the plaintiff to show to a certainty that the patient would have lived had she been hospitalized and operated on promptly."

Under the *Hamil* decision, once a plaintiff has demonstrated that defendant's acts or omissions in a situation to which §323(a) applies have increased the risk of harm to another, such evidence furnishes a basis for the fact finder to go further and find that such increased risk was in turn a substantial factor in bringing about the resultant harm. The necessary proximate cause will be established if the jury finds such cause. It is not necessary for a plaintiff to introduce evidence to establish that the negligence resulted in the injury or death, but simply that the negligence increased the risk of injury or death. The step from the increased risk to causation is one for the jury to make. . . .

Where percentage probabilities and decreased probabilities are submitted into evidence, there is simply no danger of speculation on the part of the jury. More speculation is involved in requiring the medical expert to testify as to what would have happened had the defendant not been negligent. . . .

Causing reduction of the opportunity to recover (loss of chance) by one's negligence, however, does not necessitate a total recovery against the negligent party for all damages caused by the victim's death. Damages should be awarded to the injured party or his family based only on damages caused directly by premature death, such as lost earnings and additional medical expenses, etc.

We reverse the trial court and reinstate the cause of action.

Rosellini, J., concurs.

Pearson, Justice (concurring).

I agree with the majority that the trial court erred in granting defendant's motion for summary judgment. I cannot, however, agree with the majority's reasoning in reaching this decision. . . .

We must decide whether Dr. Ostrow's testimony established that the act complained of (the alleged delay in diagnosis) "probably" or "more likely than not" caused Mr. Herskovits' subsequent disability. In order to make this determination, we must first define the "subsequent disability" suffered by Mr. Herskovits. Therein lies the crux of this case, for it is possible to define the injury or "disability" to Mr. Herskovits in at least two different ways. First, and most obviously, the injury to Mr. Herskovits might be viewed as his death. Alternatively, however, the injury or disability may be seen as the reduction of Mr. Herskovits' chance of surviving the cancer from which he suffered.

Therefore, although the issue before us is primarily one of causation, resolution of that issue requires us to identify the nature of the injury to the decedent. Our conception of the injury will substantially affect our analysis. If the injury is determined to be the death of Mr. Herskovits, then under the established principles of proximate cause plaintiff has failed to make a prima facie case. Dr. Ostrow was unable to state that probably, or more likely than not, Mr. Herskovits' death was caused by defendant's negligence. On the contrary, it is clear from Dr. Ostrow's testimony that Mr. Herskovits would have probably died from cancer even with the exercise of reasonable care by defendant. Accordingly, if we perceive the death of Mr. Herskovits as the injury in this case, we must affirm the trial court, unless we determine that it is proper to depart substantially from the traditional requirements of establishing proximate cause in this type of case.

If, on the other hand, we view the injury to be the reduction of Mr. Herskovits' chance of survival, our analysis might well be different. Dr. Ostrow testified that the failure to diagnose cancer in December 1974 probably caused a substantial reduction in Mr. Herskovits' chance of survival. . . .

I note here that two other problems are created by the latter analysis. First, we have never before considered whether the loss or reduction of a chance of survival is a compensable injury. . . .

I am persuaded [that we should adopt the approach of allowing recovery for loss of a chance] by the thoughtful discussion of a recent commentator. King, *Causation, Valuation, and Chance in Personal Injury Torts Involving Preexisting Conditions and Future Consequences*, 90 Yale L.J. 1353 (1981).

King's basic thesis is explained in the following passage, which is particularly pertinent to the case before us.

> Causation has for the most part been treated as an all-or-nothing proposition. Either a loss was caused by the defendant or it was

not. . . . A plaintiff ordinarily should be required to prove by the applicable standard of proof that the defendant caused the loss in question. What caused a loss, however, should be a separate question from what the nature and extent of the loss are. This distinction seems to have eluded the courts, with the result that lost chances in many respects are compensated either as certainties or not at all.

To illustrate, consider the case in which a doctor negligently fails to diagnose a patient's cancerous condition until it has become inoperable. Assume further that even with a timely diagnosis the patient would have had only a 30% chance of recovering from the disease and surviving over the long term. There are two ways of handling such a case. Under the traditional approach, this loss of a not-better-than-even chance of recovering from the cancer would not be compensable because it did not appear more likely [than] not that the patient would have survived with proper care. Recoverable damages, if any, would depend on the extent to which it appeared that cancer killed the patient sooner than it would have with timely diagnosis and treatment, and on the extent to which the delay in diagnosis aggravated the patient's condition, such as by causing additional pain. A more rational approach, however, would allow recovery for the loss of the chance of cure even though the chance was not better than even. The probability of long-term survival would be reflected in the amount of damages awarded for the loss of the chance. While the plaintiff here could not prove by a preponderance of the evidence that he was denied a cure by the defendant's negligence, he could show by a preponderance that he was deprived of a 30% chance of a cure.

Under the all or nothing approach . . . a plaintiff who establishes that but for the defendant's negligence the decedent had a 51 percent chance of survival may maintain an action for that death. The defendant will be liable for all damages arising from the death, even though there was a 49 percent chance it would have occurred despite his negligence. On the other hand, a plaintiff who establishes that but for the defendant's negligence the decedent had a 49 percent chance of survival recovers nothing.

This all or nothing approach to recovery is criticized by King on several grounds, First, the all or nothing approach is arbitrary. Second, it "subverts the deterrence objectives of tort law by denying recovery for the effects of conduct that causes statistically demonstrable losses. . . . A failure to allocate the cost of these losses to their tortious sources . . . strikes at the integrity of the torts system of loss allocation."

Third, the all or nothing approach creates pressure to manipulate and distort other rules affecting causation and damages in an attempt to mitigate perceived injustices. Fourth, the all or nothing approach gives certain defendants the benefit of an uncertainty which, were it not for their tortious conduct, would not exist. Finally, King argues that the loss of a less than even chance is a loss worthy of redress.

These reasons persuade me that the best resolution of the issue before us is to recognize the loss of a less than even chance as an actionable injury. Therefore, I would hold that plaintiff has established a prima facie issue of proximate cause by producing testimony that defendant probably caused a substantial reduction in Mr. Herskovits' chance of survival. . . .

Finally, it is necessary to consider the amount of damages recoverable in the event that a loss of a chance of recovery is established. Once again, King's discussion provides a useful illustration of the principles which should be applied.

> To illustrate, consider a patient who suffers a heart attack and dies as a result. Assume that the defendant-physician negligently misdiagnosed the patient's condition, but that the patient would have had only a 40% chance of survival even with a timely diagnosis and proper care. Regardless of whether it could be said that the defendant caused the decedent's death, he caused the loss of a chance, and that chance-interest should be completely redressed in its own right. Under the proposed rule, the plaintiff's compensation for the loss of the victim's chance of surviving the heart attack would be 40% of the compensable value of the victim's life had he survived (including what his earning capacity would otherwise have been in the years following death). The value placed on the patient's life would reflect such factors as his age, health, and earning potential, including the fact that he had suffered the heart attack and the assumption that he had survived it. The 40% computation would be applied to that base figure.

I would remand to the trial court for proceedings consistent with this opinion.

PREPARING FOR CLASS

1. Why, under a but-for test of actual causation, can't the widow establish that delayed diagnosis of her husband's cancer caused his death? Do some courts apply the but-for test to cases like this?

2. How is Restatement (Second) of Torts §323 relevant to this case?

3. How is *Hamil* analogous to this case? Is the analogy sufficiently tight to use the case as precedent?

4. Why do cases where the defendant failed to protect the plaintiff from harm from another source always involve a degree of speculation on causation? Is this speculation permissible?

5. Does the court choose to adopt the *Hamil* approach here? Why or why not?

6. What policies does the majority decision serve? How does the court try to be fair to both parties?

7. The concurrence refers to the traditional approach as the "all or nothing" rule. How is that an appropriate description? Some people call the majority approach "relaxed" or "proportional" causation. How are those descriptions appropriate?

8. If this is a wrongful death case, would the concurring judge find for the widow?

9. What, according to the concurring judge, was the wrong done to Mr. Herskovits?

10. How would the jury be instructed under the rule proposed by the concurring judge? How would they award damages under that instruction?

11. What are the five rationales from the King article?

Daubert v. Merrell Dow Pharm., Inc.
43 F.3d 1311 (9th Cir. 1995)

KOZINSKI, C.J.

On remand from the United States Supreme Court, we undertake "the task of ensuring that an expert's testimony both rests on a reliable foundation and is relevant to the task at hand." Daubert v. Merrell Dow Pharmaceuticals, Inc., 509 U.S. 579 (1993).

I

A. BACKGROUND

Two minors brought suit against Merrell Dow Pharmaceuticals, claiming they suffered limb reduction birth defects because their mothers had taken Bendectin, a drug prescribed for morning sickness to about 17.5 million pregnant women in the United States between 1957 and 1982. This appeal deals with an evidentiary question: whether certain expert scientific testimony is admissible to prove that Bendectin caused the plaintiffs' birth defects.

For the most part, we don't know how birth defects come about. We do know they occur in 2-3% of births, whether or not the expectant mother has taken Bendectin. . . . Limb defects are even rarer, occurring in fewer than one birth out of every 1000. But scientists simply do not know how teratogens (chemicals known to cause limb reduction defects) do their damage: They cannot reconstruct the biological chain of events that leads from an expectant mother's ingestion of a teratogenic substance to the stunted development of a baby's limbs. . . .

Not knowing the mechanism whereby a particular agent causes a particular effect is not always fatal to a plaintiff's claim. Causation can be proved even when we don't know precisely how the damage occurred, if there is sufficiently compelling proof that the agent must have caused the damage somehow. One method of proving causation in these circumstances is to use statistical evidence. If 50 people who eat at a restaurant one evening come down with food poisoning during the night, we can infer that the restaurant's food probably contained something unwholesome, even if none of the dishes is available for analysis. This inference is based on the fact that, in our health-conscious society, it is highly unlikely that 50 people who have nothing in common except that they ate at the same restaurant would get food poisoning from independent sources.

It is by such means that plaintiffs here seek to establish that Bendectin is responsible for their injuries. . . .

The opinions proffered by plaintiffs' experts do not, to understate the point, reflect the consensus within the scientific community. The FDA—an agency not known for its promiscuity in approving drugs—continues to approve Bendectin for use by pregnant women because "available data do not demonstrate an association between birth defects and Bendectin." U.S. Department of Health and Human Services News, No. P80-45 (Oct. 7, 1980). Every published study here and abroad—and there have been many—concludes that Bendectin is not a teratogen. In fact, apart from the small but determined group of scientists testifying on behalf of the Bendectin plaintiffs in this and many other cases, there doesn't appear to be a single scientist who has concluded that Bendectin causes limb reduction defects.

It is largely because the opinions proffered by plaintiffs' experts run counter to the substantial consensus in the scientific community that we affirmed the district court's grant of summary judgment the last time the case appeared before us. The standard for admissibility of expert testimony in this circuit at the time was the so-called *Frye* test: Scientific evidence was admissible if it was based on a scientific technique generally accepted as reliable within the scientific community. We found that the district court properly applied this standard, and affirmed. The Supreme Court reversed, holding that *Frye* was superseded by Federal Rule of Evidence 702, and remanded for us to consider the admissibility of plaintiffs' expert testimony under this new standard. . . .

II

A. BRAVE NEW WORLD

Federal judges ruling on the admissibility of expert scientific testimony face a far more complex and daunting task in a post-*Daubert* world than before. The judge's task under *Frye* is relatively simple: to determine whether the method employed by the experts is generally accepted in the scientific community. Under *Daubert*, we must engage in a difficult, two-part analysis. First, we must determine nothing less than whether the experts' testimony reflects "scientific knowledge," whether their findings are "derived by the scientific method," and whether their work product amounts to "good science." Second, we must ensure that the proposed expert testimony is "relevant to the task at hand," i.e., that it logically advances a material aspect of the proposing party's case. The Supreme Court referred to this second prong of the analysis as the "fit" requirement.

The first prong of *Daubert* puts federal judges in an uncomfortable position. The question of admissibility only arises if it is first established that the individuals whose testimony is being proffered are experts in a particular scientific field; here, for example, the Supreme Court waxed eloquent on the impressive qualifications of plaintiffs' experts. Yet something doesn't become "scientific knowledge" just because it's uttered by a scientist; nor can an expert's self-serving assertion that his conclusions were "derived by the scientific method" be deemed conclusive. . . .

The task before us is more daunting still when the dispute concerns matters at the very cutting edge of scientific research, where fact meets theory and certainty dissolves into probability. As the record in this case illustrates, scientists often have vigorous and sincere disagreements as to what research methodology is proper, what should be accepted as sufficient proof for the existence of a "fact," and whether information derived by a particular method can tell us anything useful about the subject under study.

Our responsibility, then, unless we badly misread the Supreme Court's opinion, is to resolve disputes among respected, well-credentialed scientists about matters squarely within their expertise, in areas where there is no scientific consensus as to what is and what is not "good science," and occasionally to reject such expert testimony because it was not "derived by the scientific method." Mindful of our position in the hierarchy of the federal judiciary, we take a deep breath and proceed with this heady task.

B. DEUS EX MACHINA. . . .

Which raises the question: How do we figure out whether scientists have derived their findings through the scientific method or whether their testimony is based on scientifically valid principles? Each expert proffered by the plaintiffs assures us that he has "utiliz[ed] the type of data that is generally and reasonably relied upon by scientists" in the relevant field, and that he has "utilized the methods and methodology that would generally and reasonably be accepted" by people who deal in these matters. The Court held, however, that federal judges perform a "gatekeeping role"; to do so they must satisfy themselves that scientific evidence meets a certain standard of reliability before it is admitted. This means that the expert's bald assurance of validity is not enough. Rather, the party presenting the expert must show that the expert's findings are based on sound science, and this will require some objective, independent validation of the expert's methodology.

While declining to set forth a "definitive checklist or test," the Court did list several factors federal judges can consider in determining whether to admit expert scientific testimony under Fed. R. Evid. 702: whether the theory or technique employed by the expert is generally accepted in the scientific community; whether it's been subjected to peer review and publication; whether it can be and has been tested; and whether the known or potential rate of error is acceptable. We read these factors as illustrative rather than exhaustive; similarly, we do not deem each of them to be equally applicable (or applicable at all) in every case. Rather, we read the Supreme Court as instructing us to determine whether the analysis undergirding the experts' testimony falls within the range of accepted standards governing how scientists conduct their research and reach their conclusions.

One very significant fact to be considered is whether the experts are proposing to testify about matters growing naturally and directly out of research they have conducted independent of the litigation, or whether they have developed their opinions expressly for purposes of testifying. That an expert testifies for money does not necessarily cast doubt on the reliability of his testimony, as few experts appear in court merely as an eleemosynary gesture. But in determining whether proposed expert testimony amounts to good science, we may not ignore the fact that a scientist's normal workplace is the lab or the field, not the courtroom or the lawyer's office. . . .

We have examined carefully the affidavits proffered by plaintiffs' experts, as well as the testimony from prior trials that plaintiffs have introduced in support of that testimony, and find that none of the experts based his testimony on preexisting or independent research. While plaintiffs' scientists are all experts in their respective fields, none claims to have studied the effect of Bendectin on limb reduction defects before being hired to testify in this or related cases.

If the proffered expert testimony is not based on independent research, the party proffering it must come forward with other objective, verifiable evidence that the testimony is based on "scientifically valid principles." One means of showing this is by proof that the research and analysis supporting the proffered conclusions have been subjected to normal scientific scrutiny through peer review and publication.

Peer review and publication do not, of course, guarantee that the conclusions reached are correct; much published scientific research is greeted with intense skepticism and is not borne out by further research. But the test under *Daubert* is not the correctness of the expert's conclusions but the soundness of his methodology. That the research is accepted for publication in a reputable scientific journal after being subjected to the usual rigors of peer review is a significant indication that it is taken seriously by other scientists, i.e., that it meets at least the minimal criteria of good science. ("[S]crutiny of the scientific community is a component of 'good science.'"). If nothing else, peer review and publication "increase the likelihood that substantive flaws in methodology will be detected."[7]

Bendectin litigation has been pending in the courts for over a decade, yet the only review the plaintiffs' experts' work has received has been by judges and juries, and the only place their theories and studies have been published is in the pages of federal and state reporters. None of the plaintiffs' experts has published his work on Bendectin in a scientific journal or solicited formal review by his colleagues. Despite the many years the controversy has been brewing, no one in the scientific community—except defendant's experts—has deemed these studies worthy of verification, refutation or even comment. It's as if there were a tacit understanding within the scientific community that what's going on here is not science at all, but litigation.[9]

Establishing that an expert's proffered testimony grows out of pre-litigation research or that the expert's research has been subjected to peer review are the two principal ways the proponent of expert testimony can show that the evidence satisfies the first prong of Rule 702. Where such evidence is unavailable, the proponent of expert scientific testimony may attempt to satisfy its burden through the testimony of its own experts. For such a showing to be sufficient, the experts must explain precisely how they went about reaching their conclusions and point to some objective source—a learned treatise, the policy statement of a professional association, a published article in a reputable scientific journal or the like—to show that they have followed the scientific method, as it is practiced by (at least) a recognized minority of scientists in their field.

Plaintiffs have made no such showing. . . . We've been presented with only the experts' qualifications, their conclusions and their assurances of reliability. Under *Daubert*, that's not enough. . . .

Were this the only question before us, we would be inclined to remand to give plaintiffs an opportunity to submit additional proof that the scientific testimony they proffer was "derived by the scientific method." *Daubert*, however, establishes two prongs to the Rule 702 admissibility inquiry. We therefore consider whether the testimony satisfies the second prong of Rule 702: Would plaintiffs' proffered scientific evidence "assist the trier of fact to . . . determine a fact in issue"?

---

7. For instance, peer review might well have brought to light the more glaring arithmetical errors in the testimony presented by plaintiffs' experts in other Bendectin cases.

9. There may well be good reasons why a scientific study has not been published. For example, it may be too recent or of insufficiently broad interest. These reasons do not apply here. Except with respect to the views expressed in this litigation, plaintiffs' experts have been well-published . . . and the opinions they proffer, if supported by sound methodology, would doubtless be greedily devoured by the machinery of peer review. A conclusion that Bendectin causes birth defects would be of significant public interest both in this country (where millions of women have taken Bendectin and the FDA continues to approve its use) and abroad (where Bendectin is still widely used). That plaintiffs' experts have been unable or unwilling to publish their work undermines plaintiffs' claim that the findings these experts proffer are "ground[ed] in the methods and procedures of science" and "derived by the scientific method."

C. NO VISIBLE MEANS OF SUPPORT

In elucidating the second requirement of Rule 702, *Daubert* stressed the importance of the "fit" between the testimony and an issue in the case: "Rule 702's 'helpfulness' standard requires a valid scientific connection to the pertinent inquiry as a precondition to admissibility." Here, the pertinent inquiry is causation. In assessing whether the proffered expert testimony "will assist the trier of fact" in resolving this issue, we must look to the governing substantive standard, which in this case is supplied by California tort law.

Plaintiffs do not attempt to show causation directly; instead, they rely on experts who present circumstantial proof of causation. Plaintiffs' experts testify that Bendectin is a teratogen because it causes birth defects when it is tested on animals, because it is similar in chemical structure to other suspected teratogens, and because statistical studies show that Bendectin use increases the risk of birth defects. Modern tort law permits such proof, but plaintiffs must nevertheless carry their traditional burden; they must prove that their injuries were the result of the accused cause and not some independent factor. In the case of birth defects, carrying this burden is made more difficult because we know that some defects—including limb reduction defects—occur even when expectant mothers do not take Bendectin, and that most birth defects occur for no known reason.

California tort law requires plaintiffs to show not merely that Bendectin increased the likelihood of injury, but that it more likely than not caused their injuries. In terms of statistical proof, this means that plaintiffs must establish not just that their mothers' ingestion of Bendectin increased somewhat the likelihood of birth defects, but that it more than doubled it—only then can it be said that Bendectin is more likely than not the source of their injury. Because the background rate of limb reduction defects is one per thousand births, plaintiffs must show that among children of mothers who took Bendectin the incidence of such defects was more than two per thousand.[13]

None of plaintiffs' epidemiological experts claims that ingestion of Bendectin during pregnancy more than doubles the risk of birth defects. . . . While plaintiffs' epidemiologists make vague assertions that there is a statistically significant relationship between Bendectin and birth defects, none states that the relative risk is greater than two. These studies thus would not be helpful, and indeed would only serve to confuse the jury, if offered to prove rather than refute causation. A relative risk of less than two may suggest teratogenicity, but

---

13. No doubt, there will be unjust results under this substantive standard. If a drug increases the likelihood of birth defects, but doesn't more than double it, some plaintiffs whose injuries are attributable to the drug will be unable to recover. There is a converse unfairness under a regime that allows recovery to everyone that may have been affected by the drug. Under this regime, all potential plaintiffs are entitled to recover, even though most will not have suffered an injury that can be attributed to the drug. One can conclude from this that unfairness is inevitable when our tools for detecting causation are imperfect and we must rely on probabilities rather than more direct proof. In any event, this is a matter to be sorted out by the states, whose substantive legal standards we are bound to apply.

it actually tends to disprove legal causation, as it shows that Bendectin does not double the likelihood of birth defects. . . .

[W]hat plaintiffs must prove is not that Bendectin causes some birth defects, but that it caused their birth defects. To show this, plaintiffs' experts would have had to testify either that Bendectin actually caused plaintiffs' injuries (which they could not say) or that Bendectin more than doubled the likelihood of limb reduction birth defects (which they did not say).

As the district court properly found below, "the strongest inference to be drawn for plaintiffs based on the epidemiological evidence is that Bendectin could possibly have caused plaintiffs' injuries." The same is true of the other testimony derived from animal studies and chemical structure analyses-these experts "testify to a possibility rather than a probability." Plaintiffs do not quantify this possibility, or otherwise indicate how their conclusions about causation should be weighted, even though the substantive legal standard has always required proof of causation by a preponderance of the evidence. Unlike these experts' explanation of their methodology, this is not a short-coming that could be corrected on remand; plaintiffs' experts could augment their affidavits with independent proof that their methods were sound, but to augment the substantive testimony as to causation would require the experts to change their conclusions altogether. Any such tailoring of the experts' conclusions would, at this stage of the proceedings, fatally undermine any attempt to show that these findings were "derived by the scientific method." Plaintiffs' experts must, therefore, stand by the conclusions they originally proffered, rendering their testimony inadmissible under the second prong of Fed. R. Evid. 702. . . .

The district court's grant of summary judgment is affirmed.

PREPARING FOR CLASS

1. What procedural path did the case take before reaching this stage?

2. How did the defendant challenge the plaintiffs' expert evidence?

3. Before the Supreme Court's ruling in *Daubert*, how had the admissibility of evidence based on scientific technique been determined? Did the plaintiffs' evidence satisfy that standard?

4. What standard applies after the Supreme Court's ruling in *Daubert*? Does the Ninth Circuit appear to approve of the new standard?

5. How does a court determine that an expert's opinions are based on sound science?

6. Is the plaintiffs' evidence sufficient under the new standard?

3. *Problems with Who Caused the Harm*

Summers v. Tice
199 P.2d 1 (Cal. 1948)

Carter, Justice.
Each of the two defendants appeals from a judgment against them in an action for personal injuries. . . .

Plaintiff's action was against both defendants for an injury to his right eye and face as the result of bring struck by bird shot discharged from a shotgun. The case was tried by the court without a jury and the court found that on November 20, 1945, plaintiff and the two defendants were hunting quail on the open range. Each of the defendants was armed with a 12 gauge shotgun loaded with shells containing 7 ½ size shot. Prior to going hunting plaintiff discussed the hunting procedure with defendants, indicating that they were to exercise care when shooting and to "keep in line." In the course of hunting plaintiff proceeded up a hill, thus placing the hunters at the points of a triangle. The view of defendants with reference to plaintiff was unobstructed and they knew his location. Defendant Tice flushed a quail which rose in flight to a ten foot elevation and flew between plaintiff and defendants. Both defendants shot at the quail, shooting in plaintiff's direction. At that time defendants were 75 yards from plaintiff. One shot struck plaintiff in his eye and another in his upper lip. Finally it was found by the court that as the direct result of the shooting by defendants the shots struck plaintiff as above mentioned and that defendants were negligent in so shooting and plaintiff was not contributorily negligent. . . .

The problem presented in this case is whether the judgment against both defendants may stand. It is argued by defendants that they are not joint tort-feasors, and thus jointly and severally liable, as they were not acting in concert, and that there is not sufficient evidence to show which defendant was guilty of the negligence which caused the injuries—the shooting by Tice or that by Simonson. . . . The one shot that entered plaintiff's eye was the major factor in assessing damages and that shot could not have come from the gun of both defendants. It was from one or the other only.

It has been held that where a group of persons are on a hunting party, or otherwise engaged in the use of firearms, and two of them are negligent in firing in the direction of a third person who is injured thereby, both of those so firing are liable for the injury suffered by the third person, although the negligence of only one of them could have caused the injury. These cases speak of the action of defendants as being in concert as the ground of decision, yet it would seem they are straining that concept and the more reasonable basis appears in Oliver v. Miles[, 110 So. 666]. There two persons were hunting together. Both shot at some partridges and in so doing shot across the highway injuring plaintiff who was travelling on it. The court stated they were acting in concert and thus both were liable. The court then stated: "We think that . . . each is liable for the resulting injury to the boy, although no one can say definitely who actually shot him. To hold otherwise would be to exonerate both from liability, although each was negligent, and the injury resulted from such negligence." . . .

When we consider the relative position of the parties and the results that would flow if plaintiff was required to pin the injury on one of the defendants only, a requirement that the burden of proof on that subject be shifted to defendants becomes manifest. They are both wrongdoers both negligent toward plaintiff. They brought about a situation where the negligence of one of them injured the plaintiff, hence it should rest with them each to absolve himself if he can. The injured party has been placed by defendants in the unfair position of pointing to which defendant caused the harm. If one can escape the other may also and plaintiff is remediless. Ordinarily defendants are in a far better position to offer evidence to determine which one caused the injury. This reasoning has recently found favor in this Court. [The court refers to Ybarra v. Spangard, 154 P.2d 687.] . . .

[T]he same reasons of policy and justice shift the burden to each of defendants to absolve himself if he can relieving the wronged person of the duty of apportioning the injury to a particular defendant, apply here where we are concerned with whether plaintiff is required to supply evidence for the apportionment of damages. If defendants are independent tortfeasors and thus each liable for the damage caused by him alone, and, at least, where the matter of apportionment is incapable of proof, the innocent wronged party should not be deprived of his right to redress. The wrongdoers should be left to work out between themselves any apportionment. . . .

The judgment is affirmed.

PREPARING FOR CLASS

1. Why, under traditional principles, was the plaintiff unable to prove causation?

2. Why does the court adopt an alternative rule? Do you think the court would have adopted or applied that rule if Simonson and Tice had not been hunting together?

3. What rule does the court adopt?

4. Can any plaintiff who cannot identify who injured him rely on this rule?

5. The court compares the case to *Ybarra v. Spangard* from Chapter 5. How are the cases similar? How are they different?

APPLYING THE LAW

Anne and Ben were partners in a law firm. They liked to spend their lunch breaks at the driving range. Both had recently bought powerful new drivers and were at the range testing them out. They saw a little girl sitting on the fence at the far end of the range and joked about whether they could drive far enough to hit her. They drove their balls simultaneously (not actually trying to hit the child) and lost track of their balls in the air. One ball hit the girl and injured her. Anne and Ben were both using range balls, so a look at the ball could not identify whose ball it was. And the girl had not been paying attention and did not know whose ball hit her. If the girl sued Anne and Ben, could she obtain a *Summers v. Tice* instruction? Assuming the instruction is given, could either Anne or Ben meet the shifted burden? What more would you want to know? (This hypothetical was inspired by a long ago Torts exam by Professor Deborah Merritt at the University of Illinois College of Law.)

Hymowitz v. Eli Lilly Co.
539 N.E. 2d 1069 (N.Y. 1989)

Wachtler, C.J.

Plaintiffs in these appeals allege that they were injured by the drug diethylstilbestrol (DES) ingested by their mothers during pregnancy. They seek relief against defendant DES manufacturers. While not class actions, these cases are representative of nearly 500 similar actions pending in the courts in this State; the rules articulated by the court here, therefore, must do justice and be administratively feasible in the context of this mass litigation. With this in mind, we now resolve the issue twice expressly left open by this court, and adopt a market share theory, using a national market, for determining liability and apportioning damages in DES cases in which identification of the manufacturer of the drug that injured the plaintiff is impossible. We also hold that the Legislature's revival for one year of actions for injuries caused by DES that were previously barred by the Statute of Limitations (see L. 1986, ch. 682, §4) is constitutional under the State and Federal Constitutions.

I.

The history of the development of DES and its marketing in this country has been repeatedly chronicled. Briefly, DES is a synthetic substance that mimics the effect of estrogen, the naturally formed female hormone. It was invented in 1937 by British researchers, but never patented.

In 1941, the Food and Drug Administration (FDA) approved the new drug applications (NDA) of 12 manufacturers to market DES for the treatment of various maladies, not directly involving pregnancy. In 1947, the FDA began approving the NDAs of manufacturers to market DES for the purpose of preventing human miscarriages; by 1951, the FDA had concluded that DES was generally safe for pregnancy use, and stopped requiring the filing of NDAs when new manufacturers sought to produce the drug for this purpose.

In 1971, however, the FDA banned the use of DES as a miscarriage preventative, when studies established the harmful latent effects of DES upon the offspring of mothers who took the drug. Specifically, tests indicated that DES caused vaginal adenocarcinoma, a form of cancer, and adenosis, a precancerous vaginal or cervical growth.

Although strong evidence links prenatal DES exposure to later development of serious medical problems, plaintiffs seeking relief in court for their injuries faced two formidable and fundamental barriers to recovery in this State; not only is identification of the manufacturer of the DES ingested in a particular case generally impossible, but, due to the latent nature of DES injuries, many claims were barred by the Statute of Limitations before the injury was discovered.

The identification problem has many causes. All DES was of identical chemical composition. Druggists usually filled prescriptions from whatever was on hand. Approximately 300 manufacturers produced the drug, with companies entering and leaving the market continuously during the 24 years that DES was sold for pregnancy use. The long latency period of a DES injury compounds the identification problem; memories fade, records are lost or destroyed, and witnesses die. Thus the pregnant women who took DES generally never knew who produced the drug they took, and there was no reason to attempt to discover this fact until many years after ingestion, at which time the information is not available. . . .

II.

In a products liability action, identification of the exact defendant whose product injured the plaintiff is, of course, generally required. In DES cases in which such identification is possible, actions may proceed under established principles of products liability. The record now before us, however, presents the question of whether a DES plaintiff may recover against a DES manufacturer when identification of the producer of the specific drug that caused the injury is impossible.

A.

As we noted in Bichler v. Lilly & Co., 436 N.E.2d 182, the accepted tort doctrines of alternative liability and concerted action are available in some personal injury cases to permit recovery where the precise identification of a wrongdoer is impossible. However, we agree with the near unanimous views of the high State courts that have considered the matter that these doctrines in their unaltered common-law forms do not permit recovery in DES cases. . . .

The paradigm of alternative liability is found in the case of Summers v. Tice, (33 Cal. 2d 80, 199 P.2d 1). In *Summers*, plaintiff and the two defendants were hunting, and defendants carried identical shotguns and ammunition. During the hunt, defendants shot simultaneously at the same bird, and plaintiff was struck by bird shot from one of the defendants' guns. The court held that where two defendants breach a duty to the plaintiff, but there is uncertainty regarding which one caused the injury, "the burden is upon each such actor to prove that he has not caused the harm" (Restatement [(Second)] of Torts §433B[3]. The central rationale for shifting the burden of proof in such a situation is that without this device both defendants will be silent, and plaintiff will not recover; with alternative liability, however, defendants will be forced to speak, and reveal the culpable party, or else be held jointly and severally liable themselves. Consequently, use of the alternative liability doctrine generally requires that the defendants have better access to information than does the plaintiff, and that all possible tortfeasors be before the court. It is also recognized that alternative liability rests on the notion that where there is a small number of possible wrongdoers, all of whom breached a duty to the plaintiff, the likelihood that any one of them injured the plaintiff is relatively high, so that forcing them to exonerate themselves, or be held liable, is not unfair.

In DES cases, however, there is a great number of possible wrongdoers, who entered and left the market at different times, and some of whom no longer exist. Additionally, in DES cases many years elapse between the ingestion of the drug and injury. Consequently, DES defendants are not in any better position than are plaintiffs to identify the manufacturer of the DES ingested in any given case, nor is there any real prospect of having all the possible producers before the court. Finally, while it may be fair to employ alternative liability in cases involving only a small number of potential wrongdoers, that fairness disappears with the decreasing probability that any one of the defendants actually caused the injury. This is particularly true when applied to DES where the chance that a particular producer caused the injury is often very remote. Alternative liability, therefore, provides DES plaintiffs no relief.

Nor does the theory of concerted action, in its pure form, supply a basis for recovery. This doctrine, seen in drag racing cases, provides for joint and several liability on the part of all defendants having an understanding, express or tacit, to participate in "a common plan or design to commit a tortious act" (Prosser and Keeton, Torts §46, at 323 [5th ed.]). As . . . the present record reflects, drug companies were engaged in extensive parallel conduct in developing and marketing DES. There is nothing in the record, however, beyond this similar conduct to show any agreement, tacit or otherwise, to market DES for pregnancy use without taking proper steps to ensure the drug's safety. Parallel activity, without more, is insufficient to establish the agreement element necessary to maintain a concerted action. Thus this theory also fails in supporting an action by DES plaintiffs.

In short, extant common-law doctrines, unmodified, provide no relief for the DES plaintiff unable to identify the manufacturer of the drug that injured her. This is not a novel conclusion; in the last decade a number of courts in other jurisdictions also have concluded that present theories do not support a cause of action in DES cases. Some courts, upon reaching this conclusion, have declined to find any judicial remedy for the DES plaintiffs who cannot identify the particular manufacturer of the DES ingested by their mothers. Other courts, however, have found that some modification of existing doctrine is appropriate to allow for relief for those injured by DES of unknown manufacture.

We conclude that the present circumstances call for recognition of a realistic avenue of relief for plaintiffs injured by DES. These appeals present many of the same considerations that have prompted this court in the past to modify the rules of personal injury liability, in order "to achieve the ends of justice in a more modern context," and we perceive that here judicial action is again required to overcome the "inordinately difficult problems of proof" caused by contemporary products and marketing techniques.

Indeed, it would be inconsistent with the reasonable expectations of a modern society to say to these plaintiffs that because of the insidious nature of an injury that long remains dormant, and because so many manufacturers, each behind a curtain, contributed to the devastation, the cost of injury should be borne by the innocent and not the wrongdoers. This is particularly so where the Legislature consciously created these expectations by reviving hundreds of DES cases. Consequently, the ever-evolving dictates of justice and fairness, which are the heart of our common-law system, require formation of a remedy for injuries caused by DES.

We stress, however, that the DES situation is a singular case, with manufacturers acting in a parallel manner to produce an identical, generically marketed product, which causes injury many years later, and which has evoked a legislative response reviving previously barred actions. Given this unusual scenario, it is more appropriate that the loss be borne by those that produced the drug for use during pregnancy, rather than by those who were injured by the use, even where the precise manufacturer of the drug cannot be identified in a particular action. We turn then to the question of how to fairly and equitably apportion the loss occasioned by DES, in a case where the exact manufacturer of the drug that caused the injury is unknown.

B.

The past decade of DES litigation has produced a number of alternative approaches to resolve this question. Thus, in a sense, we are now in an enviable position; the efforts of other courts provided examples for contending with this difficult issue, and enough time has passed so that the actual administration and real effects of these solutions now can be observed. With these useful guides in hand, a path may be struck for our own conclusion. . . .

A narrower basis for liability, tailored more closely to the varying culpableness of individual DES producers, is the market share concept. First judicially articulated by the California Supreme Court in Sindell v. Abbott Labs., [607

P.2d 924 (Cal. 1980)], variations upon this theme have been adopted by other courts. In *Sindell v. Abbott Labs.*, the court synthesized the market share concept by modifying the *Summers v. Tice* alternative liability rationale in two ways. It first loosened the requirement that all possible wrongdoers be before the court, and instead made a "substantial share" sufficient. The court then held that each defendant who could not prove that it did not actually injure plaintiff would be liable according to that manufacturer's market share. The court's central justification for adopting this approach was its belief that limiting a defendant's liability to its market share will result, over the run of cases, in liability on the part of a defendant roughly equal to the injuries the defendant actually caused.

In the recent case of Brown v. Superior Ct., 751 P.2d 470, the California Supreme Court resolved some apparent ambiguity in *Sindell v. Abbott Labs.*, and held that a manufacturer's liability is several only, and, in cases in which all manufacturers in the market are not joined for any reason, liability will still be limited to market share, resulting in a less than 100% recovery for a plaintiff. Finally, it is noteworthy that determining market shares under *Sindell v. Abbott Labs.* proved difficult and engendered years of litigation. After attempts at using smaller geographical units, it was eventually determined that the national market provided the most feasible and fair solution, and this national market information was compiled.

Four years after *Sindell v. Abbott Labs.*, the Wisconsin Supreme Court followed with Collins v. Lilly & Co., 116 Wis. 2d 166, 342 N.W.2d 37. Deciding the identification issue without the benefit of the extensive California litigation over market shares, the Wisconsin court held that it was prevented from following *Sindell* due to "the practical difficulty of defining and proving market share." Instead of focusing on tying liability closely to the odds of actual causation, as the *Sindell* court attempted, the *Collins* court took a broader perspective, and held that each defendant is liable in proportion to the amount of risk it created that the plaintiff would be injured by DES. Under the *Collins* structure, the "risk" each defendant is liable for is a question of fact in each case, with market shares being relevant to this determination. Defendants are allowed, however, to exculpate themselves by showing that their product could not have caused the injury to the particular plaintiff.

The Washington Supreme Court, writing soon after *Collins v. Lilly & Co.*, took yet another approach (see Martin v. Abbott Labs., 689 P.2d 368). The *Martin* court first rejected the *Sindell* market share theory due to the belief (which later proved to be erroneous in *Brown v. Superior Ct.*) that California's approach distorted liability by inflating market shares to ensure plaintiffs of full recovery. The *Martin* court instead adopted what it termed "market share alternative liability," justified, it concluded, because "[e]ach defendant contributed to the risk of injury to the public, and, consequently, the risk of injury to individual plaintiffs."

Under the Washington scheme, defendants are first allowed to exculpate themselves by proving by the preponderance of the evidence that they were not the manufacturer of the DES that injured plaintiff. Unexculpated defendants are presumed to have equal market shares, totaling 100%. Each defendant then has the opportunity to rebut this presumption by showing that its actual market share was less than presumed. If any defendants succeed in rebutting this presumption, the liability shares of the remaining defendants who could not prove their actual market share are inflated, so that the plaintiff received a 100% recovery. The market shares of defendants is a question of fact in each case, and the relevant market can be a particular pharmacy, or county, or State, or even the country, depending upon the circumstances the case presents.

Turning to the structure to be adopted in New York, we heed both the lessons learned through experience in other jurisdictions and the realities of the mass litigation of DES claims in this State. Balancing these considerations, we are led to the conclusion that a market share theory, based upon a national market, provides the best solution. As California discovered, the reliable determination of any market smaller than the national one likely is not practicable. Moreover, even if it were possible, of the hundreds of cases in the New York courts, without a doubt there are many in which the DES that allegedly caused injury was ingested in another State. Among the thorny issues this could present, perhaps the most daunting is the spectre that the particular case could require the establishment of a separate market share matrix. We feel that this is an unfair, and perhaps impossible burden to routinely place upon the litigants in individual cases.

Nor do we believe that the Wisconsin approach of assessing the "risk" each defendant caused a particular plaintiff, to be litigated anew as a question of fact in each case, is the best solution for this State. Applied on a limited scale this theory may be feasible, and certainly is the most refined approach by allowing a more thorough consideration of how each defendant's actions threatened the plaintiff. We are wary, however, of setting loose, for application in the hundreds of cases pending in this State, a theory which requires the fact finder's individualized and open-ended assessment of the relative liabilities of scores of defendants in every case. Instead, it is our perception that the injustices arising from delayed recoveries and inconsistent results which this theory may produce in this State outweigh arguments calling for its adoption.

Consequently, for essentially practical reasons, we adopt a market share theory using a national market. We are aware that the adoption of a national market will likely result in a disproportion between the liability of individual manufacturers and the actual injuries each manufacturer caused in this State. Thus our market share theory cannot be founded upon the belief that, over the run of cases, liability will approximate causation in this State. Nor does the use of a national market provide a reasonable link between liability and the risk created by a defendant to a particular plaintiff. Instead, we choose to apportion liability so as to correspond to the over-all culpability of each defendant, measured by the amount of risk of injury each defendant created to the public-at-large. Use of a national market is a fair method, we believe, of apportioning defendants' liabilities according to their total culpability in marketing DES for use during pregnancy. Under the circumstances, this is an equitable way to provide plaintiffs with the relief they deserve, while also rationally distributing the responsibility for plaintiffs' injuries among defendants.

To be sure, a defendant cannot be held liable if it did not participate in the marketing of DES for pregnancy use; if a DES producer satisfies its burden of proof of showing that it was not a member of the market of DES sold for pregnancy use, disallowing exculpation would be unfair and unjust. Nevertheless, because liability here is based on the over-all risk produced, and not causation in a single case, there should be no exculpation of a defendant who, although a member of the market producing DES for pregnancy use, appears not to have caused a particular plaintiff's injury. It is merely a windfall for a producer to escape liability solely because it manufactured a more identifiable pill, or sold only to certain drugstores. These fortuities in no way diminish the culpability of a defendant for marketing the product, which is the basis of liability here.[2]

Finally, we hold that the liability of DES producers is several only, and should not be inflated when all participants in the market are not before the court in a particular case. We understand that, as a practical matter, this will prevent some plaintiffs from recovering 100% of their damages. However, we eschewed exculpation to prevent the fortuitous avoidance of liability, and thus, equitably, we decline to unleash the same forces to increase a defendant's liability beyond its fair share of responsibility.

PREPARING FOR CLASS

1. What is the "identification problem" in DES cases? Why does the court think it is important to address?

2. Why not use the alternative liability approach of *Summers v. Tice* in these cases?

3. Why not use concerted action?

4. What approaches have other states taken to the identification problem in DES cases? What difficulties have these approaches presented?

5. What is the problem with allowing defendants to exculpate themselves?

6. Why does the court adopt a national market share approach?

7. Why does the court reject the risk approach?

8. How does the court justify the obvious flaws in its plan?

---

2. Various defendants argue here that although they produced DES, it was not sold for pregnancy use. If a defendant was not a member of the national market of DES marketed for pregnancy, it is not culpable, and should not be liable. Consequently, if a particular defendant sold DES in a form unsuitable for use during pregnancy, or if a defendant establishes that its product was not marketed for pregnancy use, there should be no liability. From the record before the court here, however, the facts are not developed well enough to establish that any defendants were not in the national market of DES sold for pregnancy use. Thus summary judgment cannot at this time be granted on this issue as to any defendants.

INCREASING YOUR UNDERSTANDING

Like this court, the court in Sindell v. Abbott Laboratories, 607 P.2d 924 (Cal. 1980), considered and rejected alternative liability and concert of action as approaches to the DES identification problem. In addition, the *Sindell* court looked at enterprise liability, a theory proposed in Hall v. E.I. Du Pont De Nemours & Co., Inc. 345 F. Supp. 353 (E.D.N.Y. 1972). As described in *Sindell*:

> In that case, plaintiffs were 13 children injured by the explosion of blasting caps in 12 separate incidents which occurred in 10 different states between 1955 and 1959. The defendants were six blasting cap manufacturers, comprising virtually the entire blasting cap industry in the United States, and their trade association. There were, however, a number of Canadian blasting cap manufacturers which could have supplied the caps. The gravamen of the complaint was that the practice of the industry of omitting a warning on individual blasting caps and of failing to take other safety measures created an unreasonable risk of harm, resulting in the plaintiffs' injuries. The complaint did not identify a particular manufacturer of a cap which caused a particular injury.
>
> The court reasoned as follows: there was evidence that defendants, acting independently, had adhered to an industry-wide standard with regard to the safety features of blasting caps, that they had in effect delegated some functions of safety investigation and design, such as labelling, to their trade association, and that there was industry-wide cooperation in the manufacture and design of blasting caps. In these circumstances, the evidence supported a conclusion that all the defendants jointly controlled the risk. Thus, if plaintiffs could establish by a preponderance of the evidence that the caps were manufactured by one of the defendants, the burden of proof as to causation would shift to all the defendants. The court noted that this theory of liability applied to industries composed of a small number of units, and that what would be fair and reasonable with regard to an industry of five or ten producers might be manifestly unreasonable if applied to a decentralized industry composed of countless small producers. . . .
>
> We decline to apply this theory in the present case. At least 200 manufacturers produced DES; *Hall,* which involved 6 manufacturers representing the entire blasting cap industry in the United States, cautioned against application of the doctrine espoused therein to a large number of producers. Moreover, in *Hall,* the conclusion that the defendants jointly controlled the risk was based upon allegations that they had delegated some functions relating to safety to a trade association. There are no such allegations here, and we have concluded above that plaintiff has failed to allege liability on a concert of action theory.

Thomas v. Mallett
701 N.W.2d 523 (Wis. 2005)

BUTLER, J.

Steven Thomas, by his guardian ad litem, seeks review of a published court of appeals decision that declined to extend the risk-contribution theory announced in Collins v. Eli Lilly Co., 116 Wis. 2d 166, 342 N.W.2d 37 (1984), to the defendant-respondent lead pigment manufacturers. . . .

Thomas was born on June 23, 1990. He claims that he sustained lead poisoning by ingesting lead paint from accessible painted surfaces, paint chips, and paint flakes and dust at two different houses he lived in during the early 1990's. [He suffered] cognitive deficits in perceptual organization, visual motor integration, expressive language, academic and fine motor skills coupled with an attention deficit hyperactivity disorder. . . . Thomas will require lifetime medical monitoring-surveillance for physical disorders, as he is now at a high risk for developing future medical complications, including kidney disease, peripheral neuropathy, hypertension, and cardiovascular disease. [An expert] opines that Thomas's high lead levels are exclusively derived from ingesting lead based pigments in paint.

The main policy reasons identified by *Collins* warrant extension of the risk-contribution theory here.

First, the record makes clear that the Pigment Manufacturers "contributed to the risk of injury to the public and, consequently, the risk of injury to individual plaintiffs such as" Thomas. Many of the individual defendants or their predecessors-in-interest did more than simply contribute to a risk; they knew of the harm white lead carbonate pigments caused and continued production and promotion of the pigment notwithstanding that knowledge. Some manufacturers, paradoxically, even promoted their nonleaded based pigments as alternatives that were safe in that they did not pose the risk of lead poisoning. For those that did not have explicit knowledge of the harm they were engendering, given the growing medical literature in the early part of the century, Thomas's historical experts, Markowitz and Rosner, submit that by the 1920s the entire industry knew or should have known of the dangers of its products and should have ceased producing the lead pigments, including white lead carbonate. In short, we agree with Thomas that the record easily establishes the Pigment Manufacturers' culpability for, at a minimum, contributing to creating a risk of injury to the public.

Second, as compared to Thomas, the Pigment Manufacturers are in a better position to absorb the cost of the injury. They can insure themselves against liability, absorb the damage award, or pass the cost along to the consuming public as a cost of doing business. As we concluded in *Collins*, it is better to have the Pigment Manufacturers or consumers share the cost of the injury rather than place the burden on the innocent plaintiff. . . .

One of the proof problems the *Collins* court recognized the plaintiff had was that she was unable to identify the precise producer or marketer of the DES her mother took due to, among other things, "the generic status of some DES." In different terms, this court stated that the plaintiff could not identify the drug company that caused her injury because "DES was, for the most part, produced in a 'generic' form which did not contain any clearly identifiable shape, color, or markings." This court also observed that "DES was a fungible drug produced with a chemically identical formula, and often pharmacists would fill DES prescriptions from whatever stock they had on hand, whether or not a particular brand was specified in the prescription."

There is no denying that *Collins* involved a situation where a chemically identical formula allegedly caused harm. It is also true that white lead carbonate was made from three different chemical formulas. However, *Collins* did not address whether DES was fungible because of its chemical identity, because of its interchangeability due to its generic status, or because of both. The question is, does fungibility require chemical identity? We conclude that it does not.

Chemical identity was a feature that DES apparently shared, and it was that chemical formula that created a possibility of causing harm. Here, although the chemical formulas for white lead carbonate are not the same, Thomas's toxicologist, Mushak, opines that it is the common denominator in the formulas that counts: lead. According to Mushak, the formulary differences between white lead carbonates do not affect the bioavailability of, and hence the consequences caused by, the lead pigment. Thus, the formulas for both DES and the white lead carbonate are in a sense on the same footing as being inherently hazardous. Therefore, it would be imprudent to conclude that chemical identity is a touchstone for fungibility and, in turn, for the risk-contribution theory. To prevent the triumph of form over substance, we conclude that chemical identity is not required.

But the question still remains: what does fungibility mean? It has been noted that "[w]hile 'fungibility' [has] become an obsession for courts discussing market share liability, no court has ever explained thoroughly what 'fungibility' means or why it is important." Allen Rostron, *Beyond Market Share Liability: A Theory of Proportional Share Liability for Nonfungible Products*, 52 UCLA L. Rev. 151, 163 (Oct. 2004) [hereafter Beyond Market Share Liability]. Rostron writes that a product can be fungible in at least three different senses.

First, a product can be "functionally interchangeable." Under this meaning, whether a product is fungible is a matter of degree and heavily dependent on the context of whatever "function" is at issue. . . .

Second, a product can be fungible in the sense that it is "physically indistinguishable." Because appearances can be deceiving, the degree of physical similarity required, as with functional interchangeability, depends heavily on context. . . .

Third, a product can be fungible as it presents a "uniformity of risk." Under this meaning, "[a]s a result of sharing an identical or virtually identical chemical formula, each manufacturer's product posed the same amount of risk as every other manufacturer's product." . . .

The facts presented in this case, when construed in the light most favorable to Thomas, however, establish that white lead carbonate is fungible under any of the above meanings.

First, white lead carbonate was functionally interchangeable. All forms of white lead carbonate were lead pigments, which constituted one of the two necessary components of paint (the other being the "vehicle"). The pigment is what provided the hiding power of the paint. Although there may be varying grades of hiding powers based on differing physical properties and concentrations of the particular pigments, those are differences of degree, not function.

Second, based on the summary judgment record, white lead carbonates are physically indistinguishable. . . . Although the Pigment Manufacturers contend that white lead carbonates were manufactured according to different processes, which resulted in white lead carbonates of different physical properties, these physical differences are available only on the microscopic scale. Our concern here is whether the white lead carbonates are physically indistinguishable in the context in which it is used (in paint) and to whom is using it (the consumer or injured party). We acknowledge that the physical identity in this case is markedly different from that in *Collins*. Whereas in *Collins*, the plaintiff's mother could identify certain characteristics about the particular DES pill she ingested, that type of analysis is not possible here, as pigment in paint by its nature and concentration defy more specific identification. Nevertheless, we conclude the factual circumstances of physical interchangeability that are present are still sufficiently similar to remain within *Collins'* confines.

Third, we have already noted that white lead carbonates were produced utilizing "virtually identical chemical formulas" such that all white lead carbonates were "identically defective." It is the common denominator in the various white lead carbonate formulas that matters; namely, lead.

Therefore, based on the factors identified in *Collins*, we conclude that Thomas's case is factually similar to warrant extension of the risk-contribution theory. . . .

First, the Pigment Manufacturers note that the paint Thomas allegedly ingested could have been applied at any time between construction of the two houses in 1900 and 1905 and the ban on lead paint in 1978. This significant time span greatly exceeds the nine-month window during which a plaintiff's mother would have taken DES, the Pigment Manufacturers note. Given that *Collins* attempted to strike a balance between assuring a DES plaintiff had a remedy and providing a realistic opportunity to each DES pill manufacturer to prove that it could not have caused the plaintiff's harm (by establishing its DES could not have reached the mother during her pregnancy), the Pigment Manufacturers contend that *Collins* should not be extended given that they have no reasonable ability to exculpate themselves.

We recognize that the window during which the possible injury causing white lead carbonate was placed in a house that eventually harmed Thomas is drastically larger than a nine-month window for pregnancy. However, the window will not always be potentially as large as appears in this case. Even if it routinely will be, the Pigment Manufacturers' argument must be put into perspective: they are essentially arguing that their negligent conduct should be excused because they got away with it for too long. As Thomas says, the Pigment Manufacturers "are arguing that they should not be held liable under the risk contribution doctrine because of the magnitude of their wrongful conduct."

Collins was concerned with providing possibly innocent defendants a means to exculpate themselves by establishing their product could not have caused the injury. If they could not do so, this court stated that the equities "favor placing the consequences on the defendants. Equity does not support reversing that balance simply because the Pigment Manufacturers benefited from manufacturing and marketing white lead carbonate for a significant period of time.

Next, the Pigment Manufacturers contend that the risk-contribution theory should not be extended because Thomas's lead poisoning could have been caused from many different sources. We agree that the record indicates that lead poisoning can stem from the ambient air, many foods, drinking water, soil, and dust.

Further, the Pigment Manufacturers argue that the risk-contribution theory should not be extended because lead poisoning does not produce a "signature injury." As alternate explanations for Thomas's cognitive deficits, the Pigment Manufacturers have brought forth evidence that genetics, birth complications causing damage to the central nervous system, severe environmental deprivation, inadequate parenting, parental emotional disorders, and child abuse could all, in varying ways, cause such impairments.

These arguments have no bearing on whether the risk-contribution theory should be extended to white lead carbonate claims. Harm is harm, whether it be "signature" or otherwise. Even under the risk-contribution theory, the plaintiff still retains a burden of establishing causation. To establish a negligence claim under the risk-contribution theory, this court concluded that the plaintiff nonetheless needed to prove that "DES caused the plaintiff's subsequent injuries." Similarly, on a products liability claim, the *Collins* court held that the plaintiff has to prove "that the defect was a cause of the plaintiff's injuries or damages." On whatever theory the plaintiff chooses to proceed, this causation showing must be made by a preponderance of the evidence, and ultimately "to the satisfaction of the trier of fact." The plaintiff's burden is relaxed only with respect to establishing the specific type of DES the plaintiff's mother took, which, in this case, translates into the specific type of white lead carbonate Thomas ingested. . . .

Finally, the Pigment Manufacturers argue that because they were not in exclusive control of the risk their product created, the risk-contribution model should not apply to them. We again disagree.

This was again not a distinction relevant in Collins. Further, we see no reason why it should be for at least two reasons. First, as doctors were the ones who prescribed the dosage of DES, so too were the paint manufacturers that mixed the amount of white lead carbonate in the paint. However, the paint did not alter the toxicity of the white lead carbonate anymore than the pharmacist did by filling a prescription. To the contrary, at best, the paint manufacturers actually diluted the white lead carbonate's toxicity. In other words, the inherent dangerousness of the white lead carbonate pigment existed the moment the Pigment Manufacturers created it.

Second, the record is replete with evidence that shows the Pigment Manufacturers actually magnified the risk through their aggressive promotion of white lead carbonate, even despite the awareness of the toxicity of lead. In either case, whoever had "exclusive" control over the white lead carbonate is immaterial. . . .

Applying the risk-contribution theory to Thomas's negligence claim, he will have to prove the following elements to the satisfaction of the trier of fact:

(1)   That he ingested white lead carbonate;

(2)   That the white lead carbonate caused his injuries;

(3)   That the Pigment Manufacturers produced or marketed the type of white lead carbonate he ingested; and

(4)   That the Pigment Manufacturers' conduct in producing or marketing the white lead carbonate constituted a breach of a legally recognized duty to Thomas.

Because Thomas cannot prove the specific type of white lead carbonate he ingested, he need only prove that the Pigment Manufacturers produced or marketed white lead carbonate for use during the relevant time period: the duration of the houses' existence. . . .

Once Thomas makes a prima facie case . . . the burden of proof shifts to each defendant to prove by a preponderance of the evidence that it did not produce or market white lead carbonate either during the relevant time period or in the geographical market where the house is located. However, if relevant records do not exist that can substantiate either defense, "we believe that the equities of [white lead carbonate] cases favor placing the consequences on the [Pigment Manufacturers]." In addition to these specific defenses, and unlike in the DES cases, the Pigment Manufacturers here may have ample grounds to attack and eviscerate Thomas's prima facie case, with some of those grounds including that lead poisoning could stem from any number of substances (since lead itself is ubiquitous) and that it is difficult to know whether Thomas's injuries stem from lead poisoning as they are not signature injuries.

We continue to believe that this procedure will result in a pool of defendants which can reasonably be assumed "could have caused the plaintiff's injuries." The alarmist tone of the dissents aside, our application of *Collins* here achieves *Collins'* requirement that it be shown that the defendant pigment manufacturer "reasonably could have contributed in some way to the actual injury." The procedure is not perfect and could result in drawing in some defendants who are actually innocent, particularly given the significantly larger time span at issue in this particular case. However, *Collins* declared that "we accept this as the price the defendants, and perhaps ultimately society, must pay to provide the plaintiff an adequate remedy under the law." . . .

The decision of the court of appeals is affirmed in part and reversed in part and remanded for further proceedings consistent with this opinion.

PREPARING FOR CLASS

1. What is risk-contribution theory?

2. How are the lead paint cases similar, factually and legally, to the DES cases? How are they different?

3. Why does fungibility matter? What is the argument that lead paint is fungible?

4. Why is it more difficult for pigment manufacturers to exculpate themselves in lead paint cases than pharmaceutical companies to exculpate themselves in DES cases? Is this argument persuasive to the court?

Chapter 11

Proximate Causation

The consequences of a defendant's negligence can ripple out forever. A woman negligently drops a jar of pickles on the grocery store floor. Another woman falls in the spill. A man startled by seeing the second woman fall hits a child with his grocery cart. The child has a condition called osteogenesis imperfecta, which means he has very fragile bones. The child is seriously injured and must be hospitalized for several months, and the financial and emotional distress arising from the child's injury and treatment causes the break-up of his parents' marriage. Depressed by the break-up of his marriage, the father attempts suicide by jumping from a highway overpass. His fall to the road below causes a traffic pile-up in which one person is killed and several are injured. And all this happened because a woman dropped a jar of pickles.

At some point, the consequences of a defendant's negligence have rippled too far for it to be appropriate for the defendant to be held legally responsible for them. For concerns of practicality and fairness, the proximate cause element determines which consequences are ripples too far. Proximate cause is not really a causal inquiry at all, but a legal-liability limiting principle that determines the scope of the defendant's responsibility. Proximate cause is sometimes called "legal causation," and it helps to think of it that way. Yes, defendant's negligence caused the injury. But should it be the cause with legal consequences?

A. UNEXPECTED CONSEQUENCES

Schafer v. Hoffman
831 P.2d 897 (Colo. 1992)

VOLLACK, J.

. . . On January 15, 1988, Schafer struck Hoffman, a pedestrian, with his vehicle. Schafer was under the influence of alcohol and drugs at the time of the

431

collision. As a result of the collision, Hoffman sustained numerous injuries, including a compression fracture in a spinal vertebra, a concussion with intracranial bleeding, a fractured femur in her left leg, and torn cartilage in her left knee. Hoffman also sustained other injuries to her left leg, left hand, and right elbow.

[At trial] Schafer . . . contended that Hoffman had pre-existing injuries for which he was not liable because they were not caused by his conduct. . . .

[T]he jury heard evidence introduced by Schafer that Hoffman had complained of knee pain and lower back problems prior to the accident, and that the vertebra fracture might have occurred prior to the January 15, 1988, accident. The jury also was aware that Hoffman's knee had some degeneration as a result of the normal aging process, that Hoffman might be predisposed to causalgia, and that Hoffman's knee surgery was delayed longer than the average person's because of her blood clotting condition.

At the close of trial, Hoffman submitted a "thin skull" instruction which read as follows:

> In determining the amount(s) of plaintiff's actual damages in each of the various categories set forth in Instruction No. 16, you may not refuse to award nor reduce the amount of any such damages because of any physical frailties of the plaintiff that may have made her more susceptible to injury, disability or impairment.

Schafer objected to the giving of this instruction on the grounds that the instruction told the jury that they may not refuse or reduce the amount of damages because of Hoffman's pre-existing physical ailments. Schafer contended that there was no evidence of aggravation of Hoffman's condition and thus Schafer could not be held liable for her pre-existing conditions. The district court, however, gave the challenged instruction to the jury.

The jury found for Hoffman, and Schafer appealed. The court of appeals concluded that the instruction was a proper statement of the law and that it was supported by the evidence in this case. Schafer petitions this court for a determination that the thin skull instruction is not a correct statement of law and that the court of appeals erred in holding that Hoffman was entitled to the instruction as her theory of the case. We disagree.

The term "thin skull," or "eggshell skull," is derived from illustrations appearing in English cases wherein a plaintiff with an "eggshell skull" suffers death as a result of a defendant's negligence where a normal person would only suffer a bump on the head.

The negligent defendant is liable for the resulting harm even though the harm is increased by the particular plaintiff's condition at the time of the negligent conduct. [W. Page Keeton et al., *Prosser and Keaton on the Law of Torts* §43 (Prosser)]; see also Restatement (Second) of Torts §461 cmt. a (1965) ("A negligent actor must bear the risk that his liability will be increased by reason of the actual physical condition of the other toward whom his act is negligent.").

As Prosser notes, there is almost universal agreement on this rule. Liability "beyond the risk," however, is not solely premised on the existence of ascertainable pre-existing physical conditions:

> The defendant is held liable when the defendant's negligence operates upon a concealed physical condition, such as pregnancy, or latent disease, or susceptibility to disease, to produce consequences which the defendant could not reasonably anticipate. The defendant is held liable for unusual results of personal injuries which are regarded as unforeseeable, such as tuberculosis, paralysis, pneumonia, heart or kidney disease, blood poisoning, cancer, or the loss of hair from fright.

Prosser §43. Some scholars have interpreted the thin skull doctrine to encompass the plaintiff's physical, mental, or financial condition. 4 Fowler Harper et al., *The Law of Torts* §20.3 (2d ed. 1986). "And these preexisting conditions may have the greatest bearing on the extent of the injury actually suffered by any particular plaintiff in a given case. Thus the same slight blow in the abdomen might cause only fleeting discomfort to a man but a miscarriage to a pregnant woman."

Under Colorado law, it is fundamental that a tortfeasor must accept his or her victim as the victim is found. Accordingly, under the thin skull doctrine, a tortfeasor "may not seek to reduce the amount of damages [owed to the victim] by spotlighting the physical frailties of the injured party at the time the tortious force was applied to him." A thin skull instruction is appropriately given when the defendant seeks to avoid liability by asserting that the victim's injuries would have been less severe had the victim been an average person.

Schafer contends that the foundation required for a thin skull instruction is not established. Relying on an opinion not selected for official publication, Herrera v. Nakata, 478 P.2d 706 (Colo. App. 1970), Schafer contends that a plaintiff must prove the existence of a pre-existing bodily condition before the instruction can be given. We decline to adopt such a narrow interpretation.

The thin skull doctrine has not been limited to pre-existing bodily conditions. The doctrine appropriately applies where a plaintiff may be predisposed or more susceptible to ill effects than a normal person. See City of Scottsdale v. Kokaska, 495 P.2d 1327, 1335 (Ariz. App. 1972) (plaintiff had no pre-existing injury but rather an anatomically different spine); Walton v. William Wolf Baking Co., 406 So. 2d 168, 175 (La. 1981) (holding that tortfeasor was required to take plaintiff as found, with predisposition to neurosis); Freyermuth v. Lutfy, 382 N.E.2d 1059, 1064 n. 5 (Mass. 1978) ("The established rule is that where the result of an accident is to activate a dormant or incipient disease, or one to which the person is predisposed, the negligence which caused the accident is the proximate cause of the disability.").

The challenged instruction encapsulates the fundamental thin skull doctrine. A party "is entitled to an instruction embodying his theory of the case, if there is evidence in the record to support it."

During trial, Schafer established that Dr. Rupp had prescribed Chlorinol (an anti-inflammatory) to Hoffman for knee discomfort prior to the accident. Schafer attempted to establish that Hoffman had longstanding complaints with regard to her knees. Schafer sought to prove that Hoffman's recovery process was longer than the average person's because arthroscopic surgery expedites recovery but was delayed in Hoffman's case as a result of her blood clotting condition.

Schafer also attempted to establish during cross-examination of Dr. Ceriani that chondromalacia can develop over the course of the normal aging process. Schafer elicited, through cross-examination of Hoffman's physical therapist, that Hoffman had some degeneration in her knee as a result of her age.

The testimony elicited by Schafer in this case could lead the jury to believe that Hoffman suffered frailties or was more susceptible to certain medical infirmities than the average person. The challenged instruction merely informed the jury that Schafer could not escape liability because of Hoffman's condition at the time of the accident. The trial court did not err by giving the thin skull instruction in this case. . . .

PREPARING FOR CLASS

1. What is a "thin skull" instruction? When is one given? What does it accomplish?

2. The court does not discuss policy reasons supporting the "thin skull" instruction. What do you suppose they are? How is it fair to hold defendants responsible for unforeseeable risks of their behavior?

3. Why did the defendant object to the trial court's giving the "thin skull" instruction?

4. Why does the court point out that defendant relies on an opinion not selected for official publication?

5. Why did the plaintiff request the instruction? Was it properly given? What does this mean for the plaintiff?

6. What can a defendant sued by a thin-skull plaintiff do to minimize damages?

APPLYING THE LAW

1. A taxi hit a man and threw him 20 feet into the air. His thigh was broken and his knee injured, and he was taken to the hospital, where he died two days later from delirium tremens. The man would not have had

delirium tremens if he had not been an alcoholic. In the widow's wrongful death trial, a physician testified that "He rapidly developed delirium tremens. I should say with reasonable certainty the injury precipitated his attack of delirium tremens, and understand I mean precipitated, not induced. The injury to the leg and the knee hurried up the delirium tremens." Can the widow prove that the taxi driver's negligence was the proximate cause of her husband's death from delirium tremens? (This is from McCahill v. New York Transp. Co., 94 N.E. 616 (N.Y. 1911).)

2. A real estate salesman had battled depression for years. The one thing that helped him control his depression was working out at the gym. He usually worked out for a couple of hours a day. While he was driving to an open house, his car was struck in an intersection by a negligent driver. Although he suffered no broken bones or internal injuries, he suffered soft tissue damage that made him unable to work out. Because he could not work out, he became suicidally depressed and attempted, but failed, in a suicide attempt. Is the negligent driver the proximate cause of the salesman's suicidal depression?

In re Polemis
3 K.B. 560 1921

BANKES L.J.

By a time charter party dated February 21, 1917, the respondents chartered their vessel to the appellants. . . . The vessel was employed by the charterers to carry a cargo to Casablanca in Morocco. The cargo included a quantity of benzine or petrol in cases. While discharging at Casablanca a heavy plank fell into the hold in which the petrol was stowed, and caused an explosion, which set fire to the vessel and completely destroyed her. The owners claimed the value of the vessel from the charterers, alleging that the loss of the vessel was due to the negligence of the charterers' servants. The charterers contended that . . . the damages claimed were too remote. The claim was referred to arbitration, and the arbitrators stated a special case for the opinion of the Court. Their findings of fact are as follows[: "(a) that the ship was lost by fire; (b) that the fire arose from a spark igniting petrol vapour in the hold; (c) that the spark was caused by the falling board coming into contact with some substance in the hold; (d) that the fall of the board was caused by the negligence of the Arabs . . . engaged in the work of discharging; (e) that the said Arabs were employed by the charterers or . . . on behalf of the charterers, and that the said Arabs were the servants of the charterers; (f) that the causing of the spark could not reasonably have been anticipated from the falling of the board, though some damage to the ship might reasonably have been anticipated."]

According to the one view, the consequences which may reasonably be expected to result from a particular act are material only in reference to the question whether the act is or is not a negligent act; according to the other view, those consequences are the test whether the damages resulting from the act, assuming it to be negligent, are or are not too remote to be recoverable. . . .

In the present case the arbitrators have found as a fact that the falling of the plank was due to the negligence of the defendants' servants. The fire appears to me to have been directly caused by the falling of the plank. Under these circumstances I consider that it is immaterial that the causing of the spark by the falling of the plank could not have been reasonably anticipated. The appellants' junior counsel sought to draw a distinction between the anticipation of the extent of damage resulting from a negligent act, and the anticipation of the type of damage resulting from such an act. He admitted that it could not lie in the mouth of a person whose negligent act had caused damage to say that he could not reasonably have foreseen the extent of the damage, but he contended that the negligent person was entitled to rely upon the fact that he could not reasonably have anticipated the type of damage which resulted from his negligent act. I do not think that the distinction can be admitted. Given the breach of duty which constitutes the negligence, and given the damage as a direct result of that negligence, the anticipations of the person whose negligent act has produced the damage appear to me to be irrelevant. I consider that the damages claimed are not too remote. . . .

Scrutton L.J.

. . . To determine whether an act is negligent, it is relevant to determine whether any reasonable person would foresee that the act would cause damage; if he would not, the act is not negligent. But if the act would or might probably cause damage, the fact that the damage it in fact causes is not the exact kind of damage one would expect is immaterial, so long as the damage is in fact directly traceable to the negligent act, and not due to the operation of independent causes having no connection with the negligent act, except that they could not avoid its results. Once the act is negligent, the fact that its exact operation was not foreseen is immaterial. This is the distinction laid down by the majority of the Exchequer Chamber in *Smith v. London and South Western Ry. Co.*, and by the majority of the Court in Banc in *Greenland v. Chaplin*, and approved recently by Lord Sumner in *Weld-Blundell v. Stephens* and Sir Samuel Evans in *H.M.S. London.* In the present case it was negligent in discharging cargo to knock down the planks of the temporary staging, for they might easily cause some damage either to workmen, or cargo, or the ship. The fact that they did directly produce an unexpected result, a spark in an atmosphere of petrol vapour which caused a fire, does not relieve the person who was negligent from the damage which his negligent act directly caused.

PREPARING FOR CLASS

1.   What did the arbitrators conclude? How did these conclusions limit what the judges could analyze? What part of the conclusions presents a proximate cause issue?

2.   Why was dropping the plank negligent?

3.   What distinction did "appellants' junior counsel" attempt to draw? (Whose lawyer is that?) Why did he try to make that distinction? Did Judge Bankes think the distinction was relevant?

4.   According to Judge Scrutton, on what issue is the foreseeability of consequences relevant?

5.   How does Judge Scrutton think the line for proximate cause should be drawn? Don't "cut and paste" his rule. Get it into your words. Be sure you know what "direct" means. Be sure you know what "independent" means. Think of examples that would illustrate this rule. Does foreseeability have any role in this rule?

6.   What is the result under the rule laid down in this case? What change in facts would produce a different result?

7.   Does the rule serve the tort law goal of deterrence?

APPLYING THE LAW

Professor, and later Judge, Keeton in his *Legal Cause in the Law of Torts* (1963) proposed the following hypothetical based on Larrimore v. American National Insurance Co., 89 P.2d 340 (Okla. 1939). The defendant leaves a can of rat poison on a shelf in a kitchen near a can of flour. This is negligent because someone might mistake the rat poison for flour and poison herself or someone else. But what does happen is that heat from the stove unexpectedly causes the poison to explode. Under *Polemis*, is the negligent placement of the poison the proximate cause of the explosion?

INCREASING YOUR UNDERSTANDING

This case is of more historical than practical value. As Professor Dobbs says in his hornbook, "It is very doubtful that liability unlimited by foreseeability has much contemporary support." Dan B. Dobbs, *The Law of Torts*, §185. One casebook seeking to show "considerable support" for the directly traceable rule cites one case from 1896 and another from 1928.

Overseas Tankship (U.K.) Ltd. v. Morts Dock & Engineering Co., Ltd "Wagon Mound No. 1"
Privy Council, [1961] A.C. 388

Viscount SIMONDS:

[The defendants owned the S.S. *Wagon Mound*, which negligently discharged a large quantity of furnace oil into a harbor. The oil spread and caused minor damage to the slipways of the plaintiff's wharf. After the oil was discharged, plaintiff's works manager discontinued welding operations until, based on consultation with an oil company manager and based on his own belief that furnace oil in the open was not flammable, he decided it was safe to continue welding nearby. He warned his men not to let flammable materials fall into the water. Somehow, though, cotton waste or a rag fell into the water and worked like a wick with the oil. The welding operations ignited the "wick" and a fire, fed initially by the oil, caused significant damage in the harbor. The trial judge stated, "The *raison d'être* of furnace oil is, of course, that it shall burn, but I find the defendant did not know and could not reasonably be expected to have known that it was capable of being set afire when spread on water." Plaintiff prevailed at trial, and judgment was affirmed by the Supreme Court of New South Wales. The defendant appealed.]

There can be no doubt that the decision of the Court of Appeal in *Polemis* plainly asserts that, if the defendant is guilty of negligence, he is responsible for all the consequences, whether reasonably foreseeable or not. The generality of the proposition is, perhaps, qualified by the fact that each of the lords justices refers to the outbreak of fire as the direct result of the negligent act. There is thus introduced the conception that the negligent actor is not responsible for consequences which are not "direct," whatever that may mean. . . .

Enough has been said to show that the authority of *Polemis* has been severely shaken, though lip-service has from time to time been paid to it. In their Lordships' opinion, it should no longer be regarded as good law. It is not probable that many cases will for that reason have a different result, though it is hoped that the law will be thereby simplified, and that, in some cases at least, palpable injustice will be avoided. For it does not seem consonant with current ideas of justice or morality that, for an act of negligence, however slight or venial, which results in some trivial foreseeable damage, the actor should be liable for all consequences, however unforeseeable and however grave, so long as they can be said to be "direct." It is a principle of civil liability, subject only to qualifications which have no present relevance, that a man must be considered to be responsible for the probable consequences of his act. To demand more of him is too harsh a rule, to demand less is to ignore that civilised order requires the observance of a minimum standard of behaviour.

This concept, applied to the slowly developing law of negligence, has led to a great variety of expressions which can, as it appears to their Lordships, be harmonised with little difficulty with the single exception of the so-called rule in *Polemis*. For, if it is asked why a man should be responsible for the natural or necessary or probable consequences of his act (or any other similar description of them), the answer is that it is not because they are natural or necessary or probable, but because, since they have this quality, it is judged, by the standard of the reasonable man, that he ought to have foreseen them. Thus it is that, over and over again, it has happened that, in different judgments in the same case and sometimes in a single judgment, liability for a consequence has been imposed on the ground that it was reasonably foreseeable, or alternatively on the ground that it was natural or necessary or probable. The two grounds have been treated as conterminous, and so they largely are. But, where they are not, the question arises to which the wrong answer was given in *Polemis*. For, if some limitation must be imposed on the consequences for which the negligent actor is to be held responsible — and all are agreed that some limitation there must be — why should that test (reasonable foreseeability) be rejected which, since he is judged by what the reasonable man ought to foresee, corresponds with the common conscience of mankind, and a test (the "direct" consequence) be substituted which leads to nowhere but the never ending and insoluble problems of causation. . . .

It is, no doubt, proper when considering tortious liability for negligence to analyse its elements and to say that the plaintiff must prove a duty owed to him by the defendant, a breach of that duty by the defendant, and consequent damage. But there can be no liability until the damage has been done. It is not the act but the consequences on which tortious liability is founded. Just as (as it has been said) there is no such thing as negligence in the air, so there is no such thing as liability in the air. Suppose an action brought by A for damage caused by the carelessness (a neutral word) of B, for example a fire caused by the careless spillage of oil. It may, of course, become relevant to know what duty B owed to A, but the only liability that is in question is the liability for damage by fire. It is vain to isolate the liability from its context and to say that B is or is not liable, and then to ask for what damage he is liable. For his liability is in respect of that damage and no other. If, as admittedly it is, B's liability (culpability) depends on the reasonable foreseeability of the consequent damage, how is that to be determined except by the foreseeability of the damage which in fact happened — the damage in suit? And, if that damage is unforeseeable so as to displace liability at large, how can the liability be restored so as to make compensation payable? But, it is said, a different position arises if B's careless act has been shown to be negligent and has caused some foreseeable damage to A. Their Lordships have already observed that to hold B liable for consequences, however unforeseeable, of a careless act, if, but only if, he is at the same time liable for some other damage, however trivial, appears to be neither logical nor just. This becomes more clear if it is supposed that similar unforeseeable damage is suffered by A and C, but other foreseeable damage, for which B is liable, by A only. A system of law which would hold B liable to A but not to C for the similar damage suffered by each of them could not easily be defended. Fortunately, the attempt is not necessary. For the same fallacy is at the root of the proposition. It is irrelevant to the question whether B is liable for unforeseeable damage that he is liable for foreseeable damage, as irrelevant as would the fact that he had trespassed on Whiteacre be to the question whether he had trespassed on Blackacre. Again, suppose a claim by A for damage by fire by the careless act of B. Of what relevance is it to that claim that he has another claim arising out of the same careless act? It would surely not prejudice his claim if that other claim failed; it cannot assist it if it succeeds. Each of them rests on its own bottom and will fail if it can be established that the damage could not reasonably be foreseen. We have come back to the plain common sense stated by Lord Russell of Killowen in Hay v. Young. As Denning LJ said in King v. Phillips ([1953] 1 All ER at p 623; [1953] 1 QB at p 441 "... there can be no doubt since *Hay v. Young* that the test of *liability for shock* is foreseeability of *injury by shock.*" Their Lordships substitute the word "fire" for "shock" and indorse this statement of the law. . . .

Their Lordships will humbly advise Her Majesty that this appeal should be allowed and the respondents' action so far as it related to damage caused by the negligence of the appellants be dismissed with costs. . . .

PREPARING FOR CLASS

1. Why did the plaintiff seek to have the court apply the rule from *Polemis*? Could you argue that the plaintiff would lose under *Polemis* anyway?

2. Why does the court reject the *Polemis* rule?

3. According to the court, what, instead of directness, is the most important liability-limiting principle? Why?

4. What does the court mean by, "It is not the act but the consequences on which tortious liability is founded. Just as (as it has been said) there is no such thing as negligence in the air, so there is no such thing as liability in the air"?

5. What does the court mean by, "And, if that damage is unforeseeable so as to displace liability at large, how can the liability be restored so as to make compensation payable"?

6. What was the negligence here? Why was it negligent?

7. How would you articulate the rule the court chooses to follow?

8. Under the rule, what must occur here?

9. In the rat poison hypothetical, what result with this rule?

INCREASING YOUR UNDERSTANDING

1. *Wagon Mound II.* Morts Dock wasn't the only party injured by the fire caused by the S.S. *Wagon Mound*. Owners of a destroyed ship filed suit

also, but unlike the plaintiffs in *Wagon Mound I*, they established prox-imate cause. The trial court in *Wagon Mound II* found that the defen-dants would have thought the oil was "very difficult to ignite on water" but would have recognized it was possible to ignite. The risk that occurred was thus one of those that the defendant had negligently failed to avoid. Overseas Tankship (U.K.) Ltd. v. The Miller Steamship Co., [1967] 1 A.C. 617. These different consequences highlight the predic-ament of the plaintiff in *Wagon Mound I*. Remember, the plaintiff in that case, Morts Dock, was welding, throwing sparks onto the oil in the bay. If Morts Dock put in evidence of the flammability of furnace oil on water, it would be establishing its own contributory negligence in weld-ing so close to the oil. So Morts Dock opted not to establish foreseeabil-ity and to try for a *Polemis* instruction instead. The ship owners in *Wagon Mound II* had no such problem. They could put in evidence that it was foreseeable furnace oil on water could ignite.

2. *Petition of Kinsman Transit Co.*, 338 F.2d 708, (2d Cir. 1964). Conti-nental Grain Co. owned a dock in the Buffalo River. The steamboat *Shiras*, owned by Kinsman Transit, was moored to the dock. During a thaw, large chunks of ice from a tributary came loose and piled up between the *Shiras* and the shore. The pressure caused the *Shiras* to come loose from the post (known as a "deadman") to which it had been anchored. As the *Shiras* floated downstream it collided with the *Tewks-bury* and caused it to become unmoored. The *Tewksbury* drifted into a drawbridge and brought down a tower on the bridge. The *Shiras* then drifted into that wreckage. The two ships wedged together and created a dam. Together they were about 1,000 feet long. Shortly afterward, the other bridge tower fell into the river, and the banks were flooded for several miles. One theory of negligence was that Continental Grain had negligently maintained the deadman, which permitted the *Shiras* to become unmoored and caused all the damage. At trial, Continental was held liable for a share of the flood damage asserted by 20 different plaintiffs. On this point, the court of appeals affirmed. Justice Friendly wrote the opinion:

> It was indeed foreseeable that the improper construction and lack of inspection of the "deadman" might cause a ship to break loose and damage persons and property on or near the river—that was what made Continental's conduct negligent. With the aid of hindsight one can also say that a prudent man, carefully pondering the problem, would have realized that the danger of this would be greatest under such water conditions as developed during the night of January 21, 1959, and that if a vessel should break loose under those circumstances, events might transpire as they did. But such post hoc step by step analysis would render

"foreseeable" almost anything that has in fact occurred; if the argument relied upon has legal validity, it ought not be circumvented by characterizing as foreseeable what almost no one would in fact have foreseen at the time.

The effect of unforeseeability of damage upon liability for negligence has recently been considered by the Judicial Committee of the Privy Council, Overseas Tankship (U.K.) Ltd. v. Morts Dock & Engineering Co. (The Wagon Mound), (1961) 1 All E.R. 404. The Committee there disapproved the proposition, thought to be supported by In Re Polemis and Furness, Withy & Co. Ltd., (1921) 3 K.B. 560 (C.A.), "that unforeseeability is irrelevant if damage is 'direct.'" We have no difficulty with the result of *The Wagon Mound,* in view of the finding that the appellant had no reason to believe that the floating furnace oil would burn. On that view the decision simply applies the principle which excludes liability where the injury sprang from a hazard different from that which was improperly risked. Although some language in the judgment goes beyond this, we would find it difficult to understand why one who had failed to use the care required to protect others in the light of expectable forces should be exonerated when the very risks that rendered his conduct negligent produced other and more serious consequences to such persons than were fairly foreseeable when he fell short of what the law demanded. Foreseeability of danger is necessary to render conduct negligent; where as here the damage was caused by just those forces whose existence required the exercise of greater care than was taken—the current, the ice, and the physical mass of the *Shiras,* the incurring of consequences other and greater than foreseen does not make the conduct less culpable or provide a reasoned basis for insulation. The oft encountered argument that failure to limit liability to foreseeable consequences may subject the defendant to a loss wholly out of proportion to his fault seems scarcely consistent with the universally accepted rule that the defendant takes the plaintiff as he finds him and will be responsible for the full extent of the injury even though a latent susceptibility of the plaintiff renders this far more serious than could reasonably have been anticipated.

The weight of authority in this country rejects the limitation of damages to consequences foreseeable at the time of the negligent conduct when the consequences are "direct," and the damage, although other and greater than expectable, is of the same general sort that was risked. . . . Other American courts, purporting to apply a test of foreseeability to damages, extend that concept to such unforeseen lengths as to raise serious doubt whether the concept is meaningful; indeed, we wonder whether the British courts are not finding it necessary to limit the language of *The Wagon Mound* as we have indicated.

We see no reason why an actor engaging in conduct which entails a large risk of small damage and a small risk of other and greater damage, of the same general sort, from the same forces, and to the same class of persons, should be relieved of responsibility for the latter simply because the chance of its occurrence, if viewed alone, may not have been large enough to require the exercise of care. By hypothesis, the risk of the lesser harm was sufficient to render his disregard of it actionable; the existence of a less likely additional risk that the very forces against whose action he was required to guard would produce other and greater damage than could have been reasonably anticipated should inculpate him further rather than limit his liability. This does not mean that the careless actor will always be held for all damages for which the forces that he risked were a cause in fact. Somewhere a point will be reached when courts will agree that the link has become too tenuous—that what is claimed to be consequence is only fortuity. Thus, if the destruction of the Michigan Avenue Bridge had delayed the arrival of a doctor, with consequent loss of a patient's life, few judges would impose liability on any of the parties here, although the agreement in result might not be paralleled by similar unanimity in reasoning. . . . We go only so far as to hold that where, as here, the damages resulted from the same physical forces whose existence required the exercise of greater care than was displayed and were of the same general sort that was expectable, unforeseeability of the exact developments and of the extent of the loss will not limit liability. Other fact situations can be dealt with when they arise.

Is the approach taken in *Petition of Kinsman* a *Polemis* approach or a *Wagon Mound* approach? Or is it some new American view of its own? Would the *Wagon Mound I* facts receive a different result under *Kinsman*?

APPLYING THE LAW

1. A man negligently allows his ten-year-old nephew to play with his loaded pistol. The boy takes the gun out into the yard and imitates gunslinger moves he has seen in a movie on television. As the boy is twirling the pistol on his finger, it flies out of his hand and smashes the

neighbor's window. Is the man's negligence the proximate cause of the loss of the neighbor's window?

2. A customer at a self-serve gas station left his car unattended, and it slipped into gear and ran over another customer, whose leg was broken. The injured man sued the gas station for failure to enforce its own policy prohibiting leaving cars unattended, a policy instituted because of the highly flammable properties of gasoline. Is the gas station's negligence the proximate cause of the man's injuries?

3. In United Novelty Co. v. Daniels, 42 So. 2d 395 (Miss. 1949), the teen-aged employee of the defendant was sent into an 8' x 10' room to clean coin-operated machines with gasoline. The room had a gas heater with an open flame. While the boy was working, a rat ran from under the machine he was cleaning to seek warmth under the heater. Gasoline had fallen onto the rat's coat, so when the rat ran under the heater, it caught on fire. It then ran back under the machine on which the boy was working. This ignited the gasoline fumes. The machine exploded, and the boy was killed. The theory of negligence was that the defendant had instructed the boy to use gasoline to clean machines in a room with a lit gas heater. Was this negligence the proximate cause of the boy's death?

B. INTERVENING AND SUPERSEDING CAUSES

Derdiarian v. Felix Contracting Corp.
414 N.E.2d 666 (N.Y. 1980)

COOKE, C.J.

The operator of a motor vehicle, who failed timely to ingest a dosage of medication, suffered an epileptic seizure and his vehicle careened into an excavation site where a gas main was being installed beneath the street surface. The automobile crashed through a single wooden horse-type barricade put in place by the contractor and struck an employee of a subcontractor, who was propelled into the air. Upon landing the employee was splattered by boiling liquid enamel from a kettle also struck by the vehicle. Principally at issue on this appeal is whether plaintiffs, the employee and his wife, failed to establish as a matter of law that the contractor's inadequate safety precautions on the work site were the proximate cause of the accident. . . .

To support his claim of an unsafe work site, plaintiff called as a witness Lawrence Lawton, an expert in traffic safety. According to Lawton, the usual and accepted method of safeguarding the workers is to erect a barrier around the excavation. Such a barrier, consisting of a truck, a piece of heavy equipment or a pile of dirt, would keep a car out of the excavation and protect workers from oncoming traffic. The expert testified that the barrier should cover the entire width of the excavation. He also stated that there should have been two flagmen present, rather than one, and that warning signs should have been posted advising motorists that there was only one lane of traffic and that there was a flagman ahead. . . .

Defendant Felix now argues that plaintiff was injured in a freakish accident, brought about solely by defendant Dickens' negligence, and therefore there was no causal link, as a matter of law, between Felix' breach of duty and plaintiff's injuries. . . .

The concept of proximate cause, or more appropriately legal cause, has proven to be an elusive one, incapable of being precisely defined to cover all situations. . . .

Where the acts of a third person intervene between the defendant's conduct and the plaintiff's injury, the causal connection is not automatically severed. In such a case, liability turns upon whether the intervening act is a normal or foreseeable consequence of the situation created by the defendant's negligence. If the intervening act is extraordinary under the circumstances, not foreseeable in the normal course of events, or independent of or far removed from the defendant's conduct, it may well be a superseding act which breaks the causal nexus. Because questions concerning what is foreseeable and what is normal may be the subject of varying inferences, as is the question of negligence itself, these issues generally are for the fact finder to resolve.

There are certain instances, to be sure, where only one conclusion may be drawn from the established facts and where the question of legal cause may be decided as a matter of law. Those cases generally involve independent intervening acts which operate upon but do not flow from the original negligence. Thus, for instance, we have held that where an automobile lessor negligently supplies a car with a defective trunk lid, it is not liable to the lessee who, while stopped to repair the trunk, was injured by the negligent driving of a third party. Although the renter's negligence undoubtedly served to place the injured party at the site of the accident, the intervening act was divorced from and not the foreseeable risk associated with the original negligence. And the injuries were different in kind than those which would have normally been expected from a defective trunk. In short, the negligence of the renter merely furnished the occasion for an unrelated act to cause injuries not ordinarily anticipated.

By contrast, in the present case, we cannot say as a matter of law that defendant Dickens' negligence was a superseding cause which interrupted the link between Felix' negligence and plaintiff's injuries. From the evidence in the record, the jury could have found that Felix negligently failed to safeguard the excavation site. A prime hazard associated with such dereliction is the possibility that a driver will negligently enter the work site and cause injury to a worker. That the driver was negligent, or even reckless, does not insulate Felix from liability. Nor is it decisive that the driver lost control of the vehicle through a negligent failure to take medication, rather than a driving mistake. The precise manner of the event need not be anticipated. The finder of fact could have concluded that the foreseeable, normal and natural result of the risk created by Felix was the injury of a worker by a car entering the improperly protected work area. An intervening act may not serve as a superseding cause, and relieve an actor of responsibility, where the risk of the intervening act occurring is the very same risk which renders the actor negligent.

In a similar vein, plaintiff's act of placing the kettle on the west side of the excavation does not, as a matter of law, absolve defendant Felix of responsibility. Serious injury, or even death, was a foreseeable consequence of a vehicle crashing through the work area. The injury could have occurred in numerous ways, ranging from a worker being directly struck by the car to the car hitting an object that injures the worker. Placement of the kettle, or any object in the work area, could affect how the accident occurs and the extent of injuries. That defendant could not anticipate the precise manner of the accident or the exact extent of injuries, however, does not preclude liability as a matter of law where the general risk and character of injuries are foreseeable. . . .

For the foregoing reasons, the order of the Appellate Division should be affirmed, with costs. The certified question is answered in the affirmative.

PREPARING FOR CLASS

1. Why was the defendant's manner of guarding the site negligent?

2. Was this negligence the actual cause of the plaintiff's injuries?

3. Why does the defendant think it is not liable?

4. What is an intervening cause? What is the difference between an intervening cause and a superseding cause?

5. The defective trunk example is meant to explain what "independent" means. What does it mean? Can you think of another example? How is the trunk example different from this case?

6. Was the epileptic driver a superseding cause?

INCREASING YOUR UNDERSTANDING

1. In certain recurring situations, the law is settled that the intervening act does not cut off proximate cause.

   a. The law regards the negligence of someone rescuing a person the defendant put in danger as sufficiently foreseeable that the defendant is the proximate cause of injuries from rescuer negligence. For example, the defendant's negligence causes a car accident that injures plaintiff. The ambulance driver hurrying the plaintiff to the hospital drives negligently and causes another accident. The defendant is the proximate cause of plaintiff's injuries in the second accident.

b. The law also regards medical malpractice in the treatment of negligently caused injuries as foreseeable. A dancer in a traveling troupe injures her leg because the troupe negligently failed to take a portable floor to protect her from the conditions of the stage. The doctor treating her injury malpractices and aggravates the injury to her leg. The troupe proximately caused the aggravation of the injury.

c. Negligent reactions to negligence are also foreseeable. Defendant negligently slams on his breaks. In response, the driver behind negligently jerks his steering wheel to the right and hits a bicyclist. The defendant proximately caused the injuries to the bicyclist.

2. A really interesting article by Professor Mark F. Grady, Proximate Cause Decoded, 50 UCLA L. Rev. 293 (2002), sorts the problem of intervening conduct into five categories with predictable outcomes. (As his system is about intervening conduct, it does not address intervening forces, like lightning or animals.)

a. *No intervening tort.* Here, the defendant is the proximate cause because he directly caused injury—he ran a stoplight and struck a pedestrian.

b. *Encouraged free radicals.* The defendant's negligence created a substantial and unusually tempting opportunity for irresponsible third parties to do harm. There is proximate cause here unless the third parties' behavior went beyond the defendant's encouragement. An example Professor Grady cites is a case you have read: *Weirum v. RKO.* Recall that the radio station encouraged the teenaged listeners of the radio station to race across the Los Angeles freeway system to locate "the real Don Steele." The teenagers' poor driving would not cut off proximate cause because the radio station encouraged their dangerous behavior.

c. *Dependent compliance error.* Here, the defendant's negligence exposed the plaintiff to the possibility of someone else's ordinary negligence. As Professor Grady puts it, the defendant's negligence "put[] the plaintiff in harm's way." (He does not mean, however, that the defendant put the plaintiff in the wrong place at the wrong time. Professor Grady means that the defendant made the plaintiff vulnerable specifically to negligence.) Although the risk that resulted came from an intervening cause, the possibility that the intervening cause would occur made the defendant's conduct negligent. The *Derdiarian* case fits in this category. The possibility a car would run into the site made the minimal guarding negligent. The defendant is the proximate cause here as well

d. *No corrective precaution.* Defendant was negligent, and a third party (not a free radical) comes on the scene and recognizes the risk the defendant has created. This third party also has a duty to exercise care against this risk, often because of a special relationship. The third party willfully, wantonly, or recklessly fails to prevent defendant's negligence from causing harm. This is a situation of no proximate cause. The third party's conduct is superseding. Professor Grady cites Pittsburgh Reduction Co. v. Horton, 113 S.W. 647 (Ark. 1908), in which the defendant negligently threw away live blasting caps. A child found the blasting caps, and the child's parents recognized what they were but did not confiscate them. The child then traded the caps with another child who was injured. The court held that the parents' failure to confiscate the caps cut off proximate cause.

e. *Independent intervening tort.* In this scenario, a third party commits an intervening wrong that is independent of the defendant's negligence. That tort cuts off proximate cause. In these cases, the relationship between the target defendant's negligence and the subsequent tortfeasor's act is coincidental. The target defendant's act has not made the second tort any more likely to occur, which makes that second tort independent of the target defendant's negligence. The target defendant is a bicycle shop, which negligently inflates the tires on the plaintiff's bicycle. The plaintiff blows a tire but avoids injury in the incident. As she walks her bicycle into the driveway of a nearby bicycle shop to replace the tire, she is hit by a negligent driver exiting the parking lot.

APPLYING THE LAW

1. A charter plane company negligently under-fuels a plane, forcing the pilot to land on a small island in the Pacific. There, a volcano erupts and kills a passenger. Is the negligent under-fueling the proximate cause of the death? (Although this sounds like one of those unrealistic scenarios invented by a professor, see Doss v. Big Stone Gap, 134 S.E. 563 (Va. 1926).)

2. Despite strong recommendations from the U.S. Golf Association, a golf course did not provide lightning-proof shelters at strategic places on the course, nor did it use sirens or golf marshals to warn golfers of imminent

lightning dangers. Because of this negligence a golfer was struck by lightning on the course. Is the lightning a superseding cause?

3. The defendant driver negligently ran into a power pole, cutting off electricity to a nearby traffic light. Another driver who failed to notice that the traffic light was not functioning crashed into a car in the intersection, killing the passenger. Is the second driver's negligence a superseding cause, or is the first driver's negligence the proximate cause of the death?

4. Defendant owned a bar across from a ball park. After a game one night, the assembled fans in the bar were highly intoxicated. One obviously drunken customer asked the bartender, "Hey, got a cigarette?" The bartender said, "You know you can't smoke in here, take this," and tossed the drunken customer a firecracker instead. The drunken customer lit the firecracker and tossed it to another drunken customer who tossed it to another drunken customer, who was injured when the lit firecracker finally went off. Was the defendant's negligence (in giving a firecracker to a drunken customer) the proximate cause of the third drunken customer's injuries?

5. In Central of Georgia Ry. v. Price, 32 S.E. 77 (Ga. 1898), the train conductor negligently failed to have the train stop at the plaintiff's stop. He arranged for her to stay overnight at a hotel at the next town and be taken back to her stop the following day. During the night, the negligence of the hotel led to a fire in which the plaintiff was injured. Was the conductor's negligence the proximate cause of the plaintiff's injuries?

Britton v. Wooten
817 S.W.2d 443 (Ky. 1991)

Leibson, J.
[A landlord sued a tenant after the leased property was destroyed by fire. The tenant's employees had allowed trash to pile up next to the building, which aided the spread of the fire. The trial court granted summary judgment to the tenant, and the appellate court affirmed. The landlord took this appeal.]

If the boxes and trash were piled high against the masonry wall in such a manner as to permit a fire started in the refuse access up the masonry wall to the inflammable roof of the building, undoubtedly this was a proximate cause, or a substantial factor, in the destruction of the building regardless of how the fire started. The proximate cause issue lacks substance, and the respondent really has only one argument, that "the act of the arsonist in setting the fire was a superseding cause as a matter of law." . . .

We . . . reject any all-inclusive general rule that, as respondent contends, "criminal acts of third parties . . . relieve the original negligent party from liability."

This archaic doctrine has been rejected everywhere. The only Kentucky case movant cites in support of it, Watson v. Kentucky & Indiana Bridge and R. Co., 126 S.W. 146 (Ky. 1910), [is] a case over 80 years old. In it the court draws a distinction in the railroad company's liability for a fire ignited following a train derailment and gas spillage on the basis of a fact question presented as to whether the man who ignited the gasoline did so maliciously or inadvertently. That case indeed holds that the railroad company is "not bound to anticipate the criminal act of others by which damage is inflicted and hence is not liable therefor." The question is whether that case is still viable.

Respondent cites Restatement (Second) of Torts, §448 in support of the continued viability of criminal acts, per se, as sufficient to cut the chain of causation. That section postulates that "an intentional tort or crime is a superseding cause" where the defendant's "negligent conduct" only creates "a situation which afforded an opportunity" for another to commit an intentional tort or crime, but it adds an all important caveat:

> . . . unless the actor [the defendant] at the time of his negligent conduct realized or should have realized the likelihood that such a situation might be created, and that a third person might avail himself of the opportunity to commit such a tort or crime."

Restatement (Second) of Torts, §449, expands on the meaning of §448. Section 449 postulates:

> If the likelihood that a third person may act in a particular manner is the hazard or one of the hazards which makes the actor [the defendant] negligent, such an act [by another person] whether innocent, negligent, intentionally tortious, or criminal, does not prevent the actor [the defendant] from being liable for harm caused thereby.

And these two sections, 448 and 449, also must be read in conjunction with Restatement (Second) of Torts, §302B, "Risk of Intentional or Criminal Conduct," which states:

> An act or an omission may be negligent if the actor realizes or should realize that it involves an unreasonable risk of harm to another through the conduct of the other or a third person which is intended to cause harm, even though such conduct is criminal.

The fact is that the appendices to the Restatement (Second) of Torts, §§448 and 449, are replete with numerous cases, perhaps one hundred in number, from throughout these United States, acknowledging the Restatement (Second) of Torts §§448 and 449 as authority and deciding the negligence of a defendant is actionable as a contributing cause, wherein the immediate cause is a subsequent criminal act. We will not burden this Opinion by trying to cover the field, but we will review four cases because they represent factual situations strikingly similar to the present case:

1) Arneil v. Schnitzer, 144 P.2d 707 (Ore. 1944), affirmed the liability of the property owners where litter in a junk yard created a fire hazard, and a trespasser then started a fire on the premises which spread to adjoining premises. The court states:

> The intervention of a criminal act, however, does not necessarily interrupt the relation of cause and effect between negligence and an injury. If at the time of the negligence, the criminal act might reasonably have been foreseen, the causal chain is not broken by the intervention of such act. . . . We know of no decision which holds that one who maintains his property so negligently that it menaces his neighbors, is liable for the destruction of their premises by a fire which started upon his, only in the event that he himself applied the match. To the contrary, we are satisfied that the owner's negligence is the proximate cause of the damage to the neighbor, even if a stranger communicated the spark. . . . One who suspends a sword of Damocles over the head of his neighbor must respond in damages for the consequences if another, allured by the temptation, cuts the tender cord. . . . We are satisfied that when the defendants littered their property with piles of combustible material it was their duty to anticipate trespasses by such persons as Ellis Miller, and also to anticipate that the intruders might cast about lighted tobacco.

2) d'Hedouville v. Pioneer Hotel Co., 552 F.2d 886 (9th Cir. 1977), a wrongful death action. It involved a claim against the manufacturer of acrylic fiber used in carpeting in a hotel, charging the product was highly inflammable and unreasonably dangerous, and as such a contributing cause in the rapid spread of a fire started by an arsonist. The Court states:

> Monsanto [the defendant carpet manufacturer] argues that under Arizona decisions the criminal act of a third person constitutes a superseding cause as a matter of law. While this appears to have been the rule stated in early Arizona cases, more recent decisions apply the general principle of foreseeability to intervening criminal acts.

[The third case is omitted.]

4) Hodge v. Nor-Cen, Inc., 527 N.E.2d 1157 (Ind. App. 1988), holding that the act of an arsonist in setting the fire was not an intervening event which

broke the causal connection between the landlord's negligence in failing to provide a second means of egress and the injury occasioned to tenants by inability to escape during the fire. . . . The Indiana court holds:

> While Nor-Cen correctly states the rule of [Restatement (Second) of Torts, §448], its application of the rule to these facts is faulty. . . . Fire, whether by accident or design, is not an intervening event which breaks the causal connection between the act of failing to provide a second means of egress and the injury occasioned by the inability to escape; it is merely an event in the chain of causation. . . . Because the undisputed facts do not negate the elements of a claim of negligence, appellants' claim should have survived summary judgment. . . .

The lengthy and authoritative treatise by Harper, James and Gray, *The Law of Torts*, 2d ed. (1986), addresses the point at issue as follows:

> It is often said that an actor may assume that others will act lawfully and carefully. Rightly understood this is sound enough, and no more than a corollary of the general [negligence] principle. . . . But in this connection two things must be noted. The first is that such an assumption does not always correspond to the facts. It does not in situations where a law is generally disobeyed. . . . And it does not wherever the actor's [defendant's] conduct exposes some interest to risk from a large and indeterminate group of people that will probably include some who will be negligent or commit crime, so that the likelihood of some negligence or some crime is considerable, though the number of those who will be responsible for it is relative small. . . . Perhaps the most significant trend that has taken place in this particular field, in recent years, has been the increasing liberalization in allowing the wrongs of other people to be regarded as foreseeable where the facts warrant that conclusion if they are looked at naturally and not through the lens of some artificial archaic notion.

In the present case whether the spark ignited in the trash accumulated next to the building was ignited negligently, intentionally, or even criminally, or if it was truly accidental, is not the critical issue. The issue is whether the movant can prove that the respondent caused or permitted trash to accumulate next to its building in a negligent manner which caused or contributed to the spread of the fire and the destruction of the lessor's building. If so, the source of the spark that ignited the fire is not a superseding cause under any reasonable application of modern tort law.

The Summary Judgment in the trial court is vacated, and the decision in the Court of Appeals affirming it is reversed. The within case is remanded to the trial court for further proceedings consistent with this Opinion.

PREPARING FOR CLASS

1.   For what principle did the plaintiff rely on *Watson*?

2.   For what principle did the plaintiff rely on Restatement (Second) Torts §448? What did the plaintiff overlook (or omit) in that reliance? How does that affect the plaintiff's position?

3.   How are *Arneil* and *d'Hedouville* like this case? How are those similarities legally significant? Is *Hodge* different from those two cases and the present case? In a way that matters?

4.   How does the Harper treatise criticize the logic of *Watson* and cases like it as artificial?

5.   Why does the court find it irrelevant whether the fire was started by an arsonist? Why should a party be held responsible for someone else's criminal behavior? Isn't this unfair?

6.   Does this case mean that arson will never cut off proximate cause? That intentional torts and crimes never will cut off proximate cause?

INCREASING YOUR UNDERSTANDING

Many members of the legal profession were schooled that, as a general rule, intervening crimes and intentional torts cut off proximate cause. As the *Britton* case points out, such conduct is no longer presumed unforeseeable, and foreseeability must be assessed on a case-by-case basis. Still, intervening crimes and intentional torts are more likely to be unforeseeable than intervening negligence, and the long-standing common exceptions to non-liability in such cases are helpful in determining whether the crime or intentional tort cuts off proximate cause.

1.   *Defendant had a duty to prevent crime.* Think of the landlord in *Kline v. 1500 Massachusetts Ave.* The court ruled that the landlord had a duty to protect tenants in the common areas from crime. Therefore, the landlord cannot successfully argue that when the tenant was mugged in the lobby that the mugging, as a crime, cut off proximate cause.

2.   *Defendant exposed the plaintiff to people likely to commit crimes against her.* In Hines v. Garrett, 108 S.E. 690 (Va. 1921), a train missed a station, and the conductor permitted the train to be stopped to let the plaintiff, an 18-year-old woman, get off and walk the mile back to her stop. The area where she was let off was known as "Hoboes' Hollow" and was "habitually frequented and infested by hoboes, tramps, and questionable characters." A man, dressed as a soldier, got off the train

when the plaintiff did, caught up to her, and raped her. As she was trying to rise, another man raped her. The court upheld the verdict for the plaintiff:

> No 18-year-old girl should be required to set out alone, near nightfall, to walk along an unprotected route, passing a spot which is physically so situated as to lend itself to the perpetration of a criminal assault, and which is infested by worthless, irresponsible and questionable characters known as tramps and hoboes; and no prudent man, charged with her care would willingly cause her to do so. The very danger to which this unfortunate girl fell a victim is the one to which would at once suggest itself to the average and normal mind as a danger liable to overtake her under these circumstances.

3. *Defendant destroyed or defeated plaintiff's protection against crime.* The plaintiff had a home security system. An electrician working at the home negligently severed wiring in the security system. Because the system was not working, a burglar broke into the home and caused personal injury and property damage. That crime does not cut off proximate cause.

APPLYING THE LAW

1. A bank in a high-crime neighborhood did not provide security lights or cameras by its night deposit box, and a bar manager depositing the night's receipts was stabbed by a robber. Does the stabbing cut off proximate cause?

2. A man owned several apartment buildings, and he was looking for a residential manager for one. He decided to help out a friend from his high school days. The friend had recently been released from prison, where he served time for rape. The man hired the friend for the job, which required giving the friend keys to all the residents' apartments. The friend used the keys to gain access to a tenant's apartment, where he raped her. Is the negligent hiring the proximate cause of the rape?

3. A recently convicted criminal in the hallways of a courthouse on his way to sentencing escaped because the sheriff's department was negligent. The criminal made his way to an abandoned building ten miles away. The following morning, he left his hide-out and hit a man in the head with a heavy piece of metal so that he could take his clothes and wallet. Is the sheriff's department's negligence the proximate cause of the man's injuries?

Clinkscales v. Nelson Securities, Inc.
697 N.W.2d 836 (Ia. 2005)

PER CURIAM.

. . . A marine out for a drink at a Davenport bar rushed to the scene of a gas leak at a grill on the premises. While attempting to turn off two propane gas tanks, a grease fire reignited and he was badly burned. The district court dismissed the marine's negligence claim against the bar. The court held as a matter of law the marine was solely to blame for his injuries. The court of appeals affirmed. Because a jury could find the bar's negligence proximately caused the marine's rescue attempt and injuries, we reverse the district court, vacate the court of appeals, and remand for a trial on the merits.

Late one Friday afternoon in the summer of 2002, James Clinkscales went to The Gallery Lounge, a Davenport pub. Approximately fifty people were there. Clinkscales, an active-duty marine in town as a recruiter, stationed himself at the bar next to a blonde woman known only as "Dimples." The two began to share a pitcher of beer together.

On Fridays in the summer, The Gallery regularly grilled hamburgers outside and served them to its customers. The grill stood directly outside of the bar on a patio ten feet away from where Clinkscales and Dimples sat. Two tanks of propane gas placed underneath the grill fueled it. The grill was custom-made and large enough to grill twenty burgers at a time.

The Gallery employed Joe Moser to grill the burgers. The first batch of burgers Moser placed on the grill that evening were particularly greasy. When Moser flipped them over, a fire flared up on the grill. Moser did not consider this to be a problem. All of a sudden, however, Moser heard something abnormal—"a pop and a hiss." A ball of fire erupted underneath the grill and engulfed the propane tanks.

Caroline Nelson co-owns The Gallery with her husband and regularly works there. When the fire started Nelson was standing at the patio door. Moser told Nelson to get a fire extinguisher. Nelson and Moser testified Nelson and other Gallery employees made general announcements to the patrons to leave and then one employee called the fire department. Clinkscales testified he was alerted to the fire when he saw Nelson come into the bar looking for a fire extinguisher, but did not believe Nelson said anything to him or anybody else about what was happening.

Nelson came back outside with a fire extinguisher and gave it to a patron. The patron extinguished the flame, and Moser managed to turn the knobs on the grill to the "off" position. Moser could still smell gas escaping from the tanks, however, and Moser said aloud that he wanted to shut the tanks off. Moser pulled the grill away from a wall to access the tanks, but he found the valves were too hot to touch. There were customers in the patio and adjacent bar. Clinkscales came out to the patio and asked a man holding a fire extinguisher if anyone had turned the gas off. The man told Clinkscales the handle was too hot.

Clinkscales, who had received extensive training in fire suppression in the military, recognized the situation was "very dangerous." Clinkscales took off his shirt, wrapped it around one of hands, and turned the gas off. No one asked Clinkscales to do so. He reacted instinctively:

> [I]t's like running after a kid when he runs into the street, you don't think about it, that there's a car coming, you just try to grab the child, and, you know, hope for the best. You could get killed doing it, but you just do it.

As Clinkscales was turning off the gas, the fire flared up. Clinkscales was burned on his face, neck, chest, arms, and legs.

Skin hanging from his arms, Clinkscales continued his rescue efforts by helping a frightened young woman in the patio over a fence. A frequent patron of the bar, a man named Norm, took Clinkscales to the hospital just as the fire department arrived.

Clinkscales sued The Gallery for negligence. . . .

The defendants filed a motion for summary judgment, which the district court granted. As a matter of law the district court found employees of The Gallery told Clinkscales to evacuate the premises; there was no evidence there was imminent risk to life when he turned off the gas; and "a reasonable person would not determine that the benefits of approaching a fire outweigh the risk of being seriously burned or injured." The district court ruled the defendants were not liable because (1) Clinkscales's injuries were caused by a known and obvious danger and (2) the defendants' alleged negligence was not the proximate cause of Clinkscales's injuries. . . . The court of appeals affirmed. It declined to apply the rescue doctrine and held, as a matter of law, Clinkscales "suffers from a self-inflicted wound." . . .

The rescue doctrine was forged at common law. It involves heroic people doing heroic things. The late Justice Cardozo aptly summarized the common-sense observations about human nature that led to the doctrine's widespread recognition across this nation when he wrote:

> Danger invites rescue. The cry of distress is the summons to relief. The law does not ignore these reactions of the mind in tracing conduct to its consequences. It recognizes them as normal. It places their effects within the range of the natural and probable. The wrong that imperils life is a wrong to the imperiled victim; it is a wrong also to his rescuer. The state that leaves an opening in a bridge is liable to the child that falls into the stream, but liable also to the parent who plunges to its aid. The railroad company whose train approaches without signal is a wrongdoer toward the traveler surprised between the rails, but a wrongdoer also to the bystander who drags him from the path. . . . The risk of rescue, if only it be not wanton, is born of the occasion. The

emergency begets the man. The wrongdoer may not have foreseen the coming of a deliverer. He is accountable as if he had.

Wagner v. Int'l Ry., 133 N.E. 437, 437-38 (N.Y. 1921) (citations omitted). That is, those who negligently imperil life or property may not only be liable to their victims, but also to the rescuers.

We have consistently and liberally applied the rescue doctrine in this state for over one hundred years. Historically the doctrine arose in questions of proximate cause and contributory negligence. "In other words, did the act of the injured [rescuer] so intervene as to break the chain of causation from [the] defendant's negligence, or constitute such contributory negligence as to bar recovery?" The general rule was a rescuer would not be deemed to have broken the chain of causation or charged with contributory negligence for reasonable attempts to save the life or property of another. Since the advent of comparative negligence, the doctrine has only arisen on appeal in questions of proximate cause, i.e., when, as here, the defendant claims the rescuer's actions were a superseding cause of the rescuer's injuries.

The Gallery contends its alleged negligence was not the proximate cause of Clinkscales's injuries. The Gallery asserts the facts show its employees ordered patrons to leave the premises, it had called the fire department, and at the time of the rescue attempt Moser was retrieving a rag to turn off the propane valves. The court of appeals held as a matter of law that the rescue doctrine did not apply in this case because "no one was in any danger until the plaintiff placed himself there."

It is well settled that questions of proximate cause are, absent extraordinary circumstances, for the jury to decide. The line between what is sufficiently proximate and what is too remote is a thin one:

> If upon looking back from the injury, the connection between the negligence and the injury appears unnatural, unreasonable, and improbable in the light of common experience, such negligence would be a remote rather than a proximate cause. If, however, by a fair consideration of the facts based upon common human experience and logic, there is nothing particularly unnatural or unreasonable in connecting the injury with the negligence, a jury question would be created.

Here we are concerned with Clinkscales's rescue attempt, which The Gallery characterizes as a "superseding cause" of his injuries. A superseding cause is an intervening force that "prevent[s] the defendant from being liable for harm to the plaintiff that the defendant's antecedent negligence is a substantial factor in bringing about."

When a rescue attempt is involved, matters are particularly thorny and a court should be especially wary to grant a defendant's motion for summary judgment. The rescue doctrine recognizes not all intervening forces are super-seding causes:

> If the actor's negligent conduct threatens harm to another's person, land, or chattels, the normal efforts of the other or a third person to avert the threatened harm are not a superseding cause of harm resulting from such efforts.

Restatement §445. That is, so long as the rescuer's response is "normal," the negligent actor will not escape liability for the rescuer's injuries.

What are "normal" rescue efforts? Although in [Hollingsworth v. Schminkey, 553 N.W.2d 591 (Iowa 1996)] we loosely characterized the question of "normal efforts" as one solely of foreseeability, in truth the term "normal" is not used "in the sense of what is usual, customary, foreseeable, or to be expected." Restatement §443 cmt. b; see also id. §445 cmt. b. Rather, "normal" (referred to in our pre-Restatement cases as "natural") is used as "the antithesis of abnormal, of extraordinary." Restatement §443 cmt. b.

> [T]he only inquiry should be whether the conduct of the plaintiff was "natural" under the circumstances, which is to be ascertained by a counter-chronological examination of the facts. Here the term "natural" must be taken to embrace those qualities of human nature leading to risk-taking in an effort to preserve property, to rescue other persons, or to save oneself. It necessarily includes actions which these well recognized and familiar human feelings bring about. Thus "natural" conduct includes not only cool and well-reasoned action but also the frantic, excited and apparently illogical movements which are too commonly exhibited by a large percentage of human beings in moments of stress.
>
> In these situations, the defendant may negligently have exposed the person or property of another to unreasonable risk of loss or destruction. "Natural" instincts will move some persons to make efforts at rescue. The movements of the rescuer may not be well judged and may result in harm either to the goods, to the person endangered by the defendant, or to the rescuer himself. In any such case the defendant will be held liable, for the "natural" conduct of the rescuer leaves no break or gap in the chain of causation."

Clayton [v. Blair,] 117 N.W.2d at 882 [(Iowa 1963)] (quoting Clarence M. Updegraff, *A Technique for Determining Legal Liability Based on Negligence*, 27 Iowa L. Rev. 2, 28 (1941)); accord Restatement §443 cmt. b. What constitutes normal or natural conduct depends upon the circumstances and "is in most cases a question to be decided by the jury." If the jury determines the rescuer's actions are a normal or natural result of the defendant's actions, the defendant's actions were a proximate cause of the rescuer's injuries.

We think the facts are sufficiently in conflict on the issue of proximate cause to warrant a jury determination. The dangers of fire and gas leaks are well known to all. See *Henneman*, 260 Iowa at 72, 148 N.W.2d at 454 (rescue doctrine applies not only when danger is imminent, but also when "the conduct of the rescuer is that of an ordinarily prudent person under existing circumstances"); accord Silbernagel v. Voss, 265 F.2d 390, 391-92 (7th Cir. 1959) (approving of jury instruction that was "phrased to elicit an answer as to whether the situation . . . induce[d] a reasonable belief on part of [the] plaintiff that [the victim] was in imminent peril"); *Wagner*, 133 N.E. at 438 (refuting view that rescue doctrine should not apply when, in fact, rescue attempt was futile); cf. Fullerton v. Sauer, 337 F.2d 474, 482 (8th Cir. 1964) (construing Iowa law to hold rescue doctrine did not apply when "only apparent or imminent danger" had passed). This summary-judgment record shows customers, employees, and property of The Gallery were in the vicinity of the fire and subsequent gas leak. While it is undisputed employees of The Gallery called the fire department and asked some patrons to evacuate, a jury could find Clinkscales's rescue efforts were a normal or natural reaction under the circumstances. He may have reasonably thought danger was imminent and, given his extensive training, his help was needed.

Exhortations to leave do not, as a matter of law, preclude liability in all cases. If a defendant sets into course a series of events that induces a rescue attempt, the defendant does not necessarily insulate itself from liability when it tells the rescuer to leave. In any event, in this case there is evidence no one effectively ordered Clinkscales to leave, and some evidence The Gallery enlisted the help of other customers to fight the fire. There is nothing inconsistent with an express general call to evacuate and an implicit individual invitation to help. Even if we were to assume Clinkscales was told to leave, however, this would be but one fact for the jury to consider in evaluating his rescue attempt.

We cannot say as a matter of law that the rescue doctrine does not apply to this case. A reasonable jury could find Clinkscales's rescue of Gallery employees, customers, and property was an act done in normal or natural response to the fear or emotional disturbance caused by The Gallery's negligence. Summary judgment on the issue of proximate cause was not proper. . . .

PREPARING FOR CLASS

1. Clinkscales chose to endanger himself. Why shouldn't that freely chosen risk fall on him?

2. Why is the rescue a proximate cause issue? Is it probably also a duty issue?

3. What is the rescue doctrine? What does it accomplish?

4. Does the restaurant's order to leave the premises cut off its responsibility to Clinkscales who disregarded that order?

5. Not every rescue fits within the doctrine. What requirements must the plaintiff meet to come within it?

6. Is whether the plaintiff meets the rescue doctrine a question for the judge or the jury?

7. Does this case fit within the rescue doctrine? What change in facts might change the outcome?

INCREASING YOUR UNDERSTANDING

In McCoy v. American Suzuki Motor Corp., 961 P.2d 952 (Wash. 1998), the court stated, "To achieve rescuer status one must demonstrate: (1) the defendant was negligent to the person rescued and such negligence caused the peril or appearance of peril to the person rescued; (2) the peril or appearance of peril was imminent; (3) a reasonably prudent person would have concluded such peril or appearance of peril existed; and (4) the rescuer acted with reasonable care in effectuating the rescue." Do we get the same result in *Clinkscales* with this rule statement? Do you prefer one rule to the other? Why?

APPLYING THE LAW

1. In Strickland v. Kotecki, 913 N.E.2d 80 (Ill. App. 2009), "On January 8, 2006, Janet could not find her husband, Kevin K., and feared that he was going to attempt suicide. As a result, Janet called Carrie, her sister, and requested that she and her husband, Kevin S., help her find Kevin K. The three of them inspected a fenced-in business property and saw Kevin K.'s vehicle behind a locked gate. The vehicle had a hose running from its exhaust pipe to the passenger window. When Kevin S. jumped over the fence to rescue Kevin K., he injured his right foot." Assuming that Kevin K. behaved negligently in attempting suicide, is that negligence the proximate cause of Kevin S.'s foot injury?

2. Medical malpractice by a doctor caused his patient to suffer kidney failure and require a new kidney. The patient's son was a donor match and donated his kidney to his father. The son then sued the doctor on the theory that under the rescue doctrine, his donation was foreseeable. Does the son's conduct fit within the rescue doctrine? (For two cases on point, see Moore v. Shah, 90 A.D. 2d 389 (N.Y. App. 1982), and Dabdoub v. Ochsner Clinic, 760 So. 2d 347 (La. 2000).

C. UNEXPECTED VICTIMS

Palsgraf v. Long Island R. Co.
162 N.E. 99 (N.Y. 1928)

CARDOZO, C.J.

Plaintiff was standing on a platform of defendant's railroad after buying a ticket to go to Rockaway Beach. A train stopped at the station, bound for another place. Two men ran forward to catch it. One of the men reached the platform of the car without mishap, though the train was already moving. The other man, carrying a package, jumped aboard the car, but seemed unsteady as if about to fall. A guard on the car, who had held the door open, reached forward to help him in, and another guard on the platform pushed him from behind. In this act, the package was dislodged, and fell upon the rails. It was a package of small size, about fifteen inches long, and was covered by a newspaper. In fact it contained fireworks, but there was nothing in its appearance to give notice of its contents. The fireworks when they fell exploded. The shock of the explosion threw down some scales at the other end of the platform many feet away. The scales struck the plaintiff, causing injuries for which she sues.

The conduct of the defendant's guard, if a wrong in its relation to the holder of the package, was not a wrong in its relation to the plaintiff, standing far away. Relatively to her it was not negligence at all. Nothing in the situation gave notice that the falling package had in it the potency of peril to persons thus removed. Negligence is not actionable unless it involves the invasion of a legally protected interest, the violation of a right. "Proof of negligence in the air, so to speak, will not do." Pollock, *Torts* (11th Ed.) p. 455. The plaintiff, as she stood upon the platform of the station, might claim to be protected against intentional invasion of her bodily security. Such invasion is not charged. She might claim to be protected against unintentional invasion by conduct involving in the thought of reasonable men an unreasonable hazard that such invasion would ensue. These, from the point of view of the law, were the bounds of her immunity, with perhaps some rare exceptions, survivals for the most part of ancient forms of liability, where conduct is held to be at the peril of the actor. If no hazard was apparent to the eye of ordinary vigilance, an act innocent and harmless, at least to outward seeming, with reference to her, did not take to itself the quality of a tort because it happened to be a wrong, though apparently not one involving the risk of bodily insecurity, with reference to some one else. "In every instance, before negligence can be predicated of a given act, back of the act must be sought and found a duty to the individual complaining, the observance of which would have averted or avoided the injury." McSherry, C.J., in West Virginia Central & P.R. Co. v. State, 54 A. 669. The plaintiff sues in her own right for a wrong personal to her, and not as the vicarious beneficiary of a breach of duty to another.

A different conclusion will involve us, and swiftly too, in a maze of contra-dictions. A guard stumbles over a package which has been left upon a platform. It seems to be a bundle of newspapers. It turns out to be a can of dynamite. To the eye of ordinary vigilance, the bundle is abandoned waste, which may be kicked or trod on with impunity. Is a passenger at the other end of the platform protected by the law against the unsuspected hazard concealed beneath the waste? If not, is the result to be any different, so far as the distant passenger is concerned, when the guard stumbles over a valise which a truckman or a porter has left upon the walk? The passenger far away, if the victim of a wrong at all, has a cause of action, not derivative, but original and primary. His claim to be protected against invasion of his bodily security is neither greater nor less because the act resulting in the invasion is a wrong to another far removed. In this case, the rights that are said to have been violated, are not even of the same order. The man was not injured in his person nor even put in danger. The purpose of the act, as well as its effect, was to make his person safe. It there was a wrong to him at all, which may very well be doubted it was a wrong to a property interest only, the safety of his package. Out of this wrong to property, which threatened injury to nothing else, there has passed, we are told, to the plaintiff by derivation or succession a right of action for the invasion of an interest of another order, the right to bodily security. The diversity of interests emphasizes the futility of the effort to build the plaintiff's right upon the basis of a wrong to some one else. The gain is one of emphasis, for a like result would follow if the interests were the same. Even then, the orbit of the danger as disclosed to the eye of reasonable vigilance would be the orbit of the duty. . . .

The argument for the plaintiff is built upon the shifting meanings of such words as "wrong" and "wrongful," and shares their instability. What the plain-tiff must show is "a wrong" to herself; i.e., a violation of her own right, and not merely a wrong to some one else, nor conduct "wrongful" because unsocial, but not "a wrong" to any one. We are told that one who drives at reckless speed through a crowded city street is guilty of a negligent act and therefore of a wrongful one, irrespective of the consequences. Negligent the act is, and wrongful in the sense that it is unsocial, but wrongful and unsocial in relation to other travelers, only because the eye of vigilance perceives the risk of damage. If the same act were to be committed on a speedway or a race course, it would lose its wrongful quality. The risk reasonably to be perceived defines the duty to be obeyed, and risk imports relation; it is risk to another or to others within the range of apprehension. This does not mean, of course, that one who launches a destructive force is always relieved of liability, if the force, though known to be destructive, pursues an unexpected path. "It was not necessary that the defendant should have had notice of the particular method in which an accident would occur, if the possibility of an accident was clear to the ordi-narily prudent eye." Some acts, such as shooting are so imminently dangerous to any one who may come within reach of the missile however unexpectedly, as to impose a duty of prevision not far from that of an insurer. Even today, and much oftener in earlier stages of the law, one acts sometimes at one's peril. Under this head, it may be, fall certain cases of what is known as transferred intent, an act willfully dangerous to A resulting by misadventure in injury to B. These cases aside, wrong is defined in terms of the natural or probable, at least when unintentional. The range of reasonable apprehension is at times a question for the court, and at times, if varying inferences are possible, a question for the jury. Here, by concession, there was nothing in the situation to suggest to the most cautious mind that the parcel wrapped in newspaper would spread wreckage through the station. If the guard had thrown it down knowingly and willfully, he would not have threatened the plaintiff's safety, so far as appearances could warn him. His conduct would not have involved, even then, an unreasonable probability of invasion of her bodily security. Liability can be no greater where the act is inadvertent.

Negligence, like risk, is thus a term of relation. Negligence in the abstract, apart from things related, is surely not a tort, if indeed it is understandable at all. . . .

The law of causation, remote or proximate, is thus foreign to the case before us. The question of liability is always anterior to the question of the measure of the consequences that go with liability. If there is no tort to be redressed, there is no occasion to consider what damage might be recovered if there were a finding of a tort. We may assume, without deciding, that negligence, not at large or in the abstract, but in relation to the plaintiff, would entail liability for any and all consequences, however novel or extraordinary. There is room for argument that a distinction is to be drawn according to the diversity of interests invaded by the act, as where conduct negligent in that it threatens an insignificant invasion of an interest in property results in an unforeseeable invasion of an interest of another order, as, e.g., one of bodily security. Perhaps other distinctions may be necessary. We do not go into the question now. The consequences to be followed must first be rooted in a wrong.

The judgment of the Appellate Division and that of the Trial Term should be reversed, and the complaint dismissed, with costs in all courts.

ANDREWS, J. (dissenting).

Assisting a passenger to board a train, the defendant's servant negligently knocked a package from his arms. It fell between the platform and the cars. Of its contents the servant knew and could know nothing. A violent explosion followed. The concussion broke some scales standing a considerable distance away. In falling, they injured the plaintiff, an intending passenger.

Upon these facts, may she recover the damages she has suffered in an action brought against the master? The result we shall reach depends upon our theory as to the nature of negligence. Is it a relative concept—the breach of some duty owing to a particular person or to particular persons? Or, where there is an act which unreasonably threatens the safety of others, is the doer liable for all its proximate consequences, even where they result in injury to one who would generally be thought to be outside the radius of danger? This is not a mere dispute as to words. We might not believe that to the average mind the dropping of the bundle would seem to involve the probability of harm to the plaintiff standing many feet away whatever might be the case as to the owner or to one so near as to be likely to be struck by its fall. If, however, we adopt the second hypothesis, we have to inquire only as to the relation between cause and effect. We deal in terms of proximate cause, not of negligence. . . .

But we are told that "there is no negligence unless there is in the particular case a legal duty to take care, and this duty must be not which is owed to the plaintiff himself and not merely to others." Salmond, *Torts* (6th Ed.) 24. This I think too narrow a conception. Where there is the unreasonable act, and some right that may be affected there is negligence whether damage does or does not result. That is immaterial. Should we drive down Broadway at a reckless speed, we are negligent whether we strike an approaching car or miss it by an inch. The act itself is wrongful. If is a wrong not only to those who happen to be within the radius of danger, but to all who might have been there—a wrong to the public at large. Such is the language of the street. Such the language of the courts when speaking of contributory negligence. . . .

Due care is a duty imposed on each one of us to protect society from unnecessary danger, not to protect A, B, or C alone.

It may well be that there is no such thing as negligence in the abstract. "Proof of negligence in the air, so to speak, will not do." In an empty world negligence would not exist. It does involve a relationship between man and his fellows, but not merely a relationship between man and those whom he might reasonably expect his act would injure; rather, a relationship between him and those whom he does in fact injure. If his act has a tendency to harm some one, it harms him a mile away as surely as it does those on the scene. . . .

The proposition is this: Every one owes to the world at large the duty of refraining from those acts that may unreasonably threaten the safety of others. Such an act occurs. Not only is he wronged to whom harm, might reasonably be expected to result, but he also who is in fact injured, even if he be outside what would generally be thought the danger zone. There needs be duty due the one complaining, but this is not a duty to a particular individual because as to him harm might be expected. Harm to some one being the natural result of the act, not only that one alone, but all those in fact injured may complain. We have never, I think, held otherwise. . . . Unreasonable risk being taken, its consequences are not confined to those who might probably be hurt.

. . . An overturned lantern may burn all Chicago. We may follow the fire from the shed to the last building. We rightly say the fire started by the lantern caused its destruction.

A cause, but not the proximate cause. What we do mean by the word "proximate" is that, because of convenience, of public policy, of a rough sense of justice, the law arbitrarily declines to trace a series of events beyond a certain point. This is not logic. It is practical politics. Take our rule as to fires. Sparks from my burning haystack set on fire my house and my neighbor's. I may recover from a negligent railroad [that set my haystack on fire]. He may not. Yet the wrongful act as directly harmed the one as the other. We may regret that the line was drawn just where it was, but drawn somewhere it had to be. We said the act of the railroad was not the proximate cause of our neighbor's fire. Cause it surely was. The words we used were simply indicative of our notions of public policy. Other courts think differently. . . .

Take the illustration given in an unpublished manuscript by a distinguished and helpful writer on the law of torts. A chauffeur negligently collides with another car which is filled with dynamite, although he could not know it. An explosion follows. A, walking on the sidewalk nearby, is killed. B, sitting in a window of a building opposite, is cut by flying glass. C, likewise sitting in a window a block away, is similarly injured. And a further illustration: A nursemaid, ten blocks away, startled by the noise, involuntarily drops a baby from her arms to the walk. We are told that C may not recover while A may. As to B it is a question for court or jury. We will all agree that the baby might not. Because, we are again told, the chauffeur had no reason to believe his conduct involved any risk of injuring either C or the baby. As to them he was not negligent.

But the chauffeur, being negligent in risking the collision, his belief that the scope of the harm he might do would be limited is immaterial. His act unreasonably jeopardized the safety of any one who might be affected by it. C's injury and that of the baby were directly traceable to the collision. Without that, the injury would not have happened. C had the right to sit in his office, secure from such dangers. The baby was entitled to use the sidewalk with reasonable safety.

The true theory is, it seems to me, that the injury to C, if in truth he is to be denied recovery, and the injury to the baby, is that their several injuries were not the proximate result of the negligence. And here not what the chauffeur had reason to believe would be the result of his conduct, but what the prudent would foresee, may have a bearing—may have some bearing, for the problem of proximate cause is not to be solved by any one consideration. It is all a question of expediency. There are no fixed rules to govern our judgment. There are simply matters of which we may take account. . . . There is in truth little to guide us other than common sense.

There are some hints that may help us. The proximate cause, involved as it may be with many other causes, must be, at the least, something without which the event would not happen. The court must ask itself whether there was a natural and continuous sequence between cause and effect. Was the one a substantial factor in producing the other? Was there a direct connection between them, without too many intervening causes? Is the effect of cause on result not too attentuated? Is the cause likely, in the usual judgment of mankind, to produce the result? Or, by the exercise of prudent foresight, could the result be foreseen? Is the result too remote from the cause, and here we consider remoteness in time and space. . . . Clearly we must so consider, for the greater the distance either in time or space, the more surely do other causes intervene to affect the result. When a lantern is overturned, the firing of a shed is a fairly direct consequence. Many things contribute to the spread of the conflagration—the force of the wind, the direction and width of streets, the character of intervening structures, other factors. We draw an uncertain and wavering line, but draw it we must as best we can.

Once again, it is all a question of fair judgment, always keeping in mind the fact that we endeavor to make a rule in each case that will be practical and in keeping with the general understanding of mankind.

Here another question must be answered. In the case supposed, it is said, and said correctly, that the chauffeur is liable for the direct effect of the explosion, although he had no reason to suppose it would follow a collision. "The fact that the injury occurred in a different manner than that which might have been expected does not prevent the chauffeur's negligence from being in law the cause of the injury." But the natural results of a negligent act—the results which a prudent man would or should foresee—do have a bearing upon the decision as to proximate cause. We have said so repeatedly. What should be foreseen? No human foresight would suggest that a collision itself might injure one a block away. On the contrary, given an explosion, such a possibility might be reasonably expected. I think the direct connection, the foresight of which the courts speak, assumes prevision of the explosion, for the immediate results of which, at least, the chauffeur is responsible.

If may be said this is unjust. Why? In fairness he should make good every injury flowing from his negligence. Not because of tenderness toward him we say he need not answer for all that follows his wrong. We look back to the catastrophe, the fire kindled by the spark, or the explosion. We trace the consequences, not indefinitely, but to a certain point. And to aid us in fixing that point we ask what might ordinarily be expected to follow the fire or the explosion.

This last suggestion is the factor which must determine the case before us. The act upon which defendant's liability rests is knocking an apparently harmless package onto the platform. The act was negligent. For its proximate consequences the defendant is liable. If its contents were broken, to the owner; if it fell upon and crushed a passenger's foot, then to him; if it exploded and injured one in the immediate vicinity, to him also as to A in the illustration. Mrs. Palsgraf was standing some distance away. How far cannot be told from the record—apparently 25 or 30 feet, perhaps less. Except for the explosion, she would not have been injured. We are told by the appellant in his brief, "It cannot be denied that the explosion was the direct cause of the plaintiff's injuries." So it was a substantial factor in producing the result—there was here a natural and continuous sequence—direct connection. The only intervening cause was that, instead of blowing her to the ground, the concussion smashed the weighing machine which in turn fell upon her. There was no remoteness in time, little in space. And surely, given such an explosion as here, it needed no great foresight to predict that the natural result would be to injure one on the platform at no greater distance from its scene than was the plaintiff. Just how no one might be able to predict. Whether by flying fragments, by broken glass, by wreckage of machines or structures no one could say. But injury in some form was most probable.

Under these circumstances I cannot say as a matter of law that the plaintiff's injuries were not the proximate result of the negligence. That is all we have before us. The court refused to so charge. No request was made to submit the matter to the jury as a question of fact, even would that have been proper upon the record before us.

The judgment appealed from should be affirmed, with costs.

PREPARING FOR CLASS

1. Why was the guards' behavior negligent? What did they risk?

2. Apply the rule from *Wagon Mound* to these facts. Do the facts support proximate cause?

3. Does Justice Cardozo see the unforeseeability of Mrs. Palsgraf as a proximate cause question? What is it a matter of? Why?

4. According to Justice Cardozo, on what rights is Mrs. Palsgraf basing her claim? Why can't she do that?

5. If there is transferred intent, why can't there be transferred negligence?

6. What is the rule of this case? What happens to Mrs. Palsgraf under it?

7. What is the fundamental difference in Justice Andrews's approach to the problem this case presents? Why does he view the case this way?

8. What point is Justice Andrews making with the hypothetical about the chauffeur?

9. How does Justice Andrews enhance your understanding of proximate cause? How does he apply his "hints" to the facts before him?

10. In practical terms, does it matter whether a court follows Justice Cardozo or Justice Andrews?

11. Did Mrs. Palsgraf's lawyer fail her? Was there a better theory of negligence?

D. PUBLIC POLICY

Enright by Enright v. Eli Lilly & Co.
570 N.E.2d 198 (N.Y. 1991)

WACHTLER, C.J.

The question in this case is whether the liability of manufacturers of the drug diethylstilbestrol (DES) should extend to a so-called "third generation" plaintiff, the granddaughter of a woman who ingested the drug. According to the allegations of the complaint, the infant plaintiff's injuries were caused by her premature birth, which in turn resulted from damage to her mother's reproductive system caused by the mother's in utero exposure to DES. We hold, in accord with our decision in Albala v. City of New York, 429 N.E.2d 786, that in these circumstances no cause of action accrues in favor of the infant plaintiff against the drug manufacturers. . . .

The tragic DES tale is well documented in this Court's decisions and need not be recounted here (see, e.g., Hymowitz v. Lilly & Co., supra; Bichler v. Lilly & Co., 55 N.Y.2d 571, 450 N.Y.S.2d 776, 436 N.E.2d 182). It is sufficient to note that between 1947 and 1971, the drug, a synthetic estrogen-like substance produced by approximately 300 manufacturers, was prescribed for use and ingested by millions of pregnant women to prevent miscarriages. In 1971, the Food and Drug Administration banned the drug's use for the treatment of problems of pregnancy after studies established a link between in utero exposure to DES and the occurrence in teen-age women of a rare form of vaginal and cervical cancer. Plaintiffs allege that in utero exposure to DES has since been linked to other genital tract aberrations in DES daughters, including malformations or immaturity of the uterus, cervical abnormalities, misshapen Fallopian tubes and abnormal cell and tissue growth, all of which has caused in this population a marked increase in the incidence of infertility, miscarriages, premature births and ectopic pregnancies.

The Legislature and this Court have both expressed concern for the victims of this tragedy by removing legal barriers to their tort recovery-barriers which may have had their place in other contexts, but which in DES litigation worked a peculiar injustice because of the ways in which DES was developed, marketed and sold and because of the insidious nature of its harm. . . .

More recently, this Court responded to the fact that—for a variety of reasons unique to the DES litigation context—a DES plaintiff generally finds it impossible to identify the manufacturer of the drug that caused her injuries. We held that liability could be imposed upon DES manufacturers in accordance with their share of the national DES market, notwithstanding the plaintiff's inability to identify the manufacturer particularly at fault for her injuries. . . .

In the present case, we are asked to do something significantly different. We are asked, not to remove some barrier to recovery that presents unique problems in DES cases, but to recognize a cause of action not available in other contexts simply (or at least largely) because this is a DES case.

In Albala v. City of New York, 429 N.E.2d 786, we were presented with the question "whether a cause of action lies in favor of a child for injuries suffered as a result of a preconception tort committed against the mother." There, the mother suffered a perforated uterus during the course of an abortion. Four years later, she gave birth to a brain-damaged child, whose injuries were allegedly attributable to the defendants' negligence in perforating the mother's uterus. We declined, as a matter of policy, to recognize a cause of action on behalf of the child, believing that to do so would "require the extension of traditional tort concepts beyond manageable bounds." Among other things, we were concerned with "the staggering implications of any proposition which would honor claims assuming the breach of an identifiable duty for less than a perfect birth" and the difficulty, if such a cause of action were recognized, of confining liability by other than artificial and arbitrary boundaries.

The case now before us differs from *Albala* only in that the mother's injuries in this case were caused by exposure to DES instead of by medical malpractice. A different rule is justified, therefore, only if that distinction alters the policy balance we struck in *Albala*.

The primary thrust of plaintiffs' argument and the Appellate Division's decision is that DES itself alters that balance. From the Legislature's actions in modifying the applicable Statute of Limitations and reviving time-barred DES cases and from our adoption of a market-share liability theory in *Hymo-witz*, plaintiffs perceive a public policy favoring a remedy for DES-caused injuries sufficient to overcome the countervailing policy considerations we identified in *Albala*. The implication, of course, is that the public interest in providing a remedy for those injured by DES is stronger than the public interest in providing a remedy for those injured by other means—medical malpractice, for example. We do not believe that such a preference has been established.

To be sure, recent developments demonstrate legislative and judicial solic-itude for the victims of DES, but they do not establish DES plaintiffs as a favored class for whose benefit all traditional limitations on tort liability must give way. To the extent that special rules have been fashioned, they are a response to unique procedural barriers and problems of proof peculiar to DES litigation. . . .

In the present case, however, neither plaintiffs, the Appellate Division, nor the dissent has identified any unique feature of DES litigation that justifies the novel proposition they advance—recognition of a multigenerational cause of action that we have refused to recognize in any other context. The fact that this is a DES case does not by itself justify a departure from the *Albala* rule.

Closer to the mark, though still falling short, is plaintiffs' second argument. They note that *Albala* was a negligence case and that we left open the question whether a different result might obtain under a strict products liability theory, because of the potentially different policy considerations in such a case. Hav-ing now examined the question in the context of this particular strict products liability claim, we find no basis for reaching a different conclusion than we did in *Albala*. . . .

Despite these considerations, the countervailing ones remain strong enough to preclude us from recognizing a cause of action here. To begin, the concerns we identified in *Albala* are present in equal measure here. The nature of the plaintiffs' injuries in both cases—birth defects—and their cause—harm to the mothers' reproductive systems before the children were conceived—are indis-tinguishable for these purposes. They raise the same vexing questions with the same "staggering implications." As in *Albala*, the cause of action plaintiffs ask us to recognize here could not be confined without the drawing of artificial and arbitrary boundaries. For all we know, the rippling effects of DES exposure may extend for generations. It is our duty to confine liability within manageable limits. Limiting liability to those who ingested the drug or were exposed to it in utero serves this purpose.

At the same time, limiting liability in this fashion does not unduly impair the deterrent purposes of tort liability. The manufacturers remain amenable to suit by all those injured by exposure to their product, a class whose size is commensurate with the risk created. In addition, we note that the tort system is not the only means of encouraging prescription drug safety; the Federal Food and Drug Administration has primary responsibility for that task. We do not suggest, as some have that for this reason the judicial system should abandon its traditional role. But in light of the FDA's responsibility in this area, the need for the tort system to promote prescription drug safety is at least diminished.

That the product involved here is a prescription drug raises other considerations as well. First, as in most prescription drug cases, liability here is predicated on a failure to warn of dangers of which the manufacturers knew or with adequate testing should have known. Such a claim, though it may be couched in terms of strict liability, is indistinguishable from a negligence claim. Concepts of reasonable care and foreseeability are not divorced from this theory of liability, as they may be under other strict products liability predicates. Thus, the effort to distinguish this case from *Albala* is strained.

More important, however, is recognition that public policy favors the availability of prescription drugs even though most carry some risks (see, Brown v. Superior Ct., 751 P.2d 470). That is not to say that drug manufacturers should enjoy immunity from liability stemming from their failure to conduct adequate research and testing prior to the marketing of their products. They do not enjoy such immunity, as evidenced by our recognition of liability in favor of those who have been injured by ingestion or in utero exposure to DES. But we are aware of the dangers of overdeterrence — the possibility that research will be discouraged or beneficial drugs withheld from the market. These dangers are magnified in this context, where we are asked to recognize a legal duty toward generations not yet conceived.

The dissent would have us believe that this case involves nothing but application of straightforward strict products liability doctrine. But this case is fundamentally different in the same way that *Albala* was fundamentally different from other negligence cases. In neither this case nor *Albala* was the infant plaintiff exposed to the defendants' dangerous product or negligent conduct; rather, both were injured as a consequence of injuries to the reproductive systems of their mothers. . . .

In sum, the distinctions between this case and *Albala* provide no basis for a departure from the rule that an injury to a mother which results in injuries to a later-conceived child does not establish a cause of action in favor of the child against the original tortfeasor. For this reason, we decline to recognize a cause of action on behalf of plaintiff Karen Enright. . . .

PREPARING FOR CLASS

1. The court states that the relevant precedent is *Albala*. How is that case like this one? Why does the rule in *Albala* preclude recovery here?

2. Why does the plaintiff think that her case is distinguishable from *Albala* and deserves different treatment?

3. Why does the court think that no special rules should apply to this case?

4. What public policy concerns weigh against a finding of proximate cause here? What are the "dangers of overdeterrence"?

5. Isn't proximate cause always about public policy?

Chapter 12

Defenses Based on Plaintiff's Conduct

A. CONTRIBUTORY NEGLIGENCE

Smith v. Smith
2 Pick. 621 (Mass. 1824)

This was an action on the case for an injury done to the plaintiff's horse by a wood-pile, which the defendant had placed in the highway.

At the trial, before Putnam J., it appeared, that the horse was harnessed to a wagon loaded with two barrels filled with cider, and two others which were only about two-thirds full. There was no shaft girth to the wagon; there were breech hooks and lug hooks to the shafts, and there was a crupper to the saddle. The horse was driven by one Kimball; who was a witness in the case. The wood was piled or corded up on the side of the highway. One stick projected eight inches beyond the rest of the pile. The accident happened in the night, when it was very dark, as Kimball was descending a circuitous hill. He led the horse down a part of the hill, and then got into the wagon to ride, when the shafts immediately flew up and the wagon went against the horse, which went very fast until the wagon struck the wood pile; then the wagon broke and the horse ran off with a part of the harness upon him, but clear of the wagon. The wagon rubbed for three or four feet against the pile, and then caught against the projecting stick. The horse was injured in the cords of his hind legs above the fetlocks. Kimball thought he was about twenty feet from the wood when he discovered it. He was on the right side of the road, and he thought he should have passed without injury if the wood had not been in the way.

The defendant contended, that the driver did not use ordinary care on this occasion; objecting, 1. that he overloaded the wagon; 2. that he did not put a shaft girth on; 3. that he did not drive skilfully; and 4. that the horse received the injury by kicking his hind legs against the wagon before it came in contact with the wood pile; and to those points much evidence was given and submitted to the jury, who found a verdict for the defendant.

The plaintiff moved for a new trial, because the jury were instructed, that if Kimball, who had hired and was driving the plaintiff's horse, was wanting in any respect in ordinary care, the defendant was not liable in law; whereas the plaintiff contended that the rule of law was, that even if Kimball were in some degree wanting in ordinary care, yet the defendant was the party originally in fault, by having first committed the unlawful act which occasioned the injury complained of, and was therefore liable.

The opinion of the Court was read at Ipswich. . . .

Parker C.J. [After stating the case.]

It would seem, at first, that he who does an unlawful act, such as incumbering the highway, should be answerable for any direct damages which happen to any one who is thereby injured, whether the party suffering was careful or not in his manner of driving or in guiding his vehicle, for it could not be rendered certain, whether, if the road were left free and unincumbered, even a careless traveller or team driver would meet with any injury. But on deliberation we have come to the conclusion, that this action cannot be maintained, unless the plaintiff can show that he used ordinary care; for without that, it is by no means certain that he himself was not the cause of his own injury. The party who obstructs a highway is amenable to the public in indictment, whether any person be injured or not, but not to an individual, unless it be shown that he suffered in his person or property by means of the obstruction; and where he has been careless it cannot be known whether the injury is wholly imputable to the obstruction, or to the negligence of the party complaining. And considering the indulgence shown by the public to the citizens, in many places, to occupy a part of the highway for temporary purposes, leaving ample room for travellers with ordinary care to pass uninjured, the principle which requires that degree of care in order to entitle a party to damages, may be deemed salutary and useful. That such is the law, we are fully satisfied from an examination of the authorities cited.

The case of *Butterfield v. Forrester*, 11 East, 60, is very strong to this point. The plaintiff, who was riding violently in a public highway, was thrown down with his horse, and injured by means of an obstruction placed there by the defendant. It was proved, that if the plaintiff had not been riding very hard he might have seen the obstruction and avoided it, and on this ground he failed in the action. Lord Ellenborough said, "A party is not to cast himself upon an obstruction which has been made by the fault of another, and avail himself of it, if he do not himself use common and ordinary caution to be in the right." And in the Common Pleas, in the case of *Flower v. Adam*, 2 Taunt. 314, the same principle is recognised as law, the plaintiff being prevented from recovering, because it was proved he might have avoided the obstruction, if he had managed his horse with ordinary skill and care. These cases are cited in Wheaton's edition of Selwyn's Nisi Prius, and the principle is admitted into the text, that to entitle the plaintiff to an action for damages resulting from a nuisance he must show that he acted with common and ordinary caution.

The only authority which seems to be in opposition to these, is contained in a short passage in Buller's Nisi Prius, p. 26, in these words; "If a man lay logs of wood cross a highway, though a person may with care ride safely by, yet if by means thereof my horse stumble and fling me, I may bring an action." This citation at first struck us as maintaining a principle different from that laid down in the above cited cases, but on further consideration we are satisfied that there is nothing in it repugnant to it. The meaning of the passage undoubtedly is, that notwithstanding a person using due care may possibly pass the obstruction without injury, nevertheless, if one is injured, that is, as we understand it, if one who uses this care does by misfortune suffer from the obstruction, he shall recover. And we think the court, in the case first cited, must have so understood the passage, or it would have been commented upon, it having been pressed upon their consideration by the counsel. And we are led to consider this as the true sense of the passage, also, from examining the case cited by Buller from Carthew, 194, and 451, in which we find no position which would support Buller, if he meant to say that a man might recover for an injury by an obstruction, without showing ordinary care on his part.

Whether the jury erred in their estimate of the evidence given them, which had a tendency to show a want of care on the part of the plaintiff, we are unable to say, as the case has not been reported with a view to set aside the verdict as contrary to evidence, or against the weight of it. The law was rightly stated to them, and it was their business to judge of the evidence. So that judgment must be rendered according to the verdict.

PREPARING FOR CLASS

1. What is plaintiff's chief argument?

2. What options does the court have at its disposal when addressing the issue of contributory negligence?

3. Be reminded of the goals of tort law and how the rule in this case would further or frustrate those goals.

4. Also be cognizant of the fact that negligence, unlike intentional conduct, often involves only momentary lapses in judgment.

5. What should the special verdict form look like on the "allocation of fault" question?

APPLYING THE LAW

Plaintiff (23-year-old female college student) babysits for the defendants, a married couple. Defendant-wife works nights and the couple have a two-year-old child. Defendant-husband is just lazy and not responsible enough to look out for the child while his wife is at work. One evening, husband is at home while plaintiff is babysitting and asks plaintiff to join him in drinking wine. Plaintiff does so voluntarily and eventually becomes intoxicated. Husband then sexually assaults her. Wife was aware of husband's predatory tendencies but had not shared this with babysitter. If babysitter sues wife for negligence, what is the outcome under *Smith*?

INCREASING YOUR UNDERSTANDING

1. Contributory negligence is the term that is used to describe unreasonable causal conduct of the plaintiff in a negligence case. Under the common law, the plaintiff who was determined to be contributorily negligent was barred from recovering, a rule that is often described as the "all or nothing" or "contributory negligence" rule. It mattered not the relative degrees of contribution to the plaintiff's injury; a plaintiff who was adjudged one-percent responsible was barred from recovery. A number of justifications have been offered for the "all or nothing" rule, with perhaps the most compelling being that the negligent plaintiff comes to the court with "unclean hands" and therefore is undeserving of recovery.

2. Contrary to what *Smith* might suggest, the defendant typically carries the burden of proving that the plaintiff was contributorily negligent. The court would undertake the same considerations that guided the assessment of the defendant's conduct when the topic of negligence was first discussed earlier in the term. Children will be held to the same standard as those of similar age, experience, and intelligence unless involved in an adult activity. Professionals will be held to professional standards. Customs and statutes may be relied upon to establish plaintiff's unreasonableness.

Georgia Southern & F. Ry. Co. v. Odom
263 S.E.2d 469 (Ga. App. 1979)

CARLEY, Judge.
Mrs. Ruth Odom was a guest passenger in an automobile being operated by Wayne Worley. As the automobile was proceeding across a railroad track in Arabi, Georgia, it was struck by a freight train belonging to the Georgia Southern & Florida Railway Company (railway). Both Mrs. Odom and Mr. Worley were killed. The husband and children of Mrs. Odom filed suit against the railway. The railway answered by denying liability and filed a third-party complaint for contribution against Worley's executrix on the premise that the collision was proximately caused by Worley's gross negligence.

Worley's executrix, as third-party defendant, counterclaimed against the railway. The jury returned a verdict in favor of the Odoms in the main case, against the railway on its third-party claim against Worley's executrix, and in favor of the railway on the counterclaim filed by Worley's executrix. In Case Number 58063, the railway appeals from the judgment in favor of the Odoms and the judgment in favor of the executrix of Worley on the third-party action. In Case Number 58064, Worley's executrix cross appeals from the judgment in favor of the railway on the counterclaim.

Several enumerations assign error in the giving of jury charges on the doctrine of last clear chance in connection with the main action, the third-party action and the counterclaim. The doctrine of last clear chance can be invoked "only where the defendant knows of the plaintiff's perilous situation, and realizes, or has reason to realize, the plaintiff's helpless condition, that the defendant is charged with the duty of using with reasonable care and competence his then existing ability to avoid harming the plaintiff." Southland Butane Gas Co. v. Blackwell, 211 Ga. 665, 670, 88 S.E.2d 6, 10 (1955). It is urged that there is no evidence in the instant case that at the time the train crew first became aware of the presence of the car on the tracks any action could possibly have been taken to avoid the collision. However, the testimony of the brakeman indicated that when he saw a car which successfully preceded the Worley automobile across the tracks, the train was 150 feet from the crossing and that he saw the Worley vehicle "a split second" afterwards. That the jury was authorized to conclude that the brakeman saw the Worley automobile as well as the car which negotiated the crossing without a collision is shown by the brakeman's testimony that he "thought the cars would stop, but they didn't." There was also testimony that, after the lead car passed over the tracks, the brakeman told the engineer, "Here comes another one." Thus it appears that the crew was aware of both cars and thus realized the existence of a perilous situation. Compare *Southland Butane Gas Co.*, supra; Conner v. Mangum, 132 Ga. App. 100, 207 S.E.2d 604 (1974). However, the jury was authorized to find that the train crew failed to sound either the horn or whistle. Compare Central of Ga. R. Co. v. Little, 126 Ga. App. 502, 191 S.E.2d 105 (1972). It is true that the train could not have been halted totally even had the crew taken all available remedial steps. However, there was sufficient evidence in the record to show that the train was in the eighth notch (the fastest speed) and that the crew could have "notched down." Such action would have reduced the speed of the train to some extent and a jury could have found and the verdict indicates that it did that even such a slight reduction in speed would have been sufficient to have allowed the Worley car to pass safely over the tracks. Thus, as in Central of Ga. R. Co. v. Sellers, 129 Ga. App. 811, 818, 201 S.E.2d 485, 491 (1973), "(u)nder the facts presented by this case, a jury question is presented as to whether the defendant's engineer had the 'last clear chance' of avoiding the collision with the (Worley) automobile. While the evidence conclusively shows that the train could not have been stopped prior to reaching the crossing by applying the emergency brakes when the (Worley) automobile first 'came into plain view' . . . it is entirely possible that the (Worley) automobile would have passed over the tracks without being struck by the train. . . ." See also Thompson v. Powell, 60 Ga. App. 796, 805, 5 S.E.2d 260 (1939); and Seaboard Coast L. R. Co. v. Wallace, 123 Ga. App. 490, 181 S.E.2d 542 (1971). The instructions on the last clear chance doctrine were supported by and adjusted to the evidence and were not erroneous.

Judgments affirmed.

PREPARING FOR CLASS

1. As counsel for defendant railroad, what additional facts would you want to know about the accident? Here it sought contribution from the driver and attempted to place some responsibility for the accident on Mrs. Odom.

2. Distinguish between the railroad's original negligence and its argument with respect to the "last clear chance" doctrine.

3. Articulate the last clear chance doctrine and offer possible explanations/ justifications for it.

4. Appreciate the posture the appellate court takes on appeal with respect to the "last clear chance" doctrine and how it influenced the final decision.

APPLYING THE LAW

Plaintiff ran across the expressway instead of using the crossing bridge. Defendant driver who was texting while driving unintentionally struck plaintiff causing serious injury. Discuss.

INCREASING YOUR UNDERSTANDING

1. Frustrated with the harshness of the total bar/all-or-nothing rule, many jurisdictions sought creative means to avoid its consequence. Perhaps the first response was to allow the plaintiff who was contributorily negligent to recover when the defendant had "last clear chance" to avoid causing injury. The doctrine does not absolve the plaintiff of her contribution to her own injuries but instead allows the plaintiff to recover a portion of her damages as long as the defendant was best positioned to avoid causing injury.

2. In addition to adopting the last clear chance doctrine, some jurisdictions responded to the total bar rule by prohibiting its application in strict liability cases. See Kirkland v. General Motors Corp. 521 P.2d 1353, 1355 (Okla. 1974) ("Common law defenses used in connection

with negligence and implied warranty recovery such as lack of privity, assumption of risk, and contributory negligence, used in their traditional common law sense are not applicable to Manufacturers' Products Liability recovery.") and Sandy v. Bushey, 124 Me. 320, 128 A. 513 (Supreme Judicial Court Maine 1925) (In abnormally dangerous animal strict liability case, "exclusion of negligence as the basis of liability forbids the inclusion of contributory negligence as a defense.").

B. COMPARATIVE FAULT/FAULT ALLOCATION

Coney v. J.L.G. Industries, Inc.
454 N.E.2d 197 (Ill. 1983)

THOMAS J. MORAN, Justice.

Clifford M. Jasper died as a result of injuries sustained on January 24, 1978, while operating a hydraulic aerial work platform manufactured by defendant, J.L.G. Industries, Inc. Plaintiff, Jack A. Coney, administrator of Jasper's estate, filed a two-count complaint in the circuit court of Peoria County under the wrongful death and survival acts based on a strict products liability theory. Defendant filed two affirmative defenses. The first asserted that Jasper was guilty of comparative negligence or fault in his operation of the platform. The second contended that Jasper's employer, V. Jobst & Sons, Inc., was also guilty of comparative negligence in failing to instruct and train Jasper on the operation of the platform and by failing to provide a "groundman." In these defenses, defendant requested that its fault, if any, be compared to the total fault of all parties.

On plaintiff's motion, the trial court struck the defenses, but it certified the following question for the Illinois Supreme Court:

> "Whether the doctrine of comparative negligence or fault is applicable to actions or claims seeking recovery under products liability or strict liability in tort theories?"

Traditionally in negligence actions, however, any contributory negligence by the plaintiff was an absolute defense which barred recovery. In response to the harshness of this doctrine, the court adopted comparative negligence in *Alvis v. Ribar* (1981), 85 Ill. 2d 1, 52 Ill. Dec. 23, 421 N.E.2d 886, and indicated that this concept produced "a more just and socially desirable distribution of loss" and was "demanded by today's society." In *Alvis*, we adopted the "pure" form of comparative negligence, reasoning that it "is the only system which truly apportions damages according to the relative fault of the parties and, thus, achieves total justice."

In the instant case, defendant argues that *Alvis* requires the adoption of a comparative fault system in strict products liability cases. Defendant maintains "total justice" can only be achieved where the relative fault of all the parties is considered in apportioning damages. To illustrate its argument, defendant points to the anomalous situation where, in a single case with alternate counts of negligence and strict liability, the identical conduct by the plaintiff which amounts to an assumption of the risk will completely bar recovery in the strict liability count, yet, as a result of *Alvis*, will only reduce his award under the negligence count. Moreover, if the plaintiff is only contributorily negligent, he recovers all his damages under strict liability, but his recovery is diminished under the negligence count. Defendant argues that common sense mandates an approach which is consistent in its treatment of all the parties to an action, whether founded on common law negligence or strict liability.

We are not the first to consider the impact of comparative negligence upon strict liability. Some jurisdictions have declined to apply comparative negligence or fault principles in strict liability actions. The vast majority, though, have found comparative negligence theory applicable in strict liability cases.

In the case at bar, plaintiff argues that applying comparative fault principles in strict liability actions would raise the conduct of the product user to a position equal to that of the manufacturer in regard to the prevention of injury; and that it would thereby give undue advantage to the manufacturer. The Illinois Trial Lawyers Association, in their *amicus curiae* brief, assert that comparative fault applied in this instance would undermine the policy basis that led to the imposition of strict liability. Further, they argue that reducing a plaintiff's recovery according to his fault would lessen the manufacturer's incentive to design and market a defect-free, safe product.

We believe that application of comparative fault principles in strict products liability actions would not frustrate this court's fundamental reasons for adopting strict products liability. The plaintiff will still be relieved of the proof problems associated with negligence and warranty actions. Privity and a manufacturer's negligence continue to be irrelevant. Nor would comparative fault lessen the manufacturer's duty to produce reasonably safe products. The manufacturer's liability remains strict; only its responsibility for damages is lessened by the extent the trier of fact finds the consumer's conduct contributed to the injuries.

Plaintiff and *amicus curiae* next argue that the comparison of the plaintiff's fault with the defendant's defective product is a comparison of noncomparables, an attempt to compare "apples and oranges," and that this comparison cannot be applied logically and consistently in strict products liability cases.

Although it appears theoretically difficult to balance the defendant's strict liability against the user's negligence, other courts and their juries have been able to do so. In this regard, Professor Schwartz said:

> "It is true that the jury might have some difficulty in making the calculation required under comparative negligence when defendant's responsibility is based on strict liability. Nevertheless, this obstacle is

more conceptual than practical. The jury should always be capable, when the plaintiff has been objectively at fault, of taking into account how much bearing that fault had on the amount of damage suffered and of adjusting and reducing the award accordingly. Triers of fact *are* apparently able to do this, and the benefits from the approach suggest that it be applied in all comparative negligence jurisdictions." V. Schwartz, Comparative Negligence sec. 12.7, at 208-09 (1974).

A manufacturer is under a nondelegable duty to produce a product which is reasonably safe. Defendant contends that when a manufacturer breaches this duty and places a defective product on the market, he is at "fault." Correspondingly, it argues, the plaintiff has a duty to exercise ordinary care in using the product; breach of this duty creates his "fault." Defendant maintains that these two types of "fault" should not be compared against each other in determining liability. Rather, they should be compared in terms of the causative role each played in producing the total damages sustained. Defendant postulates that once plaintiff has established his *prima facie* case and after defendant is found strictly liable, then plaintiff's recovery should be reduced by that amount which his fault contributed to the damages.

The court in *Murray v. Fairbanks Morse* (3d Cir. 1979), 610 F.2d 149, came to a similar result. The court there said the key conceptual distinction between strict products liability and negligence is that in strict liability the plaintiff need not prove faulty conduct on the part of the defendant in order to recover. The focus is on the condition of the product. In applying comparative negligence to strict products liability, the court stated a direct comparison of the defective product with the plaintiff's negligence is both conceptually and pragmatically inappropriate. "[T]he only conceptual basis for comparison is the causative contribution of each to the particular loss or injury. In apportioning damages we are really asking how much of the injury was caused by the defect in the product versus how much was caused by the plaintiff's own actions."

We believe that equitable principles require that the total damages for plaintiff's injuries be apportioned on the basis of the relative degree to which the defective product and plaintiff's conduct proximately caused them. Accordingly, we hold that the defense of comparative fault is applicable to strict liability cases.

Affirmed and remanded, with directions.

PREPARING FOR CLASS

1. Jasper was contributorily negligent. What arguments does he make to avoid it being of consequence? Is his argument more compelling as a strict liability case?

2. Though the employer could not be held liable beyond responsibility for paying workers' compensation benefits, it is likely that the employer would be listed on the special verdict. What's the strategy behind this?

McIntyre v. Balentine
833 S.W.2d 52 (Tenn. 1992)

DROWOTA, Justice.

In this personal injury action, we granted Plaintiff's application for permission to appeal in order to decide whether to adopt a system of comparative fault in Tennessee. We now replace the common law defense of contributory negligence with a system of comparative fault.

In the early morning darkness of November 2, 1986, Plaintiff McIntyre and Defendant Balentine were involved in a motor vehicle accident resulting in severe injuries to Plaintiff. The accident occurred in the vicinity of Smith's Truck Stop in Savannah, Tennessee. As Defendant was traveling south on Highway 69, Plaintiff entered the highway (also traveling south) from the truck stop parking lot. Shortly after Plaintiff entered the highway, his pickup truck was struck by Defendant's Peterbilt tractor. At trial, the parties disputed the exact chronology of events immediately preceding the accident.

Both men had consumed alcohol the evening of the accident. After the accident, Plaintiff's blood alcohol level was measured at .17 percent by weight. Testimony suggested that Defendant was traveling in excess of the posted speed limit.

Plaintiff brought a negligence action against Defendant Balentine and Defendant East-West Motor Freight, Inc. Defendants answered that Plaintiff was contributorially negligent, in part due to operating his vehicle while intoxicated. After trial, the jury returned a verdict stating: "We, the jury, find the plaintiff and the defendant equally at fault in this accident; therefore, we rule in favor of the defendant."

After judgment was entered for Defendants, Plaintiff brought an appeal alleging the trial court erred by refusing to instruct the jury regarding the doctrine of comparative negligence. The Court of Appeals affirmed, holding that comparative negligence is not the law in Tennessee.

I.

The common law contributory negligence doctrine has traditionally been traced to Lord Ellenborough's opinion in *Butterfield v. Forrester*, 11 East 60, 103 Eng. Rep. 926 (1809). There, plaintiff, "riding as fast as his horse would go," was injured after running into an obstruction defendant had placed in the road. Stating as the rule that "[o]ne person being in fault will not dispense with another's using ordinary care," plaintiff was denied recovery on the basis that he did not use ordinary care to avoid the obstruction.

The contributory negligence bar was soon brought to America as part of the common law, and proceeded to spread throughout the states. This strict bar may have been a direct outgrowth of the common law system of issue pleading; issue pleading posed questions to be answered "yes" or "no," leaving common law courts, the theory goes, no choice but to award all or nothing. A number of other rationalizations have been advanced in the attempt to justify the harshness of the "all-or-nothing" bar. Among these: the plaintiff should be penalized for his misconduct; the plaintiff should be deterred from injuring himself; and the plaintiff's negligence supersedes the defendant's so as to render defendant's negligence no longer proximate.

In Tennessee, the rule as initially stated was that "if a party, by his own gross negligence, brings an injury upon himself, or contributes to such injury, he cannot recover"; for, in such cases, the party "must be regarded as the author of his own misfortune." In subsequent decisions, we have continued to follow the general rule that a plaintiff's contributory negligence completely bars recovery. Fully entrenched in Tennessee jurisprudence are exceptions to the general all-or-nothing rule: contributory negligence does not absolutely bar recovery where defendant's conduct was intentional, where defendant's conduct was "grossly" negligent, where defendant had the "last clear chance" with which, through the exercise of ordinary care, to avoid plaintiff's injury, or where plaintiff's negligence may be classified as "remote."

In contrast, comparative fault has long been the federal rule in cases involving injured employees of interstate railroad carriers, *see* Federal Employers' Liability Act, ch. 149, §3, 35 Stat. 66 (1908) (codified at 45 U.S.C. §53 (1988)), and injured seamen.

Similarly, by the early 1900s, many states, including Tennessee, had statutes providing for the apportionment of damages in railroad injury cases. While Tennessee's railroad statute did not expressly sanction damage apportionment, it was soon given that judicial construction. In 1856, the statute was passed in an effort to prevent railroad accidents; it imposed certain obligations and liabilities on railroads "for all damages accruing or resulting from a failure to perform said dut[ies]." Apparently this strict liability was deemed necessary because "the consequences of carelessness and want of due skill [in the operation of railroads at speeds previously unknown] . . . are so frightful and appalling that the most strict and rigid rules of accountability must be applied." The statute was then judicially construed to permit the jury to consider "[n]egligence of the person injured, which caused, or contributed to cause the accident . . . in determining the amount of damages proper to be given for the injury." This system of comparative fault was utilized for almost a century until 1959 when, trains no longer unique in their "astonishing speeds," the statute was overhauled, its strict liability provision being replaced by negligence per se and the common law contributory negligence bar.

Between 1920 and 1969, a few states began utilizing the principles of comparative fault in all tort litigation. Then, between 1969 and 1984, comparative fault replaced contributory negligence in 37 additional states. In 1991, South Carolina became the 45th state to adopt comparative fault, leaving Alabama, Maryland, North Carolina, Virginia, and Tennessee as the only remaining common law contributory negligence jurisdictions. . . .

II.

Over 15 years ago, we stated, when asked to adopt a system of comparative fault:

> We do not deem it appropriate to consider making such a change unless and until a case reaches us wherein the pleadings and proof present an issue of contributory negligence accompanied by advocacy that the ends of justice will be served by adopting the rule of comparative negligence.

Street v. Calvert, 541 S.W.2d at 586. Such a case is now before us. After exhaustive deliberation that was facilitated by extensive briefing and argument by the parties, amicus curiae, and Tennessee's scholastic community, we conclude that it is time to abandon the outmoded and unjust common law doctrine of contributory negligence and adopt in its place a system of comparative fault. Justice simply will not permit our continued adherence to a rule that, in the face of a judicial determination that others bear primary responsibility, nevertheless completely denies injured litigants recompense for their damages.

We recognize that this action could be taken by our General Assembly. However, legislative inaction has never prevented judicial abolition of obsolete common law doctrines, especially those, such as contributory negligence, conceived in the judicial womb. Indeed, our abstinence would sanction "a mutual state of inaction in which the court awaits action by the legislature and the legislature awaits guidance from the court," thereby prejudicing the equitable resolution of legal conflicts.

Nor do we today abandon our commitment to *stare decisis*. While "[c]onfidence in our courts is to a great extent dependent on the uniformity and consistency engendered by allegiance to *stare decisis*, . . . mindless obedience to this precept can confound the truth and foster an attitude of contempt."

III.

Two basic forms of comparative fault are utilized by 45 of our sister jurisdictions, these variants being commonly referred to as either "pure" or "modified." In the "pure" form,[1] a plaintiff's damages are reduced in proportion to the percentage negligence attributed to him; for example, a plaintiff responsible for 90 percent of the negligence that caused his injuries nevertheless may recover 10 percent of his damages. In the "modified" form,[2] plaintiffs recover

---

1. The 13 states utilizing pure comparative fault are Alaska, Arizona, California, Florida, Kentucky, Louisiana, Mississippi, Missouri, Michigan, New Mexico, New York, Rhode Island, and Washington. *See* V. Schwartz, Comparative Negligence at §2.1 (2d ed. 1986).
2. The 21 states using the "50 percent" modified form: Connecticut, Delaware, Hawaii, Illinois, Indiana, Iowa, Massachusetts, Minnesota, Montana, Nevada, New Hampshire, New Jersey, Ohio, Oklahoma, Oregon, Pennsylvania, South Carolina, Texas, Vermont, Wisconsin, and Wyoming. The 9 states using the "49 percent"

as in pure jurisdictions, but only if the plaintiff's negligence either (1) does not exceed ("50 percent" jurisdictions) or (2) is less than ("49 percent" jurisdictions) the defendant's negligence.

Although we conclude that the all-or-nothing rule of contributory negligence must be replaced, we nevertheless decline to abandon totally our fault-based tort system. We do not agree that a party should necessarily be able to recover in tort even though he may be 80, 90, or 95 percent at fault. We therefore reject the pure form of comparative fault.

We recognize that modified comparative fault systems have been criticized as merely shifting the arbitrary contributory negligence bar to a new ground. However, we feel the "49 percent rule" ameliorates the harshness of the common law rule while remaining compatible with a fault-based tort system. We therefore hold that so long as a plaintiff's negligence remains less than the defendant's negligence the plaintiff may recover; in such a case, plaintiff's damages are to be reduced in proportion to the percentage of the total negligence attributable to the plaintiff.

In all trials where the issue of comparative fault is before a jury, the trial court shall instruct the jury on the effect of the jury's finding as to the percentage of negligence as between the plaintiff or plaintiffs and the defendant or defendants. The attorneys for each party shall be allowed to argue how this instruction affects a plaintiff's ability to recover.

IV.

Turning to the case at bar, the jury found that "the plaintiff and defendant [were] equally at fault." Because the jury, without the benefit of proper instructions by the trial court, made a gratuitous apportionment of fault, we find that their "equal" apportionment is not sufficiently trustworthy to form the basis of a final determination between these parties. Therefore, the case is remanded for a new trial in accordance with the dictates of this opinion.

V.

We recognize that today's decision affects numerous legal principles surrounding tort litigation. For the most part, harmonizing these principles with comparative fault must await another day. However, we feel compelled to provide some guidance to the trial courts charged with implementing this new system.

First, and most obviously, the new rule makes the doctrines of remote contributory negligence and last clear chance obsolete. The circumstances

---

form: Arkansas, Colorado, Georgia, Idaho, Kansas, Maine, North Dakota, Utah, and West Virginia. Two states, Nebraska and South Dakota, use a slight-gross system of comparative fault. *See* V. Schwartz, *supra*, at §2.1.

formerly taken into account by those two doctrines will henceforth be addressed when assessing relative degrees of fault.

Second, in cases of multiple tortfeasors, plaintiff will be entitled to recover so long as plaintiff's fault is less than the combined fault of all tortfeasors.

For the foregoing reasons, the judgment of the Court of Appeals is reversed in part and affirmed in part, and the case is remanded to the trial court for a new trial in accordance with the dictates of this opinion. The costs of this appeal are taxed equally to the parties.

PREPARING FOR CLASS

1. Become comfortable with the various comparative fault rules. Which is better and why?

2. What type of jury instruction should be given by the court with respect to the consequences of the fault allocation? Do you agree that the jury should be informed?

3. Which legal entity (Congress or court) is best situated to decide the "fault rules."

INCREASING YOUR UNDERSTANDING

1. *Apples and Oranges*. Often the comparative rules are unfortunately described as "comparative negligence" rules, which has allowed for plaintiffs to argue that it would be inappropriate to compare the party's conduct in any case besides a negligence one. As *Coney* illustrates, however, juries are asked to allocate fault regardless of the theory on which the fault is determined. To avoid confusion, it's best to describe the rules as "comparative fault" rules, but most have styled them as "comparative negligence" rules anyway.

2. Only a handful of jurisdictions (Alabama, Virginia, North Caroline, Maryland, and the District of Columbia) have resisted the move to comparative fault. Often these jurisdictions are described as "contributory negligence" jurisdictions, as they still may bar the plaintiff who is contributorily negligent without first comparing the plaintiff's fault to the defendant's.

3. The remainder of the jurisdictions have fashioned (most by legislation, some by court action) comparative fault rules. Before discussing them further, it should be understood that what is being compared is plaintiff's contribution to her injuries, which is almost always described as contributory negligence. The move from the "all or nothing rule" does not reflect new doctrine with respect to how plaintiff's conduct is to be

assessed but instead what the consequences of plaintiff's conduct will be. In short, instead of automatically barring the plaintiff who contributed to her own injuries, the courts will make a comparison and then decide the plaintiff's fate.

a. *Pure.* Under the "pure" rule, a plaintiff who contributes to her injuries is not barred from recovering as long as some legal fault is allocated to a defendant, even if the plaintiff's fault is greater than the defendant's. The consequence of being at fault is a reduction in recovery, not recovery elimination altogether. In other words, a plaintiff who is 99 percent at fault will still be allowed to recover 1 percent of her damages.

b. *Modified "less than" or "not as great as."* In these jurisdictions, plaintiff recovers as long as the plaintiff's fault is "less than" (which means "not as great as") the defendant's. The plaintiff who is not "less than" is barred from recovering. Plaintiffs who are not barred will have their recovery reduced by their percentage fault. Occasionally these jurisdictions will also be described as "49%" because as long as plaintiff's fault is 49 percent or less, plaintiff will be allowed to recover. Currently, there are about a dozen jurisdictions that follow this rule.

c. *Modified "not greater than."* Under this rule, plaintiff recovers as long as plaintiff's fault is not greater than the defendant's. Nearly two dozen jurisdictions follow this rule, where the plaintiff is barred from recovering should the plaintiff's fault exceed the defendant's. These jurisdictions are sometimes referred to as "50%" jurisdictions because as long as plaintiff's percentage fault is 50 percent or less, plaintiff will be allowed to recover. Again, damages are reduced by plaintiff's percentage fault.

4. Jurisdictions vary when it comes to whether the plaintiff's percentage fault is compared to the collective defendants or to individual defendants when determining the consequences of plaintiff being at fault. For example, assuming in a "less than/not as great as" state, if plaintiff's fault is 40 percent, defendant one's is 40 percent, and defendant two's is 20 percent, plaintiff will recover 60 percent of her damages if in a jurisdiction that compares to the collective defendants but recover nothing if in a jurisdiction that compares to individual defendants. See Mariuzza v. Kenower, 228 N.W.2d 702 (Wis. 1975) ("Comparison of negligence in a multiple-defendant case is required to be between plaintiff and the individual defendant, the sole exception being limited to situations where the duty involved was joint, the opportunity to protect was equal, and as a matter of law neither the obligation nor breach was divisible"); and contrast with Negley v. Massey Ferguson, Inc., 625 P.2d 472 (Kan. 1981) ("In civil action where doctrine of comparative

negligence is applicable, plaintiff's individual negligence will be compared with collective negligence of multiple defendants as found by court or jury for purpose of computing damages and negligence of party seeking damages in comparative negligence action does not bar recovery of damages so long as party's negligence is less than combined causal negligence of all parties against whom recovery is sought.").

5. *Instructing juries on consequences of their allocation.* In addition to adopting a comparative fault rule, the Tennessee Supreme Court in *McIntyre* also mandated that courts "shall instruct the jury on the effect of the jury's finding as to the percentage of negligence as between the plaintiff or plaintiffs and the defendant or defendants." Does such an instruction impermissibly transform the jury from fact finder to deal maker?

6. Does adopting comparative fault rules modify other tort doctrines? The last clear chance doctrine is now largely obsolete, as plaintiff may still be allowed to recover though at fault. Some states have relied on the adoption of comparative rules when abrogating joint and several liability. Bartell v. New Mexico, 646 P.2d 579 (N.M. App. 1982) ("Pure comparative negligence denies recovery for one's own fault; it permits recovery to the extent of another's fault; and it holds all parties fully responsible for their own respective acts to the degree that those acts have caused harm.").

C.   ASSUMPTION OF THE RISK

Heil Valley Ranch, Inc. v. Simkin
784 P.2d 781 (Colo. 1989)

Justice ERICKSON delivered the Opinion of the Court.

We granted certiorari to decide whether a release or exculpatory agreement purporting to waive "any claim [plaintiff] might state against the [defendant] as a result of physical injury incurred" while horseback riding is clear and unambiguous under *Jones v. Dressel*, 623 P.2d 370, 376-78 (Colo. 1981). The court of appeals held that the agreement in this case, which did not use the word "negligence" in its exculpatory provision, was void because it was ambiguous. We conclude that a valid release or exculpatory agreement need not invariably contain the word "negligence," and that under the facts and circumstances of this case the agreement was sufficiently clear and unambiguous to be given effect. Accordingly, we reverse the court of appeals and remand with directions to reinstate the judgment of the district court in favor of the defendant Heil Valley Ranch, Inc. (Heil Valley).

I.

On the morning of July 17, 1983, plaintiff Roane Simkin arrived at the Heil Valley Ranch in Boulder County to go horseback riding with a group of friends.[1] Before any of the participants in the ride were allowed to mount their rented horse they were required to come into the ranch's office and sign the following purported release of liability:

This is a Release of Liability

Please Read Before Signing
UPON MY ACCEPTANCE OF HORSE AND EQUIPMENT, I ACKNOWLEDGE THAT THE USE, HANDLING AND RIDING OF A HORSE INVOLVES A RISK OF PHYSICAL INJURY TO ANY INDIVIDUAL UNDERTAKING SUCH ACTIVITIES; AND THAT A HORSE, IRRESPECTIVE OF ITS TRAINING AND USUAL PAST BEHAVIOR AND CHARACTERISTICS, MAY ACT OR REACT UNPREDICTABLY AT TIMES BASED UPON INSTINCT OR FRIGHT WHICH, LIKEWISE, IS AN INHERENT RISK ASSUMED BY A HORSEBACK RIDER. THE UNDERSIGNED EXPRESSLY ASSUMES SUCH RISK AND WAIVES ANY CLAIM HESHE MIGHT STATE AGAINST THE STABLES AS A RESULT OF PHYSICAL INJURY INCURRED IN SAID ACTIVITIES. EXCEPT TO THE EXTENT SUCH CLAIM MIGHT BE BASED UPON THE SOLE AND EXCLUSIVE NEGLIGENCE OF THE STABLES, THE UNDERSIGNED FURTHER AGREES TO HOLD THE STABLES HARMLESS FOR PHYSICAL INJURY TO OTHERS, OR FOR PROPERTY DAMAGE, WHICH RESULTS FROM RIDER'S USE OF STABLES' HORSE IN VIOLATION OF ANY STABLES' RULES OR THE TERMS AND CONDITIONS OF THIS AGREEMENT.

THIS AGREEMENT SHALL BE EFFECTIVE AND BINDING UPON THE PARTIES HERETO FOR THE DATE INDICATED. THE PARTIES HERETO ACKNOWLEDGE HAVING READ AND UNDERSTOOD THIS AGREEMENT.

At a hearing, Heil Valley presented evidence that before Simkin mounted her horse, she signed the agreement in the office. In his deposition, John Hillman, a Heil Valley employee, testified that Uncle Bud, another employee, told the first woman who wanted to ride Bill that the horse needed a good rider, and she said she would wait for the next horse. Simkin said "that's the horse for

---

1. Simkin testified at a deposition and at a hearing that she does not remember anything that occurred that morning except driving to the ranch and pushing her toes into the dirt after arriving at the ranch. Except for whether or not she actually signed the release, Simkin did not dispute the facts related here.

me." Uncle Bud asked Simkin if she "knew how to ride good because [Bill] is spirited," and Simkin replied that "she worked on a dude ranch."

After Simkin mounted Bill, Hillman heard the horse walking backward and he "turned around and saw [Simkin], and saw that she had the reins tight, and I yelled at her to loosen up on the reins, and she didn't listen to me." Bill then reared up and fell backwards onto Simkin, injuring her severely.

Simkin sued Heil Valley for negligence[2] and breach of warranty.[3] Heil Valley pleaded the release as an affirmative defense, and moved for summary judgment. On August 2, 1985, the district court issued a partial summary judgment,[4] holding that the release was a valid exculpatory agreement under *Jones v. Dressel*, 623 P.2d 370, 376-78 (Colo. 1981). In particular, the court held that the language of the exculpatory portion of the release was clear and unambiguous and thus shielded Heil Valley from claims based on negligence and breach of warranty.

On appeal, the court of appeals reversed, finding that the release was not clear and unambiguous under *Jones v. Dressel*. *Simkin v. Heil Valley Ranch, Inc.*, 765 P.2d 582, 584-85 (Colo. App. 1988). Judge Babcock dissented, concluding that the language in the agreement adequately reflected Simkin's intent to release Heil Valley for liability for her injury.

---

2. Simkin's complaint alleged that Heil Valley was negligent in the following ways:

a. In inducing Plaintiff to mount the furnished horse when Defendant knew or should have known that said horse was of an uncontrollable nature and at times had an unsafe and dangerous disposition and Defendant also knew, or should have known, that said horse had on the same day of Plaintiff's accident shown such propensities by milling around, kicking, and acting in a dangerous manner.
b. In failing to provide a horse commenserate [sic] with Plaintiff's ability.
c. In providing Plaintiff with a horse which Defendant knew or should have known was unreasonably dangerous for the purpose for which said horse was provided to Plaintiff and others like Plaintiff.
d. In failing to exercise care to furnish Plaintiff with a reasonably safe horse to ride.
e. In failing to warn Plaintiff of the substantial risk of harm to Plaintiff by said horse when Defendant knew or should have known that said horse was extremely dangerous and had at times displayed an unreasonably dangerous disposition and propensity.
f. That Defendant knew or should have known that the horse was not suitable and that Defendant did not advise or otherwise assist Plaintiff in getting a different horse or controlling same horse.

3. The second claim for relief for breach of warranty stated in part:

2. That Defendant, Heil Valley Ranch, Incorporated, breached an implied warranty or express warranty and also breached a warranty of fitness for a particular purpose when Defendant furnished and supplied Plaintiff with said horse which Defendant knew or should have known was unreasonably dangerous to Plaintiff and others like Plaintiff. The Defendant further breached said warranties when the Defendant furnished and supplied Plaintiff with an unsafe and unreasonably dangerous horse and/or in failing to ascertain that such horse was in fact unsafe for the purpose intended.
3. That the horse the Plaintiff mounted to ride was not suitable for the purpose for which it was hired.
4. That as a direct and proximate consequence of Defendant's, Heil Valley Ranch, Incorporated's, breach of warranties, as aforesaid, the Plaintiff Roane Simkin, has suffered direct and consequential damages and injuries. . . .

4. The issue of whether Simkin had in fact signed the release was disputed and was reserved for trial. Because of her injuries Simkin did not remember if she signed it or not. The parties agreed to submit the issue to the court sitting without a jury. After holding a hearing, the district court concluded that Simkin had signed the release and accordingly entered a final judgment in favor of Heil Valley. Simkin has not raised the issue of signing the release on appeal.

II.

Agreements attempting to exculpate a party from that party's own negligence have long been disfavored. They stand at the crossroads of two competing principles: freedom of contract and responsibility for damages caused by one's own negligent acts.

Exculpatory agreements are not necessarily void, however, as long as one party is not "at such obvious disadvantage in bargaining power that the effect of the contract is to put him at the mercy of the other's negligence." W. Keeton, D. Dobbs, R. Keeton, & D. Owen, *Prosser and Keeton on the Law of Torts* §68, at 482 (5th ed. 1984) [hereinafter *Prosser*]. Thus, exculpatory agreements between employer and employee, and between common carriers or public utilities and members of the public are generally held invalid. *Id.* at 482-83; *see also* Restatement (Second) of Torts §496B comments f & g (1965). Such a contract is not implicated here.

Jones v. Dressel set forth the test for determining the validity of an exculpatory agreement:

> In determining whether an exculpatory agreement is valid, there are four factors which a court must consider: (1) the existence of a duty to the public; (2) the nature of the service performed; (3) whether the contract was fairly entered into; and (4) whether the intention of the parties is expressed in clear and unambiguous language.

Only the fourth factor is an issue here. "The determination of the sufficiency and validity of an exculpatory agreement is a question of law for the court to determine." Partial summary judgment on the validity of the instant agreement was therefore appropriate.

In *Jones v. Dressel*, the agreement that we upheld specifically included the word "negligence." We therefore were not required to decide whether an exculpatory agreement, in order to bar an action based on negligence, must always use the term "negligence" or words of similar import. Courts in other jurisdictions, although uniformly agreeing that exculpatory agreements must be strictly construed against the drafter, are split on whether "negligence" must be specifically mentioned, or whether more inclusive and general terms may be employed. The court of appeals majority relied on the first line of cases to find the release invalid, in which the term "negligence" or similar words are always required. In dissent, Judge Babcock believed that "use of the talismanic terms 'negligence' and 'breach of warranty' was unnecessary to render the release effective." *Simkin*, 765 P.2d at 585 (Babcock, J., dissenting).

We agree that use of the specific terms "negligence" and "breach of warranty" are not invariably required for an exculpatory agreement to shield a party from claims based on negligence and breach of warranty. The inquiry should be whether the intent of the parties was to extinguish liability and whether this intent was clearly and unambiguously expressed. In the present case, the agreement was written in simple and clear terms that were free from legal jargon. It was not inordinately long or complicated. When the agreement was read to Simkin at her deposition, she indicated that she understood it.

In addition, the first sentence of the release specifically addressed a risk that adequately described the circumstances of Simkin's injury. The record also supports the conclusion that Simkin was not a novice rider, but was instead one with some experience. The risk that a horse could rear and injure her was reasonably foreseeable to someone with her experience.

In *Harris v. Walker*, 119 Ill. 2d 542, 116 Ill. Dec. 702, 519 N.E.2d 917 (1988), the court held that a rider who fell off his rented horse when it became spooked could not sue the defendant stables for their negligence because of a release plaintiff signed. The release did not use the word "negligence," but said that "your signature shall release [defendant] and employees of any liabilities you may incur while on the premises or for any injury which may result from horseback riding." The Illinois Supreme Court stated that "when the parties adopt broad language in a release, it is reasonable to interpret the intended coverage to be as broad as the risks that are obvious to experienced participants."

Under the circumstances of this case, it is reasonable to interpret the broad language in the release to cover claims based on negligence or breach of warranty. It is difficult to imagine any claim that Simkin could have asserted against Heil Valley that would not have been based, at bottom, on negligence. It is unreasonable to interpret the agreement in a way that provides virtually no protection to Heil Valley, and renders the release essentially meaningless. We therefore hold that the district court properly found that the release was valid and enforceable.[5]

Accordingly, we reverse the judgment of the court of appeals, and remand the cause with directions to reinstate the judgment of the district court in favor of Heil Valley.

LOHR, J., dissents, and QUINN, C.J., and MULLARKEY, J., join in the dissent.

Justice LOHR dissenting:

This case presents the issue of whether a release of liability signed by the plaintiff, Roane Simkin, was effective to absolve the defendant, Heil Valley Ranch, Incorporated (Heil Valley), from liability for any negligence or breach of warranty in connection with the rental of a horse to the plaintiff for a recreational ride. The majority opinion holds that the release was clear and unambiguous, and that it was effective to release Heil Valley from liability for the

---

5. As an alternative reason for its decision reversing the district court, the court of appeals stated that even if the agreement was a valid assumption of the risk, it would still not be a total defense under comparative negligence principles. *Simkin*, 765 P.2d at 584. However, an *express* assumption of the risk by contract, as here, *does* constitute a total defense to an action based on negligence. *See Arbegast v. Board of Educ.*, 65 N.Y.2d 161, 168-70, 490 N.Y.S.2d 751, 757, 480 N.E.2d 365, 370-71 (1985); *see also* Prosser, *supra* §68, at 496 ("an express assumption of the risk by the plaintiff should continue to serve as a total bar in comparative negligence cases.").

injury suffered by Simkin when the horse she had rented reared and fell backward on her. The majority opinion therefore reverses the judgment of the Colorado Court of Appeals, which held that the release of liability was ambiguous, and directs reinstatement of the judgment issued by the district court in favor of Heil Valley. I am persuaded that the release did not clearly absolve Heil Valley from liability for the conduct alleged by Simkin, and therefore respectfully dissent.

II.

As the majority acknowledges, agreements attempting to absolve a party from liability for that party's own negligence have long been disfavored.

The release agreement begins with an acknowledgment that the "use, handling and riding of a horse" involves a risk of physical injury. It then states that a horse may act or react unpredictably based on instinct or fright notwithstanding its training and usual past behavior and that such "inherent risk" is assumed by the rider. The rider then "expressly assumes" such risk and waives any claim against the stables as a result of physical injury incurred in such activities. The risks described in the release do not extend beyond injuries resulting from the risks inherent in the nature of the activity and the unpredictableness of a horse.

Simkin, however, grounds her claims on specific negligent conduct of Heil Valley. She alleges that the defendant knew the particular horse assigned to her was uncontrollable and dangerous and that on the day of the ill-fated ride, the horse had "shown such propensities by milling around, kicking, and acting in a dangerous manner." Simkin alleged that Heil Valley failed to exercise care in providing her a reasonably safe horse to ride and in failing to furnish a horse matched to her abilities as a rider. The same alleged misconduct supplied the basis for Simkin's breach of warranty claim.

The misconduct alleged by Simkin is not referred to among the risks that the release agreement describes. That agreement simply acknowledges the existence of inherent risks because of the nature of horseback riding, including the unpredictability of the behavior of any horse. It does not purport to absolve Heil Valley from using care to provide a horse suited to the abilities of the rider or to assure that a rider is not assigned a horse that has displayed characteristics making it unsuitable for recreational riding. Accordingly, the release did not purport to absolve Heil Valley from liability for the types of negligence and breach of warranty alleged by Simkin.

Heil Valley relies upon the portion of the release stating that the rider waives "any claim" against the stables as a result of physical injury incurred in the use, handling and riding of a horse. This waiver must be read, however, in the context of the preceding language referring to risks inherent in horseback riding but making no mention of risks avoidable by the exercise of due care by the stables. This makes it at least ambiguous whether the release can be read to absolve Heil Valley from its own negligent acts in supplying a horse having characteristics unsuitable for recreational riding in general or by the person signing the release agreement in particular, as alleged by Simkin in this case. Any such ambiguity must be construed against Heil Valley, with the result that the release agreement does not provide a complete defense to Simkin's claims.

I dissent and would affirm the judgment of the court of appeals.

QUINN, C.J., and MULLARKEY, J., join in this dissent.

PREPARING FOR CLASS

1. Try to identify the risks that Simkin "assumed."

2. In what ways might Heil Valley Ranch have been negligent?

3. What would happen if Simkin had not signed the agreement?

4. What type of liability has Heil protected itself from?

APPLYING THE LAW

Plaintiff goes to hotel and, as instructed in room, decides to check in her jewelry at the main desk. She is given a claim tag, which on the back states that the hotel will not be responsible for lost or stolen items. Her jewelry is lost because of the negligence of the hotel. What result?

INCREASING YOUR UNDERSTANDING

1. *Simkin* involves what is commonly referred to as "express assumption of risk." Most jurisdictions recognize this as an affirmative defense in negligence actions and follow in some form the Restatement (Second) of Torts §496B, which states:

    > *Express Assumption of Risk*
    > A plaintiff who by contract or otherwise expressly agrees to accept a risk of harm arising from the defendant's negligent or reckless conduct cannot recover for such harm, unless the agreement is invalid as contrary to public policy.

2. *Scope of protection.* The contract between the plaintiff and defendant defines the type of conduct and the specific risks that will be excused. Heirs of the decedent may be barred from bringing a wrongful death action (Saenz v. Whitewater Voyages, Inc., 226 Cal. App. 3d 758, 276

Cal. Rptr. 672 (1st Dist. 990). Plaintiffs, who signed forms refusing blood transfusions, assumed risk of death as a consequence of refusing to permit blood transfusion. (Shorter v. Drury, 103 Wash. 2d 645, 695 P.2d 116 (Wash. 1985). Under traditional contract interpretation principles, exculpatory clauses will be strictly construed and general clauses exempting the defendant from all liability no matter the conduct "will not [be] construed to include loss or damage resulting from intentional, negligent, or reckless misconduct, unless the circumstances clearly indicate that such was the plaintiff's understanding and intention." Restatement (Second) of Torts §496B comment d. (1965).

3. In what circumstances may the court not enforce the clause? Generally courts favor contracting between parties, and thus there is no general doctrinal aversion to exculpatory agreements. As stated above, however, the court might find an exculpatory clause legally lacking because it fails in its specifics. Courts may also not enforce a clause because to do so would violate some public policy. "The courts have refused to uphold such agreements ... where one party is at such obvious disadvantage in bargaining power that the effect of the contract is to put him at the mercy of the other's negligence." Prosser and Keaton on Torts, §68 (5th ed. 1984). "Contract between employer and employee nullifying or lessening any legal duty to employee relative to safeguarding of his life, limb, safety, health, or welfare is contrary to public policy and void." (Pittsburgh, Cincinnati Chicago & St. Louis Railway Co. v. Kinney, 115 N.E. 505 (Ohio 1916). "Public utility, such as common carrier or telegraph company, cannot through use of a limitation of liability clause except itself from liability for damages resulting from its own negligence; however, when public utility has no legal or public duty to provide specific service to its customers, it may, through use of exculpatory clause, limit its liability for damages caused by its own negligence." (Richard A. Berijan, D.O., Inc. v. Ohio Bell Telephone Co., 375 N.E.2d 410 (Ohio 1978).

Nelson v. Hall
165 Cal. App. 3d 709, 211 Cal. Rptr. 668 (Cal. App. 3 Dist. 1985)

ROBIE, J.

Plaintiff Rebecca Nelson appeals from a judgment dismissing her complaint against defendants Susan and Richard Hall in an action for personal injuries, entered after the trial court granted defendants' motion for summary judgment. At issue in this appeal is (a) whether the defense of assumption of the risk is available under the "Dog Bite Statute" (Civ. Code, §3342), and (b) whether a veterinarian or veterinary assistant assumes the risk of dog bites as a matter of law while treating a dog. We hold in the affirmative.

FACTS

On January 21, 1983, plaintiff, a veterinary assistant, filed a complaint against defendants for injuries she sustained when she was bitten by defendants' dog while she assisted in its treatment at the animal hospital where she was employed. Plaintiff alleged that on or about July 30, 1982, while she was at the Skyway Pet Hospital (Skyway), defendants' dog, Amos, inflicted bites upon her head and face, causing permanent impairment, scarring, and disfigurement. Plaintiff further alleged that by reason of her injuries, she will be limited in her future employment, will require future plastic surgery, and has suffered severe emotional distress. Plaintiff brought the action under the so-called "Dog Bite Statute," Civil Code section 3342.[1] She did not allege defendants were negligent or had any knowledge of vicious propensities on Amos' part.

In answer, defendants alleged plaintiff contributed to her injuries by her own negligence and that she assumed the risk of injury. They further alleged strict liability for their dog's actions under section 3342 terminated when they delivered the dog to a qualified veterinarian and the veterinarian accepted employment.

After taking plaintiff's deposition, defendants moved for summary judgment, again contending they could not be held strictly liable under section 3342 when they delivered their dog to the veterinarian for medical treatment. Defendants submitted with the motion a portion of plaintiff's deposition and a declaration of plaintiff's employer, Mark Dunlap, D.V.M. In response to defendants' motion, plaintiff did not rebut defendants' factual evidence, but rather conceded its accuracy, arguing as a matter of law that delivery of defendants' dog to a veterinarian did not terminate their strict liability for dog-bite injuries.

Plaintiff had worked on and off as a veterinary assistant since 1966 or 1967. At that time she was studying animal husbandry and veterinary science in college. In 1980, she began working as a veterinary assistant at Skyway, which specializes in small animal treatment. There she assisted the veterinarians in all phases of veterinary medicine, including examinations, treatment, minor surgery, monitoring anesthesia, administering medication (including injections), and laboratory work.

Defendants' dog, Amos, is a black Labrador-German Shepard mix weighing approximately 100 pounds. He was first treated at the Skyway in 1974, and has been treated on a consistent basis since then. Amos was known to the hospital staff as a dog that might attempt to bite while receiving medical treatment.

---

1. Civil Code section 3342 provides: "The owner of any dog is liable for the damages suffered by any person who is bitten by the dog while in a public place or lawfully in a private place, including the property of the owner of the dog, regardless of the former viciousness of the dog or the owner's knowledge of such viciousness. A person is lawfully upon the private property of such owner within the meaning of this section when he is on such property in the performance of any duty imposed upon him by the laws of this State or by the laws or postal regulations of the United States, or when he is on such property upon the invitation, express or implied, of the owner."

On at least one occasion prior to the incident in the present case, Amos attempted to bite his handlers, and a notation of "careful" was written on his treatment card.

On July 30, 1982, defendant Susan Hall brought Amos to the hospital with a complaint of a small swelling on his right side. Plaintiff directed Mrs. Hall to bring Amos into the examination room. At the time he appeared calm. Dr. James Wadsack, a licensed veterinarian, examined Amos and determined he required minor surgery to remove a foreign object from his right lateral abdomen. After injecting Amos with a sedative, Dr. Wadsack and plaintiff moved Amos to the treatment area of the hospital.

Once there, they lifted Amos onto the treatment table and placed him on his stomach. Plaintiff was standing alongside the treatment table waiting for the sedative to take effect, her left arm placed over Amos' neck and shoulders and her right arm on his loin or rump. She was not restraining him, and he appeared calm. Without warning, Amos quickly turned and bit plaintiff in the face, causing severe injuries. She received workers' compensation benefits.

Plaintiff was not aware of any vicious propensities on the part of Amos and he did not display any such propensities while she handled him, until the time of the attack. Skyway uses muzzles on dogs who are known to be vicious, but no muzzle was used on Amos. No allegation was made that defendants were aware of any vicious propensities on Amos' part. There was no evidence that they were aware Amos had previously attempted to bite his handlers.

In his declaration, Dr. Dunlap stated it is generally accepted in the veterinary profession that any animal may react strangely or dangerously while receiving treatment, regardless of its behavior in the home environment. A veterinarian cannot assume a normally gentle dog will act gently while receiving treatment. Dog bites are an occupational hazard in the veterinary profession and Dr. Dunlap has been bitten several times. The seriousness of the hazard can be minimized through proper safety precautions. Plaintiff has received more than five minor dog bites, one of which required medical treatment. Some were received while the animals were sedated.

Discussion

(1) Although Civil Code section 3342 by its terms imposes strict liability on dog owners, it has been long established that the defense of assumption of the risk applies to actions brought under the "Dog Bite Statute".[3] The first case to so hold was *Smythe v. Schacht* in 1949, at which time the statute was uncodified. (93 Cal. App. 2d 315, 321-322 [209 P.2d 114].) In 1953, the Legislature reenacted and codified the statute without substantive modification (Stats.

---

3. "In this state, the defense of assumption of risk arises when the plaintiff voluntarily undertakes to encounter a specific known risk imposed by defendant's conduct." (*Lipson v. Superior Court* (1982) 31 Cal. 3d 362, 375, fn.8 [182 Cal. Rptr. 629, 644 P.2d 822].)

1953, ch. 37) and subsequent courts, including our Supreme Court, have reiterated the *Smythe* rule.

Even before the enactment of the "Dog Bite Statute" in 1931 (Stats. 1931, ch. 503), assumption of the risk was held to be a defense to strict liability for injuries caused by a dangerous animal. This rule still exists for animal cases as well as other instances of strict liability.

(2) In certain circumstances the defense of assumption of the risk has survived the establishment of comparative fault. Where assumption of the risk is only a form of contributory negligence—i.e., where a plaintiff *unreasonably* encounters a known risk—the doctrine has been subsumed by comparative fault is applicable to cases of strict liability. Where assumption of the risk is not merely a form of contributory negligence, it has not been subsumed and is a complete defense.

(3) Plaintiff does not dispute defendants' factual showing. Plaintiff's employer stated that dog bites are an occupational hazard in the veterinary profession and it cannot be assumed a normally gentle dog will act gently while receiving treatment. This risk logically extends to those who assist veterinarians in the treatment of dogs. Plaintiff was aware from her personal experience of the hazard involved in treating dogs, for she had been bitten several times, albeit not as seriously as in this instance. She voluntarily undertook to encounter a specific known risk. It is irrelevant that she was not aware of any particular vicious propensities on the part of Amos, for what is relevant in assumption of the risk is a person's " '. . . knowledge and appreciation of the *danger* involved and his voluntary acceptance of the risk.' " The risk of dog bites during treatment is a specific known hazard endemic to the very occupation in which plaintiff voluntarily engaged. Therefore, in voluntarily engaging in the occupation of assisting veterinarians in the medical treatment of dogs, plaintiff assumed the risk of being bitten during the course of treatment.

This is a case of "true" or "primary" assumption of the risk whereby the defendant is impliedly relieved of any duty of care by the plaintiff's acceptance of employment involving a known risk or danger. A veterinary assistant cannot be deemed to have unreasonably encountered a risk that is inherent in his or her job. Therefore, this type of assumption of the risk is not subsumed by comparative fault and, hence, is a complete defense.

Charging a plaintiff with having assumed the risks inherent in his or her occupation is not without precedent in this state. For example, it is well-established that firefighters injured while fighting a fire have no cause of action against the person whose negligence caused the fire in question. This rule applies as well to police officers injured in the course of their duties. The "fireman's rule" is based primarily upon the principle of assumption of the risk. Since firefighting is an occupation which *by its very nature* exposes them to particular hazards, firefighters cannot complain of conduct which forms the basis for their being summoned to a fire. The "fireman's rule" applies not only to negate an action based upon a defendant's negligence, but as well, an action based upon strict liability. Moreover, it is a complete defense.

The same principles apply here. A veterinarian or a veterinary assistant who accepts employment for the medical treatment of a dog, aware of the risk that *any* dog, regardless of its previous nature, might bite while being treated, has assumed this risk as part of his or her occupation. The veterinarian determines the method of treatment and handling of the dog. He or she is the person in possession and control of the dog and is in the best position to take necessary precautions and protective measures. The dog owner who has no knowledge of its particular vicious propensities has no control over what happens to the dog while being treated in a strange environment and cannot know how the dog will react to treatment. A dog owner who does no more than turn his or her dog over to a qualified veterinarian for medical treatment should not be held strictly liable when the dog bites a veterinarian or a veterinary assistant while being treated.

This does not mean dog owners could *never* be held liable for injuries to veterinarians or their assistants. We emphasize that the defense of assumption of the risk extends only to the danger which the injured person has *knowingly* assumed; i.e., the danger the dog will bite *while being treated*. Moreover, if a dog owner purposefully or negligently conceals a particular known hazard from a veterinarian, he or she would not be relieved of liability, for this would expose the injured person to an unknown risk. This question is not before us, since defendants are not accused of negligence or of knowledge of any particular vicious propensities on Amos' part.

Accordingly, we hold that assumption of the risk is a complete defense to an action by a veterinary assistant against a dog owner for damages for injuries suffered from being bitten by the owner's dog during the course of medical treatment.

DISPOSITION

The judgment is affirmed.

BLEASE, Acting, P.J., and SIMS, J., concurred.

PREPARING FOR CLASS

1. What risks should the plaintiff reasonably assume? Which ones might she not?

2. What role does the court play in this case?

3. Does the court's ruling frustrate the goals behind imposing strict liability in this context?

APPLYING THE LAW

Plaintiff attended a baseball game at Lugnut's Stadium. She occupied a seat on the first base side in an unscreened area. Plaintiff and her husband had occupied the identical seats on a previous occasion, thus she knew before entering the stadium that her seat was located in an unprotected area. Plaintiff did not request a seat in a protected area of the ballpark. During the first inning of the game a foul ball struck and injured her. Did plaintiff assume the risk as a matter of law?

INCREASING YOUR UNDERSTANDING

1. *Implied assumption of the risk.* Courts may find that the plaintiff assumed the risk of injury even in the absence of an express agreement. In these circumstances the plaintiff's voluntary conduct is viewed as entering into a tacit agreement that the defendant should not be legally responsible for harm that might stem from the defendant's conduct. Over the years, courts have recognized two forms of implied assumption of the risks: *primary* and *secondary*.

2. *Primary implied assumption of the risks; no duty.* Primary implied assumption of the risks arises in those circumstances where the court decides as a matter of law that the relationship of the parties is such that the plaintiff assumes certain risks inherent to the situation. It matters not whether the defendant acted unreasonably (risks assumed are created by the activity not the defendant's negligence) or whether the plaintiff acted unreasonably in confronting the inherent risks. In fact, under primary implied assumption of the risks the defendant does not allege that the plaintiff was negligent. So a patron struck by a baseball may be found to have assumed the risk of such injury ("One of the natural risks assumed by spectators attending professional games is that of being struck by batted or thrown balls. Management is not required to insure patrons against injury from such source. All that is required is the exercise of ordinary care to protect patrons against such injuries, and in doing so, the management is not obligated to screen all seats because many patrons prefer to sit where their view is not obscured by a screen"; Neistein v. Los Angeles, Inc., 185 Cal. App. 3d 176, 229 Cal. Rptr. 612 (Cal. 2d. Dist. 1986)), as well as a patron injured while participating in a skating game ("By taking part in skating game, skater agreed to accept risks inherent in game that were obvious and necessary, one of which was that of being knocked over and injured, and because skater voluntarily and knowingly placed himself into that area of appreciable risk and rules of game were followed, owner of skating rink did not owe duty

to skater with regard to those risks; Ridge v. Kladnick 42 Wash. App.785, 713 P.2d 1131 (Wash. 1986)).

3. Secondary implied assumption of the risks involves primarily three elements: First, the plaintiff must be aware that the risk exists; second, there must be proof that plaintiff appreciated the magnitude or severity of the risks; and third, the plaintiff must have voluntarily confronted the risks. Raising secondary assumption of the risks requires an inquiry into plaintiff's conduct in the face of defendant's negligence and as such, allows the trier of fact to assess the reasonableness of such conduct. As such, secondary assumption of the risks has a similar tone as contributory negligence, with the distinction perhaps best described as turning on the degree of "unreasonableness" involved. The line between the two is blurred, and courts have been inconsistent in their expressions of a distinction, which has only yielded more confusion. You decide whether the following articulation hits the mark: "The distinction between contributory negligence and voluntary assumption of risk is often difficult to draw in concrete cases, and under the law of this state[,] usually without importance, but it may be well to keep it in mind. Contributory negligence, of course, means negligence which contributes to cause a particular accident which occurs, while assumption of risk of accident means voluntary incurring [the risk] of an accident which may not occur, and which the person assuming the risk may be careful to avoid after starting. Contributory negligence defeats recovery because it is a proximate cause of the accident which happens, but assumption of the risk defeats recovery because it is a previous abandonment of the right to complain if an accident occurs." Prudential Securities Inc. v. E-Net, Inc., 780 A.2d 359 (Md. Ct. Spec. App. 2001).

   a. *Knowledge of risk's existence and magnitude.* "The standard to be applied is a subjective one, of what the particular plaintiff in facts sees, knows, understands and appreciates. In this it differs from the objective standard which is applied to contributory negligence." Restatement (Second) of Torts §496D comment c. (1965). General knowledge of "a danger" is insufficient; rather, plaintiff must have actual knowledge of the specific risk that injured him and appreciate its magnitude. (Garcia v. City of South Tucson, 131 Ariz. 315, 640 P.2d 1117 (Ariz. App. 1981). Whether plaintiff was aware of the risks is mostly a question of fact, and the jury may appropriately conclude that the plaintiff was aware though she may testify to the contrary. "The law would not permit passenger, injured in crash, to deny knowing that host driver was intoxicated, where the passenger had been drinking with the driver for more than three hours, where he had observed her consume at least three different types of alcoholic beverages, and where the parties had left cabin for the sole purpose of securing additional intoxicating beverages which they intended to consume." Harlow v. Connelly, 548 S.W.2d 143 (Ky. App. 1977.).

b. Did plaintiff freely and voluntarily assume the risk? One court said no when a plaintiff chose to use a negligently maintained privy (toilet housed in a small shed). Rush v. Commercial Realty Co., 7 N.J. Misc. 337, 145 A. 476 (N.J. 1929) (Plaintiff "had no choice, when impelled by the calls of nature, but to use the facilities placed at her disposal by the landlord"). Plaintiff who knew of vicious propensities of hog, which had escaped its owner's farm and was on plaintiff's farm, could have either remained a prisoner inside his farmhouse, shot hog, or risked running from farmhouse across own property to automobile to return to work, did not have free and voluntary choice in confronting risk of hog attacking him when he left house and ran to automobile. Marshall v. Ranne, 511 S.W.2d 255 (Tex. 1974). But, parent who was injured when she slipped on ice and snow covered parking lot while visiting daughter at university she attended voluntarily assumed the risk, though motivation for visit was to bring money to daughter. Morgan State University v. Walker, 397 Md. 509, 919 A.2d 21 (Md. 2007).

Duffy v. Midlothian Country Club
481 N.E.2d 1037 (Ill. App. 1 Dist. 1985)

MEJDA, Presiding Justice:

Defendants-appellants Midlothian Country Club ("Midlothian") and the Western Golf Association ("WGA") ("defendants") appeal from a jury verdict awarding plaintiff-appellee Alice Duffy ("plaintiff") $448,380 in a personal injury action. On appeal, defendants maintain 1) that the trial court improperly prevented defendants from asserting an assumption of risk defense, 2) that the trial court abused its discretion in allowing plaintiff's witness to testify as an expert, and 3) that the cumulative effect of various rulings and the improper conduct of plaintiff's counsel resulted in a jury verdict based on passion and prejudice. We affirm.

On June 29, 1973, plaintiff attended the Western Open professional golf tournament (the "tournament") as a paying spectator. The tournament was held at Midlothian and sponsored jointly by Midlothian and WGA. Plaintiff attended the tournament with her son, her son's friend, and the friend's mother, Audrey Scheufler. Upon their arrival, plaintiff and Mrs. Scheufler went to the first tee and watched a contestant tee off on the first fairway. At this time, and throughout the pertinent time period, plaintiff remained within the roped-off areas reserved for paying spectators. After watching the contestant on the first tee, plaintiff and Mrs. Scheufler walked to a concession tent (tent 1) located south of the first tee and east of a service road which ran across both the first hole and the parallel 18th hole. Not finding what they wanted, plaintiff and Mrs. Scheufler left tent 1 and walked west across the service road, between the first and 18th holes, and into a second concession tent (tent 2).

After purchasing refreshments, the two women left tent 2, walked west, and joined a group of spectators watching the first fairway. As plaintiff stood talking and eating her food, she was hit in the eye by a ball shot from the 18th tee by Dow Finsterwald ("Finsterwald") a professional golfer participating in the tournament. As a result, plaintiff has completely lost the sight in her right eye.

Plaintiff subsequently sued for injuries sustained, alleging *inter alia* that defendants 1) had failed to give plaintiff timely warning of the approaching shot, 2) had failed to restrict or warn plaintiff from a dangerous area, and 3) had failed to provide a reasonably safe environment for a professional golf tournament. Following discovery, defendants moved for summary judgment. In their motion, defendants maintained that plaintiff, an allegedly experienced golfer, appreciated the risks inherent in a professional golf tournament. Defendants consequently argued that plaintiff had voluntarily assumed a known risk and, therefore, was barred from recovery. The trial court agreed and granted defendants' motion. On appeal, this court reversed and remanded, holding that defendants had a duty of reasonable care toward spectators as business invitees. (*Duffy v. Midlothian Country Club* (1980), 92 Ill. App. 3d 193, 47 Ill. Dec. 786, 415 N.E.2d 1099.) We further ruled that the applicable standard of reasonable care was a variable question of fact for jury determination. Finally, we stated that assumption of risk could be a defense to plaintiff's claim if it could be proven that plaintiff fully appreciated the risks inherent in the situation.

On remand, the jury found that plaintiff had sustained $498,200 in damages which were proximately caused by defendants' negligence. The jury additionally determined that 10% of plaintiff's damages were attributable to her own negligence. Consequently, the award was reduced by 10% to $448,380.

OPINION

I

Defendants initially contend that the trial court improperly prevented their assertion of assumption of risk as a complete defense to plaintiff's claim. Defendants maintain that this court's decision in *Duffy v. Midlothian Country Club* (1980), 92 Ill. App. 3d 193, 47 Ill. Dec. 786, 415 N.E.2d 1099, operates as the law of the case and consequently compels this conclusion. Furthermore, defendants claim that they created no additional risk beyond those risks inherent in the situation which plaintiff, as a spectator, had assumed. Defendants specifically argue that the trial court erred in granting plaintiff's motion *in limine* to preclude defendants' use of the words "assumption of risk" and "assumed the risk." Defendants additionally argue that the trial court incorrectly refused to instruct the jury concerning assumption of risk as a complete defense.

Plaintiff, on the other hand, rejects these contentions, maintaining that the court's rulings were proper and the verdict just. Furthermore, plaintiff argues that the adoption of comparative negligence in *Alvis v. Ribar* (1981), 85 Ill. 2d 1, 52 Ill. Dec. 23, 421 N.E.2d 886, necessarily nullified implied assumption of risk as a complete defense to negligence actions. Plaintiff declares that this conclusion was expressly indicated in *Coney v. J.L.G. Industries, Inc.* (1983), 97 Ill. 2d 104, 73 Ill. Dec. 337, 454 N.E.2d 197, wherein implied assumption of risk was limited by comparative negligence in strict products liability actions. In short, plaintiff not only requests affirmance of the trial ruling and verdict below, but also an express nullification of implied assumption of risk as a defense in negligence actions.

Since its introduction into negligence law, assumption of risk has operated as a complete bar to plaintiffs' recoveries. Such drastic results were supported by the argument that plaintiff had voluntarily assumed an ascertainable risk, thus relieving defendant of all legal duties. The doctrine has subsequently developed into both express and implied forms. Under express assumption of risk, plaintiff and defendant explicitly agree, in advance, that defendant owes no legal duty to plaintiff and therefore, that plaintiff cannot recover for injuries caused either by risks inherent in the situation or by dangers created by defendant's negligence. Under the express form of the doctrine, defendants only sustain liability if their actions are construed as wanton, willful or reckless, or if damages arise from an agreement deemed contrary to public policy. Prosser, Torts §68, at 439-45 (4th ed. 1971).

Under the implied form of assumption of risk, plaintiff's willingness to assume a known risk is determined from the conduct of the parties rather than from an explicit agreement. The implied form of the doctrine has itself been subdivided into primary and secondary categories. The primary label has been applied to situations where a plaintiff has assumed known risks inherent in a particular activity or situation. The assumed risks there are not those created by defendant's negligence but rather by the nature of the activity itself. Thus, primary implied assumption of risk is, arguably, not a true negligence defense since no cause of action for negligence is ever alleged. Kionka, *Implied Assumption of the Risk: Does It Survive Comparative Fault?* 1982 S. Ill. L.J. 371.

Secondary implied assumption of risk, on the other hand, is a true defense since there plaintiff implicitly assumes the risks created by defendant's negligence. Because the secondary doctrine places greater burdens on plaintiff without his express consent, this form of implied assumption of risk has been criticized by both courts and commentators. Indeed, some courts have even refused to allow an implied assumption of risk defense in negligence actions. Until recently, however, most courts have upheld implied assumption of risk as a valid negligence defense if plaintiff's knowledge and volition could be proven.

Secondary assumption of risk has been viewed as functionally similar to contributory negligence. (See generally, Kionka, *Implied Assumption of the Risk: Does It Survive Comparative Fault?* 1982 S. Ill. L.J. 371.) This similarity is precisely the rationale used by critics arguing for abolition of the secondary doctrine. These critics maintain that comparative negligence, which effectively abolished contributory negligence, should operate similarly on secondary implied assumption of risk. Thus, comparative negligence would prevent assumption of risk from operating as a complete bar to recovery in negligence actions. This argument received support in the supreme court's decision in *Coney v. J.L.G. Industries, Inc.*(1983), 97 Ill. 2d 104, 73 Ill. Dec. 337, 454 N.E.2d 197. In *Coney*, the court held that comparative fault principles would apply to the apportionment of damages in strict products liability cases. Moreover, the court ruled that defenses of misuse and assumption of risk would no longer bar recovery in products liability actions. Instead, plaintiff's assumption or misconduct would merely be a factor in the apportionment of damages.

Here plaintiff contends that *Coney* implicitly compels the abolition of the assumption of risk defense as a complete bar to recovery in negligence actions. Additionally, plaintiff has demonstrated that a vast majority of states have abolished or severely limited the assumption of risk defense following their adoption of comparative negligence In sum, plaintiff argues that this court should follow *Coney* and the trend established in other jurisdictions by ruling that implied assumption of risk is no longer a complete bar to recovery in negligence actions.

Before adopting plaintiff's argument, however, it is important that we clarify the scope of this decision. Comparative negligence initially was introduced to ameliorate the harsh results produced by contributory negligence. Therefore, if comparative negligence affects assumption of risk, its impact should be limited to that portion of the doctrine which is functionally similar to contributory negligence. Thus, we do not find that comparative negligence affects express assumption of risk, wherein plaintiff explicitly assumes inherent dangers as well as risks created by defendant's negligence. In addition, we reach the same conclusion with regard to the primary implied assumption of risk, wherein plaintiff knowingly and voluntarily assumes the risks inherent in a particular situation. Since these branches of the assumption of risk doctrine are neither analytically nor functionally similar to contributory negligence, they arguably may be unaffected by comparative fault as amelioration for contributory negligence. We limit our ruling today to secondary implied assumption of risk and consequently hold that this doctrine is necessarily abolished by the introduction of comparative negligence into our jurisprudence. Thus, plaintiff's implied assumption of defendant's negligence will no longer operate as an absolute bar to recovery in negligence actions. Rather, as *Coney* indicates, plaintiff's assumption of risk will merely aid in the apportionment of damages.

Having so held, we refuse to disturb the verdict below since it conforms with the conclusions we have reached. We are equally unpersuaded by defendants' arguments concerning our earlier decision as the law of the case. Initially, this argument is flawed since our 1980 decision did not determine this issue, but merely raised the possibility of assumption of risk as an absolute defense.

Further, an issue may be re-examined in a subsequent appeal if, during the intervening period, a higher court has announced contrary law. Since our decision, the supreme court has introduced comparative fault and extended that concept to assumption of risk in product liability actions. Thus, a higher court has announced contrary law. Accordingly, defendants' law of the case argument fails under these facts.

We similarly reject defendants' contention that the trial court improperly granted a motion *in limine* which precluded defendants' use of the words "assumption of risk" and "assumed the risk." Defendants argue that the motion effectively and improperly restricted the presentation of their case. A motion *in limine* precluding the admission of evidence at trial should be employed with caution as it may unduly restrict the opposing party's presentation of its case. Furthermore, an *in limine* order which precludes the opponent from presenting a valid defense is an abuse of discretion by the court. Here, however, it has been determined that assumption of risk was not a valid defense to defendants' negligence. Furthermore, the trial court limited its order to the preclusion of specific words rather than an entire theory. Thus, since the order neither precluded evidence nor prevented the presentation of any theory or defense, the order was proper and not an abuse of discretion.

For the foregoing reasons, the judgment of the circuit court of Cook County is affirmed.

AFFIRMED.

Lorenz and Pincham, JJ., concur.

PREPARING FOR CLASS

1. What type of evidence should be offered by the defendant in meeting its burden on the assumption of risks defense?

2. Why was this not considered primary assumption of the risks (no duty)?

3. What's the consequence of merging assumption of the risks with comparative fault?

4. How should golf courses respond to this ruling?

INCREASING YOUR UNDERSTANDING

Duffy illustrates what many jurisdictions have chosen to do upon adopting comparative fault rules and should come as no surprise given how courts reacted to the "all or nothing" reality under the common law contributory negligence rule. Further support for merging comes from the inconsistent construction and application of secondary assumption of the risks rules/standards.

True to form, the responses have been uneven among the states that have reconsidered assumption of the risks after adopting comparative fault rules. For example, Washington has retained express and primary assumption of the risks, the latter since no duty was owed in the first. West Virginia has retained secondary assumption of the risks, but only in situations where the plaintiff's fault is greater than the combined defendants'. Wisconsin has dropped all versions of implied assumption of the risks.

TORTS II

Chapter 13

Strict Liability

Over the years American courts have moved to a fault-based system, the most prominent areas being where the defendant has acted intentionally or negligently. There are occasions, however, where liability may be imposed "strictly"—in other words, in circumstances where the defendant's conduct was neither intentional nor unreasonable. Chasing a universal definition for "strict liability" would take one on a never-ending journey. Let it suffice to say that liability is strict when the court imposes liability even though the defendant may have acted reasonably, in other words, without fault.

Before you finish with the tort classes you will have broached several topics where a court has chosen to impose strict liability—products liability, worker's compensation, defamation—to name a few. This chapter is devoted to two specific instances where liability may be strict: where the defendant has engaged in an activity that is considered "abnormally dangerous" and where liability stems from possession or ownership of a dangerous animal.

One caveat: The following case includes claims for both strict liability and negligence and was chosen for your consideration because it classically illustrates how the theories diverge substantively.

A. ANIMALS

Sinclair v. Okata
874 F. Supp. 1051 (D. Alaska 1994)

HOLLAND, Chief Judge.

Plaintiffs have moved for partial summary judgment on certain aspects of their complaint. The motion is opposed. Oral argument has been requested and heard.

On June 4, 1993, Daniel Reinhard was bitten by Anchor, a two and a half year old German Shepherd dog. Daniel was two years old when he was bitten. Daniel's five-year-old sister, Michelle Levshakoff, witnessed the attack. It is a matter of dispute whether Daniel's mother, Katherine Sinclair, was present at the time of the attack or whether she arrived shortly afterward. Katherine Sinclair, individually and on behalf of minors, Daniel and Michelle, filed suit in the Superior Court for the Third Judicial District for the State of Alaska. The named defendants included Yoshitaka Okata, Kazuyo Okata and Yoshihide Okata. Defendants removed the case to federal district court. Jurisdiction was based on diversity. Plaintiffs are Alaska citizens. The Okatas are citizens of Japan. Plaintiffs, joined by Daniel's father, filed an amended complaint with this court. In their complaint, plaintiffs asserted causes of action based on negligence, strict liability, negligent infliction of emotional distress, and for loss of society and companionship. Plaintiffs seek compensatory and punitive damages.

Although some factual issues remain in dispute, there are many areas where there is no genuine dispute. It is not genuinely disputed that the Okatas owned the dog, Anchor, at the time that Daniel Reinhard sustained his injuries. It is also undisputed that Daniel sustained his injuries when Anchor bit Daniel's face. Both sides to the dispute agree that on June 4, 1993, Yoshihide Okata, the 17-year-old son of Yoshitaka and Kazuyo Okata, arrived home without keys to enter the home he shared with his parents. With nothing else to do, Yoshihide decided to look through the owner's manuals to the new van his parents had recently purchased. While examining the manuals, Yoshihide heard the family's dog, Anchor, in the fenced backyard crying. Anchor was a two and a half year old German Shepherd. Yoshihide brought Anchor into the unfenced driveway where the van was parked and ordered the dog to "stay." The dog was not leashed, but Yoshihide stated that he believed Anchor would obey his command to stay. Yoshihide fell asleep in the van, with the dog still unleashed in the driveway. Yoshihide did not awaken until he heard Daniel Reinhard crying. He then spoke with Katherine Sinclair, Daniel's mother, who told Yoshihide that the dog bit Daniel.

There is also no dispute as to the fact that Anchor was involved in at least four previous biting incidents. On the first occasion, a young boy, Shane Perrins, was bitten after he approached Anchor in the Okata's yard. Perrins did not require medical attention, as he received only minor scratches and a small cut on his head. On another occasion, Mina Iinuma was bitten on the arm. Ms. Iinuma's injuries consisted of one or two small holes in her elbow, which did not require medical attention. The third biting incident involved Mizutaka Azuma. According to Azuma's declaration, he was bitten as he entered the Okatas' car after eating dinner with the Okatas. Azuma went to a doctor and received three stitches to his ear. A fourth incident involved Yumiko Seifert, who was bitten on her buttocks while she was a guest at the Okatas' residence. Kazuyo Okata drove Seifert to receive medical treatment. The physician's examination revealed "multiple bite marks," but there was no bleeding. Finally, there is evidence of a fifth incident involving another child, Miwa Inoue, who sustained an injury to her face requiring one stitch.

Beyond the bare facts of the four or perhaps five biting incidents, there is a marked dispute over the manner in which the incidents are characterized. Plaintiffs point to what they claim are five biting incidents to establish that Anchor had "dangerous propensities" and to establish that the Okatas had actual knowledge of Anchor's dangerousness. Defendants counter with evidence that each of the four admitted biting incidents were the result of natural instincts, not of any dangerous tendencies. They refer to the testimony of an expert who declared that each of the four biting incidents admitted to by defendants were the result of overstimulation, protective instincts and chase instincts. In Shane Perrins' case, defendants point to the fact that many children were playing near Anchor and were possibly shooting toy arrows at him when Perrins approached the dog. Defendants claim that the dog was merely excited by all the activity, and that he jumped on the boy because of the excitement, not because of any dangerous propensity. The declaration of Perrins' mother includes an opinion corroborating this characterization. Defendants next claim that the incidents involving Mina Iinuma and Mizutaka Azuma were caused by the people suddenly touching the dog. Both Iinuma and Azuma declared that they believed they were bitten because they surprised or frightened the dog. Finally, defendants claim that the incident involving Yumiko Seifert was caused by Seifert getting too close to the dog's food, then running from the dog when he barked at her. Seifert herself disputes this description of the event. She claims that she was bitten as she stood up from a table and crossed the room to examine some skis.

Further dispute exists concerning the whereabouts of plaintiff Katherine Sinclair at the time her son, Daniel Reinhard, was bitten by Anchor. In their memorandum in support of the motion for partial summary judgment, plaintiffs claim that Katherine Sinclair was in her frontyard watching and supervising her children as the children were playing outside her yard. Plaintiffs say that Ms. Sinclair was standing 10-15 feet away from her children when she saw Anchor running at Michelle and Daniel from the backside of the Okatas' van. Sinclair apparently saw the dog stop within a foot of the children, then the dog turned and began to walk away. The children disappeared behind the van. Sinclair stated that she ran towards the children yelling, "[t]hat is an unfriendly dog." While the children were behind the van, Anchor allegedly came at the children, and Michelle kicked at the dog. Sinclair then came around the backside of the van and saw Daniel on the ground. Sinclair picked up her son and began running between houses knocking on doors to get help.

Defendants deny that Sinclair was outside watching her children before the incident occurred. They point to reports of the physician and emergency room nurse who treated Daniel. The emergency report included a notation to the effect that Ms. Sinclair had stated that she was "sleeping on the couch" when the incident occurred. Dr. Hall, the attending physician, stated in deposition testimony that he clearly recalled Sinclair saying that she was sleeping on the couch when the incident occurred. Dr. Hall's memory of Sinclair's statements was corroborated by Barbara McIntire, the emergency room nurse who treated Daniel. McIntire stated that Sinclair said that she had been lying down on the couch when Daniel was bitten. Defendants also cite the deposition testimony of Tiffany (Tina) Weatherton. Weatherton lived across the street from the Okatas. She was watching the children off and on for about an hour before Daniel was bitten, and said that she did not recall seeing Sinclair outside with her children.

There is also a dispute as to the events leading up to Anchor biting Daniel. As discussed above, Katherine Sinclair has stated that the dog Anchor began running at Daniel and Michelle, but turned away. Then, as the children disappeared behind the van, Anchor is believed to have followed the children as they disappeared behind the van. This time, Michelle supposedly kicked at the dog in a defensive maneuver, and Anchor then attacked Daniel. In contrast, defendants believe that Anchor was provoked either by Michelle kicking at him or by Daniel playing with him. They believe that the children approached Anchor, not that Anchor chased after the children. They cite Weatherton's deposition testimony that she saw Daniel approach Anchor and pet him twenty minutes before Daniel was bitten. From this testimony, they infer that the children were attempting to pet the dog when Daniel was bitten.

Plaintiffs have moved for partial summary judgment on the issue of "liability." The motion does not address the plaintiffs' claims for negligent infliction of emotional distress (Counts III and IV of their complaint) nor their claims for punitive damages or compensation for loss of society (Counts V, VI and VII of their complaint).

Summary Judgment may be ordered on the issue of liability alone even though there is a genuine issue as to the amount of damages. Fed. R. Civ. Proc. 56(c). In support of the motion, plaintiffs have made three arguments: (1) that defendants are liable on a theory of strict liability; and (2) that defendants are liable under a negligence theory.

A court will grant a motion for summary judgment if the pleadings, depositions, answers to interrogatories, and admissions on file show that there is no genuine issue of material fact and that the moving party is entitled to judgment as a matter of law. Fed. R. Civ. P. 56(c). In ruling upon a motion for summary judgment, the court must first determine if "there are any genuine factual issues that properly can be resolved only by a finder of fact because they may reasonably be resolved in favor of either party." A fact is material if proof of the fact would have the effect of refuting or establishing an essential element of the plaintiff's cause of action.

A. Was Anchor a Dog of Dangerous Propensities?

In *Hale v. O'Neill*, 492 P.2d 101 (Alaska 1971), the Alaska Supreme Court referred to "the doctrine of strict liability for injuries caused by a domestic animal with known dangerous tendencies." The court in *Hale* made passing reference to the elements of an action for strict liability based on an animal's known dangerous tendencies. The court first noted that "an owner of a domestic animal becomes liable, regardless of fault, for injuries caused by the animal which stem from a vicious propensity, known to the owner." In the same paragraph, the court described the elements of such an action as being: (1) the animal's owner knew or should have known of the animal's "dangerous tendency," and (2) that the dangerous tendency resulted in an injury to the claimant. *Hale* is the only Alaskan case discussing the requirements for strict liability for injuries caused by dangerous animals. More elaboration of Alaska law is required on certain points to decide plaintiffs' motion for partial summary judgment. This court, whose subject matter jurisdiction in this case depends on diversity only, must apply the law that it believes would be applied by the Alaskan courts.

The first issue presented under this theory of strict liability is whether Anchor had a dangerous propensity. Plaintiffs point to what they believe are five prior biting incidents to establish Anchor's dangerous tendencies. Defendants' response to this point is ambiguous. On one hand, defendants seem to argue that Anchor was not dangerous because he never intended to injure any of the biting victims. They write that, "viewed in the context of the reliable, competent evidence . . . it is apparent that a reasonable jury would conclude that Anchor was not a dog with dangerous and vicious propensities." They cite declaration testimony of some of the biting victims, who believed that Anchor was not "vicious" or "aggressive." Defendants cite authority for the proposition that "the biting of a person by a dog upon provocation is not sufficient to establish a vicious disposition of the dog." Defendants also state or imply, incorrectly, that the jury decides dangerousness in a strict liability situation.[44]

Defendants' argument fails on this point because it overstates the requirements for a finding that a dog is dangerous. A dog does not have to show a tendency to inflict grievous injury for it to be dangerous. Plaintiffs note that "[a]ny knowledge of the animal's propensity to bite or attack, whether in anger or play, is sufficient [knowledge]." In *Keane v. Schroeder*, 148 Ind. App. 131, 264 N.E.2d 95 (1970), cited by defendants, the court defined the term "vicious propensity" as:

> [A] propensity or tendency of an animal to do any act which might endanger the safety of person or property in a given situation. It is the act of the animal and not the state of mind of the animal from which the effects of a dangerous propensity must be determined. A dangerous

---

44. Defendants cite authority holding that the question of whether or not an animal has a dangerous or vicious propensity is a question for the trier of fact. *Keane v. Schroeder*, 264 N.E.2d at 99; *see also, Giles v. Russell*, 255 S.C. 513, 180 S.E.2d 201, 203 (1971). As defendants point out, however, these two cases were negligence cases, not strict liability cases. In strict liability cases, the determination of whether an activity is abnormally dangerous is one for the court, not the jury. 7 Stuart M. Speiser, Charles F. Krause and Alfred W. Gans, *The American Law of Torts* §19:2 at 8 (1990). Accordingly, if the issue is relevant at a trial, the court will make the determination of whether or not Anchor had dangerous propensities abnormal to its class.

propensity may, for example, be deduced from very playful conduct. *Id.* at 103, quoting *Doe v. Barnett*, 145 Ind. App. 542, 251 N.E.2d 688, 694 (1969).

Plaintiffs cite further cases in support of the proposition that a dangerous or vicious propensity is a propensity to injure persons, whether by anger, viciousness or playfulness. This is the position taken in the Restatement of Torts as well.[49] It is likely that Alaska's courts would adopt this approach to assessing dangerousness of a domestic animal for purposes of strict liability. If Anchor did have a dangerous propensity, then it is immaterial whether this propensity was driven by anger, playfulness, affection or curiosity.

Defendants make a second type of argument which successfully raises a genuine issue of material fact on the issue of dangerousness. Throughout most of their briefing, plaintiffs engage in a qualitative analysis of the dog's behavior to determine whether the behavior was dangerous. They look to the four, perhaps five, previous biting incidents as evidence of dangerousness. This type of analysis is misplaced in a claim for strict liability. In a strict liability case, the first inquiry is always whether the activity engaged in was *abnormally* dangerous. Under the Restatement approach, "[a] possessor of a domestic animal that he knows or has reason to know has dangerous propensities *abnormal to its class*, is subject to liability for harm done by the animal to another, although he has exercised the utmost care to prevent it from doing the harm." *See, e.g., Restatement (Second) of Torts* §519(1) (1965) (stating the general principle that one who carries on an abnormally dangerous activity is liable regardless of fault for injuries caused thereby).

Again, it is likely that the Alaska courts would adopt this approach to assessing dangerousness in cases dealing with strict liability for injuries caused by domesticated animals. The question, then, becomes: is the dangerous propensity abnormal? Here, defendants are able to present a genuine question of fact. In their introduction, defendants characterize the prior biting incidents as "behavioral responses common to all dogs." Defendants' expert reviewed each of the four admitted biting incidents, and as to each one she concluded that Anchor's responses were "natural" or instinctive. Plaintiffs offer no evidence, through expert testimony or otherwise, to refute the opinion of defendants' expert. It may indeed be true that Anchor's reactions in the four or five incidents were abnormal in the sense that they were not reactions typical of domesticated dogs, but plaintiffs have not established that point beyond any reasonable dispute.

Summary judgment on Count II of plaintiffs' complaint is denied.

---

49. *See Restatement (Second) of Torts* §509 cmt. c (1965) (indicating that the doctrine of strict liability applies even when "the animal is not vicious but has a dangerous tendency that is unusual and not necessary for the purposes for which such animals are usually kept.").

B. Negligence as a Matter of Law

Plaintiffs claim that defendants were negligent as a matter of law. Plaintiffs cite *Alaskan Village, Inc. v. Smalley*, 720 P.2d 945 (Alaska 1986) as a case which outlines the framework necessary to establish negligence and which contains seven factors which establish the elements of a negligence case. A close reading of the case shows that it does not establish the elements of negligence in a dog-bite case. *Alaskan Village* addressed the question of whether the owner of a trailer park could be held liable for injuries inflicted on a tenant by the dog of another tenant. Plaintiff, a six-year-old girl, was a resident of Alaskan Village, a trailer park. Every resident of the park was required to sign a rental agreement which prohibited the tenants from keeping vicious dogs. Plaintiff's neighbor in the trailer park, Henry Scepurek, kept two pit bulls, in violation of the rental agreement. When Scepurek's dogs escaped from his yard and injured plaintiff, plaintiff sued the trailer park for negligent failure to enforce its rules prohibiting the keeping of vicious dogs by tenants. Plaintiff received a judgment against the trailer park at trial. On appeal, the issue was whether the Alaskan Village, a third party, had a duty to protect plaintiff from the dogs. The issue was not whether the dogs' owner owed plaintiff a duty, or whether the owner was negligent. Accordingly, this case does not establish the framework for negligence in a dog-bite case.

To succeed on their negligence claim, plaintiffs must satisfy the classic elements of a negligence cause of action: duty, breach, and proximate cause. Section 518 of the *Restatement (Second) of Torts* is a helpful starting point for analyzing a negligence claim in a dog-bite case. Under the Restatement approach, there is no liability for harm done by a domestic animal unless the owner of the animal intentionally causes the animal to do harm or unless the owner is negligent in failing to prevent the harm. The comments to the Restatement make it clear, however, that owners of domestic animals are "under a duty to exercise reasonable care to have them under a constant and effective control." *Id.* cmt. e. The Restatement sets the degree of care that must be exercised "commensurate with the character of the animal." *Id.* cmt. f. Of particular relevance to this case is the Restatement's language indicating that an owner is "required to realize that even ordinarily gentle animals are likely to be dangerous under particular circumstances and to exercise reasonable care to prevent foreseeable harm." *Id.* cmt. h. These principles from the Restatement provide the court with the standards by which it is possible to evaluate plaintiffs' negligence claim.

In their complaint, plaintiffs identified three acts of defendants alleged to be negligent: (1) letting the dog run loose so that it could leave the Okatas' yard and bite Daniel in another yard; (2) failing to adequately control and confine the dog; and (3) owning and retaining possession of the dog. In the memorandum in support of their motion for partial summary judgment, plaintiffs claim that the Okatas were negligent in that they left Anchor "unattended, unleashed and unsupervised" at the time Anchor bit Daniel Reinhard. Nowhere do plaintiffs distinguish among the three defendants in assessing their culpability. They merely assert that all defendants were negligent and that their negligence was the proximate cause of plaintiffs' respective injuries. The failure to assess each defendant's culpability makes resolution of the motion for partial summary judgment more difficult than it would be otherwise.

It seems clear, for example, that plaintiffs allege that Yoshihide Okata was negligent in bringing Anchor from the backyard to the frontyard, then leaving Anchor unleashed in the driveway while Yoshihide fell asleep in the van. It is unclear what Mr. and Mrs. Okata are alleged to have done that constituted negligence.

Plaintiffs have not established that Yoshitaka or Kazuyo Okata were negligent as a matter of law. To establish that Yoshitaka or Kazuyo Okata are liable for negligence, plaintiffs must show that these two were directly negligent and that their negligence was a factual and legal cause of a plaintiff's injuries. It is a well-recognized tenet of the common law that parents are not vicariously liable for the torts of their children. Plaintiffs cite no case contrary to this proposition, nor does there appear to be any Alaska law to the contrary. Plaintiffs therefore cannot claim that Mr. and Mrs. Okata are vicariously liable for Yoshihide's alleged negligence. As to other ways in which Mr. and Mrs. Okata were negligent, plaintiffs do not provide allegations detailed enough to conclude that there are no genuine issues of material fact so that plaintiffs are entitled to summary judgment as a matter of law. As to entrusting the dog to Yoshihide on the day in question, there is evidence that Yoshihide was told by his parents to keep the dog in the backyard or on a leash and that they had reason to expect that their instructions would be followed. Regarding the dog's training, there is evidence that the family took Anchor to obedience and training classes, something done by less than 10% of all dog owners in Anchorage. And while it may be said that the dog should have been terminated after the first four biting incidents, the failure to have the dog put down was not negligence as a matter of law.

Plaintiffs have made a stronger case for finding Yoshihide Okata negligent. The case against Yoshihide is stronger because it was Yoshihide who was directly responsible for taking Anchor out of the secured backyard to the unfenced driveway. As already stated, Yoshihide did not have Anchor on a leash or otherwise constrained while the dog was in the driveway. Amazingly, Yoshihide then went to sleep, leaving the dog unattended. In defense, Yoshihide claims only that he ordered the dog to "stay" and that he believed the dog would obey his command. Otherwise, Yoshihide admitted that he knew of at least one occasion where Anchor bit a child, Shane Perrins. Yoshihide also admitted that, a few days prior to the incident involving Daniel Reinhard, he was "scolded" by his mother, who was "very serious" about his "carelessness" in allowing Anchor in the frontyard alone. Yoshitaka Okata declared that he had given Yoshihide warnings about the dog after each of the other biting incidents, which indicates that Yoshihide had actual knowledge of all the other incidents. Even without actual knowledge of the prior biting incidents,

Yoshihide could be charged with constructive knowledge of the biting incidents. In short, the evidence presented in the supporting affidavits and declarations points strongly to the fact that Yoshihide failed to restrain Anchor even though he knew that Anchor had a propensity to bite humans.

Given these facts, the conclusion that Yoshihide Okata acted negligently seems inescapable. There is no genuine dispute as to the facts showing that Yoshihide Okata had a duty to control Anchor, that he failed to do so carelessly, and that this conduct was a legal cause of injury to Daniel. No reasonable juror could conclude otherwise. Yoshihide knew of four prior incidents where Anchor had bitten people, yet he brought the dog into an unsecured area then fell asleep. He was told by his parents to keep the dog in the backyard at all times, then disobeyed their instructions. It is true, as defendants claim, that it is rarely appropriate for a court to order summary judgment on the question of a party's negligence. On the other hand, where the facts are such that there can be no reasonable dispute, summary judgment is warranted. This is one of those rare cases where a defendant's conduct so clearly falls below the applicable standard of care that it is proper for the court to rule as a matter of law that the conduct was negligent.

Defendants also argue that plaintiffs' own negligence was a cause of their injuries and that, but for plaintiffs' own negligence, the injuries would not have occurred. Defendants say that plaintiffs were negligent in two respects: (1) Katherine Sinclair was negligent in allowing her children to play outside while she was asleep on the couch; and (2) Michelle was negligent in kicking at the dog. As pointed out in the plaintiffs' reply brief, however, such arguments do not prevent a finding that Yoshihide is liable for Daniel's injuries as a matter of law. In essence, defendants argue that, but for plaintiffs' negligence, Daniel would not have been bitten. This approach confuses the proximate cause element of a negligence claim. The Alaska Supreme Court held in *State v. Abbott*, 498 P.2d 712 (Alaska 1972) that a defendant's conduct could be a legal cause of the plaintiff's injuries even when the plaintiff's own negligence also contributed to the injuries. Defendants' argument does not negate the third element of a negligence claim, causation.

To conclude this section, the court finds that summary judgment against Yoshitaka and Kazuyo Okata on the issue of negligence is not appropriate because there are genuine issues of fact regarding whether Mr. and Mrs. Okata failed to conform to the standard of care imposed on them as Anchor's owners. On the other hand, the court finds that, as a matter of law, plaintiffs have established that Yoshihide Okata was negligent. As to this there is no genuine dispute as to material facts. Owners of domestic animals have a duty to exercise reasonable care to prevent their animals from harming others. No reasonable juror could find otherwise than that Yoshihide breached his duty of care when he took Anchor out of the backyard then left the dog unrestrained and fell asleep. Further, no reasonable juror could find that Yoshihide's negligence was not a legal cause of the injuries suffered by Daniel.

CONCLUSION

Plaintiffs' motion for summary judgment on their strict liability claim is denied. Plaintiffs' motion for summary judgment on their negligence claim is granted in part and denied in part. As to claims for negligence against Yoshi-taka and Kazuyo Okata, the motion for summary judgment is denied. As to the negligence claim against Yoshihide Okata, the motion for partial summary judgment on the question of liability is granted.

PREPARING FOR CLASS

1. Recall the negligence discussion from Chapter 4 in Torts I. Envision how the case would proceed under a negligence theory alone, and how strict liability as a theory is advantageous to the plaintiffs.

2. What are the defendants to do in these circumstances to avoid being sued/held liable?

3. From your read of the facts, is Anchor abnormally dangerous?

APPLYING THE LAW

Plaintiff was lawfully on private property. While there, a dog, without provocation by her, came upon the property, attacked her, and injured her. On that date, the City was the dog's owner, and the dog had been trained as a police attack dog that traveled in City police squad cars. Is the City strictly liable?

INCREASING YOUR UNDERSTANDING

1. As the case illustrates, owners of domestic animals can be held liable for personal injuries caused by such animals, and such causes of actions may be based on principles of common law strict liability or ordinary negligence. Many states have taken the common law rule of liability and adopted them by statute or ordinance, especially with respect to dogs. They are frequently referred to as "dog leash" laws. Liability often turns on whether the defendant qualifies as the owner or possessor/keeper of the animal. See Holcomb v. Colonial Associates, L.L.C. 153 N.C. App. 413, 570 S.E.2d 248 (N.C. App. 2002) (An "animal keeper" is one who, either with or without the owner's permission, undertakes to manage, control, or care for the animal as owners in general are accustomed to do); Goodman v. Kahn, 182 Ga. App. 724,

356 S.E.2d 757 (Ga. App. 1987) (Dog owner's housemate was not keeper of dog as housemate was not home on day in question and had in no way exercised supervision or control over dog); Fontecchio v. Esposito, 108 A.D.2d 780, 485 N.Y.S.2d 113 (N.Y.A.D. 1985) (Daughter of owner who was taking care of dog while owner was on vacation liable for injuries resulting from attack).

2. *First bite on the house?* An owner is only strictly responsible if she has or should have had knowledge of the animal's abnormal or unusual dangerous propensity. Although most cases involve claims that the animal was vicious, the law is more expansive and allows for liability where the animal displays dangerous tendencies that may not ordinarily be described as vicious. For example, one who possesses a large dog who he knows to "fawn violently upon children" is subject to strict liability for harm that results from the dog's playful nature. Restatement (Second) of Torts § 509, comment c. See also Groner v. Hedrick 403 Pa. 148, 169 A.2d 302 (Pa. 1961) ("Although an animal is actuated solely by mischievousness or playfulness, rather than maliciousness or ferociousness, yet, if it has a tendency to do a dangerous or harmful act, it has a vicious propensity within the meaning of the rule holding the owner or keeper liable for injuries resulting from vicious propensities of which he has knowledge."). It is the act of the animal, therefore, not its state of mind that subjects the owner to strict liability. Notice of dangerousness (constructive or actual) may arrive from behavior that is common with the animal or abhorrent, i.e., an isolated attack.

3. *Wild vs. domestic animals.* Courts have routinely suggested distinctive liability rules for animals that are "wild" as opposed to "domesticated." See Giles v. State, 106 Misc. 2d 329, 431 N.Y.S.2d 781 N.Y. Ct. Cl., 1980 (As contrasted to domestic animals, "wild animals" are those species of animals that, as a matter of common knowledge, are naturally ferocious, unpredictable, dangerous, mischievous, or not by custom devoted to the service of mankind at the time and in the place in which they are kept.); and Restatement (Second) of Torts § 506 (1) ("A wild animal is an animal that is not by custom devoted to the service of mankind at the time and in the place in which it is kept.") In contrast, a domestic animal is one that by custom is "devoted to the service of mankind at that time and in the place in which it is kept." Restatement (Second) of Torts § 506 (2). Falling within the "domestic" description would be most farm and household animals. If there is any meaningful domestic-wild distinction for strict liability purposes it is found in the law requiring notice of specific dangerousness in cases involving domestic animals but imputing such knowledge where wild animals are involved. It is, therefore, in regard to the latter, where liability is the most strict.

B. ACTIVITIES

Indiana Harbor Belt R. Co. v. American Cyanamid Co.
916 F.2d 1174 (1990)

POSNER, Circuit Judge.

American Cyanamid Company, the defendant in this diversity tort suit governed by Illinois law, is a major manufacturer of chemicals, including acrylonitrile, a chemical used in large quantities in making acrylic fibers, plastics, dyes, pharmaceutical chemicals, and other intermediate and final goods. On January 2, 1979, at its manufacturing plant in Louisiana, Cyanamid loaded 20,000 gallons of liquid acrylonitrile into a railroad tank car that it had leased from the North American Car Corporation. The next day, a train of the Missouri Pacific Railroad picked up the car at Cyanamid's siding. The car's ultimate destination was a Cyanamid plant in New Jersey served by Conrail rather than by Missouri Pacific. The Missouri Pacific train carried the car north to the Blue Island railroad yard of Indiana Harbor Belt Railroad, the plaintiff in this case, a small switching line that has a contract with Conrail to switch cars from other lines to Conrail, in this case for travel east. The Blue Island yard is in the Village of Riverdale, which is just south of Chicago and part of the Chicago metropolitan area.

The car arrived in the Blue Island yard on the morning of January 9, 1979. Several hours after it arrived, employees of the switching line noticed fluid gushing from the bottom outlet of the car. The lid on the outlet was broken. After two hours, the line's supervisor of equipment was able to stop the leak by closing a shut-off valve controlled from the top of the car. No one was sure at the time just how much of the contents of the car had leaked, but it was feared that all 20,000 gallons had, and since acrylonitrile is flammable at a temperature of 30° Fahrenheit or above, highly toxic, and possibly carcinogenic (*Acrylonitrile*, 9 International Toxicity Update, no. 3, May-June 1989, at 2, 4), the local authorities ordered the homes near the yard evacuated. The evacuation lasted only a few hours, until the car was moved to a remote part of the yard and it was discovered that only about a quarter of the acrylonitrile had leaked. Concerned nevertheless that there had been some contamination of soil and water, the Illinois Department of Environmental Protection ordered the switching line to take decontamination measures that cost the line $981,022.75, which it sought to recover by this suit.

One count of the two-count complaint charges Cyanamid with having maintained the leased tank car negligently. The other count asserts that the transportation of acrylonitrile in bulk through the Chicago metropolitan area is an abnormally dangerous activity, for the consequences of which the shipper (Cyanamid) is strictly liable to the switching line, which bore the financial brunt of those consequences because of the decontamination measures that it was forced to take. After the district judge denied Cyanamid's motion to dismiss the strict liability count, the switching line moved for summary judgment on that count—and won. The judge directed the entry of judgment for $981,022.75. The district judge [subsequently] dismissed the negligence claim with prejudice, thus terminating proceedings in the district court and clearing the way for Cyanamid to file an appeal of which we would have jurisdiction.

The question whether the shipper of a hazardous chemical by rail should be strictly liable for the consequences of a spill or other accident to the shipment en route is a novel one in Illinois, despite the switching line's contention that the question has been answered in its favor by two decisions of the Illinois Appellate Court that the district judge cited in granting summary judgment. In both *Fallon v. Indian Trail School*, 148 Ill. App. 3d 931, 934, 102 Ill. Dec. 479, 481, 500 N.E.2d 101, 103 (1986), and *Continental Building Corp. v. Union Oil Co.*, 152 Ill. App. 3d 513, 516, 105 Ill. Dec. 502, 504-05, 504 N.E.2d 787, 789-90 (1987), the Illinois Appellate Court cited the district court's first opinion in this case with approval and described it as having held that the transportation of acrylonitrile in the Chicago metropolitan area is an abnormally dangerous activity, for which the shipper is strictly liable. These discussions are dicta. The cases did not involve acrylonitrile—or for that matter transportation—and in both cases the court held that the defendant was not strictly liable.

The parties agree that the question whether placing acrylonitrile in a rail shipment that will pass through a metropolitan area subjects the shipper to strict liability is, as recommended in Restatement (Second) of Torts §520, comment *l* (1977), a question of law, so that we owe no particular deference to the conclusion of the district court. They also agree (and for this proposition, at least, there is substantial support in the *Fallon* and *Continental* opinions) that the Supreme Court of Illinois would treat as authoritative the provisions of the Restatement governing abnormally dangerous activities. The key provision is section 520, which sets forth six factors to be considered in deciding whether an activity is abnormally dangerous and the actor therefore strictly liable.

The roots of section 520 are in nineteenth-century cases. The most famous one is *Rylands v. Fletcher*, 1 Ex. 265, aff'd, L.R. 3 H.L. 300 (1868), but a more illuminating one in the present context is *Guille v. Swan*, 19 Johns. (N.Y.) 381 (1822). A man took off in a hot-air balloon and landed, without intending to, in a vegetable garden in New York City. A crowd that had been anxiously watching his involuntary descent trampled the vegetables in their endeavor to rescue him when he landed. The owner of the garden sued the balloonist for the resulting damage, and won. Yet the balloonist had not been careless. In the then state of ballooning it was impossible to make a pinpoint landing.

Guille is a paradigmatic case for strict liability. (a) The risk (probability) of harm was great, and (b) the harm that would ensue if the risk materialized could be, although luckily was not, great (the balloonist could have crashed into the crowd rather than into the vegetables). The confluence of these two factors established the urgency of seeking to prevent such accidents. (c) Yet such accidents could not be prevented by the exercise of due care; the technology of care in ballooning was insufficiently developed. (d) The activity was not a matter of common usage, so there was no presumption that it was a highly valuable activity despite its unavoidable riskiness. (e) The activity was inappropriate to the place in which it took place—densely populated New York City. The risk of serious harm to others (other than the balloonist himself, that is) could have been reduced by shifting the activity to the sparsely inhabited areas that surrounded the city in those days. (f) Reinforcing (d), the value to the community of the activity of recreational ballooning did not appear to be great enough to offset its unavoidable risks.

These are, of course, the six factors in section 520.[*] They are related to each other in that each is a different facet of a common quest for a proper legal regime to govern accidents that negligence liability cannot adequately control. The interrelations might be more perspicuous if the six factors were reordered. One might for example start with (c), inability to eliminate the risk of accident by the exercise of due care. The baseline common law regime of tort liability is negligence. When it is a workable regime, because the hazards of an activity can be avoided by being careful (which is to say, nonnegligent), there is no need to switch to strict liability. Sometimes, however, a particular type of accident cannot be prevented by taking care but can be avoided, or its consequences minimized, by shifting the activity in which the accident occurs to another locale, where the risk or harm of an accident will be less ((e)), or by reducing the scale of the activity in order to minimize the number of accidents caused by it ((f)). By making the actor strictly liable—by denying him in other words an excuse based on his inability to avoid accidents by being more careful—we give him an incentive, missing in a negligence regime, to experiment with methods of preventing accidents that involve not greater exertions of care, assumed to be futile, but instead relocating, changing, or reducing (perhaps to the vanishing point) the activity giving rise to the accident. The greater the risk of an accident ((a)) and the costs of an accident if one occurs ((b)), the more we want the actor to consider the possibility of making accident-reducing activity changes; the stronger, therefore, is the case for strict liability. Finally, if an activity is extremely common ((d)), like driving an automobile, it is unlikely either that its hazards are perceived as great or that there is no technology of care available to minimize them; so the case for strict liability is weakened.

The largest class of cases in which strict liability has been imposed under the standard codified in the Second Restatement of Torts involves the use of dynamite and other explosives for demolition in residential or urban areas. Explosives are dangerous even when handled carefully, and we therefore want blasters to choose the location of the activity with care and also to explore

---

[*][The six factors of Section 520 are: (a) existence of a high degree of risk of some harm to the person, land or chattels of others; (b) likelihood that the harm that results form it will be great; (c) inability to eliminate the risk by the exercise of reasonable care; (d) extent to which the activity is not matter of common usage; (e) inappropriateness of the activity to the place where it is carried; and (f) extent to which the value to the community is outweighed by its dangerous attributes—EDS.]

the feasibility of using safer substitutes (such as a wrecking ball), as well as to be careful in the blasting itself. Blasting is not a commonplace activity like driving a car, or so superior to substitute methods of demolition that the imposition of liability is unlikely to have any effect except to raise the activity's costs.

Against this background we turn to the particulars of acrylonitrile. Acrylonitrile is one of a large number of chemicals that are hazardous in the sense of being flammable, toxic, or both; acrylonitrile is both, as are many others. A table in the record, drawn from Glickman & Harvey, Statistical Trends in Railroad Hazardous Material Safety, 1978 to 1984, at pp. 63-65 (Draft Final Report to the Environmental & Hazardous Material Studies Division of the Association of American Railroads, April 1986) (tab. 4.1), contains a list of the 125 hazardous materials that are shipped in highest volume on the nation's railroads. Acrylonitrile is the fifty-third most hazardous on the list. Number 1 is phosphorus (white or yellow), and among the other materials that rank higher than acrylonitrile on the hazard scale are anhydrous ammonia, liquified petroleum gas, vinyl chloride, gasoline, crude petroleum, motor fuel antiknock compound, methyl and ethyl chloride, sulphuric acid, sodium metal, and chloroform. The plaintiff's lawyer acknowledged at argument that the logic of the district court's opinion dictated strict liability for all 52 materials that rank higher than acrylonitrile on the list, and quite possibly for the 72 that rank lower as well, since all are hazardous if spilled in quantity while being shipped by rail. Every shipper of any of these materials would therefore be strictly liable for the consequences of a spill or other accident that occurred while the material was being shipped through a metropolitan area. The plaintiff's lawyer further acknowledged the irrelevance, on her view of the case, of the fact that Cyanamid had leased and filled the car that spilled the acrylonitrile; all she thought important is that Cyanamid introduced the product into the stream of commerce that happened to pass through the Chicago metropolitan area. Her concession may have been incautious. One might want to distinguish between the shipper who merely places his goods on his loading dock to be picked up by the carrier and the shipper who, as in this case, participates actively in the transportation. But the concession is illustrative of the potential scope of the district court's decision.

No cases recognize so sweeping a liability. Several reject it, though none has facts much like those of the present case. With *National Steel Service Center v. Gibbons*, 693 F.2d 817 (8th Cir. 1982), which held a railroad strictly liable for transporting propane gas—but under Iowa law, which uses a different standard from that of the Restatement—we may pair *Seaboard Coast Line R.R. v. Mobil Chemical Co.*, 172 Ga. App. 543, 323 S.E.2d 849 (1984), which refused to impose strict liability on facts similar to those in this case, but again on the basis of a standard different from that of the Restatement. *Zero Wholesale Co. v. Stroud*, 264 Ark. 27, 571 S.W.2d 74 (1978), refused to hold that the delivery of propane gas was not an ultrahazardous activity as a matter of law. But the delivery in question was to a gas-storage facility, and the explosion occurred while gas was being pumped from the tank truck into a storage tank. This was a highly, perhaps unavoidably, dangerous activity.

Siegler v. Kuhlman, 81 Wash. 2d 448, 502 P.2d 1181 (1972), also imposed strict liability on a transporter of hazardous materials, but the circumstances were again rather special. A gasoline truck blew up, obliterating the plaintiff's decedent and her car. The court emphasized that the explosion had destroyed the evidence necessary to establish whether the accident had been due to negligence; so, unless liability was strict, there would be no liability—and this as the very consequence of the defendant's hazardous activity.... But when the Supreme Court of Washington came to decide the *New Meadows* case, *supra*, it did not distinguish *Siegler* on this ground, perhaps realizing that the plaintiff in *Siegler* could have overcome the destruction of the evidence by basing a negligence claim on the doctrine of res ipsa loquitur. Instead it stressed that the transmission of natural gas through underground pipes, the activity in *New Meadows*, is less dangerous than the transportation of gasoline by highway, where the risk of an accident is omnipresent.... We shall see that a further distinction of great importance between the present case and *Siegler* is that the defendant there was the transporter, and here it is the shipper.

... [W]e can get little help from precedent, and might as well apply section 520 to the acrylonitrile problem from the ground up. To begin with, we have been given no reason, whether the reason in *Siegler* or any other, for believing that a negligence regime is not perfectly adequate to remedy and deter, at reasonable cost, the accidental spillage of acrylonitrile from rail cars.... Acrylonitrile could explode and destroy evidence, but of course did not here, making imposition of strict liability on the theory of the *Siegler* decision premature. More important, although acrylonitrile is flammable even at relatively low temperatures, and toxic, it is not so corrosive or otherwise destructive that it will eat through or otherwise damage or weaken a tank car's valves although they are maintained with due (which essentially means, with average) care. No one suggests, therefore, that the leak in this case was caused by the *inherent* properties of acrylonitrile. It was caused by carelessness— whether that of the North American Car Corporation in failing to maintain or inspect the car properly, or that of Cyanamid in failing to maintain or inspect it, or that of the Missouri Pacific when it had custody of the car, or that of the switching line itself in failing to notice the ruptured lid, or some combination of these possible failures of care. Accidents that are due to a lack of care can be prevented by taking care; and when a lack of care can (unlike *Siegler*) be shown in court, such accidents are adequately deterred by the threat of liability for negligence.

It is true that the district court purported to find as a fact that there is an inevitable risk of derailment or other calamity in transporting "large quantities of anything." This is not a finding of fact, but a truism: anything can happen. The question is, how likely is this type of accident if the actor uses due care? For all that appears from the record of the case or any other sources of information that we have found, if a tank car is carefully maintained the danger of a spill of acrylonitrile is negligible. If this is right, there is no compelling reason to move to a regime of strict liability, especially one that might embrace all other hazardous materials shipped by rail as well. This also means, however, that the amici curiae who have filed briefs in support of Cyanamid cry wolf in predicting "devastating" effects on the chemical industry if the district court's decision is affirmed. If the vast majority of chemical spills by railroads are preventable by due care, the imposition of strict liability should cause only a slight, not as they argue a substantial, rise in liability insurance rates, because the incremental liability should be slight. The amici have momentarily lost sight of the fact that the feasibility of avoiding accidents simply by being careful is an argument *against* strict liability.

The district judge and the plaintiff's lawyer make much of the fact that the spill occurred in a densely inhabited metropolitan area. Only 4,000 gallons spilled; what if all 20,000 had done so? Isn't the risk that this might happen even if everybody were careful sufficient to warrant giving the shipper an incentive to explore alternative routes? Strict liability would supply that incentive. But this argument overlooks the fact that, like other transportation networks, the railroad network is a hub-and-spoke system. And the hubs are in metropolitan areas. Chicago is one of the nation's largest railroad hubs. In 1983, the latest year for which we have figures, Chicago's railroad yards handled the third highest volume of hazardous-material shipments in the nation. East St. Louis, which is also in Illinois, handled the second highest volume. Office of Technology Assessment, Transportation of Hazardous Materials 53 (1986). With most hazardous chemicals (by volume of shipments) being at least as hazardous as acrylonitrile, it is unlikely—and certainly not demonstrated by the plaintiff—that they can be rerouted around all the metropolitan areas in the country, except at prohibitive cost. Even if it were feasible to reroute them one would hardly expect shippers, as distinct from carriers, to be the firms best situated to do the rerouting. Granted, the usual view is that common carriers are not subject to strict liability for the carriage of materials that make the transportation of them abnormally dangerous, because a common carrier cannot refuse service to a shipper of a lawful commodity. Restatement, *supra*, §521. Two courts, however, have rejected the common carrier exception. . . . If it were rejected in Illinois, this would weaken still further the case for imposing strict liability on shippers whose goods pass through the densely inhabited portions of the state.

The difference between shipper and carrier points to a deep flaw in the plaintiff's case. Unlike *Guille*, and unlike *Siegler*, and unlike the storage cases, beginning with *Rylands* itself, here it is not the actors—that is, the transporters of acrylonitrile and other chemicals—but the manufacturers, who are sought to be held strictly liable. A shipper can in the bill of lading designate the route of his shipment if he likes, 49 U.S.C. §11710(a)(1), but is it realistic to suppose that shippers will become students of railroading in order to lay out the safest route by which to ship their goods? Anyway, rerouting is no panacea. Often it will increase the length of the journey, or compel the use of poorer track, or both. When this happens, the probability of an accident is increased, even if the consequences of an accident if one occurs are reduced; so the expected accident cost, being the product of the probability of an accident and the harm if the accident occurs, may rise. Glickman, Analysis of a National Policy for Routing Hazardous Materials on Railroads (Department of Transportation, Research and Special Programs Administration, Transportation Systems Center, May 1980). It is easy to see how the accident in this case might have been prevented at reasonable cost by greater care on the part of those who handled the tank car of acrylonitrile. It is difficult to see how it might have been prevented at reasonable cost by a change in the activity of transporting the chemical. This is therefore not an apt case for strict liability.

We said earlier that Cyanamid, because of the role it played in the transportation of the acrylonitrile—leasing, and especially loading, and also it appears undertaking by contract with North American Car Corporation to maintain, the tank car in which the railroad carried Cyanamid's acrylonitrile to Riverdale—might be viewed as a special type of shipper (call it a "shipper-transporter"), rather than as a passive shipper. But neither the district judge nor the plaintiff's counsel has attempted to distinguish Cyanamid from an ordinary manufacturer of chemicals on this ground, and we consider it waived. Which is not to say that had it not been waived it would have changed the outcome of the case. The very fact that Cyanamid participated actively in the transportation of the acrylonitrile imposed upon it a duty of due care and by doing so brought into play a threat of negligence liability that, for all we know, may provide an adequate regime of accident control in the transportation of this particular chemical.

In emphasizing the flammability and toxicity of acrylonitrile rather than the hazards of transporting it, as in failing to distinguish between the active and the passive shipper, the plaintiff overlooks the fact that ultrahazardous-ness or abnormal dangerousness is, in the contemplation of the law at least, a property not of substances, but of activities: not of acrylonitrile, but of the transportation of acrylonitrile by rail through populated areas. Natural gas is both flammable and poisonous, but the operation of a natural gas well is not an ultrahazardous activity. Whatever the situation under products liability law (section 402A of the Restatement), the manufacturer of a product is not considered to be engaged in an abnormally dangerous activity merely because the product becomes dangerous when it is handled or used in some way after it leaves his premises, even if the danger is foreseeable. The plaintiff does not suggest that Cyanamid should switch to making some less hazardous chemical that would substitute for acrylonitrile in the textiles and other goods in which acrylonitrile is used. Were this a feasible method of accident avoidance, there would be an argument for making manufacturers strictly liable for accidents that occur during the shipment of their products (how strong an argument we need not decide). Apparently it is not a feasible method.

The relevant activity is transportation, not manufacturing and shipping. This essential distinction the plaintiff ignores. But even if the defendant is treated as a transporter and not merely a shipper, the plaintiff has not shown that the transportation of acrylonitrile in bulk by rail through populated areas is so hazardous an activity, even when due care is exercised, that the law should seek to create — perhaps quixotically — incentives to relocate the activity to nonpopulated areas, or to reduce the scale of the activity, or to switch to transporting acrylonitrile by road rather than by rail, perhaps to set the stage for a replay of *Siegler v. Kuhlman*. It is no more realistic to propose to reroute the shipment of all hazardous materials around Chicago than it is to propose the relocation of homes adjacent to the Blue Island switching yard to more distant suburbs. It may be less realistic. Brutal though it may seem to say it, the inappropriate use to which land is being put in the Blue Island yard and neighborhood may be, not the transportation of hazardous chemicals, but residential living. The analogy is to building your home between the runways at O'Hare.

The briefs hew closely to the Restatement, whose approach to the issue of strict liability is mainly *allocative* rather than *distributive*. By this we mean that the emphasis is on picking a liability regime (negligence or strict liability) that will control the particular class of accidents in question most effectively, rather than on finding the deepest pocket and placing liability there. At argument, however, the plaintiff's lawyer invoked distributive considerations by pointing out that Cyanamid is a huge firm and the Indiana Harbor Belt Railroad a fifty-mile-long switching line that almost went broke in the winter of 1979, when the accident occurred. Well, so what? A corporation is not a living person but a set of contracts the terms of which determine who will bear the brunt of liability. Tracing the incidence of a cost is a complex undertaking which the plaintiff sensibly has made no effort to assume, since its legal relevance would be dubious. We add only that however small the plaintiff may be, it has mighty parents: it is a jointly owned subsidiary of Conrail and the Soo line.

The case for strict liability has not been made. Not in this suit in any event. We need not speculate on the possibility of imposing strict liability on shippers of more hazardous materials, such as the bombs carried in *Chavez v. Southern Pacific Transportation Co., supra,* any more than we need differentiate (given how the plaintiff has shaped its case) between active and passive shippers. We noted earlier that acrylonitrile is far from being the most hazardous among hazardous materials shipped by rail in highest volume. Or among materials shipped, period.

Ordinarily when summary judgment is denied, the movant's rights are not extinguished; the case is simply set down for trial. If this approach were followed here, it would require remanding the case for a trial on whether Cyanamid should be held strictly liable. Yet that would be a mistake. The parties have agreed that the question whether the transportation of acrylonitrile through densely populated areas is abnormally dangerous is one of law rather than of fact; and trials are to determine facts, not law. More precisely — for there is no sharp line between "law" and "fact" — trials are to determine adjudicative facts rather than legislative facts. The distinction is between facts germane to the specific dispute, which often are best developed through testimony and cross-examination, and facts relevant to shaping a general rule, which, as the discussion in this opinion illustrates, more often are facts reported in books and other documents not prepared specially for litigation or refined in its fires. Again the line should not be viewed as hard and fast. If facts critical to a decision on whether a particular activity should be subjected to a regime of strict liability cannot be determined with reasonable accuracy without an evidentiary hearing, such a hearing can and should be held, though we can find no reported case where this was done. Some courts treat the question whether an activity is abnormally dangerous as one of fact, and then there must be an evidentiary hearing to decide it. Here we are concerned with cases in which the question is treated as one of law but in which factual disputes of the sort ordinarily resolved by an evidentiary hearing may be germane to answering the question. An evidentiary hearing would be of no use in the present case, however, because the plaintiff has not indicated any facts that it wants to develop through such a hearing.

The defendant concedes that if the strict liability count is thrown out, the negligence count must be reinstated, as requested by the cross-appeal.

The judgment is reversed (with no award of costs in this court) and the case remanded for further proceedings, consistent with this opinion, on the plaintiff's claim for negligence.

REVERSED AND REMANDED, WITH DIRECTIONS.

PREPARING FOR CLASS

1. Consider the six factors in the Restatement (Second) of Torts §520 and weigh them as you would as a judge.

2. Identify the activity that is being subjected to strict liability.

APPLYING THE LAW

Two young men broke into a warehouse owned by defendant that stored explosives, set a prepared charge, and fled. The explosion caused damage to property, the closest of which was over three miles away. Is the defendant strictly liable?

INCREASING YOUR UNDERSTANDING

1. *Why strict liability?* "The liability arises out of the abnormal danger of the activity itself, and the risk that it creates, of harm to those in the

vicinity. It is founded upon a policy of the law that imposes upon anyone who for his own purposes creates an abnormal risk of harm to his neighbors, the responsibility of relieving against hat harm when it does in fact occur." Restatement (Second) of Torts §519, comment d.

2. *Weighing in on §520.* Currently, Restatement (Second) of Torts §520 forms the approach most frequently relied on by courts when considering whether an activity is "abnormally dangerous." Courts are allowed to weigh the factors as they deem appropriate and even ignore or minimize those they consider insignificant, though the Restatement encourages consideration of all six factors. And it is the court as a matter of law who determines whether the activity is abnormally dangerous, not the jury.

3. Analysis under §520 has yielded inconsistent results, except in the most extreme cases. For example, the Washington Supreme Court subjected a pyrotechnic company to strict liability for injuries inflicted during a firework display, largely relying on the "common usage" factor of §520. Klein v. Pyrodyne Corp., 117 Wash. 2d 1, 810 P.2d 917 (Wash. 1991). See ("Although fireworks are frequently and regularly enjoyed by the public, few persons set off special fireworks displays.") However, an Illinois appellate court, relying on §520 under almost identical circumstances, came to the opposite conclusion. See Cadena v. Chicago Fireworks Mfg. Co., 297 Ill. App. 3d 945, 697 N.E.2d 802 (Ill. App. 1 Dist. 1998). ("While displaying fireworks is not a common activity undertaken by a large amount of individuals, certainly many individuals view them and many municipalities display fireworks. Thus, fireworks displays *are* a matter of common usage.") Some have limited the scope of liability to cases where the danger originated from use of land; others have been more liberal (as was the case in Indiana Harbor) and subjected any claimed dangerous activity to §520 analysis.

Miller v. Civil Constructors, Inc.
272 Ill. App. 3d 263, 651 N.E.2d 239 (Ill. App. 2 Dist. 1995)

Justice BOWMAN delivered the opinion of the court:

Plaintiff, Gerald Miller, appeals from the orders of the circuit court of Stephenson County which dismissed the strict liability counts of his complaint against defendants, Civil Constructors, Inc., d/b/a Civil Constructors (Constructors) (count I), and the City of Freeport (City) (count V). Counts I and V of the complaint filed October 22, 1992, alleged essentially that defendants were strictly liable for injuries to plaintiff arising from purportedly "ultrahazardous" activity for which defendants were legally responsible either because of their control of the premises or their discharge of firearms. In each instance, plaintiff stated that the defendant, through its officers, agents or employees, knew (alternatively in count I, "or in the exercise of reasonable care should have known") that "discharging firearms is an ultrahazardous, highly dangerous activity" which was the proximate cause of plaintiff's injuries. The complaint averred that plaintiff was injured when a stray bullet ricocheted during the course of firearm target practice in a nearby gravel pit and caused him to fall from a truck. There is no legal cause of action available to plaintiff under a theory of strict liability. We affirm the orders of the circuit court.

. . . The issue before us is whether, consonant with Illinois law, the trial court properly dismissed the counts where plaintiff attempted to state a cause of action premised on a theory of strict liability by asserting that the discharge of firearms in a quarry shooting range is an ultrahazardous activity. Under the circumstances presented, we hold as a matter of law that the discharge of firearms is not an ultrahazardous activity which would support plaintiff's strict liability claims.

. . . The doctrine of strict liability, sometimes called absolute liability, has its genesis in the English rule of *Rylands v. Fletcher* (1868), 3 H.L. 330, wherein strict liability was imposed on the defendant owners of land for harm resulting from the abnormal or nonnatural use of the defendants' land which arose when water from defendants' reservoir flooded the adjoining mine of the plaintiff. Subsequent decisions interpreted the rule to be confined to things or activities which were "extraordinary," or "exceptional" or "abnormal" so that there was some special use bringing with it increased danger to others. From the decisions of the English courts, the "rule" of *Rylands* which has emerged is that "the defendant will be liable when he damages another by a thing or activity unduly dangerous and inappropriate to the place where it is maintained, in the light of the character of that place and its surroundings."

Most jurisdictions in this country have adopted the rule of *Rylands* to impose strict liability on owners and users of land for harm resulting from abnormally dangerous conditions and activities. The best-known applications of the *Rylands* rule imposing strict liability on a defendant involve the storing and use of explosives and flammable materials.

Illinois has recognized strict liability principally in two instances: (1) when, under certain circumstances, a defendant introduces a product into the community which is unreasonably dangerous to the user, consumer, or to his property (product liability cases). . . ; and (2) when a defendant engages in ultrahazardous or abnormally dangerous activity as determined by the courts, giving particular consideration, *inter alia*, to the appropriateness of the activity to the place where it is maintained, in light of the character of the place and its surroundings. . . .

We are concerned here only with determining as a matter of law whether the use of firearms is an ultrahazardous activity giving rise to strict liability.

Before we answer the question presented, we first summarize briefly what we believe is the current state of the law in this area. Plaintiff has not cited, nor have we found, any Illinois case holding that the use of a firearm which results in injury to a plaintiff is an ultrahazardous activity requiring the imposition of strict liability. Although the guns or firearms have been labeled dangerous instrumentalities..., it does not automatically follow that courts must then charge a defendant with strict liability for the use of firearms which results in harm to a plaintiff. Indeed, the prevailing rule which we have discovered in our own research is that the use of firearms ordinarily does not present a question of strict liability premised on ultrahazardous activity; rather, it ordinarily presents a question of negligence or possibly of wilful and wanton conduct.

... We return to the threshold question whether the use of firearms ought to be classified as an ultrahazardous activity. This type of inquiry is a question of law that we believe will be subjected to more rigorous, disciplined, and consistent analysis if we adopt the use of the Restatement principles and factors discussed, or at least implicitly considered, in prior decisions.

Section 519 of the Restatement states the general principle that "[o]ne who carries on an abnormally dangerous activity is subject to liability for harm to the person, land or chattels of another resulting from the activity, although he has exercised the utmost care to prevent the harm." (Restatement (Second) of Torts §519 (1977).) Section 520 of the Restatement sets forth several factors which we will consider in determining whether an activity is abnormally dangerous (ultrahazardous):

(a) existence of a high degree of risk of some harm to the person, land or chattels of others;

(b) likelihood that the harm that results from it will be great;

(c) inability to eliminate the risk by the exercise of reasonable care;

(d) extent to which the activity is not a matter of common usage;

(e) inappropriateness of the activity to the place where it is carried on; and

(f) extent to which its value to the community is outweighed by its dangerous attributes."

Restatement (Second) of Torts §520 (1977).

While all of these factors are important and should be considered, ordinarily the presence of more than one factor, but not all of them, will be necessary to declare the activity ultrahazardous as a matter of law so as to hold the actor strictly liable. The essential question is whether the risk created is so unusual, either because of its magnitude or because of the circumstances surrounding it, as to justify the imposition of strict liability even though the activity is carried on with all reasonable care. (Restatement (Second) of Torts §520, Comment *f*, at 37-38 (1977).) Considerations of public policy also enter prominently into the decisions by our courts to impose strict liability (at least in product liability cases). Particular consideration is also given to the appropriateness of the activity to the place where it is maintained, in light of the character of the place and its surroundings under the *Rylands* rule. . . .

The use of guns or firearms, even though frequently classified as dangerous or even highly dangerous, is not the type of activity that must be deemed ultrahazardous when the above-stated criteria are taken into consideration. First, the risk of harm to persons or property, even though great, can be virtually eliminated by the exercise of reasonable or even "utmost" care under the circumstances. The doctrine of strict or absolute liability is ordinarily reserved for abnormally dangerous activities for which no degree of care can truly provide safety. There is a clear distinction between requiring a defendant to exercise a high degree of care when involved in a potentially dangerous activity and requiring a defendant to insure absolutely the safety of others when engaging in ultrahazardous activity.

Second, the use of firearms is a matter of common usage and the harm posed comes from their misuse rather than from their inherent nature alone. . . . Third, the activity in this case was carried on at a firing range in a quarry located somewhere near the City of Freeport. We assume that the location was appropriate for such activity in the absence of further factual allegations in the complaint particularly describing the area as inappropriate for the target practice. Finally, the target practice is of some social utility to the community; this weighs against declaring it ultrahazardous where the activity was alleged to have been performed by law enforcement officers apparently to improve their skills in the handling of weapons.

In light of the above considerations, we conclude that plaintiff's allegations are legally insufficient to show that the activity should be declared ultrahazardous so as to subject defendants to claims premised on a theory of strict liability.

The judgment of the circuit court of Stephenson County is affirmed.

PREPARING FOR CLASS

1. Don't get confused by the court interchanging the terms "abnormally dangerous" and "ultrahazardous." Ultrahazardous was the word used under the First Restatement to describe dangerous activities subject to strict liability prior to the creation of the Second Restatement §520, and some courts were slow transitioning.

2. How might this case end up if tried under a negligence theory?

3. Recognize how the court, relying on "policy considerations," is allowed to shade or magnify reliance on the factors of §520.

INCREASING YOUR UNDERSTANDING

1. Many "abnormally dangerous" cases have involved the use of explosives or firearms. With regard to dynamiting/blasting, there is a split at least on one significant front: whether it's appropriate to impose strict liability when damage results from vibrations or concussions as opposed to direct invasions. Some courts have limited liability to where harm resulted from direct damage cause by rocks or debris. See, e.g., Coalite, Inc. v. Aldridge, 282 Ala. 137, 229 So. 2d 539 (Ala. 1969) (There is no liability for "injuries resulting from concussion or vibration, as distinguished from a trespass by casting of debris or rocks onto the land of another, where one is lawfully blasting on his own property, unless it is shown that the injury was the result of negligence in the blasting operation."). Others have held defendants strictly liable for harm that resulted from vibrations associated with blasting. See Laughon & Johnson, Inc. v. Burch, 278 S.E.2d 856 (Va. 1981) (Limiting strict liability to direct intrusions is an idea that "has been severely criticized and labeled a marriage of procedural technicality with scientific ignorance.").

2. *Ultrahazardous vs. abnormally dangerous.* Factors (a)-(c) of Restatement (Second) of Torts §520 are a carryover of the ultrahazadous concept articulated in the First Restatement. Adding factors (d)-(f) allows for courts to consider whether the activity is abnormal upon considering the utility of the conduct, its location, and commonality within the community.

C. LIMITATIONS ON STRICT LIABILITY

Foster v. Preston Mill Co.
44 Wash. 2d 440, 268 P.2d 645 (1954)

HAMLEY, Justice.

Blasting operations conducted by Preston Mill Company frightened mother mink owned by B. W. Foster, and caused the mink to kill their kittens. Foster brought this action against the company to recover damages. His second amended complaint, upon which the case was tried, sets forth a cause of action on the theory of absolute liability, and, in the laternative, a cause of action on the theory of nuisance.

After a trial to the court without a jury, judgment was rendered for plaintiff in the sum of $1,953.68. The theory adopted by the court was that, after defendant received notice of the effect which its blasting operations were having upon the mink, it was absolutely liable for all damages of that nature thereafter sustained. The trial court concluded that defendant's blasting did not constitute a public nuisance, but did not expressly rule on the question of private nuisance. Plaintiff concedes, however, that, in effect, the trial court decided in defendant's favor on the question of nuisance. Defendant appeals.

Respondent's mink ranch is located in a rural area one and one-half miles east of North Bend, in King County, Washington. The ranch occupies seven and one half acres on which are located seven sheds for growing mink. The cages are of welded wire, but have wood roofs covered with composition roofing. The ranch is located about two blocks from U.S. highway No. 10, which is a main east-west thoroughfare across the state. Northern Pacific Railway Company tracks are located between the ranch and the highway, and Chicago, Milwaukee, St. Paul & Pacific Railroad Company tracks are located on the other side of the highway about fifteen hundred feet from the ranch.

The period of each year during which mink kittens are born, known as the whelping season, begins about May 1st. The kittens are born during a period of about two and one-half weeks, and are left with their mothers until they are six weeks old. During this period, the mothers are very excitable. If disturbed by noises, smoke, or dogs and cats, they run back and forth in their cages and frequently destroy their young. However, mink become accustomed to disturbances of this kind, if continued over a period of time. This explains why the mink in question were apparently not bothered, even during the whelping season, by the heavy traffic on U.S. highway No. 10, and by the noise and vibration caused by passing trains. There was testimony to the effect that mink would even become accustomed to the vibration and noise of blasting, if it were carried on in a regular and continuous manner.

Appellant and several other companies have been engaged in logging in the adjacent area for more than fifty years. Early in May, 1951, appellant began the construction of a road to gain access to certain timber which it desired to cut. The road was located about two and one-quarter miles southwest of the mink ranch, and about twenty-five hundred feet above the ranch, along the side of what is known as Rattle-snake Ledge.

It was necessary to use explosives to build the road. The customary types of explosives were used, and the customary methods of blasting were followed. The most powder used in one shooting was one hundred pounds, and usually the charge was limited to fifty pounds. The procedure used was to set off blasts twice a day-at noon and at the end of the work day.

Roy A. Peterson, the manager of the ranch in 1951, testified that the blasting resulted in "a tremendous vibration, is all. Boxes would rattle on the cages." The mother mink would then run back and forth in their cages and many of them would kill their kittens. Peterson also testified that on two occasions the blasts had broken windows.

Appellant's expert, Professor Drury Augustus Pfeiffer, of the University of Washington, testified as to tests made with a pin seismometer, using blasts as large as those used by appellant. He reported that no effect on the delicate apparatus was shown at distances comparable to those involved in this case. He said that it would be impossible to break a window at two and one-fourth miles with a hundred-pound shot, but that it could cause vibration of a lightly-supported cage. It would also be audible. Charles E. Erickson, who had charge of the road construction for appellant in 1951, testified that there was no glass breakage in the portable storage and filing shed which the company kept within a thousand feet of where the blasting was done. There were windows on the roof as well as on the sides of this shed.

Before the 1951 whelping season had far progressed, the mink mothers, according to Peterson's estimate, had killed thirty-five or forty of their kittens. He then told the manager of appellant company what had happened. He did not request that the blasting be stopped. After some discussion, however, appellant's manager indicated that the shots would be made as light as possible. The amount of explosives used in a normal shot was then reduced from nineteen or twenty sticks to fourteen sticks.

Officials of appellant company testified that it would have been impractical to entirely cease road-building during the several weeks required for the mink to whelp and wean their young. Such a delay would have made it necessary to run the logging operation another season, with attendant expense. It would also have disrupted the company's log production schedule and consequently the operation of its lumber mill.

In this action, respondent sought and recovered judgment only for such damages as were claimed to have been sustained as a result of blasting operations conducted after appellant received notice that its activity was causing loss of mink kittens.

The primary question presented by appellant's assignments of error is whether, on these facts, the judgment against appellant is sustainable on the theory of absolute liability.

The modern doctrine of strict liability for dangerous substances and activities stems from Justice Blackburn's decision in Rylands v. Fletcher, 1 Exch. 265, decided in 1866 and affirmed two years later in Fletcher v. Rylands, L.R. 3 H.L. 330. As applied to blasting operations, the doctrine has quite uniformly been held to establish liability, irrespective of negligence, for property damage sustained as a result of casting rocks or other debris on adjoining or neighboring premises. Patrick v. Smith, 75 Wash. 407, 134 P. 1076, 48 L.R.A., N.S., 740; Schade Brewing Co. v. Chicago, M. & P.S.R. Co., 79 Wash. 651, 140 P. 897; Bedell v. Goulter, Or., 261 P.2d 842; Exner v. Sherman Power Const. Co., 2 Cir., 54 F.2d 510, 80 A.L.R. 686. But see Klepsch v. Donald, 4 Wash. 436, 30 P. 991.

There is a division of judicial opinion as to whether the doctrine of absolute liability should apply where the damage from blasting is caused, not by the casting of rocks and debris, but by concussion, vibration, or jarring. This court has adopted the view that the doctrine applies in such cases. *Patrick v. Smith*, supra. In the *Patrick* case, it was held that contractors who set off an exceedingly large blast of powder, causing the earth for a considerable distance to shake violently, were liable to an adjoining owner whose well was damaged and water supply lost, without regard to their negligence in setting off the blast, although there was no physical invasion of the property.

However the authorities may be divided on the point just discussed, they appear to be agreed that strict liability should be confined to consequences which lie within the extraordinary risk whose existence calls for such responsibility. Prosser on Torts, 458, §60; Harper, Liability Without Fault and Proximate Cause, 30 Mich. L. Rev. 1001, 1006; 3 Restatement of Torts, 41, §519. This limitation on the doctrine is indicated in the italicized portion of the rule as set forth in Restatement of Torts, supra:

> "Except as stated in §§521-4, one who carries on an ultrahazardous activity is liable to another whose person, land or chattels the actor should recognize as likely to be harmed by the unpreventable miscarringe of the activity for harm resulting thereto *from that which makes the activity ultrahazardous*, although the utmost care is exercised to prevent the harm." (Italics supplied.)

This restriction which has been placed upon the application of the doctrine of absolute liability is based upon considerations of policy. As Professor Prosser has said:

> "... It is one thing to say that a dangerous enterprise must pay its way within reasonable limits, and quite another to say that it must bear responsibility for every extreme of harm that it may cause. The same practical necessity for the restriction of liability within some reasonable bounds, which arises in connection with problems of 'proximate cause' in negligence cases, demands here that some limit be set. . . . This limitation has been expressed by saying that the defendant's duty to insure safety extends only to certain consequences. More commonly, it is said that the defendant's conduct is not the 'proximate cause' of the damage. But ordinarily in such cases no question of causation is involved, and the limitation is one of the policy underlying liability." *Prosser on Torts*, 457, §60.

Applying this principle to the case before us, the question comes down to this: Is the risk that any unusual vibration or noise may cause wild animals, which are being raised for commercial purposes, to kill their young, one of the things which make the activity of blasting ultrahazardous?

We have found nothing in the decisional law which would support an affirmative answer to this question. The decided cases, as well as common experience, indicate that the thing which makes blasting ultrahazardous is the risk that property or persons may be damaged or injured by coming into direct contact with flying debris, or by being directly affected by vibrations of the earth or concussions of the air.

Where, as a result of blasting operations, a horse has become frightened and has trampled or otherwise injured a person, recovery of damages has been upheld on the theory of negligence. But we have found no case where recovery of damages caused by a frightened farm animal has been sustained on the ground of absolute liability.

If, however, the possibility that a violent vibration, concussion, or noise might frighten domestic animals and lead to property damages or personal injuries be considered one of the harms which makes the activity of blasting ultrahazardous, this would still not include the case we have here.

The relatively moderate vibration and noise which appellant's blasting produced at a distance of two and a quarter miles was no more than a usual incident of the ordinary life of the community. See 3 Restatement of Torts, 48, §522, comment a. The trial court specifically found that the blasting did not unreasonably interfere with the enjoyment of their property by nearby land-owners, except in the case of respondent's mink ranch.

It is the exceedingly nervous disposition of mink, rather than the normal risks inherent in blasting operations, which therefore must, as a matter of sound policy, bear the responsibility for the loss here sustained. We subscribe to the view expressed by Professor Harper (30 Mich. L. Rev. 1001, 1006, supra) that the policy of the law does not impose the rule of strict liability to protect against harms incident to the plaintiff's extraordinary and unusual use of land. This is perhaps but an application of the principle that the extent to which one man in the lawful conduct of his business is liable for injuries to another involves an adjustment of conflicting interests. . . .

It may very well be that, under the facts of a particular case, recovery for damages of this kind may be sustained upon some theory other than that of absolute liability. In Hamilton v. King County, 195 Wash. 84, 79 P.2d 697, for example, recovery of such damages was sanctioned on the ground that defendant had trespassed upon plaintiff's land in doing the blasting which caused the disturbance. . . .

It is our conclusion that the risk of causing harm of the kind here experienced, as a result of the relatively minor vibration, concussion, and noise from distant blasting, is not the kind of risk which makes the activity of blasting ultrahazardous. The doctrine of absolute liability is therefore inapplicable under the facts of this case, and respondent is not entitled to recover damages.

The judgment is reversed.

PREPARING FOR CLASS

1. Recall the causation discussion from Chapter 11 in Torts I and how it would apply if the case were advanced under a traditional theory of negligence.

2. If liability is supposed to be "strict" or "absolute," why limit it?

APPLYING THE LAW

Neighbor's champion fighting pit bull jumps over the fence and darts past elderly man, frightening him, whereupon he loses his balance, falls, and breaks his hip. Is neighbor strictly liable?

INCREASING YOUR UNDERSTANDING

1. *Strict not absolute.* Most courts have followed the dictates of Restatement (Second) of Torts §519 and limited liability resulting from abnormally dangerous activities to "the kind of harm, the possibility of which makes the activity abnormally dangerous." It's misplaced (and unfortunate) therefore to describe this form of liability as "absolute," as the defendant is only strictly liable for the harm that is generally associated with the conduct from its inception.

2. In a contributory negligence jurisdiction, a defendant cannot receive a simple contributory negligence jury instruction in a strict liability case. In other words, the judge will not instruct the jury to consider whether the plaintiff failed to exercise reasonable care for his own safety. Instead, the judge must issue a stricter instruction that asks something along the lines of whether the plaintiff "unnecessarily and voluntarily put [] himself in a way to be hurt knowing the probable consequences of his act, so that he may fairly be deemed to have brought the injury upon himself." Sandy v. Bushey, 128 A. 513 (Me. 1925). This rule largely grew from judicial dissatisfaction with the common law "total bar" rule, of which currently only five jurisdictions follow in its original form. This does not mean however that a court will not, in a comparative fault jurisdiction, allow for the jury to assign fault to the plaintiff who unreasonably confronts an abnormally dangerous circumstance (animal or activity) with the prospect of recovery being denied or reduced in accordance with the mandates of the comparative rules.

3. *Intervening acts.* Some cases have found that forces of nature cut off proximate cause, for example, Golden v. Amory, 109 N.E.2d 131 (NY 1952). Under the Restatement (Second) Torts §522, however, intervening forces of nature and intervening innocent, negligent, and reckless acts of third people do not cut off proximate cause. Basically, the attitude of the Restatement is that the possibility of intervening forces and acts is part of what makes abnormally dangerous activities dangerous. The Restatement does not state that intervening intentional acts bar recovery, which means that sometimes they may defeat plaintiff's case.

Chapter 14

Vicarious Liability

Vicarious liability holds the defendant responsible for another person's tort. For example, an associate attorney driving to a deposition falls asleep behind the wheel of her car and injures the plaintiff. The law firm, because of the employer-employee relationship, will be vicariously liable for the associate's negligent driving. From the law firm's perspective, this is a kind of strict liability because the law firm will be liable without proof of any fault on its part. From the plaintiff's perspective, it feels less like strict liability because the plaintiff will still have to demonstrate the associate's underlying negligence. The employer's vicarious liability for an employee's tort is known as respondeat superior. Although it is the most common type of vicarious liability, other relationships, as we shall see, can impose vicarious liability as well.

A. RESPONDEAT SUPERIOR

Bussard v. Minimed, Inc.
129 Cal. Rptr. 2d 675 (Cal. App. 2003)

Rubin, J.

Appellant Barbara Bussard appeals from summary judgment for respondent Minimed, Inc. After review, we hold the "going-and-coming" exception to the doctrine of respondeat superior does not apply to an employee while she is driving home after becoming sick at work from exposure to pesticide fumes. . . .

On March 22, 2000, respondent Minimed hired a pest control company to spray pesticide overnight to eliminate fleas at respondent's facility. Around 7:00 A.M. the next day, Minimed clerical employee Irma Hernandez arrived for work. She noticed a funny smell similar to "Raid." By 10 o'clock, she felt ill, with a headache, nausea, and tightness in her chest. At noon, she told two supervisors she did not feel well enough to continue working and wanted to go home. One supervisor offered to send her to the company doctor, but Hernandez declined the offer, while another supervisor asked whether she felt well enough to drive home, and she said yes. (Eventually, nine workers went home early feeling ill and 22 employees sought medical care either that day or later for their exposure to the pesticide.)

Hernandez drove home shortly after noon. While in route, she rear ended appellant Barbara Bussard, who was stopped at a red light. Hernandez told the police officer who responded to the accident scene that she had felt dizzy and lightheaded before the accident.

Appellant . . . claimed respondent was vicariously liable as Hernandez's employer under the doctrine of respondeat superior because Hernandez was acting within the course and scope of her employment when she was driving home ill from pesticide exposure.

Respondent moved for summary judgment. It argued the "going-and-coming" rule meant Hernandez was not within the course and scope of her employment during her commute home. Accordingly, it should not be held vicariously liable under respondeat superior.

The court agreed. It noted the pesticide had not incapacitated Hernandez to the point of rendering her irrational. Thus, her exposure to it did not justify disregarding the going-and-coming rule to make respondent vicariously liable for her as she drove home sick. This appeal followed. . . .

Under the doctrine of respondeat superior, an employer is ordinarily liable for the injuries its employees cause others in the course of their work. Respondeat superior imposes liability whether or not the employer was itself negligent, and whether or not the employer had control of the employee. The doctrine's animating principle is that a business should absorb the costs its undertakings impose on others. . . .

The doctrine's application requires that the employee be acting within the course of her employment, which case law defines expansively. . . . Thus, acts necessary to the comfort, convenience, health, and welfare of the employee while at work, though strictly personal and not acts of service, do not take the employee outside the scope of employment. Moreover, "where the employee is combining his own business with that of his employer, or attending to both at substantially the same time, no nice inquiry will be made as to which business he was actually engaged in at the time of injury, unless it clearly appears that neither directly nor indirectly could he have been serving his employer." It is also settled that an employer's vicarious liability may extend to willful and malicious torts of an employee as well as negligence. Finally, an employee's tortious act may be within the scope of employment even if it contravenes an express company rule and confers no benefit to the employer." (Farmers Ins. Group v. County of Santa Clara (1995) 11 Cal. 4th 992, 1004, 47 Cal. Rptr. 2d 478, 906 P.2d 440.)

Despite the doctrine's wide reach, courts have not defined it so broadly as to include an employee's daily commute. "Case law has established the general rule that an employee is outside the scope of his employment while engaged in his ordinary commute to and from his place of work. This principle is known as the 'going-and-coming rule' and is based on several theories. One is that the employment relationship is suspended from the time the employee leaves his job until he returns. Another is that during the commute, the employee is not rendering services to his employer."

The going-and-coming rule is not iron-clad, however, and allows for several exceptions. One exception applies when an employee endangers others with a risk arising from or related to work. In determining whether such danger arises from or is related to work, case law applies a foreseeability test. Our Supreme Court describes this type of foreseeability, which is different from the foreseeability of negligence, as employees' conduct that is neither startling nor unusual. "'One way to determine whether a risk is inherent in, or created by, an enterprise is to ask whether the actual occurrence was a generally foreseeable consequence of the activity. . . . "[F]oreseeability" as a test for respondeat superior merely means that in the context of the particular enterprise an employee's conduct is not so unusual or startling that it would seem unfair to include the loss resulting from it among other costs of the employer's business.' . . . [Such a test is] useful because it reflects the central justification for respondeat superior: that losses fairly attributable to an enterprise—those which foreseeably result from the conduct of the enterprise—should be allocated to the enterprise as a cost of doing business."

This test has been applied to employees who got into car accidents on the way home after drinking alcohol at work. Courts have found a sufficient link between the drinking and the accidents to make the collisions neither startling nor unusual, and thus foreseeable under respondeat superior. . . .

Hernandez suffered pesticide exposure at work to which she attributed illness and impaired driving. That an employee might not be fit to drive after breathing lingering pesticide fumes for several hours is not such a startling or unusual event that we find a car accident on Hernandez's commute home was unforeseeable. Hence, the trial court erred in finding the going-and-coming rule barred appellant's claim of respondeat superior. Indeed, the going-and-coming rule was an analytical distraction. The thrust of appellant's claim for vicarious liability was that Hernandez was an "instrumentality of danger" because of what had happened to her at work. Although Hernandez's decision to drive home gave respondent an opening to raise the going-and-coming rule, the rule did not apply because her decision was a fortuity that must not obscure appellant's central claim that Hernandez's job had contributed to the accident. Thus, summary judgment for respondent was improper.

Respondent argues the foreseeability exception to the going-and-coming rule does not apply because it was not negligent. In support, respondent points to the absence of evidence that it contributed in any negligent manner to the underlying pesticide exposure. It also cites the uncontested fact that its supervisors diligently inquired into Hernandez's ability to drive before she went home. Respondent contrasts its seeming blamelessness with decisions [in other cases] imposing vicarious liability for drunken employees, suggesting liability attached to the employer in those decisions in part because the employer bore some responsibility for the employee's intoxication. Whatever merit respondent's argument might have in defeating appellant's theory that respondent was directly liable to her for ordinary negligence . . . it does not apply to vicarious liability. . . .

The judgment is reversed and the court is directed to enter a new and different order denying respondent Minimed Inc.'s motion for summary judgment. Appellant to recover her costs on appeal.

We concur: Cooper, P.J., and Boland, J.

PREPARING FOR CLASS

1. Hernandez caused the accident. Why did Bussard sue Minimed?

2. Generally, when are employers responsible for the torts of their employees?

3. How did Minimed contend that it should not be vicariously liable for Hernandez's negligent driving? What are the rationales behind the rule Minimed invoked?

4. Why did the rule invoked by Minimed not apply here? What standard did apply?

5. Did the trial court properly grant summary judgment?

6. Minimed had evidence of its reasonable care. Did that help Minimed defend the claim?

7. What policies are served by respondeat superior?

APPLYING THE LAW

1. Television station WDEF sent two employees, a reporter and a cameraman, to cover a performance by a band at a nightclub. The cameraman set his camera up so that it was blocking an exit. The band used stage fireworks, which set fire to the polyurethane soundproofing material around the stage. The fire spread quickly, and several patrons died in the fire. The negligent blocking of the exits was a cause of their deaths, and wrongful death suits have been brought against WDEF. WDEF has

moved to have the respondeat superior claims against it dismissed. Should the court grant the motion?

2. An 18-year-old high school senior worked at a fast food restaurant while maintaining high grades and a full extra-curricular schedule. He had already worked five nights in a row at the restaurant when he was asked to stay for a special clean-up project that lasted from midnight to 5 A.M. He took the extra assignment but left an hour early because he was too exhausted to continue working. On the way home, he fell asleep behind the wheel, drifted across the center lane, and crashed into an oncoming car. The driver of that car has filed a respondeat superior claim against the restaurant. The restaurant has moved for dismissal of the claim. Should the motion be granted? Even if the motion is granted, could the plaintiff have a cause of action against the restaurant?

3. A college professor had a sore throat. To soothe her throat, the professor made some tea in a common break room shared by faculty, staff, and students. While making the tea, she splashed a considerable amount of hot water on the tile floor but did not clean it up, and a student slipped on the water, fell, and broke her ankle. The student has filed a respondeat superior claim against the college. Should the college be vicariously liable?

INCREASING YOUR UNDERSTANDING

Why should a non-negligent employer, like the employer in *Bussard* who inquired into Hernandez's ability to drive and offered to have her see a doctor, be held liable for the employee's negligence? The case mentions one rationale: "A business should absorb the costs its undertakings impose on others." The idea is that employing human beings with human failings foreseeably carries some risks and those risks should be a cost of the business that brought those flawed human beings together for its benefit. In Ira S. Bushey & Sons v. United States, 398 F.2d 167 (2d. Cir. 1968), the court adopted a foreseeability approach to respondeat superior and held the Coast Guard liable when a drunken seaman returning to his ship in drydock turned the seacocks, scuttled the ship, and damaged plaintiff's drydock. Explaining how the rationales behind respondeat superior justified a foreseeability approach, Justice Friendly quoted Hartford Accident & Indemnity Co. v. Cardillo, 112 F.2d 11 (D.C. Cir. 1940) (a workers' compensation case):

> Men do not discard their personal qualities when they go to work. Into the job they carry their intelligence, skill, habits of care and rectitude. Just as inevitably they take along also their tendencies to carelessness and camaraderie, as well as emotional make-up. In bringing men

together, work brings these qualities together, causes frictions between them, creates occasions for lapses into carelessness, and for fun-making and emotional flare-up. . . . These expressions of human nature are incidents inseparable from working together. They involve risks of injury and these risks are inherent in the working environment.

Judge Friendly continued:

Put another way, [the seaman's] conduct was not so "unforeseeable" as to make it unfair to charge the Government with responsibility. We agree with a leading treatise that "what is reasonably foreseeable in this context (of respondeat superior) . . . is quite a different thing from the foreseeably unreasonable risk of harm that spells negligence . . . . The foresight that should impel the prudent man to take precautions is not the same measure as that by which he should perceive the harm likely to flow from his long-run activity in spite of all reasonable precautions on his own part. The proper test here bears far more resemblance to that which limits liability for workmen's compensation than to the test for negligence. The employer should be held to expect risks, to the public also, which arise 'out of and in the course of' his employment of labor." 2 Harper & James, *The Law of Torts* 1377-78 (1956). Here it was foreseeable that crew members crossing the drydock might do damage, negligently or even intentionally, such as pushing a Bushey employee or kicking property into the water. Moreover, the proclivity of seamen to find solace for solitude by copious resort to the bottle while ashore has been noted in opinions too numerous to warrant citation.

Other justifications for respondeat superior liability include an employer's control or right to control employees' conduct, the incentive to make sure (through careful hiring, training, supervising) that employees do not commit torts for which the employer will be held liable, and assured compensation to victims who may be unlikely to recover from employees but able to recover from an employer who can insure against risks by spreading the costs of that insurance to those who benefit from the services or goods the business provides.

Pyne v. Witmer
543 N.E.2d 1304 (Ill. 1989)

Justice STAMOS delivered the opinion of the court:

In this automobile accident case based on a theory of respondeat superior, we are asked to examine the entry of summary judgment in favor of the defendant employer. The central issue is whether a triable question of fact existed as to whether, at the time of the accident, the defendant's employee was within the scope of his employment. . . .

Briefly, this case involves an employee, defendant William E. Witmer, who, at or near the end of his scheduled work day, drove in his own vehicle from his workplace in Streamwood to Rockford in order to take an evening test that could secure his certification as an automobile mechanic. Witmer's employer, appellant D.R.W. Enterprises, Inc. (D.R.W.), which operated the gasoline station at which Witmer worked, did not pay him wages, mileage, or expenses for the trip, but D.R.W. did issue a check for the test fee. [F]or purposes of this appeal the parties are in agreement that, while taking the test, Witmer was within the scope of his employment. . . .

Generally, an employee traveling to or from work outside actual working hours is not in the scope of employment, but an exception exists for employees who are caused by their employers to travel away from a regular workplace or whose travel is at least partly for their employers' purposes rather than simply serving to convey the employees to or from a regular jobsite.

Some 2 ½ hours after he completed his test, Witmer was killed in a 10:30 P.M. automobile collision involving his vehicle and one driven by the appellee, Keith L. Pyne. According to blood-alcohol evidence, Witmer was intoxicated at the time of collision, and the appellee does not dispute this. The collision site was near Marengo, which lies between Rockford, on the one hand, and, on the other, Witmer's home in Elgin and workplace in Streamwood.

No eyewitness or physical evidence was presented as to Witmer's actual whereabouts or activities from the time he left his test location until the time of the accident. However, his widow testified in a deposition that before leaving for Rockford he had told her he would stay a little late in order to study for a second test session to be held the next evening. Witmer's former mother-in-law also swore in an affidavit that, some 10 years earlier, he had regularly commuted [in that area] for a two-year period and that at that time he had often professed to know all the back roads well.

At the time of the accident, Witmer's southbound route of travel would within two miles have led him to a T intersection with a highway, U.S. 20, that, in turn, could have led him directly east eight miles to Marengo and directly beyond to Elgin, his hometown. About 10 miles north of the accident site is Capron, where he had formerly lived. . . . The appellee argues that these facts tend to refute the contention that, at the time of accident, Witmer was so intoxicated as not to know where he was and thus was incapable of taking any steps or forming any intention to return to the scope of his employment if he had in fact left it. . . .

Summary judgment is generally inappropriate when scope of employment is at issue. Only if no reasonable person could conclude from the evidence that an employee was acting within the course of employment should a court hold as a matter of law that the employee was not so acting.

For an employer to be vicariously liable for an employee's torts under the doctrine of respondeat superior, the torts must have been committed within the scope of the employment. "No precise definition has been accorded the term 'scope of employment'" [Sunseri v. Puccia, 422 N.E.2d 925 (Ill. App. 1981)], but broad criteria have been enunciated:

(1)   Conduct of a servant is within the scope of employment if, but only if:

   (a) it is of the kind he is employed to perform;

   (b) it occurs substantially within the authorized time and space limits;

   (c) it is actuated, at least in part, by a purpose to serve the master. . . .

(2)   Conduct of a servant is not within the scope of employment if it is different in kind from that authorized, far beyond the authorized time or space limits, or too little actuated by a purpose to serve the master." (Restatement (Second) of Agency §228 (1958).) . . .

The burden is on the plaintiff to show the contemporaneous relationship between tortious act and scope of employment. . . .

A distinction between "frolic" (pursuit of an employee's personal business seen as unrelated to employment) and "detour" (an employee's deviation for personal reasons that is nonetheless seen as sufficiently related to employment) was long ago noted. Once an employee abandons a frolic and reenters the scope of employment, the employer will be vicariously liable for injuries caused by the employee's negligence after reentry. [Prince v. Atchison, Topeka & Santa Fe Ry. Co., 395 N.E.2d 592 (Ill. App. 1979).] An employee may combine personal business with the employer's business at the time of negligence, yet the employer will not necessarily be relieved of liability on that account [Flood v. Bitzer, 40 N.E.2d 557 (Ill. App. 1942)], and the fact that an employee is not immediately and single-mindedly pursuing the employer's business at the time of negligence but has deviated somewhat therefrom or that the employee's conduct was not authorized does not necessarily take the employee out of the scope of employment.

Where an employee's deviation from the course of employment is slight and not unusual, a court may find as a matter of law that the employee was still executing the employer's business. [Boehmer v. Norton, 65 N.E.2d 212 (Ill. App. 1946)]. Conversely, when a deviation is exceedingly marked and unusual, as a matter of law the employee may be found to be outside the scope of employment. But in cases falling between these extremes, where a deviation is uncertain in extent and degree, or where the surrounding facts and circumstances leave room for legitimate inferences as to whether, despite the deviation, the employee was still engaged in the employer's business, the question is for the jury. [Gundich v. Emerson-Comstock Co., 171 N.E.2d 60 (Ill. 1960).]

Though D.R.W. insists that the appellee offered no evidence on what Witmer was doing in the time between his test and his accident, and hence no evidence on whether he was within the scope of his employment, the fact is that evidence was offered. The evidence was not direct, but it was circumstantial; its strength would be a matter for the trier of fact. . . .

The appellee cites evidence of Witmer's familiarity with Marengo-area roads, his position on a road that within two miles would meet a highway leading homeward, his intention to study after the test, his freedom to return at his own pace, and his reporting time for work the next day, all in an effort to show that, before the accident, Witmer arguably remained within or returned to the scope of employment. . . . [W]hen viewed in the light most favorable to the appellee, the evidence tended to prove that Witmer was within rather than outside the scope of employment.

Furthermore, a jury might be entitled, in view of the timing of events and the jury's experience with the affairs of life to consider the possibility that Witmer had stopped for refreshment (and drinks) after the test. If, because of the hour and the fact that he was away from his home kitchen, the jury were to find that he had stopped for refreshment en route rather than simply having chosen to indulge in what D.R.W. characterizes as a drinking bout, the jury might then more easily find him to have remained within the scope of employment. . . .

Because pertinent evidence was presented on both sides of the scope-of-employment issue, this case differs from Murphy v. Urso [430 N.E.2d 1079 (Ill. 1981)], which D.R.W. cites. In *Murphy*, the evidence was uncontradicted that an erstwhile bus driver was moving furniture for friends at the time of an accident and that moving friends' furniture was outside the scope of employment even if the driver were to be considered still employed at the time; accordingly, summary judgment was proper. Here, the appellee's evidence does contradict D.R.W.'s as to whether Witmer was within the scope of employment at the time of the accident. Moreover, a current employee's returning from a test that was authorized by an employer and that arguably benefits the employer's business is not comparable to a past or present employee's using employer equipment to perform unauthorized services for personal friends. Hence, *Murphy* does not support summary judgment for D.R.W.

D.R.W. contends that, on the "real issue in this case" in regard to its liability, it proved the "irrefutable fact" of Witmer's frolic; that it then became the appellee's burden to prove Witmer's reentry to the scope of employment; and that the appellee offered no evidence of reentry. To the contrary, as noted by the appellate court majority, "it is not clear that Witmer was ever on a frolic." For all we know, Witmer could have done his drinking before or during the test as well as after, or as part of a normal post-test stop for rest or a meal while on the road to home; he could have had car trouble after leaving Rockford; he could have stayed late in Rockford studying. The mere passage of time did not necessarily mean frolic, and Witmer's route of travel might be found reasonably direct.

As D.R.W. acknowledges, it was D.R.W.'s burden to go forward with evidence tending to show frolic. On a motion for summary judgment, however, the present appellee was not required actually to prove reentry or disprove frolic, any more than D.R.W. was required actually to prove frolic; the parties were merely called on to offer sufficient evidence to raise a triable question of fact that was material to the frolic issue. If such a question remained after the appellee responded to D.R.W.'s motion, summary judgment would be precluded.

A jury would not be required to accept D.R.W.'s frolic evidence, rather than the appellee's contrary evidence. If no frolic were found, then at trial the appellee would not need to have shown reentry to a scope that Witmer would be found never to have left. In other words, D.R.W.'s concern with whether at the summary-judgment stage the appellee "proffered any evidence that [Witmer] had reentered the scope of his employment" would then prove moot. D.R.W. asserts at one point that the question of proffering reentry evidence was "the only issue before the appellate court." If so, D.R.W. deservedly failed in that court to avoid reversal of summary judgment; the question was immaterial, because a jury might find no frolic in the first place. Rather, to avoid summary judgment, all that the appellee had to do was to show a genuine question of material fact as to frolic, not reentry. This the appellee did. . . .

Since . . . reasonable persons could draw divergent inferences from the evidence presented, summary judgment was improperly entered. . . .

Justice Ryan, dissenting:

The majority opinion cites all the correct propositions of law, but comes to the wrong conclusion by not properly applying them. I, therefore, dissent.

No other inferences can be logically drawn than that the deceased was not in the course of his employment at the time of the accident, but was on a "frolic" of his own. He was sent to Rockford to take a test. As agreed by the parties, it is not disputed that he would have been in the course of his employment during the taking of the test and during travel incident thereto. However, the accident happened 2 ½ hours after the test was completed, and at a place where his employment would not have taken him. The most direct route between Rockford and the deceased's home is Interstate Highway 90. The next most direct route is U.S. Highway 20. The deceased was on neither of these highways at the time of the accident. The majority opinion seems to imply that he was traveling in an area he could be expected to travel on his way home from Rockford. He was not. He was traveling south on a country road, two miles north of U.S. Highway 20. He was coming from the north and not from Rockford, which is directly west of the scene of the accident. The country road on which he was traveling is not a shortcut to Rockford. In fact, it does not even lead to Rockford. Rather, it is directly south of Capron, Illinois, the town in which the deceased formerly lived. One need only look at a road map of Illinois to be convinced that the deceased's employment did not place him at the scene of the accident. Travel incident to the employment in which the deceased was engaged would have taken him to Rockford and then back to his home. It would not have taken him on a tour of northern Illinois.

Furthermore, at the time of the accident, the deceased's blood-alcohol content was .187, nearly twice the legal limit for driving of .10. Possibly a beer or two, or even a slight overindulgence alone, would not have jeopardized the deceased's course-of-employment status. However, he so deviated from his assigned mission that he became intoxicated to the extent that he was committing a serious criminal act by driving. That, coupled with the deviation in time and travel, prevents me from agreeing with the majority's conclusion that there exists a question of fact as to whether the deceased was in the course of his employment. Summarizing, the accident happened 2 ½ hours after the test was completed, at a place where the deceased's employment did not take him, and he was so intoxicated that he could not lawfully drive.

This was not a case of a slight deviation from the deceased's employment. He had so departed from his assigned purposed that as a matter of law, it cannot be said he was performing within the course of his employment. He was, instead, serving solely his own personal purpose. The mere fact that he was driving in the general direction of his home did not bring him back within the scope of his employment. An employer may be liable to a third person for the acts of his employee when such acts are committed in the course of employment and in furtherance of the business of the employer. However, the employer is not liable to an injured third party where the acts complained of were committed solely for the benefit of the employee.

For the above reasons, I dissent.

MILLER, J., joins in this dissent.

PREPARING FOR CLASS

1. The parties agree that while Witmer was taking the test, he was in the scope of employment. If he had driven directly towards home from the test and been in an accident on the way, would the parties have agreed that he was in the scope of employment?

2. Is scope of employment generally a question for the judge or the jury?

3. What is the difference between frolic and detour—both in definition and consequence?

4. Why does the majority find that summary judgment was improper? Why was the question of whether Witmer had reentered the scope of employment irrelevant to that decision?

5. What flaws does the dissent find in the majority's logic?

6. What do you think the jury decided?

INCREASING YOUR UNDERSTANDING

Generally, slight deviations are treated as detours and substantial deviations as frolics. "Several factors have been identified as helpful in determining whether an employee has embarked on a slight or substantial deviation. They include: (1) the employee's intent; (2) the nature, time, and place of the deviation; (3) the time consumed in the deviation; (4) the work for which the employee was hired; (5) the incidental acts reasonably expected by the employer; and (6) the freedom allowed the employee in performing his job responsibilities." O'Shea v. Welch, 350 F.3d 1101 (10th Cir. 2003). In *O'Shea*, an Osco store manager, driving from his store to the district office, decided on the spur of the moment to pull into a service station for an estimate and hit O'Shea's car as he turned left in front of it. Was this a slight deviation or a substantial one? (1) intent: the estimate was for maintenance on the car he used for work, a mixed work/personal purpose; (2) time/place: mere minutes and feet from the direct route to the district office, still on the road, not even in the station, hadn't yet abandoned work; (3) time consumed: moments; (4/5/6): kind of job, what to expect, freedom: he's a manager, probably has freedom to attend to personal matters, and Osco might reasonably expect that while driving from store to store he would do personal things. So, as long as the trip to the district office was within the scope of employment, the accident was within the scope.

APPLYING THE LAW

1.   The manager of an apartment complex had been concerned that people were breaking into the pool after hours, so she asked two maintenance employees to stay late for a week to police the pool area. By the second night, the employees were bored with this assignment. On the third night, they brought a 12-pack of beer and proceeded to get very drunk. To amuse themselves, they decided to reenact a movie scene involving an underwater escape. In doing so, one of the drunken employees smashed the drain cover with a rock. The powerful suction of swimming pool pumps makes it critical that drain covers on swimming pools be unbroken and secure. Because the drain cover was broken, a boy swimming down to the bottom of the pool to retrieve his goggles became caught in the suction and was seriously injured. Would the apartment complex owner be vicariously liable for the employees' negligence?

2.   A life insurance salesman was required by his office to go to the insurance company's annual week-long convention. The salesmen were to provide their own transportation and then seek reimbursement. The salesman chose to drive his own car. Throughout the week, scheduled events included dinners and cocktail parties, and the salesmen were encouraged to mix freely with insurance experts who were attending the convention as guests. Sometimes the scheduled gatherings led to informal gatherings at a popular local bar five miles from the convention center. On the final night, the salesman fell asleep in his room after a cocktail party. He awoke at 11:00 P.M. and decided to go to the bar

where people from the convention had been gathering through the week. He hoped to connect with some of the salesmen from other offices and insurance experts one more time before everyone left the next day. When he arrived at the bar, no one was there. Returning to the hotel, he was in an automobile accident. Did this accident occur in the scope of his employment?

Baker v. St. Francis Hospital
126 P.3d 602 (Okla. 2005)

Per Curiam:

[Amy Davis, an employee of the daycare center at St. Francis Hospital, intentionally struck the head of two-month-old Summer Baker against the side of a cubby—twice. The child suffered skull fractures and traumatic brain injury. Davis pled guilty to injury of a minor and was convicted and sentenced to ten years. Summer's parents sued the hospital under a respondeat superior theory. The trial court granted summary judgment to the hospital, and the appellate court affirmed.]

The issue is whether [Davis's] employer, the appellee, may be held liable in damages for this intentional wrongful act.

To hold an employer responsible for the tort of an employee, the tortious act must be committed in the course of the employment and within the scope of the employee's authority. As a general rule, an assault on a third person is not within the scope of an employee's authority. The exception to the general rule is well established. An employer may be held responsible for the tort committed by the employee where the act is incidental to and done in furtherance of the business of the employer even though the servant or agent acted in excess of the authority or willfully or maliciously committed the wrongs. This is not to say that the commission of the tort was within the scope of the employee's authority, for no authority for such commission could be conferred, but where the employee was acting within the scope of authority to do the particular thing rightfully that was subsequently done in a wrongful manner. *Rodebush* [infra] summarized the exception to the general rule as applying where the act is "fairly and naturally incident to the business," and is done "while the servant was engaged upon the master's business and . . . done, although mistakenly or ill advisedly, with a view to further the master's interest, or from some impulse of emotion which naturally grew out of or was incident to the attempt to perform the master's business." *Rodebush* added that: "An employee's act is within the scope of employment if it is incident to some service being performed for the employer or arises out of an emotional response to actions being taken for the employer."

The appellee asserts, "It is self-evident that the act of smashing a child's head against a shelf does not accomplish the assigned work of caring for, protecting, and nurturing." That mischaracterizes the law concerning liability of an employer for the tort of an employee. Where an employee of a daycare center is responsible for the care of infants, some type of stress-induced temporary loss of control over one's behavior (or other psychological malfunction) over a crying baby and/or babies [is foreseeable] and the act(s) of Davis in hitting Summer's head against a shelf (the cubby) arguably involve "an emotional response to actions being taken for the employer," if her motivation and purpose in doing so was, in whole or in part, an attempt to quiet the crying infant. Thus, the act(s) may have been an attempt to do a rightful thing (i.e., quiet a crying child) "in a wrongful manner."

Oklahoma case law provides examples of cases involving torts for which the employer was held liable and those in which the employer was not held liable. Early in statehood the Court held that a railroad company was liable for the actions of the train auditor, who falsely imprisoned a passenger arising out of a controversy over the payment of a fare. The Court stated the general rule that a corporation, like an individual, is liable for any tort committed by its agent in the course of his employment, "even though the act is done wantonly and recklessly, or was against the express orders of the company." Chicago R.I. & P. Ry. Co. v. Radford, 129 P. 834, 837 (Okla. 1913). Other cases holding the employer liable for the tort of the employee include: Ada-Konawa Bridge Co. v. Cargo, 21 P.2d 1 (Okla. 1932) (the servant of the toll bridge company shot an automobile driver when he drove past the toll gate and failed to pay the toll); Russell-Locke Super-Service v. Vaughn, 40 P.2d 1090 (Okla. 1935) (the servant of a corporation selling and servicing automobile batteries injured the plaintiff in a fight after the servant tried to repossess a battery from the plaintiff's vehicle); Mistletoe Express Service v. Culp, 353 P.2d 9 (Okla. 1959) (the servant for a common carrier of freight assaulted the plaintiff when he refused to accept a television tube after the common carrier denied the plaintiff's claim for damage in transit); and Rodebush v. Oklahoma Nursing Homes, Ltd., 867 P.2d 1241 (Okla. 1993) (the employee of a nursing home forcefully slapped a combative male Alzheimer's patient while bathing the patient).

Cases holding the employer was not liable for the tort of the employee include: Hill v. McQueen, 230 P.2d 483 (Okla. 1951) (the manager of a seed company assaulted a former independent sales contractor after the two got into an argument over a disputed debt); Oklahoma Ry. Co. v. Sandford, 258 P.2d 604 (Okla. 1953) (bus driver for bus company left his bus parked and assaulted the driver of an automobile and held him for arrest after the bus driver concluded he was drunk); Tulsa General Drivers, Warehousemen, and Helpers Union, Local No. 523 v. Conley, 288 P.2d 750 (Okla. 1955) (the agent of the union was picketing a business but left to follow the plaintiff four and one-half blocks to beat him with a board studded with nails, because he had crossed the picket line); Allison v. Gilmore, Gardner & Kirk, Inc., 350 P.2d 287 (Okla. 1960) (a gasoline truck driver was employed by the defendant to drive a truck and deliver gasoline, and while fulfilling those duties, assaulted the plaintiff who was climbing on the gasoline truck); and N.H. v. Presbyterian Church (U.S.A.), 998 P.2d 592 (Okla. 1999) (a Presbyterian minister molested minors, including the plaintiff, during recreational activities aimed at recruiting new members and their families).

The Court in *N.H. v. Presbyterian Church (U.S.A.)* distinguished the facts in that case from those in *Rodebush*. The Court observed that the attendant who was bathing the Alzheimer's patient acted impulsively when he slapped the combative patient, but that the impulse naturally arose from the situation he had been placed in by the employer, which was to complete the patient's bath. But the minister acted for his own personal gratification rather than for any religious purpose.

In the *Hill* case, the Court distinguished it from the *Ada-Konawa Bridge* and *Radford* cases. It was the employee's duty to obtain payment of the toll, in *Ada-Konawa Bridge*, and the train fare in *Radford*. The employee was to withhold the enjoyment of the right or privilege, if payment was not obtained. Since successful performance involved some type of immediate action in opposition to the will of the other, the employer could have anticipated the wrongful acts taken. In contrast, the Court held that McQueen's assault on Hill could not be properly contemplated as an incident to the exercise of ordinary authority to collect indebtedness.

The question of whether or not a servant should be considered to have been acting within the line of duty sufficient to support respondeat superior liability is normally a question of fact to be determined by the jury from all the surrounding circumstances. . . . Only when one reasonable conclusion can be drawn from the facts is it appropriate for a court to rule on a respondeat superior issue as a matter of law. Of course, it is a plaintiff's burden to show that the employee was acting within the scope of employment.

In the instant case, the answer to the respondeat superior issue primarily lies in determining whether Davis had stepped aside from her employment at the time of the offending tortious act(s) on some mission or conduct to serve her own personal needs, motivations or purposes. Our view of the instant matter is consistent with Rest. 2d Agency §245 (1958), comment f at 541, which provides

> f. Servant actuated by personal motives. The liability of a master for the use of force by a servant is not prevented by the fact that the servant acts in part because of a personal motive, such as revenge. The master, however, is relieved from liability under the rule stated in this Section if the servant has no intent to act on his master's behalf, although the events from which the tortious act follows arise while the servant is acting in the employment and the servant becomes angry because of them. The fact that the servant acts in an outrageous manner or inflicts a punishment out of all proportion to the necessities of his master's business is evidence indicating that the servant has departed from the scope of employment in performing the act.

In our view, a jury, as fact-finder (assuming the parties do not waive a jury trial) must decide if Davis's acts were so far removed from any work-related endeavor and geared, instead, toward a personal course of conduct unrelated to her work so that it would no longer be appropriate to hold her employer responsible for her act(s). Therefore, the purpose or motivation behind Davis's act(s) is an important, and potentially an overriding, consideration permeating resolution of arriving at a correct answer to the respondeat superior question. The statement on the plea document does not unequivocally answer the motivation question. In other words, one cannot tell from the words used in the plea document ("I hit Summers (sic) head against the cubby; she was crying she wouldn't stop crying") the purpose or motivation underpinning the act(s) of hitting the infant's head against the shelf (i.e., the cubby). Was it in whole or in part a misguided attempt to quiet the infant or, was it a conscious attempt to harm or injure the child because of Davis's own personal irritation or annoyance at the child? If the latter, the employer would not be liable under the doctrine of respondeat superior; if the former a jury (under appropriate instructions), as fact-finder, might be warranted in finding employer liable under the respondeat superior doctrine.

We hold the issue concerning appellee's respondeat superior liability for the act(s) of Davis in hitting Summer's head against the shelf (the cubby) is not one subject to determination as a matter of law on the instant summary judgment record. We also hold that the issue regarding any injury resulting from a fall remains in controversy and summary judgment on it was improper. Accordingly, the judgment of the trial court is reversed and the cause is remanded for proceedings not inconsistent with this opinion.

[Lavender, Hargrave, Opala, Kauger, and Edmondson concurred. Watt, Winchester, Taylor, and Colbert dissented.]

PREPARING FOR CLASS

1. Generally, employers are not vicariously liable for the intentional torts of their employees. Why is that?

2. When will an employer be vicariously liable for an employee's intentional tort? What do the Oklahoma cases finding such liability have in common? How are they different from the cases where no vicarious liability was found?

3. The court found the pleading documents not sufficiently clear to find no vicarious liability as a matter of law. What facts would help the defendant at trial? What facts would help the plaintiff at trial?

APPLYING THE LAW

1. A bouncer at a bar tosses an abusive, drunken patron out onto the curb and kicks him. Is the bar vicariously liable for the battery?

2. A big-box store employee sees his former high school algebra teacher whom he despises. He falsely accuses the teacher of shoplifting and detains him for 30 minutes. Is the store vicariously liable for the false imprisonment?

3. A big-box store employee mistakenly believes a customer put merchandise inside her sweatshirt. He detains her for longer than is reasonable. Is the store vicariously liable for the false imprisonment?

B. INDEPENDENT CONTRACTORS

Mavrikidis v. Petullo
707 A.2d 977 (N.J. 1998)

GARIBALDI, J.

In this case, we revisit the parameters of the vicarious liability doctrine as it pertains to whether a contractee may be vicariously liable for the negligence of its independent contractor. . . .

I

This case arose from an automobile accident that resulted in severe injury to plaintiff Alice Mavrikidis (Mavrikidis or plaintiff), including second- and third-degree burns over twenty-one percent of her body. On September 11, 1990, the intersection collision occurred after defendant Gerald Petullo, operating a dump truck registered to Petullo Brothers, Inc. (Petullo Brothers), drove through a red light, struck plaintiff's car, hit a telephone pole, and then overturned, spilling the truck's contents onto Mavrikidis's car. At the time of the accident, Gerald was transporting 10.99 tons of hot asphalt, which had been loaded onto the truck by Newark Asphalt Corporation (Newark Asphalt), to his job site at Clar Pine Servicenter (Clar Pine), a retail gasoline and automotive repair shop in Montclair.

Prior to the accident, Clar Pine's owner, Karl Pascarello (Pascarello), decided to renovate the station because he was switching gasoline brands from Getty to Gulf Oil. Those renovations included the installation of new pumps and canopies. . . .

Because Pascarello had no experience in the construction or paving business, he hired Gerald's father, Angelo Petullo, to perform the asphalt and concrete work as part of the renovation of his service station. Pascarello had known Angelo since 1972 and, prior to hiring him, Pascarello examined other paving jobs that Angelo had completed. Pascarello hired Angelo by verbal agreement to participate in the station's renovations based on Angelo's reputation as an excellent mason and, to a lesser extent, the debt owed Clar Pine under the Petullo Brothers' account. Over the years, Angelo and Gerald had charged gas and small repairs to their company account. In exchange for the asphalt work, both parties orally agreed that the Petullos would receive a $6,800 credit toward a $12,000 to $20,000 debt that Petullo Brothers had accumulated. . . .

The Petullos supplied the labor, equipment, concrete, and most of the asphalt needed for the job, until Angelo "ran out of money" in the midst of the renovations. As a result, Pascarello provided him with a blank check made out to Newark Asphalt to purchase the asphalt on the day of the accident. Pascarello testified that he supplied Angelo with a check because he "[was] the type of person you don't give cash to." Nevertheless, it is undisputed that Pascarello was not involved in supervising the Petullos' work on a daily basis. Other than general supervision and periodic consultation, Pascarello's limited participation in the asphalt work consisted of payment for three loads of asphalt, including the one involved in this accident, as well as his direction to lay the asphalt in front of the service station's bay doors first to enable him to continue his automotive repairs while the gas station was out of service. As part of its regular course of business, Clar Pine repaired cars and small trucks. During completion of the paving job, Clar Pine remained open for business, servicing cars but not selling gasoline.

II

The first question is whether Clar Pine is vicariously liable for plaintiff's injuries. As we explained in [Majestic Realty Associates, Inc. v. Toti Contracting Co., 30 N.J. 425, 153 A.2d 321 (1959)] the resolution of this issue must be approached with an awareness of the long settled doctrine that ordinarily where a person engages a contractor, who conducts an independent business by means of his own employees, to do work not in itself a nuisance (as our cases put it), he is not liable for the negligent acts of the contractor in the performance of the contract.

See also Bahrle v. Exxon Corp., 145 N.J. 144, 156, 678 A.2d 225 (1996) ("Ordinarily, an employer that hires an independent contractor is not liable for the negligent acts of the contractor in the performance of the contract."); Baldasarre v. Butler, 132 N.J. 278, 291, 625 A.2d 458 (1993) ("Generally . . . the principal is not vicariously liable for the torts of the independent contractor if the principal did not direct or participate in them.").

The initial inquiry in our analysis is to examine the status of the Petullos in relation to Clar Pine. Despite plaintiff's alternate theories to the contrary, the Petullos were independent contractors rather than servants of Clar Pine.

> The important difference between an employee and an independent contractor is that one who hires an independent contractor "has no right

of control over the manner in which the work is to be done, it is to be regarded as the contractor's own enterprise, and he, rather than the employer is the proper party to be charged with the responsibility for preventing the risk, and administering and distributing it."

[*Baldasarre, supra,* 132 N.J. at 291, 625 A.2d 458 (*quoting* W. Page Keeton, *Prosser & Keeton on the Law of Torts* §71 (5th ed. 1984)).]

In contrast, a servant is traditionally one who is "employed to perform services in the affairs of another, whose physical conduct in the performance of the service is controlled, or is subject to a right of control, by the other." W. Page Keeton, *Prosser & Keeton, supra,* §70 at 501.

In determining whether a contractee maintains the right of control, several factors are to be considered. The Restatement (Second) of Agency sets forth these factors, including:

(a) the extent of control which, by the agreement, the master may exercise over the details of the work;

(b) whether or not the one employed is engaged in a distinct occupation or business;

[The court omits factor c, which considers whether the person was hired to do the kind of work that in that locale is usually done by unsupervised specialists or by employees under an employer's direction.]

(d) the skill required in the particular occupation;

(e) whether the employer or the workman supplies the instrumentalities, tools, and the place of work for the person doing the work;

(f) the length of time for which the person is employed;

(g) the method of payment, whether by the time or by the job;

(h) whether or not the work is a part of the regular business of the employer; [and]

(i) whether or not the parties believe they are creating the relation of master and servant. . . .

[Restatement (Second) of Agency §220(2) (1958).]

Applying those Restatement factors, it is evident that neither Angelo nor Gerald was a servant of Clar Pine. The masonry work required a skilled individual. Although Pascarello paid for three loads of asphalt, the Petullos provided their own tools and the remainder of the needed materials, other than bolts and plywood supplied by Pascarello to install the canopies. Their work did not involve the regular business of Clar Pine. In addition, the period of employment spanned only the time it took to lay the asphalt and concrete. Following the accident, the Petullos continued the job for which they were hired, which was approved by the Building Inspector of Montclair. In exchange for their services, the Petullos were not paid by the hour or month; instead, they received a discharge of the portion of their debt.

Based on that threshold determination, we now must determine whether this case falls within any exceptions to the general rule of nonliability of principals/contractees for the negligence of their independent contractors. There are three such exceptions, as delineated by the *Majestic* Court: "(a) where the landowner [or principal] retains control of the manner and means of the doing of the work which is the subject of the contract; (b) where he engages an incompetent contractor; or (c) where . . . the activity contracted for [is inherently dangerous]."

III

We now discuss each of the *Majestic* exceptions in turn. Under the first *Majestic* exception, the reservation of control "of the manner and means" of the contracted work by the principal permits the imposition of vicarious liability. "In such a case the employer is responsible for the negligence of the independent contractor even though the particular control exercised and its manner of exercise had no causal relationship with the hazard that led to the injury, just as in the case of a simple employer-employee situation." Bergquist v. Penterman, 46 N.J. Super. 74, 85, 134 A.2d 20 (App. Div.), certif. denied, 25 N.J. 55, 134 A.2d 832 (1957). Under that test, the reservation of control over the equipment to be used, the manner or method of doing the work, or direction of the employees of the independent contractor may permit vicarious liability. Trecartin v. Mahony-Troast Constr. Co., 18 N.J. Super. 380, 387, 87 A.2d 349 (App. Div. 1952), aff'd, 21 N.J. 1, 120 A.2d 733 (1956).

However, supervisory acts performed by the contractee will not give rise to vicarious liability under that exception. As indicated by the language of the exception, application of principles of respondeat superior are not warranted where the contractee's "supervisory interest relates [only] to the result to be accomplished, not to the means of accomplishing it." *Majestic, supra*, 30 N.J. at 431, 153 A.2d 321; *see also* Marion v. Public Serv. Elec. & Gas Co., 72 N.J. Super. 146, 154-55, 178 A.2d 57 (App. Div. 1962) (explaining that retention of broad supervisory power rather than "right to direct and control" did not subject contractee to vicarious liability for independent contractor's actions); *Trecartin*, supra, 18 N.J. Super. at 386, 87 A.2d 349 (recognizing that "[a] general contractor . . . exercising only such general superintendence as is necessary to see that the subcontractor performs the contract, ordinarily has no duty to protect an employee of the subcontractor").

Pascarello's actions did not exceed the scope of general supervisory powers so as to subject Clar Pine to vicarious liability for Gerald's negligence. Providing blueprints, paying for some of the asphalt, and directing that a portion of the concrete be completed first are clearly within the scope of a contractee's broad supervisory powers. . . .

IV

Under the second *Majestic* exception, a principal may be held liable for injury caused by its independent contractor where the principal hires an incompetent contractor. As the Appellate Division explained in this case, "[t]he gravamen of th[is] exception is selection of a contractor who is incompetent. The selection of a competent contractor who negligently causes injury, does not render a [principal] liable." No presumption as to the negligence of an employer in hiring an independent contractor arises from the fact that, after being hired, the contractor is negligent in the performance of his duties and injures the person or property of another. *See* Reuben I. Friedman, Annotation, *When is Employer Chargeable with Negligence in Hiring Careless, Reckless, or Incompetent Independent Contractor*, 78 A.L.R.3d 910, 919 (1977). . . .

Because the second *Majestic* prong may include causes of action for both direct and vicarious liability, there is no reason to set out a separate tort for negligently hiring an independent contractor. To hold an employer liable under the second Majestic exception to the general rule of nonliability of principals for the negligence of their independent contractors, it is necessary to show both (1) that the contractor was incompetent or unskilled to perform the job for which he was hired, and (2) that the principal knew or had reason to know of the contractor's incompetence. The Petullos were skilled and experienced paving contractors. There is no evidence that the Petullos were unqualified to perform the masonry work for which they were hired. In fact, Pascarello visited other job sites that Angelo had paved in order to check the quality of his work. Viewing the evidence most favorably to plaintiffs, we find that the evidence does not support a finding that the Petullos were incompetent to perform the paving work for which they were engaged; hence, there is no basis for holding Clar Pine liable, either vicariously or directly, for plaintiff's injuries. . . .

V

Next, we consider the application of the third *Majestic* exception — whether the work engaged in by Petullo Brothers was inherently dangerous. In formulating this exception, the *Majestic* Court explained,

> where work is to be done that may endanger others, there is no real hardship in holding the party for whom it is done responsible for neglect in doing it. Though he may not be able to do it himself, or intelligently supervise it, he will nevertheless be the more careful in selecting an agent to act for him.
>
> We observed that . . . work can be considered to be inherently dangerous if it is an activity which can be carried on safely only by the exercise of special skill and care, and which involves grave risk of danger

to persons or property if negligently done. The term signifies that danger inheres in the activity itself at all times, so as to require special precautions to be taken with regard to it to avoid injury. It means more than simply danger arising from the casual or collateral negligence of persons engaged in it under particular circumstances.

The definition of inherently dangerous set forth in *Majestic* comports with the discussion in sections 413, 416, and 427 of the Restatement (Second) of Torts (1965) regarding a contractee's nondelegable duty to take special precautions against dangers that arise from inherently dangerous work. The comments and illustrations following those sections explain that in cases in which the work relates to the transport of materials, the contractee is not responsible for the ordinary risks or dangers associated with faulty brakes or poor driving. In discussing the meaning of "[p]eculiar risk and special precautions," comment b to section 413 states:

> It is obvious that an employer of an independent contractor may always anticipate that if the contractor is in any way negligent toward third persons, some harm to such persons may result. Thus one who hires a trucker to transport his goods must, as a reasonable man, always realize that if the truck is driven at an excessive speed, or with defective brakes, some collision or other harm to persons on the highway is likely to occur.... [Routine] precautions are the responsibility of the contractor....

A peculiar risk is different "from the common risks to which persons in general are commonly subjected by the ordinary forms of negligence." Id. §416 comment d. As a result, "the [contractee] is not liable for the contractor's failure to inspect the brakes on his truck, or for his driving in excess of the speed limit, because the risk is in no way a peculiar one, and only an ordinary precaution is called for."

In Ek v. Herrington, 939 F.2d 839 (9th Cir.1991), the Ninth Circuit applied the three sections of the Restatement (Second) of Torts discussed above. In that case, decedent's heirs sued an independent contractor, who was hired to haul logs, and the owner of the logging operation, after the logs broke loose from the truck, landing on decedent's vehicle and causing her death. There, the brakes on the truck were defective and the truck was overloaded by at least 10,000 pounds. Addressing the issue of whether vicarious liability should be imposed on the logging operation for the hauler's negligence, the court held:

> We accept the Restatement's suggestion that the risk posed by malfunctioning brakes is an ordinary one that an employer of an independent contractor has no duty to provide against. Similarly, we hold that the risk posed by overloading a logging truck is not a peculiar

risk that arises in the normal course of logging and for which special precautions must be taken. It is a risk that would not arise, but for the independent contractor's negligence, and which can be avoided by the ordinary precaution of not overloading the truck. An employer of an independent contractor is justified in presuming that a careful contractor will not create that risk. . . . The duty rests solely on the shoulders of the independent contractor.

Moreover, in a case with facts almost identical to those presented here, a California appellate court refused to impose vicarious liability on a contractee whose independent contractor struck and killed the plaintiff's decedent with his dump truck, which was loaded with asphalt. A. Teichert & Son, Inc. v. Superior Court, 179 Cal. App. 3d 657, 225 Cal. Rptr. 10 (1986). In its decision, the court noted that "[the truck driver's] negligence, if any, entailed nothing more than ordinary failure to exercise due care in the operation of a motor vehicle. This is not sufficient to invoke the 'special risk' exception to the rule of non-liability for the negligence of an independent contractor." . . .

PREPARING FOR CLASS

1. Why is the first issue whether the Petullos were independent contractors or employees of Clar Pine?

2. How do courts distinguish between employees and independent contractors? Must a plaintiff trying to establish an employee-employer relationship establish all the factors from the Restatement of Agency?

3. Why were the Petullos independent contractors?

4. What kind of reservation of control will impose vicarious liability on the principal who hires an independent contractor?

5. How is the second exception, hiring an incompetent contractor, like a direct negligence action?

6. What must the plaintiff prove to demonstrate that the defendant comes within the second exception? Could the plaintiff demonstrate that here?

7. What must the plaintiff demonstrate to satisfy the third exception — inherently dangerous activity? What is the difference between a common risk and a peculiar one, and why does the difference matter? Why was the risk in *Ek* merely common?

8. Was hauling the asphalt inherently dangerous?

9. Why do you suppose hiring the independent contractor to perform an inherently dangerous activity is one of the exceptions to the no-liability rule?

INCREASING YOUR UNDERSTANDING

The principal who hires an independent contractor is generally not liable for the torts of the independent contractor. The *Mavrikidis* case, however, has pointed out some exceptions to that rule. Another exception is when the principal has hired the agent to carry out a statutory duty of the principal. Statutory duties are also non-delegable. For example, in Maloney v. Rath, 445 P.2d 513 (Cal. 1968), the plaintiff was injured in an automobile accident caused by the failure of the defendant's brakes. Three months before the accident a mechanic had overhauled the defendant's brakes, and the accident was due to his negligence, not the defendant's. The mechanic was a classic independent contractor (run through the factors from *Mavrikidis* and see why), but the defendant was nonetheless vicariously liable for his negligent brake repair because the California vehicle code required car owners to keep their brakes "in good working order." Although the defendant could delegate the work—she didn't have to repair her own brakes—she could not delegate the financial responsibility for poor brake repair to her independent contractor.

APPLYING THE LAW

1. Davis owns the Desert View Apartments and four other apartment complexes. Years ago, when his brother-in-law, Ben, was out of work, Davis told Ben, "Get some training, and you can do the pool maintenance at my apartments." Ben took a Certified Pool Operator course, which Davis paid for. For a couple of years, Ben worked only at apartments owned by Davis. But after awhile, Ben hired an assistant and began servicing a few other pools in the area as well. Because pools require daily attention, many apartment complexes, hotels, motels, and clubs in the area train their own employees to maintain pools and supplement their work with occasional visits from pool service companies. No one at Desert View oversees Ben's work. He is expected to keep the pool clean and the pH balance correct and to watch out for and repair any damaged parts of the pool. Ben is paid a monthly fee for caring for the five swimming pools. He receives no benefits. Ben noticed that the drain cover in the pool was broken, but he did not replace it. This negligence led to serious injuries to a boy who was caught in the strong suction of the pool pump. The boy has sued Davis in respondeat superior. How will the boy's lawyer contend that Ben is an employee? How will Davis contend that Ben is an independent contractor?

2. A man kept a pair of tigers in a pen on a two-acre compound. He retained an independent contractor, an exotic pet sitting service, to feed and otherwise tend to the tigers. One day, the pet sitters negligently

left the cage door ajar, and a tiger escaped and mauled a child on the neighboring property. Would the man be vicariously liable for the negligence of the pet sitting service?

3.   The aging rock band, You Brutus, was reduced to gigs at county fairs and small clubs. They were booked for a weekend run at The Gallery, a nightclub in Springfield, Michiana. The booking contract paid You Brutus $1,500 per night and specified only "2 70-minute sets per night, must include at least 2 hit songs per set and stage fireworks—must follow local and state regulations." Michiana state fire statutes required all owners of public venues that displayed interior fireworks to use only licensed pyrotechnicians and to follow various specified safety guidelines. On Friday evening, in the final song of the first set, Yale Brown, tour manager for the band, set off stage fireworks, which he had purchased and brought to the gig. Brown was not a licensed pyrotechnician, and he did not follow the interior-fireworks guidelines established by Michiana statutes. The fireworks created sparks behind the stage, and the sparks ignited the polyurethane-foam panels on the ceiling and walls surrounding the stage. Within minutes, the entire building was on fire and more than 200 people were struggling to escape the crowded, dark, and smoky club. Several of the exits were blocked. There was no fire extinguisher. There were no sprinklers—state law did not require them for this building. Fifty people died. More than 100 were injured. Many of the injured and survivors of the dead have filed lawsuits against The Gallery. Many of those suits have counts seeking to hold The Gallery vicariously liable for the band's negligence. The Gallery is seeking to have those counts dismissed. What is The Gallery's argument against vicarious liability? What is the plaintiffs' response?

C. JOINT ENTERPRISE

Blackburn v. Columbia Medical Center
58 S.W.3d 263 (Tex. App. 2001)

GARDNER, J.

[The plaintiff, Blackburn, sought to hold Columbia Medical Center vicariously liable for the medical malpractice of Dr. Noss, a radiologist furnished by Medical Imaging under a contract with Columbia. The trial court granted summary judgment to Columbia, and the plaintiff appealed.]

Generally, a hospital is not liable for injuries resulting from the negligence of a physician who is an independent contractor rather than an employee or servant of the hospital. Whether a physician is an independent contractor rather than an employee depends upon whether the employer has the right to control the progress, details, and methods of operation of the physician's work. The employer must control not only the end result but also the means and details of the accomplishment of the result. Generally, the diagnoses and performance of medical procedures are within the province of the physician's judgment and not subject to a hospital's control. The fact that a physician has staff privileges and agrees to abide by the hospital's policies and procedures while utilizing its equipment and facilities does not affect the physician's status as an independent contractor.

Blackburn does not contend that Dr. Noss was acting as an employee of Columbia so as to invoke the doctrine of respondeat superior. Instead, Blackburn seeks to impose vicarious liability on Columbia by imputing the liability of Dr. Noss to Medical Imaging and, in turn, imputing Medical Imaging's liability to Columbia under the theory of joint enterprise. We disagree with Blackburn, however, that the summary judgment evidence provided raises the issue of joint enterprise.

Joint enterprise liability, as applied to joint undertakings, makes "each party thereto the agent of the other and thereby . . . hold[s] each responsible for the negligent act of the other." Tex. Dep't of Transp. v. Able, 35 S.W.3d 608, 613 (Tex. 2000); Shoemaker v. Estate of Whistler, 513 S.W.2d 10, 14 (Tex. 1974). Although earlier Texas cases had applied a broad interpretation of the doctrine of joint enterprise including situations involving family or friendly cooperation and accommodation, in *Shoemaker*, the Texas Supreme Court limited the doctrine to the definition in comment c of the Restatement (Second) of Torts section 491. Comment c expressly sets forth four essential elements for the doctrine of joint enterprise, and limits application of the doctrine to enterprises having a business or commercial purpose. The Restatement states, in pertinent part:

> [t]he elements which are essential to a joint enterprise are commonly stated to be four: (1) an agreement, express or implied, among the members of the group; (2) a common purpose to be carried out by the group; (3) a community of pecuniary interest in that purpose, among the members; and (4) an equal right to a voice in the direction of the enterprise, which gives an equal right of control.

1. AGREEMENT, EXPRESS OR IMPLIED, AMONG THE MEMBERS OF THE GROUP

The first element of the theory of joint enterprise, as adopted in *Shoemaker*, requires that the two entities involved have an agreement, either express or implied. It is undisputed that Medical Imaging and Columbia had an agreement. Prior to Blackburn's treatment at Columbia, Medical Imaging and Columbia executed a diagnostic radiology agreement under which Medical Imaging became obligated to provide physicians specializing in radiology, referred to as "Associates," to perform radiology services on patients in Columbia's radiology department. . . . The summary judgment evidence demonstrates that there was an express agreement between the parties.

2. A COMMON PURPOSE TO BE CARRIED OUT BY THE GROUP

A joint enterprise also requires that the two entities involved have a common purpose. As evidenced by the written agreement between Columbia and Medical Imaging, the purpose of the department of radiology at Columbia was to provide radiological services for patients of the hospital. . . .

3. COMMUNITY OF PECUNIARY INTEREST IN THE COMMON PURPOSE

A community of pecuniary interest is essential to the existence of a joint enterprise. The supreme court has limited the element of "common purpose" to those endeavors in which the parties share a "community of pecuniary interest" involving a business or pecuniary purpose. "Common" in this context means sharing without special or distinguishing characteristics.

On the one hand, Blackburn contends that . . . deposition excerpts of Dr. Railey and Dr. Chacko . . . support . . . her argument that the summary judgment record establishes the existence of a commercially and financially "symbiotic" relationship between the two entities.

Columbia, on the other hand, argues that the summary judgment record wholly fails to show evidence of a community of pecuniary interest between Columbia and Medical Imaging because there was no evidence that they agreed to share in profits and losses. In this regard, Columbia relies principally upon statements from cases discussing sharing of financial "benefits and costs." See *Shoemaker*, 513 S.W.2d at 14 (quoting Prosser, *Law of Torts* §69, 458 (4th ed. 1971)) (finding that a joint venture exists "[w]here the enterprise is for some commercial or business purpose, and particularly where the parties have agreed to share profits and losses."). However, we decline to accept such a narrow interpretation of the element of community of pecuniary interest.

A. NO REQUIREMENT TO SHOW SHARING OF PROFITS AND LOSSES

We are mindful that the doctrines of partnership, joint venture, and joint enterprise are closely related and that those doctrines each spring from the roots of partnership law. Those doctrines, however, are not without distinction. The *Shoemaker* court described the distinction between a partnership, a joint venture, and a joint enterprise, as follows:

> By way of history, we know that the law of partnership and the principles of agency serve as a foundation for the doctrine of joint enterprise.

A step away from partnership is joint venture, a concept that is generally more limited in time and in purpose than a partnership. While a joint venture encompasses fewer objectives than a partnership, both exist in a business or commercial setting. Joint enterprise, which may be considered a third stage of development, is an unique creation of American jurisprudence. American courts have applied this doctrine almost solely in the field of automobile law; in interpreting joint enterprise, some courts have retained the business character of joint venture as a requirement, while others have manifested a broader view of the doctrine. The pecuniary interest requirement has been most often imposed in the context of imputed contributory negligence and it has been said that this is the direction toward which the courts are tending to move.

After making this distinction, the *Shoemaker* court went on to adopt the commercial characterization of joint enterprise as set forth in the Restatement (Second) of Torts, effectively limiting the traditionally broad application of joint enterprise liability to enterprises having a business or pecuniary purposes.

As a general rule, joint venture is governed by the same rules as a partnership and vice versa. According to the Texas Supreme Court, to establish a partnership or joint venture, a party must establish each of the following elements: (1) a community of interest in the venture; (2) an agreement to share profits; (3) an agreement to share losses; and (4) a mutual right of control or management of the enterprise. Sharing in profits and losses is an essential element of a joint venture.

As characterized by the supreme court in *Shoemaker*, joint enterprise is not the same as joint venture and is not governed by the rules applicable to joint ventures. As noted above, the supreme court has established a separate set of elements for joint enterprise that are similar to, but different from, the elements of joint venture enterprise. Sharing of profits and losses is not listed as one of the essential elements of joint enterprise. The court of appeals' decision in *Able*, affirmed by the supreme court, noted that "the elements required to establish a joint enterprise, as distinguished from a joint venture, do not require proof of the sharing of profits and losses." Tex. Dep't Transp. v. Able, 981 S.W.2d 765, 769 (Tex. App.-Houston [1st Dist.] 1998), aff'd, 35 S.W.3d 608 (Tex. 2000).

In *Able*, the supreme court held that sufficient evidence supported the jury's finding that the Texas Department of Transportation ("TxDOT") and the Houston Metropolitan Transit Authority were engaged in a joint enterprise as to a particular highway project. In reaching its decision as to the element of community pecuniary interest, the court looked to evidence that the master agreement between TxDOT and the transit authority plainly recognized that the project contemplated a joint effort that utilized federal, state, and local funds; shared resources in furtherance of the ultimate purposes of providing mass transit; and realized an economic gain on the investment. The court also found it noteworthy that monetary and personnel savings produced from pooling of resources might have been substantial and that the project was not a matter of mere friendly or family cooperation and accommodation.

Citing its prior decision in *Shoemaker*, the *Able* court reaffirmed that there must be a community of pecuniary interest in the purpose of the joint undertaking –not necessarily in the sharing of profits and losses. As noted above, the *Able* court relied principally on the "Master Agreement," which contained a specific provision contemplating a joint investment of resources by both entities in furtherance of the ultimate purposes of providing mass transit and realizing economic gain on the investment.

We fully acknowledge that the common purpose to be carried out by the group may certainly include making profits. *Shoemaker* expressly noted that some courts have articulated the element of community of pecuniary interest in terms "such as a 'common business purpose,' a 'common pecuniary objective,' or a 'venture for profit.' . . ." However, we do not read *Shoemaker* as requiring sharing of profits and losses in every case in order to establish the pecuniary interest element. Just because an agreement does not contemplate sharing of profits and losses, as a common purpose to be carried out by the group, does not mean that the pecuniary interest prerequisite is not met. . . .

We must, therefore, determine whether the summary judgment record contains any other evidence of a community of pecuniary interest in the common purpose to be carried out by the group, absent an agreement to share profits and losses, which raises an issue of material fact on this element to preclude summary judgment.

B. NO EVIDENCE OF COMMUNITY OF PECUNIARY INTEREST

The agreement between Columbia and Medical Imaging . . . places upon Medical Imaging the exclusive responsibility for payment of its respective income tax, vacation pay, sick leave, unemployment insurance, worker's compensation, retirement benefits, disability benefits, and any other employee benefits. The agreement expressly states that Medical Imaging and its Associates shall not incur any financial obligation on behalf of Columbia without prior written approval by Columbia's president/chief executive officer. The agreement makes Medical Imaging responsible for all personnel and professional expenses of its Associates.

Columbia is exclusively responsible for employing or assigning all non-physician personnel necessary for the operation of the Radiology Department and is, likewise, exclusively responsible for providing their salaries, wages, taxes, insurance, worker's compensation insurance, and other expenses and benefits incidental to their employment. Medical Imaging is expressly forbidden to bill hospital patients for any care rendered by Columbia's non-physician personnel. During the term of the agreement, Columbia provides the space, utilities, equipment, supplies, and services necessary for the proper operation of the Radiology

Department. The hospital has the responsibility to maintain the necessary equipment in good order and repair. Finally, Medical Imaging is responsible for establishing its own schedule of fees and services and its sole source of compensation is its own collection of fees from its patients. . . .

Both Dr. Railey and Dr. Chacko testified regarding the same symbiotic relationship. Columbia benefitted from its agreement with Medical Imaging by staffing its radiology department in-house, eliminating the need for patients to obtain radiological services off premises, and Medical Imaging benefitted by letting the hospital provide the facilities and equipment for Medical Imaging physicians to provide radiological services. However, evidence of such general benefits does not establish a community of pecuniary interest in the common purpose to be carried out by the group. . . .

In determining whether a community of pecuniary interest existed such as to give rise to a joint enterprise, the supreme court in *Able* focused upon evidence showing pooling of efforts and monetary resources between entities to achieve common purposes, namely reduction in costs and contemplation of economic gain by approaching the project as a joint undertaking. The master agreement in *Able* clearly acknowledged these purposes and was relied upon by the court in holding that some evidence of a joint enterprise existed between the contracting parties. *Able* confirms that more is required for a community of pecuniary interest than a generally shared business purpose.

Here, there was absolutely no evidence regarding either party's pecuniary or monetary interest in the agreement, much less a community of pecuniary interest. In fact, the summary judgment evidence provided conclusively disproves any community of pecuniary interest, as it supports an independent contractor relationship. Further, there was no evidence to show a sharing of resources, pooling of funds, monetary investment, costs or benefits to either party. Nothing more than limited evidence of mere convenience to the parties arising from the arrangement and a shared general business interest is shown. . . .

Viewing the summary judgment record in the light most favorable to Blackburn, the party against whom summary judgment was rendered, and disregarding all contrary evidence and inferences, we believe that Blackburn failed to bring forward more than a scintilla of probative evidence that raises a genuine issue of material fact regarding the existence of a community of pecuniary interest between Columbia and Medical Imaging.

We hold that the trial court properly granted . . . summary judgment[] in favor of Columbia on the ground of lack of a community of pecuniary interest. . . .

PREPARING FOR CLASS

1. Why did Blackburn attempt to prove a joint enterprise—why was that a necessary strategy?

2. How are joint ventures and joint enterprises related to each other? How are they different? How does the difference matter to a plaintiff?

3. What are the elements of a joint enterprise? Does the case suggest that the rule might be different elsewhere?

4. Could Blackburn satisfy the first two elements of joint enterprise?

5. What does "community of pecuniary interest in the common purpose" mean? Does it require sharing profits and losses? Where did that idea come from?

6. What was Blackburn's evidence of the community of pecuniary interest? Was this adequate to reach a jury? Why or why not?

Triplex Communications, Inc. v. Riley
900 S.W.2d 716 (Tex. 1995)

Spector, Justice, delivered the opinion of the Court, in which all Justices join. . . .

For about seven years, KZZB-95 FM (B-95), a Beaumont radio station, and the Cowboy Palace, Inc. (the Palace) collaborated on a weekly event known as "B-95 Ladies Night at the Palace." B-95 advertised that Thursday night was Ladies' Night at the Palace, meaning that women aged twenty-one years or older would be admitted at no charge. The Palace pre-screened the radio advertisements, except for occasional promotional spots that it could later change. Consistent with the law and at the Palace's request, B-95 indicated in its spots that persons aged eighteen to twenty would be admitted into the establishment. The Palace's Thursday night bar drinks were ninety-five cents, a price set to correspond with B-95's 95.1 FM frequency.

B-95 and the Palace worked closely to make "B-95 Ladies' Night" successful. The Palace sought to increase patronage and B-95 sought advertising revenue. Toward this end, B-95 assigned a disc jockey to the Palace for live remote broadcasts during Ladies' Night. The on-site disc jockey was responsible for making announcements over the public address system informing patrons of drink specials and other promotions. The announcements encouraged patrons to go to the bar. There was evidence that B-95's disc jockey witnessed people becoming intoxicated at the Palace and was aware of underage drinking at the club. Over the seven-year relationship, there were a number of other promotional activities, including the appearance of B-95's mascot, the "Super Bee," at the Palace during Ladies' Night.

On the evening of June 30, 1988, Michael Edward Poupart, an underage patron of the Palace, was served ten alcoholic beverages. After leaving the Palace on the evening in question, Poupart was involved in a serious automobile accident caused by his intoxication. The Beaumont police responded, and officers James Riley and Mary Gray were responsible for directing traffic off of the freeway approximately 300 to 400 yards north of the accident.

During that same evening, Joseph Wayne Stephens arrived at the Palace sometime between 8:30 and 9:00 P.M. Vernis T. Dartez, a Palace bartender, served Stephens either sixteen or seventeen mixed drinks. Stephens, a regular at the Palace, exhibited signs that he was highly intoxicated while he was being served alcoholic beverages.

Stephens was on his way home and travelling at a high rate of speed when his car hit another car that had stopped at the scene of Poupart's accident. Stephens' car ricocheted off the other car and struck Riley and Gray. Stephens' blood-alcohol content was later determined to be substantially above the legal limit, and it is undisputed that Stephens caused the accident.

Officers Riley and Gray brought this action against the Palace, Dartez, and B-95/Triplex. [The trial court refused to instruct the jury on joint enterprise, and the plaintiffs lost.] The court of appeals reversed the judgment of the trial court, concluding that the trial court erred by failing to submit [the] questions on joint enterprise. . . .

Triplex . . . argues that the court of appeals erred in holding that Riley and Gray were entitled to a jury question on the issue of joint enterprise. We agree. . . .

Here, while Riley and Gray may have properly pleaded joint enterprise liability, the evidence adduced at trial was legally insufficient to support the submission of their tendered question.

Riley's and Gray's requested question asked whether B-95 and the Palace had: (1) an express agreement; (2) a common purpose; (3) a common pecuniary interest; and (4) an equal right to control the enterprise. Even if the evidence adduced at trial satisfied the first three prongs of this test, there is no evidence of an equal right to direct and control the enterprise to justify the imposition of joint enterprise liability.

Riley and Gray suggest that we define enterprise broadly, to encompass all of the business dealings between the Palace and B-95 relating to Ladies' Night. They argue that this expansive definition would reveal that B-95 exercised some control over the relationship, giving rise to some evidence of a joint enterprise. See *Shoemaker*, 513 S.W.2d at 15 (equal right of control means that each member of the joint venture must have an authoritative voice, or "must have some voice and right to be heard"); Restatement (Second) of Torts §491 (1965). Triplex, on the other hand, prefers to characterize its relationship with the Palace as one in which a radio station, through advertising and promotions, conducted ordinary business with a client. Under either characterization, however, whether there was a joint business venture or a simple advertiser-client relationship, there is no evidence that B-95 had an equal right of control that would give rise to joint enterprise liability.

To establish that B-95 exercised an equal right to control the business relationship, Riley and Gray place great emphasis on the fact that drink prices corresponded with B-95's FM frequency. Yet, it is undisputed that the

Palace—not B-95—set drink prices. Drinks were 95 cents on all nights except KYKR night, when they were 93 cents to correspond with that station's FM frequency.

The Palace, which was licensed to sell alcohol, maintained absolute control over the provision of all drinks. The proprietors of the Palace decided who was admitted and ejected from the Palace, controlled how much liquor was served and to whom it was served, and were best positioned to monitor the amount of liquor that patrons consumed. There was no evidence that B-95 had a contractual right of control, or exercised any right of control, over who was served, admitted, or ejected. Similarly, the Palace had no right to control the operation of the radio station.

At most, the evidence at trial indicated that B-95 could make suggestions that the Palace could adopt or reject. There was no evidence that B-95 had a voice in, or an equal right to control, the provision of the alcohol. The evidence of B-95's general participation in the event is legally insufficient to support the submission of a question regarding joint enterprise. . . .

PREPARING FOR CLASS

1. The court does not discuss the first three elements of joint enterprise. Do you think they were met?

2. What is required by the control element? What is it that the members must have the equal right to control? Must responsibilities be equally shared? Must it be equal control over the activity that caused the injury?

3. Could the plaintiffs establish that the radio station had the requisite control?

APPLYING THE LAW

1. Amber was a contestant in an "adult" beauty pageant held at The Delta, a night club. Fancy Promotions (Fancy) promoted the pageant. Based on rumors about Amber's attempts to rig the competition, The Delta banned Amber from its premises, which effectively eliminated her from the pageant. Amber sued The Delta for slander and tortious interference with business relations and sought to hold Fancy liable as well, under a joint enterprise theory.

    The Delta and Fancy were separate corporations. They had a written agreement regarding the pageant. Under the agreement The Delta had certain specified duties for the pageant, including providing the premises, keeping the stage clean, decorating, selecting the judges, providing dressing rooms and door prizes, providing a person to witness the tallying of votes, prohibiting disqualified contestants from entering the premises during the competition, and using their best efforts to ensure the pageant's success.

Under the agreement Fancy was required to give The Delta 50 percent of the profits from on-premises events, provide "audience favorite" ballots, provide emcees and coordinators, select most of the contestants (Delta was to provide two), provide prizes for the winners, and establish the contest rules. Also, Fancy was responsible for disqualifying contestants.

Should Fancy be vicariously liable for any torts committed by The Delta with regard to the pageant?

2. A 21-year-old pitcher for the Michiana State University (MSU) Falcons was struck in the temple by a line drive off the bat of a player for the Western Michiana University (WMU) Badgers and seriously injured. The WMU batter whose ball struck the pitcher was using an aluminum alloy bat, the Krebco Attacker. As part of an endorsement agreement with the WMU Athletic Department, the manufacturer, Krebco, provided the Attackers free to WMU and also compensated the WMU baseball program for using the Attackers exclusively. Such agreements are common. The MSU Falcons have an endorsement deal with Kentuckyville Swatters to use its Bomber II exclusively. The pitcher has brought a products liability claim against Krebco, claiming that the bat design was defectively dangerous because it produced exit speeds faster than human reaction time. The pitcher has also sought to hold WMU vicariously liable as a joint enterpriser with Krebco. Will that work?

Chapter 15

Products Liability

A. INTRODUCTION: PATHWAY TO MODERN PRODUCTS LIABILITY LAW

Thomas v. Winchester
6 N.Y. 397, (N.Y. 1852)

RUGGLES, Ch. J. delivered the opinion of the court.

This is an action brought to recover damages from the defendant for negligently putting up, labeling and selling as and for the extract of *dandelion*, which is a simple and harmless medicine, a jar of the extract of *belladonna*, which is a deadly poison; by means of which the plaintiff Mary Ann Thomas, to whom, being sick, a dose of dandelion was prescribed by a physician, and a portion of the contents of the jar, was administered as and for the extract of dandelion, was greatly injured, &c.

The facts proved were briefly these: Mrs. Thomas being in ill health, her physician prescribed for her a dose of dandelion. Her husband purchased what was believed to be the medicine prescribed, at the store of Dr. Foord, a physician and druggist in Cazenovia, Madison county, where the plaintiffs reside.

A small quantity of the medicine thus purchased was administered to Mrs. Thomas, on whom it produced very alarming effects; such as coldness of the surface and extremities, feebleness of circulation, spasms of the muscles, giddiness of the head, dilation of the pupils of the eyes, and derangement of mind. She recovered however, after some time, from its effects, although for a short time her life was thought to be in great danger. The medicine administered was *belladonna, and not dandelion*. The jar from which it was taken was labeled "*½ lb. dandelion, prepared by A. Gilbert, No. 108, John-street, N. Y. Jar 8 oz.*" It was sold for and believed by Dr. Foord to be the extract of dandelion as labeled. Dr. Foord purchased the article as the extract of dandelion from Jas. S. Aspinwall, a druggist at New-York. Aspinwall bought it of the defendant as extract of dandelion, believing it to be such. The defendant was engaged at No. 108 John-street, New-York, in the manufacture and sale of certain vegetable extracts for medicinal purposes, and in the purchase and sale of others. The extracts manufactured by him were put up in jars for sale, and those which he purchased were put up by him in like manner. The jars containing extracts manufactured by himself and those containing extracts purchased by him from others, were labeled alike. Both were labeled like the jar in question, as "prepared by A. Gilbert." Gilbert was a person employed by the defendant at a salary, as an assistant in his business. The jars were labeled in Gilbert's name because he had been previously engaged in the same business on his own account at No. 108 John-street, and probably because Gilbert's labels rendered the articles more salable. The extract contained in the jar sold to Aspinwall, and by him to Foord, was not manufactured by the defendant, but was purchased by him from another manufacturer or dealer. The extract of dandelion and the extract of belladonna resemble each other in color, consistence, smell and taste; but may on careful examination be distinguished the one from the other by those who are well acquainted with these articles. Gilbert's labels were paid for by Winchester and used in his business with his knowledge and assent.

The defendants' counsel moved for a nonsuit on the [ground that] the action could not be sustained, as the defendant was the remote vendor of the article in question: and there was no connection, transaction or privity between him and the plaintiffs, or either of them.

The judge among other things charged the jury, that if they should find from the evidence that either Aspinwall or Foord was guilty of negligence in vending as and for dandelion, the extract taken by Mrs. Thomas, or that the plaintiff Thomas, or those who administered it to Mrs. Thomas, were chargeable with negligence in administering it, the plaintiffs were not entitled to recover; but if they were free from negligence, and if the defendant Winchester was guilty of negligence in putting up and vending the extracts in question, the plaintiffs were entitled to recover, provided the extract administered to Mrs. Thomas was the same which was put up by the defendant and sold by him to Aspinwall and by Aspinwall to Foord. . . .

The action was properly brought in the name of the husband and wife for the personal injury and suffering of the wife; and the case was left to the jury with the proper directions on that point.

The case depends on the first point taken by the defendant on his motion for a nonsuit; and the question is, whether the defendant, being a remote vendor of the medicine, and there being no privity or connection between him and the plaintiffs, the action can be maintained.

If, in labeling a poisonous drug with the name of a harmless medicine, for public market, no duty was violated by the defendant, excepting that which he owed to Aspinwall, his immediate vendee, in virtue of his contract of sale, this action cannot be maintained. If A. build a wagon and sell it to B., who sells it to C., and C. hires it to D., who in consequence of the gross negligence of A. in building the wagon is overturned and injured, D. cannot recover damages against A., the builder. A.'s obligation to build the wagon faithfully arises solely out of his contract with B. The public have nothing to do with it. Misfortune to third persons, not parties to the contract, would not be a natural and necessary consequence of the builder's negligence; and such negligence is not an act imminently dangerous to human life.

So, for the same reason, if a horse be defectively shod by a smith, and a person hiring the horse from the owner is thrown and injured in consequence of the smith's negligence in shoeing; the smith is not liable for the injury. The smith's duty in such case grows exclusively out of his contract with the owner of the horse; it was a duty which the smith owed to him alone, and to no one else. And although the injury to the rider may have happened in consequence of the negligence of the smith, the latter was not bound, either by his contract or by any considerations of public policy or safety, to respond for his breach of duty to any one except the person he contracted with.

This was the ground on which the case of *Winterbottom v. Wright*, (10 *Mees. & Welsb.* 109,) was decided. A. contracted with the postmaster general to provide a coach to convey the mail bags along a certain line of road, and B. and others, also contracted to horse the coach along the same line. B. and his co-contractors hired C., who was the plaintiff, to drive the coach. The coach, in consequence of some latent defect, broke down; the plaintiff was thrown from his seat and lamed. It was held that C. could not maintain an action against A. for the injury thus sustained. The reason of the decision is best stated by Baron Rolfe. A.'s duty to keep the coach in good condition, was a duty to the postmaster general, with whom he made his contract, and not a duty to the driver employed by the owners of the horses.

But the case in hand stands on a different ground. The defendant was a dealer in poisonous drugs. Gilbert was his agent in preparing them for market. The death or great bodily harm of some person was the natural and almost inevitable consequence of the sale of belladonna by means of the false label.

Gilbert, the defendant's agent, would have been punishable for manslaughter if Mrs. Thomas had died in consequence of taking the falsely labeled medicine. Every man who, by his culpable negligence, causes the death of another, although without intent to kill, is guilty of manslaughter. (2 *R.S.* 662, §19.) A chemist who negligently sells laudanum in a phial labeled as paregoric, and thereby causes the death of a person to whom it is administered, is guilty of manslaughter. (*Tessymond's case*, 1 *Lewin's Crown Cases*, 169.) "So highly does the law value human life, that it admits of no justification wherever life has been lost and the carelessness or negligence of one person has contributed to the death of another. (*Regina v. Swindall*, 2 *Car. & Kir.* 232-3.) And this rule applies not only where the death of one is occasioned by the negligent act of another, but where it is caused by the negligent omission of a duty of that other. (2 *Car. & Kir.* 368, 371.) Although the defendant Winchester may not be answerable criminally for the negligence of his agent, there can be no doubt of his liability in a civil action, in which the act of the agent is to be regarded as the act of the principal.

In respect to the wrongful and criminal character of the negligence complained of, this case differs widely from those put by the defendant's counsel. No such imminent danger existed in those cases. In the present case the sale of the poisonous article was made to a dealer in drugs, and not to a consumer. The injury therefore was not likely to fall on him, or on his vendee who was also a dealer; but much more likely to be visited on a remote purchaser, as actually happened. The defendant's negligence put human life in imminent danger. Can it be said that there was no duty on the part of the defendant, to avoid the creation of that danger by the exercise of greater caution? or that the exercise of that caution was a duty only to his immediate vendee, whose life was not endangered? The defendant's duty arose out of the nature of his business and the danger to others incident to its mismanagement. Nothing but mischief like that which actually happened could have been expected from sending the poison falsely labeled into the market; and the defendant is justly responsible for the probable consequences of the act. The duty of exercising caution in this respect did not arise out of the defendant's contract of sale to Aspinwall. The wrong done by the defendant was in putting the poison, mislabeled, into the hands of Aspinwall as an article of merchandise to be sold and afterwards used as the extract of dandelion, by some person then unknown. The owner of a horse and cart who leaves them unattended in the street is liable for any damage which may result from his negligence. The owner of a loaded gun who puts it into the hands of a child by whose indiscretion it is discharged, is liable for the damage occasioned by the discharge. The defendant's contract of sale to Aspinwall does not excuse the wrong done to the plaintiffs. It was a part of the means by which the wrong was effected. The plaintiffs' injury and their remedy would have stood on the same principle, if the defendant had given the belladonna to Dr. Foord without price, or if he had put it in his shop without his knowledge, under circumstances which would probably have led to its sale on the faith of the label.

In *Longmeid v. Holliday,* (6 *Law and Eq. Rep.* 562,) the distinction is recognized between an act of negligence imminently dangerous to the lives of others, and one that is not so. In the former case, the party guilty of the negligence is liable to the party injured, whether there be a contract between them or not; in the latter, the negligent party is liable only to the party with whom he contracted, and on the ground that negligence is a breach of the contract. . . .

The defendant, by affixing the label to the jar, represented its contents to be dandelion; and to have been "prepared" by his agent Gilbert. The word "prepared" on the label, must be understood to mean that the article was manufactured by him, or that it had passed through some process under his hands, which would give him personal knowledge of its true name and quality. Whether Foord was justified in selling the article upon the faith of the defendant's label, would have been an open question in an action by the plaintiffs against him, and I wish to be understood as giving no opinion on that point. But it seems to me to be clear that the defendant cannot, in this case, set up as a defense, that Foord sold the contents of the jar as and for what the defendant represented it to be. The label conveyed the idea distinctly to Foord that the contents of the jar was the extract of dandelion; and that the defendant knew it to be such. So far as the defendant is concerned, Foord was under no obligation to test the truth of the representation. The charge of the judge in submitting to the jury the question in relation to the negligence of Foord and Aspinwall, cannot be complained of by the defendant. . . .

Judgment affirmed.

PREPARING FOR CLASS

1. Limitations on recovery based on whether one was in privity stems in part from the reluctance to expand liability—especially in contract—to those who might be viewed as strangers to the defendant. Contract remedies for breach have intentionally and historically been limited to those most proximate to contracting, i.e., in privity, as a means of encouraging contracting. Imagine all to which the defendant could be liable here and how it might respond to a rule that expands liability to those it was not directly involved with.

2. Note that the defendant does not deny culpability, just liability for lack of duty reasons.

3. How might the holding be limited?

INCREASING YOUR UNDERSTANDING

The cited *Winterbottom* case was an unfortunate one as it infused contract principles into tort law. The requirement of privity in contract has long been recognized (at least in contract actions) but the goals of tort law, to compensate and deter, would be significantly frustrated should the court limit liability to those directly involved with the defendant. *Winchester* sparked a major move in product liability cases, though much more rule construction remained.

MacPherson v. Buick Motor Co.
217 N.Y. 382, 111 N.E. 1050, (N.Y. 1916)

CARDOZO, J.

The defendant is a manufacturer of automobiles. It sold an automobile to a retail dealer. The retail dealer resold to the plaintiff. While the plaintiff was in the car, it suddenly collapsed. He was thrown out and injured. One of the wheels was made of defective wood, and its spokes crumbled into fragments. The wheel was not made by the defendant; it was bought from another manufacturer. There is evidence, however, that its defects could have been discovered by reasonable inspection, and that inspection was omitted. There is no claim that the defendant knew of the defect and willfully concealed it. The case, in other words, is not brought within the rule of Kuelling v. Lean Mfg. Co. (183 N.Y. 78). The charge is one, not of fraud, but of negligence. The question to be determined is whether the defendant owed a duty of care and vigilance to any one but the immediate purchaser.

The foundations of this branch of the law, at least in this state, were laid in Thomas v. Winchester (6 N.Y. 397). A poison was falsely labeled. The sale was made to a druggist, who in turn sold to a customer. The customer recovered damages from the seller who affixed the label. "The defendant's negligence," it was said, "put human life in imminent danger." A poison falsely labeled is likely to injure any one who gets it. Because the danger is to be foreseen, there is a duty to avoid the injury. Cases were cited by way of illustration in which manufacturers were not subject to any duty irrespective of contract. The distinction was said to be that their conduct, though, negligent, was not likely to result in injury to any one except the purchaser. We are not required to say whether the chance of injury was always as remote as the distinction assumes. Some of the illustrations might be rejected to-day. The principle of the distinction is for present purposes the important thing.

. . . *Thomas v. Winchester* became quickly a landmark of the law. In the application of its principle there may at times have been uncertainty or even error. There has never in this state been doubt or disavowal of the principle itself. . . .

[The] early cases suggest a narrow construction of the rule. Later cases, however, evince a more liberal spirit. First in importance is Devlin v. Smith (89 N.Y. 470). The defendant, a contractor, built a scaffold for a painter. The painter's servants were injured. The contractor was held liable. He knew that the scaffold, if improperly constructed, was a most dangerous trap. He knew that it was to be used by the workmen. He was building it for that very purpose. Building it for their use, he owed them a duty, irrespective of his contract with their master, to build it with care.

. . . *Thomas v. Winchester* was followed [most recently] by Statler v. Ray Mfg. Co. (195 N.Y. 478, 480). [In *Statler*] the defendant manufactured a large coffee urn. It was installed in a restaurant. When heated, the urn exploded and injured the plaintiff. We held that the manufacturer was liable. We said that the urn "was of such a character inherently that, when applied to the purposes for which it was designed, it was liable to become a source of great danger to many people if not carefully and properly constructed." It may be that *Devlin v. Smith* and *Statler v. Ray Mfg. Co.* have extended the rule of *Thomas v. Winchester.* If so, this court is committed to the extension. The defendant argues that things imminently dangerous to life are poisons, explosives, deadly weapons—things whose normal function it is to injure or destroy. But whatever the rule in *Thomas v. Winchester* may once have been, it has no longer that restricted meaning. A large coffee urn (*Statler v. Ray Mfg. Co.,* supra) may have within itself, if negligently made, the potency of danger, yet no one thinks of it as an implement whose normal function is destruction. . . .

We hold, then, that the principle of *Thomas v. Winchester* is not limited to poisons, explosives, and things of like nature, to things which in their normal operation are implements of destruction. If the nature of a thing is such that it is reasonably certain to place and limb in peril when negligently made, it is then a thing of danger. Its nature gives warning of the consequences to be expected. If to the element of danger there is added knowledge that the thing will be used by persons other than the purchaser, and used without new tests then, irrespective of contract, the manufacturer of this thing of danger is under a duty to make it carefully. That is as far as we are required to go for the decision of this case. There must be knowledge of a danger, not merely possible, but probable. It is possible to use almost anything in a way that will make it dangerous if defective. That is not enough to charge the manufacturer with a duty independent of his contract. Whether a given thing is dangerous may be sometimes a question for the court and sometimes a question for the jury. There must also be knowledge that in the usual course of events the danger will be shared by others than the buyer. Such knowledge may often be inferred from the nature of the transaction. But it is possible that even knowledge of the danger and of the use will not always be enough. The proximity or remoteness of the relation is a factor to be considered. We are dealing now with the liability of the manufacturer of the finished product, who puts it on the market to be used without inspection by his customers. If he is negligent, where danger is to be foreseen, a liability will follow.

From this survey of the decisions, there thus emerges a definition of the duty of a manufacturer which enables us to measure this defendant's liability. Beyond all question, the nature of an automobile gives warning of probable danger if its construction is defective. This automobile was designed to go fifty miles an hour. Unless its wheels were sound and strong, injury was almost certain. It was as much a thing of danger as a defective engine for a railroad. The defendant knew the danger. It knew also that the care would be used by persons other than the buyer. This was apparent from its size; there were seats for three persons. It was apparent also from the fact that the buyer was a dealer in cars, who bought to resell. The maker of this car supplied it for the use of purchasers from the dealer just as plainly as the contractor in *Devlin v. Smith* supplied the scaffold for use by the servants of the owner. The dealer was indeed the one person of whom it might be said with some approach to certainly that by him the car would not be used. Yet the defendant would have us say that he was the one person whom it was under a legal duty to protect. The law does not lead us to so inconsequent a conclusion. Precedents drawn from the days of travel by stage coach do not fit the conditions of travel today. The principle that the danger must be imminent does not change, but the things subject to the principle do change. They are whatever the needs of life in a developing civilization require them to be. . . .

We think the defendant was not absolved from a duty of inspection because it bought the wheels from a reputable manufacturer. It was not merely a dealer in automobiles. It was a manufacturer of automobiles. It was responsible for the finished product. It was not at liberty to put the finished product on the market without subjecting the componet parts to ordinary and simple tests (Richmond & Danville R.R. Co. v. Elliot, 149 U.S. 266, 272). Under the charge of the trial judge nothing more was required of it. The obligation to inspect must vary with the nature of the thing to be inspected. The more probable the danger, the greater the need of caution. . . .

Other rulings complained of have been considered, but no error has been found on them.

The judgment should be affirmed.

WILLARD BARTLETT, Ch. J., dissenting.

. . . The theory upon which the case was submitted to the jury by the learned judge who presided at the trial was that, although an automobile is not an inherently dangerous vehicle, it may become such if equipped with a weak wheel; and that if the motor car in question, when it was put upon the market was in itself inherently dangerous by reason of its being equipped with a weak wheel, the defendant was chargeable with a knowledge of the defect so far as it might be discovered by a reasonable inspection and the application of reasonable tests. This liability, it was further held, was not limited to the original vendee, but extended to a subvendee like the plaintiff, who was not a party to the original contract of sale.

. . . The late Chief Justice Cooley of Michigan, one of the most learned and accurate of American law writers, states the general rule thus: "The general rule is that a contractor, manufacturer, vendor, or furnisher of an article is not liable to third parties who have no contractual relations with him for negligence in the construction, manufacture, or sale of such article." (2 Cooley on Torts (3d ed.), 1486.) . . .

. . . [I] vote for a reversal of this judgment.

PREPARING FOR CLASS

1. What recourse would plaintiff have should the court place no liability on Buick?

2. Pay special attention to the reference to *Winchester* and how the lawyers involved may have presented it to the *MacPherson* court.

3. Keep the circumstances of and arguments in *MacPherson* close as related discussions will take place once we start defining the product defects, and settle generally on rules governing liability.

INCREASING YOUR UNDERSTANDING

MacPherson makes clear that privity of contract is not a condition to tort liability, no matter how inherently dangerous the product may not have been. Simply put, *MacPherson* keeps alive the negligence claim because it creates a duty. Plaintiff, however, is still burdened with the responsibility of proving that the defendant acted unreasonably, which, particularly in the case of component part defects, might be difficult. The next case provides an assist.

Baxter v. Ford Motor Co.
168 Wash. 456, 12 P.2d 409 (Wash. 1932)

HERMAN, J.

During the month of May, 1930, plaintiff purchased a model A Ford town sedan from defendant St. John Motors, a Ford dealer, who had acquired the automobile in question by purchase from defendant Ford Motor Company. Plaintiff claims that representations were made to him by both defendants that the windshield of the automobile was made of nonshatterable glass which would not break, fly, or shatter. October 12, 1930, while plaintiff was driving the automobile through Snoqualmie pass, a pebble from a passing car struck the windshield of the car in question, causing small pieces of glass to fly into plaintiff's left eye, resulting in the loss thereof. Plaintiff brought this action for damages for the loss of his left eye and for injuries to the sight of his right eye. The case came on for trial, and, at the conclusion of plaintiff's testimony, the court took the case from the jury and entered judgment for both defendants. From that judgment, plaintiff appeals.

The principal question in this case is whether the trial court erred in refusing to admit in evidence, as against respondent Ford Motor Company, the catalogues and printed matter furnished by that respondent to respondent St. John Motors to be distributed for sales assistance. Contained in such printed matter were statements which appellant maintains constituted representations or warranties with reference to the nature of the glass used in the windshield of the car purchased by appellant. A typical statement, as it appears in appellant's exhibit for identification No. 1, is here set forth:

> "Triplex Shatter-Proof Glass Windshield. All of the new Ford cars have a Triplex shatter-proof glass windshield—so made that it will not fly or shatter under the hardest impact. This is an important safety factor because it eliminates the dangers of flying glass—the cause of most of the injuries in automobile accidents. In these days of crowded, heavy traffic, the use of this Triplex glass is an absolute necessity. Its extra margin of safety is something that every motorist should look for in the purchase of a car—especially where there are women and children."

Respondent Ford Motor Company contends that there can be no implied or express warranty without privity of contract, and warranties as to personal property do not attach themselves to, and run with, the article sold.

Mazetti v. Armour & Co., 75 Wash. 622, 135 P. 633, 634, 48 L.R.A. (N.S.) 213, Ann. Cas. 1915C, 140, was a case brought against Armour & Co. by proprietors of a restaurant. The complaint alleged that in the course of their business they purchased from the Seattle Grocery Company a carton of cooked tongue, relying upon the representations of Armour & Co. that its goods were pure, wholesome, and fit food for human beings; that in the center of the carton was a foul, filthy, nauseating, and poisonous substance; that during the due course of trade plaintiffs served one of their patrons a portion of the tongue, the customer ate of it, became sick and nauseated, and proceeded publicly to denounce service of such foul and poisonous food; that the incident became generally known; that plaintiffs had no knowledge of or means of learning the character of the food served; that its condition could not be discovered until it was served for use; and that, as a result thereof, plaintiffs were damaged. The trial court sustained a demurrer to the complaint. In the course of an opinion reversing the case, the court said:

> "It has been accepted as a general rule that a manufacturer is not liable to any person other than his immediate vendee; that the action is necessarily one upon an implied or express warranty, and that without privity of contract no suit can be maintained; that each purchaser must resort to his immediate vendor. To this rule certain exceptions have been recognized: (1) Where the thing causing the injury is of a noxious or dangerous kind. (2) Where the defendant has been guilty of fraud or deceit in passing off the article. (3) Where the defendant has been negligent in some respect with reference to the sale or construction of a thing not imminently dangerous. . . .
>
> "Although the cases differ in their reasoning, all agree that there is a liability in such cases irrespective of any privity of contract in the sense of immediate contract between the parties. . . .
>
> "To the old rule that a manufacturer is not liable to third persons who have no contractual relations with him for negligence in the manufacture of an article should be added another exception, not one arbitrarily worked by the courts, but arising, as did the three to which we have heretofore alluded, from the changing conditions of society. An exception to a rule will be declared by courts when the case is not an isolated instance, but general in its character, and the existing rule does not square with justice. Under such circumstances a court will, if free from the restraint of some statute, declare a rule that will meet the full intendment of the law. No case has been cited that is squarely in point with the instant case; but there is enough in the adjudged cases to warrant us in our conclusion. . . .

"We would be disposed to hold on this question that, where sealed packages are put out, and it is made to appear that the fault, if any, is that of the manufacturer, the product was intended for the use of all those who handle it in trade as well as those who consume it."

In the case at bar the automobile was represented by the manufacturer as having a windshield of nonshatterable glass "so made that it will not fly or shatter under the hardest impact." An ordinary person would be unable to discover by the usual and customary examination of the automobile whether glass which would not fly or shatter was used in the windshield. In that respect the purchaser was in a position similar to that of the consumer of a wrongly labeled drug, who has bought the same from a retailer, and who has relied upon the manufacturer's representation that the label correctly set forth the contents of the container. For many years it has been held that, under such circumstances, the manufacturer is liable to the consumer, even though the consumer purchased from a third person the commodity causing the damage. Thomas v. Winchester, 6 N.Y. 397, 57 Am. Dec. 455. The rule in such cases does not rest upon contractual obligations, but rather on the principle that the original act of delivering an article is wrong, when, because of the lack of those qualities which the manufacturer represented it as having, the absence of which could not be readily detected by the consumer, the article is not safe for the purposes for which the consumer would ordinarily use it.

The vital principle present in the case of *Mazetti v. Armour & Co.*, supra, confronts us in the case at bar. In the case cited the court recognized the right of a purchaser to a remedy against the manufacturer because of damages suffered by reason of a failure of goods to comply with the manufacturer's representations as to the existence of qualities which they did not in fact possess, when the absence of such qualities was not readily discoverable, even though there was no privity of contract between the purchaser and the manufacturer.

Since the rule of caveat emptor was first formulated, vast changes have taken place in the economic structures of the English-speaking peoples. Methods of doing business have undergone a great transition. Radio, billboards, and the products of the printing press have become the means of creating a large part of the demand that causes goods to depart from factories to the ultimate consumer. It would be unjust to recognize a rule that would permit manufacturers of goods to create a demand for their products by representing that they possess qualities which they, in fact, do not possess, and then, because there is no privity of contract existing between the consumer and the manufacturer, deny the consumer the right to recover if damages result from the absence of those qualities, when such absence is not readily noticeable.

"An exception to a rule will be declared by courts when the case is not an isolated instance, but general in its character, and the existing rule does not square with justice. Under such circumstances a court will, if free from the restraint of some statute, declare a rule that will meet the full intendment of the law." *Mazetti v. Armour & Co.*, supra.

We hold that the catalogues and printed matter furnished by respondent Ford Motor Company for distribution and assistance in sales (appellant's exhibits for identification Nos. 1, 2, 3, 4 and 5) were improperly excluded from evidence, because they set forth representations by the manufacturer that the windshield of the car which appellant bought contained Triplex nonshatterable glass which would not fly or shatter. The nature of nonshatterable glass is such that the falsity of the representations with reference to the glass would not be readily detected by a person of ordinary experience and reasonable prudence. Appellant, under the circumstances shown in this case, had the right to rely upon the representations made by respondent Ford Motor Company relative to qualities possessed by its products, even though there was no privity of contract between appellant and respondent Ford Motor Company.

The trial court erred in taking the case from the jury and entering judgment for respondent Ford Motor Company. It was for the jury to determine, under proper instructions, whether the failure of respondent Ford Motor Company to equip the windshield with glass which did not fly or shatter was the proximate cause of appellant's injury.

Reversed, with directions to grant a new trial with reference to respondent Ford Motor Company; affirmed as to respondent St. John Motors.

PREPARING FOR CLASS

1. Misrepresentation will be discussed later in the term, and the cause of action will take on some familiarity to the claim in *Baxter*. Fraudulent misrepresentation, though, requires proof of lying, and there is nothing to suggest that Ford lied about the capabilities of its windshields.

2. On what basis did the trial court take the case from the jury? If it was because of lack of duty, that decision should have been made well before trial.

3. It matters not whether Ford was reasonable in making the promise, only whether the promise runs to Baxter. With that issue resolved by the appellate court, what will the focus be on retrial? For example, should Baxter have to prove the he relied on the defendant's representations when making the purchase?

APPLYING THE LAW

Tire manufacturer represents to automobile dealers that its tires will never contribute to spin-out in wintery conditions. Plaintiff purchases car from GM dealer with the aforementioned tires attached, though unfamiliar with the no spin-out claims. Plaintiff is later involved in an accident while driving on "black ice." Is tire manufacturer potentially liable under *Baxter*? Is dealer potentially liable under *MacPherson*?

INCREASING YOUR UNDERSTANDING

1. *Products liability and misrepresentation.* Misrepresentation as a tort claim will be discussed later in the term and imposes liability as a means of removing the incentive from lying, though courts have also created rules that may hold the negligent or innocent misrepresenter responsible as well. As a tort claim, misrepresentation is most significant as it allows for recovery of simple economic loss alone whereas most tort actions require some type of harm to person or property as a predicate for recovery. When it comes to products liability, many states allowed for misrepresentation principles to govern responsibility as well, a position that has been summarized in the most recent Restatement of Torts. Restatement (Third) of Torts §9, Liability of Commercial Product Seller or Distributor for Harm Caused by Misrepresentation, states:

   > One engaged in the business of selling or otherwise distributing products who, in connection with the sale of a product, makes a fraudulent, negligent, or innocent misrepresentation of material fact concerning the product is subject to liability for harm to persons or property caused by the misrepresentation.

   Perhaps most significant about the ALI's position is the relaxation of the requirement that a defect be proved by the plaintiff; the fact that a promise has been broken is enough.

2. *Express warranties and the Uniform Commercial Code.* Uniform Commercial Code §2-313 defines and governs the law with respect to express warranties and generally describes them as being created by:

   a. Any affirmation of fact or promise made by the seller which relates to the goods and becomes part of the basis of the bargain creates an express warranty that the goods shall conform to the affirmation or promise.

   b. Any description of the goods which is made part of the basis of the bargain creates an express warranty that the goods shall conform to the description.

   c. Any sample or model that is made part of the basis of the bargain creates an express warranty that the whole of the goods shall conform to the sample or model.

The UCC also allows sellers of goods to limit their responsibility to those who are injured, thus potentially frustrating the governing principles of products liability laws. *Henningsen* dissipated any tension, real or fanciful.

Henningsen v. Bloomfield Motors, Inc.
32 N.J. 358, 161 A.2d 69 (N.J. 1960)

FRANCIS, J.

Plaintiff Clause H. Henningsen purchased a Plymouth automobile, manufactured by defendant Chrysler Corporation, from defendant Bloomfield Motors, Inc. His wife, plaintiff Helen Henningsen, was injured while driving it and instituted suit against both defendants to recover damages on account of her injuries. Her husband joined in the action seeking compensation for his consequential losses. The complaint was predicated upon breach of express and implied warranties and upon negligence. At the trial the negligence counts were dismissed by the court and the cause was submitted to the jury for determination solely on the issues of implied warranty of merchantability. Verdicts were returned against both defendants and in favor of the plaintiffs. Defendants appealed and plaintiffs cross-appealed from the dismissal of their negligence claim. The matter was certified by this court prior to consideration in the Appellate Division.

The facts are not complicated, but a general outline of them is necessary to an understanding of the case.

On May 7, 1955 Mr. and Mrs. Henningsen visited the place of business of Bloomfield Motors, Inc., an authorized De Soto and Plymouth dealer, to look at a Plymouth. They wanted to buy a car and were considering a Ford or a Chevrolet as well as a Plymouth. They were shown a Plymouth which appealed to them and the purchase followed. The record indicates that Mr. Henningsen intended the car as a Mother's Day gift to his wife. He said the intention was communicated to the dealer. When the purchase order or contract was prepared and presented, the husband executed it alone. His wife did not join as a party. . . .

The reverse side of the contract contains 8 ½ inches of fine print. . . . The page is headed "Conditions" and contains ten separate paragraphs consisting of 65 lines in all. The paragraphs do not have headnotes or margin notes denoting their particular subject, as in the case of the "Owner Service Certificate" to be referred to later. In the seventh paragraph, about two-thirds of the way down the page, the warranty, which is the focal point of the case, is set forth. It is as follows:

> "7. It is expressly agreed that there are no warranties, express or implied, Made by either the dealer or the manufacturer on the motor vehicle, chassis, of parts furnished hereunder except as follows.

"The manufacturer warrants each new motor vehicle (including original equipment placed thereon by the manufacturer except tires), chassis or parts manufactured by it to be free from defects in material or workmanship under normal use and service. Its obligation under this warranty being limited to making good at its factory any part or parts thereof which shall, within ninety (90) days after delivery of such vehicle to the original purchaser or before such vehicle has been driven 4,000 miles, whichever event shall first occur, be returned to it with transportation charges prepaid and which its examination shall disclose to its satisfaction to have been thus defective; This warranty being expressly in lieu of all other warranties expressed or implied, and all other obligations or liabilities on its part, and it neither assumes nor authorizes any other person to assume for it any other liability in connection with the sale of its vehicles. . . ."

The new Plymouth was turned over to the Henningsens on May 9, 1955. . . . Thereafter, it was used for short trips on paved streets about the town. It had no servicing and no mishaps of any kind before the event of May 19. That day, Mrs. Henningsen drove to Asbury Park. On the way down and in returning the car performed in normal fashion until the accident occurred. She was proceeding north on Route 36 in Highlands, New Jersey, at 20-22 miles per hour. The highway was paved and smooth, and contained two lanes for northbound travel. She was riding in the right-hand lane. Suddenly she heard a loud noise "from the bottom, by the hood." It "felt as if something cracked." The steering wheel spun in her hands; the car veered sharply to the right and crashed into a highway sign and a brick wall. No other vehicle was in any way involved. A bus operator driving in the left-hand lane testified that he observed plaintiffs' car approaching in normal fashion in the opposite direction; "all of a sudden (it) veered at 90 degrees . . . and right into this wall." As a result of the impact, the front of the car was so badly damaged that it was impossible to determine if any of the parts of the steering wheel mechanism or workmanship or assembly were defective or improper prior to the accident. The condition was such that the collision insurance carrier, after inspection, declared the vehicle a total loss. It had 468 miles on the speedometer at the time.

The insurance carrier's inspector and appraiser of damaged cars, with 11 years of experience, advanced the opinion, based on the history and his examination, that something definitely went "wrong from the steering wheel down to the front wheels" and that the untoward happening must have been due to mechanical defect or failure; "something down there had to drop off or break loose to cause the car" to act in the manner described.

As has been indicated, the trial court felt that the proof was not sufficient to make out a Prima facie case as to the negligence of either the manufacturer or the dealer. The case was given to the jury, therefore, solely on the warranty theory, with results favorable to the plaintiffs against both defendants.

I. The Claim of Implied Warranty Against the Manufacturer

In the ordinary case of sale of goods by description an implied warranty of merchantability is an integral part of the transaction. R.S. 46:30-20, N.J.S.A. If the buyer, expressly or by implication, makes known to the seller the particular purpose for which the article is required and it appears that he has relied on the seller's skill or judgment, an implied warranty arises of reasonable fitness for that purpose. R.S. 46:30-21(1), N.J.S.A. The former type of warranty simply means that the thing sold is reasonably fit for the general purpose for which it is manufactured and sold. . . .

The uniform act codified, extended and liberalized the common law of sales. The motivation in part was to ameliorate the harsh doctrine of Caveat emptor, and in some measure to impose a reciprocal obligation on the seller to beware. The transcendent value of the legislation, particularly with respect to implied warranties, rests in the fact that obligations on the part of the seller were imposed by operation of law, and did not depend for their existence upon express agreement of the parties. And of tremendous significance in a rapidly expanding commercial society was the recognition of the right to recover damages on account of personal injuries arising from a breach of warranty. The particular importance of this advance resides in the fact that under such circumstances strict liability is imposed upon the maker or seller of the product. Recovery of damages does not depend upon proof of negligence or knowledge of the defect. . . .

As the Sales Act and its liberal interpretation by the courts threw this protective cloak about the buyer, the decisions in various jurisdictions revealed beyond doubt that many manufacturers took steps to avoid these ever increasing warranty obligations. Realizing that the act governed the relationship of buyer and seller, they undertook to withdraw from actual and direct contractual contact with the buyer. They ceased selling products to the consuming public through their own employees and making contracts of sale in their own names. Instead, a system of independent dealers was established; their products were sold to dealers who in turn dealt with the buying public, ostensibly solely in their own personal capacity as sellers. In the past in many instances, manufacturers were able to transfer to the dealers burdens imposed by the act and thus achieved a large measure of immunity for themselves. But, as will be noted in more detail hereafter, such marketing practices, coupled with the advent of large scale advertising by manufacturers to promote the purchase of these goods from dealers by members of the public, provided a basis upon which the existence of express or implied warranties was predicated, even though the manufacturer was not a party to the contract of sale. . . .

Putting aside for the time being the problem of the efficacy of the disclaimer provisions contained in the express warranty, a question of first importance to be decided is whether an implied warranty of merchantability by

Chrysler Corporation accompanied the sale of the automobile to Claus Henningsen. . . .

Chrysler points out that an implied warranty of merchantability is an incident of a contract of sale. It concedes, of course, the making of the original sale to Bloomfield Motors, Inc., but maintains that this transaction marked the terminal point of its contractual connection with the car. Then Chrysler urges that since it was not a party to the sale by the dealer to Henningsen, there is no privity of contract between it and the plaintiffs, and the absence of this privity eliminates any such implied warranty.

There is no doubt that under early common-law concepts of contractual liability only those persons who were parties to the bargain could sue for a breach of it. In more recent times a noticeable disposition has appeared in a number of jurisdictions to break through the narrow barrier of privity when dealing with sales of goods in order to give realistic recognition to a universally accepted fact. The fact is that the dealer and the ordinary buyer do not, and are not expected to, buy goods, whether they be foodstuffs or automobiles, exclusively for their own consumption or use. Makers and manufacturers know this and advertise and market their products on that assumption; witness, the "family" car, the baby foods, etc. The limitations of privity in contracts for the sale of goods developed their place in the law when marketing conditions were simple, when maker and buyer frequently met face to face on an equal bargaining plane and when many of the products were relatively uncomplicated and conducive to inspection by a buyer competent to evaluate their quality. See, Freezer, "Manufacturer's Liability for Injuries Caused by His Products," 37 Mich. L. Rev. 1 (1938). With the advent of mass marketing, the manufacturer became remote from the purchaser, sales were accomplished through intermediaries, and the demand for the product was created by advertising media. In such an economy it became obvious that the consumer was the person being cultivated. Manifestly, the connotation of "consumer" was broader than that of "buyer." He signified such a person who, in the reasonable contemplation of the parties to the sale, might be expected to use the product. Thus, where the commodities sold are such that if defectively manufactured they will be dangerous to life or limb, then society's interests can only be protected by eliminating the requirement of privity between the maker and his dealers and the reasonably expected ultimate consumer. In that way the burden of losses consequent upon use of defective articles is borne by those who are in a position to either control the danger or make an equitable distribution of the losses when they do occur. As Harper & James put it, "The interest in consumer protection calls for warranties by the maker that Do run with the goods, to reach all who are likely to be hurt by the use of the unfit commodity for a purpose ordinarily to be expected." 2 Harper & James, supra 1571, 1572; also see, 1535; Prosser, supra, 506-511. As far back as 1932, in the well known case of Baxter v. Ford Motor Co., 168 Wash. 456, 12 P.2d 409 (Sup. Ct. 1932), affirmed 15 P.2d 1118, 88 A.L.R. 521 (Sup. Ct. 1932), the

Supreme Court of Washington gave recognition to the impact of then existing commercial practices on the strait jacket of privity, saying:

> "It would be unjust to recognize a rule that would permit manufacturers of goods to create a demand for their products by representing that they possess qualities which they, in fact, do not possess, and then, because there is no privity of contract existing between the consumer and the manufacturer, deny the consumer the right to recover if damages result from the absence of those qualities, when such absence is not readily noticeable."

12 P.2d at page 412.

. . . Although only a minority of jurisdictions have thus far departed from the requirement of privity, the movement in that direction is most certainly gathering momentum. Liability to the ultimate consumer in the absence of direct contractual connection has been predicated upon a variety of theories. Some courts hold that the warranty runs with the article like a covenant running with land; others recognize a third-party beneficiary thesis; still others rest their decision on the ground that public policy requires recognition of a warranty made directly to the consumer. . . .

Most of the cases where lack of privity has not been permitted to interfere with recovery have involved food and drugs. . . .

We see no rational doctrinal basis for differentiating between a fly in a bottle of beverage and a defective automobile. The unwholesome beverage may bring illness to one person, the defective car, with its great potentiality for harm to the driver, occupants, and others, demands even less adherence to the narrow barrier of privity. . . .

Accordingly, we hold that under modern marketing conditions, when a manufacturer puts a new automobile in the stream of trade and promotes its purchase by the public, an implied warranty that it is reasonably suitable for use as such accompanies it into the hands of the ultimate purchaser. Absence of agency between the manufacturer and the dealer who makes the ultimate sale is immaterial.

II. The Effect of the Disclaimer and Limitation of Liability Clauses on the Implied Warranty of Merchantability

. . . In view of the cases in various jurisdictions suggesting the conclusion which we have now reached with respect to the implied warranty of merchantability, it becomes apparent that manufacturers who enter into promotional activities to stimulate consumer buying may incur warranty obligations of either or both the express or implied character. These developments in the law inevitably suggest the inference that the form of express warranty made part of the Henningsen purchase contract was devised for general use in the automobile industry as a possible means of avoiding the consequences of the growing judicial acceptance of the thesis that the described express or implied warranties run directly to the consumer.

In the light of these matters, what effect should be given to the express warranty in question which seeks to limit the manufacturer's liability to replacement of defective parts, and which disclaims all other warranties, express or implied? In assessing its significance we must keep in mind the general principle that, in the absence of fraud, one who does not choose to read a contract before signing it, cannot later relieve himself of its burdens. And in applying that principle, the basic tenet of freedom of competent parties to contract is a factor of importance. But in the framework of modern commercial life and business practices, such rules cannot be applied on a strict, doctrinal basis. The conflicting interests of the buyer and seller must be evaluated realistically and justly, giving due weight to the social policy evinced by the Uniform Sales Act, the progressive decisions of the courts engaged in administering it, the mass production methods of manufacture and distribution to the public, and the bargaining position occupied by the ordinary consumer in such an economy. This history of the law shows that legal doctrines, as first expounded, often prove to be inadequate under the impact of later experience. In such case, the need for justice has stimulated the necessary qualifications or adjustments.

In these times, an automobile is almost as much a servant of convenience for the ordinary person as a household utensil. For a multitude of other persons it is a necessity. Crowded highways and filled parking lots are a commonplace of our existence. There is no need to look any farther than the daily newspaper to be convinced that when an automobile is defective, it has great potentiality for harm. . . .

What influence should these circumstances have on the restrictive effect of Chrysler's express warranty in the framework of the purchase contract? As we have said, warranties originated in the law to safeguard the buyer and not to limit the liability of the seller or manufacturer. It seems obvious in this instance that the motive was to avoid the warranty obligations which are normally incidental to such sales. The language gave little and withdrew much. In return for the delusive remedy of replacement of defective parts at the factory, the buyer is said to have accepted the exclusion of the maker's liability for personal injuries arising from the breach of the warranty, and to have agreed to the elimination of any other express or implied warranty. An instinctively felt sense of justice cries out against such a sharp bargain. But does the doctrine that a person is bound by his signed agreement, in the absence of fraud, stand in the way of any relief? . . .

The warranty before us is a standardized form designed for mass use. It is imposed upon the automobile consumer. He takes it or leaves it, and he must take it to buy an automobile. No bargaining is engaged in with respect to it. In fact, the dealer through whom it comes to the buyer is without authority to alter it; his function is ministerial — simply to deliver it. The form warranty is not only standard with Chrysler but, as mentioned above, it is the uniform warranty of the Automobile Manufacturers Association. Members of the Association are: General Motors, Inc., Ford, Chrysler, Studebaker-Packard, American Motors, (Rambler), Willys Motors, Checker Motors Corp., and International Harvester Company. Automobile Facts and Figures (1958 Ed., Automobile Manufacturers Association) 69. Of these companies, the "Big Three" (General Motors, Ford, and Chrysler) represented 93.5% of the passenger-car production for 1958 and the independents 6.5%. Standard & Poor (Industrial Surveys, Autos, Basic Analysis, June 25, 1959) 4109. And for the same year the "Big Three" had 86.72% of the total passenger vehicle registrations. Automotive News, 1959 Almanac (Slocum Publishing Co., Inc.) p. 25.

The gross inequality of bargaining position occupied by the consumer in the automobile industry is thus apparent. There is no competition among the car makers in the area of the express warranty. Where can the buyer go to negotiate for better protection? Such control and limitation of his remedies are inimical to the public welfare and, at the very least, call for great care by the courts to avoid injustice through application of strict common-law principles of freedom of contract. Because there is no competition among the motor vehicle manufacturers with respect to the scope of protection guaranteed to the buyer, there is no incentive on their part to stimulate good will in that field of public relations. Thus, there is lacking a factor existing in more competitive fields, one which tends to guarantee the safe construction of the article sold. Since all competitors operate in the same way, the urge to be careful is not so pressing. . . .

The task of the judiciary is to administer the spirit as well as the letter of the law. On issues such as the present one, part of that burden is to protect the ordinary man against the loss of important rights through what, in effect, is the unilateral act of the manufacturer. The status of the automobile industry is unique. Manufacturers are few in number and strong in bargaining position. In the matter of warranties on the sale of their products, the Automotive Manufacturers Association has enabled them to present a united front. From the standpoint of the purchaser, there can be no arms length negotiating on the subject. Because his capacity for bargaining is so grossly unequal, the inexorable conclusion which follows is that he is not permitted to bargain at all. He must take or leave the automobile on the warranty terms dictated by the maker. He cannot turn to a competitor for better security. . . .

The trial court sent the case to the jury against Chrysler on the theory that the evidence would support a finding of breach of an implied warranty of merchantability. In fact, at one point in his charge he seemed to say that as a matter of law such a warranty existed. He also told them that:

> "A provision in a purchase order for an automobile that an express warranty shall exclude all implied warranties will not be given effect so as to defeat an implied warranty that the machine shall be fit for the purposes for which it was intended unless its inclusion in the contract was fairly procured or obtained."

Thereafter, the court charged that when the car was sold a warranty arose that it was reasonably suited for ordinary use, and that if they found that it was defective and "not reasonably suited for ordinary driving" liability would exist "provided . . . you find there was an implied warranty and a breach thereof." The reasonable inference to be drawn from the whole context is that a preliminary finding against the binding effect of the disclaimer would have to be made, i.e., that the disclaimer was not "fairly procured," before an implied warranty could be deemed to exist. Even assuming that the duty to make such a finding was not as explicit as it should have been, in view of our holding that the disclaimer is void as a matter of law, the charge was more favorable to the defendant than the law required it to be. The verdict in favor of the plaintiffs and against Chrysler Corporation establishes that the jury found that the disclaimer was not fairly obtained. Thus, this defendant cannot claim to have been prejudiced by a jury finding on an aspect of the case which the court should have disposed of as a matter of law.

IV. Proof of Breach of the Implied Warranty of Merchantability

Both defendants argue that the proof adduced by plaintiffs as to the happening of the accident was not sufficient to demonstrate a breach of warranty. Consequently, they claim that their motion for judgment should have been granted by the trial court. We cannot agree. In our view, the total effect of the circumstances shown from purchase to accident is adequate to raise an inference that the car was defective and that such condition was causally related to the mishap. Thus, determination by the jury was required.

The proof adduced by the plaintiffs disclosed that after servicing and delivery of the car, it operated normally during the succeeding ten days, so far as the Henningsens could tell. They had no difficulty or mishap of any kind, and it neither had nor required any servicing. It was driven by them alone. The owners service certificate provided for return for further servicing at the end of the first 1,000 miles—less than half of which had been covered at the time of Mrs. Henningsen's injury.

The facts, detailed above, show that on the day of the accident, ten days after delivery, Mrs. Henningsen was driving in a normal fashion, on a smooth highway, when unexpectedly the steering wheel and the front wheels of the car went into the bizarre action described. Can it reasonably be said that the circumstances do not warrant an inference of unsuitability for ordinary use against the manufacturer and the dealer? Obviously there is nothing in the proof to indicate in the slightest that the most unusual action of the steering wheel was caused by Mrs. Henningsen's operation of the automobile on this day, or by the use of the car between delivery and the happening of the incident. Nor is there anything to suggest that any external force or condition unrelated to the manufacturing or servicing of the car operated as an inducing or even concurring factor. . . .

Circumstantial evidence sufficient to create a jury question as to the negligence of a manufacturer or dealer would clearly justify the same result where the issue is breach of warranty. As the late Chief Justice Vanderbilt said, in *Simon v. Graham Bakery*, supra, liability would exist notwithstanding all care was used to prevent a breach.

V. The Defense of Lack of Privity Against Mrs. Henningsen

Both defendants contend that since there was no privity of contract between them and Mrs. Henningsen, she cannot recover for breach of any warranty made by either of them. On the facts, as they were developed, we agree that she was not a party to the purchase agreement. Her right to maintain the action, therefore, depends upon whether she occupies such legal status thereunder as to permit her to take advantage of a breach of defendants' implied warranties. . . .

[I]t is our opinion that an implied warranty of merchantability chargeable to either an automobile manufacturer or a dealer extends to the purchaser of the car, members of his family, and to other persons occupying or using it with his consent. It would be wholly opposed to reality to say that use by such persons is not within the anticipation of parties to such a warranty of reasonable suitability of an automobile for ordinary highway operation. Those persons must be considered within the distributive chain.

Under all of the circumstances outlined above, the judgments in favor of the plaintiffs and against the defendants are affirmed.

PREPARING FOR CLASS

1. UCC §2-316, "Exclusion or Modification of Warranties," provides in part that:

    (2) Subject to subsection (3), to exclude or modify the implied warranty of merchantability or any part of it in a consumer contract the language must be in a record, be conspicuous, and state "The seller undertakes no responsibility for the quality of the goods except as otherwise provided in this contract," and in any other contract the language must mention merchantability and in case of a record must be conspicuous. . . .

    (3) Notwithstanding subsection (2):

    (a) unless the circumstances indicate otherwise, all implied warranties are excluded by expressions like "as is", "with all faults" or other language that in common understanding calls the buyer's attention to the exclusion of warranties, makes plain that there is no implied warranty, and, in a consumer contract evidenced by a record, is set forth conspicuously in the record;

(b) if the buyer before entering into the contract has examined the goods or the sample or model as fully as desired or has refused to examine the goods after a demand by the seller there is no implied warranty with regard to defects that an examination in the circumstances should have revealed to the buyer; and. . . .

(4) Remedies for breach of warranty may be limited in accordance with Sections 2-718 and 2-719.

§2-719, "Contractual Modification or Limitation of Remedy," states in part:

(3) Consequential damages may be limited or excluded unless the limitation or exclusion is unconscionable. Limitation of consequential damages for injury to the person in the case of consumer goods is prima facie unconscionable but limitation of damages where the loss is commercial is not.

2. The UCC gave states options when it came to who could properly bring a breach of warranty claim. §2-318, "Third Party Beneficiaries of Warranties Express or Implied," provides:

(States to select one alternative.)

ALTERNATIVE A
A seller's warranty whether express or implied extends to any natural person who is in the family or household of his buyer or who is a guest in his home if it is reasonable to expect that such person may use, consume or be affected by the goods and who is injured in person by breach of the warranty. A seller may not exclude or limit the operation of this section.

ALTERNATIVE B
A seller's warranty whether express or implied extends to any natural person who may reasonably be expected to use, consume or be affected by the goods and who is injured in person by breach of the warranty. A seller may not exclude or limit the operation of this section.

ALTERNATIVE C
A seller's warranty whether express or implied extends to any person who may reasonably be expected to use, consume or be affected by the goods and who is injured by breach of the warranty. A seller may not exclude or limit the operation of this section with respect to injury to the person of an individual to whom the warranty extends.

Alternative A limits horizontal and vertical liability; only the immediate seller ("of his buyer") is liable.

The only distinction between B and C is the latter allows for business entities as well as individuals to bring suit.

3. Note the Henningsens were allowed to recover, though they never proved what was particularly wrong (defective) about the vehicle and though the negligence claims were dismissed. Liability was indeed strict.

INCREASING YOUR UNDERSTANDING

1. Prior to *Henningsen*, most of the cases where liability for breach of warranty was imposed involved drug or food products, extending liability to a more common product signaled a major move in the law. No longer would manufacturers find sanctuary in the lack of privity or the absence of any agency between it and the dealer. Holding that liability was rooted in tort rendered any act of disclaiming responsibility pursuant to rules of sales meaningless.

2. *Remnants of warranty.* The *Henningsen* court did not disavow warranty as a theory of liability, instead it clarified any misunderstanding on the origins of the implied promises that manufactures of products make to the public, dispelled any notion that liability for personal injury could be disclaimed, and embraced one of the UCC privity rules. Reliance on warranty as a theory continued to allow the product liability cases to be mired with UCC verbiage and dictates. A liberated Justice Traynor, next in *Greenman*, almost single handedly buried warranty as a tort theory of liability.

Greenman v. Yuba Power Products, Inc.
59 Cal.2d 57, 377 P.2d 897 (Cal. 1963)

TRAYNOR, Justice.

Plaintiff brought this action for damages against the retailer and the manufacturer of a Shopsmith, a combination power tool that could be used as a saw, drill, and wood lathe. He saw a Shopsmith demonstrated by the retailer and studied a brochure prepared by the manufacturer. He decided he wanted a Shopsmith for his home workshop, and his wife bought and gave him one for Christmas in 1955. In 1957 he bought the necessary attachments to use the Shopsmith as a lathe for turning a large piece of wood he wished to make into a chalice. After he had worked on the piece of wood several times without difficulty, it suddenly flew out of the machine and struck him on the forehead, inflicting serious injuries. About ten and a half months later, he gave the retailer and the manufacturer written notice of claimed breaches of warranties and filed a complaint against them alleging such breaches and negligence.

After a trial before a jury, the court ruled that there was no evidence that the retailer was negligent or had breached any express warranty and that the manufacturer was not liable for the breach of any implied warranty. Accordingly, it submitted to the jury only the cause of action alleging breach of implied warranties against the retailer and the causes of action alleging negligence and breach of express warranties against the manufacturer. The jury returned a verdict for the retailer against plaintiff and for plaintiff against the manufacturer in the amount of $65,000. The trial court denied the manufacturer's motion for a new trial and entered judgment on the verdict. The manufacturer and plaintiff appeal. Plaintiff seeks a reversal of the part of the judgment in favor of the retailer, however, only in the event that the part of the judgment against the manufacturer is reversed.

Plaintiff introduced substantial evidence that his injuries were caused by defective design and construction of the Shopsmith. His expert witnesses testified that inadequate set screws were used to hold parts of the machine together so that normal vibration caused the tailstock of the lathe to move away from the piece of wood being turned permitting it to fly out of the lathe. They also testified that there were other more positive ways of fastening the parts of the machine together, the use of which would have prevented the accident. The jury could therefore reasonably have concluded that the manufacturer negligently constructed the Shopsmith. The jury could also reasonably have concluded that statements in the manufacturer's brochure were untrue, that they constituted express warranties, and that plaintiff's injuries were caused by their breach.

The manufacturer contends, however, that plaintiff did not give it notice of breach of warranty within a reasonable time and that therefore his cause of action for breach of warranty is barred by section 1769 of the Civil Code. Since it cannot be determined whether the verdict against it was based on the negligence or warranty cause of action or both, the manufacturer concludes that the error in presenting the warranty cause of action to the jury was prejudicial.

Section 1769 of the Civil Code provides: "In the absence of express or implied agreement of the parties, acceptance of the goods by the buyer shall not discharge the seller from liability in damages or other legal remedy for breach of any promise or warranty in the contract to sell or the sale. But, if, after acceptance of the goods, the buyer fails to give notice to the seller of the breach of any promise or warranty within a reasonable time after the buyer knows, or ought to know of such breach, the seller shall not be liable therefor."

Like other provisions of the uniform sales act Civ. Code, §§1721-1800), section 1769 deals with the rights of the parties to a contract of sale or a sale. It does not provide that notice must be given of the breach of a warranty that arises independently of a contract of sale between the parties. Such warranties are not imposed by the sales act, but are the product of common-law decisions that have recognized them in a variety of situations. It is true that in many of these situations the court has invoked the sales act definitions of warranties (Civ. Code, §§1732, 1735) in defining the defendant's liability, but it has done so, not because the statutes so required, but because they provided appropriate standards for the court to adopt under the circumstances presented.

The notice requirement of section 1769, however, is not an appropriate one for the court to adopt in actions by injured consumers against manufacturers with whom they have not dealt. "As between the immediate parties to the sale (the notice requirement) is a sound commercial rule, designed to protect the seller against unduly delayed claims for damages. As applied to personal injuries, and notice to a remote seller, it becomes a booby-trap for the unwary. The injured consumer is seldom 'steeped in the business practice which justifies the rule,' (James, Product Liability, 34 Texas L. Rev. 44, 192, 197) and at least until he has had legal advice it will not occur to him to give notice to one with whom he has had no dealings." It is true that in Jones v. Burgermeister Brewing Corp., 198 Cal. App. 2d 198, 202-203, 18 Cal. Rptr. 311; Perry v. Thrifty Drug Co., 186 Cal. App. 2d 410, 411 ,9 Cal. Rptr. 50; Arata v. Tonegato, 152 Cal. App. 2d 837, 841, 314 P.2d 130, and Maecherlein v. Sealy Mattress Co., 155 Cal. App. 2d 275, 278, 302 P.2d 331, the court assumed that notice of breach of warranty must be given in an action by a consumer against a manufacturer. Since in those cases, however, the court did not consider the question whether a distinction exists between a warranty based on a contract between the parties and one imposed on a manufacturer not in privity with the consumer, the decisions are not authority for rejecting the rule of the *La Hue* and *Chapman* cases, supra. We conclude, therefore, the even if plaintiff did not give timely notice of breach of warranty to the manufacturer, his cause of action based on the representations contained in the brochure was not barred.

Moreover, to impose strict liability on the manufacturer under the circumstances of this case, it was not necessary for plaintiff to establish an express warranty as defined in section 1732 of the Civil Code. A manufacturer is strictly liable in tort when an article he places on the market, knowing that it is to be used without inspection for defects, proves to have a defect that causes injury to a human being. Recognized first in the case of unwholesome food products, such liability has now been extended to a variety of other products that create as great or greater hazards if defective.

Although in these cases strict liability has usually been based on the theory of an express or implied warranty running from the manufacturer to the plaintiff, the abandonment of the requirement of a contract between them, the recognition that the liability is not assumed by agreement but imposed by law, and the refusal to permit the manufacturer to define the scope of its own responsibility for defective products (Henningsen v. Bloomfield Motors, Inc., 32 N.J. 358, 161 A.2d 69, 84-96; General Motors Corp. v. Dodson, 47 Tenn. App. 438, 338 S.W.2d 655, 658-661; State Farm Mut. Auto. Ins. Co. v. Anderson-Weber, Inc., 252 Iowa 1289, 110 N.W.2d 449, 455-456; Pabon v. Hackensack Auto Sales, Inc., 63 N.J. Super. 476, 164 A.2d 773, 778; Linn v. Radio Center Delicatessen, 169 Misc. 879, 9 N.Y.S. 2d 110, 112) make clear that the liability is not one governed by the law of contract warranties but by the law of strict liability in tort. Accordingly, rules defining and governing warranties that were developed to meet the needs of commercial transactions cannot properly be invoked to govern the manufacturer's liability to those injured by their defective products unless those rules also serve the purposes for which such liability is imposed.

We need not recanvass the reasons for imposing strict liability on the manufacturer. They have been fully articulated in the cases cited above. The purpose of such liability is to insure that the costs of injuries resulting from defective products are borne by the manufacturers that put such products on the market rather than by the injured persons who are powerless to protect themselves. Sales warranties serve this purpose fitfully at best. In the present case, for example, plaintiff was able to plead and prove an express warranty only because he read and relied on the representations of the Shopsmith's ruggedness contained in the manufacturer's brochure. Implicit in the machine's presence on the market, however, was a representation that it would safely do the jobs for which it was built. Under these circumstances, it should not be controlling whether plaintiff selected the machine because of the statements in the brochure, or because of the machine's own appearance of excellence that belied the defect lurking beneath the surface, or because he merely assumed that it would safely do the jobs it was built to do. It should not be controlling whether the details of the sales from manufacturer to retailer and from retailer to plaintiff's wife were such that one or more of the implied warranties of the sales act arose. (Civ. Code, §1735.) "The remedies of injured consumers ought not to be made to depend upon the intricacies of the law of sales." (Ketterer v. Armour & Co., D.C., 200 F. 322, 323; Klein v. Duchess Sandwich Co., 14 Cal. 2d 272, 282, 93 P.2d 799.) To establish the manufacturer's liability it was sufficient that plaintiff proved that he was injured while using the Shopsmith in a way it was intended to be used as a result of a defect in design and manufacture of which plaintiff was not aware that made the Shopsmith unsafe for its intended use.

The judgment is affirmed.

PREPARING FOR CLASS

1. Verdict forms often contain multiple theories of liability; here the form contained claims against manufacturer sounding in both warranty and negligence. Consider how the claims would be prosecuted individually. In other words, what facts would be relied upon to establish liability under each claim in this case, and how are they distinct?

2. Become familiar with the rationales behind imposing strict liability.

3. The UCC has a tort statute of limitation equivalent requiring that notice of a breach be provided to the seller within a "reasonable period" or the plaintiff loses the right to recover. A typical statute of limitations on the other hand articulates a specific period that governs the right to bring a lawsuit. Which controls is determined by where the cause of action resides.

INCREASING YOUR UNDERSTANDING

1. The Restatement (Second) of Torts §402A soon followed the *Greenman* decision and is perhaps the most cited Restatement in the history of torts law. Without any reference to warranty as the basis for liability being strict, it pronounced liability rules that would, at least initially, govern products liability cases advanced under a strict liability theory. It states:

   §402A. SPECIAL LIABILITY OF SELLER OF PRODUCT FOR PHYSICAL HARM TO USER OR CONSUMER
   (1) One who sells any product in a defective condition unreasonably dangerous to the user or consumer or to his property is subject to liability for physical harm thereby caused to the ultimate user or consumer, or to his property, if
   (a) the seller is engaged in the business of selling such a product, and
   (b) it is expected to and does reach the user or consumer without substantial change in the condition in which it is sold.
   (2) The rule stated in Subsection (1) applies although
   (a) the seller has exercised all possible care in the preparation and sale of his product, and
   (b) the user or consumer has not bought the product from or entered into any contractual relation with the seller.

2. What's a defect? Under products liability law, courts came to recognize three defects: manufacturing, design, and warning/instruction. As will be developed in the following cases, courts were inconsistent in the methods employed when establishing defects — at least for liability purposes. It all purportedly started with the desire to impose strict liability, but many of the rules eventually took on a negligence tenor. In an effort to clarify some of the matters created through misinterpretation and/or misapplication of §402A in 1998, §402A was superseded by the Restatement (Third) of Torts: Products Liability.

3. Over the years, several justifications have been offered for making liability strict. Some of them are listed below.

   a. The injured party may find it difficult to prove negligence. This is especially true in circumstances where the damage to the product is such where it's hard to identify a specific defect or where a component part is defective and a reasonable inspection would not have discovered it.

   b. By making products available for purchase, manufacturers make certain representations related to the safety of the products, with consumers relying on those representations.

    c. Non-manufacturer distributors who are held strictly liable can exert pressure on the manufacturer to make safer products or seek indemnity.

    d. Distributors are uniquely positioned to absorb any costs that the imposition of liability creates by rolling them into the cost of the product or purchasing insurance.

    e. Imposing strict liability is necessary to create the necessary incentive to make safe products, an incentive that the prospect of negligence liable was insufficient to generate.

Restatement (Third) of Torts: Products Liability

§2. Categories of Product Defect

A product is defective when, at the time of sale or distribution, it contains a manufacturing defect, is defective in design, or is defective because of inadequate instructions or warnings. A product:

    (a) contains a manufacturing defect when the product departs from its intended design even though all possible care was exercised in the preparation and marketing of the product;

    (b) is defective in design when the foreseeable risks of harm posed by the product could have been reduced or avoided by the adoption of a reasonable alternative design by the seller or other distributor, or a predecessor in the commercial chain of distribution, and the omission of the alternative design renders the product not reasonably safe;

    (c) is defective because of inadequate instructions or warnings when the foreseeable risks of harm posed by the product could have been reduced or avoided by the provision of reasonable instructions or warnings by the seller or other distributor, or a predecessor in the commercial chain of distribution, and the omission of the instructions or warnings renders the product not reasonably safe.

B. MANUFACTURING DEFECTS

Rix v. General Motors Corp.
222 Mont. 318, 723 P.2d 195 (Mont. 1986)

Weber, Justice.

In 1978, Michael Rix was injured when the pickup he was driving was hit from behind by a 1978 General Motors Corporation (GMC) two ton chassis-cab, which had been equipped with a water tank after sale by the GMC dealer. Plaintiff sued GMC on a theory of strict liability in the Yellowstone County District Court. Following a jury verdict for GMC, plaintiff appeals. We reverse and remand for new trial.

ISSUE[]:

1. Did the trial court properly instruct the jury on strict liability?

The pertinent portion of the revised pretrial order contained the following stipulated facts:

1. That on the 4th day of August, 1978, on the Shepherd Road, near mile post number 1, in the County of Yellowstone, State of Montana, JOHN STANLEY FISHER was driving a 1978 GMC, two ton chassis-cab equipped with a water tank when it collided with the rear of the 1968 GMC pickup truck being operated by MICHAEL RIX and in which Michael Eaton was a passenger.

2. That at the time and date of the . . . accident, the 1978 GMC two ton chassis-cab equipped with a water tank was 4-6 weeks old, having been purchased and delivery taken on or about June 28, 1978.

3. GENERAL MOTORS CORPORATION designed, manufactured in part, assembled, and sold the certain 1978 two ton chassis-cab. . . .

4. [G]ENERAL MOTORS CORPORATION designed, manufactured in part, and assembled the . . . vehicle at its plant in Pontiac, Michigan.

5. That on or about May 25, 1978, Town and Country GMC, an authorized dealer of General Motors Corporation took delivery of the aforesaid chassis-cab at the Silverdome in Pontiac, Michigan, and brought it to Billings.

6. The failure of a brake line carrying hydraulic fluid was a cause of the brake failure occurring on the aforesaid vehicle on August 4, 1978.

7. The 1978 two ton chassis-cab . . . was equipped with a single brake system offered as the standard system and not a split (dual) system.

8. At the time the . . . 1978 two ton chassis-cab . . . was designed, manufactured in part, and assembled, . . . GENERAL MOTORS CORPORATION had the knowledge, capacity, and capability to incorporate a split (dual) brake system, and in fact did so as optional equipment, if ordered by purchaser. . . .

Plaintiff contends he was injured by an unreasonably dangerous 1978 two ton chassis-cab, which had been placed in the stream of commerce by GMC. Premised on a theory of strict liability, he maintains the product was unreasonably dangerous because of both manufacturing and design defects.

The parties stipulated that the accident occurred because of brake failure. Expert testimony from both parties established that the fluids necessary to the braking system had escaped when a brake tube came out of a nut where it fastened to the top of the Hydrovac, a booster unit. Witnesses also testified that the brake tube came out of the nut either because the tube broke or was improperly flared.

Plaintiff contends that the tube broke because there was a manufacturing defect in the tube, basically a bad flare, when the truck came off the assembly line. Plaintiff also contends that the brake system on the truck, a single system, was defectively designed, and argues that GMC's knowledge of available technology coupled with the foreseeable use of the vehicle should have mandated a dual braking system, which provides extra braking power. Plaintiff maintains the accident would have been less severe or would not have happened had the truck been equipped with a dual system.

GMC agreed that the brake tube was defective, but contended that the tube had been altered after it left the GMC assembly line, so that the defective tube was not GMC's responsibility. GMC also contended that the single system was neither a design defect nor unreasonably dangerous, and that the accident would have occurred even if the truck had been equipped with a dual brake system.

I

Did the trial court properly instruct the jury on strict liability?

INSTRUCTION NO. 10

I will now define the doctrine of strict liability to you. Keep in mind that this is only a general definition, and must be considered along with the specific instructions on the same topic which follow. The general principle of strict liability as it applies in the State of Montana is:

(1) One who sells any product in a defective condition unreasonably dangerous to the user or consumer or to his property is subject to liability for physical harm thereby caused to the ultimate user or consumer, or to his property, if:

(a) the seller is engaged in the business of selling such a product, and

(b) it is expected and does reach the user or consumer without substantial change in the condition in which it is sold.

(2) The rule stated in Subsection (1) applies although

(a) the seller has exercised all possible care in the preparation and sale of his product, and

(b) the user or consumer has not bought the product from or entered into any contractual relation with the seller.

INSTRUCTION NO. 11

The plaintiff must establish three essential elements in order to recover under his theory of strict liability. They are as follows:

First, that the defendant General Motors Corporation manufactured and sold a product which at the time General Motors sold it was in a defective condition unreasonably dangerous to the consumer or user;

Second, that the product was expected to and did reach the ultimate consumer without substantial change in the condition it was in at the time it was sold; and

Third, that the defective condition in the product proximately caused injury to the plaintiff.

Jury instruction #10 is the same as §402A Restatement (Second) of Torts (1965). Plaintiff did not make an objection at the time the instruction was offered. Plaintiff objected to jury instruction #11 "on the grounds that the second standard improperly states Montana law regarding tracing requirement back to the manufacturer."

. . . Under a manufacturing defect theory, the essential question is whether the product was flawed or defective because it was not constructed correctly by the manufacturer:

> [M]anufacturing defects, by definition, are "imperfections that inevitably occur in a typically small percentage of products of a given design as a result of the fallibility of the manufacturing process. A [defectively manufactured] product does not conform in some significant aspect to the intended design, nor does it conform to the great majority of products manufactured in accordance with that design." Stated differently, a defectively manufactured product is flawed because it is misconstructed without regard to whether the intended design of the manufacturer was safe or not. Such defects result from some mishap in the manufacturing process itself, improper workmanship, or because defective materials were used in construction.

Restatement (Second) of Torts, §402A (1965) has been adopted by this Court as the applicable law with regard to strict liability under a manufacturing defect theory. The Restatement view is contained in Instruction #10, previously quoted in this opinion. In the context of strict liability under a manufacturing defect theory, we conclude that Instructions #10 and #11, as given by the District Court, are adequate. On retrial if the plaintiff presents a manufacturing defect theory, Instructions #10 and #11 must be limited so that they apply only to the manufacturing defect aspect of the case.

We reverse and remand for a new trial in conformity with this opinion.

[A new trial was ordered mainly because of issues involving the design claim.]

PREPARING FOR CLASS

1. The plaintiff claims both manufacturing and design defects. The pleading rules allow for alternative theories of liability to be pled,

and the operation of statutes of limitations force plaintiffs to bring legal actions within a certain period or lose the right to do so. The factual support for each claim is largely similar; the arguments for defectiveness diverge. See how the claims can co-exist without contradiction.

2. The fact that GMC agreed that the brake tube was defective is of little significance; its defense to the manufacturing claims lies in a different argument. Get comfortable with the factual and legal support for the argument; it is a common one for defendants involved in manufacturing defect lawsuits. Remember that the plaintiff carries the burden on defectiveness, and the operative jury instruction parrots §402A.

3. The fact that Rix was neither the purchaser or user of the truck should make manifest the total abolishment of any privity related argument in products cases.

APPLYING THE LAW

Defendant manufactures and sells widgets. One, allegedly suffering from a manufacturing defect, injures plaintiff, resulting in a lawsuit sounding in strict liability. Defendant's quality control program has won the industry's top award for five consecutive years. Is evidence of the quality control accolades admissible in the instant case?

INCREASING YOUR UNDERSTANDING

1. *Liability is strict not absolute.* GMC is not potentially liable simply because it made the truck; its liability is contingent on plaintiff proving that the truck was defective when it left GMC as it deviated from its intended design. Manufacturing defects are flaws or imperfections in products as a result of the limitations of the manufacturing process, and often many of them are not remotely attributable to any act of negligence. But courts have not hesitated holding manufacturers liable when their products don't measure up to what was originally intended. As such, among the three types of defects, this is where liability is most strict notwithstanding the legal verbiage that might be used to describe the type of liability; the manufacturer is declared strictly liable or negligent per se, and the plaintiff meets her burden on defectiveness when she convinces the court that it left the control of the manufacturer in an unintended condition.

2. *Food products.* Food products don't fit neatly within any category of defectiveness; some might view them as manufacturing defects, others

as design. Two rules have emerged when food products are involved: the Foreign Natural and Consumer Expectation Tests.

a. Foreign Natural: Under the foreign natural test, the jury is asked to determine whether the alleged defect in the food product was "foreign" or "natural" to the food product; strict liability will follow only if the defect is unnatural to the product. The simplicity of the test made it attractive during a time when courts were most interested in ridding their dockets of litigation, especially cases where liability could be easily determined. (David G. Owen, Products Liability Law, §7.5 (2005).) Under the test, if the defect results from a foreign object, the defendant is strictly liable; if from something natural, the jury is asked to determine if the defendants conduct amounted to negligence. Under this test, a gum manufacturer who left a screw in a piece of gum was liable to the plaintiff who broke a tooth while chewing the gum (Hickman v. Wm. Wrigley, Jr. Co., Inc. 768 So. 2d 812 (La. App. 2 Cir. 2000)), but a restaurant that served a bowl of fish chowder containing a bone, which on consumption led to the plaintiff's throat being obstructed, was not (Webster v. Blue Ship Tea Room, Inc. 347 Mass. 421, 198 N.E.2d 309 (Mass. 1964)).

b. Consumer Expectation: Dissatisfied with some of the uneven results under the foreign natural test, courts turned to this test as it better furthered the pro-consumer goal of the judiciary and introduced some flexibility into the analysis. Under this test, the question is whether the community of consumers would find the food product more dangerous than what would ordinarily be associated with the consumption of the product. "A strong majority of courts have applied the 'reasonable consumer expectations test' in deciding whether an ingredient that caused the plaintiff's harm is an unanticipated adulteration or is an inherent aspect of the product." Restatement (Third) of Torts: Products Liability §7 comment b(1).

C. DESIGN DEFECTS

Potter v. Chicago Pneumatic Tool Co.
241 Conn. 199, 694 A.2d 1319 (Conn. 1997)

KATZ, Associate Justice.

This appeal arises from a products liability action brought by the plaintiffs[1] against the defendants, Chicago Pneumatic Tool Company (Chicago

---

1. For purposes of this opinion, the plaintiffs are Joseph Gladu, David Thompson, Roy Tutt, Thomas Brayman and Jaime Irizarry. They are among more than 400 individuals pursuing claims against the

Pneumatic), Stanley Works and Dresser Industries, Inc. (Dresser). The plaintiffs claim that they were injured in the course of their employment as shipyard workers at the General Dynamics Corporation Electric Boat facility (Electric Boat) in Groton as a result of using pneumatic hand tools manufactured by the defendants. Specifically, the plaintiffs allege that the tools were defectively designed because they exposed the plaintiffs to excessive vibration, and because the defendants failed to provide adequate warnings with respect to the potential danger presented by excessive vibration.

The defendants appeal from the judgment rendered on jury verdicts in favor of the plaintiffs, claiming [among other things that]: the trial court should have rendered judgment for the defendants notwithstanding the verdicts because (a) there was insufficient evidence that the tools were defective in that the plaintiffs had presented no evidence of a feasible alternative design. . . .

The trial record reveals the following facts, which are undisputed for purposes of this appeal. The plaintiffs were employed at Electric Boat as "grinders," positions which required use of pneumatic hand tools to smooth welds and metal surfaces.[2] In the course of their employment, the plaintiffs used various pneumatic hand tools, including chipping and grinding tools, which were manufactured and sold by the defendants. The plaintiffs' use of the defendants' tools at Electric Boat spanned approximately twenty-five years, from the mid-1960s until 1987. The plaintiffs suffer from permanent vascular and neurological impairment of their hands, which has caused blanching of their fingers, pain, numbness, tingling, reduction of grip strength, intolerance of cold and clumsiness from restricted blood flow. As a result, the plaintiffs have been unable to continue their employment as grinders and their performance of other activities has been restricted. The plaintiffs' symptoms are consistent with a diagnosis of hand arm vibration syndrome. Expert testimony confirmed that exposure to vibration is a significant contributing factor to the development of hand arm vibration syndrome, and that a clear relationship exists between the level of vibration exposure and the risk of developing the syndrome.

In addition to these undisputed facts, the following evidence, taken in favor of the jury's verdict, was presented. Ronald Guarneri, an industrial hygienist at Electric Boat, testified that he had conducted extensive testing of tools used at the shipyard in order to identify occupational hazards. This testing revealed that a large number of the defendants' tools violated the limits for vibration exposure established by the American National Standards Institute (institute),

---

defendants. The named plaintiff, John Potter, is not a party to this appeal, the action as it pertained to him having been withdrawn prior to trial.

2. One expert witness explained the design and purpose of these pneumatic tools: "[T]he machines are connected to an air hose that has air pressure, and you squeeze some kind of a valve and the air pressure is released into what's called an air motor, which is a turbine of sorts. The air propels the motor and rotates the grinding device and you apply the grinding wheel or attachment to the metal that you want to grind."

and exceeded the threshold limit promulgated by the American Conference of Governmental and Industrial Hygienists (conference).

Richard Alexander, a mechanical engineering professor at Texas A & M University, testified that because machinery vibration has harmful effects on machines and on people, engineers routinely research ways to reduce or to eliminate the amount of vibration that a machine produces when operated. Alexander discussed various methods available to control vibration, including isolation (the use of springs or mass to isolate vibration), dampening (adding weights to dampen vibrational effects), and balancing (adding weights to counterbalance machine imbalances that cause vibration). Alexander testified that each of these methods has been available to manufacturers for at least thirty-five years.

Alexander also stated that, in 1983, he had been engaged by another pneumatic tool manufacturer to perform testing of methods by which to reduce the level of vibration in its three horsepower vertical grinder. The vertical grinder had a live handle, which contained hardware for the air power, and a dead handle, which vibrated significantly more than the live handle because it weighed less. Alexander modified the design by inserting rubber isolation mounts between the handles and the housing, and by adding an aluminum rod to the dead handle to match the weight of the two handles. As a result of these modifications, which were published in 1987, Alexander achieved a threefold reduction in vibration levels.

The plaintiffs also presented the testimony of Charles Suggs, a research engineer at North Carolina State University, who has been investigating machinery vibration reduction since the 1960s. In 1968, Suggs published the first of several papers in which he discussed his success in reducing vibration hazards in chain saws by inserting rubber mounts between the handle and chain saw body. In the 1970s, he also published a series of articles reporting how he had reduced vibration by 70 percent in tools without handles by wrapping the tools with a resilient foam rubber material and a metal sleeve. Additionally, in 1988, Suggs tested the defendants' die grinders and, by applying the same technique, reduced the levels of vibration by between 35 and 60 percent. Additional facts will be presented as warranted.

After a six week trial, the trial court rendered judgment on jury verdicts in favor of the plaintiffs. Finding that the defendants' tools had been defectively designed so as to render them unreasonably dangerous, the jury awarded the plaintiffs compensatory damages.

I

We first address the defendants' argument that the trial court improperly failed to render judgment for the defendants notwithstanding the verdicts because there was insufficient evidence for the jury to have found that the tools had been defectively designed. Specifically, the defendants claim that, in order to establish a prima facie design defect case, the plaintiffs were required to prove that there was a feasible alternative design available at the time that the defendants put their tools into the stream of commerce. We disagree.

In order properly to evaluate the parties' arguments, we begin our analysis with a review of the development of strict tort liability, focusing specifically on design defect liability. At common law, a person injured by a product had no cause of action against the manufacturer of the product unless that person was in privity of contract with the manufacturer. This rule, established in *Winterbottom v. Wright*, 152 Eng. Rep. 402 (1842), made privity a condition precedent to actions against manufacturers grounded in negligence. American courts widely adopted this rule and, for the next one-half century, the privity requirement remained steadfast in American jurisprudence.

The evolution of modern products liability law began with the landmark case of *MacPherson v. Buick Motor Co.*, 217 N.Y. 382, 111 N.E. 1050 (1916), in which the New York Court of Appeals extended the manufacturer's duty to all persons in fact harmed by products that were reasonably certain to cause injury when negligently made. As Justice Cardozo wrote in *MacPherson*, "[i]f the nature of a thing is such that it is reasonably certain to place life and limb in peril when negligently made, it is then a thing of danger. Its nature gives warning of the consequences to be expected. If to the element of danger there is added knowledge that the thing will be used by persons other than the purchaser, and used without new tests, then, irrespective of contract, the manufacturer of this thing of danger is under a duty to make it carefully." *Id.*, at 389, 111 N.E. 1050. The *MacPherson* reasoning eventually was accepted by nearly all American courts.

Similarly, the New Jersey Supreme Court in *Henningsen v. Bloomfield Motors, Inc.*, 32 N.J. 358, 161 A.2d 69 (1960), imposed "strict liability" upon the manufacturer of a defective product, but on a warranty basis. Discarding the antiquated notions of privity of contract, the court imposed upon the manufacturer an implied warranty of merchantability to a third party. The *Henningsen* court stated: "We are convinced that the cause of justice in this area of the law can be served only by recognizing that [the third party] is such a person who, in the reasonable contemplation of the parties to the warranty, might be expected to become a user of the [product]. Accordingly, [the third party's] lack of privity does not stand in the way of prosecution of the injury suit against the [manufacturer]." *Id.*, at 413, 161 A.2d 69.

The next major development in products liability law did not attempt to modify the negligence rule any further, but, rather, urged its replacement. In *Escola v. Coca Cola Bottling Co. of Fresno*, 24 Cal. 2d 453, 461, 150 P.2d 436 (1944). Justice Roger Traynor, in a now famous concurring opinion, first suggested that courts should hold manufacturers liable without fault when defective products cause personal injury. Justice Traynor asserted that strict liability would serve several policy justifications: (1) manufacturers could readily absorb or pass on the cost of liability to consumers as a cost of doing business; (2) manufacturers would be deterred from marketing defective products; and (3) injured persons, who lack familiarity with the manufacturing process, would no longer shoulder the burden of proving negligence. *Id.*, at 462, 150 P.2d 436 (Traynor, J., concurring).

Although Justice Traynor's argument did not prevail in *Escola*, nearly twenty years later he wrote for the majority in *Greenman v. Yuba Power Products, Inc.*, 59 Cal. 2d 57, 62, 377 P.2d 897, 27 Cal. Rptr. 697 (1963), holding a manufacturer strictly liable because its defective product caused injury to the plaintiff. The *Greenman* court stated that "[a] manufacturer is strictly liable in tort when an article he places on the market, knowing that it is to be used without inspection for defects, proves to have a defect that causes injury to a human being." *Id.* The court explained that the purpose of this rule "is to insure that the costs of injuries resulting from defective products are borne by the manufacturers that put such products on the market rather than by the injured persons who are powerless to protect themselves." *Id.*, at 63, 27 Cal. Rptr. 697, 377 P.2d 897.

Two years later, §402A of the Restatement (Second) of Torts adopted, with slight variation, the doctrine of strict tort liability espoused in *Greenman*. Section 402A provides:

> "(1) One who sells any product in a defective condition unreasonably dangerous to the user or consumer or to his property is subject to liability for physical harm thereby caused to the ultimate user or consumer, or to his property, if
>
> "(a) the seller is engaged in the business of selling such a product, and
>
> "(b) it is expected to and does reach the user or consumer without substantial change in the condition in which it is sold.
>
> "(2) The rule stated in Subsection (1) applies although
>
> "(a) the seller has exercised all possible care in the preparation and sale of his product, and
>
> "(b) the user or consumer has not bought the product from or entered into any contractual relation with the seller." 2 Restatement (Second), Torts §402A (1965).

Products liability law has thus evolved to hold manufacturers strictly liable for unreasonably dangerous products that cause injury to ultimate users. Nevertheless, strict tort liability does not transform manufacturers into insurers, nor does it impose absolute liability. As the Wisconsin Supreme Court has pointed out, "[f]rom the plaintiff's point of view the most beneficial aspect of the rule is that it relieves him of proving specific acts of negligence and protects him from the defenses of notice of breach, disclaimer, and lack of privity in the implied warranty concepts of sales and contracts." *Dippel v. Sciano*, 37 Wis. 2d 443, 460, 155 N.W.2d 55 (1967). Strict tort liability merely relieves the plaintiff from proving that the manufacturer was negligent and allows the plaintiff to establish instead the defective condition of the product as the principal basis of liability

Although courts have widely accepted the concept of strict tort liability, some of the specifics of strict tort liability remain in question. In particular, courts have sharply disagreed over the appropriate definition of defectiveness in design cases. As the Alaska Supreme Court has stated: "Design defects present the most perplexing problems in the field of strict products liability because there is no readily ascertainable external measure of defectiveness. While manufacturing flaws can be evaluated against the intended design of the product, no such objective standard exists in the design defect context."

Section 402A imposes liability only for those defective products that are "unreasonably dangerous" to "the ordinary consumer who purchases it, with the ordinary knowledge common to the community as to its characteristics." 2 Restatement (Second), supra, §402A, comment (i). Under this formulation, known as the "consumer expectation" test, a manufacturer is strictly liable for any condition not contemplated by the ultimate consumer that will be unreasonably dangerous to the consumer.

Some courts, however, have refused to adopt the "unreasonably dangerous" definition, determining that it injects a concept of foreseeability into strict tort liability, which is inappropriate in such cases because the manufacturer's liability is not based upon negligence. See *Caterpillar Tractor Co. v. Beck*, supra, 593 P.2d at 882-83 (articulating that "unreasonably dangerous" narrows scope of recovery and unduly increases plaintiff's burden); *Cronin v. J.B.E. Olson Corp.*, 8 Cal. 3d 121, 133, 501 P.2d 1153, 104 Cal. Rptr. 433 (1972) ("[w]e think that a requirement that a plaintiff also prove that the defect made the product 'unreasonably dangerous' places upon him a significantly increased burden and represents a step backward").

In *Barker v. Lull Engineering Co.*, 20 Cal. 3d 413, 435, 573 P.2d 443, 143 Cal. Rptr. 225 (1978), the California Supreme Court established two alternative tests for determining design defect liability: (1) the consumer expectation analysis; and (2) a balancing test that inquires whether a product's risks outweigh its benefits. Under the latter, otherwise known as the "risk-utility," test, the manufacturer bears the burden of proving that the product's utility is not outweighed by its risks in light of various factors.[8] Three other jurisdictions have subsequently adopted California's two-pronged test, including the burden-shifting risk-utility inquiry.[9]

---

8. In evaluating the adequacy of a product's design, the *Barker* court stated that "a jury may consider, among other relevant factors, the gravity of the danger posed by the challenged design, the likelihood that such danger would occur, the mechanical feasibility of a safer alternative design, the financial cost of an improved design, and the adverse consequences to the product and to the consumer that would result from an alternative design."

9. Additionally, other states have adopted *Barker*-type alternative tests, but have declined to shift the burden of proving the product's risks and utility to the manufacturer.

Other jurisdictions apply only a risk-utility test in determining whether a manufacturer is liable for a design defect. To assist the jury in evaluating the product's risks and utility, these courts have set forth a list of nonexclusive factors to consider when deciding whether a product has been defectively designed.[10]

With this history in mind, we turn to the development of strict products liability law in Connecticut. In *Garthwait v. Burgio*, 153 Conn. 284, 289-90, 216 A.2d 189 (1965), this court recognized a products liability cause of action sounding in tort and became one of the first jurisdictions to adopt the rule provided in §402A. In *Garthwait*, the court stated: "Where the liability is fundamentally founded on tort rather than contract there appears no sound reason why the manufacturer should escape liability simply because the injured user, a party in the normal chain of distribution, was not in contractual privity with it by purchase and sale." This court has further held that "[i]n order to recover under the doctrine of strict liability in tort the plaintiff must prove that: (1) the defendant was engaged in the business of selling the product; (2) the product was in a defective condition unreasonably dangerous to the consumer or user; (3) the defect caused the injury for which compensation was sought; (4) the defect existed at the time of the sale; and (5) the product was expected to and did reach the consumer without substantial change in condition."

This court has long held that in order to prevail in a design defect claim, "[t]he plaintiff must prove that the product is unreasonably dangerous." We have derived our definition of "unreasonably dangerous" from comment (i) to §402A, which provides that "the article sold must be dangerous to an extent beyond that which would be contemplated by the ordinary consumer who purchases it, with the ordinary knowledge common to the community as to its characteristics." 2 Restatement (Second), supra, §402A, comment (i). This "consumer expectation" standard is now well established in Connecticut strict products liability decisions.

The defendants propose that it is time for this court to abandon the consumer expectation standard and adopt the requirement that the plaintiff must

---

10. These factors are typically derived from an influential article by Dean John Wade, in which he suggested consideration of the following factors:

"1. The usefulness and desirability of the product-its utility to the user and to the public as a whole.

"2. The safety aspects of the product-the likelihood that it will cause injury, and the probable seriousness of the injury.

"3. The availability of a substitute product which would meet the same need and not be as unsafe.

"4. The manufacturer's ability to eliminate the unsafe character of the product without impairing its usefulness or making it too expensive to maintain its utility.

"5. The user's ability to avoid danger by the exercise of care in the use of the product.

"6. The user's anticipated awareness of the dangers inherent in the product and their avoidability, because of general public knowledge of the obvious condition of the product, or of the existence of suitable warnings or instructions.

"7. The feasibility, on the part of the manufacturer, of spreading the loss by setting the price of the product or carrying liability insurance." J. Wade, "On the Nature of Strict Tort Liability for Products," 44 Miss. L.J. 825, 837-38 (1973).

prove the existence of a reasonable alternative design in order to prevail on a design defect claim. We decline to accept the defendants' invitation.

In support of their position, the defendants point to the second tentative draft of the Restatement (Third) of Torts: Products Liability (1995) (Draft Restatement [Third]), which provides that, as part of a plaintiff's prima facie case, the plaintiff must establish the availability of a reasonable alternative design. Specifically, §2(b) of the Draft Restatement (Third) provides: "[A] product is defective in design when the foreseeable risks of harm posed by the product could have been reduced or avoided by the adoption of a reasonable alternative design by the seller or other distributor, or a predecessor in the commercial chain of distribution, and the omission of the alternative design renders the product not reasonably safe." The reporters to the Draft Restatement (Third) state that "[v]ery substantial authority supports the proposition that [the] plaintiff must establish a reasonable alternative design in order for a product to be adjudged defective in design." Draft Restatement (Third), supra, §2, reporters' note to comment (c), p. 50.

We point out that this provision of the Draft Restatement (Third) has been a source of substantial controversy among commentators. Contrary to the rule promulgated in the Draft Restatement (Third), our independent review of the prevailing common law reveals that the majority of jurisdictions *do not* impose upon plaintiffs an absolute requirement to prove a feasible alternative design.

In our view, the feasible alternative design requirement imposes an undue burden on plaintiffs that might preclude otherwise valid claims from jury consideration.[12] Such a rule would require plaintiffs to retain an expert witness even in cases in which lay jurors can infer a design defect from circumstantial evidence. Connecticut courts, however, have consistently stated that a jury may, under appropriate circumstances, infer a defect from the evidence without the necessity of expert testimony.

Moreover, in some instances, a product may be in a defective condition unreasonably dangerous to the user even though no feasible alternative design is available. In such instances, the manufacturer may be strictly liable for a design defect notwithstanding the fact that there are no safer alternative designs in existence.

Although today we continue to adhere to our long-standing rule that a product's defectiveness is to be determined by the expectations of an ordinary consumer, we nevertheless recognize that there may be instances involving complex product designs in which an ordinary consumer may not be able

---

12. Indeed, as one commentator has pointed out: "Apparently, without expert evidence in [the] plaintiff's prima facie case, [the] defendant would be entitled to a directed verdict. This is despite the advice in comment d [of the Draft Restatement (Third), supra] that, due to [the] plaintiff's limited access to relevant data, [the] plaintiff should not be required to make a detailed showing. Moreover, it is clear that defendants will hold plaintiffs to their burden of showing the alternative design to be reasonable considering the 'overall safety of the entire product.' In short, the proposed standard requires the plaintiff to put on a case to the judge supporting a product the defendant did not make. Only then will the plaintiff be permitted to place the merits of his or her case before the jury. Worse yet, due to the added cost and risk of a directed verdict, some plaintiffs with meritorious claims will not reach the jury, and others may not find representation at all." P. Corboy, supra, 61 Tenn. L. Rev. 1095-96.

to form expectations of safety. In such cases, a consumer's expectations may be viewed in light of various factors that balance the utility of the product's design with the magnitude of its risks. We find persuasive the reasoning of those jurisdictions that have modified their formulation of the consumer expectation test by incorporating risk-utility factors into the ordinary consumer expectation analysis. Thus, the modified consumer expectation test provides the jury with the product's risks and utility and then inquires whether a reasonable consumer would consider the product unreasonably dangerous. As the Supreme Court of Washington stated in *Seattle-First National Bank v. Tabert*, supra, at 154, 542 P.2d 774, "[i]n determining the reasonable expectations of the ordinary consumer, a number of factors must be considered. The relative cost of the product, the gravity of the potential harm from the claimed defect and the cost and feasibility of eliminating or minimizing the risk may be relevant in a particular case. In other instances the nature of the product or the nature of the claimed defect may make other factors relevant to the issue. Accordingly, under this modified formulation, the consumer expectation test would establish the product's risks and utility, and the inquiry would then be whether a reasonable consumer would consider the product design unreasonably dangerous.

In our view, the relevant factors that a jury *may* consider include, but are not limited to, the usefulness of the product, the likelihood and severity of the danger posed by the design, the feasibility of an alternative design, the financial cost of an improved design, the ability to reduce the product's danger without impairing its usefulness or making it too expensive, and the feasibility of spreading the loss by increasing the product's price. The availability of a feasible alternative design is a factor that the plaintiff may, rather than must, prove in order to establish that a product's risks outweigh its utility.

Furthermore, we emphasize that our adoption of a risk-utility balancing component to our consumer expectation test does not signal a retreat from strict tort liability. In weighing a product's risks against its utility, the focus of the jury should be on the product itself, and not on the conduct of the manufacturer.[16]

Although today we adopt a modified formulation of the consumer expectation test, we emphasize that we do not require a plaintiff to present evidence relating to the product's risks and utility in every case. As the California Court of Appeals has stated: "There are certain kinds of accidents—even where fairly complex machinery is involved—[that] are so bizarre that the average juror, upon hearing the particulars, might reasonably think: 'Whatever the user may have expected from that contraption, it certainly wasn't that.'" *Akers v. Kelley Co.*, 173 Cal. App.3d 633, 651, 219 Cal. Rptr. 513 (1985). Accordingly, the ordinary consumer expectation test is appropriate when the everyday experience of the particular product's users permits the inference that the

---

16. As Dean Keeton has stated, "[t]he change in the substantive law as regards the liability of makers of products and other sellers in the marketing chain has been from fault to defect. The plaintiff is no longer required to impugn the maker, but he is required to impugn the product." P. Keeton, "Product Liability and the Meaning of Defect," 5 St. Mary's L.J. 30, 33 (1973).

product did not meet minimum safety expectations. See *Soule v. General Motors Corp.*, 8 Cal. 4th 548, 567, 882 P.2d 298, 34 Cal. Rptr. 2d 607 (1994).

Conversely, the jury should engage in the risk-utility balancing required by our modified consumer expectation test when the particular facts do not reasonably permit the inference that the product did not meet the safety expectations of the ordinary consumer. Furthermore, instructions based on the ordinary consumer expectation test would not be appropriate when, as a matter of law, there is insufficient evidence to support a jury verdict under that test. In such circumstances, the jury should be instructed solely on the modified consumer expectation test we have articulated today.

In this respect, it is the function of the trial court to determine whether an instruction based on the ordinary consumer expectation test or the modified consumer expectation test, or both, is appropriate in light of the evidence presented. In making this determination, the trial court must ascertain whether, under each test, there is sufficient evidence as a matter of law to warrant the respective instruction.

With these principles in mind, we now consider whether, in the present case, the trial court properly instructed the jury with respect to the definition of design defect for the purposes of strict tort liability. The trial court instructed the jury that a manufacturer may be strictly liable if the plaintiffs prove, among other elements, that the product in question was in a defective condition, unreasonably dangerous to the ultimate user. The court further instructed the jury that, in determining whether the tools were unreasonably dangerous, it may draw its conclusions based on the reasonable expectations of an ordinary user of the defendants' tools. Because there was sufficient evidence as a matter of law to support the determination that the tools were unreasonably dangerous based on the ordinary consumer expectation test, we conclude that this instruction was appropriately given to the jury.

"Whether a product is unreasonably dangerous is a question of fact to be determined by the jury. . . . [T]he jury can draw their own reasonable conclusions as to the expectations of the ordinary consumer and the knowledge common in the community at large." (Citation omitted; internal quotation marks omitted.) *Giglio v. Connecticut Light & Power Co.*, supra, 180 Conn. at 235, 429 A.2d 486. . . .

The judgment is reversed and the case is remanded for a new trial on the design defect claim based on various other errors committed by the trial court.

PREPARING FOR CLASS

1. The original version of the "consumer expectations" test can be found in comment (i) to §402A. The operative language is as follows: To be defective "the article sold must be dangerous to an extent beyond that which would be contemplated by the ordinary consumer who purchases it, with the ordinary knowledge common to the community as to

its characteristics." The test found favor particularly in pro-strict liability jurisdictions as the test shifted the focus from an assessment of the manufacturer's conduct to a standard that would allow the public to control how defects would be determined.

2. Plaintiffs claim defects in the design of a product whenever a product causes injury not attributable to a manufacturing or warning/instruction defect. In short, a design defect claim arises in circumstances where the product is made as intended but use of the product has caused an injury allowing for an argument that the product is not "sufficiently safe."

3. Plaintiffs often plead warning claims with design claims as an alternative theory of liability. As such, they are not mutually exclusive.

INCREASING YOUR UNDERSTANDING

1. "The approaches for determination of the meaning of 'defect' in design cases fall into four general categories. The first, usually associated with Dean Wade, employs a negligence risk-utility analysis, but focuses upon whether the manufacturer would be judged negligent if it had known of the product's dangerous condition at the time it was marketed. The second, associated with Dean Keeton, compares the risk and utility of the product at the time of trial. The third focuses on consumer expectations about the product. The fourth combines the *risk-utility and consumer-expectation tests*." See Prentis v. Yale Mfg. Co., 421 Mich. 670, 365 N.W.2d 176 (Mich. 1984). Each "approach" will be discussed separately below.

    a. *Risk utility negligence*: Under this test, the jury is asked to consider and weigh various aspects of the subject product and eventually decide whether the product was defective, i.e., whether the manufacturer was unreasonable in designing the product. Over the years, courts have varied in what the jury would be required to balance (footnote 3 in *Potter*), but the "Wade" factors (footnote 5 in *Potter*) are often cited by courts in whole or in part. In some quarters it is described as a negligence test, as it relies on factors known to the manufacturer at the time the product was produced. Others might describe the test as strict depending on whether the factors are viewed as focusing on the product as opposed to the manufacturer's conduct. In short, courts describe the test in conformance with the preferred doctrine.

    b. *Risk utility . . . time of trial*: This test is a variant of the above with one key distinction; the facts balanced or considered are those known at the time of trial as opposed to those known at the time the product was produced. Under this question the jury might be asked: "Would the defendant be considered negligent if it designed the product as it did with the knowledge that currently exists about the product?" This test in essence imputes facts to the manufacturer that may not have existed at the time of design and therefore expresses the purest form of strict liability as among the four approaches.

c. *Consumer expectation test*: Rooted in comment (i) in §402A, this test is particularly appealing in those jurisdictions that draw a discernable line between negligence and strict liability. As illustrated in *Potter*, it can be defined by simple regurgitation of the language in comment (i) or take on a more complicated definition with an infusion of many of the aspects of the risk-utility test.

d. *Combination of risks utility and consumer expectation tests*: Support for this combination test is best derived from the §402A suggestion that strict liability was limited to products sold in a "defective condition unreasonably dangerous to the user or consumer."

2. Does plaintiff have to prove the existence of a safer alternative design? Notwithstanding statements to the contrary in *Potter*, most states seem to require that plaintiff offer an alternative design by which the subject product can be compared before liability will be had against a defendant in a design case. This does not require for trial purposes that the plaintiff construct a prototype of the safer design, but simply offer credible testimony that one was practical and feasible at the time the subject product was sold. There are at least two circumstances where the court will relax this requirement: in cases involving obvious product malfunctions, and where the subject product failed to meet government or industry standards. See Restatement (Third) of Torts: Products Liability §2 comment b, §3, and §4.

3. *Special rules for prescription drugs.* There has been considerable debate over whether drug manufacturers should be subject to strict liability for injuries caused by prescription drugs. Since the American Law Institute release of §402A, much of the debate has centered on comment *k*, spawning various interpretations and considerable criticism. In short, comment *k* provides that strict liability should not be imposed on manufacturers of products described as "unavoidably unsafe" and contains a reference to a vaccination used to treat rabies. William Prosser, the reporter who drafted comment *k* explains: "The argument that industries producing potentially dangerous products should make good the harm, distribute it by liability insurance, and add the cost to the price of the product, encounters reason to pause, when we consider that two of the greatest boons to the human race, penicillin and cortisone, both have their dangerous side effects, and

that drug companies might well have been deterred from producing and selling them." W. Prosser, Handbook of the law of Torts Fourth Edition §99 at 661 (1971). Under comment *k*, immunity from strict liability is conditioned on the drug being properly prepared and accompanied with proper warnings. Most courts have responded to comment *k* by limiting its grant of immunity to truly "unavoidably unsafe" products", a determination made on a case-by-case basis. D. Owen, Products Liability Law §8.10 at 554 (2005).

4. *Duty to recall.* Often manufacturers become aware of hazards associated with the use of their products after there has been experience with their use post-distribution. Arguments have been advanced that in certain circumstances a manufacturer should have a duty to recall the product, either to remove it entirely from the market or to make it safe by redesigning/retrofitting it. Most courts have rejected the invitation to impose a common law duty on manufacturers to recall their products, finding such a burden too onerous and the court's ability to define the circumstances in which the duty would arise too arbitrary and/or difficult.

D. WARNING DEFECTS

Geressy v. Digital Equipment Corp.
980 F. Supp. 640 (E.D.N.Y. 1997)

Weinstein, Senior District Judge:
In suits commenced on March 16, 1994, plaintiffs Geressy, Jackson and Rotolo claimed that use of Digital's LK201 computer keyboard caused repetitive stress injuries (RSI). Their husbands alleged loss of consortium. The jury returned a verdict in favor of all plaintiffs on failure to warn claims, rejecting negligent design claims and declining to award punitive damages.

Defendant moved in all cases for judgment as a matter of law, a new trial and remittitur.

II. Facts

A. Patricia Geressy

Ms. Geressy worked as a secretary at the Port Authority for five years in the 1960s and again from 1984 until the present. She used defendant's keyboard and did other secretarial work. She had never been told that use of the keyboard might cause RSI.

She testified that the first manifestation of her condition "was [in] the summer of 1991. I started waking up at night with numbness, tingling in my hands, burning in my wrists, I didn't think much of it at the time."

Initially, Ms. Geressy's most severe problems were with her left wrist and hand. She underwent surgery for that wrist and hand in December of 1991. Because her first surgery was not successful, Ms. Geressy had a second operation in May of 1992. The second operation also gave no relief. She then started to experience pain in her right wrist and hand, her neck, and her shoulders. By the time the failure of her first two operations was known, the problems throughout her upper extremities had intensified. A third operation, on her neck, was recommended and eventually performed. By the end of 1994 her then treating doctor recommended surgery for her right hand.

After four operations and other therapy, Ms. Geressy's condition has continued to deteriorate. She has very little use of either hand.

Plaintiffs' experts testified that these problems were due to use of defendant's keyboard which presented ergonomic dangers requiring warnings to the user. Defendant's experts testified to the contrary, attributing plaintiff's physical symptoms to natural causes, finding no keyboard dangers, and no need to warn.

B. JILL M. JACKSON

In the 1980s Ms. Jackson worked intensively at one of defendant's computers without warnings of dangers. Some time around Christmas of 1989 she experienced "a pinching pain in [her] left elbow one day at work." She was treated with cortisone. She had elbow pain again a few months later in 1990 and sought the advice of another doctor. In filling out preliminary medical forms, she included in her complaints "lower back pain, right hip pain after sitting," and pain in the "upper right back shoulder area."

From 1990 on she has experienced debilitating pain in her elbows, forearms and hands, as well as a severe loss of strength in her upper extremities. In 1994 her disabilities forced her to leave her position as a legal secretary and to begin training in a new field.

C. JEANNETTE ROTOLO

Ms. Rotolo—married on May 15, 1993—has a short history of poor health. Until the onset of RSI, she was a "very athletic person," involved in such sports as karate and horseback riding. In April of 1993, Ms. Rotolo, a secretary using defendant's keyboard, first experienced symptoms of RSI. At work, she began to notice that her hands were "cold and stiff" and that she made an undue number of mistakes in typing. By June she began dropping things. Eventually the pain became constant.

In the years since her first symptoms, Ms. Rotolo has been diagnosed with a variety of specific RSIs. She has tried numerous treatments, from physical therapy to surgery on her wrists and hands. Since September of 1993, Ms. Rotolo has not been able to return to clerical work, although she has been able to do some lower-paid child care work that does not exacerbate her condition.

III. LAW AND ITS APPLICATION . . .

C. WARNINGS

1. Law

A "manufacturer's knowledge of special risks of harm attendant upon normal use of his product imposes a duty upon the manufacturer to warn adequately those using his product of those risks." . . .

The nature of the failure to warn tort in New York is fairly straight forward. *See* 1 N.Y. Pattern Jury Instructions—Civil §2:135 (1974) ("The manufacturer of a product which is reasonably certain to be dangerous if used in a way which he should reasonably foresee it would be used is under a duty to exercise reasonable care to give reasonable and adequate warning of any dangers known to him or which in the exercise of reasonable care he should have known and which the user of the product ordinarily would not discover. Reasonable care means that degree of care which a reasonably prudent person would exercise under the same circumstances."); IA N.Y. Pattern Jury Instructions—Civil §2:135 (3d ed. 1996). *See also* Restatement (Third) of Torts §2(c) (Draft adopted at May 1997 meeting of American Law Institute) ("A product is defective when, at the time of sale or distribution, it contains a manufacturing defect, is defective in design, or is defective because of inadequate instructions or warnings. A product . . . is defective because of inadequate instructions or warnings when the foreseeable risks of harm posed by the product could have been reduced or avoided by the provision of reasonable instructions or warnings by the seller or other distributor, or a predecessor in the commercial chain of distribution and the omission of the instructions or warnings renders the product not reasonably safe.").

Whether it is reasonably safe "when marketed" depends in part on what the manufacturer knew or should have known at the time of marketing—i.e., the state of the art. The manufacturer may be found to be unreasonable even after the product has been marketed if it should have been aware of dangers and it was reasonable to try to bring them to the attention of users of the product in the field.

The relevant portions of the charge, without substantial objection, became the law of the case:

> . . . A failure to warn or an inadequate warning about dangers attendant upon the use of the product may make the product not reasonably safe

and therefore defective even if it was otherwise properly designed, manufactured and sold.

A manufacturer of a product which is likely to be dangerous if utilized in an intended or reasonably foreseeable manner is under a duty to give adequate warning which would be useful to the user of any known dangers or dangers which in the exercise of reasonable care it should have known and which those foreseeably exposed to these products ordinarily would not discover. It is sufficient that a reasonable manufacturer which knew of the product's potential for causing injury would have concluded that the product should not have been marketed without suitable warnings.

When we talk of exercising "reasonable care" to give a warning, we mean that degree of care which a reasonably prudent person would exercise under the same circumstances.

The manufacturer must keep informed of knowledge of the effect of its products gained through research, reports, scientific literature and other available methods. It must, when reasonable, take such steps as are reasonably necessary to bring that knowledge to the attention of those foreseeably exposed to its products; that is, it must take reasonable steps to adequately warn them. In deciding what is reasonable you may consider the special circumstances of the case including the degree of hazard and whether it would reasonably be expected to be known to the user, the likelihood and severity of harm, and the feasibility of actually getting a warning to the plaintiff and the effectiveness of a warning, and whether the danger was not obvious to the user and whether the product causes immediate symptoms. A manufacturer does not have a duty to warn the user of a danger obvious to the user.

The duty to warn extends to dangers or defects about which the manufacturer either actually knew or should have known. "Should have known" means that a manufacturer is held to that level of knowledge which knowledge people in the particular industry had, and in view of the state of medical and scientific knowledge, and technology in general, and in the manufacturer's own experience in particular, reasonably should have had at the time the product was marketed. You may consider what was known or should have been known about the dangers of the product and the effects of a failure to take adequate precautions in its use.

You must decide, based on all the evidence that you have heard and seen during this trial, whether the plaintiff has proved that the defendant actually was, or should have been aware that its products, when used as the manufacturer would reasonably foresee that products would be used, could cause injury to those who used the products.

The precise disease suffered by a plaintiff need not have been foreseeable by the defendant. It is sufficient that the defendant knew or should have known that some serious injury could result from use of its products.

Each plaintiff had a right to decide for herself whether to work and what she would require as protection before continuing to work. The fact that another worker might have done the job does not negate the obligation of the defendant to a particular worker. If, however, as defendant claims, a plaintiff would have done her work the same way whether or not the defendant gave warnings, then there was no cause of the injuries from the failure to warn.

You may find that a warning must specifically and clearly identify each of the potential dangers involved in the products' uses including those dangers which might affect only some users, but not all users.

A defendant's duty to use reasonable care in giving adequate warning is nondelegable. That means that a defendant may not rely on others to issue an adequate warning. It was the duty of defendant to issue warnings, if any, that you find were necessary to those who might be exposed to the defendant's products.

The duty to warn does not terminate when an item produced by the manufacturer is sold. It continues to exist and be a responsibility of a defendant even after the product was sold, if it becomes known or reasonably should have become known to the manufacturer that persons who use the product may be harmed.

2. Application of Law to Facts

Plaintiffs produced sufficient evidence to make out a classic product liability case for failure to warn under New York law. They successfully persuaded the jury to find in their favor on all of the elements of such a case. Based on the evidence, the jury could have found that: defendant had a duty to plaintiffs to warn of the dangers inherent in its product, the LK201 keyboard; defendant breached that duty by not issuing appropriate warnings; and defendant's failure to warn was the proximate cause of all three plaintiffs' RSIs.

PREPARING FOR CLASS

1. In addition to requiring that products be properly manufactured and reasonably designed, courts require manufacturers to provide reasonable warnings/instructions to product users/consumers. Two reasons have been primarily advanced for imposing this duty: First, warnings are appropriate as a means of assisting the consumer in the decision to purchase the product, and second, warnings are valuable when it comes to risks/injury avoidance.

2. Manufacturer's strike a delicate balance when it comes to discharging their legal duty to warn and marketing the product in a way that

encourages its acquisition. In other words, concerns with turning a profit may dictate against affixing warnings to a product that might intimidate to the point of discouraging purchase. What should Digital have done here?

INCREASING YOUR UNDERSTANDING

1. Warnings are a relatively inexpensive way to instruct on how to avoid injury, certainly less expensive than implementing the redesign of a product. Courts generally assess the need to warn and the sufficiency of a warning under a reasonableness standard regardless of the theory upon which the case is advanced. In other words, the great majority of courts only require the manufacturer to warn of risks associated with the use of their products that they are aware of or should have been aware of.

2. *What makes for a good warning?* Generally courts focus on two aspects of a warning when assessing it for reasonableness: The process in delivering the warning and the substance of the information contained in it. Procedurally, warning should be attention-grabbing, so located in a conspicuous area of the product, and styled in a way that promotes respectful reading. Substantively, at a minimum a warning should identify the risks associated with a product's use, describe how the risks could be avoided, and give guidance on steps that should be taken should an injury occur. The warning should be detailed but not to the extent that excessive verbiage discourages the user from reading it all. The law requires reasonableness not perfection. The determination of whether the manufacturer acted reasonably is most often made by the jury.

3. Most states take the position that manufacturers are only obligated to warn of non-obvious (i.e., latent) risks associated with a product's use. Sometimes this position is stated as an affirmative defense, but most often it goes to the core of the underlying charge; for liability to follow there must be proof that the warning defect caused the plaintiff's injury, and a plaintiff who confronts an obvious risk is unlikely to be deterred by a warning. Of course, whether a risk is obvious is subject to debate, and any manufacturer hedging its decision to warn on the belief that the risk is legally obvious faces the reality that the jury may decide otherwise.

4. *"Adverse allergy or idiosyncratic reactions."* Once again the rule of reasonableness governs. There is no universal legal threshold that instructs when a manufacturer must take on the responsibility to warn those who might experience an allergic response upon using a product. In this area a manufacturer should be guided primarily by the percentage of users who suffer an adverse reaction to use and the severity of the reaction.

5. *Post-sale duty to warn.* Increasingly courts have been willing to impose a duty on manufacturers to provide warnings to consumers after the product has been sold. This sentiment is expressed in §10 of the Restatement (Third) of Torts: Products Liability, which provides:

(a) One engaged in the business of selling or otherwise distributing products is subject to liability for harm to persons or property caused by the seller's failure to provide a warning after the time of sale or distribution of a product if a reasonable person in the seller's position would provide such a warning.

(b) A reasonable person in the seller's position would provide a warning after the time of sale if:

(1) the seller knows or reasonably should know that the product poses a substantial risk of harm to persons or property; and

(2) those to whom a warning might be provided can be identified and can reasonably be assumed to be unaware of the risk of harm; and

(3) a warning can be effectively communicated to and acted on by those to whom a warning might be provided; and

(4) the risk of harm is sufficiently great to justify the burden of providing a warning.

Unlike retrofitting/designing after sale, courts have found obliging a manufacturer to provide a warning post-sale acceptable, provided the conditions of (b) can be met. But see Lewis v. Ariens Co. 434 Mass. 643, 751 N.E.2d 862 (Mass. 2001) (Second-hand purchaser of snowblower, acquired 16 years after originally sold, not owed a post-sale duty to warn as he is a "member of a universe too diffuse and too large for manufacturers or sellers of original equipment to identify."), and Modelski v. Navistar Intern. Transp. Corp.

302 Ill. App.3d 879, 707 N.E.2d 239 (Ill. App. 1 Dist.1999) (Illinois law "does not contemplate placing the onerous duty on manufacturers to subsequently warn all foreseeable users of products based on increased design or manufacture expertise that was not present at the time the product left its control. If such a duty were imposed, it might well "discourage manufacturers from developing safer products.").

MacDonald v. Ortho Pharmaceutical Corp.
394 Mass. 131, 475 N.E.2d 65 (Mass. 1985)

ABRAMS, Justice.

This products liability action raises the question of the extent of a drug manufacturer's duty to warn consumers of dangers inherent in the use of oral contraceptives. The plaintiffs brought suit against the defendant, Ortho Pharmaceutical Corporation (Ortho), for injuries allegedly caused by Ortho's birth control pills, and obtained a jury verdict in their favor. The defendant moved for a judgment notwithstanding the verdict. The judge concluded that the defendant did not owe a duty to warn the plaintiffs, and entered judgment for Ortho. The plaintiffs appealed. We transferred the case to this court on our own motion and reinstate the jury verdict.

We summarize the facts. In September, 1973, the plaintiff Carole D. Mac-Donald (MacDonald), who was twenty-six years old at the time, obtained from her gynecologist a prescription for Ortho-Novum contraceptive pills, manufactured by Ortho. As required by the then effective regulations promulgated by the United States Food and Drug Administration (FDA), the pill dispenser she received was labeled with a warning that "oral contraceptives are powerful and effective drugs which can cause side effects in some users and should not be used at all by some women," and that "[t]he most serious known side effect is abnormal blood clotting which can be fatal."[3] The warning also referred MacDonald to a booklet which she obtained from her gynecologist, and which was distributed by Ortho pursuant to FDA requirements. The booklet contained detailed information about the contraceptive pill, including the increased risk to pill users that vital organs such as the brain may be damaged by abnormal blood clotting.[4] The word "stroke" did not appear on the dispenser warning or in the booklet.

MacDonald's prescription for Ortho-Novum pills was renewed at subsequent annual visits to her gynecologist. The prescription was filled annually. On July 24, 1976, after approximately three years of using the pills, MacDonald suffered an occlusion of a cerebral artery by a blood clot, an injury

---

3. FDA regulations in effect during the time period relevant to this litigation required that the following warning be included in or with the pill dispenser:

"Do Not Take This Drug Without Your Doctor's Continued Supervision.

"The oral contraceptives are powerful and effective drugs which can cause side effects in some users and should not be used at all by some women. The most serious known side effect is abnormal blood clotting which can be fatal.

"Safe use of this drug requires a careful discussion with your doctor. To assist him in providing you with the necessary information, (Firm name) has prepared a booklet (or other form) written in a style understandable to you as the drug user. This provides information on the effectiveness and known haxards of the drug including warnings, side effects and who should not use it. Your doctor will give you this booklet (or other form) if you ask for it and he can answer any questions you may have about the use of this drug.

"Notify your doctor if you notice any unusual physical disturbance or discomfort."

4. . . . Ortho's booklet contained the following information:

"About blood clots

"Blood clots occasionally form in the blood vessels of the legs and the pelvis of apparently healthy people and may threaten life if the clots break loose and then lodge in the lung or if they form in other vital organs, such as the brain. It has been estimated that about one woman in 2,000 on the pill each year suffers a blood clotting disorder severe enough to require hospitalization. The estimated death rate from abnormal blood clotting in healthy women under 35 not taking the pill is 1 in 500,000; whereas for the same group taking the pill it is 1 in 66,000. For healthy women over 35 not taking the pill, the rate is 1 in 200,000 compared to 1 in 25,000 for pill users. Blood clots are about three times more likely to develop in women over the age of 34. For these reasons it is important that women who have had blood clots in the legs, lungs or brain not use oral contraceptives. Anyone using the pill who has severe leg or chest pains, coughs up blood, has difficulty breathing, sudden severe headache or vomiting, dizziness or fainting, disturbances of vision or speech, weakness or numbness of an arm or leg, should call her doctor immediately and stop taking the pill."

commonly referred to as a stroke. The injury caused the death of approximately twenty per cent of MacDonald's brain tissue, and left her permanently disabled. She and her husband initiated an action in the Superior Court against Ortho, seeking recovery for her personal injuries and his consequential damages and loss of consortium.

MacDonald testified that, during the time she used the pills, she was unaware that the risk of abnormal blood clotting encompassed the risk of stroke, and that she would not have used the pills had she been warned that stroke is an associated risk. The case was submitted to a jury on the plaintiffs' theories that Ortho was negligent in failing to warn adequately of the dangers associated with the pills and that Ortho breached its warranty of merchantability. These two theories were treated, in effect, as a single claim of failure to warn. The jury returned a special verdict, finding no negligence or breach of warranty in the manufacture of the pills. The jury also found that Ortho adequately advised the gynecologist of the risks inherent in the pills;[7] the jury found, however, that Ortho was negligent and in breach of warranty because it failed to give MacDonald sufficient warning of such dangers. The jury further found that MacDonald's injury was caused by Ortho's pills, that the inadequacy of the warnings to MacDonald was the proximate cause of her injury, and that Ortho was liable to MacDonald and her husband.[8]

After the jury verdict, the judge granted Ortho's motion for judgment notwithstanding the verdict, concluding that, because oral contraceptives are prescription drugs, a manufacturer's duty to warn the consumer is satisfied if the manufacturer gives adequate warnings to the prescribing physician, and that the manufacturer has no duty to warn the consumer directly.

The narrow issue, on appeal, is whether, as the plaintiffs contend, a manufacturer of birth control pills owes a direct duty to the consumer to warn her of the dangers inherent in the use of the pill. We conclude that such a duty exists under the law of this Commonwealth.

1. *Extent of duty to warn.* Ordinarily, "a manufacturer of a product, which the manufacturer knows or should know is dangerous by nature or is in a dangerous condition," is under a duty to give warning of those dangers to "persons who it is foreseeable will come in contact with, and consequently be endangered by, that product." The element of privity being long discarded, a manufacturer's warning to the immediate purchaser will not, as a general matter, discharge this duty. However, "there are limits to that principle." *Carter v. Yardley & Co.*, 319 Mass. 92, 98, 64 N.E.2d 693 (1946). Thus, "a

---

7. MacDonald stated at trial that her gynecologist had informed her only that oral contraceptives might cause bloating, and had not advised her of the increased risk of stroke associated with consumption of birth control pills. The physician was not joined as a defendant in this action, and no questions relating to any potential liability on his part are before us.

MacDonald further testified at trial that she had read both the warning on the Dialpak tablet dispenser as well as the booklet which she received from her gynecologist.

8. The only issue before us concerns the scope of Ortho's duty to the plaintiffs. The defendant does not contest the damages but relies solely on its claim that it owes no duty to warn the plaintiffs directly.

manufacturer may be absolved from blame because of a justified reliance upon . . . a middleman." *Id.* at 99, 64 N.E.2d 693. This exception is applicable only in the limited instances in which the manufacturer's reliance on an intermediary is reasonable. See Restatement (Second) of Torts §388, comment n (1965). In such narrowly defined circumstances, the manufacturer's immunity from liability if the consumer does not receive the warning is explicable on the grounds that the intermediary's failure to warn is a superseding cause of the consumer's injury, or, alternatively, that, because it is unreasonable in such circumstances to expect the manufacturer to communicate with the consumer, the manufacturer has no duty directly to warn the consumer.

The rule in jurisdictions that have addressed the question of the extent of a manufacturer's duty to warn in cases involving prescription drugs is that the prescribing physician acts as a "learned intermediary" between the manufacturer and the patient, and "the duty of the ethical drug manufacturer is to warn the doctor, rather than the patient, [although] the manufacturer is directly liable to the patient for a breach of such duty." *McEwen v. Ortho Pharmaceutical Corp.*, 270 Or. 375, 386-387, 528 P.2d 522 (1974). Oral contraceptives, however, bear peculiar characteristics which warrant the imposition of a common law duty on the manufacturer to warn users directly of associated risks. Whereas a patient's involvement in decision-making concerning use of a prescription drug necessary to treat a malady is typically minimal or nonexistent, the healthy, young consumer of oral contraceptives is usually actively involved in the decision to use "the pill," as opposed to other available birth control products, and the prescribing physician is relegated to a relatively passive role.[10]

Furthermore, the physician prescribing "the pill," as a matter of course, examines the patient once before prescribing an oral contraceptive and only annually thereafter. At her annual checkup, the patient receives a renewal prescription for a full year's supply of the pill.[11] Thus, the patient may only seldom have the opportunity to explore her questions and concerns about the medication with the prescribing physician. Even if the physician, on those occasions, were scrupulously to remind the patient of the risks attendant on continuation of the oral contraceptive, "the patient cannot be expected to remember all of the details for a protracted period of time."

Last, the birth control pill is specifically subject to extensive Federal regulation. The FDA has promulgated regulations designed to ensure that the choice of "the pill" as a contraceptive method is informed by comprehensible warnings of potential side effects. These regulations, and subsequent amendments, have their basis in the FDA commissioner's finding, after hearings, that "[b]ecause oral contraceptives are ordinarily taken electively by

---

10. According to the American Medical Association, "the medical profession regards the pill, in most cases, as a convenience rather than a traditional medication." These distinguishing features have been recognized by legal commentators as well as by the medical profession.

11. MacDonald saw her gynecologist once in the summer of 1973, once in the summer of 1974, and once in August of 1975. At each appointment, she received a prescription for birth control pills. Thus, eleven months had elapsed between her last gynecological checkup and her stroke in July, 1976.

healthy women who have available to them alternative methods of treatment, and because of the relatively high incidence of serious illnesses associated with their use, . . . users of these drugs should, without exception, be furnished with written information telling them of the drug's benefits and risks." The FDA also found that the facts necessary to informed decisions by women as to use of oral contraceptives are "too complex to expect the patient to remember everything told her by the physician," and that, in the absence of direct written warnings, many potential users of "the pill" do not receive the needed information "in an organized, comprehensive, understandable, and handy-for-future-reference form."

The oral contraceptive thus stands apart from other prescription drugs in light of the heightened participation of patients in decisions relating to use of "the pill"; the substantial risks affiliated with the product's use; the feasibility of direct warnings by the manufacturer to the user; the limited participation of the physician (annual prescriptions); and the possibility that oral communications between physicians and consumers may be insufficient or too scanty standing alone fully to apprise consumers of the product's dangers at the time the initial selection of a contraceptive method is made as well as at subsequent points when alternative methods may be considered. We conclude that the manufacturer of oral contraceptives is not justified in relying on warnings to the medical profession to satisfy its common law duty to warn, and that the manufacturer's obligation encompasses a duty to warn the ultimate user. Thus, the manufacturer's duty is to provide to the consumer written warnings conveying reasonable notice of the nature, gravity, and likelihood of known or knowable side effects, and advising the consumer to seek fuller explanation from the prescribing physician or other doctor of any such information of concern to the consumer.[13]

2. *Adequacy of the warning.* Because we reject the judge's conclusion that Ortho had no duty to warn MacDonald, we turn to Ortho's separate argument, not reached by the judge, that the evidence was insufficient to warrant the jury's finding that Ortho's warnings to MacDonald were inadequate. Ortho contends initially that its warnings complied with FDA labeling requirements, and that those requirements preempt or define the bounds of the common law duty to warn. We disagree. The regulatory history of the FDA requirements belies any objective to cloak them with preemptive effect. In response to concerns raised by drug manufacturers that warnings required and drafted by the FDA might be deemed inadequate by juries, the FDA commissioner specifically noted that the boundaries of civil tort liability for failure to warn are controlled by applicable State law. 43 Fed. Reg. 4214 (1978). Although the common law duty we today recognize is to a large degree coextensive with the regulatory duties imposed by the FDA, we are persuaded that, in instances

---

13. This opinion does not diminish the prescribing physician's duty to "disclose in a reasonable manner all significant medical information that the physician possesses or reasonably should possess that is material to an intelligent decision by the patient whether to" take "the pill." *Harnish v. Children's Hosp. Medical Center*, 387 Mass. 152, 155, 439 N.E.2d 240 (1982).

where a trier of fact could reasonably conclude that a manufacturer's compliance with FDA labeling requirements or guidelines did not adequately apprise oral contraceptive users of inherent risks, the manufacturer should not be shielded from liability by such compliance. Thus, compliance with FDA requirements, though admissible to demonstrate lack of negligence, is not conclusive on this issue, just as violation of FDA requirements is evidence, but not conclusive evidence, of negligence. We therefore concur with the plaintiffs' argument that even if the conclusion that Ortho complied with FDA requirements were inescapable, an issue we need not decide, the jury nonetheless could have found that the lack of a reference to "stroke" breached Ortho's common law duty to warn.

The common law duty to warn, like the analogous FDA "lay language" requirement, necessitates a warning "comprehensible to the average user and . . . convey[ing] a fair indication of the nature and extent of the danger to the mind of a reasonably prudent person." Whether a particular warning measures up to this standard is almost always an issue to be resolved by a jury; few questions are "more appropriately left to a common sense lay judgment than that of whether a written warning gets its message across to an average person." A court may, as a matter of law, determine "whether the defendant has conformed to that standard, in any case in which the jury may not reasonably come to a different conclusion," Restatement (Second) of Torts §328B(d) and comment g (1965), but judicial intrusion into jury decision-making in negligence cases is exceedingly rare. Further, we must view the evidence in the light most favorable to the plaintiffs. The test is whether "anywhere in the evidence, from whatever source derived, any combination of circumstances could be found from which a reasonable inference could be drawn in favor of the plaintiff."

Ortho argues that reasonable minds could not differ as to whether MacDonald was adequately informed of the risk of the injury she sustained by Ortho's warning that the oral contraceptives could cause "abnormal blood clotting which can be fatal" and further warning of the incremental likelihood of hospitalization or death due to blood clotting in "vital organs, such as the brain." We disagree. "The fact finder may find a warning to be unreasonable, hence inadequate, in its factual content, its expression of the facts, or the method or form in which it is conveyed. . . . The adequacy of such warnings is measured not only by what is stated, but also by the manner in which it is stated. A reasonable warning not only conveys a fair indication of the nature of the dangers involved, but also warns with the degree of intensity demanded by the nature of the risk. A warning may be found to be unreasonable in that it was unduly delayed, reluctant in tone or lacking in a sense of urgency." We cannot say that this jury's decision that the warning was inadequate is so unreasonable as to require the opposite conclusion as a matter of law. The jury may well have concluded, in light of their common experience and MacDonald's testimony, that the absence of a reference to "stroke" in the warning unduly minimized the warning's impact or failed to make the nature of the risk reasonably comprehensible to the average consumer. Similarly, the jury may have concluded that there are fates worse than death, such as the permanent disablement suffered by MacDonald, and that the mention of the risk of death did not, therefore, suffice to apprise an average consumer of the material risks of oral contraceptive use.

Ortho's argument that, as a matter of law, there was insufficient evidence that MacDonald's injury was proximately caused by a deficiency in the warnings is substantially similar to its argument on the issue of the adequacy of the warnings, and is likewise unavailing. Relying on *Harnish v. Children's Hosp. Medical Center*, 387 Mass. 152, 439 N.E.2d 240 (1982), for the proposition that MacDonald had the burden of proving causation by showing that "had the proper information been provided neither [s]he nor a reasonable person in similar circumstances" would have accepted Ortho's pills as a contraceptive method, *id.* at 158, 439 N.E.2d 240, Ortho argues that "[t]here was no evidence that a reasonable person, having been informed of the risk of death by abnormal blood clotting and having chosen to assume the risk, would have acted differently if informed of the risk of 'stroke.'" The jury were free, however, to credit MacDonald's testimony that she would not have used the pills had she been advised of the danger of "stroke," and to infer that an explicit reference to the risk of stroke might tip the balance in a reasonable person's choice of a contraceptive method. Ortho also asserts that evidence that MacDonald did not ask her gynecologist for an explanation of the meaning of "abnormal blood clotting" or inform him of two episodes of numbness in her hand subsequent to her initiation of oral contraceptive use indicates that MacDonald was not disposed to heed Ortho's warnings, and, consequently, that the evidence did not permit an inference that a different warning by Ortho would have affected MacDonald's decision to use Ortho's pills. These arguments raise the issue of the plaintiff Carole MacDonald's comparative negligence. That issue was not raised below and thus is not before us.

We reverse the judgment, which the judge ordered notwithstanding the verdict, and remand the case to the Superior Court for the entry of judgment for the plaintiffs.

So ordered.

O'CONNOR, Justice (dissenting).

The court reverses the judgment below and holds Ortho Pharmaceutical Corporation (Ortho) liable to Carole and Bruce MacDonald even though the jury found that Ortho adequately informed Carole MacDonald's physician of the risks associated with the use of its contraceptive pills, and regardless of whether Ortho complied with the applicable Federal Food and Drug Administration (FDA) regulations governing the provision of printed information to users of oral contraceptives. I would hold that, as a matter of law, by adequately informing physicians of the risks associated with its product and by complying with applicable FDA regulations, a contraceptive pill manufacturer fulfils the duty to warn that it owes consumers. Therefore, because the jury found that Ortho adequately warned Carole MacDonald's physician of the risks associated with its contraceptive pills and because the MacDonalds presented no evidence that Ortho failed to comply with FDA regulations, I would affirm the judgment for Ortho.

. . . Before prescribing any drug, whether on the doctor's initiative or at the patient's request, the doctor must exercise professional judgment as to the medical propriety of that patient's taking that drug and, in exercising that judgment, the doctor must conform to the standards of good medical practice laid down in *Brune v. Belinkoff*, 354 Mass. 102, 109, 235 N.E.2d 793 (1968).

. . . Unless doctors have current, accurate, and complete information about a drug's risks, they cannot properly perform their vital role. Therefore, courts have imposed on drug manufacturers the duty to provide doctors with that information. A drug manufacturer who fails properly to fulfill that duty must respond in damages to a patient who suffers an injury as a result.

. . . Doctors, unlike printed warnings, can tailor to the needs and abilities of an individual patient the information that that patient needs in order to make an informed decision whether to use a particular drug. Manufacturers are not in position to give adequate advice directly to those consumers whose medical histories and physical conditions, perhaps unknown to the consumers, make them peculiarly susceptible to risk. Prescription drugs—including oral contraceptives—differ from other products because their dangers vary widely depending on characteristics of individual consumers. Exposing a prescription drug manufacturer to liability based on a jury's determination that, despite adequately informing physicians of the drug's risks and complying with FDA regulations, the manufacturer failed reasonably to warn a particular plaintiff-consumer of individualized risks is not essential to reasonable consumer protection and places an unfair burden on prescription drug manufacturers.

. . . The court attempts to distinguish contraceptive pills from other prescription drugs by comparing the relative involvement of doctor and patient in the prescribing process. "Whereas a patient's involvement in decision-making concerning use of a prescription drug necessary to treat a malady is typically minimal or nonexistent," the court asserts, "the healthy, young consumer of oral contraceptives is usually actively involved in the decision to use 'the pill,' as opposed to other available birth control products, and the prescribing physician is relegated to a relatively passive."

. . . Furthermore, even if there be a common law duty necessitating a direct warning to the consumer with respect to the "nature and extent of the danger" of contraceptive pills, as the court declares, the MacDonalds presented no evidence that Ortho failed to fulfil that duty. The court states only that the jury "could have found that the lack of a reference to 'stroke' breached Ortho's common law duty to warn." Surely, the statement in Ortho's booklet that the contraceptive pill could cause life threatening blood clots to form in the brain, even though it did not contain the word "stroke," satisfied the court's requirement that Ortho provide "written warnings conveying reasonable notice of the nature, gravity, and likelihood of known or knowable side effects." I would affirm the judgment for Ortho.

PREPARING FOR CLASS

1. Normally a manufacturer is charged with the duty to directly warn the consumer, but there are some circumstances where it may be impractical to do so. Consider what products might be of such a nature where a manufacturer might be unable to deliver the message that warnings typically convey.

2. On what facts does the *MacDonald* decision rest? What other drugs might qualify for similar treatment?

3. MacDonald argued that, had the word stroke been employed, she would have avoided taking the birth control pills. Do you believe her?

4. Get comfortable with the rationale behind the learned intermediary rule. It remains prominent notwithstanding the decision here.

APPLYING THE LAW

Consumer who suffers from allergies sees commercial on television for allergy medication and promptly makes an appointment to see his allergist. During the visit consumer asks doctor for a prescription for the aforementioned allergic medication, to which the doctor favorably responds without additional discussion. Shortly after taking the medication, consumer suffers an adverse reaction. Can consumer successfully prosecute a failure to warn claim against the manufacturer of the allergy medication?

INCREASING YOUR UNDERSTANDING

1. *MacDonald* is largely an aberration. In the case of prescription drugs, most jurisdictions allow drug manufacturers to rely on the learned intermediary doctrine when discharging their duty to warn. Three justifications have generally been offered in support of the rule: (1) The reluctance to interfere/undermine the doctor-patient relationship; (2) The inability of drug manufacturers to communicate directly with patients; and (3) A positioned intermediary who is both willing and capable. However, the increased use of social media by drug companies to reach consumers has given some courts cause to reverse their earlier position. Such was the position taken by the New Jersey Supreme

Court in *Perez v. Wyeth Laboratories Inc.*, 161 N.J. 1, 734 A.2d 1245 (N.J. 1999).

> "First, the fact that manufacturers are advertising their drugs and devices to consumers suggests that consumers are active participants in their health care decisions, invalidating the concept that it is the doctor, not the patient, who decides whether a drug or device should be used. Second, it is illogical that requiring manufacturers to provide direct warnings to a consumer will undermine the patient-physician relationship, when, by its very nature, consumer-directed advertising encroaches on that relationship by encouraging consumers to ask for advertised products by name. Finally, consumer-directed advertising rebuts the notion that prescription drugs and devices and their potential adverse effects are too complex to be effectively communicated to lay consumers."

Perez at 1256.

2. Causation and warnings. Carole MacDonald convinced the court that had she been sufficiently warned she would not have taken the birth control pills, and the jury believed her. As is the case with whether a warning is adequate, whether a defect in a product caused plaintiff's harm is almost always a question of fact. Procedurally, many courts have a heeding presumption in warning cases, which relieves the plaintiff of having to prove causation. The assumption is that had plaintiff been adequately warned, she would have acted consistently with it. The presumption is most acceptable in circumstances where the defect in the warning stems from a failure to mandate that something not be done, i.e., "don't use product close to a flame." The presumption, however, is rebuttable and allows for the defendant to offer testimony that even the proposed warning would have been ignored. See Gosewisch v. Am. Honda Motor Co., 153 Ariz. 400, 737 P.2d 376 (Az. 1987) (In claim that an all-terrain cycle warning was inadequate, as it failed to sufficiently warn of vehicle instability, the court held that the heeding presumption was rebutted by evidence that plaintiff ignored existing warnings about carrying passengers and wearing a helmet).

E. MISCELLANEOUS PRODUCTS LIABILITY ISSUES: THE INTERPLAY BETWEEN DESIGN AND WARNING CLAIMS, PREEMPTION AND DEFENSES

Uniroyal Goodrich Tire Co. v. Martinez
977 S.W.2d 328 (Tex. 1998)

PHILLIPS, Chief Justice, delivered the opinion of the Court

We must decide whether a manufacturer who knew of a safer alternative product design is liable in strict products liability for injuries caused by the use of its product that the user could have avoided by following the product's warnings. The court of appeals held that the mere fact that a product bears an adequate warning does not conclusively establish that the product is not defective. Because we agree, we affirm the judgment of the court of appeals.

I

Roberto Martinez, together with his wife and children, sued Uniroyal Goodrich Tire Company ("Goodrich"), The Budd Company, and Ford Motor Company for personal injuries Martinez suffered when he was struck by an exploding 16″ Goodrich tire that he was mounting on a 16.5″ rim. Attached to the tire was a prominent warning label containing yellow and red highlights and a pictograph of a worker being thrown into the air by an exploding tire. The label stated conspicuously:

DANGER
NEVER MOUNT A 16″ SIZE DIAMETER TIRE ON A 16.5″ RIM. Mounting a 16″ tire on a 16.5″ rim can cause severe injury or death. While it is possible to pass a 16″ diameter tire over the lip or flange of a 16.5″ size diameter rim, it cannot position itself against the rim flange. If an attempt is made to seat the bead by inflating the tire, the tire bead will break with explosive force.
* * *
NEVER inflate a tire which is lying on the floor or other flat surface. Always use a tire mounting machine with a hold-down device or safety cage or bolt to vehicle axle.
NEVER inflate to seat beads without using an extension hose with gauge and clip-on chuck.

NEVER stand, lean or reach over the assembly during inflation.
* * *
Failure to comply with these safety precautions can cause the bead to break and the assembly to burst with sufficient force to cause serious injury or death.

Unfortunately, Martinez ignored every one of these warnings. While leaning over the assembly, he attempted to mount a 16″ tire on a 16.5″ rim without a tire mounting machine, a safety cage, or an extension hose. Martinez explained, however, that because he had removed a 16″ tire from the 16.5″ rim, he believed that he was mounting the new 16″ tire on a 16″ rim. Moreover, the evidence revealed that Martinez's employer failed to make an operable tire-mounting machine available to him at the time he was injured, and there was no evidence that the other safety devices mentioned in the warning were available.

In their suit, the Martinezes did not claim that the warnings were inadequate, but instead alleged that Goodrich, the manufacturer of the tire, Budd, the manufacturer of the rim, and Ford, the designer of the rim, were each negligent and strictly liable for designing and manufacturing a defective tire and rim. Budd and Ford settled with the Martinezes before trial, and the case proceeded solely against Goodrich.

At trial, the Martinezes claimed that the tire manufactured by Goodrich was defective because it failed to incorporate a safer alternative bead design that would have kept the tire from exploding. This defect, they asserted, was the producing cause of Martinez's injuries. Further, they alleged that Goodrich's failure to adopt this alternative bead design was negligence that proximately caused Martinez's injury.

The bead is the portion of the tire that holds the tire to the rim when inflated. A bead consists of rubber-encased steel wiring that encircles the tire a number of times. When the tire is placed inside the wheel rim and inflated, the bead is forced onto the bead-seating ledge of the rim and pressed against the lip of the rim, or the wheel flange. When the last portion of the bead is forced onto this ledge, the tire has "seated," and the air is properly sealed inside the tire. The bead holds the tire to the rim because the steel wire, unlike rubber, does not expand when the tire is inflating. The tire in this case was a 16″ bias-ply light truck tire with a 0.037″ gauge multi-strand weftless bead, or tape bead, manufactured in 1990. A tape bead consists of several strands of parallel unwoven steel wires circling the tire with each layer resting on top of the last, similar to tape wound on a roll. After a number of layers have been wound, the end of the bead is joined, or spliced, to the beginning of the same bead to form a continuous loop.

The Martinezes' expert, Alan Milner, a metallurgical engineer, testified that a tape bead is prone to break when the spliced portion of the bead is the last portion of the bead to seat. This is commonly called a hang-up. Milner testified that an alternative bead design, a 0.050″ gauge single strand programmed bead, would have prevented Martinez's injuries because its strength and uniformity make it more resistant to breaking during a hang-up. Milner explained that the 0.050″ single strand programmed bead is stronger because it is 0.013″ thicker and that it is uniform because it is wound, or programmed, by a computer, eliminating the spliced portion of the bead that can cause the tire to explode during a hang-up.

. . . In 1966, 16.5″ wheel rims were first introduced into the American market. Milner testified that Uniroyal, Inc. and B.F. Goodrich Company, who in 1986 merged to form Goodrich, soon became aware that mismatching their 16″ tires with the new wheel rims often caused hang-ups that resulted in broken beads. The minutes of a 1972 meeting of the Rubber Manufacturers Association ("RMA"), of which both Uniroyal, Inc. and B.F. Goodrich were members, provided:

> Mounting of LT [light truck] tires. Attention was drawn to reports that there have been instances where 16″ LT tires have been mounted on 16.5″ rims and 14″ tires on 14.5″ rims. It was proposed and approved to request the Service Managers Committee to add a cautionary statement to RMA documents.

Similarly, the minutes from a 1972 meeting of the Tire and Rim Association, of which Uniroyal, Inc. and B.F. Goodrich were both members, provided:

> It was reported that there have been incidents where 14″ and 16″ tires have been mounted on 14.5″ and 16.5″ rims that have resulted in broken beads. The Rim Subcommittee of the Technical Advisory Committee was requested to consider some method of marking 15″ Drop Center rims and wheels to avoid this practice.

. . . Milner explained that the computer technology required to manufacture the programmed bead was developed in 1972 and widely available by 1975. Milner testified that Goodyear began using a 0.051″ gauge single strand programmed bead in its radial light truck tires in 1977, and that Yokohama began using a single strand programmed bead in its radial light truck tires in 1981. Milner also testified that General Tire began using a single strand programmed bead in its bias-ply light truck tires in 1982. Finally, Milner testified that Goodrich itself began using the single strand programmed bead in its 16″ radial light truck tires in 1991. Based upon this evidence and his expert opinion, Milner testified that the tire manufactured by Goodrich with a tape bead was defective and unreasonably dangerous. Because Goodrich had also been sued in thirty-four other lawsuits alleging accidents caused by mismatching Goodrich tires, Milner asserted that Goodrich was grossly negligent in failing to adopt the 0.050″ single strand programmed bead in it bias-ply 16″ light truck tires.

The jury found that Goodrich's conduct was the sole proximate cause of Martinez's injuries and that Goodrich was grossly negligent. Furthermore, the jury found that the tire manufactured by Goodrich was defective, while the wheel rim designed by Ford and manufactured by Budd was not defective. The jury allocated 100% of the producing cause of Martinez's injuries to the acts and omissions of Goodrich.

The jury awarded the Martinezes $5.5 million in actual damages and $11.5 million in punitive damages. After reducing the award of actual damages by $1.4 million pursuant to a settlement agreement between the Martinezes, Ford, and Budd, reducing the punitive damages to the amount of actual damages pursuant to a pretrial agreement between Goodrich and the Martinezes, and awarding prejudgment interest, the trial court rendered judgment for the Martinezes for $10,308,792.45.

The court of appeals affirmed the award of actual damages, holding that there was legally sufficient evidence to support the finding of a design defect based upon its examination of the following factors: (1) the availability of safer design alternatives; (2) similar accidents involving the same product; [and] (3) subsequent changes or modifications in design. The court rejected Goodrich's argument that Martinez's failure to heed the product's warnings was a complete defense to the product defect claim.

. . . Only Goodrich applied to this Court for writ of error. As in the court of appeals, Goodrich's principal argument here is that no evidence supports the jury finding that the tire was defective because "the tire bore a warning which was unambiguous and conspicuously visible (and not claimed to be inadequate); the tire was safe for use if the warning was followed; and the cause of the accident was mounting and inflating a tire in direct contravention of those warnings."

II

A

This Court has adopted the products liability standard set forth in section 402A of the Restatement (Second) of Torts.

The newly released Restatement (Third) of Torts: Products Liability carries forward this focus on reasonable alternative design. *See* Restatement (Third) of Torts: Products Liability §2(b). Section 2(b) provides:

> A product . . . is defective in design when the foreseeable risks of harm posed by the product could have been reduced or avoided by the adoption of a reasonable alternative design by the seller or other distributor, or a predecessor in the commercial chain of distribution, and the omission of the alternative design renders the product not reasonably safe.

To determine whether a reasonable alternative design exists, and if so whether its omission renders the product unreasonably dangerous (or in the words of the new Restatement, not reasonably safe), the finder of fact may weigh various factors bearing on the risk and utility of the product. One of these factors is whether the product contains suitable warnings and instructions. The new Restatement likewise carries forward this approach:

> A broad range of factors may be considered in determining whether an alternative design is reasonable and whether its omission renders a product not reasonably safe. The factors include, among others, the magnitude and probability of the foreseeable risks of harm, *the instructions and warnings accompanying the product*, and the nature and strength of consumer expectations regarding the product, including expectations arising from product portrayal and marketing. . . . The relative advantages and disadvantages of the product as designed and as it alternatively could have been designed may also be considered. Thus, the likely effects of the alternative design on production costs; the effects of the alternative design on product longevity, maintenance, repair, and esthetics; and the range of consumer choice among products are factors that may be taken into account. . . .

Restatement (Third) of Torts: Products Liability §2 cmt. f (emphasis added).

  Goodrich urges this Court to depart from this standard by following certain language from Comment j of the Restatement (Second) of Torts. Comment j provides in part:

> Where warning is given, the seller may reasonably assume that it will be read and heeded; and a product bearing such a warning, which is safe for use if it is followed, is not in defective condition, nor is it unreasonably dangerous.

Restatement (Second) of Torts §402A cmt. j (1965). The new Restatement, however, expressly rejects the Comment j approach:

> Reasonable designs and instructions or warnings both play important roles in the production and distribution of reasonably safe products. In general, when a safer design can reasonably be implemented and risks can reasonably be designed out of a product, adoption of the safer design is required over a warning that leaves a significant residuum of such risks. For example, instructions and warnings may be ineffective because users of the product may not be adequately reached, may be likely to be inattentive, or may be insufficiently motivated to follow the instructions or heed the warnings. However, when an alternative design to avoid risks cannot reasonably be implemented, adequate instructions and warnings will normally be sufficient to render the product reasonably safe. *Compare* Comment *e*. *Warnings are not, however, a substitute for the provision of a reasonably safe design.*

Restatement (Third) of Torts: Products Liability §2 cmt. *l* (emphasis added).

The drafters of the new Restatement provide the following illustration for why courts have overwhelmingly rejected Comment j:

> Jeremy's foot was severed when caught between the blade and compaction chamber of a garbage truck on which he was working. The injury occurred when he lost his balance while jumping on the back step of the garbage truck as it was moving from one stop to the next. The garbage truck, manufactured by XYZ Motor Co., has a warning in large red letters on both the left and right rear panels that reads "DANGER—DO NOT INSERT ANY OBJECT WHILE COMPACTION CHAMBER IS WORKING—KEEP HANDS AND FEET AWAY." The fact that adequate warning was given does not preclude Jeremy from seeking to establish a design defect under Subsection (b). The possibility that an employee might lose his balance and thus encounter the shear point was a risk that a warning could not eliminate and that might require a safety guard. Whether a design defect can be established is governed by Subsection (b).

Restatement (Third) of Torts: Products Liability §2 cmt. *l*, illus. 14. In fact, Goodrich recognized at trial that warnings are an imperfect means to remedy a product defect. In response to a question posed by the Martinezes' attorney, Goodrich engineer Stanley Lew answered:

> Q: Is that why designs of a product are more important than warnings on a product because people may not see warnings but they are always going to encounter the design?
> A: Yes, that's correct. It's the products they deal with.

For these reasons we refuse to adopt the approach of Comment j of the superseded Restatement (Second) of Torts section 402A.

III

Goodrich argues that even if its Comment j argument does not prevail, it is still entitled to judgment as a matter of law because no safer alternative was available. In response, the Martinezes point to the evidence that Goodrich's competitors, and eventually Goodrich itself, adopted the safer 0.050″ single strand programmed bead. Goodrich counters that this alternative design is not in fact safer because if the tire is matched to the wrong size rim the bead will never seat on the rim and it will inevitably explode during use.

We agree with the general proposition that a manufacturer should not be liable for failing to adopt an alternative design that would, under other circumstances, impose an equal or greater risk of harm. To prevail in a design defect case, a plaintiff should be required to show that the safety benefits from its proposed design are foreseeably greater than the resulting costs, including any diminished usefulness or diminished safety. As the new Restatement explains:

> When evaluating the reasonableness of a design alternative, the overall safety of the product must be considered. It is not sufficient that the alternative design would have reduced or prevented the harm suffered by the plaintiff if it would also have introduced into the product other dangers of equal or greater magnitude.

Restatement (Third) of Torts: Products Liability §2 cmt. f.

The Martinezes, however, offered some evidence that their alternative design not only would have prevented the injury to Martinez, but also that it would not have introduced other dangers of equal or greater magnitude. . . .

This evidence does not conclusively prove that the programmed bead would have introduced into the product other dangers of equal or greater magnitude. There was thus a fact issue regarding whether a reasonable alternative design existed, which the jury resolved in favor of the Martinezes.

V

Goodrich also argues that the evidence conclusively establishes that Martinez was negligent and that he contributed to his own injuries. Specifically, Goodrich argues that unless some defect in the warning hinders a plaintiff's ability to see and heed it, the failure to see and heed a warning is conclusive proof of contributory negligence.

In reviewing a conclusive evidence point, we must determine whether the proffered evidence as a whole rises to a level that reasonable people could not differ in their conclusions. The jury was asked to decide whether Martinez was negligent, that is, whether he failed to exercise ordinary prudence. Both Martinez and his co-worker Ramundo Regalado testified that, because they had removed 16″ tires from the rims on which they were working, they assumed that the rims were also 16″. Also, although there was a tire-changing machine on the premises, the evidence was conflicting as to whether Martinez could have used it to secure the tire. Rene Vera, Martinez and Regalado's employer, testified that the tire-changing machine, although inoperable for dismounting tires, could have nonetheless been used to secure the tire during inflation. Regalado testified, however, that the tire-changing machine did not work, despite his repeated requests to the safety foreman to have it repaired, and that had it worked he and Martinez would have been using it on the day of the accident to secure the tire. Thus, Goodrich failed to conclusively prove that Martinez was negligent in failing to use the machine. There is no evidence that the other safety devices referenced in the tire warning—a safety cage or an extension hose—were available to Martinez. Further, Goodrich offered no evidence as to whether it was practical or feasible under the circumstances for Martinez to bolt the rim to a vehicle axle in order to inflate the tire and seat the bead. Both Martinez and Regalado testified that the manner in which Martinez was inflating the tire was customary in their shop. Based upon this evidence, we cannot conclude that reasonable people could not differ about whether Martinez failed to exercise ordinary prudence under the circumstances.

Because we conclude that Goodrich did not conclusively establish that Martinez was negligent, we do not address Goodrich's argument that there is no evidence to support the jury's allocation of causation.

VI

Goodrich next argues that even if it is not entitled to a rendition of judgment, it is entitled to a new trial because of [two] reversible evidentiary rulings. These rulings were: (1) the admission of evidence of thirty-four other lawsuits against Goodrich involving mismatched tires and (2) the admission of evidence that Goodrich had subsequently redesigned its radial light truck tires to incorporate the single strand programmed bead.

First, as to the other lawsuits, Goodrich asserts that thirty-three of these thirty-four lawsuits involved tires without pictographic warnings. Therefore, they were not substantially similar and were admitted without proper predicate. Evidence of earlier accidents that occurred under reasonably similar but not necessarily identical circumstances is admissible. Like this case, the earlier accidents resulted from mounting a 16″ Goodrich tire with a tape bead on a 16.5″ rim. The absence of pictographic warnings on the tires does not render the accidents so dissimilar as to preclude their admission, but merely goes to the weight of the evidence. The trial court did not commit error by admitting evidence of the thirty-four earlier accidents caused by mismatching Goodrich tires.

Goodrich next complains that the trial court erred by admitting evidence that Goodrich subsequently redesigned its radial light truck tires to incorporate the single strand programmed bead, because radial tires are fundamentally different from the bias-ply tire that injured Martinez, and the bead change was not made in the radial tires for safety reasons. Goodrich first argues that, under these circumstances, the evidence regarding radial tires violates Texas Rule of Civil Evidence 407(a).

Rule 407(a) states:

> Subsequent Remedial Measures. When, after an event, measures are taken which, if taken previously, would have made the event less likely to occur, evidence of the subsequent remedial measures is not admissible to prove negligence or culpable conduct in connection

with the event. This rule does not require the exclusion of evidence of subsequent remedial measures when offered for another purpose, such as proving ownership, control or feasibility of precautionary measures, if controverted, or impeachment. *Nothing in this rule shall preclude admissibility in products liability cases based on strict liability.*

Tex. R. Civ. Evid. 407(a) (emphasis added). Goodrich argues that this rule only permits the admission of subsequent remedial measures involving the product at issue, and that such measures must have been made for safety reasons. However, the rule does not contain these limitations. Rather, under the express language emphasized above, Rule 407(a) simply does not apply in products liability cases based on strict liability. Thus, the trial court did not violate Rule 407(a).

* * *

Because we conclude that there is some evidence to support the judgment of the court below on the theory of products liability, we need not consider Goodrich's claim that there is no evidence as to negligence. For the foregoing reasons, we affirm the judgment of the court of appeals.

PREPARING FOR CLASS

1. Human Factors is an established science, and professionals within this area are eminently qualified to provide knowledge with respect to the interactions between product and user, especially in regard to human capabilities and limitations. As such, they are often employed in product liability design and warning cases to give testimony on any matter that might speak to how, where, and why injuries occur, as well as to how they can be avoided. In general, they work from the trilogy of thought when it comes to how reasonable manufacturers respond to risks associated with the use of their product. First, if practical, the manufacturer should attempt to design out the risk. Second, if entirely designing out the problem is impossible or impractical, the manufacturer should attempt to protect the user by locating the risk in an area where the user is less likely to confront it. If the first or second options are impractical, the manufacturer should protect the user by warning about the risk. In short, reasonable manufacturers view warnings as the last resort when protecting users from risks. Goodrich's argument relying on comment j makes human science relevant. Grasp the origins of the argument and appreciate the court's response to it.

2. Martinez was found not to be contributorily negligent? Do you agree?

3. Read Texas Rule of Civil Evidence 407(a) closely and be prepared to articulate the policy behind the rule and its application, especially in products cases.

4. Plaintiffs carry the burden on defectiveness and often resort to other similar accidents to meet this obligation. See how such evidence might be used to satisfy the risk-utility test or generally cast the manufacturer as negligent.

INCREASING YOUR UNDERSTANDING

Subsequent remedial measures. Texas Rule of Civil Evidence 407 parrots Federal Rule of Civil Procedure 407. The main policy behind the rule is the desire to encourage the taking of safety measures in an effort to avoid further injuries. The belief is that remedial steps won't be taken by a defendant if it knows that such efforts might be turned against it at trial. As such, the rule generally prohibits the plaintiff from introducing evidence of remedial actions taken by the defendant, at least for the purpose of establishing negligence. In a jurisdiction that recognizes both negligence and strict liability, a court may require the plaintiff to drop the negligence claim if the plaintiff is insistent on introducing evidence of remedial actions taken by the defendant as a limiting instruction to the jury (that it may consider the evidence with respect to the strict liability claim but should ignore it when deliberating on negligence).

Baccelleri v. Hyster Co.
287 Or. 3, 597 P.2d 351 (Or. 1979)

DENECKE, Chief Justice.

The jury returned a verdict for the defendant in this products liability action brought to recover damages for injuries plaintiff incurred when a forklift truck manufactured by the defendant backed over the plaintiff's legs. Plaintiff appeals and we reverse.

Plaintiff worked as a checker on the docks in Portland. He was checking thirty-foot-long bundles of angle iron which had been unloaded from a ship and placed on the dock by the forklift operator. Plaintiff was kneeling down checking a bundle which was between six to twenty feet from the forklift. The forklift operator had just deposited another bundle and was backing the forklift when he ran over plaintiff's legs.

Plaintiff contends the forklift was unreasonably dangerous and defective because it lacked both visual and audible warning alarms to alert persons that the machine was backing.

Plaintiff submitted his case on the theory of strict liability in tort. Over plaintiff's objection, the trial court instructed the jury that assumption of risk was a complete defense. *Hornbeck v. Western States Fire Apparatus*, 280 Or. 647, 572 P.2d 620 (1977), decided after the trial of this case, held that assumption of the risk as a complete bar had been abolished.

. . . If this case is retried, a different aspect of the issue of assumption of the risk is almost certain to arise, and we conclude that in the interest of litigation efficiency we should resolve that issue now.

As is true of many legal problems, the problem is one of the meaning of words, semantics. The phrase, "assumption of the risk," is a common legal phrase which has been loosely used to express several results flowing from several courses of conduct. In Ritter v. Beals, 225 Or. 504, 510-521, 358 P.2d 1080 (1961), we dissected the meaning of the phrase. We observed that some conduct which is pleaded as the defense of assumption of the risk is in reality contributory negligence and evidence of such conduct is admissible if it is pleaded as contributory negligence. In other instances assumption of the risk describes a situation in which the defendant is free from fault. Hunt v. Portland Baseball Club, 207 Or. 337, 296 P.2d 495 (1956), was thought to be an example of the latter category.

In 1975 the legislature enacted a statute providing: "The doctrine of implied assumption of the risk is abolished." ORS 18.475(2), Oregon Laws 1975, ch. 599. Our general question is, what did the legislature intend to abolish by enacting that statute? This statute was enacted during the statutory evolution of comparative fault.

In 1971, ORS 18.470 enacted the law of comparative negligence to replace the court-made law that any contributory negligence on the part of plaintiff was a bar to plaintiff's recovery:

> "Contributory negligence, including assumption of the risk, shall not bar recovery in an action by any person or his legal representative to recover damages for negligence resulting in death or injury to person or property if such negligence contributing to the injury was not as great as the negligence of the person against whom recovery is sought, but any damages allowed shall be diminished in the proportion to the amount of such negligence attributable to the person recovering."

In 1975, ORS 18.470 was amended to take the form that is applicable to the present case. It now provides:

> "Contributory negligence shall not bar recovery in an action by any person or his legal representative to recover damages for death or injury to person or property if the fault attributable to the person seeking recovery was not greater than the combined fault of the person or persons against whom recovery is sought, but any damages allowed shall be diminished in the proportion to the percentage of fault attributable to the person recovering. This section is not intended to create or abolish any defense."

In the same chapter making this amendment the section was enacted abolishing the doctrine of assumption of the risk. . . .

This statute poses the question: Did this latter statute prohibit comparing the conduct of the defendant with conduct of the plaintiff, which conduct was sometimes labeled assumption of the risk but was in reality a species of contributory negligence? The words of the statute are not free from doubt but the legislative history makes it quite clear that the legislature did not intend to prohibit the comparison with such conduct.

Senate Bill 797 became ORS 18.475. A memorandum dated May 28, 1975, from State Representative David Frohnmayer to the House Judiciary Committee contains this comment on §5 of Senate Bill No. 797:

> "Section 5 abolishes the doctrine of implied assumption of the risk. Ritter v. Beals, 225 Or. 504 (358 P.2d 1080) (1961) subsumed under contributory negligence the form of assumption of the risk in which plaintiff voluntarily and unreasonably encounters a known risk; This type of assumption of the risk is unaffected by Section 5 and should be pled as contributory negligence." (Emphasis added.)

The House version of this bill, HB 2879, was accompanied by this observation from the Judiciary Committee:

> "However, contributory negligence, assumption of the risk, and other defenses overlap and a plaintiff's conduct may often be characterized in a number of ways. . . . Therefore, contributory negligence as used in the statute should be broadly construed to include: ' . . . the form of contributory negligence which consists of involuntarily (sic) and unreasonably proceeding to encounter a known danger and commonly passes under the name of assumption of the risk. . . .' HB 2879 (Appendix D, House Judiciary Committee. 4/3/75.) [8]
>
> "In addition, the minutes of this Committee for April 17, 1975, contain this comment at p. 11:
>
> "Vice Chairman Stults, who was presiding at this point . . . asked Mr. Rike if he was satisfied it would be safe to take out the assumption of risk situation. Mr. Rike said this was handled in section 4. As long as it was clear that contributory negligence includes any unreasonable conduct on the part of the plaintiff, there should be no problem."

This history is clearly to the effect that at least House Judiciary was informed that the section abolishing the doctrine of assumption of the risk did not prohibit the trier of fact from weighing the plaintiff's conduct which formerly was a subspecies of contributory negligence called assumption of the risk and comparing it with defendant's fault.

We hold that conduct which was sometimes labeled assumption of the risk but which is a subspecies of contributory negligence can be compared in the apportionment of damages.

A further question remains: Can this form of contributory negligence be used for comparison in apportioning damages when plaintiff is proceeding on the theory of strict liability in tort?

Conceptually, applying the doctrine of comparative fault in action based upon strict liability in tort offers some problems. This court, however, has answered part of the problem and held that contributory negligence can be a bar in strict liability cases.

Now that contributory negligence is not a bar but the plaintiff's fault is compared to the defendant's fault and damages apportioned accordingly, a further conceptual problem is present.

Two courts have recently confronted this problem and reached the conclusion that despite the forfeiture of a "degree of semantic symmetry," comparative fault was applicable in strict liability in tort. Daly v. General Motors Corp., 20 Cal. 3d 725, 734-736, 144 Cal. Rptr. 380, 575 P.2d 1162, 1169 (1978); Butaud v. Suburban Marine & Sport. Goods, Inc., 555 P.2d 42, 45 (Alaska 1976).

Whether these decisions reach the most preferable results is immaterial. It is a feasible result and one which the legislature could reasonably adopt. The question, therefore, is did the Oregon Legislature intend to apply comparative fault in strict liability cases?

Again, the legislative history is informative. The memorandum from State Representative Frohnmayer, previously quoted, stated:

> "Finally Section 1 provides for apportionment to the extent that plaintiff's conduct may be characterized as contributory negligence and would otherwise completely bar recovery. Section 1 is not intended to create new defenses. (However, see section 2.) Specifically, this Act is not meant to require apportionment of those types of contributory negligence held not to constitute a defense to strict liability. (This statement is followed by footnote 5, which reads: 'Findlay v. Copeland Lumber, 265 Or. 300, 500 P.2d 28 (1973), adopts Restatement (Second) Torts, Section 402A, Comment n, which reads in part, "contributory negligence of a plaintiff is not a defense when such negligence consists merely in a failure to discover the defect in the product, or to guard against the possibility of its existence."....'"

We realize that this kind of legislative history has its limitations in attempting to discern the intent of the legislature. It consists of a memorandum from one legislator and another memorandum probably prepared by the staff of the committee, whereas, a majority of 60 House members and 30 Senators, for reasons unknown and unexplained to us, voted to pass the legislation. However, in this instance we are of the opinion that the history is persuasive. The subject of the legislation was extremely technical and the terminology involved has caused lawyers and judges much difficulty. In such instances the careful distinctions drawn by one knowledgeable legislator and the committee staff would be of particular influence on the passage of the legislation.

. . . We hold that Oregon statutes provide that comparative fault is applicable in strict liability in tort. Whether defendant has adequately pleaded or proved that kind of contributory negligence which can qualify as comparative fault in a strict liability case was not in issue on this appeal. If a new trial is held those issues will be decided upon the state of the pleadings and proof at the new trial.

Plaintiff has made other assignments of error; however, none of these will necessarily arise at a new trial if one is held; therefore, we will not consider them.

Reversed and remanded for a new trial.

PREPARING FOR CLASS

1. Another illustration of how strict does not mean absolute liability; a plaintiff's recovery may be denied or reduced depending on the jurisdiction's contributory negligence/comparative fault rule. The adoption of comparative fault rules required courts to revisit traditional defenses to determine current suitability, especially cases sounding in strict liability.

2. What rule should be adopted in strict liability cases when there is evidence that the plaintiff was partially at fault for her injuries?

INCREASING YOUR UNDERSTANDING

1. A majority of courts have not hesitated to reduce plaintiff's recovery when there is evidence that plaintiff was at fault, even in strict liability cases. See Duncan v. Cessna Aircraft Co., 665 S.W.2d 414, 425 (Tex. 1984) ("Unfairness . . . is not the only serious flaw of virtually ignoring plaintiff and third party misconduct in strict products liability actions. The failure to allocate costs in proportion to the parties' relative abilities to prevent or reduce those costs is economically inefficient. . . ."), rev'd on other grounds, and Smith v. Goodyear Tire & Rubber Co., 600 F. Supp. 1561 (D. Vt. 1985) ("Although we would be reluctant to completely excuse defendants simply because *some* of a plaintiff's injuries might have resulted from his own actions, it also does not seem fair to allow a negligent plaintiff, who may have contributed to as much as fifty percent of his injuries, to pay for none of them and to recover as much as a plaintiff who had taken all precautions reasonable under the circumstances.").

2. *Relationship of contributory negligence to misuse.* A manufacturer has a legal duty to produce a product that will be safe for its intended

and foreseeable use. The courts are varied in how conduct constituting misuse should impact the underlying case: some have it bear on whether the product is defective in the first; others treat it as an affirmative defense, much along the same lines as contributory negligence; others limit the consideration to when causation is determined. See Ellsworth v. Sherne Lingerie, Inc. 303 Md. 581, 495 A.2d 48 (Md. 1985) ("Because defectiveness and causation are elements which must be proved by the plaintiff, we conclude that misuse is not an affirmative defense. Misuse, therefore, is a 'defense' only in the sense that proof of misuse negates one or more essential elements of a plaintiff's case, and may thereby defeat recovery.") As an affirmative defense, misuse is deemed in some courts to be an absolute bar to recovery, but only if the misuse was unintended/unforeseeable. "The question is always one of whether he (the party initially liable) is to be relieved of responsibility, and his liability superseded, by the subsequent event. In general, this has been determined by asking whether the intervention of the later cause is a significant part of the risk involved in the defendant's conduct, or is so reasonably connected with it that the responsibility should not be terminated. It is therefore said that the defendant is to be held liable if, but only if, the intervening cause is foreseeable." Prosser, Law of Torts §44, at 272 (1971).

Bruesewitz v. Wyeth LLC
131 S. Ct. 1068 (2011)

Justice SCALIA delivered the opinion of the Court.

We consider whether a preemption provision enacted in the National Childhood Vaccine Injury Act of 1986 (NCVIA) bars state-law design-defect claims against vaccine manufacturers.

I

A

For the last 66 years, vaccines have been subject to the same federal premarket approval process as prescription drugs, and compensation for vaccine-related injuries has been left largely to the States. Under that regime, the elimination of communicable diseases through vaccination became "one of the greatest achievements" of public health in the 20th century. But in the 1970's and 1980's vaccines became, one might say, victims of their own success. They had been so effective in preventing infectious diseases that the public became much less alarmed at the threat of those diseases, and much more concerned with the risk of injury from the vaccines themselves.

Much of the concern centered around vaccines against diphtheria, tetanus, and pertussis (DTP), which were blamed for children's disabilities and developmental delays. This led to a massive increase in vaccine-related tort litigation. Whereas between 1978 and 1981 only nine product-liability suits were filed against DTP manufacturers, by the mid-1980's the suits numbered more than 200 each year. This destabilized the DTP vaccine market, causing two of the three domestic manufacturers to withdraw; and the remaining manufacturer, Lederle Laboratories, estimated that its potential tort liability exceeded its annual sales by a factor of 200. Vaccine shortages arose when Lederle had production problems in 1984.

Despite the large number of suits, there were many complaints that obtaining compensation for legitimate vaccine-inflicted injuries was too costly and difficult. A significant number of parents were already declining vaccination for their children, and concerns about compensation threatened to depress vaccination rates even further. This was a source of concern to public health officials, since vaccines are effective in preventing outbreaks of disease only if a large percentage of the population is vaccinated.

To stabilize the vaccine market and facilitate compensation, Congress enacted the NCVIA in 1986. The Act establishes a no-fault compensation program "designed to work faster and with greater ease than the civil tort system." A person injured by a vaccine, or his legal guardian, may file a petition for compensation in the United States Court of Federal Claims, naming the Secretary of Health and Human Services as the respondent. A special master then makes an informal adjudication of the petition within (except for two limited exceptions) 240 days. The Court of Federal Claims must review objections to the special master's decision and enter final judgment under a similarly tight statutory deadline. At that point, a claimant has two options: to accept the court's judgment and forgo a traditional tort suit for damages, or to reject the judgment and seek tort relief from the vaccine manufacturer.

The *quid pro quo* for this, designed to stabilize the vaccine market, was the provision of significant tort-liability protections for vaccine manufacturers. The Act requires claimants to seek relief through the compensation program before filing suit for more than $1,000. Manufacturers are generally immunized from liability for failure to warn if they have complied with all regulatory requirements (including but not limited to warning requirements) and have given the warning either to the claimant or the claimant's physician. They are immunized from liability for punitive damages absent failure to comply with regulatory requirements, "fraud," "intentional and wrongful withholding of information," or other "criminal or illegal activity." And most relevant to the present case, the Act expressly eliminates liability for a vaccine's unavoidable, adverse side effects:

> "No vaccine manufacturer shall be liable in a civil action for damages arising from a vaccine-related injury or death associated with the administration of a vaccine after October 1, 1988, if the injury or death

resulted from side effects that were unavoidable even though the vaccine was properly prepared and was accompanied by proper directions and warnings."

B

The vaccine at issue here is a DTP vaccine manufactured by Lederle Laboratories. It first received federal approval in 1948 and received supplemental approvals in 1953 and 1970. Respondent Wyeth purchased Lederle in 1994 and stopped manufacturing the vaccine in 1998.

Hannah Bruesewitz was born on October 20, 1991. Her pediatrician administered doses of the DTP vaccine according to the Center for Disease Control's recommended childhood immunization schedule. Within 24 hours of her April 1992 vaccination, Hannah started to experience seizures. She suffered over 100 seizures during the next month, and her doctors eventually diagnosed her with "residual seizure disorder" and "developmental delay." Hannah, now a teenager, is still diagnosed with both conditions.

In April 1995, Hannah's parents, Russell and Robalee Bruesewitz, filed a vaccine injury petition in the United States Court of Federal Claims, alleging that Hannah suffered from on-Table residual seizure disorder and encephalopathy injuries. A Special Master denied their claims on various grounds, though they were awarded $126,800 in attorney's fees and costs. The Bruesewitzes elected to reject the unfavorable judgment, and in October 2005 filed this lawsuit in Pennsylvania state court. Their complaint alleged (as relevant here) that defective design of Lederle's DTP vaccine caused Hannah's disabilities, and that Lederle was subject to strict liability, and liability for negligent design, under Pennsylvania common law.

Wyeth removed the suit to the United States District Court for the Eastern District of Pennsylvania, which granted Wyeth summary judgment on the strict-liability and negligence design-defect claims, holding that the Pennsylvania law providing those causes of action was preempted by 42 U.S.C. §300aa-22(b)(1).

II

A

We set forth again the statutory text at issue:

"No vaccine manufacturer shall be liable in a civil action for damages arising from a vaccine-related injury or death associated with the administration of a vaccine after October 1, 1988, if the injury or death resulted from side effects that were unavoidable even though the vaccine was properly prepared and was accompanied by proper directions and warnings."

The "even though" clause clarifies the word that precedes it. It delineates the preventative measures that a vaccine manufacturer *must* have taken for a side-effect to be considered "unavoidable" under the statute. Provided that there was proper manufacture and warning, any remaining side effects, including those resulting from design defects, are deemed to have been unavoidable. State-law design-defect claims are therefore preempted.

If a manufacturer could be held liable for failure to use a different design, the word "unavoidable" would do no work. A side effect of a vaccine could *always* have been avoidable by use of a differently designed vaccine not containing the harmful element. The language of the provision thus suggests that the *design* of the vaccine is a given, not subject to question in the tort action. What the statute establishes as a complete defense must be unavoidability (given safe manufacture and warning) *with respect to the particular design*. Which plainly implies that the design itself is not open to question.[35]

A further textual indication leads to the same conclusion. Products-liability law establishes a classic and well known triumvirate of grounds for liability: defective manufacture, inadequate directions or warnings, and defective design. If all three were intended to be preserved, it would be strange to mention specifically only two, and leave the third to implication. It would have been much easier (and much more natural) to provide that manufacturers would be liable for "defective manufacture, defective directions or warning, and defective design." It seems that the statute fails to mention design-defect liability "by deliberate choice, not inadvertence."

B

The dissent's principal textual argument is mistaken. We agree with its premise that "'side effects that were unavoidable' must refer to side effects caused by a vaccine's *design*." We do not comprehend, however, the second step of its reasoning, which is that the use of the conditional term "if" in the introductory phrase "if the injury or death resulted from side effects that were unavoidable" "plainly implies that some side effects stemming from a vaccine's design are 'unavoidable,' while others are avoidable." That is not so. The "if" clause

---

35. The dissent advocates for another possibility: "[A] side effect is 'unavoidable' . . . where there is no feasible alternative design that would eliminate the side effect of the vaccine without compromising its cost and utility." The dissent makes no effort to ground that position in the text of §300aa-22(b)(1). We doubt that Congress would introduce such an amorphous test by implication when it otherwise micromanages vaccine manufacturers. We have no idea how much more expensive an alternative design can be before it "compromis[es]" a vaccine's cost or how much efficacy an alternative design can sacrifice to improve safety. Neither does the dissent. And neither will the judges who must rule on motions to dismiss, motions for summary judgment, and motions for judgment as a matter of law. Which means that the test would probably have no real-world effect.

makes total sense whether the design to which "unavoidable" refers is (as the dissent believes) any feasible design (making the side effects of the design used for the vaccine at issue avoidable), or (as we believe) the particular design used for the vaccine at issue (making its side effects unavoidable). Under the latter view, the condition established by the "if" clause is that the vaccine have been properly labeled and manufactured; and under the former, that it have been properly *designed*, labeled, and manufactured. Neither view renders the "if" clause a nullity. Which of the two variants must be preferred is addressed by our textual analysis, and is in no way determined by the "if" clause.

. . . Petitioners and the dissent contend that the interpretation we propose would render part of §300aa-22(b)(1) superfluous: Congress could have more tersely and more clearly preempted design-defect claims by barring liability "if . . . the vaccine was properly prepared and was accompanied by proper directions and warnings." The intervening passage ("the injury or death resulted from side effects that were unavoidable even though") is unnecessary. True enough. But the rule against giving a portion of text an interpretation which renders it superfluous does not prescribe that a passage which could have been more terse does not mean what it says. The rule applies only if verbosity and prolixity can be eliminated by giving the offending passage, or the remainder of the text, a competing interpretation. That is not the case here.[48] To be sure, petitioners' and the dissent's interpretation gives independent meaning to the intervening passage (the supposed meaning of comment *k*); but it does so only at the expense of rendering the remainder of the provision superfluous. Since a vaccine is not "quite incapable of being made safer for [its] intended use" if manufacturing defects could have been eliminated or better warnings provided, the entire "even though" clause is a useless appendage.[49] It would suffice to say "if the injury or death resulted from side effects that were unavoidable"—full stop.

III

. . . The structure of the NCVIA and of vaccine regulation in general reinforces what the text of §300aa-22(b)(1) suggests. A vaccine's license spells out the manufacturing method that must be followed and the directions and warnings that must accompany the product. Manufacturers ordinarily must obtain the Food and Drug Administration's (FDA) approval before modifying either.[51] Deviations from the license thus provide objective evidence of manufacturing defects or inadequate warnings. Further objective evidence

---

48. Because the dissent has a superfluity problem of its own, its reliance on Bates v. Dow Agrosciences LLC, 544 U. S. 431 (2005), is misplaced. See id., at 449 (adopting an interpretation that was "the only one that makes sense of each phrase" in the relevant statute).

49. That is true regardless of whether §300aa-22(b)(1) incorporates comment k. See Restatement §402A, Comment k, pp. 353, 354 (noting that "unavoidably unsafe products" are exempt from strict liability "with the qualification that they are properly prepared and marketed, and proper warning is given").

51. See §601.12.

comes from the FDA's regulations—more than 90 of them—that pervasively regulate the manufacturing process, down to the requirements for plumbing and ventilation systems at each manufacturing facility. Material noncompliance with any one of them, or with any other FDA regulation, could cost the manufacturer its regulatory-compliance defense.

Design defects, in contrast, do not merit a single mention in the NCVIA or the FDA's regulations. Indeed, the FDA has never even spelled out in regulations the criteria it uses to decide whether a vaccine is safe and effective for its intended use. And the decision is surely not an easy one. Drug manufacturers often could trade a little less efficacy for a little more safety, but the safest design is not always the best one. Striking the right balance between safety and efficacy is especially difficult with respect to vaccines, which affect public as well as individual health. Yet the Act, which in every other respect micromanages manufacturers, is silent on how to evaluate competing designs. Are manufacturers liable only for failing to employ an alternative design that the FDA has approved for distribution (an approval it takes years to obtain)? Or does it suffice that a vaccine design has been approved in other countries? Or could there be liability for failure to use a design that exists only in a lab? Neither the Act nor the FDA regulations provide an answer, leaving the universe of alternative designs to be limited only by an expert's imagination.

Jurors, of course, often decide similar questions with little guidance, and we do not suggest that the absence of guidance alone suggests preemption. But the lack of guidance for design defects combined with the extensive guidance for the two grounds of liability specifically mentioned in the Act strongly suggests that design defects were not mentioned because they are not a basis for liability.

And finally, the Act's structural *quid pro quo* leads to the same conclusion: The vaccine manufacturers fund from their sales an informal, efficient compensation program for vaccine injuries; in exchange they avoid costly tort litigation and the occasional disproportionate jury verdict. But design-defect allegations are the most speculative and difficult type of products liability claim to litigate. Taxing vaccine manufacturers' product to fund the compensation program, while leaving their liability for design defect virtually unaltered, would hardly coax manufacturers back into the market.

* * *

For the foregoing reasons, we hold that the National Childhood Vaccine Injury Act preempts all design-defect claims against vaccine manufacturers brought by plaintiffs who seek compensation for injury or death caused by vaccine side effects. The judgment of the Court of Appeals is affirmed.

It is so ordered.

Justice BREYER, concurring.

I join the Court's judgment and opinion. In my view, the Court has the better of the purely textual argument. But the textual question considered alone is a close one. Hence, like the dissent, I would look to other sources, including legislative history, statutory purpose, and the views of the federal administrative agency, here supported by expert medical opinion. Unlike the dissent, however, I believe these other sources reinforce the Court's conclusion.

II

In considering the NCVIA, Congress found that a sharp increase in tort suits brought against whooping cough and other vaccine manufacturers between 1980 and 1985 had "prompted manufacturers to question their continued participation in the vaccine market." Indeed, two whooping cough vaccine manufacturers withdrew from the market, and other vaccine manufacturers, "fac[ing] great difficulty in obtaining [product liability] insurance," told Congress that they were considering "a similar course of action." Childhood Immunizations 68-70. The Committee Report explains that, since there were only one or two manufacturers of many childhood vaccines, "[t]he loss of any of the existing manufacturers of childhood vaccines . . . could create a genuine public health hazard"; it "would present the very real possibility of vaccine shortages, and, in turn, increasing numbers of unimmunized children, and, perhaps, a resurgence of preventable diseases." At the same time, Congress sought to provide generous compensation to those whom vaccines injured-as determined by an expert compensation program.

Given these broad general purposes, to read the pre-emption clause as preserving design-defect suits seems anomalous. The Department of Health and Human Services (HHS) decides when a vaccine is safe enough to be licensed and which licensed vaccines, with which associated injuries, should be placed on the Vaccine Injury Table. To allow a jury in effect to second-guess those determinations is to substitute less expert for more expert judgment, thereby threatening manufacturers with liability (indeed, strict liability) in instances where any conflict between experts and nonexperts is likely to be particularly severe-instances where Congress intended the contrary. That is because potential tort plaintiffs are unlikely to bring suit unless the specialized compensation program has determined that they are not entitled to compensation (say, because it concludes that the vaccine did not cause the injury). . . . It is difficult to reconcile these potential conflicts and the resulting tort liabilities with a statute that seeks to diminish manufacturers' product liability while simultaneously augmenting the role of experts in making compensation decisions.

Justice SOTOMAYOR, with whom Justice GINSBURG joins, dissenting.

Vaccine manufacturers have long been subject to a legal duty, rooted in basic principles of products liability law, to improve the designs of their vaccines in light of advances in science and technology. Until today, that duty was enforceable through a traditional state-law tort action for defective design. In holding that §22(b)(1) of the National Childhood Vaccine Injury Act of 1986 (Vaccine Act or Act), 42 U.S.C. §300aa-22(b)(1), pre-empts all design defect claims for injuries stemming from vaccines covered under the Act, the Court imposes its own bare policy preference over the considered judgment of Congress. In doing so, the Court excises 13 words from the statutory text, misconstrues the Act's legislative history, and disturbs the careful balance Congress struck between compensating vaccine-injured children and stabilizing the childhood vaccine market. Its decision leaves a regulatory vacuum in which no one ensures that vaccine manufacturers adequately take account of scientific and technological advancements when designing or distributing their products. Because nothing in the text, structure, or legislative history of the Vaccine Act remotely suggests that Congress intended such a result, I respectfully dissent.

PREPARING FOR CLASS

1. There are two forms of preemption, expressed and implied. Federal and state law are to exist independently of each other as long as state law assists or complements federal law. Conversely, if state law frustrates or interferes with federal law, the Supremacy Clause of the U.S. Constitution allows for federal law to trump or supersede state law. This can be accomplished either because Congress has "expressly" articulated an intent to be the final authority when it comes to certain matters or where, because of the nature of Congress' involvement, it can be inferred that Congress would have wanted federal laws to govern when an irreconcilable conflict with states law arises. Amid the preemption discussion is the oft-cited belief that state law serves as a regulatory compliment to federal law and also provides a necessary avenue to compensation where federal law is deficient. The paramount issue in any preemption case is Congress' intent because the Court is not empowered to substitute its judgment, in other words, implement its own version of "tort reform."

2. *The politics of preemption.* The U.S. Supreme Court was relatively inactive on the preemption front prior to Cippollone v. Liggett Goup, Inc., 505 U.S. 504, which was decided in 1992. Since *Cipplolone*, the Court has been much more interested in taking on preemption cases but what has resulted, at least when it comes to a predictably consistent analytical process, is a bog of confusion. Rarely an entity that shies from stating what the law is or should be, the American Law Institute when it came to preemption and the Restatement Third of Torts politely begged off: "The complex set of rules and standards for resolving questions of federal preemption are beyond the scope

of this Restatement." Restatement (Third) of Torts: Products Liability §4 comment e.

3. In theory, state law should only expressly be preempted by Congress where its intention to do so is clearly manifest. In theory, ambiguous statutory language would fail to establish a clear intent. And in theory, express preemption cases should never make their way to the Supreme Court, let alone yield a divided court. When it came to liability, what do you believe Congress intended when it created the Vaccine Act?

4. Since its implementation, nearly two billion dollars have been paid to claimants under the Act (U.S. Dept. of Health & Human Services National Vaccine Injury Compensation Program: Vaccine Injury Compensation Trust Fund.) Funding for the Compensation Fund comes from taxes paid by vaccine manufacturers on each vial of vaccine sold.

Wyeth v. Levine
555 U.S. 555, 129 S. Ct. 1187 (2009)

Justice STEVENS delivered the opinion of the Court.

Directly injecting the drug Phenergan into a patient's vein creates a significant risk of catastrophic consequences. A Vermont jury found that petitioner Wyeth, the manufacturer of the drug, had failed to provide an adequate warning of that risk and awarded damages to respondent Diana Levine to compensate her for the amputation of her arm. The warnings on Phenergan's label had been deemed sufficient by the federal Food and Drug Administration (FDA) when it approved Wyeth's new drug application in 1955 and when it later approved changes in the drug's labeling. The question we must decide is whether the FDA's approvals provide Wyeth with a complete defense to Levine's tort claims. We conclude that they do not.

I

Phenergan is Wyeth's brand name for promethazine hydrochloride, an antihistamine used to treat nausea. The injectable form of Phenergan can be administered intramuscularly or intravenously, and it can be administered intravenously through either the "IV-push" method, whereby the drug is injected directly into a patient's vein, or the "IV-drip" method, whereby the drug is introduced into a saline solution in a hanging intravenous bag and slowly descends through a catheter inserted in a patient's vein. The drug is corrosive and causes irreversible gangrene if it enters a patient's artery.

Levine's injury resulted from an IV-push injection of Phenergan. On April 7, 2000, as on previous visits to her local clinic for treatment of a migraine headache, she received an intramuscular injection of Demerol for her headache and Phenergan for her nausea. Because the combination did not provide relief, she returned later that day and received a second injection of both drugs. This time, the physician assistant administered the drugs by the IV-push method, and Phenergan entered Levine's artery, either because the needle penetrated an artery directly or because the drug escaped from the vein into surrounding tissue (a phenomenon called "perivascular extravasation") where it came in contact with arterial blood. As a result, Levine developed gangrene, and doctors amputated first her right hand and then her entire forearm. In addition to her pain and suffering, Levine incurred substantial medical expenses and the loss of her livelihood as a professional musician.

After settling claims against the health center and clinician, Levine brought an action for damages against Wyeth, relying on common-law negligence and strict-liability theories. Although Phenergan's labeling warned of the danger of gangren eand amputation following inadvertent intra-arterial injection, Levine alleged that the labeling was defective because it failed to instruct clinicians to use the IV-drip method of intravenous administration instead of the higher risk IV-push method. . . .

Based on this regulatory history, the trial judge instructed the jury that it could consider evidence of Wyeth's compliance with FDA requirements but that such compliance did not establish that the warnings were adequate. He also instructed, without objection from Wyeth, that FDA regulations "permit a drug manufacturer to change a product label to add or strengthen a warning about its product without prior FDA approval so long as it later submits the revised warning for review and approval."

Answering questions on a special verdict form, the jury found that Wyeth was negligent, that Phenergan was a defective product as a result of inadequate warnings and instructions, and that no intervening cause had broken the causal connection between the product defects and the plaintiff's injury. It awarded total damages of $7,400,000, which the court reduced to account for Levine's earlier settlement with the health center and clinician.

On August 3, 2004, the trial court filed a comprehensive opinion denying Wyeth's motion for judgment as a matter of law. After making findings of fact based on the trial record (supplemented by one letter that Wyeth found after the trial), the court rejected Wyeth's pre-emption arguments. It determined that there was no direct conflict between FDA regulations and Levine's state-law claims because those regulations permit strengthened warnings without FDA approval on an interim basis and the record contained evidence of at least 20 reports of amputations similar to Levine's since the 1960's. The court also found that state tort liability in this case would not obstruct the FDA's work because the agency had paid no more than passing attention to the question whether to warn against IV-push administration of Phenergan. In addition, the court noted that state law serves a compensatory function distinct from federal regulation.

The Vermont Supreme Court affirmed. It held that the jury's verdict "did not conflict with FDA's labeling requirements for Phenergan because [Wyeth] could have warned against IV-push administration without prior FDA approval, and because federal labeling requirements create a floor, not a ceiling, for state regulation." In dissent, Chief Justice Reiber argued that the jury's verdict conflicted with federal law because it was inconsistent with the FDA's conclusion that intravenous administration of Phenergan was safe and effective.

The importance of the pre-emption issue, coupled with the fact that the FDA has changed its position on state tort law and now endorses the views expressed in Chief Justice Reiber's dissent, persuaded us to grant Wyeth's petition for certiorari. . . . The question presented by the petition is whether the FDA's drug labeling judgments "preempt state law product liability claims premised on the theory that different labeling judgments were necessary to make drugs reasonably safe for use."

II

Wyeth makes two separate pre-emption arguments: first, that it would have been impossible for it to comply with the state-law duty to modify Phenergan's labeling without violating federal law, . . . and second, that recognition of Levine's state tort action creates an unacceptable "obstacle to the accomplishment and execution of the full purposes and objectives of Congress,". . . because it substitutes a lay jury's decision about drug labeling for the expert judgment of the FDA. As a preface to our evaluation of these arguments, we identify two factual propositions decided during the trial court proceedings, emphasize two legal principles that guide our analysis, and review the history of the controlling federal statute.

III

. . . Wyeth first argues that Levine's state-law claims are pre-empted because it is impossible for it to comply with both the state-law duties underlying those claims and its federal labeling duties. The FDA's premarket approval of a new drug application includes the approval of the exact text in the proposed label. See 21 U.S.C. §355; 21 CFR §314.105(b) (2008). Generally speaking, a manufacturer may only change a drug label after the FDA approves a supplemental application. There is, however, an FDA regulation that permits a manufacturer to make certain changes to its label before receiving the agency's approval. Among other things, this "changes being effected" (CBE) regulation provides that if a manufacturer is changing a label to "add or strengthen a contraindication, warning, precaution, or adverse reaction" or to "add or strengthen an instruction about dosage and administration that is intended to increase the safe use of the drug product," it may make the labeling change upon filing its supplemental application with the FDA; it need not wait for FDA approval. §§314.70(c)(6)(iii)(A), (C).

. . . Wyeth argues that if it had unilaterally added such a warning, it would have violated federal law governing unauthorized distribution and misbranding. Its argument that a change in Phenergan's labeling would have subjected it to liability for unauthorized distribution rests on the assumption that this labeling change would have rendered Phenergan a new drug lacking an effective application. But strengthening the warning about IV-push administration would not have made Phenergan a new drug.

. . . Impossibility pre-emption is a demanding defense. On the record before us, Wyeth has failed to demonstrate that it was impossible for it to comply with both federal and state requirements. The CBE regulation permitted Wyeth to unilaterally strengthen its warning, and the mere fact that the FDA approved Phenergan's label does not establish that it would have prohibited such a change.

IV

Wyeth also argues that requiring it to comply with a state-law duty to provide a stronger warning about IV-push administration would obstruct the purposes and objectives of federal drug labeling regulation. Levine's tort claims, it maintains, are pre-empted because they interfere with "Congress's purpose to entrust an expert agency to make drug labeling decisions that strike a balance between competing objectives." We find no merit in this argument, which relies on an untenable interpretation of congressional intent and an overbroad view of an agency's power to pre-empt state law.

Wyeth contends that the FDCA establishes both a floor and a ceiling for drug regulation: Once the FDA has approved a drug's label, a state-law verdict may not deem the label inadequate, regardless of whether there is any evidence that the FDA has considered the stronger warning at issue. The most glaring problem with this argument is that all evidence of Congress' purposes is to the contrary. Building on its 1906 Act, Congress enacted the FDCA to bolster consumer protection against harmful products. Congress did not provide a federal remedy for consumers harmed by unsafe or ineffective drugs in the 1938 statute or in any subsequent amendment. Evidently, it determined that widely available state rights of action provided appropriate relief for injured consumers. It may also have recognized that state-law remedies further consumer protection by motivating manufacturers to produce safe and effective drugs and to give adequate warnings.

If Congress thought state-law suits posed an obstacle to its objectives, it surely would have enacted an express pre-emption provision at some point during the FDCA's 70-year history. But despite its 1976 enactment of an express pre-emption provision for medical devices, see §521, 90 Stat. 574 (codified at 21 U.S.C. §360k(a)), Congress has not enacted such a provision for prescription drugs. Its silence on the issue, coupled with its certain awareness of the prevalence of state tort litigation, is powerful evidence that Congress did not intend FDA oversight to be the exclusive means of ensuring drug safety and effectiveness. As Justice O'Connor explained in her opinion for a unanimous Court: "The case for federal pre-emption is particularly weak where Congress has indicated its awareness of the operation of state law in a field of federal interest, and has nonetheless decided to stand by both concepts and to tolerate whatever tension there [is] between them." *Bonito Boats, Inc. v. Thunder Craft Boats, Inc.*, 489 U.S. 141, 166-167, 109 S. Ct. 971, 103 L. Ed. 2d 118 (1989) (internal quotation marks omitted).

Despite this evidence that Congress did not regard state tort litigation as an obstacle to achieving its purposes, Wyeth nonetheless maintains that, because the FDCA requires the FDA to determine that a drug is safe and effective under the conditions set forth in its labeling, the agency must be presumed to have performed a precise balancing of risks and benefits and to have established a specific labeling standard that leaves no room for different state-law judgments. In advancing this argument, Wyeth relies not on any statement by Congress, but instead on the preamble to a 2006 FDA regulation governing the content and format of prescription drug labels. In that preamble, the FDA declared that the FDCA establishes "both a 'floor' and a 'ceiling,'" so that "FDA approval of labeling . . . preempts conflicting or contrary State law." It further stated that certain state-law actions, such as those involving failure-to-warn claims, "threaten FDA's statutorily prescribed role as the expert Federal agency responsible for evaluating and regulating drugs."

. . . In prior cases, we have given "some weight" to an agency's views about the impact of tort law on federal objectives when "the subject matter is technica[l] and the relevant history and background are complex and extensive." Even in such cases, however, we have not deferred to an agency's *conclusion* that state law is pre-empted. Rather, we have attended to an agency's explanation of how state law affects the regulatory scheme. While agencies have no special authority to pronounce on pre-emption absent delegation by Congress, they do have a unique understanding of the statutes they administer and an attendant ability to make informed determinations about how state requirements may pose an "obstacle to the accomplishment and execution of the full purposes and objectives of Congress." . . . The weight we accord the agency's explanation of state law's impact on the federal scheme depends on its thoroughness, consistency, and persuasiveness.

Under this standard, the FDA's 2006 preamble does not merit deference. When the FDA issued its notice of proposed rulemaking in December 2000, it explained that the rule would "not contain policies that have federalism implications or that preempt State law." . . . In 2006, the agency finalized the rule and, without offering States or other interested parties notice or opportunity for comment, articulated a sweeping position on the FDCA's preemptive effect in the regulatory preamble. The agency's views on state law are inherently suspect in light of this procedural failure.

In keeping with Congress' decision not to pre-empt common-law tort suits, it appears that the FDA traditionally regarded state law as a complementary form of drug regulation. The FDA has limited resources to monitor the 11,000 drugs on the market, and manufacturers have superior access to information about their drugs, especially in the postmarketing phase as new risks emerge. State tort suits uncover unknown drug hazards and provide incentives for drug manufacturers to disclose safety risks promptly. They also serve a distinct compensatory function that may motivate injured persons to come forward with information. Failure-to-warn actions, in particular, lend force to the FDCA's premise that manufacturers, not the FDA, bear primary responsibility for their drug labeling at all times. Thus, the FDA long maintained that state law offers an additional, and important, layer of consumer protection that complements FDA regulation. The agency's 2006 preamble represents a dramatic change in position.

. . . In short, Wyeth has not persuaded us that failure-to-warn claims like Levine's obstruct the federal regulation of drug labeling. Congress has repeatedly declined to pre-empt state law, and the FDA's recently adopted position that state tort suits interfere with its statutory mandate is entitled to no weight. Although we recognize that some state-law claims might well frustrate the achievement of congressional objectives, this is not such a case.

V

We conclude that it is not impossible for Wyeth to comply with its state and federal law obligations and that Levine's common-law claims do not stand as an obstacle to the accomplishment of Congress' purposes in the FDCA. Accordingly, the judgment of the Vermont Supreme Court is affirmed.

It is so ordered.

Justice THOMAS, concurring in the judgment.

I agree with the Court that the fact that the Food and Drug Administration (FDA) approved the label for petitioner Wyeth's drug Phenergan does not preempt the state-law judgment before the Court. That judgment was based on a jury finding that the label did not adequately warn of the risk involved in administering Phenergan through the IV-push injection method. Under federal law, without prior approval from the FDA, Wyeth could have "add[ed] or strengthen[ed]" information on its label about "a contraindication, warning, precaution, or adverse reaction, or "about dosage and administration that is intended to increase the safe use of the drug product," in order to "reflect newly acquired information," including "new analyses of previously submitted data," about the dangers of IV-push administration of Phenergan. It thus was possible for Wyeth to label and market Phenergan in compliance with federal law while also providing additional warning information on its label beyond that previously approved by the FDA. In addition, federal law does not give drug manufacturers an unconditional right to market their federally approved drug at all times with the precise label initially approved by the FDA. The Vermont court's judgment in this case, therefore, did not directly conflict with federal law and is not pre-empted.

I write separately, however, because I cannot join the majority's implicit endorsement of far-reaching implied pre-emption doctrines. In particular, I have become increasingly skeptical of this Court's "purposes and objectives" pre-emption jurisprudence. Under this approach, the Court routinely invalidates state laws based on perceived conflicts with broad federal policy objectives, legislative history, or generalized notions of congressional purposes that are not embodied within the text of federal law. Because implied pre-emption doctrines that wander far from the statutory text are inconsistent with the Constitution, I concur only in the judgment.

Justice ALITO, with whom THE CHIEF JUSTICE and Justice SCALIA join, dissenting.

This case illustrates that tragic facts make bad law. The Court holds that a state tort jury, rather than the Food and Drug Administration (FDA), is ultimately responsible for regulating warning labels for prescription drugs. That result cannot be reconciled with *Geier v. American Honda Motor Co.*, 529 U.S. 861, 120 S. Ct. 1913, 146 L. Ed. 2d 914 (2000), or general principles of conflict pre-emption. I respectfully dissent.

B

1

. . . Where the FDA determines, in accordance with its statutory mandate, that a drug is on balance "safe," our conflict pre-emption cases prohibit any State from countermanding that determination.

PREPARING FOR CLASS

1. There are three types of implied preemption, two of which are argued unsuccessfully by Wyeth. They are: (1) field preemption, where the government's degree of regulation is so extensive that there is little

doubt that Congress intended to preclude intrusion by state courts; (2) conflict preemption, where it is impossible to comply with both federal and state law; and (3) where preemption arises when the imposition of state law would "obstruct purpose and objectives" of the federal law. Many of the preemption cases have involved medical devices and drugs, areas where federal regulations often may invade into a state's product liability common law.

2.   Justice Thomas' concurrence illustrates why implied preemption has been met with claims that much of the "doctrine" is driven by politics. Regardless of what motivates, the Court's unwillingness to establish consistent rules and analytical standards has largely made litigation in this area a crapshoot.

INCREASING YOUR UNDERSTANDING

Compliance with government regulations or standards. Assuming preemption is off the table, a majority of courts hold that violations of product safety statutes or regulations render products defective as a matter of law. See Orthopedic Equip. Co., Inc. v. Eutsler, 276 F.2d 455, 461 (4th Cir. 1960) ("The majority of American courts which have passed on this question, in cases arising under state laws resembling the Federal Act, have held violations [of The Federal Food, Drug, and Cosmetic Act] to be negligence per se."). Compliance with an applicable regulation or statute, however, does not generally immunize the manufacturer from product liability. See Plenger v. Alza Corp., 13 Cal. Rptr. 2d 811, 819 n.7 (1992) citing Stevens v. Parke, Davis & Co., 9 Cal. 3d 51, 507 P.2d 653 (Cal. 1973) ("[M]ere compliance with regulations or directives as to warnings, such as those issued by the United States Food and Drug Administration here, may not be sufficient to immunize the manufacturer or supplier of the drug from liability. The warnings required by such agencies may be only minimal in nature and when the manufacturer or supplier knows of, or has reason to know of, greater dangers not included in the warning, its duty to warn may not be fulfilled."); See also, Restatement (Third) of Torts: Products Liability §4(b) ("[A] product's compliance with an applicable product safety statute or administrative regulation is properly considered in determining whether the product is defective with respect to the risks sought to be reduced by the statute or regulation, but such compliance does not preclude as a matter of law a finding of product defect."). But see Miller v. Lee Apparel Co., Inc., 881 P.2d 576 (Kan. App. 1994) (compliance with safety regulation supports a statutory presumption of nondefectiveness).

F.   WHO IS IN THE BUSINESS OF SELLING?

Restatement (Third) of Torts: Products Liability

§1. Liability of Commercial Seller or Distributor for Harm Caused
by Defective Products

One engaged in the business of selling or otherwise distributing products
who sells or distributes a defective product is subject to liability for harm to
persons or property caused by the defect.

Tillman v. Vance Equipment Co.
286 Or. 747, 596 P.2d 1299 (Or. 1979)

Denecke, Chief Justice.

Plaintiff brought this action based upon the theory of strict liability in tort to
recover for personal injuries caused by a 24-year-old crane sold by defendant, a
used equipment dealer, to plaintiff's employer, Durametal. The court tried the
case without a jury and found for the defendant. The plaintiff appeals and
we affirm.

Durametal asked the defendant to locate a crane for purchase by Durametal. Defendant found one that looked suitable; Durametal inspected and
approved it. The defendant purchased the crane and immediately resold it
to Durametal. Defendant prepared documents making the sale "as is."

Durametal assigned plaintiff to operate the crane, including greasing it.
Plaintiff believed the greasing of the gears could not be done properly without
removing the gear cover and applying the grease while the gears were moving.
While he was so greasing the gears, plaintiff's hand was drawn into them and
he was injured.

Plaintiff alleged the defendant seller was liable because the crane was defectively designed in that it could not be properly greased without removing the
protective gear covering and for failing to provide warnings of the danger. The
trial court found for the defendant because the crane was a used piece of
equipment and sold "as is."

The parties disagree about the effect of the "as is" disclaimer in the documents of sale. The issues raised include whether that disclaimer has any effect
in an action of strict liability in tort, and whether, if so, it is effective to disclaim
liability for a design defect as distinguished from a defect in the condition of
the individual product. We do not answer these questions because we conclude that the trial court was correct in holding that a seller of used goods is not
strictly liable in tort for a defect in a used crane when that defect was created by
the manufacturer.

While we have decided cases in which the sale of a used product was
involved, we have not decided the issue presented in this case.

In Tucker v. Unit Crane & Shovel Corp., 256 Or. 318, 473 P.2d 862 (1970), we held the manufacturer liable for a death caused by a defect created at manufacture in a nine-year-old crane which had been purchased used by one Eldridge and then leased to the decedent's employer. The case is not a precedent for this case because it was brought against the manufacturer, who the trier of fact found had created the defect at the time of manufacture.

In Markle v. Mulholland's, Inc., 265 Or. 259, 509 P.2d 529 (1973), the plaintiff was injured by the blowout of a recapped tire sold to plaintiff by the defendant retailer. The defect was in the casing, which is the used portion of a recapped tire. The sale of a recapped tire therefore is partially the sale of used goods. However, the majority of the court in *Markle* was of the opinion that the sale was not an ordinary sale of used goods.

> ". . . Nevertheless, the manufacturer selected this casing from among all available casings to retread and this implies something concerning its condition. Tread was put upon it which was capable of lasting more than 5,000 or 6,000 miles. This indicates that there is reason to believe that the manufacturer intended and the purchaser had a right to expect a quality of performance from the casing greater than that which it gave. . . ." Id. at 271, 509 P.2d at 535.

In Cornelius v. Bay Motors, 258 Or. 564, 484 P.2d 299 (1971), the plaintiff was struck by an automobile sold as a used car by defendant and which had defective brakes. We expressly reserved ruling upon the potential strict liability in tort of a dealer in used vehicles and upheld a jury verdict for the defendant dealer.

In order to determine whether the defendant seller may be held liable we are required to re-examine why we arrived at the decision that a seller "who is free from fault in the usual legal sense" should be held strictly liable for a defective product.

> ". . . Usually liability has been predicated on a breach of an implied warranty without explaining why the warranty was judicially implied. When the action was brought by the buyer against his immediate seller, it seemed enough that the plaintiff and defendant were parties to a contract, the warranty being born in some mysterious way out of the contractual relationship even in the absence of any promise express or implied in fact made by the seller. . . . . ."

Because of the impediments accompanying a contractual remedy, including the requirement of privity, we evolved the tort of strict liability. Redfield v. Mead, Johnson & Co., 266 Or. 273, 285, 512 P.2d 776 (1973) (specially concurring). Strict liability could be imposed upon a party with whom the plaintiff was not in privity. For this reason the manufacturer who created the defect could be sued directly. The injured party could usually obtain personal jurisdiction over the manufacturer by the use of the long-arm statutes. Because of the circumstances, there was no longer any urgent necessity to continue a cause of action against the seller who had not created the defect.

Nevertheless, courts did impose strict liability on the nonmanufacturer sellers of new goods as summarized in a recent study:

> "Over time most courts extended the rationale of these cases to both retailers and distributors. . . . Courts extended strict liability to retailers and distributors, in part, on the assumption that these groups would place pressure on the manufacturer to produce safe products. Courts also believed that retailers and distributors might be more accessible to suit than manufacturers."

As Mr. Justice Traynor said in Vandermark v. Ford Motor Company, 61 Cal. 2d 256, 37 Cal. Rptr. 896, 899, 391 P.2d 168, 171 (1964):

> "Retailers like manufacturers are engaged in the business of distributing goods to the public. They are an integral part of the overall producing and marketing enterprise that should bear the cost of injuries resulting from defective products. (See Greenman v. Yuba Power Products, Inc., 59 Cal. 2d 57, 63, 27 Cal. Rptr. 697, 377 P.2d 897). In some cases the retailer may be the only member of that enterprise reasonably available to the injured plaintiff. In other cases the retailer himself may play a substantial part in insuring that the product is safe or may be in a position to exert pressure on the manufacturer to that end; the retailer's strict liability thus serves as an added incentive to safety. . . . ."

This court has never been willing to rely on enterprise liability alone as a justification for strict liability for defective products. See *Markle v. Mulholland's, Inc.*, supra, 265 Or. at 265, 509 P.2d 529. Instead, we have identified three justifications for the doctrine:

> ". . . (C)ompensation (ability to spread the risk), satisfaction of the reasonable expectations of the purchaser or user (implied representational aspect), and over-all risk reduction (the impetus to manufacture a better product). . . ." Fulbright v. Klamath Gas Co., 271 Or. 449, 460, 533 P.2d 316, 321 (1975).

While dealers in used goods are, as a class, capable like other businesses of providing for the compensation of injured parties and the allocation of the cost of injuries caused by the products they sell, we are not convinced that the other two considerations identified in Fulbright weigh sufficiently in this class of cases to justify imposing strict liability on sellers of used goods generally.

. . . We conclude that holding every dealer in used goods responsible regardless of fault for injuries caused by defects in his goods would not only affect the prices of used goods; it would work a significant change in the very nature of used goods markets. Those markets, generally speaking, operate on the apparent understanding that the seller, even though he is in the business of selling such goods, makes no particular representation about their quality simply by offering them for sale. If a buyer wants some assurance of quality, he typically either bargains for it in the specific transaction or seeks out a dealer who routinely offers it (by, for example, providing a guarantee, limiting his stock of goods to those of a particular quality, advertising that his used goods are specially selected, or in some other fashion). The flexibility of this kind of market appears to serve legitimate interests of buyers as well as sellers.

We are of the opinion that the sale of a used product, without more, may not be found to generate the kind of expectations of safety that the courts have held are justifiably created by the introduction of a new product into the stream of commerce.

As to the risk-reduction aspect of strict products liability, the position of the used-goods dealer is normally entirely outside the original chain of distribution of the product. As a consequence, we conclude, any risk reduction which would be accomplished by imposing strict liability on the dealer in used goods would not be significant enough to justify our taking that step. The dealer in used goods generally has no direct relationship with either manufacturers or distributors. Thus, there is no ready channel of communication by which the dealer and the manufacturer can exchange information about possible dangerous defects in particular product lines or about actual and potential liability claims.

In theory, a dealer in used goods who is held liable for injuries caused by a design defect or manufacturing flaw could obtain indemnity from the manufacturer. This possibility supports the argument that permitting strict liability claims against dealers in used goods will add to the financial incentive for manufacturers to design and build safe products. We believe, however, that the influence of this possibility as a practical factor in risk prevention is considerably diluted where used goods are involved due to such problems as statutes of limitation and the increasing difficulty as time passes of locating a still existing and solvent manufacturer.

Both of these considerations, of course, are also obstacles to injured parties attempting to recover directly from the manufacturer. However, although the provision of an adequate remedy for persons injured by defective products has been the major impetus to the development of strict product liability, it cannot provide the sole justification for imposing liability without fault on a particular class of defendants.

For the reasons we have discussed, we have concluded that the relevant policy considerations do not justify imposing strict liability for defective products on dealers in used goods, at least in the absence of some representation of quality beyond the sale itself or of a special position vis-à-vis the original manufacturer or others in the chain of original distribution.

We have suggested, although we have never had occasion to rule on the question, that those who are in the business of leasing products to others may be strictly liable for injuries caused by defective products on the same basis as sellers of new products. *Fulbright v. Klamath Gas Co.*, supra, 271 Or. at 455-458, 459, 533 P.2d 316. It has been urged that recognizing such a liability on the part of lessors while refusing to hold sellers of used goods liable would be logically inconsistent, because most leased goods are used when they reach the lessee. We see no such inconsistency when the focus of analysis is not on the status of the product but on that of the potential defendant. The lessor chooses the products which he offers in a significantly different way than does the typical dealer in used goods; the fact that he offers them repeatedly to different users as products he has selected may constitute a representation as to their quality; and it may well be that he has purchased them, either new or used, from a dealer who is directly related to the original distribution chain. Our rationale in the present case leaves the question of a lessor's strict liability an open one in this jurisdiction.

Affirmed.

PREPARING FOR CLASS

1. Restatement (Second) of Torts §402A imposed strict liability on "one who sells . . . [or] who is engaged in the business of selling such a product." The Restatement (Third) seems to expand liability to include those that are in the business of distributing, though this largely reflects how the law of §402A had been interpreted since 1965. The question that arises in *Tillman* is not whether it could be liable at all but whether it could be held strictly liable. Revisit the goals behind the strict liability doctrine, and see how they shape the arguments by counsel for both sides.

2. One other reason why courts have deemed it fair to impose strict liability on those within the original chain of distribution is the availability of indemnification. Typically, manufacturers in direct business relationships with distributors will indemnify the distributor as long as liability stems from something the manufacturer did. That's good business. The used-product dealer lacks the status to command such protection.

APPLYING THE LAW

Smitty sells used cars. Plaintiff purchases a vehicle from Smitty that will start in drive, which is contrary to how the car is supposed to operate. Smitty is unaware of this flaw as is the plaintiff. Several days after purchase, plaintiff inadvertently starts the car while in drive and plows through his garage, causing considerable property damage. Is Smitty strictly liable?

INCREASING YOUR UNDERSTANDING

1. Most courts are in accord with the principle case and do not impose strict liability on sellers of used products. One notable exception to this rule appears in cases where the product sold suffers from a manufacturing defect. In this respect, the used product seller stands on the same liability grounds as the person who distributed it new.

2. Similarly, traditional rules don't impose strict liability on those not in the business of distributing products. Thus the garage salesperson is not subject to strict liability, though negligence liability may loom. Furthermore, strict liability is limited to those who are in the business of selling or otherwise distributing the *injury causing product*. See Restatement (Third) of Torts: Products Liability §1 comment c. Usually, the question of whether a defendant is a commercial seller is a matter of law. Id.

3. *Hybrid sales/service cases.* The liability rules in this chapter apply to those who sell products, not those who primarily provide sellers. When an injuring-causing product has been sold incident to a service being provided, courts had to decide whether the seller was subject to strict liability, i.e., in the business of selling. Though the results have been inconsistent, in one respect, the provision of blood products, the great majority of states through legislation have barred the application of traditional products liability rules to blood and blood products. See Greif, Hospital and Blood Bank Liability to Patients Who Contract AIDS Through Blood Transfusions, 23 San Diego L. Rev. 875, 882 n.36 (July-Aug. 1986).

Chapter 16

Damages

A. INTRODUCTION

It might be difficult to fully appreciate the discussion in this chapter without a general understanding of the process that leads to recovery. After a lawsuit is threatened or filed, parties have the opportunity to informally mediate the dispute, where the discussion of recovery or a remedy is initially addressed. Remedies in tort actions are varied; the law may afford the aggrieved party an injunction, restitution, or damages depending on the nature of the claim and the rights infringed. The substantive and remedial aspects of restitution—which focus on the ill-gotten gain by the wrongdoer as opposed to the harm caused by the wrongful conduct—will be thoroughly covered in the Equity and Remedies class, as will the law with respect to injunctions. This chapter focuses exclusively on damages as a remedy in torts—damages intended to compensate as well as punish.

Historically in tort cases courts have recognized three types of damages: nominal, compensatory, and punitive. The majority of case law that has developed typically resulted from cases where some issue arose with respect to compensatory damages, whether related to the propriety of the award or how the amount was determined. The right to be compensated stems from the common law's desire to compensate victims and deter tortious conduct. The trier of fact (jury unless a bench trial) is typically the entity that is vested with the authority to calculate the loss, allowing for unpredictable results. In personal injury cases, money often serves as a substitute for the actual loss; indeed, there is no pretense that the affection of a loved one can be bought in the market. Instead the hope is that money as compensation will somehow serve as an appropriate proxy for the actual loss.

The tenor of the discussion changes when we turn to punitive damages, as the focus switches from what is needed to compensate the plaintiff to whether the defendant should feel the wrath of society. Again, it is the jury who at least initially determines if and to what extent the defendant should be punished. The judicial oversight of any punitive award, however, is more complex, as the U.S. Constitution has been interpreted as limiting a court's ability to punish.

At the completion of this chapter, you should have a strong familiarity with the various types of tort damages and the process that leads to their recovery.

Johnson v. Valu Food, Inc.
751 A.2d 19 (Md. 2000)

This appeal stems from a dismissal of appellant Lakesha Johnson's amended complaint for failure to state a claim upon which relief could be granted. On January 17, 1997, appellant, a minor, by her mother Celia Cotten, filed suit in the Circuit Court for Baltimore City against appellee Valu Food, Inc., alleging false imprisonment and battery. Upon appellee's request to change venue, the case was transferred to the Circuit Court for Anne Arundel County on May 29, 1997. During the jury trial, which commenced in the circuit court on August 13, 1998, appellee moved for summary judgment arguing that appellant, in her complaint for battery, failed to allege damages suffered by her as a result of appellee's conduct.

> Did the trial court err by dismissing appellant's amended complaint, which contained general pleas of damages resulting from the torts of false imprisonment and battery?

For the reasons set forth herein, we answer appellant's question in the affirmative and reverse the judgment of the trial court.

On May 5, 1996, appellant was a business invitee on the retail premises of appellee located at 2655 Old Annapolis Road, Hanover, Maryland. Appellant accompanied her mother, who had gone to appellee's store, Valu Food, in order to purchase groceries for dinner. While in the supermarket, according to Dawn Lohman, one of appellee's employees, she saw appellant take gum from the candy stand and place it in her purse. Suspicious that she had observed appellant shoplifting, Lohman approached her to question her about the gum; Lohman then proceeded to detain her against her will. Specifically, appellant alleges that Lohman put her arm around her and led her down the aisle toward the back of the store. As a result of Lohman's actions, appellant filed a complaint in the Circuit Court for Baltimore City against appellee. Count I of appellant's complaint alleges that being detained against her will constituted the tort of false imprisonment; Count II alleges the tort of battery as a result of her physical contact and restraint by Lohman.

Appellant contends that the trial court erred by dismissing her complaint for failure properly to plead damages in accordance with Maryland law. In support of her claim, she argues that the intentional torts of false imprisonment and battery do not require a separately pleaded element of damages. Rather, appellant asserts that a general plea of damages is sufficient to sustain claims involving intentional torts. She further urges that the sufficiency of pleading general damages in a complaint is recognized by Maryland common law and legal authorities on Maryland civil procedure. Her complaint states in relevant part:

COUNT 1—FALSE IMPRISONMENT

1. On or about May 5, 1996, [appellant], [sic] was an invitee on the retail premises of the [appellee] at its store located at 2655 Old Annapolis Road, Hanover, Maryland 21076.
2. While on said premises, [appellant] was detained against her will by an agent, servant, and[/]or employee of [appellee], without probable cause, and accused of theft. The agent, servant, and[/]or employee put her arm around [appellant] and escorted her down an aisle in the store and interrogated [appellant] concerning the theft of merchandise from [appellee].

WHEREFORE, this suit is brought and [appellant], [sic] claims the sum of Twenty-five Thousand Dollars ($25,000.00) compensatory damages and One Hundred Thousand Dollars ($100,000.00) punitive damages against [appellee].

COUNT 2—BATTERY
. . .

5. The allegation contained in paragraphs 1 through 3, are adopted by reference with the same effect as if herein fully set forth.
6. Such actions by the agent, servant, and/or employee constituted an offensive, intentional touching of [appellant] and was without the consent of [appellant].

WHEREFORE, this suit is brought and [appellant], [sic] claims the sum of Twenty-five Thousand Dollars ($25,000.00) compensatory damages and One Hundred Thousand Dollars ($100,000) punitive damages against [appellee].

Appellant contends that her general plea of damages in her complaint is sufficient. We agree. It is well settled that Maryland Rule 2-303(b) (2000) governs the form of pleadings and states in pertinent part:

(b) Contents. Each averment of a pleading shall be simple, concise, and direct. No technical forms of pleadings are required. A pleading shall contain only such statements of fact as may be necessary to show the pleader's entitlement to relief or ground of defense. It shall not include argument, unnecessary recitals of law, evidence, or documents, or any immaterial, impertinent, or scandalous matter.

In examining the purpose of pleadings, the Court of Appeals, in *Scott*, observed that

> pleading plays four distinct roles in our system of jurisprudence. It (1) provides notice to the parties as to the nature of the claim or defense; (2) states the facts upon which the claim or defense allegedly exists; (3) defines the boundaries of litigation; and (4) provides for the speedy resolution of frivolous claims and defenses.

The Maryland Court of Appeals, in *Bugg v. Brown*, 251 Md. 99, 104, 246 A.2d 235 (1968), noted that there is a fundamental distinction between intentional and non-intentional torts:

> While it is necessary to prove actual damages to obtain a recovery in negligence actions, the same rule does not apply to intentional torts. For example, a plaintiff who proves a prima facie case for an intentional tort, but fails to prove damages, will always be allowed to obtain at least a nominal recovery. . . .

Richard J. Gilbert & Paul T. Gilbert, Maryland Tort Law Handbook §1.5 (2d ed. 1992). In the instant case, the record demonstrates that appellant pled the intentional torts of battery and false imprisonment. Because a plaintiff need not prove damages in intentional torts, unlike non-intentional torts, appellant is only required to plead general damages in her complaint. Moreover, the Court of Appeals observed that "damages which necessarily result from the wrong complained of may be shown under a general allegation, and, ordinarily, only special damages need be more particularly set forth." *See Rein v. Koons Ford, Inc.*, 318 Md. 130, 141, 567 A.2d 101 (1989) (citations omitted). Although the record demonstrates that appellant's amended complaint failed to articulate the nature and the harm or loss that she suffered, merely stating that the harm she suffered flowed from the specific alleged torts is sufficient and she will be allowed to obtain nominal damages. We hold, therefore, that the trial court erred by dismissing appellant's claim and we remand the case for trial.

JUDGMENT OF THE CIRCUIT COURT FOR ANNE ARUNDEL COUNTY REVERSED; CASE REMANDED FOR FURTHER PROCEEDINGS CONSISTENT WITH THIS OPINION.

PREPARING FOR CLASS

1. What role does the complaint play in this litigation?

2. Why isn't plaintiff required to be more particular with regard to the amount of damages sought?

3. What types of harm might you expect to result from the circumstances, and what type of evidence might be offered to support the claim of harm?

4. As it relates to 3 (above), might the court be reluctant to allow recovery for policy reasons?

INCREASING YOUR UNDERSTANDING

1. *Nominal damages in tort.* Nominal damages are rarely awarded in tort claims, as the substantive law usually requires that the defendant caused some type of harm before liability will ensue. There are occasions (intentional torts, constitutional/civil rights violations), however, where, because of the nature of the right infringed, courts have allowed the recovery of nominal damages.

2. *Nominal award as predicate for punitive damages.* Most courts allow for recovery of punitive damages upon an award of nominal damages. See Bains LLC d/b/a/Flying B v. Arco Peoducts Company, 220 F. Supp. 2d 1193 (W.D. Washington 2002). (Award of $5.0 million punitive damages on §1981 race discrimination claim was reasonably related to actual damages suffered, although jury awarded only $1 of nominal damages; conduct at issue had potential to harm other victims. Some, however, find a nominal award insufficient to support an award of punitive damages, relying primarily on the substantive law's requirement of harm before any liability will be imposed. See Weinberg v. Mauch, 890 P.2d 277 (Hawaii 1995) ("Punitive damages can be returned in Hawai[']i based on nominal damages only. . . . However, the [a]ppellate [c]ourt decisions which state the elements of interference with contract consistently state damages as an essential element of interference with contract, without which there is no cause of action.").

B. ESTABLISHING THE PAIN AND SUFFERING ENTITLEMENT: THE "PER DIEM" ARGUMENT

Debus v. Grand Union Stores of Vermont
621 A.2d 1288 (Vt. 1993.)

JOHNSON, Justice.
Defendant Grand Union appeals from a jury verdict and award of personal injury damages made to plaintiff on her premises-liability claim. Defendant

contends the trial court erred by allowing plaintiff to make a per diem damage argument to the jury, and claims that such arguments are overly prejudicial and should not be allowed. We disagree, and affirm. Defendant also appeals on five other grounds, which shall be taken in turn, each affirmed.

Plaintiff was injured while shopping at defendant's store on August 23, 1985, when a pallet of boxes, piled high and imbalanced, toppled over and fell upon her. The boxes, containing cans of pet food, tumbled off the pallet and onto plaintiff when a store clerk, engaged in routine shelf-restocking, attempted to move the overloaded pallet. Plaintiff suffered injuries resulting in a 20% permanent disability. The jury awarded plaintiff damages of $346,276.23.

I.

During closing argument, plaintiff suggested that the jury think about plaintiff's injury in terms of daily pain and suffering, and then determine what amount of damages would be appropriate compensation for each day of suffering. An average daily figure was suggested to the jury, which it could then multiply by the number of days plaintiff would live, counting from the day of the accident until the end of her life expectancy, some thirty-five years. The jury was told to consider the figure only if it found the calculations useful in quantifying plaintiff's damages. Defendant contends that such per diem arguments are unduly prejudicial and should have been disallowed by the trial court. Defendant further contends that if per diem arguments are permissible, the court should give cautionary instructions.

A per diem argument is a tool of persuasion used by counsel to suggest to the jury how it can quantify damages based on the evidence of pain and suffering presented. The principal reason advanced against per diem arguments is that a jury's verdict must be based on the evidence before it, and a per diem figure, which is not in evidence, allows the jury to calculate damages based solely on the argument of counsel. Further, courts have reasoned that a per diem argument unfairly assumes that pain is constant, uniform, and continuous, and that the pain will prevail for the rest of plaintiff's life. Therefore, it creates an "illusion of certainty" in a disability that is more likely to be subject to great variation. Finally, some courts conclude that the jury will be too easily misled by the plaintiff's argument.

On the other hand, jurisdictions that have allowed per diem arguments counter that sufficient safeguards exist in the adversarial system to overcome the objections to its use. They point out that a plaintiff's hypothesis on damages, even if presented on a per diem basis, must be reasonable or suffer serious and possibly fatal attack by opposing counsel; further, the notion that pain is constant and uniform may be easily rebutted by reference to the evidence or the jury's own experience. Most importantly, they note that juries are entitled to draw inferences from the evidence before them and that the extent of damages attributable to pain and suffering is a permissible inference.

After review of the arguments and authorities, we are persuaded that there is nothing inherently improper or prejudicial about per diem arguments if they are made under the ordinary supervision and control of the trial court. In cases where claims for pain and suffering are made, juries are forced to equate pain with damages. The jury can benefit by guidance offered by counsel in closing argument as to how they can construct that equation. We permit counsel reasonable latitude in this phase of the trial to summarize the evidence, to persuade the jury to accept or reject a plaintiff's claim, and to award a specific lump sum. If a lump sum is to be suggested to the jury, it cannot be impermissible to explain how the lump sum was determined.

Nor do we agree with defendant that per diem arguments must be accompanied by specific instructions. Juries are routinely instructed that arguments and suggestions by counsel are not evidence, whether or not a party makes a per diem argument. It may well be that other instructions may be required when per diem arguments are used, but we leave to the trial courts the fashioning of instructions and controls appropriate to the cases before them.

Our holding should not be taken to grant the plaintiff carte blanche to depart from any reasonable view of the evidence. Rather, it reflects our confidence that the defendant's opportunity to refute the plaintiff's closing argument will ensure that an absurd hypothesis will be rejected. Even if it is not, and a verdict is excessive, the trial court has adequate mechanisms, such as remittitur, to deal with it.

The question remains as to whether the per diem argument in the present case was improper. In closing argument, plaintiff's counsel told the jury the per diem figure was only a suggestion for its consideration, and that determining a fair amount would be entirely up to the jury. He did not argue that plaintiff's pain was constant, uniform, and easy to quantify on a daily basis. In fact, counsel told the jury that pain fluctuates and that he was only suggesting an average figure for their consideration, and told them to "[d]isregard it if it is not helpful." Defendant had a full opportunity to rebut the per diem argument and did so. We cannot conclude that this argument invaded the province of the jury.

The case was submitted to the jury with appropriate instructions. The trial court cautioned the jury that "the arguments of the attorneys and any statements which they made in their arguments or in their summation is not evidence and will not be considered by you as evidence," and that "it is your recollection of the witness's testimony and not the attorney's statements which shall control you in reaching your decision."

The court made it clear to the jury that the final determination of damages was to be made on the evidence alone and not on persuasive arguments for any particular formulas. That the jury was able to make this distinction between presented evidence and suggested formulas is demonstrated by their arriving at a total damages award $166,194 below the figure suggested by plaintiff's counsel, which figure counsel calculated in part by using the per diem formula. There was no error.

Affirmed.

ALLEN, Chief Justice, dissenting.

The majority reasons that if a lump sum award may be suggested to a jury, it cannot be impermissible to explain how the lump sum was determined. The difficulty with this rationale, however, is that, until today, it has been improper in Vermont to mention to the jury the lump sum being sought. *Mattison v. Smalley*, 122 Vt. 113, 118, 165 A.2d 343, 347-48 (1960). As stated in *Mattison*, the amount which the plaintiff hopes to recover is not evidence, proof of the amount due, or a standard for estimating the damages.

It is unnecessary here to set forth the various arguments in favor of or against per diem arguments as they have been thoroughly and exhaustively discussed in opinions from virtually every other jurisdiction over the past thirty years. I believe the better answer is to permit counsel to argue to the trier of fact the appropriateness of employing a time-unit calculation technique for fixing damages for pain and suffering, but to prohibit any suggestion by counsel of specific monetary amounts either on a lump sum or time-unit basis. This approach was suggested in *King v. Railway Express Agency*, 107 N.W.2d 509, 517 (N.D.1961), and adopted by rule in New Jersey. Rule 1:7-1(b), New Jersey Rules of Court.

The ultimate objective should be to aid the jury in determining what sum of money will reasonably compensate the plaintiff for the pain and suffering endured. The attainment of this goal is not enhanced by counsel arguing the dollar amounts that they desire to have a jury return. The fair and practical solution is to permit the jury to hear about the methodology and to apply its dollar amounts from the evidence rather than sums suggested in argument.

I further disagree with the majority in its reluctance to require a specific cautionary instruction, beyond the general language offered that "the arguments of the attorneys and any statements which they made in their arguments or in their summation [are] not in evidence and will not be considered by you as evidence." The instruction approved by the majority may be adequate to deal with remarks of an attorney that are plainly argumentative. The difficulty is that remarks regarding numbers or dollar amounts may not appear to be argument, but rather evidence itself. Hence, an instruction not to consider argument as evidence does not cure the problem.

As the Hawaii Supreme Court said in overruling an earlier case and allowing per diem arguments:

> With proper guidance by the trial judge the objections advanced in [an earlier holding] can be avoided and formula arguments can be usefully made by both sides. The trial judge should make it clear that the formula is just that, *argument*, and no more. He should emphasize that it is part of counsel's function as an advocate to persuade the jury and that formulas are but illustrations which serve only to focus the inquiry on the issue which the jury must ultimately resolve, the extent of money damages.

Barretto v. Akau, 51 Hawaii 383, 461, 463 P.2d 917, 923-24 (1969) (citations omitted) (emphasis in original).

> When a per diem argument is used,
>   [t]he trial judge should tell the jury that they are not to be governed by the amount of damages suggested by counsel for whatever unit of time counsel employed, that this argument does not constitute evidence but is merely an approach to the damages issue which the jury may consider but need not adopt, and that the jury's ultimate obligation is to arrive at a lump sum amount which, in its view, is supported by the evidence and is fair and just to both the plaintiff and the defendant.

Weeks v. Holsclaw, 306 N.C. 655, 295 S.E.2d 596, 601 (1982).
   The majority relies on the proposition that "[i]n closing argument, plaintiff's counsel told the jury the per diem figure was only a suggestion for its consideration, and that determining a fair amount would be entirely up to the jury." The majority is overly generous. Counsel's remarks are at best ambiguous and come at the beginning of a lengthy and detailed mathematical presentation. That presentation, stated in part, follows:

> What award will it take to tell Grand Union what accountability means and that this is what the people in Bennington County think a human life and human suffering is worth[?]
>   Now, let's just take one element. We have talked about pain and suffering. What would be fair compensation for pain and suffering? *Entirely up to you.* I have a suggestion. If you think about what it is like for Susanne to go through one day with the pain that she has and think about what would be fair compensation for that one day, what do you think it would be? Would it be $100 to go through that in a day? Would it be $75? Would it be $50, $40?
>   Ladies and gentlemen, we want to be scrupulously fair about our request to you. So I am going to suggest to you that you award Susanne $30 a day for the loss of those three elements: pain and suffering, mental anguish, and loss of enjoyment of life. That is $10 a day for each one. *I put it to you for your consideration to follow that through.*
>   You would do it this way, there are 365 days a year. I am just going to put here pain and suffering, mental anguish, loss of enjoyment of life. Now there are 365 days in a year. And Susanne's six years she has already suffered in these ways and 29 more, that is 35 years total that she should be compensated for. And if you multiply 35 times 365, there are 12,775 days. And if you multiply that figure by the $30 per day I just suggested, it comes out to $383,250—sorry. $383,250.
>   Now, another way of thinking of that is if you divide 35 years into this figure of $383,250 it comes out to slightly under $11,000 a year.

Maybe that would be a help to think for you $11,000 a year to live the way she lives, to lose what she has lost. *Perhaps that would be a help for you; I don't know.* (Emphasis added.)

The caveats in this argument are nearly invisible, and an additional statement in rebuttal is no better. The residue is a set of specific numbers that are, by the majority's holding, proper, but which at least deserve a specific cautionary instruction. Yet the majority would substitute counsel's at best ambiguous message for a clear instruction from the bench about the use of the numbers.

I would not, and I dissent.

PREPARING FOR CLASS

1. As a juror, what evidence would most persuade you should you be asked to quantify pain and suffering damages?

2. How much deference should the court give the testimony given by the plaintiff?

3. Is it realistic to effectively instruct a jury that arguments by lawyers should not be considered as anything but advisory?

4. What's a possible alternative to a per diem argument accompanied with a specific number?

5. Distinguish between determining whether an award is excessive and whether the argument leading to the award was improper. *Debus* involves the latter.

INCREASING YOUR UNDERSTANDING

1. *Burden of proof.* Plaintiff carries the burden of proof in most tort actions, on most tort issues. When it comes to seeking damages, the argument begins with showing a nexus between the defendant's conduct and the alleged harm. When it comes to harm of a general nature (pain and suffering, hedonic, disability, loss of relationships, etc.), there are no universal guidelines, tables, or resources that can be legitimately relied upon to calculate the loss. That being the case, it is in this context where the skill of the lawyer may be most palpable.

2. *Split on per diem.* There is a split among the states on whether a per diem argument is proper. If allowed, the jury is typically given a cautionary or limiting instruction, with the court counseling on the lack of evidentiary value of the plaintiff's lawyer's arguments. It's rare that

the court will delve into the basis upon which the per diem amount was established.

C. APPEAL OF COMPENSATORY AWARD

Ming Yu He v. Miller
983 A.2d 1164, 411 N.J. Super. 15 (App. Div. 2009)

FISHER, J.A.D.

We again review an order granting remittitur or, upon its rejection, a new trial on damages. We previously reversed, but the Supreme Court summarily reversed in part and remanded for the trial judge's complete and searching analysis, including an assessment of comparable jury verdicts, to be followed by our reconsideration. Having reexamined the matter, we again reverse and reinstate the jury's verdict.

I

The complaint filed by plaintiff Ming Yu He, and her husband, Jinfang He, against defendant Enilma Miller, was tried to a jury over four days in February 2008. The jury found defendant to have been negligent and awarded plaintiff $1,000,000 for pain and suffering, $110,000 for past lost wages, and $500,000 for future lost wages; the jury also awarded plaintiff's husband $100,000 on his loss of consortium claim.

Defendant filed a post-verdict motion seeking a new trial or, in the alternative, a remittitur. The trial judge granted the motion in part. He found the pain and suffering award, as well as the per quod award, to be excessive and shocking to the conscience. He granted a remittitur of the pain and suffering award to $200,000 and the per quod claim to $10,000. The judge also ordered a new trial on damages if plaintiffs rejected the remittitur. Plaintiffs rejected the remittitur and moved for leave to appeal.

We granted leave to appeal and subsequently reversed by way of an unpublished opinion. The Supreme Court granted defendant's petition for certification, summarily reversed our judgment in part and remanded the matter to the trial judge "for a complete and searching analysis under [*Johnson v. Scaccetti*, 192 N.J. 256, 927 A.2d 1269 (2007)], including a 'factual analysis of how the award is different or similar to others to which it is compared.'" The [Supreme] Court also directed that we reconsider our judgment "in light of the findings developed on remand."

On August 12, 2009, the trial judge rendered a decision further explaining and adhering to his finding of excessiveness. The parties have since filed briefs relating to the trial judge's most recent decision, and we have again heard the oral argument of counsel.

II

In our earlier unpublished opinion, we canvassed the evidence adduced at trial. To summarize, plaintiff Ming Yu He was injured when, on October 28, 2003, her motor vehicle was struck head-on by defendant's vehicle. Plaintiff was rendered unconscious by the impact and transported by ambulance to a nearby hospital. X-rays revealed no fractures and she was discharged. However, due to continuing pain, she visited a chiropractor on three occasions, but received no relief.

On November 6, 2003, plaintiff was examined by Dr. Robert Kramberg, who found a limited range of motion in plaintiff's cervical spine and lower back, back spasms, bruising and abnormal nerve sensation. Dr. Kramberg prescribed various medications, including painkillers. He also started a program of physical therapy.

A few weeks later, in light of plaintiff's continued complaints of pain in her neck, lower back and left knee, Dr. Kramberg ordered magnetic resonance imaging (MRI) of plaintiff's cervical and lumbar spine. The MRI revealed that plaintiff had four herniated or ruptured discs, located at C4-C5, C5-C6, L4-L5 and L5-S1. An electromyography determined that the herniated discs were causing compression of the nerves, which affected plaintiff's arms, legs and back. Dr. Kramberg concluded that plaintiff was suffering from radiculitis or radiculopathy from the herniated discs in both the cervical and lumbosacral spine.

The physical therapy program failed to produce satisfactory results. As a result, Dr. Kramberg referred plaintiff to Dr. Jay Lee, who performed over thirty acupuncture treatments on plaintiff's hands, neck, waist and back. These treatments only provided temporary relief.

Epidural injections of cortisone brought about no significant improvement. Indeed, plaintiff experienced a bad reaction from the cervical epidurals, and the lumbar epidural injections caused plaintiff's leg to become swollen. Consequently, plaintiff received no further injections.

Dr. Kramberg referred plaintiff to a neurosurgeon. MRIs taken at that time were consistent with the earlier findings. The neurosurgeon did not recommend surgery, explaining that "whether or not a spinal patient is referred to surgery depends on the particular patient and particular injury." Dr. Kramberg also observed that

> not all patients do well with surgery. And once you have a failed surgery, there's nothing else you can do for the patient. They wind up on lifetime narcotic pain medication.

Dr. Kramberg testified at trial that after five years of unavailing treatment, plaintiff's pain was "chronic [and] permanent." As we explained in our earlier opinion, Dr. Kramberg opined that plaintiff

> continued to have limited range of motion, and he believed she was medically incapable of performing her job as a housekeeper at a hotel. He continued to prescribe pain medication (Vicodin) to plaintiff and she last saw him in January 2008. In Dr. Kramberg's opinion, based upon the MRI and EMG results, the physical examination, plaintiff's complaints, and the fact that plaintiff had been completely asymptomatic prior to the accident, her injuries were causally related to the October 28, 2003 accident.

Dr. Kramberg also acknowledged that testing revealed plaintiff had "a little bit of arthritic degeneration on the vertebrae," which he determined was part of the "normal aging process" and "pretty much consistent with her age, being in her [forties]." Defendant's expert, an orthopedic surgeon, opined that "there's a good suspicion that a lot" of the MRI and EMG findings "are degenerative and preexisting," but acknowledged "there's really no way of ascertaining, based on these films, whether or not the disc herniations are a result of the degenerative changes or not."

Plaintiff, her husband and their daughter also testified about the injury and its sequelae, which we summarized in our earlier opinion in the following way:

> Plaintiff testified as to how the accident and her resulting injuries impacted upon her activities of daily living. She indicated that she experienced neck and back pain "on a daily basis[,]" which often spread and caused headaches and pain in the legs and hands, and sometimes caused her to lose her grip and drop things. She was no longer able to work at the job she held for thirteen years and could not perform most normal household duties such as grocery shopping, cooking a full meal, gardening, vacuuming, cleaning, or participating in activities with her children. She also testified she was no longer able to swim or ride a bicycle.
>
> Plaintiff's husband and daughter provided similar testimony as to plaintiff's home life. Both plaintiff and her husband testified that they brought their parents to the United States from China so that they would not have to work in their old age and their daughter could take care of them, in accordance with the Chinese custom of filial piety. Now, according to plaintiffs, the situation had been reversed, with the grandparents taking care of plaintiff by helping out with the chores she could no longer perform. They both also testified that they have been completely unable to have sexual relations since the accident because their attempts to do so were continually foiled by the onset of back and neck pain for plaintiff. Plaintiff told the jury that since the accident, she felt "useless."

III

Defendant moved for a new trial or, in the alternative, for a remittitur. Among other things, defendant argued that the $1,000,000 pain and suffering award was shockingly high because of verdicts rendered in other purportedly similar cases. Based on references in defendant's moving papers to the verdicts in thirteen other cases, defendant contended that a proper award should have fallen within a range between $50,000 and $100,000.

The judge denied the motion insofar as it related to liability, the past lost wage award of $110,000, and the future lost wage award of $500,000. He did, however, conclude that the pain and suffering award of $1,000,000 and the per quod award of $100,000 were shocking to the conscience and warranted relief, explaining:

> Based upon the fact that surgery was never recommended for [plaintiff], that she has degenerative dis[c] disease, that she is able to care for herself, drive a motor vehicle and perform light housekeeping, as well as the fact that she did not appear to be experiencing pain and suffering during the course of the trial and was able to sit for long periods of time during the trial, I find that the jury award of $1M to [plaintiff] for her injuries constitutes a manifest injustice that shocks the judicial conscience.

In so ruling, the judge made no mention of verdicts in other cases of a similar nature.

Plaintiff rejected the remittitur and moved for leave to appeal. At the same time, the judge issued a written amplification of his oral decision, pursuant to *Rule* 2:5-1(b), which mainly explained why, if remittitur was rejected, a new trial on all elements of damages, and not just the remitted components, was required. The judge found that "in the case at bar, there is an interrelationship" between the awards he found excessive and those he found were not excessive.

Although the trial judge's initial decision and subsequent amplification made no reference to comparable jury verdicts in finding parts of this verdict to be shockingly high, following the Supreme Court's mandate the judge rendered a written decision in which he identified certain verdicts he thought were relevant.

Specifically, the judge referred to two cases over which he presided. The first, *Morales v. Keith*, was an action brought by a thirty-four-year old male plaintiff who, as a result of an auto accident, was diagnosed with one herniated disc and one disc bulge. The plaintiff in *Morales* was also diagnosed with bilateral carpal tunnel syndrome, which required surgery. The jury awarded $2500, which was increased by stipulation of the parties to nearly $50,000.

The second, *Ziza v. Romanelli*, was an action commenced by a fifty-five-year old female plaintiff who suffered a hairline fracture of an ankle, and torn ligaments, as a result of a fall-down accident. A disputed issue at trial related to plaintiff's claim of reflex sympathetic dystrophy (RSD); she was treated for the alleged RSD through surgical implantation of a spinal cord stimulator. According to the trial judge,

> despite some degree of relief from the stimulator, plaintiff still experienced pain. In addition, the facts revealed that plaintiff's lifestyle and her relationship with her husband were affected by the injuries. Further, plaintiff was unable to continue working in the family bakery business where she had worked for many years.

The jury awarded the plaintiff in *Ziza* $200,000; her husband received $25,000.

The trial judge summed up the significance of these verdicts in the following way:

> Although the injuries sustained in the above-noted cases were not identical to those sustained by [p]laintiff in this case, the cases provided a basis for comparison to the matter involved herein, as they involved spinal and/or other serious injuries which had a significant impact on the lives of the plaintiffs. The [c]ourt found it particularly noteworthy that even in a case which required the permanent implantation of a spinal stimulator and ligament reconstructionsurgery, the jury award did not exceed $200,000.00.

Not only, as the judge recognized, were the injuries sustained in these two cases different from those sustained by plaintiff here, but the cases involved persons of different ages who led different lives.

IV

The Supreme Court's mandate in this case requires that we reconsider our earlier decision "in light of the findings developed on remand." Having carefully examined the trial judge's remand decision, we find no cause to alter our earlier judgment. In reaching that conclusion, we consider (a) the applicable principles for determining the excessiveness of a damages award, (b) the judge's examination of what he found were other comparable verdicts, and (c) the judge's description of the relevant facts and his "feel of the case."

A

A trial court's role in assessing a verdict is to ensure that damages awarded "encompass no more than the amount that will make the plaintiff whole, that is, the actual loss." "Although '[t]he judicial role in reviewing jury verdicts . . . is essential to a rational system of justice,' the authority to set aside damages awards on grounds of excessiveness is 'limited,' and should only occur "in clear cases.".

To put these principles in perspective, we must recognize that juries are routinely instructed that to reach a reasonable measure of damages "[t]he law does not provide you with any table, schedule or formula by which a person's pain and suffering[,] disability, loss of enjoyment of life may be measured in terms of money." Jurors are told that the proper measure of damages is "left to [their] sound discretion," based on their common experiences regarding "the nature of pain and suffering, disability, impairment and loss of enjoyment of life" and the "function of money," and that

> [t]he task of equating the two so as to arrive at a fair and reasonable award of damages requires a high order of human judgment. For this reason, the law can provide no better yardstick for your guidance than your own impartial judgment and experience.

As a result, following its recognition of the broad discretion that is "uniquely reposed in the jury's good judgment," our Supreme Court has directed that "to justify judicial interference [t]he verdict must be wide of the mark and pervaded by a sense of wrongness."

In assessing excessiveness, the Supreme Court has determined that the trial judge's review "must be grounded substantially in the 'totality of the evidence' in the record." That evidence must be "viewed in a light most favorable to the plaintiff." This evaluation must encompass

> the nature and extent of the injury, the medical treatment that the plaintiff underwent and may be required to undergo in the future, the impact of the injury on the plaintiff's life from the date of injury through the date of trial, and the projected impact of the injury on the plaintiff in the future.

The Supreme Court has also held that the trial judge "may look beyond the record to judicial 'experience with other injury verdicts.'" The Court mentioned, however, that if a judge goes outside the record to consider other verdicts, "it must give a factual analysis of how the award is different or similar to others to which it is compared." A verdict "should not be overthrown except upon the basis of a carefully reasoned and factually supported (and articulated) determination, after canvassing the record and weighing the evidence, that the continued viability of the judgment would constitute a manifest denial of justice." As a result, even if "generous," a jury verdict having "reasonable support in the record" must "be regarded as final."

The appellate standard of review employs the same principles utilized in the trial court with the exception that the appellate court must afford "due deference" to the trial judge's "feel of the case" with regard "to the assessment of intangibles, such as witness credibility."

B

As we have observed, the Supreme Court mandated our reconsideration following the trial judge's further examination "including 'a factual analysis of how the award is different or similar to others to which it is compared.'" We, thus, turn to the judge's discussion of comparable verdicts in his remand decision.

As recounted earlier, the judge relied on the verdicts in two cases over which he presided. These comparables possess little similarity to the case at hand. In the first, *Morales v. Keith*, plaintiff suffered a disc herniation, as well as a disc bulge, but it was the carpal tunnel syndrome that required surgery. Even at that, the jury only awarded $2500, which-from the information provided in the judge's opinion-might be more likely to suggest the verdict was shockingly low, as revealed by the parties' stipulation that increased the award to nearly $50,000. The second, *Ziza v. Romanelli*, involved a plaintiff who sustained a hairline ankle fracture and torn ligaments; it also included a dispute between the parties regarding a diagnosis of RSD. The plaintiff in *Ziza* underwent surgery for the implantation of a spinal cord stimulator. She received a $200,000 award. There apparently was a lost wage claim in that case as well, but we assume from the judge's remand decision that the jury was only asked to provide a single verdict for all the components of that plaintiff's injuries. *Ziza's* husband received a per quod award of $25,000.

From what the trial judge has said about these cases there are obvious significant differences. Only *Morales* dealt with a herniated disc (and not, as here, four herniated discs) and that case generated a verdict less than two percent of the amount to which the trial judge remitted the pain-and-suffering verdict in the case at hand. The *Ziza* case involved injuries that required spinal surgery, but it also involved an injured ankle and the verdict apparently lumped all the elements of damages together. The plaintiff in *Ziza* was fifty-five years old; plaintiff here was forty-six years old at the time of trial.

The judge also referred to verdicts in other cases where the plaintiffs sustained spinal injuries: in *Astarita*, plaintiff sustained two herniated discs, underwent alaminotomy, and was awarded $200,000; in *Regan*, plaintiff sustained two herniated discs, was treated conservatively, and awarded $150,000; in *Shamosh*, plaintiff sustained two disc herniations, underwent decompression surgery and was awarded $50,000; in *Fernandez*, plaintiff sustained three herniated discs and one disc bulge, and was awarded $100,000; in *Hossain*, plaintiff sustained one herniated disc and was awarded $50,000; in *Boghdady*, the plaintiff sustained three herniated discs and one disc bulge, and was awarded $40,000.

These cases provide some superficial support for the judge's conclusion, but what the judge has said about these cases reveals little about those particular plaintiffs and their own unique lives. The judge's discussion of those cases does not inform us of the plaintiffs' ages or how their particular injuries—undoubtedly similar to plaintiff's injuries here—impacted upon their lives. In other words, it may be fair to compare the injuries sustained by plaintiff with the injuries sustained by these other plaintiffs but we question how can it be said without more that the pain and suffering of those others, as well as the way in which their enjoyment of life was lost or impaired, is sufficiently similar to warrant comparison.

Comparing the injuries sustained by individuals is not the same as comparing damages to automobiles. If a jury was asked to determine the value of a 2004 Ford Focus, which was totaled in an accident, it could safely consider the value of any other 2004 Ford Focus with similar mileage. But we are not dealing with the damage done to mechanical things—we are dealing with human beings, all of whom are in many ways similar but in many ways different from all other human beings. We can generally predict, based on past experiences in similar cases, what a reasonable jury might award for a particular type of injury, but we should not expect that all juries ought to produce the same or similar verdict. The task of a jury in such a matter is to resolve complex issues regarding the monetary value of a particular person's pain and suffering and loss of the enjoyment of life. In examining such verdicts for excessiveness, courts should not expect or require the type of exactitude that seems to form the basis for the judge's decision in this case.

Given very limited information from the trial judge as to the facts and circumstances of these purported comparable verdicts, we reject the notion that they provide adequate support for the judge's finding of excessiveness.

C

In his decision following the Supreme Court's summary order in this matter, the trial judge also referred to his "feel of the case" in concluding that the pain and suffering and per quod awards were excessive. In this respect, the judge relied upon his observations of plaintiff during the course of the four-day trial, noting that she

> was able to sit for long periods of time without any visible signs of pain or discomfort. She was able to enter and exit the courtroom without assistance or any apparent difficulty. Plaintiff's gait and appearance did not appear to be in any way affected by her injuries. Overall, there were no outward signs of pain or discomfort observable during the course of the trial.

The judge also sought to minimize plaintiff's injuries by referring to the facts that: plaintiff's treating doctors did not recommend surgery; "there was undisputed evidence of degenerative disc disease which preexisted the accident"; and, although she claimed a significant limitation in her daily activities, plaintiff "is able to care for herself, continues to perform light cleaning work, and is able to drive a motor vehicle."

We emphasize that the trial judge is not "a thirteenth and decisive juror," and "may not substitute his judgment for that of the jury." We pay deference to the trial judge's "feel of the case" mainly because a judge's observations are helpful in understanding a jury's findings. Those observations are not, however, to supplant the jury's findings when the evidence—viewed in the light most favorable to plaintiff—indicates the jury possessed a different view of the case. Indeed, a trial judge's "feel of the case" is entitled to "minimal" weight when based on things observed by the jury.

Here, it is interesting to observe that the trial judge found nothing excessive or shocking about the jury's award of future lost wages of $500,000. We gather from the jury's verdict on that aspect of damages, and the judge's finding that it was not excessive, that the jury found—as was its right—that plaintiff would remain permanently unable to return to work. The judge also determined, in amplifying his initial decision prior to our earlier opinion, that "there is an interrelationship between the pain and suffering and per quod damage awards and the lost wage awards." That being the case, we find incongruous the judge's determination that the pain and suffering award—although, as the judge held, not "fairly separable" from the lost wage award—was excessive whereas the lost wage award was not. In our earlier opinion, we provided the following comments, which remain applicable:

> [W]hile the factors upon which the court focused led it to conclude the pain and suffering and per quod awards were excessive, those same factors apparently did not lead the court to conclude that the jury's verdict relative to past and future lost wages was excessive. At their core, past and future loss of wages requires proof that plaintiff's injuries are causally related to plaintiff's inability to engage in her pre-accident employment responsibilities. Thus, plaintiff's inability to work is inextricably linked to the nature of injuries and the effect those injuries have upon continued employment. Consequently, we find it difficult to understand that the court could accept the jury's award for past and future lost earnings but not its award for pain and suffering and the per quod verdict.

In carefully examining the record on appeal, we conclude that the judge mistakenly failed to appreciate that the jury's view of the case—that is, the jury's findings regarding plaintiff's injuries, the duration and intensity of her pain and suffering, and the impact those injuries and the consequent pain had on her enjoyment of life—differed substantially from his own. While the judge determined from his own observations of plaintiff in the courtroom that she did not appear to be as limited as claimed, the jury had the same opportunity to observe plaintiff and clearly found otherwise. And the judge, in his initial oral decision, concluded from his view of the evidence that plaintiff "has degenerative disk [sic] disease." Although plaintiff's expert indicated that the MRI studies revealed "degenerative problems" in places along her spine, that expert rejected the assertion that the herniated discs were causally related to any degenerative problems due to age. Again, in light of the jury's entire verdict, including those aspects the judge found were not excessive, we must assume the jury found plaintiff's expert credible. In exalting these "degenerative problems," as a means for minimizing the extent of plaintiff's pain and suffering, the judge failed to view the evidence "in a light most favorable to the plaintiff." In concluding as we must that the jury found persuasive all aspects of plaintiff's claim, including the intensity and chronicity of her pain, the permanency of her injuries, and the severe blow these injuries dealt to her enjoyment of life, we reject the judge's own personal view of the evidence as an appropriate yardstick by which to measure defendant's claim of excessiveness.

V

To summarize, we have reconsidered the matter in light of the judge's written decision following the Supreme Court's remand. We conclude that the judge's additional findings regarding comparable verdicts and his "feel of the case" are inconsistent with the principles set forth in *Johnson, supra*, 192 N.J. at 281, 927 A.2d 1269. Moreover, the findings are plainly insufficient to establish that the verdict constituted the manifest denial of justice required to overthrow the jury's determination.

In the final analysis, we find the trial judge's decision to be erroneous because he viewed as excessive a verdict that did not meet his vision of what lawyers or insurance adjusters might expect a jury to award to a plaintiff who has suffered certain injuries. In reversing, we can assume—although we think he was more conservative than warranted—that the judge was correct when he estimated the likely range of pain-and-suffering verdicts to be $40,000 to $200,000 in cases involving these types of injuries, treated in a similar way and with similar results. Finding such a range and ascertaining whether the verdict fell outside its borders, however, is not determinative of whether an award is excessive. It would indeed be strange if the law required that we instruct juries that there is no yardstick against which to measure a proper award of damages and then permit trial judges to use such a yardstick to determine excessiveness. Instead, determining what might be a predictable award in a particular case is only a starting point in such an analysis.

That is, verdicts that fall outside a predictable range are not per se excessive. For example, in *Jastram, supra*, 197 N.J. at 235, 962 A.2d 503, the Court reinstated a jury verdict, stating: "To be sure . . . this was a high verdict, but that does not mean it was excessive." Likewise, in *Johnson, supra*, 192 N.J. at 283, 927 A.2d 1269, the Court found a jury's award to be "undoubtedly high, perhaps overly generous," but concluded it was not "so grossly excessive that it shocks the conscience." In short, it is a mistake to conclude that a verdict is excessive and shocking because it was greater than what an experienced practitioner or judge might expect in similar circumstances. The question is not whether the verdict "missed the mark" but whether it was "wide of the mark." When the predictable range for the damages in a case has been exceeded—even when "high" or "overly generous"—the verdict must still be sustained unless it can be held and adequately articulated that the award was "so grossly excessive" as to permit a conclusion—clearly and convincingly reached—that permitting the award to stand would constitute a manifest miscarriage of justice.

Having reexamined the matter in light of the trial judge's additional findings, we again recognize that this is a close case. It is not unreasonable to conclude that the pain and suffering award missed the mark. It may even lie around the edges of what might constitute a grossly excessive award. But, as our Supreme Court has said, a "tie must go to the jury," because "[i]n the American system of justice the presumption of correctness of a verdict by a jury has behind it the wisdom of centuries of common law merged into our constitutional framework."

The order under review is reversed and the matter remanded for reinstatement of the jury's verdict.

PREPARING FOR CLASS

1. What damages were lowered, and what was the basis for doing so?

2. What did the trial court do that was improper, and what criticism did the court of appeal have? Has the appellate court finally satisfied the Supreme Court?

3. Do you agree with the decision to reverse, or would you have sustained the trial court? If your answer is "well I need more facts" then you've started the process of understanding how the record limits the ability to give adequate review to the matters that transpired at trial.

4. At what point should the judges simply defer to the jurors?

INCREASING YOUR UNDERSTANDING

1. *Remititurs.* Courts vary on the standards they articulate when responding to requests to remit the jury's award. "Shock the conscience," "monsterously excessive," verdict a clear "result of prejudice or passion," etc., have all been offered as standards employed by a court when assessing whether the award should be lowered. Despite varying verbiage, they all enjoy a common thread: the reviewing court is ostensibly showing deference to the jury's finding, otherwise the review would be *de novo*. Giving deference to the original award is rooted in the desire to preserve the plaintiff's right to have the jury decide her fate.

2. *Additurs.* In contrast, a plaintiff disappointed with the amount of the award may in some jurisdictions request that the judge increase the award. Additurs in federal courts have been found violative of

the Seventh Amendment right to a jury trial and therefore unavailable. U.S. Dimick v. Schiedt, 293 U.S. 474 (1935).

3.   Standards for recovering damages and the categories:

   a.   *Standards.* Courts require that plaintiff show a relationship between the loss and the defendant's conduct with reasonable certainty. It's unusual for the parties to stipulate to some of the hard damages like lost wages and medical expenses to avoid the matters being litigated at trial. That's if the parties agree that the amounts are reasonable and need.

   b.   *Categories.* Those that practice in the area of personal injury customarily divide compensatory damages into two categories: economic (i.e., "hard" or "special") and noneconomic (i.e., "soft" or "general"). It's typical for practitioners to "value" the noneconomic damages by reference to the economic ones. The implication is, for example, that the more the medical expenses the greater the suffering. In addition, pleading rules may require the economic damages to be pled in the complaint with particularity while allowing for the noneconomic damages to be generally pled.

   c.   Economic:

      i.   Lost wages and impaired earning capacity. Injured parties (including children) often have to miss time from work, and courts allow them to recover the income they would have earned had they not been injured. Depending on the situation, there can be wages that were lost before trial and those that are expected to be lost after the trial is concluded. Quantifying the loss requires reference to the wages that were earned by the plaintiff (assuming employment) and the amount of time the plaintiff is expected to be unable to work. The impaired earning capacity stems from the premise that some injured parties' real wage loss cannot be appropriately measured by the real wages they lost as they may have been unemployed, at the time of injury or limited (by injury) in their ability to enter other, more lucrative employment. See, Wal-Mart Stores v. Cordova, 856 S.W.2d 768 (Tex. App. El Paso 1993) ("Evidence supported award for customer's loss-of-earning capacity as result of injury in store, even though customer was not gainfully employed during year in which accident occurred; customer was employed as cook in year before accident and had also worked as factory worker and in janitorial services, and economist testified as to customer's capacity to earn money in future based on degree of impairment and minimum wage.").

ii. *Medical expenses.* Courts allow for injured parties to recover past and future medical expenses incurred as a result of being injured, provided they were reasonable and necessary. Often expert testimony is required to support the claim of necessity; though on occasion, where the losses are not in dispute, the parties may stipulate to the amount.

iii. *Present day value adjustments.* It may be expected that the plaintiff will incur losses after the trial is completed, which is often the case where, because of the injuries, plaintiff will be required to seek medical care and/or will experience some impairment in the ability to earn income. For example, a 30-year-old adult involved in an automobile accident that renders her a paraplegic may require medical attention well beyond the trial. Experts will testify as to the future loss, the need for assistance, and the cost of medical care. Working from this number, the court will have to determine what amount should be awarded today to cover for the future loss, taking into consideration that today's award could be invested with a considerable return. The goal is not to over-compensate nor short the plaintiff, so the court will guestimate as to what amount today, if reasonably invested, will yield the amount needed in the future based on testimony from economists. In other words, the eventual award will reflect "present day" dollars if the court is convinced that the failure to do so will lead to a windfall for the plaintiff.

d. Noneconomic:

i. There is no universally accepted definition for what constitutes pain and suffering. Generally, it refers to the variety of sensations one experiences after being subjected to bodily injury. Emotional distress, loss of enjoyment of life (hedonic damages, discussed below), phantom pain suffered by those who are paralyzed or amputees, fear of contracting future disease, disability, etc., have all been described at one time or the other as falling within the definition. As illustrated in the principal case, there is no accepted yardstick for quantifying pain and suffering, yet courts routinely find it compensable.

"The jury must impartially determine pain and suffering damages based upon evidence specific to the plaintiff, as opposed to statistical data concerning the public at large. The only person whose pain and suffering is relevant in calculating a general damage award is the plaintiff. . . . Translating pain and anguish into dollars can, at least, be only an arbitrary allowance, and not a process of measurement, and consequently the judge can, in his instructions, give the jury no standard to go by; he can also tell them to allow such amount as in their general discretion they may consider reasonable. . . . The chief reliance for reaching reasonable results in attempting to value in terms of money must be the restraint and common sense of the jury." Loth v. Truck-A-Way Corporation et al., 70 Cal. Rptr. 2d 571, 576 (1998).

ii. "Hedonic" damages are another subset of noneconomic damages and have been described as "an award that compensates for the limitations, resulting from defendant's negligence, on the injured person's ability to participate in and derive pleasure from the normal activities of daily life, or for the individuals inability to pursue his talents, recreations, interests, hobbies or avocation." Boan v. Blackwell, 541 S.E.2d 242, 244 (S.C. 2001). Courts that allow recovery of hedonic damages follow one of two approaches: integrated and segregated. Those that integrate combine for the jury the aforementioned physical or visceral pain and suffering with loss of enjoyment of life into one damage category described as "pain and suffering." Those that segregate instruct the jury on each item of suffering individually. See Flannery v. United States, 297 S.E.2d 433, 437 (1982) (The loss associated with the "capacity to enjoy life" does not depend on pain and suffering. For example, "one can lose his eyesight or a limb and be without physical pain" and yet have a diminished ability to enjoy life's pleasure.).

iii. Loss of society and companionship (including consortium) "embraces a broad range of mutual benefits each family member receives from the others' continued existence, including love, affection, care, attention, companionship, comfort, and protection." U.S. Sea-Land Servs. v. Gaudet, 414 U.S. 573 (1974). Though courts vary on whether parents can recover for the companionship loss ("filial") when a child is injured and whether a child can be compensated for relationship losses when a parent has been injured, almost all states allow for spouses to recover for the harm to the marriage resulting from a spouse being injured.

Restatement (Second) of Torts §693, "Action by One Spouse for Harm Caused by Tort Against Other Spouse," provides:

> (1) One who by reason of his tortious conduct is liable to one spouse for illness or other bodily harm is subject to liability to the other spouse for the resulting loss of the

society and services of the firs spouse, including impairment of capacity for sexual intercourse, and for reasonable expense incurred by the second spouse in providing medical treatment.

e. Nearly half of the states have attempted to reform tort law by enacting statutory caps on damages awards. Each act of legislation has been subjected to challenge, primarily constitutional, with opponents having varying degrees of success. A primary motivation behind the perceived need to cap damages has been the "medical malpractice" crisis born of rising costs to secure medical malpractice insurance. If caps are instituted they most often apply to noneconomic damages, as legislatures are convinced that juries are too often arbitrary in their dispensing and calculation. Statutory caps on damages will be discussed in more detail in Equity and Remedies, but other attempts at limiting liability have also been implemented by states. They include:

—Eliminating joint and several liability

—Modifying the collateral source rule

—Restricting the right to contribution among tortfeasors

—Shortening the statute of limitations

—Recognizing more affirmative defenses

—Strict adherence to the "economic loss doctrine"

—Limiting or disallowing punitive damages.

D. DUTY TO MITIGATE

Dohmann v. Richard
282 So. 2d 789 (La. Ct. App. 1973)

DOMENGEAUX, Judge.

Plaintiff-Appellee J. Gervais Dohmann, Sr., a salesman employed by Bordelon Chevrolet, Inc., brought this suit for damages, alleging that he, a pedestrian, was struck by a one-half ton pickup truck being driven by Ronald C. Richard on the parking lot of his employer in Opelousas, Louisiana, on January 29, 1968, at approximately 11:30 A.M. Made defendants were Richard, the latter's employer, Dimmick Supply Company, Incorporated, and the insurer of the truck, State Farm Mutual Automobile Insurance Company.

After a trial on the merits, judgment was rendered by the trial court in favor of plaintiff and against all defendants in the sum of $60,401.02, which represented $40,000.00 for loss of earnings, $18,000.00 for physical and mental pain and suffering and mental anguish, and $2,401.02 for medical expenses.

Defendants have appealed devolutively to this court claiming that the trial judge erred in failing to find that plaintiff failed to mitigate his damages.

From the time of the accident to the time of trial, he was examined and/or treated by Dr. R. Luke Bordelon, an orthopaedic surgeon; Dr. Daniel L. Buller, a surgeon; Dr. S.J. Rozas, a General Practitioner and his family physician; Dr. Joseph M. Edelman, a neurosurgeon; and Dr. William E. McCray, a psychiatrist.

Plaintiff's complaints after the accident were of pain in the left leg, left hip, back, head, neck, and testicles. He was treated conservatively and placed in various types of traction, as it was evident that he received some physical injuries consisting of contusions and sprains, but obviously his physical injuries were not overly serious and should have been of a moderate duration. Accordingly most of the aforementioned doctors who treated him found that his difficulty was not of a significant organic type, but that he had enough difficulty to focus on, and act as, a stimulus for a psychological state. He was finally referred by his family physician to Dr. William E. McCray.

Doctor McCray first saw plaintiff on April 16, 1969, treated him rather extensively with high doses of tranquilizing and antidepressant medication, saw him regularly over a period of months and was of the opinion that plaintiff had developed a psychotic state known as a depression. Although he could not say definitely that the accident was the cause of the psychotic depression, he was emphatic that it was a precipitating factor in the development of the illness. The doctor held no hope for improvement of plaintiff's mental condition even with the medication he had prescribed. He considered him totally unemployable.

The record is replete with testimony from members of his family, neighbors, friends, his former employer, and his family physician, that prior to the accident plaintiff was an outgoing, industrious, hard-working, individual, who was close to his family and friends; but that since the accident he constantly complains of various physical ailments, blackouts, spells, difficulty with memory and concentration, and is very nervous and moody. He wants to be alone at all times, and has no patience, or interest in the outside world. In sort, he had a complete personality change. He has lost interest in hunting and outdoor recreation, tending his garden, lawn, etc., all of which he participated in and enjoyed before the accident.

We are satisfied that the record shows that the plaintiff is totally and permanently disabled as a result of the accident sued on herein in his present condition. However, appellants contend that plaintiff has not fulfilled his responsibility to take all reasonable steps to mitigate his injuries and as such his award for damages should be limited or decreased. This they base on plaintiff's refusal to subject himself to electro-shock treatments as recommended by Dr. McCray.

In this connection it is true that Dr. McCray recommended electro-shock treatments and opined that they would in all probability improve plaintiff's condition. The doctor explained to the plaintiff and his family the involvements of receiving such therapy. He indicated that there was some danger in the process although he thought it was minimal as compared to some risks that are prevalent in the administration of certain medicines and surgery. He indicated that the administering of shock treatments results in a convulsion very similar to an epileptic fit, and that the treatment carries with it the risk of fractures and dislocations because of the convulsions resulting therefrom.

The doctor thought that there was an approximate 80% to 90% chance of improvement if plaintiff would take the treatment, although of course, he could not guarantee the results.

It is evident that the plaintiff and his family were extremely frightened of the prospect of electro-shock treatments. In fact it is obvious that the plaintiff himself feigned improvement in his condition as an excuse not to submit himself to such treatments.

Appellants have cited us some cases in our jurisprudence, and correctly so, to the effect that where an injured person unreasonably refuses to minimize his damages by accepting non-dangerous and customary medical treatment which is recommended by his physicians, the damages against a tortfeasor may be limited to that which the injured person would have reasonably recovered if he had undergone the recommended treatment. The cases cited and others which we have found through our independent research have to do with operations and the administration of regimens of treatment concerning physical injuries. None have to do, nor have we been able to discover any which may be applicable in cases of mental illness and the administration of electro-shock treatment. In the case at bar we are dealing with what is perhaps the most misunderstood field of medicine, i.e., treatment of the mind. Plaintiff is not being asked to have a fractured bone placed in a cast, a hernia repaired, or any other conventional form of surgery. Instead it is proposed that he subject himself to electro-shock, a form of treatment designed to work a change in his personality. Furthermore we bear in mind that our society has not progressed to a point in which it accepts mental illnesses, and particularly the drastic treatment thereof by such measures as shock therapy, with the same tolerance that it now regards physical surgery or treatment. Accordingly we cannot disregard the effect that such treatment, given the present attitudes of our society, is likely to have on plaintiff's future relations with his peers. In so stating we do not intend to in any way demean the value of such treatments or to question the effectiveness with which they are generally credited within the medical profession, but refer only to the attitudes held towards them by the public at large. As testified to by Dr. McCray the treatment is of undoubted value and benefit in many cases and may very well be so in the case at bar. However, for the reasons given we are not prepared to hold at this time that psychiatric therapy of this sort falls within the spirit, or the letter, of that line of jurisprudence which requires injured persons to mitigate their damages.

Accordingly in view of all the facts and circumstances present in this case we are unable to hold that the plaintiff's refusal to submit to the electro-shock therapy is unreasonable.

For the above and foregoing reasons the judgment of the district court is affirmed.

PREPARING FOR CLASS

1. What is the primary argument of the defendant and how does the plaintiff respond?

2. What standard does the court employ when addressing the failure to mitigate?

3. What would be the result if the defendant was successful in its argument?

APPLYING THE LAW

Plaintiff, while working at a construction site, gets injured operating a defective piece of equipment manufactured by defendant. Specifically, plaintiff suffers a broken back, which requires considerable rehabilitation. Though almost back to normal, plaintiff believes he can no longer return to construction work because of physical limitations. He sues the defendant. As counsel for the defendant, what additional facts would assist you in making your failure-to-mitigate arguments, and what is the nature of each argument?

INCREASING YOUR UNDERSTANDING

1. The duty to mitigate (or avoid consequences) after injury should be distinguished from contributory negligence, which instead asks whether plaintiff's unreasonableness was a contributor to the original injury. An injured party is denied the right to recover damages she could have avoided through her own reasonable efforts or diligence. How an injured party is expected to act post-injury is dictated by the circumstances of the specific case:

   > The jury must look at all the circumstances of the case, the medical advice received, the need for action, and the precautions taken during the doing of it. The injured person need not act with perfect knowledge and ideal wisdom, but, upon the other hand, cannot claim damages for such injuries as are really due to wanton, heedless, or careless conduct on his own part. If what is

done reasonably does augment the injuries, that may be regarded as a natural consequence of the accident. Jones v. Watney, Combe Reid & Co., (Eng) 28 Times L 399.

2. What if plaintiff declines medical treatment because of religious beliefs? The courts are split, and the answer to the question depends on the extent the court is willing to conform the duty to mitigate to the specific attributes of the plaintiff. See Williams v. Bright, 167 Misc. 2d 312, 326, 327. 632 N.Y.S.2d 760 (Sup. Ct. 1995). ("When we consider the condition of a plaintiff as she is, while it is true the doctrine is generally construed in the light of pre-existing physical or physiological conditions, it can also extend to latent mental instability and mind-sets, i.e. psychological conditions. There is no compelling reason other than potential fraud) to draw the line there and hold that we may not consider other aspects of an individual person. Conscience and religious belief are not passing whims, but guide human beings to life and death decisions.").

3. *Lost wages and employment.* Assuming an ability to return to work, the law requires that plaintiff accept "substantially similar" employment opportunities in discharging her duty to mitigate her wage loss damages. What qualifies as substantially similar is influenced by plaintiff's work history, education, geographic location, and generally her skill set. Expenses associated with a job search, even if unsuccessful, may be recoverable.

E. COLLATERAL SOURCE RULE

Helfend v. Southern Cal. Rapid Transit Dist.
465 P.2d 61 (Cal. 1970)

TOBRINER, Acting Chief Justice.

Plaintiff filed a tort action against the Southern California Rapid Transit District, a public entity, and Mitchell, an employee of the transit district. At trial plaintiff claimed slightly more than $2,700 in special damages, including $921 in doctor's bills, a $336.99 hospital bill, and about $45 for medicines. Defendant requested permission to show that about 80 percent of the plaintiff's hospital bill had been paid by plaintiff's Blue Cross insurance carrier and that some of his other medical expenses may have been paid by other insurance. The superior court thoroughly considered the then very recent case of City of Salinas v. Souza & McCue Construction Company (1967) 424 P.2d 921, distinguished the *Souza* case on the ground that *Souza* involved a contract setting, and concluded that the judgment should not be reduced to the extent of the amount of insurance payments which plaintiff received. The court ruled that defendants should not be permitted to show that plaintiff had received medical coverage from any collateral source.

After the jury verdict in favor of plaintiff in the sum of $16,300, defendants appealed, claiming that the trial court committed prejudicial error in refusing to allow the introduction of evidence to the effect that a portion of the plaintiff's medical bills had been paid from a collateral source.

We must decide whether the collateral source rule applies to tort actions involving public entities and public employees in which the plaintiff has received benefits from his medical insurance coverage.

The Supreme Court of California has long adhered to the doctrine that if an injured party receives some compensation for his injuries from a source wholly independent of the tortfeasor, such payment should not be deducted from the damages which the plaintiff would otherwise collect from the tortfeasor. As recently as August 1968 we unanimously reaffirmed our adherence to this doctrine, which is known as the "collateral source rule."

Although the collateral source rule remains generally accepted in the United States, nevertheless many other jurisdictions have restricted or repealed it. In this country most commentators have criticized the rule and called for its early demise. In *Souza* we took note of the academic criticism of the rule, characterized the rule as "punitive," and held it inapplicable to the governmental entity involved in that case.

Although *Souza's* reasoning as to punitive damages might appear to apply to private tortfeasors as well as public entities and to torts as well as contract actions, we did not there consider the collateral source rule in contexts different from the specific contractual setting and particular relationship of the parties involved. We distinguish the present case from *Souza* on the ground that in *Souza* the plaintiff received payments from his subcontractor which, in the contractual setting of that case, did not constitute a truly independent source. Obviously, such a "source" differs entirely from the instant one, which derives from plaintiff's payment of insurance premiums. Here plaintiff received benefits from his medical insurance coverage only because he had long paid premiums to obtain them. Such an origin does constitute a completely independent source. Hence, although we reaffirm the holding in *Souza*, we do not believe that its reasoning either compels the abolition of the collateral source rule in all cases or requires an unwarranted exemption from the rule of public entities and their employees involved in tort actions. *Souza* does not even suggest that public employees should be charged with the extra liability which an exemption for public entities might imply.

The collateral source rule as applied here embodies the venerable concept that a person who has invested years of insurance premiums to assure his medical care should receive the benefits of his thrift. The tortfeasor should not garner the benefits of his victim's providence.

The collateral source rule expresses a policy judgment in favor of encouraging citizens to purchase and maintain insurance for personal injuries and for other eventualities. Courts consider insurance a form of investment, the benefits of which become payable without respect to any other possible source of funds. If we were to permit a tortfeasor to mitigate damages with payments from plaintiff's insurance, plaintiff would be in a position inferior to that of having bought no insurance, because his payment of premiums would have earned no benefit. Defendant should not be able to avoid payment of full compensation for the injury inflicted merely because the victim has had the foresight to provide himself with insurance.

Some commentators object that the above approach to the collateral source rule provides plaintiff with a "double recovery," rewards him for the injury, and defeats the principle that damages should compensate the victim but not punish the tortfeasor. [However], insurance policies increasingly provide for either subrogation or refund or benefits upon a tort recovery, and such refund is indeed called for in the present case. Hence, the plaintiff receives no double recovery; the collateral source rule simply serves as a means of by-passing the antiquated doctrine of non-assignment of tortious actions and permits a proper transfer of risk from the plaintiff's insurer to the tortfeasor by way of the victim's tort recovery. The double shift from the tortfeasor to the victim and then from the victim to his insurance carrier can normally occur with little cost in that the insurance carrier is often intimately involved in the initial litigation and quite automatically receives its part of the tort settlement or verdict.

Even in case in which the contract or the law precludes subrogation or refund of benefits, or in situations in which the collateral source waives such subrogation or refund, the rule performs entirely necessary functions in the computation of damages. For example, the cost of medical care often provides both attorneys and juries in tort cases with an important measure for assessing the plaintiff's general damages. To permit the defendant to tell the jury that the plaintiff has been recompensed by a collateral source for his medical costs might irretrievably upset the complex, delicate, and somewhat indefinable calculations which result in the normal jury verdict.

We also note that generally the jury is not informed that plaintiff's attorney will receive a large portion of the plaintiff's recovery in contingent fees or that personal injury damages are not taxable to the plaintiff and are normally deductible by the defendant. Hence, the plaintiff rarely actually receives full compensation for his injuries as computed by the jury. The collateral source rule partially serves to compensate for the attorney's share and does not actually render 'double recovery' for the plaintiff. Indeed, many jurisdictions that have abolished or limited the collateral source rule have also established a means for assessing the plaintiff's costs for counsel directly against the defendant rather than imposing the contingent fee system. In sum, the plaintiff's recovery for his medical expenses from both the tortfeasor and his medical insurance program will not usually give him "double recovery," but partially provides a somewhat closer approximation to full compensation for his injuries.

If we consider the collateral source rule as applied here in the context of the entire American approach to the law of torts and damages, we find that the rule presently performs a number of legitimate and even indispensable functions. Without a thorough revolution in the American approach to torts and the consequent damages, the rule at least with respect to medical insurance benefits has become so integrated within our present system that its precipitous judicial nullification would work hardship. In this case the collateral source rule lies between two systems for the compensation of accident victims: the traditional tort recovery based on fault and the increasingly prevalent coverage based on non-fault insurance. Neither system possesses such universality of coverage or completeness of compensation that we can easily dispense with the collateral source rule's approach to meshing the two systems. The reforms which many academicians propose cannot easily be achieved through piecemeal common law development; the proposed changes, if desirable, would be more effectively accomplished through legislative reform. In any case, we cannot believe that the judicial repeal of the collateral source rule, as applied in the present case, would be the place to begin the needed changes.

Defendants would have this court create a special form of sovereign immunity as a novel exception to the collateral source rule for tortfeasors who are public entities or public employees. We see no justification for such special treatment. In the present case the nullification of the collateral source rule would simply frustrate the transfer of the medical costs from the medical insurance carrier, Blue Cross, to the public entity. The public entity or its insurance carrier is in at least as advantageous a position to spread the risk of loss as is the plaintiff's medical insurance carrier. To deprive Blue Cross of repayment for its expenditures on plaintiff's behalf merely because he was injured by a public entity rather than a private individual would constitute an unwarranted and arbitrary discrimination.

Affirmed.

PREPARING FOR CLASS

1. What damages is the defendant challenging recovery off?

2. Consider what the implications are should the defendant be successful with its argument.

3. To what "sources" might the collateral source rule apply in general?

4. Do the particulars of this case form the basis for an exception to the rule?

APPLYING THE LAW

Paula is injured in an automobile accident that requires physical therapy. In lieu of going to the rehabilitation facility at the health club, Paula is treated at home by her fiancée, who is a licensed physical therapist. He, of course, only asks for her continued companionship in return. If Paula sues because of the auto accident, is the defendant liable for the reasonable value of fiancée's physical therapy services?

INCREASING YOUR UNDERSTANDING

1. Under the common law, the defendant was precluded from admitting into evidence the value of benefits provided by "collateral sources." Various policy justifications have been offered for the rule in this form:

    a. Plaintiff does not realize a windfall, as in many cases she is required to pay back the party who provided the benefit.

    b. Particularly in the case of medical assistance, the actual value of the charges, as opposed to only those that were paid personally by the plaintiff, best represents the value of the entire claim (including pain and suffering) to the plaintiff, as often jurors correlate pain and suffering with medical expenses/lost wages.

    c. The plaintiff, who had the vision to purchase insurance, should be favored, not the defendant.

    d. Laws should promote recovery and liability to further the goal of deterring tortious conduct.

2. The collateral source rule has been found to apply to just about any benefit provided by a party other than the defendant, for example, Medicare and Medicaid benefits, private medical and life insurance benefits, worker's compensation and disability benefits, etc.

3. In those jurisdictions that have modified the collateral source rule, as a means of tort reform, many would still allow the plaintiff to recover the insurance premiums paid by the plaintiff.

4. *The collateral source rule: liens/subrogation and legal malpractice trap.* Courts that follow the collateral source rule stated in *Helfend* arrive at the decision by citing the practice of many collateral source providers to seek reimbursement of what has previously been provided. For example, in the case of medical insurance, it's not unusual for the contract with the plaintiff to require reimbursement should the plaintiff recover monies from a tortfeasor reflecting benefits that have already been fronted. Even in the absence of contractual language, courts may require/allow reimbursement through legal/equitable subrogation. Most plaintiffs are unaware of the responsibility to reimburse and must be advised of it by counsel. Many providers are willing to negotiate their interest and eventually accept a percentage of the original amount.

F. PUNITIVE DAMAGES

State Farm Mut. Auto. Ins. Co. v. Campbell
538 U.S. 408 (2003)

In 1981, Curtis Campbell (Campbell) was driving with his wife, Inez Preece Campbell, in Cache County, Utah. He decided to pass six vans traveling ahead of them on a two-lane highway. Todd Ospital was driving a small car approaching from the opposite direction. To avoid a head-on collision with Campbell, who by then was driving on the wrong side of the highway and toward oncoming traffic, Ospital swerved onto the shoulder, lost control of his automobile, and collided with a vehicle driven by Robert G. Slusher. Ospital was killed, and Slusher was rendered permanently disabled. The Campbells escaped unscathed.

In the ensuing wrongful death and tort action, Campbell insisted he was not at fault. Early investigations did support differing conclusions as to who caused the accident, but "a consensus was reached early on by the investigators and witnesses that Mr. Campbell's unsafe pass had indeed caused the crash." Campbell's insurance company, petitioner State Farm Mutual Automobile Insurance Company (State Farm), nonetheless decided to contest liability and declined offers by Slusher and Ospital's estate (Ospital) to settle the claims for the policy limit of $50,000 ($25,000 per claimant). State Farm also ignored the advice of one of its own investigators and took the case to trial, assuring the Campbells that "their assets were safe, that they had no liability for the accident, that [State Farm] would represent their interests, and that they did not need to procure separate counsel." To the contrary, a jury determined that Campbell was 100 percent at fault, and a judgment was returned for $185,849, far more than the amount offered in settlement.

At first State Farm refused to cover the $135,849 in excess liability. Its counsel made this clear to the Campbells: " 'You may want to put for sale signs on your property to get things moving.' " Nor was State Farm willing to post a supersedeas bond to allow Campbell to appeal the judgment against him. Campbell obtained his own counsel to appeal the verdict. During the pendency of the appeal, in late 1984, Slusher, Ospital, and the Campbells reached an agreement whereby Slusher and Ospital agreed not to seek satisfaction of their claims against the Campbells. In exchange the Campbells agreed to pursue a bad faith action against State Farm and to be represented by Slusher's and Ospital's attorneys. The Campbells also agreed that Slusher and Ospital would have a right to play a part in all major decisions concerning the bad-faith action. No settlement could be concluded without Slusher's and Ospital's approval, and Slusher and Ospital would receive 90 percent of any verdict against State Farm.

In 1989, the Utah Supreme Court denied Campbell's appeal in the wrongful-death and tort actions. State Farm then paid the entire judgment, including the amounts in excess of the policy limits. The Campbells nonetheless filed a complaint against State Farm alleging bad faith, fraud, and intentional infliction of emotional distress. The trial court initially granted State Farm's motion for summary judgment because State Farm had paid the excess verdict, but that ruling was reversed on appeal. On remand State Farm moved *in limine* to exclude evidence of alleged conduct that occurred in unrelated cases outside of Utah, but the trial court denied the motion. At State Farm's request the trial court bifurcated the trial into two phases conducted before different juries. In the first phase the jury determined that State Farm's decision not to settle was unreasonable because there was a substantial likelihood of an excess verdict.

Before the second phase of the action against State Farm we decided *BMW of North America, Inc. v. Gore*, 517 U.S. 559, 116 S. Ct. 1589, 134 L. Ed. 2d 809 (1996), and refused to sustain a $2 million punitive damages award which accompanied a verdict of only $4,000 in compensatory damages. Based on that decision, State Farm again moved for the exclusion of evidence of dissimilar out-of-state conduct. The trial court denied State Farm's motion.

The second phase addressed State Farm's liability for fraud and intentional infliction of emotional distress, as well as compensatory and punitive damages. The Utah Supreme Court aptly characterized this phase of the trial:

> "State Farm argued during phase II that its decision to take the case to trial was an 'honest mistake' that did not warrant punitive damages. In contrast, the Campbells introduced evidence that State Farm's decision to take the case to trial was a result of a national scheme to meet corporate fiscal goals by capping payouts on claims company wide. This scheme was referred to as State Farm's 'Performance, Planning and Review,' or PP & R, policy. To prove the existence of this scheme, the trial court allowed the Campbells to introduce extensive expert testimony regarding fraudulent practices by State Farm in its nation-wide operations.

The jury awarded the Campbells $2.6 million in compensatory damages and $145 million in punitive damages, which the trial court reduced to $1 million and $25 million respectively. Both parties appealed.

The Utah Supreme Court sought to apply the three guideposts we identified in *Gore*, and it reinstated the $145 million punitive damages award. Relying in large part on the extensive evidence concerning the PP & R policy, the court concluded State Farm's conduct was reprehensible. The court also relied upon State Farm's "massive wealth" and on testimony indicating that "State Farm's actions, because of their clandestine nature, will be punished at most in one out of every 50,000 cases as a matter of statistical probability," and concluded that the ratio between punitive and compensatory damages was not unwarranted. Finally, the court noted that the punitive damages award was not excessive when compared to various civil and criminal penalties State Farm could have faced, including $10,000 for each act of fraud, the suspension of its license to conduct business in Utah, the disgorgement of profits, and imprisonment. We granted certiorari.

KENNEDY, J., delivered the opinion of the Court, in which REHNQUIST, C.J., and STEVENS, O'CONNOR, SOUTER, and BREYER, JJ., joined.

II

We recognized in Cooper Industries, Inc. v. Leatherman Tool Group, Inc., 532 U.S. 424 (2001), that in our judicial system compensatory and punitive damages, although usually awarded at the same time by the same decision-maker, serve different purposes. Compensatory damages "are intended to redress the concrete loss that the plaintiff has suffered by reason of the defendant's wrongful conduct." (citing Restatement (Second) of Torts §903, pp. 453-454 (1979)). By contrast, punitive damages serve a broader function; they are aimed at deterrence and retribution. ("Punitive damages may properly be imposed to further a State's legitimate interests in punishing unlawful conduct and deterring its repetition") ("Punitive damages are imposed for purposes of retribution and deterrence").

While States possess discretion over the imposition of punitive damages, it is well established that there are procedural and substantive constitutional limitations on these awards. The Due Process Clause of the Fourteenth Amendment prohibits the imposition of grossly excessive or arbitrary punishments on a tortfeasor. The reason is that "[e]lementary notions of fairness enshrined in our constitutional jurisprudence dictate that a person receive fair notice not only of the conduct that will subject him to punishment, but also of the severity of the penalty that a State may impose." . . . To the extent an award is grossly excessive, it furthers no legitimate purpose and constitutes an arbitrary deprivation of property.

Although these awards serve the same purposes as criminal penalties, defendants subjected to punitive damages in civil cases have not been accorded the protections applicable in a criminal proceeding. This increases our concerns over the imprecise manner in which punitive damages systems are administered. We have admonished that "[p]unitive damages pose an acute danger of arbitrary deprivation of property. Jury instructions typically leave the jury with wide discretion in choosing amounts, and the presentation of evidence of a defendant's net worth creates the potential that juries will use their verdicts to express biases against big businesses, particularly those without strong local presences." . . .

In light of these concerns, in *Gore*, we instructed courts reviewing punitive damages to consider three guideposts: (1) the degree of reprehensibility of the defendant's misconduct; (2) the disparity between the actual or potential harm suffered by the plaintiff and the punitive damages award; and (3) the difference between the punitive damages awarded by the jury and the civil penalties authorized or imposed in comparable cases. We reiterated the importance of these three guideposts in *Cooper Industries* and mandated appellate courts to conduct *de novo* review of a trial court's application of them to the jury's award. Exacting appellate review ensures that an award of punitive damages is based upon an " 'application of law, rather than a decisionmaker's caprice.' "

III

Under the principles outlined in *BMW of North America, Inc. v. Gore*, 517 U.S. 559 (1996), this case is neither close nor difficult. It was error to reinstate the jury's $145 million punitive damages award. We address each guidepost of *Gore* in some detail.

A

"[T]he most important indicium of the reasonableness of a punitive damages award is the degree of reprehensibility of the defendant's conduct." We have instructed courts to determine the reprehensibility of a defendant by considering whether: the harm caused was physical as opposed to economic; the tortious conduct evinced an indifference to or a reckless disregard of the health or safety of others; the target of the conduct had financial vulnerability; the conduct involved repeated actions or was an isolated incident; and the harm was the result of intentional malice, trickery, or deceit, or mere accident. The existence of any one of these factors weighing in favor of a plaintiff may not be sufficient to sustain a punitive damages award; and the absence of all of them renders any award suspect. It should be presumed a plaintiff has been made whole for his injuries by compensatory damages, so punitive damages should only be awarded if the defendant's culpability, after having paid compensatory damages, is so reprehensible as to warrant the imposition of further sanctions to achieve punishment or deterrence.

Applying these factors in the instant case, we must acknowledge that State Farm's handling of the claims against the Campbells merits no praise. The trial court found that State Farm's employees altered the company's records to make Campbell appear less culpable. State Farm disregarded the overwhelming likelihood of liability and the near-certain probability that, by taking the case to trial, a judgment in excess of the policy limits would be awarded. State Farm amplified the harm by at first assuring the Campbells their assets would be safe from any verdict and by later telling them, postjudgment, to put a for-sale sign on their house. While we do not suggest there was error in awarding punitive damages based upon State Farm's conduct toward the Campbells, a more modest punishment for this reprehensible conduct could have satisfied the State's legitimate objectives, and the Utah courts should have gone no further. . . .

A State cannot punish a defendant for conduct that may have been lawful where it occurred. Nor, as a general rule, does a State have a legitimate concern in imposing punitive damages to punish a defendant for unlawful acts committed outside of the State's jurisdiction. . . .

For a more fundamental reason, however, the Utah courts erred in relying upon this and other evidence: The courts awarded punitive damages to punish and deter conduct that bore no relation to the Campbells' harm. A defendant's dissimilar acts, independent from the acts upon which liability was premised, may not serve as the basis for punitive damages. A defendant should be punished for the conduct that harmed the plaintiff, not for being an unsavory individual or business. Due process does not permit courts, in the calculation of punitive damages, to adjudicate the merits of other parties' hypothetical claims against a defendant under the guise of the reprehensibility analysis, but we have no doubt the Utah Supreme Court did that here.

B

Turning to the second *Gore* guidepost, we have been reluctant to identify concrete constitutional limits on the ratio between harm, or potential harm, to the plaintiff and the punitive damages award. ("[W]e have consistently rejected the notion that the constitutional line is marked by a simple mathematical formula, even one that compares actual *and potential* damages to the punitive award") We decline again to impose a bright-line ratio which a punitive damages award cannot exceed. Our jurisprudence and the principles it has now established demonstrate, however, that, in practice, few awards exceeding a single-digit ratio between punitive and compensatory damages, to a significant degree, will satisfy due process. In *Haslip*, in upholding a punitive damages award, we concluded that an award of more than four times the amount of compensatory damages might be close to the line of constitutional impropriety. We cited that 4-to-1 ratio again in *Gore*. The Court further referenced a long legislative history, dating back over 700 years and going forward to today, providing for sanctions of double, treble, or quadruple damages to deter and punish. While these ratios are not binding, they are instructive. They demonstrate what should be obvious: Single-digit multipliers are more likely to comport with due process, while still achieving the State's goals of deterrence and retribution, than awards with ratios in range of 500 to 1, or, in this case, of 145 to 1.

Nonetheless, because there are no rigid benchmarks that a punitive damages award may not surpass, ratios greater than those we have previously upheld may comport with due process where "a particularly egregious act has resulted in only a small amount of economic damages." The converse is also true, however. When compensatory damages are substantial, then a lesser ratio, perhaps only equal to compensatory damages, can reach the outermost limit of the due process guarantee. The precise award in any case, of course, must be based upon the facts and circumstances of the defendant's conduct and the harm to the plaintiff.

In sum, courts must ensure that the measure of punishment is both reasonable and proportionate to the amount of harm to the plaintiff and to the general damages recovered. In the context of this case, we have no doubt that there is a presumption against an award that has a 145-to-1 ratio. The compensatory award in this case was substantial; the Campbells were awarded $1 million for a year and a half of emotional distress. This was complete compensation. The harm arose from a transaction in the economic realm, not from some physical assault or trauma; there were no physical injuries; and State Farm paid the excess verdict before the complaint was filed, so the Campbells suffered only minor economic injuries for the 18-month period in which State Farm refused to resolve the claim against them. The compensatory damages for the injury suffered here, moreover, likely were based on a component which was duplicated in the punitive award. Much of the distress was caused by the outrage and humiliation the Campbells suffered at the actions of their insurer; and it is a major role of punitive damages to condemn such conduct. Compensatory damages, however, already contain this punitive element.

C

The third guidepost in *Gore* is the disparity between the punitive damages award and the "civil penalties authorized or imposed in comparable cases." We note that, in the past, we have also looked to criminal penalties that could be imposed. The existence of a criminal penalty does have bearing on the seriousness with which a State views the wrongful action. When used to determine the dollar amount of the award, however, the criminal penalty has less utility. Great care must be taken to avoid use of the civil process to assess criminal penalties that can be imposed only after the heightened protections of a criminal trial have been observed, including, of course, its higher standards of proof. Punitive damages are not a substitute for the criminal process, and the remote possibility of a criminal sanction does not automatically sustain a punitive damages award.

Here, we need not dwell long on this guidepost. The most relevant civil sanction under Utah state law for the wrong done to the Campbells appears to be a $10,000 fine for an act of fraud, an amount dwarfed by the $145 million punitive damages award. . . .

IV

An application of the *Gore* guideposts to the facts of this case, especially in light of the substantial compensatory damages awarded (a portion of which contained a punitive element), likely would justify a punitive damages award at or near the amount of compensatory damages. The punitive award of $145 million, therefore, was neither reasonable nor proportionate to the wrong committed, and it was an irrational and arbitrary deprivation of the property of the defendant. The proper calculation of punitive damages under the principles we have discussed should be resolved, in the first instance, by the Utah courts.

The judgment of the Utah Supreme Court is reversed, and the case is remanded for further proceedings not inconsistent with this opinion.

Justice SCALIA, dissenting.

I adhere to the view expressed in my dissenting opinion in *BMW*, that the Due Process Clause provides no substantive protections against "excessive" or "'unreasonable'" awards of punitive damages. I am also of the view that the punitive damages jurisprudence which has sprung forth from *BMW v. Gore* is insusceptible of principled application; accordingly, I do not feel justified in giving the case *stare decisis* effect. I would firm the judgment of the Utah Supreme Court.

Justice GINSBURG, dissenting

The large size of the award upheld by the Utah Supreme Court in this case indicates why damages-capping legislation may be altogether fitting and proper. Neither the amount of the award nor the trial record, however, justifies this Court's substitution of its judgment for that of Utah's competent decisionmakers. . . .

When the Court first ventured to override state-court punitive damages awards, it did so moderately. The Court recalled that "[i]n our federal system, States necessarily have considerable flexibility in determining the level of punitive damages that they will allow in different classes of cases and in any particular case." Today's decision exhibits no such respect and restraint. No longer content to accord state-court judgments "a strong presumption of validity," the Court announces that "few awards exceeding a single-digit ratio between punitive and compensatory damages, to a significant degree, will satisfy due process." Moreover, the Court adds, when compensatory damages are substantial, doubling those damages "can reach the outermost limit of the due process guarantee." In a legislative scheme or a state high court's design to cap punitive damages, the handiwork in setting single-digit and 1-to-1 benchmarks could hardly be questioned; in a judicial decree imposed on the States by this Court under the banner of substantive due process, the numerical controls today's decision installs seem to me boldly out of order.

PREPARING FOR CLASS

1. State Farm is requesting what here?

2. How does the fact tha this involves punitive damages affect the courts consideration of defendant's request?

3. What was State Farm punished for?

4. How does the ruling impact the *Gore* decision?

5. What factual support did Campbell have for his compensatory award?

6. Justices Scalia, Ginsburg, and Thomas have consistently taken the position that there is no basis under the federal constitution to challenge a state's award of punitive damages. Their position is fundamental and not dependent on the size of the award.

7. Eventually an award of a little over nine million dollars was upheld by the courts. Campbell passed before the legal odyssey concluded.

APPLYING THE LAW

How would you begin to frame an argument asking that the court sustain a jury award that had a double digit punitive/compensatory ratio?

INCREASING YOUR UNDERSTANDING

1. Not until *BMW v. Gore* did the U.S. Supreme Court strike down as unconstitutional a punitive damage award. Gore sued BMW after discovering that the "new" BMW he purchased had been previously damaged and repainted. BMW failed to inform Gore of previous damage or that the car had been repainted. After trial, Gore was awarded $4.0 million in punitive damages and $4,000 in compensatory damages. There was evidence that BMW had on approximately 1,000 other occasions sold previously damaged cars to customers nationwide, and so the jury seemingly arrived at the $4 million figure by multiplying 1,000 by $4,000, which represented the decreased value of the cars. The Alabama Supreme Court reduced the punitives to $2 million, and BMW appealed to the U.S. Supreme Court. While declaring the punitive award unconstitutional, the Supreme Court articulated the "guideposts" that should be employed by courts when responding to the argument that a punitive award is unconstitutionally excessive. The Court in *Gore*, however, refused to articulate concrete constitutional limits on the ratio between harm, or potential harm, to the plaintiff and the punitive damage award. *Campbell* signals a major move in punitive jurisprudence, strongly suggesting that "in practice, few awards exceeding a single-digit ratio between punitive and compensatory damages, to a significant degree, will satisfy due process."

2. Unlike requests for remitters of compensatory awards, where the court is required to be largely deferential to the jury's award determination, a

review by the court as to whether a punitive award transgresses constitutional limits is done de novo, which means that the court is not bound by the jury's decision and must undertake an independent evaluation of the award.

3. Common law malice is typically the standard that courts instruct juries with when punitive damages are sought. Common law malice is best described as intending injury or acting with reckless disregard as to whether injury would occur. Thus under the common law, malice is a dual standard, describing two distinct types of conduct that warrant punishment:

> The first type is that in which the defendant desires to cause the harm sustained by the plaintiff, or believes that the harm is substantially certain to follow his conduct. With the second type of conduct the defendant knows, or should have reason to know, not only that his conduct creates an unreasonable risk of harm, but also that there is a strong probability, although not a substantial certainty, that the harm will result but, nevertheless, he proceeds with his conduct in reckless or conscious disregard of the consequences. Neither form of conduct, therefore, involves mere, inadvertence or what, in the traditional sense, would be called ordinary negligence. Loveridge v. Chartier, 468 N.W.2d 146, 159 (Wis. 1991).

4. Municipalities are typically immune from liability for punitive damages for primarily two reasons: the concern with compromising the municipality's financial ability to provide services and the lack of any deterrent impact as taxpayers eventually bear the burden of the award.

5. Should an employer be vicariously liable for punitive damages when an employee acts maliciously and injures another while within the scope of employment? Again, courts are split, with some imposing liability on the employer under the same standard as an award of compensatory damages; others, however, require some evidence that the employer authorized or ratified the employee's conduct.

6. *Insurability of punitive damages.* Often, insurance contracts refer to paying "all sums" an insured might be liable for as damages. Absent express exclusions in insurance contracts, many courts allow for a punitive judgment to be covered by an insurance contract. This follows the general rule that ambiguities in contracts be construed in favor of the policy holder. See Harrell v. Travelers Insurance Co., 567 P.2d 1013, 1015 (Or. 1977) ("Defendant insurance company could have removed this ambiguity easily by including an express exclusion from liability for punitive damages, but apparently chose not to do so . . . there is nothing

in the insuring clause that would forewarn an insured that such was to be the intent of the parties,' if indeed, such was the intent of the insurance company.").

7. In tort cases, evidence of the defendant's financial status is almost always withheld from the jury's consideration, as courts consider any reference to the defendant's financial status too prejudicial and lacking in probative value. Most courts, however, allow for evidence of the defendant's finances to assist a jury when it comes to the amount necessary to impose a proper punishment on the defendant. See Capstick v. Allstate Ins. Co., 998 F.2d 810, 822, 823 (Tenth Cir. 1993) ("Under Oklahoma law the purpose of a punitive award is to punish and deter a wrongdoer. In order to have a deterrent effect, the damage award must be sufficient to attract the attention of the defendant in order to assure that oppressive practices do not continue . . . While the Due Process Clause requires that punitive damages not be grossly excessive, it does not require that punitive damages be ineffectual and impotent.").

8. To limit the prejudice associated with the jury being informed of the defendant's wealth, some jurisdictions either require or allow (at the trial court's discretion) the trial to be bifurcated into two phases. In the first phase, the jury will decide whether the evidence supports an award of punitive damages (i.e., whether malice has been shown), and if the jury finds in the plaintiff's favor, a second phase will be conducted (before the same jury) where evidence of the defendant's wealth will be offered to assist in setting the punitive award.

Exxon Shipping Co. v. Baker
554 U.S. 471 (2008)

Justice SOUTER delivered the opinion of the Court.

I

On March 24, 1989, the supertanker *Exxon Valdez* grounded on Bligh Reef off the Alaskan coast, fracturing its hull and spilling millions of gallons of crude oil into Prince William Sound. The owner, petitioner Exxon Shipping Co. (now SeaRiver Maritime, Inc.), and its owner, petitioner Exxon Mobil Corp. (collectively, Exxon), have settled state and federal claims for environmental damage, with payments exceeding $1 billion, and this action by respondent Baker and others, including commercial fishermen and native Alaskans, was brought for economic losses to individuals dependent on Prince William Sound for their livelihoods.

A

The tanker was over 900 feet long and was used by Exxon to carry crude oil from the end of the Trans-Alaska Pipeline in Valdez, Alaska, to the lower 48 States. On the night of the spill it was carrying 53 million gallons of crude oil, or over a million barrels. Its captain was one Joseph Hazelwood, who had completed a 28-day alcohol treatment program while employed by Exxon, as his superiors knew, but dropped out of a prescribed followup program and stopped going to Alcoholics Anonymous meetings. According to the District Court, "[t]here was evidence presented to the jury that after Hazelwood was released from [residential treatment], he drank in bars, parking lots, apartments, airports, airplanes, restaurants, hotels, at various ports, and aboard Exxon tankers." The jury also heard contested testimony that Hazelwood drank with Exxon officials and that members of the Exxon management knew of his relapse. See *ibid.* Although Exxon had a clear policy prohibiting employees from serving onboard within four hours of consuming alcohol, Exxon presented no evidence that it monitored Hazelwood after his return to duty or considered giving him a shoreside assignment. Witnesses testified that before the *Valdez* left port on the night of the disaster, Hazelwood downed at least five double vodkas in the waterfront bars of Valdez, an intake of about 15 ounces of 80-proof alcohol, enough "that a non-alcoholic would have passed out."

The ship sailed at 9:12 P.M. on March 23, 1989, guided by a state-licensed pilot for the first leg out, through the Valdez Narrows. At 11:20 P.M., Hazelwood took active control and, owing to poor conditions in the outbound shipping lane, radioed the Coast Guard for permission to move east across the inbound lane to a less icy path. Under the conditions, this was a standard move, which the last outbound tanker had also taken, and the Coast Guard cleared the *Valdez* to cross the inbound lane. The tanker accordingly steered east toward clearer waters, but the move put it in the path of an underwater reef off Bligh Island, thus requiring a turn back west into the shipping lane around Busby Light, north of the reef.

Two minutes before the required turn, however, Hazelwood left the bridge and went down to his cabin in order, he said, to do paperwork. This decision was inexplicable. There was expert testimony that, even if their presence is not strictly necessary, captains simply do not quit the bridge during maneuvers like this, and no paperwork could have justified it. And in fact the evidence was that Hazelwood's presence was required, both because there should have been two officers on the bridge at all times and his departure left only one, and because he was the only person on the entire ship licensed to navigate this part of Prince William Sound. To make matters worse, before going below Hazelwood put the tanker on autopilot, speeding it up, making the turn trickier, and any mistake harder to correct.

As Hazelwood left, he instructed the remaining officer, third mate Joseph Cousins, to move the tanker back into the shipping lane once it came abeam of

Busby Light. Cousins, unlicensed to navigate in those waters, was left alone with helmsman Robert Kagan, a nonofficer. For reasons that remain a mystery, they failed to make the turn at Busby Light, and a later emergency maneuver attempted by Cousins came too late. The tanker ran aground on Bligh Reef, tearing the hull open and spilling 11 million gallons of crude oil into Prince William Sound.

After Hazelwood returned to the bridge and reported the grounding to the Coast Guard, he tried but failed to rock the *Valdez* off the reef, a maneuver which could have spilled more oil and caused the ship to founder. The Coast Guard's nearly immediate response included a blood test of Hazelwood (the validity of which Exxon disputes) showing a blood-alcohol level of .061 11 hours after the spill. Extrapolating backward, an expert testified that Hazelwood at the time of the spill must have had a blood-alcohol level of around .241.

In the aftermath of the disaster, Exxon spent around $2.1 billion in cleanup efforts, $25 million in criminal fines plus restitution of $100 million. A civil action by the United States and the State of Alaska for environmental harms ended with a consent decree for Exxon to pay at least $900 million toward restoring natural resources, and it paid another $303 million in voluntary settlements with fishermen, property owners, and other private parties.

The remaining civil cases were consolidated into this one against Exxon, Hazelwood, and others. The District Court for the District of Alaska divided the plaintiffs seeking compensatory damages into three classes: commercial fishermen, Native Alaskans, and landowners. At Exxon's behest, the court also certified a mandatory class of all plaintiffs seeking punitive damages, whose number topped 32,000.

In Phase II the jury awarded $287 million in compensatory damages to the commercial fishermen. After the Court deducted released claims, settlements, and other payments, the balance outstanding was $19,590,257. Meanwhile, most of the Native Alaskan class had settled their compensatory claims for $20 million, and those who opted out of that settlement ultimately settled for a total of around $2.6 million.

In Phase III, the jury heard about Exxon's management's acts and omissions arguably relevant to the spill. At the close of evidence, the court instructed the jurors on the purposes of punitive damages, emphasizing that they were designed not to provide compensatory relief but to punish and deter the defendants. The court charged the jury to consider the reprehensibility of the defendants' conduct, their financial condition, the magnitude of the harm, and any mitigating facts. The jury awarded $5,000 in punitive damages against Hazelwood and $5 billion against Exxon.

On appeal, the Ninth Circuit remanded twice for adjustments in light of this Court's due process cases before ultimately itself remitting the award to $2.5 billion.

We granted certiorari to consider whether the punitive damages awarded against Exxon in this case were excessive as a matter of maritime common law.

IV

Finally, Exxon raises an issue of first impression about punitive damages in maritime law, which falls within a federal court's jurisdiction to decide in the manner of a common law court, subject to the authority of Congress to legislate otherwise if it disagrees with the judicial result. See U.S. Const., Art. III, §2, cl. 1; see, e.g., *Edmonds v. Compagnie Generale Transatlantique*, 443 U.S. 256, 259, 99 S. Ct. 2753, 61 L. Ed. 2d 521 (1979) ("Admiralty law is judge-made law to a great extent"); *Romero v. International Terminal Operating Co.*, 358 U.S. 354, 360-361, 79 S. Ct. 468, 3 L. Ed. 2d 368 (1959) (constitutional grant "empowered the federal courts . . . to continue the development of [maritime] law"). In addition to its resistance to derivative liability for punitive damages and its preemption claim already disposed of, Exxon challenges the size of the remaining $2.5 billion punitive-damages award. Other than its preemption argument, it does not offer a legal ground for concluding that maritime law should never award punitive damages, or that none should be awarded in this case, but it does argue that this award exceeds the bounds justified by the punitive-damages goal of deterring reckless (or worse) behavior and the consequently heightened threat of harm. The claim goes to our understanding of the place of punishment in modern civil law and reasonable standards of process in administering punitive law, subjects that call for starting with a brief account of the history behind today's punitive damages.

A

The modern Anglo-American doctrine of punitive damages dates back at least to 1763, when a pair of decisions by the Court of Common Pleas recognized the availability of damages "for more than the injury received." *Wilkes v. Wood, Lofft 1, 18, 98 Eng. Rep. 489, 498 (1763)* (Lord Chief Justice Pratt). In *Wilkes v. Wood*, one of the foundations of the Fourth Amendment, exemplary damages awarded against the Secretary of State, responsible for an unlawful search of John Wilkes's papers, were a spectacular £4,000. In *Wilkes*, the same judge who is recorded in *Wilkes* gave an opinion upholding a jury's award of £300 (against a government officer again) although "if the jury had been confined by their oath to consider the mere personal injury only, perhaps [£20] damages would have been thought damages sufficient."

Awarding damages beyond the compensatory was not, however, a wholly novel idea even then, legal codes from ancient times through the Middle Ages having called for multiple damages for certain especially harmful acts. But punitive damages were a common law innovation untethered to strict numerical multipliers, and the doctrine promptly crossed the Atlantic, to become widely accepted in American courts by the middle of the 19th century.

Early common law cases offered various rationales for punitive-damages awards, which were then generally dubbed "exemplary," implying that these verdicts were justified as punishment for extraordinary wrongdoing, as in

Wilkes's case. Sometimes, though, the extraordinary element emphasized was the damages award itself, the punishment being "for example's sake," "to deter from any such proceeding for the future."

A third historical justification, which showed up in some of the early cases, has been noted by recent commentators, and that was the need "to compensate for intangible injuries, compensation which was not otherwise available under the narrow conception of compensatory damages prevalent at the time."). As the century progressed, and "the types of compensatory damages available to plaintiffs . . . broadened," the consequence was that American courts tended to speak of punitive damages as separate and distinct from compensatory damages.

Regardless of the alternative rationales over the years, the consensus today is that punitives are aimed not at compensation but principally at retribution and deterring harmful conduct. This consensus informs the doctrine in most modern American jurisdictions, where juries are customarily instructed on twin goals of punitive awards.

C

State regulation of punitive damages varies. A few States award them rarely, or not at all. Nebraska bars punitive damages entirely, on state constitutional grounds. Four others permit punitive damages only when authorized by statute: Louisiana, Massachusetts, and Washington as a matter of common law, and New Hampshire by statute codifying common law tradition. Michigan courts recognize only exemplary damages supportable as compensatory, rather than truly punitive, while Connecticut courts have limited what they call punitive recovery to the "expenses of bringing the legal action, including attorney's fees, less taxable costs."

As for procedure, in most American jurisdictions the amount of the punitive award is generally determined by a jury in the first instance, and that "determination is then reviewed by trial and appellate courts to ensure that it is reasonable." Many States have gone further by imposing statutory limits on punitive awards, in the form of absolute monetary caps, a maximum ratio of punitive to compensatory damages, or, frequently, some combination of the two, see. The States that rely on a multiplier have adopted a variety of ratios, ranging from 5:1 to 1:1.

Despite these limitations, punitive damages overall are higher and more frequent in the United States than they are anywhere else. In England and Wales, punitive, or exemplary, damages are available only for oppressive, arbitrary, or unconstitutional action by government servants; injuries designed by the defendant to yield a larger profit than the likely cost of compensatory damages; and conduct for which punitive damages are expressly authorized by statute. Even in the circumstances where punitive damages are allowed, they are subject to strict, judicially imposed guidelines.

D

American punitive damages have been the target of audible criticism in recent decades, but most recent studies tend to undercut much of it. A survey of the literature reveals that discretion to award punitive damages has not mass-produced runaway awards, and although some studies show the dollar amounts of punitive-damages awards growing over time, even in real terms, by most accounts the median ratio of punitive to compensatory awards has remained less than 1:1. Nor do the data substantiate a marked increase in the percentage of cases with punitive awards over the past several decades. The figures thus show an overall restraint and suggest that in many instances a high ratio of punitive to compensatory damages is substantially greater than necessary to punish or deter.

The real problem, it seems, is the stark unpredictability of punitive awards. Courts of law are concerned with fairness as consistency, and evidence that the median ratio of punitive to compensatory awards falls within a reasonable zone, or that punitive awards are infrequent, fails to tell us whether the spread between high and low individual awards is acceptable. The available data suggest it is not. A recent comprehensive study of punitive damages awarded by juries in state civil trials found a median ratio of punitive to compensatory awards of just 0.62:1, but a mean ratio of 2.90:1 and a standard deviation of 13.81. Even to those of us unsophisticated in statistics, the thrust of these figures is clear: the spread is great, and the outlier cases subject defendants to punitive damages that dwarf the corresponding compensatories. The distribution of awards is narrower, but still remarkable, among punitive damages assessed by judges: the median ratio is 0.66:1, the mean ratio is 1.60:1, and the standard deviation is 4.54.

Starting with the premise of a punitive-damages regime, these ranges of variation might be acceptable or even desirable if they resulted from judges' and juries' refining their judgments to reach a generally accepted optimal level of penalty and deterrence in cases involving a wide range of circumstances, while producing fairly consistent results in cases with similar facts. But anecdotal evidence suggests that nothing of that sort is going on. One of our own leading cases on punitive damages, with a $4 million verdict by an Alabama jury, noted that a second Alabama case with strikingly similar facts produced "a comparable amount of compensatory damages" but "no punitive damages at all." See *BMW, Inc. v. Gore*, 517 U.S., 559, 565, n.8. As the Supreme Court of Alabama candidly explained, "the disparity between the two jury verdicts . . . [w]as a reflection of the inherent uncertainty of the trial process." We are aware of no scholarly work pointing to consistency across punitive awards in cases involving similar claims and circumstances.

Our review of punitive damages today, then, considers not their intersection with the Constitution, but the desirability of regulating them as a common law remedy for which responsibility lies with this Court as a source of judge-made law in the absence of statute. Whatever may be the constitutional significance of the unpredictability of high punitive awards, this feature of happenstance is in tension with the function of the awards as punitive, just because of the implication of unfairness that an eccentrically high punitive verdict carries in a system whose commonly held notion of law rests on a sense of fairness in dealing with one another. Thus, a penalty should be reasonably predictable in its severity, so that even Justice Holmes's "bad man" can look ahead with some ability to know what the stakes are in choosing one course of action or another. And when the bad man's counterparts turn up from time to time, the penalty scheme they face ought to threaten them with a fair probability of suffering in like degree when they wreak like damage. The common sense of justice would surely bar penalties that reasonable people would think excessive for the harm caused in the circumstances.

F

1

With that aim ourselves, we have three basic approaches to consider, one verbal and two quantitative. As mentioned before, a number of state courts have settled on criteria for judicial review of punitive-damages awards that go well beyond traditional "shock the conscience" or "passion and prejudice" tests. Maryland, for example, has set forth a nonexclusive list of nine review factors under state common law that include "degree of heinousness," "the deterrence value of [the award]," and "[w]hether [the punitive award] bears a reasonable relationship to the compensatory damages awarded." Alabama has seven general criteria, such as "actual or likely harm [from the defendant's conduct]," "degree of reprehensibility," and "[i]f the wrongful conduct was profitable to the defendant."

These judicial review criteria are brought to bear after juries render verdicts under instructions offering, at best, guidance no more specific for reaching an appropriate penalty. In Maryland, for example, which allows punitive damages for intentional torts and conduct characterized by "actual malice," juries may be instructed that

> "[a]n award for punitive damages should be:
>   "(1) In an amount that will deter the defendant and others from similar conduct.
>   "(2) Proportionate to the wrongfulness of the defendant's conduct and the defendant's ability to pay.
>   "(3) But not designed to bankrupt or financially destroy a defendant."

In Alabama, juries are instructed to fix an amount after considering "the character and degree of the wrong as shown by the evidence in the case, and the necessity of preventing similar wrongs."

These examples leave us skeptical that verbal formulations, superimposed on general jury instructions, are the best insurance against unpredictable outliers. Instructions can go just so far in promoting systemic consistency when awards are not tied to specifically proven items of damage (the cost of medical treatment, say), and although judges in the States that take this approach may well produce just results by dint of valiant effort, our experience with attempts to produce consistency in the analogous business of criminal sentencing leaves us doubtful that anything but a quantified approach will work. A glance at the experience there will explain our skepticism.

The points of similarity are obvious. "[P]unitive damages advance the interests of punishment and deterrence, which are also among the interests advanced by the criminal law."

It is instructive, then, that in the last quarter century federal sentencing rejected an "indeterminate" system, with relatively unguided discretion to sentence within a wide range, under which "similarly situated offenders were sentenced [to], and did actually serve, widely disparate sentences." Instead it became a system of detailed guidelines tied to exactly quantified sentencing results, under the authority of the Sentencing Reform Act of 1984.

The importance of this for us is that in the old federal sentencing system of general standards the cohort of even the most seasoned judicial penalty-givers defied consistency. Judges and defendants alike were "[l]eft at large, wandering in deserts of uncharted discretion, which is very much the position of those imposing punitive damages today, be they judges or juries, except that they lack even a statutory maximum; their only restraint beyond a core sense of fairness is the due process limit. This federal criminal-law development, with its many state parallels, strongly suggests that as long as there are no punitive-damages guidelines, corresponding to the federal and state sentencing guidelines, it is inevitable that the specific amount of punitive damages awarded whether by a judge or by a jury will be arbitrary."

2

This is why our better judgment is that eliminating unpredictable outlying punitive awards by more rigorous standards than the constitutional limit will probably have to take the form adopted in those States that have looked to the criminal-law pattern of quantified limits. One option would be to follow the States that set a hard dollar cap on punitive damages, a course that arguably would come closest to the criminal law, rather like setting a maximum term of years. The trouble is, though, that there is no "standard" tort or contract injury, making it difficult to settle upon a particular dollar figure as appropriate across the board. And of course a judicial selection of a dollar cap would carry a serious drawback; a legislature can pick a figure, index it for inflation, and revisit its provision whenever there seems to be a need for further tinkering, but a court cannot say when an issue will show up on the docket again.

The more promising alternative is to leave the effects of inflation to the jury or judge who assesses the value of actual loss, by pegging punitive to compensatory damages using a ratio or maximum multiple. As the earlier canvass of state experience showed, this is the model many States have adopted, and Congress has passed analogous legislation from time to time, as for example in providing treble damages in antitrust, racketeering, patent, and trademark actions. And of course the potential relevance of the ratio between compensatory and punitive damages is indisputable, being a central feature in our due process analysis.

Still, some will murmur that this smacks too much of policy and too little of principle. But the answer rests on the fact that we are acting here in the position of a common law court of last review, faced with a perceived defect in a common law remedy. Traditionally, courts have accepted primary responsibility for reviewing punitive damages and thus for their evolution, and if, in the absence of legislation, judicially derived standards leave the door open to outlier punitive-damages awards, it is hard to see how the judiciary can wash its hands of a problem it created, simply by calling quantified standards legislative.

Although the legal landscape is well populated with examples of ratios and multipliers expressing policies of retribution and deterrence, most of them suffer from features that stand in the way of borrowing them as paradigms of reasonable limitations suited for application to this case. While a slim majority of the States with a ratio have adopted 3:1, others see fit to apply a lower one, and a few have gone higher. Judgments may differ about the weight to be given to the slight majority of 3:1 States, but one feature of the 3:1 schemes dissuades us from selecting it here. With a few statutory exceptions, generally for intentional infliction of physical injury or other harm, the States with 3:1 ratios apply them across the board (as do other States using different fixed multipliers). That is, the upper limit is not directed to cases like this one, where the tortious action was worse than negligent but less than malicious, exposing the tortfeasor to certain regulatory sanctions and inevitable damages actions; the 3:1 ratio in these States also applies to awards in quite different cases involving some of the most egregious conduct, including malicious behavior and dangerous activity carried on for the purpose of increasing a tortfeasor's financial gain. We confront, instead, a case of reckless action, profitless to the tortfeasor, resulting in substantial recovery for substantial injury. Thus, a legislative judgment that 3:1 is a reasonable limit overall is not a judgment that 3:1 is a reasonable limit in this particular type of case.

3

There is better evidence of an accepted limit of reasonable civil penalty, however, in several studies mentioned before, showing the median ratio of punitive to compensatory verdicts, reflecting what juries and judges have considered reasonable across many hundreds of punitive awards. We think it is fair to assume that the greater share of the verdicts studied in these comprehensive collections reflect reasonable judgments about the economic penalties appropriate in their particular cases.

These studies cover cases of the most as well as the least blameworthy conduct triggering punitive liability, from malice and avarice, down to recklessness, and even gross negligence in some jurisdictions. The data put the median ratio for the entire gamut of circumstances at less than 1:1, meaning that the compensatory award exceeds the punitive award in most cases. In a well-functioning system, we would expect that awards at the median or lower would roughly express jurors' sense of reasonable penalties in cases with no earmarks of exceptional blameworthiness within the punishable spectrum (cases like this one, without intentional or malicious conduct, and without behavior driven primarily by desire for gain, for example) and cases (again like this one) without the modest economic harm or odds of detection that have opened the door to higher awards. It also seems fair to suppose that most of the unpredictable outlier cases that call the fairness of the system into question are above the median; in theory a factfinder's deliberation could go awry to produce a very low ratio, but we have no basis to assume that such a case would be more than a sport, and the cases with serious constitutional issues coming to us have naturally been on the high side. On these assumptions, a median ratio of punitive to compensatory damages of about 0.65:1 probably marks the line near which cases like this one largely should be grouped. Accordingly, given the need to protect against the possibility (and the disruptive cost to the legal system) of awards that are unpredictable and unnecessary, either for deterrence or for measured retribution, we consider that a 1:1 ratio, which is above the median award, is a fair upper limit in such maritime cases.

The dissent also suggests that maritime tort law needs a quantified limit on punitive awards less than tort law generally because punitives may mitigate maritime law's less generous scheme of compensatory damages. But the instructions in this case did not allow the jury to set punitives on the basis of any such consideration. And this Court has long held that "[p]unitive damages by definition are not intended to compensate the injured party, but rather to punish the tortfeasor . . . and to deter him and others from similar extreme conduct." Indeed, any argument for more generous punitive damages in maritime cases would call into question the maritime applicability of the constitutional limit on punitive damages as now understood, for we have tied that limit to a conception of punitive damages awarded entirely for a punitive, not quasi-compensatory, purpose.

. . . In *State Farm v. Mutual Auto. Ins. Co. v. Campbell*, 538 U.S. 408 (2003), we said that a single-digit maximum is appropriate in all but the most exceptional of cases, and "[w]hen compensatory damages are substantial, then a lesser ratio, perhaps only equal to compensatory damages, can reach the outermost limit of the due process guarantee."

Applying this standard to the present case, we take for granted the District Court's calculation of the total relevant compensatory damages at $507.5 million. A punitive-to-compensatory ratio of 1:1 thus yields maximum punitive damages in that amount.

We therefore vacate the judgment and remand the case for the Court of Appeals to remit the punitive-damages award accordingly.

It is so ordered.

PREPARING FOR CLASS

1. How reliant was the Court on precedent established in *Gore* and *Campbell*?

2. Assess the proposition that a compensatory award could serve as punishment.

INCREASING YOUR UNDERSTANDING

1. *Exxon's reach.* Unlike the Court's posture in *Campbell v. State*, where the Court tested the constitutional propriety of the punitive award, in *Exxon* the Court sat as the creator of the common law with respect to punitive damages in maritime actions. At least initially in actions (state or federal) where, because of lack of legislation, courts are charged with the responsibility to set the parameters for punitive awards, *Exxon* may have influence. But that is just the first cut, as even if a punitive award is allowed by the common law, it remains subject to constitutional scrutiny should the defendant find the award excessive.

   Most courts have responded to *Exxon* by distinguishing the circumstance, see Allstate Insurance Co. v. Dodson, __S.W.3d__ (Ark. 2011) (*Exxon* decision limited to cases where there is a considerable compensatory award), or being guided when establishing the common law parameters for a punitive award, especially under federal laws. See Bridgeport Harbor Place I, LLC v. Ganim, 2008 WL 4926925 (Conn. Super 2008) ("Although the plaintiff is unquestionably correct that *Exxon Shipping* is not controlling, the reasoning of the Supreme Court's decision is very persuasive in identifying certain factors relevant to determining the amount of a punitive damages award, even in a CUTPA case.").

2. Many courts require that there be a reasonable relationship between the punitive and compensatory awards. This is rooted in the belief that the degree of punishment should be gauged by the extent of harm actually caused. Some states have formalized this concept by statute and fix the punitive by a multiplier of the compensatory award; others have flatly rejected the concept of a predetermined acceptable ratio. The Supreme Court in *Gore* takes this concept and incorporates it as one of the guideposts when a constitutional challenge is brought.

Chapter 17

Liability in Cases Involving Multiple Tortfeasors

———————————————

Cases involving multiple defendants create unique issues beyond the causation issues discussed previously in Chapters 10 and 11 of Torts I. This chapter covers how courts have responded when confronted with cases where multiple parties have contributed to harming the plaintiff.

A. JOINT AND SEVERAL LIABILITY

Bierczynski v. Rogers
239 A.2d 218 (Del. 1968)

HERRMANN, Justice:

This appeal involves an automobile accident in which the plaintiffs claim that the defendant motorists were racing on the public highway, as the result of which the accident occurred.

The plaintiffs Cecil B. Rogers and Susan D. Rogers brought this action against Robert C. Race and Ronald Bierczynski, ages 18 and 17 respectively, alleging concurrent negligences in that they violated various speed statutes and various other statutory rules of the road, and in that they failed to keep a proper lookout and failed to keep their vehicles under proper control. The jury, by answer to interrogatories in its special verdict, expressly found that Race and Bierczynski were each negligent and that the negligence of each was a proximate cause of the accident. Substantial verdicts were entered in favor of the plaintiffs against both defendants jointly. The defendant Bierczynski appeals therefrom. The defendant Race does not appeal; rather, he joins with the plaintiffs in upholding the judgment below.[*]

———————————

[*] Bierczynski does not deny negligence. He admits driving 45 m.p.h. in a 25 m.p.h. zone.

Bierczynski and Race worked at the same place, located a short distance east of Governor Printz Boulevard near Lore Avenue. They lived near each other in the southerly part of Wilmington. On the day before the accident, Bierczynski drove Race to work. On the day of the accident, Bierczynski intended to pick Race up again; but, upon meeting, Race told Bierczynski he would take his own automobile too, because he intended to leave work early. Thereupon, one following the other, they drove toward their place of employment northerly across Wilmington to Lore Avenue in a suburban area of Brandywine Hundred. The accident occurred on Lore Avenue about 300 feet east of its intersection with River Road. Lore Avenue runs east and west and River Road north and south. Lore Avenue was 18 feet wide, macadam surfaces, without a marked center line, and was lined by guard rails at various places. For a distance of about 1,000 feet west of its intersection with River Road, Lore Avenue is a moderately steep hill; after crossing River Road, it levels off. The speed limit at the scene was 25 m.p.h.

Cecil Rogers testified as follows: He was returning from a Girl Scout trip with his daughter, headed for their home located about three blocks from the scene of the accident. He entered Lore Avenue from Governor Printz Boulevard, thus driving in a westerly direction on Lore Avenue. At a point about 300 feet east of River Road, Rogers' car was struck by Race's car which approached him sideways, moving in an easterly direction on the westbound lane. Rogers saw Race's car coming at him; he stopped in the westbound lane; but he was unable to move out of the way because there was a guard rail along that part of the road and no shoulder. Rogers first saw the Race vehicle when it was about 550 feet up Lore Avenue-or about 250 feet west of River Road. At that point, the Race car was being driven easterly on Lore Avenue in the westbound lane, almost along-side the Bierczynski car which was moving easterly in the eastbound lane. The front bumper of the Race car was opposite the back bumper of the Bierczynski car. Both cars were moving at about 55 or 60 m.p.h. down the hill. Before reaching River Road, Race swerved back into the eastbound lane behind Bierczynski, who was about a car length in front. As it crossed River Road, the Race automobile "bottomed on the road"; and it "careened down against the pavement and gave an impression of an explosion"; dust "flew everywhere" sufficiently to obscure the Race car momentarily from Rogers' view. At that point, the Race and Bierczynski automobiles were only "inches apart." The Race car then emerged from behind the Bierczynski car and careened sideways, at about 70 m.p.h., a distance of about 300 feet to the Rogers car standing in the westbound lane. The left side of the Race car struck the front of the Rogers car. Meanwhile, the Bierczynski car was brought to a stop in the eastbound lane, about 35 feet from the area of impact. The Bierczynski car did not come into contact with the Rogers vehicle.

A reasonable inference capable of being drawn from the above testimony of Rogers, in the light of the surrounding circumstances, is that Race and Bierczynski were engaged in a speed contest as they came down the hill of

Lore Avenue approaching its intersection with River Road. It is unimportant whether it was technically a "race," in the terminology of the defendants who deny that they were "racing." Clearly, the inference of a deliberate and intentional speed competition, as they came down the hill practically side-by-side at twice the legal speed, was permissible from Rogers' testimony; clearly, the inference that Bierczynski maintained his greatly excessive speed deliberately to prevent Race from passing him, was also permissible from Rogers' testimony. We classify both of these courses of conduct as improper racing on the highway. In either of the latter situations, the issue of whether Bierczynski's conduct was a proximate cause of Race's loss of control and collision with Rogers, was a proper issue for the jury.

In many States, automobile racing on a public highway is prohibited by statute, the violation of which is negligence Per se. Delaware has no such statute. Nevertheless, speed competition in automobiles on the public highway is negligence in this State, for the reason that a reasonably prudent person would not engage in such conduct. This conclusion is in accord with the general rule, prevailing in other jurisdictions which lack statutes on the subject, that racing motor vehicles on a public highway is negligence.

It is also generally held that all who engage in a race on the highway do so at their peril, and are liable for injury or damage sustained by a third person as a result thereof, regardless of which of the racing cars directly inflicted the injury or damage. The authorities reflect generally accepted rules of causation that all parties engaged in a motor vehicle race on the highway are wrongdoers acting in concert, and that each participant is liable for harm to a third person arising from the tortious conduct of the other, because he has induced and encouraged the tort.

We subscribe to those rules; and hold that, as a general rule, participation in a motor vehicle race on a public highway is an act of concurrent negligence imposing liability on each participant for any injury to a non-participant resulting from the race. If, therefore, Race and Bierczynski were engaged in a speed competition, each was liable for the damages and injuries to the plaintiffs herein, even though Bierczynski was not directly involved in the collision itself. Bierczynski apparently concedes liability if a race had, in fact, been in progress.

We find no error as asserted by the appellant. The judgments below are affirmed.

PREPARING FOR CLASS

1. What is Bierczynski's chief argument? Do you find it compelling? What is the consequence of the court rejecting it?

2. What does Race hope to accomplish by joining the plaintiffs on appeal?

APPLYING THE LAW

A is a passenger in B's car when involved in an accident with C. Both B and C were negligent. A suffers a concussion as a result of the accident. B drives A to the hospital for care and while walking through the emergence room, A slips on a recently cleaned floor and breaks his leg. Assume negligence on the part of the hospital. Who is potentially responsible for what and are any of the parties jointly liable?

INCREASING YOUR UNDERSTANDING

1. *Joint and several liability.* Under this theory, plaintiff is allowed to recover from each of the defendants severally based on their proportionate liability or to recover the entire judgment from one of the joint defendants. The plaintiff is favored with each option and typically will take the path of least resistance, i.e., collect the entire amount from the defendant with the most financial resources. Among the many justifications for the rule are:

    a. As between an innocent plaintiff and wrongdoers, the burden of an insolvent defendant should fall on the less culpable party, and courts are particularly loath to deny recovery to an "innocent" plaintiff in this instance.

    b. Joint liability promotes recovery and furthers the policy of deterring tortious conduct.

    c. The defendant that pays more than her fair share has the right to seek reimbursement (contribution) from the party who doesn't pay.

2. *Circumstances appropriate for imposing joint liability.* Acting in concert, as illustrated in *Bierczynski*, is one of three situations where courts will hold defendants jointly or severally liable. The others are:

    a. *Where the defendants have acted individually yet caused an indivisible harm.* The classic example is the auto accident case where two negligent drivers collided and a passenger in one of the cars is injured. While a jury asked to assess fault may assign different percentages, the harm is singular and neither is able to avoid responsibility for the entire harm simply because another party was involved.

    b. *Where the defendants owe a common duty to the plaintiff.* "Where two or more persons are under a common duty and failure to perform it amounts to tortuous conduct, each is subject to liability for the entire harm resulting from failure to perform the duty." Restatement (Second) of Torts §878 (1965). This rule makes the employer sued under a theory of vicarious liability jointly liable with the employee, and the co-owners of a business obligated to provide a safe environment are jointly liable though one may have been particularly assigned the responsibility of safety and maintenance. See comment a to Restatement (Second) of Torts §878.

3. Can a plaintiff recover punitive damages in a case involving joint tortfeasors? Maybe. It should first be noted that it is the rare case where defendants will share joint liability for the punitive award, as a punitive award is unique to each defendant and as such does not involve an "indivisible" damage or actual loss. "While a defendant who is least culpable may remain liable for all the compensatory damages suffered by plaintiff, given the purpose of a punitive award, there is no justice in allowing similar recovery of such damages in an action against several defendants based upon evidence of the wealth and blameworthiness of one other than he who must pay the exemplary award." Embrey v. Holly, 293 Md. 128, 442 A.2d 966 (Md. 1982). Courts, however, have individually allocated punitive awards to defendants with the amounts varying based on degree of culpability and financial resources. See Edquest v. Tripp & Dragstedt Co., 93 Mont. 446, 19 P.2d 637 (Mont. 1933) ("The jury may take into consideration the difference in financial condition of the defendants and impose different amounts as punishment upon them in case the conclusion is reached that both ought to be penalized"), and Taylor v. Compere, 230 S.W.3d 606 (Mo. App. S.D. 2007) ("Establishing a conspiracy will make all defendants jointly and severally liable for actual damages, but it does not change the rule that punitive damages are to be assessed against each tortfeasor depending, among other factors, upon his degree of culpability."). Other courts, however, have rejected awards of punitive damages in "joint liability" cases where the trial court had allocated a punitive award against a single defendant but not all. "The jury should have been instructed, as respects exemplary damages . . . to assess them according to the acts of the most innocent of the defendants, and if any defendant was not liable for exemplary damages, none should be included in the verdict, for the question was as to the motives of the defendants." MacHolme v. Cochenour, 109 Pa. Super. 563, 167 A. 647 (Pa. Super. 1933).

Bartlett v. New Mexico Welding Supply, Inc.
98 N.M. 152, 646 P.2d 579 (N.M. Ct. App. 1982)

Wood, Judge.

This comparative negligence case presents two issues: (1) whether a tortfeasor is liable for all of the damages caused by concurrent tortfeasors under a theory of joint and several liability; and (2) whether the percentage of fault of a non-party concurrent tortfeasor is to be determined by the fact finder.

The automobile accident involved three vehicles. The car in front of plaintiffs' car signaled a right hand turn. This lead car turned into and then pulled out of a service station in a very fast motion. Plaintiff Jane Bartlett slammed on her brakes to avoid hitting the lead car. Defendant's truck was behind plaintiffs' car. Defendant's driver applied his brakes; however, the truck skidded into the rear of plaintiffs' car.

The driver of the lead car is unknown. Plaintiffs sued defendant on a theory of negligence. Defendant contended that the negligence of the unknown driver "caused or contributed to cause" the accident and resulting damages.

The trial court instructed the jury:

> If you find for the plaintiff but also find that the negligence of the plaintiff and/or the unknown third party contributed to cause the accident and resulting damages, then you must decide how much each party was at fault. The defendant is liable only for defendant's percentage of fault in causing the accident and any resulting damages and the total amount of damages to which plaintiff would otherwise be entitled shall be reduced in proportion to the percentage of plaintiff's negligence and/or the negligence of the unknown third party.

The jury answered "special questions." It determined that plaintiffs' damages were $100,000.00, that plaintiffs were not negligent, that defendant was negligent, that defendant's negligence contributed to the accident and plaintiffs' damages to the extent of 30%, that the unknown driver was negligent and this negligence contributed to the accident and plaintiffs' damages to the extent of 70%.

Plaintiffs moved that judgment be entered in their favor in the amount of $100,000.00. This motion was not granted. Instead, the trial court ordered a new trial. The trial court was of the view that: (a) the above quoted instruction should not have been given; (b) that the case should not have been tried between plaintiffs, defendant, and the unknown driver; (c) that defendant is jointly and severally liable for the damages to plaintiffs caused by defendant and the unknown driver; and (d) "that a different result would have occurred had the jury known that this Defendant would have been responsible for the total damages under joint and several liability."

We granted defendant's application for an interlocutory appeal.

JOINT AND SEVERAL LIABILITY

In this case, in using the term "joint and several liability," we mean that either of two persons whose concurrent negligence contributed to cause plaintiffs' injury and damage may be held liable for the entire amount of the damage caused by them. It is not disputed that this is a common law rule which existed in New Mexico prior to Scott v. Rizzo, 96 N.M. 682, 634 P.2d 1234 (1981), which adopted the opinion of the Court of Appeals in *Claymore v. City of Albuquerque*. In *Claymore*, this Court adopted pure comparative negligence. *Claymore* is reported immediately following the Supreme Court opinion in *Scott* and without a separate citation. Our references to *Scott* and *Claymore* are to be found in the opinion reported under the above citation. It is not disputed that defendant and the unknown driver were concurrent tortfeasors.

The question is whether, in a comparative negligence case, a concurrent tortfeasor is liable for the entire damage caused by concurrent tortfeasors. In answering this question, we do not consider situations where one of the tortfeasors would not be subject to any liability; such situations might arise under either statutory or common law provisions. The premise for the question to be answered is that, under the common law rule, either the defendant or the unknown driver could be held liable for the damage caused by their combined negligence.

The question has been answered in several states; most of these decisions are not helpful because the answer depended upon the contents of a comparative negligence statute.

The retention of joint and several liability ultimately rests on two grounds; neither ground is defensible.

The first ground is the concept that a plaintiff's injury is "indivisible." The California Supreme Court, in American Motorcycle Ass'n v. Super. Ct. Etc., 65 Cal. App. 3d 694, 135 Cal. Rptr. 497 (1977), followed this ground when it stated:

> (T)he simple feasibility of apportioning fault on a comparative negligence basis does not render an indivisible injury "divisible" for purposes of the joint and several liability. . . . In other words, the mere fact that it may be possible to assign some percentage figure to the relative culpability of one negligent defendant as compared to another does not in any way suggest that each defendant's negligence is not a proximate cause of the entire indivisible injury.

Thus, under the California Supreme Court decision, a concurrent tortfeasor, 1% at fault, is liable for 100% of the damage caused by concurrent tortfeasors, on the basis that the tortfeasor, 1% at fault, caused the entire damage. A practical answer, in this case, is that the jury found that defendant was 30% at fault and caused 30% of the damage.

Prosser, Law of Torts, 4th Edition, §41, p. 241, states: "The law of joint tortfeasors rests very largely upon recognition of the fact that each of two or more causes may be charged with a single result."

Prosser, "Joint Torts and Several Liability," 25 Cal. L. Rev. 413 (1936-37), states that the rule holding a concurrent tortfeasor for the entire loss "grew out of the common law concept of the unity of the cause of action; the jury could not be permitted to apportion the damages, since there was but one wrong." The "unity" concept, in turn was based on common law rules of pleading and joinder. Prosser, Law of Torts, supra, ch. 8. The article "Torts—Liability of Joint Tort-Feasors—Apportionment of Damages Between Joint Tort-Feasors by Verdict of Jury," 14 Va. L. Rev. 677 (1927-28), at p. 680-81, states that the cases which retain joint and several liability under relaxed American rules of joinder and in cases where causes of injury are concurrent, rather than concerted:

> seem to consider the question, not from the standpoint of whether it is just and reasonable to hold a person liable for all the damages occasioned by a joint tort in which his individual part may have resulted in little or no damage, but rather from the viewpoint of the unity of a cause in the old technical common law sense. That as the tortfeasors committed the tort together, and a single writ was brought against them, and they were sued in a single action and found guilty, then the damages should be rendered in a single sum. For, as the action was a unit and all found guilty of the same wrong, they must be equally guilty of the same amount of wrong. . . . But with the broadening in modern times of the legal conceptions regarding real consistency in the law as distinguished from mere technicality, the reasoning which appeared so persuasive to the old English jurists has lost much, if not all, of its force.

The article states that the doctrine "cannot be said to be based on any sound reason." "The few attempts by American authorities to justify the rule on reason cannot be said to be absolutely satisfactory."

The California Court of Appeal stated in *American Motorcycle Ass'n*, supra: "Li [v. Yellow Cab Company of California, 13 Cal. 3d 804, 119 Cal. Rptr. 8585, 532 P.2d 1226 (1975)], (where pure comparative negligence was adopted) accepts the ability of the fact finding process to apportion degrees of negligence. In so doing, it eliminates the previously assumed inability to apportion fault among tortfeasors as the foundation of joint and several liability." We are unwilling, as was the California Supreme Court, to say that although fault may be apportioned, causation cannot. If the jury can do one, it can do the other. See, 14 Va. L. Rev., supra, p. 682.

Joint and several liability is not to be retained in our pure comparative negligence system on a theory of one indivisible wrong. The concept of one indivisible wrong, based on common law technicalities, is obsolete, and is not to be applied in comparative negligence cases in New Mexico. See, *Scott v. Rizzo*, supra.

The second ground is that joint and several liability must be retained in order to favor plaintiffs; a plaintiff should not bear the risk of being unable to collect his judgment. We fail to understand the argument. Between one plaintiff and one defendant, the plaintiff bears the risk of the defendant being insolvent; on what basis does the risk shift if there are two defendants, and one is insolvent? In our case, the risk factor arises because the concurrent tortfeasor, 70% at fault, is unknown.

We agree with Adler, "Allocation of Responsibility After *American Motorcycle Association v. Superior Court*," 6 Pepperdine L. Rev. 1 (1978), when, in reference to the California Supreme Court decisions, it states:

> In this final quarter of the twentieth century, it seems startling to find that plaintiffs, as a class, have a greater claim upon the court's sympathy than defendants. In contrast, the court in Li had mandated that each person's allocable responsibility for an incident would be determined by the finder of fact, whether that tortfeasor is labeled a "plaintiff" or a "defendant."
>
> The thrust of the comparative negligence doctrine is to accomplish (1) apportionment of fault between or among negligent parties whose negligence proximately causes any part of a loss or injury, and (2) apportionment of the total damages resulting from such loss or injury in proportion to the fault of each party.... In multiple party cases, interrogatories will address the question of liability between each plaintiff and each defendant, to reflect such apportionment.
>
> Pure comparative negligence denies recovery for one's own fault; it permits recovery to the extent of another's fault; and it holds all parties fully responsible for their own respective acts to the degree that those acts have caused harm.

Joint and several liability is not to be retained in our pure comparative negligence system on the basis that a plaintiff must be favored.

We hold that defendant is not liable for the entire damage caused by defendant and the unknown driver. Defendant, as a concurrent tortfeasor, is not liable on a theory of joint and several liability.

NON-PARTY CONCURRENT TORTFEASOR

Heft and Heft Comparative Negligence Manual (1978), §8.131, states:

> It is accepted practice to include all tortfeasors in the apportionment question. This includes nonparties who may be unknown tortfeasors, phantom drivers, and persons alleged to be negligent but not liable in damages to the injured party such as in the third party cases arising in the workmen's compensation area.

"The jury must ascertain the percentage of negligence of all participants to an occurrence." Bd. of Cty. Com'rs of Cty., Etc. v. Ridenour, 623 P.2d 1174 (Wyo. 1981).

The trial court properly instructed the jury to consider the negligence and damage resulting from the negligence of the unknown driver.

The order granting a new trial is reversed. The cause is remanded with instructions to enter judgment in favor of plaintiffs, against defendant, for the 30% of plaintiffs' damages caused by defendant.

IT IS SO ORDERED.

PREPARING FOR CLASS

1. Identify whether the case falls within one of the circumstances where joint and several liability would be imposed and, if so, be reminded of the articulated goals in imposing joint liability.

2. Recall the comparative fault rules.

INCREASING YOUR UNDERSTANDING

Styled as tort reform, most states took the adoption of comparative fault rules as an opportunity to reconsider many common law doctrines, including joint and several liability. New Mexico is one such state; though subsequent to *Bartlett*, the New Mexico Legislature (N.M.S.A. 1978, §41-3A-1) revived joint and several liability, applying it:

> (1) to any person or persons who acted with the intention of inflicting injury or damage;
>
> (2) to any persons whose relationship to each other would make one person vicariously liable for the acts of the other, but only to that portion of the total liability attributed to those persons;
>
> (3) to any persons strictly liable for the manufacture and sale of a defective product, but only to that portion of the total liability attributed to those persons; or
>
> (4) to situations not covered by any of the foregoing and having a sound basis in public policy.

Below are samplings from other states:

Colorado: Liability is several only except when "there is a common plan to commit a tortuous act." C.R.S. §13-21-111.5.

Connecticut: No joint and several liability unless judgment is uncollectable. C.G.S. §52-572(c).

Florida: Joint and several liability for all cases less than $25,000 but otherwise abolished except "to any party whose percentage of fault equals or exceeds that of a particular claimant, the court shall enter judgment with respect to economic damages against the party on the basis of the doctrine of joint and several liability." F.S. §768.81.

Louisiana: "Joint tortfeasors of a negligent offense are jointly liable except for the first 50 percent of plaintiff's recoverable damages." L.C.C. Article 2324.

Washington: Joint and several liability eliminated in cases where the plaintiff is at fault, though liability may be joint in certain product liability and hazardous waste cases.

B. CONTRIBUTION AND INDEMNITY

Bervoets v. Harde Ralls Pontiac-Olds, Inc.
891 S.W.2d 905 (Tenn. 1994)

Drowota, Justice.

Adanac, Inc. (d/b/a Cactus Jack's) appeals from the holding of the Court of Appeals denying its motion to dismiss and requiring the contribution action brought against it by Safeco Insurance Company to be tried under the principles of the Uniform Contribution Among Tortfeasors Act (UCATA)—Tenn. Code Ann. §29-11-101—29-11-106—instead of the principles of comparative fault as announced in *McIntyre v. Balentine*, 833 S.W.2d 52 (Tenn. 1992). After carefully considering the arguments of the parties, we modify the decision of the Court of Appeals and hold that this contribution action shall be tried pursuant to the principles of comparative fault.

Facts and Procedural History

The underlying lawsuit upon which this action for contribution is predicated arose on July 5, 1980 when Lee Jackson, after consuming alcoholic beverages at Cactus Jack's restaurant, wrecked his car in which Michael Bervoets was a passenger, causing Bervoets to suffer severe and permanent injuries. After the accident, Bervoets brought a negligence action against Jackson and his parents. Thereafter, the Jacksons and their insuror, Safeco, filed a third party complaint against Adanac, alleging that because Lee Jackson was a minor for the purpose of purchasing alcoholic beverages at the time of the accident, Adanac was guilty of negligence *per se* for serving the alcoholic beverages to him, and that this negligence proximately caused the plaintiff Bervoets' injuries.

On May 11, 1983, Jackson and Safeco entered into a settlement with Bervoets in the amount of $1,250,000; this settlement served to release all Bervoets' claims against all defendants. Safeco then pursued its third party complaint in contribution under the UCATA against Adanac. The first trial in the matter resulted in a verdict for Adanac; this verdict was, however, set aside by the trial court. The second trial resulted in a verdict for Safeco; but this judgment was reversed by the Court of Appeals because of the trial court's erroneous "dynamite charge" and misconduct on the part of one of the jurors.

After the matter had been continued several times, this Court released its decision in *McIntyre v. Balentine*, 833 S.W.2d 52 (Tenn. 1992) on May 4, 1992. Thereafter Safeco filed an amended third party complaint, alleging that Adanac was liable to it on theories of contribution and common law indemnity. Adanac filed a motion to dismiss the complaint; and the trial court granted the motion as to the common law indemnity claim but denied it as to the contribution claim.

Adanac appealed from the trial court's decision pursuant to Rule 9 of the Tennessee Rules of Appellate Procedure. The Court of Appeals affirmed the judgment of the trial court, denying the motion to dismiss and holding that the contribution claim was to be determined with reference to the principles of the Uniform Contribution Among Tortfeasors Act despite our decision in *McIntyre*. We granted Adanac's Rule 11 application in order to clarify this situation.

ANALYSIS

Adanac's basic argument is that because this Court abolished the doctrine of joint and several liability in *McIntyre*, and because contribution can be had under the UCATA only if the parties are jointly and severally liable for a judgment, the Court effectively abolished the remedy of contribution in Tennessee. Moreover, Adanac points out that we unequivocally stated in *McIntyre* that the principles of comparative fault adopted in that case are to apply to "all cases tried or retried after the date of this opinion." Therefore, Adanac concludes, Safeco cannot now maintain an action against it for contribution, and the third party complaint, which has been pending for several years, is without foundation and should be dismissed.

We must reject this sweeping argument because it extends our *McIntyre* decision beyond its permissible and intended bounds. Although we stated in *McIntyre* that "today's holding renders the doctrine of joint and several liability obsolete," and thus did abolish the doctrine of joint and several liability to the extent that it allows a plaintiff to sue and obtain a full recovery against any one or more of several parties against whom liability could be established, it does not follow that we abolished the remedy of contribution. In fact we did not, and could not, completely abolish the remedy of contribution in *McIntyre* because that remedy was granted to the parties by the legislature. Moreover, our statements in *McIntyre* with regard to the effect of our adoption of a scheme of comparative fault on the remedy of contribution make it clear that we did not intend to deprive litigants of the right to pursue a claim for contribution in an appropriate case:

> [B]ecause a particular defendant will henceforth be liable only for the
> percentage of a plaintiff's damages occasioned by that defendant's

> negligence, situations where a defendant has paid more than his "share" of a judgment will no longer arise, and therefore the Uniform Contribution Among Tortfeasors Act, T.C.A. §29-11-101—106 (1980) *will no longer determine the apportionment of liability between co-defendants.*

Although we certainly did not intend in *McIntyre* to totally abolish the remedy of contribution, it is obvious from the above-quoted passage that we did intend that the "pro rata share of damages" approach of the UCATA,[4] which provides that the fault of the parties is not to be considered in determining each party's share of damages, should not continue to be utilized after the *McIntyre* decision was released. Because we intended to adopt a comprehensive scheme of comparative fault in *McIntyre*, and because the "pro rata share" approach set forth in the UCATA is in direct conflict with such a scheme, we felt it necessary to explicitly provide such guidance to the trial courts charged with the duty of trying tort cases in this state.

Although Safeco readily admits that the "pro rata share" approach to contribution is inconsistent with the principles of comparative fault, it contends that our substantial dictum regarding contribution in *McIntyre* should not apply to the retrial in this case for two basic reasons. First, Safeco contends that it had an expectation that it would be able to pursue a UCATA-type contribution claim against Adanac at the time it entered into the settlement agreement, that this expectation constituted an accrued or vested right, and that it is therefore impermissible to retroactively apply the principles of *McIntyre* so as to deprive it of that vested right. We are not convinced, however, that the retroactive application of *McIntyre* in fact serves to *deprive* Safeco of any "right," vested or otherwise. In fact, it is entirely possible that Safeco could actually obtain a better result under the principles of comparative fault than it could under the UCATA approach. Nor do we find persuasive Safeco's second argument—that our holding in *McIntyre*, while not totally abolishing the remedy of contribution, nevertheless constitutes an impermissible nullification of constitutionally valid legislation because it changed the method by which contribution is determined. Other jurisdictions that have both the UCATA and comparative fault schemes have interpreted the UCATA to require contribution to be made on the basis of the relative fault of the parties.

Therefore, we today reaffirm *McIntyre* and hold that actions for contribution that are to be tried or retried after May 4, 1992, are to be tried in accordance with the principles of comparative fault. Because this case unquestionably fits in this category, on retrial the jury will determine the percentage of fault attributable to each of the defendants, and contribution will be ordered accordingly.

---

4. Tenn. Code Ann. §29-11-103(1) (1980). Under the "pro rata share" approach, damages are apportioned on the basis of the number of defendants against whom liability has been established. For example, if two defendants are found to be liable, each is responsible for 50% of the damages; if three are found to be liable, each is responsible for 33.33%; and so on.

The judgment of the Court of Appeals is modified and the case remanded for proceedings consistent with this opinion.

O'BRIEN, C.J., and REID, ANDERSON and BIRCH, JJ., concur.

OPINION ON PETITION TO REHEAR

Both parties in this case have filed petitions for rehearing. Because this case marks the first time we have addressed the relationship between the Uniform Contribution Among Tortfeasors Act and our system of comparative fault, several procedural issues have arisen for which there is no guidance either in the Act or in our decisions dealing with comparative fault. Therefore, we grant the parties' petitions to rehear in order to provide this necessary guidance.

The petitions present three issues for our determination: (1) whether on retrial the jury may consider the fault of the plaintiff; (2) whether on retrial the jury may consider awarding punitive damages; and (3) since Tenn. Code Ann. §29-11-102(d) provides that a settling tortfeasor may not recover contribution from another tortfeasor for any amount of the settlement "in excess of what was reasonable," whether the jury should be told the amount of the settlement and asked to determine its reasonableness, or whether the jury should be asked to determine damages anew.

We are of the opinion that on the retrial of this case the jury should first be informed of the amount of the settlement, and then asked to determine if that settlement was reasonable according to the principles of comparative fault. The jury may consider the fault of the plaintiff Bervoets and the defendants Jackson (Safeco Insurance Company) and Adanac Inc. in making this determination. If the jury finds that the settlement amount was reasonable, it shall proceed to determine the percentage of fault attributable to each of the defendants, and contribution will be ordered accordingly. If however, the jury finds that the settlement was, according to the principles of comparative fault, "in excess of what was reasonable," this same jury will then determine the proper amount of damages; and the jury may consider the fault of plaintiff and the two defendants in making this determination. Once the jury has determined the proper amount of damages, it shall then determine the fault attributable to each of the defendants. If the jury finds that the third-party defendant was at fault, contribution shall be ordered from that defendant commensurate with its percentage of fault.

The jury may not consider punitive damages in either scenario. This action is for contribution; therefore, the defendant Jackson (Safeco) is essentially attempting to recover the amount paid by him in excess of his proportional share of liability. *See* Tenn. Code Ann. §29-11-102(b). Thus, once the jury finds how much of the settlement amount (if any) exceeds Jackson's proportional share of liability, his recovery is limited to that amount, as it is settled that a contribution plaintiff may only recover punitive damages from other tortfeasors if he has been held liable for punitive damages.

This case in remanded to the trial court for retrial in accordance with this opinion.

PREPARING FOR CLASS

1. This is a cause of action for contribution by Safeco against Adanac, dealing with issues that would have been litigated in the original lawsuit had neither of the defendants entered into a settlement with the plaintiff. As such, if there was evidence that Bervoets was contributorily negligent, it will be a point of emphasis by Adanac as it tries to limit how much liability the jury will assign to it. Adanac will, of course, also try to color Safeco's clients as the principle wrongdoers for similar reasons. Ultimately, the jury will decide who is at fault and to what extent when it is asked through its special verdict to allocate fault for the harm.

2. Distinguish the arguments in favor of abolishing joint and several liability and those offered (one way or the other) where the right of contribution is being addressed. In some respects the arguments overlap; they are, though, distinct issues. Here, the abolition of joint and several liability afforded Adanac a unique opportunity.

APPLYING THE LAW

Working with the scenario from the case (except, for purposes of simplifying the math, assume that Safeco had settled for $1.0 million), the jury assigns no fault to the plaintiff, 40 percent to Safeco, and 60 percent to Adanac. What, if anything, does Safeco recover in the contribution action? Now assume the jury assigns 20 percent to plaintiff, 40 percent to Safeco, and 40 percent to Adanac. Same question as before.

INCREASING YOUR UNDERSTANDING

1. *Right to contribution.* "Where two or more persons become jointly or severally liable in tort for the same injury to person or property or for the same wrongful act, there is a right of contribution among them even though judgment has not been recovered against all or any of them." Uniform Contribution Among Tortfeasors Act §1(a) (1955). This right to seek contribution is triggered once the party seeking contribution has covered by payment of an obligation owed by another, and liability for contribution is limited to the amount paid in excess of the party's

proportionate liability to the plaintiff. The party from whom contribution is sought is required to pay no more than what would have been owed to the plaintiff.

2. *Not much "safe" about Safeco.* Ordinarily a defendant who settles has no claim of contribution from a non-settling defendant, as in most cases a settling defendant does not agree to cover the obligation of the non-settling defendant. For example, had Safeco settled and the agreement only allowed for a release in favor of Safeco, Adanac would have remained exposed to liability to the plaintiffs, so Safeco would not have been allowed to seek recovery through contribution from Adanac. So what went into Safeco's decision to settle the case on both its and Adanac's behalf? Initially, Safeco had a settlement number in mind that it was willing to pay to avoid the risk associated with the jury returning a much larger number. Once the settlement discussion entered into the range of reasonableness, both Safeco and the plaintiffs had to iron out the other parameters, i.e., who would be released. At the time it settled, the "pro rata" law allowed for Safeco to recover 50 percent of the amount it paid no matter how much fault would have been allocated to Adanac. What Safeco could not have anticipated was the *McIntyre* decision, which, depending on what happens at retrial, may significantly increase or decrease what it recoups from Adanac.

3. There is a divide over whether intentional tortfeasors will be allowed to seek contribution from those they are in joint liability with. The most recent version of the Uniform Contribution Among Tortfeasors Act (1955, §1(c)) denies the right to those who acted intentionally, which is further described as acting in a willful or wanton fashion. The Restatement (Third) of Torts §23 ("Apportionment Liability") comment l allows for it.

Yellow Cab Co. of D.C. v. Dreslin
181 F.2d 626 (D.C. Cir. 1950)

Proctor, Circuit Judge.

The question here concerns contribution between tortfeasors where the judgment creditor is the wife of the tortfeasor against whom contribution is sought.

A taxicab of appellant (hereinafter called "Cab Co."), driven by its agent, and an automobile, driven by appellee (hereafter called "Dreslin"), collided. Dreslin's wife and others in his car were injured. They sued the Cab Co. for damages. Dreslin joined with them, claiming for loss of consortium, medical expenses for Mrs. Dreslin and damages to his automobile. Among its defenses, the Cab Co. pleaded contributory negligence of Dreslin. It also cross-claimed against him for damages to the taxicab and for contribution for any sums recovered by the other plaintiffs against it. The jury's verdict established the collision to have been caused by concurrent negligent operation of the two cars. Accordingly judgments for varying amounts were entered in favor of all plaintiffs except Dreslin. In addition a declaratory judgment was entered allowing the Cab Co. contribution against Dreslin upon the several judgments except that of Mrs. Dreslin. This was disallowed because, as the Court held, "the right to contribution arises from a joint liability," and as Dreslin was not liable in tort to his wife, there was no joint liability between him and the Cab Co. as to her. This appeal is confined to that single question.

We agree with the conclusion of the trial court. Neither husband nor wife is liable for tortious acts by one against the other. That is the common law rule. It prevails today in the District of Columbia unaffected by 30 D.C. Code (1940) §208 (Mar. 3, 1901, 31 Stat. 1374, ch. 854, Sec. 1155; May 28, 1926, 44 Stat. 676, ch. 419).

The right of contribution arises out of a common liability. The rule "hinges on the doctrine that general principles of justice require that in the case of a common obligation, the discharge of it by one of the obligors without proportionate payment from the other, gives the latter an advantage to which he is not equitably entitled." George's Radio, Inc., v. Capital Transit Co., 1942, 75 U.S. App. D.C. 187, 189, 126 F.2d 219, 221. Contribution, then, depends upon joint liability. An injured party plaintiff in the suit from which a right of contribution develops must have had a cause of action against the party from whom contribution is sought. Here there was no liability by Dreslin to his wife,- no right to action against him and the Cab Co., hence nothing to which a right of contribution could attach.

The argument that it would be inequitable to allow Mrs. Dreslin to be "enriched" at the sole expense of the Cab Co., permitting her husband, equally at fault, to escape any of the burden, overlooks the fact that preservation of domestic peace and felicity is the policy upon which the rule of immunity between husband and wife is based. The judgment is Affirmed.

PREPARING FOR CLASS

1. Recall the various forms of immunity and the rational for recognizing them.

2. Distinguish between Mr. Dreslin's right to recover and his potential liability to the other plaintiff's and Yellow Cab, and consider how his presence as a defendant influences the disposition of the lawsuit.

APPLYING THE LAW

Employee is injured on the job by a defective product manufactured by company. Employee initially receives workers' compensation benefits from employer and later sues company. Who is liable to whom?

INCREASING YOUR UNDERSTANDING

1. *The liability/immunity door swings both ways.* The right to contribution exists only from a party who shares *common liability* with the defendant seeking it. As such, if the law (or facts) denies liability to the plaintiff as against a defendant, the defendant is not allowed to be otherwise held liable by way of contribution claimed by another.

2. *Preserving the right to contribution.* Had Mr. Dreslin not joined the suit as a plaintiff, the Federal Rules of Civil Procedure (Rule 14 (a)(1)) would have allowed Yellow Cab to bring him in as a third party for contribution purposes: "A defending party may, as third-party plaintiff, serve a summons and complaint on a nonparty who is or may be liable to it for all or part of the claim against it." In most circumstances, the plaintiff would have initially sued all potentially responsible parties but where the plaintiff has chosen not to, a defendant may.

3. What becomes of the immune party's liability? It depends. Many courts allow for "all parties" responsible for plaintiff's injuries to be included on the verdict form; this includes those who never were sued for whatever reason, as well as those who were sued but later found to be immune from liability. If fault is eventually to allocated to an immune party, courts have chosen from one of three rules: (1) Apportion the immune party's fault as among both plaintiff(s) and defendants(s); (2) Apportion the immune party's fault among the defendant(s) only; or (3) Apportion the fault among the plaintiff(s) only.

National Health Laboratories, Inc. v. Ahmadi
596 A.2d 555 (D.C. 1991)

STEADMAN, Associate Judge:
The plaintiff in this litigation suffered permanent paralysis as a result of misdiagnosis of her ailment. She brought a malpractice action against the two appellants, one the medical group that was treating the plaintiff and the other a laboratory which improperly conducted a blood test. A jury found both appellants negligent. The principal issue in these consolidated appeals is whether the trial court erred in refusing to hold either appellant solely responsible for the judgment, either by way of indemnification or superseding cause as a matter of law, and instead imposing on each appellant an equal, fifty percent contribution to the judgment. We affirm.

I

On June 30, 1986, Pari Ahmadi, the plaintiff below and appellee in the instant appeals, came to the Neurology Center (the "NC") with a history of numbness in her lower extremities and other symptoms. She was about thirty years old. Her first NC physician, Dr. Elliott Wilner, performed an examination which led him tentatively to conclude that Ahmadi suffered from a spinal cord lesion caused either by (1) vitamin B-12 deficiency; (2) multiple sclerosis ("MS"); or (3) mass lesion from a tumor or ruptured disk.

To narrow the diagnosis, Wilner ordered various tests, including a vitamin B-12 level test to rule out B-12 deficiency. Although Wilner was quickly able to exclude the tumor or ruptured disk alternatives, he could not so easily exclude either MS or B-12 deficiency by the other tests that the NC administered. Since the NC did not have the capability to perform the vitamin B-12 level test on Ahmadi, blood was drawn on July 7 and sent to the National Health Laboratories (the "NHL") for such a test. The NHL conducted the B-12 test on July 8. Because of an admitted error in the testing methodology, the NHL technicians incorrectly reached a normal-range finding, which was accordingly reported to Dr. Wilner and the NC on July 11.

On July 8, Ahmadi had been admitted to George Washington University Hospital ("GW") by another NC physician, Dr. Phillip Pulaski, for further workups due to increased symptomatology. On admission, a GW resident ordered a second vitamin B-12 level test, unaware of the first apparently normal result which had not yet been reported to Wilner and the NC. The hospital staff never carried out the new test, and Pulaski testified that he relied on the normal-range result of the NHL's test to rule out B-12 deficiency; he thereby made the probable diagnosis of MS. Pulaski did admit, however, that her symptoms were consistent not only with MS but also with B-12 deficiency.

Ahmadi marginally improved with outpatient treatment by the NC's Dr. Richard Edelson from the end of July to November, when she worsened again. The NC again ruled out vitamin B-12 deficiency without conducting a new B-12 level test, instead suggesting risky drug treatment for MS. Finally, in February, while on a trip to see her sister in California, Ahmadi suffered a serious bladder infection for which she went to see Dr. Bruce Spertell at Stanford University Medical Center. Over the next few days, she became much weaker, and, on the verge of paralysis, went to Stanford on an emergency basis, again seeing Dr. Spertell. Spertell diagnosed B-12 deficiency even before the results of a new B-12 test came back at a dangerously low level. Ahmadi has remained paralyzed from the waist down ever since.

Ahmadi brought suit against the NC for negligence and medical malpractice; against the NHL, for negligent failure to perform the B-12 test properly and for falsely reporting a normal result; and against GW for negligence in failing to complete a second B-12 test and failure to diagnose. The jury exonerated GW, but found for Ahmadi as against the NC and NHL, rendering a $10 million verdict against both. Previously filed cross-claims for contribution and indemnity by each liable defendant against the other were argued in a bench hearing. The trial court ruled that while each was entitled to contribution of 50% from the other, neither was entitled to indemnification under District law. The NC has since settled its share of the judgment with Ahmadi.

II

In its appeal, the NC challenges the trial court's refusal to order the NHL to indemnify it for its half share of liability for Ahmadi's injuries. The NC argues that indemnification by the NHL is required as a matter of law.

At common law, there existed no right of contribution between joint tortfeasors who contributed to a single injury, and until the passage of specific statutes about twenty years ago, the great majority of American courts followed this rule. The District of Columbia, however, was one of nine American jurisdictions to come to the contrary conclusion without legislation. W. Prosser, D. Dobbs, R. Keeton, & D. Owen, Prosser and Keeton on The Law of Torts §50, at 336-37 (5th ed. 1984) (hereafter "Prosser"). In *Knell v. Feltman*, 85 U.S. App. D.C. 22, 174 F.2d 662 (1949), the court rejected the common law rule and permitted contribution in such circumstances.

Thus, ordinarily, when two tortfeasors jointly contribute to harm to a plaintiff, both are potentially liable to the injured party for the entire harm. As between themselves, however, through the principle of contribution, they share equally in satisfaction of the judgment. Such equal contribution by the NHL and NC was what the trial court ordered here, from which they both appeal.

Under certain circumstances, however, a trial court may require that one of the two tortfeasors bear, as against the other, sole responsibility for satisfaction of the judgment. One of the common bases for such a right of indemnity is the existence of an express contractual duty to indemnify. [6] Another is where one is held responsible solely by operation of law because of a relation to the original wrongdoer, such as the liability of an employer for acts of his employee or an owner of an automobile for acts of the driver. Likewise, one who is wrongfully directed or induced by another to do the negligent act may be entitled to indemnity from the other.

It may be seen from these examples that the right to indemnity depends essentially upon the relationship between the parties, which may be expressly contractual or may be such that an obligation to indemnify, in a sense quasi-contractual in nature, [7] may be fairly imposed. So it is that while indeed a right to indemnity may extend to those personally at fault, it is granted in such circumstances normally only where "a duty to indemnify may . . . be implied 'out of a relationship between the parties,' to prevent a result 'which is regarded as unjust or unsatisfactory.'" *East Penn Mfg. Co. v. Pineda*, 578 A.2d 1113, 1126 (D.C. 1990), quoting from *Myco, supra* note 6, 565 A.2d at 297. As noted in *Myco*, this concept in the main "is based on the well-established theory that if one [tortfeasor] breaches a duty owed to another and the breach causes

---

6. Since neither party disputes that "there exists no such contractual provision in the case before us, we need not further discuss the issue."*Myco v. Super Concrete*, 565 A.2d 293, 297 (D.C. 1989).

7. "Indemnity . . . sounds in contract and is founded not on either party's obligation to the victim, but on the indemnitor's obligation to the indemnitee (distinct from their coincident obligations to the victim)."*Eagle-Picher Industries, Inc. v. United States*, 937 F.2d 625, 635 (D.C. Cir. 1991).

injury, the former should compensate the latter." 565 A.2d at 298. "In order to establish the right to this particular type of implied indemnity, the obligation must arise out of a specific duty of defined nature—separate from the injury to the [plaintiff]—owed to the third party . . . ," and there must be evidence of a special legal relationship between the tortfeasors. 565 A.2d at 299. The fact that one joint tortfeasor was more or less actively negligent than the other does not alone warrant indemnification. We have rejected the "active/passive" theory of implied indemnity.

We have recently upheld an award of implied indemnity flowing from a relationship between the parties involving justified reliance where the joint tortfeasors stood in a manufacturer-retailer relationship. There, we found an implied duty on the manufacturer of a battery to indemnify the retailer where the retailer's "only fault" was to rely on the manufacturer's skill and experience in its duplication of the wording of the manufacturer's warning label.

The NC contends that the same principle entitles it to indemnification. It argues that the NHL "had a critical relationship with the [NC] which preexisted its negligence, and which gave rise to a duty . . . to render accurate, complete information regarding Pari Ahmadi's blood test results" to the NC. The NC then argues that the NHL breached this duty to it by failing both to provide a correct test result and to warn it that the test result was unreliable where its employees knowingly failed to follow proper testing protocols.

We think the trial court was correct in rejecting these arguments and concluding that whatever the duty or relationship of the NHL to the NC may have been initially, over time the NC could no longer rely reasonably on the test result. As the trial court found, the NC pursued a "misdiagnosis that initially perhaps was a difficult one . . . but which over the passage of time, perhaps soon after the report of the test from the [NHL], should have . . . caused [it] to doubt the accuracy of the laboratory result in favor of the clinical symptoms which were consistent with vitamin B-12 deficiency . . ." and "the [NC] doctors [were] independently negligent and actively negligent in failing to reopen the whole question of what the correct diagnosis was and to pursue that new inquiry . . . by ordering another . . . B-12 test." Certainly the different NC neurologists could at least collectively be expected to rely on their own clinical impressions as much as on the expertise of the testers where the B-12 test result itself represented only one piece of the diagnostic mosaic according to the standard of care of the profession.[11]

Neither *East Penn* nor *Myco* entitles the NC to indemnity here. In *Myco*, an employer assertedly had modified certain equipment furnished by Myco which resulted in injury to an employee. We rejected the concept that the

---

11. As counsel for the NHL argued at oral argument, the ongoing and lengthy nature of the NC's negligence distinguishes this case from one where, for example, an improper testing procedure missed the presence of a severe bacterial infection and the patient thereby died before the doctors could diagnose and treat the illness from clinical or other indicators. In such a situation, the doctors may have relied reasonably on the laboratory's duty to provide a correct result (or inform them otherwise), assuming, of course, that the clinical symptoms of the patient were consistent with something other than the wrongly diagnosed illness.

user of a product has a responsibility to a manufacturer to use the product in such a way as not to bring liability upon the manufacturer, and that the duty of proper care by the user, the employer in that case, extends solely to his employees. 565 A.2d at 300. That case, involving an unsuccessful attempt by the prior joint tortfeasor to obtain indemnity from the subsequent tortfeasor, implicated the reverse of the NC's efforts here.

East Penn does involve a situation in which a subsequent tortfeasor sought indemnity but is clearly distinguishable. The sole involvement of the retailer there was to rely upon the manufacturer's warning label. It had no independent reason to suspect error or impetus to investigate further. Here, the NC was an active and ongoing participant, indeed the chief participant, in the effort to diagnose a mysterious ailment. The NHL's negligent test was only a part of the overall mosaic of the NC's activity. As the trial court reasoned, while the NC may have initially relied on the NHL's duty to provide it with accurate test results, the NC could not properly have relied on these results over the entire seven-month period. Any "independent duty" that the NHL may have had to the NC was thus dissipated for purposes of seeking indemnity.[13]

The trial court quite properly denied the NC's indemnification claim against the NHL. We now turn to the arguments made by the NHL on appeal.

III.

Any indemnity claim by the NHL against the NC must be judged by the same principles applicable to the NC's like claim against the NHL and found wanting for substantially the same reasons. The NHL as a prior tortfeasor can establish no duty imposed on the NC arising out of the relationship. The NC's responsibility ran to the plaintiff to render her competent medical service. There can be no legitimate claim that the NC had a separate duty to the NHL to discover that the NHL had made an error in its blood test. As we said in *Myco, supra* note 6, "imposition of such a duty would stand 'indemnity on its head.'" 565 A.2d at 300 (citation omitted). Moreover, given that indemnification is founded in principles of equity, we can find no difference in the relative fault of the NHL and the NC of such a "kind" or "quality" as to have required the trial court to make the NC bear the entire cost of their dual negligence.

Perhaps realizing that it would not be able to succeed on an indemnification argument, the NHL instead stresses an argument that the damages should be

---

13. Appellant also argues that the trial court's factual findings were clearly erroneous because the court (1) failed to address "independent duty," (2) could not locate in time specifically when the negligence of the NC occurred or which NC doctor was negligent, and (3) erred in finding the doctors "actively negligent." The first two issues are essentially those of law, and were adequately dealt with. There was ample evidence to support the trial court's findings that a "tandem" tort mutually resulted in the harm, and that the NC was "actively" negligent.

"apportioned" as between itself and the NC favorably to it. On the facts here, this is essentially an argument for adopting comparative negligence, which as already mentioned has never been the law in the District.

In sum, we find no ground for reversal in the trial court's ultimate conclusion that "based on the necessary facts decided by the jury by which . . . I am bound," this was a "classic case for contribution between joint tortfeasors." We uphold the trial court's award of 50% contribution by each appellant, and in all other respects affirm the judgment appealed from.

Affirmed.

PREPARING FOR CLASS

Both defendants are requesting that the other be responsible for the judgment rendered against them. Note how the argument is common with those made with respect to vicarious liability. Also note the distinction between contribution and indemnity.

APPLYING THE LAW

Company manufactures and distributes above-ground pools. The distribution is through dealers who have exclusive rights to distribute the pools. The agreement requires the dealers to place warning labels on the pools at the time of installation so their placement can be tailored to the particulars of the purchaser. Dealer fails to place a "do not dive, shallow area" warning on pool, and subsequently there is an injury leading to a products liability failure-to-warn claim against both the manufacturer and the dealer. Both parties brings crossclaims seeking indemnity. How should the court rule?

INCREASING YOUR UNDERSTANDING

1. Parties seeking indemnity are requesting that another step in and assume its liability. As the principle case indicates, often parties in contract with one another will include indemnifying as part of the expected performances. Absent a contractual provision, courts remain free to require indemnification where fairness and equity require that they do so. Indemnity, therefore, "shifts the loss from one tortfeasor who has been compelled to pay it to the shoulders of another who should bear it instead." Suvada v. White Motor Co., 32 Ill. 2d 612, 210 N.E.2d 182 (1965).

2. *Distinguishing contribution and indemnity.* Conceptually, contribution and indemnity are rooted in a similar command; one party is requesting

that another shoulder a responsibility forced on it. The requests, however, differ in one key respect: A party seeking indemnity is asking that another take on the full obligation that has been (or is attempting to be) forced on it, while contribution is a request for reimbursement measured by other's fault that the party requesting contribution has previously discharged. In its simplest form, indemnification can be seen as a request coming from an innocent whose liability is solely predicated on the wrongdoing of another. So the distributor of a defectively designed product seeks indemnity from the product manufacturer upon being sued, and the employer who is held liable through vicarious liability has the right to claim indemnity from the employee who actually did the injuring. See Restatement (Second) of Torts §886B (2)(a), (d) (1979).

C.   CONSEQUENCE OF SETTLEMENTS ON REMAINING LIABILITY

Patricia C. Roland v. Ronald A. Bernstein, M.D.
171 Ariz. 96 (1991), 828 P.2d 1237 (Ariz. Ct. App. 1991)

LIVERMORE, Chief Judge.

Plaintiff brought a medical malpractice complaint against Ronald Bernstein, a neurosurgeon, his professional corporation, Desert Neurosurgery, Joseph Marcinkowski, an anesthesiologist, and Tucson General Hospital. Tucson General and Marcinkowski settled the claim for $700,000 each and the case proceeded to trial against Bernstein and his corporation. The jury found plaintiff's damages to be $1,965,000 and the degree of fault to be 47% for Bernstein, 28% for Marcinkowski, and 25% for Tucson General Hospital. The question then arose whether under A.R.S. §12-2504 the amount Bernstein had to pay should be reduced by the amount of the pre-existing settlements. The trial court held that it should and thus entered a judgment for $565,000 rather than for $923,550 (47% of $1,965,000). This appeal followed. We reverse.

When more than one defendant caused plaintiff's injuries the rule originally was that each such defendant was liable for the whole injury, that recovery against one eliminated the claim against the others, and that no right of contribution existed among defendants. See generally W. Prosser & W. Keeton, Torts §§46-52 (5th ed. 1984). Over time the rigor of these rules was relaxed, permitting settlement by one of the defendants without eliminating rights against the others, so long as double recovery did not occur, and contribution among tortfeasors. That result was accomplished in Arizona by passage of the Uniform Contribution Among Tortfeasors Act, A.R.S. §12-2501 et seq.

Section 12-2504, at issue in this case, provides that a settlement with "one of two or more persons liable in tort for the same injury . . . does not discharge any of the other tortfeasors from liability for the injury . . . but it reduces the claim against the others" by the amount of the settlement. If that section were applicable here the trial judge's ruling would be correct because the $1,400,000 settlement would be deducted from the $1,965,000 verdict to arrive at a $565,000 judgment against Bernstein.

We conclude, however, that §12-2504 does not apply because it was enacted as part of a statute permitting contribution between defendants liable for the entire amount of damages caused by the concurrent negligence of each of them. It was not designed for this case which was tried under A.R.S. §12-2506, a more recently enacted statute. Section 12-2506 abolished joint and several liability, limiting recovery against any defendant to that percentage of a plaintiff's total injuries representing that defendant's degree of fault. Because recovery is so limited, contribution can never occur. Section 12-2504, passed as part of a statute regulating contribution, therefore, is not, obviously, applicable to a situation where there is no right to contribution.

This result can be easily squared with the statutory language. Section 12-2504 applies when "two or more persons [are] liable in tort for the same injury." Section 12-2506, on the contrary, provides that "the liability of each defendant for damages is several only and is not joint." In short, each defendant is liable only for the portion of the injury he caused, not the whole injury; no two are liable for the same injury.

In addition, we believe that it would be anomalous to give the benefit of an advantageous settlement, not to the plaintiff who negotiated it, but to the non-settling tortfeasor. Had plaintiff made a disadvantageous settlement, she would have borne that consequence because her recovery against Bernstein would have been limited to $923,550. At a minimum, symmetry requires that if the disadvantage of settlement is hers so ought the advantage be. Beyond that, we see no reason why a non-settling tortfeasor ought to escape the liability that is his by reason of the faulty assessment of probabilities by a settling tortfeasor. Indeed, such a rule might well discourage settlement by the last tortfeasor on the reasoning that his exposure is limited to his degree of fault and even that might be reduced by reason of pre-existing settlements. These considerations have led most courts considering this question to apply the rule we are adopting.

The judgment is reversed and the matter remanded for the entry of a judgment in plaintiff's favor for $923,550 effective December 19, 1990, with interest on the unpaid balance from that date until paid.

PREPARING FOR CLASS

1. Most lawsuits are disposed of partially or entirely before trial, with settlements forming the basis for much of the pretrial dispositions. There

exist various motivations for settling; perhaps the most compelling is the desire to buy peace of mind going forward. In addition, complex tort cases require substantial funding to prosecute, so a party who is eager and willing to settle might assist in providing the funding necessary to take the case to trial against those not willing or interested in settling.

2. Understand why settlements are not subject to the collateral source rule.

3. Consider how courts might fashion rules that encourage settling.

APPLYING THE LAW

Plaintiff settles with *D1* before trial for $50,000 and proceeds to trial against *D2*. After trial, the jury returns the following verdict: Damages award of $500,000; fault allocation, *P* 10 percent, *D1* 40 percent, and *D2* 50 percent. What does *D2* pay? How much does plaintiff recover in total?

INCREASING YOUR UNDERSTANDING

1. *Can we make a deal?* Settlements reflect a compromise: Plaintiffs receive something from tortfeasors (typically money, but might also involve promises to cease offending conduct, apologies, etc.) and the defendant is released from liability. Under the common law, an over-compensation-averse judiciary viewed a release of a single tortfeasor as a release of all others who potentially were liable to the plaintiff, though that may not have been the intention of the settling parties. The notion was that the plaintiff should only be "satisfied" once; multiple "satisfactions" would over-compensate the plaintiff and be a waste of both societal and judicial resources. Many courts and legislators eventually viewed the "single satisfaction" mandate as too harsh and inflexible, and now most courts will determine the consequence of settling by the intent of the settling parties. In other words, if the plaintiff only intended to release from liability the party named in the settlement agreement, that will be the court's construction, allowing the plaintiff to seek additional recovery against unnamed tortfeasors.

2. In addition to being released from liability (past and future) to the plaintiff, the great majority of settlement rules protect the settling party by disallowing contribution claims by other tortfeasors, with some conditioning this protection on the settlement having been made in "good faith." Furthermore, settlements are often styled as "confidential" (amounts paid are not to be revealed, only fact that suit has been settled can be disclosed publicly), require that plaintiff indemnify the settling party against third-party claims (contribution by other tortfeasors or

subrogation by parties who have previously provided compensation to plaintiff for injuries related to the incidents that gave rise to the claim in the first), and as stated above, require upon accepting payment that the plaintiff release the settling party from all liability related to the incidents that gave rise to the claim. This includes liability for harm that had manifested itself, as well as harm that hadn't.

3. *Liability consequences for non-settling parties.* Courts have generally adopted one of two approaches when addressing the effect that a settlement will have on remaining liability issues—"pro rata" or "pro tanto"—with the majority of courts embracing a form of the pro rata rule.

   a. *Pro rata.* Pursuant to this rule, the consequence of settling is determined per something, either per party or per fault allocation. For example, in a pro rata jurisdiction, fault may be allocated evenly among all defendants (if two defendants, each is 50% liable without regard to specific facts) or as determined by the jury's allocation. Upon settling, the plaintiff is viewed as discharging or satisfying the pro rata share of liability assigned to the settling party. This moots any consideration of contribution as no non-settling tortfeasor is required to pay any portion of the settling party's share. Most jurisdictions follow this rule, which, as illustrated in *Ahmadi*, places the burden of a bad settlement (and thus "discourages sweetheart deals") on the plaintiff but advantages the plaintiff who makes a good one.

   b. *Pro tanto.* Under the pro tanto rule (rejected in *Ahmadi*), the settlement reduces any remaining claims against non-settling parties by the settlement amount, with the non-settling parties required to make up the difference regardless of their allocated fault. Thus there is potential for non-settling parties to pay more than their "fair share," which is why some who follow this rule allow for contribution from the settling party.

Chapter 18

Wrongful Death and Survival

———————————

Under the common law, a cause of action against a tortfeasor was extinguished when the injured person died. The English were the first to make any significant inroads into this doctrine with Lord Campbell's Act, which established a cause of action by statute. American states followed, passing legislation in each state to recognize a cause of action even after death. These statutes were often narrowly construed but did establish a legal action for the wronged decedent.

For the victim of a tort who dies as a result of the tort, there are two causes of action. Wrongful death statutes create an action for surviving relatives who suffer loss as a result of the decedent's death. The recovery in these cases belongs to the survivors, not the estate of the decedent, so the proceeds of the action are not available to creditors of the decedent. Survival actions, on the other hand, continue the decedent's case against the tortfeasor for loss during the decedent's life. Survival actions address the common law rule that lawsuits die with the decedent. Under the survival statutes, the decedent's case for loss during his lifetime continues but the decedent's estate is substituted for the decedent. The recovery under the survival statutes goes to the estate and is, therefore, available to the creditors after distribution.

Hypothetical

Thomas and his wife, Susan, were driving to the grocery store on Saturday morning. Susan was driving the car when an oncoming truck of General Corporation crossed the centerline by about a foot. Thomas yelled to Susan and tried to grab the wheel to steer away from the truck but Susan was seeking a different station on the radio so she did not react at all. The truck hit the left front of Thomas's and Susan's car spinning it down the road and into the ditch. Susan was fine after the accident but Thomas sustained substantial injuries. Thomas was taken to the hospital where doctors tried to save him for over three weeks, but he finally died. Thomas incurred $50,000 of medical bills, lost $3,000 of wages, and lost a car worth $10,000.

Susan comes to your law office to discuss filing an action against General Corporation. The police have investigated this accident and believe that the General truck driver was 70 percent at fault, Susan was 20 percent at fault, and Thomas was 10 percent at fault. Susan says that Thomas left a brother and two parents surviving him. Susan thinks she may now be pregnant with Thomas's child. Thomas was employed making $1,000 per week.

Write a memo about how to proceed with this case.

A.   SURVIVAL/WRONGFUL DEATH ACTIONS

Gandy v. United States
437 F. Supp. 2d 1085 (D. Ariz. 2006)

TEILBORG, District Judge.
Pending before this Court is Defendant's Motion in Limine ("Motion") regarding loss of future earnings. The Court now rules on this motion.

I. BACKGROUND

On June 27, 2003, Sally Robbins ("Decedent") filed a Complaint in the United States District Court for the District of Arizona. Ms. Robbins brought the Complaint under the Federal Torts Claims Act ("FTCA"), alleging medical negligence on the part of the Defendant, United States of America. The Complaint alleged that Ms. Robbins suffered permanent injury to her pancreas and resulting pain and suffering, loss of wages, medical expenses, and permanent physical disability due to an endoscopic retrograde cholangiopancreatogram ("ERCP") negligently performed by the Veterans Administration Medical Center on September 9, 1999.

On May 22, 2005, approximately three weeks before trial, Ms. Robbins passed away. The medical examiner concluded that Ms. Robbins' death was the result of a toxic level of combined prescription medications, some of which Ms. Robbins was taking because of her pancreatic problems. Ms. Robbins is survived by her children, Renee and Paul Montz, as well as her parents, Darrell and Helen Robbins. Troy Gandy ("Plaintiff") was subsequently appointed as the personal representative of Sally Robbins' estate with the consent of her surviving children.

On February 14, 2006, this Court issued the Order granting Plaintiff's Motion to Amend Complaint. The Order ruled that Troy Gandy, Personal

Representative of Ms. Robbins' estate, may bring a survival claim on the estate's behalf. The Amended Complaint, filed on February 21, 2006, includes a survival claim and a wrongful death claim on behalf of all statutory beneficiaries.

The Amended Complaint alleges wrongful death damages including loss of Decedent's companionship, comfort, and guidance; and anguish, sorrow, stress, mental suffering, grief, shock, and other recoverable damages. The Amended Complaint also alleges economic damages for Ms. Robbins' lost earnings in the amount of $522,117.00 under the survival statute.

Defendant has moved to limit all evidence in the survival claim relating to loss of Decedent's future earnings to the amount that Decedent actually lost between the time of her injury, September 9, 1999, and her death, May 22, 2005.

II. Legal Standard and Analysis

The Court will address the pending motion to limit the time frame for economic damages recoverable under Arizona's survival statute. This is a medical malpractice case under the FTCA. Under the FTCA, tort liability of the United States is determined "in accordance with the law of the place where the act or omission occurred." In this case, the substantive law of Arizona controls.

A wrongful death claim and a survival claim are separate claims arising from the same incident. Barragan v. Superior Court of Pima County, 12 Ariz. App. 402, 404, 470 P.2d 722, 724 (1970) (holding that a claim under the survival statute permits recovery for the wrong to the injured person, and the wrongful death statute confines recovery to the loss suffered by the beneficiaries). Remedies provided in the survival and wrongful death statutes are not mutually exclusive.

The survival statute provides that:

> Every cause of action, except a cause of action for damages for breach of promise to marry, seduction, libel, slander, separate maintenance, alimony, loss of consortium or invasion of the right of privacy, shall survive the death of the person entitled thereto or liable therefore, and may be asserted by or against the personal representative of such person, provided that upon the death of the person injured, damages for pain and suffering of such injured person shall not be allowed.

A.R.S. §14-3110. The survival statute provides for recovery of damages sustained by the decedent from the time of injury until her death. The claim passes from the decedent to the personal representative, and becomes an asset of the estate. The purpose of the survival statute is "to prevent the tortfeasor's liability from ceasing upon the injured person's death." The survival statute, does not create a new claim, but rather allows the personal representative to enforce the decedent's claim.

The wrongful death statute provides that:

> When death of a person is caused by wrongful act, neglect or default, and the act, neglect or default is such as would, if death had not ensued, have entitled the party injured to maintain an action to recover damages in respect thereof, then, and in every such case, the person who or the corporation which would have been liable if death had not ensued shall be liable to an action for damages, notwithstanding the death of the person injured, and although the death was caused under such circumstances as amount in law to murder in the first or second degree or manslaughter.

A.R.S. §12-611. A wrongful death claim is neither continuation of the decedent's claim, nor continuation of the survival claim. A wrongful death claim compensates statutory beneficiaries for their injuries, as opposed to a survival claim which compensates the decedent's estate. When both survival and wrongful death claims are asserted, recovery cannot be duplicative.

To avoid duplication of the damages, Defendant has moved to exclude evidence of economic damages for loss of Decedent's future earnings in the survival claim. While enumerating which causes of action do not survive the death of the plaintiff, the survival statute is silent as to which compensatory damages, including damages for loss of future earnings, are allowed. Further, there is no Arizona case addressing loss of future earnings in a survival claim. In support of Defendant's Motion requesting that damages for Decedent's future earnings in the survival claim be limited, many jurisdictions, as well as the Restatement (Second) of Torts, find that recovery in survival claims is limited to damages accruing before the injured person's death.

In its Motion, Defendant cites several jurisdictions which hold that state survival statutes do not entitle beneficiaries to recover damages for decedent's loss of future earnings. Many jurisdictions hold that when damages are recoverable under both survival and wrongful death statutes, the damages recoverable under the survival statute do not include the loss of decedent's future earnings.

Defendant cites Jones v. Flood, 351 Md. 120, 716 A.2d 285 (1998) as evidence of limited recovery in survival statutes. The Maryland Supreme Court in *Jones* addressed the issue that is presently before this Court, and held that when a statute is silent as to the recovery of loss of decedent's future earnings, then the recovery will be limited to the time of injury through the time of death. The Maryland Supreme Court based its ruling on the interaction between the wrongful death and survival statutes, and stated "'[t]he wrongful death damages begin with the death of the person wronged. The survival claim damages end with the death of the person wronged. There is no overlap or duplication of damages.'" The court's rationale in *Jones* is similar to the Arizona Supreme Court's interpretation of claims under Arizona wrongful death and survival statutes. To prevent double recovery under the wrongful death and survival statutes, recovery for Decedent's loss of future earnings in the survival claim is limited to the time between her injury, September 9, 1999, to her death, May 22, 2005.

In the absence of prior decisions or authority to the contrary, the Arizona Supreme Court consistently follows the Restatement of Torts where applicable. The Restatement of Torts supports granting Defendant's Motion. The Restatement does not allow the estate in a survival claim to recover decedent's loss of future earnings. Restatement (Second) of Torts §926(a) (1979) (providing an exception that limits "damages for loss or impairment of earning capacity ... to harms suffered before the death [of injured person]"). The policy behind this limitation is to prevent overlapping recovery between wrongful death and survival statutes. Loss of future income is recoverable under Arizona's wrongful death statute, therefore in order to prevent double recovery, as a policy matter, damages for loss of earnings in the survival matter must be limited to those incurred between Decedent's injury and her death.

The Court grants Defendant's Motion to limit all evidence concerning the loss of Decedent's earnings to the amount that Decedent actually lost between the time of her injury and her death for purposes of the survival claim. Accordingly,

PREPARING FOR CLASS

1. Assume that actions under the survival statute and the wrongful death statute have been filed as a result of the decedent's death in an automobile accident. Which cause of action will claim the following damages?

    a. Damages to the decedent's car.

    b. Decedent's loss of anticipated earnings after death.

    c. Decedent's medical bills.

    d. Decedent's funeral bills.

2. The decedent's creditors have filed claims against the estate. Which of the above items of damages may be used to pay creditors?

UNDERSTANDING THE LAW

1. The Michigan Wrongful Death Act is typical of the wrongful death statutes across the United States. It provides that the wrongful death cause of action shall be brought by the personal representative of the estate. Therefore, the plaintiff must first go to the probate court and have someone appointed as personal representative of the estate, and then must prove at the trial that the probate court has appointed a personal

representative and that that person is bringing the cause of action on behalf of the decedent's relatives. (M.C.L.A. 600.2922).

2. The Michigan Wrongful Death Act provides that the spouse, children, descendants, parents, brothers and sisters, the children of the deceased's spouse, and devisees under the will are all entitled to notice of the wrongful death action and, therefore, to claim part of the proceeds of the lawsuit. (M.C.L.A. 600.2922). Notice who is not entitled to notice or to share in the proceeds, i.e., unmarried couples who have been living together. Unless they are provided for in the will, they do not have a right to notice or hearing about the distribution of the proceeds.

3. The Michigan Wrongful Death Act provides that the personal representative of the estate shall file a petition with the court for authority to distribute the proceeds of the estate and shall give notice to all the named beneficiaries set forth in the statute. (M.C.L.A. 600.3924). Most of the time, the family meets to agree on how the proceeds shall be distributed and the judge approves of the family's plan of distribution.

4. The Michigan Wrongful Death Act is a little different than most wrongful death statutes in providing that the proceeds of a wrongful death action shall be used to pay the decedent's reasonable medical, hospital, and burial expenses for which the estate is liable. (M.C.L.A. 700.3924 (2)(d)).

APPLYING THE LAW

1. If you were representing the defendant in a wrongful death cause of action in Michigan, would you accept a release from the mother and father of the decedent to settle the case?

2. Would the illegitimate child of a deceased father be entitled to notice of settlement and to a share of the proceeds of the settlement?

Greene v. Texeira
505 P.2d 1169 (Haw. 1973)

This appeal arises out of consolidated actions brought by Florence Greene, the appellant herein, in her individual capacity and as administratrix of the estate of her son, Michael T. Greene, against John and Maxine Texeira, parents of Ronald Texeira, a minor, pursuant to HRS §§633-3[2]

---

2. HRS §633-3 provides:

> Death by wrongful act. When the death of a person is caused by the wrongful act, neglect, or default of any person or corporation, the deceased's legal representative, or any of the persons hereinafter enumerated,

and 633-7.[3] The claims were the result of an automobile accident involving a single vehicle driven by Ronald Texeira. Michael T. Greene, a passenger in the car, sustained injuries from which he died following 45 days of hospitalization. Michael was 19 years of age, unmarried, and a college freshman at the time of his death.

On April 27, 1970, verdicts were returned. The jury awarded the mother $30,000 under the Wrongful Death Act, HRS §663-3, and $5,000 under the Survival Statute, HRS §663-7. Judgment was entered in accordance with the verdicts on April 30, 1970. The Wrongful Death Act judgment was satisfied, but the administratrix appealed from the judgment under the Survival Statute.

The first three specifications of error alleged by the appellant concern the probable future earnings of the decedent, in excess of the probable cost of his own maintenance and the provision he would have made for his family and dependents during the time he would likely have lived but for the accident. That such earnings are a proper item of damages in an action under HRS §663-7 was determined by this court in Rohlfing v. Akiona, 45 Haw. 373, 369 P.2d 96 (1961).

In the present case, appellant at trial had full opportunity to present his facts on all issues concerning damages. Overruling *Rohlfing* by this court merely rendered trial of one issue, that concerning decedent's excess earnings, superfluous. The great importance to the public of a proper interpretation of Hawaii's Survival Statute is obvious. Thus, we will consider the issue whether the decedent's excess earnings are a proper item of damages under HRS §633-7.

Under HRS §663-7 there survives in favor of the decedent's legal representative only such cause of action as the decedent himself had at the moment of his death. Rohlfing v. Akiona, 45 Haw. at 377, 400, 369 P.2d 96. The crux of the majority opinion in *Rohlfing* was that an injured person has a

---

may maintain an action against the person or corporation causing the death or against the person or corporation responsible for the death, on behalf of the persons hereinafter enumerated.

In any action under this section, such damages may be given as under the circumstances shall be deemed fair and just compensation, with reference to the pecuniary injury and loss of love and affection, including (1) loss of society, companionship, comfort, consortium, or protection, (2) loss of marital care, attention, advice, or counsel, (3) loss of filial care or attention or (4) loss of parental care, training, guidance, or education suffered as a result of the death of the person by the surviving spouse, children, father, mother, and by any person wholly or partly dependent upon the deceased person. The jury or court sitting without jury shall allocate the damages to the persons entitled thereto in its verdict or judgment, and any damage recovered under this section, except for reasonable expenses of last illness and burial, shall not constitute a part of the estate of the deceased. If an action is brought pursuant to this section and a separate action brought pursuant to section 663-7, such actions may be consolidated for trial on the motion of any interested party, and a separate verdict, report, or decision may be rendered as to each right of action. Any action brought under this section shall be commenced within two years from the date of death of the injured person.

3. HRS §663-7 provides:

Survival of actions. A cause of action arising out of a wrongful act, neglect, or default, except actions for defamation and malicious prosecution, shall not abate by reason of the death of the injured person. The action shall survive in favor of the legal representative of the person and any damage recovered shall form part of the estate of the deceased.

right to recovery of all future earnings lost as a result of his injury and that the intervention of death should not divest the decedent's estate of that right.

We have come to the conclusion that the minority opinion in *Rohlfing* presents the most sound position on this issue; that an injured plaintiff is not entitled to recover damages "for any earnings he might be supposed to make, if living, in that part of his life lost by reason of his injuries." Kraskowski v. Aurora, Elgin & Chicago R.R., 167 Ill. App. 469, 472-473 (1912). As the decedent would not have been entitled to recover such earnings in his lifetime, it follows that his representative is not entitled to recover such earnings in a later survival action under HRS §663-7.

Our interpretation of HRS §663-7 is in accordance with the view of most states with statutes such as ours. In the majority of jurisdictions with both Survival and Wrongful Death statutes, recovery for lost earnings under the Survival Statute is not permitted beyond the time of death. McCormick, Damages, §94 (1935); Prosser, Torts, §127 (4th Ed. 1971).

Our interpretation of HRS §663-7 recognizes that the aim of the statutes in this area of the law is compensation for loss rather than punishment. Our wrongful death statute, HRS §663-3, compensates a deceased's survivors for economic loss and deprivation of love, affection and companionship. Decedent's mother has already been awarded $30,000 under HRS §663-3. To press HRS §663-7 into service to further compensate the decedent's survivors for the loss of their loved one would result in excess damages, justifiable only on a theory of punishment, rather than compensation.

Our holding that future excess earnings are not an element of damages in an action under HRS §663-7 renders irrelevant the first three specifications of error alleged by appellant, all of which concern the measure of decedent's future excess earnings. We turn now to appellant's fourth allegation.

Reversed and remanded for a new trial on the issue of the amount of damages accrued between the time of decedent's injury and the time of his death.

LEVINSON, Justice, dissenting, with whom KOBAYASHI, Justice, joins.

I dissent because I think that Rohlfing v. Moses Akiona, Ltd., 45 Haw. 373, 369 P.2d 96 (1961), was decided correctly.

I.

Rohlfing held, in effect, that those jurisdictions which have both survival and wrongful death statutes and which allow damages to be cut off at the date of death are misinterpreting the statutes, and I agree. The *Rohlfing* majority accurately characterized the source of an action under the survival statute as the injury rather than the loss of life:

> Hence, under the survival statute the cause of action arises out of the injury. The injury may manifest itself in the loss of life instantly or

subsequently, but the loss of life is not what gives rise to the cause of action. In contrast, an action under (the wrongful death statute) arises out of the death. (45 Haw. at 383, 369 P.2d at 101.)

The court further elaborated on this principle:

> The touchstone is the right that was vested in the injured person at the moment of his death. It seems to us that a person mortally wounded cannot have less than the right to the present value of the sum, if any, that with due regard to his own cost of living and the care of his loved ones, would have been at his disposal during his lifetime had he been permitted to live it normally. If that is not a sound proposition then one can with equal justice urge that an injured person, alone in the world, who lies in a coma in a hospital and will never recover from it, has only a right to such sum as will maintain him in the hospital and nothing for lost earnings because, forsooth, he will not in future be able to spend anything; or that in any instance in which a person's earnings are more than he is ever likely to spend in his lifetime there should be no recovery for the excess since it will only go to his heirs anyway. (45 Haw. at 390, 369 P.2d at 105.)

While the issue of duplication of damages was not directly before the Rohlfing court on the facts of that case because that action was brought under the survival statute only, the court recognized this as a genuine problem and discussed it at length. It concluded that the legislature provided against this possibility by merging the common law wrongful death action into its statutory successor and by providing for consolidation of wrongful death and survival actions arising from the same incident.

The *Rohlfing* approach was noted with approval by Professor John G. Fleming in The Lost Years: A Problem in the Computation and Distribution of Damages, 50 Calif. L. Rev. 598, 606-07 (1962):

> The standard solution (to the conflict between wrongful death claims of the survivors and those of the heirs under survival statutes) is to allow the dependents the value of their expectancy and to allot the estate, as representing the decedent, his probable earnings limited to the span between injury and death. This disposition offers the tortfeasor adequate protection against double liability (even when the actions are not consolidated), but incidentally confers on him a disguised windfall by not mulcting him for the difference between the present worth of the decedent's likely earnings during his lost years, reduced by the probable cost of his maintenance, and the amount awarded to the dependents. In recognizing the estate's legitimate claim to such "excess earnings," Pennsylvania and Hawaii are thus far alone in offering a commendable departure from the customary formula. (Footnotes omitted.)

In contrast to *Rohlfing*, the majority in the present case is attempting to reconcile the wrongful death and survival statutes on the theory that duplication of damages can be avoided by the simple device of limiting recovery in the survival action to the date of death, with the wrongful death action then picking up any loss of earning capacity from death to the date of life expectancy prior to the injury. Unfortunately, in its headlong rush to avoid what it labels 'punishment,' the majority has lost sight of such considerations as the true goals of compensation, the fact that our statutory scheme already avoids duplication, and the impact of its decision upon the distribution of damages.

The goals of compensation have been set forth with clarity in prior decisions of this court: The general rule in measuring damages is to award such sum of money to the injured person as will restore him to the position he would have been in had the injury not occurred. Lost future earnings are one element of damages commonly arising from personal injuries which are properly chargeable against the tortfeasor. If the injury results in a permanent destruction of the ability to earn income, the wage loss may form a large portion of the total injury suffered, and evidence of this future loss is properly admissible for consideration by the jury. The sum of these goals, that injured parties must be compensated by the wrongdoer for the totality of their losses, has been overlooked by the majority in its narrow concentration on the problem of 'punishment.'

Under the Hawaii statutory scheme duplication of damages is easily avoided. The problem, of course, is certainly one which cannot be ignored. But the functional result under *Rohlfing* is that a dependent's recovery is limited to his net pecuniary loss, because any support which he would have received must be deducted from that part of the estate to which he is entitled as an heir. This constitutes a built-in prevention of any double recovery. Again, this feature is commended by Professor Fleming:

> (A) more sophisticated disposition has recently been suggested which would actually offer him some measure of participation in the fund notionally represented by his lost years. According to this recommendation by the Hawaii court, it would be wholly proper to allow him the difference between his probable earnings during that period and the amount to which his dependents could lay a subsequent claim for loss of their expected support. Recognition of the decedent's title to such "excess earnings" has the undoubted advantage of forestalling the tortfeasor from any disguised windfall, insignificant though it may be in most cases, besides emphasizing that recovery based on normal life expectancy should be qualified only to the extent irreducibly necessary for sparing the tortfeasor from double liability. (50 Cal. L. Rev. at 613).

Perhaps the most important shortcoming of the majority's position is its refusal to acknowledge the impact of its broad-ranging language upon the distribution of damages. To rule that the probable future excess earnings of the decedent are not a proper item of damages in this case allows future defendants to obtain a windfall from their own actions. A benefit will be reaped when a victim is killed rather than injured.

There are a number of readily conceivable situations in which a tortfeasor will benefit under the majority's holding when an injury results in death rather than disability, thereby allowing the wrongdoer to escape all or part of his liability. Any situation in which a decedent has beneficiaries under his will or heirs who do not fall within those categories empowered to bring actions under the wrongful death statute, that is, any heir or beneficiary not supported by, or beneficiary not related to, the decedent, would result in the complete loss of an otherwise compensable damage. The fact that a dependent spouse, parent, or child has a valid action under the wrongful death statute offers no consolation to those who, in spite of an otherwise compensable interest, are now foreclosed from protecting it, especially in view of the fact that duplication of damages is already prevented in this jurisdiction.

Other interested parties, although they may appear with less frequency, are creditors and the state. The majority's opinion has a detrimental effect upon the interest of the creditors of an estate by virtue of the fact that lost future earnings would likely be the largest single damage item; nor does our wrongful death statute list creditors among those groups empowered to use it. Also, any advantage accruing to the state under the escheat statute would be lost, resulting in a loss of revenue.

The inevitable conclusion is that, as a result of the majority's balancing of the two statutes, distribution is by item of damages rather than upon any considered policy decision as to the extent of the damage interest. This, in my opinion, is patently unfair to those who have been damages by the wrongdoing of others.

II.

Because I believe the *Rohlfing* decision was correct, it is necessary to address the other issues raised on appeal, for the reason that the legislature may now choose to amend the survival statute or the court may one day return to the proper interpretation.

A. THE DEDUCTION OF FEDERAL AND STATE INCOME TAX FROM AWARD OF DAMAGES FOR LOSS OF PROBABLE NET EXCESS EARNINGS.

At trial, the circuit court instructed the jury that future federal and state income tax payments should be deducted from the present value of the decedent's likely earnings in determining the loss to his estate of probable net excess earnings. This instruction reflected the obvious fact that, had the decedent lived, his future gross earnings would have been taxable.[1]

In my opinion, the circuit court erred in so instructing the jury. I agree with the well-reasoned opinion of Chief Judge Friendly in McWeeney v. New York, New Haven & Hartford Railroad Company, 282 F.2d 34, 36-39 (2d Cir. 1960), cert. denied, 364 U.S. 870, 81 S. Ct. 115, 5 L. Ed. 2d 93 (1960), that the pitfalls of presenting the jury with a task of such 'delusive simplicity' outweigh whatever utility there might be. Even assuming that the jury could estimate with any degree of accuracy the number of the decedent's probable exemptions, the dates when they would come into being, the rates to which the decedent would be subject, the deductions to which he would variously be entitled, and the particular state tax structures under which he would incur liability during his lifetime, the instruction fails to credit the decedent's estate with a number of offsetting factors. First, the theoretical measure of the loss of the plaintiff's earning capacity is that sum of money which if invested at a fair rate of return will yield annually the amount by which the plaintiff's earning capacity has been lessened and which will at the end of the plaintiff's life expectancy be reduced to zero. This takes account of the fact that money earns interest each year; and it should be remembered that this interest is taxable. Therefore, if a court is going to use income after taxes as a measure of plaintiff's loss, it must add back the taxes which would be due on the interest earned—else the award would not fully compensate for the loss.

Second, such an instruction exacerbates the role of inflation and attorneys' contingency fees in diminishing the real recovery to a decedent's estate. A trial court should not permit the introduction of testimony relating to the likely incidence of tax liability which a decedent would have encountered but for his death or instruct the jury that such tax should be deducted from the measure of probable net excess earnings.[2]

B. THE HYPOTHETICAL WIFE AND CHILDREN

In Rohlfing v. Moses Akiona, Ltd., 369 P.2d 96, 106 (1961), this court declared the necessity of reducing an award to a decedent's estate for loss of excess earnings in such a way as "to eliminate the expenditures for decedent's own cost of living and the care of his family and dependents." With this caveat

---

1. The appellant relies upon Kawamoto v. Yasutake, 49 Haw. 42, 51, 410 P.2d 976, 981 (1966), for the proposition that "the incidence of taxation is not a proper fact for a jury's consideration since '(i)t introduces a wholly collateral matter into the damage issue.'" The principle underlying that case is not applicable to the issue presented in the instant appeal, since it dealt with an attempt to have the jury told, in fixing damages for personal injury, that the award is not taxable. Here, the question is whether the jury should properly be instructed to take into account the fact that future earnings would be taxable.

2. I am aware of the warning in *McWeeney* that an added benefit might be bestowed upon the estates of decedents whose income levels were extraordinarily high. However, this possibility is counterbalanced by the salutary effect of the rule upon "the great mass of litigation at the lower or middle reach of the income scale, where future income is fairly predictable, added exemptions or deductions drastically affect the tax and, for the reasons indicated, the plaintiff is almost certain to be under compensated for loss of earning power in any event."

in mind, the Apelles introduced evidence at trial, over the appellant's objection, that the decedent, had he lived, would probably have married and had two children, and that the cost of maintaining this hypothetical family over his life expectancy would have eliminated his excess earnings. The appellant contends that the circuit court's failure to exclude this evidence and to instruct the jury that it could not properly consider the effect of maintaining a hypothetical family upon a decedent's probable net excess earnings resulted in a disproportionately low jury award.

The appellees counter by urging that speculation is inevitable when excess earnings are at issue. They point to numerous instances in the record where the appellant resorted to such speculation in establishing the decedent's probable level of future income. They argue additionally that the circuit court's instruction to the jury did not require the jury to deduct the cost of maintaining a hypothetical wife and two children from the excess earnings credited to the decedent's estate.

The appellee's arguments, however, misconceive the injunction of the *Rohlfing* case. Under *Rohlfing*, support money actually awarded to a widow or children under HRS §663-3 must be deducted from the excess earnings to be credited under HRS §663-7 to the decedent's estate, in order to prevent a double recovery by the decedent's dependents and heirs. But there can be no double recovery by a widow or by children who do not in fact exist. To deduct the cost of maintaining a hypothetical family from the award to which a decedent's estate is entitled would give a windfall to the defendant and literally make it cheaper to kill a single man than a married man with a family. Such a course of action is inconsistent with the policies articulated in *Rohlfing*.

I would hold that in connection with the award under HRS §663-7 it was error for the circuit court to permit the jury to consider the cost of maintaining a hypothetical family. On the other hand, under HRS §663-3 the jury awarded $30,000 to the appellant for pecuniary injury an loss of love and affection. This sum has been paid. Of course, there is no way of knowing how much of it, if any, was to compensate for pecuniary injury, i.e., loss of support, and how much was to compensate for loss of love and affection. In any event, retrial of the appellant's claim under HRS §663-7, which would be the only claim to be retried, poses no threat of double recovery; whatever sum the trier of fact finds would have been spent by the decedent in support of the appellant will by definition be excluded from the measure of probable net excess earnings.

C. THE HYPOTHETICAL QUESTIONS

The appellant's expert economist testified on direct examination that, in his opinion, the present value of the decedent's probable excess earnings should be determined on the basis of a 4% discount factor, the average yield of U.S. government bonds over a 50-year period. Over the appellant's objection and subsequent motion to strike, the appellees were permitted to elicit an estimate from the witness based on a discount rate of 6%. The appellant argues that the assumption that 6% was a proper discount rate was unsupported by any evidence adduced at trial; she therefore maintains that to question the witness on that basis contravened the mandate of Barretto v. Akau, 51 Haw. 383, 388, 463 P.2d 917, 921 (1969), wherein we stated that:

> While the authorities are divided on this issue, we think that in cross-examining an expert witness a question aimed at demonstrating an alternative theory or contesting a substantive element of the case may be based on (1) those facts already in evidence, (2) those facts which are the proper subject of judicial notice, and (3) those facts which the cross-examiner in good faith anticipates he will establish later in the trial. If the cross-examiner fails to prove the facts assumed in his hypothetical question, then a motion to strike by opposing counsel is appropriate to cure the defect. (Citations omitted.)

I think that a proper foundation was laid for calculation of present value based on a 6% discount rate, and that therefore the circuit court did not err in permitting the questions. The expert witness testified on cross-examination that several varieties of investments would currently yield greater than a 6% return. Although he maintained that to reduce future excess earnings to present value at that rate would not be economically "rational," in light of the risk which an investor would be required to taken in order to obtain that rate of return, the question was ultimately one for the trier of fact to resolve on the basis of the evidence presented.

I am in agreement with the majority's opinion on this issue.

PREPARING FOR CLASS

1. Does this decision mean that the relatives of the decedent will not be able to recover for the decedent's future loss of earnings? Explain your answer.

2. How will this decision affect the position of the creditors of the decedent?

3. The decedent was 19 years old, unmarried, and a college freshman. Do his parents have any financial loss from his death? Remember that his girlfriend is not listed as a beneficiary under the statute, even if she has been living with him.

4. Would Michael's grades in college affect the amount of recovery in the case? If your answer is yes, explain how.

5. What if Michael lost his arm in the accident and sustained separate injuries that caused his death. Would the damages for the loss of his arm have to be reduced because he only lost his arm for a limited period of time?

INCREASING YOUR UNDERSTANDING

1. The courts use a number of different measures of the damages in a wrongful death case.

    a. A majority allow recovery for the financial support lost by the decedent's dependents. This approach would allow the plaintiff to recover the financial support lost by the dependents.

    b. Another approach is to measure the loss to the estate. These courts allow the recovery of the amount the decedent would have added to their estate if they had not died earlier.

    c. Some courts measure both the loss to dependents and the loss of the heirs. These courts add the loss of support to the dependents to any savings the decedent would have accrued and left to his heirs, essentially combining the losses in (a) and (b). See Dan Dobbs, The Law of Torts, pp. 808-810.

2. The original wrongful death statutes allowed for recovery of financial loss only. This left the wrongful death claim for children, housewives, and retirees in doubt. Most states now allow recovery for companionship, love, advice, and guidance.

3. If the court allows recovery for companionship and love, should it allow the defendant to show that the police had been summoned to the home of the decedent for domestic violence on the surviving spouse?

4. If the court allows recovery for companionship and love, should it allow the defendant to show that the parents of the deceased only child have had another child? How about allowing the defendant to show that the surviving spouse has remarried? Should the court allow the defendant to refer to the surviving spouse as "Mrs." if she has remarried?

APPLYING THE LAW

1. Describe the loss to your survivors if you should die as a result of a tort today. Does it make any difference whether you use the loss to the estate, the loss to the dependents, or both the loss to the dependents and the loss to the heirs approach?

2. Will recovery under the wrongful death statute be subject to state inheritance taxes? Explain.

B. MEASURING THE RECOVERY IN WRONGFUL DEATH CASES

Weigel v. Lee
752 N.W.2d 618 (N.D. 2008)

CROTHERS, Justice.

Darla Weigel, Melody Frieson, Diana Seney and Lorna Strand (collectively "the Weigels") appeal from the district court's judgment for dismissal of their wrongful death claims against Dr. Lane Lee and Trinity Hospital (collectively "Lee"). The Weigels argue the district court misconstrued the wrongful death statutes. We conclude a decedent's children are able to seek recovery of non-economic damages in a wrongful death action and therefore this case was improperly dismissed. We reverse and remand.

I

On May 6, 2004, Darlyne Rogers arrived at the emergency room of St. Luke's Hospital in Crosby, North Dakota, complaining of abdominal pain, nausea and vomiting. X-rays revealed Rogers suffered from pneumonia and a bowel obstruction. A doctor at St. Luke's Hospital contacted Dr. Lane Lee who agreed to treat Rogers. Rogers was transferred as Lee's patient to Trinity Hospital in Minot. Rogers, despite being critically ill, was admitted to a room on the "regular" floor of the hospital. Three and one-half hours later, Rogers began vomiting bodily waste and aspirating it into her lungs. Rogers ultimately died.

Rogers' adult children, the Weigels, brought a suit on their own behalf against Lee and Trinity Hospital, alleging negligence. The complaint stated,

> "This is an action to recover damages for the wrongful death of Darlyne Rogers ... pursuant to N.D.C.C. Chapter 32-21. ... [T]he Plaintiffs have sustained injuries and damages, both economic and non-economic. ... The Plaintiffs have sustained mental and emotional anguish as a result of the Defendants' negligence and their mother's death. Furthermore, the Plaintiffs have been denied the society, comfort, counsel and companionship of Darlyne Rogers."

The Weigels' case was tried to a jury. After testimony concluded on April 7, 2006, the parties disagreed over jury instructions, leading the district court to examine Butz v. World Wide, Inc., 492 N.W.2d 88 (N.D. 1992). The district court determined that under *Butz*, children do not have a cause of action for loss of parental consortium. The district court announced its intention to dismiss the Weigels' loss of consortium claim. Because the Weigels could not prove economic damages, and because the court was persuaded the remaining mental and emotional anguish claim was inseparable from the loss of consortium claim, the court dismissed the entire case and discharged the jury.

In its written order dated April 21, 2006, the district court reconsidered its opinion, instead deciding sufficient evidence existed for the case to have gone to the jury on the mental and emotional anguish claim under N.D.C.C. ch. 32-21 and N.D.C.C. §32-03.2-04. Thus, the district court determined the Weigels were entitled to a new trial.

On September 6, 2006, the district court granted the Weigels' motion for a new trial. However, the order stated the reasoning in the April 21, 2006 order was flawed. The court wrote, "Rather than allowing the jury to consider awarding damages for mental anguish/emotional distress allegedly sustained by the surviving children of the decedent . . . the jury should instead be allowed to consider awarding compensation for non-economic damages — such as, pain, suffering, mental anguish, emotional distress or humiliation — allegedly sustained by the decedent herself, prior to her death. . . . Otherwise stated, Darlyne Rogers' surviving heirs . . . 'step into her shoes' in terms of the cause of action available against the Defendants in this matter."

On January 18, 2007, the Weigels filed a Motion for Reconsideration of Order, arguing the district court misconstrued the wrongful death statute. On April 24, 2007, the court reaffirmed the order for a new trial, commenting that much of the court's and counsel's confusion was due to a failure to distinguish between a wrongful death action under N.D.C.C. §32-21-01 and a survival action under N.D.C.C. §28-01-26.1. Ultimately, the court determined *Butz* is dispositive and children are not entitled to non-economic damages on their own behalf for the death of a parent.

On May 2, 2007, the Weigels informed the court they sought only non-economic damages resulting from Rogers' death. Lee moved to dismiss, and because the Weigels sought only a remedy the court previously determined improper, Lee's motion was granted on May 31, 2007. The Weigels appeal the judgment of dismissal, contending the district court's interpretation of the wrongful death act is erroneous. We agree.

II

"Statutory interpretation is a question of law, fully reviewable on appeal." Chamley v. Khokha, 730 N.W.2d 864.

The district court erred by blending three distinct claims for tortious conduct. At various points in its orders, the district court discussed (1) loss of consortium claims arising out of personal injury actions, (2) survival actions and (3) wrongful death actions. This Court and North Dakota's statutes distinguish between these three claims, as we explain below.

First, English common law recognized an action for loss of consortium arising out of tortious conduct that resulted in personal injury. Historically, "a husband's right to recover for the loss of his wife's consortium was considered a property right" with a loss of consortium being defined as "love, companionship, affection, society, comfort, solace, support, sexual relations, and services." Under this original approach, "only a husband could recover for the loss of [his wife's] consortium." The contemporary interpretation of this common law concept includes recovery for wives as well as for husbands. This Court has acknowledged both spouses' right to recover for loss of consortium, but refused to extend this type of recovery to children who suffer the loss of a parent's consortium Nonetheless, this is not the basis of the Weigels' action, and as this Court importantly clarified in *Hastings*, the inability of children to recover for loss of consortium arising out of personal injury to a parent "should not be construed to prohibit recovery where a parent dies and recovery is allowed under the Wrongful Death Act."

The distinction between loss of consortium in personal injury and in wrongful death actions is important here because Lee argues this Court's decision in *Butz* indicates a decedent's children are not entitled to damages in a wrongful death action. Lee misapplies *Butz*. *Butz* was not a claim under the wrongful death act because the tortious conduct resulted in severe injury, not in death. This Court acknowledged the loss of consortium claim made in *Butz* was like that made in Hastings, arising out of the common law. Because *Butz* does not address claims made under the wrongful death statutes, it is not applicable to the Weigels' claim.

Second, N.D.C.C. §28-01-26.1 provides for survival actions: "No action or claim for relief, except for breach of promise, alienation of affections, libel, and slander, abates by the death of a party or of a person who might have been a party had such death not occurred." For example, in Nodak Mut. Ins. Co. v. Stegman, 647 N.W.2d 133, an individual was seriously injured in an automobile accident. He underwent hospital treatment, but died approximately two weeks later. This Court stated, "Clearly a personal injury action existed on behalf of [the injured party] against [the tortfeasor] for various damages, including the medical expenses occasioned by the accident, and that action survived [the injured party's] death." Survival statutes "are remedial in nature, and are intended to permit recovery by the representatives of the deceased for damages the deceased could have recovered had he lived. . . . A survival action merely continues in existence an injured person's claim after death as an asset of his estate." Sheets v. Graco, Inc., 292 N.W.2d 63, 66-67 (N.D. 1980). Although they could have, the Weigels' complaint indicates they are not seeking damages on Rogers' behalf as part of a survival action. Instead, the Weigels brought a wrongful death action for their own injuries: "The Plaintiffs have sustained mental and emotional anguish as a result of the Defendants' negligence and their mother's death. Furthermore, the Plaintiffs have been denied the society, comfort, counsel and companionship of Darlyne Rogers, all to their injury and damage."

Third, N.D.C.C. ch. 32-21 provides for wrongful death actions. The Weigels offer the wrongful death act as the legal basis for their claim. We conclude the Weigels are entitled to seek compensation for Rogers' wrongful death for the reasons stated below.

There was no wrongful death claim at common law. Early wrongful death statutes severely limited compensable damages. Generally, only pecuniary losses were awarded, with no compensation available for mental anguish or loss of companionship. Contemporary wrongful death statutes tend to address a broader scope of injuries, including those considered non-pecuniary.

> "Wrongful death actions are intended to compensate the survivors of the deceased for the losses they have sustained as a result of a wrongful killing. Dependent upon the specific statutory language, losses recoverable by survivors in wrongful death actions often include the prospective loss of earnings and contribution; prospective expenses; loss of services; loss of companionship, comfort, and consortium; and mental anguish and grief."

Sheets, 292 N.W.2d at 66 (emphasis added).

North Dakota's wrongful death act, N.D.C.C. ch. 32-21, provides:

> "Whenever the death of a person shall be caused by a wrongful act, neglect, or default, and the act, neglect, or default is such as would have entitled the party injured, if death had not ensued, to maintain an action and recover damages in respect thereof, then and in every such case the person who, or the corporation, limited liability company, or company which, would have been liable if death had not ensued, shall be liable to an action for damages, notwithstanding the death of the person injured or of the tortfeasor, and although the death shall have been caused under such circumstances as amount in law to felony."

N.D.C.C. §32-21-01. This statute "is not a survival statute intended to increase the estate of the deceased, but its purpose is to give a measure of protection to those persons within a fixed degree of relationship to and dependency on the deceased because of actual injury sustained by them by reason of the wrongful killing of the deceased." *Sheets*, 292 N.W.2d at 65 (quoting *Satterberg*, 19 N.D. at 41, 121 N.W. at 71). Damages under the wrongful death act are "based on the loss suffered by the beneficiaries, and not on the loss sustained by the decedent's estate." A jury determines the quantity of damages and "shall give such damages as it finds proportionate to the injury resulting from the death to the persons entitled to the recovery." N.D.C.C. §32-21-02.

Compensable damages available in wrongful death actions are enumerated in N.D.C.C. §32-03.2-04:

> "In any civil action for damages for wrongful death or injury to a person and whether arising out of breach of contract or tort, damages may be awarded by the trier of fact as follows:
>
> 1. Compensation for **economic damages**, which are **damages** arising from medical expenses and medical care, rehabilitation services, custodial care, loss of earnings and earning capacity, loss of income or support, burial costs, cost of substitute domestic services, loss of employment or business or employment opportunities and other monetary losses.
> 2. Compensation for noneconomic damages, which are damages arising from pain, suffering, inconvenience, physical impairment, disfigurement, mental anguish, emotional distress, fear of injury, loss or illness, loss of society and companionship, loss of consortium, injury to reputation, humiliation, and other nonpecuniary damage."

(Emphasis added.)

Section 32-21-04, N.D.C.C., clarifies that intended recipients of damages under the wrongful death act are "the decedent's heirs at law." This Court has determined "heirs at law" for purposes of this statute are "those persons who by the laws of descent would succeed to the property of the decedent in case of intestacy, but in addition, that if members of a preferred class are precluded from recovery for reasons other than death those next entitled to inherit may be considered beneficiaries." A decedent's descendants are designated by the Uniform Probate Code to share in portions of the intestate estate and are therefore able to seek recovery of damages under the wrongful death act. See N.D.C.C. §30.1-04-03.

Persons entitled to recover damages under the wrongful death act should not be confused with persons statutorily authorized to bring an action. Section 32-21-03, N.D.C.C., states:

> "The action shall be brought by the following persons in the order named:
>
> 1. The surviving husband or wife, if any.
> 2. The surviving children, if any.
> 3. The surviving mother or father.
> 4. A surviving grandparent.
> 5. The personal representative.
> 6. A person who has had primary physical custody of the decedent before the wrongful act.

"If any person entitled to bring the action refuses or neglects so to do for a period of thirty days after demand of the person next in order, that person may bring the action."

The distinction between persons eligible to seek damages from wrongful death actions and those entitled to bring such actions is important because the trial judge is charged with splitting the recovery among eligible heirs. Section 32-21-04, N.D.C.C., states:

"The amount recovered shall not be liable for the debts of the decedent, but shall inure to the exclusive benefit of the decedent's heirs at law in such shares as the judge before whom the case is tried shall fix in the order for judgment, and for the purpose of determining such shares, the judge after the trial may make any investigation which the judge deems necessary."

In specific wrongful death actions, overlap will likely exist between plaintiffs bringing the action under N.D.C.C. §32-21-03 and those entitled to any damages. However, those with authority to bring the action do "not have an absolute right to the damages recovered, and, instead, bring[ ] the action in a representative capacity for the exclusive benefit of the persons entitled to recover." The wrongful death act "thus differentiate[s] between the capacity to bring an action and the right to share in the damages recovered." Id. at 306-07; see also N.D.C.C. §32-21-06 ("The person entitled to bring the action may compromise the same, or the right thereto, and such compromise shall be binding upon all persons authorized to bring the action or to share in the recovery."). Surviving children are eligible to bring a wrongful death action under N.D.C.C. §32-21-03(2) if the decedent had no eligible spouse or if the spouse fails to bring an action for thirty days after the children made a demand. But this issue is separate from the children's ability to recover damages in a wrongful death action.

Because the wrongful death act does not exclude the decedent's children from parties entitled to damages and because the damages requested are permitted under N.D.C.C. §32-03.2-04, the Weigels' claim should not have been dismissed.

III

We conclude a decedent's children are entitled to seek recovery of damages in a wrongful death action and this case was improperly dismissed. We reverse the district court's judgment and remand for further proceedings.

PREPARING FOR CLASS

1. What is a claim for loss of consortium? How does it differ from a wrongful death claim?

2. How could there be no cause of action for loss of consortium of parents but recovery for loss of companionship of parents in wrongful death cases?

3. If the surviving husband of the deceased brings the cause of action, who is entitled to recover the proceeds of the lawsuit?

4. Would there be a claim for loss of companionship of parents in a survival action?

INCREASING YOUR UNDERSTANDING

1. Most states have ruled that the survivor's loss of companionship, society, advice, and guidance has pecuniary value and is, therefore, recoverable in a wrongful death case. See Dan Dobbs, *The Law of Torts*, p. 812.

2. Alabama bases recovery in wrongful death cases on punitive damages. But most wrongful death statutes do not mention punitive damages, so punitive damages are rare in these cases.

APPLYING THE LAW

1. Assume you are engaged in the practice of law and you are contacted by the father of an adult killed in an automobile accident in North Dakota. The father wants to retain you for the wrongful death case. What questions, if any, do you have for the father? Will you sign a contingency fee contract with the father?

2. The opinion states that there "was no wrongful death claim at common law." What difference does that make in wrongful death cases?

C. DEFENSES TO WRONGFUL DEATH ACTIONS

Teeter vs. Missouri Highway & Transp. Comm'n
891 S.W.2d 817 (Mo. 1995)

COVINGTON, Chief Justice.

Pamela F. Teeter and her former husband, Darien Teeter, the plaintiffs in a wrongful death action filed after the death of their daughter Ashley, appealed the judgment of the trial court imputing Mrs. Teeter's negligence to Mr. Teeter. The Missouri Court of Appeals, Southern District, reversed and remanded. This Court granted transfer. Reversed and remanded.

The facts are not in dispute. The Teeters' marriage was dissolved in 1981. Mrs. Teeter was awarded custody of the children of the marriage, including Ashley Teeter. On June 30, 1987, Ashley was killed when Mrs. Teeter's car collided with a vehicle driven by Diana L. Hurlbut at the intersection of U.S. Highway 54 and Missouri Highway 73 in Camden County, Missouri.

Mrs. Teeter filed a wrongful death action against Ms. Hurlbut and the Missouri Highway and Transportation Commission ("MHTC"). Mrs. Teeter alleged that MHTC was negligent in designing and maintaining the road where the collision occurred and that Ms. Hurlbut was negligent in the operation of her vehicle. Mr. Teeter intervened in the wrongful death action, alleging that Ms. Hurlbut, MHTC, and Mrs. Teeter were negligent in causing Ashley's death.

The trial court approved settlements in which payments were made on behalf of Ms. Hurlbut in the amount of $25,000 and on behalf of Mrs. Teeter, in her capacity as a defendant, in the amount of $23,000.

After the settlements, the trial court granted the Teeters' joint motion for realignment of the parties. Mr. Teeter was designated a plaintiff. After the realignment, the action was between the Teeters as plaintiffs and MHTC as the sole remaining defendant.

At trial, the jury returned a verdict assessing the Teeters' damages at $500,000. The jury assessed ninety percent of the fault for Ashley's death to Mrs. Teeter and ten percent to MHTC.

In its judgment the trial court allowed MHTC credit for the $48,000 paid in settlement on behalf of Ms. Hurlbut and Mrs. Teeter. The court held that Mrs. Teeter's fault should be imputed to Mr. Teeter. The court then reduced the remaining $452,000 by ninety percent, the percentage of fault the jury assessed to Mrs. Teeter. The court entered judgment in favor of Mr. and Mrs. Teeter and against MHTC in the amount of $45,200. The court apportioned seventy percent of the judgment to Mrs. Teeter and thirty percent to Mr. Teeter. On appeal the Teeters contend that the trial court erred in imputing the comparative fault of Mrs. Teeter to Mr. Teeter.

To address the Teeters' contention that the trial court erred in imputing the comparative fault of Mrs. Teeter to Mr. Teeter, this Court must first address the larger issue of whether a defendant's liability can be reduced on account of the fault of one of several beneficiaries of a wrongful death action. A wrongful death defendant "may plead and prove as a defense any defense which the defendant would have had against the deceased in an action based on the same [facts], and which action for damages the deceased would have been entitled to bring had death not ensued." The comparative fault of the decedent is such a defense. Although the fault of a decedent may be assessed against the beneficiaries in a wrongful death action, no appellate court of this state has held that comparative fault applies to reduce the award in a wrongful death case in proportion to the fault of one of the beneficiaries.

To reduce a defendant's liability by the percentage of fault of one of several beneficiaries is inconsistent with the nature of the wrongful death cause of action.[4] Unlike tort actions, in which the plaintiffs have individual causes of action, wrongful death actions are indivisible—only one action may be brought against any one defendant for the death of any one person. Any recovery in a wrongful death action is for the benefit of those who sue or are entitled to sue and of whom the court has notice. The individual interests of the beneficiaries become separable only after the indivisible cause of action becomes merged in a judgment. Under the wrongful death statutes, it is impossible to reduce a defendant's liability to one of several claimants prior to judgment because no claimant has an individual interest until apportioned one by the court. Apportionment takes place only after judgment is entered against the defendant. §537.095.3. Where there are multiple beneficiaries, therefore, the wrongful death statutes cannot logically coexist with comparative fault, for it is impossible to "[diminish] proportionately the amount awarded as compensatory damages . . . attributable to the claimant's contributory fault."

In spite of the inability logically to apply comparative fault in a wrongful death action with multiple beneficiaries, the function of comparative fault is served by contribution among joint tortfeasors. Section 537.060 provides, in pertinent part:

> Defendants in a judgment founded on an action for the redress of a private wrong shall be subject to contribution, and all other consequences of such judgment, in the same manner and to same extent as defendants in a judgment in an action founded on contract. When an agreement by release, covenant not to sue or not to enforce a judgment is given in good faith to one of two or more persons liable in tort for the same injury or wrongful death, such agreement shall not discharge any of the other tortfeasors for the damage unless the terms of the agreement so provide; however such agreement shall reduce the claim by the stipulated amount of the agreement, or in the amount of consideration paid, whichever is greater. The agreement shall discharge the tortfeasor to whom it is given from all liability for contribution or noncontractual indemnity to any other tortfeasor.

The doctrine of comparative fault and the policy enunciated in §537.060 stand on similar principles. Comparative fault reduces the defendant's liability in proportion to the plaintiff's negligence. Section 537.060 permits the defendant's liability to be reduced by the amounts of settlements by joint tortfeasors. The theory underlying both rules is the principle of fairness. Both seek to ensure that the defendant is not forced to bear an unfair burden.

---

4. The present case does not concern, and the Court does not address, the applicability of comparative fault to a wrongful death action with one beneficiary.

A defendant, therefore, has no need to invoke comparative fault principles when a plaintiff in a wrongful death case with multiple beneficiaries is also a joint tortfeasor. The defendant's interests are protected by the law of contribution. If comparative fault were also applied to limit the defendant's liability, the defendant would twice obtain the benefit of the plaintiff's fault. The principle of fairness is served by applying the law of contribution among joint tortfeasors alone.

Contribution affords no relief, however, to MHTC in the present case. MHTC failed to take any steps to protect its right to contribution from Mrs. Teeter. Mrs. Teeter entered into a settlement. Section 537.060 provides that defendants who go to trial may not seek contribution from joint tortfeasors who reach good faith settlements with the plaintiff, but instead are entitled to have their liability reduced by the amount of the settlement. The section, the applicability of which the parties do not contest, "permits alleged tortfeasors to buy their peace by good faith settlements with the claimant." MHTC relinquished any claim for contribution; it neither sought to have the trial court disapprove Mrs. Teeter's settlement, §537.095.1, nor contested the good faith nature of the settlement, §537.060. MHTC, therefore, is not entitled to contribution from Mrs. Teeter.

PREPARING FOR CLASS

1. Consider the Hypothetical from the beginning of this chapter. If the Hypothetical took place in Missouri and the Missouri wrongful death act said that Susan would share equally in the wrongful death recovery with her child, how much, if anything, would Susan recover? How much would the child recover?

2. What if the court appointed you as the guardian ad litem for Susan's child and the jury determines that there is $1.0 million of damages from Thomas's death? What is the child likely to recover if Missouri law makes the surviving spouse and child equal beneficiaries under the wrongful death act?

INCREASING YOUR UNDERSTANDING

1. Most jurisdictions have held that if the decedent settled the case during his or her lifetime by signing a release of liability then that release bars the wrongful death action also.

2. Many wrongful death statutes have a separate time period in which to bring the action for wrongful death. In those jurisdictions, that statutory time limit applies rather than the general statute of limitations time limit. In addition, the tolling provisions of the general statute of

limitations generally do not apply to the wrongful death limitations period. See Moreno v. Sterling Drug Inc., 787 S.W.2d 348 (Tex. 1990).

3. In comparative negligence jurisdictions, the jury considers the fault of the decedent with the fault of the decedent, as if the decedent were the plaintiff in the action.

4. The conduct of the deceased may even bar a wrongful death case when it would bar a cause of action if the decedent were alive, for example, assumption of the risk, contributory negligence, and self defense. When one of several beneficiaries is contributorily negligent or has engaged in any other act that would bar the cause of action, the majority of courts allow the case to continue with a reduction in recovery for the barred beneficiary.

Chapter 19

Statutes of Limitations and Immunities

A. WHEN DOES THE STATUTE OF LIMITATIONS BEGIN TO RUN?

Locke v. Johns-Manville Corp.
221 Va. 951, 275 S.E.2d 900 (Va. 1981)

COMPTON, Justice.

In this products liability case, we consider only a statute of limitations question. We must determine when plaintiff's cause of action accrued in this personal injury suit alleging that the disease of mesothelioma resulted from inhalation of asbestos particles. According to the record, this disease is a cancerous tumor most often found in the pleura, or lining, of the victim's lung.

Appellant Douglas T. Locke, the plaintiff below, filed this action on July 24, 1978, against appellees Johns-Manville Corporation, Johns-Manville Sales Corporation, Keene Building Products Corporation, The Celotex Corporation, Unarco Industries, Inc., Eagle-Picher Industries, Inc., Armstrong-Cork Company and Norport Supply Company, Inc. In an amended motion for judgment, plaintiff alleged defendants were engaged in the business of mining, manufacturing, processing, importing, converting, selling and supplying asbestos and asbestos insulation materials and products. Plaintiff further alleged that during the period from 1948 to 1972 he inhaled asbestos fibers and dust as the result of his exposure to various asbestos products which were manufactured, sold and supplied by "some or all" of defendants. He also alleged that due to defendants' negligence and breach of warranty, and because of the inhalation of asbestos particles, he contracted mesothelioma, a disabling and fatal disease. Plaintiff sought recovery of compensatory damages in the amount of $1 million and punitive damages of $500,000.

Defendants' responsive pleadings included pleas of the two-year statute of limitations. Following pre-trial discovery proceedings, defendants filed motions for summary judgment also asserting the action was time-barred. Upon consideration of the allegations in plaintiff's amended motion for judgment, plaintiff's testimony contained in de bene esse depositions, a response to request for admissions, a written proffer of medical evidence filed by plaintiff, and argument of counsel, the trial court sustained the several motions and entered judgment for the defendants in the November 1978 order appealed from.

The record shows that since approximately 1948 plaintiff had been employed as an industrial electrician by various contractors at sites in Virginia, New York and North Carolina. For example, he worked: during 1948 and 1949 on the construction of the cruiser U.S.S. Newport News, at the Newport News Shipbuilding and Drydock Company; during 1954 and 1955 on a "power plant job" at Wilmington, North Carolina; in 1957 at a power plant location near the George Washington Bridge in New York City; during 1971-1972 on the Virginia Electric and Power Company "nuclear power house" in Surry County; and during 1972 at that company's Bremo Bluff power plant. Plaintiff asserts that at intervals during the period from 1948 to 1972 he breathed asbestos fibers and dust from defendants' various asbestos insulation products, with the last exposure being in September of 1972.

The plaintiff further alleged that before November of 1977 he was "in excellent health and physical condition," having had no symptoms of lung disease or abnormality. At that time plaintiff was 49 years of age and weighed 220 pounds. On November 1, plaintiff began experiencing impairment of lung function and thereafter sought medical attention. But prior to early 1978 he had no clinical or other medical evidence of mesothelioma, or any other lung-related abnormality or disease. Chest X-rays performed on April 14, 1978, were normal and "negative for disease," according to plaintiff's contention. Pain and other symptoms in the chest persisted, however.

On May 22, 1978, another X-ray was taken of plaintiff's chest and, for the first time, "an abnormality" was noted. A subsequent X-ray taken four days later "was markedly more abnormal" than the previous one. On May 26, 1978, plaintiff was hospitalized with a tentative diagnosis of pneumonia. Chest surgery was performed seven days later on June 2 and lung tissue was removed. This led to a diagnosis of mesothelioma located in the pleura of plaintiff's lungs. By the time this suit was filed in July of 1978, plaintiff's weight was below 180 pounds and his medical condition was rapidly deteriorating.

Plaintiff's proffer of medical evidence states that if permitted to go to trial on the merits his proof will show the following facts. Asbestos is a carcinogenic chemical, known by experts since at least the 1930s to be a "cancer producer." Asbestos is the "only known cause" of mesothelioma, but not all persons exposed to asbestos fibers will contract the disease. There is no method, "medically or otherwise," to determine in advance which persons exposed to asbestos fibers will develop the disease.

The proffer further discloses that in those persons who contract mesothelioma, the tumor "begins at some time later" than the exposure to the fibers and "there is no clinical or medical evidence of any injury until some time elapses" after such exposures. Additionally, the dates of the victim's exposures to asbestos fibers, and particularly the date of last exposure, bear no medical relationship to when and if a mesothelioma will occur in that person. Also, the disease is always fatal, death normally occurring within three to 18 months of the time the victim first suffers symptoms.

The proffer also states that plaintiff's case of mesothelioma was caused by occupational exposures to asbestos fibers; that the date of plaintiff's last exposure to asbestos in 1972 "bears no relationship medically as to when his mesothelioma occurred"; and, finally, that no "clinical, medical, X-ray or other evidence of the occurrence of mesothelioma" in plaintiff existed before 1978.

To support the charge of negligence, plaintiff asserts, inter alia, that defendants failed to warn him of known dangers connected with use of the asbestos products, failed to inform him of what would be safe protective clothing and equipment to be used while being exposed to asbestos products, failed to inform him about safe and proper methods of handling and using defendants' products, and failed to test the asbestos products to ascertain the danger involved. Contending also that defendants were guilty of breaches of express and implied warranties that caused his personal injuries, plaintiff alleged, inter alia, defendants failed to properly label the products and sold defective products that were "unreasonably unsafe."

The parties do not dispute that the statute of limitations here is governed by Code §§8.01-243(A) and -230. Section 8.01-243(A) provides, in pertinent part, that "every action for personal injuries, whatever the theory of recovery . . . shall be brought within two years next after the cause of action shall have accrued." The relevant part of §8.01-230 provides that "(i)n every action for which a limitation period is prescribed, the cause of action shall be deemed to accrue and the prescribed limitation period shall begin to run from the date the injury is sustained in the case of injury to the person. . . ." (accent added).

The trial court held, relying principally on Street v. Consumers Mining Corp., 185 Va. 561, 39 S.E.2d 271 (1946), that the cause of action accrued no later than September of 1972 when plaintiff was last exposed to asbestos dust caused by defendants' products. The court accordingly decided that the suit filed in 1978 was untimely.

Plaintiff's main argument on appeal is that his injury was sustained subsequent to defendants' tortious conduct. Thus, he contends, the statute of limitations began to run at the time of injury and not when the wrongful act was done. Plaintiff says that the right to maintain a tort action for personal injuries does not "accrue," within the meaning of the pertinent statutes, until the claimant has a "legally provable injury." He argues that when the word "injury" as used in §8.01-230 is applied to the disease in question, the plaintiff has sustained an injury only when "the cancer manifests itself with sufficient certainty to be subject to proof in court." To rule otherwise, plaintiff asserts, would mean that a mesothelioma victim would be required to bring his suit at a time when it would have been impossible for him to have maintained it. Plaintiff argues that the purpose of a general statute of limitations, as here, is to regulate the remedy, not to destroy the right of action before it accrues or can be sued upon.

Defendants maintain that the trial court properly ruled that plaintiff's cause of action accrued no later than the date of his last alleged injurious exposure to an asbestos-containing product "and not upon his, or his physician's, discovery of resulting damage." Defendants say that the "purported legal basis" for plaintiff's lawsuit is that defendants failed to test properly their products and failed to warn adequately the plaintiff, prior to exposure, of any detrimental effects from their use. Defendants point out that plaintiff's proffer of medical evidence states that his disease was caused only by pre-1973 occupational exposure to and inhalation of airborne asbestos fibers. Yet, according to defendants, plaintiff also asserts that a discovery rule of accrual should apply because his exposure bears no relationship to when the cancer was capable of diagnosis. But plaintiff's cause of action, defendants urge, "rests on alleged harmful occupational exposure," that is, "the injurious event or series of injurious events complained of." And, defendants argue, their breach of any duties to test or warn "necessarily preceded, or at best were coextensive, with these injurious events." Relying upon *Street v. Consumers Mining Corp.*, supra; defendants exclaim that a decision reversing the lower court in this case "would run counter to all relevant legal and statutory precedent, and would represent a clear departure from Virginia's longstanding limitations principles." We reject defendants' contentions. We think this action was timely.

The broad issue to be decided here is whether the plaintiff's right to bring his action accrued no later than 1972, when he was last exposed to the asbestos fibers from defendants' products, or whether his right accrued at some subsequent time, and if it did arise later, at what time did the right, in fact, accrue.

In order to reach the core of the problem raised by this all-inclusive question, a review first must be made of the ingredients of a cause of action. Then, the specific language of the instant statute of limitations must be studied, in light of the nature and purpose of statutes of limitations in general. That exercise will result in a focus upon the crucial question in the case, which will then be answered, first, by an examination of these unique facts, especially the medical evidence, and, second, by application of the pertinent law to those facts.

There is no right of action until there is a cause of action. Caudill v. Wise Rambler, 210 Va. 11, 13, 168 S.E.2d 257, 259 (1969). The essential elements of a cause of action, whether based on a tortious act or breach of contract, are (1) a legal obligation of a defendant to the plaintiff, (2) a violation or breach of that duty or right, and (3) harm or damage to the plaintiff as a proximate consequence of the violation or breach. Id. See Sides v. Richard Machine Works, Inc., 406 F.2d 445, 446 (4th Cir. 1969). A cause of action does not evolve unless all of these factors are present. Specifically, without injury or damage to the plaintiff, no right of action accrues; stated differently, a plaintiff's right of action for damages for bodily injuries does not accrue until he is hurt. Id.; Barnes v. Sears, Roebuck & Co., 406 F.2d 859, 861 (4th Cir. 1969).

The provisions of the statute of limitations under discussion, enacted in 1977 as a part of the wholesale revision of former Title 8 of the Code of Virginia, are not only consistent with the foregoing case law but are also compatible with the nature and purpose of such a general statute of limitations. They are intended to require prompt assertion of an accrued right of action, not to bar such a right before it has accrued.

Code §8.01-230 specifies that a cause of action for personal injuries shall be deemed to accrue and the prescribed limitation period shall commence to run from the date the injury is sustained. We construe the statutory word "injury" to mean positive, physical or mental hurt to the claimant, not legal wrong to him in the broad sense that his legally protected interests have been invaded. Thus, the running of the time is tied to the fact of harm to the plaintiff, without which no cause of action would come into existence; it is not keyed to the date of the wrongful act, another ingredient of a personal injury cause of action.

The crucial question in this case thus becomes: When was the plaintiff hurt? Was he hurt when he breathed defendants' particles of asbestos no later than 1972 or was he hurt at some subsequent date, and, if then, was the date within two years of July 24, 1978, when suit was filed? The answer to these questions must, in the main, be found in the medical evidence.

Although having breathed asbestos fibers from 1948 to 1972, plaintiff was in excellent health and physical condition until November of 1977. Prior to 1978 there was absolutely no medical evidence he had any lung-related abnormality or disease.

The medical expert opinion (uncontradicted at this stage of the proceedings), reasonably construed, shows that the cancerous tumor in question does not begin to form contemporaneously with exposure to asbestos dust; the malignancy is born afterwards. During the period between exposure and formation of the tumor "there is no clinical or medical evidence of any injury until some time elapses" (emphasis added), just how much time not being revealed by the proffer. Moreover, many persons exposed to asbestos particles never develop mesothelioma. And, the dates of exposure bear no medical relationship to when and if the malignant tumor will occur in the person exposed to asbestos dust.

Thus, according to the medical evidence before us, and keeping in mind that the burden to prove facts necessary to establish an application of the statute of limitations is upon a defendant, Louisville and Nashville Railroad v. Saltzer, 151 Va. 165, 168, 144 S.E. 456, 457 (1928), we are confronted in this case with a medical condition that does not arise at a specific point of time, as does a broken bone; mesothelioma results over a period of time, the beginning of the period being unknown. In other words, the cancer the hurt the harm the injury did not spring up at infliction of the wrongful act, that is, when the dust was inhaled no later than 1972. Rather, the tumor the hurt the harm the injury manifestly occurred before June of 1978 when the mesothelioma was diagnosed; the time it began to form before that date not being shown by the evidence. Simply put, legally and medically there was no injury upon inhalation of defendants' asbestos fibers.

Consequently, based on the record in this case, we hold the plaintiff's injury was not sustained and the cause of action did not accrue in 1972 or before, within the meaning of Code §§8.01-230 and -243(A). We further hold the cause of action accrued and the statute of limitations began to run from the time plaintiff was hurt. The "time plaintiff was hurt" is to be established from available competent evidence, produced by a plaintiff or a defendant, that pinpoints the precise date of injury with a reasonable degree of medical certainty.

Under the scant evidence in this case, the foregoing point in time would coincide with either the November 1977 date when plaintiff first experienced impairment of lung function or the date of the May 1978 X-ray when a lung abnormality was noted. Thus, we do not hold that the foregoing rule means the limitation period does not begin to run until the initial diagnosis is communicated to the victim or even until the first diagnosis is actually made. We merely conclude that the accrual point is when damage occurs. Under this rule, it is conceivable that when the disease manifests itself by symptoms, such as pain, discomfort or impairment of function, expert medical testimony will demonstrate the injury occurred weeks, months or even years before onset of the symptoms. Thus, the cause of action would accrue and the limitations period would run from the earlier and not the later time.

Contrary to defendants' argument, the rule we have just articulated is not a so-called "discovery" rule, and plaintiff does not advocate that we embrace such a theory. We adhere to our belief, expressed in Virginia Military Institute v. King, 217 Va. at 760, 232 S.E.2d at 900, that adoption of a discovery rule, which triggers the running of the statute only when the injury is discovered or should have been discovered in the exercise of reasonable diligence, must be accomplished by the General Assembly. But, as we shall shortly demonstrate, in all of our prior decisions that reject the discovery rule, the injury or damage existed at the time of the wrongful act; it had merely not been discovered in a timely manner. Here, however, there was no injury at the time of the wrongful act. A disease like this cancer must first exist before it is capable of causing injury. To hold otherwise would result in the inequity of barring the mesothelioma plaintiff's cause of action before he sustains injury.

The rule we adopt today is but an application of our prior decisions, such as *Caudill* and *Saltzer*, to the facts of the present case. In the latter case, Saltzer sued the railroad company to recover for damage to his land resulting from defendant's action in changing the channel of a river flowing through the property. Defendant's plea of the applicable five-year statute of limitations raised the question: When did the right of action accrue? Defendant contended it arose at the time the channel was changed in 1891 which was followed by erosion of soil. Plaintiff argued that no appreciable damage occurred until there was "high water" in 1918, and the right of action accrued then. In affirming the trial court's decision overruling the plea, based on a jury's finding that the damage occurred in 1918, this court said, apropos the present case:

> "(W)here the damage . . . arises from a cause not then immediately effective, . . . the cause of action does not arise until the injury can be shown. The reason and justice of this is perfectly apparent, for a plaintiff who merely feared ultimate damage . . . under such circumstances would invite defeat if he only relied upon his fears and was unable to prove any actual damage. So the courts have formulated the general rule thus: Whenever any injury, however slight it may be, is complete at the time the (act or omission) is completed, the cause of action then accrues; but, whenever the (act or omission) is not legally injurious, there is no cause of action until such injurious consequences occur, and it accrues at the time of such consequential injury. . . ."

151 Va. at 170-71, 144 S.E. at 457, quoting Southern Ry. Co. v. Leake, 140 Va. 438, 441, 125 S.E. 314, 315 (1924).

Likewise, in *Caudill*, this court held that plaintiff's cause of action for personal injury arose at the time of the 1967 injury and not in 1964 when she purchased the defective automobile causing the injury. There, we decided that when plaintiff purchased the vehicle, the breach of an implied warranty of fitness occurred and plaintiff's cause of action for property damage arose. At the same time, the court said, plaintiff had a potential cause of action for personal injuries which did not accrue until she was injured. Thus, her personal injury action filed within two years of the date of injury was timely. There we also said:

> Obviously, since the plaintiff had not been injured at the time she purchased the car, she could not then maintain an action for her injuries. To say, then, that her right of action accrued before her injuries were received is to say that she was without remedy to recover damages for her alleged injuries. Such an unjust and inequitable result is not the purpose of statutes of limitation.

210 Va. at 12-13, 168 S.E.2d at 259.

In *Caudill*, we relied on the decisions of the United States Court of Appeals for the Fourth Circuit in *Sides v. Richard Machine Works, Inc.*, supra, and *Barnes v. Sears, Roebuck & Co.*, supra. In *Sides*, the Court of Appeals held that plaintiff's right of action for personal injuries accrued when he was injured and not at the time of the earlier purchase of the defective locomotive that caused his injuries. The court analyzed Virginia law and the language of the former personal injury statute of limitations, which provided, without defining the accrual point, that actions for personal injury "shall be brought within two years next after the right to bring the same shall have accrued," Code §8-24 (Cum. Supp. 1976). Holding there was no actionable tort until the plaintiff was hurt, the court said:

> Before (plaintiff was hurt), of course, a duty, an act or failure to act in violation of the duty, and negligence were outstanding, but no tort was then in being; it was no more than a potentiality or threat. If harm had not ensued, there would have been no tort and nothing to sue on.

406 F.2d at 446. In *Barnes*, the same court on similar facts reached a like result, applying identical reasoning.

The following cases relied upon by defendants, applying the limitations bar, are all factually inapposite. In Street v. Consumers Mining Corp., 185 Va. 561, 39 S.E.2d 271 (1946), the victim's disease, caused by breathing silica dust, had existed "from 10 to 15 years" although there was "no definite evidence to show at what time (the) silicosis was contracted." 185 Va. at 565, 39 S.E.2d at 272. There, the injury was complete and the cause of action accrued many years before the plaintiff's wrongful death action was instituted.

In Richmond Redevelopment and Housing Authority v. Laburnum Construction Corp., 195 Va. 827, 80 S.E.2d 574 (1954), a 1948 explosion stemming from an improper gas-pipe union caused the property damage sued for. The defective gas line was installed by defendant's subcontractor not later than 1943. In holding the suit filed in 1949 time-barred under a five-year statute of limitations, the court held the cause of action accrued at the time the line was constructed and not when the explosion occurred. The basis of the claim was for defective materials and improper workmanship and, according to the court, the hurt the injury alleged was the harm done to the pipe line upon installation. Thus, the injury was complete and the cause of action accrued no later than 1943, although the injury was not discovered until the subsequent explosion, which caused consequential damage.

Also in Hawks v. DeHart, 206 Va. 810, 146 S.E.2d 187 (1966), the cause of action for medical malpractice accrued in 1946 when a surgical needle was negligently left in plaintiff's neck by the defendant physician. Thus the 1963 personal injury suit was untimely even though plaintiff did not discover the wrong until 1962. There, plaintiff was hurt and harmed when the needle was allowed to remain in her body. The injury was complete in 1946 when the wrong was committed.

Finally, in Virginia Military Institute v. King, 217 Va. 751, 232 S.E.2d 895 (1977), V.M.I. sued a firm of architects for alleged improper design of a building. We held the cause of action accrued when the plans were finally approved no later than February of 1968 and not when evidence of deterioration of the building's stonework was first noticed in December of 1969. Thus, the January 1974 suit was barred by the applicable five-year statute of limitations. There we pointed out that at the time the plans were approved in 1968, "if defects had been discovered, V.M.I. could have initiated legal proceedings against the architects" because "a cause of action for defective plans arose upon tender of the plans by the architect to the owner." Consequently, the injury was complete in 1968 because the owner had suffered harm when the erroneous drawings were submitted.

For the reasons assigned, we conclude the trial court erred in determining this action was time-barred. Accordingly, the judgment appealed from will be reversed. The case will be remanded for further proceedings not inconsistent with the views expressed in this opinion, without prejudice to the interests of the plaintiff, his estate, his personal representative or the decedent's statutory beneficiaries under the Virginia Death by Wrongful Act statutes.

Reversed and remanded.

PREPARING FOR CLASS

Distinguish between when the harm was first inflicted and when it was first discovered. Here the court defened adopting the discovery rule, deeming it more appropriate for legislative consideration. The discovery rule will be addressed more in the following case. Understand and appreciate the consequences of having a limitation period on the right to bring a cause of action. In other words, who is advantaged by having a statute of limitations and what goals or policies are furthered by their implementation?

APPLYING THE LAW

Plaintiff is seriously injured in a car accident on May, 24 2009. Plaintiff is initially in a coma as a result of the accident but comes out of it on August 4, 2009. The applicable statute of limitation is 2 years. Plaintiff files a lawsuit on August 2, 2011. Defendant moves for dismissal arguing that the claim is untimely. Who wins?

INCREASING YOUR UNDERSTANDING

1. Statutes of limitations prescribe the time period in which a cause of action must be filed. Failure to file the lawsuit within the statutory period may preclude the plaintiff from realizing any recovery. The period typically starts to run when the plaintiff is injured, but some statutes may describe the period as beginning to run at the time of the defendant's wrongful act. In most cases the wrongful act causes an immediate obvious injury so there is little controversy over when the statute starts to run. Regardless, *Locke* articulates the position that most courts take when interpreting statutory language; the limitations

period starts to run after there has been a wrong and an injury, as there is no claim without both.

2. States vary on the period of time a party may have to bring a cause of action. The nature of the underlying claim (contracts/torts) and who the defendant is (doctor/governmental entities) are a couple of factors that might influence the prescribed period. A longer limitation period promotes recovery, a shorter one might be preferred in situations where there is interest in shielding the defendant from liability. In cases where the cause of action fails to fit squarely within a described category the court will ultimately decide the theory upon which the claim is premised and therefore what the appropriate limitation period is, not the parties.

3. *Continuing torts.* Occasionally the underlying claim stems from a series of wrongful acts, which then makes unsettled when the limitations period commences. In the medical malpractice context some courts have relied on the "the continuous course of treatment doctrine" to toll the limitations period from running until the treatment for a particular condition is terminated. See Cunningham v. Huffman, 154 Ill. 2d 398, 609 N.E.2d 321 (Ill. 1993) (To prevail under a continuous course of negligence theory, plaintiff "must demonstrate: (1) that there was a continuous and unbroken course of *negligent* treatment, and (2) that the treatment was so related as to constitute one continuing wrong."

4. Statues of limitations usually provide for the tolling (statute does not start running) in cases involving minors or those who may suffer from an "incapacity" (mental or physical infirmity/incarceration, etc.) until the minor reaches the age of majority or the incapacity is removed. Similarly, the defendant whose fraudulent conduct has prevented the plaintiff from realizing the existence of a cause of action may be estopped from relying on a running of the statute of limitations, which is tantamount to finding that the period doesn't start to run until the plaintiff has been relieved of the fraud.

B. THE DISCOVERY RULE

O'Brien v. Eli Lilly & Co.
668 F.2d 704 (3d Cir. 1981)

ALDISERT, Circuit Judge.
The question for decision in this appeal from a summary judgment in favor of four defendant pharmaceutical manufacturers in a diversity action is

whether the district court properly applied the Pennsylvania "discovery rule," which modifies the personal injury statute of limitations. The district court determined that, if she had exercised due diligence, appellant Ann O'Brien reasonably could have discovered in February 1976 that her mother had taken Diethylstilbestrol (commonly known as Stilbestrol or DES) during her 1956 pregnancy and that the drug arguably caused appellant's subsequent cancer. She did not file her complaint until December 31, 1979; accordingly, the district court concluded that the suit was barred by the two-year statute of limitations. Appellant contends that whether she possessed the knowledge necessary in 1976 to start the running of the statute was a jury question. Conceding that this is a close case, we nevertheless find no genuine issue of material fact and affirm the grant of summary judgment.

I.

The relevant Pennsylvania statute of limitations for personal injury actions states:

> The following actions and proceedings must be commenced within two years:
> ... (2) An action to recover damages for injuries to the person or for the death of an individual caused by the wrongful act or neglect or unlawful violence or negligence of another.

42 Pa. Cons. Stat. Ann. §5524(2). The district court applied this statute in granting appellees' motion for summary judgment.

Statutes of limitation express the legislatures' public policy judgments of how long a plaintiff may delay suit without being unfair to a defendant. "These and similar legislative enactments are expressive of the feeling of mankind that where there are wrongs to be redressed, they should be redressed without unreasonable delay, and where there are rights to be enforced, they should be enforced without unreasonable delay."

Nevertheless, Pennsylvania courts have recognized the potential harshness inherent in a rigid application of the statute and long ago carved out an exception: ignorance of an injury may delay the running of the statute of limitations. Lewey v. Fricke Coke Co., 166 Pa. 536, 31 A. 261 (1895). The judicially created "discovery rule" announced in *Lewey* has been expanded to except the plaintiff who is aware of his injury but not its cause. Federal courts in this circuit have helped to refine the precept. Our district courts have noted that the rule delays the accrual of a cause of action from the time of a defendant's tortious conduct to a time when the injury and its cause become known or knowable, Gemignani v. Philadelphia Phillies Nat'l League Baseball Club, 287 F. Supp. 465, 467 (E.D. Pa. 1967), that it is a rule intended to benefit plaintiffs in that it avoids potential injustice caused where an injury is "inherently unknowable" at the time of a defendant's conduct, . . . and that the legislatively declared desirability for repose and judicial administrative expediency will not be unduly affected by the small number of "inherently unknowable" injuries. . . . Moreover, this court, in Bayless v. Philadelphia Nat'l League Club, 579 F.2d 37 (3d Cir. 1978), and DaMato v. Turner & Newall, Ltd., 651 F.2d 908 (3d Cir. 1981) (per curiam), adopted the reasoning and the precept announced by our colleague A. Leon Higginbotham, Jr. (then a district judge) in *Gemignani*: in a personal injury action under Pennsylvania law, the period of limitations begins to run "from the time the plaintiff, through the exercise of reasonable diligence, should have learned both the facts in question and that those facts bore some causative relationship to the injury." In further refining the test, Pennsylvania courts have developed a precise analysis defining the elements of the discovery rule. We will discuss this analysis in detail in Part III of this opinion.

We use the discovery rule to measure the facts adduced in the summary judgment proceedings below. We are not presented with a question of choice or interpretation of the precept; rather the dispute is over the application of the precept to the facts presented to the district court. We will review the facts in detail and in the light most favorable to the appellant, essentially as set forth in her brief.

II.

In July 1956, Mary Ann O'Brien, appellant's mother, consulted Dr. Kenneth L. Cooper, a gynecologist and obstetrician, concerning her pregnancy with appellant Ann O'Brien, who was born on February 18, 1957. Because Mrs. O'Brien's previous pregnancy had terminated in a miscarriage, Dr. Cooper on July 26, 1956, prescribed 25 milligrams of Stilbestrol. In her deposition Mrs. O'Brien recalled that Dr. Cooper had prescribed some medication during this pregnancy, but she did not know the specific kind. She did recall taking a "red pill" or "white pill" during her pregnancy with appellant. Mrs. O'Brien testified: "I took whatever he prescribed and never questioned . . . it, I simply took it, if he prescribed it, I took it."

During the summer of 1971, when she was fourteen years old, appellant experienced unusual vaginal bleeding. In September of that year, upon examination by a gynecologist, Dr. Carl Dorko, and following a recommendation by her pediatrician, Dr. Frank Procopio, she was admitted to the Harrisburg Hospital for diagnosis. Dr. Dorko discovered a tumor and performed a biopsy. In addition to the pathology report prepared by the Harrisburg Hospital pathologist, the biopsy slides were sent for evaluation to Dr. Robert Scully, a pathologist at Massachusetts General Hospital.

Dr. Scully responded that the tumor "fits into the category of clear cell carcinoma occurring in young women that we have found to be frequently associated with maternal Stilbestrol administration." Dr. Dorko informed Mr. and Mrs. O'Brien of the biopsy results and referred their daughter for treatment to Dr. John Mikuta, a gynecologist and oncologist at the Hospital of the University of Pennsylvania. There, in October 1971, appellant underwent a radical hysterectomy, lymph node dissection, and partial vaginectomy. She received radiation therapy for six weeks.

Appellant's parents requested that she not be told that her tumor was malignant. All doctors participating in her diagnosis and treatment cooperated with that wish and her parents did not themselves tell her of the malignancy.

Shortly before appellant's surgery, in the fall of 1971, her mother met with Dr. Mikuta. During this meeting, Dr. Mikuta asked Mrs. O'Brien whether she had ever taken diethylstilbestrol to prevent a miscarriage. Mrs. O'Brien denied taking the medication.

In 1971, Dr. Scully and Dr. Arthur Herbst of Massachusetts General Hospital reported in the medical literature an association between maternal ingestion of diethylstilbestrol during pregnancy and clear cell adenocarcinoma in the female offspring of that pregnancy. As a means of centralizing data obtained from such cases, Drs. Herbst and Scully established a Registry for Adenocarcinoma of the Genital Tract in Young Women. Dr. Mikuta was familiar with the work of Drs. Herbst and Scully. He discussed appellant's case with Dr. Herbst as well as with Drs. Cooper and Dorko in late 1971 and early 1972.

In October 1971, Dr. Herbst wrote to Dr. Dorko, enclosing two questionnaire forms pertaining to appellant, her treatment, medical history, and family history. Following a telephone conversation with Mrs. O'Brien in January 1972, Dr. Dorko sent her one of the forms asking her to "fill out as much of it as you can." The form included the question, "Did mother take hormones during pregnancy?" Mrs. O'Brien has stated, in an affidavit, that the answer "No" on the form is in her handwriting and was placed there in late January 1972. The form also asked for "Other medications taken during pregnancy (name, dosage, and when taken)." Diethylstilbestrol is not among the medicines Mrs. O'Brien listed in response.

Shortly before her regular appointment with Dr. Mikuta in February 1976, appellant read an article in a January 1976 issue of *Newsweek*. At this time she knew that her mother had suffered a miscarriage before appellant was born. She also knew that Dr. Cooper was her mother's obstetrician.

In her deposition, Ann recollected the article ["Daughters of DES, Newsweek, January 26, 1976"] and her subsequent discussion with Dr. Mikuta:

> A. Well, the article talked about a girl whose mother had taken DES and the girl had cancer. And the article talked about the procedure, the surgical procedure . . . that she had gone through. And what happened to her after that and she died.

And everything about the procedure that she had gone through—or almost everything—was what I had gone through. And it was all too close, the cancer, and this was my concern, not DES at that point. And I was quite upset with Doctor Mikuta, I was very adamant that I wanted an answer from him whether I had cancer or not. And he said that I did.

Q. Did you ask him whether it was in any way DES related?
A. Yes. And he said that it pointed to that but they were not sure.
Q. It pointed to DES but they were not sure?
A. Not sure. And we continued to talk about cancer.
Q. Did he tell you why it pointed to DES?
A. No.
Q. Did he tell you why they were not sure?
A. No.
Q. Did Doctor Mikuta indicate to you why he responded that the cancer pointed to DES?
A. Because of the type of cancer that it is or was.
Q. Did he say that to you?
A. Yes.
Q. Did he ever say to you that it pointed to DES because your mother had taken it?
A. I don't think so.

In April 1976, Ann O'Brien confronted her mother about concealing the truth about the tumor. She was very upset with her parents and dissatisfied with Mrs. O'Brien's explanation for withholding the information. During the course of that confrontation, appellant also asked her mother whether she had taken DES during her pregnancy. Her mother denied taking the drug. Although Mrs. O'Brien does not remember her daughter asking prior to September 1979 whether she had taken DES, appellant's recollection of the 1976 conversation is very clear.

Three years later, in the summer of 1979, appellant became aware of additional magazine and newspaper articles on the relationship of DES ingestion by pregnant women to the incidence of cancer in female offspring. Although the record does not set forth the content or text of these articles, she testified that again she was struck by the similarity between her own medical history and the type of cancer and treatment described.

In September 1979, appellant again asked her mother if she had taken DES while pregnant, and Mrs. O'Brien again replied that she had not. This time, however, appellant insisted that her mother call Drs. Cooper and Mikuta in order to determine if in fact she had taken the drug. According to appellant, both doctors confirmed that it had been prescribed for Mrs. O'Brien. Mrs. O'Brien also contacted the Kolb Pharmacy in an attempt to identify the manufacturer of the diethylstilbestrol she had purchased there, but found that any records the pharmacy might have maintained were destroyed in the Hurricane "Agnes" flood of 1972. Thereafter, on December 31, 1979, appellant filed her complaint against four leading manufacturers of DES.

III.

In DaMato v. Turner & Newall, Ltd., 651 F.2d 908 (3d Cir. 1981) (per curiam), we noted Pennsylvania's acceptance of a standard for defining the level of knowledge a plaintiff must have before the period of limitations will start to run. As set forth by Pennsylvania Common Pleas Court Judge Takiff in Volpe v. Johns-Manville Corp., 4 P.C.R. 290 (Phila. C.P. 1980), the standard has three elements:

> With the question of "reasonableness" as a constant qualification running through the decisional law, the principle emerges that three independent phases of knowledge must be known or knowable to plaintiff before the limitations period commences: (1) knowledge of the injury; (2) knowledge of the operative cause of the injury; and (3) knowledge of the causative relationship between the injury and the operative conduct.

Measuring the instant facts against this three-part standard, we are persuaded that in 1976, when Ann O'Brien was told that she had had cancer, she acquired knowledge of her injury; and that when she read the Newsweek article and consulted with Dr. Mikuta she acquired knowledge from which, by the exercise of due diligence, she could have discovered both the alleged operative cause of her injury—her mother's ingestion of DES—and the causal relationship between the operative conduct and her injury.

Appellant concedes the first element, knowledge of injury by 1976, but she contends that there was sufficient controversy regarding the second and third elements to require submission to a factfinder the issue of when she could have acquired information about the causal relation to DES by the exercise of due diligence. We do not agree. There is no dispute to be resolved by a factfinder. The question is solely whether from the facts presented a jury could reasonably conclude that appellant, if she had exercised due diligence, could not have discovered the operative cause of her injury and the causal relationship in 1976.

Appellant argues that because she did not know that her mother had taken DES until September 1979, she did not acquire actual knowledge of the cause of her injury until then. The acquisition of actual knowledge, however, is not the trigger for the running of the limitations period under Pennsylvania law. The correct inquiry, as appellant recognizes, is not whether she had actual knowledge of all three *Volpe* elements before 1979, but "whether (she) should reasonably be charged with that knowledge before that time." We held in Bayless v. Philadelphia Nat'l League Club, 579 F.2d 37 (3d Cir. 1978) that the statute runs "from the time the plaintiff, through the exercise of due diligence, should have learned" the facts and their relationship. The policy enunciated by Judge Takiff in *Volpe* is also applicable:

> Plaintiff's ignorance of his injury or its cause may render knowledge of his cause of action unknown and unknowable. But once he possesses the salient facts concerning the occurrence of his injury and who or what caused it, he has the ability to investigate and pursue his claim. Postponing the commencement of the limitations period until he has actually done so would nullify the justifiable rationale of the statute of limitations and permit the prosecution of stale claims.

Volpe, 4 P.C.R. at 303-04. Although *Volpe* dealt with the relationship of the discovery rule to ignorance of a legal cause of action, the same considerations are present in a case in which a plaintiff has facts sufficient to prompt an investigation but does not investigate.

The flaw in appellant's case is her failure to present evidence sufficient to permit a jury to find that she could not reasonably have possessed "the salient facts concerning the occurrence of (her) injury and who or what caused it" before 1979. The facts recited in Part II of this opinion demonstrate that in 1976 appellant knew the facts necessary to complete her investigation: (1) that her mother had miscarried prior to appellant's birth, (2) that appellant's medical history had a marked similarity to the medical history of other young women whose cancers had been linked to DES ingestion by mothers who had previously miscarried, (3) that her doctors believed her medical history pointed in the direction of DES, and (4) the identity of her mother's obstetrician.

The district court's conclusion that as a matter of law appellant unreasonably delayed investigating is underscored by the similarity of appellant's knowledge in 1976 to her knowledge in 1979. The record shows only two historical events of 1979 supplementing the basic factual matrix of 1976: (1) appellant read some additional articles on DES and (2) she insisted that her mother ask Dr. Cooper if he had prescribed DES to her during her pregnancy. The record does not indicate that appellant acquired knowledge from her reading about the DES-cancer relationship in 1979 that she had not previously acquired in 1976.

The record as to the new information gained from Drs. Cooper and Mikuta in 1979 also compels our conclusion that the crucial information on causation was available upon reasonable inquiry in 1976. The 1976 Newsweek article was specific and presented a case history that paralleled appellant's in many ways. The record fails to show that the articles read by appellant after 1976 contained any new information about either the operative cause or the causal relationship between the operative conduct and the injury that was not contained in the 1976 Newsweek article. Similarly, appellant's mother provided information in 1976 that, in effect, she merely repeated in 1979.

When asked by her daughter in 1976, the mother denied having taken DES. When asked again in 1979, the mother persisted in the denial. Given the foregoing circumstances, there appears to be no persuasive reason why appellant in 1976 could not, "through the exercise of due diligence," have requested her mother to call Dr. Cooper then to learn "both the facts in question and that those facts bore some causative relationship to the injury."

The polestar of the Pennsylvania discovery rule is not a plaintiff's actual acquisition of knowledge but whether the knowledge was known or, through the exercise of diligence, knowable to plaintiff. We agree with the district court that, as a matter of law, the crucial knowledge was knowable to the appellant in 1976 and could have been obtained through the exercise of due diligence. Therefore, its conclusion that the action is barred by the statute of limitations must be affirmed.

PREPARING FOR CLASS

1. What does the plaintiff have to discover before the statute of limitations starts to run?

2. Would this issue best be resolved by the jury?

3. Be reminded of the primary purpose behind the creation of statutes of limitations and how it might influence a courts willingness to extend it by adopting a discovery rule.

APPLYING THE LAW

Deceased is murdered by an employee while employee is on the job. Applicable statute of limitations for wrongful death action is two years. The identity of the assailant and the fact that he was working at the time of the murder are not known until he is convicted four years after the crime. Would a wrongful death action against the employer be untimely if brought immediately after the criminal trial concluded?

INCREASING YOUR UNDERSTANDING

1. The principal case relies on what has been commonly referred to as the "discovery rule." The rule originated in the common law but has recently found its way into legislation. And while the justification for the rule is grounded in fairness, it is not without controversy as it potentially extends the period for plaintiff to bring a claim indefinitely. Perhaps there is no more visible critic of the rule, at least without legislative approval, than Justice Scalia: "The injury-discovery rule . . . . is bad wine of recent vintage." TRW Inc. v. Andrews 534

U.S. 19, 122 S. Ct. 441 (2001). See also Trentadue v. Buckler Lawn Sprinkler 479 Mich. 378, 738 N.W.2d 664 (2007). In *Trentadue*, the deceased was raped and murdered in 1986. DNA evidence established in 2002 that an employee of the defendant had committed the crimes. Acting on this revelation the plaintiffs initiated a wrongful death lawsuit, which in Michigan was governed by a three-year statute of limitations. Held: Supreme Court would not use equity to toll wrongful death statute's three-year statute of limitations until 16 years after murder merely because personal representative could not reasonably discover facts underlying potential negligence of the defendants.

2. What does the plaintiff have to discover? *O'Brien* is explicit in the showing that plaintiff has to make in order to prevail under the discovery rule. Other courts however aren't as articulate, let alone consistent. Some suggest that discovering the injury is enough, while others may require that both injury and the cause of the injury must be discovered before the limitations clock begins to run. Where the identity of the defendant is unknown, some states allow for plaintiffs to sue fictitious parties as a way of avoiding the consequence attendant to bringing an untimely suit.

3. Repose within a limitation period? An unconditional adoption of the discovery rule extends the period for bringing a cause of action indefinitely; the clock doesn't start to run on bringing the cause of action until plaintiff discovers that she has been injured. To ameliorate the harshness associated with a literal application of the discovery rule, some jurisdictions have incorporated a repose period within their statute of limitations. For example, Wisconsin has incorporated the discover rule in its statute of limitations for medical malpractice actions (Wis. Stat. §893.55 (1m)(b)), and it states that causes of actions must be brought "one year from the date the injury was discovered or, in the exercise of reasonable diligence should have been discovered, except that an action may not be commenced under this paragraph more than 5 years from the date of the act or omission."

C.   STATUTE OF REPOSE

Trinity River Authority v. URS Consultants, Inc.—Texas
889 S.W.2d 259 (Tex. 1994)

PHILLIPS, Chief Justice, delivered the opinion of the Court.
Texas Civil Practice and Remedies Code section 16.008 bars suits against architects or engineers for defective design of an improvement to real property unless brought within ten years after the improvement is completed, regardless

of when the defect is discovered. The issue presented is whether this statute of repose violates either the Texas or United States Constitution. We hold that, as applied in this case, it does not, and therefore we affirm the judgment of the court of appeals.

I

In May 1972, respondent URS Consultants, Inc. ("URS") contracted with petitioner Trinity River Authority ("Trinity") to design improvements to a sewage treatment plant operated by Trinity. An equalizer basin wall designed by URS was completed and put into service at the plant in 1976. On March 11, 1990, the basin wall collapsed, spilling a large amount of raw sewage and causing extensive property damage to the plant and surrounding area. Contending that the basin wall was negligently designed, Trinity brought suit for damages against URS on March 6, 1992.

URS subsequently moved for summary judgment on the basis of Texas Civil Practice and Remedies Code section 16.008, which bars such suits against architects or engineers brought more than ten years after the improvement is completed. The motion for summary judgment was based solely on Trinity's pleadings, which indicated on their face that more than ten years had elapsed since completion of the basin wall. The trial court rendered summary judgment for URS, and the court of appeals affirmed.

II

Texas Civil Practice and Remedies Code section 16.008 provides in pertinent part as follows:

> (a) A person must bring suit for [personal injury or property damage] against a registered or licensed architect or engineer in this state, who designs, plans, or inspects the construction of an improvement to real property or equipment attached to real property, not later than 10 years after the substantial completion of the improvement or the beginning of operation of the equipment in an action arising out of a defective or unsafe condition of the real property, the improvement, or the equipment.

This statute, which bars claims against an architect or engineer after ten years even if the alleged design defect was undiscoverable before that time, is commonly referred to as a "statute of repose." Unlike traditional limitations provisions, which begin running upon accrual of a cause of action, a statute of repose runs from a specified date without regard to accrual of any cause of action. One court has characterized statutes of repose as "a substantive definition of, rather than a procedural limitation on, rights." Statutes similar to section 16.008 have been enacted in a majority of states in response to a perceived need to protect designers and builders from the threat of claims arising many years after completion of a project.

Trinity does not contest that URS is a design professional covered by section 16.008. The sole issue, therefore, is whether the statute is constitutional. Trinity raises challenges under the Texas constitutional guarantees of open courts, equal protection, and due course of law, as well as the federal equal protection and due process clauses.

IV

Trinity argues that section 16.008 violates its right to substantive due process under the Texas and United States Constitutions. The principal Texas due process guarantee provides as follows:

> No citizen of this State shall be deprived of life, liberty, property, privileges or immunities, or in any manner disfranchised, except by the due course of the law of the land.

Tex. Const. art. I, §19. Although Texas courts have not been consistent in articulating a standard of review under the due course clause, under any cognizable test section 16.008 passes constitutional muster.

We start with the unassailable premise that statutes of limitation, in general, serve a public function. They "compel the exercise of a right of action within a reasonable time so that the opposing party has a fair opportunity to defend while witnesses are available and the evidence is fresh in their minds." As recognized in *Rosenberg v. Town of North Bergen*, 61 N.J. 190, 293 A.2d 662, 667-68 (1972):

> There comes a time when [the defendant] ought to be secure in his reasonable expectation that the slate has been wiped clean of ancient obligations, and he ought not to be called on to resist a claim "when evidence has been lost, memories have faded, and witnesses have disappeared."

(quoting *Developments in the Law: Statutes of Limitations*, 63 Harv. L. Rev. 1177, 1185 (1950)).

Statutes of repose differ from traditional limitations, of course, in that they potentially cut off a right of action before it accrues. As to real estate improvements, however, where a claim may arise many years after the designer's involvement with the project has ceased, the statute must operate in this manner if it is to serve its purpose. URS correctly notes that potential liability could extend for "50 or even 60 years," throughout the designer's lifetime.

This Court's decision in *Robinson v. Weaver*, 550 S.W.2d 18 (Tex. 1977), illustrates the important public purpose underlying statutes of repose. We held in that case that the discovery rule does not apply to cases of medical misdiagnosis. Unlike malpractice based on leaving a foreign object in the patient's body, or negligently performing a vasectomy, there is often no physical evidence establishing a misdiagnosis, thus increasing the risk of stale or even fraudulent claims. The Court thus concluded that the public purpose of limitations—protecting defendants from having to defend stale claims—should be served even though some meritorious claims might be barred:

> Statutes of limitations are not directed to the merits of any individual case, they are a result of the legislative assessment of the merits of cases in general. The fact that a meritorious claim might thereby be rendered nonassertible is an unfortunate, occasional by-product of the operation of limitations. All statutes of limitations provide *some* time period during which the cause of action is assertible. However, preclusion of a legal remedy alone is not enough to justify a judicial exception to the statute. The primary purpose of limitations, to prevent litigation of stale or fraudulent claims, must be kept in mind.

The Court noted that application of the discovery rule would subject physicians to the expense of litigation "however great may have been the lapse of time between the date of cessation of the doctor-patient relationship and the formal prosecution of the claim."

Defending against allegations of negligent structural design many years after completion of a building also presents substantial evidentiary problems. The passage of time not only fades memories, but also increases "[t]he possibility of third-party neglect, abuse, poor maintenance, mishandling, improper modification, or unskilled repair." We believe that the ten year repose period chosen by the Legislature strikes a fair balance between the legislative purpose of protecting against stale claims and the rights of litigants to obtain redress for injuries.

For the reasons discussed above in connection with the Texas due course of law guarantee, section 16.008 also does not violate Trinity's right to due process of law under the United States Constitution.

The judgment of the court of appeals is accordingly affirmed.

DOGGETT, J., joins in the judgment only.

PREPARING FOR CLASS

1. What circumstances might compel a state to create a statute of repose?

2. Is there room for a discovery rule along with a repose rule?

3. See the interplay between the statutes of limitations and repose and how they coexist.

APPLYING THE LAW

Defendant sells asbestos-containing product in 2000. State has a ten-year statute of repose for product liability actions, a two-year statute of limitations, and has adopted the discovery rule. Plaintiff is exposed to asbestos between 2005 and 2009 but doesn't discover that he has asbestosis until 2011, when he promptly brings lawsuit against the defendant. Should the court dismiss the case?

INCREASING YOUR UNDERSTANDING

1. As the principal case illustrates, statutes of reposes were first created to shield architects and engineers from liability that might stem from injuries caused by defects or conditions created by their work. Subsequently, lawyers and lobbyists for other enterprises (product manufacturers, doctors, accountants, etc.) were successful in convincing legislators in some states that they too should be protected from long-term liability. Over the years, the justifications for enacting repose periods have largely remained the same, all that has changed is the context.

2. *Getting things started*. While every state has a statute of limitations that governs recognizable tort claims, not every state has adopted a statute of repose. As previously stated, statutes of limitations typically begin to run at the time of injury. In contrast, repose periods start to run upon an event unrelated to injury. The running of either will defeat a plaintiff's claim.

D. SOVEREIGN IMMUNITY

Hicks v. State
88 N.M. 588, 544 P.2d 1153 (N.M. 1975)

Montoya, Justice.

This appeal arises from an order of the Santa Fe County District Court granting the motion of defendant State of New Mexico to dismiss on the ground that the action of plaintiff Ron E. Hicks was barred by the doctrine of sovereign immunity.

Suit was originally brought in the District Court of Santa Fe County on August 6, 1973, to recover damages for the wrongful death of plaintiff's wife and minor daughter due allegedly to the negligence of the State Highway Department. These deaths were the result of an accident near Fort Summer, New Mexico, on December 26, 1972, when a school bus collided with a cattle truck on a narrow bridge constructed and maintained by the State Highway Department. Subsequently, defendant filed a motion to dismiss. After a hearing, the motion was granted by order of the trial court on May 31, 1974. On June 21, 1974, plaintiff filed a notice of appeal.

In a memorandum decision, the district court stated that the doctrine of sovereign immunity was a long-standing common law principle which could now be changed only by legislative action. We do not agree that a change in this age-old doctrine can only be made by the legislature.

As recognized by the district court, the doctrine of sovereign immunity is one of common law, judicially created. This court stated in the case of Dougherty v. Vidal, 37 N.M. 256, 257-58, 21 P.2d 90, 91 (1933), that:

> " 'It is a fundamental doctrine at common law and everywhere in America that no sovereign state can be sued in its own courts or in any other without its consent and permission.' State ex rel. Evans v. Field, 27 N.M. 384, 201 P. 1059, 1060 (1921). . . ." (Emphasis added.)

Over the years, we have tenaciously retained this archaic principle in spite of changing circumstances. Not until 1941 did the legislature enact any law directly relating to the matter of sovereign immunity. [These] statutory schemes were in harmony with the common law doctrine of sovereign immunity, but had the effect of lessening, to a certain extent, the oftentimes harsh results of that doctrine. They definitely did not, as argued by defendants, create statutory sovereign immunity.

The legislature itself recognizes that sovereign immunity is a common law doctrine and this should dispel the argument or contention that sovereign immunity was statutorily created, either by the repealed statutes, supra, or by the statute adopting the common law in New Mexico. See §21-3-3, N.M.S.A., 1953 (Repl. Vol. 4, 1970).

The original justification for the doctrine of sovereign immunity was the archaic view that "the sovereign can do no wrong." It is hardly necessary for this court to spend time to refute this feudalistic contention. This and all other rationalizations which have been advanced to justify continued adherence to this doctrine are no longer valid in New Mexico. The argument has been presented that the elimination of sovereign immunity will result in an intolerable financial burden upon the State. We believe it is safe to say that adequate insurance can be secured to eliminate that possible burden in a satisfactory manner. In addition, it would appear that placing the financial burden upon the State, which is able to distribute its losses throughout the populace, is more just and equitable than forcing the individual who is injured to bear the entire burden alone. There are presently in New Mexico no conditions or circumstances which could rationally support the doctrine of sovereign immunity. We have long recognized that the doctrine is not applicable to municipalities when engaged in a proprietary function . . . .

Several times in the recent past this court has cast aspersions upon sovereign immunity:

> "As to sovereign immunity, that doctrine, insofar as it has been created by courts, seems headed for a deserved repose. Courts and scholars can find little reason for it, and its historical basis is of doubtful validity. . . ."

City of Albuquerque v. Garcia, 84 N.M. 776, 778, 508 P.2d 585, 587 (1973).

> ". . . We are thus not concerned with the outmoded medievalisms embedded in our jurisprudence in the form of judicially-created sovereign immunity."

State ex rel. N.M. Water Qual. C.C. v. City of Hobbs, 86 N.M. 444, 445, 525 P.2d 371, 372 (1974). But unfortunately, in those cases, the issue was not squarely before us, as it is today. Thus, we take this opportunity to rid the State of this legal anachronism. Common law sovereign immunity may no longer be interposed as a defense by the State, or any of its political subdivisions, in tort actions. Sovereign immunity was born out of the judicial branch of government, and it is the same branch which may dispose of the doctrine. It can no longer be justified by existing circumstances and has long been devoid of any valid justification. In so doing, we join the growing number of States which have judicially abolished it.

We recognize that this is a far-reaching decision which, at first blush, does violence to the doctrine of "stare decisis." However, we do not feel that "stare decisis" should be used to perpetuate the harsh and unjust results which blind adherence to sovereign immunity rules mandated. We concede that there was ample authority which influenced our predecessors in adopting and upholding the doctrine of sovereign immunity. We also say that there is better reasoned authority to overturn it. We simply conclude that its continuance is causing a great degree of injustice.

In today's world, we cannot discount the extent of governmental intervention and actions which affect the conduct of human affairs. We agree with the reasoning of the Supreme Court of Pennsylvania in its discussion of the doctrine in Ayala v. Philadelphia Board of Public Education, 453 Pa. 584, 592, 305 A.2d 877, 881-82 (1973), when it stated:

> "Today we conclude that no reasons whatsoever exist for continuing to adhere to the doctrine of governmental immunity. Whatever may have been the basis for the inception of the doctrine, it is clear that no public policy considerations presently justify its retention.
>
> "Governmental immunity can no longer be justified on 'an amorphous mass of cumbrous language about sovereignty. . . .' Leflar and

Kantrowitz, Tort Liability of the States, 29 N.Y.U. L. Rev. 1363, 1364 (1954). As one court has stated:

"'... it is almost incredible that in this modern age of comparative sociological enlightenment, and in a republic, the medieval absolutism supposed to be implicit in the maxim, "the King can do no wrong," should exempt the various branahes of the government from liability for their torts, and that the entire burden of damage resulting from the wrongful acts of the government should be imposed upon the single individual who suffers the injury, rather than distributed among the entire community constituting the government, where it could be borne without hardship upon any individual, and where it justly belongs.' Barker v. City of Santa Fe, 47 N.M. 85, 136 P.2d 480, 482. Likewise, we agree with the Supreme Court of Florida that in preserving the sovereign immunity theory, courts have overlooked the fact that the Revolutionary War was fought to abolish that 'divine right of kings' on which the theory is based"

"Moreover, we are unwilling to perpetuate the notion that 'it is better that an individual should sustain an injury than that the public should suffer an inconvenience.' This social philosophy of nonliability is 'an anachronism in the law of today.' As has been noted:

> "'The social climate which fostered the growth of absolutism and the divine right of kings in England has long since been tempered with the warm winds of humanitarianism and individual freedom. The changes which have occurred in the last century with respect to the imposition of liability upon private corporate enterprises of any kind are well-known. Workmen's compensation laws have replaced the old theories which permitted the corporate organizations to escape liability under the fellow-servant rule or the doctrine of assumption of risk. Liability may now be predicated without fault merely on grounds that potential injuries to individuals must be calculated as a part of the cost of doing business, and must be paid for by the business enterprise. There is widespread acceptance of a philosophy that those who enjoy the fruits of the enterprise must also accept its risks and attendant responsibilities.'"

"Recently, this Court reiterated the prevailing philosophy that liability follows tortious conduct. In Niederman v. Brodsky, 436 Pa. 401, 403, 261 A.2d 84, 85 (1970), we said:

> "'It is fundamental to our common law system that one may seek redress for every sustantial wrong. "The best statement of the rule is that a wrongdoer is responsible for the natural and proximate consequences of his misconduct. ...'"

"Appellee offers no reason—and we are unable to discern one—for permitting governmental units to escape the effect of this fundamental principle."

Though the foregoing case decided by the Pennsylvania Supreme Court related to liability of a local school board, we believe that the principles and reasoning enunciated therein apply equally to a State agency.

We, therefore, conclude that the ancient doctrine of sovereign immunity has lost its underpinnings by the social and governmental changes which have occurred. This view was expressed with great clarity by Justice Cardozo in the following words:

"'A rule which in its origins was the creation of the courts themselves, and was supposed in the making to express the mores of the day, may be abrogated by the courts when the mores have so changed that perpetuation of the rule would do violence to the social conscience.' Cardozo, The Growth of the Law 136-37 (1924)."

Ayala v. Philadelphia Board of Public Education, supra, 453 Pa. at 602, 305 A.2d at 886.

Accordingly all prior cases wherein governmental immunity from tort liability was recognized are expressly overruled and shall no longer be considered precedents in tort actions filed against governmental agencies.

Since this action involves a significant and major change in tort liability for governmental agencies, the question of its applicability to past, pending and future cases must be determined. The factors to be considered concerning retroactivity of court decisions are set out in Linkletter v. Walker, 381 U.S. 618, 85 S. Ct. 1731, 14 L. Ed. 2d 601 (1965). The United States Supreme Court there concluded that no distinction is drawn between civil and criminal litigation. It further held that there are no constitutional requirements concerning retroactivity, and that in each case the court may determine whether retroactive or prospective application is appropriate. After considering the factors as announced in *Linkletter v. Walker,* supra, it is our considered opinion that the rule of law announced herein shall have modified prospectivity. Consequently, the decision we announce herein applies to the case at bar, all similar pending actions and all cases which may arise in the future.

Consequently, the order of the district court is reversed. This matter is remanded to the district court with instructions to proceed with the action initiated by plaintiff in accordance with the views expressed herein.

It is so ordered.

OPINION ON MOTION FOR REHEARING

McMANUS, Justice.

By Order effective January 5, 1976, we modified our decision in Hicks v. State, 88 N.M. 588, 544 P.2d 1153, filed September 26, 1975, by holding that it is not to take effect nor apply to the case at bar or to any other cause or action in tort against any governmental agency if the alleged tort has occurred or occurs prior to July 1, 1976. We based this modification upon the briefs and arguments presented in the rehearing which we granted to the State. The rehearing was limited to the issue of whether the *Hicks* decision should apply: (1) only to cases arising in the future; (2) to cases arising in the future and to the case at bar; or (3) to cases arising in the future, to the case at bar and to all similar pending actions.

In the original *Hicks* decision we selected the third option. The briefs and arguments presented on rehearing developed this issue much more fully than had been done in the briefs and arguments on the appeal. We now conclude that the *Hicks* decision should apply only to cases arising in the future.

Many courts abolishing sovereign immunity have applied their decisions to cases arising in the future and to the case under consideration (the second option mentioned above).

At least two other courts have abolished sovereign immunity on a purely prospective basis, denying relief even to the plaintiffs who brought the action. Williams v. City of Detroit, 364 Mich. 231, 111 N.W.2d 1 (1961); Spanel v. Mounds View School District No. 621, 264 Minn. 279, 118 N.W.2d 795 (1962). In support of their decision the Minnesota Supreme Court in *Spanel* quoted Mr. Justice Cardozo from an article at 109 Pa. L. Rev. 13, as follows:

> "The rule that we are asked to apply is out of tune with the life about us. It has been made discordant by the forces that generate a living law. We apply it to this case because the repeal might work hardship to those who have trusted to its existence. We give notice, however, that any one trusting to it hereafter will do so at his peril." 264 Minn. at 294, 118 N.W.2d at 804.

The Minnesota court went on to conclude:

> "It may appear unfair to deprive the present claimant of his day in court. However, we are of the opinion it would work an even greater injustice to deny defendant and other units of government a defense on which they have had a right to rely. We believe that it is more equitable if they are permitted to plan in advance by securing liability insurance or by creating funds necessary for self-insurance. In addition, provision must be made for routinely and promptly investigating personal injury and other tort claims at the time of their occurrence in order that defendants may marshal and preserve whatever evidence is available for the proper conduct of their defense." 264 Minn. at 294-95, 118 N.W.2d at 804.

We find this reasoning persuasive.

It is so ordered.

MONTOYA, Justice (dissenting).

I respectfully disagree with the conclusion reached by the majority on rehearing, that the ruling previously made in this case should not take effect until July 1, 1976. The "modified prospectivity" rule, as announced in our opinion, is in accord with well-recognized principles of justice. The terms "similar pending actions" and "causes arising in the future," alleged to be ambiguous, have a definite legal meaning and are not subject to interpretation as claimed. It recognizes the oft-stated principle of law that all citizens should have access to the courts in seeking redress for every substantial wrong. The spectre that the effects of this ruling will bankrupt the State is, at best, based on pure conjecture and speculation. Before the State can be held liable for any claim the liability must be established and the damages proven in a court of law. I do not believe that reliance, convenience or expediency should outweigh the just objective that an aggrieved party be compensated for injuries suffered when incurred through the negligence of the State or any of its political subdivisions.

The least this Court should do is to apply the ruling to the case at bar where, through the efforts of the appellant, we have been afforded an opportunity to change an outmoded and unjust rule of law. The majority of cases dealing with the problem, excepting two, have applied the ruling to the case which resulted in the abolishment of the doctrine of sovereign immunity. To do otherwise would prevent case law or decisions from keeping up with the changing needs of society, when we deprive the litigant who was successful in making the change possible of the opportunity to completely litigate his claim on the merits. To be left only with the distinction of causing a change in the rule of law seems manifestly unfair.

The majority feeling otherwise, I respectfully dissent from the order on rehearing for the reasons above stated.

PREPARING FOR CLASS

1. Try mightily to identify the change in circumstances that this court relied upon in reaching the decision to abolish sovereign immunity. Do you find them persuasive? What would have to happen to give the New Mexico Supreme Court cause to reconsider and perhaps reverse its decision in *Hicks*?

2. Pay special attention to how the case advanced procedurally, especially with regard the application of the court's new rule.

INCREASING YOUR UNDERSTANDING

1. Most states have modified the sovereign immunity it once enjoyed— some totally abolishing the doctrine, others in a more limited fashion. The New Mexico Supreme Court in *Hicks* relied on the following chart:

The columns are as follows: (1) General abolition of immunity, subject to the normal exceptions, (2) Partial abolition, (3) Abolition (or waiver) in case of insurance, and (4) Full retention of immunity.

"§895B

Abolished	Partial	Insurance	Immunity
Alaska	Conn.	Ga.	Ala.
J Ariz.	Ky.	Kan.	Ark.
J Cal.	Mich.	Me.	Del.
J Colo.	Minn.	Mont.	Fla.
Haw.	Tenn.	N.H.	Md.
J Ida.	N.C.	N.M.	Mass.
Ill.	S.C.	N.D.	Miss.
J Ind.	Tex.	Okla.	Mo.
Ia.	W.Va.		Ohio
La.			Pa.
Neb.			S.D.
Nev.			Va.
J N.J.			Wyo.
N.Y.			
Ore.			
R.I.			
UtahVt.			
Wash.			
J Wis.			
J D.C.			
21 (8 J)	9	8	13 "

[A "J" in front of a state means thatchange was made judicially.]

Source: Restatement (Second) Torts, Special Note §895B at 21 (Tent. Draft No. 19, March 30, 1973).

Subsequently, Kansas, Pennsylvania, and West Virginia judicially abolished governmental immunity as to all or some governmental agencies.

2. Where a form of immunity has been retained.

a. Municipalities (and other state governmental entities) are typically immune from liability for punitive damages. See, e.g., Fisher v. Miami, 172 So. 2d 455 (Fla. 1965); and Williams v. City of Minneola, 619 So. 2d 983 (Fla. Dist. Ct. App. 5th Dist. 1993) (Municipality could not be liable for punitive damages based on malicious or reckless conduct of police officers under sovereign immunity statue barring liability of municipality for malicious or reckless acts of its employees.).

b. Absolute immunity. For the most part, federal officers and employees, working within the scope of their office or employment at the time of injury, are absolutely immune from tort liability unless the claim against the officer or employee alleges a violation of the U.S. Constitution or a federal statute. Assuming the claim does not allege a violation of the U.S. Constitutional or a federal statute, the exclusive remedy is limited to what is afforded under the Federal Tort Claim Act (FTCA), discussed in the following case. Under the FTCA, the U.S. government (not the officer or employee) is named as the defendant and the attorney general is responsible for representing the government. 28 U.S.C.A. §2679. Similarly, many states have chosen to immunize absolutely high-ranking (judges, legislators, attorneys, etc.) officers or employees, provided they were working within the scope of their official responsibilities at the time of causing injury.

c. Qualified immunity. State employees who aren't cloaked with absolute immunity may nevertheless be protected from tort liability in a limited or qualified sense. In these circumstances, as long as the employee was acting in good faith and performing an act where discretion is allowed (i.e., a non-ministerial act), the employee may be immune from liability. This will be further developed next in *McCloskey*.

E. THE FEDERAL TORT CLAIMS ACT

McCloskey v. Mueller
385 F. Supp. 2d 74 (D. Mass. 2005)

LINDSAY, District Judge.
Before me is a motion of Robert S. Mueller, III ("Mueller"), in his capacity as Director of the Federal Bureau of Investigation (the "FBI"); the FBI; William H. Anderson ("Anderson"), in his capacity as an employee of the FBI; and the United States of America (collectively the "Federal Defendants") to dismiss the complaint filed against them by Thomas S. McCloskey and Kevin P. McCloskey (collectively "the Plaintiffs"). The defendant, Gary Lee Sampson ("Sampson") has filed a separate motion to dismiss all claims against him and for the appointment of counsel to represent him in this matter.

I. BACKGROUND

A. FACTUAL BACKGROUND

The complaint, as amended, makes the following allegations.
On July 23, 2001, Anderson, who worked as a personnel security specialist at the Boston office of the FBI, covered the switchboard of the Boston office

during lunch. Anderson took a call from Sampson, who identified himself and told Anderson that he "was a fugitive, wanted for several bank robberies and that he was in the town of Abington[, Massachusetts,] and wanted the [FBI] to come and take him into custody." Anderson disconnected the call; Sampson did not call back. Anderson neither reported the call to an agent or a supervisor, nor took steps to trace or track the call. Either the equipment Anderson was using did not permit him to track and trace the call, or Anderson was not properly trained in the use of the equipment. The FBI did not supervise Anderson or regularly monitor or scrutinize records.

On July 24, 2001, Sampson car-jacked Philip McCloskey ("McCloskey") and murdered him. Before being apprehended on July 31, 2001, in Vermont, Sampson also murdered two other persons. After he was arrested, Sampson reported that he called the FBI's Boston office on July 23, 2001, seeking to surrender himself to the FBI. Sampson, who was tried and received the death penalty for the murder of McCloskey, is currently an inmate in the care, custody, and control of the Federal Bureau of Prisons.

B. PROCEDURAL BACKGROUND

The Plaintiffs, who are the executors of the estate of McCloskey, have sued Sampson and the Federal Defendants. They seek compensatory and punitive damages, together with costs and expenses. The ten-count complaint contains six counts against the Federal Defendants and four counts against Sampson. Counts I and II assert a negligence claim under the Federal Tort Claims Act, 28 U.S.C. §§2671-80 (the "FTCA"), and a civil rights claim under 42 U.S.C. §1983 ("Section 1983"), respectively. Both claims are based on Anderson's conduct in disconnecting Sampson's call and failing subsequently to trace, track, or report the call to his supervisors to ensure Sampson's capture. Count III alleges that the Federal Defendants violated McCloskey's civil rights under Section 1983 by their "clear indifference and pattern of deliberate indifference coupled with inadequate training, supervision and use of inadequate technology." Counts IV and V set forth state law negligence claims and seek compensatory damages and damages against the Federal Defendants for McCloskey's conscious pain and suffering. Count VI asserts a state law claim for punitive damages against the Federal Defendants. Counts VII, VIII, IX, and X assert Massachusetts state law claims against Sampson for McCloskey's wrongful death and conscious pain and suffering and for punitive damages.

II. DISCUSSION

For the purposes of a Rule 12(b)(6) motion to dismiss, the court must "accept as true the well-pleaded factual allegations of the complaint, draw all reasonable inferences there from in the plaintiff's favor and determine whether the complaint, so read, sets forth facts sufficient to justify recovery on any cognizable theory."

A. THE TORT CLAIMS AGAINST THE FEDERAL DEFENDANTS (COUNTS I, IV, V, AND VI)

Citing *Kentucky v. Graham*, 473 U.S. 159, 165, 105 S. Ct. 3099, 87 L. Ed. 2d 114 (1985), the Federal Defendants explain that the Plaintiffs' claims against federal agencies or federal employees, acting in their official capacities, are in reality claims against the United States. This assertion of the Federal Defendants is not entirely correct, as applied to the amended complaint in this case. The *Graham* case stands for the proposition that official-capacity suits must be treated as suits against the federal entity. Therefore, a suit against Mueller and Anderson in their respective official capacities is to be treated as a suit against the FBI, but the suit against the FBI itself will not be treated as a suit against the United States.

Citing *Bennett v. Federal Bureau of Investigation*, 278 F. Supp. 2d 104, 121 (D. Mass. 2003), the Federal Defendants point out that the FTCA expressly prohibits lawsuits against individual federal agencies like the FBI. Citing 28 U.S.C. §2679(d) and 28 C.F.R. §15.3, they further explain that where, as here, the Attorney General has certified that individual federal employees (Mueller and Anderson), sued in their official capacity, acted within the scope of their employment at all relevant times, the United States must be substituted as the party defendant in their stead. The Federal Defendants point out that, because the United States is already a named defendant in this case, no substitution is required, and that the court should dismiss all counts directed against Mueller, Anderson, and the FBI.

a. Claims against Mueller and Anderson

I dismiss counts I, IV, V, and VI, to the extent that they set forth claims against Mueller and Anderson. The FTCA, 28 U.S.C. §2679(b)(1) provides that "[t]he remedy against the United States provided by [28 U.S.C. §§1346(b) and 2672] for . . . personal injury or death arising or resulting from the negligent or wrongful act or omission of any employee of the Government while acting within the scope of his office or employment is *exclusive of any other civil action or proceeding for money damages by reason of the same subject matter against the employee* whose act or omission gave rise to the claim or against the estate of such employee" (emphasis added). Section 2679(b)(1) further provides that "[a]ny other civil action or proceeding for money damages arising out of or relating to the same subject matter against the employee . . . is precluded without regard to when the act or omission occurred." Accordingly, the Plaintiffs' claims against Anderson and Mueller set forth in counts I, IV, V, and VI, are dismissed.

b. Claims against the FBI

I also dismiss counts I, IV, V, and VI, to the extent that they set forth claims against the FBI. The FTCA makes it clear that individual agencies of the United States may not be sued in tort for personal injuries or death caused by "the negligent or wrongful act or omission" of any federal employee acting within the scope of his or her employment. 28 U.S.C. §1346(b).

c. Claims against the United States—the discretionary function exception

The United States may be sued only if it has consented to be sued. *Lehman v. Nakshian*, 453 U.S. 156, 160, 101 S. Ct. 2698, 69 L. Ed. 2d 548 (1981) (explaining that "the United States, as sovereign, 'is immune from suit save as it consents to be sued . . . and the terms of its consent to be sued in any court define that court's jurisdiction to entertain the suit'"). The Federal Defendants agree that the FTCA is a limited consent to suit.

The Federal Defendants argue that this court does not have subject matter jurisdiction of the Plaintiffs' claims against the United States because: (1) the challenged actions fall within the discretionary function exception to the FTCA; and/or (2) a private person would not be liable in like circumstances under Massachusetts law.

The Federal Defendants further argue that the United States is liable neither for Anderson's alleged negligence in disconnecting Sampson's call, nor for the FBI's alleged negligence in training or supervising Anderson because, under Massachusetts law, a private person would not be liable in like circumstances. Alternatively, the Federal Defendants argue that the complaint does not establish that the United States owed McCloskey a duty of care. They cite *Leidy v. Borough of Glenolden*, 277 F. Supp. 2d 547, 569-70 (E.D. Pa. 2003), in support of the proposition that there is no general duty to protect victims of crimes.

For their part, the Plaintiffs assert that, in the context of a motion to dismiss, it is not proper for this court to determine whether a purely "discretionary act" is involved here. They assert that further discovery is needed to determine whether, in disconnecting Sampson's call and failing to inform his supervisors of the call, Anderson violated any applicable policy, rule, or regulation.

The "discretionary function exception" to the FTCA, set forth in 28 U.S.C. §2680(a), protects the government from lawsuits "based upon the exercise or performance or the failure to exercise or perform a discretionary function or duty on the part of a federal agency or an employee of the Government, whether or not the discretion involved be abused." The exception is intended to prevent the courts from second-guessing "legislative and administrative decisions grounded in social, economic and political policy through the medium of an action in tort." The Supreme Court has described a discretionary function as one "in which there exists an 'element of judgment or choice,'" and the court must dismiss any claim "covered by the discretionary function exception . . . for lack of subject matter jurisdiction."

There is a two-prong test to determine whether particular conduct falls within the discretionary function exception: (1) "whether the challenged action was a matter of choice for the acting official"; and (2) "whether the official's discretion was based on considerations of public policy." With regard to the first prong, the court must focus on "the nature of the conduct, rather than the status of the actor," and determine "whether the action is a matter of choice for the acting employee." An action is outside the scope of the discretionary function exception "if a federal statute, regulation or policy specifically prescribes a course of action for [an official] to follow, because [the official] has no rightful option but to adhere to the directive.").

With regard to the second prong, the inquiry must center "not on the agent's subjective intent in exercising the discretion . . . , but on the nature of the actions taken and on whether they are susceptible to policy analysis." There exists a presumption that if "there is an exercise of discretion, that exercise is based on considerations of public policy." If an action "meets both prongs of this test . . . and is thus within the discretionary function exception, even an abuse or negligent exercise of discretion is not actionable."

I hold that under the principles set forth above, Anderson's actions in dealing with Sampson's call fall within the discretionary function exception. The FBI's broad discretion to decide whether to investigate and/or apprehend a particular individual, encompasses the discretion of an individual officer like Anderson to report or not report a particular call. Therefore, the first prong of the discretionary function test is met.

The second prong of the test is also met here, because, in deciding which cases to bring to his supervisors' attention, an officer like Anderson "necessarily weighs the benefit to society" in preventing future crime against the limited nature of law enforcement resources.

To the extent that the Plaintiffs' claim is based on the assumption that, if notified of Sampson's call, the FBI would have immediately arrested Sampson, thereby preventing McCloskey's death, their claim also falls within the discretionary function exception to the FTCA. Furthermore, to the extent that the Plaintiffs' FTCA claim against the United States is based on the FBI's failure to use particular technology, that claim also falls within the discretionary function exception and must, therefore, be dismissed for lack of subject matter jurisdiction.

Even if the conduct at issue were not protected by the discretionary function exception, this court still would not have subject matter jurisdiction of the Plaintiffs' FTCA claim against the United States. Under the FTCA, district courts have jurisdiction to hear claims against the United States for money damages arising out of "personal injury or death caused by the negligent or wrongful act or omission of any employee of the Government while acting within the scope of his office or employment, *under the circumstances where the United States, if a private person, would be liable to the claimant in accordance with the law of the place where the act or omission occurred* (emphasis added)." 28 U.S.C. §1346(b)(1). Thus, to hold the United States liable for

Anderson's conduct in disconnecting Sampson's telephone call and for the FBI's alleged negligent supervision and training of Anderson, the Plaintiffs must show that, under Massachusetts law, a private person in similar circumstances would be liable.

To prevail on a negligence claim under Massachusetts law, the plaintiff must establish that (1) the defendant owed the plaintiff a legal duty, (2) the defendant breached that duty, (3) proximately or legally causing (4) the plaintiff's actual injury or damages. . . . In the context of an FTCA claim, a legal duty of care exists where there is "some relationship between the governmental employee[s] and the plaintiff to which state law would attach a duty of care in purely private circumstances."

In defining the duty of care in tort actions, Massachusetts follows the Restatement (Second) of Torts §315 (1965) ("Section 315"). Section 315 "recognizes two types of special relationships that may form the basis of an exception to the general principle that a person has no duty to control the conduct of a third person."

The first arises where "a special relation exists between the actor [i.e., the person whose duty is at issue] and the third person which imposes a duty upon the actor to control the third person's conduct." Restatement (Second) of Torts §315. Such relationships include parent-child, master-servant, possessor of land or chattels-licensee. Restatement (Second) of Torts §§316-18 (1965). In addition, if one "takes charge" of a person having dangerous propensities, he is under a duty to control that person's conduct if he knows or should know of the person's dangerous propensities. *See*, Restatement (Second) of Torts §319 (1965).

The second exception arises where "a special relation exists between the actor and the other [i.e., the potential plaintiff] which gives to the other a right to protection." Restatement (Second) of Torts §315. This second kind of a special relation exists between (1) a common carrier and its passengers, (2) an innkeeper and his guests, (3) a possessor of land who holds the land open to the public and members of the public who enter the land in response to his invitation, and (4) one who "is required by law to take or who voluntarily takes the custody of another" in a way that deprives that person "of his normal opportunities for protection" and the other person. Restatement (Second) of Torts §314A (1965).

If neither of the two special relationships described above exists, "the actor is not subject to liability if he fails, either intentionally or through inadvertence, to exercise his ability so to control the actions of third persons as to protect another from even the most serious harm." Restatement (Second) of Torts §315 cmt. b (emphasizing that the actor is not liable even if he "realizes that he has the ability to control the conduct of a third person, and could do so with only the most trivial of efforts and without any inconvenience to himself").

In sum, nothing in this case suggests that a special relationship existed between the Federal Defendants and Sampson that would obligate the Federal Defendants to control Sampson's conduct. Sampson had not been in federal custody before he murdered McCloskey, he had not been an FBI informant, and he had not been supervised by the FBI in any way. Furthermore, under the Restatement (Second) of Torts §314A, no special relationship existed between the Federal Defendants and McCloskey, obligating the Federal Defendants to protect McCloskey from foreseeable harm. Because, under Massachusetts law, a private person would not be liable to the Plaintiffs under like circumstances, no claim lies against the United States.

C. CLAIM FOR PUNITIVE DAMAGES (COUNT VI)

Count VI purports to state a claim for punitive damages against the Federal Defendants. The FTCA provides that the United States "shall not be liable . . . for punitive damages." 28 U.S.C. §2674. Because the FTCA is the only basis for this court's jurisdiction of the Plaintiffs' claims against the United States, I dismiss count VI to the extent that it asserts a claim for punitive damages against the United States. I also dismiss count VI to the extent that it seeks punitive damages against Anderson and Mueller, because, as noted earlier, Section 2679(b)(1) of the FTCA precludes "[a]ny other civil action or proceeding for money damages arising out of or relating to the same subject matter against the employee[s]" of the United States, whose act or omission gave rise to the FTCA claim.

III. CONCLUSION

For the foregoing reasons, I GRANT the Federal Defendants' motion to dismiss and decline to exercise jurisdiction over the Plaintiffs' claims against Sampson.
SO ORDERED

PREPARING FOR CLASS

1. Note that the failure to immunize does not create a cause of action for the plaintiff. The common law will dictate what has to be proven for the plaintiff to be successful as well as the types of damages that might be recoverable.

2. Recall the circumstances where a party might owe a duty of protection to another.

INCREASING YOUR UNDERSTANDING

1. Congress passed the Federal Tort Claims Act (FTCA) in 1946 and in doing so waived sovereign immunity and allowed the federal

government to be sued "if a private person, would be liable to the claimant in accordance with the law of the place where the act or omission occurred." 28 U.S.C.A §1346. As such, a plaintiff bringing a tort claim action under the FTCA must meet the requirements of the common law and be subjected to the same defenses and limitations that a suit against a private person would. Ultimately the plaintiff's action is against the government not the employee whose conduct may have given rise to the claim.

2. Congress gives and takes. The FTCA didn't totally abandon the concept of immunity and carried with it a limited form for those acts described as "discretionary," which is more specifically and awkwardly referred to as the "discretionary function exception to liability." Section 2680 (a) in part provides that excepted from liability is "any claim based upon an act or omission of an employee of the Government, exercising due care, in the execution of a statute or regulation . . . or based on the exercise or performance or the failure to exercise or perform a discretionary function." In short, there will no liability for negligent acts where the employee had the discretion to be negligent. In 1998, the Supreme Court established a step-by-step test for courts to use when determining whether the government would be immune from liability pursuant to the discretionary function exception. Courts must determine: (1) whether a government employee or agency had discretion, i.e., the authority to make a choice at all; and (2) whether Congress intended to immunize the type of discretion from liability. Berkovitz v. U.S. 486 U.S. 531, 108 S. Ct. 1954 (1988).

3. Other FTCA notables:

   a. §1346: United States as defendant.
   "(b)(1) [T]he district courts . . . shall have exclusive jurisdiction of civil actions on claims against the United States, for money damages, accruing on and after January 1, 1945 . . . ."

   b. §2401: Time for commencing action against United States.
   "(a) Except as provided by [chapter 71 of title 41], every civil action commenced against the United States shall be barred unless the complaint is filed within six years after the right of action first accrues. The action of any person under legal disability or beyond the seas at the time the claim accrues may be commenced within three years after the disability ceases.

   "(b) A tort claim against the United States shall be forever barred unless it is presented in writing to the appropriate Federal agency within two years after such claim accrues or unless action is begun within six months after the date of mailing, by certified or registered mail, of notice of final denial of the claim by the agency to which it was presented."

c. §2402: Jury trial in actions against the United States.
    "[A]ny action against the United States under section 1346 shall be tried by the court without a jury . . . ."

d. §2674: Liability of United States.
    "The United States shall be liable, respecting the provisions of this title relating to tort claims, in the same manner and to the same extent as a private individual under like circumstances, but shall not be liable for interest prior to judgment or for punitive damages."

    This provision has been relied upon to deny recovery for injuries sustained incident to military service. "We know of no American law which ever has permitted a soldier to recover for negligence, against either his superior officers or the Government he is serving." Feres v. United States, 340 U.S. 135, 141, 71 S. Ct. 153, 157 (1950).

e. §2678: Attorney fees; penalty.
    "No attorney shall charge, demand, receive, or collect for services rendered, fees in excess of 25 per centum of any judgment rendered pursuant to section 1346(b) of this title or any settlement made pursuant to section 2677 of this title, or in excess of 20 per centum of any award, compromise, or settlement made pursuant to section 2672 of this title.

    "Any attorney who charges, demands, receives, or collects for services rendered in connection with such claim any amount in excess of that allowed under this section, if recovery be had, shall be fined not more than $2,000 or imprisoned not more than one year, or both."

f. §2680: Exceptions (In addition to the discretionary function exception).
    "The provisions of this chapter and section 1346(b) of this title shall not apply to—

    "(h) Any claim arising out of assault, battery, false imprisonment, false arrest, malicious prosecution, abuse of process, libel, slander, misrepresentation, deceit, or interference with contract rights: *Provided*, That, with regard to acts or omissions of investigative or law enforcement officers of the United States Government, the provisions of this chapter and section 1346(b) of this title shall apply to any claim arising, on or after the date of the enactment of this proviso, out of assault, battery, false imprisonment, false arrest, abuse of process, or malicious prosecution. For the purpose of this subsection, "investigative or law enforcement officer" means any officer of the United States who is empowered by law to execute searches, to seize evidence, or to make arrests for violations of Federal law."

F. NO-DUTY RULE

Riss v. City of New York
22 N.Y.2d 579, 240 N.E.2d 860 (1968)

[The facts are taken from Judge Keating's dissenting opinion]

Linda Riss, an attractive young woman, was for more than six months terrorized by a rejected suitor well known to the courts of this State, one Burton
Pugach. This miscreant, masquerading as a respectable attorney, repeatedly
threatened to have Linda killed or maimed if she did not yield to him: "If I
can't have you, no one else will have you, and when I get through with you, no
one else will want you." In fear for her life, she went to those charged by law
with the duty of preserving and safeguarding the lives of the citizens and residents of this State. Linda's repeated and almost pathetic pleas for aid were
received with little more than indifference. Whatever help she was given
was not commensurate with the identifiable danger. On June 14, 1959
Linda became engaged to another man. At a party held to celebrate the
event, she received a phone call warning her that it was her "last chance."
Completely distraught, she called the police, begging for help, but was refused.
The next day Pugach carried out his dire threats in the very manner he had
foretold by having a hired thug throw lye in Linda's face. Linda was blinded in
one eye, lost a good portion of her vision in the other, and her face was permanently scarred. After the assault the authorities concluded that there was
some basis for Linda's fears, and for the next three and one-half years, she was
given around-the-clock protection.

BREITEL, Judge.

This appeal presents, in a very sympathetic framework, the issue of the liability of a municipality for failure to provide special protection to a member of
the public who was repeatedly threatened with personal harm and eventually
suffered dire personal injuries for lack of such protection. The facts are amply
described in the dissenting opinion and no useful purpose would be served by
repetition. The issue arises upon the affirmance by a divided Appellate Division of a dismissal of the complaint, after both sides had rested but before
submission to the jury.

It is necessary immediately to distinguish those liabilities attendant upon
governmental activities which have displaced or supplemented traditionally
private enterprises, such as are involved in the operation of rapid transit systems, hospitals, and places of public assembly. Once sovereign immunity was
abolished by statute the extension of liability on ordinary principles of tort law
logically followed. To be equally distinguished are certain activities of government which provide services and facilities for the use of the public, such as
highways, public buildings and the like, in the performance of which the
municipality or the State may be liable under ordinary principles of tort

law. The ground for liability is the provision of the services or facilities for the direct use by members of the public.

In contrast, this case involves the provision of a governmental service to protect the public generally from external hazards and particularly to control the activities of criminal wrongdoers. The amount of protection that may be provided is limited by the resources of the community and by a considered legislative-executive decision as to how those resources may be deployed. For the courts to proclaim a new and general duty of protection in the law of tort, even to those who may be the particular seekers of protection based on specific hazards, could and would inevitably determine how the limited police resources of the community should be allocated and without predictable limits. This is quite different from the predictable allocation of resources and liabilities when public hospitals, rapid transit systems, or even highways are provided.

Before such extension of responsibilities should be dictated by the indirect imposition of tort liabilities, there should be a legislative determination that that should be the scope of public responsibility

It is notable that the removal of sovereign immunity for tort liability was accomplished after legislative enactment and not by any judicial arrogation of power (Court of Claims Act, §8). It is equally notable that for many years, since as far back as 1909 in this State, there was by statute municipal liability for losses sustained as a result of riot (General Municipal Law, §71). Yet even this class of liability has for some years been suspended by legislative action (New York State Defense Emergency Act (L.1951, ch. 784, §113, subd. 3; §121, as last amd. by L. 1968, ch. 115)), a factor of considerable significance.

When one considers the greatly increased amount of crime committed throughout the cities, but especially in certain portions of them, with a repetitive and predictable pattern, it is easy to see the consequences of fixing municipal liability upon a showing of probable need for and request for protection. To be sure these are grave problems at the present time, exciting high priority activity on the part of the national, State and local governments, to which the answers are neither simple, known, or presently within reasonable controls. To foist a presumed cure for these problems by judicial innovation of a new kind of liability in tort would be foolhardy indeed and an assumption of judicial wisdom and power not possessed by the courts.

Nor is the analysis progressed by the analogy to compensation for losses sustained. It is instructive that the Crime Victims Compensation and "Good Samaritan" statutes, compensating limited classes of victims of crime, were enacted only after the most careful study of conditions and the impact of such a scheme upon governmental operations and the public fisc (Executive Law, art. 22, §620 et seq. (L.1966, ch. 894); Administrative Code of City of New York, ch. 3, tit. A, §67-3.2). And then the limitations were particular and narrow.

For all of these reasons, there is no warrant in judicial tradition or in the proper allocation of the powers of government for the courts, in the absence of legislation, to carve out an area of tort liability for police protection to members of the public. Quite distinguishable, of course, is the situation where the police authorities undertake responsibilities to particular members of the public and expose them, without adequate protection, to the risks which then materialize into actual losses.

Accordingly, the order of the Appellate Division affirming the judgment of dismissal should be affirmed.

KEATING, Judge (dissenting).

Certainly, the record in this case, sound legal analysis, relevant policy considerations and even precedent cannot account for or sustain the result which the majority have here reached. For the result is premised upon a legal rule which long ago should have been abandoned, having lost any justification it might once have had. Despite almost universal condemnation by legal scholars, the rule survives, finding its continuing strength, not in its power to persuade, but in its ability to arouse unwarranted judicial fears of the consequences of overturning it.

No one questions the proposition that the first duty of government is to assure its citizens the opportunity to live in personal security. And no one who reads the record of Linda's ordeal can reach a conclusion other than that the City of New York, acting through its agents, completely and negligently failed to fulfill this obligation to Linda.

Linda has turned to the courts of this State for redress, asking that the city be held liable in damages for its negligent failure to protect her from harm. With compelling logic, she can point out that, if a stranger, who had absolutely no obligation to aid her, had offered her assistance, and thereafter Burton Pugach was able to injure her as a result of the negligence of the volunteer, the courts would certainly require him to pay damages. (Restatement, 2d, Torts, §323.) Why then should the city, whose duties are imposed by law and include the prevention of crime (New York City Charter, §435) and, consequently, extend far beyond that of the Good Samaritan, not be responsible? If a private detective acts carelessly, no one would deny that a jury could find such conduct unacceptable. Why then is the city not required to live up to at least the same minimal standards of professional competence which would be demanded of a private detective?

Linda's reasoning seems so eminently sensible that surely it must come as a shock to her and to every citizen to hear the city argue and to learn that this court decides that the city has no duty to provide police protection to any given individual. What makes the city's position particularly difficult to understand is that, in conformity, to the dictates of the law, Linda did not carry any weapon for self-defense (former Penal Law, §1897). Thus, by a rather bitter irony she was required to rely for protection on the City of New York which now denies all responsibility to her.

It is not a distortion to summarize the essence of the city's case here in the following language: "Because we owe a duty to everybody, we owe it to nobody." Were it not for the fact that this position has been hallowed by much ancient and revered precedent, we would surely dismiss it as preposterous. To say that there is no duty is, of course, to start with the conclusion. The question is whether or not there should be liability for the negligent failure to provide adequate police protection.

The foremost justification repeatedly urged for the existing rule is the claim that the State and the municipalities will be exposed to limitless liability. The city invokes the specter of a "crushing burden" if we should depart from the existing rule and enunciate even the limited proposition that the State and its municipalities can be held liable for the negligent acts of their police employees in executing whatever police services they do in fact provide.

The fear of financial disaster is a myth. The same argument was made a generation ago in opposition to proposals that the State waive its defense of 'sovereign immunity'. The prophecy proved false then, and it would now. The supposed astronomical financial burden does not and would not exist. No municipality has gone bankrupt because it has had to respond in damages when a policeman causes injury through carelessly driving a police car or in the thousands of other situations where, by judicial fiat or legislative enactment, the State and its subdivisions have been held liable for the tortious conduct of their employees. That Linda Riss should be asked to bear the loss, which should properly fall on the city if we assume, as we must, in the present posture of the case, that her injuries resulted from the city's failure to provide sufficient police to protect Linda is contrary to the most elementary notions of justice.

What has existed until now is that the City of New York and other municipalities have been able to engage in a sort of false bookkeeping in which the real costs of inadequate or incompetent police protection have been hidden by charging the expenditures to the individuals who have sustained often catastrophic losses rather than to the community where it belongs, because the latter had the power to prevent the losses.

No doubt in the future we shall have to draw limitations just as we have done in the area of private litigation, and no doubt some of these limitations will be unique to municipal liability because the problems will not have any counterpart in private tort law. But if the lines are to be drawn, let them be delineated on candid considerations of policy and fairness and not on the fictions or relics of the doctrine of 'sovereign immunity'. Before reaching such questions, however, we must resolve the fundamental issue raised here and recognize that, having undertaken to provide professional police and fire protection, municipalities cannot escape liability for damages caused by their failure to do even a minimally adequate job of it.

FULD, C.J., and BURKE, SCILEPPI, BERGAN and JASEN, JJ., concur with BREITEL, JJ.

KEATING, J., dissents and votes to reverse in a separate opinion.

PREPARING FOR CLASS

1. *Riss* is not an immunity case; the case turns on whether there is a duty, a discussion only required because the state no longer immunized police in this instance.

2. Why no duty here, and in what circumstance might there be?

3. Fashion a duty-creating rule that would protect the Riss's of the world yet not offend the majority of the court.

4. Revisit the duty establishing rules especially with respect to nonfeasance and "special" relationships

APPLYING THE LAW

Resident calls 911 complaining of a person breaking into her home. The 911 operator informs the resident that she will dispatch a police officer to the home immediately. Operator, though, gets distracted by conversation with co-employee and forgets to dispatch officer. Resident is found murdered later that evening. In the ensuing lawsuit, does *Riss* apply?

INCREASING YOUR UNDERSTANDING

1. Courts generally have adopted the rule that there can be no tort liability on the part of a city/municipality for failure to provide police protection where the original duty was owed only to the public and not to any particular person. And while the "no-duty" rule results in a finding of no liability, it is a distinction from governmental immunity, which would excuse responsibility even in the presence of a duty. Describing the duty as one owed generally to the public allows only the "public" to sue when there has been a breach; no single person has standing to sue for individual harm as there was no obligation to any single person.

2. At some point most states abolished the sovereign immunity it once enjoyed, which then required state courts (or legislators) to fashion liability rules for the first time in cases involving government actors. Often courts would rely on parallel cases brought against private individuals when framing these new rules, but sometimes the cases would involve circumstances unique to the provision of traditional governmental services such as police protection. From these unique circumstances came the "no-duty" rule, and though it was not limited to police protection cases, it is the *Riss*-type case where the rule has generated the most debate. Dissatisfaction with the "no-duty" rule led to legislation by many states that ostensibly would require police officer intervention in some domestic cases, such as when there is evidence that one party has violated a restraining order. Colorado is one such state. Colorado Revised Statutes Annotated §18-6-803.5 sec. 3(b) provides that:

(b) A peace officer shall arrest, or, if an arrest would be impractical under the circumstances, seek a warrant for the arrest of a restrained person when the peace officer has information amounting to probable cause that:

(I)   The restrained person has violated or attempted to violate any provision of a protection order; and

(II) The restrained person has been properly served with a copy of the protection order or the restrained person has received actual notice of the existence and substance of such order.

Colorado citizen, Jessica Gonzalez, brought suit against the town of Castle Rock after her husband, who was subjected to a restraining order, killed their three children. Prior to murdering the children, Gonzalez had informed the police that her husband was in violation of the restraining order. The case made its way to the U.S. Supreme Court where it held in favor of the Town, finding that in its law Colorado had not created a personal entitlement to enforcement of restraining orders as it didn't make enforcement of the retraining law mandatory; "A well-established tradition of police discretion has long coexisted with apparently mandatory arrest statutes." Town of Castle Rock, Colo. v. Gonzales 545 U.S. 748, 749, 125 S. Ct. 2796 (2005). Did the Colorado legislature not contemplate that its restraining order laws would form the basis for civil liability or has the U.S. Supreme Court contravened its desire to give more substance to its restraining order law?

3. *Crazy in love or both?* After being convicted for participating in the assault of Linda Riss, Burton Pugach went to jail for 14 years, during which time he remained in contact with Riss. Upon release in 1974, Pugach and Riss resumed their relationship and married soon after. They co-wrote a book in 1976 titled *A Very Different Love Story*. In 1997, after Pugach was accused of threatening another woman with whom he allegedly was having an affair, Riss testified on his behalf and reportedly described him as a "wonderful, caring husband." And In 2007, their story went to the big screen with the movie *Crazy Love*. The movie won several documentary awards.

G.   CHARITABLE IMMUNITY

Collopy v. Newark Eye & Ear Infirmary
27 N.J. 29, 141 A.2d 276 (N.J. 1958)

JACOBS, J.

The plaintiff's complaint alleges that he entered the defendant hospital on March 21, 1957 for the purpose of having surgery performed upon his eyes;

that after the surgery was completed he remained at the hospital as a post-operative patient and wore protective bandages over his eyes; that on March 28, 1957 he was, through the negligence of the defendant in failing to provide suitable guard railings, permitted to fall out of bed with great force and with resulting serious injuries; that the defendant delayed in taking X-rays until March 30, 1957 and then negligently informed him that he had not sustained any injuries from his fall and discharged him from the hospital; and that subsequently he was obliged to undergo further hospitalization for the treatment of the injuries sustained in his fall. Before answering, the defendant moved to dismiss the complaint, asserting that since it is a nonprofit eleemosynary corporation (R.S. 15:1-1 et seq., N.J.S.A.) it possesses an absolute immunity from any responsibility to the plaintiff for injuries resulting from its alleged negligent conduct. The trial court granted the motion and entered summary judgment in favor of the defendant. Thereafter the plaintiff appealed to the Appellate Division and we certified under R.R. 1:10-1(a).

The immunity upon which the defendant relies was first declared in our courts in 1925 as a judicial expression of the State's public policy; however, the reasonable demands and expectations of innocent persons who were injured through the fault of others soon brought about a far-reaching exception and in recent years many of our judges have pointedly suggested that sound concepts of right, justice and morality require outright rejection of the immunity. In the case before us the single issue presented by the parties is whether the last vestiges of the judicially declared immunity should at this time be erased.

In Heaven v. Pender, (1883) 11 Q.B. 503, 509, the court expressed the general rule of negligence in the following well-known language:

> "Whenever one person is placed by circumstances in such a position with regard to another that every one of ordinary sense who did think would at once recognize that if he did not use ordinary care and skill in his own conduct with regard to those circumstances he would cause danger of injury to the person or property of the other, a duty arises to use ordinary care and skill to avoid such danger."

This common law duty of due care, with tort liability for its breach, prevails generally throughout the law although it occasionally comes into conflict with immunities which must find independent support for their continued recognition in their own historical and social justifications. Historically the immunity of eleemosynary institutions (such as the defendant) has little basis. In Duncan v. Findlater, 6 Cl. & Fin. 894, 7 Eng. Rep. 934 (1839), and The Feoffees of Heriot's Hospital v. Ross, 12 Cl. & Fin. 507, 8 Eng. Rep. 1508 (1846), there were dicta by Lord Cottenham supporting the immunity, although neither case involved a tort action for personal injuries resulting from the negligent operation of a nongovernmental eleemosynary institution. In Holliday v. St. Leonard, Shoreditch, 11 C.B. (N.S.) 192, 142 Eng. Rep. 769 (1861), the court followed the dictum in the *Duncan* case and held the vestry of a parish to be immune from tort responsibility, but this holding was quickly overturned, and later English cases have given no recognition to the immunity.

A highly significant rejection of the immunity was the 1957 decision by the New York Court of Appeals in Bing v. Thunig (St. John's Episcopal Hospital), . . . which held that a hospital was liable for its negligent injury of a patient. The court, after describing the manifold business operations of present-day hospitals, expressed the view that they should fairly "shoulder the responsibilities borne by everyone else"; it rejected the illogical distinctions which had been made in earlier New York decisions and flatly discarded the immunity as being wholly at variance with the needs of today and with "concepts of justice and fair dealing." In 1956 the Supreme Court of Ohio and in 1953 the Supreme Court of Washington had reached similar conclusions in full opinions which pointed out that since liability insurance was available to charitable institutions they were in no position to urge that their subjection to ordinary tort responsibilities for their wrongdoings might endanger the continuance of their highly worthy endeavors. And in 1950 the Supreme Court of Vermont in Foster v. Roman Catholic Diocese of Vermont . . . rejected the immunity in an opinion which stressed (1) the differences between conditions when the immunity was first judicially embraced and present-day conditions, and (2) the idleness of suggestions that donations would "dry up if the charity is held to respond for its torts" or that charitable donations are given with the expectation that the charity "will not be responsible like other institutions for negligent injury."

Professorial and student writings overwhelmingly oppose the immunity. Although these writings are free from the restraints of judicial responsibilities, they are worthy of careful consideration for they embody thoughtful and high-minded endeavors to stimulate the movement of our law towards the ever-present goal of obtaining a higher measure of justice for all people. A quarter of a century ago Professor Harper expressed the pertinent policy views which have been long entertained by legal scholars and have been strongly re-enforced by the passage of time:

> "The immunity of charitable corporations in tort is based upon very dubious grounds. It would seem that a sound social policy ought, in fact to require such organizations to make just compensation for harm legally caused by their activities under the same circumstances as individuals before they carry on their charitable activities. The policy of the law requiring individuals to be just before generous seems equally applicable to charitable corporations. To require an injured individual to forego compensation for harm when he is otherwise entitled thereto, because the injury was committed by the servants of a charity, is to require him to make an unreasonable contribution to the charity, against his will, and a rule of law imposing such burdens

cannot be regarded as socially desirable nor consistent with sound policy."

Harper, Law of Torts, §294, p. 657 (1933).

Haynes v. Presbyterian Hospital Ass'n., supra [241 Iowa 1269, 45 N.W.2d 154]:

> "The law's emphasis generally is on liability, rather than immunity, for wrongdoing. Charity is generally no defense. It is for the legislature, not the courts, to create and grant immunity. The fact that the courts may have at an early date, in response to what appeared good as a matter of policy, created an immunity, does not appear to us a sound reason for continuing the same, when under all legal theories, it is basically unsound and especially so, when the reasons upon which it was built, no longer exist."

Professor Scott has extensively discussed three possible grounds which have been suggested for the exemption of charitable institutions from tort liability. See 4 Scott, Trusts 2894 (2d ed. 1956). The first is that where trust funds are devoted to charitable objects they should not be diverted from those objects and that payment of tort claims would amount to such diversion; but this legalistic view would deny liability in all tort cases. The second rests on an alleged waiver by the injured party; but such waiver would be wholly fictitious and a figment of the imagination. The third rests on the inapplicability of the doctrine of Respondeat superior; but adoption of this approach would deny liability in all tort cases and would seem to disregard the true ground for vicarious liability in our law.

The contention has been advanced that even though the former public policy notions have been strongly altered, the elimination of the immunity should be left exclusively to the Legislature. There is no doubt that within constitutional limits the Legislature may at any time, if it so chooses, explicitly fix the State's policy as to the immunity of charitable institutions from tort responsibilities. But the Legislature has not done so; it has broadly empowered nonprofit corporations to sue "and be sued" (R.S. 15:1-4, N.J.S.A.; see Taylor v. New Jersey Highway Authority, 22 N.J. 454, 467, 126 A.2d 313 (1956)); and it has never in any form voiced approval of the immunity of charitable institutions though it has expressly legislated for immunities in other fields.

The unmistakable fact remains that judges of an earlier generation declared the immunity simply because they believed it to be a sound instrument of judicial policy which would further the moral, social and economic welfare of the people of the State. When judges of a later generation firmly reach a contrary conclusion they must be ready to discharge their own judicial responsibilities in conformance with modern concepts and needs. It should be borne in mind that we are not dealing with property law or other fields of the law where stability and predictability may be of the utmost concern. We are dealing with the law of torts where there can be little, if any, justifiable reliance and where the rule of Stare decisis is admittedly limited. Dean Pound has had this to say as to the applicability of the rule of Stare decisis in the particular situation before us:

> "Again Stare decisis has no legitimate application to doctrines of the law of torts built upon a mistaken foundation persisting in the books after that foundation has been undermined, which are out of accord with general principles recognized today, so that if they are rejected the general law is clarified rather than unsettled. Such, for example, is the doctrine of immunity of charitable hospitals and like institutions. This immunity for wrong ran counter to general principles of law. In this country it was based upon Dicta in English cases which were rejected in England before taken over in the United States. It has been given up by the courts in twenty states but is adhered to still in twenty-six. Anomalies of this sort ought not to be protected by Stare decisis." 13 N.A.C.C.A.L.J., at 23.

See also Judge Fuld's comments in Bing v. Thunig (St. John's Episcopal Hospital), supra (2 N.Y.2d 656, 163 N.Y.S.2d 11):

> "The rule of nonliability is out of tune with the life about us, at variance with modern-day needs and with concepts of justice and fair dealing. It should be discarded. To the suggestion that Stare decisis compels us to perpetuate it until the legislature acts, a ready answer is at hand. It was intended, not to effect a 'petrifying rigidity,' but to assure the justice that flows from certainty and stability. If, instead, adherence to the precedent offers not justice but unfairness, not certainty but doubt and confusion, it loses its right to survive, and no principle constrains us to follow it. On the contrary, as this court, speaking through Judge Desmond in Woods v. Lancet, 303 N.Y. 349, 355, 102 N.E.2d 691, 694, 27 A.L.R.2d 1250, declared, we would be abdicating 'our own function, in a field peculiarly nonstatutory,' were we to insist on legislation and 'refuse to reconsider an old and unsatisfactory court-made rule.'"

. . . In State v. Culver, 23 N.J. 495, 503 (1957), certiorari denied, 354 U.S. 925, 77 S. Ct. 1387, 1 L. Ed. 2d 1441 (1957), this court, through Chief Justice Vanderbilt, recently held that the term "otherwise" appropriately included not only legislative alterations but also alterations by the process of change "inherent in the common law"; and as to this process the Chief Justice said:

> "One of the great virtues of the common law is its dynamic nature that makes it adaptable to the requirements of society at the time of its application in court. There is not a rule of the common law in force today that has not evolved from some earlier rule of common rule,

gradually in some instances, more suddenly in others, leaving the common law of today when compared with the common law of centuries ago as different as day is from night. The nature of the common law requires that each time a rule of law is applied it be carefully scrutinized to make sure that the conditions and needs of the times have not so changed as to make further application of it the instrument of injustice. Dean Pound posed the problem admirably in his Interpretations of Legal History (1922) when he stated, 'Law must be stable, and yet it cannot stand still.' And what has been done in the past is but one of the factors determinative of the present course of our law—a truism which has not gone unrecognized among the great thinkers of the legal profession."

The primary function of the law is justice and when a principle of the law no longer serves justice it should be discarded; here the law was embodied not in any controlling statute but in a judicial principle of the law of torts; it had no sound English common law antecedents and found its way into American law through a misconception; it runs counter to widespread principles which fairly impose liability on those who wrongfully and negligently injure others; it operates harshly and disregards modern concepts of justice and fair dealing; it has been roundly and soundly condemned here and elsewhere and the time has come for its elimination by the very branch of government which brought it into our system. Since the dismissal of the plaintiff's complaint was grounded entirely on the defendant's alleged immunity which we now repudiate, the judgment below must be:

Reversed, with direction for a new trial.

PREPARING FOR CLASS

1.   What purpose would protecting "charities" serve?

2.   Familiarize yourself with the significance of stare decisis and how uncomfortable the court was with changing the legal landscape.

3.   What should we expect going forward now that charities are no longer immune?

INCREASING YOUR UNDERSTANDING

1.   In Heriot's Hospital v. Ross, 12 C. & F. 507, 8 Eng. Rep. 1508, a court in England first articulated immunity for a charitable institution when it held that a charity's funds could not be used to satisfy a judgment, as that would require a diversion of funds contrary to the wishes of the donor. Soon after *Heriot's*, the charitable immunity doctrine made its way to

the United States and was recognized by most American courts in some form.

2. *Justifications for immunity. Heriot's,* supra, based its decision to recognize charitable immunity on the concern that donated money might be used for a purpose inconsistent with the donor's wishes. Other justifications have been that the beneficiary of charitable services "assumes the risk" of substandard care and the belief that it would be inappropriate to impose vicarious liability on an entity that derives no gain from the services the employee provided. See Restatement (Second) of Torts §895E, comment c(2),(3).

3. *Abrogation.* Inconsistent application of unsettled rules and dissatisfaction with how charities were conducting themselves encouraged courts to take a critical look at the doctrine, with most now rejecting it entirely.

H. PARENTAL IMMUNITY

Gelbman v. Gelbman
23 N.Y.2d 434, 245 N.E.2d 192 (N.Y. 1969)

BURKE, Judge.

Plaintiff Adele Gelbman was the passenger in an automobile owned by her and operated by her unemancipated 16-year-old son. This vehicle collided with the automobile owned and driven by one Herman Rudder while proceeding along a major thoroughfare in White Plains. Plaintiff, seriously injured in the accident, has commenced separate negligence actions against both drivers. The Rudder litigation has not yet been concluded, and is not now before the court. An insurance company, representing her son in the second action, has interposed as an affirmative defense the fact that defendant is the unemancipated son of plaintiff. The trial court, relying on prior decisions of this court, responded by dismissing the complaint. That determination was unanimously affirmed by the Appellate Division.

In this appeal, plaintiff requests that we review and then revoke a rule of this State prohibiting child-parent suits for nonwillful torts, first established in 1928 (Sorrentino v. Sorrentino, 248 N.Y. 626, 162 N.E. 551) and twice reaffirmed (Cannon v. Cannon, 287 N.Y. 425, 40 N.E.2d 236; Badigian v. Badigian, 9 N.Y.2d 472, 215 N.Y.S.2d 35, 174 N.E.2d 718). While those cases dealt with suits by minors against parents, the converse of the present situation, the underlying policy considerations which influenced those decisions—if presently viable—should be equally determinative of this appeal.

The majority in *Badigian* proffered three reasons for maintaining the intrafamily immunity doctrine, barring suits for nonwillful torts. Thus, it was noted that no other jurisdiction had seen fit to abolish the immunity doctrine. This inactivity was attributed, at least in part, to the belief that a suit by a child against a parent would have serious consequences upon the unity of that family. The immunity rule was characterized as "a concept that cannot be rejected without changing the whole fabric of our society, a fundamental idea that is at the bottom of all community life." Because of the changes envisioned by a repudiation of the rule, and because of the unprecedented disposition requested, it was suggested that the Legislature take the initiative in the area.

Seven years have passed since that decision. During that period, there has been a judicial erosion of the intrafamily immunity doctrine for nonwillful torts by courts of sister States. During that same interval, legislative intervention has not been forthcoming. While I agreed with the majority in *Badigian* that the doctrine should be abrogated by the Legislature, I no longer adhere to that view. As the courts of other States have indicated in abandoning it, the doctrine of intrafamily immunity for nonwillful torts was a court-created rule and, as such, the courts can revoke it. The inactivity of the Legislature since the time of our decision in *Badigian* illustrates the fact that the rule will be changed, if at all, by a decision of this court.

It is now apparent that the *Sorrentino* decision can again be reaffirmed only if we conclude that the doctrine is essential for the purpose of preserving family unity. However, the invocation of that argument is not persuasive, as it would require us to conclude that family unity is promoted when a parent is prohibited from suing a child. It seems obvious that family unity can only be preserved in this case by permitting the present action. As one commentator noted, "If the action of the parent against the child is viewed as a manifestation of the parent's right to discipline and punish his child" then such an action would be a proper exercise of parental authority, which authority should not be impaired by the doctrine of intrafamily tort immunity.

A more difficult but not insoluble question is presented when the child is suing his parent. However, as Judge Fuld stated in his dissenting opinion in *Badigian*, "A rule which so incongruously shields conceded wrongdoing bears a heavy burden of justification." Rather than repeat the convincing arguments advanced by Judge Fuld in his comprehensive dissent in *Badigian*, I would merely summarize the many points advanced therein for the abolition of the immunity rule.

First, the doctrine does not apply if the child is of legal age. Moreover, the tolling provisions of the Civil Practice Law and Rules would seem to protect the right of the child to maintain the action upon reaching majority. The doctrine is also inapplicable where the suit is for property damage. Thus, suits have been successfully maintained involving contracts, wills and inheritances.

Another anomaly permitted the unemancipated minor to maintain an action for personal injuries willfully or intentionally inflicted (e.g., Cannon v. Cannon, 287 N.Y. 425, 427, 429, 40 N.E.2d 236, 237, 238, supra). Finally, there were exceptions even in those instances where the child's suit arose as the result of an automobile accident. As Judge Fuld indicated, it was a common case for the child to sue his parent's employer, even though that parent might subsequently be required to indemnify said employer. Also, it was noted that other jurisdictions had permitted suits where the unemancipated child's injuries were caused by the parent's negligent operation of a vehicle being used in connection with a business. These exceptions neither permit reconciliation with the family immunity doctrine, nor provide a meaningful pattern of departure from the rule. Rather, they attest the primitive nature of the rule and require its repudiation. We, therefore, overrule our decisions in *Sorrentino*, *Cannon* and *Badigian*.

The parties recognize, as we must, that there is compulsory automobile insurance in New York. Such insurance effectively removes the argument favoring continued family harmony as a basis for prohibiting this suit. The present litigation is, in reality, between the parent passenger and her insurance carrier. Viewing the case in this light, we are unable to comprehend how the family harmony will be enhanced by prohibiting this suit.

The argument has been advanced that, by permitting suits between parent and child for nonwillful negligent acts, we will be encouraging fraudulent lawsuits. The argument fails to explain how the possibility of fraud would be magically removed merely by the child's attainment of legal majority. Nor does the argument pretend to present the first instance in which there is the possibility of a collusive and fraudulent suit. There are analogous situations in which we rely upon the ability of the jury to distinguish between valid and fraudulent claims. The effectiveness of the jury system will pertain in the present situation. The definite and vital interest of society in protecting people from losses resulting from accidents should remain paramount.

By abolishing the defense of intrafamily tort immunity for nonwillful torts, we are not creating liability where none previously existed. Rather, we are permitting recovery, previously denied, after the liability has been established. We, therefore, conclude that the present decision should be applied retrospectively to matters which have not gone to final judgment.

The order appealed from should be reversed, the complaint reinstated, and the motion to strike the affirmative defense granted.

PREPARING FOR CLASS

1. How does compulsory automobile insurance assist in framing the argument?

2. Which historical justifications listed by the court for parental immunity do you find most compelling? Did the court miss some?

3. Track the gradual erosion of the doctrine.

INCREASING YOUR UNDERSTANDING

1. Parental immunity originated in America; it failed to find a place in English common law. Gibson v. Gibson, 3 Cal. 3d 914, 92 Cal. Rptr. 288, 479 P.2d 648 (1971). Perhaps the seminal case for the doctrine was Hewlett v. George, 68 Miss. 703, 911 So. 885 (1891), where the Mississippi Supreme Court held that a child could not hold her mother liable for false imprisonment after the mother had her confined in an insane asylum. *Hewlett* was followed by McKelvey v. McKelvey, 111 Tenn. 388, 77 S.W. 664 (1903) (suit by child against father and stepmother alleging cruel and inhuman), and Roller v. Roller, 37 Wash. 242, 79 P. 788 (1905) (suit brought by daughter against father who raped her), where the Tennessee and Washington Supreme Courts both relied on parental immunity to dismiss the child's claims. *Hewlett*, *McKelvey*, and *Roller* comprised the trilogy of cases that most states referenced when they came to recognize the parental immunity doctrine. See Broadbent v. Broadbent, 184 Ariz. 74, 907 P.2d 43 (Ariz. 1995).

2. *General abrogation. Gelbman* is no anomaly; most jurisdictions have, through exceptions, stripped the doctrine of its original significance or abolished it all together.

I. SPOUSAL IMMUNITY

Waite v. Waite
618 So. 2d 1360 (Fla. 1993)

KOGAN, Justice.
We have for review *Waite v. Waite*, 593 So. 2d 222 (Fla. 3d DCA 1991), which certified the following question of great public importance:

> Whether *Sturiano v. Brooks*, 523 So. 2d 1126 (Fla. 1988), permits a claim by a former spouse for battery against the other spouse, committed during the marriage, and prior to the effective date of section 741.235, Florida Statutes (1985), where the claim is limited to the extent of insurance coverage, the spouse was convicted of attempted first degree murder stemming from the battery, and the egregious nature of the injuries demonstrates that the policy considerations enunciated in *Sturiano*—"fear of disruption of the family or other marital discord, or the possibility of fraud or collusion"—were not present when the battery was committed.

We rephrase the question as follows:

> Does the doctrine of interspousal immunity remain a part of Florida's common law?

In 1984, Joyce Waite and other members of her family were attacked by her husband, who inflicted substantial injuries upon them with a machete. He subsequently was convicted of several crimes, including attempted murder. Joyce Waite divorced him. Later, she filed suit seeking a recovery of damages against a homeowner's insurance policy. On the husband's motion, the trial court dismissed the cause as being barred by the doctrine of interspousal immunity. *See Raisen v. Raisen*, 379 So. 2d 352 (Fla. 1979), *modified*, *Sturiano v. Brooks*, 523 So. 2d 1126 (Fla. 1988). The Third District reversed based on *Sturiano*.

In *Sturiano*, 523 So. 2d at 1128, we held that the doctrine of interspousal immunity no longer is applicable when the public policy reasons for applying it do not exist. These policy reasons are judicial avoidance of acts that could disrupt the family or foster marital discord, or where there is a strong possibility of fraud or collusion between husband and wife. Based on this holding, we found in *Sturiano* that the doctrine did not bar a wife's claim filed against the insurer of a deceased husband when the factual claim before us arose from the same accident in which the husband died and when the claim did not exceed the limits of liability.

Since *Sturiano* was issued, this Court and its advisory commissions have had an opportunity to review legal issues relevant to the doctrine of interspousal immunity. As a result of that review, we now find that there no longer is a sufficient reason warranting a continued adherence to the doctrine of interspousal immunity. As we previously have held, the common law will not be altered or expanded by this Court unless demanded by public necessity or to vindicate fundamental rights. Here, we find that both public necessity and fundamental rights require judicial abrogation of the doctrine.

First, we find no reason to believe that married couples are any more likely to engage in fraudulent conduct against insurers than anyone else. An otherwise meritorious claim should not be foreclosed simply because a person is married to a wrongdoer.

The fact is that when couples collude in a fraud, many devices exist to detect the deception whether or not the couples are married. Insurance companies can and do hire their own lawyers and investigators to examine suspicious claims. When testifying, the claimants are subject to impeachment and discrediting because of their own financial stake in the outcome. They are subject to the court's contempt power, to the criminal laws for perjury and various forms of fraud, to civil lawsuit, and even to the racketeering and forfeiture statutes authorizing (among other things) the seizure of property used to further their crimes. If these other devices are adequate for unmarried couples, then we believe they also must be equally adequate for those with a marriage license.

Second, we do not believe that the types of lawsuits prohibited by the doctrine of interspousal immunity, if allowed, are likely to foster unwarranted marital discord. Under present law, for example, an abused spouse still might file criminal charges against the abuser, can sue in equity over property interests, and can file for an injunction for protection. We believe that marital disharmony will not be increased merely because of the addition of a lawsuit for the various types of personal injury at issue here.

Finally, we note that thirty-two states have abrogated the doctrine of interspousal immunity completely, *Waite v. Waite*, 593 So. 2d 222, 225, 229-31 (Gersten, J., dissenting), leaving Florida in a shrinking minority. The doctrine also has been resoundingly rejected by the single most respected authority on American tort law. W. Page Keeton et al., *Prosser and Keeton on the Law of Torts* § 122, at 902-04 (5th ed. 1984). We particularly agree with Keeton's observation that the very act of creating exceptions to the doctrine, as this Court repeatedly has done, renders the doctrine increasingly less justifiable. *Id.* at 904. We also find absolutely no evidence that fraud and collusion have been promoted or encouraged to any undue extent in the majority of states that have abrogated the doctrine, some many decades ago.

For the foregoing reasons, the result reached below is approved and the certified question as rephrased here is answered in the negative.

It is so ordered.

HARDING, Justice, concurring.

Justices Grimes and McDonald raise the specter of a proliferation of lawsuits between spouses upon the abrogation of the doctrine of interspousal immunity. However, limiting litigation has never been the stated policy for the doctrine. Rather, the doctrine is based upon the dual public policies of fostering marital harmony and avoiding possible collusion or fraud between spouses.

The Legislature has already statutorily abrogated the doctrine with regard to the intentional tort of battery. Section 741.235, Fla. Stat. (1991). Florida law also permits a spouse to file a criminal complaint against a spouse, to seek an injunction for protection from that spouse's violence, and to sue in equity over property interests. If the preservation of marital harmony is the compelling reason for maintaining interspousal immunity as to other personal tort actions, then that rationale should apply with equal force to these legal actions that the law permits one spouse to maintain against the other. Certainly, it is difficult to make any rational argument for interspousal immunity as to these permitted legal actions. Yet, such actions are just as likely, if not even more likely, to foster marital discord than are the personal tort actions that are barred by the doctrine of interspousal immunity.

Moreover, if the overriding concern is to prevent fraud or collusion by spouses in bringing such an action, then the remedy should be to expose the fraud rather than to discard all the honest claims along with the bad ones. As the majority notes, legal devices exist to detect possible collusion or fraud whether the parties are married or not. Thus, this policy does not warrant the continuation of the interspousal immunity doctrine.

KOGAN, J., concurs.

McDONALD, Justice, concurring in result only.

The majority now accepts the position urged by the dissent in *Raisen v. Raisen*, 379 So. 2d 352 (Fla. 1979). As I did in *Raisen*, I continue to believe that there are societal advantages of maintaining interspousal immunity as a concept. I am willing to, and have, examined particular circumstances to determine in a given situation whether an exception to this historical doctrine should be made. The question as certified by the district court of appeal is such a situation. I do not agree, however, that the doctrine should be completely abolished.

I am firmly convinced that the unfettered ability of one spouse to sue the other can, and likely will, place an undue strain on a marriage relationship. A spouse's threat to file such an action can equally do so. Finally, if a marriage does culminate in divorce, I can foresee multiple counts for damages being claimed by each spouse against the other for events that occurred during their marriage. The fault concept which was discarded in no fault dissolution proceedings will have a rebirth in a different form.

The step the majority takes is entirely too broad. The Legislature has abolished spousal immunity in intentional battery cases. Section 741.235, Fla. Stat. (1985). Had the Legislature felt it desirable to completely abolish the doctrine, it could have done so then. In any event, because of the action of the majority, I invite the Legislature to reexamine this issue and take whatever action it deems appropriate.

I would allow Joyce Waite's suit to proceed because this was an intentional battery, now legislatively excepted from immunity, and because the parties are now divorced.

OVERTON, J., concurs.

GRIMES, Justice, concurring in part, dissenting in part.

I agree with the abolition of interspousal immunity for intentional torts and therefore concur with the result reached in this case. However, I believe that the doctrine continues to serve a useful purpose in negligence actions.

This Court has emphasized that the purpose of interspousal immunity is to protect family harmony and resources. *Hill v. Hill*, 415 So. 2d 20 (Fla. 1982). If one spouse sues another to obtain damages for negligent injuries and there is no liability insurance, how can it be said that such a lawsuit will not severely disrupt family harmony? While family harmony may suffer less when liability insurance is involved, the temptation for collusion will dramatically increase.

Compensation for injuries caused by the negligence of a person's spouse should come from medical and disability insurance or some other form of first-party insurance so that the question of fault does not become involved.

While discussions of interspousal immunity usually focus on personal injury actions, I also foresee a spate of lawsuits between spouses covering a wide range of torts including defamation, conversion, fraud, and property damage, and perhaps more creatively the negligent infliction of a disease, such as AIDS.

Despite continued academic criticism of the doctrine of interspousal immunity, the Legislature has declined to intervene, except for the passage of a recent statute abolishing the doctrine with respect to battery. I would prefer to leave the question of whether one spouse can sue another in negligence to the Legislature which is better equipped to consider the ramifications which may result from permitting it.

OVERTON, J., concurs.

PREPARING FOR CLASS

1. Note the similarities in the policies behind spousal and parental immunity.

2. Does *Waite* potentially change the marriage dynamic in an acceptable way, if at all?

3. Are legislators better positioned to resolve this issue?

APPLYING THE LAW

Stan Focker is allegedly seriously injured (organic brain disease, which is incapable of objective diagnosis) after he slipped on some steps and hit his head while visiting his in-laws. Stan claims that the accident resulted from the step being defective, and his wife, Laurin Focker, pushing him. He brings suit against all the responsible Fockers and their insurance carriers. Does he get past a motion for summary judgment?

INCREASING YOUR UNDERSTANDING

1. *"You're a big girl now."* Spousal immunity was partially born out of a desire to clean up or avoid an awkward dilemma. Way back when, upon being married, the wife's existence merged with the husband, such that she had no legal identity independent of him. She couldn't lease a property on contract without his co-signature and any suit brought by her against him (or him against her) would be tantamount to him suing

himself. Recognizing spousal immunity avoided the legal conundrum. Over the years, married women became more independent as the law began to vest to them rights that would eventually elevate them to an equivalent legal position as men, which, of course, included the right to sue their husbands.

2.   *General abrogation.* The first act of reforming spousal immunity was to create exceptions to its application in cases involving intentional torts and other personal injury actions not involving property. Today, a great majority of the states have abolished it altogether.

Chapter 20

Defamation

Imagine a college football player on a Big Ten team falsely (but, initially, convincingly) accused of rape. Think for a moment of what will happen to that player. (Do it. Make a list.) Will he have academic consequences? Career consequences? Will the Nancy-Grace types vilify him for weeks on their television shows? How will people treat him? How will he feel? Even when he's cleared, will he ever fully shake off being the Big Ten player accused of rape? Will some people always believe he did it?

Reputations are powerful. The regard in which we are generally held affects the quality of our social and emotional lives and our ability to earn a living. Recognizing the importance of the dignitary and financial aspects of reputation, defamation law protects reputation against false, harmful statements. Of course, false statements are also speech, which the Constitution protects under the First Amendment. Any defamation case will involve the competing concerns of the plaintiff's reputational rights and the defendant's Free Speech rights. Beginning with New York Times v. Sullivan, 376 U.S. 254 (1964), courts have struggled to balance these concerns correctly, and this can be a tangled area of the law. If at any point you are struggling with untangling it, the authors recommend that you take a look at *Law of Defamation* by Rod Smolla.

Also, as you read the cases, consider the following problem:

Parker vs. Davis

Agents of the Bureau of Alcohol, Tobacco, and Firearms (ATF) raided a fortified compound occupied by members of Red Bliss, a religious sect, which had stockpiled large quantities of illegal weapons. The compound was in rural Michiana, outside Springfield. The two Springfield television stations, WINX and WREM, learned from various sources that the

---

raid would occur at the Red Bliss compound that morning. WINX dispatched reporter Prentice Parker to report on the event.

When the ATF agents attempted to enter the compound dormitory, a gunfight broke out. During the gunfight, three agents and four sect members were killed. Many others, in both groups, were injured. Parker and his cameraman were the only media representatives to follow the agents onto the compound, and Parker reported live from the sidelines of the firefight. Parker's reports were broadcast worldwide, and he himself was subsequently interviewed by other reporters about his daring coverage and his role in helping wounded ATF agents despite what Parker described as "great personal risk."

Soon after the raid, media reports began to criticize the ATF's handling of the raid. Denise Davis, a journalist for the *Michiana Times*, appeared on *Nightline*, the ABC late-night news show, and discussed the role of the media in the ATF raid. Davis said that ATF agents believed they were set up. Davis said:

> Many agents blame the local media for the tragedy. They believe the local television station and the local newspaper were at the compound, hiding in the bushes, before the ATF got there. This was their first hint that they'd been set up and a Springfield reporter had tipped off Red Bliss to get permission to be on the compound and cover the story.

Davis never mentioned Parker by name, but immediately after the *Nightline* broadcast ended, WINX began to receive calls criticizing his role in the raid. Since the *Nightline* broadcast, Parker has received over 400 pieces of hate mail as well as vicious messages on his answering machine. The station has stood by Parker throughout this experience.

A review of all footage shot that day and an interview with the lead ATF agents have made clear that Parker was not at the Red Bliss compound before ATF agents, and no evidence has been produced to demonstrate that Parker tipped off members of the Red Bliss sect for access to their compound.

Davis based her comments on an interview with the secretary at the regional ATF office that covers the Springfield area. The secretary told Davis what she claimed to have heard from agents who participated in the raid after they returned to the field office. Davis did not attempt to speak directly to any ATF agents because they were under orders not to comment to the press on the raid. Davis did call WINX and leave a message requesting an interview with Parker, but in the aftermath of the Red Bliss raid, Parker was receiving over 30 interview requests a day and did not return her call.

Parker has sued Davis for defamation.

A. DEFAMATORY MEANING

Evel Knievel v. ESPN
393 F.3d 1068 (9th Cir. 2005)

TASHIMA, C.J.

Famed motorcycle stuntman Evel Knievel and his wife Krystal were photographed when they attended ESPN's Action Sports and Music Awards in 2001. The photograph depicted Evel, who was wearing a motorcycle jacket and rose-tinted sunglasses, with his right arm around Krystal and his left arm around another young woman. ESPN published the photograph on its "extreme sports" website with a caption that read "Evel Knievel proves that you're never too old to be a pimp." The Knievels brought suit against ESPN . . . contending that the photograph and caption were defamatory because they accused Evel of soliciting prostitution and implied that Krystal was a prostitute. ESPN . . . moved to dismiss for failure to state a claim. . . . The court granted ESPN's motion on the ground that the photograph and its caption were not defamatory as a matter of law. We . . . affirm. . . .

B. THE PHOTOGRAPH AND CAPTION WERE NOT DEFAMATORY AS A MATTER OF LAW

. . . In order to survive ESPN's motion to dismiss, the Knievels must . . . establish that the photograph and caption about which they complain are "reasonably capable of sustaining a defamatory meaning". . . .

When evaluating the threshold question of whether a statement is reasonably capable of sustaining a defamatory meaning, we must interpret that statement "from the standpoint of the average reader, judging the statement not in isolation, but within the context in which it is made." . . .

Although the word "pimp" may be reasonably capable of a defamatory meaning when read in isolation, we agree with the district court's assessment that "the term loses its meaning when considered in the context presented here." As discussed in more detail herein, the term "pimp" as used on the EXPN.com website was not intended as a criminal accusation, nor was it reasonably susceptible to such a literal interpretation. Ironically, it was most likely intended as a compliment. . . .

The First Amendment protects "statements that cannot 'reasonably [be] interpreted as stating actual facts' about an individual." Courts have extended First Amendment protection to such statements in recognition of "the reality that exaggeration and non-literal commentary have become an integral part of social discourse." By protecting speakers whose statements cannot reasonably be interpreted as allegations of fact, courts "provide[ ] assurance that public debate will not suffer for lack of 'imaginative expression' or the 'rhetorical hyperbole' which has traditionally added much to the discourse of our Nation."

When determining whether a statement can reasonably be interpreted as a factual assertion, we must examine the "totality of the circumstances in which it was made."

First, we look at the statement in its broad context, which includes the general tenor of the entire work, the subject of the statements, the setting, and the format of the work. Next we turn to the specific context and content of the statements, analyzing the extent of figurative or hyperbolic language used and the reasonable expectations of the audience in that particular situation. Finally, we inquire whether the statement itself is sufficiently factual to be susceptible of being proved true or false.

The context in which the statement appears is paramount in our analysis, and in some cases it can be dispositive. . . .

Because the reasonable interpretation of a word can change depending on the context in which it appears, not all statements that could be interpreted in the abstract as criminal accusations are defamatory. In Greenbelt Coop. Publ'g Ass'n v. Bresler, 398 U.S. 6 (1970), newspaper articles reporting on the contents of a public meeting regarding a pending development permit stated that some people at the meeting characterized the developer's negotiating position as "blackmail." The developer recovered in state court for libel on the ground that the articles accused him of the crime of blackmail. The Supreme Court reversed, holding that the statement was protected First Amendment speech because "[n]o reader could have thought that either the speakers at the meetings or the newspaper articles reporting their words were charging [the developer] with the commission of a criminal offense." On the contrary, it held, "even the most careless reader must have perceived that the word was no more than rhetorical hyperbole, a vigorous epithet used by those who considered [the developer's] negotiating position extremely unreasonable."

A speaker's use of "loose, figurative" language can also determine whether his or her statement can reasonably be interpreted as a factual allegation. In Standing Comm. on Discipline of the United States Dist. Court v. Yagman, 55 F.3d 1430 (9th Cir. 1995), we held that an attorney could not be sanctioned for accusing a district judge of being "dishonest" because the other terms the attorney used to describe the judge—"ignorant," "ill-tempered," "buffoon," "sub-standard human," and "right-wing fanatic"—made it clear that the attorney intended only to signal his general contempt for the judge, rather than to accuse him of corruption. . . . On the other hand, we held that Yagman could be sanctioned for accusing Judge Keller of being "drunk on the bench" because he made that accusation on a separate occasion and there was "nothing relating to the context in which this statement was made that tends to negate the literal meaning of the words he used." . . .

2. *The Use of "Loose, Figurative" Language*

Our first inquiry is into the "broad context" of the statement, which includes "the general tenor of the entire work, the subject of the statements, the setting, and the format of the work." The district court found, and we agree, that the content of the EXPN.com main page is lighthearted, jocular, and intended for a youthful audience. It is equally clear that the subject matter of the page is not merely extreme sports themselves, but the youth culture and style associated with extreme sports. The page directs the viewer to "[c]heck out what the rock-stars and prom queens were wearing," and offers a "behind the scenes look at all the cool kids, EXPN-style." Most importantly, however, we observe that the page features slang phrases such as "[d]udes rollin' deep" and "[k]ickin' it with much flavor," neither of which is susceptible to a literal interpretation, and neither of which one would expect to hear uttered by anyone but a teenager or young adult. A reasonable viewer exposed to the main page would expect to find precisely that type of youthful, non-literal language on the rest of the site.

Next, we examine the "specific context and content of the statements, ana-lyzing the extent of figurative or hyperbolic language used and the reasonable expectations of the audience in that particular situation." Again, the over-whelming presence of slang and non-literal language guides our inquiry. The web pages immediately preceding and following the Knievel photo use slang words such as "hardcore" and "scoping," and slang phrases such as "throwing down a pose," "put a few back," and "hottie of the year," none of which is intended to be interpreted literally, if indeed they have a literal mean-ing at all. We think that any reasonable viewer would have interpreted the word "pimp" in the same loose, figurative sense as well.

But even if a viewer had interpreted the word "pimp" literally, he or she would have certainly interpreted the photograph and caption, in the context in which they were published, as an attempt at humor. . . .

For the foregoing reasons, we affirm the judgment of the district court.

BEA, C.J., dissenting.

Shakespeare's Iago said it best:

> Good name in man and woman, dear my lord,
> Is the immediate jewel of their souls.
> Who steals my purse steals trash;
> 'Tis something, nothing;
> 'Twas mine, 'tis his, and has been slave to thousands;
> But he that filches from me my good name
> Robs me of that which not enriches him,
> And makes me poor indeed.

William Shakespeare, *Othello*, Act III, scene iii (1604).

With considerable less lilt than Iago, but with perhaps the same desire to poison the mind not of a Moor—but of millions—defendant ESPN wrote below a photograph of Knievel, his attractive wife and a younger woman: "Evel Knievel proves you are never too old to be a pimp."

. . . Because I believe that a reasonable person could view this photo and its caption as defamatory of the Knievels, I respectfully dissent. . . .

The issue is not "whether the court regards the language as libelous, but whether it is reasonably susceptible of such a construction." Indeed, "[t]his court may not . . . interfere with the jury's role by treating as nondefamatory a statement that a reasonable juror may fairly read in context as defamatory."

In determining whether the "reasonable juror" would find a particular statement defamatory, courts have held that "words charged to be defamatory are to be taken in their natural meaning and that the courts will not strain to interpret them in their mildest and most inoffensive sense to hold them nonlibelous." (A court must "place itself in the position of the . . . reader, and determine the sense of meaning of the statement according to its natural and popular construction" and the "natural and probable effect [it would have] upon the mind of the average reader").

Moreover, if the language at issue is "capable of both a defamatory and a nondefamatory meaning, there exists a question of fact for the jury."

To determine whether a statement is defamatory, courts should first look at the publication in which the statement appears. . . .

[H]ere the EXPN website is not an overtly non-factual, satirical publication, nor does ESPN contend that it is. Here, there was nothing to suggest satire. ESPN was not holding up the "vices" of anyone to "ridicule or contempt," the function of satire. Second, it is not inherently unbelievable that a daredevil attract, and perhaps exploit, women. Last, there has not been a semblance of a disclaimer, then or now. [The dissent is distinguishing a case where statement was held not defamatory as a matter of law.]

Second, in analyzing the broad context in which the photo and caption appear, the Majority's analysis of the "broad context" was erroneously narrowed by its acceptance of defendant's argument that to determine "broad context" all that matters is to whom the publication is targeted. . . .

Since the EXPN.com event and website are targeted at the hip, young and irreverent who revel in slang and do not take statements "seriously," the Majority reasons "no harm, no foul." However, the case law does not allow a court to judge whether a statement is defamatory by asking who was intended to read or hear it. The true test is "who did read or hear it." The general law of defamation is that a publisher is liable for the unintended results of his publication. . . .

What about those dowdy corporate bourgeois who are Knievel's clients and who allegedly have abandoned him because of the photograph and caption? Put another way, one cannot judge the liability of a defamer by the composition of what he claims is his targeted audience. One also has to consider not only who was targeted, but who was hit.

a. Slang v. Dictionary Definition of Term "Pimp"

The Majority concludes that the definition of the word assigned by Plaintiffs is not the only definition and therefore that the term is not capable of defamatory meaning. . . .

This analysis is a classic example of circular reasoning. To conclude that the slang definition is the correct reference point is to decide the issue. Not so fast.

Even were the hip usage—a sharp-dressing dude—widespread, even ESPN does not claim such meaning is unanimous amongst "average persons. That is as it should be, since "pimp's" pejorative meaning made it into *Webster's Collegiate Dictionary*, but not Appellees' hip offering nor, with respect, the Majority's application of the term. . . .

Indeed, in a recent case, the California Court of Appeals held that the term "pimp," allegedly used "in jest" was reasonably capable of defamatory meaning. In [Hughes v. Hughes, 122 Cal. App. 4th 931 (2004)], the plaintiff alleged that he was defamed by his sons' statement, published in the *Vanity Fair* magazine, that "[o]ur dad's a pimp." The court concluded that the term "pimp" was capable of defamatory meaning and the case was properly tried to a jury. In so holding, the court noted that "the dictionary definition of pimp is a man who solicits clients for a prostitute" and reasoned that, "[s]o long as the statement 'our dad's a pimp' can reasonably be understood to mean that plaintiff had at one time engaged in pimping activity, it was for the jury to determine if that is how the statement should be understood."

b. "Loose, Figurative or Hyperbolic" Language

The Majority next reasons that the term "pimp" is "loose, figurative or hyperbolic" language and is therefore not capable of defamatory meaning. Not so.

First, there is nothing "loose, figurative or hyperbolic" about the term "pimp." The noun describes criminal activity in Montana, and should be especially loathsome to the "hip" who sometimes espouse political correctness, for it connotes despicable sexist conduct of domination and exploitation.

Second, the terms used to describe the other individuals ESPN displayed in the photo gallery implicitly allude to an individual's promiscuity ("share the love"; "hottie"), conceit and self-centeredness ("throwing down a pose"), drinking prowess ("put a few back"), attitude ("hardcore") and general hipness ("give a shout out to EXPN"). Slang is used to describe being left alone, greeting someone or drinking beer. These terms are aptly deemed "loose, figurative and hyperbolic" phrases.

On the other hand, the description of Knievel is unique. While all the others are described in terms implying fun-filled misconduct of one sort or another, only Knievel was described as a criminal, per dictionary definition. For example, the promiscuous women are called "hotties," not "whores" or "sluts"; the beer-drinkers are not called "public drunks." None of the other terms describes any criminal activity, much less the loathsome anti-feminist characteristics of a "pimp."

The "loose, figurative and hyperbolic" language used to describe the other individuals actually highlights the fact that while all others are described as sexy, hip and with-it, the hard, factual description of plaintiff as a criminal and abuser of women is reserved for Knievel. Courts have recognized that "[s]tatements that could reasonably be understood as imputing specific criminal or other wrongful acts are not entitled to constitutional protection merely because they are phrased in the form of an opinion." . . .

Is it so "unreasonable" to conceive of an executive of a certain age, concerned with his market share of "average person" consumers, believing that a reputed daredevil has decided to supplement his income by living off "his ladies," a couple of which are shown in the photo? Again, so long as a reasonable interpretation is defamatory, plaintiff has stated a claim for relief.

Accordingly, I respectfully dissent.

PREPARING FOR CLASS

1. As counsel for the Knievels, what key points would you have made in your appeal?

2. As counsel for ESPN, what key points would you have made in your response brief?

3. What are the roles of judge and jury on the question of defamatory meaning?

INCREASING YOUR UNDERSTANDING

1. The California legislature provides a fairly common definition of defamatory meaning. A defamatory statement "exposes any person to hatred, contempt, ridicule, or obloquy, or . . . causes him to be shunned or avoided, or . . . has a tendency to injure him in his occupation." Cal. Civ. Code §45. Courts will often cite the definition from the Prosser hornbook: "Defamation is rather that which tends to injure 'reputation' in the popular sense; to diminish the esteem, respect, goodwill or confidence in which the plaintiff is held, or to excite adverse, derogatory or unpleasant feelings or opinions against him." Prosser, Keeton, Dobbs, and Keeton, *Prosser and Keeton on Torts*, 773, 5th edition.

2. Epithets, name-calling, obscenity, and other verbal abuse are not considered defamatory. In a sense, they reflect more on the person who is speaking than they do on the person who is being spoken about. Moreover, such words are generally not taken literally and do not cause harm. To defeat an argument that the statement is mere name-calling or verbal abuse, the plaintiff would have to show that, in context, the statement communicates something factual (and ultimately false) about him.

APPLYING THE LAW

1. Are the following at least capable of a defamatory meaning so that the jury should hear the case?

   a. A doctor performs legal abortions. A member of a right-to-life group referred to the doctor as a "murderer" in a letter to the editor.

    b.   A well-known lawyer was hired to speak to a state bar association. He was offered a low speaking fee plus payment of his hotel bill. A news article reported that the lawyer, so as to be adequately compensated, ran up the hotel bill by making purchases in the hotel boutiques.

    c.   A blog referred to a Chicago alderwoman as a "nut job" and "loud mouthy bitch."

    d.   A political candidate called an opponent "racist."

    e.   A newspaper article about a child's death stated that the parents were too poor to afford a funeral.

    f.   A celebrity's unauthorized biography stated that she was raped when she was 16.

2.   In the Parker vs. Davis problem, would a judge find the statement capable of a defamatory meaning? Would a jury find he was defamed?

Grant v. Reader's Digest Ass'n
151 F.2d 733 (2d Cir. 1946)

HAND, C.J.

This is an appeal from a judgment dismissing a complaint in libel for insufficiency in law upon its face. The complaint alleged that the plaintiff was a Massachusetts lawyer, living in that state; that the defendant, a New York corporation, published a periodical of general circulation, read by lawyers, judges and the general public; and that one issue of the periodical contained an article entitled "I Object To My Union in Politics," in which the following passage appeared:

> And another thing. In my state the Political Action Committee has hired as its legislative agent one, Sidney S. Grant, who but recently was a legislative representative for the Massachusetts Communist Party.

The innuendo then alleged that this passage charged the plaintiff with having represented the Communist Party in Massachusetts as its legislative agent, which was untrue and malicious. Two questions arise: (1) What meaning the jury might attribute to the words; (2) whether the meaning so attributed was libelous. . . . The innuendo added nothing to the meaning of the words, and, indeed, could not. However, although the words did not say that the plaintiff was a member of the Communist Party, they did say that he had acted on its behalf, and we think that a jury might in addition find that they implied that he was in general sympathy with its objects and methods. The last conclusion does indeed involve the assumption that the Communist Party would not retain as its "legislative representative" a person who was not in general accord with its purposes; but that inference is reasonable and was pretty plainly what the author wished readers to draw from his words. The case therefore turns upon whether it is libelous in New York to write of a lawyer that he has acted as agent of the Communist Party, and is a believer in its aims and methods.

The interest at stake in all defamation is concededly the reputation of the person assailed; and any moral obliquity of the opinions of those in whose minds the words might lessen that reputation, would normally be relevant only in mitigation of damages. A man may value his reputation even among those who do not embrace the prevailing moral standards; and it would seem that the jury should be allowed to appraise how far he should be indemnified for the disesteem of such persons. That is the usual rule.

The New York decisions define libel, in accordance with the usual rubric, as consisting of utterances which arouse "hatred, contempt, scorn, obloquy or shame," and the like. However, the opinions at times seem to make it a condition that to be actionable the words must be such as would so affect "right-thinking" people. . . . Be that as it may, in New York if the exception covers more than such a case, it does not go far enough to excuse the utterance at bar. Katapodis v. Brooklyn Spectator, Inc.[, 38 N.E.2d 112 (N.Y. 1941),] . . . held that the imputation of extreme poverty might be actionable; although certainly "right-thinking" people ought not shun, or despise, or otherwise condemn one because he is poor. Indeed, the only declaration of the Court of Appeals (Moore v. Francis, 121 N.Y. 199) leaves it still open whether it is not libellous to say that a man is insane. . . . We do not believe, therefore, that we need say whether "right-thinking" people would harbor similar feelings toward a lawyer, because he had been an agent for the Communist Party, or was a sympathizer with its aims and means. It is enough if there be some, as there certainly are, who would feel so, even though they would be "wrong-thinking" people if they did. . . .

The lower courts in New York have passed on almost the same question in three cases. In Garriga v. Richfield, 20 N.Y.S.2d 544, Pecora, J., held that it was not libelous to say that a man was a Communist; in the next year in Levy v. Gelber, 25 N.Y.S.2d 148, Hofstadter, J., held otherwise. That perhaps left the answer open; but Boudin v. Tishman, 35 N.Y.S.2d 760, was an unescapable ruling, although no opinion was written. Being the last decision of the state courts, it is conclusive upon us, unless there is a difference between saying that a man is a Communist and saying that he is an agent for the Party or sympathizes with its objects and methods. Any difference is one of degree only: those who would take it ill of a lawyer that he was a member of the Party, might no doubt take it less so if he were only what is called a "fellow-traveler"; but, since the basis for the reproach ordinarily lies in some supposed threat to our institutions, those who fear that threat are not likely to believe that it is limited to party members. Indeed, it is not uncommon for them to feel less concern at avowed propaganda than at what they regard as the insidious spread of the dreaded doctrines by those who only dally and coquette with them, and have not the courage openly to proclaim themselves.

Judgment reversed; cause remanded.

PREPARING FOR CLASS

1. Why did the trial court dismiss the case?

2. What is the argument that right-thinking people do not think less of Communists, their representatives, or their sympathizers?

3. What does the court mean by "any moral obliquity of the opinions of those in whose minds the words might lessen that reputation, would normally be relevant only in mitigation of damages"?

4. In the mid-1940s in the United States, did people think less of or avoid Communists or their sympathizers? Could being branded a Communist or Communist sympathizer have been harmful?

5. What is wrong with imposing a right-thinking person standard? If you are having difficulty with that question, consider this hypothetical: A magazine in the state of Michiana annually publishes a list of doctors in the state who will perform legal abortions. The editors approve of the doctors on the list and intend inclusion on the list to express that approval. A Michiana doctor who does *not* perform abortions is accidentally included in the list. Could this harm her reputation? What would be wrong with having a Michiana trial court judge determine whether right-thinking people would think less of or avoid a physician for being on that list?

6. In whose eyes must the statement be defamatory?

INCREASING YOUR UNDERSTANDING

1. Justice Holmes, considering a case brought by a woman whose photograph was used in a testimonial advertisement about the benefits of drinking whiskey, wrote, "If the advertisement obviously would hurt the plaintiff in the estimation of an important and respectable part of the community, liability is not a question of majority vote. . . . That it will be known by a large number and will lead an appreciable fraction of that number to regard the plaintiff with contempt is enough to do her practical harm." Peck v. Tribune Co., 214 U.S. 185 (1909).

2. *Inducement and Innuendo.* Sometimes the defamatory meaning of a statement will not be clear on its face. In such a case, the plaintiff must plead inducement and innuendo. The inducement provides the extrinsic facts—facts outside the defamatory statement—that would explain why the statement could have a defamatory meaning. The innuendo is the alleged defamatory meaning. For example, a Scottish newspaper published a false report that the plaintiff had given birth to twins. Many readers knew that the plaintiff had been

married only one month. Morrison v. Ritchie & Co., 39 Scot. L. Rep. 432 (1902). On the face of it, the report was congratulatory, not defamatory. But the inducement—she was married only a month—created the innuendo that she was an unchaste woman who had become pregnant before marriage.

3. *Falsity*. A defamatory statement must also be false to be actionable. For a long time, the common law presumed that defamatory statements were false and put the burden of proving truth on the defendant. This truth defense is known as "justification." (Some states have placed limitations on the truth defense, such as restricting it to situations where the defendant published the statement in good faith and for a justifiable purpose.) Today, the justification defense is greatly eroded. Later in this chapter you will read New York Times Co. v. Sullivan, 376 U.S. 254 (1964), which recognized that defamation law must balance the reputational rights of plaintiffs against the Free Speech rights of defendants and implied that truth should no longer be a defense and that falsity, instead, should be an element of a plaintiff's case, at least if the plaintiff has brought an action against a public official. When we move into the constitutional section of this chapter, we will see that the implication in *New York Times* has been adopted as law and that in many cases, not just those involving public officials, plaintiffs will have the burden of proving falsity, rather than defendants having the burden of proving truth.

Whether the defendant must prove truth or the plaintiff must prove falsity, a defamatory statement is treated as true if it is substantially true. The U.S. Supreme Court has explained it this way:

> The common law of libel ... overlooks minor inaccuracies and concentrates upon substantial truth. As in other jurisdictions, California law permits the defense of substantial truth and would absolve a defendant even if she cannot "justify every word of the alleged defamatory matter; it is sufficient if the substance of the charge be proved true, irrespective of slight inaccuracy in the details." 5 B. Witkin, Summary of California Law §495 (9th ed. 1988). In this case, of course, the burden is upon petitioner to prove falsity. The essence of that inquiry, however, remains the same whether the burden rests upon plaintiff or defendant. Minor inaccuracies do not amount to falsity so long as "the substance, the gist, the sting, of the libelous charge be justified." Put another way, the statement is not considered false unless it "would have a different effect on the mind of the reader from that which the pleaded truth would have produced."

Masson v. New Yorker Magazine, 501 U.S. 496, 516-17 (1991).

The "substance, the gist, the sting" of a specific libelous charge will not be justified, however, by an allegation of the plaintiff's general bad deeds or poor reputation. If specific allegations are made against the plaintiff, those specific allegations must be true for the defendant to escape liability. For example, in the case of Kilian v. Doubleday & Co., 79 A.2d 657 (Pa. 1951), the plaintiff was a commanding officer at a replacement depot in England in World War II. He filed a defamation case regarding an article that portrayed him as committing a number of specific inhumane acts towards prisoners in his charge. Witnesses did testify to harsh conduct by the plaintiff but not to the specific acts alleged in the story, and although the plaintiff had been convicted of neglect of prisoners, he had not been convicted of any intentional wrongdoing. Thus, the evidence did not justify the comments in the story.

> Defendant produced as witnesses three soldiers who were at Lichfield, who testified to punishments inflicted on them or observed by them as imposed on others, but none of the incidents they described tended to prove that a single one of the events narrated in the O'Connell article actually occurred; therefore such testimony was not properly admissible to prove the truth of the publication. While, in order to support a defense of truth, it is necessary merely to prove that it was substantially true, and while, therefore, if the testimony of those witnesses had shown a variance merely in the details of the events described in the article it would nevertheless have been admissible as giving support to the plea of truth, it furnished no such support by proving that other and wholly different incidents occurred although these also may have been equally blameworthy. If, for instance, one were to assert that A had embezzled $50 from the X Bank he would not support the truth of such allegation by testimony that A embezzled $100 from the Y Bank, especially if he were also falsely to state that he actually saw A committing this other embezzlement. "Specific charges cannot be justified by showing the plaintiff's general bad character; and if the accusation is one of particular misconduct, such as stealing a watch from A, it is not enough to show a different offense, even though it be a more serious one, such as stealing a clock from A, or six watches from B." *Prosser on Torts*, p. 855, §95. . . . None of defendant's testimony showed any instances at the camp, as alleged in O'Connell's article, of lashing, of cursing prisoners, of having a soldier whose fingers were missing act as a stretcher bearer, of ordering a badly wounded veteran on a ten-mile hike. . . . It is obvious that there was not a shred of testimony presented at the trial to prove either that the author of the article saw any of the events he narrated, or that those events or even

substantially similar ones occurred, or that plaintiff was aware of any such happenings, or that he sanctioned them, or that he was a "dictator," or that in his very appearance he looked like a man who would enjoy seeing another man suffer. The court, therefore, was in error in submitting to the jury, as it did, the question whether the publication was substantially true.

APPLYING THE LAW

In Warner v. Monk, 22 Media L. Rep. (BNA) 1667 (Cal. Ct. App. 1994), the plaintiff, a former bodyguard for Sid Vicious, filed a defamation suit over his portrayal in a book about touring with the Sex Pistols.

> On page 66 of the book was recounted what may have been plaintiff's first meeting with his protégé, at a dinner party. This momentous drama was set in a restroom. Vicious was skinny and "shaky drunk." Plaintiff was big and brawny and "hung out with bikers for the better part of a decade." Vicious challenged plaintiff to fight. Undesirous of fighting the person he was employed to protect, plaintiff let Vicious hit him, thinking a wiry drunk's punches could not hurt much. But Vicious packed a wallop and inflicted real pain on plaintiff. Plaintiff announced, "That was your turn, you [expletive] limey. Now it's my turn." Plaintiff grabbed Vicious by the hair and banged Vicious's head hard against the sink half a dozen times. Vicious slumped to the floor, saying "OK, OK, enough. You're good enough. I like you. Now we can be friends." Plaintiff exited, leaving Vicious crumpled on the floor. Soon Vicious staggered out of the restroom and challenged Camel, another security man, to fight. Camel refused to fight and pushed Vicious aside. Later that night, after plaintiff reported these events to defendant Monk, Monk approached Vicious, who was suffering from serious heroin withdrawal. Vicious told Monk, "I like D.W. He's a good man. He can fight. That's the kind of guy I want around me."

What is the argument that this is not capable of defaming? What is the argument that it is? Which argument prevails?

B. OF AND CONCERNING THE PLAINTIFF

The defamation lawsuit remedies harms to the plaintiff's reputation, but a defamatory statement cannot harm a plaintiff's reputation if people do not think it was about her. Therefore, a defamation plaintiff must prove that she was reasonably believed to be the subject of the defamatory statement. She must prove it was "of and concerning" her. Often, this will be simple. The statement will explicitly refer to the plaintiff. When the statement does not explicitly identify the plaintiff, she must plead and prove "colloquium," which includes the allegation that the statement is about her and extrinsic facts that support the allegation.

For example, Joni Mitchell wrote a song, "Not to Blame," which appeared on her 1994 album, *Turbulent Indigo*. The song accuses someone (Mitchell says it is no one specific) of domestic abuse and of driving someone to suicide, and many people have speculated that the song is about Mitchell's former boyfriend, Jackson Browne. Browne is never named in the song, however. If he had sued Mitchell for defamation, he would have had the burden of pleading and proving colloquium. In the lyrics, a three-year-old boy whose mother committed suicide suggests that he and his father go out looking for girls. Jackson Browne's complaint would point out that, like the man in the song, he had a wife who committed suicide when his son was three. The lyrics describe the discrepancy between the man's charitable acts and his fist marks on a beauty's face. Jackson Browne would point out that he was known for environmental activism, and the beauty could be interpreted as Darryl Hannah, the actress Browne dated, whom the tabloids said he beat up. The fact that Browne and Mitchell had a failed relationship might also cause reasonable people to interpret the song to be an attack on him because of bitter feelings from that relationship.

Now, think of the Parker vs. Davis problem. Will the case involve special pleading requirements? Is the statement of and concerning Parker?

The cases in this section look at other situations that create "of and concerning" problems.

McCullough v. Cities Service Co.
676 P.2d 833 (Ok. 1984)

Lavender, J.

[The plaintiff was one of 19,686 Doctors of Osteopathy practicing in the United States. The defendant's publication advised people that they should have medical doctors as their family physicians and not doctors of osteopathy because medical doctors have superior education and post-graduate training.]

Finally, plaintiff alleges that the trial court misconstrued our holding in Fawcett Publications, Inc. v. Morris, 377 P.2d 42 (1962), cert. denied, 376 U.S. 513 (1964) or, in the alternative, that *Fawcett* should be overruled as a minority view, in the trial court's determination that the Plaintiff's petition states a cause of action for group libel maintainable by the plaintiff individually. . . .

In *Fawcett*, the plaintiff brought a libel action in his own name and on his own personal behalf against defendant publishing company which published an article stating that the entire 1956 University of Oklahoma football team ingested amphetamines illegally during football games. There were sixty or seventy members of the 1956 team and the libelous publication made no personal reference to any particular member of the team. Thus, as in the case before us, the action was one for group libel where the opprobrium attributable to the plaintiff was confined to plaintiff's membership in the group. In *Fawcett*, the group consisted of sixty to seventy members; in the case before us, the group consists of 19,686 members.

In *Fawcett* we said:

> While there is substantial precedent from other jurisdictions to the effect that a member of a "larger group" may not recover in an individual action for a libelous publication unless he is referred to personally, we have found no substantial reason why size alone should be conclusive. We are not inclined to follow such a rule where, as here, the complaining member of the group is as well known and identified in connection with the group as was the plaintiff in this case. In 34 Columbia Law Review 1322, supra, in considering group libel, it said, with good reason:
>
> > . . . the primary consideration would properly seem to be whether the plaintiff was in fact defamed, although not specifically designated. Considerations adduced in support of the absolute denial of recovery are inconclusive, as against the desirability of providing a remedy for actual injury.
> >
> > A more realistic approach would recognize that even a general derogatory reference to a group does affect the reputation of every member, and would adopt as its test the intensity of the suspicion cast upon the plaintiff.

A careful review of the reported cases before and after *Fawcett* has furnished no enlightenment which impels us to retreat from the two principles therein enunciated with reference to group libel actions wherein the opprobrium of the publication attributable to the individual plaintiff arises solely by reason of his membership in the group: (1) Size of the group alone is not conclusive although the size of the group is to be considered, and (2) the intensity of suspicion cast upon the plaintiff is the true test in determining a plaintiff's right to maintain a personal action for group libel.

The so-called "majority rule" is tersely summarized in Restatement, Torts, 2nd §564A in the following language:

DEFAMATION OF A GROUP OR CLASS
One who publishes defamatory matter concerning a group or class of persons is subject to liability to an individual member of it, but only if,
(a) the group or class is so small that the matter can reasonably be understood to refer to the member, or
(b) the circumstances of publication reasonably give rise to the conclusion that there is a particular reference to the member.

The failure in every reported case which has come to our attention to announce the precise numerical dividing line between groups which are "too large" and groups which are "small" enough to permit a plaintiff to recover, demonstrates the weakness of slavish reliance upon the general rule which relies upon numbers alone. Indeed, the Restatement, Torts 2nd Ed. §564A states:

> It is not possible to set definite limits as to the size of the group or class, but the cases in which recovery has been allowed usually involved numbers of 25 or fewer.

Yet no reported case has undertaken to announce that 26 is "too large" to permit an individual plaintiff to recover, and in *Fawcett* the number was sixty to seventy, a group determined not to be "too large" to permit recovery.

In the case of Brady v. Ottaway Newspapers, Inc., 84 A.D.2d 226, 445 N.Y.S.2d 786 (1981) the New York Supreme Court, Appellate Division, critically analyzed our holding in *Fawcett*, rejected the "majority rule" as solely determinative, adopted and applied the "intensity of suspicion" test and concluded that under the facts then before the Court, a cause of action by one of a group of at least 53 was legally maintainable.

From the teaching of *Brady*, we glean the following principles to which we subscribe:

1. The "of and concerning" element in defamation actions requires that the allegedly defamatory comment refer to the plaintiff.

2. Generally, an impersonal reproach of an indeterminate class is not actionable. The underlying premise of this principle is that the larger the collectivity named in the libel, the less likely it is that a reader would understand it to refer to a particular individual. The rule was designed to encourage frank discussions of matters of public concern under the First Amendment guarantees. Thus the incidental and occasional injury to the individual resulting from the defamation of large groups is balanced against the public's right to know.

3. In contrast to the treatment of an individual in a large group which has been defamed, an individual belonging to a small group may maintain an action for individual injury resulting from a defamatory comment about the group, by showing that he is a member of the group. Because the group is small and includes few individuals, reference to the individual plaintiff reasonably follows from the statement and the question of reference is left for the jury.

4. Size alone is too narrow a focus to determine the issue of individual application in group defamation.

5. The intensity of suspicion test recognizes that even a general derogatory reference to a group may affect the reputation of every member. In order to determine personal application it requires that a factual inquiry be made to determine the degree that the group accusation focuses on each individual member of the group. The numerical size of the group is a consideration, but is not the only factor to be considered. One element to be considered is

the prominence of the group and the prominence of the individual within the group.

In applying the above principles to the case before us, we hold that plaintiff's action is not maintainable.

The publication constitutes an impersonal reproach of an indeterminate class. There are some 19,686 D.O.'s in the United States. Since it is conceded no particular or personal reference is made to the plaintiff, there can be no intensity of suspicion cast upon the plaintiff. Whatever aspersions are cast by the publication fall upon the profession of osteopathy, and not upon a small or identifiable group within the class of osteopaths.

The Order of the trial court overruling Defendant's demurrer to plaintiff's petition is reversed.

PREPARING FOR CLASS

1. Why do courts have special rules for determining "of and concerning" when the allegedly defamatory statement criticizes a group the plaintiff belongs to?

2. What are the competing rules for determining "of and concerning" in group defamation? Why/how is this court critical of the majority rule? Which approach do you prefer?

3. Imagine the arguments of the plaintiff and the defendant in *Fawcett*.

4. Why did the court conclude that defamation of a group of 60-70 football players was of and concerning each and every player on that team? Would a court applying the majority rule have reached a different result?

5. If the plaintiff in this case could point to lost patients and lost esteem in the community directly traceable to the defendant's article, would the outcome in this case be the same? Why or why not?

APPLYING THE LAW

1. The Bradys were going to adopt a baby. State law required that they go through an interview process with Children's Social Services. In the interview they said their religion was "The Way International" (TWI). When the interviewing social worker's supervisor reviewed her report, he told her that TWI is a cult that uses mind control techniques. The social worker terminated the adoption process. The Bradys sued the supervisor for defamation. He argued that his statements were about TWI, a religion with approximately 10,000 members, and were not of and concerning the Bradys. Will this argument succeed?

2. A television panelist discussing religion in America denounced TWI as a cult that used mind control techniques. Several members of TWI sued him for defamation. Was the statement of and concerning them?

INCREASING YOUR UNDERSTANDING

The Restatement's 25-member threshold is defended in Stern, The Certainty Principle as Justification for the Group Defamation Rule, 40 Ariz. St. L.J. 951 (Fall 2008).

Smith v. Stewart
660 S.E.2d 822 (Ga. App. 2008)

Ellington, J.

In this appeal, Haywood Smith, author of a book entitled *The Red Hat Club*, and St. Martin's Press, LLC, publisher of the book, appeal from the trial court's denial of summary judgment in a defamation suit brought by Vickie Stewart. . . .

Vickie Stewart is a 60-year-old woman who grew up in the Buckhead area of Atlanta and graduated from Northside High School. She met Anne Haywood Pritchett (now known as "Haywood Smith") as a child when she moved to Cottage Lane, just down the street from Smith. As an adult, Stewart got married and had two children, including a daughter she named "Mindunn." Stewart's first husband was killed in a car accident, and she received a substantial insurance settlement. She subsequently became engaged to Harold Stewart ("Harold"); at the time, she did not know that Harold was also engaged to another woman. Harold owned several nursing homes in Florida. In 1983, Stewart married Harold, but they divorced after Harold moved to Florida, stole her insurance money, and transferred his assets to his mistress. A Fulton County judge awarded Stewart $750,000 in the divorce, but Stewart was unable to collect on the award. She placed advertisements in a Florida newspaper offering a reward to anyone who provided information about when Harold was in Georgia so he could be held in contempt of the court's order. Then, in 1998, when Stewart was over 50 years old, she became a flight attendant.

Haywood Smith is an author who has known Stewart for over 50 years. Smith was familiar with Stewart's background, and Stewart had talked to Smith about her (Stewart's) first marriage, her relationship with Harold, the circumstances of their divorce, and Stewart's efforts to collect the court's $750,000 award. Smith believed that Stewart's stories were "really good" and decided to include them in a book she was writing. In 2002, Smith wrote a novel about five middle-aged women who lived in Buckhead, were life-long friends, and were members of a group called the "Red Hat Club." One of the women was "Susan Virginia McIntyre Harris Cates" and was nicknamed "SuSu." According to the book, SuSu moved to Cottage Circle in Atlanta, near the book's narrator, and attended Northside High School. SuSu got married and had two children, including a daughter named "Mignon." SuSu's first husband was killed in a car accident, and she received a large insurance settlement. SuSu became engaged to a man who owned nursing homes in Florida and was already secretly engaged to another woman. He eventually stole all of SuSu's money from the insurance settlement, moved to Florida, and transferred all of his assets to a "bimbo" with whom he was having an affair. A Georgia court subsequently awarded SuSu $750,000, but she was unable to collect the money because the man "skipped out to Florida." SuSu became obsessed with collecting the money and eventually placed an advertisement in a newspaper and created "Wanted" posters offering a reward to anyone who could lure the man back into Georgia. SuSu later became a flight attendant, and her friends jokingly referred to her as the "world's oldest stewardess."

The book also portrayed SuSu as an unrehabilitated alcoholic who secretly drank alcohol before and during flights and frequently became intoxicated—even "smashed"—in public. SuSu was very promiscuous, regularly engaging in one-night stands with passengers she met on flights, affairs with married men, and casual sex with young "stud puppies." . . . The book also described SuSu as foul-mouthed, insensitive and ill-mannered, a "right-wing reactionary" and atheist, and a "loose cannon" with a bad temper. . . .

St. Martin's Press published the hardcover edition of Smith's book in 2003, and it reached number 15 on the *New York Times* bestseller list. . . . [Many people recognized Stewart and gossiped about her, wondering whether she was, indeed, a promiscuous alcoholic. She filed a defamation suit against Smith and her publisher. This is an appeal of the trial court's denial of summary judgment for the defendants.]

Regarding the first element of a defamation claim, that is, whether the publication could be found to be "a false and defamatory statement concerning the plaintiff," "the allegedly defamatory words must refer to some ascertained or ascertainable person, and that person must be the plaintiff." Stated differently, the plaintiff has the burden of showing, inter alia, that "the publication was about the plaintiff, that is, whether it was of and concerning her as a matter of identity." The "of and concerning" test for works of fiction is essentially the same as that for nonfiction. "The test is whether persons who knew or knew of the plaintiff could reasonably have understood that the fictional character was a portrayal of the plaintiff." "It is not necessary that all the world should understand the libel; it is sufficient if those who knew the plaintiff can make out that [she] is the person meant." Consequently, the defendants are only entitled to summary judgment on this issue if, on the undisputed facts, no jury could reasonably conclude that the character of SuSu was a portrayal of Stewart.

In this case, in addition to the numerous unique facts about Stewart which Smith used to create SuSu's character and background, as outlined above, the book includes many other references to distinct, albeit more common, similarities between Stewart and SuSu. These similarities include their propensity for being chronically late, their hair color (red/auburn), their chain-smoking and smoker's cough, and the descriptions of their parents' occupations and their childhood homes, as well as other facts about Stewart that were not matters of public knowledge until the publication of the book. In fact, the trial court found at least twenty-six specific examples of similarities between the two. As noted above, these similarities led many readers to immediately conclude that SuSu was based on Stewart.

Further, the defendants have conceded that SuSu was inspired by and based in part on Stewart, that there are numerous similarities between Stewart and SuSu, and that SuSu is recognizable as Stewart. The defendants argue, however, that there are also many differences between Stewart and SuSu, such as their names and the names of their friends, and the fact that, unlike SuSu, Stewart was not a high school cheerleader or a member of a sorority and does not belong to a group called The Red Hat Club. Those differences, however, merely create a jury issue as to whether the character of SuSu was a portrayal of Stewart.

Under these circumstances, Stewart should be allowed the opportunity to prove that, despite the fictional label, the character of SuSu bears such a close resemblance to Stewart that a jury could reasonably conclude that the character was intended to portray her. Whether the book was actually understood by third parties to be about Stewart is, of course, a question of fact for the jury.

Thus, the trial court properly denied summary judgment to the defendants on the issue of whether the character of SuSu was a portrayal of Stewart. . . .

The defendants also contend that the court erred in finding that the allegedly defamatory excerpts from the book could reasonably be understood as stating actual facts about Stewart. They argue that the book is "clearly and unambiguously a work of fiction," that the book contains a disclaimer ["This novel is a work of fiction about a group of women who belong to a group like the Red Hat Society. It has not been authorized or endorsed by the Red Hat Society."] . . . and that the book is simply a "light-hearted romp that tells a thoroughly fantastic tale about five middle-aged women . . . undertaking an over-the-top scheme for revenge on a philandering husband."

The test to be applied in determining whether an allegedly defamatory statement constitutes an actionable statement of fact requires that the court examine the statement in its totality in the context in which it was uttered or published. It is not unusual to protect false statements of fact where, because of the context, they would have been understood as part of a satire or fiction. Although the fictional or humorous nature of a publication will not necessarily insulate it from a libel claim, if the allegedly defamatory statement could not be reasonably understood as describing actual facts about the plaintiff or actual events in which he participated, the publication will not be libelous.

The defendants contend that certain passages in the book are so "whimsically outlandish" and "implausible" that no reader could reasonably believe that "the novel is relating real-life events" about any real person, including

Stewart. Pretermitting whether those specific passages, read in isolation, could be deemed implausible, those passages must be read in context with the entire book. The record shows that Smith based much of the book upon true stories, some of which actually involved Stewart, that she set the action in actual restaurants, hotels, clubs, and other buildings located in and around the city of Atlanta, and that she researched the details of the book to ensure their accuracy and to add "credibility" to the book. And the book is not just a "light-hearted romp" that simply describes a few "implausible" antics by the main characters; it also includes stories about real adult issues, including adultery, divorce, spousal abuse, mid-life crises, deceit, disappointment, and regret. . . .

Throughout the book, Smith portrays SuSu as a middle-aged flight attendant who is an alcoholic and drinks on the job, and who regularly engages in lewd public behavior, one night stands, secret affairs with married men, and brief sexual relationships with younger men. This negative depiction is commingled with specific references to SuSu's background, references which Smith admits were drawn directly from Stewart's life. Considering the allegedly defamatory assertions in context with the rest of the book, we cannot say that the assertions are so implausible, fanciful or ridiculous that no one could reasonably interpret them as stating actual facts. Instead, they are sufficiently plausible and factual that they could be proven true or false. Whether they are actually true or false is a question for the jury.

Further, to the extent that the defendants argue that merely because a book is labeled as "fiction" or a "novel" it is automatically protected from being considered defamatory, such argument lacks merit. Simply because a book is labeled "fiction" does not mean that it may not be defamatory. In other words, the test for libel "is not whether the story is or is not characterized as 'fiction,' or 'humor,' but whether the charged portions, in context, could be reasonably understood as describing actual facts about the plaintiff or actual events in which she participated." Further, when an author uses the real names of people and places in order to give the book a sense of historical accuracy, simply labeling the book "a novel" or "a work of fiction" will not prevent its readers from reasonably believing the book is something other than a purely fictional work.

Accordingly, because the allegedly defamatory portions of the book could be reasonably understood as describing actual facts about Stewart or actual events in which she participated, the defendants were not entitled to summary judgment on this issue. . . .

Judgment affirmed in part and reversed in part, and case remanded with direction.

PREPARING FOR CLASS

1. The author changed key characteristics to make SuSu different from Stewart. She included a disclaimer that the book was just fiction. How,

then, did the court find that a reasonable jury could find the book to be "of and concerning" Stewart? What more should the author have done to avoid liability?

2. If those disclaimers don't prevent liability, why include them?

3. What hurdles will the plaintiff alleging she is defamed in fiction face other than showing she's recognizable as the character? Why might this sometimes be a difficult hurdle—indeed, more difficult for plaintiffs of good reputation and with more to lose than for plaintiffs with bad reputations and less to lose? How did the defendants in this case try to show the plaintiff could not jump that hurdle? Why did their argument fail?

APPLYING THE LAW

Melanie Geisler and Orlando Petrocelli worked together at the same small publishing house for a short while and knew each other on a casual, business basis. Petrocelli later wrote a steamy book about corruption in women's professional tennis and named the main character "Melanie Geisler." The character, like Geisler, was young, petite, attractive, and honey blonde. The fictional Geisler was a female transsexual (born male) tennis player, who hid this fact and was involved with unscrupulous people who sabotaged her opponents. Initially naïve, the fictional Geisler was lured into corruption and "untoward sexual conduct which is graphically portrayed." The real life Geisler was not a corrupt, transsexual, sexually adventurous tennis player. She was "purportedly an upstanding individual and the mother of two." Geisler sued Petrocelli for defamation. The Southern District of New York dismissed the case, and the Second Circuit reversed. Why do you suppose the trial court dismissed the suit? Why do you suppose the appellate court reversed? Figure it out before looking at Geisler v. Petrocelli, 616 F.2d 636 (2d Cir. 1980).

C.   PUBLICATION

A plaintiff's reputation cannot be damaged by a defamatory statement if it is not communicated to someone other than the plaintiff. If an employer calls an employee into his office, closes his door, and falsely accuses the employee, in front of no one, of thieving from the petty cash, the employee does not have a defamation cause of action. His feelings may be injured, but no one else heard the accusation, so no one else thinks less of him. The employer must negligently or intentionally communicate the accusation to someone other than the employee. One other person is enough. If the employer leaves his office door open and makes the accusation loudly so that it is overheard by a client passing in the hallway, the employer has negligently communicated the accusation to the client. Additionally, publication requires that the third person understand the communication. If the employer and the employee both speak Russian and the employer, with the door open, loudly makes the accusation in Russian so that it is overheard by a client who does not speak Russian, the accusation is not published.

Hellar v. Bianco
244 P.2d 757 (Cal. App. 1952)

Van Dyke, J.

Appellant brought this action against respondents, seeking to recover damages for a libelous publication. At the trial she made proof as follows: Respondents were the proprietors of a public tavern and for the convenience of patrons maintained a toilet room for men on the wall of which there appeared on May 4, 1950 libelous matter indicating that appellant was an unchaste woman who indulged in illicit amatory ventures. The writer recommended that anyone interested should call a stated telephone number, which was the number of the telephone in appellant's home and "ask for Isabelle," that being appellant's given name. At about nine o'clock on the evening of that day a man, unknown to appellant, called the number and appellant answered. The caller requested permission to visit her and when in the course of the conversation it developed that a meeting could not be arranged he told her "there is some of the most terrible writing over here on the wall of the men's toilet about you, that is where I got your telephone number and your name." He suggested that she look into it and told her he was calling from respondents' tavern. Appellant informed her husband of the conversation and he called the tavern and talked with the bartender who was shown to have been in charge of the tavern during the absence of respondents. He told the bartender that his attention had been called to some writing on the walls of the men's toilet regarding his wife, that he would give the bartender just 30 minutes to take it off the wall and that he was coming out to investigate. The bartender replied that he was busy and alone and would remove the writing when he got around to it. Appellant's husband thereupon called a constable and after some delay arrived at the tavern where, in company with several people, including the bartender, he went to the toilet and found the libelous matter still on the wall. Falsity of the libel was shown and its defamatory nature is conceded. In fact it was shocking. The husband, constable and other persons present when the group went to the toilet and found the defamatory writing still upon the wall were shown to have understood the appellant was person referred to in the writing and the writing itself was sufficient to be understood by anyone knowing about it that it was written concerning her. After introduction of the foregoing proof, appellant rested her case and upon motion of the defendants was nonsuited. She appeals from the judgment thereafter entered and based upon the order of nonsuit.

Appellant contends that from the facts shown publication by respondents could be sufficiently inferred and therefore that the nonsuit was improper. "Publication of defamatory matter is its communication intentionally or by a negligent act to one other than the person defamed." Restatement of the Law of Torts, Sec. 577. Persons who invite the public to their premises owe a duty to others not to knowingly permit their walls to be occupied with defamatory matter. . . . The theory is that by knowingly permitting such matter to remain after reasonable opportunity to remove the same the owner of the wall or his lessee is guilty of republication of the libel. . . . Republication occurs when the proprietor has knowledge of the defamatory matter and allows it to remain after a reasonable opportunity to remove it. While there is in the record no evidence of actual knowledge on the part of the defendants the knowledge of an agent, while acting in the scope of his authority, is imputed to the principal. From the testimony given the jury could have found that the bartender, to whom appellant's husband imparted knowledge of the existence of the slanderous matter and of its location, was in general control of the establishment, with the duty of supervising the premises, including the rest rooms. While he was not told of the exact terminology of the writing, undoubtedly because neither appellant nor her husband had been given that terminology by the stranger who called appellant on the phone, yet the bartender was told enough about the defamatory nature of it to put him upon inquiry and to charge him with the duty of removing the writing from respondents' wall. This knowledge of the bartender, acquired within the scope of his authority, is chargeable to the respondents. It was also a question for the jury whether, after knowledge of its existence, respondents negligently allowed the defamatory matter to remain for so long a time as to be chargeable with its republication, occurring when the husband and the group with him visited the rest room and saw the writing.

The judgment appealed from is reversed.

PREPARING FOR CLASS

1. How did the defendant publish the statement? How does the court explain this nonfeasance as publication?

2. Does this holding mean that the defendant is liable?

APPLYING THE LAW

1. In Scott v. Hull, 259 N.E.2d 160 (Ohio App. 1970), the plaintiff brought a defamation suit against the defendant because graffiti defaming her

was painted in large letters on the exterior wall of a building the defendant owned. The plaintiff did not allege that the defendant painted the graffiti, but she contended that he was nonetheless the publisher of the graffiti because he had been notified of its existence and yet permitted it to remain on the wall for three months. How could the plaintiff argue that *Hellar* supports liability? How would the defendant distinguish the case? Who is likely to prevail?

2.   Was the statement about Parker published?

INCREASING YOUR UNDERSTANDING

Notice that the publisher in *Hellar* did not write or speak the defamatory words. They were on his wall, and he allowed them to remain. A magazine, book, or newspaper is like that wall. Someone who takes out a personal ad in a magazine or newspaper posts it on the wall, and the owner of the wall, even though it did not create the content of the ad, will be considered a publisher under defamation law. A book publisher is also a publisher, in the defamation sense, of defamatory statements in its books, even though the publisher did not write or speak those words. The words are on the publisher's wall. And, of course, calling these instances publications makes even more sense than the publication in *Hellar* because the magazine, book, or newspaper publisher is not merely someone who allowed the words to remain. It actively printed the words of the other. Similarly, radio and television outlets are publishers of words spoken in their broadcasts, whether their employees speak those words or not.

Carafano v. Metrosplash.com, Inc.
339 F.3d 1119 (9th Cir. 2003)

Thomas, C.J.

This is a case involving a cruel and sadistic identity theft. In this appeal, we consider to what extent a computer match making service may be legally responsible for false content in a dating profile provided by someone posing as another person. Under the circumstances presented by this case, we conclude that the service is statutorily immune pursuant to 47 U.S.C. §230(c)(1).

I

Matchmaker.com is a commercial Internet dating service. For a fee, members of Matchmaker post anonymous profiles and may then view profiles of other members in their area, contacting them via electronic mail sent through the Matchmaker server. A typical profile contains one or more pictures of the subject, descriptive information such as age, appearance and interests, and answers to a variety of questions designed to evoke the subject's personality and reason for joining the service.

Members are required to complete a detailed questionnaire containing both multiple-choice and essay questions. In the initial portion of the questionnaire, members select answers to more than fifty questions from menus providing between four and nineteen options. Some of the potential multiple choice answers are innocuous; some are sexually suggestive. In the subsequent essay section, participants answer up to eighteen additional questions, including "anything that the questionnaire didn't cover." Matchmaker policies prohibit members from posting last names, addresses, phone numbers or e-mail addresses within a profile. Matchmaker reviews photos for impropriety before posting them but does not review the profiles themselves, relying instead upon participants to adhere to the service guidelines.

On October 23, 1999, an unknown person using a computer in Berlin posted a "trial" personal profile of Christianne Carafano in the Los Angeles section of Matchmaker. (New members were permitted to post "trial" profiles for a few weeks without paying.) The posting was without the knowledge, consent or permission of Carafano. The profile was listed under the identifier "Chase529."

Carafano is a popular actress. Under the stage name of Chase Masterson, Carafano has appeared in numerous films and television shows, such as "Star Trek: Deep Space Nine," and "General Hospital." Pictures of the actress are widely available on the Internet, and the false Matchmaker profile "Chase529" contained several of these pictures. Along with fairly innocuous responses to questions about interests and appearance, the person posting the profile selected "Playboy/Playgirl" for "main source of current events" and "looking for a one-night stand" for "why did you call." In addition, the open-ended essay responses indicated that "Chase529" was looking for a "hard and dominant" man with "a strong sexual appetite" and that she "liked sort of be [ ]ing controlled by a man, in and out of bed." The profile text did not include a last name for "Chase" or indicate Carafano's real name, but it listed two of her movies (and, as mentioned, included pictures of the actress).

In response to a question about the "part of the LA area" in which she lived, the profile provided Carafano's home address. The profile included a contact e-mail address, cmla2000@yahoo.com, which, when contacted, produced an automatic e-mail reply stating, "You think you are the right one? Proof it !!" [sic], and providing Carafano's home address and telephone number.

Unaware of the improper posting, Carafano soon began to receive messages responding to the profile. Although she was traveling at the time, she checked her voicemail on October 31 and heard two sexually explicit messages. When she returned to her home on November 4, she found a highly threatening and sexually explicit fax that also threatened her son. Alarmed, she contacted the police the following day. As a result of the profile, she also received numerous phone calls, voicemail messages, written correspondence, and e-mail from fans through her professional e-mail account. Several men expressed concern that she had given out her address and phone number (but simultaneously expressed an interest in meeting her). Carafano felt unsafe in her home, and she and her son stayed in hotels or away from Los Angeles for several months.

Sometime around Saturday, November 6, Siouxzan Perry, who handled Carafano's professional website and much of her e-mail correspondence, first learned of the false profile through a message from "Jeff." Perry exchanged e-mails with Jeff, visited the Matchmaker site, and relayed information about the profile to Carafano. Acting on Carafano's instructions, Perry contacted Matchmaker and demanded that the profile be removed immediately. The Matchmaker employee indicated that she could not remove the profile immediately because Perry herself had not posted it, but the company blocked the profile from public view on Monday morning, November 8. At 4:00 A.M. the following morning, Matchmaker deleted the profile.

Carafano filed a complaint in California state court against Matchmaker and its corporate successors, alleging . . . defamation. . . . The defendants removed the case to federal district court. The district court granted the defendants' motion for summary judgment in a published opinion. Carafano v. Metrosplash.com, Inc., 207 F. Supp. 2d 1055 (C.D. Cal. 2002). The court rejected Matchmaker's argument for immunity under 47 U.S.C. §230(c)(1) after finding that the company provided part of the profile content. However, the court rejected Carafano's . . . claim[] for defamation . . . because she failed to show that Matchmaker had acted with actual malice.

Carafano timely appealed. America Online, eBay, and two coalitions of online businesses intervened to challenge the district court's construction of §230(c)(1). Several privacy advocacy groups and two organizations representing entertainers intervened in support of Carafano.

II

The dispositive question in this appeal is whether Carafano's claims are barred by 47 U.S.C. §230(c)(1), which states that "[n]o provider or user of an interactive computer service shall be treated as the publisher or speaker of any information provided by another information content provider." Through this provision, Congress granted most Internet services immunity from liability for publishing false or defamatory material so long as the information was provided by another party. As a result, Internet publishers are treated differently from corresponding publishers in print, television and radio. See Batzel v. Smith, 333 F.3d 1018, 1026-27 (9th Cir. 2003).

Congress enacted this provision as part of the Communications Decency Act of 1996 for two basic policy reasons: to promote the free exchange of information and ideas over the Internet and to encourage voluntary monitoring for offensive or obscene material. . . . Congress incorporated these ideas into the text of §230 itself, expressly noting that "interactive computer services have flourished, to the benefit of all Americans, with a minimum of government regulation," and that "[i]ncreasingly Americans are relying on interactive media for a variety of political, educational, cultural, and entertainment services." 47 U.S.C. §230(a)(4), (5). Congress declared it the "policy of the United States" to "promote the continued development of the Internet and other interactive computer services," "to preserve the vibrant and competitive free market that presently exists for the Internet and other interactive computer services," and to "remove disincentives for the development and utilization of blocking and filtering technologies." 47 U.S.C. §230(b)(1), (2), (4).

In light of these concerns, reviewing courts have treated §230(c) immunity as quite robust, adopting a relatively expansive definition of "interactive computer service" and a relatively restrictive definition of "information content provider." Under the statutory scheme, an "interactive computer service" qualifies for immunity so long as it does not also function as an "information content provider" for the portion of the statement or publication at issue.

We recently considered whether §230(c) provided immunity to the operator of an electronic newsletter who selected and published an allegedly defamatory e-mail over the Internet. *Batzel*, 333 F.3d at 1030-32. We held that the online newsletter qualified as an "interactive computer service" under the statutory definition and that the selection for publication and editing of an e-mail did not constitute partial "creation or development" of that information within the definition of "information content provider." Although the case was ultimately remanded for determination of whether the original author intended to "provide" his e-mail for publication, the *Batzel* decision joined the consensus developing across other courts of appeals that §230(c) provides broad immunity for publishing content provided primarily by third parties. . . .

The fact that some of the content was formulated in response to Matchmaker's questionnaire does not alter this conclusion. Doubtless, the questionnaire facilitated the expression of information by individual users. However, the selection of the content was left exclusively to the user. The actual profile "information" consisted of the particular options chosen and the additional essay answers provided. Matchmaker was not responsible, even in part, for associating certain multiple choice responses with a set of physical characteristics, a group of essay answers, and a photograph. Matchmaker cannot be considered an "information content provider" under the statute because no profile has any content until a user actively creates it.

As such, Matchmaker's role is similar to that of the customer rating system at issue in Gentry v. eBay, Inc., 121 Cal. Rptr. 2d 703 (Cal. App. 2002). In that case, the plaintiffs alleged that eBay "was an information content provider in that it was responsible for the creation of information, or development of information, for the online auction it provided through the Internet." Specifically, the plaintiffs noted that eBay created a highly structured Feedback Forum, which categorized each response as a "Positive Feedback," a "Negative

Feedback," or a "Neutral Feedback." In addition, eBay provided a color coded star symbol next to the user name of a seller who had achieved certain levels of "Positive Feedback" and offered a separate "Power Sellers" endorsement based on sales volume and Positive Feedback ratings. The court concluded that §230 barred the claims:

> Appellants' negligence claim is based on the assertion that the information is false or misleading because it has been manipulated by the individual defendants or other co-conspiring parties. Based on these allegations, enforcing appellants' negligence claim would place liability on eBay for simply compiling false and/or misleading content created by the individual defendants and other coconspirators. We do not see such activities transforming eBay into an information content provider with respect to the representations targeted by appellants as it did not create or develop the underlying misinformation.

Similarly, the fact that Matchmaker classifies user characteristics into discrete categories and collects responses to specific essay questions does not transform Matchmaker into a "developer" of the "underlying misinformation."

We also note that, as with eBay, Matchmaker's decision to structure the information provided by users allows the company to offer additional features, such as "matching" profiles with similar characteristics or highly structured searches based on combinations of multiple choice questions. Without standardized, easily encoded answers, Matchmaker might not be able to offer these services and certainly not to the same degree. Arguably, this promotes the expressed Congressional policy "to promote the continued development of the Internet and other interactive computer services." 47 U.S.C. §230(b)(1).

Carafano responds that Matchmaker contributes much more structure and content than eBay by asking 62 detailed questions and providing a menu of "pre-prepared responses." However, this is a distinction of degree rather than of kind, and Matchmaker still lacks responsibility for the "underlying misinformation."

Further, even assuming Matchmaker could be considered an information content provider, the statute precludes treatment as a publisher or speaker for "any information provided by another information content provider." 47 U.S.C. §230(c)(1) (emphasis added). The statute would still bar Carafano's claims unless Matchmaker created or developed the particular information at issue. As the *Gentry* court noted,

> [T]he fact appellants allege eBay is an information content provider is irrelevant if eBay did not itself create or develop the content for which appellants seek to hold it liable. It is not inconsistent for eBay to be an interactive service provider and also an information content provider; the categories are not mutually exclusive. The critical issue is whether eBay

acted as an information content provider with respect to the information that appellants claim is false or misleading.

In this case, critical information about Carafano's home address, movie credits, and the e-mail address that revealed her phone number were transmitted unaltered to profile viewers. Similarly, the profile directly reproduced the most sexually suggestive comments in the essay section, none of which bore more than a tenuous relationship to the actual questions asked. Thus Matchmaker did not play a significant role in creating, developing or "transforming" the relevant information.

Thus, despite the serious and utterly deplorable consequences that occurred in this case, we conclude that Congress intended that service providers such as Matchmaker be afforded immunity from suit. Thus, we affirm the judgment of the district court, albeit on other grounds.

PREPARING FOR CLASS

1. If someone placed a false personal ad for Carafano in a newspaper, the paper would be a publisher of that ad. Why doesn't this principle apply to Internet service providers?

2. What policies does the Communications Decency Act promote? How does barring recovery for a persecuted victim like Carafano promote those policies?

3. What is the point of the eBay analogy? Is it an apt analogy?

Overcast v. Billings Mutual Ins. Co.
11 S.W.3d 62 (Mo. 2000)

WOLFF, J.
[Overcast's home burned down, and he filed a claim for insurance benefits. The insurance company performed an investigation and concluded that the fire was the result of arson.]

After this investigation, Cobb [the agent for the defendant insurance company] sent Overcast a letter denying his claim for coverage, stating: "the loss resulted from an intentional act committed by you or at your direction." Cobb testified that the letter was addressed solely to Overcast and sent by registered mail, return receipt requested. He did so, Cobb said, to avoid "publishing" the arson charge to other persons.

Cobb testified that he knew the contents of the letter would affect Overcast's ability to obtain insurance policies from other companies. Overcast attempted to get an insurance policy for his farm buildings through All Risk Insurance Agency in Springfield, Missouri. The agent asked Overcast if he had a claim that had ever been denied. After Overcast showed the Cobb letter to the agent, the agent told Overcast that she would not be able to issue a policy. Overcast attempted to get insurance from other companies, but was asked the same question as to the reason for the denial of the claim. He was unable to get coverage.

[Overcast filed multiple counts against Billings Mutual Insurance, one of which was defamation. He won the defamation case at trial, and Billings appealed.]

Billings Mutual contends that because the letter was addressed registered mail, return receipt requested, deliver to addressee Overcast only, there was no publication; thus, Overcast was not defamed.

Under Missouri case law, there was sufficient evidence of publication to support the jury's verdict. Communication of defamatory matter only to the plaintiff who then discloses it to third parties ordinarily does not subject defendant to liability. However, an exception, which applies here, is recognized by this Court where "the utterer of the defamatory matter intends, or has reason to suppose, that in the ordinary course of events the matter will come to the knowledge of some third person." Herberholt v. DePaul Community Health Center, 625 S.W.2d at 624-625. There was testimony that Cobb was concerned that he would be sued for defamation. His sending the letter registered mail, return receipt requested, deliver to addressee only, was his unsuccessful attempt to avoid a publication to third parties. There was testimony by agents from other insurance companies that insurance applications ask if the applicant had ever had a claim denied and the reasons for the denial. The evidence was sufficient to show that in the ordinary course of business, Cobb was aware that the allegation that Overcast was an arsonist would need to be published and would be published to third parties. . . .

The judgment of the trial court is affirmed.

PREPARING FOR CLASS

1. If Cobb sent the letter, why is the lawsuit against the insurance company? Would the insurance company's liability be affected by whether Cobb negligently or intentionally published the arson charge?

2. As a general rule, can people repeat what others have said about them and thereby self-publish defamatory statements? Why or why not?

3. In this case, why does the court not follow the general rule?

APPLYING THE LAW

1. An employee was fired. In the exit interview, his employer said, "You have a poor work ethic, and your demeanor makes the female

staff uncomfortable." When the employee interviewed for other jobs and was asked why he left his previous employment he said, "I was fired for having a poor work ethic and making the female staff uncomfortable." When he was unable to find another job, he sued his former employer for defamation. The employer moved for a dismissal on the grounds that he had not published the statement. Should the motion be granted?

2. A woman received a letter from a former boyfriend. The last two sentences were written in Spanish, but the woman does not speak Spanish, and the boyfriend knew that. She took the letter to a friend who did speak Spanish, and the friend translated them. The final sentences described the woman in defamatory terms. If she sues the former boyfriend for defamation, can she establish publication to the friend who translated the letter?

D. LIBEL AND SLANDER

Standifer v. Val Gene Mgmt. Servs., Inc.
527 P.2d 28 (Ok. App. 1974)

BRIGHTMIRE, P.J.

This is a slander action. The trial court disposed of it by granting defendant a summary judgment. Whether he was correct in doing so is the only issue presented for review. We think he was and affirm.

In her petition, plaintiff stated that through the mouth of its agent, 24-year-old redheaded Sharon Gayle Wright, defendant corporation maliciously spoke and published to several people certain slanderous, false and defamatory words about plaintiff, "to-wit: That the plaintiff was a constant troublemaker; that the plaintiff was not a fit tenant; that the plaintiff was harassing her; that the plaintiff had 'cussed her out'; that the plaintiff was disruptive in nature and was bothering the other tenants; and various and numerous statements tending to degrade the plaintiff . . . and . . . spoken . . . to blacken and injure the honesty, virtue, integrity, morality and reputation of . . . plaintiff and to thereby expose her to public contempt and ridicule." As a "direct . . . result" of all this she "was compelled to move from her residence of many years and incurred (these) actual damages . . . Moving expense—$375.00; Telephone—$15.00; Automobile expense—$20.00; and additional rent—$80.00." She asked for these amounts plus $5,000 general damages and $25,000 punitive damages. . . .

[D]efendant filed a motion for summary judgment stating . . . that . . . "assuming that all the statements said to have been made by defendant were in fact made, they are insufficient as a matter of law to be the foundation for recovery."

A short time later the court agreed. . . .

This [appeal] involves consideration of one or two more basic issues: (1) is the alleged publication slanderous *per se*: or if not, (2) has special resulting damage been adequately alleged?

To start our probe of these points we quote the statute defining slander—12 O.S.1971 s 1442:

> Slander is a false and unprivileged publication, other than libel, which:
>
> 1. Charges any person with crime, or with having been indicted, convicted or punished for crime.
>
> 2. Imputes in him the present existence of an infectious, contagious or loathsome disease.
>
> 3. Tends directly to injure him in respect to his office, profession, trade or business, either by imputing to him general disqualification in those respects which the office or other occupation peculiarly requires, or by imputing something with reference to his office, profession, trade or business that has a natural tendency to lessen its profit.
>
> 4. Imputes to him impotence or want of chastity; or,
>
> 5. Which, by natural consequences, causes actual damage.

We can dismiss from consideration those paragraphs numbered one through four as being irrelevant because not alleged by plaintiff.

Slander is one of the two torts comprising the law of defamation. In general it is an oral publication while its mate, libel, is generally a written one. The distinction between the two developed haphazardly in old English courts from as far back as Runnymede. Their decisional expediencies were influenced considerably by the rise and fall in popularity of the actions at various points in time and—during the 14th and 15th centuries—by the ecclesiastical courts' punishment of defamation as a "sin." A jurisdictional dispute between church and common law courts was temporarily resolved by allowing the latter tribunals to act if "temporal" damage could be proved and if not then the defamation was deemed a "spiritual" matter for the church to handle. In its early development slander was thought to be within the province of ecclesiastical law prompting secular courts to hold the action would not lie without proof of "temporal" damages. Eventually proof of actual damage became an essential element of slander. Then in deference to reality courts began to recognize various exceptions such as imputations of a crime, of a loathsome disease, and those adversely affecting plaintiff's trade, business, or profession—exceptions which required no proof of damages. This historical distinction between libel and slander eventually found its way into the statutory law of this area while Oklahoma was still Indian Territory, along with—as can be seen above—the addition of a fourth category regarding imputation of unchastity or impotency to one.

To compare our libel statute with the one defining slander is to dramatize the distinction and underscore the former's much larger "temporal" base. It is 12 O.S.1971 §1441 and reads:

> Libel is a false or malicious unprivileged publication by writing, printing, picture, or effigy or other fixed representation to the eye, which exposes any person to public hatred, contempt, ridicule or obloquy, or which tends to deprive him of public confidence, or to injure him in his occupation. . . .

At once it can be seen libel has quite a bit broader statutory definition than slander. That the historical basis for the difference is irrational is beside the point. The statute being what it is must determine human rights until otherwise legally changed.

Turning now to the case at bar, it is conceded that plaintiff has not attempted to plead or complain of any statement which would be actionable slander without proof of damages under the first four numbered paragraphs of §1442. . . . Thus if an action she has it must be in terms of paragraph five requiring pleading and proof of "actual damage."

The words said to have been spoken by defendant's agent were, we think, defamatory on their face in that they have a clear tendency to injure plaintiff's reputation. By natural import they diminish the esteem, respect, and confidence in which she is held by others. They would, had the publication been written, be actionable without proof of damages.

But it was not written and so—because they neither charge a crime, impute disease or sexual irregularity, nor tend to injure plaintiff in respect to any known office or calling—it matters not how grossly defamatory or insulting the words may be they are actionable only upon proof of "special damage."

The next question then is does plaintiff claim actual damages which the slander "by natural consequences" caused?

The phrase "by natural consequences" is another way of saying there must be a causal connection between the slanderous statement and the damage sought—one that is reasonably direct.

As mentioned earlier the special damages plaintiff says she sustained as a "direct result" of the defamation were various items relating to moving from defendant's apartment to another.

The only conceivable basis upon which the moving expenses could be the natural consequences of the alleged slander would be that the defamation published to plaintiff's fellow tenants caused them to react toward and treat her in such a manner as to significantly interfere with the enjoyment of her habitation and effectuate a constructive ouster therefrom.

Such causal connection is not perceptible on the face of plaintiff's petition. And since this would not necessarily foreclose proof of the consequence at trial we will examine the record to see if it discloses any admission by plaintiff fatally inconsistent with a cause and effect relationship between the slander and the move. . . .

Interpreting [plaintiff's deposition testimony] in a light most favorable to plaintiff we can see no way the alleged defamation could have caused the move for the simple reason plaintiff was unaware of it until after she vacated defendant's apartment where she presumably would still be had she not been asked to move. The cause of the move was a request by the manager to do so—a request involving neither a tortious nor anti-contractual act—not the defamation. Injured reputation there may have been but unless it in some way precipitated the change of apartments the latter could not be a natural consequence of the former.

We therefore hold the facts admitted by plaintiff disclose she is without an actionable cause for lack of special damages hence the trial court did not err in awarding defendant a summary judgment.

Affirmed.

PREPARING FOR CLASS

1.   Why is this a case of slander and not libel? Why does it matter?

2.   What is the historical basis for the different treatment that libel and slander cases receive? The court comments that the historical basis is "irrational." Why besides tradition might courts still honor the distinction?

3.   What qualities do the categories of slander *per se* share?

4.   If the slander does not fall into a *per se* category, what kind of damages must a plaintiff allege and prove? Can you think of examples?

5.   The defendant appears to have conducted quite a smear campaign against the plaintiff. Why did she get away with it?

INCREASING YOUR UNDERSTANDING

1.   *Defamacasts.* Broadcasts are oral, yet they have the wide distribution, permanency, and power of written defamation. So what are they? Libel or slander? The answer is, "It depends upon where you live." Some jurisdictions treat "defamacasts" as libel, while others—often through legislation most likely inspired by broadcast media lobbyists—treat them as slander.

2.   *Libel* per se *and libel* per quod. In some states, even libel cases require special damages if the statement is not defamatory *per se*. Those cases are referred to as libel *per quod*. Maddeningly, though, those states do not define libel *per se* as libel within the four categories supporting slander *per se*. Instead, libel *per se* refers to cases where the defamatory

meaning is clear on the face of the statement and extrinsic evidence is not necessary to establish the defamatory meaning. Libel *per quod* refers to cases where the defamatory meaning is not clear without extrinsic facts. In other words, in states that distinguish between libel *per se* and libel *per quod*, if inducement is necessary, so are special damages. How, then, do these jurisdictions treat slander? Slanders within the traditional four categories are slander *per se* and do not require special damages. Slanders outside the four categories are *per quod* and require special damages. The question of extrinsic facts does not figure into slander analysis.

APPLYING THE LAW

Apply the principles learned in this section to the Parker vs. Davis problem.

E. CONSTITUTIONAL LIMITATIONS

1. *Balancing Free Speech with Reputational Rights*

New York Times Co. v. Sullivan
376 U.S. 254 (1964)

Justice BRENNAN delivered the opinion of the court.

We are required in this case to determine for the first time the extent to which the constitutional protections for speech and press limit a State's power to award damages in a libel action brought by a public official against critics of his official conduct.

Respondent L.B. Sullivan is one of the three elected Commissioners of the City of Montgomery, Alabama. He testified that he was "Commissioner of Public Affairs and the duties are supervision of the Police Department, Fire Department, Department of Cemetery and Department of Scales." He brought this civil libel action against the four individual petitioners, who are Negroes and Alabama clergymen, and against petitioner the New York Times Company, a New York corporation which publishes the New York Times, a daily newspaper. A jury in the Circuit Court of Montgomery County awarded him damages of $500,000, the full amount claimed, against all the petitioners, and the Supreme Court of Alabama affirmed.

Respondent's complaint alleged that he had been libeled by statements in a full-page advertisement that was carried in the New York Times on March 29, 1960. Entitled "Heed Their Rising Voices," the advertisement began by stating that "As the whole world knows by now, thousands of Southern Negro students are engaged in widespread non-violent demonstrations in positive affirmation of the right to live in human dignity as guaranteed by the U.S. Constitution and the Bill of Rights." It went on to charge that "in their efforts to uphold these guarantees, they are being met by an unprecedented wave of terror by those who would deny and negate that document which the whole world looks upon as setting the pattern for modern freedom. . . ." Succeeding paragraphs purported to illustrate the "wave of terror" by describing certain alleged events. The text concluded with an appeal for funds for three purposes: support of the student movement, "the struggle for the right-to-vote," and the legal defense of Dr. Martin Luther King, Jr., leader of the movement, against a perjury indictment then pending in Montgomery.

The text appeared over the names of 64 persons, many widely known for their activities in public affairs, religion, trade unions, and the performing arts. . . .

Of the 10 paragraphs of text in the advertisement, the third and a portion of the sixth were the basis of respondent's claim of libel. They read as follows:

Third paragraph:

"In Montgomery, Alabama, after students sang 'My Country, 'Tis of Thee' on the State Capitol steps, their leaders were expelled from school, and truckloads of police armed with shotguns and tear-gas ringed the Alabama State College Campus. When the entire student body protested to state authorities by refusing to re-register, their dining hall was padlocked in an attempt to starve them into submission."

Sixth paragraph:

"Again and again the Southern violators have answered Dr. King's peaceful protests with intimidation and violence. They have bombed his home almost killing his wife and child. They have assaulted his person. They have arrested him seven times-for 'speeding,' 'loitering' and similar 'offenses.' And now they have charged him with 'perjury' – a felony under which they could imprison him for *ten years*. . . ."

Although neither of these statements mentions respondent by name, he contended that the word "police" in the third paragraph referred to him as the Montgomery Commissioner who supervised the Police Department, so that he was being accused of "ringing" the campus with police. He further claimed that the paragraph would be read as imputing to the police, and hence to him, the padlocking of the dining hall in order to starve the students into submission. As to the sixth paragraph, he contended that since arrests are ordinarily made by the police, the statement "They have arrested (Dr. King) seven times" would be read as referring to him; he further contended that the "They" who did the arresting would be equated with the "They" who committed the other described acts and with the "Southern violators." Thus, he argued, the paragraph would be read as accusing the Montgomery police, and hence him, of answering Dr. King's protests with "intimidation and violence," bombing his home, assaulting his person, and charging him with perjury. Respondent and six other Montgomery residents testified that they read some or all of the statements as referring to him in his capacity as Commissioner.

It is uncontroverted that some of the statements contained in the two paragraphs were not accurate descriptions of events which occurred in Montgomery. Although Negro students staged a demonstration on the State Capital steps, they sang the National Anthem and not "My Country, 'Tis of Thee." Although nine students were expelled by the State Board of Education, this was not for leading the demonstration at the Capitol, but for demanding service at a lunch counter in the Montgomery County Courthouse on another day. Not the entire student body, but most of it, had protested the expulsion, not by refusing to register, but by boycotting classes on a single day; virtually all the students did register for the ensuing semester. The campus dining hall was not padlocked on any occasion, and the only students who may have been barred from eating there were the few who had neither signed a preregistration application nor requested temporary meal tickets. Although the police were deployed near the campus in large numbers on three occasions, they did not at any time "ring" the campus, and they were not called to the campus in connection with the demonstration on the State Capitol steps, as the third paragraph implied. Dr. King had not been arrested seven times, but only four; and although he claimed to have been assaulted some years earlier in connection with his arrest for loitering outside a courtroom, one of the officers who made the arrest denied that there was such an assault.

On the premise that the charges in the sixth paragraph could be read as referring to him, respondent was allowed to prove that he had not participated in the events described. Although Dr. King's home had in fact been bombed twice when his wife and child were there, both of these occasions antedated respondent's tenure as Commissioner, and the police were not only not implicated in the bombings, but had made every effort to apprehend those who were. Three of Dr. King's four arrests took place before respondent became Commissioner. Although Dr. King had in fact been indicted (he was subsequently acquitted) on two counts of perjury, each of which carried a possible five-year sentence, respondent had nothing to do with procuring the indictment. . . .

The trial judge submitted the case to the jury under instructions that the statements in the advertisement were "libelous per se" and were not privileged, so that petitioners might be held liable if the jury found that they had published the advertisement and that the statements were made "of and concerning" respondent. . . .

Under Alabama law as applied in this case . . . [o]nce "libel per se" has been established, the defendant has no defense as to stated facts unless he can persuade the jury that they were true in all their particulars. His privilege of "fair comment" for expressions of opinion depends on the truth of the facts upon which the comment is based. . . .

The First Amendment, said Judge Learned Hand, "presupposes that right conclusions are more likely to be gathered out of a multitude of tongues, than through any kind of authoritative selection. To many this is, and always will be, folly; but we have staked upon it our all." United States v. Associated Press, 52 F. Supp. 362, 372 (S.D.N.Y. 1943). Mr. Justice Brandeis, in his concurring opinion in Whitney v. California, 274 U.S. 357, 375-376, gave the principle its classic formulation:

> Those who won our independence believed that public discussion is a political duty; and that this should be a fundamental principle of the American government. They recognized the risks to which all human institutions are subject. But they knew that order cannot be secured merely through fear of punishment for its infraction; that it is hazardous to discourage thought, hope and imagination; that fear breeds repression; that repression breeds hate; that hate menaces stable government; that the path of safety lies in the opportunity to discuss freely supposed grievances and proposed remedies; and that the fitting remedy for evil counsels is good ones. Believing in the power of reason as applied through public discussion, they eschewed silence coerced by law—the argument of force in its worst form. Recognizing the occasional tyrannies of governing majorities, they amended the Constitution so that free speech and assembly should be guaranteed.

Thus we consider this case against the background of a profound national commitment to the principle that debate on public issues should be uninhibited, robust, and wide-open, and that it may well include vehement, caustic, and sometimes unpleasantly sharp attacks on government and public officials. The present advertisement, as an expression of grievance and protest on one of the major public issues of our time, would seem clearly to qualify for the constitutional protection. The question is whether it forfeits that protection by the falsity of some of its factual statements and by its alleged defamation of respondent.

Authoritative interpretations of the First Amendment guarantees have consistently refused to recognize an exception for any test of truth—whether administered by judges, juries, or administrative officials—and especially one that puts the burden of proving truth on the speaker. The constitutional protection does not turn upon "the truth, popularity, or social utility of the ideas and beliefs which are offered." N.A.A.C.P. v. Button, 371 U.S. 415, 445. As Madison said, "Some degree of abuse is inseparable from the proper use of every thing; and in no instance is this more true than in that of the press." . . .

If neither factual error nor defamatory content suffices to remove the constitutional shield from criticism of official conduct, the combination of the two elements is no less inadequate. [The Court then discussed the Sedition Act of 1798, which criminalized defamation against high officers of the United States, and concluded the Act was unconstitutional.]

What a State may not constitutionally bring about by means of a criminal statute is likewise beyond the reach of its civil law of libel. The fear of damage awards under a rule such as that invoked by the Alabama courts here may be markedly more inhibiting than the fear of prosecution under a criminal statute. . . . Presumably a person charged with violation of this statute enjoys ordinary criminal-law safeguards such as the requirements of an indictment and of proof beyond a reasonable doubt. These safeguards are not available to the defendant in a civil action. . . .

The constitutional guarantees require, we think, a federal rule that prohibits a public official from recovering damages for a defamatory falsehood relating to his official conduct unless he proves that the statement was made with "actual malice"—that is, with knowledge that it was false or with reckless disregard of whether it was false or not. An oft-cited statement of a like rule, which has been adopted by a number of state courts, is found in the Kansas case of Coleman v. MacLennan, 98 P. 281 (Kan. 1908). The State Attorney General, a candidate for re-election and a member of the commission charged with the management and control of the state school fund, sued a newspaper publisher for alleged libel in an article purporting to state facts relating to his official conduct in connection with a school-fund transaction. . . . In answer to a special question, the jury found that he plaintiff had not proved actual malice, and a general verdict was returned for the defendant. On appeal the Supreme Court of Kansas, in an opinion by Justice Burch, reasoned as follows:

> [I]t is of the utmost consequence that the people should discuss the character and qualifications of candidates for their suffrages. The importance to the state and to society of such discussions is so vast, and the advantages derived are so great that they more than counterbalance the inconvenience of private persons whose conduct may be involved, and occasional injury to the reputations of individuals must yield to the public welfare, although at times such injury may be great. The public benefit from publicity is so great and the chance of injury to private character so small that such discussion must be privileged.

The court thus sustained the trial court's instruction as a correct statement of the law, saying: "In such a case the occasion gives rise to a privilege qualified to this extent. Any one claiming to be defamed by the communication must show actual malice, or go remediless. This privilege extends to a great variety of subjects and includes matters of public concern, public men, and candidates for office." . . .

We hold today that the Constitution delimits a State's power to award damages for libel in actions brought by public officials against critics of their official conduct. Since this is such an action, the rule requiring proof of actual malice is applicable. . . .

[W]e consider that the proof presented to show actual malice lacks the con-vincing clarity which the constitutional standard demands, and hence that it would not constitutionally sustain the judgment for respondent under the proper rule of law. The case of the individual petitioners requires little discussion. Even assuming that they could constitutionally be found to have authorized the use of their names on the advertisement, there was no evidence whatever that they were aware of any erroneous statements or were in any way reckless in that regard. The judgment against them is thus without constitutional support.

As to the Times, we similarly conclude that the facts do not support a finding of actual malice. The statement by the Times' Secretary that, apart from the padlocking allegation, he thought the advertisement was "substantially correct," affords no constitutional warrant for the Alabama Supreme Court's conclusion that it was a "cavalier ignoring of the falsity of the advertisement (from which), the jury could not have but been impressed with the bad faith of The Times, and its maliciousness inferable therefrom." The statement does not indicate malice at the time of the publication; even if the advertisement was not "substantially correct"—although respondent's own proofs tend to show that it was—that opinion was at least a reasonable one, and there was no evidence to impeach the witness' good faith in holding it. The Times' failure to retract upon respondent's demand, although it later retracted upon the demand of Governor Patterson, is likewise not adequate evidence of malice for constitutional purposes. Whether or not a failure to retract may ever constitute such evidence, there are two reasons why it does not here. *First*, the letter written by the Times reflected a reasonable doubt on its part as to whether the advertisement could reasonably be taken to refer to respondent at all. *Second*, it was not a final refusal, since it asked for an explanation on this point—a request that respondent chose to ignore. Nor does the retraction upon the demand of the Governor supply the necessary proof. It may be doubted that a failure to retract which is not itself evidence of malice can retroactively become such by virtue of a retraction subsequently made to another party. But in any event that did not happen here, since the explanation given by the Times' Secretary for the distinction drawn between respondent and the Governor was a reasonable one, the good faith of which was not impeached.

Finally, there is evidence that the Times published the advertisement without checking its accuracy against the news stories in the Times' own files. . . . We think the evidence against the Times supports at most a finding of negligence in failing to discover the misstatements, and is constitutionally insufficient to show the recklessness that is required for a finding of actual malice. . . .

We also think the evidence was constitutionally defective in another respect: it was incapable of supporting the jury's finding that the allegedly libelous statements were made "of and concerning" respondent. . . .

There was no reference to respondent in the advertisement, either by name or official position. A number of the allegedly libelous statements . . . did not even concern the police. . . .

Although the statements may be taken as referring to the police, they do not on their face make even an oblique reference to respondent as an individual. . . .

This . . . has disquieting implications for criticism of governmental conduct. For good reason, "no court of last resort in this country has ever held, or even suggested, that prosecutions for libel on government have any place in the American system of jurisprudence." City of Chicago v. Tribune Co., 139

N.E. 86, 88 (Ill. 1923). The present proposition would sidestep this obstacle by transmuting criticism of government, however impersonal it may seem on its face, into personal criticism, and hence potential libel, of the officials of whom the government is composed. . . . We hold that such a proposition may not constitutionally be utilized to establish that an otherwise impersonal attack on governmental operations was a libel of an official responsible for those operations. . . .

The judgment of the Supreme Court of Alabama is reversed, and the case is remanded to that court for further proceedings not inconsistent with this opinion.

[Justices Black and Goldberg submitted concurring opinions, and Justice Douglas joined both opinions.]

PREPARING FOR CLASS

1.   What is the argument that the defamatory statements were not of and concerning Sullivan? Why didn't the Supreme Court simply dispense with the case by concluding that the defamation did not refer to Sullivan?

2.   If Sullivan had been a private citizen allegedly defamed by the advertisement, do you think the Supreme Court would have taken the case?

3.   How did defamation law, prior to *New York Times*, make Sullivan's case easy?

4.   What interests did this ease threaten?

5.   The Court quotes Justice Brandeis in his *Whitney* concurrence. Brandeis wrote that the founders "[b]eliev[ed] in the power of reason as applied through public discussion." As public discussion (arguably) grows more strident and uninformed, does our society really benefit? Should the constitutional protections afforded defamers be reevaluated?

6.   What competing interests does a defamation case present? How does the Court balance the competing interests a defamation case affects?

7.   The *New York Times* had in its own files stories that contradicted some of the false statements in the advertisement. Why did that not satisfy the actual malice requirement?

INCREASING YOUR UNDERSTANDING

Public Officials. In Rosenblatt v. Baer, 383 U.S. 75 (1966), the Supreme Court provided a test for public official status. The question is whether "the position in government has such apparent importance that the public has an independent interest in the qualifications and performance of the person who holds it, beyond the general public interest in the qualifications and performance of all governmental employees." The rule applies to candidates for political office. Monitor Patriot Co. v. Roy, 401 U.S. 265 (1971). Although Chief Justice Burger cautioned in Hutchinson v. Proxmire, 443 U.S. 111 (1979), that public official status "cannot be thought to include all public employees," according to Rod Smolla, "there are relatively few examples of government-related defamation plaintiffs who are held *not* to be public officials subject to the *New York Times* standard. Those government-related plaintiffs held not to be public officials usually have a peripheral or transient connection to governmental activity, or are extremely low in the organizational hierarchy." Rod Smolla, *Law of Defamation*, §2:100.

2.   *Actual Malice*

St. Amant v. Thompson
39 U.S. 727 (1968)

Mr. Justice WHITE delivered the opinion of the Court.

The question presented by this case is whether the Louisiana Supreme Court, in sustaining a judgment for damages in a public official's defamation action, correctly interpreted and applied the rule of New York Times Co. v. Sullivan, 376 U.S. 254 (1964), that the plaintiff in such an action must prove that the defamatory publication "was made with 'actual malice'—that is, with knowledge that it was false or with reckless disregard of whether it was false or not."

On June 27, 1962, petitioner St. Amant, a candidate for public office, made a televised speech in Baton Rouge, Louisiana. In the course of this speech, St. Amant read a series of questions which he had put to J.D. Albin, a member of a Teamsters Union local, and Albin's answers to those questions. [Those answers falsely accused plaintiff Thompson, a deputy sheriff, with criminal behavior.]

Thompson promptly brought suit for defamation. . . . The case was tried prior to the decision in *New York Times Co. v. Sullivan*. The trial judge ruled in Thompson's favor and awarded $5,000 in damages. Thereafter, in the course of entertaining and denying a motion for a new trial, the Court considered the ruling in *New York Times*, finding that rule no barrier to the judgment already entered. The Louisiana Court of Appeal reversed because the record failed to show that St. Amant had acted with actual malice, as required by *New York Times*. The Supreme Court of Louisiana reversed the intermediate appellate court. In its view, there was sufficient evidence that St. Amant recklessly disregarded whether the statements about Thompson were true or false. We granted a writ of certiorari.

For purposes of this case we accept the determinations of the Louisiana courts that the material published by St. Amant charged Thompson with criminal conduct, that the charge was false, and that Thompson was a public official and so had the burden of proving that the false statements about Thompson were made with actual malice as defined in *New York Times Co. v. Sullivan* and later cases. We cannot, however, agree with either the Supreme Court of Louisiana or the trial court that Thompson sustained this burden.

The Louisiana Supreme Court concluded, after considering state law, that a deputy sheriff has "substantial responsibility for or control over the conduct of governmental affairs," the test established by Rosenblatt v. Baer, 383 U.S. 75, 85, 86 S. Ct. 669, 675, 15 L. Ed. 2d 597 (1966), "at least where law enforcement and police functions are concerned."

Purporting to apply the *New York Times* malice standard, the Louisiana Supreme Court ruled that St. Amant had broadcast false information about Thompson recklessly, though not knowingly. Several reasons were given for this conclusion. St. Amant had no personal knowledge of Thompson's activities; he relied solely on Albin's affidavit although the record was silent as to Albin's reputation for veracity; he failed to verify the information with those in the union office who might have known the facts; he gave no consideration to whether or not the statements defamed Thompson and went ahead heedless of the consequences; and he mistakenly believed he had no responsibility for the broadcast because he was merely quoting Albin's words.

These considerations fall short of proving St. Amant's reckless disregard for the accuracy of his statements about Thompson. "Reckless disregard," it is true, cannot be fully encompassed in one infallible definition. Inevitably its outer limits will be marked out through case-by-case adjudication, as is true with so many legal standards for judging concrete cases, whether the standard is provided by the Constitution, statutes, or case law. Our cases, however, have furnished meaningful guidance for the further definition of a reckless publication. In *New York Times*, the plaintiff did not satisfy his burden because the record failed to show that the publisher was aware of the likelihood that he was circulating false information. In Garrison v. State of Louisiana, 379 U.S. 64 (1964), also decided before the decision of the Louisiana Supreme Court in this case, the opinion emphasized the necessity for a showing that a false publication was made with a "high degree of awareness of . . . probable falsity." Mr. Justice Harlan's opinion in Curtis Publishing Co. v. Butts, 388 U.S. 130, 153 (1967), stated that evidence of either deliberate falsification or reckless publication "despite the publisher's awareness of probable falsity" was essential to recovery by public officials in defamation actions. These cases are clear that reckless conduct is not measured by whether a reasonably prudent man would have published, or would have investigated before publishing. There must be sufficient evidence to permit the conclusion that the defendant in fact entertained serious doubts as to the truth of his publication. Publishing with such doubts shows reckless disregard for truth or falsity and demonstrates actual malice.

It may be said that such a test puts a premium on ignorance, encourages the irresponsible publisher not to inquire, and permits the issue to be determined by the defendants testimony that he published the statement in good faith and unaware of its probable falsity. Concededly the reckless disregard standard may permit recovery in fewer situations than would a rule that publishers must satisfy the standard of the reasonable man or the prudent publisher. But *New York Times* and succeeding cases have emphasized that the stake of the people in public business and the conduct of public officials is so great that neither the defense of truth nor the standard of ordinary care would protect against self-censorship and thus adequately implement First Amendment policies. Neither lies nor false communications serve the ends of the First Amendment, and no one suggests their desirability or further proliferation. But to insure the ascertainment and publication of the truth about public affairs, it is essential that the First Amendment protect some erroneous publications as well as true ones. We adhere to this view and to the line which our cases have drawn between false communications which are protected and those which are not.

The defendant in a defamation action brought by a public official cannot, however, automatically insure a favorable verdict by testifying that he published with a belief that the statements were true. The finder of fact must determine whether the publication was indeed made in good faith. Professions of good faith will be unlikely to prove persuasive, for example, where a story is fabricated by the defendant, is the product of his imagination, or is based wholly on an unverified anonymous telephone call. Nor will they be likely to prevail when the publisher's allegations are so inherently improbable that only a reckless man would have put them in circulation. Likewise, recklessness may be found where there are obvious reasons to doubt the veracity of the informant or the accuracy of his reports.

By no proper test of reckless disregard was St. Amant's broadcast a reckless publication about a public officer. Nothing referred to by the Louisiana courts indicates an awareness by St. Amant of the probable falsity of Albin's statement about Thompson. Failure to investigate does not in itself establish bad faith. . . .

Because the state court misunderstood and misapplied the actual malice standard which must be observed in a public official's defamation action, the judgment is reversed and the case remanded for further proceedings not inconsistent with this opinion.

[Justices Black and Douglas concurred, and Justice Fortas dissented.]

PREPARING FOR CLASS

1. Why did *New York Times* apply?

2. Why did the Louisiana Supreme Court find that Thompson proved actual malice?

3. Why do "these considerations fall short of proving St. Amant's reckless disregard for the accuracy of his statements"?

4. Does this holding mean that defendants can simply take the stand and assert, with convincing delivery, that they believed what they published and escape liability?

Harte-Hanks Commc'ns, Inc. v. Connaughton
491 U.S. 657 (1989)

Justice STEVENS delivered the opinion of the Court.

A public figure may not recover damages for a defamatory falsehood without clear and convincing proof that the false "statement was made with 'actual malice'—that is, with knowledge that it was false or with reckless disregard of whether it was false or not." New York Times Co. v. Sullivan, 376 U.S. 254, 279-280 (1964). In Bose Corp. v. Consumers Union of United States, Inc., 466 U.S. 485 (1984), we held that judges in such cases have a constitutional duty to "exercise independent judgment and determine whether the record establishes actual malice with convincing clarity." In this case the Court of Appeals affirmed a libel judgment against a newspaper without attempting to make an independent evaluation of the credibility of conflicting oral testimony concerning the subsidiary facts underlying the jury's finding of actual malice. We granted certiorari to consider whether the Court of Appeals' analysis was consistent with our holding in Bose.

Respondent, Daniel Connaughton, was the unsuccessful candidate for the office of Municipal Judge of Hamilton, Ohio, in an election conducted on November 8, 1983. Petitioner is the publisher of the Journal News, a local newspaper that supported the reelection of the incumbent, James Dolan. A little over a month before the election, the incumbent's Director of Court Services resigned and was arrested on bribery charges. A grand jury investigation of those charges was in progress on November 1, 1983. On that date, the Journal News ran a front-page story quoting Alice Thompson, a grand jury witness, as stating that Connaughton had used "dirty tricks" and offered her and her sister jobs and a trip to Florida "in appreciation" for their help in the investigation. . . .

After listening to six days of testimony and three taped interviews—one conducted by Connaughton and two by Journal News reporters—and reviewing the contents of 56 exhibits, the jury was given succinct instructions accurately defining the elements of public figure libel and directed to answer three special verdicts. It unanimously found by a preponderance of the evidence that the November 1 story was defamatory and that it was false. It also found by clear and convincing proof that the story was published with actual malice. After a separate hearing on damages, the jury awarded Connaughton $5,000 in compensatory damages and $195,000 in punitive damages. Thereafter, the District Court denied a motion for judgment notwithstanding the verdict, and petitioner appealed. . . .

The Court of Appeals affirmed. . . . It separately considered the evidence supporting each of the jury's special verdicts, concluding that neither the finding that the article was defamatory nor the finding that it was false was clearly erroneous.

II

Petitioner contends that the Court of Appeals made two basic errors. First, while correctly stating the actual malice standard announced in *New York Times*, the court actually applied a less severe standard that merely required a showing of "'highly unreasonable conduct constituting an extreme departure from the standards of investigation and reporting ordinarily adhered to by responsible publishers.'" (quoting Curtis Publishing Co. v. Butts, 388 U.S., at 155 (opinion of Harlan, J.)). Second, the court failed to make an independent de novo review of the entire record and therefore incorrectly relied on subsidiary facts implicitly established by the jury's verdict instead of drawing its own inferences from the evidence.

There is language in the Court of Appeals' opinion that supports petitioner's first contention. For example, the Court of Appeals did expressly state that the Journal News' decision to publish Alice Thompson's allegations constituted an extreme departure from professional standards. Moreover, the opinion attributes considerable weight to the evidence that the Journal News was motivated by its interest in the reelection of the candidate it supported and its economic interest in gaining a competitive advantage over the Cincinnati Enquirer, its bitter rival in the local market. Petitioner is plainly correct in recognizing that a public figure plaintiff must prove more than an extreme departure from professional standards and that a newspaper's motive in publishing a story — whether to promote an opponent's candidacy or to increase its circulation — cannot provide a sufficient basis for finding actual malice. . . .

It also is worth emphasizing that the actual malice standard is not satisfied merely through a showing of ill will or "malice" in the ordinary sense of the term. Indeed, just last Term we unanimously held that a public figure "may not recover for the tort of intentional infliction of emotional distress . . . without showing . . . that the publication contains a false statement of fact which was made . . . with knowledge that the statement was false or with reckless disregard as to whether or not it was true." Hustler Magazine, Inc. v. Falwell, 485 U.S. 46, 56 (1988). Nor can the fact that the defendant published the defamatory material in order to increase its profits suffice to prove actual malice. The allegedly defamatory statements at issue in the *New York Times* case were themselves published as part of a paid advertisement. If a profit motive could somehow strip communications of the otherwise available constitutional protection, our cases from *New York Times* to *Hustler Magazine* would be little more than empty vessels. Actual malice, instead, requires at a minimum that the statements were made with a reckless disregard for the truth. And although the concept of "reckless disregard" "cannot be fully encompassed in one infallible definition," St. Amant v. Thompson, 390 U.S. 727, 730 (1968), we have made clear that the defendant must have made the false publication with a "high degree of awareness of . . . probable falsity," or must have "entertained serious doubts as to the truth of his publication." . . .

[W]hen the [court of appeals] opinion is read as a whole, it is clear that the conclusion concerning the newspaper's departure from accepted standards and the evidence of motive were merely supportive of the court's ultimate conclusion that the record "demonstrated a reckless disregard as to the truth or falsity of Thompson's allegations and thus provided clear and convincing proof of 'actual malice' as found by the jury." Although courts must be careful not to place too much reliance on such factors, a plaintiff is entitled to prove the defendant's state of mind through circumstantial evidence, and it cannot be said that evidence concerning motive or care never bears any relation to the actual malice inquiry. Thus, we are satisfied that the Court of Appeals judged the case by the correct substantive standard.

The question whether the Court of Appeals gave undue weight to the jury's findings—whether it failed to conduct the kind of independent review mandated by our opinion in Bose—requires more careful consideration. A proper answer to that question must be prefaced by additional comment on some of the important conflicts in the evidence. [The opinion then reviews the evidence.]

V

The question whether the evidence in the record in a defamation case is sufficient to support a finding of actual malice is a question of law. This rule is not simply premised on common-law tradition, but on the unique character of the interest protected by the actual malice standard. Our profound national commitment to the free exchange of ideas, as enshrined in the First Amendment, demands that the law of libel carve out an area of "'breathing space'" so that protected speech is not discouraged. *Gertz*, 418 U.S., at 342. The meaning of terms such as "actual malice"—and, more particularly, "reckless disregard"—however, is not readily captured in "one infallible definition." St. Amant v. Thompson, 390 U.S., at 730. Rather, only through the course of case-by-case adjudication can we give content to these otherwise elusive constitutional standards. *Bose, supra*, 466 U.S., at 503. Moreover, such elucidation is particularly important in the area of free speech for precisely the same reason that the actual malice standard is itself necessary. Uncertainty as to the scope of the constitutional protection can only dissuade protected speech—the more elusive the standard, the less protection it affords. Most fundamentally, the rule is premised on the recognition that "[j]udges, as expositors of the Constitution," have a duty to "independently decide whether the evidence in the record is sufficient to cross the constitutional threshold that bars the entry of any judgment that is not supported by clear and convincing proof of 'actual malice.'" *Bose, supra*, at 511, 104 S. Ct., at 1965.

There is little doubt that "public discussion of the qualifications of a candidate for elective office presents what is probably the strongest possible case for application of the *New York Times* rule," Ocala Star-Banner Co. v. Damron, 401 U.S. 295, 300 (1971), and the strongest possible case for independent review. As Madison observed in 1800, just nine years after ratification of the First Amendment:

> Let it be recollected, lastly, that the right of electing the members of the government constitutes more particularly the essence of a free and responsible government. The value and efficacy of this right depends on the knowledge of the comparative merits and demerits of the candidates for public trust, and on the equal freedom, consequently, of examining and discussing these merits and demerits of the candidates respectively. 4 J. Elliot, *Debates on the Federal Constitution* 575 (1861).

This value must be protected with special vigilance. When a candidate enters the political arena, he or she "must expect that the debate will sometimes be rough and personal," Ollman v. Evans, 750 F.2d 970, 1002 (D.C. Cir. 1984) (en banc) (Bork, J., concurring), cert. denied, 471 U.S. 1127 (1985), and cannot "'cry Foul!' when an opponent or an industrious reporter attempts to demonstrate" that he or she lacks the "sterling integrity" trumpeted in campaign literature and speeches, Monitor Patriot Co. v. Roy, 401 U.S. 265, 274 (1971). Vigorous reportage of political campaigns is necessary for the optimal functioning of democratic institutions and central to our history of individual liberty.

We have not gone so far, however, as to accord the press absolute immunity in its coverage of public figures or elections. If a false and defamatory statement is published with knowledge of falsity or a reckless disregard for the truth, the public figure may prevail. See Curtis Publishing Co. v. Butts, 388 U.S., at 162 (opinion of Warren, C.J.). A "reckless disregard" for the truth, however, requires more than a departure from reasonably prudent conduct. "There must be sufficient evidence to permit the conclusion that the defendant in fact entertained serious doubts as to the truth of his publication." *St. Amant*, 390 U.S., at 731. The standard is a subjective one—there must be sufficient evidence to permit the conclusion that the defendant actually had a "high degree of awareness of . . . probable falsity." Garrison v. Louisiana, 379 U.S., at 74. As a result, failure to investigate before publishing, even when a reasonably prudent person would have done so, is not sufficient to establish reckless disregard. In a case such as this involving the reporting of a third party's allegations, "recklessness may be found where there are obvious reasons to doubt the veracity of the informant or the accuracy of his reports." *St. Amant.*

In determining whether the constitutional standard has been satisfied, the reviewing court must consider the factual record in full. Although credibility determinations are reviewed under the clearly-erroneous standard because the trier of fact has had the "opportunity to observe the demeanor of the witnesses," *Bose*, the reviewing court must "'examine for [itself] the statements in issue and the circumstances under which they were made to see . . . whether they are of a character which the principles of the First Amendment . . . protect,'" *New York Times*. Based on our review of the entire record, we agree with the Court of Appeals that the evidence did in fact support a finding of actual malice. Our approach, however, differs somewhat from that taken by the Court of Appeals. In considering the actual malice issue, the Court of Appeals identified 11 subsidiary facts that the jury "could have" found. The court held that such findings would not have been not clearly erroneous, and, based on its independent review, that when considered cumulatively they provide clear and convincing evidence of actual malice. We agree that the jury may have found each of those facts, but conclude that the case should be decided on a less speculative ground.

Given the trial court's instructions, the jury's answers to the three special interrogatories, and an understanding of those facts not in dispute, it is evident that the jury must have rejected (1) the testimony of petitioner's witnesses that Stephens was not contacted simply because Connaughton failed to place her in touch with the newspaper; (2) the testimony of Blount that he did not listen to the tapes simply because he thought they would provide him with no new information; and (3) the testimony of those Journal News employees who asserted that they believed Thompson's allegations were substantially true. When these findings are considered alongside the undisputed evidence, the conclusion that the newspaper acted with actual malice inexorably follows.

There is no dispute that Thompson's charges had been denied not only by Connaughton, but also by five other witnesses before the story was published. Thompson's most serious charge—that Connaughton intended to confront the incumbent judge with the tapes to scare him into resigning and otherwise not to disclose the existence of the tapes—was not only highly improbable, but inconsistent with the fact that Connaughton had actually arranged a lie detector test for Stephens and then delivered the tapes to the police. These facts were well known to the Journal News before the story was published. Moreover, because the newspaper's interviews of Thompson and Connaughton were captured on tape, there can be no dispute as to what was communicated, nor how it was said. The hesitant, inaudible, and sometimes unresponsive and improbable tone of Thompson's answers to various leading questions raise obvious doubts about her veracity. Moreover, contrary to petitioner's contention that the prepublication interview with Connaughton confirmed the factual basis of Thompson's statements, review of the tapes makes clear that Connaughton unambiguously denied each allegation of wrongful conduct. Connaughton's acknowledgment, for instance, that his wife may have discussed with Stephens and Thompson the possibility of working at an ice cream store that she might someday open, hardly confirms the allegations that Connaughton had promised to buy a restaurant for the sister's parents to operate, that he would provide Stephens with a job at the Municipal Court, or even that he would provide Thompson with suitable work. It is extraordinarily unlikely that the reporters missed Connaughton's denials simply because he confirmed certain aspects of Thompson's story.

It is also undisputed that Connaughton made the tapes of the Stephens interview available to the Journal News and that no one at the newspaper took the time to listen to them. Similarly, there is no question that the Journal News was aware that Patsy Stephens was a key witness and that they failed to make any effort to interview her. Accepting the jury's determination that petitioner's explanations for these omissions were not credible, it is likely that the newspaper's inaction was a product of a deliberate decision not to acquire knowledge of facts that might confirm the probable falsity of Thompson's charges. Although failure to investigate will not alone support a finding of actual malice, the purposeful avoidance of the truth is in a different category.

There is a remarkable similarity between this case—and in particular, the newspaper's failure to interview Stephens and failure to listen to the tape recording of the September 17 interview at Connaughton's home—and the facts that supported the Court's judgment in *Curtis Publishing Co. v. Butts*. In *Butts* the evidence showed that the Saturday Evening Post had published an accurate account of an unreliable informant's false description of the Georgia athletic director's purported agreement to "fix" a college football game. Although there was reason to question the informant's veracity, just as there was reason to doubt Thompson's story, the editors did not interview a witness who had the same access to the facts as the informant and did not look at films that revealed what actually happened at the game in question. This evidence of an intent to avoid the truth was not only sufficient to convince the plurality that there had been an extreme departure from professional publishing standards, but it was also sufficient to satisfy the more demanding *New York Times* standard . . .

As in *Butts*, the evidence in the record in this case, when reviewed in its entirety, is "unmistakably" sufficient to support a finding of actual malice. The judgment of the Court of Appeals is accordingly affirmed.

PREPARING FOR CLASS

1. What is the burden of proof for actual malice?

2. What two basic errors does the petitioner contend the Court of Appeals made?

3. Will an extreme departure from professional journalistic standards establish actual malice? What about a profit motive?

4. Why does the petitioner fail/succeed on the first basis of appeal?

5. Why does speech like the speech in this case generally deserve protection? When does that protection end?

6. Is actual malice an objective standard?

7. What kind of review must an appellate court make in a case like this? Why?

8.   Did the evidence in this case support the jury's finding of actual malice? Why or why not?

9.   After reading *St. Amant* and *Harte-Hanks*, can you make a list of behaviors that might persuade a court to find sufficient evidence of actual malice?

APPLYING THE LAW

How will Parker argue that Davis had actual malice? How will she argue that she did not?

3.   *Categorizing the Plaintiff and the Subject Matter*

In *New York Times v. Sullivan*, the Supreme Court adopted an actual malice standard for defamation suits brought by public officials. Three years later, with opinions in Curtis Publishing Co. v. Butts, 388 U.S. 130 (1967), and Associated Press v. Walker, 389 U.S. 889 (1967), the Court extended the actual malice standard to public figures. Judge Lawrence of the Southern District of Georgia wrote, "How and where do we draw a line between public figures and private individuals? They are nebulous concepts. Defining public figures is much like trying to nail a jellyfish to the wall." Rosanova v. Playboy Enterprises, Inc., 411 F. Supp. 440 (1976). The question of plaintiff status has become even more slippery since Judge Lawrence wrote that opinion. In addition to public officials, courts recognize all-purpose public figures, limited-purpose public figures (both voluntary and involuntary), private plaintiffs defamed on public matters, and private plaintiffs defamed on private matters. Different combinations of status and subject matter impose different requirements on defamation plaintiffs.

Gertz v. Robert Welch, Inc.
418 U.S. 323 (1974)

Justice POWELL delivered the opinion of the Court.

I

In 1968 a Chicago policeman named Nuccio shot and killed a youth named Nelson. The state authorities prosecuted Nuccio for the homicide and ultimately obtained a conviction for murder in the second degree. The Nelson family retained petitioner Elmer Gertz, a reputable attorney, to represent them in civil litigation against Nuccio.

Respondent publishes American Opinion, a monthly outlet for the views of the John Birch Society. Early in the 1960's the magazine began to warn of a nationwide conspiracy to discredit local law enforcement agencies and create in their stead a national police force capable of supporting a Communist dictatorship. As part of the continuing effort to alert the public to this assumed danger, the managing editor of American Opinion commissioned an article on the murder trial of Officer Nuccio. For this purpose he engaged a regular contributor to the magazine. In March 1969 respondent published the resulting article under the title "FRAME-UP: Richard Nuccio And The War On Police." The article purports to demonstrate that the testimony against Nuccio at his criminal trial was false and that his prosecution was part of the Communist campaign against the police.

In his capacity as counsel for the Nelson family in the civil litigation, petitioner attended the coroner's inquest into the boy's death and initiated actions for damages, but he neither discussed Officer Nuccio with the press nor played any part in the criminal proceeding. Notwithstanding petitioner's remote connection with the prosecution of Nuccio, respondent's magazine portrayed him as an architect of the "frame-up." According to the article, the police file on petitioner took "a big, Irish cop to lift." The article stated that petitioner had been an official of the "Marxist League for Industrial Democracy, originally known as the Intercollegiate Socialist Society, which has advocated the violent seizure of our government." It labeled Gertz a "Leninist" and a "Communist-fronter." It also stated that Gertz had been an officer of the National Lawyers Guild, described as a Communist organization that "probably did more than any other outfit to plan the Communist attack on the Chicago police during the 1968 Democratic Convention."

These statements contained serious inaccuracies. The implication that petitioner had a criminal record was false. Petitioner had been a member and officer of the National Lawyers Guild some 15 years earlier, but there was no evidence that he or that organization had taken any part in planning the 1968 demonstrations in Chicago. There was also no basis for the charge that petitioner was a "Leninist" or a "Communist-fronter." And he had never been a member of the "Marxist League for Industrial Democracy" or the "Intercollegiate Socialist Society."

The managing editor of American Opinion made no effort to verify or substantiate the charges against petitioner. Instead, he appended an editorial introduction stating that the author had "conducted extensive research into the Richard Nuccio Case." And he included in the article a photograph of petitioner and wrote the caption that appeared under it: "Elmer Gertz of Red Guild harasses Nuccio." Respondent placed the issue of American Opinion containing the article on sale at newsstands throughout the country and distributed reprints of the article on the streets of Chicago.

Petitioner filed a diversity action for libel in the United States District Court for the Northern District of Illinois.

[The defendant filed a motion to dismiss, which the District Court denied. Determining that Gertz was neither a public official nor a public figure, the court submitted the case to the jury, which awarded Gertz $50,000. The District Court subsequently reevaluated its position and decided that the *New York Times* standard did apply and entered judgment for the defendant notwithstanding the verdict. The Seventh Circuit affirmed this ruling, citing Rosenbloom v. Metromedia, Inc., 403 U.S. 29 (1971), which had been decided after the trial.]

II

The principal issue in this case is whether a newspaper or broadcaster that publishes defamatory falsehoods about an individual who is neither a public official nor a public figure may claim a constitutional privilege against liability for the injury inflicted by those statements. The Court considered this question on the rather different set of facts presented in *Rosenbloom v. Metromedia, Inc.* . . . .

III

We begin with the common ground. Under the First Amendment there is no such thing as a false idea. However pernicious an opinion may seem, we depend for its correction not on the conscience of judges and juries but on the competition of other ideas. But there is no constitutional value in false statements of fact. Neither the intentional lie nor the careless error materially advances society's interest in "uninhibited, robust, and wide-open" debate on public issues. They belong to that category of utterances which "are no essential part of any exposition of ideas, and are of such slight social value as a step to truth that any benefit that may be derived from them is clearly outweighed by the social interest in order and morality." Chaplinsky v. New Hampshire, 315 U.S. 568, 572 (1942).

Although the erroneous statement of fact is not worthy of constitutional protection, it is nevertheless inevitable in free debate. As James Madison pointed out in the Report on the Virginia Resolutions of 1798: "Some degree of abuse is inseparable from the proper use of every thing; and in no instance is this more true than in that of the press." 4 J. Elliot, *Debates on the Federal Constitution of 1787*, p. 571 (1876). And punishment of error runs the risk of inducing a cautious and restrictive exercise of the constitutionally guaranteed freedoms of speech and press. Our decisions recognize that a rule of strict liability that compels a publisher or broadcaster to guarantee the accuracy of his factual assertions may lead to intolerable self-censorship. Allowing the media to avoid liability only by proving the truth of all injurious statements does not accord adequate protection to First Amendment liberties. As the Court stated in *New York Times Co. v. Sullivan*: "Allowance of the defense of truth, with the burden of proving it on the defendant, does not mean that only false speech will be deterred." The First Amendment requires that we protect some falsehood in order to protect speech that matters.

The need to avoid self-censorship by the news media is, however, not the only societal value at issue. If it were, this Court would have embraced long ago the view that publishers and broadcasters enjoy an unconditional and indefeasible immunity from liability for defamation. Such a rule would, indeed, obviate the fear that the prospect of civil liability for injurious falsehood might dissuade a timorous press from the effective exercise of First Amendment freedoms. Yet absolute protection for the communications media requires a total sacrifice of the competing value served by the law of defamation.

The legitimate state interest underlying the law of libel is the compensation of individuals for the harm inflicted on them by defamatory falsehood. . . . The protection of private personality, like the protection of life itself, is left primarily to the individual States under the Ninth and Tenth Amendments. But this does not mean that the right is entitled to any less recognition by this Court as a basic of our constitutional system.

Some tension necessarily exists between the need for a vigorous and uninhibited press and the legitimate interest in redressing wrongful injury. . . . In our continuing effort to define the proper accommodation between these competing concerns, we have been especially anxious to assure to the freedoms of speech and press that "breathing space" essential to their fruitful exercise. To that end this Court has extended a measure of strategic protection to defamatory falsehood.

The *New York Times* standard defines the level of constitutional protection appropriate to the context of defamation of a public person. Those who, by reason of the notoriety of their achievements or the vigor and success with which they seek the public's attention, are properly classed as public figures and those who hold governmental office may recover for injury to reputation only on clear and convincing proof that the defamatory falsehood was made with knowledge of its falsity or with reckless disregard for the truth. This standard administers an extremely powerful antidote to the inducement to media self-censorship of the common-law rule of strict liability for libel and slander. And it exacts a correspondingly high price from the victims of defamatory falsehood. Plainly many deserving plaintiffs, including some intentionally subjected to injury, will be unable to surmount the barrier of the *New York Times* test. Despite this substantial abridgment of the state law right to compensation for wrongful hurt to one's reputation, the Court has concluded that the protection of the *New York Times* privilege should be available to publishers and broadcasters of defamatory falsehood concerning public officials and public figures. We think that these decisions are correct, but we do not find their holdings justified solely by reference to the interest of the press and broadcast media in immunity from liability. Rather, we believe that the

New York Times rule states an accommodation between this concern and the limited state interest present in the context of libel actions brought by public persons. For the reasons stated below, we conclude that the state interest in compensating injury to the reputation of private individuals requires that a different rule should obtain with respect to them.

Theoretically, of course, the balance between the needs of the press and the individual's claim to compensation for wrongful injury might be struck on a case-by-case basis. . . . But this approach would lead to unpredictable results and uncertain expectations, and it could render our duty to supervise the lower courts unmanageable. Because an ad hoc resolution of the competing interests at stake in each particular case is not feasible, we must lay down broad rules of general application. . . .

With that caveat we have no difficulty in distinguishing among defamation plaintiffs. The first remedy of any victim of defamation is self-help—using available opportunities to contradict the lie or correct the error and thereby to minimize its adverse impact on reputation. Public officials and public figures usually enjoy significantly greater access to the channels of effective communication and hence have a more realistic opportunity to counteract false statements then private individuals normally enjoy. Private individuals are therefore more vulnerable to injury, and the state interest in protecting them is correspondingly greater.

More important than the likelihood that private individuals will lack effective opportunities for rebuttal, there is a compelling normative consideration underlying the distinction between public and private defamation plaintiffs. An individual who decides to seek governmental office must accept certain necessary consequences of that involvement in public affairs. He runs the risk of closer public scrutiny than might otherwise be the case. And society's interest in the officers of government is not strictly limited to the formal discharge of official duties. As the Court pointed out in Garrison v. Louisiana, 379 U.S., at 77, the public's interest extends to "anything which might touch on an official's fitness for office. . . . Few personal attributes are more germane to fitness for office than dishonesty, malfeasance, or improper motivation, even though these characteristics may also affect the official's private character."

Those classed as public figures stand in a similar position. Hypothetically, it may be possible for someone to become a public figure through no purposeful action of his own, but the instances of truly involuntary public figures must be exceedingly rare. For the most part those who attain this status have assumed roles of especial prominence in the affairs of society. Some occupy positions of such persuasive power and influence that they are deemed public figures for all purposes. More commonly, those classed as public figures have thrust themselves to the forefront of particular public controversies in order to influence the resolution of the issues involved. In either event, they invite attention and comment.

Even if the foregoing generalities do not obtain in every instance, the communications media are entitled to act on the assumption that public officials and public figures have voluntarily exposed themselves to increased risk of injury from defamatory falsehood concerning them. No such assumption is justified with respect to a private individual. He has not accepted public office or assumed an "influential role in ordering society." Curtis Publishing Co. v. Butts, 388 U.S., at 164, 87 S. Ct., at 1996 (Warren, C.J., concurring in result). He has relinquished no part of his interest in the protection of his own good name, and consequently he has a more compelling call on the courts for redress of injury inflicted by defamatory falsehood. Thus, private individuals are not only more vulnerable to injury than public officials and public figures; they are also more deserving of recovery.

For these reasons we conclude that the States should retain substantial latitude in their efforts to enforce a legal remedy for defamatory falsehood injurious to the reputation of a private individual. The extension of the *New York Times* test proposed by the *Rosenbloom* plurality would abridge this legitimate state interest to a degree that we find unacceptable. And it would occasion the additional difficulty of forcing state and federal judges to decide on an ad hoc basis which publications address issues of "general or public interest" and which do not—to determine, in the words of Mr. Justice Marshall, "what information is relevant to self-government." Rosenbloom v. Metromedia, Inc., 403 U.S., at 79. We doubt the wisdom of committing this task to the conscience of judges. Nor does the Constitution require us to draw so thin a line between the drastic alternatives of the *New York Times* privilege and the common law of strict liability for defamatory error. . . .

We hold that, so long as they do not impose liability without fault, the States may define for themselves the appropriate standard of liability for a publisher or broadcaster of defamatory falsehood injurious to a private individual. This approach provides a more equitable boundary between the competing concerns involved here. It recognizes the strength of the legitimate state interest in compensating private individuals for wrongful injury to reputation, yet shields the press and broadcast media from the rigors of strict liability for defamation. At least this conclusion obtains where, as here, the substance of the defamatory statement "makes substantial danger to reputation apparent." . . .

IV

Our accommodation of the competing values at stake in defamation suits by private individuals allows the States to impose liability on the publisher or broadcaster of defamatory falsehood on a less demanding showing than that required by *New York Times*. This conclusion is not based on a belief that the considerations which prompted the adoption of the *New York Times* privilege for defamation of public officials and its extension to public figures are wholly inapplicable to the context of private individuals. Rather, we endorse this approach in recognition of the strong and legitimate state interest in compensating private individuals for injury to reputation. But this countervailing state interest extends no further than compensation for actual injury. For the reasons stated below, we hold that the States may not permit recovery of presumed or punitive damages, at least when liability is not based on a showing of knowledge of falsity or reckless disregard for the truth.

The common law of defamation is an oddity of tort law, for it allows recovery of purportedly compensatory damages without evidence of actual loss. Under the traditional rules pertaining to actions for libel, the existence of injury is presumed from the fact of publication. Juries may award substantial sums as compensation for supposed damage to reputation without any proof that such harm actually occurred. The largely uncontrolled discretion of juries to award damages where there is no loss unnecessarily compounds the potential of any system of liability for defamatory falsehood to inhibit the vigorous exercise of First Amendment freedoms. Additionally, the doctrine of presumed damages invites juries to punish unpopular opinion rather than to compensate individuals for injury sustained by the publication of a false fact. More to the point, the States have no substantial interest in securing for plaintiffs such as this petitioner gratuitous awards of money damages far in excess of any actual injury.

We would not, of course, invalidate state law simply because we doubt its wisdom, but here we are attempting to reconcile state law with a competing interest grounded in the constitutional command of the First Amendment. It is therefore appropriate to require that state remedies for defamatory falsehood reach no farther than is necessary to protect the legitimate interest involved. It is necessary to restrict defamation plaintiffs who do not prove knowledge of falsity or reckless disregard for the truth to compensation for actual injury. We need not define "actual injury," as trial courts have wide experience in framing appropriate jury instructions in tort actions. Suffice it to say that actual injury is not limited to out-of-pocket loss. Indeed, the more customary types of actual harm inflicted by defamatory falsehood include impairment of reputation and standing in the community, personal humiliation, and mental anguish and suffering. Of course, juries must be limited by appropriate instructions, and all awards must be supported by competent evidence concerning the injury, although there need be no evidence which assigns an actual dollar value to the injury.

We also find no justification for allowing awards of punitive damages against publishers and broadcasters held liable under state-defined standards of liability for defamation. In most jurisdictions jury discretion over the amounts awarded is limited only by the gentle rule that they not be excessive. Consequently, juries assess punitive damages in wholly unpredictable amounts bearing no necessary relation to the actual harm caused. And they remain free to use their discretion selectively to punish expressions of unpopular views. Like the doctrine of presumed damages, jury discretion to award punitive damages unnecessarily exacerbates the danger of media self-censorship, but, unlike the former rule, punitive damages are wholly irrelevant to the state interest that justifies a negligence standard for private defamation actions. They are not compensation for injury. Instead, they are private fines levied by civil juries to punish reprehensible conduct and to deter its future occurrence. In short, the private defamation plaintiff who establishes liability under a less demanding standard than that stated by *New York Times* may recover only such damages as are sufficient to compensate him for actual injury.

V

Notwithstanding our refusal to extend the *New York Times* privilege to defamation of private individuals, respondent contends that we should affirm the judgment below on the ground that petitioner is either a public official or a public figure. . . . Respondent admits this but argues that petitioner's appearance at the coroner's inquest rendered him a "de facto public official." Our cases recognized no such concept. Respondent's suggestion would sweep all lawyers under the *New York Times* rule as officers of the court and distort the plain meaning of the "public official" category beyond all recognition. We decline to follow it.

Respondent's characterization of petitioner as a public figure raises a different question. That designation may rest on either of two alternative bases. In some instances an individual may achieve such pervasive fame or notoriety that he becomes a public figure for all purposes and in all contexts. More commonly, an individual voluntarily injects himself or is drawn into a particular public controversy and thereby becomes a public figure for a limited range of issues. In either case such persons assume special prominence in the resolution of public questions.

Petitioner has long been active in community and professional affairs. He has served as an officer of local civic groups and of various professional organizations, and he has published several books and articles on legal subjects. Although petitioner was consequently well known in some circles, he had achieved no general fame or notoriety in the community. None of the prospective jurors called at the trial had ever heard of petitioner prior to this litigation, and respondent offered no proof that this response was atypical of the local population. We would not lightly assume that a citizen's participation in community and professional affairs rendered him a public figure for all purposes. Absent clear evidence of general fame or notoriety in the community, and pervasive involvement in the affairs of society, an individual should not be deemed a public personality for all aspects of his life. It is preferable to reduce the public-figure question to a more meaningful context by looking to the nature and extent of an individual's participation in the particular controversy giving rise to the defamation.

In this context it is plain that petitioner was not a public figure. He played a minimal role at the coroner's inquest, and his participation related solely to his representation of a private client. He took no part in the criminal prosecution of Officer Nuccio. Moreover, he never discussed either the criminal or civil litigation with the press and was never quoted as having done so. He plainly did not thrust himself into the vortex of this public issue, nor did he engage the public's attention in an attempt to influence its outcome. We are persuaded that the trial court did not err in refusing to characterize petitioner as a public figure for the purpose of this litigation.

We therefore conclude that the *New York Times* standard is inapplicable to this case and that the trial court erred in entering judgment for respondent. Because the jury was allowed to impose liability without fault and was permitted to presume damages without proof of injury, a new trial is necessary. We reverse and remand for further proceedings in accord with this opinion.

It is ordered.

Reversed and remanded.

[Justices Stewart, Marshall, Blackmun, and Rehnquist, joined in the opinion, and Justices Burger, Douglas, and White dissented.]

PREPARING FOR CLASS

1. If Gertz is neither a public official nor a public figure, why does regulating speech about him raise constitutional concerns?

2. What concerns must be balanced against the Free Speech concerns the case raises?

3. How does the court define public figures and distinguish them from private ones? What two types of public figures does the court seem to identify? Can people be involuntary public figures?

4. What kind of figure is Gertz? Does the court categorize him by subject matter?

5. Why and how does the balance of competing interests shift when plaintiff is someone like Gertz? Does *New York Times* apply to him? If not, what rule does?

INCREASING YOUR UNDERSTANDING

Plaintiff's voluntary involvement in an activity likely to invite attention and comment is an important factor in determining that the plaintiff was a "vortex" or limited-purpose public figure. Nonetheless, courts have found some plaintiffs to be involuntary limited-purpose public figures. The relatives of highly famous or notorious people have been found to be involuntary public figures—the wife of Johnny Carson in Carson v. Allied News Co., 529 F.2d 206 (7th Cir. 1976) and the sons of Ethel and Julius Rosenberg in Meeropol v. Nizer, 381 F. Supp. 29 (S.D.N.Y. 1974), aff'd in relevant part, 560 F.2d 1061 (2d Cir. 1977), cert. den., 434 U.S. 1013 (1978). The D.C. Circuit also ruled that the sole air traffic controller on duty the day of a major air disaster was a limited-purpose public figure with regard to that event because he had played a central role in a major news event and had become closely identified with that event. Dameron v. Washington Magazine, Inc. 779 F.2d 736 (D.C. Cir. 1985).

Dun & Bradstreet, Inc. v. Greenmoss Builders, Inc.
472 U.S. 749 (1985)

Justice POWELL announced the judgment of the Court and delivered an opinion, in which Justice REHNQUIST and Justice O'CONNOR joined.

In Gertz v. Robert Welch, Inc., 418 U.S. 323, we held that the First Amendment restricted the damages that a private individual could obtain from a publisher for a libel that involved a matter of public concern. More specifically, we held that in these circumstances the First Amendment prohibited awards of presumed and punitive damages for false and defamatory statements unless the plaintiff shows "actual malice," that is, knowledge of falsity or reckless disregard for the truth. The question presented in this case is whether this rule of *Gertz* applies when the false and defamatory statements do not involve matters of public concern.

[Dun & Bradstreet provided credit ratings reports to subscribers. A 17-year-old high-school student working for Dun & Bradstreet reviewed Vermont bankruptcy proceedings and mistakenly attributed to Greenmoss Builders a bankruptcy petition filed by a former Greenmoss employee, and Dun & Bradstreet negligently failed to catch this error. Therefore, five subscribers were informed that Greenmoss had filed for bankruptcy. Dun & Bradstreet sent out correction reports when notified of the mistake but refused to reveal the identities of the subscribers because of its confidentiality policy. Greenmoss successfully sued for defamation and was awarded $50,000 in presumed, compensatory damages and $300,000 in punitive damages.]

In *Gertz*, we held that the fact that expression concerned a public issue did not by itself entitle the libel defendant to the constitutional protections of *New York Times*. These protections, we found, were not "justified solely by reference to the interest of the press and broadcast media in immunity from liability." Rather, they represented "an accommodation between [First Amendment] concern[s] and the limited state interest present in the context of libel actions brought by public persons." In libel actions brought by private persons we found the competing interests different. Largely because private persons have not voluntarily exposed themselves to increased risk of injury from defamatory statements and because they generally lack effective opportunities for rebutting such statements, we found that the State possessed a "strong and legitimate . . . interest in compensating private individuals for injury to reputation." Balancing this stronger state interest against the same First Amendment interest at stake in *New York Times*, we held that a State could not allow recovery of presumed and punitive damages absent a showing of "actual malice." Nothing in our opinion, however, indicated that this same balance would be struck regardless of the type of speech involved. . . .

We have never considered whether the *Gertz* balance obtains when the defamatory statements involve no issue of public concern. To make this determination, we must employ the approach approved in *Gertz* and balance the State's interest in compensating private individuals for injury to their reputation against the First Amendment interest in protecting this type of expression. This state interest is identical to the one weighed in *Gertz*. There we found that it was "strong and legitimate." A State should not lightly be required to abandon it. . . .

The First Amendment interest, on the other hand, is less important than the one weighed in *Gertz*. We have long recognized that not all speech is of equal First Amendment importance. It is speech on "'matters of public concern'" that is "at the heart of the First Amendment's protection." First National Bank of Boston v. Bellotti, 435 U.S. 765, 776 (1978). . . .

In contrast, speech on matters of purely private concern is of less First Amendment concern. As a number of state courts, including the court below, have recognized, the role of the Constitution in regulating state libel law is far more limited when the concerns that activated *New York Times* and *Gertz* are absent. . . .

While . . . speech [on matters not of public concern] is not totally unprotected by the First Amendment, its protections are less stringent. In *Gertz*, we found that the state interest in awarding presumed and punitive damages was not "substantial" in view of their effect on speech at the core of First Amendment concern. This interest, however, is "substantial" relative to the incidental effect these remedies may have on speech of significantly less constitutional interest. The rationale of the common-law rules has been the experience and judgment of history that "proof of actual damage will be impossible in a great many cases where, from the character of the defamatory words and the circumstances of publication, it is all but certain that serious harm has resulted in fact." As a result, courts for centuries have allowed juries to presume that some damage occurred from many defamatory utterances and publications. This rule furthers the state interest in providing remedies for defamation by ensuring that those remedies are effective. In light of the reduced constitutional value of speech involving no matters of public concern, we hold that the state interest adequately supports awards of presumed and punitive damages-even absent a showing of "actual malice." . . .

The only remaining issue is whether petitioner's credit report involved a matter of public concern. In a related context, we have held that "[w]hether . . . speech addresses a matter of public concern must be determined by [the expression's] content, form, and context . . . as revealed by the whole record." Connick v. Myers, supra, 461 U.S., at 147-148. These factors indicate that petitioner's credit report concerns no public issue. It was speech solely in the individual interest of the speaker and its specific business audience. This particular interest warrants no special protection when—as in this case—the speech is wholly false and clearly damaging to the victim's business reputation. Moreover, since the credit report was made available to only five subscribers, who, under the terms of the subscription agreement, could not disseminate it further, it cannot be said that the report involves any "strong interest in the free flow of commercial information." There is simply no credible argument that this type of credit reporting requires special protection to ensure that "debate on public issues [will] be uninhibited, robust, and wide-open." New York Times Co. v. Sullivan, 376 U.S., at 270.

In addition, the speech here, like advertising, is hardy and unlikely to be deterred by incidental state regulation. It is solely motivated by the desire for profit, which, we have noted, is a force less likely to be deterred than others. Arguably, the reporting here was also more objectively verifiable than speech deserving of greater protection. In any case, the market provides a powerful incentive to a credit reporting agency to be accurate, since false credit reporting is of no use to creditors. Thus, any incremental "chilling" effect of libel suits would be of decreased significance.

We conclude that permitting recovery of presumed and punitive damages in defamation cases absent a showing of "actual malice" does not violate the First Amendment when the defamatory statements do not involve matters of public concern.

Accordingly, we affirm the judgment of the Vermont Supreme Court.

[Chief Justice Burger and Justice White concurred. The dissenting justices would have extended *Gertz* to all private plaintiff cases.]

PREPARING FOR CLASS

1. How is the key issue here different from that in *Gertz?*

2. How is the balance of competing concerns different in this case from the balance in *Gertz?*

3. What kind of subject matter does this case involve? Do you agree with the court's assessment of the type of subject matter?

4. With this category of plaintiff and subject matter, what must plaintiff prove?

5. Is the presumed damages concept any clearer than it was when you read *Gertz?*

INCREASING YOUR UNDERSTANDING

In analyzing a defamation problem, you will have to categorize the plaintiff and, in some cases, the subject matter of the defamation, so that you know what level of fault the plaintiff must prove. This subsection has covered each of the following categories. See if you can define each and identify what level of fault each must establish.

1. Public official (awaiting a case that tells us otherwise, we are assuming their matters are always public)

2. All-purpose public figure (again, their lives are public, not private matters)

3. Limited-purpose public figure defamed on the issue for which she is public

4. Involuntary limited-purpose public figure defamed on the issue for which she is public

5. Limited-purpose public figure defamed on a private issue

6. Private figure defamed on a matter of public concern

7. Private figure defamed on a private issue

APPLYING THE LAW

What status did Parker have? What fault level will he have to prove?

4. *Falsity and Opinion*

Philadelphia Newspapers v. Hepps
475 U.S. 767 (1986)

[Maurice Hepps sued the defendant's newspaper for an article that said he had links to organized crime. The trial court instructed the jury that Hepps had the burden of demonstrating falsity. Adhering to the rule that placed the burden of truth on the defendant, the Pennsylvania Supreme Court reversed. The Supreme Court, in an opinion by Justice O'Connor, reversed.]

There will always be instances when the factfinding process will be unable to resolve conclusively whether the speech is true or false; it is in those cases that the burden of proof is dispositive. Under a rule forcing the plaintiff to bear the burden of showing falsity, there will be some cases in which plaintiffs cannot meet their burden despite the fact that the speech is in fact false. The plaintiff's suit will fail despite the fact that, in some abstract sense, the suit is meritorious. Similarly, under an alternative rule placing the burden of showing truth on defendants, there would be some cases in which defendants could not bear their burden despite the fact that the speech is in fact true. Those suits would succeed despite the fact that, in some abstract sense, those suits are unmeritorious. Under either rule, then, the outcome of the suit will sometimes be at variance with the outcome that we would desire if all speech were either demonstrably true or demonstrably false.

This dilemma stems from the fact that the allocation of the burden of proof will determine liability for some speech that is true and some that is false, but *all* of such speech is *unknowably* true or false. Because the burden of proof is the deciding factor only when the evidence is ambiguous, we cannot know how much of the speech affected by the allocation of the burden of proof is true and how much is false. In a case presenting a configuration of speech and plaintiff like the one we face here, and where the scales are in such an uncertain balance, we believe that the Constitution requires us to tip them in favor of protecting true speech. To ensure the true speech on matters of public concern is not deterred, we hold that the common-law presumption that defamatory speech is false cannot stand when a plaintiff seeks damages against a media defendant for speech of public concern. . . .

We recognize that requiring the plaintiff to show falsity will insulate from liability some speech that is false, but unprovably so. Nonetheless, the Court's previous decisions on the restrictions that the First Amendment places upon the common law of defamation firmly support our conclusion here with respect to the allocation of the burden of proof. In attempting to resolve related issues in the defamation context, the court has affirmed that "[t]he First Amendment requires that we protect some falsehood in order to protect speech that matters." *Gertz*, 418 U.S., at 341. Here the speech concerns the legitimacy of the political process, and therefore clearly "matters." . . .

We note that our decision adds only marginally to the burdens that the plaintiff must already bear as a result of our earlier decisions in the law of defamation. The plaintiff must show fault. A jury is obviously more likely to accept a plaintiff's contention that the defendant was at fault in publishing the statements at issue if convinced that the relevant statement were false. As a practical matter, then, evidence offered by plaintiffs on the publisher's fault in adequately investigating the truth of the published statements will generally encompass evidence of the falsity of the matters asserted.

PREPARING FOR CLASS

1. Why will the burden of proof on falsity sometimes determine the outcome of a case?

2. Why does the Court abandon, for cases like this one, the common law presumption that defamatory speech is false?

3. The Court limits the holding to cases involving media defendants and public concerns. Does this limitation make sense? Do you think the limitation would withstand a challenge?

4. Why does the decision "add[] marginally to the burdens that plaintiff must already bear"?

Milkovich v. Lorain Journal Co.
497 U.S. 1 (1990)

CHIEF JUSTICE REHNQUIST delivered the opinion of the Court.

Respondent J. Theodore Diadiun authored an article in an Ohio newspaper implying that petitioner Michael Milkovich, a local high school wrestling coach, lied under oath in a judicial proceeding about an incident involving petitioner and his team which occurred at a wrestling match. Petitioner sued Diadiun and the newspaper for libel, and the Ohio Court of Appeals affirmed a lower court entry of summary judgment against petitioner. This judgment was based in part on the grounds that the article constituted an "opinion" protected from the reach of state defamation law by the First Amendment to the United States Constitution. We hold that the First Amendment does not prohibit the application of Ohio's libel laws to the alleged defamations contained in the article.

This lawsuit is before us for the third time in an odyssey of litigation spanning nearly 15 years. Petitioner Milkovich, now retired, was the wrestling coach at Maple Heights High School in Maple Heights, Ohio. In 1974, his team was involved in an altercation at a home wrestling match with a team from Mentor High School. Several people were injured. In response to the incident, the Ohio High School Athletic Association (OHSAA) held a hearing at which Milkovich and H. Don Scott, the Superintendent of Maple Heights Public Schools, testified. Following the hearing, OHSAA placed the Maple Heights team on probation for a year and declared the team ineligible for the 1975 state tournament. OHSAA also censured Milkovich for his actions during the altercation. Thereafter, several parents and wrestlers sued OHSAA in the Court of Common Pleas of Franklin County, Ohio, seeking a restraining order against OHSAA's ruling on the grounds that they had been denied due process in the OHSAA proceeding. Both Milkovich and Scott testified in that proceeding. The court overturned OHSAA's probation and ineligibility orders on due process grounds.

The day after the court rendered its decision, respondent Diadiun's column appeared in the News-Herald, a newspaper which circulates in Lake County, Ohio, and is owned by respondent Lorain Journal Co. The column bore the heading "Maple beat the law with the 'big lie,'" beneath which appeared Diadiun's photograph and the words "TD Says." The carryover page headline announced ". . . Diadiun says Maple told a lie." The column contained the following passages:

> . . . [A] lesson was learned (or relearned) yesterday by the student body of Maple Heights High School, and by anyone who attended the Maple-Mentor wrestling meet of last Feb. 8.
>
> A lesson which, sadly, in view of the events of the past year, is well they learned early.
>
> It is simply this: If you get in a jam, lie your way out.

If you're successful enough, and powerful enough, and can sound sincere enough, you stand an excellent chance of making the lie stand up, regardless of what really happened.

The teachers responsible were mainly head Maple wrestling coach, Mike Milkovich, and former superintendent of schools H. Donald Scott. . . .

Anyone who attended the meet, whether he be from Maple Heights, Mentor, or impartial observer, knows in his heart that Milkovich and Scott lied at the hearing after each having given his solemn oath to tell the truth.

But they got away with it.

Is that the kind of lesson we want our young people learning from their high school administrators and coaches?

I think not.

. . . Superintendent Scott had been pursuing a separate defamation action through the Ohio courts. Two years after its Milkovich decision, in considering Scott's appeal, the Ohio Supreme Court reversed its position on Diadiun's article, concluding that the column was "constitutionally protected opinion." *Scott v. News-Herald*, 496 N.E.2d 699, 709 (Ohio 1986). Consequently, the court upheld a lower court's grant of summary judgment against Scott.

The *Scott* court decided that the proper analysis for determining whether utterances are fact or opinion was set forth in the decision of the United States Court of Appeals for the District of Columbia Circuit in Ollman v. Evans, 750 F.2d 970 (D.C. Cir. 1984), cert. denied, 471 U.S. 1127 (1985). Under that analysis, four factors are considered to ascertain whether, under the "totality of circumstances," a statement is fact or opinion. These factors are: (1) "the specific language used"; (2) "whether the statement is verifiable"; (3) "the general context of the statement"; and (4) "the broader context in which the statement appeared." The court found that application of the first two factors to the column militated in favor of deeming the challenged passages actionable assertions of fact. That potential outcome was trumped, however, by the court's consideration of the third and fourth factors. With respect to the third factor, the general context, the court explained that "the large caption 'TD Says' . . . would indicate to even the most gullible reader that the article was, in fact, opinion." As for the fourth factor, the "broader context," the court reasoned that because the article appeared on a sports page—"a traditional haven for cajoling, invective, and hyperbole"—the article would probably be construed as opinion.

Subsequently, considering itself bound by the Ohio Supreme Court's decision in *Scott*, the Ohio Court of Appeals in the instant proceedings affirmed a trial court's grant of summary judgment in favor of respondents, concluding that "it has been decided, as a matter of law, that the article in question was constitutionally protected opinion." The Supreme Court of Ohio dismissed petitioner's ensuing appeal for want of a substantial constitutional question. We granted certiorari to consider the important questions raised by the Ohio courts' recognition of a constitutionally required "opinion" exception to the application of its defamation laws. We now reverse.

... As the common law developed in this country, apart from the issue of damages, one usually needed only allege an unprivileged publication of false and defamatory matter to state a cause of action for defamation. The common law generally did not place any additional restrictions on the type of statement that could be actionable. Indeed, defamatory communications were deemed actionable regardless of whether they were deemed to be statements of fact or opinion. *See,* e.g., Restatement of Torts, §§565-567. As noted in the 1977 Restatement (Second) of Torts §566, Comment a:

> Under the law of defamation, an expression of opinion could be defamatory if the expression was sufficiently derogatory of another as to cause harm to his reputation, so as to lower him in the estimation of the community or to deter third persons from associating or dealing with him. ... The expression of opinion was also actionable in a suit for defamation, despite the normal requirement that the communication be false as well as defamatory. ... This position was maintained even though the truth or falsity of an opinion—as distinguished from a statement of fact—is not a matter that can be objectively determined and truth is a complete defense to a suit for defamation.

However, due to concerns that unduly burdensome defamation laws could stifle valuable public debate, the privilege of "fair comment" was incorporated into the common law as an affirmative defense to an action for defamation. "The principle of 'fair comment' afford[ed] legal immunity for the honest expression of opinion on matters of legitimate public interest when based upon a true or privileged statement of fact." 1 F. Harper & F. James, *Law of Torts* §5.28, p. 456 (1956) (footnote omitted). As this statement implies, comment was generally privileged when it concerned a matter of public concern, was upon true or privileged facts, represented the actual opinion of the speaker, and was not made solely for the purpose of causing harm. See Restatement of Torts, supra, §606. "According to the majority rule, the privilege of fair comment applied only to an expression of opinion and not to a false statement of fact, whether it was expressly stated or implied from an expression of opinion." Restatement (Second) of Torts, supra, §566, Comment a. Thus under the common law, the privilege of "fair comment" was the device employed to strike the appropriate balance between the need for vigorous public discourse and the need to redress injury to citizens wrought by invidious or irresponsible speech.

[The Court then reviewed the case law regarding constitutional limitations on defamation suits.]

Respondents would have us recognize, in addition to the established safeguards discussed above, still another First-Amendment-based protection for defamatory statements which are categorized as "opinion" as opposed to "fact." For this proposition they rely principally on the following dictum from our opinion in *Gertz*:

> Under the First Amendment there is no such thing as a false idea. However pernicious an opinion may seem, we depend for its correction not on the conscience of judges and juries but on the competition of other ideas. But there is no constitutional value in false statements of fact.

Judge Friendly appropriately observed that this passage "has become the opening salvo in all arguments for protection from defamation actions on the ground of opinion, even though the case did not remotely concern the question." Cianci v. New Times Publishing Co., 639 F.2d 54, 61 (2d. Cir. 1980). Read in context, though, the fair meaning of the passage is to equate the word "opinion" in the second sentence with the word "idea" in the first sentence. Under this view, the language was merely a reiteration of Justice Holmes' classic "marketplace of ideas" concept. See Abrams v. United States, 250 U.S. 616, 630 (1919) (dissenting opinion) ("[T]he ultimate good desired is better reached by free trade in ideas . . . the best test of truth is the power of the thought to get itself accepted in the competition of the market").

Thus, we do not think this passage from *Gertz* was intended to create a wholesale defamation exemption for anything that might be labeled "opinion." . . . Not only would such an interpretation be contrary to the tenor and context of the passage, but it would also ignore the fact that expressions of "opinion" may often imply an assertion of objective fact.

If a speaker says, "In my opinion John Jones is a liar," he implies a knowledge of facts which lead to the conclusion that Jones told an untruth. Even if the speaker states the facts upon which he bases his opinion, if those facts are either incorrect or incomplete, or if his assessment of them is erroneous, the statement may still imply a false assertion of fact. Simply couching such statements in terms of opinion does not dispel these implications; and the statement, "In my opinion Jones is a liar," can cause as much damage to reputation as the statement, "Jones is a liar." As Judge Friendly aptly stated: "[It] would be destructive of the law of libel if a writer could escape liability for accusations of [defamatory conduct] simply by using, explicitly or implicitly, the words 'I think.'" It is worthy of note that at common law, even the privilege of fair comment did not extend to "a false statement of fact, whether it was expressly stated or implied from an expression of opinion." Restatement (Second) of Torts, §566, Comment a (1977).

Apart from their reliance on the *Gertz* dictum, respondents do not really contend that a statement such as, "In my opinion John Jones is a liar," should be protected by a separate privilege for "opinion" under the First Amendment. But they do contend that in every defamation case the First Amendment mandates an inquiry into whether a statement is "opinion" or "fact," and that only the latter statements may be actionable. They propose that a number of factors developed by the lower courts (in what we hold was a mistaken reliance on the *Gertz* dictum) be considered in deciding which is which. But we think the "'breathing space'" which "'[f]reedoms of expression require in order to survive,'" (*Hepps*, supra, quoting *New York Times*, supra) is adequately secured by existing constitutional doctrine without the creation of an artificial dichotomy between "opinion" and fact.

Foremost, we think *Hepps* stands for the proposition that a statement on matters of public concern must be provable as false before there can be liability under state defamation law, at least in situations, like the present, where a media defendant is involved. Thus, unlike the statement, "In my opinion Mayor Jones is a liar," the statement, "In my opinion Mayor Jones shows his abysmal ignorance by accepting the teachings of Marx and Lenin," would not be actionable. *Hepps* ensures that a statement of opinion relating to matters of public concern which does not contain a provably false factual connotation will receive full constitutional protection.

Next, the *Bresler-Letter Carriers-Falwell* line of cases provides protection for statements that cannot "reasonably [be] interpreted as stating actual facts" about an individual. *Falwell*, 485 U.S., at 50, 108 S. Ct., at 879. This provides assurance that public debate will not suffer for lack of "imaginative expression" or the "rhetorical hyperbole" which has traditionally added much to the discourse of our Nation.

The *New York Times-Butts-Gertz* culpability requirements further ensure that debate on public issues remains "uninhibited, robust, and wide-open." *New York Times*. Thus, where a statement of "opinion" on a matter of public concern reasonably implies false and defamatory facts regarding public figures or officials, those individuals must show that such statements were made with knowledge of their false implications or with reckless disregard of their truth. Similarly, where such a statement involves a private figure on a matter of public concern, a plaintiff must show that the false connotations were made with some level of fault as required by *Gertz*. Finally, the enhanced appellate review required by *Bose Corp*. provides assurance that the foregoing determinations will be made in a manner so as not to "constitute a forbidden intrusion of the field of free expression."

We are not persuaded that, in addition to these protections, an additional separate constitutional privilege for "opinion" is required to ensure the freedom of expression guaranteed by the First Amendment. The dispositive question in the present case then becomes whether a reasonable factfinder could conclude that the statements in the Diadiun column imply an assertion that petitioner Milkovich perjured himself in a judicial proceeding. We think this question must be answered in the affirmative. . . . This is not the sort of loose, figurative, or hyperbolic language which would negate the impression that the writer was seriously maintaining that petitioner committed the crime of perjury. Nor does the general tenor of the article negate this impression.

We also think the connotation that petitioner committed perjury is sufficiently factual to be susceptible of being proved true or false. A determination whether petitioner lied in this instance can be made on a core of objective evidence by comparing, inter alia, petitioner's testimony before the OHSAA board with his subsequent testimony before the trial court. As the *Scott* court noted regarding the plaintiff in that case: "[W]hether or not H. Don Scott did indeed perjure himself is certainly verifiable by a perjury action with evidence adduced from the transcripts and witnesses present at the hearing. Unlike a subjective assertion the averred defamatory language is an articulation of an objectively verifiable event." So too with petitioner Milkovich.

The numerous decisions discussed above establishing First Amendment protection for defendants in defamation actions surely demonstrate the Court's recognition of the Amendment's vital guarantee of free and uninhibited discussion of public issues. But there is also another side to the equation; we have regularly acknowledged the "important social values which underlie the law of defamation," and recognized that "[s]ociety has a pervasive and strong interest in preventing and redressing attacks upon reputation." Rosenblatt v. Baer, 383 U.S. 75, 86 (1966). Justice Stewart in that case put it with his customary clarity:

> The right of a man to the protection of his own reputation from unjustified invasion and wrongful hurt reflects no more than our basic concept of the essential dignity and worth of every human being—a concept at the root of any decent system of ordered liberty. . . .
>
> The destruction that defamatory falsehood can bring is, to be sure, often beyond the capacity of the law to redeem. Yet, imperfect though it is, an action for damages is the only hope for vindication or redress the law gives to a man whose reputation has been falsely dishonored.

We believe our decision in the present case holds the balance true. The judgment of the Ohio Court of Appeals is reversed, and the case is remanded for further proceedings not inconsistent with this opinion.

Reversed.

[Justice Marshall joined Justice Brennan in a dissent.]

PREPARING FOR CLASS

1. Why did the Ohio Supreme Court protect the sports column?

2. What does "there is no such thing as a false idea" mean in terms of defamation law?

3. How can it be difficult to separate fact from opinion? How could it be harmful to try?

4. How are defendants who think their opinions should be protected speech protected without an opinion privilege?

5. What rule does the court adopt? Is the column still protected under it?

F. DAMAGES

1. *Nominal Damages*

Sometimes the jury will award the defamation plaintiff only nominal damages—a trivial amount, such as $1.00. Sometimes this will be what the plaintiff has requested because the plaintiff's purpose in litigating the case has been to clear his name and not to be financially compensated. Other times, this will be what the jury has deemed appropriate because, although the plaintiff has demonstrated the necessary elements, he has not suffered significant reputational harm. Lawyers have also asked for nominal damages as a "peg" for punitive damages, which cannot be awarded unless some compensatory amount has been awarded. In light of *State Farm v. Campbell*, does this still make sense?

[handwritten margin note: / good rep \ bad rep]

2. *Compensatory Damages*

Defamation can damage a person in a variety of ways. The tort compensates successful plaintiffs not only for their reputational losses but for their emotional and dignitary losses as well. And it compensates them for general, non-pecuniary losses as well as monetary losses, known as special damages. Damages supported with proof are actual damages. As you recall, the *Gertz* case addressed the necessary fault to recover presumed damages. These are damages not supported with proof, and they are general damages only, not special.

So this means that a plaintiff could recover:

Actual, general damages for reputational losses: Plaintiff proves that he has been shunned by members of his social group and that he lost the presidency of a club he belongs to because of the defamation.

Actual, general damages for emotional/dignitary losses: Plaintiff proves that he has been depressed and sleepless as a result of the cruel, false things said about him and the response of others to those things.

Actual, special damages for reputational losses: Plaintiff proves that he lost his job because of the defamation. Plaintiff proves that he was not awarded a contract because of the defamation.

Actual, special damages for emotional/dignitary losses: Plaintiff proves that he has been seeing a psychiatrist because of the emotional harm from the defamation and that he is on anti-depressants because of the defamation. He can recover those medical costs. (Important note: This class of special damages would not be enough to help a slander case make it to the jury. The special damages necessary to take a slander case before a jury are those that demonstrate reputational harm.)

Presumed, general damages for reputational losses: With evidence of what was said and how broadly it was disseminated, the jury may presume that the plaintiff suffered reputational losses he cannot demonstrate in court. (Not all states permit recovery of these damages.)

3.   Punitive Damages

No matter what status a plaintiff has, she must demonstrate common law malice to recover punitive damages. This means that the defendant has made the statement with ill will or spite or for revenge. In addition to common law malice, the plaintiff must meet whatever constitutional requirements attach to her status.

APPLYING THE LAW

What damages could Parker recover?

G.   DEFENSES

1.   Absolute Privilege

Hawkins v. Harris
661 A.2d 284 (N.J. 1995)

O'HERN, J.
Plaintiff alleges that in the course of her personal injury action against two motorists, she was subjected to repeated indignities by private investigators acting on behalf of an insurance company and a law firm representing one of the motorists. . . . We agree with the majority of the Appellate Division panel that the absolute privilege does extend to statements made by private investigators. We affirm the judgment below.

. . . One member of the Appellate Division panel dissented from the part of the decision affirming the dismissal of plaintiff's defamation claims against the investigator-defendants. He found three allegations in the amended complaint especially troubling: (1) investigator-defendants contacted an attendant at Mrs. Hawkins' health club and asked him how long he had been having an affair with her; (2) investigator-defendants twice contacted Mrs. Hawkins' minister and informed him that she and her husband were committing insurance fraud; and (3) investigator-defendants contacted Mrs. Hawkins' housekeeper and asked her how much money Mrs. Hawkins was paying her to lie.

Those words, portraying plaintiff as an unfaithful spouse, insurance cheat, and as a suborner of perjury, could amount to actionable defamation unless privileged. . . .

Although defamatory, a statement will not be actionable if it is subject to an absolute or qualified privilege. A statement made in the course of judicial, administrative, or legislative proceedings is absolutely privileged and wholly immune from liability. That immunity is predicated on the need for unfettered expression critical to advancing the underlying government interest at stake in those settings.

The trouble with privileges is that they are granted to good and bad alike. A legislator has an absolute privilege on the floor of a chamber to revile, to defame, or to distort the truth. Invoking the Speech and Debate Clause, U.S. Const. art. I, §6, a lawmaker may use this provision "as a cloak of immunity from prosecution while he [is] smearing the reputations and characters of American citizens whom the Bill of Rights [had] been designed to protect." Albert Coates, *Preserving the Constitution: The Autobiography of Senator Sam Ervin*, 63 N.C. L. Rev. 993, 994 (1985) (book review). We accept such a privilege because it is more important to allow a lawmaker to speak and vote freely on matters of public concern than it is to punish the lawmaker as a rogue. The Speech and Debate Clause protects the integrity of the legislative process by preventing the "intimidation of legislators by the Executive and accountability before a possibly hostile judiciary." Gravel v. United States, 408 U.S. 606 (1972).

A corresponding privilege extends to members of the judiciary in the performance of judicial duties. Few doctrines were more solidly established at common law than the immunity of judges from liability for damages for acts committed within their judicial jurisdiction. . . . This immunity applies even when the judge is accused of acting maliciously and corruptly, and it "is not for the protection or benefit of a malicious or corrupt judge, but for the benefit of the public, whose interest it is that the judges should be at liberty to exercise their functions with independence and without fear of consequences." "The principle of judicial immunity has remained viable in the face of challenges in some very emotionally and politically charged cases."

The extension of an absolute privilege to jurors, witnesses, and parties and their representatives is grounded in similar public-policy concerns. In Fenning v. S.G. Holding Corp., 135 A.2d 346 (App. Div. 1957), the late Chief Justice Hughes, then sitting in the Appellate Division, explained our adherence to the doctrine of litigation immunity:

> The doctrine that an absolute immunity exists in respect of statements, even those defamatory and malicious, made in the course of proceedings before a court of justice, and having some relation thereto, is a principle firmly established, and is responsive to the supervening

public policy that persons in such circumstances be permitted to speak and write freely without the restraint of fear of an ensuing defamation action, this sense of freedom being indispensable to the due administration of justice. . . .

The California Supreme Court set forth a useful formulation of the litigation privilege in Silberg v. Anderson, 786 P.2d 365 (1990). Although California's litigation privilege has been codified, the underlying principles are substantially the same as those underlying the New Jersey privilege. The absolute privilege applies to "any communication (1) made in judicial or quasi-judicial proceedings; (2) by litigants or other participants authorized by law; (3) to achieve the objects of the litigation; and (4) that have some connection or logical relation to the action." Whether a defendant is entitled to the privilege is a question of law. Because the most difficult question in this case is whether investigator-defendants should be considered "litigants" or "other participants authorized by law," we will address that issue last.

1. Were the investigator-defendants' statements made in the course of judicial proceedings?

The litigation privilege is not limited to statements made in a courtroom during a trial; "it extends to all statements or communications in connection with the judicial proceeding." For example, the privilege covers statements made during settlement negotiations. The privilege also protects a person while engaged in a private conference with an attorney regarding litigation. Such application of the privilege affords litigants and witnesses "the utmost freedom of access to the courts without fear of being harassed subsequently by derivative tort actions."

Thus, the privilege extends to "preliminary conversations and interviews between a prospective witness and an attorney if they are in some way related to or connected with a pending or contemplated action." One purpose of the privilege is to encourage "open channels of communication and the presentation of evidence" in judicial proceedings. Such open communication is "a fundamental adjunct to the right of access to judicial and quasi-judicial proceedings." The reason has been well explained:

A witness' apprehension of subsequent damages liability might induce two forms of self-censorship. First, witnesses might be reluctant to come forward to testify. And once a witness is on the stand, his testimony might be distorted by the fear of subsequent liability. Even within the constraints of the witness' oath there may be various ways to give an account or to state an opinion. These alternatives may be more or less detailed and may differ in emphasis and certainty. A witness who knows that he might be forced to defend a subsequent lawsuit, and perhaps to pay damages, might be inclined to shade his testimony in favor of the potential plaintiff, to magnify uncertainties, and thus to deprive the finder of fact of candid, objective, and undistorted evidence. But the truthfinding process is better served if the witness' testimony is submitted to "the crucible of the judicial process so that the factfinder may consider it, after cross-examination, together with the other evidence in the case to determine where the truth lies." Imbler v. Pachtman, 424 US 409 (1976) (White, J., concurring in judgment).

Just as we wish witnesses to have absolute freedom to express the truth as they view it, we wish parties to have an unqualified opportunity to explore the truth of a matter without fear of recrimination.

We are satisfied that the pretrial discussions between the investigator-defendants and the witnesses were made in the course of the underlying personal injury litigation.

2. Were the investigator-defendants' statements made to achieve the objects of the litigation?

Pretrial investigation is "necessary to a thorough and searching investigation of the truth," Van V. Veeder, *Absolute Immunity in Defamation: Judicial Proceedings*, 9 Colum. L. Rev. 463, 477 (1909), and, therefore, essential to the achievement of the objects of litigation. In *Devlin*, 147 N.J. Super. at 458, the court implicitly recognized that the statements of a private investigator made during the course of the proceeding would be covered by the privilege, but found that in the circumstances of that case the investigation was too remote from any anticipated litigation.

The evaluation and investigation of facts and opinions for the purpose of determining what, if anything, is to be raised or used in pending litigation is as integral a part of the search for truth and therefore of the judicial process as is the presentation of such facts and opinions during the course of the trial, either in filed documents or in the courtroom itself.

Pretrial communications by parties and witnesses are protected "to promote the development and free exchange of information and to foster judicial and extra-judicial resolution of disputes."

The investigations took place in the course of the underlying automobile accident litigation. The disputes therefrom were not resolved before trial, but they might have been. We are satisfied that the investigations were undertaken to achieve the objects of the litigation. Whether the statements were made to achieve the objects of the litigation depends on their relationship to the investigation.

3. Did the investigator-defendants' statements have some connection or logical relation to the action?

To be privileged, a defamatory statement must have some relation to the course of the proceedings. "The pertinency thus required is not a technical legal relevancy, such as would, necessarily, justify insertion of the matter in a pleading or its admission into evidence, but rather a general frame of reference and relationship to the subject matter of the action."

That requirement "was never intended as a test of a participant's motives, morals, ethics or intent." So, too, the morals, ethics, and values of the investigators here cannot resolve the issue of relatedness. The question is whether the three statements at issue were in any way relevant to the proceedings. The allegedly defamatory statements concerning insurance fraud and the subornation of a witness were clearly relevant to the underlying litigation. However, we are less certain about the relevance to the proceedings of plaintiff's claimed infidelity. "[E]xtrajudicial defamatory allegations relating to a party's honesty are not sufficiently 'pertinent' to a judicial proceeding to clothe them with an absolute privilege, when the only basis alleged for finding the allegations pertinent is that the defamed party's credibility was at issue." We shall return to the issue of relevancy in our disposition.

4. Were the investigator-defendants "other participants authorized by law"?

Whether investigators are "other participants authorized by law" is the crucial issue. Had an insurance company for the defendants in the underlying litigation conducted the investigations, the company would have been regarded as a participant authorized by law because of its undoubted interest in the outcome of the proceedings. The immunity that attends judicial proceedings "protects both counsel and other representatives who are employed to assist a party in the course of litigation." The privilege protects an attorney's agents and employees in what they do at the attorney's request. Thus, in *Middlesex Concrete Products*, 68 N.J. Super. at 92, the court found that the litigation privilege immunized accusations made by an engineering consultant working for a defendant in a pending lawsuit.

The closest case on point is Leavitt v. Bickerton, 855 F. Supp. 455 (D. Mass. 1994). In that case, the mother of a brain-damaged child had sued the birthing physician for malpractice. During the malpractice action, the mother's attorney sent a letter about the suit to the medical school where the birthing physician taught. The physician, in turn, sued the mother and her attorney for libel. While investigating the libel case, a private investigator working for the physician's attorney interviewed the mother's former employers and suggested that she had used alcohol during the pregnancy. The mother sued the doctor's attorney and investigator for defamation and intentional infliction of emotional distress. The court acknowledged that the investigator "could have used a more tactful method of inquiry or otherwise saved Mrs. Leavitt humiliation and grief," but it concluded that to be privileged the statement "need only be made in the course of judicial proceedings and be, in some way, related to those proceedings." The private investigator's inquiries met those requirements and were therefore privileged. The court concluded:

> Finally, it is of little significance that the statements made to Mrs. Leavitt's former employers were made by a private investigator and not by an attorney. The privilege conferred upon attorneys relates to their function as an advocate on behalf of their client, as is evidenced by the requirement that statements be made in the context of pending or ongoing litigation. Thus, insofar as [the investigator] was engaged in a function which would be protected had it been undertaken by an attorney, he is entitled to absolute immunity while acting as an agent of an attorney.

We believe that that is the correct legal analysis. . . . Just as the legislative privilege extends to the aide of the legislator, *Gravel*, supra, the litigation privilege should extend to the aide of an attorney in the course of legal proceedings.

Because of their extraordinary scope, absolute privileges "have been limited to situations in which authorities have the power both to discipline persons whose statements exceed the bounds of permissible conduct and to strike such statements from the record." Moore v. Smith, 578 P.2d 26, 29 (Wash. 1978). The absolute privilege "does not extend to statements made in situations for which there are no safeguards against abuse." *Demopolis*, supra, 796 P.2d at 430. *See also* Rainier's Dairies v. Raritan Valley Farms, Inc. 117 A.2d 889 (N.J. 1955) ("[I]n strictly judicial proceedings the potential harm which may result from the absolute privilege is somewhat mitigated by the formal requirements such as notice and hearing, the comprehensive control exercised by the trial judge whose action is reviewable on appeal, and the availability of retarding influences such as false swearing and perjury prosecutions. . . .";) "Binkewitz v. Allstate Ins. Co., 537 A.2d 723 (N.J. App.) ("Judges and lawyers answer to their oaths and are subject to discipline for misconduct in court; parties and witnesses speak under oath or similar restraint, and may be punished for irresponsible speech."), certif. denied, 550 A.2d 481 (N.J. 1988). A corresponding burden, then, that flows from the benefits of the privilege is an attorney's ethical and professional responsibility for the conduct of aides. Cf. In re Opinion No. 24, 607 A.2d 962 (N.J. 1992) (reminding attorneys of their responsibility to supervise paralegals, whether employees or independent contractors).

We are satisfied that the privilege should extend to the relevant statements of investigators made in the course of pretrial discovery. Courts have the power and authority to impose sanctions (for example, the suppression of improperly adduced evidence) on parties for an abuse of the discovery process. In addition, some private investigators will be subject to State licensure procedures. Finally, an attorney may be held professionally responsible for a lack of supervision of such investigators.

This litigation immunity, of fourteenth century origin, protects lawyers, judges, witnesses, parties, and jurors. Judith Kilpatrick, *Regulating the Litigation Immunity: New Power and a Breath of Fresh Air for the Attorney Discipline System*, 24 Ariz. St. L.J. 1069, 1072 (1992). "In providing this protection, English courts were concerned that justice would be impaired if those involved in court proceedings could be sued for statements made 'in the discharge of their public duties or in pursuing their rights.'"

Given the importance to our justice system of ensuring free access to the courts, promoting complete and truthful testimony, encouraging zealous advocacy, giving finality to judgments, and avoiding unending litigation, it is not surprising that . . . the litigation privilege[ ] has been referred to as "the backbone to an effective and smoothly operating judicial system."

Those values are at least as important today as they were when the privilege originated 600 years ago. There must be an end to litigation.

The litigation privilege is not, however, a license to defame. A statement is privileged only if it has some relation to the proceeding. Because of the unusual procedural posture of this case, the trial court may not have fully considered the relevance to the underlying litigation of the investigator's alleged suggestion of plaintiff's adultery. That issue is not before us on this appeal.

The judgment of the Appellate Division is affirmed.

PREPARING FOR CLASS

1. What is the effect of an absolute privilege?

2. Broadly, when do absolute privileges arise? What do the various absolute privileges have in common?

3. When does the litigation privilege arise?

4. Could the defendant meet each part of the test for the litigation privilege?

5. How is this case like *Leavitt v. Bickerton*?

6. If the privileges are absolute, do they have no limitations?

INCREASING YOUR UNDERSTANDING

1. *The legislative privilege.* As mentioned in *Hawkins*, the legislative privilege is based on the "Speech and Debate Clause" of the U.S. Constitution. The Supreme Court has interpreted this privilege to extend beyond speech and debate on the floor of Congress. Members of the U.S. Congress are absolutely privileged to make defamatory statements in their legislative activities. In the *Gravel* case, also referred to in *Hawkins*, the Court stated that the Speech and Debate Clause reaches matters that are "an integral part of the deliberative and communicative processes by which Members participate in committee and House proceedings with respect to the consideration and passage or rejection of proposed legislation or with respect to other matters which the Constitution places within the jurisdiction of either house." Gravel v. United States, 408 U.S. 606 (1972).

    The legislative privilege did and did not protect Senator William Proxmire when he was sued for awarding a "Golden Fleece of the Month Award" to a research scientist for wasteful use of government funding. When the Senator read his speech awarding the "prize" to the scientist on the Senate floor, he was privileged. But when he circulated that speech to the media and in a newsletter to his constituents, he was not. The press release and newsletter were not "essential to the deliberations of the Senate" nor were they "part of the deliberative process." Hutchinson v. Proxmire, 443 U.S. 111 (1979).

2. *The executive privilege.* The Federal Torts Claims Act immunizes individual federal government employees for torts in the scope of their employment. Although the Act substitutes the government as a defendant for the individual employees, the Act also contains a list of torts for which the federal government is itself immune. That list includes libel and slander. 28 U.S.C. §2680(h). States take a variety of approaches to the executive privilege for state officials. Some do not recognize immunity. Others limit the immunity to high-ranking officials. Yet others shield employees for defamation that occurs within the "outer perimeter" of their duties. See Kendrick v. Fox Television, 659 A.2d 814 (D.C. Ct. App. 1995).

2. *Conditional Privilege*

Gohari v. Darvish
767 A.2d 321 (Md. 2001)

HARRELL, J.

[The plaintiff, Gohari, was senior vice president of Darcars Automotive Group, owned by Darvish, the defendant. Gohari quit his job and entered into an agreement to buy his own Toyota dealership, which would be a competitor with a Toyota dealership owned by Darvish. To complete the transaction, Gohari needed the approval of Central Atlantic Toyota Distributors (CATD). CATD sought out Darvish for his input on Gohari's qualifications to operate a franchise. Darvish described Gohari as unqualified because of inexperience, unprofessional behavior, dishonesty, and lack of people skills, among other considerations. As a result, CATD refused to approve the contract unless Gohari recruited a qualified general manager, and the deal fell through because Gohari could not do so in time. At trial, Gohari won defamation and interference with contract claims against Darvish, who appealed. The appellate court reversed, stating that Darvish was entitled to assert the qualified privilege defense at trial. That decision led to Gohari's appeal.]

Petitioner contends that no qualified privilege protects a business owner's defamatory statements about a former employee who seeks to enter a directly competitive business arrangement with a third party, in this case a potential common franchisor. Respondent argues that the Court of Special Appeals "correctly held that the common law affords a qualified privilege to a franchisee who gives information about a former employee to his franchisor at the franchisor's request, just as it protects communications in other business and employment-related contexts." We agree with Respondent and the Court of Special Appeals.

A defendant, in a defamation suit, may assert a qualified, or conditional, privilege. See generally Dan B. Dobbs, *The Law of Torts*, §§413-414 (2000) [hereinafter *The Law of Torts*]. As the Court of Special Appeals succinctly stated, "[t]here are circumstances in which a person will not be held liable for a defamatory statement because the person is acting 'in furtherance of some interest of social importance, which is entitled protection.'"

In Marchesi v. Franchino, 283 Md. 131, 387 A.2d 1129 (1978), we explained:

> The common law conditional privileges rest upon the notion that a defendant may escape liability for an otherwise actionable defamatory statement, if publication of the utterance advances social policies of greater importance than the vindication of a plaintiff's reputational interest. . . . Specifically, the common law recognized that a person ought to be shielded against civil liability for defamation where, in good faith, he publishes a statement in furtherance of his own legitimate interests, or those shared in common with the recipient or third parties, or where his declaration would be of interest to the public in general.

. . . The Court of Special Appeals also was correct in concluding that the common law qualified privilege applied in the present case. The common law conditional privilege is broad and may apply to "an infinite variety of factual circumstances." . . . Though we have not recognized before a qualified privilege applicable to communications in a franchisor/franchisee relationship, we determine, taking into consideration the breadth of the privilege, that it is available as a defense in such circumstances.

According to one scholar, there are four basic common law qualified privileges:

> (1) The public interest privilege, to publish materials to public officials on matters within their public responsibility; (2) the privilege to publish to someone who shares a common interest, or, relatedly, to publish in defense of oneself or in the interest of others; (3) the fair comment privilege; and (4) the privilege to make a fair and accurate report of public proceedings.

The Law of Torts §413, at 1158. . . .

The conditional privilege at issue in the present case involves Professor Dobbs's subsection, supra, (2) "the privilege to publish to someone who shares a common interest, or, relatedly, to publish in defense of oneself or in the interest of others." The standard for common interest is the following:

> An occasion is conditionally privileged when the circumstances are such as to lead any one of several persons having a common interest in a particular subject matter correctly or reasonably to believe that facts exist which another sharing such common interest is entitled to know.

Hanrahan, 305 A.2d at 156. In determining what qualifies as a common interest, we have stated that a common interest may include "interests in property, business and professional dealings," and can "inhere in business dealings between the publisher and the recipient." Dobbs has elaborated:

> Common interests are usually found among members of identifiable groups in which members share similar goals or values or cooperate in a single endeavor. . . . The idea is to promote free exchange of relevant information among those engaged in a common enterprise or activity and to permit them to make appropriate internal communications and share consultations without fear of suit. . . . The privilege does not arise in the first place unless the communication relates in some degree to the common interest, and once the privilege arises it is lost if it is abused by malice or excessive publication.

The Law of Torts, §414, at 1160-61.

The record in the present case demonstrates a common interest shared by CATD/franchisor and Darvish/franchisee for they share in "business and professional dealings." It was undoubtedly in CATD's business interest to receive an accurate, full, and truthful assessment of the qualifications of a proposed franchisee candidate to operate one of its franchises. A logical person to give such an assessment might be someone like Darvish-Gohari's former employer and an existing franchisee of Toyota, CATD's principal. Furthermore, conceptually it would be in Darvish's professional interest to answer candidly as Darvish must deal with CATD and Toyota on an ongoing basis as a Toyota franchisee. For example, Darvish "reports his sales to CATD and requests inventory from CATD, and it is CATD which, as in this case, holds approval power over the potential sale or transfer of a Toyota franchise." Thus, there is a common interest in maintaining a candid business relationship in furtherance of the franchisee's individual success and the overall success of the franchisor.

We perceive also that a need "to publish . . . in the interest of others" arguably is present in this case. The rule regarding the protection of interest of the recipient or a third person has been explained as follows:

> (1) An occasion makes a publication conditionally privileged if the circumstances induce a correct or reasonable belief that
>
> > (a) there is information that affects a sufficiently important interest of the recipient or a third person, and
> > (b) the recipient is one to whom the publisher is under a legal duty to publish the defamatory matter or is a person to whom its publication is otherwise within the generally accepted standards of decent conduct.
>
> (2) In determining whether a publication is within generally accepted standards of decent conduct it is an important factor that

(a) the publication is made in response to a request rather than volunteered by the publisher or

(b) a family or other relationship exists between the parties.

Restatement (Second) of Torts §595.

It seems patent that information regarding Gohari's qualifications would be important to CATD and Toyota. The information supplied by Darvish also appears to have been supplied within generally accepted standards of decent conduct. The comment regarding subsection (1) of the Restatement states that "a statement made for the protection of a lawful business, professional, property or other pecuniary interest . . . comes within the rule stated in this Section." Restatement (Second) of Torts §595, at 270. Additionally, the comment states that "[i]t is enough that the circumstances are such as to lead to the reasonable belief that the third person's interest is in danger." The statements made by Darvish regarding Gohari's abilities to operate a Toyota franchise fall here.

When considering whether Darvish acted within generally accepted standards of decent conduct, it is important to look at the circumstances of the present case and "[t]he social value of the particular interest of the third person that is believed to be imperiled, the value of the communication as a means of protection if the defamatory matter is true, the probable harm to the person defamed if the defamatory matter is false, and the fact that the publication is made in response to a request." The fact that the communication is made in response to a request is of particular importance:

> The fact that the recipient has made the request is an indication that he, at least, regards the matter in respect to which information is desired as sufficiently important to justify the publication of any defamatory matter than may be involved in response to the request. In that case, the person requested to give information is not required nicely to evaluate the interest that the person making the request seeks to protect, nor to make that comparison otherwise required of him, between the harm likely to be done to the other's reputation if the defamatory matter is false and the harm likely to be done to the third person's interest if the it should prove true.

Restatement (Second) of Torts §595, at 273-74.

In the present case, Darvish was approached by CATD to provide his assessment of his former employee's, Gohari's, qualifications as the prospective owner-operator of a Toyota dealership. CATD approached Darvish after receiving Gohari's express permission to do so. Moreover, Gohari's Toyota dealership application permitted CATD to obtain information from other sources about his "character, general reputation and credit history" and to "obtain and share information . . . from and with any of its affiliated entities." . . .

Lastly, Petitioner argues that there can be no qualified privilege because "Darvish, as Gohari's potential competitor, had a powerful interest in destroying Gohari's chances of entering into the same sort of contract with CATD and acquiring his own Toyota dealership," and thus, "[n]o 'social polic[ies]' . . . are advanced by applying a qualified privilege under such circumstances; to the contrary, a qualified privilege would only injure competition and protect individuals whose self-interest lies in defaming innocent parties." We agree that the potential competitive interest of Darvish should not be disregarded. . . .

Whether Respondent made the statements, assuming them to be false for present analysis, because of his competitive interest becomes part of the evaluation concerning whether the qualified privilege has been abused. The Court of Special Appeals correctly reasoned that

> appellee "has the right notwithstanding the privileged character of the communication to go to the jury, if there be evidence tending to show actual malice, as where the words unreasonably impute crime, or the occasion of their utterance is such as to indicate, by its unnecessary publicity or otherwise, a purpose wrongfully to defame the plaintiff. . . . Or, malice may be established by showing that the publication contained matter not relevant to the occasion. . . . Expressions in excess of what the occasion warrants do not per se take away the privilege, but such evidence may be excess of malice. . . ."

Furthermore, "[w]hile the question of whether a defamatory communication enjoys a conditional privilege is one of law for the court, whether it has been forfeited by malice is usually a question for the jury." Therefore, any competitive interest bias, if supported by evidence, could be the subject of a jury instruction and jury determination as to whether Respondent abused his qualified privilege. . . . In short, Respondent may lose the qualified privilege recognized here if Petitioner demonstrates that "the publication is made for a purpose other than to further the social interest entitled to protection . . . or can prove malice on the part of the publisher." . . .

Judgment of the Court of Special Appeals affirmed; Petitioner to pay the costs.

PREPARING FOR CLASS

1. How are qualified (or conditional) privileges different from absolute privileges?

2. Generally, when do qualified privileges arise?

3. Which kind of qualified privilege is at issue in this case? Could the defendant establish it?

4. What other qualified privilege might be relevant? Could the defendant establish it?

5. How are qualified privileges lost? Does the plaintiff have an argument that this privilege was lost?

6. What are the roles of judge and jury on the issue of qualified privileges?

APPLYING THE LAW

1. A law professor received a letter from the Michiana State Bar asking whether John Doe had the requisite character and fitness to practice law. The professor remembered a John Doe who was in her class and who had sexually harassed a classmate and been suspended for a term for cheating on an exam, and she reported this to the Michiana State Bar, which did not admit John Doe. The professor had had two John Does in class, a year apart. The professor's statements were accurate regarding one of the John Does, just not the one she was asked to comment on. As to him, they were false. The professor had forgotten there was a different John Doe. Could the professor successfully raise a conditional privilege defense against a defamation suit from the John Doe she prevented from being admitted to the Michiana Bar?

2. Believing (incorrectly, as it turned out) that a middle-manager had been pilfering from petty cash and engaging in other improper activities, a mid-sized manufacturing business fired him. The business was concerned that other middle-managers would interpret the firing as a sign that cut-backs in middle-management were ahead because of hard economic times and that this would affect the morale of the middle-managers and their job performance. Therefore, the business called a company-wide meeting to explain why the middle-manager had been fired. At the meeting were factory employees, secretaries, accountants, janitors, and sales representatives, as well as the middle-managers. The fired middle-manager sued for defamation. Were the statements at the meeting privileged?

3. Statute of Limitations

Nationwide Bi-Weekly Admin., Inc. v. Belo Corp.
512 F.3d 137 (5th Cir. 2007)

DeMoss, C.J.

Nationwide Bi-Weekly Administration ("Nationwide") brought defamation and related claims against Belo Corp., The Dallas Morning News, and writer Scott Burns (collectively referred to as "Belo") based on an allegedly defamatory article that appeared in The Dallas Morning News. The district court granted Belo's Rule 12(b)(6) motion to dismiss on statute of limitations grounds and Nationwide appealed to this court. For the reasons stated below, we affirm.

On July 29, 2003, The Dallas Morning News published an article criticizing a particular mortgage program offered by Nationwide. The article first appeared in a financial column written by Scott Burns in the newspaper's print edition and was subsequently made available on its website. The Dallas Morning News website is readily accessible on the Internet by entering the proper Internet address or by using a standard Internet search engine. . . .

Texas has adopted a one-year statute of limitations for libel claims. See Tex. Civ. Prac. & Rem. Code §16.002(a). The one-year limitations period begins to run when publication of the libelous statement is complete, which is "the last day of the mass distribution of copies of the printed matter." Holloway v. Butler, 662 S.W.2d 688, 692 (Tex. App.—Houston [14th Dist.] 1983, writ ref'd n.r.e.). "On that date, the publisher of the statement has made the libelous matter available to his intended audience and the tort is complete." Stephan v. Baylor Med. Ctr. at Garland, 20 S.W.3d 880, 889 (Tex. App.—Dallas 2000, no pet.). Because the period begins to run on the date the publication is complete, this rule is commonly referred to as the "single publication rule."

An important purpose of the single publication rule is to prevent plaintiffs from bringing stale and repetitive defamation claims against publishers. As a result, retail sales of individual copies after the publication date and sales of back issues do not trigger a new limitations period. However, separate printings of the original content are considered subsequent publications. *Stephan*, 20 S.W.3d at 889 (reasoning that in the case of separate printings "it is apparent that the publisher intends to reach different audiences and this intention justifies a new cause of action").

It is uncontested that The Dallas Morning News published the allegedly defamatory article in its July 29, 2003 print edition, and that Nationwide filed its complaint on July 28, 2004—within the allowed period. However, "the mere [timely] filing of a suit will not interrupt or toll the running of a statute of limitation; to interrupt the statute, the use of diligence in procuring the issuance and service of citation is required." Nationwide failed to serve Belo until June 2005, more than 10 months after filing suit. The district court, citing this lengthy and unexplained delay, found that Nationwide failed to exercise due diligence in serving Belo and dismissed the suit on statute of limitations grounds. . . .

On appeal, Nationwide does not appear to challenge the proposition that, if its claim rested solely on publication of the article in the print edition, its claim is barred. Nationwide instead argues that the article's availability on The Dallas Morning News website mandates a different result. This is so, according to Nationwide, because each time a viewer accesses the article from the website a "republication" occurs for statute of limitations purposes. This concept, widely argued but virtually always rejected, is referred to as the "continuous publication rule." . . .

Texas courts have not yet considered whether the single publication rule should apply to Internet publications. . . . In considering decisions from other jurisdictions, we have found only one that applied the continuous publication rule. *See* Swafford v. Memphis Individual Practice Ass'n, 1998 WL 281935 (Tenn. Ct. App. June 2, 1998). Nationwide believes the Texas Supreme Court would be inclined to follow *Swafford's* lead and hold that each time a reader accesses the article on The Dallas Morning News website a new publication occurs. However, our reading of *Swafford* and subsequent cases fails to persuade us that Texas would adopt its holding here.

Swafford involved a restricted-access online database containing information about individual doctors. The database allegedly provided defamatory information about an individual doctor to health care facilities who requested his information. The Tennessee Court of Appeals, reasoning that the database limited access to authorized users and only released information in response to "an affirmative request by a hospital," refused to apply the single publication rule. The court noted that no "aggregate publication" occurs when users of the database request information, and thus, "the justification for the single publication rule, a vast multiplicity of lawsuits resulting from a mass publication, is simply not present."

Swafford is factually distinguishable from the case at bar. The information at issue in *Swafford* was not publicly available and "could hardly be considered an aggregate communication comparable to typical Internet publication." Oja v. U.S. Army Corps of Eng'rs, 440 F.3d 1122, 1133 (9th Cir. 2006) (discussing *Swafford*). In contrast, the article at issue here was undisputably posted on the website and made widely available to the public via the Internet. This distinction is material because, as *Swafford* itself noted, a primary purpose of the single publication rule is to prevent the multiplicity of suits that may follow widespread dissemination.

In addition to this factual distinction, we are influenced by the fact that apparently no court has followed *Swafford*. However, a number of cases have refused to follow *Swafford* and have applied the single publication rule to Internet publications. Of these, perhaps the most influential is Firth v. State, 775 N.E.2d 463, 466 (N.Y. App. 2002).

In *Firth*, the plaintiff sued the publisher of an investigative report that was published on the Internet. The plaintiff argued that because the report was constantly available on the Internet, each day resulted in a new publication of the report. The New York Court of Appeals, after considering the competing policy arguments, held that "a multiple publication rule would implicate an even greater potential for endless retriggering of the statute of limitations, multiplicity of suits and harassment of defendants." Further, the court recognized that if it applied the continuous publication rule "[i]nevitably, there would be a serious inhibitory effect on the open, pervasive dissemination of information and ideas over the Internet, which is, of course, its greatest beneficial promise." Thus, the court held the single publication rule applies to Internet publications.

Every court to consider the issue after *Firth* has followed suit in holding that the single publication rule applies to information widely available on the Internet. Given that every case to consider the issue has applied the single publication rule to publicly available Internet articles, it is clearly the majority approach. Furthermore, we find the rationale behind the widespread acceptance of the single publication rule in the Internet context persuasive.

For example, some courts have reasoned that the "functional similarities between print and Internet publication" support application of the single publication rule to both types of media. As one court noted, "A statement electronically located on a server which is called up when a web page is accessed, is no different from a statement on a paper page in a book lying on a shelf which is accessed by the reader when the book is opened." *Mitan*, 243 F. Supp. 2d at 724. While we recognize that important differences exist between print media and the Internet, we agree that the similarities between the two media support application of a consistent rule.

Nationwide attempts to distinguish Internet publication, where editors can easily alter or remove content, from print media where publishers "relinquish all right of control, title, and interest in the printed matter" upon publication. In *Oja*, the Ninth Circuit rejected a similar argument:

> It is true that an Internet publisher may have greater control over the availability of content posted on its server than a print publisher has over its printed stock; however, that fact alone does not corrupt the analogy between Internet and print publication, given that the single publication rule generally applies to books in a publisher's stock that could have been withdrawn following their initial availability for sale but were not.

In other words, a website's control over its content is akin to a publisher's control over its stock. When a publisher continues to make an allegedly defamatory book available from its stock, courts have held that action does not constitute republication, even though the publisher could have withdrawn the book. Likewise, the continued availability of an article on a website should not result in republication, despite the website's ability to remove it.

Perhaps more important than the similarities between print media and the Internet, strong policy considerations support application of the single publication rule to information publicly available on the Internet. See *Firth*, 775 N.E.2d at 466 (discussing the "potential for endless retriggering of the statute of limitations, multiplicity of suits and harassment of defendants" and warning of a corresponding chilling effect on Internet communication). We agree that these policy considerations favor application of the single publication rule here and we note that application of the rule in this context appears consistent with the policies cited by Texas courts in adopting and applying the single publication rule to print media: to support the statute of limitations and to prevent the filing of stale claims.

Nationwide points out several competing public policy arguments. First, "the publication of defamatory and private information on the web has the potential to be vastly more offensive and harmful than it might otherwise be in a more circumscribed publication." To the extent this argument is based on the fact that more people will be exposed to Internet publications because those publications are likely accessible for a potentially indefinite period, we feel it is outweighed by the competing policy interests of enforcing the statute of limitations and preventing stale claims. To the extent this argument is premised on the fact that an Internet publication has the potential to reach more people because of broader readership (without any temporal component), it is likely relevant only to the issue of damages, not to the triggering of the statute of limitations. . . .

Based on the near unanimity of the large number of courts to apply the single publication rule to Internet publications, the fact that the only case to hold otherwise (*Swafford*) is distinguishable, and because sound policy reasons support its application in this context, we hold that the Texas Supreme Court would likely adopt the single publication rule for Internet publications.

Applying the single publication rule here, the statute of limitations began to run on July 29, 2003, the date the initial print publication was complete. . . .

Affirmed.

PREPARING FOR CLASS

1. What was Nationwide's lawyer's biggest mistake? How did the lawyer try to avoid the consequences of that mistake?

2. Let's ignore for a moment the issue raised by the Internet publication. Without it, when would the statute of limitations have run on the case? What if a company that did business with Nationwide did not read the article until a month after it ran—would the clock start ticking then?

3. What is the single-publication rule? What are the policies behind it?

4. How did Nationwide argue that the single-publication rule did not apply? If it did not apply, what would that mean for Nationwide?

5. Why does the court find *Swafford* inapplicable?

6. Why is *Firth* the better analogy?

INCREASING YOUR UNDERSTANDING

The First Restatement of Torts had followed the English rule that every time a copy of a newspaper, book, or magazine was sold a distinct publication occurred, creating a separate cause of action with its own statute of limitations period. By the time the Second Restatement of Torts was written, the majority of American courts had rejected the English rule and followed the single-publication rule described in the *Nationwide* case, and the Restatement followed suit. The rule does not only create one statute of limitations period, it creates one cause of action. So when the plaintiff is defamed in the defendant's magazine, which is published in all 50 United States, plaintiff has one case. Republication of the defamatory matter, though, creates a new cause of action with a statute of limitations that begins running with the republication. Therefore, the morning and evening editions of a newspaper are two separate publications, as are the 6:00 P.M. and 10:00 P.M. airings of a news story on television. When the paperback edition of a hardcover book is released, that is a new publication. When a new printing of a book occurs, that is a new publication.

Chapter 21

Invasion of Privacy

Four torts come under the invasion-of-privacy umbrella: public disclosure of private facts, intrusion into seclusion, false light, and appropriation. Courts trace the origin of a right to be let alone to an 1890 Harvard Law Review article by Louis Brandeis and Samuel Warren, who, as Professor Dobbs has said, "proposed a new tort to protect privacy against the trashier interests of both the press and its readers." Dan B. Dobbs, *The Law of Torts*, p. 1197. The Warren and Brandeis article did not, however, propose the four distinct torts. Credit for that goes to Dean Prosser in Privacy, 48 Calif. L. Rev. 381 (1960). As you read this chapter, consider whether the torts provide relief for Piper Paxton against Del Dawson on the facts in the following problem:

Paxton vs. Dawson

Piper Paxton was one of the victims of a tragic nightclub fire that injured more than a 100 people and killed 50. She suffers from permanent lung damage, hair loss, and severe scarring on the right side of her body, including her face. Once beautiful, she is now extremely self-conscious of how she looks. She is a plaintiff in two lawsuits arising from the fire.

Del Dawson has created a Web site, www.remembergallery.com, devoted to the tragedy. One section profiles people who were injured or died in the fire. Del has sold banner advertising on these pages to an insurance company and a home health-care provider.

Piper's profile includes past and current photographs of her. Del obtained the past photograph by finding Piper's high-school yearbook picture in the library. He obtained the current photograph by parking outside the courthouse on the day of an important hearing. (He was able to photograph many key figures at once that way.) With his telephoto lens, Del snapped several pictures of Piper. He used the one in which a breeze lifted the hair in her wig away from her face and fully revealed her startling scars.

Piper's profile also includes a brief biography, which includes this statement: "Piper was a vibrant woman, but now she is utterly helpless." Del based this on following Piper around for a few days and noticing that she never drove herself, was always attached to a portable oxygen tank, and always had a companion to help her with her errands. Although Piper is quite weak and needs help, she also continues to do bookkeeping from her home, tends to all her personal hygiene without assistance, and does her own light housework.

A. PUBLIC DISCLOSURE OF PRIVATE FACTS

Shulman v. Group W Productions, Inc.
955 P.2d 469 (Cal. 1998)

Werdergar, J.

More than 100 years ago, Louis Brandeis and Samuel Warren complained that the press, armed with the then recent invention of "instantaneous photographs" and under the influence of new "business methods," was "overstepping in every direction the obvious bounds of propriety and of decency." (Warren & Brandeis, *The Right to Privacy* (1890) 4 Harv. L. Rev. 193, 195-196.) Even more ominously, they noted the "numerous mechanical devices" that "threaten to make good the prediction that 'what is whispered in the closet shall be proclaimed from the house-tops.'" Today, of course, the newspapers of 1890 have been joined by the electronic media; today, a vast number of books, journals, television and radio stations, cable channels and Internet content sources all compete to satisfy our thirst for knowledge and our need for news of political, economic and cultural events — as well as our love of gossip, our curiosity about the private lives of others, and "that weak side of human nature which is never wholly cast down by the misfortunes and frailties of our neighbors." Moreover, the "devices" available for recording and transmitting what would otherwise be private have multiplied and improved in ways the 19th century could hardly imagine.

Over the same period, the United States has also seen a series of revolutions in mores and conventions that has moved, blurred and, at times, seemingly threatened to erase the line between public and private life. While even in their day Brandeis and Warren complained that "the details of sexual relations are spread broadcast in the columns of the daily papers," today's public discourse is particularly notable for its detailed and graphic discussion of intimate personal and family matters — sometimes as topics of legitimate public concern, sometimes as simple titillation. More generally, the dominance of the visual image in contemporary culture and the technology that makes it possible to capture and, in an instant, universally disseminate a picture or sound allows us, and leads us to expect, to see and hear what our great-grand-parents could have known only through written description.

The sense of an ever-increasing pressure on personal privacy notwith-standing, it has long been apparent that the desire for privacy must at many points give way before our right to know, and the news media's right to inves-tigate and relate, facts about the events and individuals of our time. . . .

On June 24, 1990, plaintiffs Ruth and Wayne Shulman, mother and son, were injured when the car in which they and two other family members were riding on interstate 10 in Riverside County flew off the highway and tumbled down an embankment into a drainage ditch on state-owned property, coming to rest upside down. Ruth, the [more] seriously injured of the two, was pinned under the car. Ruth and Wayne both had to be cut free from the vehicle by the device known as "the jaws of life."

A rescue helicopter operated by Mercy Air was dispatched to the scene. The flight nurse, who would perform the medical care at the scene and on the way to the hospital, was Laura Carnahan. Also on board were the pilot, a medic and Joel Cooke, a video camera operator employed by defendants Group W Productions, Inc., and 4MN Productions. Cooke was recording the rescue operation for later broadcast.

Cooke roamed the accident scene, videotaping the rescue. Nurse Carnahan wore a wireless microphone that picked up her conversations with both Ruth and the other rescue personnel. Cooke's tape was edited into a piece approx-imately nine minutes long, which, with the addition of narrative voice-over, was broadcast on September 29, 1990, as a segment of *On Scene: Emergency Response.* . . .

While Ruth is still trapped under the car, Carnahan asks Ruth's age. Ruth responds, "I'm old." On further questioning, Ruth reveals she is 47, and Car-nahan observes that "it's all relative. You're not that old." During her extrica-tion from the car, Ruth asks at least twice if she is dreaming. At one point she asks Carnahan, who has told her she will be taken to the hospital in a helicopter: "Are you teasing?" At another point she says: "This is terrible. Am I dreaming?" She also asks what happened and where the rest of her family is, repeating the questions even after being told she was in an accident and the other family members are being cared for. While being loaded into the helicopter on a stretcher, Ruth says: "I just want to die." Carnahan reassures her that she is "going to do real well," but Ruth repeats: "I just want to die. I don't want to go through this."

Ruth and Wayne are placed in the helicopter, and its door is closed. . . . Carnahan, speaking into what appears to be a radio microphone, transmits some of Ruth's vital signs and states that Ruth cannot move her feet and has no sensation. The video footage during the helicopter ride includes a few seconds of Ruth's face, covered by an oxygen mask. Wayne is neither shown nor heard.

The helicopter lands on the hospital roof. With the door open, Ruth states while being taken out: "My upper back hurts." Carnahan replies: "Your upper back hurts. That's what you were saying up there." Ruth states: "I don't feel that great." Carnahan responds: "You probably don't."

Finally, Ruth is shown being moved from the helicopter into the hospital. . . .

The accident left Ruth a paraplegic. When the segment was broadcast, Wayne phoned Ruth in her hospital room and told her to turn on the television because "Channel 4 is showing our accident now." Shortly afterward, several hospital workers came into the room to mention that a videotaped segment of her accident was being shown. Ruth was "shocked, so to speak, that this would be run and I would be exploited, have my privacy invaded, which is what I felt had happened." She did not know her rescue had been recorded in this manner and had never consented to the recording or broadcast. . . . Asked at deposition what part of the broadcast material she considered private, Ruth explained: "I think the whole scene was pretty private. It was pretty gruesome, . . . and it's not for the public to see this trauma that I was going through."

Ruth and Wayne sued the producers of *On Scene: Emergency Response*, as well as others. The first amended complaint included two causes of action for invasion of privacy, one based on defendants' unlawful intrusion by videotaping the rescue in the first instance and the other based on the public disclosure of private facts, i.e., the broadcast. . . .

The trial court granted the media defendants' summary judgment motion, basing its ruling on plaintiffs' admissions that the accident and rescue were matters of public interest and public affairs. . . .

The Court of Appeal reversed and remanded for further proceedings, but on limited grounds and as to some causes of action only. . . .

Influenced by Dean Prosser's analysis of the tort actions for invasion of privacy (Prosser, *Privacy* (1960) 48 Cal. L. Rev. 381) and the exposition of a similar analysis in the Restatement Second of Torts sections 652A-652E (further references to the Restatement are to the Restatement Second of Torts), California courts have recognized both of the privacy causes of action pleaded by plaintiffs here: (1) public disclosure of private facts, and (2) intrusion into private places, conversations or other matters. . . .

I. Publication of Private Facts

The claim that a publication has given unwanted publicity to allegedly private aspects of a person's life is one of the more commonly litigated and well-defined areas of privacy law. In Diaz v. Oakland Tribune, Inc., 139 Cal. App. 3d at page 126, 188 Cal. Rptr. 762, the appellate court accurately discerned the following elements of the public disclosure tort: "(1) public disclosure (2) of a private fact (3) which would be offensive and objectionable to the reasonable person and (4) which is not of legitimate public concern." That formulation does not differ significantly from the Restatement's, which provides that "[o]ne who gives publicity to a matter concerning the private life of another is subject to liability to the other for invasion of his privacy, if the matter publicized is of a kind that (a) would be highly offensive to a reasonable person, and (b) is not of legitimate concern to the public." (Rest. 2d Torts, §652D.) . . .

Diaz . . . expressly makes the lack of newsworthiness part of the plaintiff's case in a private facts action. . . .

We therefore agree with defendants that under California common law the dissemination of truthful, newsworthy material is not actionable as a publication of private facts. If the contents of a broadcast or publication are of legitimate public concern, the plaintiff cannot establish a necessary element of the tort action, the lack of newsworthiness. To so state, however, is merely to begin the necessary legal inquiry, not to end it. It is in the determination of newsworthiness—in deciding whether published or broadcast material is of legitimate public concern—that courts must struggle most directly to accommodate the conflicting interests of individual privacy and press freedom.

Although we speak of the lack of newsworthiness as an element of the private facts tort, newsworthiness is at the same time a constitutional defense to, or privilege against, liability for publication of truthful information. Indeed, the danger of interference with constitutionally protected press freedom has been and remains an ever-present consideration for courts and commentators struggling to set the tort's parameters, and the requirements of tort law and the Constitution have generally been assumed to be congruent. Little is to be gained, therefore, in attempting to keep rigorously separate the tort and constitutional issues as regards newsworthiness, and we have not attempted to do so here. Tort liability, obviously, can extend no further than the First Amendment allows; conversely, we see no reason or authority for fashioning the newsworthiness element of the private facts tort to preclude liability where the Constitution would allow it.

Delineating the exact contours of the constitutional privilege of the press in publication of private facts is, however, particularly problematic, because this privilege has not received extensive attention from the United States Supreme Court. The high court has considered the issue in only one case involving the common law public disclosure tort, Cox Broadcasting Corp. v. Cohn (1975) 420 U.S. 469, and its holding in that case was deliberately and explicitly narrow. In *Cox Broadcasting*, a criminal court clerk, during a recess in court proceedings relating to a rape-murder case, allowed a television reporter to see the indictment, which contained the name of the victim. The television station broadcast an account of the court proceedings, using the victim's name; the victim's father alleged the broadcast to be a tortious publication of private facts. The Georgia Supreme Court, relying on a Georgia statute prohibiting publication or broadcast of a rape victim's identity, held the broadcast of the victim's name was not privileged as newsworthy; the court viewed the statute as showing that the victim's identity was not a matter of legitimate public concern. The state court further held the statute did not itself infringe on the station's First Amendment rights.

The federal high court reversed, but—recognizing the important interests on both sides of the newsworthiness question—proceeded cautiously and on limited grounds. "Rather than address the broader question of whether truthful publications may ever be subjected to civil or criminal liability consistently with the First and Fourteenth Amendments, or to put it another way, whether the State may ever define and protect an area of privacy free from unwanted publicity in the press, it is appropriate to focus on the narrower interface between press and privacy that this case presents, namely, whether the State may impose sanctions on the accurate publication of the name of a rape victim obtained from public records—more specifically, from judicial records which are maintained in connection with a public prosecution and which themselves are open to public inspection. We are convinced that the State may not do so." . . . [T]he high court's decisions . . . establish that truthful reporting on current judicial proceedings, using material drawn from public records, is generally within the scope of constitutional protection. The decisions do not, however, enunciate a general test of newsworthiness applicable to other factual circumstances or provide a broad theoretical basis for discovery of such a general constitutional standard.

Newsworthiness—constitutional or common law—is also difficult to define because it may be used as either a descriptive or a normative term. "Is the term 'newsworthy' a descriptive predicate, intended to refer to the fact there is widespread public interest? Or is it a value predicate, intended to indicate that the publication is a meritorious contribution and that the public's interest is praiseworthy?" (Comment, *The Right of Privacy: Normative-Descriptive Confusion in the Defense of Newsworthiness* (1963) 30 U. Chi. L. Rev. 722, 725.) A position at either extreme has unpalatable consequences. If "newsworthiness" is completely descriptive—if all coverage that sells papers or boosts ratings is deemed newsworthy—it would seem to swallow the publication of private facts tort, for "it would be difficult to suppose that publishers were in the habit of reporting occurrences of little interest." At the other extreme, if newsworthiness is viewed as a purely normative concept, the courts could become to an unacceptable degree editors of the news and self-appointed guardians of public taste.

The difficulty of finding a workable standard in the middle ground between the extremes of normative and descriptive analysis, and the variety of factual circumstances in which the issue has been presented, have led to considerable variation in judicial descriptions of the newsworthiness concept. . . .

First, the analysis of newsworthiness does involve courts to some degree in a normative assessment of the "social value" of a publication. All material that might attract readers or viewers is not, simply by virtue of its attractiveness, of *legitimate* public interest. Second, the evaluation of newsworthiness depends on the degree of intrusion and the extent to which the plaintiff played an important role in public events, and thus on a comparison between the information revealed and the nature of the activity or event that brought the plaintiff to public attention. "Some reasonable proportion is . . . to be maintained between the events or activity that makes the individual a public figure and the private facts to which publicity is given. Revelations that may properly be made concerning a murderer or the President of the United States would not be privileged if they were to be made concerning one who is merely injured in an automobile accident." (Rest. 2d Torts, §652D, com. h.)

Courts balancing these interests in cases similar to this have recognized that, when a person is involuntarily involved in a newsworthy incident, not all aspects of the person's life, and not everything the person says or does, is thereby rendered newsworthy. . . .

[N]o mode of analyzing newsworthiness can be applied mechanically or without consideration of its proper boundaries. To observe that the newsworthiness of private facts about a person involuntarily thrust into the public eye depends, in the ordinary case, on the existence of a logical nexus between the newsworthy event or activity and the facts revealed is not to deny that the balance of free press and privacy interests may require a different conclusion when the intrusiveness of the revelation is greatly disproportionate to its relevance. Intensely personal or intimate revelations might not, in a given case, be considered newsworthy, especially where they bear only slight relevance to a topic of legitimate public concern. . . .

Turning now to the case at bar, we consider whether the possibly private facts complained of here—broadly speaking, Ruth's appearance and words during the rescue and evacuation—were of legitimate public interest. If so, summary judgment was properly entered. . . .

We agree at the outset with defendants that the subject matter of the broadcast as a whole was of legitimate public concern. Automobile accidents are by their nature of interest to that great portion of the public that travels frequently by automobile. The rescue and medical treatment of accident victims is also of legitimate concern to much of the public, involving as it does a critical service that any member of the public may someday need. The story of Ruth's difficult extrication from the crushed car, the medical attention given her at the scene, and her evacuation by helicopter was of particular interest because it highlighted some of the challenges facing emergency workers dealing with serious accidents.

The more difficult question is whether Ruth's appearance and words as she was extricated from the overturned car, placed in the helicopter and transported to the hospital were of legitimate public concern. Pursuant to the analysis outlined earlier, we conclude the disputed material was newsworthy as a matter of law. One of the dramatic and interesting aspects of the story as a whole is its focus on flight nurse Carnahan, who appears to be in charge of communications with other emergency workers, the hospital base and Ruth, and who leads the medical assistance to Ruth at the scene. Her work is portrayed as demanding and important and as involving a measure of personal risk (e.g., in crawling under the car to aid Ruth despite warnings that gasoline may be dripping from the car). The broadcast segment makes apparent that this type of emergency care requires not only medical knowledge, concentration and courage, but an ability to talk and listen to severely traumatized patients. One of the challenges Carnahan faces in assisting Ruth is the confusion, pain and fear that Ruth understandably feels in the aftermath of the accident. For that reason the broadcast video depicting Ruth's injured physical state (which was not luridly shown) and audio showing her disorientation and despair were substantially relevant to the segment's newsworthy subject matter.

Plaintiffs argue that showing Ruth's "intimate private, medical facts and her suffering was not necessary to enable the public to understand the significance of the accident or the rescue as a public event." The standard, however, is not necessity. That the broadcast could have been edited to exclude some of Ruth's words and images and still excite a minimum degree of viewer interest is not determinative. Nor is the possibility that the members of this or another court, or a jury, might find a differently edited broadcast more to their taste or even more interesting. The courts do not, and constitutionally could not, sit as superior editors of the press.

The challenged material was thus substantially relevant to the newsworthy subject matter of the broadcast and did not constitute a "morbid and sensational prying into private lives for its own sake." (Rest. 2d Torts, §652D, com. h.) Nor can we say the broadcast material was so lurid and sensational in emotional tone, or so intensely personal in content, as to make its intrusiveness disproportionate to its relevance. Under these circumstances, the material was, as a matter of law, of legitimate public concern. Summary judgment was therefore properly entered against Ruth on her cause of action for publication of private facts. As to Wayne, he is glimpsed only fleetingly in the broadcast video and is never heard. The broadcast includes no images or information regarding him that could be offensive to a reasonable person of ordinary sensibilities. Summary judgment was therefore also proper on Wayne's cause of action for publication of private facts. . . .

PREPARING FOR CLASS

1. Have the privacy concerns expressed by Warren and Brandeis in their famous article become greater today than in 1890? Or are they just different?

2. What do you suppose led Ruth and Wayne to sue?

3. What must a plaintiff prove to establish public disclosure of private facts?

4. What kinds of private facts can be disclosed without liability? Why?

5. Is lack of newsworthiness an element of the plaintiff's case, or is newsworthiness a defense?

6. What's the difference between a descriptive and a normative term? Which is "newsworthiness," and why does it matter?

7. Did Ruth have a cause of action? Why or why not?

8. Why did the father in *Cohn* think his private facts had been disclosed? He was not, after all, the crime victim. Why was he unable to recover?

INCREASING YOUR UNDERSTANDING

1. *The publicity requirement.* In Yath v. Fairview Clinics, 767 N.W.2d 34 (Minn. App. 2009), the plaintiff appealed the dismissal of her public-disclosure-of-private-facts cause of action. The trial court had held that the plaintiff could not establish the requisite publicity. The appellate court disagreed:

> "Publicity," for the purposes of an invasion-of-privacy claim, means that "the matter is made public, by communicating it to the public at large, or to so many persons that the matter must be regarded as substantially certain to become one of public knowledge." In other words, there are two methods to satisfy the publicity element of an invasion-of-privacy claim: the first method is by proving a single communication to the public, and the second method is by proving communication to individuals in such a large number that the information is deemed to have been communicated to the public.
>
> The supreme court's analysis and application in Bodah v. Lakeville Motor Express, 649 N.W.2d 859 (Minn. Sup. 2003) [are] illuminating. The *Bodah* court held that the publicity element was not satisfied when an employer disseminated employee names and social security numbers to sixteen managers in six states. The employer disseminated the information by private means, specifically, by facsimile. The private rather than public nature of this communication caused the *Bodah* court to consider whether the communication was to a large enough number of recipients to support a determination of "publicity" under the second method. It held that dissemination of information to the relatively small group of individuals did not satisfy the publicity element because the disseminated information could not "be regarded as substantially certain to become public."
>
> But in reaching the conclusion, the supreme court explained the type of communication that would constitute publicity under the first method. It approvingly acknowledged the Restatement of Torts explanation that "any publication in a newspaper or a

magazine, even of small circulation . . . or any broadcast over the radio, or statement made in an address to a large audience," would meet the publicity element of an invasion-of-privacy claim. It also relied on the Restatement for the proposition that posting private information in a shop window viewable by passers-by constitutes "publicity." The Restatement explains that "[t]he distinction . . . is one between private and public communication." This explanation informs our judgment that the challenged communication here constitutes publicity under the first method, or publicity per se. Unlike *Bodah*, where the private information went through a private medium to reach a finite, identifiable group of privately situated recipients, Yath's private information was posted on a public MySpace.com webpage for anyone to view. This Internet communication is materially similar in nature to a newspaper publication or a radio broadcast because upon release it is available to the public at large.

The district court appears to have accepted [the defendants'] argument that the publicity element was not satisfied because [plaintiff] proved only that a small number of people actually viewed the MySpace.com webpage and that the webpage was available only 24 to 48 hours. A similar argument could be made about a newspaper having only a small circulation, or a radio broadcast at odd hours when few were listening. The district court therefore mistakenly analyzed "publicity" using the second method, which applies only to privately directed communication and requires an assessment based on the number of actual viewers. But when the communication is made by offering the information in a public forum, the first method applies and the tort is triggered when the discloser makes the private information publicly available, not when some substantial number of individuals actually get the information. Like the temporary posting of information in a shop window, the MySpace.com webpage put the information in view of any member of the public—in large or small numbers—who happened by. The number of actual viewers is irrelevant.

Nonetheless, the plaintiff lost because she could not prove that either defendant created the MySpace page.

2. *The offensiveness requirement.* In Harris v. Easton Publishing, Co., 483 A.2d 1377 (Pa. Super. 1984), the Department of Public Welfare distributed to various newspapers, as part of a regular column from the department, a minimally fictionalized account of the plaintiff-appellant's conversations with a department employee as she applied for food

stamps and medical assistance. Despite being "disguised," plaintiff and the other family members for whom she sought help (also plaintiffs) were readily recognizable. Of their public-disclosure-of-private-facts causes of action, the court wrote:

> The third element requires that a reasonable person of ordinary sensibilities would find such publicity highly offensive. In making this determination, the customs of the time and place, occupation of the plaintiff and habits of his neighbors and fellow citizens are material. Restatement (Second) of Torts §652D, comment c. The act which constitutes the tortious invasion of privacy must be committed in such a manner as to outrage or cause mental suffering, shame or humiliation to a person of ordinary sensibilities. . . .
>
> In Aquino v. Bulletin Company, 190 Pa. Super. at 533-34, 154 A.2d at 426, this court stated that:
>
>> The rule does not depend for its validity upon a breach of confidence, nor upon the untruth of the statements. The liability exists only if the defendant's conduct was such that he should have realized that it would be offensive to persons of ordinary sensibilities. It is only where the intrusion has gone beyond the limits of decency that liability accrues. These limits are exceeded where intimate details of the life of one who has never manifested a desire to have publicity are exposed to the public. On the other hand, there is no invasion of a right of privacy in the description of the ordinary goings and comings of a person, or of weddings, even though intended to be entirely private, or of other publications to which people do not ordinarily seriously object. . . .

The third element requires the publicity given to private facts be highly offensive to a reasonable person. This element finds support from both the protection afforded welfare applicants pursuant to [a statutory ban on disclosing names of those on public assistance] and from a commonsense analysis of the type of information at issue. . . .

The statutory ban . . . is a clear recognition and directive by the Legislature that the privacy of the recipient is a fundamental need worthy of protection. This Court is bound to give great deference to this sound legislative judgment. . . .

Applicants for welfare benefits would be justifiably appalled at having the confidential and highly personal information they provide publicized in a newspaper. . . . [Disseminating this information] to the general public was highly offensive, particularly in light of the statutory protection afforded to them pursuant to the Public Welfare Code. . . .

APPLYING THE LAW

1. Does Piper have a public-disclosure-of-private-facts case against Del?

2. An anti-abortion activist flirts at a bar with the receptionist for a doctor who performs legal abortions and manages to get her to reveal the doctor's home address and work, church, and gym schedules and locations. The activist then posts that information on an anti-abortion Web site, and the post leads to stalking and harassment of the doctor. Is the activist liable to the doctor for public disclosure of private facts?

3. A student who was dismissed from law school applies for readmission. A professor who learns that the student has reapplied sends a memo to the readmission committee stating that when she spoke privately with the student, he disclosed that he had problems with an uncontrollable temper and that he was physically abusive of his girlfriend and had been physically abusive of his former wife. Is the professor liable to the student for public disclosure of private facts?

B. INTRUSION INTO SECLUSION

Shulman v. Group W Productions, Inc.
955 P.2d 469 (Cal. 1998)

[See Section A, supra, for the facts and procedural history of this case.]

Of the four privacy torts identified by Prosser, the tort of intrusion into private places, conversations or matter is perhaps the one that best captures the common understanding of an "invasion of privacy." It encompasses unconsented-to physical intrusion into the home, hospital room or other place the privacy of which is legally recognized, as well as unwarranted sensory intrusions such as eavesdropping, wiretapping, and visual or photographic spying. (See Rest. 2d Torts, §652B, com. b.) It is in the intrusion cases that invasion of privacy is most clearly seen as an affront to individual dignity. "[A] measure of personal isolation and personal control over the conditions of its abandonment is of the very essence of personal freedom and dignity, is part of what our culture means by these concepts. A man whose home may be entered at the will of another, whose conversations may be overheard at the will of another, whose marital and familial intimacies may be overseen at the will of another, is less of a man, has less human dignity, on that account. He who may intrude upon another at will is the master of the other and, in fact, intrusion is a primary weapon of the tyrant." (Bloustein, *Privacy as an Aspect of Human Dignity: An Answer to Dean Prosser* (1964) 39 N.Y.U. L. Rev. 962, 973-974.)

Despite its conceptual centrality, the intrusion tort has received less judicial attention than the private facts tort, and its parameters are less clearly defined.

The leading California decision is Miller v. National Broadcasting Co., 187 Cal. App. 3d 1463, 232 Cal. Rptr. 668. *Miller*, which like the present case involved a news organization's videotaping the work of emergency medical personnel, adopted the Restatement's formulation of the cause of action: "One who intentionally intrudes, physically or otherwise, upon the solitude or seclusion of another or his private affairs or concerns, is subject to liability to the other for invasion of his privacy, if the intrusion would be highly offensive to a reasonable person." (Rest. 2d Torts, §652B.)

As stated in *Miller* and the Restatement, therefore, the action for intrusion has two elements: (1) intrusion into a private place, conversation or matter, (2) in a manner highly offensive to a reasonable person. We consider the elements in that order.

We ask first whether defendants "intentionally intrude[d], physically or otherwise, upon the solitude or seclusion of another," that is, into a place or conversation private to Wayne or Ruth. "[T]here is no liability for the examination of a public record concerning the plaintiff. . . . [Or] for observing him or even taking his photograph while he is walking on the public highway. . . ." (Rest. 2d Torts, §652B, com. C.) To prove actionable intrusion, the plaintiff must show the defendant penetrated some zone of physical or sensory privacy surrounding, or obtained unwanted access to data about, the plaintiff. The tort is proven only if the plaintiff had an objectively reasonable expectation of seclusion or solitude in the place, conversation or data source. (Rest. 2d, §652B, com. c., p. 379; *see*, e.g., People for the Ethical Treatment of Animals v. Bobby Berosini, Ltd., 895 P.2d 1269, 1280-1281 (Nev. 1995) [plaintiff animal trainer had no expectation of seclusion or solitude in backstage preparation area]; Frankel v. Warwick Hotel (E.D. Pa. 1995) 881 F. Supp. 183, 188 [father's meddling in son's marriage not intrusion where there was no "physical or sensory penetration of a person's zone of seclusion"].)

Cameraman Cooke's mere presence at the accident scene and filming of the events occurring there cannot be deemed either a physical or sensory intrusion on plaintiffs' seclusion. Plaintiffs had no right of ownership or possession of the property where the rescue took place, nor any actual control of the premises. Nor could they have had a reasonable expectation that members of the media would be excluded or prevented from photographing the scene; for journalists to attend and record the scenes of accidents and rescues is in no way unusual or unexpected.

Two aspects of defendants' conduct, however, raise triable issues of intrusion on seclusion. First, a triable issue exists as to whether both plaintiffs had an objectively reasonable expectation of privacy in the interior of the rescue helicopter, which served as an ambulance. Although the attendance of reporters and photographers at the scene of an accident is to be expected, we are aware of no law or custom permitting the press to ride in ambulances or enter hospital rooms during treatment without the patient's consent. (Other than the two patients and Cooke, only three people were present in the helicopter, all Mercy Air staff.) As the Court of Appeal observed, "[i]t is neither the custom nor the habit of our society that any member of the public at large or its media representatives may hitch a ride in an ambulance and ogle as paramedics care for an injured stranger."

Second, Ruth was entitled to a degree of privacy in her conversations with Carnahan and other medical rescuers at the accident scene, and in Carnahan's conversations conveying medical information regarding Ruth to the hospital base. Cooke, perhaps, did not intrude into that zone of privacy merely by being present at a place where he could hear such conversations with unaided ears. But by placing a microphone on Carnahan's person, amplifying and recording what she said and heard, defendants may have listened in on conversations the parties could reasonably have expected to be private.

The Court of Appeal held plaintiffs had no reasonable expectation of privacy at the accident scene itself because the scene was within the sight and hearing of members of the public. The summary judgment record, however, does not support the Court of Appeal's conclusion; instead, it reflects, at the least, the existence of triable issues as to the privacy of certain conversations at the accident scene, as in the helicopter. The videotapes (broadcast and raw footage) show the rescue did not take place "on a heavily traveled highway," as the Court of Appeal stated, but in a ditch many yards from and below the rural superhighway, which is raised somewhat at that point to bridge a nearby cross-road. From the tapes it appears unlikely the plaintiffs' extrication from their car and medical treatment at the scene could have been observed by any persons who, in the lower court's words, "passed by" on the roadway. Even more unlikely is that any passersby on the road could have heard Ruth's conversation with Nurse Carnahan or the other rescuers.

As to those gathered at the rescue site itself, it is unclear from the record, and therefore unripe for decision on summary judgment, whether any of those present—other than cameraman Cooke—were mere spectators. Most were clearly law enforcement personnel, firefighters or paramedics. . . . Finally, it is unclear from the tapes if anyone other than those involved was able to hear Ruth's conversation with the nurse and paramedics. . . .

Whether Ruth expected her conversations with Nurse Carnahan or the other rescuers to remain private and whether any such expectation was reasonable are, on the state of the record before us, questions for the jury. We note, however, that several existing legal protections for communications could support the conclusion that Ruth possessed a reasonable expectation of privacy in her conversations with Nurse Carnahan and the other rescuers. A patient's conversation with a provider of medical care in the course of treatment including emergency treatment, carries a traditional and legally well-established expectation of privacy. [The court cites and discusses provisions of the evidence and penal codes and case law.]

Ruth's claim, of course, does not require her to prove a statutory violation, only to prove that she had an objectively reasonable expectation of privacy in her conversations. Whether the circumstances of Ruth's extrication and helicopter rescue would reasonably have indicated to defendants, or to their agent, Cooke, that Ruth would desire and expect her communications to Carnahan and the other rescuers to be confined to them alone, and therefore not to be electronically transmitted and recorded, is a triable issue of fact in this case. . . . We cannot say, as a matter of law, that Cooke should not have perceived he might be intruding on a confidential communication when he recorded a seriously injured patient's conversations with medical personnel.

We turn to the second element of the intrusion tort, offensiveness of the intrusion. In a widely followed passage, the *Miller* court explained that determining offensiveness requires consideration of all the circumstances of the intrusion, including its degree and setting and the intruder's "motives and objectives." (*Miller*, 187 Cal. App. 3d at pp. 1483-1484, 232 Cal. Rptr. 668.) The *Miller* court concluded that reasonable people could regard the camera crew's conduct in filming a man's emergency medical treatment in his home, without seeking or obtaining his or his wife's consent, as showing "a cavalier disregard for ordinary citizens' rights of privacy" and, hence, as highly offensive.

We agree with the *Miller* court that all the circumstances of an intrusion, including the motives or justification of the intruder, are pertinent to the offensiveness element. Motivation or justification becomes particularly important when the intrusion is by a member of the print or broadcast press in the pursuit of news material. Although, as will be discussed more fully later, the First Amendment does not immunize the press from liability for torts or crimes committed in an effort to gather news, the constitutional protection of the press does reflect the strong societal interest in effective and complete reporting of events, an interest that may—as a matter of tort law—justify an intrusion that would otherwise be considered offensive. While refusing to recognize a broad privilege in newsgathering against application of generally applicable laws, the United States Supreme Court has also observed that "without some protection for seeking out the news, freedom of the press could be eviscerated." (Branzburg v. Hayes (1972) 408 U.S. 665, 681.)

In deciding, therefore, whether a reporter's alleged intrusion into private matters (i.e., physical space, conversation or data) is "offensive" and hence actionable as an invasion of privacy, courts must consider the extent to which the intrusion was, under the circumstances, justified by the legitimate motive of gathering the news. Information collecting techniques that may be highly offensive when done for socially unprotected reasons—for purposes of harassment, blackmail or prurient curiosity, for example—may not be offensive to a reasonable person when employed by journalists in pursuit of a socially or politically important story. . . .

The mere fact the intruder was in pursuit of a "story" does not, however, generally justify an otherwise offensive intrusion; offensiveness depends as well on the particular method of investigation used. At one extreme, "'routine . . . reporting techniques,'" such as asking questions of people with information ("including those with confidential or restricted information") could rarely, if ever, be deemed an actionable intrusion. (Nicholson v. McClatchy Newspapers, 223 Cal. Rptr. 58.) At the other extreme, violation of well-established legal areas of physical or sensory privacy—trespass into a home or tapping a personal telephone line, for example—could rarely, if ever, be justified by a reporter's need to get the story. Such acts would be deemed highly offensive even if the information sought was of weighty public concern; they would also be outside any protection the Constitution provides to newsgathering.

Between these extremes lie difficult cases, many involving the use of photographic and electronic recording equipment. Equipment such as hidden cameras and miniature cordless and directional microphones are powerful investigative tools for newsgathering, but may also be used in ways that severely threaten personal privacy. California tort law provides no bright line on this question; each case must be taken on its facts.

On this summary judgment record, we believe a jury could find defendants' recording of Ruth's communications to Carnahan and other rescuers, and filming in the air ambulance, to be "'highly offensive to a reasonable person.'" With regard to the depth of the intrusion, a reasonable jury could find highly offensive the placement of a microphone on a medical rescuer in order to intercept what would otherwise be private conversations with an injured patient. In that setting, as defendants could and should have foreseen, the patient would not know her words were being recorded and would not have occasion to ask about, and object or consent to, recording. Defendants, it could reasonably be said, took calculated advantage of the patient's "vulnerability and confusion." Arguably, the last thing an injured accident victim should have to worry about while being pried from her wrecked car is that a television producer may be recording everything she says to medical personnel for the possible edification and entertainment of casual television viewers.

For much the same reason, a jury could reasonably regard entering and riding in an ambulance—whether on the ground or in the air—with two seriously injured patients to be an egregious intrusion on a place of expected seclusion. Again, the patients, at least in this case, were hardly in a position to keep careful watch on who was riding with them, or to inquire as to everyone's business and consent or object to their presence. A jury could reasonably believe that fundamental respect for human dignity requires the patients' anxious journey be taken only with those whose care is solely for them and out of sight of the prying eyes (or cameras) of others.

Nor can we say as a matter of law that defendants' motive—to gather usable material for a potentially newsworthy story—necessarily privileged their intrusive conduct as a matter of common law tort liability. A reasonable jury could conclude the producers' desire to get footage that would convey the "feel" of the event—the real sights and sounds of a difficult rescue—did not justify either placing a microphone on Nurse Carnahan or filming inside the rescue helicopter. Although defendants' purposes could scarcely be regarded as evil or malicious (in the colloquial sense), their behavior could, even in light of their motives, be thought to show a highly offensive lack of sensitivity and respect for plaintiffs' privacy. A reasonable jury could find that defendants, in placing a microphone on an emergency treatment nurse and recording her conversation with a distressed, disoriented and severely injured patient, without the patient's knowledge or consent, acted with highly offensive disrespect for the patient's personal privacy comparable to, if not quite as extreme as, the disrespect and insensitivity demonstrated in *Miller*.

Turning to the question of constitutional protection for newsgathering, one finds the decisional law reflects a general rule of nonprotection: the press in its newsgathering activities enjoys no immunity or exemption from generally applicable laws. . . .

Courts have impliedly recognized that a generally applicable law might, under some circumstances, impose an "impermissible burden" on news-gathering. *Miller*, 187 Cal. App. 3d at 1493, 232 Cal. Rptr. 668, 685. No basis exists, however for concluding that . . . the intrusion tort places such a burden on the press, either in general or under the circumstances of this case. . . . More specifically, nothing in the record or briefing here suggests that reporting on automobile accidents and medical rescue activities depends on secretly recording accident victims' conversations with rescue personnel or on filming inside an occupied ambulance . . .

[T]he constitutional protection accorded newsgathering, if any, is far narrower than the protection surrounding the publication of truthful material; consequently, the fact that a reporter may be seeking "newsworthy" material does not in itself privilege the investigatory activity. The reason for the difference is simple: the intrusion tort, unlike that for publication of private facts, does not subject the press to liability for the contents of its publications. Newsworthiness, as we stated earlier, is a complete bar to liability for publication of private facts and is evaluated with a high degree of deference to editorial judgment. The same deference is not due, however, when the issue is not the media's right to publish or broadcast what they choose, but their right to intrude into secluded areas or conversations in pursuit of publishable material. At most, the Constitution may preclude tort liability that would "place an impermissible burden on newsgatherers" by depriving them of their "'indispensable tools.'" . . .

In contrast to the broad privilege the press enjoys for publishing truthful, newsworthy information in its possession, the press has no recognized constitutional privilege to violate generally applicable laws in pursuit of material. Nor, even absent an independent crime or tort, can a highly offensive intrusion into a private place, conversation, or source of information generally be justified by the plea that the intruder hoped thereby to get good material for a news story. Such a justification may be available when enforcement of the tort or other law would place an impermissibly severe burden on the press, but that condition is not met in this case.

In short, the state may not intrude into the proper sphere of the news media to dictate what they should publish and broadcast, but neither may the media play tyrant to the people by unlawfully spying on them in the name of newsgathering. Summary judgment for the defense was proper as to plaintiffs' cause of action for publication of private facts (the second cause of action), but improper as to the cause of action for invasion of privacy by intrusion (the first cause of action).

PREPARING FOR CLASS

1. What are the elements of the intrusion tort?

2. What aspects of defendant's conduct do not raise triable issues? Why not?

3. What aspects of defendant's conduct do raise triable issues? Why?

4. How was the reporter's use of electronic devices significant?

5. Was the intrusion offensive? Does it matter that the intrusion was meant to serve the public interest?

6. Newsworthiness precluded the public-disclosure-of-private-facts cause of action in this case. Why doesn't it bar the intrusion claim? Moreover, how can it be tortious to record the conversation but not tortious to broadcast the tortiously recorded conversation?

APPLYING THE LAW

1. Does Piper have an intrusion claim against Del?

2. Perry Poster played basketball for the University of Michiana and was voted most valuable player of the 2007 NCAA Final Four. He is now a guard for the Chicago Bulls. The *Chicago Tribune* ran an article about Poster titled "MVP Made Grade Only on the Court." An employee in the University of Michiana Registrar's Office had leaked Poster's academic transcripts (which, under federal law, are not to be released without the student's permission) to a *Tribune* reporter, and the transcripts revealed that Poster had been on academic probation almost his entire college playing career. Poster sued the university employee and the reporter for intrusion into seclusion. Can he win?

C. FALSE LIGHT

Crump v. Beckley Newspapers, Inc.
320 S.E.2d 70 (W. Va. 1983)

McGRAW, C.J. . . . .
On December 5, 1977, the defendant published an article in one of its newspapers concerning women coal miners. Photographs of the plaintiff, a miner with the Westmoreland Coal Company, taken with her knowledge and consent, were used by the defendant in conjunction with the article. Her name was specifically mentioned, and her picture appeared. . . . [T]he

defendant did not request permission to use her picture or name in any other newspaper article.

On September 23, 1979, an article entitled "Women Enter 'Man's' World" appeared in one of the defendant's newspapers. The article generally addressed some of the problems faced by women miners, and by women who desire employment in the mining industry. The article related incidents in which two Kentucky women were "'stripped, greased and sent out of the mine' as part of an initiation rite"; in which a woman miner in southwestern Virginia was physically attacked twice while underground; and in which one Wyoming woman "was dangled off a 200-foot water tower accompanied by the suggestion that she quit her job. She did." The article also discussed other types of harassment and discrimination faced by women miners. Although Crump's name was not mentioned in the article, her 1977 photograph was used, accompanied by a caption which read, "Women are entering mines as a regular course of action."

As a result of the unauthorized publication of Crump's photograph in conjunction with the article, she states in an affidavit submitted below that she was questioned by friends and acquaintances concerning the incidents contained in the article and concerning whether she had been the subject of any harassment by her employer or by fellow employees. She had, in fact, experienced no such harassment. Crump also states that the article caused one reader to ask her whether she had ever been "stripped, greased and sent out of the mine." She alleges that the unfavorable attention precipitated by the publication of her photograph in conjunction with the article has damaged her reputation and caused her a great deal of embarrassment and humiliation. Therefore, she seeks recovery from the defendant for damages resulting from their unauthorized publication of her photograph.

[Crump filed a suit against the defendant "alleging, in substance, defamation and invasion of privacy." The trial court granted summary judgment to the defendant, and this opinion finds that the trial court made three errors in doing so, including failure to consider invasion of privacy as an alternative theory of recovery. The appeal and opinion addressed both appropriation and false light. The court's discussion of the former is omitted here.]

The second privacy theory of recovery which Crump advances is that of false light. . . . [P]ublicity which unreasonably places another in a false light before the public is an actionable invasion of privacy. One form in which false light invasions of privacy often appears is the use of another's photograph to illustrate an article or book with which the person has no reasonable connection, and which places the person in a false light. For example, in Leverton v. Curtis Pub. Co., 192 F.2d 974 (3d Cir. 1951), a photograph of a child being helped to her feet after nearly being struck by an automobile through no fault of her own was initially published in a local newspaper. Approximately twenty months later, however, in an article published in the *Saturday Evening Post* on the role of pedestrian carelessness in traffic accidents, the plaintiff's photograph was used as an illustration of such carelessness. The Third Circuit affirmed the jury verdict for the plaintiff, holding that her privacy had been invaded because she had been presented in a false light. Other examples of communications which have been held to constitute false light invasions of privacy include where a photograph of an honest taxi driver was used to illustrate an article on unscrupulous taxi drivers, Peay v. Curtis Pub. Co., 78 F. Supp. 305 (D.D.C. 1948); where a photograph of a husband and wife in an affectionate pose taken without their permission or knowledge was used to illustrate an article which stated that "love at first sight" was founded upon one hundred percent sex attraction and would be followed by divorce, Gill v. Curtis Pub. Co., 239 P.2d 630 (1952); publication of a photograph depicting the plaintiff as a member of a gang of juvenile delinquents, Metzger v. Dell Pub. Co., 136 N.Y.S.2d 888 (1955); and where the plaintiff posed as a model for fashion pictures to appear in the defendant's *Ebony* magazine, but where the defendant used her picture to illustrate a story entitled "Man Hungry" appearing in an issue of *Tan* magazine, Martin v. Johnson Pub. Co., 157 N.Y.S.2d 409 (N.Y. Sup. 1956).

There are obviously a number of similarities between actions for false light invasion of privacy and actions for defamation. The most prominent characteristic shared by the two causes of action is that the matter publicized as to the plaintiff must be untrue. Additionally, "[i]n a false light privacy action, as in a defamation action, a court should not consider words or elements in isolation, but should view them in the context of the whole article to determine if they constitute an invasion of privacy." Rinsley v. Brandt, 700 F.2d at 1310. Therefore, courts and commentators have consistently treated false light privacy claims in essentially the same manner as they have treated defamation.

Despite the similarities between defamation and false light causes of action, there are also a number of important differences. First, "each action protects different interests: privacy actions involve injuries to emotions and mental suffering, while defamation actions involve injury to reputation." Second, "[t]he false light need not be defamatory, although it often is, but it must be such as to be offensive to a reasonable person." Finally, although widespread publicity is not necessarily required for recovery under a defamation cause of action, it is an essential ingredient to any false light invasion of privacy claim. Therefore, false light invasion of privacy is a distinct theory of recovery entitled to separate consideration and analysis.

The United States Supreme Court first considered false light invasions of privacy in Time, Inc. v. Hill, [385 U.S. 374 (1967)]. There, in analyzing New York's statutory right of privacy in light of important first amendment considerations, it held that, "the constitutional protections for speech and press preclude the application of the New York statute to redress false reports of matters of public interest in the absence of proof that the defendant published the report with knowledge of its falsity or in reckless disregard of the truth." Therefore, the Court held that when matters of "public interest" are involved, the *New York Times* "actual malice" standard is applicable in invasion of privacy actions. Subsequent decisions by the United States Supreme

Court indicate, however, that the *Hill* "actual malice" requirement is no longer applicable in privacy actions, at least where private individuals are involved.

Shortly after its decision in *Hill*, the Court in Curtis Pub. Co. v. Butts, 388 U.S. 130 (1967), utilized the *Hill* "public interest" analysis to extend the *New York Times* "actual malice" requirement to cases involving public figures as well as public officials. Later, in Rosenbloom v. Metromedia, Inc., 403 U.S. 29 (1971), the Court's protection of media defendants from defamation liability reached its apex when it again used the *Hill* public interest analysis to extend the *New York Times* rule to private individuals in certain circumstances. Shortly thereafter, however, as the Court began its gradual shift away from its staunch protection of the media, and returned to a more status oriented approach, it held in Gertz v. Robert Welch, Inc., 418 U.S. 323, 348 (1974), that, "Our accommodation of the competing values at stake in defamation suits by private individuals allows the States to impose liability on the publisher or broadcaster of defamatory falsehood on a less demanding showing than that required by *New York Times*." Therefore, a private individual need only show negligence in an action for defamation against a media defendant in the absence of an otherwise privileged communication.

In Cantrell v. Forest City Pub. Co., 419 U.S. 245 (1974) and Cox Broadcasting Corp. v. Cohn, 420 U.S. 469 (1975), the Court avoided the opportunity to address the issue of whether *Gertz* had, in effect, overruled *Hill* to the extent of requiring "actual malice" in privacy cases involving private individuals. In *Cantrell*, the Court consciously abstained from addressing the validity of *Hill* by finding "actual malice" to be present as a matter of fact, thereby negating the necessity of deciding whether a lesser degree of fault would be sufficient. In *Cohn* the Court again managed to avoid the issue since the information published was a matter of public record, and therefore was absolutely privileged.

Section 652E of the Restatement (Second) of Torts (1977) retains the *Hill* approach, it provides that a false light invasion of privacy occurs if

> (a) the false light in which the other was placed would be highly offensive to a reasonable person, and (b) the actor had knowledge of or acted in reckless disregard as to the falsity of the publicized matter and the false light in which the other would be placed.

In a caveat to this section, however, the American Law Institute states,

> The Institute takes no position on whether there are any circumstances under which recovery can be obtained under this Section if the actor did not know of or act with reckless disregard as to the falsity of the matter publicized and the false light in which the other would be placed but was negligent in regard to these matters.

Expanding upon the uncertainty in this area of the law, comment d to this section states,

> The effect of the *Gertz* decision upon the holding in ... *Hill* has ... been left in a state of uncertainty. ... If *Time v. Hill* is modified along the lines of *Gertz v. Robert Welch*, then the reckless-disregard rule would apparently apply [only] if the plaintiff is a public official or public figure and the negligence rule will apply to other plaintiffs.

Although a number of courts have applied the Restatement rule, few have given any consideration to the constitutional issues involved in determining the degree of fault required.

Despite this unwillingness on the part of the majority of jurisdictions and the Restatement to recognize the invalidity of *Hill* in light of *Gertz*, several commentators and at least one federal district court have concluded that the "actual malice" standard no longer applies to privacy actions involving private individuals.

Cantrell and *Cohn* notwithstanding, subsequent Supreme Court decisions are indicative of the trend towards moving away from *Hill*. In Zacchini v. Scripps-Howard Broadcasting Co., 433 U.S. at 571-75, the Supreme Court emphasized the striking similarities between false light and defamation actions in holding that the *Hill* standard does not apply to non-false light "right of publicity" actions. In Time, Inc. v. Firestone, 424 U.S. 448 at 452-57 (1976), the Court downplayed the role of the first amendment in defamation actions where private individuals are involved in holding that a prominent socialite, involved in a celebrated divorce, who had held news conferences about the divorce proceedings, was not a public figure, and could recover for emotional distress caused by the alleged false defamatory statements.

Due to the pronounced overlap of defamation and false light invasion of privacy, particularly in the area of their first amendment implications, we conclude that the existing inconsistency between *Hill* and *Gertz* will eventually be resolved in favor of *Gertz*. In the absence of a privileged communication, the test to be applied in a false light invasion of privacy action by a private individual against a media defendant is what a reasonably prudent person would have done under the same or similar circumstances. Of course, as in defamation actions, if a privileged communication is involved, the "actual malice" or abuse of privilege standard will apply.

This negligence standard need not present any potential for a "chilling effect" on the press. First, as the United States Supreme Court stated in *New York Times*, 376 U.S. at 270, we have a "profound national commitment to the principle that debate on public issues should be uninhibited, robust, and wide open. ..." Therefore, when public officials, public figures, or legitimate matters of public interest are involved, plaintiffs may recover only upon proof of knowledge of falsity or reckless disregard for the truth. Second, the price of the license granted by the first amendment to the press to engage in robust activity is the necessity of every citizen of having some thickness of skin. Therefore, a plaintiff in a false light invasion of privacy action may not recover unless the false light in which he was placed would be highly offensive to a reasonable person. Restatement (Second) of Torts §652E(a) (1977). This requirement ensures that liability will not attach for the publication of information so innocuous that notice of potential harm would not be present. The childhood idiom "sticks and stones may break my bones, but names can never hurt me" provides a cultural sense of the community standard on de minimus misrepresentations. Third, the recognition of retraction or apology as mitigating factors in the assessment of damages furnishes media defendants with an institutional mechanism for avoiding or minimizing unnecessary liability. Finally, when a media defendant is involved in a privacy action, the "reasonably prudent person" standard becomes, in effect, a "liberal professional newsperson" standard. The "same or similar circumstances" portion of this test will allow a media defendant to interject such considerations as "chilling effect," the need for robusticity, standards within the profession, and the role of the press in society. All of these factors contribute to our determination that negligence, indeed, is the proper standard to be applied when a nonprivileged false light action by a private individual is involved.

Turning to the facts surrounding the present case, it is clear that genuine issues of material fact remain which preclude the granting of summary judgment for the defendant on the false light invasion of privacy cause of action. First, as in the appellant's defamation cause of action, whether the statements in the article involved referred to the appellant with regards to her privacy cause of action is a question of fact for the jury. Second, when the communication involved in a false light case does not clearly favor one construction over another, the determination of what light it places the plaintiff is for the jury. This consideration is related to the first in that the key factual issue upon remand is whether the article implied that Crump had suffered harassment in the course of her employment, thereby either defaming her or placing her in a false light before the public. Finally, the issue of abuse of privilege, as in the defamation portion of the appellant's action, will be an issue for the jury in the false light portion if the trial court finds upon remand that a qualified privilege or privileges existed.

Accordingly, the trial court's order granting summary judgment for the defendant is reversed, and the plaintiff's defamation and false light causes of action are remanded for a trial on the merits. . . .

PREPARING FOR CLASS

1. In what ways are false light claims similar to defamation? How are they different? Is false light just defamation lite?

2. What did the court hold in *Time, Inc. v. Hill*? Why? What is the argument that *Gertz* limits or changes the holding in *Hill*? What is the Restatement's answer to this question? What is the answer of this court?

3. What fault standard does the court adopt for cases like this one? And what are "cases like this one"? How does the court address concerns that this standard could have a chilling effect on speech?

4. What are the elements of a false light case? Can plaintiff establish them?

INCREASING YOUR UNDERSTANDING

The Warren Spahn litigation. Milton Shapiro wrote an unauthorized biography for the juvenile market about Warren Spahn, a famous baseball player. He did not communicate with Spahn, or his family, or the Milwaukee Braves, for whom Spahn played. Instead, he read newspaper and magazine clippings and made almost no attempt to verify the facts he found in them. In fact, when Shapiro discovered facts contrary to the narrative he was concocting, he ignored them. Two chapters of the book were dedicated to Spahn's heroics in World War II—heroics that did not occur.

> The book mistakenly states that Warren Spahn had been decorated with the Bronze Star. In truth, Spahn had not been the recipient of this award, customarily bestowed for outstanding valor in war. Yet the whole tenor of the description of Spahn's war experiences reflects this basic error. Plaintiff thus clearly established that the heroics attributed to him constituted a gross non-factual and embarrassing distortion as did the description of the circumstances surrounding his being wounded. Sergeant Spahn was not in charge of "supervision of the repairs" (p. 10) of the Bridge at Remagen; Spahn did not go "from man to man, urging them on" (p. 9); Sergeant Spahn did not go "into the town of Remagen to check with his company commander on his orders for the day" (p. 11) and, consequently, the whole description thereof is imaginary; Spahn had not "raced out into the teeth of the enemy barrage" (p. 13); and in addition to other untruthful statements surrounding his being wounded, Spahn was not "rolled . . . onto a stretcher" (p. 14); but remained ambulatory at all times after treatment in the First Aid Station.

Spahn v. Julian Messner, Inc., 250 N.Y.S.2d (N.Y. Sup. Ct. 1964).

Spahn sued Shapiro and his publisher for invasion of privacy. The gist of his suit was false light, although some of the opinions, as the case went up and down through the court system, also addressed appropriation. In all the various opinions, the bone of contention was never whether a plaintiff could recover for a laudatory false light. Think for a moment how Spahn would feel wronged by being portrayed as a war hero and what would cause him to sue. Can you see how false praise could satisfy the requirements of the false light tort?

Ray Yasser, a sports law professor at the University of Tulsa College of Law, once met Spahn, who said he had been embarrassed by Shapiro's glorification of his war experiences and worried that people might think he planted the story in an attempt to appear heroic. Professor Yasser has written an article on Spahn's long litigation of his privacy claim, *Warren Spahn's Legal Legacy: The Right to be Free from False Praise*, 18 Seton Hall J. Sports & Ent. L. 49 (2008).

In the final installment of the *Spahn* litigation, the court, on remand from the U.S. Supreme Court, considered the case in light of *Time, Inc. v. Hill*:

> We hold . . . that, before recovery by a public figure may be had for an unauthorized presentation of his life, it must be shown, in addition to the other requirements of the statute, that the presentation is infected with material and substantial falsification and that he work was published with knowledge of such falsification or with a reckless disregard for the truth.
>
> An examination of the undisputed findings of fact below as well as the defendants' own admission that "(i)n writing this biography, the author used the literary techniques of invented dialogue, imaginary incidents, and attributed thoughts and feelings" clearly indicates that the test of *New York Times Co. v. Sullivan* and *Time, Inc. v. Hill* has been met here. The Trial Judge found gross errors of fact and "all-pervasive distortions, inaccuracies, invented dialogue, and the narration of happenings out of context." [The appellate court] wrote:
>
>> (I)t is conceded that use was made of imaginary incidents, manufactured dialogue and a manipulated chronology. In short, defendants made no effort and had no intention to follow the facts concerning plaintiff's life, except in broad outline and to the extent that the facts readily supplied a dramatic portrayal attractive to the juvenile reader. This liberty . . . was exercised with respect to plaintiff's childhood, his relationship with his father, the courtship of his wife, important events during their marriage, and his military experience.
>
> Exactly how it may be argued that the "all-pervasive" use of imaginary incidents—incidents which the author knew did not take place—invented dialogue—dialogue which the author knew had never occurred—and attributed thoughts and feelings—thoughts and feelings which were likewise the figment of the author's imagination—can be said not to constitute knowing falsity is not made clear by the defendants. Indeed, the arguments made here are, in essence, not a denial of knowing falsity but a justification for it.

Thus the defendants argue that the literary techniques used in the instant biography are customary for children's books. . . .

To hold that this research effort entitles the defendants to publish the kind of knowing fictionalization presented here would amount to granting a literary license which is not only unnecessary to the protection of free speech but destructive of an individual's right—albeit a limited one in the case of a public figure—to be free of the commercial exploitation of his name and personality. . . .

Spahn v. Julian Messner, Inc., 233 N.E.2d 840 (N.Y. 1967).

APPLYING THE LAW

1. Does Piper have a false light claim against Del?

2. A reporter in Springfield, Michiana, went to a local grade school to interview third graders about the craze for reading the *FearTown* series of horror novels written for children. The article stated, "Third-grader Electra Antrobus says, 'My mom won't let me read them. She says it freaks me out.'" Electra did say this, but it was not true. Electra's mother let her read whatever she wanted. But little Electra, remembering what fun it had been to be quoted in the paper as a second grader on her thoughts on the presidential election, said what she thought she needed to say to get quoted in the story. The reporter did not check with Electra's mother to see if Electra's comment was true. In the story, Electra's comment was immediately followed by, "Dave Eckley, himself a parent of a third grader, says, 'Parents like these are ridiculous and narrow-minded. They are limiting their children's growth.'" Electra's mother, Ada Antrobus, a local physician, is considering suing the newspaper for false light. How would you advise her?

D. Appropriation

Joe Dickerson & Associates, LLC v. Dittmar
34 P.3d 995 (Colo. 2001)

Justice BENDER delivered the Opinion of the Court. . . .

II. FACTS AND PROCEEDINGS BELOW

Defendants Joe Dickerson & Associates, LLC and Joe Dickerson were hired during a child custody dispute to investigate plaintiff Rosanne Marie (Brock)

Dittmar. During the course of this investigation, Dickerson noticed inconsistencies in the way Dittmar came to possess certain bearer bonds. He reported the results of his investigation to authorities. Thereafter, Dittmar was charged with and convicted of felony theft of these bonds.

Dickerson publishes a newsletter called "The Dickerson Report," which is sent free of charge to law enforcement agencies, financial institutions, law firms, and others. This report contains articles about financial fraud investigations, tips for avoiding fraud, activities of private investigator boards, information about upcoming conferences, and the like. Dickerson ran a series of articles in the report under the heading "Fraud DuJour." This column included such articles as "Fraud DuJour—Wireless Cable Investments," "Fraud DuJour—Prime Bank Instruments," and the article at issue here, "Fraud—DuJour Five Cases, 100%+ Recovery."

In this article, Dickerson related the role his firm played in five cases in recovering 100%—and in one case more than 100%—of the value of stolen assets. Dittmar's case was discussed first. Dickerson's article detailed how Dittmar, who worked as a secretary at a brokerage firm, stole a customer's bearer bonds from her place of employment and cashed them for personal use. In addition, the article described Dickerson's investigation of Dittmar, the fact that the jury convicted Dittmar of theft, and how the court ordered her to pay restitution to the theft victim. This article appears on the front page of The Dickerson Report, mentions Dittmar by name, and includes her photograph.

Dittmar sued Dickerson on a number of tort theories including defamation, outrageous conduct, and invasion of privacy by appropriation of another's name or likeness. The trial court granted summary judgment for Dickerson on all claims. With respect to Dittmar's claim for invasion of privacy by appropriation of another's name or likeness, the only claim relevant to this appeal, the trial court noted that Colorado has not explicitly recognized this tort. The trial court granted Dickerson's motion for summary judgment because, even assuming the tort was cognizable under Colorado law, Dittmar "present[ed] no evidence that her name or likeness had any value." The trial court noted that, under the definition of the tort in the Second Restatement of Torts, appropriation requires more than mere publication of the plaintiff's name or likeness:

> The value of a plaintiff's name is not appropriated by mere mention of it, or by reference to it in connection with legitimate mention of his public activities; nor is the value of his likeness appropriated when it is published for purposes other than taking advantage of his reputation, prestige, or other value associated with him, for purposes of publicity.

Restatement (Second) of Torts §652C, cmt. d (1976).

Dittmar appealed the trial court's dismissal of her appropriation claim. The court of appeals agreed with the trial court that this tort requires the defendant to appropriate certain values associated with the plaintiff's name or likeness:

"In order for liability to exist, the defendant must have appropriated to his or her own use or benefit the reputation, prestige, social or commercial standing, public interest or other values of the plaintiff's name or likeness." The court of appeals concluded, however, that the plaintiff raised issues of material fact regarding different aspects of the tort, namely the purpose of the publication and whether the use benefited Dickerson. These issues of fact, the court of appeals reasoned, precluded summary judgment in favor of Dickerson. Hence, that court reversed the trial court's grant of summary judgment.

Dickerson petitioned this court for certiorari on three issues: (1) whether the tort of invasion of privacy based on appropriation of another's name or likeness is cognizable under Colorado law; (2) if so, whether an appropriation claim requires evidence that the plaintiff's name has an exploitable value; and (3) whether the article constituted constitutionally protected speech.

We agree with the court of appeals' recognition of this tort but we disagree that a plaintiff must provide evidence of the value of her name and likeness when she seeks only personal damages. Because we find that the defendant's publication of the plaintiff's name and likeness in the context of an article about her crime and felony conviction is privileged under the First Amendment, we hold that the defendant is entitled to summary judgment as a matter of law.

III. ANALYSIS

A. OVERVIEW OF THE APPROPRIATION TORT

In 1890, an influential law review article outlined the contours of the tort of invasion of privacy. Samuel D. Warren & Louis D. Brandeis, *The Right To Privacy*, 4 Harv. L. Rev. 193 (1890). Warren and Brandeis suggested that increased abuses by the press required a remedy that would protect private individuals from mental distress and anguish. They proposed that the right of privacy would protect a person's rights in their appearance, sayings, acts, and personal relations. To Warren and Brandeis, the right of privacy did not involve property so much as the "more general immunity of the person—the right to one's personality." In short, they desired to protect the individual's right "to be let alone."

Over the years, almost every state has recognized, either statutorily or by case law, that one way that an individual's privacy can be invaded is when a defendant appropriates a plaintiff's name or likeness for that defendant's own benefit. While the exact parameters of this tort of invasion of privacy by appropriation of identity vary from state to state, it has always been clear that a plaintiff could recover for personal injuries such as mental anguish and injured feelings resulting from an appropriation.

There has been a great deal of debate, however, over the ability of a plaintiff to recover for pecuniary loss resulting from an unauthorized commercial exploitation of her name or likeness. Courts initially had difficulty reconciling how a celebrity, well-known to the public, could recover under the misleading heading of "privacy." Such plaintiffs often sought damages for commercial injury that resulted when defendants used plaintiffs' identities in advertising.

Therefore, in the context of pecuniary damages, some courts and commentators have resorted by analogy to property law and have recognized a "right of publicity" which permits plaintiffs to recover for injury to the commercial value of their identities.

In a seminal law review article, William Prosser described invasion of privacy as a complex of four related torts: (1) unreasonable intrusion upon the seclusion of another; (2) publicity that places another in a false light before the public; (3) public disclosure of embarrassing private facts about another; and (4) appropriation of another's name or likeness. The first three of these four torts protect only personal interests. But, perhaps in response to the simmering legal debate about the scope of the protection afforded by the appropriation tort, Prosser defined the appropriation tort as protective of both personal and economic interests. In doing so, Prosser emphasized the proprietary nature of the appropriation tort without removing it from the framework of privacy: "The interest protected is not so much a mental as a proprietary one, in the exclusive use of the plaintiff's name and likeness as an aspect of his identity."

Thus, Prosser's formulation of the appropriation tort subsumed the two types of injuries—personal and commercial—into one cause of action that existed under the misleading label of "privacy." The privacy label is misleading both because the interest protected (name and/or likeness) is not "private" in the same way as the interests protected by other areas of privacy law and because the appropriation tort often applies to protect well-known "public" persons. Despite these problems, Prosser's view of the appropriation tort was ultimately incorporated into the Second Restatement of Torts. Restatement (Second) of Torts §652C.

Prosser's emphasis on the property-like aspects of the tort has led to a great deal of confusion in the law of privacy. Some courts have partially rejected the Prosser formulation, choosing to distinguish claims for injury to personal feelings caused by an unauthorized use of a plaintiff's identity ("right of privacy") from claims seeking redress for pecuniary damages caused by an appropriation of the commercial value of the identity ("right of publicity"). Thus, in those jurisdictions, the right of publicity is viewed as an independent doctrine distinct from the right of privacy. . . .

Some jurisdictions attempt to follow Prosser's formulation of the tort and provide relief for both personal and commercial harm through a single common law or statutory cause of action.

In other states, however, the parameters or even the existence of the appropriation tort remain undetermined. Such is the case in Colorado.

B. COLORADO'S RECOGNITION OF THE APPROPRIATION TORT

A brief review of the development of the tort of invasion of privacy in Colorado demonstrates that recognition of the appropriation tort is a natural outgrowth of our earlier precedent.

We have recognized that invasion of privacy is a cognizable tort under Colorado law. Rugg v. McCarty, 476 P.2d 753, 755 (Colo. 1970). In *Rugg*, we held that a plaintiff may assert a claim for invasion of privacy where a creditor unreasonably attempts collection of a debt in a manner that will foreseeably result in extreme mental anguish and embarrassment to the debtor. In reaching this decision, we relied both on a Colorado statute that protected a privacy right and the fact that a majority of jurisdictions had recognized the tort of invasion of privacy. We did not, however, "attempt to comprehensively define the right of privacy, nor to categorize the character of all invasions which may constitute a violation of such right."

Recently, we recognized the tort of invasion of privacy by unreasonable publicity given to another's private life. Ozer v. Borquez, 940 P.2d 371, 377 (Colo. 1997). As in *Rugg*, we relied upon the fact that a majority of jurisdictions have recognized this tort.

Similarly, the tort of invasion of privacy by appropriation of a plaintiff's name or likeness has been recognized throughout most of the United States, either statutorily or through the common law. Further, neither the plaintiff nor the defendant in this case disputes that such a tort is cognizable in Colorado. We now hold that Colorado recognizes the tort of invasion of privacy by appropriation of an individual's name or likeness.

C. ELEMENTS OF THE TORT

Having recognized that the invasion of privacy by appropriation of name or likeness tort is recognized in Colorado, we now consider the elements of this tort.

The Second Restatement of Torts articulates the tort of appropriation of another's name or likeness, stating: "One who appropriates to his own use or benefit the name or likeness of another is subject to liability to the other for invasion of his privacy." Restatement (Second) of Torts §652C. The Colorado Civil Jury Instructions divide the tort into five distinct elements: (1) the defendant used the plaintiff's name or likeness; (2) the defendant sought to take advantage of the plaintiff's reputation, prestige, social or commercial standing, or any other value attached to the plaintiff's name, likeness, or identity; (3) the use of the plaintiff's name or likeness was for the defendant's own purposes or benefit, commercially or otherwise; (4) damages; and (5) causation. CJI-Civ. 4th 28:4 (2000).

The dispute in this case centers around the second element listed above, that defendant must appropriate "the reputation, prestige, social or commercial standing, or other value associated with the plaintiff's name or likeness." The defendant, Dickerson, argues that summary judgment in his favor is appropriate because the plaintiff, Dittmar, has presented no evidence that her name and likeness had any value.

The Colorado Civil Jury Instructions were developed from the comments to section 652C of the Second Restatement of Torts. Comment c implies that one element that a plaintiff must prove is that the plaintiff's identity has value, stating that "the defendant must have appropriated to his own use or benefit the reputation, prestige, social or commercial standing, public interest or other values of the plaintiff's name or likeness." Restatement (Second) of Torts §652C, cmt. c. Based on this and other comments to section 652C, some courts that follow the Restatement have explicitly required that one element of the tort is that the plaintiff's identity must have had pre-existing commercial value.

However, as discussed above, the Restatement takes a property-oriented approach to the law of appropriation, an approach not wholly embraced in all jurisdictions. In the context of damages intended to remedy a proprietary injury to the plaintiff's commercial interests, it may make sense to require a plaintiff to prove the value of her identity, either as part of her proof of damages or as an element of the tort. This does not necessarily mean that the value of the plaintiff's identity is relevant when the plaintiff seeks damages only for her mental anguish.

It appears illogical to require the plaintiff to prove that her identity has value in order for her to recover for her personal damages. The market value of the plaintiff's identity is unrelated to the question of whether she suffered mental anguish as a result of the alleged wrongful appropriation. A plaintiff whose identity had no commercial value might still experience mental anguish based on an unauthorized use of her name and likeness. Of the numerous cases that have considered the tort of invasion of privacy by appropriation of the plaintiff's name or likeness, few have suggested that there is any requirement that the plaintiff prove the value of her identity as a prerequisite to recovery for mental suffering. Rather, a more typical summary of the law is found in *Motschenbacher v. R.J. Reynolds Tobacco Co.*, where the 9th Circuit attempted to reconcile the relationship between commercial damages, mental anguish damages, and the requirement of value, stating:

> It is true that the injury suffered from an appropriation of the attributes of one's identity may be "mental and subjective"—in the nature of humiliation, embarrassment and outrage. However, where the identity appropriated has a commercial value, the injury may be largely, or even wholly, of an economic or material nature.

498 F.2d 821, 824 (9th Cir. 1974).

Consistent with this approach, we decline to include the second element of value, as described by the Colorado Civil Jury Instructions, as a required element of the tort. Hence, we hold that the elements of an invasion of privacy by appropriation claim are: (1) the defendant used the plaintiff's name or likeness; (2) the use of the plaintiff's name or likeness was for the defendant's own purposes or benefit, commercially or otherwise; (3) the plaintiff suffered damages; and (4) the defendant caused the damages incurred.

Applying these elements in this case, we conclude that Dittmar, the plaintiff, alleged sufficient facts to satisfy each of the required elements. We do not require the plaintiff, who seeks only personal damages, to prove the value of her identity. Thus, her failure to do so is not fatal to her claim.

We note that the plaintiff does not seek commercial damages. Hence, we do not reach the question of whether Colorado permits recovery for commercial damages under either the rubric of privacy or under the right of publicity, or the question of whether the plaintiff must prove the value of her identity when she seeks commercial damages.

Thus, we hold that the trial court erred by granting summary judgment to the defendant on the grounds that the plaintiff failed to provide evidence of the value of her name or likeness.

D. NEWSWORTHINESS PRIVILEGE

Having defined the elements of the tort of invasion of privacy by appropriation of name or likeness, we now consider the defendant's argument that the trial court properly granted summary judgment in his favor because his publication of the plaintiff's name and picture was constitutionally protected speech as a matter of law. We note, as discussed below, that our review is de novo because this is a question of law.

Dickerson, the defendant, argues that his article relates to a matter of legitimate public concern and that, therefore, it is constitutionally protected speech. The plaintiff agrees that the circumstances surrounding her arrest and conviction are newsworthy and of legitimate public concern. She does not object to the fact that a local newspaper wrote articles regarding her crime, arrest, trial, and conviction, or that these articles identified her by name. Instead, she argues that the defendant's republication of these same facts in his newsletter, in conjunction with her name and picture, constitutes an invasion of her privacy. She characterizes Dickerson's newsletter as an "infomercial" that is "designed to promote Dickerson's private investigation firm and to attract business for the firm." Hence, she argues that the character of the defendant's article is primarily commercial and that it should not receive the protection of the First Amendment. Under the particular facts of this case, we disagree with the plaintiff's argument.

In the context of invasion of privacy by appropriation of name and likeness, there is a First Amendment privilege that permits the use of a plaintiff's name or likeness when that use is made in the context of, and reasonably relates to, a publication concerning a matter that is newsworthy or of legitimate public concern. This privilege exists because dissemination of information regarding matters of public concern is necessary for the maintenance of an informed public.

In many situations, however, it is not altogether clear whether a particular use of a person's name or likeness is made for the purpose of communicating news or for the purpose of marketing a product or service. After all, many advertisements incorporate factual information as part of their sales message. *See* McCarthy, supra, §8:16 ("[A]s every marketer knows, the best way to sell is to slip the message 'buy me' in between informing and entertaining the prospective customer. Thus, almost all 'advertising' both entertains and informs.").

To resolve this question, courts must determine whether the character of the publication is primarily noncommercial, in which case the privilege will apply, or primarily commercial, in which case the privilege will not apply. Under this test, an article that has commercial undertones may still be protected if it concerns a legitimate matter of public concern. The question of whether a use of plaintiff's identity is primarily commercial or noncommercial is ordinarily decided as a question of law.

Because the defendant's article has aspects of both commercial and noncommercial speech, we must determine which type of speech predominates. The facts of this case are unusual. We have found no precedent where a convicted felon has brought a tort claim of wrongful appropriation of her identity based upon the defendant's republication of truthful information about her conviction.

To determine whether the defendant's use of the plaintiff's name and likeness was for a primarily commercial or noncommercial purpose, we must first define "commercial speech." Commercial speech is speech that proposes a commercial transaction. It is the content of the speech, not the motivation of the speaker, which determines whether particular speech is commercial.

A profit motive does not transform a publication regarding a legitimate matter of public concern into commercial speech. Id. ("Some of our most valued forms of fully protected speech are uttered for a profit."). Many news publishers, including newspapers and magazines, are motivated by their desire to make a profit. Courts have repeatedly held that, in order to be actionable, the use of a plaintiff's identity must be more directly commercial than simply being printed in a periodical that operates for profit. A contrary rule would preclude the publication of much news and other matters of legitimate public concern.

Applying the above principles to the instant case, we conclude that the defendant's publication was primarily noncommercial because it related to a matter of public concern, namely the facts of the plaintiff's crime and felony conviction. The defendant's article detailed how the plaintiff, who worked as a secretary at a brokerage firm, stole a customer's bearer bonds from her place of employment and cashed them for personal use. In addition, the article described the defendant's investigation of the plaintiff, the fact that the jury convicted the plaintiff of theft, and how the court ordered her to pay restitution to the theft victim. There can be no question that these details about the plaintiff's crime and conviction are matters of legitimate public concern. In Cox

Broadcasting Corp. v. Cohn, 420 U.S. 469, 492 (1975), the United States Supreme Court stated, "The commission of crime, prosecutions resulting from it, and judicial proceedings arising from the prosecutions . . . are without question events of legitimate concern to the public." In the context of a discussion of the plaintiff's crime and felony conviction, which are legitimate matters of public concern, the use of her name and picture cannot be described as a primarily commercial usage of her identity.

The fact that the defendant's article did not appear in a traditional newspaper does not change this result. We have previously stated that "[i]t is . . . well established that freedom of the press is not confined to newspapers or periodicals, but is a right of wide import and 'in its historic connotation comprehends every sort of publication which affords a vehicle of information and opinion.'" This means that if the contents of an article are newsworthy when published by a local newspaper, then they do not cease to be newsworthy when subsequently communicated by a different sort of publisher.

Further, the fact that the defendant's reason for publishing the newspaper may have been his own commercial benefit does not necessarily render the speech "commercial." As noted above, a magazine or newspaper article is protected despite the fact that a publisher may publish a particular article in order to make a profit. Similarly, the defendant's speech is protected even if he intends it to result in profit to him, so long as the contents of the speech qualify for protection.

The defendant's profit motive does not affect the fact that the article relates to the arrest and circumstances of a felony conviction, which are matters of legitimate public concern. Therefore, we conclude that the defendant's publication was predominately a noncommercial publication. We hold that the publication of a plaintiff's name and likeness in connection with a truthful article regarding the plaintiff's felony conviction is privileged. As such, the plaintiff's claim of invasion of privacy by appropriation of name or likeness cannot prevail.

IV. CONCLUSION

Since the defendant's use of the plaintiff's name and picture is privileged under the First Amendment, we reverse the court of appeals and return this case to that court with directions to reinstate the trial court's order granting summary judgment to the defendant.

PREPARING FOR CLASS

1. Why did the trial court dismiss Dittmar's claim?

2. What different interests does the appropriation tort protect? Which interest is the basis of Dittmar's suit?

3. What is the argument that having an identity with some value is essential to a cause of action? What is the argument that it is not?

4. Does the court accept or reject the rule as stated in the Colorado Civil Jury Instructions? Why or why not?

5. How could Dittmar argue that she has satisfied the relevant rule?

6. What are the requirements of the newsworthiness privilege? Could the defendant here satisfy them?

APPLYING THE LAW

1. Does Piper have an appropriation cause of action against Del?

2. Mary Kay Letourneau became notorious when she was convicted of statutory rape for having an affair with one of her middle-school students whose child she bore. Eventually, the couple married. The singer/songwriter Jill Sobule wrote a song about Mary Kay (and we don't want to pay for the permission to quote it, so Google it), which appeared on her *Pink Pearl* album. Was this appropriation?

White v. Samsung Electronics America, Inc. (*White I*)
971 F.2d 1395 (9th Cir. 1992)

GOODWIN, C.J. . . .
Plaintiff Vanna White is the hostess of "Wheel of Fortune," one of the most popular game shows in television history. An estimated forty million people watch the program daily. Capitalizing on the fame which her participation in the show has bestowed on her, White markets her identity to various advertisers.

The dispute in this case arose out of a series of advertisements prepared for Samsung by Deutsch. The series ran in at least half a dozen publications with widespread, and in some cases national, circulation. Each of the advertisements in the series followed the same theme. Each depicted a current item from popular culture and a Samsung electronic product. Each was set in the twenty-first century and conveyed the message that the Samsung product would still be in use by that time. By hypothesizing outrageous future outcomes for the cultural items, the ads created humorous effects. For example, one lampooned current popular notions of an unhealthy diet by depicting a raw steak with the caption: "Revealed to be health food. 2010 A.D." Another depicted irreverent "news"-show host Morton Downey Jr. in front of an American flag with the caption: "Presidential candidate. 2008 A.D."

The advertisement which prompted the current dispute was for Samsung video-cassette recorders (VCRs). The ad depicted a robot, dressed in a wig, gown, and jewelry which Deutsch consciously selected to resemble White's hair and dress. The robot was posed next to a game board which is instantly recognizable as the Wheel of Fortune game show set, in a stance for which White is famous. The caption of the ad read: "Longest-running game show. 2012 A.D." Defendants referred to the ad as the "Vanna White" ad. Unlike the other celebrities used in the campaign, White neither consented to the ads nor was she paid.

[White sued Samsung and Deutsch on various theories including a violation of her common law right of publicity. The district court awarded summary judgment to Samsung, and White appealed.]

White . . . argues that the district court erred in granting summary judgment to defendants on White's common law right of publicity claim. In Eastwood v. Superior Court, 198 Cal. Rptr. 342 (Cal. App. 1983), the California court of appeal stated that the common law right of publicity cause of action "may be pleaded by alleging (1) the defendant's use of the plaintiff's identity; (2) the appropriation of plaintiff's name or likeness to defendant's advantage, commercially or otherwise; (3) lack of consent; and (4) resulting injury." Id. at 342 (citing Prosser, *Law of Torts* (4th ed. 1971) §117, pp. 804-807). The district court dismissed White's claim for failure to satisfy *Eastwood*'s second prong, reasoning that defendants had not appropriated White's "name or likeness" with their robot ad. We agree that the robot ad did not make use of White's name or likeness. However, the common law right of publicity is not so confined. . . .

The "name or likeness" formulation referred to in Eastwood originated not as an element of the right of publicity cause of action, but as a description of the types of cases in which the cause of action had been recognized. The source of this formulation is Prosser, *Privacy*, 48 Cal. L. Rev. 383, 401-07 (1960), one of the earliest and most enduring articulations of the common law right of publicity cause of action. In looking at the case law to that point, Prosser recognized that right of publicity cases involved one of two basic factual scenarios: name appropriation, and picture or other likeness appropriation.

Even though Prosser focused on appropriations of name or likeness in discussing the right of publicity, he noted that "[i]t is not impossible that there might be appropriation of the plaintiff's identity, as by impersonation, without the use of either his name or his likeness, and that this would be an invasion of his right of privacy." At the time Prosser wrote, he noted however, that "[n]o such case appears to have arisen."

Since Prosser's early formulation, the case law has borne out his insight that the right of publicity is not limited to the appropriation of name or likeness. In Motschenbacher v. R.J. Reynolds Tobacco Co., 498 F.2d 821 (9th Cir. 1974), the defendant had used a photograph of the plaintiff's race car in a television commercial. Although the plaintiff appeared driving the car in the photograph, his features were not visible. Even though the defendant had not appropriated the plaintiff's name or likeness, this court held that plaintiff's California right of publicity claim should reach the jury.

In *Midler* [v. Ford Motor Co., 849 F.2d 460 (9th Cir. 1988)], this court held that, even though the defendants had not used Midler's name or likeness, Midler had stated a claim for violation of her California common law right of publicity because "the defendants . . . for their own profit in selling their product did appropriate part of her identity" by using a Midler sound-alike.

In Carson v. Here's Johnny Portable Toilets, Inc., 698 F.2d 831 (6th Cir.1983), the defendant had marketed portable toilets under the brand name "Here's Johnny"—Johnny Carson's signature "Tonight Show" introduction—without Carson's permission. The district court had dismissed Carson's Michigan common law right of publicity claim because the defendants had not used Carson's "name or likeness." In reversing the district court, the sixth circuit found "the district court's conception of the right of publicity . . . too narrow" and held that the right was implicated because the defendant had appropriated Carson's identity by using, inter alia, the phrase "Here's Johnny."

These cases teach not only that the common law right of publicity reaches means of appropriation other than name or likeness, but that the specific means of appropriation are relevant only for determining whether the defendant has in fact appropriated the plaintiff's identity. The right of publicity does not require that appropriations of identity be accomplished through particular means to be actionable. It is noteworthy that the *Midler* and *Carson* defendants not only avoided using the plaintiff's name or likeness, but they also avoided appropriating the celebrity's voice, signature, and photograph. The photograph in *Motschenbacher* did include the plaintiff, but because the plaintiff was not visible the driver could have been an actor or dummy and the analysis in the case would have been the same.

Although the defendants in these cases avoided the most obvious means of appropriating the plaintiffs' identities, each of their actions directly implicated the commercial interests which the right of publicity is designed to protect. . . .

It is not important how the defendant has appropriated the plaintiff's identity, but whether the defendant has done so. . . . A rule which says that the right of publicity can be infringed only through the use of nine different methods of appropriating identity merely challenges the clever advertising strategist to come up with the tenth.

Indeed, if we treated the means of appropriation as dispositive in our analysis of the right of publicity, we would not only weaken the right but effectively eviscerate it. The right would fail to protect those plaintiffs most in need of its protection. Advertisers use celebrities to promote their products. The more popular the celebrity, the greater the number of people who recognize her, and the greater the visibility for the product. The identities of the most popular celebrities are not only the most attractive for advertisers, but also the easiest to evoke without resorting to obvious means such as name, likeness, or voice. . . .

Viewed separately, the individual aspects of the advertisement in the present case say little. Viewed together, they leave little doubt about the celebrity the ad is meant to depict. The female-shaped robot is wearing a long gown, blond wig, and large jewelry. Vanna White dresses exactly like this at times, but so do many other women. The robot is in the process of turning a block letter on a game-board. Vanna White dresses like this while turning letters on a game-board but perhaps similarly attired Scrabble-playing women do this as well. The robot is standing on what looks to be the Wheel of Fortune game show set. Vanna White dresses like this, turns letters, and does this on the Wheel of Fortune game show. She is the only one. Indeed, defendants themselves referred to their ad as the "Vanna White" ad. We are not surprised.

Television and other media create marketable celebrity identity value. Considerable energy and ingenuity are expended by those who have achieved celebrity value to exploit it for profit. The law protects the celebrity's sole right to exploit this value whether the celebrity has achieved her fame out of rare ability, dumb luck, or a combination thereof. We decline Samsung and Deutch's invitation to permit the evisceration of the common law right of publicity through means as facile as those in this case. Because White has alleged facts showing that Samsung and Deutsch had appropriated her identity, the district court erred by rejecting, on summary judgment, White's common law right of publicity claim. . . .

IV. THE PARODY DEFENSE

In defense, defendants cite a number of cases for the proposition that their robot ad constituted protected speech. The only cases they cite which are even remotely relevant to this case are Hustler Magazine v. Falwell, 485 U.S. 46 (1988) and L.L. Bean, Inc. v. Drake Publishers, Inc., 811 F.2d 26 (1st Cir. 1987). Those cases involved parodies of advertisements run for the purpose of poking fun at Jerry Falwell and L.L. Bean, respectively. This case involves a true advertisement run for the purpose of selling Samsung VCRs. The ad's spoof of Vanna White and Wheel of Fortune is subservient and only tangentially related to the ad's primary message: "buy Samsung VCRs." Defendants' parody arguments are better addressed to non-commercial parodies. The difference between a "parody" and a "knock-off" is the difference between fun and profit. . . .

In remanding this case, we hold only that White has pleaded claims which can go to the jury for its decision.

White v. Samsung Electronics America, Inc. (*White II*)
989 F.2d 1512 (9th Cir. 1993)

[The court declined to rehear the case en banc. Judge Kozinski dissented.]
Saddam Hussein wants to keep advertisers from using his picture in unflattering contexts. Clint Eastwood doesn't want tabloids to write about him.

Rudolf Valentino's heirs want to control his film biography. The Girl Scouts don't want their image soiled by association with certain activities. George Lucas wants to keep Strategic Defense Initiative fans from calling it "Star Wars." Pepsico doesn't want singers to use the word "Pepsi" in their songs. Guy Lombardo wants an exclusive property right to ads that show big bands playing on New Year's Eve. Uri Geller thinks he should be paid for ads showing psychics bending metal through telekinesis. Paul Prudhomme, that household name, thinks the same about ads featuring corpulent bearded chefs. And scads of copyright holders see purple when their creations are made fun of. [Judge Kozinski provided cites for all of these statements.] . . .

Something very dangerous is going on here. Private property, including intellectual property, is essential to our way of life. It provides an incentive for investment and innovation; it stimulates the flourishing of our culture; it protects the moral entitlements of people to the fruits of their labors. But reducing too much to private property can be bad medicine. Private land, for instance, is far more useful if separated from other private land by public streets, roads and highways. Public parks, utility rights-of-way and sewers reduce the amount of land in private hands, but vastly enhance the value of the property that remains.

So too it is with intellectual property. Overprotecting intellectual property is as harmful as underprotecting it. Creativity is impossible without a rich public domain. Nothing today, likely nothing since we tamed fire, is genuinely new: Culture, like science and technology, grows by accretion, each new creator building on the works of those who came before. Overprotection stifles the very creative forces it's supposed to nurture.

The panel's opinion is a classic case of overprotection. Concerned about what it sees as a wrong done to Vanna White, the panel majority erects a property right of remarkable and dangerous breadth: Under the majority's opinion, it's now a tort for advertisers to remind the public of a celebrity. Not to use a celebrity's name, voice, signature or likeness; not to imply the celebrity endorses a product; but simply to evoke the celebrity's image in the public's mind. This Orwellian notion withdraws far more from the public domain than prudence and common sense allow. It conflicts with the Copyright Act and the Copyright Clause. It raises serious First Amendment problems. It's bad law, and it deserves a long, hard second look. . . .

Consider how sweeping this new right is. What is it about the ad that makes people think of White? It's not the robot's wig, clothes or jewelry; there must be ten million blond women (many of them quasi-famous) who wear dresses and jewelry like White's. It's that the robot is posed near the "Wheel of Fortune" game board. Remove the game board from the ad, and no one would think of Vanna White. But once you include the game board, anybody standing beside it—a brunette woman, a man wearing women's clothes, a monkey in a wig and gown—would evoke White's image, precisely the way the robot did. It's the "Wheel of Fortune" set, not the robot's face or dress or jewelry that evokes White's image. The panel is giving White an exclusive right not in what she looks like or who she is, but in what she does for a living.

This is entirely the wrong place to strike the balance. Intellectual property rights aren't free: They're imposed at the expense of future creators and of the public at large. Where would we be if Charles Lindbergh had an exclusive right in the concept of a heroic solo aviator? If Arthur Conan Doyle had gotten a copyright in the idea of the detective story, or Albert Einstein had patented the theory of relativity? If every author and celebrity had been given the right to keep people from mocking them or their work? Surely this would have made the world poorer, not richer, culturally as well as economically.

This is why intellectual property law is full of careful balances between what's set aside for the owner and what's left in the public domain for the rest of us: The relatively short life of patents; the longer, but finite, life of copyrights; copyright's idea-expression dichotomy; the fair use doctrine; the prohibition on copyrighting facts; the compulsory license of television broadcasts and musical compositions; federal preemption of overbroad state intellectual property laws; the nominative use doctrine in trademark law; the right to make soundalike recordings. All of these diminish an intellectual property owner's rights. All let the public use something created by someone else. But all are necessary to maintain a free environment in which creative genius can flourish.

The intellectual property right created by the panel here has none of these essential limitations: No fair use exception; no right to parody; no idea-expression dichotomy. It impoverishes the public domain, to the detriment of future creators and the public at large. Instead of well-defined, limited characteristics such as name, likeness or voice, advertisers will now have to cope with vague claims of "appropriation of identity," claims often made by people with a wholly exaggerated sense of their own fame and significance. Future Vanna Whites might not get the chance to create their personae, because their employers may fear some celebrity will claim the persona is too similar to her own. The public will be robbed of parodies of celebrities, and our culture will be deprived of the valuable safety valve that parody and mockery create.

Moreover, consider the moral dimension, about which the panel majority seems to have gotten so exercised. Saying Samsung "appropriated" something of White's begs the question: Should White have the exclusive right to something as broad and amorphous as her "identity"? Samsung's ad didn't simply copy White's schtick—like all parody, it created something new. True, Samsung did it to make money, but White does whatever she does to make money, too; the majority talks of "the difference between fun and profit," but in the entertainment industry fun is profit. Why is Vanna White's right to exclusive for-profit use of her persona—a persona that might not even be her own creation, but that of a writer, director or producer—superior to Samsung's right to profit by creating its own inventions? Why should she have such absolute rights to control the conduct of others, unlimited by the idea-expression dichotomy or by the fair use doctrine?

To paraphrase only slightly *Feist Publications, Inc. v. Rural Telephone Service Co.*, 499 U.S. 340 (1991), it may seem unfair that much of the fruit of a creator's labor may be used by others without compensation. But this is not some unforeseen byproduct of our intellectual property system; it is the system's very essence. Intellectual property law assures authors the right to their original expression, but encourages others to build freely on the ideas that underlie it. This result is neither unfair nor unfortunate: It is the means by which intellectual property law advances the progress of science and art. We give authors certain exclusive rights, but in exchange we get a richer public domain. The majority ignores this wise teaching, and all of us are the poorer for it. . . .

PREPARING FOR CLASS

1. *White I*

    a. What are the elements of appropriation?

    b. Why did the trial court dismiss the case? How does the Ninth Circuit criticize the trial court's interpretation of the law?

    c. What must be appropriated? How can appropriation occur?

    d. What policies support recognizing the appropriation tort?

    e. What does Vanna White's case have to do with privacy?

    f. Could White establish her claim?

    g. Did Samsung have a parody defense?

2. *White II*

    a. Why does Judge Kozinski describe the panel's opinion as "a classic case of overprotection"?

    b. In what way is intellectual property law "full of careful balances"? How does the ruling arguably upset these balances?

    c. What is Judge Kozinski's moral argument?

    d. How, according to Judge Kozinski, are we left poorer by the majority opinion?

INCREASING YOUR UNDERSTANDING

Name as a symbol of identity. T.J. Hooker was a professional woodcarver from Woodstock, Illinois. He specialized in carving ducks, and in that niche market did well for himself. He claimed to be "internationally renowned." "T.J. Hooker" was also a policeman portrayed by William Shatner in a television series by the same name. The producers of the show had never heard of the duck-carving T.J. Hooker, who himself admitted that the name was probably just a coincidence, but sued them for appropriation nonetheless. The court wrote:

> In order to state a claim for relief based on this theory, it is vital that some "appropriation" be alleged. See W. Prosser, *Law of Torts* §117 at 804-07 (4th ed. 1971). "Appropriation" in this context means more than the mere coincidental use of a name that happens to be the same as that of the plaintiff. Dean Prosser explained this as follows:
>
>> It is the plaintiff's name as a symbol of his identity that is involved here, and not as a mere name. Unless there is some tortious use made of it, there is no such thing as an exclusive right to the use of a name; and any one can be given or assume any name he likes. It is only when he makes use of the name to pirate the plaintiff's identity for some advantage of his own . . . that he becomes liable. . . . It is therefore not enough that a name which is the same as the plaintiff's is used in a novel, or the title of a corporation, unless the context or the circumstances indicate that the name is that of the plaintiff. . . .
>
> [I]t is apparent that plaintiff has failed to allege a tortious appropriation of his name. Plaintiff does allege that "[d]efendants' . . . use of plaintiff's name appropriates the right of publicity in plaintiff's celebrated name." But this broad, conclusory allegation cannot substitute for allegations of facts showing that the defendants used the name "T.J. Hooker" as a means of pirating plaintiff's identity. By his own admission, the commercial value of plaintiff's name is in the field of wildlife art. Hunters, sportsmen, and collectors identify plaintiff's name with fine carvings of ducks and other fowl. There is nothing in the complaint which can be construed as an allegation that the defendants adopted the name "T.J. Hooker" in order to avail themselves of plaintiff's reputation as an extraordinary woodcarver.

Hooker v. Columbia Pictures Industries, Inc., 551 F. Supp. 1060 (N.D. Ill. 1982).

APPLYING THE LAW

During the 2010 Super Bowl, E-Trade ran one of its popular talking-babies commercials. In the commercial, a female baby asked her boyfriend baby whether "that milkaholic Lindsay" had visited him. Another female baby then appeared and said in a drunken voice: "Milk-a-what?" The actress Lindsay Lohan sued E-Trade for appropriation. The case was brought under a New York statute, but consider whether, under the common law principles in the *White* case, Lohan had a claim. (E-Trade settled the case as "a business decision.")

Martin Luther King, Jr., Center for Social Change, Inc. v. American Heritage Products, Inc.
296 S.E.2d 697 (Ga. 1982)

HILL, J.

The plaintiffs are the Martin Luther King, Jr. Center for Social Change (the Center), Coretta Scott King, as administratrix of Dr. King's estate, and Motown Record Corporation, the assignee of the rights to several of Dr. King's copyrighted speeches. Defendant James F. Bolen is the sole proprietor of a business known as B & S Sales, which manufactures and sells various plastic products as funeral accessories. Defendant James E. Bolen, the son of James F. Bolen, developed the concept of marketing a plastic bust of Dr. Martin Luther King, Jr., and formed a company, B & S Enterprises, to sell the busts, which would be manufactured by B & S Sales. B & S Enterprises was later incorporated under the name of American Heritage Products, Inc.

Although Bolen sought the endorsement and participation of the Martin Luther King, Jr. Center for Social Change, Inc., in the marketing of the bust, the Center refused Bolen's offer. Bolen pursued the idea, nevertheless, hiring an artist to prepare a mold and an agent to handle the promotion of the product. Defendant took out two half-page advertisements in the November and December 1980 issues of *Ebony* magazine, which purported to offer the bust as "an exclusive memorial" and "an opportunity to support the Martin Luther King, Jr., Center for Social Change." The advertisement stated that "a contribution from your order goes to the King Center for Social Change." Out of the $29.95 purchase price, defendant Bolen testified he set aside 3% or $.90, as a contribution to the Center. The advertisement also offered "free" with the purchase of the bust a booklet about the life of Dr. King entitled "A Tribute to Dr. Martin Luther King, Jr." . . .

Defendant James E. Bolen testified that he created a trust fund for that portion of the earnings which was to be contributed to the Center. The trust fund agreement, however, was never executed. . . . Also, the district court found that, as of the date of the preliminary injunction, the defendants had sold approximately 200 busts and had outstanding orders for 23 more.

[The plaintiffs filed a complaint requesting various forms of injunctive relief.]

In ruling on the third request for injunction, the court confronted the plaintiffs' claim that the manufacture and sale of the busts violated Dr. King's right of publicity which had passed to his heirs upon Dr. King's death. The defendants contended that no such right existed, and hence, an injunction should not issue. The district court concluded that it was not necessary to determine whether the "right of publicity" was devisable in Georgia because Dr. King did not commercially exploit this right during his lifetime. As found by the district court, the evidence of exploitation by Dr. King came from his sister's affidavit which stated that he had received "thousands of dollars in the form of honorariums from the use of his name, likeness, literary compositions, and speeches." The district court further found that "Dr. King apparently sold his copyrights in several speeches to Motown Records Corporation."

On plaintiffs' appeal of the partial denial of the preliminary injunction, the Eleventh Circuit Court of Appeals has certified the following questions:

> (1) Is the "right of publicity" recognized in Georgia as a right distinct from the right of privacy?
> (2) If the answer to question (1) is affirmative, does the "right to publicity" survive the death of its owner? Specifically, is the right inheritable and devisable?
> (3) If the answer to question (2) is also affirmative, must the owner have commercially exploited the right before it can survive his death?
> (4) Assuming the affirmative answers to questions (1), (2) and (3), what is the guideline to be followed in defining commercial exploitation and what are the evidentiary prerequisites to a showing of commercial exploitation? . . .

The right of publicity may be defined as a celebrity's right to the exclusive use of his or her name and likeness. The right is most often asserted by or on behalf of professional athletes, comedians, actors and actresses, and other entertainers. This case involves none of those occupations. As is known to all, from 1955 until he was assassinated on April 4, 1968, Dr. King, a Baptist minister by profession, was the foremost leader of the civil rights movement in the United States. He was awarded the Nobel Prize for Peace in 1964. Although not a public official, Dr. King was a public figure, and we deal in this opinion with public figures who are neither public officials nor entertainers. Within this framework, we turn to the questions posed.

[The court answered Question 1 in the affirmative.]

2. Does the "right of publicity" survive the death of its owner (i.e., is the right inheritable and devisable)?

Although the *Pavesich* court [Pavesich v. New England Life Ins. Co, 50 S.E. 68 (1905)] expressly did not decide this question, the tenor of that opinion is that the right to privacy at least should be protectable after death.

The right of publicity is assignable during the life of the celebrity, for without this characteristic, full commercial exploitation of one's name and likeness is practically impossible. That is, without assignability the right of publicity could hardly be called a "right." Recognizing its assignability, most commentators have urged that the right of publicity must also be inheritable.

The courts that have considered the problem are not as unanimous. In Price v. Hal Roach Studios, Inc., [400 F. Supp. 836, S.D.N.Y. 1975] the court reasoned that since the right of publicity was assignable, it survived the deaths of Stanley Laurel and Oliver Hardy. Other decisions from the Southern District of New York recognize the descendibility of the right of publicity, which has also been recognized by the Second Circuit Court of Appeals.

In Factors Etc., Inc. v. Pro Arts, Inc., 579 F.2d 215 (2d Cir. 1978), Elvis Presley had assigned his right of publicity to Boxcar Enterprises, which assigned that right to Factors after Presley's death. Defendant Pro Arts published a poster of Presley entitled "In Memory." In affirming the grant of injunction against Pro Arts, the Second Circuit Court of Appeals said, "The identification of this exclusive right belonging to Boxcar as a transferable property right compels the conclusion that the right survives Presley's death. The death of Presley, who was merely the beneficiary of an income interest in Boxcar's exclusive right, should not in itself extinguish Boxcar's property right. Instead, the income interest, continually produced from Boxcar's exclusive right of commercial exploitation, should inure to Presley's estate at death like any other intangible property right. To hold that the right did not survive Presley's death, would be to grant competitors of Factors, such as Pro Arts, a windfall in the form of profits from the use of Presley's name and likeness. At the same time, the exclusive right purchased by Factors and the financial benefits accruing to the celebrity's heirs would be rendered virtually worthless."

In Lugosi v. Universal Pictures, 603 P.2d 425 (Cal. 1979), the Supreme Court of California, in a 4 to 3 decision, declared that the right of publicity expires upon the death of the celebrity and is not descendible. . . .

In Memphis Development Foundation v. Factors Etc., Inc., 616 F.2d 956 (6th Cir. 1980), Factors, which had won its case against Pro Arts in New York, lost against the Memphis Development Foundation under the Court of Appeals for the Sixth Circuit's interpretation of Tennessee law. There, the Foundation, a non-profit corporation, planned to erect a statue of Elvis Presley in Memphis and solicited contributions to do so. Donors of $25 or more received a small replica of the proposed statue. The Sixth Circuit reversed the grant of an injunction favoring Factors, holding that a celebrity's right of publicity was not inheritable even where that right had been exploited during the celebrity's life.[4] The court reasoned that although recognition of the right of publicity during life serves to encourage effort and inspire creative endeavors, making the right inheritable would not. The court also was concerned with unanswered legal questions which recognizing inheritability would create. We note, however, that the court was dealing with a non-profit foundation attempting to promote Presley's adopted home-place, the City of Memphis. The court was not dealing, as we do here, with a profit making endeavor.

In Estate of Presley v. Russen, [513 F. Supp. 1339 (D.N.J. 1981)], the court found in favor of descendibility, quoting from Chief Justice Bird's dissent in

---

4. The Second Circuit has now accepted the Sixth Circuit's interpretation of Tennessee law. Factors Etc., Inc. v. Pro Arts, Inc., 652 F.2d 278 (2d Cir. 1981).

Lugosi v. Universal Pictures, supra, 603 P.2d at 434, and saying: "If the right is descendible, the individual is able to transfer the benefits of his labor to his immediate successors and is assured that control over the exercise of the right can be vested in a suitable beneficiary. 'There is no reason why, upon a celebrity's death, advertisers should receive a windfall in the form of freedom to use with impunity the name or likeness of the deceased celebrity who may have worked his or her entire life to attain celebrity status. The financial benefits of that labor should go to the celebrity's heirs. . . . '"

For the reasons which follow we hold that the right of publicity survives the death of its owner and is inheritable and devisable. Recognition of the right of publicity rewards and thereby encourages effort and creativity. If the right of publicity dies with the celebrity, the economic value of the right of publicity during life would be diminished because the celebrity's untimely death would seriously impair, if not destroy, the value of the right of continued commercial use. Conversely, those who would profit from the fame of a celebrity after his or her death for their own benefit and without authorization have failed to establish their claim that they should be the beneficiaries of the celebrity's death. Finally, the trend since the early common law has been to recognize survivability, notwithstanding the legal problems which may thereby arise. We therefore answer question 2 in the affirmative.

3. Must the owner of the right of publicity have commercially exploited that right before it can survive?

Exploitation is understood to mean commercial use by the celebrity other than the activity which made him or her famous, e.g., an inter vivos transfer of the right to the use of one's name and likeness.

The requirement that the right of publicity be exploited by the celebrity during his or her lifetime in order to render the right inheritable arises from the case involving Agatha Christie, Hicks v. Casablanca Records, [464 F. Supp. 426 (S.D.N.Y. 1978)] [but the cited cases were not apt]. Moreover, the *Hicks* court held that the fictional account of Agatha Christie's 11-day disappearance was protected by the first amendment. Thus, the finding that exploitation during life was necessary to inheritability was actually unnecessary to that decision.

Nevertheless, the *Hicks* dicta has been relied upon. *See* Groucho Marx Productions, Inc. v. Day & Night Co., 523 F. Supp. 485, 490 (S.D.N.Y. 1981). However, in this case, involving the Marx brothers, it was found that, although Leo and Adolpho Marx ("Chico" and "Harpo") had not made inter vivos or specific testamentary dispositions of their rights, they had earned their livelihoods by exploiting the unique characters they created and thus had exploited their rights to publicity so as to make such rights descendible. Thus, even in the Southern District of New York where the requirement arose, exploitation beyond the "activity which made him or her famous" is not now required.

The cases which have considered this issue involved entertainers. The net result of following them would be to say that celebrities and public figures have the right of publicity during their lifetimes (as others have the right of privacy), but only those who contract for bubble gum cards, posters and tee shirts have a descendible right of publicity upon their deaths. That we should single out for protection after death those entertainers and athletes who exploit their personae during life, and deny protection after death to those who enjoy public acclamation but did not exploit themselves during life, puts a premium on exploitation. Having found that there are valid reasons for recognizing the right of publicity during life, we find no reason to protect after death only those who took commercial advantage of their fame.

Perhaps this case more than others brings the point into focus. A well known minister may avoid exploiting his prominence during life because to do otherwise would impair his ministry. Should his election not to take commercial advantage of his position during life ipso facto result in permitting others to exploit his name and likeness after his death? In our view, a person who avoids exploitation during life is entitled to have his image protected against exploitation after death just as much if not more than a person who exploited his image during life.

Without doubt, Dr. King could have exploited his name and likeness during his lifetime. That this opportunity was not appealing to him does not mean that others have the right to use his name and likeness in ways he himself chose not to do. Nor does it strip his family and estate of the right to control, preserve and extend his status and memory and to prevent unauthorized exploitation thereof by others. Here, they seek to prevent the exploitation of his likeness in a manner they consider unflattering and unfitting. We cannot deny them this right merely because Dr. King chose not to exploit or commercialize himself during his lifetime.

Question 3 is answered in the negative, and therefore we need not answer question 4. . . .

PREPARING FOR CLASS

Imagine that you are in a state that has not addressed Questions 2 and 3 from this case.

1. As plaintiff's counsel, how would you argue those questions to your state supreme court?

2. As defendant's counsel, how would you argue them?

3. As a judge, how would you rule?

Chapter 22

Misrepresentation

A. INTRODUCTION

In this chapter we deal with the tort of misrepresentation. A misrepresentation is a false statement of fact made with the intention that the listener will rely on it. There are various causes of action for misrepresentation. In the context of contract law, a false statement may give rise to an action to set the contract aside, i.e., rescission, or those statements may be warranties that could bring about a cause of action for breach of warranty or contract. A false statement may also give rise to an action for negligence. A person who told a child "you can cross the road now" before the person had checked for oncoming traffic, causing the child to be struck by a car, would be sued for negligence. But in this chapter we are dealing with the tort of misrepresentation. The victims of these misrepresentations have been damaged as a result of relying on the false statements of someone. They seek not necessarily the return of their property but money damages for the loss caused when they relied on the false statement.

Hypothetical

The Campbell Corporation (Campbell) has decided to move its high-tech factory to China. But Campbell desperately needs to recruit highly educated engineers for the last four months of operating its business in Chicago. Campbell runs advertisements in a major Chicago technical journal that say:

Fabulous Opportunity
Chance of a Lifetime
Campbell Corporation Is Hiring
Run Don't Walk To Apply

Campbell also retained an engineering professor, Paul Davis. Davis was retained primarily to recruit engineers from the engineering school where he taught. Professor Davis wrote a letter to the best graduates of his school saying, "I've been around this business quite a while. The Campbell opportunity is one of the best I've ever seen." Professor Davis had talked to Campbell engineering executives about their job offerings but had never asked about their plans to stay in the region. Campbell thought the Davis letter was helpful, so they sent a copy to everyone they recruited.

Campbell hired 20 highly qualified engineers, all of whom had read Professor Davis's letter, but only five of whom were from his engineering school and had received the letter directly from him.

After three months of work, the engineers were given one month notice that they must either move to China with Campbell or lose their jobs. Campbell says that it was very careful to never represent to any applicant the length of their expected employment.

Most of the engineers were making $1,000 per month in their previous jobs but left them because Campbell was promising $1,500 per month.

A) The five engineers from Professor Davis's school want to sue Davis and Campbell. What are the issues, and how would you expect the court to rule? Explain your answer.

B) The 15 engineers who did not graduate from Professor Davis's school, and so were not in his classes and did not receive his letter directly from him, also want to sue Davis and Campbell. How would you expect a court to rule? Explain your answer.

B. FRAUD

The common law recognized a cause of action for intentional misrepresentation or deceit. Modern courts have been willing to go one or two steps further to award the victim of a negligent misrepresentation, or even, in some cases, an innocent misrepresentation.

Bortz v. Noon
729 A.2d 555 (Pa. 1999)

NEWMAN, Justice.
This is an appeal by Coldwell Banker Real Estate (Coldwell Banker) from an Order of the Superior Court, which affirmed the determination of the

Court of Common Pleas of Allegheny County (Chancellor). Coldwell Banker was held liable to the buyer of residential property for a misrepresentation made by its agent relating to a third party's repairs of the on-site sewage disposal system (septic system) located on the property. Coldwell Banker raises the sole issue of whether the actions of its agent amounted to fraudulent misrepresentation. For the reasons that follow, we reverse the Superior Court and hold that a real estate broker cannot be liable for the misrepresentation of its agent, innocently made, under circumstances where the agent had no reason to know that her statement was false, and the agent had no duty to verify the accuracy of the third party report.

I. FACTS

On July 27, 1986, Albert M. Bortz (the Buyer) and his former wife entered into an Agreement of Sale with Patrick J. Noon and Virginia R. Noon (collectively Sellers), to buy the Sellers' home on Woodland Road in Pittsburgh, Pennsylvania. Coldwell Banker, through its agent, Renee Valent (the Agent), was the selling agent for the property. The Buyer had used the Agent as a selling agent for his previous home, and testified at the hearing of this matter that he considered the Agent as his representative for the Woodland Road transaction for the purchase of the Woodland Road home, the Agent referred the Buyer to a lender, Coldwell Banker Residential Mortgage Services, Inc. (the Lender). There is no evidence to suggest that the Lender was affiliated with Coldwell Banker. For the Buyer to receive a mortgage commitment from the Lender, the septic system had to pass a dye test before closing, and the Agent informed the Buyer that the septic system needed to pass this test before the closing. The Agent referred the Buyer to a contractor to conduct the test. On August 14, 1986, the contractor performed the dye test, and the septic system failed.[1] The contractor told the Agent that the septic system failed the dye test and the Agent then informed the Buyer. The Agent did not give the Buyer a copy of this report, and apparently, the Buyer did not ask for one.

Following the failed dye test, the Agent told the Buyer that the Sellers had the option of repairing the septic system, and they had chosen another contractor, J.J. Nolte (Nolte), to do the work. There is no evidence that the Agent had any dealings with Nolte nor played any part in the selection of Nolte as a contractor. The Agent informed the Buyer that settlement would be delayed until a dye test was successful. The Buyer argues that the Agent represented to him that the problem with the septic system would be repaired. During the period that Nolte was working on the septic system, the Buyer and his father-in-law went to the home, observed Nolte, and seemingly had the opportunity to ask questions about the repairs to the septic system.

---

1. This dye test is not at issue in this appeal, as the Chancellor found no misrepresentation related to it.

At some point in September of 1986, a woman from Suburban Settlement Services, Inc. (the Title Company) told the Agent that "the dye test passed and now we can set closing." The Agent conveyed this information to the Buyer, and then set a settlement closing date. Neither the Agent nor the Buyer reviewed a written Nolte report evidencing a satisfactory dye test. The closing on the house was on September 26, 1986, at the offices of the Title Company, but apparently, the proceedings were delayed for ten to twenty minutes. The Agent believed that the closing was delayed because of "Mr. Nolte's inspection—you know, everything was supposed to be fine a week before the closing, so I assume they had this paperwork." In addition, the Agent testified that she believed that the County was inspecting Nolte's work on the day of closing, and she in turn told the Buyer that the County would inspect the septic system.

When the closing finally occurred, the settlement officer from the Title Company, Christopher Abernathy, told everyone present, including the Agent and the Buyer, that the dye test on the septic system had passed. Apparently, however, neither the Agent nor the Buyer was given any written materials to verify this statement, and neither asked to review the report. Following the closing, the Buyer and his former wife discovered that the septic tank had not actually passed a dye test. In fact, the former wife of the Buyer testified that she received a call from the Title Company and was advised that it had "forgotten to do the dye test." The Title Company then scheduled a new dye test for October 22, 1986. The septic system failed the test and the system could not be repaired. The only alternative was to connect into the public sewer system at a cost of more than $15,000.

In an equity proceeding, the Buyer then sued Coldwell Banker, the Title Company, and the Sellers seeking monetary damages and rescission of the Agreement of Sale. The Buyer claimed that all defendants made affirmative misstatements regarding repairs on the septic system and reported that the septic system was functioning properly. The Sellers joined Nolte. After a hearing in the matter, the Chancellor entered an order in favor of the Buyer and against Coldwell Banker, concluding that Coldwell Banker, "through [its agent], made material misrepresentations to [the Buyer] by failing to disclose the conflicting septic test results and making affirmative representations that the septic system was repaired and properly functioning." The Chancellor denied a rescission of the sale, but entered a decree nisi in favor of the Buyer and against Coldwell Banker for $15,300 plus pre-judgment interest. The Chancellor held that neither Nolte nor the Title Company owed a duty to the Buyer and thus could not be liable for misrepresentation. Coldwell Banker filed motions for post-trial relief, alleging that it could not be liable for misrepresentation, which the trial court denied. Coldwell Banker then filed an appeal to the Superior Court.

On the appeal of Coldwell Banker, the Superior Court affirmed in part and reversed in part the decision of the Chancellor. The Superior Court agreed with the conclusion of the Chancellor that Coldwell Banker was liable to the

Buyer for misrepresentation because the Agent had a duty to ascertain whether the septic system had actually passed the dye test, and her failure to do so constituted a misrepresentation under the circumstances of this case. However, the Superior Court reversed the finding of the Chancellor regarding Nolte and the Title Company, and held that both could be liable to the Buyer for misrepresentation. Judge Johnson dissented. While Judge Johnson agreed that Nolte and the Title Company were liable to the Buyer for misrepresentation, he disagreed that Coldwell Banker was liable.[2]

We granted allocator limited to the question of whether the Superior Court was correct in its conclusions that the Agent had a duty to ascertain whether the septic system had actually passed the dye test and if her failure to do so amounted to a misrepresentation to the Buyer. There is no appeal docketed regarding the determination of the Superior Court that Nolte and the Title Company owed a duty to the Buyer, and we do not address that portion of the Superior Court's opinion in this appeal.

II. ANALYSIS

Coldwell Banker argues that it can not be liable for fraudulent misrepresentation because the Agent made no affirmative misrepresentation, she had no duty to disclose Nolte's reports, and she had no knowledge that the septic system was not working properly. Coldwell Banker further asserts that at most the Agent made a statement concerning a future event that the septic system would be repaired, a statement that can not support a cause of action for fraudulent misrepresentation.

The Buyer counters that the Agent indeed misrepresented material facts when she misrepresented that the dye test was clear, coupled with a promise of a future event that the septic system would pass a dye test and function properly before closing. Moreover, she scheduled and attended the closing; failed to advise the Buyer that she was unaware of whether the original representation was actually true; and failed to ascertain whether the facts originally represented continued to be true. Thus, the Agent is liable for misrepresenting a material fact on which the Buyer relied in closing on the property. Therefore, she had a duty both to correct this misrepresentation and to disclose the report of Nolte to the Buyer.

A. FACT FINDING OF THE CHANCELLOR

After a hearing in this matter, the Chancellor found that the Agent made "affirmative misrepresentations that the septic system was repaired and properly functioning." A review of the record reasonably reflects this conclusion.

---

2. Judge Johnson explained that the Lender required the septic system test and the Agent gave the Buyer all of the information that she had about the test.

In particular, the Agent testified that in the days preceding the closing, she told the Buyer that the septic system had passed the dye test. This representation was not accurate, and was followed by conduct that reinforced the affirmative statement that the septic system had passed the dye test. The Agent set up the closing date, which strengthened the perception that the septic system was acceptable because the mortgage could not be approved without such a test. Additionally, at the closing, the proceedings were delayed on the assumption the dye test information was delivered to the closing. These acts, together with the affirmative statement of the Agent before the closing, support the determination of the Chancellor that the Agent made an affirmative misrepresentation. We now turn to the question of whether, under the facts presented here, the Agent had a duty to disclose the written report and whether the law in this Commonwealth allows the Buyer to recover against Coldwell Banker for the Agent's affirmative misrepresentation regarding the dye test.

B. LEGAL LIABILITY FOR MISREPRESENTATION

Generally, a misrepresentation may be actionable pursuant to three theories: Intentional Misrepresentation, Negligent Misrepresentation, and Innocent Misrepresentation.

1. Intentional Misrepresentation

The elements of intentional misrepresentation are as follows:

(1) A representation;

(2) which is material to the transaction at hand;

(3) made falsely, with knowledge of its falsity or recklessness as to whether it is true or false;

(4) with the intent of misleading another into relying on it;

(5) justifiable reliance on the misrepresentation; and,

(6) the resulting injury was proximately caused by the reliance.

Gibbs v. Ernst, 538 Pa. 193, 207, 647 A.2d 882, 889 (1994), citing, Restatement (Second) of Torts §525 (1977). The tort of intentional non-disclosure has the same elements as intentional misrepresentation "except in the case of intentional non-disclosure, the party intentionally conceals a material fact rather than making an affirmative misrepresentation." We have recognized the tort of intentional misrepresentation and intentional concealment in the context of real estate broker liability to the buyer of residential property.

Here, there is no evidence supporting a conclusion that the Agent intentionally misrepresented any facts to the Buyer, nor intended to deceive the Buyer by failing to give him copies of the septic system reports, which she herself did not have. While the Agent made an affirmative misrepresentation that the dye test was clear, there is no finding that the Agent made any misrepresentation with knowledge that it was false. Instead, the Agent was giving information to the Buyer that she received from the Title Company, an apparently reputable company, so that she could schedule the closing. The Agent had no agency relationship with the Title Company or Nolte, and she had not selected Nolte to perform the septic tank repairs nor asked him to do the dye test. The Chancellor did not find that the Agent acted with knowledge that the septic tank had not passed the dye test, nor that she acted recklessly. Moreover, there was no evidence in the record that the Agent intended to mislead the Buyer in any way, a required element of intentional misrepresentation. Thus, the Record does not support any conclusion that the Agent could be liable to the Buyer for an intentional fraudulent misrepresentation or concealment.

2. Negligent Misrepresentation

Negligent misrepresentation requires proof of: (1) a misrepresentation of a material fact; (2) made under circumstances in which the misrepresenter ought to have known its falsity; (3) with an intent to induce another to act on it; and; (4) which results in injury to a party acting in justifiable reliance on the misrepresentation. The elements of negligent misrepresentation differ from intentional misrepresentation in that the misrepresentation must concern a material fact and the speaker need not know his or her words are untrue, but must have failed to make a reasonable investigation of the truth of these words. Moreover, like any action in negligence, there must be an existence of a duty owed by one party to another. This Court has not specifically recognized this cause of action in the situation of a real estate broker, but the Superior Court has applied a negligence standard in a number of cases.

Moreover, many other states recognize that a real estate broker may be liable for negligent misrepresentations when the broker fails to use reasonable care in ascertaining the truth of a representation. Generally, these courts have expanded liability of real estate brokers for failing independently to verify facts that the seller represents to the broker, and which the broker then passes on to the buyer. In these cases, the courts have found that because of the relationship among the buyer, seller, and broker, the broker is in a better position to verify the statements of the seller than is the buyer.

Here, neither the Chancellor nor the Superior Court specifically articulated the exact legal theory supporting their ultimate finding of liability. However, although not specifically labeled, it appears that both the Chancellor and the Superior Court found Coldwell Banker liable based upon either a negligent or innocent misrepresentation, for the Agent's misstatement to the Buyer that the septic system passed the dye test and for negligently failing to provide him with Nolte's written reports. In his Adjudication of the matter, the Chancellor discussed Section 323 of the Restatement (Second) of Torts, apparently concluding that the Agent had assumed a duty to the Buyer. In denying post-trial motions, the Chancellor opined that the Agent "so positioned [herself] as to be liable to the Buyer in money damages" and "had the duty to be sure that when the closing of title occurred the circumstances conformed with the Buyer's expectations or risk the consequences." He also determined that the Agent:

> took no action to be sure that the Nolte report was, in fact, a "clear septic test". . . . It was careless (or worse) of Valent to either rely wholly on Abernathy's interpretation of the report, and not to examine it herself. . . . At the very least, Valent should have seen to it that Bortz had both the Ross and Nolte reports available for his review. Valent did none of the above and proceeded in reckless disregard of the expectations and attendant rights of Bortz.

The Superior Court essentially agreed with the Chancellor and determined that the Agent and Coldwell Banker were liable to the Buyer because the Agent had a duty to make an independent inquiry to determine whether the septic tank actually had passed the dye test, by reviewing either the report herself, or checking County records.

While we recognize that there is no reason to per se omit a real estate broker or its agent from liability for negligence or misrepresentations negligently made, a reasonable review of the record in this matter does not support the conclusion that the Agent made a negligent misrepresentation, or negligently failed to disclose the Nolte report, because there is not an adequate record of evidence to support a conclusion that the Agent had a duty to investigate the accuracy of the dye test, or that she had a duty to provide the Buyer with a written copy of Nolte's report. First, there was no testimony or introduction of other evidence to establish that in 1986, the standard of care in the real estate brokerage business required an agent independently to verify or disclose test results that the broker had not ordered and were not part of the sales purchase agreement. Second, under the circumstances of this case, the Agent would have no reason to know that the representatives from the Title Company failed to confirm that the dye test was properly executed, before telling her that the test was clean. Third, there was no special relationship among the Buyer, the Agent, the Title Company and the Lender that would require the Agent to undertake such investigation, or that would place the Agent in a superior position to the Buyer in verifying the accuracy of the third party reports of the dye test. The dye test was part of the requirement of the Lender's mortgage and it was the Title Company that on two occasions misrepresented facts to both the Agent and the Buyer that the dye test was clear.

The Agent was not acting as a source of information from Sellers or other entity with whom she had an agency relationship and which might then trigger a duty to physically transfer the reports to the Buyer and verify the accuracy of statements that were material to the sales transaction. She had not assumed the duty of arranging, verifying or investigating the test, and did not act with the pretense of knowledge that the dye test was in fact clear. Instead, the Agent acted as the innocent conduit of information from an apparently reliable source, who said that the dye test was "clear," and the Agent repeated this statement solely in the context of scheduling the closing.

While the Agent did state to the Buyer that there was a clean septic dye test, she had no knowledge to the contrary and she did not know that the representative from the Title Company was providing misinformation. There was nothing in the relationship among the parties that would place the Agent on notice that the information was incorrect and she had no duty to engage in any independent inquiry. There is no record evidence that the Agent had specialized knowledge of septic systems, that she pretended to have such knowledge, or that she assumed the obligation of guaranteeing or providing this information to the Buyer.

We believe that imposing upon the Agent the duty to investigate, in the unique circumstance of this case, would place too high a burden on real estate agents. It would be an unreasonable burden on them because it would make it their responsibility to guarantee the accuracy of pre-closing tests done by persons with whom they have no relationship. Thus, we hold that a real estate broker has no duty to make an independent investigation of a contractor's report, where the real estate broker did not have any agency or contractual relationship with the third party.

3. Innocent Misrepresentation

A claim for an "innocent" misrepresentation has been recognized in this Commonwealth in order to rescind a real estate transaction that is based upon a material misrepresentation, even if the misrepresentation is innocently made. However, we have found no cases in which this Court adopted this theory as a basis to award monetary damages for tort recovery. . . . In *De Joseph*, we set aside a sale because of termite infestation that was concealed from the purchaser. We formulated the cause of action for fraud as follows:

> Where a party is induced to enter into a transaction with another by means of the latter's fraud or material misrepresentation; such a transaction can be avoided by the innocent party. Fraud arises where the misrepresentation is knowingly false, where there is concealment calculated to deceive, or where there is non-privileged failure to disclose. Fraud renders a transaction voidable even where the misrepresentation is not material; on the other hand, a misrepresentation made innocently is not actionable unless it is material, and in such case there must be a right to reliance.

139 A.2d at 647. . . .

In La Course v. Kiesel, 366 Pa. 385, 77 A.2d 877 (1951), we also set aside a sale, although neither the seller nor the real estate broker intentionally misrepresented facts to the buyer. In *La Course*, the sellers of real estate engaged an auction company to act as their agent in advertising and selling real estate. One of the sellers told the broker that the property was zoned R-5, which permitted apartments, and the broker advertised the property as "splendid for apartments." Prospective buyers entered an agreement of sale for the property and then learned that the building lot was not appropriately zoned for apartments. They thus sought an action in equity to cancel the agreement of sale and for a return of their deposit money. The Chancellor entered an Order in favor of the buyers. This Court affirmed although there was no evidence that either the brokers or the owners knew of the restriction on the zoning. We held that:

> whether the auctioneer or owners knew that the representation was false has been repeatedly held in this jurisdiction to be a matter of no consequence. A vendor has no right to make a statement of which he has no knowledge.
>
> * * *
>
> A material misrepresentation of an existing fact confers on the party who relies on it the right to rescind whether the defendant here actually knew the truth or not, especially where as here, they had means of knowledge from which they were bound to ascertain the truth before making the representation.

A claim for a misrepresentation, innocently made, to the extent recognized in this Commonwealth, is an equitable doctrine based upon contract principles supporting equitable rescission to make a contract voidable by the innocent party, where appropriate, as set forth in *DeJoseph*, supra and *La Course*, supra. Here, we have not been asked to address the issue of whether this doctrine was viable here, because the Chancellor denied rescission, and that determination was not appealed. However, we decline to extend these equitable principles to establish legal tort liability for an innocent misrepresentation of the Agent, where she had no duty to ascertain the accuracy of test results of a third party with whom she had no agency or other relationship. Such strict liability would place too high a burden on the real estate broker.

III. Conclusion

For the reasons set forth in this Opinion, we reverse the Superior Court's determination and hold that Coldwell Banker is not liable to the Buyer for the affirmative misrepresentations of the Agent. The remainder of the Superior Court's Opinion governing the liability of the Title Company and Nolte was not at issue in this appeal.

PREPARING FOR CLASS

1. The court said that there was no evidence that the Agent knew that the dye test had not been performed. Is there any other way that the Agent could be responsible for intentional misrepresentation? (See Note 6 in Increasing Your Understanding, below.) Are there any facts that support this argument?

2. The court said that there was "no testimony or introduction of other evidence to establish that in 1986, the standard of care in the real estate brokerage business required an agent independently to verify or disclose test results that the broker had not ordered and were not part of the sales purchase agreement." What is the standard of care for a real estate broker? Is it the standard of care in the real estate brokerage industry at the time of the act? How does the court know what that standard of care is?

3. There are many documents in a real estate closing, for example, surveys, various affidavits of the buyer and seller, etc. Why wouldn't the closing company or the Agent require a document that they had previously delayed the closing for? Isn't that negligence?

4. The court says that the Agent has no "special relationship" that would require her to investigate or place her in a superior position to verify the results of the dye testing. The Agent is a licensed real estate professional who often is responsible for closings for clients. This agent had represented the plaintiffs in the past. Doesn't that give her a "superior position" to investigate or verify necessary facts? Wouldn't you expect a real estate agent to verify important facts in the closing of your home?

5. The court said that there is no precedent for awarding damages for innocent misrepresentation. But should there be; i.e., shouldn't the court consider whether there are public policy reasons for awarding damages for innocent misrepresentation? Can you think of any?

INCREASING YOUR UNDERSTANDING

1. One of the original common law cases of misrepresentation was Derry v. Peek, 14 App. Cas. 337 (1889). That case clearly rejected liability for negligent or innocent misrepresentation. Since recovery has been denied for pure economic loss in negligence cases, the courts have been reluctant to expand liability for the misrepresentation tort into areas of economic loss.

2. As *Bortz v. Noon* points out, the modern trend is toward expanding liability for negligent and even innocent misrepresentation.

3. Liability for negligent misrepresentation has been confined to people who make representations in the course of business or transactions in which the speaker has a financial interest and supplies information for the guidance of others. Restatement (Second) of Torts §552.

4. Most courts have agreed with the Pennsylvania court above and refused to extend liability for money damages to innocent misrepresentation. However, a definite minority of jurisdictions, including the Restatement, have found that damages may be awarded for innocent misrepresentation made in the course of a sale, rental, or exchange of property. Restatement (Second) of Torts §552C.

5. The courts have always been willing to allow rescission of a contract for negligent or innocent misrepresentation. Even *Derry v. Peek* said, "Where rescission is claimed it is only necessary to prove that there was misrepresentation; then, however honestly it may have been made, however free from blame the person who made it, the contract, having been obtained by misrepresentation, cannot stand."

6. The Restatement would find "scienter" when the defendant knew or believed that he was not telling the truth, did not have the confidence in the accuracy of his statement that he stated or implied that he did, or knew that he did not have the ground for his statement that he stated or implied the he had. Restatement (Second) of Torts §526. That is a broad definition of scienter, which includes many situations that would appear to be negligent misrepresentation.

APPLYING THE LAW

1. Alice notarizes a deed for a person signing as John Smith. Unfortunately, the person signing the deed was not John Smith but an imposter. Alice did not know John Smith and did not ask for identification from the person who identified himself as Smith. The deed was duly recorded, and the imposter was able to sell the property to an unsuspecting buyer. Would the notary be liable for misrepresentation? What kind of misrepresentation?

2. Jack, a veterinarian, certified that the horse, Sea Biscuit, was sound, without lameness. Jack had been busy so he signed the certification without examining Sea Biscuit. Jack had talked to Sea Biscuit's owner about the horse and was convinced that the horse must be sound. The owners used Jack's certification to sell Sea Biscuit. The new owners have discovered that Sea Biscuit is lame. What kind of misrepresentation is this? Would Jack be liable?

3. Sylvia owned a home that she wanted to sell. Sylvia ordered a survey of her property, which showed the house and garage within the boundary

lines of the property. Sylvia sold the property to Mitch. Mitch had another survey done, which showed the house was partially on the neighbor's property. Mitch likes the property and thinks he can work out a deal with the neighbor but thinks that Sylvia should also pay. Could Sylvia be liable to Mitch in this situation? What kind of misrepresentation would this be?

C. NONDISCLOSURE AND NEGLIGENT MISREPRESENTATION

In re Agribiotech
291 F. Supp. 2d 1186 (Nev. 2003)

Pro, Chief Judge.

I. Background

This case arises out of the bankruptcy of Agribiotech, Inc. ("Agribiotech" or "ABT"). The Trustee brought the lawsuit in federal court against various individual and corporate Defendants, based on the rights assigned pursuant to the First Amended Joint Plan of Reorganization. In the Growers' First Amended Complaint ("Complaint"), at issue here, the Trustee asserts claims of fraud and negligent misrepresentation against, among others, Ingram and Fisher.

As discussed in the October order, the Complaint seeks to hold Ingram and Fisher liable for fraud and negligence arising out of two occurrences. First, Ingram and Fisher attended the Growers meeting held on September 2, 1999, at which ABT Chief Executive Officer Richard Budd ("Budd") allegedly made misrepresentations and failed to disclose to the Growers various material pieces of information. The Complaint alleges Ingram and Fisher attended this meeting in their official capacities as ABT's Chief Financial Officer and General Counsel, but does not identify any statements Ingram or Fisher made at the meeting. Second, the Complaint alleges Ingram and Fisher "reviewed and approved" the "Dear ABT Growers" letter Budd sent to Growers following the September 2 meeting. The letter, signed only by Budd, stated:

> [O]n Tuesday night, September 2, 1999, ABT assembled eight large alfalfa growers . . . to meet with me and two other senior officers of ABT (Randy Ingram who is our Chief Financial Officer and Doug Fisher who is our Chief Legal Officer and head of communication) . . . to hear their thoughts and concerns first hand. I felt it was an extremely

productive meeting, and we want to share the highlights of the information which was provided. . . .

[F]or a number of reasons, ABT's ability to pay growers is improving.

The Trustee alleges the statement that ABT's ability to pay the Growers was improving was false because Budd knew ABT's ability to pay the Growers was deteriorating rather than improving. The Trustee further alleges Ingram and Fisher "reviewed and approved" this letter, even though they also knew ABT's ability to pay was deteriorating rather than improving.

III. ANALYSIS

Nevada has adopted the Restatement (Second) of Torts definition of negligent misrepresentation. Under this theory of liability:

> One who, in the course of his business, profession or employment, or in any other action in which he has a pecuniary interest, supplies false information for the guidance of others in their business transactions, is subject to liability for pecuniary loss caused to them by their justifiable reliance upon the information, if he fails to exercise reasonable care or competence in obtaining or communicating the information.

Restatement (Second) Torts §552 (1977) (emphasis added).

Ingram and Fisher move, pursuant to Federal Rule of Civil Procedure 12(b)(6), to dismiss the Complaint's negligent misrepresentation claim for failure to state a claim upon which relief may be granted. According to Ingram and Fisher, negligent misrepresentation by its nature requires a positive assertion, and they personally made no affirmative representations. The Trustee responds that Ingram and Fisher made misrepresentations through their conduct by attending the September 2 meeting and reviewing and approving the letter. The Trustee also argues several states have recognized negligent misrepresentation by omission, especially where coupled with a duty to disclose.

This Court finds Ingram and Fisher's conduct as alleged in the Complaint, without more, does not constitute "supplying" misinformation for purposes of a negligent misrepresentation claim. But the Court also finds Nevada would recognize the tort of negligent misrepresentation by nondisclosure, a cause of action based on an actor's negligent failure to disclose material information where there is a duty to disclose. Under this alternative theory, the Complaint states a claim for which relief may be granted.

A. SUPPLYING INFORMATION

The Trustee argues Ingram and Fisher made positive assertions through their conduct when they attended the September 2 meeting and when they reviewed and approved the "Dear ABT Growers" letter. Nevada has not addressed circumstances like those alleged in the Complaint, nor do its opinions offer any insight as to whether Ingram and Fisher's alleged conduct might constitute "supplying" false information.

A review of decisions outside of Nevada reveals that a majority of courts would not consider attendance at a meeting or review and approval of a letter to be "supplying" information. Federal courts examining when a party "makes" a misrepresentation under Section 10(b) of the Securities Exchange Act and Rule 10b-5 generally have concluded that reviewing and approving another actor's statements does not constitute "making" a misrepresentation. Even courts that construe more broadly the term "making" a misrepresentation have required substantial participation in the drafting of a misrepresentation such that an unnamed actor could be considered a co-author of the statement.

Most courts would hold Ingram and Fisher's "review and approval" of the letter and mere silent attendance at the meeting do not constitute "making" misrepresentations or, for purposes of negligent misrepresentation under the Restatement, "supplying" false information. The Complaint alleges only that Ingram and Fisher attended a meeting and reviewed and approved a letter. The Complaint does not allege that either Ingram or Fisher had a hand in preparing Budd's statements at the meeting or advised Budd not to make various disclosures at the meeting. With respect to the letter, the Complaint does not allege that either Ingram or Fisher was the source of the alleged misrepresentation in the letter, or that they participated in drafting or editing the letter.

Following the wave of corporate and accounting scandals that have swept the American business community over the past few years, Nevada ultimately may adopt a standard under which Ingram and Fisher's alleged conduct would support a negligent misrepresentation claim. But Nevada has yet to signal this sort of move. Absent further direction from Nevada, this Court cannot hold that Ingram and Fisher's attendance at the meeting and "review and approval" of the letter, without more, constitute making a misrepresentation or supplying false information.

B. NEGLIGENT MISREPRESENTATION BY NONDISCLOSURE

Although attending a meeting and reviewing and approving a letter do not constitute "supplying" information for purposes of a negligent misrepresentation claim, this Court is convinced that Nevada would adopt the Restatement's formulation that silence coupled with a duty to speak does constitute "supplying" information. Furthermore, the Court finds Ingram and Fisher's conduct, as alleged in the Complaint, would constitute "supplying" misinformation so as to form the basis of a negligent misrepresentation by nondisclosure claim.

1. Federal Court Determination of State Law

"When interpreting state law, federal courts are bound by decisions of the state's highest court." If the state has not addressed the particular issue, a federal court must use its best judgment to predict how the highest state court would resolve it "using intermediate appellate court decisions, decisions from other jurisdictions, statutes, treatises, and restatements as guidance." Id. (quotation omitted). "In making that prediction, federal courts look to existing state law without predicting potential changes in that law." Although federal courts should not predict changes in a state's law, they "are not precluded from affording relief simply because neither the state Supreme Court nor the state legislature has enunciated a clear rule governing a particular type of controversy."

2. Negligent Misrepresentation by Nondisclosure

The parties agree Nevada has not considered whether one can "supply" false information through silence to support a negligent misrepresentation claim. Courts in other jurisdictions are divided on the issue.

Because Nevada generally has adopted the Restatement in developing its common law governing deceit torts, the Court determines Nevada would recognize the tort of negligent misrepresentation by nondisclosure as outlined in the Restatement (Second) of Torts. Under the theory of negligent misrepresentation by nondisclosure as described in §§551 and 552:

> (1) One who fails to disclose to another a fact that he knows may justifiably induce the other to act or refrain from acting in a business transaction is subject to the same liability to the other as though he had represented the nonexistence of the matter that he has failed to disclose, if, but only if, he is under a duty to the other to exercise reasonable care to disclose the matter in question.
>
> (2) One party to a business transaction is under a duty to exercise reasonable care to disclose to the other before the transaction is consummated,. . . .
>
> (e) facts basic to the transaction, if he knows that the other is about to enter into it under a mistake as to them, and the other, because of the relationship between them, the customs of the trade or other objective circumstances, would reasonably expect a disclosure of those facts.

Restatement (Second) of Torts §551 (1977). Pursuant to §551, silence about material facts basic to the transaction, when combined with a duty to speak, is the functional equivalent of a misrepresentation or "supplying false information" under Restatement §552.

In addition to generally following the Restatement, Nevada already has recognized a cause of action for fraud by nondisclosure where a special relationship between the parties imposes a duty to speak. See *Epperson*, 719 P.2d at 804 (holding defendant owes a duty to disclose "where the defendant alone has knowledge of material facts which are not accessible to the plaintiff"); Mackintosh v. Jack Matthews and Co., 109 Nev. 628, 855 P.2d 549, 553 (1993) (noting failure to disclose is equivalent to fraudulent concealment any time parties are not on equal footing and one party reposes confidence in the other due to the other's position); The Court concludes Nevada, if given the opportunity, also would extend tort liability to those who negligently fail to disclose material facts where a special relationship imposes a duty to disclose.

In addition to showing a duty to disclose under §551, a plaintiff alleging negligent misrepresentation under §552 must show particular circumstances warranting imposition of tort liability. The Restatement takes this position because "the fault of the maker of [a negligent] misrepresentation is sufficiently less [than that of the maker of a fraudulent misrepresentation] to justify a narrower responsibility for its consequences." Restatement (Second) of Torts §552, cmt. a (1977). The Restatement confines a tortfeasor's liability for negligent misrepresentations to only those persons to whom he knows the information will be supplied, and only for losses incurred in the kind of transaction in which the misrepresentation is expected to influence them. See id. §552, cmt. i.

The Court previously ruled that in the context of fraudulent nondisclosure, Ingram and Fisher owed a duty to disclose due to the Growers placing confidence in Ingram and Fisher because of their positions as CFO and General Counsel of ABT. The Court determined that Ingram and Fisher, as CFO and General Counsel of ABT, could not sit silent while Budd made various alleged misrepresentations about ABT's financial health where Ingram and Fisher allegedly knew the statements were false. The Growers meeting was called, and the "Dear ABT Growers" letter written. for the specific purpose of assuring the Growers ABT could pay for their seed and with the express goal of inducing the Growers to turn over their seed to ABT. Budd's statements to the Growers about ABT's financial health allegedly were bolstered by the silent acquiescence of ABT's CFO and General Counsel, two professionals whom the Growers allegedly trusted based on their positions and specialized knowledge of ABT's financial health. The Complaint alleges the Growers relied to their detriment on the overall presentation, including Ingram and Fisher's alleged tacit approval through silence.

These facts give rise to a duty to speak under a negligent misrepresentation theory. Under §551(2)(e) of the Restatement, a party is under a duty to exercise reasonable care to disclose "facts basic to the transaction" if he knows the other party is about to enter into the transaction under a mistake as to the basic facts, and, "because of the relationship between them, the customs of the trade or other objective circumstances," the other party reasonably would expect the alleged tortfeasor to disclose those facts. Restatement (Second) of Torts §551(2)(e) (1977).

Here, ABT's ability to pay for the Growers' seed is a fact basic to the transaction. The Complaint alleges Ingram and Fisher knew the assurances the Growers received that ABT would be able to pay for the seed were mistaken or false. As discussed above, the relationship between the parties and the objective circumstances of the campaign gave rise to a duty on the part of Ingram and Fisher to exercise reasonable care to disclose accurate information.

The Complaint's allegations also fall within the narrow confines of negligent misrepresentation liability. Ingram and Fisher knew the meeting was aimed at eight specific Growers, and the letter was directed at "ABT Growers." Thus, they knew the limited target audience at which the communications were directed. Ingram and Fisher also knew the purpose of the meeting and letter: to induce the Growers to turn over their seed. The Complaint seeks redress for misrepresentations that allegedly achieved their purpose when the Growers turned over their seed and suffered financial losses as a result.

Accordingly, the Court concludes Nevada would recognize negligent misrepresentation by nondisclosure where a special relationship created a duty to disclose. Viewing the Complaint's allegations in the light most favorable to the Trustee, it does not appear beyond doubt that the Trustee can prove no set of facts in support of a negligent misrepresentation by nondisclosure claim which would entitle it to relief. Because the Complaint states a claim for which relief may be granted, the Court will deny Ingram and Fisher's motion to dismiss the negligent misrepresentation by nondisclosure claim.

PREPARING FOR CLASS

1. Why did the complaint allege negligent misrepresentation rather than intentional misrepresentation?

2. What if Ingram and Fisher were optimistic people who believed Budd's statements even though a reasonable person would have known that Budd was incorrect? Would Ingram's and Fisher's good faith be a defense?

3. What should Ingram and Fisher have done to avoid liability in this situation?

4. While the CFO of a company would certainly know about the company's financial condition, a general counsel would not necessarily know. Do you agree? If so, do the growers have a right to rely on the general counsel, Fisher?

5. Don't the growers who are about to rely on the silence of Ingram and Fisher have a duty to ask them what they think? What does the court think about that?

INCREASING YOUR UNDERSTANDING

1. Consider the following paragraph from the opinion:

   1. Federal Court Determination of State Law

   "When interpreting state law, federal courts are bound by decisions of the state's highest court." If the state has not addressed the particular issue, a federal court must use its best judgment to predict how the highest state court would resolve it "using intermediate appellate court decisions, decisions from other jurisdictions, statutes, treatises, and restatements as guidance." Id. (quotation omitted). "In making that prediction, federal courts look to existing state law without predicting potential changes in that law. Although federal courts should not predict changes in a state's law, they "are not precluded from affording relief simply because neither the state Supreme Court nor the state legislature has enunciated a clear rule governing a particular type of controversy."

Notice that this case is a federal court hearing a case and applying state, rather than federal, law. You will learn more about this in Civil Procedure.

2. The Court says:

Following the wave of corporate and accounting scandals that have swept the American business community over the past few years, Nevada ultimately may adopt a standard under which Ingram and Fisher's alleged conduct would support a negligent misrepresentation claim.

Should the law change because there have been scandals? Who would change the law, the courts or the legislature?

3. The courts have also found a duty to disclose (1) when there is a fiduciary relationship, (2) when the speaker had previously made a statement that was true at the time but has now become false, and (3) when the speaker has made a statement that is only partially true. Dan Dobbs, *The Law of Torts*, p. 1375.

4. The duty to speak in the *Agribiotech* case is usually confined to latent, not patent, facts, i.e., the speaker doesn't have a duty to speak about obvious or easily observable facts.

APPLYING THE LAW

1. A horse seller told the buyer that the horse had some lameness in the right front leg. Is the seller obligated to disclose that the seller has treated the left rear leg for lameness?

2. Would a lawyer who sells his or her house have an obligation to disclose that the house is being sold for double its fair market value? Must the lawyer disclose the meaning of an easement to a buyer who chooses not to be represented by counsel?

D.   REASONABLE RELIANCE

Terra Securities ASA Konkursbo v. Citigroup, Inc.
740 F. Supp. 2d 441 (S.D.N.Y. 2010)

Victor MARRERO, District Judge.

B. FACTUAL ALLEGATIONS

The operative facts and events underlying the Terra Complaint are largely set forth in the February 2010 Decision, familiarity with which is assumed. Here, the Court will briefly review additional facts relevant to this motion to dismiss, as well as factual background and allegations derived from the Banca Carige Complaint.

1. Plaintiffs' Fund-Linked Investments

In May and June of 2007, Defendants sold over $115 million in securities to the Municipalities through Terra, a Norwegian securities firm. The securities constituted fund-linked notes ("FLNs") linked to the Citi Tender Option Bond Fund (the "Citi TOB Fund"). The FLNs were arranged by Defendants, issued by Banque AIG and Starling Finance, PLC, and purchased by Terra "for the benefit of the investing Municipalities."

Similarly, in or around January 2007, Defendants sold 10 million euros worth of FLNs linked to Defendants' Offshore Tender Option Bond Fund (the "Offshore TOB Fund," together with the Citi TOB Fund, the "Funds") to Banca Carige, and entered into a fund-linked "Total Return Swap" (the "TRS") agreement with Banca Carige.

2. Marketing Materials

In or about April 2007, Defendants began marketing the FLNs to the Municipalities through Terra. In May and June of 2007, Terra entered into distribution agreements (the "Distribution Agreements") with Defendants, which governed the terms of their FLN distribution, and mandated distribution of marketing materials, including the presentation (the "Presentation") that Plaintiffs allege contained material misstatements and omissions of fact. On two separate occasions, Defendants allegedly provided the Presentation to Terra with full knowledge and intention that it would be transmitted to the Municipalities and/or would serve as the basis for Terra's advice to the Municipalities with respect to their investment in the FLNs.

Similarly, Banca Carige alleges that Defendants provided it with the Presentation along with other materials marketing the Offshore TOB Fund beginning in or around November 2006.

The Presentation marketed the Funds by describing the Funds' investment strategy, detailing their structure, and purporting to demonstrate the historical performance of municipal yields hedged with interest rate swap agreements. The Presentation described the Funds' investment strategy as an arbitrage opportunity for investors, whereby the Funds take advantage of the relative steepness of the long-term, nontaxable, municipal curve as against a taxable London Interbank Offered Rate ("LIBOR") curve (the "Hedging Strategy"). The Funds purported to hedge against a drop in municipal bond values with LIBOR swap agreements that traded a fixed interest rate for a floating rate, and Defendants represented that the net amount long-term municipal bonds pay over the cost of short-term LIBOR loans (the "Arbitrage") was consistent over time.

Both the Terra and Banca Carige Complaints rely primarily on allegations that Defendants materially misrepresented the Hedging Strategy by portraying the correlation between long-term municipal bond rates and LIBOR swap rates as "virtually perfect, with a factor of almost .97 out of a possible 1." Specifically, Plaintiffs rely on a graph contained in the Presentation entitled "Correlation Between Municipal and LIBOR rates" (the "Graph"), which purports to represent a regression analysis of the taxable and non-taxable rates over the last thirty years. Defendants represented that the Arbitrage was the result of "market inefficiency due to investor preference for shorter term municipal maturities, the risk of changes in tax law, and the lack of any short market on municipal bonds."

Plaintiffs allege that the correlation presented in the Graph was "blatantly false and misleading." The Graph incorrectly compared levels of interest rates and not rates of change, and thereby generated the misrepresentative, near-perfect correlation. Plaintiffs also condemn statistical flaws that led to the misrepresentative Graph, including an unacceptable standard error. By contrast to the Graph's representation, Plaintiffs allege that if more accurate correlation analyses for the hedging strategy were employed, the result would have been a significantly lower correlation factor-as low as .562 or .27 out of a possible 1, depending on the municipal benchmark used. As a result, Plaintiffs allege that Defendants misrepresented the risk associated with the FLNs and the TRS, and that they relied on these misrepresentations to their financial detriment.

3. Failure to Disclose Credit and Liquidity Risk

Plaintiffs allege that the Presentation materially omitted to disclose two additional risk factors: (1) credit risk-the risk that municipal borrowers may become less creditworthy; and (2) liquidity risk-the risk that investors may become increasingly concerned about the liquidity of their long-term municipal bonds. Plaintiffs assert that the risk that insurers to the municipal debt offerings would falter could not be effectively hedged with interest rate swap agreements and thus should have been disclosed in the Presentation.

4. Financial Loss

Six weeks after the Municipalities' purchase of the FLNs, Defendants' representations regarding the high correlation between municipal and

LIBOR rates were proven "demonstrably false, and those rates began to dramatically diverge." As the rates diverged, the Citi TOB Fund's assets, and thus correspondingly the Municipalities' FLNs, lost value. Municipal bond yields increased, causing the value of long-term municipal bonds to fall, but the Funds' taxable LIBOR swap agreements did not offset the non-taxable losses. Instead, "as investors worried about credit and liquidity risk," yields fell on taxable instruments, and thus both assets held by the Citi TOB Fund fell in value.

Ultimately, at the request of Defendants and Terra, the Municipalities sold their FLNs in late 2007 and early 2008. Combined, the Municipalities lost approximately $90 million, and these investment losses also allegedly resulted in Terra's financial ruin. Following the precipitous decline of the FLNs, Norway's Financial Supervisory Agency launched an investigation into Terra, which forced Terra to cease operations and declare bankruptcy.

For its part, Banca Carige alleges damages in excess of $47 million resulting from Defendants' alleged fraud. In or about the spring of 2008, after their fund-linked investments had suffered losses, Defendants contacted Banca Carige and assured them that the Offshore TOB Fund was stabilizing. Later that year, in December 2008, Banca Carige retained an Italian law firm to evaluate their fund-linked investments, an evaluation which ultimately prompted the instant action.

Plaintiffs allege that where they lost, Defendants gained: the fund-linked investments were set up to provide insurance for Defendants' investments in the Funds, as well as hefty advisory and dealing fees.

III. DISCUSSION

B. COMMON LAW FRAUD

In addition to their federal securities fraud claims, Plaintiffs bring common law fraud claims arising out of the same allegedly fraudulent conduct. To state a claim for common law fraud under New York law, a plaintiff must allege: "(1) a material representation or omission of fact; (2) made with knowledge of its falsity; (3) with an intent to defraud; and (4) reasonable reliance on the part of the plaintiff, (5) that causes damage to the plaintiff."

Defendants argue that Plaintiffs fail to plead two elements of their common law fraud claims: (1) reasonable reliance upon the alleged material misstatements, and (2) that the reliance caused their alleged injuries.

1. Reasonable Reliance

New York law requires that plaintiffs alleging common law fraud establish reasonable reliance on a material misrepresentation. A plaintiff must demonstrate that there was some basis for it to have relied on the alleged misstatement or omission. To determine, on a motion to dismiss, whether a plaintiff has alleged reasonable reliance, a court may "consider the entire context of the transaction, including . . . the sophistication of the parties, and the content of any agreements between them."

a. Sophisticated Investors

The reasonableness of a claim of reliance must be considered in light of the plaintiff's sophistication. "It is well established that where sophisticated businessmen engaged in major transactions enjoy access to critical information but fail to take advantage of that access, New York courts are particularly disinclined to entertain claims of justifiable reliance." Sophisticated investors must "investigate the information available to them with the care and prudence expected from people blessed with full access to information."

Defendants argue that, as sophisticated investors, Terra and Banca Carige had a duty to investigate and inquire regarding any purported misrepresentations, and any reliance on their part was thus unreasonable as a matter of law. Plaintiffs counter that reasonableness of reliance is a question of fact, generally not properly resolved on a motion to dismiss. Even if properly considered here, Plaintiffs argue that Defendants' misrepresentations and omissions were not discoverable from "available information" provided to them prior to their investments.

As an initial matter, the Court notes that the reasonableness of reliance is properly considered at the motion to dismiss stage.

The Court thus turns to consideration of whether Terra and Banca Carige are sophisticated financial entities that, as a matter of law, could not have reasonably relied on the alleged misrepresentations. Representations by a plaintiff that it had "knowledge and experience in financial and business matters and that it could readily evaluate the risks of the transaction" can indicate sophistication for the purposes of this analysis.

In their respective Complaints and agreements relevant to this dispute, Terra and Banca Carige acknowledge their own sophistication as investors. In their Complaints, Terra indicates that it is a "Norwegian securities brokerage firm" and Banca Carige identifies itself as a "full-service Italian bank . . . [that] managed the investment portfolios" of its subsidiary insurance companies. In addition, as noted above, Terra entered into Distribution Agreements with Citigroup to market and distribute the FLNs at issue here. The Distribution Agreements provide, in pertinent part: "Terra has sufficient knowledge, experience, and professional advice to make its own evaluation of the merits and risks of a transaction of this type," and "The Distributor represents and warrants . . . that . . . it is experienced in distributing structured products and understands the risks inherent in them. . . ." Likewise, Banca Carige, in the TRS agreement, avowed that "[i]t is capable of evaluating and understanding (on its own behalf or through independent professional advice), and understands and accepts, the terms, conditions, and risks of [the transaction.]"

Terra and Banca Carige assert that the information underlying the alleged misrepresentations was within the peculiar knowledge of Defendants and unavailable to them. However, Plaintiffs mischaracterize what constitutes available information for the purposes of the present inquiry. The availability of information in this context is not whether the requisite material was made available to Plaintiffs by Defendants. Rather, available in this context denotes accessible-would the information necessary to unmask the alleged fraud have been accessible to the sophisticated party through minimal diligence.

Terra and Banca Carige cite *E*Trade Fin. Corp. v. Deutsche Bank AG* to argue that a plaintiff's reliance is unreasonable only where "'it has been put on notice of the existence of material facts which have not been documented'. . . . No authority holds reliance to be unreasonable unless the plaintiff saw red flags or other circumstances existed that made reliance unquestionably unreasonable."

While Plaintiffs correctly articulate the applicable standard—a heightened degree of diligence is required of sophisticated plaintiffs only where red flags or other circumstances existed that made reliance unreasonable—they misapply it to the facts at issue here. The Court finds that Terra and Banca Carige knew or should have known that they were in a position to acquire additional information regarding the alleged misrepresentations.

First, the full context of the Presentation should have flagged for Terra and Banca Carige that an independent appraisal of the Graph and the Hedging Strategy was warranted. The Presentation provides an explicit risk disclosure (the "Risk Disclosure") addressing the Hedging Strategy and the Graph: "[T]he Fund may experience substantial volatility due to dissentions in the relationship of the municipal bond investments and the hedging instruments." Plaintiffs contend that this cautionary language about the possible future divergence of the taxable and non-taxable rates does not inoculate the plausible marketing power of a misrepresentation about historical performance of those rates. To an untrained eye this may hold true, but the Graph and Risk Disclosure, when viewed in tandem by a sophisticated appraiser, should have resulted in a dissonant picture that looked decisively like a red flag.

The Court finds that Terra and Banca Carige's respective Complaints also reveal additional hints of misstatement that render their alleged reliance unreasonable. Among the reasons Terra and Banca Carige set forth to allege that the Graph fraudulently misrepresented the Hedging Strategy are that Defendants "failed to set forth a standard error for its statistical analysis," and relied on municipal bond data that did not correspond, in significant part, with the class of municipal bonds in the Funds. Both of these flaws are readily apparent from the Presentation: there is no standard error indicated for the Graph, and the data source, which Plaintiffs now maintain fraudulently misrepresented the Funds' bond investments, is indicated below the Graph. Viewing Plaintiffs in light of their sophistication as investors, the Court finds that Terra and Banca Carige cannot now in hindsight rely on these statistical flaws and characterize them as misrepresentations when they were sufficiently on notice of them and their potential implications before investing in the FLNs. Terra and Banca Carige knew or should have known that they were in a position to acquire additional information regarding the statistical analysis portrayed in the Graph, as well as the precise nature of the bond investments in the Funds.

Finally, neither Banca Carige nor Terra allege that the statistical information underpinning the allegedly misleading Graph, or the existence of any credit or liquidity risk, was inaccessible or non-public information. The main premise of Plaintiffs' lawsuit-that an alternative representation of the relationship between taxable and non-taxable rates would not have been misleading-itself demonstrates that the information was public and readily available to them before their entering the securities transactions at issue. Indeed, Terra and Banca Carige now rely on "market research" to claim that Defendants' representations in the Graph were false and misleading. While it is true that the reliance requirement is not "designed to shield perpetrators of fraud by forcing investors to conduct exhaustive research every time they invest money," it is also true that this doctrine generally applies to ordinary purchasers of securities, not to sophisticated investors, and especially not to financial entities like Terra and Banca Carige that hold themselves out to the public as experienced investment managers, bankers and brokers, and do conduct exhaustive research in connection with the services they provide to their customers. Here, the Court is not persuaded that Banca Carige and Terra had no duty to conduct an independent appraisal of a statistical representation based on publicly-available interest rates.

Accordingly, the Court finds that Terra and Banca Carige's reliance on the Presentation to be unreasonable as a matter of law and grants Defendants' motion to dismiss Terra and Banca Carige's common law fraud claims.

PREPARING FOR CLASS

1. Would this case be dismissed if the plaintiffs were not sophisticated investors?

2. What makes the plaintiffs sophisticated investors?

3. Would anyone who purchases $110 million of securities be a sophisticated investor?

4. Weren't the defendants also sophisticated in financial markets? How does that influence the analysis of this case? Aren't the plaintiffs entitled to rely on a sophisticated seller?

INCREASING YOUR UNDERSTANDING

1. Notice the nature of this element. The defendant can acknowledge that he lied but allege that the plaintiff had no right to believe him. What is the rationale for the reliance requirement?

2. In a cause of action for misrepresentation, the plaintiff must, in fact, rely on the representation as well as reasonably rely. Thus, if the plaintiff knows the representation is false or did not know of the representation, there can be no misrepresentation.

3. Sometimes a salesperson's representations are "puffing," i.e., exaggerated sales statements that are common and not to be believed. For example, a car salesman's statements that this car is the finest car you will ever own are puffing, and the buyer may not justifiably rely on them.

4. Sometimes the buyer is obligated to investigate further. That may include an obligation to read the terms of the contract.

5. The plaintiff must also justifiably rely on a *material* misrepresentation. The parties may say many things while negotiating a transaction, but only the material statements can give rise to a cause of action for misrepresentation. A material misrepresentation is one that a reasonable person would consider in deciding whether to enter into the deal.

APPLYING THE LAW

A person is selling her car on the Internet. Which of the following statements could the buyer justifiably rely on?

1. This car is the fastest car you will ever own.

2. This car has only been driven by a grandmother over 70 years old.

3. This car has been driven 36,000 miles.

4. The former driver of this car is a good, Christian gentleman.

5. This is the best model of Chevrolet produced in the last ten years.

Nelson v. Taff
499 N.W.2d 685 (Ct. App. Wisc. 1993)

DYKMAN, Judge.

James Taff and Taff & Taff Builders, Inc. appeal from a judgment for $1,514,326 plus costs and attorneys' fees of approximately $22,000, and from an order denying relief under sec. 806.07, Stats., from that judgment. Taff asserts that the trial court erred by refusing to direct a verdict, by refusing to give a requested instruction and by denying relief from the judgment. We affirm.

In 1978, Peter Dwyer, Tilman Christianson and Donald Raffel formed the PDT Partnership to develop land at the corner of North Sherman and Aberg

Avenues in Madison. James Taff became involved with the partnership, and Taff & Taff became the general contractor for the project known as "Maple Wood Condominium Homes." Various witnesses testified that James Taff was a partner in the project and that the entity formed was a general partnership and that James Taff was well aware that the partnership was not a limited partnership.

Between June 1978 and April 1979, PDT brought in ten "investors" who each contributed $10,000 to the project. There was conflicting testimony, but the jury believed Fred Nelson, who testified that in February 1979, he and his wife had a meeting with James Taff, at Poole's supper club, just across the street from the project. Nelson and his wife were interested in the project but they quizzed Taff on the nature of the interest they could buy. Taff told them that they would be purchasing a limited partnership interest. Nelson pressed Taff on the subject, inquiring as to what would happen if the project failed. Taff explained that the project would not fail because of his experience and reputation, but that if it did, the Nelsons' exposure would be limited to their $10,000 investment.

Maple Wood failed. The partnership filed a petition in bankruptcy. The partnership's bankruptcy trustee sued Nelson, alleging that Nelson was a partner in Maple Wood and liable for its debts. Ultimately, the trustee obtained a judgment against Nelson for nearly $400,000. Unable to pay the judgment, Nelson began this action against James Taff and Taff & Taff, alleging fraud, violations of the Racketeer Influenced and Corrupt Organizations Act (RICO), 18 U.S.C. §§1961-1968, and the Wisconsin Organized Crime Control Act, secs. 946.80-946.88, Stats.

The jury found that James Taff either knowingly made a false representation to Nelson, or he did so recklessly, without caring whether it was untrue. It found that Taff intended to deceive Nelson, and that Taff made the statement to induce Nelson to act on it. The jury decided that Nelson believed Taff's false representation and relied on it to his detriment. Taff had stipulated that Nelson was damaged in the amount of the $400,000 judgment, and the jury found additional damages of $105,000. As required by RICO, the trial court trebled the jury's verdict and entered judgment against James Taff and Taff & Taff for $1,514,326 plus costs and Nelson's actual attorneys' fees.

After judgment was entered, Nelson negotiated a settlement of the trustee's judgment against him. In exchange for paying $16,000 and relinquishing a $700 claim against PDT, Nelson received a satisfaction of the $400,000 judgment. James Taff and Taff & Taff moved for relief under sec. 806.07(1)(f)-(h), Stats. The trial court denied the motion, and this appeal resulted.

DIRECTED VERDICT

James Taff asserts that any statements he made concerning the nature of the partnership were representations of law and, therefore, not actionable. He concludes that the trial court erred by not granting him a directed verdict at the end of the plaintiff's case.

Misrepresentations of law are generally not actionable as fraud. But there are exceptions to this rule. Ritchie v. Clappier, 109 Wis. 2d 399, 402, 326 N.W.2d 131, 133 (Ct. App. 1982).

> "It is not . . . universally true that a misrepresentation of the law is not binding upon the party who made it. . . . Where one who has had superior means of information professes a knowledge of the law, and thereby obtains an unconscionable advantage of another who is ignorant and has not been in a situation to become informed, the injured party is entitled to relief as well as if the misrepresentation had been concerning [a] matter of fact."

Other authority also holds that the general rule is not as rigid as Taff suggests. In Sawyer v. Pierce, 580 S.W.2d 117, 125 (Tex. Civ. App. 1979), the court said:

> One notable exception to the general rule is that where one party who possesses superior knowledge as to the law takes advantage of the other party's ignorance in that respect, and intentionally makes a misrepresentation concerning the law for the purpose of deceiving the other party and actually succeeds in that respect, [the person making the fraudulent misrepresentation] may be held responsible for his conduct.

In Miller v. Osterlund, 154 Minn. 495, 191 N.W. 919, 919 (1923), the court said:

> But it is not always easy to classify representations as of law or fact, often they are of mixed law and fact, and courts should not be too indulgent of defendants who have made misrepresentations as to matters of which they should be expected to have knowledge, and of which the other party ordinarily would not have knowledge. A misrepresentation though involving [a] matter of law will be held actionable if it amounts to an implied assertion that facts exist that justifies the conclusion of law which is expressed.

In National Conversion Corp. v. Cedar Bldg. Corp., 23 N.Y.2d 621, 298 N.Y.S.2d 499, 246 N.E.2d 351 (1969), the court commented on the modern trend that requires frauds to suffer the consequences of their acts:

> Most important it is that the law has outgrown the over-simple dichotomy between law and fact in the resolution of issues in deceit. It has been said that "a statement as to the law, like a statement as to anything else, may be intended and understood either as one of fact or one of opinion only, according to the circumstances of the case." . . .

Moreover, the modern rule extends even further to cover a false opinion of law if misrepresented as a sincere opinion, as in the case of any other opinion, where there is reasonable reliance.

Id. at 504, 246 N.E.2d at 355 (citations omitted).

Restatement (Second) of Torts §545 (1977) also recognizes that misrepresentations of law are actionable:

(1) If a misrepresentation as to a matter of law includes, expressly or by implication, a misrepresentation of fact, the recipient is justified in relying upon the misrepresentation of fact to the same extent as though it were any other misrepresentation of fact.

(2) If a misrepresentation as to a matter of law is only one of opinion as to the legal consequences of facts, the recipient is justified in relying upon it to the same extent as though it were a representation of any other opinion.

Professor Prosser notes:

The present tendency is strongly in favor of eliminating the distinction between law and fact as "useless duffle of an older and more arbitrary day," and recognizing that a statement as to the law, like a statement as to anything else, may be intended and understood either as one of fact or one of opinion only, according to the circumstances of the case. Most courts still render lip service to the older rule, but they have been inclined whenever possible to find statements of fact "implied" in representations as to the law.

W. Prosser, *Law of Torts* §109, at 725 (4th ed. 1971) (footnotes omitted).

We conclude that whether the changing view as to the remedy for fraudulent misrepresentation of law is viewed as an exception to the general rule, as we noted in *Ritchie*, or an elimination of the law-fact difference as noted by Prosser and the Restatement, the result is the same. One who misrepresents the law after professing knowledge of the law will not be able to escape the consequences of his or her misrepresentation by asserting that the misrepresentation was one of law only.

A case should be taken from the jury and a verdict directed only if the evidence gives rise to no dispute as to material issues, or when the evidence is so clear and convincing that unbiased and impartial minds could reasonably come to but one conclusion. We therefore examine the evidence that Nelson produced to determine whether, under the standard we have just discussed, there was a complete lack of evidence that James Taff misrepresented to the Nelsons the nature of the partnership developing Maple Wood.

James Taff admitted that on June 8, 1978, Taff & Taff builders signed a contract with PDT for the construction of Maple Wood. He signed the contract. PDT's partnership agreement, dated June 5, 1978, was signed in Taff's office. Taff read the partnership agreement and asked whether it was a limited or a general partnership. He was told that the partnership was a general partnership, and he believed that it was a general partnership. We have already discussed Nelson's testimony as to James Taff's statements to him and his wife in February 1979. We conclude that the trial court did not err when it denied James Taff's motion for a directed verdict at the end of Nelson's case.

PREPARING FOR CLASS

1. What is the misrepresentation of fact made by James Taff?

2. Could Nelson justifiably rely on the legal statements of James Taff, who was not a lawyer and never trained in the law?

3. Would it make any difference if Taff said, "I think it's a limited partnership"?

4. Would it make any difference if Taff had told the Nelsons that they should retain an attorney to review the documents?

5. Would it make any difference if Taff gave Nelson a copy of the general partnership agreement that he had just signed? What if Taff gave Nelson a copy of the general partnership agreement a week before he signed it?

6. Why shouldn't a person be able to rely on representations of law?

INCREASING YOUR UNDERSTANDING

1. Many statements about the law are opinions, and many opinions imply facts that are false. When James Taff told Nelson that he was investing in a "limited partnership," Taff was implying that the agreement Nelson was to sign had words establishing that legal relationship. Since the agreement did not contain those words but rather words of general partnership, Taff was making a misrepresentation.

2. Some statements about the law are nothing more than mere opinion. If Taff had said to Nelson that the courts preferred this type of investment, that would be understood as opinion and not the sort of statement that supports a case for misrepresentation.

3. Obviously, statements by non-lawyers that would not be misrepresentation as mere opinion may be actionable if stated by a lawyer or even by you, a legally trained person.

APPLYING THE LAW

1. The seller of a pickup with large tires says "that truck is street legal." That's a legal opinion, isn't it? Does that legal opinion imply facts? The buyer purchases the truck and later is stopped by a police officer because the tires on the pickup are too large. Does the buyer have a cause of action for misrepresentation? Can the buyer keep the truck and sue for misrepresentation?

2. The seller of a rental house says that it is "up to code." It isn't; the electrical service is inadequate. The buyer is going to have to pay over $3,000 to install "code" electrical service. The seller says that he isn't a lawyer and the buyer had no right to rely on his estimates. Could these statements support a cause of action for misrepresentation?

Republic Bank & Trust Co. v. Bear, Stearns & Co., Inc.
707 F. Supp. 2d 702, (W.D. Ky. 2010)

CHARLES R. SIMPSON III, District Judge.

In 2003 and 2006, Republic Bank & Trust Company bought from Bear Stearns several securities that it now recognizes to be, in the parlance of our times, "toxic assets." Republic admits to not reading the relevant prospectuses prior to its purchases, but it has nevertheless sued Bear Stearns, its parent companies, and an employee for fraud, negligent misrepresentation, and violations of Kentucky's Blue Sky Law. The defendants now move to dismiss the complaint pursuant to Fed. R. Civ. P. 12(b)(6). For the reasons that follow, we will grant that motion in full.

I

The following facts are drawn from the face of the complaint (the allegations of which we must take as true for present purposes), as well as the prospectuses and prospectus supplements ("prosupps") (collectively, the "offering documents") for the securities in question. Bear, Stearns & Company ("Bear Stearns"), a wholly-owned subsidiary of The Bear Stearns Companies ("Bear Stearns Companies"), employed Frederick W. Barney, Jr. as a senior manager. In that role, Barney solicited the business of Republic Bank & Trust Company ("Republic") and convinced it to purchase several residential-mortgage-backed securities. Specifically, on March 31, 2003, Bear Stearns sold Republic a number of mortgage pass-through certificates issued by ABFS Mortgage Loan Trust 2003-1 for $20 million. Then on October 2, 2006, Republic bought from Bear Stearns additional mortgage pass-through certificates, issued by Bear Stearns ALTA Trust 2005-10, Bear Stearns ARM Trust 2006-2, Bear

Stearns ARM Trust 2006-4, and IndyMac INDX Mortgage Loan Trust 2006-AR11, for a total price of more than $32 million.

There are two reasons an investor might buy this particular sort of asset (which was not labeled "toxic" until years after these securities were issued). Primarily, the holder of a pass-through certificate is entitled to a monthly distribution of principal and interest as homeowners make payments on the mortgage loans that underlie the security. Alternately, one might buy a mortgage-backed security with the expectation that its market value will appreciate, allowing the holder to sell it for a profit at some future date. Republic does not allege that the stream of income from any of the securities has been unexpectedly low. Nor does it claim that it sold the certificates, or that it attempted to do so. Rather, it complains that because it held the certificates on its balance sheet and was required to revise their value to reflect market prices, it recorded on-paper losses of some $14.2 million as of December 31, 2008. Basically, the certificates are not now worth as much as Republic expected they would be.

This decline in nominal value is not in Republic's view solely the fault of the recent global financial crisis and ensuing recession. Instead, the bank alleges that Bear Stearns, through Barney, made a series of misrepresentations and omissions in the run-up to its decisions to buy the securities, and that but for those misrepresentations it would not have bought the certificates and thus would not have had to write down the value of its assets. Thus it sued Bear Stearns, its salesman (Barney), its former parent (Bear Stearns Companies), and its new parent (JP Morgan Chase & Co., which bought the Bear Stearns Companies in March 2008), seeking to hold them responsible for deceiving Republic into buying now-troubled financial products.

II

A claim of fraud or mistake creates a "high risk of abusive litigation and therefore must satisfy a still more stringent pleading standard under Fed. R. Civ. P. 9(b). At a minimum, the complaint must (1) specify the allegedly fraudulent statements, (2) identify the speaker, (3) state where and when the statements were made, and (4) explain why the statements were fraudulent. And while mental states "may be alleged generally," Fed. R. Civ. P. 9(b), the allegations "must be made with sufficient particularity and with a sufficient factual basis to support an inference that they were knowingly made." With these standards in mind, we turn to the allegations of the complaint.

III

A

Count I is titled "Fraud and Deceit," and contains two distinct causes of action: fraud by misrepresentation and fraud by omission.

1

Common-law fraud in Kentucky requires proof of six elements: (1) that the declarant (the defendant or its agent) made a material representation to the plaintiff; (2) that this representation was false; (3) that the declarant knew the representation was false or made it with reckless disregard for its truth or falsity; (4) that the declarant intended to induce the plaintiff to act upon the misrepresentation; (5) that the plaintiff reasonably relied upon the misrepresentation; and (6) that the misrepresentation caused injury to the plaintiff. The misrepresentation in question "must relate to a past or present material fact." A statement of opinion or prediction about investment prospects or future sales performance generally cannot form the basis of a fraud claim. Kentucky recognizes an exception to this rule against predictions where the proffered opinion "either incorporates falsified past or present facts or is so contrary to the true current state of affairs that the purported prediction is an obvious sham," but an experienced institutional investor like Republic nonetheless remains under a duty to exercise "common sense" to protect itself. "'[M]ere commendation, or even false representation by the seller of stock as to its value, when the purchaser has an opportunity to ascertain for himself such value by ordinary vigilance or inquiry, has no legal effect on the rights of the contracting parties, even when made with the intention to deceive.'" The exception is limited to cases where the defendant has misrepresented objective data or its own present intentions; "'forward-looking recommendations and opinions are not actionable . . . merely because they are misguided, imprudent or overly optimistic.'" The complaint contains three subjects on which the defendants allegedly made false statements.

a. "Reasonably Safe Investment Products"

Republic complains that "[d]efendants represented that the certificates were reasonably safe investment products backed by mortgage loans made according to reasonably prudent underwriting standards." This allegation fails. We agree with the defense: to say that an investment is "reasonably safe" or that it was based on "reasonably prudent" mortgages is only to offer an opinion, from which no fraud action can originate. Whether something is reasonably safe is an inherently subjective question. Different investors have different levels of tolerance for risk and uncertainty, so whether an investment is "reasonable" or a loan is "prudent" will depend on an individual's strategy and preferences. This is something that each investor must assess for himself. Bear Stearns, we now know, had an unusually high risk tolerance. This earned it huge returns on its investments, but also led to a precipitous collapse two years ago. It apparently thought its investments were reasonable, and was willing to accept the risk of loss. If it told Republic that the investment products were reasonably safe, it can only have been expressing its opinion. Republic cannot expect another party to take Republic's subjective assessment of its own risk-averseness into account in discerning whether or not a product is "reasonably safe."

To make out an actionable fraud claim, Republic would have had to allege a statement like, "Barney told us there was only a 10% chance of a write-down, but we later learned that there was in fact a 75% chance of a write-down." It has not done anything like that, and its allegations are therefore insufficient. They will be dismissed.

b. Intent to Make a Secondary Market

Paragraph 32.h alleges that "Bear Stearns stated in the prospectuses or prospectus supplements that it intended to make a secondary market for the certificates," but that in fact it lacked the ability to do so due to its own financial weakness. We are told that this is relevant, notwithstanding Republic's admission that it "did not have or review the offering documents until after it purchased the certificates," because it "relied upon [the offering documents] in continuing to hold the certificates." This argument comes close to disproving itself. If Bear Stearns intended to create a secondary market for the certificates, we can suppose that no such market existed at the outset, and that therefore by the time Republic read the offering documents it was already too late for it to "choose" to hold the certificates. Absent a secondary market, it could not have readily sold them if it had wanted to.

But set that aside; perhaps Republic could have found a buyer on its own. Its claim nonetheless fails because an alleged "intent" to do something is not an actionable statement. It is not a "past or present material fact," but rather a forward-looking statement about what a party may do in the future. Furthermore, the prosupps amply warn of the possibility that Bear Stearns would be incapable of following through on its intention, and expressly disclaim any obligation to do so.[2] So even if the intentions were statements of fact, Republic could not have reasonably relied on them. It cannot prove fraud.

PREPARING FOR CLASS

1. How does the court's example, "Barney told us there was only a 10% chance of a write-down, but we later learned that there was in fact a 75% chance of a write-down," differ from the representations that the court dismissed, i.e., the investments were reasonably safe investment products?

2. Is there any way that Bear Stearns's future intention to make a market can be a misrepresentation? What if, as the complaint stated, Bear Stearns was so financially weak that it had no ability to create a market in the foreseeable future?

---

2. For this reason we will also dismiss Republic's allegation that Bear Stearn[s] failed to state that its financial weakness precluded creation of a secondary market.

INCREASING YOUR UNDERSTANDING

1. Predictions or representations of the future are opinions, and many opinions imply current facts. For instance, the statement "that stock will double in value in the next year" is opinion and does not imply any current facts. On the other hand, the statement "my research indicates that stock will double in value in the next year" implies that the speaker has done research that supports the statement in some way.

2. A statement of intention implies that someone has that intention but does not imply that the person with the intention will not change his or her mind. Thus, any party who relies on that intention has a difficult burden to show that the person never, in fact, had the intention.

APPLYING THE LAW

1. The seller of a hotel in the mountains of Montana says "that hotel will double in value in the next year or so since the railroad is going to be stopping a quarter mile away." What facts are implied from that statement? Could those facts support a cause of action for misrepresentation?

2. Would the following statements support a cause of action for misrepresentation? If so, under what circumstances?

   a. I'm sure the government wants to buy this land.

   b. As this paint ages, it becomes more beautiful.

   c. I promise to pay you $20 on March 1 of next year.

   d. The market is going to go up over the next several months.

E. THIRD-PARTY RELIANCE

Nycal Corp. v. KPMG Peat Marwick LLP
688 N.E.2d 1368 (Mass. 1998)

GREANEY, Justice.

On May 24, 1991, the plaintiff, allegedly in reliance on an auditors' report of the 1990 financial statements of Gulf Resources & Chemical Corporation (Gulf) prepared by the defendant, entered into a stock purchase agreement with the controlling shareholders of Gulf and, on July 12, 1991, the sale was completed. Gulf filed for bankruptcy protection in October, 1993, rendering the plaintiff's investment worthless. The plaintiff filed a civil complaint against the defendant seeking damages and costs incurred as a result of its alleged reliance on the auditors' report. The plaintiff claimed that the report materially misrepresented the financial condition of Gulf,[1] and should have included a "going concern" qualification. After applying the liability standard embodied in §552 of the Restatement (Second) of Torts (1977), a judge in the Superior Court granted summary judgment for the defendant. We granted the parties' applications for direct appellate review of the final judgment. We conclude that the defendant did not breach any legal duty owed to the plaintiff and, accordingly, we affirm the judgment.

The following material facts are undisputed. Gulf retained the defendant to audit its 1990 financial statements. At that time, Gulf was listed on the New York Stock Exchange, and was controlled by several of its officers and directors who held their Gulf shares through two other entities (Inoco P.L.C. and Downshire N.V.). The financial statements were prepared by, and were the responsibility of, Gulf's management.

In February, 1990, D.S. Kennedy & Co. (Kennedy) reported to the Securities and Exchange Commission (SEC) that it had acquired 2,033,600 shares of Gulf common stock, and that it intended to acquire a controlling interest in Gulf. The defendant was aware of Kennedy's SEC filing. Gulf's controlling shareholders responded to the filing by increasing Inoco P.L.C.'s holdings in Gulf through purchasing and exercising warrants. Gulf management discussed with the defendant the potential for purchasing Kennedy's shares. Thus, the defendant was aware of Kennedy's interest in acquiring a controlling interest in Gulf and that Gulf intended to treat Kennedy as a hostile takeover threat.

The minutes of a September 14, 1990, meeting of Gulf's board of directors (board) reflect that the board discussed a possible sale to Aviva Petroleum, Inc. (Aviva). The minutes of an October 4, 1990, meeting indicates that the board discussed acquiring a 17% interest in Aviva, and adoption of a "poison pill" to defend against a hostile takeover by Aviva. Gulf ultimately purchased Aviva stock. The defendant reviewed the minutes from the board's meetings in preparing the audit report, and was aware of Gulf's purchase of Aviva stock.

The defendant's completed auditors' report was included in Gulf's 1990 annual report, which became publicly available on February 22, 1991. In March, 1991, the plaintiff entered into discussions with Gulf concerning the possible purchase of a large block of Gulf shares, and during the course of those discussions, Gulf provided the plaintiff with a copy of its 1990 annual report. Thereafter, the plaintiff purchased 3,626,775 shares of Gulf (approximately 35% of the outstanding shares) in exchange for $16,000,000 in cash and

---

1. The plaintiff asserted that the report failed to take into account recurring substantial losses from operations, the extent of liability for environmental clean-up costs, inadequate accruals of pension and retirement obligations, and restrictions on transfers in certain bank covenants.

$18,000,000 in the plaintiff's stock. The acquisition gave the plaintiff operating control of Gulf.

The defendant first learned of the transaction between the plaintiff and Gulf a few days prior to the July 12, 1991, closing. Until that time, the defendant did not know that any transaction between the plaintiff and Gulf had been contemplated.

We have not addressed the scope of liability of an accountant to persons with whom the accountant is not in privity. Three tests have generally been applied in other jurisdictions, either by common law or by statute, to determine the duty of care owed by accountants to nonclients. These include the foreseeability test, the near-privity test, and the test contained in §552 of the Restatement.

The plaintiff urges our adoption of the broad standard of liability encompassed in the foreseeability test. Pursuant to this test, which is derived from traditional tort law concepts as first enunciated in Palsgraf v. Long Island R.R., 344, 162 N.E. 99 (1928), an accountant may be held liable to any person whom the accountant could reasonably have foreseen would obtain and rely on the accountant's opinion, including known and unknown investors. This test is generally disfavored, having been adopted by courts in only two jurisdictions. See Touche Ross & Co. v. Commercial Union Ins. Co., 514 So. 2d 315 (Miss. 1987); Citizens State Bank v. Timm, Schmidt & Co., 335 N.W.2d 361 (Wisc. 1983).

Our cases draw a distinction between the duty owed by a professional to a third party for personal injuries and that owed to a third party for pecuniary loss due to a professional's negligence. While we apply traditional tort law principles in cases involving the former, we have not done so in cases concerning the latter. Such principles are particularly unsuitable for application to accountants where, "regardless of the efforts of the auditor, the client retains effective primary control of the financial reporting process." Bily v. Arthur Young & Co., 834 P.2d 745 (Calif. 1992). The auditor prepares its report from statements and information supplied by the client, and once the report is completed and provided to the client, the client controls its dissemination. If we were to apply a foreseeability standard in these circumstances, "a thoughtless slip or blunder, the failure to detect a theft or forgery beneath the cover of deceptive entries, may expose accountants to a liability in an indeterminate amount for an indeterminate time to an indeterminate class." Ultramares Corp. v. Touche, 174 N.E. 441 (N.Y. 1931). We refuse to hold accountants susceptible to such expansive liability, and conclude that Massachusetts law does not protect every reasonably foreseeable user of an inaccurate audit report.

The near-privity test, which originated in Chief Judge Cardozo's decision in *Ultramares Corp. v. Touche*, supra, and was modified by Credit Alliance Corp. v. Arthur Andersen & Co., 483 N.E.2d 110 (N.Y. 1985), limits an accountant's liability exposure to those with whom the accountant is in privity or in a relationship "sufficiently approaching privity." Under this test, an accountant may be held liable to noncontractual third parties who rely to their detriment on an inaccurate financial report if the accountant was aware that the report was to be used for a particular purpose, in the furtherance of which a known party (or parties) was intended to rely, and if there was some conduct on the part of the accountant creating a link to that party, which evinces the accountant's understanding of the party's reliance. *Id.* 483 N.E.2d 110.

The defendant professes that the near-privity test is consistent with the standard we have previously applied to other professionals in the absence of privity. We disagree. A review of the relevant cases demonstrates that the first two elements of the near-privity test—reliance by the third party and knowledge that the party intended to rely—have analogs in our case law, but the third element—conduct by the accountant providing a direct linkage to the third party—does not.

The leading case in Massachusetts on the duty owed by a professional to persons with whom the professional is not in privity is Craig v. Everett M. Brooks Co., 222 N.E.2d 752 (Mass. 1967). In *Craig,* the plaintiff, a general contractor, and the defendant, a civil engineer and surveyor, each had a contract with the same real estate developer. The defendant placed stakes on the developer's real estate to enable the plaintiff to build roads. The defendant knew that the plaintiff was the contractor, and that the work which the plaintiff was contracted to perform would be in accordance with the defendant's stakes. Because the defendant knew the plaintiff's identity, and the precise purpose for which the work was to be performed, as well as that the plaintiff would be relying on the work, we held that there would be recovery despite the lack of a contractual relation. The rule in *Craig* has been referred to as "the *Craig* principle of foreseeable reliance," Page v. Frazier, 445 N.E.2d 148 (1983), and subsequent cases rely on *Craig* for the proposition that recovery for negligent misrepresentation is limited to situations where the defendant knew that a particular plaintiff would rely on the defendant's services.

We believe that the third test, taken from §552 of the Restatement (Second) of Torts (1977), comports most closely with the liability standard we have applied in other professional contexts. Section 552 describes the tort of negligent misrepresentation committed in the process of supplying information for the guidance of others as follows:

> "(1) One who, in the course of his business, profession or employment, or in any other transaction in which he has a pecuniary interest, supplies false information for the guidance of others in their business transactions, is subject to liability for pecuniary loss caused to them by their justifiable reliance upon the information, if he fails to exercise reasonable care or competence in obtaining or communicating the information."

That liability is limited to:

> "loss suffered (a) by the person or one of a limited group of persons for whose benefit and guidance he intends to supply the information or

knows that the recipient intends to supply it; and (b) through reliance upon it in a transaction that he intends the information to influence or knows that the recipient so intends or in a substantially similar transaction."

Id.

The attendant comments explain the policy behind §552 as follows:

"[T]he duty of care to be observed in supplying information for use in commercial transactions implies an undertaking to observe a relative standard, which may be defined only in terms of the use to which the information will be put, weighed against the magnitude and probability of loss that might attend that use if the information proves to be incorrect. A user of commercial information cannot reasonably expect its maker to have undertaken to satisfy this obligation unless the terms of the obligation were known to him. Rather, one who relies upon information in connection with a commercial transaction may reasonably expect to hold the maker to a duty of care only in circumstances in which the maker was manifestly aware of the use to which the information was to be put and intended to supply it for that purpose."

Id. comment a, at 128.

The comments explain with regard to the requirement that the plaintiff be a member of a "limited group of persons for whose benefit and guidance" the information is supplied as follows:

"[I]t is not required that the person who is to become the plaintiff be identified or known to the defendant as an individual when the information is supplied. It is enough that the maker of the representation intends it to reach and influence either a particular person or persons, known to him, or a group or class of persons, distinct from the much larger class who might reasonably be expected sooner or later to have access to the information and foreseeably to take some action in reliance upon it. . . . It is sufficient, in other words, insofar as the plaintiff's identity is concerned, that the maker supplies the information for repetition to a certain group or class of persons and that the plaintiff proves to be one of them, even though the maker never had heard of him by name when the information was given. It is not enough that the maker merely knows of the ever-present possibility of repetition to anyone, and the possibility of action in reliance upon it, on the part of anyone to whom it may be repeated."

Id. comment h, at 132-133.

We concur with the California Supreme Court's conclusion in Bily v. Arthur Young & Co., 834 P.2d 745 (Calif. 1992), that the Restatement test properly balances the indeterminate liability of the foreseeability test and the restrictiveness of the near-privity rule. Section 552 "recognizes commercial realities by avoiding both unlimited and uncertain liability for economic losses in cases of professional mistake and exoneration of the auditor in situations where it clearly intended to undertake the responsibility of influencing particular business transactions involving third persons." Id. at 834 P.2d 745.

Although the Restatement standard has been widely adopted by other jurisdictions, courts differ in their interpretations of the standard. The better reasoned decisions interpret §552 as limiting the potential liability of an accountant to noncontractual third parties who can demonstrate "actual knowledge on the part of accountants of the limited—though unnamed—group of potential [third parties] that will rely upon the [report], as well as actual knowledge of the particular financial transaction that such information is designed to influence." The accountant's knowledge is to be measured "at the moment the audit [report] is published, not by the foreseeable path of harm envisioned by [litigants] years following an unfortunate business decision."

The plaintiff argues that, by limiting §552 to allow recovery only by those persons, or limited group of persons, that an accountant actually knows will receive and rely on an audit report, we will be rewarding an accountant's efforts to "remain blissfully unaware" of the report's proposed distribution and uses. We are unpersuaded by this argument. The axiom we have applied in other contexts applies to accountants as well: the Restatement standard will not excuse an accountant's "wilful ignorance" of information of which the accountant would have been aware had the accountant not consciously disregarded that information.

The judge correctly concluded under §552, that the undisputed facts failed to show that the defendant knew (or intended) that the plaintiff, or any limited group of which the plaintiff was a member, would rely on the audit report in connection with an investment in Gulf. To the contrary, the record suggests that the defendant did not prepare the audit report for the plaintiff's benefit and that the plaintiff was not a member of any "limited group of persons" for whose benefit the report was prepared. At the time the audit was being prepared, the plaintiff was an unknown, unidentified potential future investor in Gulf. The defendant was not aware of the existence of the transaction between the plaintiff and Gulf until after the stock purchase agreement had been signed and only a few days before the sale was completed.

The summary judgment record further indicates that the defendant neither intended to influence the transaction entered into by the plaintiff and Gulf nor knew that Gulf intended to influence the transaction by use of the audit report. While the defendant was aware of the circumstances surrounding the Kennedy and Aviva transactions, which had occurred prior to the completion of the audit report, the plaintiff's purchase of Gulf stock did not resemble either of those transactions, and it occurred subsequent to the issuance of the defendant's report. Furthermore, contrary to the plaintiff's contention, the Kennedy and Aviva transactions did not indicate to the defendant that Gulf's controlling shareholders intended to use the audit report to locate a purchaser for their stock. In fact, the record reveals that at the time the report was being prepared, Gulf's controlling shareholders were responding to expressions of interest in acquiring their stock by aggressively rejecting those advances and taking actions to defend against a hostile takeover.

Moreover, the record suggests that the defendant's audit report was prepared for inclusion in Gulf's annual report and not for the purpose of assisting Gulf's controlling shareholders in any particular transaction. The record does not exhibit that the defendant knew of any particular use that would be made of its audit report.

The rule we adopt today will preclude accountants from having to ensure the commercial decisions of nonclients where, as here, the accountants did not know that their work product would be relied on by the plaintiff in making its investment decision.

Judgment affirmed.

PREPARING FOR CLASS

1. Why is the law so concerned about the scope of liability of an accounting firm? If an accounting firm is negligent, why shouldn't it be responsible to all who are harmed as a result?

2. What sort of additional facts can you imagine that would make KPMG Peat Marwick liable?

INCREASING YOUR UNDERSTANDING

1. New York is an important jurisdiction for accountant liability since so many major accounting firms, stock exchanges, and companies are located there. In Ultramares Corporation v. Touche, 174 N.E.2d 441 (N.Y. 1931), Justice Cardozo, writing for New York's highest court, said that an accounting firm owed no duty to third parties who relied upon the accounting firm's negligently prepared statements to lend money to the audited company. But in an earlier case, Glanzer v. Shepard, 135 N.E. 275 (N.Y. 1922), the court had ruled that a weighmaster who negligently provided an erroneous statement of weight to the seller, realizing that it would be used to verify the weight to a buyer, could be held liable because the weighmaster had clear knowledge of the reliance of the seller and stood in virtual privity with the plaintiff. So, the New York Court of Appeals had to decide how to reconcile these two cases, i.e., the no liability decision of *Ultramares* and the liability decision of *Glanzer*. The court reconciled these decisions in *Credit Alliance v. Arthur*

Anderson, mentioned in the opinion above. The *Credit Alliance* court required some conduct (linkage) on the part of the party to be held liable to show that the defendant knew that the plaintiff or its group would rely on the negligent statement.

2. Other courts, such as the Supreme Court of Wisconsin, have followed the ordinary negligence law analysis and found liability if the negligent representor, for example, the accounting firm, could reasonably foresee reliance by a third party. Citizens State Bank v. Timm, Schmidt & Co., 335 N.W.2d 361 (Wisc. 1983).

APPLYING THE LAW

1. Able Corporation (Able) borrows money from General Bank every year. The loans of General Bank are on Able's books and are most of the debt of Able. Classic Accounting audits the books of Able and made a mistake in auditing Able's receivables so that they are significantly overstated. Able fails shortly thereafter, defaulting on General Bank's loans. General Bank wants to sue Classic Accounting since they read and relied upon Classic's auditing statements before making the loans. Will General Bank be able to sue Classic Accounting? Explain.

2. A farmer brought an abstract of title, i.e., copies of all documents filed with the Register of Deeds office affecting the farmer's property, to a lawyer. The farmer asked the lawyer to prepare a written title opinion. The lawyer prepared a title opinion determining that the farmer owned the farm free and clear of all liens. The lawyer made a mistake and did not notice a large mortgage on the farm. The farmer sold the property to a buyer who relied on the lawyer's opinion in making the deal. Now the buyer has discovered the mortgage. The buyer wants to sue the lawyer for negligence. Will the buyer have a cause of action? Explain.

F. DAMAGES FOR MISREPRESENTATION

BDO Seidman, LLP v. Mindis Acquisition Corp.
578 S.E.2d 400 (Ga. 2003)

FLETCHER, Chief Justice.
We granted certiorari in this case to consider the proper measure of damages in a negligent misrepresentation case. Because the Court of Appeals improperly utilized a fraud standard of damages for this negligence cause of action, we reverse.

Mindis Acquisition Corporation was formed to purchase Mindis Corporation. After the purchase was complete, MAC discovered that the inventory value of Mindis was less than what appeared on Mindis's financial statements. MAC then sued Mindis's accountants, BDO Seidman, LLP, for negligent misrepresentation, contending that BDO was negligent in its audit of Mindis's financial statements. The trial court instructed the jury that damages were to be determined by the standard used in fraud and deceit cases, a benefit-of-the-bargain standard.[1] The jury found in favor of MAC and awarded $44 million. The Court of Appeals rejected BDO's contention that the jury was charged on an improper fraud standard of damages and affirmed the jury's verdict.

In Robert & Co. v. Rhodes-Haverty Partnership, 300 S.E.2d 503 (1983), this Court first recognized a claim for negligent misrepresentation and adopted the liability standard set forth in section 552 of the Restatement (Second) of Torts. This Court again considered negligent misrepresentation in Hardaway Co. v. Parsons, Brinckerhoff, Quade & Douglas, Inc., 479 S.E.2d 727 (1997), and agreed with the Court of Appeals that the proper statute of limitations for a negligent misrepresentation case must be determined by applying principles of negligence law. Consistent with our prior cases treating this cause of action as one sounding in negligence, we now conclude that the damages standard for a negligent misrepresentation claim is the traditional negligence standard, which is also set forth in the Restatement (Second) §552. Under Restatement (Second) of Torts §552B, the amount of damages awarded for negligent misrepresentation is measured by an "out-of-pocket" standard:

> The damages recoverable for a negligent misrepresentation are those necessary to compensate the plaintiff for the pecuniary loss to him of which the misrepresentation is a legal cause, including (a) The difference between the value of what he has received in the transaction and its purchase price or other value given for it; and (b) Pecuniary loss suffered otherwise as a consequence of the plaintiff's reliance upon the representation.

The out-of-pocket measure of damages is consistent with Georgia's general measure of damages in negligence cases, which seeks to place the injured party in the same place it would have been had there been no injury or breach of duty. It is also consistent with our prior decision in *Robert & Co.*, supra, in which we recognized that the important distinction between cases of intentional misrepresentation and cases of negligent misrepresentation is the culpability of the defendant. As noted in the commentary to section 552B, an out-of-pocket measure of damages is commensurate with the culpability of the tortfeasor, who acted negligently, rather than intentionally or

---

1. Kunzler Enterprises v. Rowe, 438 S.E.2d 365 (1993) (damages for fraudulent misrepresentation are difference between the value of the thing sold at the time of delivery and what would have been its value if the representations made by the defendants had been true).

maliciously. Furthermore, utilizing the out-of-pocket standard for negligent misrepresentation and the benefit-of-the-bargain standard for fraudulent misrepresentation is a middle position that is consistent with our statement in Badische Corp. v. Caylor, 356 S.E.2d 198 (1987), that our adoption of section 552 represents a "middle ground" standard. Finally, a majority of jurisdictions favor the Restatement position.

In adopting the benefit-of-the-bargain standard, the Court of Appeals failed to recognize how this standard is related to the culpability of the defendant. A benefit-of-the-bargain standard gives the wronged party the benefit of the contract he made, but it also ensures that the fraudfeasor does not enjoy any fruits of his misdeeds. The dual purposes of this standard have no application in a negligence misrepresentation case where there was no privity because the defendant was not a party to the transaction and thus, has not been unjustly enriched.

After considering the measure of damages, the Court of Appeals ruled that BDO had waived this enumeration by failing to properly object to the jury charge. Our review of the record, however, demonstrates that the issue was preserved. Therefore, a new trial utilizing the proper measure of damages is required.

Judgment reversed.

PREPARING FOR CLASS

1. Assume that BDO sent a new auditor to Mindis Corporation. The new auditor did extensive checking at Mindis but forgot to check the inventory. BDO's audit said, among other things, that it had audited the inventory. Would a party who relied on that representation to its detriment be entitled to benefit-of-the-bargain or out-of-pocket damages?

2. How does the benefit-of-the-bargain measure of damages "ensure that the fraudfeasor does not enjoy any fruits of his misdeeds"?

INCREASING YOUR UNDERSTANDING

1. Damages are not the only remedy for misrepresentation.

    a. A party may seek reformation of a contract when the writing does not reflect the agreement of the parties due to fraud or mistake.

    b. Often a party will want to rescind a contract that was brought about by fraud, negligent misrepresentation, or even innocent misrepresentation.

2. The Restatement provides for out-of-pocket damages for innocent misrepresentation. Innocent misrepresentation may also be either a contractual warranty or a mistake justifying rescission of the contract.

3. If the transaction would have resulted in a loss, then out-of-pocket damages will exceed benefit-of-the-bargain damages. The victim of intentional misrepresentation will then seek out-of-pocket damages.

APPLYING THE LAW

Jason Company represents to Moreau Co. that its only asset, its oil reserves, are worth $100 million. Jason Company is wrong; it has oil reserves worth only $75 million. Moreau Co., believing Jason Company's statements, paid $70 million for Jason Company. Moreau Co. has now discovered the shortfall in oil reserves and wants to sue Jason Company.

1. How much will Moreau Co. recover if the court concludes that Jason Company intentionally misrepresented the size of the oil reserves?

2. How much will Moreau Co. recover if the court concludes that Jason Company negligently misrepresented the size of the oil reserves?

Chapter 23

Alternatives to Tort—No-Fault Systems

The tort system has been found lacking in areas of frequent and predictable injury. When this occurs, the legislature has looked to noneconomic, pain-and-suffering damages as an area to cut in return for more predictable payment of lost wages and medical bills. In the area of employee injuries, the workers' compensation system was set up to pay employees their lost wages and medical bills but, in return, the employer would not be responsible for pain-and-suffering damages. This is a theory of enterprise liability, i.e., the enterprise should pay the costs of worker injury as a cost of doing business or a cost of producing that product. The employer would be strictly liable, i.e., liable regardless of fault for all injuries that "arise out of and in the course of employment."

A. WORKERS' COMPENSATION

Davis v. Rockwell International Corp.
596 F. Supp. 780 (N.D. Ohio 1984)

ANN ALDRICH, District Judge.
This Memorandum and Order sets forth the reasons for this Court's September 25, 1984 Order denying defendant Rockwell International Corporation's ("Rockwell") motion for summary judgment.

I.

Robert B. Davis was formerly employed as a mixer machine operator at Rockwell's Reinforced Plastics Division ("the Division") plant located in Ashtabula, Ohio. On May 28, 1980, his hand was partially crushed when it became caught between two power-driven rollers which are parts of a fiberglass molding machine. The injury occurred when, in the normal course of employment, Davis was attempting to clean the machine.

Davis applied for and collected workers' compensation benefits under the Ohio Workers' Compensation Act ("OWCA"), Rockwell, a self-insured employer complied with the law and has paid the administratively-determined amount of benefits to Davis and his doctors. Davis has also filed an "Application for Additional Award for Violation of Specific Requirement" as provided for by the Ohio Constitution.

On May 28, 1982, Davis and his wife Emilie commenced this action against Rockwell, the Division, and eight other defendants. The first three counts of the complaint concern the mixer machine and are not relevant to this motion. The fourth cause of action, however, states that the mixer was provided by Rockwell and the Division "for the use and operation by plaintiff and other employees in a dangerous and/or hazardous condition, thereby proximately causing his injuries." Davis further "states that these defendants had knowledge of the dangerous and hazardous condition of the machine and failed to correct and warn with respect thereto." Providing the mixer in such a condition and failing to correct it and warn employees of it "constituted intentional and malicious conduct and was in willful and wanton disregard of the health and safety of the plaintiff, and which proximately caused his injuries. . . ." Davis seeks $600,000 in compensatory damages and $1,000,000 in punitive damages.

In the fifth cause of action, Emilie Davis seeks $150,000 in compensatory damages and $300,000 in punitive damages for loss of her husband's services.

II.

Rockwell claims that its participation in the workers' compensation system protects it from suit over an employee's work-related injury. It further contends that Davis' decision to collect workers' compensation benefits constitutes an election of remedies which precludes him from bringing a civil action for intentional tort.

III.

A. THE CONSTITUTIONAL AND STATUTORY SCHEME

Workers' compensation statutes, such as the OWCA, generally provide that benefits recoverable under the statute are the exclusive remedy available to an employee injured in the course of employment. . . . Section 35, Article II of the Ohio Constitution establishes the groundwork for the OWCA. In pertinent part, it provides:

> For the purpose of providing compensation to workmen and their dependents, for death, injuries or occupational disease, occasioned in the

course of such workmen's employment, laws may be passed establishing a state fund to be created by compulsory contribution thereto by employers, and administered by the state, determining the terms and conditions upon which payment shall be made therefrom. Such compensation shall be in lieu of all other rights to compensation, or damages, for such death, injuries, or occupational disease, and any employer who pays the premium or compensation provided by law, passed in accordance herewith, shall not be liable to respond in damages at common law or by statute for such death, injuries or occupational disease. . . .

Implementing the constitutional mandate, the Ohio legislature passed the OWCA. Ohio Rev. Code §4123.74 provides:

Employers [in compliance with the OCWA] shall not be liable to respond in damages at common law or by statute for any injury, or occupational disease, or bodily condition, received or contracted by an employee in the course of or arising out of his employment. . . .

For an injury resulting from an employer's violation of a specific safety standard, an employee may be granted an additional award of up to fifty per cent of the maximum award. The award is in the form of a penalty against the employer. Ohio Constitution, Section 35, Article II. . . .

The Ohio legislature also established a rule of construction, Ohio Rev. Code §4123.95, which has been termed "clearly of assistance in determining the scope of employer immunity." The section reads:

[The Ohio Workers Compensation Act] shall be liberally construed in favor of employees and the dependents of deceased employees.

The constitution and code reflect a legislated compromise between the interest of the employees and the concerns of the employers. On both sides, there is a quid pro quo. In return for a greater assurance of recovery, the employees relinquish their common law remedy and accept lower benefits. Employers sacrifice their common law defenses and, in turn, are protected from unlimited liability.

B. INTENTIONAL TORT

Workers' compensation statutes, designed to improve the plight of the injured worker, do not, however, afford an employer immunity for its intentionally tortious behavior. As the Ohio Supreme Court held:

An employee is not precluded by Section 35, Article II of the Ohio Constitution, or (The Ohio Workers Compensation Act) from enforcing his common law remedies against his employer for an intentional tort.

Blankenship, 69 Ohio St. 2d at 608 (syllabus). While plain reading of the syllabus alone appears to indicate that Rockwell's motion must be denied, the issue is complicated by the need to define an intentional tort and to resolve the election of remedies issues not decided in *Blankenship*.[3]

Several reasons have been advanced to explain the intentional tort exception to the exclusive remedy provisions of workers' compensation statutes. The most persuasive is that an employer who commits an intentional wrong should not be permitted to argue that the resulting injury was accidental and within the exclusivity terms of the act. Following Delamotte v. Midland Ross, 411 N.E.2d 814 (Lucas County, Ohio, 1978), *Blankenship* allowed an intentional tort claim because "the substance of the claim is not an injury . . . received or contracted by any employee in the course of or arising out of his employment within the meaning of R.C. 4123.74." The court also stated that one of the avowed purposes of the act, promoting a safe and injury free work environment, would not be fulfilled if an employer could commit an intentional tort with impunity having only to worry about its workers' compensation premiums rising.

The majority of courts adopting the intentional tort exception have held that even egregious or reckless employer conduct that falls short of demonstrating a deliberate intent to injure will not permit an employee to overcome the exclusivity provision. For example, an employee who merely alleges constructive intent is limited to workers' compensation remedies and cannot resort to a common law action.[4] Employer misconduct that does not fall within the intentional tort exception includes: knowingly permitting a hazardous work condition to exist; willfully failing to furnish a safe place to work; intentionally failing to warn the employee of the dangers and health hazard to which he could be exposed; and willfully and unlawfully violating a safety statute.,

---

3. It should be noted here that intentional tort is not the only exception to the general rule that workers' compensation provides an exclusive forum and sole remedy. Other exceptions recognized under Ohio and federal law include: the dual capacity theory, 378 N.E.2d 488 (1978) (injured hospital employee's suit not barred where employer hospital occupies second or dual capacity as administering hospital); the parent and sibling corporation exception, Boggs v. Blue Diamond Coal Co., 590 F.2d 655, 663 (6th Cir. 1979) (without exception corporation could contract within itself for safety services and create immunity); third party suits for contribution and indemnity from employers, Ryan Stevedoring Co. v. Pan-Atlantic S.S. Corp., 350 U.S. 124, (1956) (creates de facto exception to exclusive remedy rule) and allowing pursuit of Longshoremen's and Harbor Workers' Compensation Act ("LHWCA") claims after recourse to state compensation, Landry v. Carlson Mooring Service, 643 F.2d 1080, 1087-88,(5th Cir.1981) (complementary claims may be pursued successively by litigant).

4. In describing intentionally tortuous conduct Dean Prosser states:

> Intent is the word commonly used to describe the desire to bring about the physical consequences [of an act]. . . . Intent, however, is broader than a desire to bring about physical results. It must extend not only to those consequences which are desired, but also to those which the actor believes are substantially certain to follow from what he does.

Prosser, Law of Torts, §8 (4th ed. 1971). Likewise, the Restatement (Second) of Torts §8A, comment (a), states that "intent" refers to the consequences of an act rather than to the act itself.

The Ohio Supreme Court, however, has taken a slightly different approach to this question. In *Blankenship*, employees and their spouses sued in tort for an employer's intentional use of chemicals it allegedly knew were harmful, and for its failure to warn and to report the dangerous conditions to federal and state agencies as required. The complaint alleged that, within the scope of their employment, the employees were exposed to fumes and other noxious characteristics of several chemicals. Like Davis, the employees further alleged that notwithstanding the employer's knowledge that hazardous conditions existed, it "failed to correct said conditions, failed to warn ... [employees] of the dangers and conditions that existed ... [and] such failure on the part of the [employer] was intentional, malicious and in willful and wanton disregard of the health of [the employees]." In reversing the lower court's dismissal of the action, the Ohio Supreme Court did not define an intentional tort.[5] Rather it concluded:

> ... it is for the trier of fact to initially determine whether the alleged conduct constitutes an intentional injury. In the instant case, the facts will demonstrate whether an intentional tort occurred or whether the injuries received by [the employees] were incurred in the course of and arising from ... employment such that worker's [sic] compensation would be exclusive.

Some guidance is provided by the court's reliance upon Mandolidis v. Elkins Industries, 246 S.E.2d 907 (W.V. 1978). *Mandolidis* held that "the workers' compensation system completely supplanted the common law tort system only with respect to negligently caused industrial accidents." While the opinion included willful, wanton and reckless conduct within the category of unprotected employer activity, *Mandolidis* emphasized that "conduct removing the immunity bar must be undertaken with a knowledge and an appreciation of the high degree of risk of physical harm to another created thereby. ... Liability will require 'a strong probability that harm may result." The *Blankenship* court's reliance on *Mandolidis* implies that a plaintiff need only satisfy this lesser standard of proof to adequately allege deliberate intent and avoid the exclusivity of remedy doctrine.[6]

The decision in Nayman v. Kilbane, 439 N.E.2d 888 (Ohio1982), offers some further guidance through the muddled state of Ohio law. In *Nayman*, an employee injured his hand while adjusting a punch press at his place of

---

5. Even though the court failed to define what acts constitute an intentional tort, Larson calls the *Blankenship* holding a "distinctly out-of-line view."

6. The quasi-legislative language of the *Blankenship* majority and concurring opinions conceivably supports an even broader interpretation, which this Court does not adopt. The majority opinion can be read as holding that an intentional failure to warn employees of dangerous conditions is by itself a "deliberate" intent to injure. Moreover, the statement that the OWCA affords protection for negligent acts, and the reliance on *Mandolidis*, could be read together to hold that intentional conduct comprises all that conduct beyond mere negligence, such as recklessness, willful and wanton behavior, even when entered into with presumed knowledge of the likely result but without specific intent to cause injury.

employment. He filed for, and was awarded, workers' compensation benefits. He then sued his employer, alleging that his injuries resulted from intentionally tortious acts. The trial judge denied the employer's motion for summary judgment and set the case for trial. The employer filed a complaint for a writ of prohibition in the Court of Appeals, which denied the requested relief. In a narrow holding based on its decision in *Blankenship*, the Ohio Supreme Court affirmed. It held that the Court of Common Pleas possessed subject matter jurisdiction over a suit in which an employee alleged that he had been intentionally injured by his employer.

While neither *Blankenship* nor *Nayman* deals precisely with the summary judgment issue presented by Rockwell's motion, this Court is persuaded that, construing the evidence in a light most favorable to Davis, the Ohio Supreme Court would hold that the alleged intentional tort states a cause of action sufficient to withstand a motion for summary judgment. Rockwell's attempt to draw a distinction between the single incident of injury suffered by Davis and the lengthy exposure to fumes alleged in Blankenship is immaterial. Under Ohio's liberal definition of the intentional tort exception to the exclusive remedy doctrine contained in the OWCA, there is a genuine issue of material fact as to whether Davis' injury was the result of an intentional tort or was incurred in the course of and arising from his employment.

This Court notes that another federal court in this state, in a lengthy and careful opinion, recently has reached the same conclusion. In Gross v. Kenton Structural & Ornamental Ironworks, 581 F. Supp. 390 (S.D. Ohio 1984), Judge Spiegel concluded that "*Blankenship* does not require that the plaintiff prove an actual intent to injure. . . . [U]nder *Nayman* and *Blankenship* failure to warn of a known danger may amount to intentional tortious conduct." Citing *Blankenship*'s admonition that "it is for the trier of fact to initially determine whether the alleged conduct constitutes an intentional injury," he denied a motion for summary judgment and permitted the plaintiff a jury trial to resolve the factual disputes.

C. ELECTION OF REMEDIES

Rockwell's second contention is that Davis has elected his remedy—first by applying for and receiving workers' compensation, and further by pursuing a claim for violation of a specific safety requirement. Rockwell argues that Davis cannot logically claim that his injury was caused by his employer's intentional tort—and thus, under *Blankenship*, did not arise out of his employment—after his injury was found compensable under OCWA. Under Rockwell's theory, Davis' successful pursuit of his statutory remedy acts as an election which bars the pursuit of a common law action for intentional tort.

The Ohio Supreme Court has not yet addressed the election of remedies issue in the context of *Blankenship* actions. Traditionally, one purpose of the doctrine of election of remedies is to prevent double recovery and preclude a litigant from pursuing a remedy which, in a previous action, he rejected in favor of an alternative and inconsistent remedy. Another purpose is to prevent needless experimentation with the remedies afforded by law. The prerequisites to application of the doctrine are: (1) the existence of two or more remedies; (2) the inconsistency of such remedies; and (3) a choice of one of them.

Nevertheless, the election of remedies doctrine is a harsh and technical rule of procedure that is not favored in Ohio. Moreover, in the absence of an express legislative declaration to the contrary, courts have been reluctant to extend this harsh doctrine.

The jurisdictions which have decided the issue posed by Rockwell's motion are, not surprisingly, divided. Some courts have applied the election of remedies doctrine when an employee filed for and collected workmen's compensation benefits and then attempted to sue his employer in intentional tort. Other courts, however, have allowed an employee to sue his employer for personal injuries sustained in an attack by a fellow employee even though workers' compensation benefits already had been accepted.

After a thorough examination of the current state of Ohio workers' compensation law, the best judgment of this Court is that the Ohio Supreme Court, consistent with *Blankenship* and *Nayman*, would not permit an employer to shield itself behind the election of remedy doctrine when an intentional tort is alleged. The same court that expanded an employee's right to sue in intentional tort is not likely to nullify that right through a rigid and expansive application of the election of remedies doctrine. Moreover, the election of remedies rule urged by Rockwell would not relieve employers of their obligations under the OWCA nor free them from the need to insure themselves against intentional tort claims that are filed prior to the receipt of benefits. Employers would still have to be covered for both possible routes that their employees could take. Furthermore, noting again that workers' compensation statutes must be construed liberally in favor of the employees, this Court observes that the rule urged by Rockwell would unfairly thrust employees back into the jurisdictional conundrum that the OWCA was enacted to alleviate. With no express legislative or judicial declaration to the contrary, this Court concludes that Davis must be allowed to pursue his remedies successively.

In summary, we conclude that the Blankenship action should be viewed as a supplemental remedy, rather than as an exclusive remedy, where an employee alleges injury resulting from his employer's intentional tort. Accordingly, we hold that an injured employee who files for and accepts workers' compensation benefits is not barred from proceeding with a common law action against the employer.

D. DOUBLE RECOVERY

While the issue of double recovery has not been briefed by the parties, it is elementary that the claimant should not be allowed to keep the entire amount of his compensation award as well as his common law damage recovery, if any. Ohio follows a collateral source rule which permits an employee to recover the full amount of damages in a negligence action against a third party tortfeasor without deducting awards made under the compensation system. There is, however, ample precedent in the Ohio workers' compensation statutes themselves to enable Rockwell to set off any damages awarded to Davis against payments already made in the form of workers' compensation. If the trier of fact determined that an intentional tort occurred, Rockwell should be able to offset the benefits previously paid. Double recovery would thus be avoided.

IV.

Workmens' compensation is social legislation designed to benefit the injured employee and does not prevent that employee from seeking out the true wrongdoer whenever possible. For the reasons set forth above, the motion for summary judgment is denied.

IT IS SO ORDERED.

PREPARING FOR CLASS

1. What kind of damages is Davis seeking in this case?

2. Does knowledge of the dangerous condition of a machine constitute an intentional tort? Explain.

3. Doesn't this decision give the employee two opportunities to collect?

4. How is there an offset if workers' compensation is covered by the collateral benefits rule?

INCREASING YOUR UNDERSTANDING

1. Workers' compensation laws originated in Germany as Bismarck's defense against Marxism and quickly came to New York and the rest of the United States.

2. Workers' Compensation laws require employers to pay for an employee disability that arises out of and in the course of employment. The employer is required to purchase insurance or participate in a state-managed insurance fund to pay for an injury that arises out of and in the course of employment.

3. The employer in a workers' compensation case is strictly liable, so the traditional defenses of contributory negligence, assumed risk, and the fellow servant rule do not apply. The employer pays the medical bills and two-thirds of the lost wages, up to a maximum, but does not pay for pain-and-suffering damages. Contested cases are heard by an

administrative law judge and not before a jury or judge. Generally, workers' compensation benefits are the exclusive remedy of the employee, so the employee cannot sue the employer in tort.

APPLYING THE LAW

1. What if an angry fellow employee slugs the claimant? Would the claimant be able to sue in court for an intentional tort? Would the claimant be able to collect workers' compensation benefits? Would it make a difference if the fellow employee was the president of the company?

2. If workers' compensation is the exclusive remedy for a claim for lost wages, could an employee sue for state employment discrimination, or would that claim be precluded by the workers' compensation act?

Whetro v. Awkerman
174 N.W.2d 783 (Mich. 1970)

T.G. KAVANAGH, Justice.
These cases were consolidated pursuant to our order of September 5, 1968 wherein we granted leave to appeal prior to decision by the Court of Appeals in the case of Emery v. Huge Company (1968), 381 Mich. 774.

They turn on the same question, for the damages for which workmen's compensation was awarded in each case were caused by the Palm Sunday 1965 tornadoes which devastated parts of Southern Michigan.

Carl Whetro was injured when the tornado destroyed the residence wherein he was working for his employer and seeks reimbursement for his medical expenses. Henry E. Emery was killed when the motel in which he was staying while on a business trip for his employer was destroyed by the tornado, and his widow seeks compensation for his death.

In each case the hearing referee found that the employee's injury arose out of and in the course of his employment. The award was affirmed by the appeal board in each case and by the Court of Appeals in the *Whetro* case.

The defendant-appellants in both cases base their defense on the assertion that tornadoes are "acts of God" or acts of nature and injuries which are caused by them do not arise "out of" the employment and hence are not compensable under the Workman's Compensation Act. For this reason they maintain that the cases were erroneously decided as a matter of law and the awards should be set aside.

The appellants in each case maintain that the injury did not arise 'out of' the employment because that phrase as it is used in the act refers to a causal connection between the event which put in motion the forces which caused the injury and the work itself or the conditions under which it is required to be performed.

Employment as a caretaker-gardener or salesman, they argue, does not include tornadoes as incidents or conditions of the work, and the path of injury is determined by the tornado, not the employment.

Appellants cite a series of Michigan decisions involving injury by lightning; in which compensation was denied and assert that a tornado is like lightning in that it acts capriciously, leaving its victims and the untouched side by side. The decisions in all of these "lightning cases" denied compensation on the ground that the injury did not arise "out of" the employment because the employment did not expose the workman to any increased risk or to a more hazardous situation than faced by others in the area.

The Court of Appeals was able to distinguish between a tornado and a bolt of lightning as a causative force of injury and base its decision affirming the award for Carl Whetro on the reasoning of the Massachusetts supreme court in *Caswell's* Case (Mass. 1940), 26 N.E.2d 328, wherein recovery was allowed for injuries received when a brick wall of the employer's factory was blown down on workmen during a hurricane. This "contact with the premises" met the requirement that the injury arise "out of" the employment in the mind of the Court of Appeals.

We are unable to accept the distinction drawn between a tornado and bolt of lightning when viewed as the cause of an injury. As we see it, a tornado, no less than a bolt of lightning or an earthquake or flood is an "act of God" and if the phrase "out of" the employment in the Workmen's Compensation Act necessarily entails the notion of proximate causality, no injury received because of an 'act of God' should be compensable.

But we are satisfied that it is no longer necessary to establish a relationship of proximate causality between employment and an injury in order to establish compensability. Accordingly we no longer regard an "act of God" whether it be a tornado, lightning, earthquake, or flood as a defense to a claim for a work connected injury. Such a defense retains too much of the idea that an employer should not pay compensation unless he is somehow at fault. This concept from the law of tort is inconsistent with the law of workmen's compensation.

The purpose of the compensation act as set forth in its title, is to promote the welfare of the people of Michigan relating to the liability of employers for injuries or death sustained by their employees. The legislative policy is to provide financial and medical benefits to the victims of work connected injuries in an efficient, dignified and certain form. The act allocates the burden of such payments to the most appropriate source of payment, the consumer of the product.

Fault has nothing to do with whether or not compensation is payable. The economic impact on an injured workman and his family is the same whether the injury was caused by the employer's fault or otherwise.

We hold that the law in Michigan today no longer requires the establishment of a proximately causal connection between the employment and the injury to entitle a claimant to compensation. The cases which have allowed recovery for street risks, increased risks, and on the premises accidents were made without consideration of the proximate causal connection between the nature of the employment and the injury. They have brought the law in Michigan to the point where it can be said today that if the employment is the occasion of the injury, even though not the proximate cause, compensation should be paid.

Such a development of the Michigan law is paralleled by the development of the law in England and Massachusetts—the two jurisdictions which served as Michigan's model in the original legislative drafting and judicial construction of the Workmen's Compensation Act.

The early Michigan case of Hopkins v. Michigan Sugar Co. (Mich. 1915), 150 N.W. 325, imported the "causality" concept into the requirement that the injury must arise "out of" the employment. The court drew this interpretation from the English case of Fitzgerald v. Clark & Son (1908), 2 KB 796, both of these jurisdictions have since adopted the doctrine of positional risk. The Massachusetts court said in *Baran's* Case, p. 344, 145 N.E.2d p. 727: "We think that they (recent cases) disclose the development of a consistent course which is a departure from the earlier view expressed, for example in (*McNicol's* Case). . . . The injury 'need not arise out of the nature of the employment. . . . The question is whether his employment brought him in contact with the risk that in fact caused his death.'"

The English court, in *Powell*, supra, held that if the work required the employee to be at the place of injury the accident arose "out of" his employment.

Accordingly, we hold that the employment of Carl Whetro and Henry E. Emery in each case was the occasion of the injury which they suffered and therefore the injuries arose "out of" and in the course of their employment.

The award in each case is affirmed.

T.M. Kavanagh and Adams, JJ., concurred with T.G. Kavanagh, J.

Brennan, Chief Justice.

The function of the workmen's compensation act is to place the financial burden of industrial injuries upon the industries themselves, and spread that cost ultimately among the consumers.

This humane legislation was developed because the industrialization of our civilization had left in its wake a trail of broken bodies.

Employers were absolved from general liability for negligence, in exchange for the imposition of more certain liability under the act.

But it is a mistake to say that employers were absolved from fault. Liability is the basis of legal remedy. Fault is the basis of moral responsibility.

The workmen's compensation law is society's expression of the moral responsibility of employers and consumers to the workmen whose health and whose lives are sacrificed to industrial and commercial progress and production.

Fault is not the same thing as proximate cause. The compensation law does not use the word *cause*. Rather, it expresses the concept of employer and consumer responsibility in the phrase 'arising out of and in the course of' the employment.

The terms "arising out of" and "in the course of" are not redundant. They mean two different things. An adulterous cobbler shot at his last by his jealous wife may be "in the course of" his employment. But the injury does not "arise out of" his job. On what basis of moral responsibility should his injuries be paid for by his employer? By what logic would society decree that his disability should add a farthing to the price of shoes?

The workmen's compensation law is not a utopian attempt to put a price tag on all human suffering and incorporate it into the cost of living.

Lightning, flood, tornados and estranged wives will always be with us, in this vale of tears. They were the occasion of human injury when our forebears were tilling the soil with sharp sticks. They are not a byproduct of the industrial revolution, nor are they in any sense the moral responsibility of those who profit by or enjoy the fruits of, our modern industrialized society.

I would reverse without apology for the precedents.

DETHMERS and KELLY, JJ., concurred with T.E. BRENNAN, C.J.

PREPARING FOR CLASS

1. Liability for workers' compensation benefits comes about when an injury to an employee arises out of and in the course of employment. Which one of these requirements is at issue in the *Whetro* case?

2. Is it fair to allocate the possibility of injury by an "Act of God" to the consumer of the product?

3. What do you think of Justice Brennan's dissent? Does workers' compensation liability require fault? Should it?

4. Why would a man staying in a hotel be covered by workers' compensation?

INCREASING YOUR UNDERSTANDING

1. The "course of employment" begins when the employee arrives at work, not when driving or commuting to work, unless the employee is on special assignment and is not reporting to a regular workplace. The "course of employment" is primarily a time and place requirement.

2. The "arise out of employment" is a scope of risk requirement, but the risk need not be negligently created. Workers' compensation is a strict liability system. Do you agree that the risk of injury from a tornado "arises out of" the employment of the injured employee?

APPLYING THE LAW

1. Beatrice is attacked by a stranger while she is working at a store. Would the injuries she sustains be covered by workers' compensation? Explain.

2. Beatrice is attacked by her former boyfriend while she is working at a store. Would the injuries she sustains be covered by workers' compensation? Explain.

3. Beatrice is attacked by a former boyfriend while working at a store. The boyfriend had been looking for Beatrice but could not find her because she was hiding. The boyfriend did know where Beatrice worked, though, so he found her there. Would Beatrice's injuries be covered by workers' compensation?

B. AUTOMOBILE NO-FAULT

In the early 1960s, automobile accident litigation became ubiquitous. It was clogging the courts, causing unnecessary delays in collecting insurance, and failing its essential purposes. State governments were seeking broad coverage for all automobile accidents so, like the workers' compensation system, the lawmakers went to the same place to find the money for the broad coverage of automobile accidents as they did for injured workers, i.e., noneconomic or pain-and-suffering damages. Following groundbreaking studies in the 1970s and a proposed uniform law for accident reparations, the legislatures of several states adopted a no-fault automobile reparations system. Automobile no-fault insurance would provide broad coverage—coverage for everyone regardless of fault—but limit noneconomic damages. But contrary to the workers' compensation system, where pain-and-suffering damages were eliminated altogether, noneconomic damages were retained in certain prescribed situations in the automobile no-fault systems.

Hypothetical

Ron was going to drive to the General Grocery store to pick up a six-pack of beer. Tom wanted to go too but Tom wanted to ride in the back of the pickup to "catch some air." Ron and Tom argued about Tom riding in the back but Ron finally relented. Tom jumped into the bed of the pickup and stood up to catch the air coming over the top of the cab.

Ron drove his pickup to the front of General Grocery. Unfortunately, General Grocery had a low-hanging awning, which hit Tom in the head, knocking him from the pickup. Tom was taken to the hospital where he remained for five days. Tom also incurred $15,000 in medical expenses and was out of work for a year (Tom was making $5,000 per month at the time of his injury.). Tom had a five-inch scar on his fore-head where his head hit the awning but no other permanent medical problems.

Tom comes to your law office for legal advice. He has the following questions:

1. Will Tom's accident be covered by his no-fault insurance? The accident happened in a no-fault insurance state.

2. If the accident is covered by no-fault insurance, how much will Tom be able to recover, if any, from the no-fault insurance policy on his car?

3. If the accident is covered by no-fault insurance, how much, if any, will Tom be able to recover from General Grocery for its negligence in constructing and maintaining the awning?

1. Injuries Arising Out of the Use of an Automobile

An automobile accident often causes personal injury to the driver, resulting in lost wages and medical bills. The accident will also cause property damage to the motor vehicles involved in the accident. And finally, from the driver's perspective, the accident may cause liability under the tort system to other drivers, pedestrians, and motor vehicles involved in the accident. In the traditional tort system, the consumer was primarily concerned with liability to anyone who he or she might injure. Consumers in these systems purchased policies to protect against that liability. The essential innovation of the no-fault system is to mandate first–party—against one's own insurance company—coverage of economic damages, i.e., lost wages and medical expenses of the insured.

The first-party insurance system partially replaces the right to sue the tort-feasor abolished by no-fault. Some states maintain the traditional tort system but require insurance companies to add on no-fault coverage or, at least, to offer first-party no-fault coverage. The apparent purpose of these add-on policies is to provide the injured party with some minimum coverage regardless of fault and thus minimize the necessity of a tort suit.

Other states, like Michigan, require every driver to have first-party no-fault insurance. These states eliminate the right to sue the negligent tortfeasor unless the driver is seriously injured. But that brings about the question of whether the accident arises out of the use of a motor vehicle. If it does, then the injured party is covered for first-party benefits but must show that the injury is serious to sue the negligent tortfeasor. Consider the following case that dealt with that issue in Michigan.

Morosini v. Citizens Ins. Co. of America
586 N.W.2d 400 (Mich. 1998)

PER CURIAM.

After a minor traffic accident, the plaintiff was assaulted by the driver of the other car. The lower courts granted no-fault benefits to the plaintiff, but we reverse and remand the case to the district court for entry of a judgment in favor of the defendant.

I

This case arises from an incident that took place in January 1993. It was submitted to the district court on stipulated facts, which the court summarized in this fashion:

On the date stated in the complaint, the

> Plaintiff was an operator of a motor vehicle on a public highway, I believe, leaving the Silverdome or the Palace or something like that, and he was struck from the rear by a motorist who was operating a motor vehicle.
>
> It was a minor impact, and the impact, per se, itself, caused no injury whatsoever to Mr. Kenneth Morosini. However, it was an impact which would give rise to the requirement to determine if property damage had occurred, and if property damage had occurred, it would be necessary, under the rules of a-for vehicle operators, for the operators to exchange identification information, such as driver's license and insurance and registration information.
>
> Mr. Morosini exited his vehicle, was in the process of examining the area where he believed a slight impact had occurred, and he was assaulted by the driver of the other vehicle resulting in injuries.
>
> He has brought this action against Citizens Insurance Company, who is Mr. Morosini's own personal-injury protection carrier, for recoupment of medical expenses arising out of the treatment for the assault.

The parties further stipulated that Mr. Morosini's damages, if liability were found, would be $2,500.

The question before the district court was whether Mr. Morosini's insurer—Citizens

Insurance Company of America—was obliged to pay first-party no-fault benefits. More specifically, the question is whether the facts of this case give rise to liability under M.C.L. §500.3105(1), which reads:

> Under personal protection insurance an insurer is liable to pay benefits for accidental bodily injury arising out of the ownership, operation,

maintenance or use of a motor vehicle as a motor vehicle, subject to the provisions of this chapter.

The district court granted judgment to Mr. Morosini, finding a sufficient nexus between the injuries and the use of a motor vehicle as a motor vehicle. The court reasoned that the traffic accident gave rise to a statutory obligation to stop and exchange information, and that the assault occurred as Mr. Morosini was "in the process of fulfilling his obligations as an operator of a motor vehicle. . . ." Accordingly, the district court entered judgment in favor of Mr. Morosini, in the amount of $2,500.

The circuit court affirmed, saying that "[t]he accident precipitated the assault, and the assault occurred as an integral part of the continuum of the accident."

Citizens took a further appeal to the Court of Appeals. However, the result was another affirmance. The Court of Appeals said that Mr. Morosini's "injuries arose out of the use of his motor vehicle as a motor vehicle because his getting out of his car—thus exposing himself to the risk of an assault—to determine whether there was an accident resulting in damage was in compliance with his statutory obligations." The Court said that "what is critical for the purpose of determining whether plaintiff's injuries were compensable under the no-fault act is whether his injuries arose from an activity normally associated with the use of a vehicle as a motor vehicle." The Court of Appeals then went on to explain why its conclusion "is supported by public policy."

Citizens applied to this Court for leave to appeal. In lieu of granting leave, we remanded the case to the Court of Appeals for reconsideration in light of McKenzie v. ACIA, 580 N.W.2d 424 (Mich. 1998).

On remand, the Court of Appeals issued a short opinion adhering to its earlier conclusion.

Once again, Citizens has applied to this Court for leave to appeal.

II

As one readily can see from the first opinion of the Court of Appeals, there is a substantial body of case law concerning the meaning of the phrase "use of a motor vehicle as a motor vehicle." Among these decisions, several pertain specifically to situations in which a driver has been assaulted.

In Thornton v. Allstate Ins. Co., 391 N.W.2d 320 (Mich. 1986), this Court considered a suit brought by a Flint taxi driver who had been assaulted by a person who pretended to be a fare. As the driver pulled away from the curb, the passenger drew a pistol and shot the driver in the neck. The robbery netted $15 in change, and left the driver paralyzed from the neck down. As this Court explained, however, the Legislature did not extend coverage to this situation: "The connection in this case between the debilitating injuries suffered by Mr. Thornton and the use of the taxicab as a motor vehicle is no more than incidental, fortuitous, or 'but for.'" The cab "was not the instrumentality of the injuries," but "was merely the situs of the armed robbery—the injury could have occurred whether or not Mr. Thornton used a motor vehicle as a motor vehicle."

Marzonie v. ACIA, 495 N.W.2d 788 (1992), likewise illustrates the decisions made by the Legislature in this realm. In *Marzonie*, a dispute erupted between the occupants of two vehicles. One driver drove home, followed by the other. In the moments after the second car arrived, the first driver emerged from his house with a shotgun. Later claiming that he had intended to shoot the second car, not its driver, the first driver discharged his shotgun. Again, the result was permanent and serious injury. The no-fault act did not cover this situation, either, since "[t]he involvement of the automobiles was incidental and fortuitous"—"the shooting arose out of a dispute between two individuals, one of whom happened to be occupying a vehicle at the moment of the shooting."

Bourne v. Farmers Ins. Exchange, 534 N.W.2d 491, (Mich. 1995), involved a claim brought by a man who entered his parked car, only to find two men in the back seat. They forced him at gunpoint to drive to a parking lot a mile away, where he was struck in the face and thrown to the ground. His injuries included several facial fractures and a broken ankle. Building on *Thornton* and *Marzonie*, this Court found that "there was not a sufficient causal connection between plaintiff's injuries and the use of his motor vehicle as a motor vehicle to find liability on the part of defendant."

Finally, there is *McKenzie*, which was decided after the Court of Appeals issued its first opinion in the present case. In *McKenzie*, two men were hospitalized after inhaling carbon monoxide fumes from a propane heater in a camper/trailer that was attached to the back of a pickup truck. Examining closely the syntax selected by the Legislature, this Court observed that "the phrase 'use of a motor vehicle as a motor vehicle' would appear to invite contrasts with situations in which a motor vehicle is not used as a motor vehicle." Noting that a motor vehicle can be used for other purposes, this Court explained that "when we are applying the statute, the phrase 'as a motor vehicle' invites us to determine if the vehicle is being used for transportational purposes." Discussing *Thornton* and *Bourne*, and overruling an earlier decision involving a cement truck that was being unloaded, this Court held that "whether an injury arises out of the use of a motor vehicle 'as a motor vehicle' under [MCL 500.3105(1)] turns on whether the injury is closely related to the transportational function of motor vehicles." Applying that test to the *McKenzie* facts, this Court again concluded that the Legislature excluded coverage.

III

Each of these decisions is instructive, and each supports our conclusion that the Legislature crafted the no-fault statute in a manner that excludes the facts of the present case. From these decisions we learn:

- Coverage is not mandated by the fact that the injury occurred within a moving vehicle, or by the fact that the driver believed that the passenger entered the vehicle for the purpose of being transported. *Thornton*.

- The focus is on the relationship between the injury and the use of a motor vehicle as a motor vehicle, not on the intent of the assailant. *Marzonie.*

- Incidental involvement of a motor vehicle does not give rise to coverage under the language enacted by the Legislature, even if assaultive behavior occurred at more than one location, and the vehicle was used to transport the victim from one place to the other. *Bourne.*

- The statute authorizes coverage in the event of an assault only if it is "closely related to the transportational function of motor vehicles." *McKenzie.*

These cases can lead only to the conclusion that the facts of the present case are not within the coverage intended by the Legislature. In the mind of the second motorist, the assault may have been motivated by closely antecedent events that involved the use of a motor vehicle as a motor vehicle, but the assault itself was a separate occurrence. The plaintiff was not injured in a traffic accident—he was injured by another person's rash and excessive response to these events. The assault in this case was not "closely related to the transportational function of motor vehicles."

For these reasons, we reverse the judgments of the Court of Appeals, the circuit court, and the district court, and we remand this case to the district court for entry of a judgment in favor of defendant Citizens Insurance Company.

WEAVER, C.J., and TAYLOR, CORRIGAN, YOUNG, and MARKMAN, JJ., concurred.

[Justice Cavanagh filed a concurring opinion and Justice Kelly filed a dissent.]

PREPARING FOR CLASS

1. Don't you think that the common understanding arising out of the use of a motor vehicle would include an altercation that arose out of a traffic accident? Why would the court reach a more restrictive result?

2. What is the essential function of the "arising out of" requirement?

3. Morosini is not going to get no-fault Personal Injury Protection benefits as a result of this case. What are the implications for Morosini? Can Morosini recover his medical expenses and lost wages any other place? Could this decision benefit Morosini? Explain.

4. Would the result in this case change if the angry assailant had not gotten out of his car but fired a gun that hit Morosini?

INCREASING YOUR UNDERSTANDING

1. Insurance for tort liability to an injured party is often called third-party insurance. Insurance that is carried by and covers the injured party directly is called first-party insurance. Automobile no-fault insurance is primarily first-party insurance, i.e., the injured party's own insurance covers medical and wage loss.

2. Third-party insurance is more expensive than first-party. Third-party requires plaintiff and defense lawyers, expert witnesses, and court time and resources to resolve disputes. A first-party, strict liability system cuts down on most of these expenses.

3. The model for the no-fault system was developed by Professors Keeton and O'Connell in 1965 (Keeton & O'Connell, Basic Protection for the Traffic Victim). This plan required that each auto owner have insurance for first-party and third-party insurance. The first-party, no-fault insurance would pay the owner, passengers, and pedestrians injured by that automobile for wage loss and medical bills but not pain and suffering. Third-party insurance would pay pain and suffering and wage loss not covered by first-party insurance if there was a tort.

4. Fortunately, most automobile accident claims are small claims that are handled by the auto owner's own insurance company.

APPLYING THE LAW

1. A truck driver owned a truck, which he used for his fuel delivery business. The driver arrived at a customer's house, connected the fuel oil delivery hose to the customer's tank, and turned on the delivery system when the hose exploded. The truck driver was sitting in the truck and was badly burned by the explosion. The truck driver has claimed personal injury protection benefits from the insurer of the truck. What will the truck driver argue? The personal injury protection insurer will move for summary disposition of the case. How should the court rule?

2. A homeowner wanted to clean the eaves troughs of his house but his ladder was not long enough to reach the eaves. He decided to back his pickup up to the house so he could place his ladder on it and reach the eaves troughs. He was on the ladder on the pickup when it slipped, and the homeowner fell to the ground and was seriously injured. He wants to claim personal injury protection benefits from the insurance on his pickup. What result?

2. *The No-Fault Threshold*

The early Canadian no-fault systems adopted in the late 1940s completely abolished the liability of the negligent tortfeasor, but none of the U.S. systems have gone that far. All of the states that have adopted no-fault insurance have established some sort of threshold to a suit for negligence. Some states have monetary thresholds to a tort suit, i.e., a minimum monetary amount of damages suffered by the victim before suing in tort. Massachusetts, the first state to adopt no-fault automobile insurance, required the victim to suffer at least $2,000 of economic damages before suing for tort. These set statutory minimums require the state to readjust the amount of the threshold over time or they would lose their effectiveness.

Other states, like Michigan, require a certain level of seriousness defined by the statute before the victim can sue in tort. But there is always the question about what these thresholds, which are necessarily ambiguous, mean and who will determine whether the threshold has been met. Michigan has been struggling with these questions since no-fault has been adopted. Consider the following case.

McCormick v. Carrier
487 Mich. 180 (Mich. 2010)

MICHAEL F. CAVANAGH, J.

The issue in this case is the proper interpretation of the "serious impairment of body function" threshold for non-economic tort liability under MCL 500.3135. We hold that Kreiner v. Fischer, 683 N.W.2d 611 (2004), was wrongly decided because it departed from the plain language of MCL 500.3135, and is therefore overruled. We further hold that, in this case, as a matter of law, plaintiff suffered a serious impairment of a body function. Accordingly, we reverse and remand the case to the trial court for proceedings consistent with this opinion.

I. FACTS AND PROCEEDINGS

This case arises out of an injury that plaintiff, Rodney McCormick, suffered while working as a medium truck loader at a General Motors Corporation (GM) plant. Plaintiff's job mainly consisted of assisting in the loading of trucks, which required climbing up and around trucks and trailers, standing, walking, and heavy lifting. He generally worked nine-to ten-hour shifts, six days a week.

On January 17, 2005, a coworker backed a truck into plaintiff, knocking him over, and then drove over plaintiff's left ankle. Plaintiff was immediately taken to the hospital, and x-rays showed a fracture of his left medial malleolus. Plaintiff was released from the hospital that day, and two days later metal hardware was surgically inserted into his ankle to stabilize plaintiff's bone fragments.

Plaintiff was restricted from weight-bearing activities for one month after the surgery and then underwent multiple months of physical therapy. The metal hardware was removed in a second surgery on October 21, 2005.

At defendant's request, plaintiff underwent a medical evaluation with Dr. Paul Drouillard in November 2005. He indicated that plaintiff could return to work but was restricted from prolonged standing or walking. On January 12, 2006, the specialist who performed plaintiff's surgeries cleared him to return to work without restrictions. The specialist's report noted that plaintiff had an "excellent range of motion," and an x-ray showed "solid healing with on [sic] degenerative joint disease of his ankle."

Beginning on January 16, 2006, plaintiff returned to work as a medium truck loader for several days, but he had difficulty walking, climbing, and crouching because of continuing ankle pain. He requested that his job duties be restricted to driving, but defendant directed him to cease work.

Defendant required plaintiff to undergo a functional capacity evaluation (FCE) in March 2006. The FCE determined that plaintiff was unable to perform the range of tasks his job required, including stooping, crouching, climbing, sustained standing, and heavy lifting. This was due to ankle and shoulder pain, a moderate limp, and difficulty bearing weight on his left ankle. The report stated that plaintiff's range of motion in his left ankle was not within normal limits and that difficulty climbing and lifting weights had been reported and observed.

In May 2006, Dr. Drouillard examined plaintiff again and reported that plaintiff could return to work. Dr. Drouillard's report stated that plaintiff complained of ankle and foot pain, but the doctor found "no objective abnormality to correspond with his subjective complaints." In June 2006, plaintiff also underwent a magnetic resonance imaging (MRI) test, which showed some postoperative scar and degenerative tissue formation around his left ankle. At plaintiff's request, another FCE was performed on August 1, 2006, which affirmed that plaintiff could return to work without restriction and was capable of performing the tasks required for his job. The report stated that plaintiff complained of "occasional aching" and tightness in his ankle, but it did not appear to be aggravated by activities such as prolonged standing or walking. It also noted that plaintiff's range of motion in his left ankle was still not within normal limits, although it had improved since the March 2006 FCE.

Plaintiff returned to work on August 16, 2006, 19 months after he suffered his injury. He volunteered to be assigned to a different job, and his pay was not reduced. He has been able to perform his new job since that time.

On March 24, 2006, plaintiff filed suit, seeking recovery for his injuries under MCL 500.3135. In his October 2006 deposition, plaintiff testified that at the time of the incident, he was a 49-year-old man and his normal life before the incident mostly consisted of working 60 hours a week as a medium-duty truck loader. He stated that he also was a "weekend golfer" and frequently fished in the spring and summer from a boat that he owns. He testified that he was fishing at pre-incident levels by the spring and summer of 2006, but he has only golfed once since he returned to work. He stated that he can drive and take care of his personal needs without assistance and that his relationship with his wife has not been affected. He stated that he has not sought medical treatment for his ankle since January 2006, when he was approved to return to work without restriction. He further testified that his life is "painful, but normal," although it is "limited," and he continues to experience ankle pain.

The trial court granted defendant's motion for summary disposition on the basis that plaintiff had recovered relatively well and could not meet the serious impairment threshold provided in MCL 500.3135(1). The Court of Appeals affirmed, with one judge dissenting. The majority held that, under *Kreiner*, plaintiff's impairment did not affect his ability to lead his normal life because he is able to care for himself, fish and golf, and work at the same rate of pay. The dissent disagreed, arguing that two doctors had determined that the impairment would cause problems over plaintiff's entire life and his employer had determined that he could not perform his work duties, the main part of his "normal" life.

After initially denying leave to appeal, this Court granted plaintiff's motion for reconsideration, vacated its prior order, and granted the application for leave to appeal.

III. Analysis

The issue presented in this case is the proper interpretation of MCL 500.3135. We hold that *Kreiner* incorrectly interpreted MCL 500.3135 and is overruled because it is inconsistent with the statute's plain language and this opinion. Further, under the proper interpretation of the statute, plaintiff has demonstrated that, as a matter of law, he suffered a serious impairment of body function.

A. Overview of MCL 500.3135

In 1973, the Michigan Legislature adopted the no-fault insurance act, MCL 500.3101 *et seq*. The act created a compulsory motor vehicle insurance program under which insureds may recover directly from their insurers, without regard to fault, for qualifying economic losses arising from motor vehicle incidents. In exchange for ensuring certain and prompt recovery for economic loss, the act also limited tort liability. MCL 500.3135. The act was designed to remedy problems with the traditional tort system as it relates to automobile accidents. These included that "[the contributory negligence liability scheme] denied benefits to a high percentage of motor vehicle accident victims, minor injuries were overcompensated, serious injuries were undercompensated, long payment delays were commonplace, the court system was overburdened, and those with low income and little education suffered discrimination." Shavers v. Attorney General, 267 N.W.2d 72 (Mich. 1978).

Under the act, tort liability for non-economic loss arising out of the owner-ship, maintenance, or use of a qualifying motor vehicle is limited to a list of enumerated circumstances. MCL 500.3135(3). The act creates threshold requirements in MCL 500.3135(1), which has remained unchanged in all key aspects since the act was adopted. That subsection currently provides that "[a] person remains subject to tort liability for noneconomic loss caused by his or her ownership, maintenance, or use of a motor vehicle only if the injured person has suffered death, serious impairment of body function, or permanent serious disfigurement."

The threshold requirement at issue in this case is whether plaintiff has suf-fered "serious impairment of body function." The act did not originally define this phrase. Accordingly, it initially fell to this Court to do so, and the result was a series of differing opinions. In Cassidy v. McGovern, 330 N.W.2d 22 (1982), this Court held that whether the serious impairment threshold is met is a question of law for the court to decide where there is no material disputed fact. It further held that in order to meet the threshold, the plaintiff must show an objectively manifested injury and an impairment of an important body function, which it defined as "an objective standard that looks to the effect of an injury on the person's general ability to live a normal life." This Court later in part modified and in part affirmed *Cassidy* in DiFranco v. Pick-ard, 398 N.W.2d 896 (Mich. 1986). The *DiFranco* Court agreed that a plaintiff had to suffer an objectively manifested injury, but it rejected the *Cassidy* Court's determination that the impairment needed to be "important" and its definition of "important." The *DiFranco* Court further held that whether the threshold is met is a question of law for the court only if there are no material disputed facts and the facts could not support conflicting inferences.

In 1995, however, the Legislature intervened. It amended MCL 500.3135 to define a "serious impairment of body function" as "an objectively manifested impairment of an important body function that affects the person's general ability to lead his or her normal life." MCL 500.3135(7). The Legislature also expressly provided that whether a serious impairment of body function has occurred is a "question[ ] of law" for the court to decide unless there is a factual dispute regarding the nature and extent of injury and the dispute is relevant to deciding whether the standard is met. MCL 500.3135(2)(a). Thus, the Legislature incorporated some language from *DiFranco* and *Cassidy* but also made some significant changes.

This Court interpreted the amended provisions in 2004, in *Kreiner*. The question before this Court is whether the *Kreiner* majority properly interpreted the statute, and, if not, whether its interpretation should be overruled.

B. INTERPRETATION OF MCL 500.3135

The primary goal of statutory construction is to give effect to the Legisla-ture's intent. This Court begins by reviewing the language of the statute, and, if the language is clear and unambiguous, it is presumed that the Legislature intended the meaning expressed in the statute. Judicial construction of an unambiguous statute is neither required nor permitted. When reviewing a statute, all non-technical "words and phrases shall be construed and understood according to the common and approved usage of the language," and, if a term is not defined in the statute, a court may consult a dictionary to aid it in this goal. A court should consider the plain meaning of a statute's words and their "'placement and purpose in the statutory scheme.'" "Where the language used has been subject to judicial interpretation, the legislature is presumed to have used particular words in the sense in which they have been interpreted."

1. *A Question of Law or Fact Under MCL 500.3135(2)*

The first step in interpreting MCL 500.3135 is to determine the proper role of a court in applying MCL 500.3135(1) and (7). The Legislature addressed this issue in the amended MCL 500.3135(2)(a), which states in relevant part:

> The issues of whether an injured person has suffered serious impairment of body function or permanent serious disfigurement are questions of law for the court if the court finds either of the following:
>
> (i) There is no factual dispute concerning the nature and extent of the person's injuries.
>
> (ii) There is a factual dispute concerning the nature and extent of the person's injuries, but the dispute is not material to the determination as to whether the person has suffered a serious impairment of body function or permanent serious disfigurement.

Under the plain language of the statute, the threshold question whether the person has suffered a serious impairment of body function should be determined by the court as a matter of law as long as there is no factual dispute regarding "the nature and extent of the person's injuries" that is material to determining whether the threshold standards are met. If there is a material factual dispute regarding the nature and extent of the person's injuries, the court should not decide the issue as a matter of law. Notably, the disputed fact does not need to be outcome determinative in order to be material, but it should be "significant or essential to the issue or matter at hand." Black's Law Dictionary (8th ed.) (defining "material fact").

2. *A "Serious Impairment of Body Function" Under MCL 500.3135(1) and (7)*

In those cases where the court may decide whether the serious impairment threshold is met as a matter of law, the next issue is the proper interpretation of MCL 500.3135(7). It provides that, for purposes of the section, a "serious impairment of body function" is "an objectively manifested impairment of an important body function that affects the person's general ability to lead his or her normal life." On its face, the statutory language provides three prongs that are necessary to establish a "serious impairment of body function": (1) an objectively manifested impairment (2) of an important body function that (3) affects the person's general ability to lead his or her normal life.

Overall, because we conclude that each of these prongs' meaning is clear from the plain and unambiguous statutory language, judicial construction is neither required nor permitted. Notably, however, a dictionary may aid the Court in giving the words and phrases in MCL 500.3135(7) their common meaning, and where the language used in MCL 500.3135(7) was originally adopted and interpreted in *Cassidy* and *DiFranco*, it may be presumed that the Legislature intended the previous judicial interpretation to be relevant. As will be discussed within, where the *Kreiner* majority's interpretation of these prongs is inconsistent with the clear language of the statute, we hold that *Kreiner* was wrongly decided. Most significantly, its interpretation of the third prong deviates dramatically from the statute's text.

a. An Objectively Manifested Impairment

Under the first prong, it must be established that the injured person has suffered an objectively manifested impairment of body function. The common meaning of "an objectively manifested impairment" is apparent from the unambiguous statutory language, with aid from a dictionary, and is consistent with the judicial interpretation of "objectively manifested" in *Cassidy* and *DiFranco*. To the extent that the *Kreiner* majority's interpretation of this prong differs from this approach, it was wrongly decided.

To begin with, the adverb "objectively" is defined as "in an objective manner," Webster's Third New International Dictionary (1966), and the adjective "objective" is defined as "1. Of or having to do with a material object as distinguished from a mental concept. 2. Having actual existence or reality. 3. a. Uninfluenced by emotion, surmise, or personal prejudice. b. Based on observable phenomena; presented factually. . . ." The American Heritage Dictionary, Second College Edition (1982). It is defined specifically in the medical context as "[i]ndicating a symptom or condition perceived as a sign of disease by someone other than the person afflicted." The verb "manifest" is defined as "1. To show or demonstrate plainly; reveal. 2. To be evidence of; prove." *Id.* Overall, these definitions suggest that the common meaning of "objectively manifested" in MCL 500.3135(7) is an impairment that is evidenced by actual symptoms or conditions that someone other than the injured person would observe or perceive as impairing a body function. In other words, an "objectively manifested" impairment is commonly understood as one observable or perceivable from actual symptoms or conditions.

Notably, MCL 500.3135(7) does not contain the word "injury," and, under the plain language of the statute, the proper inquiry is whether the *impairment* is objectively manifested, not the injury or its symptoms. This distinction is important because "injury" and "impairment" have different meanings. An "injury" is "1. Damage of or to a person . . . 2. A wound or other specific damage." The American Heritage Dictionary, Second College Edition (1982). "Impairment" is the "state of being impaired," Webster's Third New International Dictionary

(1966), and to be "impaired" means being "weakened, diminished, or damaged" or "functioning poorly or inadequately." Random House Webster's Unabridged Dictionary (1998). These definitions show that while an injury is the actual damage or wound, an impairment generally relates to the effect of that damage. Accordingly, when considering an "impairment," the focus "is not on the injuries themselves, but how the injuries affected a particular body function." *DiFranco*.

Further, the pre-existing judicial interpretation of "objectively manifested" is consistent with the plain language of the later-adopted statute. In *Cassidy*, this Court explained that the serious impairment threshold was not met by pain and suffering alone, but also required "injuries that affect the functioning of the body," i.e., "objectively manifested injuries." *Cassidy*. In other words, *Cassidy* defined "objectively manifested" to mean affecting the functioning of the body. *DiFranco* affirmed this and further explained that the "objectively manifested" requirement signifies that plaintiffs must "introduce evidence establishing that there is a physical basis for their subjective complaints of pain and suffering" and that showing an impairment generally requires medical testimony.

The *Kreiner* majority's interpretation of this language was only partially consistent with the plain language of the statute. It addressed this issue briefly, stating that "[s]ubjective complaints that are not medically documented are insufficient [to establish that an impairment is objectively manifested]." *Kreiner*. To the extent that this is inconsistent with *DiFranco's* statement that medical *testimony* will *generally* be required to establish an impairment, it is at odds with the legislative intent expressed by the adoption of the "objectively manifested" language from *DiFranco* and *Cassidy*. Thus, to the extent that *Kreiner* could be read to *always* require medical documentation, it goes beyond the legislative intent expressed in the plain statutory text, and was wrongly decided.

b. Of an Important Body Function

If there is an objectively manifested impairment of body function, the next question is whether the impaired body function is "important." The common meaning of this phrase is expressed in the unambiguous statutory language, although reference to a dictionary and limited reference to *Cassidy* is helpful.

The relevant definition of the adjective "important" is "[m]arked by or having great value, significance, or consequence." The American Heritage Dictionary, Second College Edition (1982). See also Random House Webster's Unabridged Dictionary (1998), defining "important" in relevant part as "of much or great significance or consequence," "mattering much," or "prominent or large." Whether a body function has great "value," "significance," or "consequence" will vary depending on the person. Therefore, this prong is an inherently subjective inquiry that must be decided on a case-by-case basis, because what may seem to be a trivial body function for most people may be subjectively important to some, depending on the relationship of that function to the person's life.

The "important body function" language was originally adopted in *Cassidy*, where the Court stated that an "important" body function is not *any* body function but also does not refer to the entire body function. *Cassidy*. This pre-existing judicial construction of "important body function" is consistent with the common meaning of "important."

For this prong, the *Kreiner* majority's interpretation appears to be consistent with the plain language of the statute, as it only briefly stated that "[i]t is insufficient if the impairment is of an unimportant body function." *Kreiner*. If, however, the *Kreiner* majority's position has been construed in a manner that is inconsistent with this opinion, then we disapprove of those constructions.

c. That Affects the Person's General Ability to Lead His or Her Normal Life

Finally, if the injured person has suffered an objectively manifested impairment of body function, and that body function is important to that person, then the court must determine whether the impairment "affects the person's general ability to lead his or her normal life." The common meaning of this phrase is expressed by the unambiguous statutory language, and its interpretation is aided by reference to a dictionary, reading the phrase within its statutory context, and limited reference to *Cassidy*.

To begin with, the verb "affect" is defined as "[t]o have an influence on; bring about a change in." The American Heritage Dictionary, Second College Edition (1982). An "ability" is "[t]he quality of being able to do something," *id.*, and "able" is defined as "having sufficient power, skill, or resources to accomplish an object." Merriam-Webster Online Dictionary, [http://www.merriam-webster.com] (accessed May 27, 2010). The adjective "general" means:

> 1. Relating to, concerned with, or applicable to the whole or every member of a class or category. 2. Affecting or characteristic of the majority of those involved; prevalent: *a general discontent*. 3. Being usually the case; true or applicable in most instances but not all. 4. a. Not limited in scope, area, or application: *as a general rule*. b. Not limited to one class of things: *general studies*. 5. Involving only the main features of something rather than details or particulars. 6. Highest or superior in rank." [The American Heritage Dictionary, Second College Edition (1982).]

The sixth definition is obviously irrelevant, and the first definition of "general" does not make sense in this context because a person's "whole" ability to live his or her normal life is surely not affected short of complete physical and mental incapacitation, which is accounted for in a different statutory threshold: death. The other definitions, however, more or less convey the same meaning: that "general" does not refer to only one specific detail or particular part of a thing, but, at least some parts of it. Thus, these definitions illustrate that to "affect" the person's "general ability" to lead his or her normal life is to influence some of the person's power or skill, i.e., the person's capacity, to lead a normal life.

The next question is the meaning of "to lead his or her normal life." The verb "lead," in this context, is best defined as "[t]o pass or go through; live."

The American Heritage Dictionary, Second College Edition (1982). Although the verb "lead" has many definitions, some of which have similar nuances, this definition is the most relevant because it expressly applies in the context of leading a certain type of life. Indeed, other dictionaries provide a similar definition with the same context, using a "type of life" as an example. Similarly, "life" has multiple meanings, but one specifically references the context of leading a particular type of life, which is "[a] manner of living: *led a good life.*" Other definitions are similar, such as "[t]he physical, mental, and spiritual experiences that constitute a person's existence," or "[h]uman existence or activity in general." Given the contextual examples used in the dictionary, the common understanding of "to lead his or her normal life" is to live, or pass life, in his or her normal manner of living.

Therefore, the plain text of the statute and these definitions demonstrate that the common understanding of to "affect the person's ability to lead his or her normal life" is to have an influence on some of the person's capacity to live in his or her normal manner of living. By modifying "normal life" with "his or her," the Legislature indicated that this requires a subjective, person- and fact-specific inquiry that must be decided on a case-by-case basis. Determining the effect or influence that the impairment has had on a plaintiff's ability to lead a normal life necessarily requires a comparison of the plaintiff's life before and after the incident.

There are several important points to note, however, with regard to this comparison. First, the statute merely requires that a person's general ability to lead his or her normal life has been *affected*, not destroyed. Thus, courts should consider not only whether the impairment has led the person to completely cease a pre-incident activity or lifestyle element, but also whether, although a person is able to lead his or her pre-incident normal life, the person's general ability to do so was nonetheless affected.

Second, and relatedly, "general" modifies "*ability*," not "affect" or "normal life." Thus, the plain language of the statute only requires that some of the person's *ability* to live in his or her normal manner of living has been affected, not that some of the person's normal manner of living has itself been affected. Thus, while the extent to which a person's general ability to live his or her normal life is affected by an impairment is undoubtedly related to what the person's normal manner of living is, there is no quantitative minimum as to the percentage of a person's normal manner of living that must be affected.

Third, and finally, the statute does not create an express temporal requirement as to how long an impairment must last in order to have an effect on "the person's general ability to live his or her normal life." To begin with, there is no such requirement in the plain language of the statute. Further, MCL 500.3135(1) provides that the threshold for liability is met "if the injured person has suffered death, serious impairment of body function, or permanent serious disfigurement." While the Legislature required that a "serious disfigurement" be "permanent," it did not impose the same restriction on a "serious impairment of body function." Finally, to the extent that this prong's language reflects a legislative intent to adopt this portion of *Cassidy* in some measure, *Cassidy* expressly rejected a requirement of permanency to meet the serious impairment threshold. (noting that "two broken bones, 18 days of hospitalization, 7 months of wearing casts during which dizzy spells further affected his mobility, and at least a minor residual effect one and one-half years later are sufficiently serious to meet the threshold requirement of serious impairment of body function") . . . .

[The court then goes on to criticize the dissent.]

4. Summary of Legislative Test

On the basis of the foregoing, the proper interpretation of the clear and unambiguous language in MCL 500.3135 creates the following test.

To begin with, the court should determine whether there is a factual dispute regarding the nature and the extent of the person's injuries, and, if so, whether the dispute is material to determining whether the serious impairment of body function threshold is met. MCL 500.3135(2)(a)(*i*) and (*ii*). If there is no factual dispute, or no material factual dispute, then whether the threshold is met is a question of law for the court.

If the court may decide the issue as a matter of law, it should next determine whether the serious impairment threshold has been crossed. The unambiguous language of MCL 500.3135(7) provides three prongs that are necessary to establish a "serious impairment of body function": (1) an objectively manifested impairment (observable or perceivable from actual symptoms or conditions) (2) of an important body function (a body function of value, significance, or consequence to the injured person) that (3) affects the person's general ability to lead his or her normal life (influences some of the plaintiff's capacity to live in his or her normal manner of living).

The serious impairment analysis is inherently fact- and circumstance-specific and must be conducted on a case-by-case basis. As stated in the *Kreiner* dissent, "[t]he Legislature recognized that what is important to one is not important to all[;] a brief impairment may be devastating whereas a near permanent impairment may have little effect." As such, the analysis does not "lend itself to any bright-line rule or imposition of [a] nonexhaustive list of factors," particularly where there is no basis in the statute for such factors. Accordingly, because "[t]he Legislature avoided drawing lines in the sand . . . so must we."

C. APPLICATION OF MCL 500.3135

Under the facts of this case, we hold that plaintiff has met the serious impairment threshold as a matter of law.

To begin with, there is no factual dispute that is material to determining whether the serious impairment threshold is met. The parties do not dispute that plaintiff suffered a broken ankle, was completely restricted from bearing weight on his ankle for a month, and underwent two surgeries over a 10-month period and multiple months of physical therapy. The parties do dispute the extent to which plaintiff continues to suffer a residual impairment and the potential for increased susceptibility to degenerative arthritis.

Plaintiff has provided at least some evidence of a physical basis for his subjective complaints of pain and suffering, but defendant disputes whether there is persuasive evidence of impairment beyond plaintiff's subjective complaints. This dispute is not significant or essential to determining whether the serious impairment threshold is met in this case, however, because plaintiff has not alleged that the residual impairment, to the extent that it exists, continues to affect his general ability to lead his pre-incident "normal life,"[29] the third prong of the analysis. Moreover, it is not necessary to establish the first two prongs. Therefore, the dispute is not material and does not prevent this Court from deciding whether the threshold is met as a matter of law under MCL 500.3135(2)(a).

The other facts material to determining whether the serious impairment threshold is met are also undisputed. Before the incident, plaintiff's "normal life" consisted primarily of working 60 hours a week as a medium truck loader. Plaintiff also frequently fished in the spring and summer and was a weekend golfer. After the incident, plaintiff was unable to return to work for at least 14 months and did not return for 19 months. He never returned to his original job as a medium truck loader, but he suffered no loss in pay because of the change in job. He was able to fish at pre-incident levels by the spring of 2006 and is able to take care of his personal needs at the same level as before the incident. There is no allegation that the impairment of body function has affected his relationship with his significant other or other qualitative aspects of his life.

Next, in light of the lack of a factual dispute that is material to determining whether the threshold is met, under MCL 500.3135(2)(a), this Court should decide as a matter of law whether plaintiff suffered a serious impairment of body function under the three prongs in MCL 500.3135(7).

With regard to the first prong, plaintiff has shown an objectively manifested impairment of body function. There is no dispute that plaintiff has presented evidence that he suffered a broken ankle and actual symptoms or conditions that someone else would perceive as impairing body functions, such as walking, crouching, climbing, and lifting weight. Even 14 months after the incident, an FCE report observed that ankle pain and a reduced range of motion inhibited these body functions. Thus, plaintiff has satisfied this prong.

With regard to the second prong, the impaired body functions were important to plaintiff. His testimony establishes that being unable to walk and perform other functions were of consequence to his ability to work. Thus, the second prong of MCL 500.3135(7) is met.

The next question in this case is whether the third prong is met, but we hold that plaintiff has shown that the impairment affected his general ability to lead

---

29. Plaintiff stated that his life is "painful, but normal." He does not allege that any residual impairment has a significant effect on his ability to participate in or enjoy activities to the extent that he could before the accident.

his normal life because it influenced some of his capacity to live in his normal, pre-incident manner of living. Before the incident, plaintiff's normal manner of living consisted primarily of working, for 60 hours a week, and secondarily his hobbies of fishing and golfing. After the incident, at least some of plaintiff's capacity to live in this manner was affected. Specifically, for a month after the incident, plaintiff could not bear weight on his left ankle. He underwent two surgeries over a period of 10 months and multiple months of physical therapy. Moreover, his capacity to work, the central part of his pre-incident "normal life," was affected. Whereas before the incident he spent most of his time working, after the incident he was unable to perform functions necessary for his job for at least 14 months, and he did not return to work for 19 months. On the basis of these facts, we conclude that some of plaintiff's capacity to live in his pre-incident manner of living was affected, and the third prong of MCL 500.3135(7) is satisfied.

Because all three prongs of MCL 500.3135(7) are satisfied, we hold, as a matter of law, that plaintiff has met the serious impairment threshold requirement under MCL 500.3135(1).

[Marilyn Kelly, C.J., and Weaver (except for part III(B)(3)) and Hathaway concurred. Markman, Corrigan, and Young dissented.]

PREPARING FOR CLASS

1. The Michigan Supreme Court has been evenly split between justices friendly to the claimant and justices friendly to the defendant and insurance companies. This split causes the continual changing of positions on the contested areas like the threshold for no-fault. The above opinion was a 4-3 opinion. Since the time of this opinion, Justice Weaver has retired from the court and been replaced by a gubernatorial appointee who was not elected in the 2010 election. A justice supported by the business and insurance interests won election. So now the court favors the defense. Anticipate a reversal of the *McCormick* decision soon.

2. Why is the no-fault threshold such a controversial area? How does this decision favor the plaintiffs in auto accident litigation?

3. Is there a better legislative definition of the no-fault threshold that would avoid this controversy?

4. The statute says the issue of whether the threshold has been reached is a matter of law. What does that mean? What are the consequences of that statute?

5. If the language of the statute is plain and unambiguous as stated by the majority, why would the court consult a dictionary and face a dissent from three justices?

INCREASING YOUR UNDERSTANDING

1. Not every no-fault statute is the same. One of the areas where the statutes vary is in the threshold to file a tort suit. The concept of no-fault requires first-party, no-fault insurance to cover the minor auto accidents while a cause of action for tort is preserved for the more serious injuries. Some states established a quantitative threshold, i.e., the injured party could sue after suffering a certain amount of economic loss. If economic damages exceeded the economic loss set forth in the statute, then the claim was "serious" and the injured party could proceed in tort. Michigan, on the other hand, established a definitional threshold, i.e., death, serious impairment of a bodily function, or permanent and serious disfigurement. Do you think there is as much disagreement about the quantitative threshold as there is with the Michigan threshold? Do the quantitative thresholds serve their purpose as well as the Michigan threshold?

2. Social security disability is another major no-fault system like workers' compensation and automobile no-fault. This system is like workers' compensation in providing for strict liability for disability, which pays according to a schedule. Like workers' compensation, an administrative law judge and not a jury decides these claims. Social security disability is not like social security benefits, which begin at a certain age. These benefits begin, regardless of age, when the claimant becomes disabled from working. Many personal injury lawyers are now seeking social security disability cases.

APPLYING THE LAW

1. Anthony injures his right wrist in an automobile accident. Although he did not seek immediate medical attention, he soon experienced swelling and pain in his wrist. Two weeks later, x-rays revealed arthritic changes to his wrist aggravated by the trauma of the automobile accident. Anthony was totally disabled for six weeks and then partially disabled as the arthritis continued to worsen. Wrist surgery was finally performed, and a joint prosthesis was implanted. Is Anthony entitled to sue the negligent tortfeasor?

2. Ben was driving his car on a sunny Saturday afternoon when it collided with a motorcycle. Ben stopped the car as quickly as possible but the motorcycle, its rider, and passenger skidded under the car for over 100 feet. The motorcycle passenger died at the scene. The rider was convicted of reckless driving. About six months after the accident, Ben had a heart attack, which he says was caused by the trauma of the accident. The cardiologist said that was entirely possible. The cardiologist said Ben

suffered significant heart damage, which will restrict his activity for six months. Will Ben be able to sue the motorcycle rider in tort? Explain.

3. *The Michigan No-Fault Statute*

There are three fundamental questions in auto no-fault legislation: (1) What accidents are covered by the no-fault system; (2) what benefits are provided to those that are covered; and (3) when, if ever, can an injured party sue a negligent party in tort for noneconomic damages? Michigan has one of the most pure no-fault systems in the United States. Familiarity with the Michigan system helps to understand no-fault insurance in other states. Following are selected sections of the Michigan no-fault insurance statute:

SEC. 3105. PERSONAL PROTECTION BENEFITS; ACCIDENTAL BODILY INJURY

(1) Under personal protection insurance an insurer is liable to pay benefits for accidental bodily injury arising out of the ownership, operation, maintenance or use of a motor vehicle as a motor vehicle, subject to the provisions of this chapter.

(2) Personal protection insurance benefits are due under this chapter without regard to fault.

(3) Bodily injury includes death resulting therefrom and damage to or loss of a person's prosthetic devices in connection with the injury.

(4) Bodily injury is accidental as to a person claiming personal protection insurance benefits unless suffered intentionally by the injured person or caused intentionally by the claimant. Even though a person knows that bodily injury is substantially certain to be caused by his act or omission, he does not cause or suffer injury intentionally if he acts or refrains from acting for the purpose of averting injury to property or to any person including himself.

SEC. 3107. PERSONAL PROTECTION INSURANCE BENEFITS; ALLOWABLE EXPENSES, WORK LOSS, PERSONAL SERVICES, WAIVERS OF COVERAGE

(1) Except as provided in subsection (2), personal protection insurance benefits are payable for the following:

(a) Allowable expenses consisting of all reasonable charges incurred for reasonably necessary products, services and accommodations for an injured person's care, recovery, or rehabilitation. Allowable expenses within personal protection insurance coverage shall not include charges for a hospital room in excess of a reasonable and customary charge for semiprivate accommodations except if the injured person requires special or intensive care, or for funeral and burial expenses in the amount set forth in the policy which shall not be less than $1,750.00 or more than $5,000.00.

(b) Work loss consisting of loss of income from work an injured person would have performed during the first 3 years after the date of the accident if he or she had not been injured. Work loss does not include any loss after the date on which the injured person dies. Because the benefits received from personal protection insurance for loss of income are not taxable income, the benefits payable for such loss of income shall be reduced 15% unless the claimant presents to the insurer in support of his or her claim reasonable proof of a lower value of the income tax advantage in his or her case, in which case the lower value shall apply. Beginning March 30, 1973, the benefits payable for work loss sustained in a single 30-day period and the income earned by an injured person for work during the same period together shall not exceed $1,000.00, which maximum shall apply pro rata to any lesser period of work loss. Beginning October 1, 1974, the maximum shall be adjusted annually to reflect changes in the cost of living under rules prescribed by the commissioner but any change in the maximum shall apply only to benefits arising out of accidents occurring subsequent to the date of change in the maximum.

(c) Expenses not exceeding $20.00 per day, reasonably incurred in obtaining ordinary and necessary services in lieu of those that, if he or she had not been injured, an injured person would have performed during the first 3 years after the date of the accident, not for income but for the benefit of himself or herself or of his or her dependent.

(2) A person who is 60 years of age or older and in the event of an accidental bodily injury would not be eligible to receive work loss benefits under subsection (1)(b) may waive coverage for work loss benefits by signing a waiver on a form provided by the insurer. An insurer shall offer a reduced premium rate to a person who waives coverage under this subsection for work loss benefits. Waiver of coverage for work loss benefits applies only to work loss benefits payable to the person or persons who have signed the waiver form.

Sec. 3121. Personal protection benefits; property damage, accidental damage; measure of benefits; maximum benefits

(1) Under property protection insurance an insurer is liable to pay benefits for accidental damage to tangible property arising out of the ownership, operation, maintenance, or use of a motor vehicle as a motor vehicle subject to the provisions of this section and sections 3123, 3125, and 3127. However, accidental damage to tangible property does not include accidental damage to tangible property, other than the insured motor vehicle, that occurs within the course of a business of repairing, servicing, or otherwise maintaining motor vehicles.

(2) Property protection insurance benefits are due under the conditions stated in this chapter without regard to fault.

(3) Damage to tangible property consists of physical injury to or destruction of the property and loss of use of the property so injured or destroyed.

(4) Damage to tangible property is accidental, as to a person claiming property protection insurance benefits, unless it is suffered or caused intentionally by the claimant. Even though a person knows that damage to tangible property is substantially certain to be caused by his or her act or omission, he or she does not cause or suffer such damage intentionally if he or she acts or refrains from

acting for the purpose of averting injury to any person, including himself or herself, or for the purpose of averting damage to tangible property.

(5) Property protection insurance benefits consist of the lesser of reasonable repair costs or replacement costs less depreciation and, if applicable, the value of loss of use. However, property protection insurance benefits paid under 1 policy for damage to all tangible property arising from 1 accident shall not exceed $1,000,000.00.

SEC. 3135. TORT LIABILITY FOR NONECONOMIC LOSS, CAUSE OF ACTION FOR DAMAGES; TORT LIABILITY FROM OWNERSHIP, MAINTENANCE, OR USE OF A MOTOR VEHICLE, ABOLITION, EXCEPTIONS, DAMAGES; SERIOUS IMPAIRMENT OF BODILY FUNCTION, DEFINED

(1) A person remains subject to tort liability for noneconomic loss caused by his or her ownership, maintenance, or use of a motor vehicle only if the injured person has suffered death, serious impairment of body function, or permanent serious disfigurement.

(2) For a cause of action for damages pursuant to subsection (1) filed on or after July 26, 1996, all of the following apply:

(a) The issues of whether an injured person has suffered serious impairment of body function or permanent serious disfigurement are questions of law for the court if the court finds either of the following:

(i) There is no factual dispute concerning the nature and extent of the person's injuries

(ii) There is a factual dispute concerning the nature and extent of the person's injuries, but the dispute is not material to the determination as to whether the person has suffered a serious impairment of body function or permanent serious disfigurement. However, for a closed-head injury, a question of fact for the jury is created if a licensed allopathic or osteopathic physician who regularly diagnoses or treats closed-head injuries testifies under oath that there may be a serious neurological injury.

(b) Damages shall be assessed on the basis of comparative fault, except that damages shall not be assessed in favor of a party who is more than 50% at fault.

(c) Damages shall not be assessed in favor of a party who was operating his or her own vehicle at the time the injury occurred and did not have in effect for that motor vehicle the security required by section 3101 at the time the injury occurred.

(3) Notwithstanding any other provision of law, tort liability arising from the ownership, maintenance, or use within this state of a motor vehicle with respect to which the security required by section 3101 was in effect is abolished except as to:

(a) Intentionally caused harm to persons or property. Even though a person knows that harm to persons or property is substantially certain to be caused by his or her act or omission, the person does not cause or suffer that harm intentionally if he or she acts or refrains from acting for the purpose of averting injury to any person, including himself or herself, or for the purpose of averting damage to tangible property.

(b) Damages for noneconomic loss as provided and limited in subsections (1) and (2).

(c) Damages for allowable expenses, work loss, and survivor's loss as defined in sections 3107 to 3110 in excess of the daily, monthly, and 3-year limitations contained in those sections. The party liable for damages is entitled to an exemption reducing his or her liability by the amount of taxes that would have been payable on account of income the injured person would have received if he or she had not been injured.

(d) Damages for economic loss by a nonresident in excess of the personal protection insurance benefits provided under section 3163(4). Damages under this subdivision are not recoverable to the extent that benefits covering the same loss are available from other sources, regardless of the nature or number of benefit sources available and regardless of the nature or form of the benefits.

(e) Damages up to $500.00 to motor vehicles, to the extent that the damages are not covered by insurance. An action for damages pursuant to this subdivision shall be conducted in compliance with subsection (4).

(4) In an action for damages pursuant to subsection (3)(e):

(a) Damages shall be assessed on the basis of comparative fault, except that damages shall not be assessed in favor of a party who is more than 50% at fault.

(b) Liability shall not be a component of residual liability, as prescribed in section 3131, for which maintenance of security is required by this act.

(5) Actions under subsection (3)(e) shall be commenced, whenever legally possible, in the small claims division of the district court or the municipal court. If the defendant or plaintiff removes the action to a higher court and does not prevail, the judge may assess costs.

(6) A decision of a court made pursuant to subsection (3)(e) is not res judicata in any proceeding to determine any other liability arising from the same circumstances as gave rise to the action brought pursuant to subsection (3)(e).

(7) As used in this section, "serious impairment of body function" means an objectively manifested impairment of an important body function that affects the person's general ability to lead his or her normal life.

PREPARING FOR CLASS

1. How will these statutes affect Tom's (from the hypothetical at the beginning of this chapter) ability to recover personal injury protection benefits?

2. How will these statutes affect Tom's ability to recover from General Grocery?

3. Look at §3135 (2). Is that section consistent with *Morosini v. Citizens Ins. Co. of America*, which you just read? If not, what happened? Why would the legislature limit §3135 (2) to causes of actions filed after July 26, 1996?

4. Does Michigan no-fault insurance cover damage to the automobile? What section, if any, covers an automobile?

5. The act preserves liability for negligent damage to a motor vehicle for a deductible up to $500 (§3135(3)(e)). This is sometimes called the "mini-tort" and is filed in small claims court. Who will pay for repair of the motor vehicle that exceeds $500?

6. Who will pay for the lost wages that exceed the work loss benefits in §3107(1)(b)?

INDEX